I0817459

In *The Story of Jesus Continues*, Douglas Huffman has produced a remarkably comprehensive yet accessible survey of the book of Acts. The many supplemental charts and diagrams both inform and engage, providing commentary and background to a well-written text. Highly recommended for both college and seminary-level courses and for anyone interested in the history of early Christianity.

MARK STRAUSS, university professor of New Testament, Bethel Seminary

Good texts contain useful information, but great textbooks compel the student to read and appreciate the content. Doug Huffman is a well-informed and enthusiastic advocate for the importance of the book of Acts, and his enthusiasm comes through on every page. Huffman offers strong support for Acts as a historically reliable narrative of the growth and development of the early church as it spread the message of Jesus to the Jewish and then the gentile worlds. The narrative is compelling, fully supported by useful and informative sidebars, bibliographies, and other helpful information.

STANLEY E. PORTER, president, dean, professor of New Testament,
and Roy A. Hope Chair in Christian Worldview, McMaster Divinity College

Douglas Huffman's engaging prose, beautiful photos, and helpful organization make *The Story of Jesus Continues* a perfect fit for the classroom and pastor's study. Drawing on decades of scholarship, Huffman provides a thorough and lively discussion of key issues within Acts and offers insightful suggestions to apply its teachings today.

LYNN COHICK, distinguished professor of New Testament
and director of Houston Theological Seminary

A beautifully produced volume chock-full of insight, information, and instructional aids for studying the book of Acts. An ideal resource for students and teachers alike, stimulating and supporting in-depth analysis of this exciting New Testament writing. Huffman clearly and carefully unfolds the continuing story of Jesus in Acts. Along the way, he illuminates the interpretive journey with a wide array of primary materials from the ancient world and literary and theological commentary from modern scholars. As a bonus, far from being a sterile textbook, this work is written in a warm evangelical spirit—appropriate to the Spirit's dynamic role in Acts!—blending solid academic analysis with thoughtful spiritual application. Perfect for use in Christian colleges and seminaries.

F. SCOTT SPENCER, New Testament general editor for *The SBL Study Bible* and
former professor at Wingate University and Baptist Theological Seminary

It's my privilege to commend this excellent introduction, suitable for courses on the book of Acts. It is well-informed and thorough, presenting fairly a range of positions; it is also well organized and designed for optimal learning outcomes.

CRAIG S. KEENER, F. M. and Ada Thompson Professor
of Biblical Studies, Asbury Theological Seminary

Talk about one-stop shopping! This book has everything an instructor in an advanced undergraduate or beginning seminary class on the book of Acts could realistically want. The scholarship is completely up-to-date without neglecting the classics. This volume is attractively laid out and straightforward to read, with sidebars, charts, maps, photos, definitions of key terms, and even suggested assignments to help teachers and their students do superior work. Theologically evangelical and exegetically astute, Huffman's work should command assent in almost all respects. A gem of a gift for the church of Jesus Christ and our contemporary world!

CRAIG L. BLOMBERG, distinguished professor emeritus of New Testament, Denver Seminary

Academically rigorous and masterfully written, this book is an asset to both the church and the academy. Drawing on the genre of storytelling, Douglas S. Huffman himself weaves a clear and compelling treatment of the biblical account of the early church. Huffman's name will become synonymous with the study of Acts.

DANIEL K. ENG, assistant professor of New Testament language and literature, Western Seminary

Doug Huffman has put together an amazing textbook for students on the book of Acts. It is informative yet accessible, scholarly without being dry, and full of helpful charts, photos, tables, and diagrams to make it very pictorial. Huffman explains to readers how Jesus continued to work in and through the apostles and how the gospel spread from Jerusalem to the ends of the earth. A terrific guide to Luke's story of Jesus and the early church!

REV. DR. MICHAEL F. BIRD, deputy principal at Ridley College, Melbourne, Australia

Professor Huffman has provided students, scholars, pastors, and general readers with a brilliant survey of the book of Acts that is focused both on the details of the text and on theological insights relevant for the church, well informed of scholarship, and written in a very accessible style. It is a privilege and pleasure to recommend this book for readers who seek reliable information about the world in which the earliest Christians worshiped the one true God and Jesus Messiah and proclaimed the gospel.

ECKHARD SCHNABEL, Mary F. Rockefeller Distinguished Professor of New Testament Studies Emeritus, Gordon-Conwell Theological Seminary

The Story of Jesus Continues is an extraordinary accomplishment, resulting from a career and vocation of teaching the book of Acts. This textbook will prove valuable for a generation because of its lucidity, pedagogical awareness, theological sensitivity, as well of its agility in the literary nature of Acts, its historical connections, and its value for pastors and churches today.

SCOT MCKNIGHT, visiting professor of New Testament, Houston Theological Seminary and Westminster Theological Centre (UK)

This outstanding textbook is well researched, clearly written, and beautifully presented. Douglas Huffman is a master teacher who expertly situates Acts in its first-century context and effectively engages readers today with its enduring theological message. Highly recommended!

BRIAN TABB, president and professor of biblical studies,
Bethlehem College and Seminary

Dr. Huffman's excellent and highly informative textbook is a delight for students and teachers of the New Testament. It is a privilege for students, pastors, scholars, and many others to explore the book of Acts through this meticulously methodical and practical course book. It provides a comprehensive overview of current Acts scholarship, helping students understand the book of Acts in both its ancient and contemporary contexts. The study features lucid presentations of the book's content, cautious judgments on critical introductory questions and exegetical issues, stimulating questions to deepen understanding, extensive background information, and much practical wisdom. As adventurous as the book of Acts itself, Huffman's work is to teachers and students what Keener's is to exegetes and researchers. What a joy to read this book! Highly recommended!

ARIE ZWIEP, professor of hermeneutics and vice dean faculty
of religion and theology, Vrije Universiteit Amsterdam

Huffman has written the perfect textbook for all professors teaching seminary and upper-level undergraduate courses on the Acts of the Apostles. Simultaneously comprehensive and accessible, this work will help readers attain a thorough grasp of how the risen Jesus was—and is—at work in the life of the church and his followers.

JOSHUA W. JIPP, professor of New Testament, Trinity International University

This book is an impressive achievement. It is a thorough, faithful, and balanced survey of Acts that covers everything from introductory issues to a close analysis of the text. I was pleased with how much material Huffman was able to cover and his awareness of modern advances in the study of Acts. His interactions were appropriate, his conclusions were nuanced, and his historical and textual work were skilled. I wish this book had been available when I wrote my commentary on Acts and will be requiring it for many future students who wish to hear the continuing story of Jesus in the book of Acts.

PATRICK SCHREINER, associate professor of New Testament and
biblical theology, Midwestern Baptist Theological Seminary

With solid detail and an eye on all the options, this survey of Acts is far more than an overview of the book. It is a deep dive into the many facets of this pivotal New Testament book. Huffman has done us all a service, and students will surely benefit from it as a regular resource on Luke's strategic volume on the early church.

DARRELL L. BOCK, executive director for cultural engagement and senior
research professor of New Testament Studies, Dallas Theological Seminary

A wonderful, deep dive into Acts with an eye to living its message today. Huffman illuminates and contextualizes Acts in its historical context with colorful graphics and sidebars, outlines sound options for interpretation, and interacts with a wealth of primary and secondary literature. Here is a tremendous resource for students of Acts and the pastor's shelf.

BRANDON CROWE, professor of New Testament,
Westminster Theological Seminary

Professor Huffman has written a thorough and helpful introduction to the Acts of the Apostles made accessible by his helpful outlines, chapter introductions and summaries, theological observations, vocabulary lists, charts, illustrations, and photographs. While this book is primarily a critical introduction to Acts, it is also a useful resource for spiritual formation, ministerial training, and personal spiritual growth. Anyone, whether general reader, student, pastor, or scholar, who reads this important book carefully will benefit from the author's admirable scholarship and unmistakable faith that support and undergird this work.

MELVIN STORM, professor of New Testament and Greek,
Rochester University

Acts is both an exciting and inspiring account of the spread of the gospel throughout the Mediterranean world. Doug Huffman's wonderfully presented introduction to and survey of Acts will enhance your appreciation of Acts all the more. Drawing on his many years of research on Acts and his experience of teaching through the book numerous times, Huffman provides a trove of historical information that illuminates the text and brings it to life. The many photographs, charts, maps, and diagrams will help readers visualize the context and appreciate how Acts fits into its cultural and historical setting. Huffman's volume should be the starting point for anyone preaching a series on Acts, leading a Bible study, or simply seeking to understand the book better.

CLINTON E. ARNOLD, research professor of New Testament,
Talbot School of Theology, Biola University

THE STORY OF JESUS CONTINUES

A Survey of the Acts of the Apostles

DOUGLAS S. HUFFMAN

ZONDERVAN ACADEMIC

The Story of Jesus Continues

Published in Grand Rapids, Michigan, by Zondervan. Zondervan is a registered trademark of The Zondervan Corporation, L.L.C., a wholly owned subsidiary of HarperCollins Christian Publishing, Inc.

Requests for information should be addressed to customercare@harpercollins.com.

Zondervan titles may be purchased in bulk for educational, business, fundraising, or sales promotional use. For information, please email SpecialMarkets@Zondervan.com.

Library of Congress Cataloging-in-Publication Data

Names: Huffman, Douglas S., 1961– author.
Title: The story of Jesus continues : a survey of the Acts of the Apostles / Douglas S. Huffman.
Description: Grand Rapids, Michigan : Zondervan Academic, [2024] | Includes bibliographical references and index.
Identifiers: LCCN 2024009791 (print) | LCCN 2024009792 (ebook) | ISBN 9780310514794 (hardcover) | ISBN 9780310514800 (ebook)
Subjects: LCSH: Bible. Acts. | Jesus Christ.
Classification: LCC BS2625.53 .H69 2024 (print) | LCC BS2625.53 (ebook) | DDC 226.6/06—dc23/eng/20240627
LC record available at https://lccn.loc.gov/2024009791
LC ebook record available at https://lccn.loc.gov/2024009792

Cover design: Tammy Johnson
Cover photography: public domain; courtesy National Gallery of Art, Washington
Interior design: Kait Lamphere

Printed in the United States of America

---

25 26 27 28 29 30 31 32 33 34 35 36 37 38 /TRM/ 19 18 17 16 15 14 13 12 11 10 9 8 7 6 5 4 3 2

CONTENTS

Abbreviations ix
Acknowledgments xix
Introduction xxi

Part 1: Introduction to the Acts of the Apostles

1. The People of Acts. 3
2. The Genre and Purpose of Acts 38
3. Storytelling in Acts 73
4. Interpreting and Applying Acts. 107
5. The Setting of Acts 142

Part 2: The Story of Jesus Reaching the Jewish World—Acts 1–12

6. The Story of Jesus Continues (Acts 1:1–2:41). 193
7. The Story of the Church in Its Earliest Days (Acts 2:42–6:7). 227
8. Three Key Non-Apostle Characters in the Story (Acts 6:8–9:31). 265
9. The Story Advances in Palestine (Acts 9:32–12:25) 295

Part 3: The Story of Jesus Reaching the Gentile World—Acts 13–28

10. The Story of the First Missionary Campaign (Acts 13:1–14:28). 335
11. The Central Interlude in the Story: The Jerusalem Council (Acts 15:1–35). 375
12. The Story of the Second Missionary Campaign (Acts 15:36–18:22) 405
13. The Story of the Third Missionary Campaign (Acts 18:23–21:17) 453
14. The Story Moves in Prison in Jerusalem and Caesarea (Acts 21:18–26:32). 485
15. The Story in Rough Waters on the Way to Rome (Acts 27:1–28:31). 527

Part 4: The Story of Jesus Reaching Your World

16. Conclusion: Continuing the Story of Jesus Unhindered 565

Glossary 609
Scripture Index 629
Extrabiblical Sources Index 653
Subject Index 659
Author Index 675

Abbreviations

Generally speaking, abbreviations in this volume utilize the pattern of abbreviations customary in English academia and the theological disciplines; readers can consult *The SBL Handbook of Style*, 2nd ed., ed. Billie Jean Collins et al. (Atlanta: SBL Press, 2014). The following categorized lists of abbreviations cover most of those used in this volume. Unless otherwise noted, English quotations of the Bible come from the NIV translation.

ABBREVIATIONS FOR BIBLICAL DIVISIONS AND VERSIONS

CEV	Contemporary English Version (1995)
CSB	Christian Standard Bible (2017)
ESV	English Standard Version (2001)
KJV	King James Version (1611)
LXX	Septuagint, Alfred Rahlfs, ed., *Septuaginta* (2 vols. in 1, 1979)
NASB	New American Standard Bible (1995)
NET	New English Translation (2006)
NIV	New International Version (2011)
NLT	New Living Translation (2015)
NT	New Testament (usually as an adjective, e.g., "NT authors")
OT	Old Testament (usually as an adjective, e.g., "OT passage")

ABBREVIATIONS FOR ANCIENT EXTRABIBLICAL REFERENCES

From Septuagint, Apocrypha, and Pseudepigraphic Works

1 Macc	1 Maccabees

2 Macc	2 Maccabees
3 Macc	3 Maccabees
4 Macc	4 Maccabees
4 Ezra	4 Ezra
Jdt	Judith
Jos. Asen.	Joseph and Aseneth
Jub.	Jubilees
Pss. Sol.	Psalms of Solomon
Sir	Sirach
Tob	Tobit
Wis	Wisdom

Other Ancient Texts

1QM	DSS Milḥamah or War Scroll
1QS	DSS Serek haYaḥad or Rule of the Community
Abraham	Philo, *On the Life of Abraham*
Ag.	Aeschylus, *Agamemnon*
Ag. Ap.	Josephus, *Against Apion*
Alleg. Interp.	Philo, *Allegorical Interpretation*
Ann.	Tacitus, *Annals*
Ant.	Josephus, *Jewish Antiquities*
Ant. rom.	Dionysius of Halicarnassus, *Antiquitates romanae* (a.k.a. *Roman Antiquities*)
Apol.	Plato, *Apology*
Aug.	Suetonius, *Divus Augustus*
b. ʿAbod. Zar.	Babylonian Talmud, ʿAbodah Zarah
b. Ber.	Babylonian Talmud, Berakot
b. Git.	Babylonian Talmud, Gittin
b. Meg.	Babylonian Talmud, Megillah
b. Menah.	Babylonian Talmud, Menahot
b. Sanh.	Babylonian Talmud, Sanhedrin
b. Tem.	Babylonian Talmud, Temurah
b. Yebam.	Babylonian Talmud, Yebamot
b. Yoma	Babylonian Talmud, Yoma
Brut.	Cicero, *Brutus* (a.k.a. *De Claris oratoribus*)
Busybody	Plutarch, *Moralia: On Being a Busybody*
CD	DSS Cairo Genizah copy of the Damascus Document
Claud.	Suetonius, *Divus Claudius*
Comm. Matt.	Jerome, *Commentariorum in Matthaeum libri IV*

Cor.	Demosthenes, *De Corona* (a.k.a. *On the Crown*)
Decl.	Quintilian, *Declamationes*
Deipn.	Athenaeus, *Deipnosophistae* (a.k.a. *Learned Banqueters*)
Demon.	Lucian, *Demonax*
DSS	Dead Sea Scrolls
El.	Sophocles, *Electra*
Epist.	Jerome, *Epistulae*
Eum.	Aeschylus, *Eumenides*
Exp. Luc.	Ambrose, *Expositio evangelii secundum Lucan*
Haer.	Irenaeus, *Adversus haereses* (a.k.a. *Against Heresies*)
Hel.	Euripides, *Helen*
Hermot.	Lucian, *Hermotimus* (a.k.a. *Concerning Sects*)
Hist.	Herodotus, *Histories* (a.k.a. *The Persian Wars*)
Hist.	Tacitus, *Histories*
Hist. eccl.	Eusebius, *Ecclesiastical History*
Hom. Act.	John Chrysostom, *Homiliae in Acta apostolorum* (a.k.a. *Commentary on Acts*)
Hom. Matt.	John Chrysostom, *Homiliae in Matthaeum* (a.k.a. *Commentary on Matthew*)
Hyp.	Clement of Alexandria, *Hypotyposes*
Il.	Homer, *Illiad*
Joseph	Philo, *On the Life of Joseph*
J.W.	Josephus, *Jewish War*
Life	Josephus, *The Life of Josephus*
m. Naz.	Mishnah, Nazir
m. 'Ohal.	Mishnah, 'Ohalot
m. Tehar.	Mishnah, Teharot
Mem.	Xenophon, *Memorabilia*
Migration	Philo, *On the Migration of Abraham*
Mor.	Plutarch, *Moralia*
Moses	Philo, *On the Life of Moses*
Nat.	Pliny the Elder, *Natural History*
Pis.	Cicero, *In Pisonem*
Pomp.	Dionysius of Halicarnassus, *Epistula ad Pompeium Geminum* (a.k.a. *Letter to Gnaeus Pompeius*)
Quis div.	Clement of Alexandria, *Quis dives salvetur* (a.k.a. *Salvation of the Rich*)
Salt.	Lucian, *De saltatione* (a.k.a. *The Dance*)
Strom.	Clement of Alexandria, *Stromateis* (a.k.a. *Miscellanies*)

Tit.	Suetonius, *Divus Titus*
Verr.	Cicero, *In Verrem* (a.k.a. *The Verrine Orations*)
Vit. Apoll.	Philostratus, *Vita Apollonii* (a.k.a. *The Life of Apollonius of Tyana*)
Vir. ill.	Jerome, *De viris illustribus*
y. Meg.	Jerusalem Talmud, Megillah

SECONDARY SOURCE ABBREVIATIONS

AB	Anchor Bible
ABD	*Anchor Bible Dictionary*. Edited by David Noel Freedman. 6 vols. New York: Doubleday, 1992.
AcBib	Academia Biblica
AJEC	Ancient Judaism and Early Christianity
AJPS	*Asian Journal of Pentecostal Studies*
AnBib	Analecta Biblica
ANF	*Ante-Nicene Fathers*
ANRW	*Aufstieg und Niedergang der römischen Welt: Geschichte und Kultur Roms im Spiegel der neueren Forschung*. Part 2, *Principat*. Edited by Hildegard Temporini and Wolfgang Haase. Berlin: de Gruyter, 1972–.
ANTC	Abingdon New Testament Commentaries
ASMS	American Society of Missiology Series
ASNU	Acta Seminarii Neotestamentici Upsaliensis
AUSTR	American University Studies, Series 7: Theology and Religion
BA	*The Biblical Archaeologist*
BAFCS	The Book of Acts in Its First Century Setting
BAR	*Biblical Archaeological Review*
BBR	*Bulletin for Biblical Research*
BDAG	Danker, Frederick W., Walter Bauer, William F. Arndt, and F. Wilbur Gingrich. *A Greek-English Lexicon of the New Testament and Other Early Christian Literature*, 3rd ed. Chicago: University of Chicago Press, 2000.
BEB	*Baker Encyclopedia of the Bible*. Edited by Walter A. Elwell. 4-vol. ed. Grand Rapids: Baker, 1997.
BECNT	Baker Exegetical Commentary on the New Testament
BETL	Bibliotheca Ephemeridum Theologicarum Lovaniensium
Bib	*Biblica*
BIBD	*The Baker Illustrated Bible Dictionary*. Edited by Tremper Longman III. Grand Rapids: Baker, 2013.

BibInt — Biblical Interpretation Series
BJRL — *Bulletin of the John Rylands Library*
BNP — *Brill's New Pauly: Encyclopedia of the Ancient World*. Edited by Hubert Cancik. 22 vols. Leiden: Brill, 2002–2011.
BR — *Biblical Research*
BRev — *Bible Review*
BSac — *Bibliotheca Sacra*
BTB — *Biblical Theological Bulletin*
BZ — *Biblische Zeitschrift*
BZNW — Beihefte zur Zeitschrift für die neutestamentliche Wissenschaft
CBET — Contributions to Biblical Exegesis and Theology
CBQ — *Catholic Biblical Quarterly*
CEJ — *Christian Education Journal*
CIG — *Corpus Inscriptionum Graecarum*. Edited by August Boeckh. 4 vols. Berlin: Reimer, 1828–1877.
CIL — *Corpus Inscriptionum Latinarum*. Berlin: de Gruyter/Reimer, 1862–.
CurBR — *Currents in Biblical Research*
DJG[1] — *Dictionary of Jesus and the Gospels*. Edited by Joel B. Green, Scot McKnight, and I. Howard Marshall. Downers Grove, IL: InterVarsity Press, 1992.
DJG[2] — *Dictionary of Jesus and the Gospels*. Edited by Joel B. Green, Jeannine K. Brown, and Nicholas Perrin. 2nd ed. Downers Grove, IL: InterVarsity Press, 2013.
DLNT — *Dictionary of the Later New Testament and Its Developments*. Edited by Ralph P. Martin and Peter H. Davids. Downers Grove, IL: InterVarsity Press, 1997.
DMOA — Documenta et Monumenta Orientis Antiqui
DNTB — *Dictionary of New Testament Background*. Edited by Craig A. Evans and Stanley E. Porter. Downers Grove, IL: InterVarsity Press, 2000.
DOTPent — *Dictionary of the Old Testament Pentateuch*. Edited by T. Desmond Alexander and David W. Baker. Downers Grove, IL: InterVarsity Press, 2003.
DOTProph — *Dictionary of the Old Testament Prophets*. Edited by Mark J. Boda and J. Gordon McConville. Downers Grove, IL: InterVarsity Press, 2012.
DPL — *Dictionary of Paul and His Letters*. Edited by Gerald F. Hawthorne and Ralph P. Martin. Downers Grove, IL: InterVarsity Press, 1993.
DSS — Dead Sea Scrolls

DTIB	*Dictionary for Theological Interpretation of the Bible*. Edited by Kevin J. Vanhoozer, Craig G. Bartholomew, Daniel J. Treier, and N. T. Wright. Grand Rapids: Baker Academic, 2005.
ECL	Early Christianity and Its Literature
EDB	*Eerdmans Dictionary of the Bible*. Edited by David Noel Freedman et al. Grand Rapids: Eerdmans, 2000.
EDBT	*Evangelical Dictionary of Biblical Theology*. Edited by Walter A. Elwell. Baker Reference Library. Grand Rapids: Baker, 1996.
EDT[2]	*Evangelical Dictionary of Theology*. Edited by Walter A. Elwell. 2nd ed. Baker Reference Library. Grand Rapids: Baker Academic, 2001.
ESEC	Emory Studies in Early Christianity
EvJ	*Evangelical Journal*
EvQ	*Evangelical Quarterly*
ExpTim	*Expository Times*
FC	Fathers of the Church
FF	Foundations and Facets
FRLANT	Forschungen zur Religion und Literatur des Alten und Neuen Testaments
GBS	Guides to Biblical Scholarship
GNS	Good News Studies
Historia	*Historia: Zeitschrift für Alte Geschichte*
HJP	*A History of the Jewish People in the Time of Jesus Christ*, by Emil Schürer. 5 vols. 2nd ed. Edinburgh: T&T Clark, 1885–1890. Rev. ed., *The History of the Jewish People in the Age of Jesus Christ (175 B.C.–A.D. 135)*. Edited by Geza Vermes et al. 4 vols. Edinburgh: T&T Clark, 1973–1987.
HTR	*Harvard Theological Review*
HTS	Harvard Theological Studies
ICC	International Critical Commentary
IDBSup	*The Interpreter's Dictionary of the Bible: Supplementary Volume*. Edited by Keith Crim. Nashville: Abingdon, 1976.
IG	*Inscriptiones Graecae. Editio Minor*. Berlin: de Gruyter, 1924–.
IGR	*Inscriptiones Graecae ad res romanas pertinentes*. Edited by René Cagnat et al. 4 vols. Paris: Leroux, 1911–1927.
ILS	*Inscriptiones Latinae Selectae*. Edited by Hermann Dessau. 3 vols. in 5. Berlin: Weidmann, 1892–1916.
Int	*Interpretation*
JAOS	*Journal of the American Oriental Society*
JBL	*Journal of Biblical Literature*

JETS	*Journal of the Evangelical Theological Society*
JGRChJ	*Journal of Greco-Roman Christianity and Judaism*
JPT	*Journal of Pentecostal Theology*
JPTSup	Journal of Pentecostal Theology Supplement
JRS	*Journal of Roman Studies*
JSJ	*Journal for the Study of Judaism*
JSNT	*Journal for the Study of the New Testament*
JSNTSup	Journal for the Study of the New Testament Supplement Series
JSOTSup	Journal for the Study of the Old Testament Supplement Series
JSPSup	Journal for the Study of the Pseudepigrapha Supplement Series
JTS	*Journal of Theological Studies*
LCL	Loeb Classical Library
LEC	Library of Early Christianity
LNTS	The Library of New Testament Studies
MNTC	Moffatt New Testament Commentary
NAC	New American Commentary
NCBC	New Century Bible Commentary
NDBT	*New Dictionary of Biblical Theology: Exploring the Unity & Diversity of Scripture*. Edited by Brian S. Rosner, T. Desmond Alexander, Graeme Goldsworthy, and D. A. Carson. Downers Grove, IL: InterVarsity Press, 2000.
NEAEHL	*The New Encyclopedia of Archaeological Excavations in the Holy Land*. Edited by Ephraim Stern. 5 vols. New York: Simon & Schuster, 1993.
Neot	*Neotestamentica*
NIBCNT	New International Biblical Commentary on the New Testament
NICNT	New International Commentary on the New Testament
NIDB	*The New Interpreter's Dictionary of the Bible*. Edited by Katharine Doob Sakenfeld. 5 vols. Nashville: Abingdon, 2006–2009.
NIDNTT	*New International Dictionary of New Testament Theology*. Edited by Colin Brown. 4 vols. Grand Rapids: Zondervan, 1986.
NIDNTTE	*New International Dictionary of New Testament Theology and Exegesis*. 2nd ed. Revised and edited by Moisés Silva. 5 vols. Grand Rapids: Zondervan, 2014.
NIGTC	New International Greek Testament Commentary
NovT	*Novum Testamentum*
NovTSup	Supplements to Novum Testamentum
NPNF^{1}	*Nicene and Post-Nicene Fathers*, Series 1
NPNF^{2}	*Nicene and Post-Nicene Fathers*, Series 2

NSBT	New Studies in Biblical Theology
NTG	New Testament Guides
NTL	New Testament Library
NTOA	Novum Testamentum et Orbis Antiquus
NTS	*New Testament Studies*
OEAGR	*The Oxford Encyclopedia of Ancient Greece & Rome*. Edited by Michael Gagarin et al. 7 vols. New York: Oxford University Press, 2010.
OEANE	*The Oxford Encyclopedia of Archaeology in the Near East*. Edited by Eric M. Meyers. 5 vols. Oxford: Oxford University Press, 1997.
OEBB	*The Oxford Encyclopedia of the Books of the Bible*. Edited by Michael D. Coogan. 2 vols. New York: Oxford University Press, 2011.
OGIS	*Orientis Graeci Inscriptiones Selectae*. Edited by Wilhelm Dittenberger. 2 vols. Leipzig: Hirzel, 1903–1905.
OTP	*The Old Testament Pseudepigrapha*. Edited by James H. Charlesworth. 2 vols. Garden City, NY: Doubleday, 1983–1985.
PSB	*Princeton Seminary Bulletin*
PTMS	Pittsburgh Theological Monograph Series
RevExp	*Review and Expositor*
RTR	*Reformed Theological Review*
SBFA	Studium Biblicum Franciscanum Analecta
SBG	Studies in Biblical Greek
SBL	Society of Biblical Literature
SBLDS	Society of Biblical Literature Dissertation Series
SBLMS	Society of Biblical Literature Monograph Series
SBLRBS	Society of Biblical Literature Resources for Biblical Studies
SBLSP	Society of Biblical Literature Seminar Papers
SBLSymS	Society of Biblical Literature Symposium Series
SE	*Studia Evangelica*
SNTA	Studiorum Novi Testamenti Auxilia
SNTSMS	Society for New Testament Studies Monograph Series
SNTW	Studies of the New Testament and Its World
SP	Sacra Pagina
StBibLit	Studies in Biblical Literature (Lang)
SUNT	Studien zur Umwelt des Neuen Testaments
SwJT	*Southwestern Journal of Theology*
TDNT	*Theological Dictionary of the New Testament*. Edited by Gerhard Kittel and Gerhard Friedrich. Translated by Geoffrey W. Bromiley. 10 vols. Grand Rapids: Eerdmans, 1964–1976.

TENTS	Text and Editions for New Testament Study
TGST	Tesi Gregoriana, Serie Teologia
TNTC	Tyndale New Testament Commentaries
TPINTC	TPI New Testament Commentaries
TynBul	*Tyndale Bulletin*
VL	Vestus Latina: Die Reste der altlateinischen Bibel
WBC	Word Biblical Commentary
WBD	*Wycliffe Bible Dictionary*. Edited by Charles F. Pfeiffer, Howard F. Vos, and John Rea. Peabody, MA: Hendrickson, 1998.
WGRW	Writings from the Greco-Roman World
WUNT	Wissenschaftliche Untersuchungen zum Neuen Testament
WW	*Word and World*
ZEB	*The Zondervan Encyclopedia of the Bible*. Rev. ed. Edited by Merrill C. Tenney and Moisés Silva. 5 vols. Grand Rapids: Zondervan, 2009.
ZECNT	Zondervan Exegetical Commentary on the New Testament
ZIBBCNT	*Zondervan Illustrated Bible Backgrounds Commentary: New Testament*. Edited by Clinton E. Arnold. 5 vols. Grand Rapids: Zondervan, 2002–2019.
ZNW	*Zeitschrift für die neutestamentiche Wissenschaft und die Kunde der älteren Kirche*

ACKNOWLEDGMENTS

As is often noted in the opening pages of books, such volumes as this one seldom come together without the assistance of many people. Friends, family, research assistants, editors, publishers, students, colleagues—these and others too numerous to name all make possible the publication of books today. For this project, the following must be mentioned:

- This book is one that follows in a particular line of such survey books published by Zondervan Academic, and it has benefited from these prior volumes. See *Four Portraits, One Jesus: A Survey of Jesus and the Gospels* by Mark L. Strauss (2007; 2nd ed. 2020); *The Message of the Prophets: A Survey of the Prophetic and Apocalyptic Books of the Old Testament* by J. Daniel Hays (2010); *The Writings of John: A Survey of the Gospel, Epistles, and Apocalypse* by C. Marvin Pate (2011); *Letters to the Church: A Survey of Hebrews and the General Epistles* by Karen H. Jobes (2011); and *Thinking through Paul: A Survey of His Life, Letters, and Theology* by Bruce W. Longenecker and Todd D. Still (2014). Thank you for these fine models of excellent survey presentations.
- Working on this book during the turbulent years of the worldwide COVID-19 pandemic (amid other political, social, and moral dilemmas in America) added some complexities to this project. Zondervan Academic's vice president and publisher, Katya Covrett, has not only made it possible for me to contribute to this line of books, but she has been instrumental in helping me overcome the writing ailments of "audience amnesia" (i.e., forgetting my intended readership) and "authorial laryngitis" (i.e., losing my own scholarly voice). Thank you for seeing potential in me, for working to improve my writing, and for waiting with extreme patience for the completion of this project.
- My colleagues in the Division of Biblical and Theological Studies at Biola University's Talbot School of Theology have helped me read, research, and write

with greater excellence. I sometimes wonder if I can keep up with them. In particular, this book has benefited from some of the New Testament department members who have engaged in conversations about this material and encouraged me in these efforts. Thank you, Ken Berding, Jeannine Hanger, Joanne Jung, Michelle Lee-Barnewall, Darian Lockett, Jon Lunde, James Petitfils, Jeanette Hagen Pifer, and Matt Williams.

- My fellow leadership colleagues at Talbot School of Theology have also been supportive, particularly by covering for me in my absence during sabbaticals and research leaves. I am grateful to Ed Stetzer (dean), Clint Arnold (former dean and now research professor of New Testament), Scott Rae (dean of faculty), Doug Geringer (associate dean), Joanne Jung (associate dean), Dave Talley and Charlie Trimm (chairs of Old Testament), Matt Williams and Jeannine Hanger (chairs of New Testament), Erik Thoennes and Uche Anizor (chairs of Theology), and Dave Keehn (chair of Christian Ministries).
- Hundreds of students studying Luke or Acts with me over the course of thirty years at two institutions (University of Northwestern–St. Paul and Biola University) have helped me see more and learn to communicate better. Thank you for teaching me.
- Several students serving as my teaching assistants have been especially helpful with this project. These include Jordan Cardenas, Jacob Sorenson, and Jake Edwards.
- Two additional friends have been persistent encouragers and prayer supporters on my behalf. Thank you, Jeff Bradbury and Dave Browning.
- And as always, my wife Deb has been ever supportive of my work in all its (sometimes strained and straining) diversity. Thank you for suffering with me (in both the "alongside me" sense and the "because of me" sense).

Now, let's get started in our study of the story of Acts!

INTRODUCTION

THE STORY OF JESUS CONTINUES

The book known as the Acts of the Apostles—or simply Acts, for short—is unique in the canon of the New Testament. There are four gospels, twenty-one epistles (thirteen ascribed to Paul and eight "general letters"), and one apocalypse (although it is worth noting that the book of Revelation also has several epistolary elements). But there is only one book of Acts. Particularly interesting about this observation is that the book of Acts comes from the same pen as one of the gospels: the Gospel of Luke. This author felt the need to keep writing. That is, while the other gospels—Matthew, Mark, and John—cease their recounting of the story about Jesus with the resurrection, the author of Luke and Acts (or Luke-Acts, as the corpus is often referenced) felt the need to continue the story of Jesus for his readership. We have no Acts According to Matthew, Acts According to Mark, or Acts According to John.[1] But as indicated in the prologue to Acts, this book is connected to its author's "former book" (Acts 1:1). In this sense, the New Testament book of Acts alone reads as a continuation of the Jesus story.

The Gospel of Luke ends with the ascension of Jesus into heaven (Luke 24:50–53), and Acts begins by repeating that report (Acts 1:9–11). So it is doubly clear that Jesus, in an important sense, is gone as the story continues. Nevertheless, the reader discovers that the story remains about Jesus (e.g., the name of Jesus occurs more than sixty times in Acts) and that Jesus himself is still an actor in the story (e.g., Acts 1:1–11; 7:55–59; 9:3–6, 34; 16:7; 18:9–10; 23:11). Thus, even with Jesus in heaven, Acts remains a continuation of the Jesus story.

1. There are several other "Acts" books dating to the second century AD. But not only are these extrabiblical writings too late to be canonical, none of them reads quite like the New Testament book we call the Acts of the Apostles. On noncanonical "Acts," see esp. Hans-Josef Klauck, *The Apocryphal Acts of the Apostles: An Introduction*, trans. Brian McNeil (Waco, TX: Baylor University Press, 2008); see also chapter 16 in this book.

The author of the Acts of the Apostles—let's call him Luke—is an excellent storyteller, but there is more to Luke's writing than merely a longer story of Jesus. While Luke's writing style in the prologue to the Gospel of Luke demonstrates that he could have written his volumes in a cultivated literary Greek style, he chose to write instead with a less formal but nevertheless an educated approach. Not only does he write in a good storytelling manner, but Luke's style is also reminiscent of the old Greek translation of the Hebrew Bible known as the Septuagint (abbreviated LXX). So then, the story in Acts is not only a continuation of the story of Jesus, it is also the continuation of the story of the Hebrew Scriptures.[2] Luke sees Jesus as the Messiah fulfilling God's plan in keeping with the Hebrew Scriptures, a plan that encompasses all of creation and invites the compliance of everyone. For Luke, the story of Jesus and his followers is a continuation of God's purposes in the world.[3]

Moreover, in another sense, the mission of the church is itself a continuation of the Jesus story. Grounded in the Hebrew Scriptures and in Jesus's own work, the ongoing mission of the church continues the scriptural story from God's promises to Abraham, through the ancient Israelites, to and through Jesus, to reach all of humanity.[4] Jesus continues his ministry through his disciples in Acts and in the world today as well.[5] So Luke's report about the spread of the gospel message in Acts calls his readers to participate in the spread of the gospel message in the world.

Christopher Wright has observed that, from a missional point of view, the whole Bible can be considered as a *product* of God's mission in the world, as the supreme *witness* to God's mission in the world, and as the *tool* of God's mission in the world. That is, the Bible is the result of God's work in the world, the record of God's work in history, and the resource for continuing God's work into the future.[6] As part of the Bible, the Acts of the Apostles fits this description, and the purpose of this textbook is to study the Acts of the Apostles not only as the result of God's mission in the world

---

2. See esp. H. Douglas Buckwalter, "Luke as Writer of Sacred History," *EvJ* 14 (1996): 86–99; cf. Jacob Jervell, *The Theology of the Acts of the Apostles*, New Testament Theology (Cambridge: Cambridge University Press, 1996), 18–43; Joel B. Green, "Learning Theological Interpretation from Luke," pp. 55–78 in *Reading Luke: Interpretation, Reflection, Formation*, ed. Craig G. Bartholomew, Joel B. Green, and Anthony C. Thiselton, Scripture and Hermeneutics 6 (Grand Rapids: Zondervan, 2005), 66–72; Luke Timothy Johnson, *The Gospel of Luke*, SP 3 (Collegeville, MN: Liturgical, 1991), 10; Brian S. Rosner, "Acts and Biblical History," in *The Book of Acts in its Ancient Literary Setting*, ed. Bruce W. Winter and Andrew D. Clarke, BAFCS 1 (Grand Rapids: Eerdmans, 1993; Carlisle: Paternoster, 1993), 65–82; and Gregory E. Sterling, *Historiography and Self-Definition: Josephos, Luke-Acts and Apologetic Historiography*, NovTSup 64 (Leiden: Brill, 1992), 363.

3. Scott Shauf, *The Divine in Acts and in Ancient Historiography* (Minneapolis: Fortress, 2015), 246.

4. Andreas J. Köstenberger and Richard D. Patterson, *Invitation to Biblical Interpretation: Exploring the Hermeneutical Triad of History, Literature, and Theology*, Invitation to Theological Studies (Grand Rapids: Kregel, 2011), 221.

5. Karl Allen Kuhn, *The Kingdom according to Luke and Acts: A Social, Literary, and Theological Introduction* (Grand Rapids: Baker Academic, 2015), 165.

6. Christopher J. H. Wright, "The Missional Nature and Role of Theological Education," pp. 225–54 in *Evangelical Scholarship, Retrospects and Prospects: Essays in Honor of Stanley N. Gundry*, ed. Dirk R. Buursma, Katya Covrett, and Verlyn D. Verbrugge (Grand Rapids: Zondervan, 2017), 225–26.

up to the time of the first century and as the record of God's mission in the early church during the first century but also as a resource for learning how God's mission can continue in the twenty-first century. We want to investigate Luke's Scripture-based message to us about the continuing mission of Jesus. We want to understand the message, be impacted by it, and participate in it.

EXAMINING THE STORY LUKE TELLS

For the sake of clarity, let me make plain that the word *story* in this book refers to the narrative nature of the writing. Acts is not a mere chronicle listing of past events pertaining to the first-century church; it is a meaningful story that Luke tells with intention.[7] While some people might use the term *story* to refer to fabricated narratives, the term is used here without that pejorative sense; indeed, I think of Acts as a true story. For many people the examination of the story Luke tells is motivated by their belief that his report is not a work of fiction but a meaningful account of historical events that can affect the stories of our own lives going forward.

Storytelling is an important literary art form. It involves various elements, like characters, settings, and plots. While technically not a whole-hearted literary approach to the book of Acts,[8] this survey of the book of Acts as the continuation of the Jesus story is laid out with some opening chapters discussing these kinds of literary elements (chapters 1–5). After these opening chapters, the story itself is surveyed by going through the book of Acts section by section, following a storytelling outline for Acts introduced in chapter 3. It traces the story of Jesus reaching the Jewish world (chapters 6–9) and the story of Jesus reaching the gentile world (chapters 10–15). A brief final chapter discusses how the Jesus story continues even in our own time and places today (chapter 16).

Each of the chapters of this book has basically the same structure. Each chapter begins with a list of its goals, a brief overview, and a listing of key verses pertaining to the content. After addressing the content material, each chapter has some concluding remarks, followed by a list of key people, places, and terms (which are given definitions in the glossary at the end of the book). Each chapter closes with a list of review or discussion questions, a list of optional assignments, and a bibliography of items for further reading and research.

The reader who already knows something about the New Testament will likely come across many familiar things in working through this survey of Acts. But I suspect they will discover much new material as well. And, as readers of the Bible—scholars

7. David R. Bauer, *The Book of Acts as Story: A Narrative-Critical Study* (Grand Rapids: Baker Academic, 2021), 2–3.

8. For an introduction to literary approaches to the interpretation of Scripture, see Douglas Mangum and Douglas Estes, eds. *Literary Approaches to the Bible*, Lexham Methods Series (Bellingham, WA: Lexham, 2017). For Acts in particular, see Bauer, *The Book of Acts as Story*.

and lay people alike—can attest, new insights and applications are regularly uncovered even in the study of familiar material. Indeed, that has been my experience in putting this survey together.

OPTIONAL ASSIGNMENTS

Some additional explanation may be in order for the section on optional assignments at the close of each chapter. Five kinds of assignments are offered:

1. **Text Reflection Project**—*Relating the concepts discussed in the chapter to another biblical text.* This assignment involves learning through research and reflective writing.
2. **Interview Project**—*Inquiring of others their views concerning the concepts discussed in the chapter.* This assignment involves learning through listening, perhaps with a reflective writing dimension or classroom reporting activity.
3. **Service-Learning Project**—*Applying the concepts discussed in the chapter in some form of service to others outside the class.* This assignment involves learning through doing, perhaps with a reflective writing dimension.
4. **Prayer Project**—*Talking with God about the concepts discussed in the chapter.* This assignment involves learning through writing a prayer that reflects on some of the concepts discussed in the chapter.
5. **Testimony Project**—*Telling others about the concepts discussed in the chapter.* This assignment involves learning through telling, perhaps with a reflective writing dimension.

Thus, these various projects suggest a variety of ways for students to continue their interaction with—and perhaps their application of—the material discussed in the chapter. No one professor using this textbook will want to utilize all the assignments in every chapter. Conversely, some of the assignments have thematic connections and may well be clustered together into larger student assignments. Thus, in regard to these optional assignments (as always!), students should heed the directions of their professor.

REGARDING BIBLIOGRAPHIES

In addition to the bibliographic footnotes found throughout this work, each of the chapters has its own categorized bibliography citing various journal articles, monographs, and reference volumes germane to that chapter's discussion. Unless otherwise marked, the ancient works referenced in this volume utilize the published editions of the *ANF*, LCL, *NPNF*[1], *NPNF*[2], *OTP*, and www.sefaria.org (for rabbinic writings).

Part 1

INTRODUCTION TO THE ACTS OF THE APOSTLES

In the study of any book of the Bible, it is common practice to devote some time and energy to the discussion of some basic background material helpful for properly understanding the book. This information regularly includes such things as the author and the intended recipient(s) of the book, proposed dates for when the book was written, the genre and purpose of the book, the structure and themes of the book, and any other issues for proper interpretation of the book. The first five chapters of this textbook are devoted to such introductory matters for understanding the Acts of the Apostles. While by no means as comprehensive as other works, five chapters may nevertheless seem like a lot for introducing one book of the New Testament.[1] Indeed, this might be too much information for some, but the way this introductory material is divided into specific portions will make selective use of it much easier (see sidebar).

The chapters cover the following areas of introduction: "Chapter 1: The People of Acts" covers the issues of the author and recipient(s) of the book of Acts, along with a brief discussion of some of the book's main characters. "Chapter 2: The Genre and Purpose of Acts" engages with the scholarly debates about the genre of the book of Acts, the various proposals for the book's intended purposes, and the trustworthiness of Acts as a historical record. "Chapter 3: Storytelling in Acts" addresses various suggested outlines for the book of Acts as well as some of the main techniques used in Acts for delivery of its message. This chapter also discusses some of the key theological themes of Acts. "Chapter 4: Interpreting and Applying Acts" continues the discussion of properly understanding the book of Acts, with more emphasis on bridging the two-thousand-year span and applying the principles in Acts. "Chapter 5: The Setting of Acts" focuses on understanding the historical-political, religious, and sociocultural background material that is helpful for reading Acts.

Covering Introductory Matters for Acts

Author: Section 1.1
Recipient(s): Section 1.2
Genre: Sections 2.1, 2.2, and 2.3
Purpose: Section 2.4
Historicity: Section 2.5
Structure: Section 3.1
Writing Techniques: Section 3.2
Theological Themes: Section 3.3
Dates: Section 4.1
Sources: Section 4.2
Text-Critical Issues: Section 4.3
Use of the Hebrew Bible: Section 4.4
Interpretation Issues: Section 4.5
Historical-Political Setting: Section 5.1
Religious Setting: Section 5.2
Sociocultural Setting: Section 5.3

1. Craig S. Keener, *Acts: An Exegetical Commentary*, 4 vols. (Grand Rapids: Baker Academic, 2012–2015), 1:1–638 has eighteen chapters of introductory material!

1 The People of Acts

Chapter Goals

After reading this chapter, you should be able to:

- Discuss who Luke is and why he is thought to be the writer of Acts.
- Appreciate Luke as an accurate, artistic first-century writer with an important message.
- Say something about the intended readership of Acts.
- Consider the book of Acts as written to impact real readers with its important message.
- Reflect on who the story of Acts is really about.
- Reflect on how the message of Acts is meant to impact you and your church.

Chapter Overview

1.1 The Storyteller of Acts: Who Is the Author of Acts?
1.2 The Recipients of Acts: Who Is Theophilus, and What about Us?
1.3 The Characters of Acts: Who Is the Story of Acts About?
1.4 Concluding Remarks
1.5 Key People, Places, and Terms
1.6 Questions for Review and Discussion
1.7 Optional Assignments
1.8 Bibliography for Going Further

Key Verses

Many have undertaken to draw up an account of the things that have been fulfilled among us, just as they were handed down to us by those who from the first were eyewitnesses and servants of the word. With this in mind, since I myself have carefully investigated everything from the beginning, I too decided to write an orderly account for you, most excellent Theophilus, so that you may know the certainty of the things you have been taught. (Luke 1:1–4)

In my former book, Theophilus, I wrote about all that Jesus began to do and to teach until the day he was taken up to heaven, after giving instructions through the Holy Spirit to the apostles he had chosen. (Acts 1:1–2)

My fellow prisoner Aristarchus sends you his greetings, as does Mark, the cousin of Barnabas. (You have received instructions about him; if he comes to you, welcome him.) Jesus, who is called Justus, also sends greetings. These are the only Jews among my co-workers for the kingdom of God, and they have proved a comfort to me. Epaphras, who is one of you and a servant of Christ Jesus, sends greetings. He is always wrestling in prayer for you, that you may stand firm in all the will of God, mature and fully assured. I vouch for him that he is working hard for you and for those at Laodicea and Hierapolis. Our dear friend Luke, the doctor, and Demas send greetings. (Col 4:10–14)

Do your best to come to me quickly, for Demas, because he loved this world, has deserted me and has gone to Thessalonica. Crescens has gone to Galatia, and Titus to Dalmatia. Only Luke is with me. Get Mark and bring him with you, because he is helpful to me in my ministry. I sent Tychicus to Ephesus. When you come, bring the cloak that I left with Carpus at Troas, and my scrolls, especially the parchments. (2 Tim 4:9–13)

Epaphras, my fellow prisoner in Christ Jesus, sends you greetings. And so do Mark, Aristarchus, Demas and Luke, my fellow workers. (Phlm 23–24)

INTRODUCTION

The author of the Acts of the Apostles shows himself to be particularly people oriented. He mentions some 110 names of individual people in Acts, besides over forty various people groups. There is not time and space here to work through the stories of all these individuals mentioned in Acts, but there are several key figures on whom to focus in this first chapter. These include the author of Acts, the named recipient of the book and the unnamed hearers and (later) readers of Acts, and the question of the main characters in the story.

1.1 THE STORYTELLER OF ACTS: WHO IS THE AUTHOR OF ACTS?

The author of the Acts of the Apostles is traditionally held to be the same person who authored the Third Gospel: Paul's "dear friend ***Luke***, the doctor" (Col 4:14, emphasis added), his "fellow worker" (Phlm 24), and his devoted companion ("Only Luke is with me"; 2 Tim 4:11). Neither of the books actually name Luke as the author; as with the other gospels, the title The Gospel According to Luke is not original to the writing but was added later. Although both the Third Gospel and Acts are unsigned, several pieces of internal (from within the two books) and external evidence (from outside the Third Gospel and Acts) support the traditional authorship claim. In the description of the author of Acts here, I address several areas of investigation and make appeals first primarily to several areas of internal evidence and then later more specifically to external evidence.

The NT Contributions of Different Writers

Percent of NT	Individual Authors' Contributions to the NT
27%	**Luke** (2 books): The Gospel of Luke and Acts
23%	**Paul** (13 letters): Romans, 1-2 Corinthians, Galatians, Ephesians, Philippians, Colossians, 1-2 Thessalonians, 1-2 Timothy, Titus, and Philemon
21%	**John** (2 books and 3 letters): The Gospel of John, 1-3 John, and Revelation
29%	**Other Writers** (2 books and 5 letters): The Gospel of Matthew, The Gospel of Mark, Hebrews, James, 1-2 Peter, Jude

By word count, the author of Luke-Acts contributes more material to the New Testament than any other writer. Paul comes close, but Luke still has a little more. Luke-Acts has 37,965 words in the Greek text; Paul (Romans-Philemon) has 32,440 words. Even if the anonymous Epistle to the Hebrews was written by Paul, it would add only 4,956 words to the Pauline count, so Luke has still written more (and some suspect that Luke wrote Hebrews!). Nevertheless, the friends and coworkers for the gospel Luke and Paul together contribute about half of the NT material.

1.1.1 THE AUTHOR'S WRITTEN WORKS

There is virtually universal agreement that the author of the Acts of the Apostles is also the author of the third canonical gospel, known now as the Gospel of Luke. Some have questioned the authorial connection between these two books of the New Testament, but those voices are overwhelmingly in the minority.[1] While not pointing

1. See Patricia Walters, *The Assumed Authorial Unity of Luke and Acts: A Reassessment of the Evidence*, SNTSMS 145 (Cambridge: Cambridge University Press, 2009).

us directly to Luke the physician, very strong internal evidence supports the claim that the Gospel of Luke and the book of Acts have the same author, i.e., the prologues, the themes, and the language and style of the two books.

Comparing the prologue to the Gospel of Luke (1:1–4) with the prologue to Acts (1:1–2), the reader easily sees four connections between the two volumes: (1) both books are dedicated to someone named Theophilus, (2) the author of Acts refers to having written a "former book" (1:1), (3) he summarizes the contents of his previous volume as being written about "all that Jesus began . . . until the day he was taken up" (1:1–2)—an apt summary of the Third Gospel, and (4) the preface to Acts bleeds into a narrative of Jesus's postresurrection days on earth up to his ascension, which fittingly overlaps with where the Third Gospel ends. These literary observations are often enough to convince readers that the two books have the same author; some even claim that these prologues (a.k.a. prefaces) suggest that the two books are actually two halves of one book, a single two-volume work that scholars sometimes call Luke-Acts (see the discussion in chapter 2).

The Third Gospel and the book of Acts share several common interests. In addition to the more obvious storyline themes in these two books (e.g., the life and ministry of Jesus the risen king, the completion of God's plan and purposes, the coming and work of the Holy Spirit, the calling and growing faith of Jesus's followers, etc.), the observant reader will note other similar themes such as gentiles, women, prayer, government officials, poverty and riches, etc. Furthermore, the collections of stories in Acts that parallel stories in the Third Gospel look like the intentional efforts of a single author (more on this in chapter 3).

Like the rest of the New Testament, the Third Gospel and Acts were written in Greek. Greek was the commonly utilized international language (or *lingua franca*) of the first-century world. While not as evident in our English translations, the various NT writers all display their own particular writing styles, and, as is well noted by scholars, the Third Gospel and Acts have some of the finest Greek in the New Testament (along with the Epistle to the Hebrews).[2] The cultivated Greek writing style of Luke and Acts is not properly called ***classical Greek*** (i.e., the Greek language as utilized in approximately 500–330 BC). While it still exhibits the features of ***Koine Greek*** (or Hellenistic Greek, i.e., the Greek language utilized as the "common" [*koinē*] international language throughout the world in 330 BC–AD 330), Luke's wide-ranging writing ability displays more refinement than that of the everyday style used in most of

---

2. See, for example, Albert Wifstrand, "Luke and Greek Classicism" and "Luke and the Septuagint" in *Epochs and Styles: Selected Writings on the New Testament, Greek Language and Greek Culture in the Post-Classical Era*, ed. Lars Rydbeck and Stanley E. Porter, trans. Denis Searby, WUNT 179 (Tübingen: Mohr Siebeck, 2005): 17–27 and 28–45, respectively, where Wifstrand remarks, "Luke has long been known and recognized as the most careful stylist among the four evangelists" (p. 17) and, "After the author of the Epistle to the Hebrews, Luke is regarded as the most literary of the authors of the New Testament" (p. 29).

the rest of the New Testament. Some of Luke's formal style is perhaps more attributable to his imitation of the style of the ***Septuagint*** than it is to his supposed imitation of the style of classical Greek authors.[3]

Various external evidence supports the tradition that the Third Gospel and Acts were authored by the same person (see section 1.1.8). But even by itself, this evidence from within the two books affirms the conclusion that they have one author.

1.1.2 The Author's Educational Background and Career

While not immediately evident by simply reading Luke-Acts, suggestions for the author's career or profession have included medical doctor and priest. The suggestion that the author of Luke-Acts was a priest will perhaps surprise some readers, but it is built on observing that his scriptural writing style displays an interest in the themes of the Hebrew Scriptures in the tradition of other priestly writers. Rick Strelan cautiously suggests that the author of Luke-Acts is best pictured in the mold of the OT author of 1–2 Chronicles (Ezra?) and the first-century Jewish historian Josephus, who were priests (see Ezra 7:1–10 and Josephus, *Ag. Ap.* 1.10 §§54–55), or even the Qumran figure who was dubbed the Teacher of Righteousness.[4] The Jewish priesthood was closely connected to the written Law and to the writing process, so if Luke was a priest, it would make sense for him to provide a written record of Jesus's interpretation of the Law and its impact on Jesus's followers.[5] Similarly, noting that the priests functioned as the preservationists of Israelite tradition, James Dawsey suggests that Luke writes with a comparable identity in his desire to pass on traditions about Jesus.[6] Nevertheless, such suggestive observations are hardly convincing that Luke was one of the Jewish ***priests***.[7]

The traditional view that Luke authored both the Third Gospel and the book of Acts points to Colossians 4:14 to demonstrate that Luke was a physician. Given Paul's evident health issues (e.g., Gal 4:13–15; cf. 2 Cor 12:7–10), Luke may well have served as Paul's personal physician.[8] On the other hand, in keeping with his proposal that Luke was a Jewish priest, Strelan argues that the label "physician" is used metaphorically,

---

3. See Wifstrand, "Luke and Greek Classicism," esp. 23.

4. Rick Strelan, *Luke the Priest: The Authority of the Author of the Third Gospel* (Burlington, VT: Ashgate, 2008; repr., New York: Routledge, 2016), esp. 17–19.

5. Ibid., 32.

6. James M. Dawsey, *The Lukan Voice: Confusion and Irony in the Gospel of Luke* (Macon: Mercer University Press, 1986), 109.

7. See the critique by L. Daniel Chrupcata, "Luke the Jew? Current Trajectories of Scholarship," pp. 1–22 in *Everyone Will See the Salvations of God: Studies in Lukan Theology*, SBFA 83 (Milan: Edizioni Terra Santa, 2015); Chrupcata suggests that using the same hermeneutical procedure could lead a person to conclude that Luke was a politician, a soldier, a sailor, or a geographer (p. 22).

8. See Adolf von Harnack, *Luke the Physician: The Author of the Third Gospel and the Acts of the Apostles*, trans. J. R. Wilkinson, New Testament Studies I (London: Williams and Norgate, 1908; New York: Putnam, 1909; repr., Eugene, OR: Wipf & Stock, 2009), 3n2; cf. William Kirk Hobart, *The Medical Language of St. Luke: A Proof from Internal Evidence*, Dublin University Press Series (Dublin: Hodges, Figgis, & Co., 1882), 292–97.

i.e., that Paul (and others) looked to Luke when they needed a diagnosis of their spiritual condition, their grasp of Scripture, or their understanding of the gospel.[9] Such a metaphorical reading, however, seems like an unnecessary stretch. Some have championed the idea that the medical terms in Luke and Acts support the idea of their author being a physician (e.g., Luke 4:35; 5:18; 9:38–39; 10:30–35; 18:25; Acts 3:7–8; 8:7; 9:33; 13:11; 14:8; 28:8–9), but such a thesis proves inconclusive because other ancient writers, including nonmedical professionals and literary authors, used the same sorts of medical language.[10] Nevertheless, the use of medical terminology by nonmedical writers is hardly conclusive proof that Luke the doctor was not the author of the Third Gospel and Acts.[11] On the contrary, these observations on the sophistication of his vocabulary and writing indicate that the author of these two volumes was most likely an educated person—which would include the possibility of a physician.[12]

Indeed, the training of a physician in antiquity was not limited to simple medical symptoms and possible cures; it included a wide variety of scientific information and sociological studies. According to A. H. N. Green-Armytage, a first-class doctor in Hellenistic times (i.e., in the world of 330 BC–AD 330, which had been thoroughly influenced by Greek language and culture) was likely better informed than any other class of educated people and also more capable of properly interpreting his information.[13] While Luke's writing evidences possible training in rhetoric and history,[14] Loveday Alexander's analysis of Luke's prologues places them by style and content into the scientific tradition more so than the historiography tradition (although the categories need not be mutually exclusive; see more on this in chapter 2).[15] As already noted, with Luke's comprehensive style and extensive vocabulary, the book of Acts along with

---

9. Strelan, *Luke the Priest*, 70.

10. See Hobart, *The Medical Language of St. Luke*, and the counter argument by Henry Joel Cadbury, *The Style and Literary Method of Luke*, 2 vols., HTS 6 (Cambridge: Harvard University Press, 1919–20).

11. Mikeal Parsons notes, "His students used to jest that Cadbury earned his doctorate by taking Luke's away. Still, we should not claim more for Cadbury's evidence than does Cadbury himself. Cadbury is careful to say that the so-called medical language cannot be used to prove that the author of the Third Gospel was a physician, but neither, he asserts, should Cadbury's own analysis be used to 'prove' that he was not. Subsequent critical scholarship has often heard the first caveat but not the second"; Mikeal C. Parsons, *Luke: Storyteller, Interpreter, Evangelist* (Peabody, MA: Hendrickson, 2007), 6.

12. Thus, Harnack offers a similar conclusion that "this great historical work was composed by a writer who either was a physician or was quite intimately acquainted with medical language and science"; Harnack, *Luke the Physician*, 14.

13. A. H. N. Green-Armytage, *A Portrait of St. Luke* (London: Burns and Oates, 1955; Chicago Henry Regnery, 1955), 34–35.

14. Noted, for example, by Jacob Jervell, "The Future of the Past: Luke's Vision of Salvation History and Its Bearing on His Writing of History," pp. 104–26 in *History, Literature and Society in the Book of Acts*, ed. Ben Witherington III (Cambridge: Cambridge University Press, 1996), 125. For an exhaustive study, see Steve Reece, *The Formal Education of the Author of Luke-Acts*, LNTS 669 (New York: T&T Clark, 2022).

15. See Loveday C. A. Alexander, *The Preface to Luke's Gospel: Literary Convention and Social Context in Luke 1.1–4 and Acts 1.1*, SNTSMS 78 (Cambridge: Cambridge University Press, 1993) and idem, "Luke's Preface in the Pattern of Greek Preface-Writing," *NovT* 28 (1986): 48–74 (esp. p. 69).

the Gospel of Luke displays some of the best Greek in the New Testament. Thus, the author of Luke-Acts shows himself to be well educated, and he is likewise concerned to educate his audience well. In this way the traditional suggestion that the author of Luke-Acts was a physician seems to fit agreeably with the evidence.

1.1.3 Where the Author Was From

Various attempts at identifying the author of Luke and Acts have made suggestions as to where he was from or where he was residing when he wrote these books. Among the various hometown theories, a more persistent and somewhat ancient tradition claims that the author of Luke-Acts was a gentile from ***Antioch of Syria***, which (according to Josephus, *J.W.* 3.2.4 §29) was the third largest city in the first-century world. A set of second-century introductory notes to the Gospels called the ***Anti-Marcionite Prologues*** (see section 1.1.8) introduces the Gospel of Luke with the words, "The holy Luke is an Antiochene, Syrian by race . . ." Similarly, the fourth-century bishop Eusebius reports that Luke was "of Antiochian parentage" (*Hist. eccl.* 3.4.7). Further hints at this tradition come from within the book of Acts itself, particularly passages with certain emphases on the city of Antioch (e.g., Acts 6:5; 11:19–30; 13:1–3; 14:26–28; 15:35–40; and 18:22–23).[16] An expansion of Acts 11:28 into a "we section" in the Western text also suggests at least Luke's presence in Antioch on that occasion if not also lending support to the tradition that Antioch was Luke's place of origin.

Various suggestions have also been made for where the author of Luke and Acts resided when he wrote these two books. These include Boeotia in Achaia (Greece), Caesarea, Corinth, Ephesus, Macedonia, Syrian Antioch, and Rome. Some have suggested that the Gospel of Luke was written in the east (perhaps in Antioch or during Paul's two-year imprisonment in Caesarea) and that Acts was written in Rome.[17] Indeed, given that the story of Acts comes to such an abrupt end in Rome—with Paul under house arrest and awaiting trial—this seems to be a good guess as to where Acts was finally composed. While we do not know this for sure, this view has the support of Irenaeus (ca. AD 130–200), Eusebius (ca. AD 260–340), and Jerome (ca. AD 347–420).[18]

1.1.4 The Author's Ethnic Background

Most scholars consider Luke a gentile, especially given his thematic interest in gentiles in both the Third Gospel and Acts. This is a fitting understanding of Paul's

16. See Richard T. Glover, "'Luke the Antiochene' and Acts," *NTS* 11 (1964): 97–106.

17. The issue of two different editions of Luke and Acts is caught up in this discussion as well. See, for example, Friedrich Blass, "The Question of the Double Text in St. Luke's Gospel and in the Acts," pp. 96–112 in *Philology of the Gospels* (London: Macmillan, 1898; repr., Chicago: Argonaut, 1969), esp. 100–104.

18. See Irenaeus, *Haer* 3.1.1; 3.14.1; Eusebius, *Hist. eccl.* 2.22.6; and Jerome, *Vir. ill.* 7; *Epist.* 53.9. See more on the abrupt ending of Acts in chapter 15.

description of Luke as someone outside those "of the circumcision group" in Colossians 4:10–14 (see NIV notes). If Luke were a native of Syrian Antioch, then many assume he had to have been a gentile, but this need not be the case. Antioch had a sizable Jewish community in the first century, and Josephus notes that "Jewish residents in Antioch are called Antiochenes" (*Ag. Ap.* 2.4 §39; cf. *Ant.* 12.3.1 §§119–24).

Indeed, a few scholars have suggested that Luke was a ***Jew***, and this suggestion has early representation in the third century (e.g., Hippolytus, *On the Seventy Apostles*, 15) and the fourth century (Epiphanius of Salamis, *Panarion*, 51.11.6–7). John Wenham has utilized several such ancient suggestions to make an extended argument that the author of the Third Gospel and Acts may well have been a man of Jewish birth (see the sidebar). The internal evidence supporting the potential Jewish nationality of the author of Luke-Acts includes his familiarity with Israel's sacred tradition, his ability to mimic the Hebrew Scriptures, his concern for some level of scriptural piety, and the possibility that he was acquainted with some of the writings found among the Dead Sea Scrolls.[19]

Nevertheless, a writer's firm understanding of Judaism and sympathy for Jewish interests do not necessitate that he be of Jewish birth (any more than facility in the use of the Greek language proves him to be a gentile). In fact, in Acts 1:19 the author seems to identify himself as non-Jewish when he gives the Semitic name of Judas's field and comments that it is in "their" language, i.e., the language of the Jews and not his own.[20]

The Author of Luke-Acts as One of the Seventy (or Seventy-Two) Disciples?

John Wenham has made an extended argument that the author of the Third Gospel and Acts may well have been a Hellenistic Jew among the seventy (or seventy-two) disciples sent by Jesus in Luke 10. He makes several other NT connections in his suggested description of the author of Luke-Acts. But in the end, however, Wenham admits, "I make no pretence to have proved my case, but to me it is a substantial one" ("The Identification of Luke," 44).

Wenham suggests that Luke was:

- Luke the physician (in Col 4:14; Phlm 24; 2 Tim 4:11),
- a Hellenistic Jew who was one of the seventy sent-out disciples (in Luke 10),
- one of the disciples on the road to Emmaus (in Luke 24),
- the same person as Lucius the Cyrene (in Acts 13:1),
- a relative of the apostle Paul ("kinsmen" [ESV], not mere "fellow Jews" [NIV], in Rom 16:21), and
- the "brother" responsible for a written (not merely preached) gospel (in 2 Cor 8:18–19).

See John Wenham, "The Identification of Luke," *EvQ* 63 (1991): 3–44; cf. idem, *Redating Matthew, Mark & Luke: A Fresh Assault on the Synoptic Problem* (London: Hodder & Stoughton, 1991), 234–36.

19. Kuhn, *The Kingdom according to Luke and Acts*, 60–63; cf. idem, *Luke: The Elite Evangelist*, Paul's Social Network: Brothers and Sisters in Faith (Collegeville, MN: Liturgical Press, 2010), 102–3.

20. Darrell L. Bock, "Luke, Gospel of," *DJG*[1], 496.

Furthermore, if the author of Luke-Acts is indeed the physician Luke of Colossians 4:10–14, it seems that he was most likely a ***gentile***, for the smoothest way to take this passage is to understand Luke as apart from those among Paul's coworkers identified as being Jewish. That is, Paul names several people present with him—Aristarchus, Mark, and Justus—remarking that they "are the only Jews among my co-workers for the kingdom of God" (Col 4:10–11). Then in the next three verses, Paul lists several additional coworkers present with him—Epaphras, Luke the doctor, and Demas—who are apparently not Jewish (Col 4:12–14).[21] Rather than prove him Jewish, Luke's tremendous familiarity with Judaism and the Hebrew Scriptures evidences his good education and perhaps even his affiliation with those called God-fearers (i.e., gentiles who wanted to worship the God of the Jews).

1.1.5 The Author's Relationship to the Apostle Paul

The traditional view is that the author of Luke-Acts accompanied the apostle Paul on several of his missionary travels. By far the most palpable internal evidence in Acts that supports a connection between its author and the apostle Paul is the presence of several ***"we sections."*** While narrating the story of Paul, in several places (i.e., Acts 16:10–17; 20:5–15; 21:1–18; 27:1–28:16) the author unexpectedly switches from using third person pronouns (e.g., they went there, he said this, etc.) to using first person plural pronouns (e.g., we decided this, then we went there, etc.). While various literary theories have been developed to explain this phenomenon (see chapter 4), the simplest and oldest explanation is that they indicate the writer was a companion of Paul at these points in the story.

Paul had a number of companions other than Luke who might have authored the Third Gospel and Acts. These include those mentioned in the Pauline epistles: e.g., Timothy (Rom 16:21; Phil 1:1; Col 1:1; 1 Thess 1:1; 2 Thess 1:1; Phlm 1); Lucius, Jason, and Sosipater (Rom 16:21); Gaius (Rom 16:23; 1 Cor 1:14); Sosthenes (1 Cor 1:1); Silas (2 Cor 1:19; 1 Thess 1:1; 2 Thess 1:1); Titus (2 Cor 8:23 et al.; Gal 2:1; 2 Tim 4:10); Tychicus (Eph 6:21; Col 4:7; 2 Tim 4:12; Titus 3:12); Epaphroditus (Phil 2:25; 4:18); Epaphras (Col 1:7; 4:12; Phlm 23); Aristarchus (Col 4:10; Phlm 24); Mark the cousin of Barnabas (Col 4:10; 2 Tim 4:11; Phlm 24); Jesus called Justus (Col 4:11); Demas (Col 4:14; 2 Tim 4:10; Phlm 24); Crescens (2 Tim 4:10); and Trophimus (2 Tim 4:20). Some of these are easy to eliminate from consideration. For example, the author of Acts mentions Aristarchus (Phlm 24; Col 4:10) as "with us" (Acts 27:2),

21. Countering this reading, some scholars have suggested that the men "of the circumcision" in Col 4:10–14 might have been ritually strict Jewish Christians and that those not "of the circumcision" were less strict Jews; see Strelan, *Luke the Priest*, 105; Edward Carus Selwyn, *St. Luke the Prophet* (London: Macmillan, 1901), 37n1, 38n1; cf. xxiii; idem, "The Carefulness of Luke the Prophet," *Expositor* 7 (1909): 547–58; Edward Earle Ellis, *The Gospel of Luke*, rev. ed. NCBC (London: Marshall, Morgan & Scott, 1974; repr., Grand Rapids: Eerdmans, 1981), 52–53; and Ralph P. Martin, *Colossians: The Church's Lord and the Christian's Liberty* (Exeter: Paternoster, 1972), 146.

and thus the two are distinct. Likewise, in Acts 16:19, Paul and Silas are thrown in the Philippian jail, but the author does not use the authorial "we" of vv. 10–17. Similarly, Sopater, Aristarchus, Secundus, Gaius, Timothy, Tychicus, and Trophimus went on ahead "and waited for us at Troas" (Acts 20:4–5), which rules out each of them as the author. Conversely, Demas deserted Paul "because he loved this world" (2 Tim 4:10) and is thus not likely a NT writer. It seems that all of Paul's leading associates can be eliminated in this fashion except for Titus and Luke, as neither are named in Acts (see sidebar).[22] While arguably less notable than Titus, Aristarchus is named no less than three times in Acts and is twice named with Luke in Paul's letters. This observation leads some scholars to favor Luke over Titus as the sometimes coworker of Paul who authored Acts.[23]

The conclusion that the author of Acts was actually one of Paul's fellow workers troubles many scholars. They notice that the presentation of Paul in Acts does not always match up well with the presentation Paul offers of himself in his epistles. But this need not mean that the author of Luke-Acts did not know Paul. As writers with different purposes and with different genres, it is not surprising that Luke and Paul would have different focuses. On the contrary, there are several commonalities of themes and even of language between Luke-Acts and Paul's letters (see the sidebar on this in chapter 4). So the differences between the Paul of Acts and the Paul of the Epistles may be differences of what is included and emphasized, but such differences do not necessitate contradictions.

1.1.6 The Author's Social Location

Where did the author of Luke-Acts fit in the social setting of his world? He seems to place himself among the second generation of believers. That is, while the "we sections" of Acts indicate that he accompanied Paul in some of his missionary travels, the prologue to the Gospel of Luke draws a distinction between the author and the original eyewitnesses to the life and ministry of Jesus. There he indicates that testimony to the ministry of Jesus was "handed down to us by those who from the first were eyewitnesses and servants of the word" (Luke 1:2). In other words, the author himself is clear that he was not a firsthand witness to the earthly life and ministry of Jesus, but he learned these things in hearing from those who were firsthand witnesses as he conducted his research. And so the author of Luke-Acts indicates his apostolicity. Scholars today use the term *apostolicity* to refer to the connection NT books have with the apostolic generation. Some books were written by members of the original Twelve, including Matthew (his gospel), John (his gospel, three letters, and Revelation), and Peter (two letters).

22. Wilber T. Dayton, "Luke," *ZEB* 3:1125 notes further that some scholars suspect that Luke and Titus were brothers (see 2 Cor 8:17–18; 12:18), which would help explain the silence of Acts about Titus.

23. See Harnack, *Luke the Physician*, 12.

Ministry Companions Mentioned in Acts and Paul's Letters

This list of gospel ministers is similar to, but more extensive than, the listing in Keener, *Acts*, 1:243; cf. the very different charting in E. Earle Ellis, "Coworkers, Paul and His," *DPL*, 184.

People	Acts	Pauline Letters
Peter/Cephas	1–12 passim; 15:7–11	1 Cor 1:12; 3:22; 9:5; 15:5; Gal 1:18; 2:7–11, 14
John	1:13; 3:1–11; 4:6, 13, 19; 8:14; 12:2	Gal 2:9
Barnabas	9:27; 11:22, 30; 12:25–15:38	1 Cor 9:6; Gal 2:1, 9, 13; Col 4:10
John Mark	12:12, 25; 13:5, 13; 15:37–39	Col 4:10; Phlm 24; 2 Tim 4:11
James, brother of Jesus	12:17; 15:13; 21:18	1 Cor 15:7; Gal 1:19; 2:9, 12
Lucius	13:1	Rom 16:21
Silas/Silvanus	15:22–18:5	2 Cor 1:19; 1 Thess 1:1; 2 Thess 1:1
Timothy	16:1; 17:14–15; 18:5; 19:22; 20:4	Rom 16:21; 1 Cor 4:17; 16:10; 2 Cor 1:1, 19; Phil 1:1; 2:19–23; Col 1:1; 1 Thess 1:1; 2 Thess 1:1; passim
Jason	17:5–9	Rom 16:21
Aquila & Priscilla/ Prisca	18:2, 18, 26	Rom 16:3; 1 Cor 16:19; 2 Tim 4:19
Crispus	18:8	1 Cor 1:14
Sosthenes	18:17	1 Cor 1:1
Apollos	18:24, 27; 19:1	1 Cor 1:12; 3:4–6, 22; 4:6; 16:12; Titus 3:13
Erastus	19:22	Rom 16:23; 2 Tim 4:20
Gaius	19:29; 20:4	Rom 16:23; 1 Cor 1:14
Aristarchus	19:29; 20:4; 27:2	Col 4:10; Phlm 24
Tychicus	20:4	Eph 6:21; Col 4:7; 2 Tim 4:12; Titus 3:12
Sopater/Sosipater	20:4	Rom 16:21
Trophimus	20:4; 21:29	2 Tim 4:20

Ministry Companions of Paul Not Mentioned in Acts

Achaicus	1 Cor 16:17	*Luke*	Col 4:14; Phlm 24; 2 Tim 4:11
Andronicus	Rom 16:7	*Mary*	Rom 16:6
Apphia	Phlm 2	*Onesimus*	Col 4:9; Phlm 10
Archippus	Col 4:17; Phlm 2	*Persis*	Rom 16:12
Artemas	Titus 3:12	*Philemon*	Phlm 1
Claudia	2 Tim 4:21	*Phoebe*	Rom 16:1
Clement	Phil 4:3	*Pudens*	2 Tim 4:21
Crescens	2 Tim 4:10	*Quartus*	Rom 16:23
Demas	Col 4:14; Phlm 24; cf. 2 Tim 4:10	*Stephanas*	1 Cor 1:16; 16:15, 17
Epaphras	Col 1:7; 4:12; Phlm 23	*Syntyche*	Phil 4:2
Epaphroditus	Phil 2:25; 4:18	*Tertius*	Rom 16:22
Eubulus	2 Tim 4:21	*Titus*	Gal 2:1–3; 2 Cor 2:13; 7:6–16; 8:6, 16–24; 12:18; 2 Tim 4:10; Titus 1:4
Euodia	Phil 4:2		
Fortunatus	1 Cor 16:17	*Tryphena*	Rom 16:12
Junia	Rom 16:7	*Tryphosa*	Rom 16:12
Jesus Justus	Col 4:11	*Urbanus*	Rom 16:9
Linus	2 Tim 4:21	*Zenas*	Titus 3:13

Some books were written by believers closely affiliated with the apostles: Mark, Luke, Paul, James, Jude, and the anonymous author of Hebrews.[24]

Nevertheless, the author of Luke-Acts writes as more than a mere gatherer of stories told by others. Rather, he claims some authoritative role as a writer who has researched his material well (cf. Luke 1:1–4), and his scriptural writing style (mentioned previously) seems to indicate an intention to write the continuation of biblical history. Pointing to the significant "witness" theme in Luke-Acts fanning out from the prologue of Luke 1:1–4, Michael Kruger outlines five points of evidence indicating the author's awareness that his written records hold authentic apostolic authority in the life of the church.[25] This evidence includes (a) the ***inclusio***—i.e., the literary device where an author states an idea at both the beginning and the end of a section—of references to witnesses in the gospel (Luke 1:2; 24:48); (b) the parallel descriptions of the apostles as

24. For more on the formation of the NT canon, see esp. the works of Michael J. Kruger, including *Canon Revisited: Establishing the Origins and Authority of the New Testament Books* (Wheaton, IL: Crossway, 2012), and idem, *The Question of Canon: Challenging the Status Quo in the New Testament Debate* (Downers Grove, IL: InterVarsity Press, 2013). For a brief survey treatment, see Kenneth Berding, "New Testament Canon: Recognizing the Authoritative Writings," in *What the New Testament Authors Really Cared About: A Survey of Their Writings*, ed. Kenneth Berding and Matt Williams, 2nd ed. (Grand Rapids: Kregel, 2015), 315–20. I address Acts becoming part of the NT canon in chapter 16.

25. Kruger, *The Question of Canon,* 121; my paragraph here summarizes Kruger's five-point argument on pp. 139–43.

Luke's Location in the Second Generation of Christians

In the prologue to his gospel, Luke acknowledges that he gets much of his information from those who were "eyewitnesses" to the events. This puts Luke in the second generation of Jesus followers, passing the information on to those in his own and succeeding generations. In the book of Acts, however, several times Luke utilizes the first person personal pronoun *we*, indicating his presence at some of the events (see Acts 16:10-17; 20:5-15; 21:1-18; 27:1-28:16; these "we sections" are examined further in chapter 4).

Luke 1:1-4

Many have undertaken to draw up an account of the things that have been fulfilled among us, just as they were handed down to us by those who from the first were eyewitnesses and servants of the word. With this in mind, since I myself have carefully investigated everything from the beginning, I too decided to write an orderly account for you, most excellent Theophilus, so that you may know the certainty of the things you have been taught.

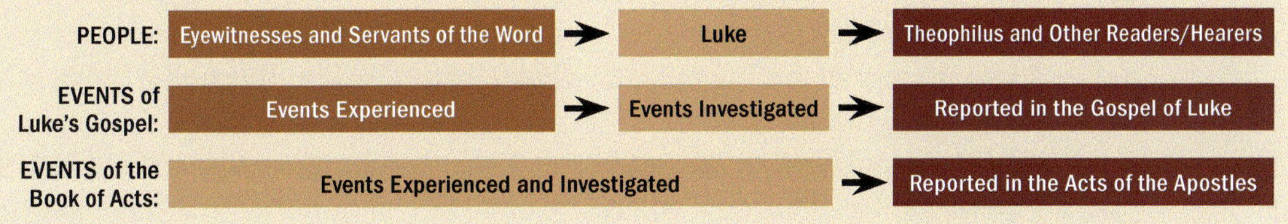

witnesses from the beginning (Luke 1:2; Acts 1:22; cf. 10:36–43); (c) the commission of Paul as a "servant and as a witness," forming something of a grand *inclusio* across all of Luke-Acts (Luke 1:2; Acts 26:16); (d) the description of the apostles as those devoted to "the ministry of the word" echoing their description as "servants of the word" (Luke 1:2; Acts 6:4);[26] and (e) the "handed down" family of terms (Luke 1:2 has the Greek *paradidōmi*; cf. *paradosis*) is regularly used elsewhere in the New Testament to reference the passing along of apostolic tradition (e.g., 1 Cor 11:2, 23; 15:3; 2 Thess 2:15; 3:6; Jude 3). All this suggests a self-consciousness on the part of the author of Luke-Acts to be writing with some sense of authority as he records the continuation of biblical history.[27]

26. Note that the term "the word" (*ho logos*) is regularly used in the New Testament in referring to the authoritative apostolic message; see Michael W. Pahl, "The 'Gospel' and the 'Word': Exploring Some Early Christian Patterns," *JSNT* 29 (2006): 211–27; cf. Joseph A. Fitzmyer, *The Gospel According to Luke: Introduction, Translation, and Notes*, 2 vols., AB 28 (New York: Doubleday, 1982, 1985), 1:295.

27. See also Strelan, *Luke the Priest*, 21–25, who summarizes, "Luke sees himself doing what these others have done—delivering the tradition. He does so in written form. He claims an authority equal to that of the 'eyewitnesses and ministers of the word'" (pp. 23–24). See also Nils Dahl, "The Story of Abraham in Luke-Acts," pp. 139–58 in *Studies in Luke-Acts: Essays Presented in Honor of Paul Schubert*, ed. Leander E. Keck and Louis J. Martyn (Nashville: Abingdon, 1966; repr., Philadelphia: Fortress, 1980), 152–53; and Craig A. Evans, "Gospels and Midrash: And Introduction to Luke and Scripture: The Question of Genre," in *Luke and Scripture: The Function of Sacred Tradition in Luke-Acts*, ed. Craig A. Evans and James A. Sanders (Minneapolis: Fortress, 1993), 1–4.

In first-century society, the author of Luke-Acts is undoubtedly in the small percentage of literate citizens (around 10 percent).[28] Furthermore, in addition to his general literary expertise, many of the nuances of his writing—particularly his portrayal of the Roman elite—betray the author's intimate familiarity with the upper crust of society.[29] Moreover, the production of Luke-Acts would have been a costly process given first-century book publishing practices. These two books—amounting to more than 25 percent of the New Testament—would have each taken a whole scroll of handwritten work. Thus, this writer somehow had access to the necessary funding or influence for such an expensive undertaking.[30]

None of these observations necessitates the conclusion that the writer himself held a social status among the elite of his day or that he himself was rich.[31] Rather, his written work suggests that he had connections in those realms, and an interesting implication of this is how the author of Luke-Acts chose to invest himself as a Jesus follower in his particular network. The central place of written Scripture and other literature in Christian communities seems to have eventually resulted in a certain appeal among some of the Roman elite who highly valued reading and writing.[32] And instead of leveraging his acquaintances to support the status quo and to maintain a thoroughly tiered society, the author of Luke-Acts evidences a concern that the gospel message cross these tiers and that Christian communities function unencumbered by them. As a gentile making a significant literary contribution early in the Jewish Christian movement, the author can be of great encouragement and hope for those who feel marginalized in today's church.[33] As with his relationship to the apostles and eyewitnesses before him, whatever his connections with society's elite, the author utilized his associations in service of the spread of the gospel.[34]

---

28. See William V. Harris, *Ancient Literacy* (Cambridge: Harvard University Press, 1989), 173, 284. Catherine Hezser suggests that the literacy rates in first-century Palestine were even lower than the 10 percent estimate for general Roman society; Catherine Hezser, *Jewish Literacy in Roman Palestine*, Texts and Studies in Ancient Palestine 81 (Tübingen: Mohr Siebeck, 2001), 496–504; cf. 188.

29. Kuhn, *The Kingdom according to Luke and Acts*, 59–60; cf. idem, *Luke: The Elite Evangelist*, 71–73.

30. So Strelan, *Luke the Priest*, 55. On the costs associated with ancient book production and writing see, for example, Arthur G. Patzia, *The Making of the New Testament: Origin, Collection, Text, and Canon*, 2nd ed. (Downers Grove, IL: InterVarsity Press, 2011), 197–98.

31. The highly stratified social domains in the first-century Greco-Roman world were complex and sometimes involved competing valuations along such lines as honor and shame, wealth and poverty, power and submission, etc. Thus, while some generalizations might be helpful as broad guidelines, care must be taken with terms like *class* and *status* so as not to reduce them to simplistic suppositions that, for example, a person of "high status" was necessarily wealthy or that a person with "good connections" was also politically powerful. See chapter 5 for more detail.

32. John S. Kloppenborg, "The Attraction of Roman Élite to the Christ Movement," pp. 263–80 in *Talking God in Society: Multidisciplinary (Re)Constructions of Ancient (Con)Texts, Festschrift Peter Lampe*, vol. 1: *Theories and Applications*, ed. Ute Eva Eisen and Heidrun E. Mader, NTOA/SUNT 120a (Göttingen: Vandenhoeck & Ruprecht, 2021), 274–76.

33. E.g., see Esau McCaulley, *Reading While Black: African American Biblical Interpretation as an Exercise in Hope* (Downers Grove, IL: IVP Academic, 2020), 74–77.

34. For an extended discussion of this idea, see Dominique DuBois Gilliard, *Subversive Witness: Scripture's Call to Leverage Position* (Grand Rapids: Zondervan Reflective, 2021).

1.1.7 The Author as Artist

There is a long-standing tradition that the author of Luke and Acts was an artistic painter, and some ancient paintings have been attributed to his hand. While the origins of this tradition are unclear, Heidi Hornik and Mikeal Parsons suggest two factors that may have contributed to this connection with the visual arts.[35] First, the writer's unmistakable literary artistry—i.e., his skillful use of language, his colorful commentary in the midst of realistic reporting, his ability to provide both detailed descriptions and smooth, flowing summaries—may imply that the author of Luke-Acts also had talents in more literal productions of art.[36] Second, all the paintings attributed to "Luke" are images of Mary; thus, as the NT author who says more about Mary than any other, the author of Luke-Acts was a natural candidate for someone who would have known what Mary actually looked like. A third factor is related to the artistic aspects of the medical field in which the proposed author of Luke-Acts was involved, for drawing may well have been part of ancient medical training.[37]

As it is, hundreds of images of Mary with the Christ child have been attributed to "Luke," even though these works of art most often date to centuries after Luke's lifetime. They are purported copies of Luke's original work and (perhaps analogous to copies of the written works of an author) are nevertheless attributed to the first-century author-artist himself. Furthermore, the tradition that this man was the original Christian painter and inventor of iconography has led to Luke being recognized as the patron saint of artists.

Theotokos of Tikhvin (ca. AD 1300)

A Copy of the Hodegetria ("She Who Shows the Way")

Luke is thought to have been the inventor of painted icons featuring the Virgin Mary with the Christ child. One such painting has Mary gesturing to an adult-looking infant. The supposed original *Hodegetria* ("she who shows the way") has been lost, but hundreds of copies, similar to this one from the Russian city of Tikhvin, are nonetheless still attributed to Luke.

Theotokos of Tikhvin (ca. AD 1300), a copy of the Hodegetria ("She Who Shows the Way")
BAHADIR YENICERI/stock.adobe.com

35. Heidi J. Hornik and Mikeal C. Parsons, "Luke the Physician, Painter, Patron Saint," pp. 11–27 in *The Infancy Narrative in Italian Renaissance Painting*, vol. 1 of *Illuminating Luke* (Harrisburg, PA: Trinity Press International, 2003), 19; cf. Michele Bacci, *Il pennello dell'Evangelista: Storia delle immagini sacre attribuite a san Luca*, Piccola Biblioteca Gisem 14 (Pisa: Gisem, 1998); and Giordana Canova Mariani, ed., *Luca Evangelista: Parola e Immagine tra Oriente e Occidente* (Padova: Il Poligrafo, 2000).

36. Robert J. Karris gives a nod to Luke's literary artistry in the title of his book, *Luke, Artist and Theologian: Luke's Passion Account as Literature*, Theological Inquiries (New York: Paulist, 1985).

37. See Green-Armytage, *A Portrait of St. Luke*, 34.

Icon of the Blessed Virgin Mary (ca. AD 300s)

Credited to Luke and on display at the Syriac Orthodox Monastery of Saint Mark in Jerusalem, this painting has Mary holding a miniaturized adult Jesus on her lap. Dating to the fourth century AD, the painting has since been adorned with several gold features. Miracles and miraculous signs are reported to have taken place as people have prayed in the presence of the icon. Noteworthy is that this Monastery of Saint Mark is so named because tradition claims it is located on the site of the house owned by John Mark's mother where the early believers gathered to pray for Peter to be released (Acts 12:12).

Public domain

St. Luke Portraying the Virgin (ca. AD 1435–1440)

This oil and tempera on oak panel painting by Rogier van der Weyden is thought to have been commissioned for the chapel of the painters' guild, Cathedral of St. Michael and St. Gudula in Brussels (where Van der Weyden is buried). As known from his other self-portrait work, the artist put his own image on the face of Luke in this painting! It is now housed in the Museum of Fine Arts, Boston.

St. Luke Portraying the Virgin (ca. AD 1435–40)
INTERFOTO / Alamy Stock Photo

During the Renaissance period, a popular subject matter for paintings was the image of Luke painting or drawing a portrait of Mary posing with the Christ child. Sometimes these paintings were intended to be hung above altars maintained by artists at their local church sanctuaries.[38] Moreover, some artists even painted the face of Luke with their own image in its place, demonstrating their pride in being associated with

38. Craig Harbison, *The Mirror of the Artist: Northern Renaissance Art in Its Historical Context* (New York: Harry N. Abrams, 1995), 10.

Paintings of Luke Painting (ca. AD 1300s)

The tradition of Luke as the original painter of icons led to Luke being a favorite subject of paintings in the art world. Many of these feature Luke painting his signature icon of the Virgin Mary with the Christ child. Note the similarities between the *Hodegetria* and the artwork on the easel in this fourteenth-century painting.

The Picture Art Collection / Alamy Stock Photo

St. Luke Painting the Virgin (ca. AD 1565)

This fresco by Giorgio Vasari is in the artists' chapel, the Cappella di San Luca, in Santissima Annunziata, a church in Florence, Italy. Note the traditional ox image representing Luke. Vasari (like others before him) painted his own image on the face of Luke.

St. Luke Painting the Virgin (ca. AD 1565)

Sailko/CC BY 3.0

this particular evangelist and perhaps their desire to emulate him.[39] The Renaissance painters of Florence, who belonged to the guild of doctors and pharmacists, further congealed the connection of traditions about the artistic and medical background of the author of Luke-Acts. This pairing of professions was due in part to the shared practice of grinding materials (i.e., for the artists' paint colors and for the pharmacists' medicines) but also in part to them sharing Luke as their patron saint.[40] A statue of St. Luke stands in a niche of Orsanmichele, the fourteenth-century chapel of Florence's craft and trade guilds.

39. Hornik and Parsons, "Luke the Physician, Painter, Patron Saint," 17; cf. Harbison, *The Mirror of the Artist*, 10, 102.

40. Hornik and Parsons, "Luke the Physician, Painter, Patron Saint," 19.

A Sculpture of Luke (AD 1601)

A (copy of a) bronze statue of St. Luke sculpted by Giambologna (AD 1601) is positioned in a niche of Orsanmichele, the chapel of craft and trade guilds in Florence, Italy. There Luke is noted as the patron saint of the guild of magistrates and notaries.

A Sculpture of Luke by Giambologna (AD 1601). Orsanmichele Church and Museum, Florence.
ArTono/Shutterstock.com

How historical is the tradition that the author of Luke and Acts was also a painter? For our purposes here, the internal evidence of the Gospel of Luke and the book of Acts demonstrates only the author's literary artistry, which is far more important to our immediate project than determining his status as a painter. While legends make claims that the author of Luke-Acts was a painter, our focus here is his written record of the truth about Jesus and the early church in Acts.[41]

1.1.8 External Evidence

Several pieces of authorship evidence outside the Third Gospel and Acts have already been mentioned in the previous discussion, but a few more comments are worth mentioning. These are all additional literary references that point specifically to Luke the physician as author of the Third Gospel and Acts. This external evidence can be grouped into four categories: a canon list, a prologue identification, manuscript evidence, and references by early church fathers.

The ***Muratorian Canon*** is a list of books from the latter part of the second century (dating to AD 170–180) that discusses the writings of the New Testament.[42] It is preserved in Latin translation in a fragmentary seventh- or eighth-century document.[43] This list attributes both the Third Gospel and Acts to Luke. Some have questioned the second-century dating of the Muratorian Canon,[44] but the Lukan authorship of the Third Gospel and Acts has the support of several other, independent second-century testimonies.

41. Similarly, Dayton, "Luke," *ZEB* 3:1125.

42. The term *canon* means "measure" and refers to the list of books recognized by the church as measuring up to be God's authoritative word to humanity. The Muratorian Canon is an example of an early list of NT books.

43. The Latin text of the Muratorian Canon can be readily accessed in Kurt Aland, ed., *Synopsis Quattuor Evangeliorum*, 13th ed. (Stuttgart: Deutsche Bibelgesellschaft, 1985), 538.

44. See Albert C. Sundberg Jr., "Canon Muratori: A Fourth-Century List," *HTR* 66 (1973): 1–41; idem., "Muratorian Fragment," *IDBSup*, 609–10; and Geoffrey Mark Hahneman, *The Muratorian Fragment and the Development of the Canon* (Oxford: Clarendon, 1992); cf. Gregory Allen Robbins, "Muratorian Canon," *NIDB* 4:165. But in favoring the earlier, second-century dating, see the devastating response of Everett Ferguson, "Canon Muratori: Date and Provenance," *Studia Patristica* 17 (1982): 677–83; cf. Harry Y. Gamble, *The New Testament Canon: Its Making and Meaning*, GBS (Philadelphia: Fortress, 1985), 32. See also Bruce M. Metzger, *The Canon of the New Testament: Its Origin, Development, and Significance* (Oxford: Clarendon, 1987), 191–201.

The Muratorian Canon on Luke and Acts

Discovered in the Ambrosian Library in Milan by Ludovico Antonio Muratori (1672–1750), this list of NT books in a fragmentary document of eighty-five lines in Latin represents a translation of an original document that dates back to as early as the late second century AD. This list comments on the various NT books and identifies Luke the physician as author of the Third Gospel (in lines 2–8) and the Acts of the Apostles (in lines 34–39). The translation here of the portions pertaining to Luke and Acts is from Harry Y. Gamble, *The New Testament Canon: Its Making and Meaning*, GBS (Philadelphia: Fortress, 1985), 93–94.

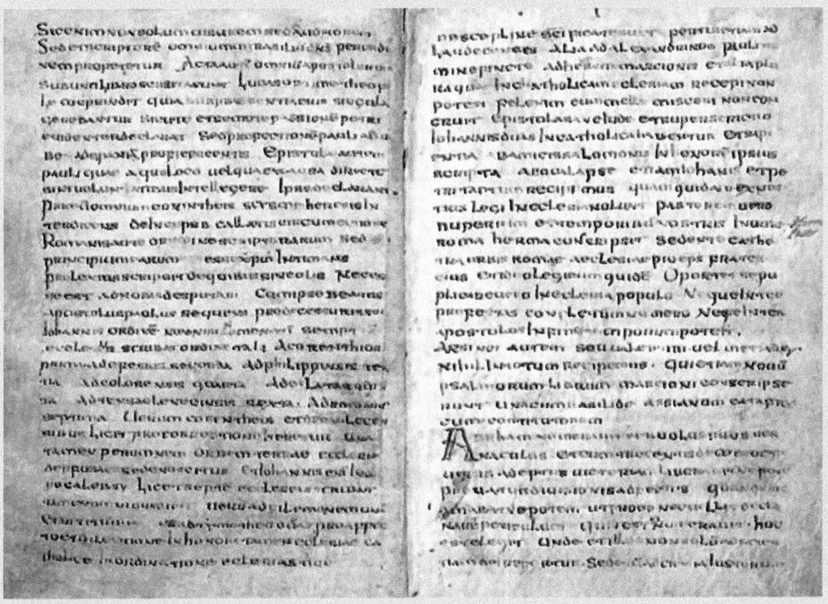

The Muratorian Canon

The Picture Art Collection / Alamy Stock Photo

The third Gospel book, that according to Luke.

This physician Luke after Christ's ascension,

since Paul had taken him with him as a companion of his travels,

composed it in his own name

according to his thinking. Yet neither did he himself

see the Lord in the flesh, and thus as he was able to ascertain it,

so he also begins to tell the story from the birth of John.

. . .

The acts of all the apostles, however,

were written in one volume. Luke summarized "for most excellent Theophilus"

particular things which happened in his own presence,

as he also clearly indicates by omitting the martyrdom of Peter

as well as the departure of Paul from the city

[of Rome] as he proceeded to Spain.

The Anti-Marcionite Prologue to the Third Gospel

This introduction to the Third Gospel is preserved in Latin and Greek documents; the English translation here is that of Ben C. Smith, accessed February 13, 2024, http://prenicea.net/doc2/29951-en-01.pdf (page 10).

> The holy Luke is an Antiochene, Syrian by race, physician by trade. As his writings indicate, of the Greek speech he was not ignorant. He was a disciple of the apostles, and afterward followed Paul until his confession, serving the Lord undistractedly, for he neither had any wife nor procreated sons. [A man] of eighty-four years, he slept in Thebes, the metropolis of Boeotia, full of the holy spirit. He, when the gospels were already written down, that according to Matthew in Judea, but that according to Mark in Italy, instigated by the holy spirit, in parts of Achaea wrote down this gospel, he who was taught not only by the apostle, who was not with the Lord in the flesh, but also by the other apostles, who were with the Lord, even making clear this very thing himself in the preface, that the others were written down before his, and that it was necessary that he accurately expound for the gentile faithful the entire economy in his narrative, lest they, detained by Jewish fables, be held by a sole desire for the law, or lest, seduced by heretical fables and stupid instigations, they slip away from the truth. It being necessary, then, immediately in the beginning we receive report of the nativity of John, who is the beginning of the gospel, who was the forerunner of our Lord Jesus Christ, and a partaker in the perfecting of the people, and also in the induction of baptism, and a partaker of his passion and of the fellowship of the spirit. Zechariah the prophet, one of the twelve, made mention of this economy. And indeed afterward this same Luke wrote the Acts of the Apostles. And later John the apostle from the twelve first wrote down the apocalypse on the isle of Patmos, then the gospel in Asia.

From roughly the same time period as the Muratorian Canon comes some introductory remarks prefaced to copies of the Gospels. Because they speak against the interpretations of Marcion, these are referred to as ***Anti-Marcionite Prologues***, and only those for Mark, Luke, and John are extant. Originally composed in Greek, these extrabiblical prologues might be compared to such introductions in modern study Bibles; they are not intended to be understood as part of the original texts of the biblical books but as introductions to them. The Anti-Marcionite Prologue to the Third Gospel refers to the writer of the Third Gospel and Acts as Luke, a Syrian from Antioch, a physician by profession, a disciple of the apostles, and a follower of Paul (see sidebar).

Manuscript P^{75}: Bodmer Papyrus XIV–XV

This papyrus codex, dating to AD 175–225, is the oldest extant Greek manuscript of the Third Gospel and has the first occurrence of the title Gospel According to Luke:

ΕΥΑΓΓΕΛΙΟΝ
ΚΑΤΑ
ΛΟΥΚΑΝ

This is interestingly placed at the end of the book and immediately before the title and subsequent text of the Gospel of John.

The manuscript P^{75} is made of ***papyrus***, i.e., an ancient kind of paper made from strips of the papyrus reed. It is a ***codex***, i.e., a manuscript with leaf pages in book form rather than a scroll form or single pages. It is written in ***Koine Greek***, i.e., the Greek "common" to the era between ancient (or classical) and modern Greek. And even those who don't know Greek can see that it is written in a style known as ***scripta continua***, i.e., with no spaces or markings between the words and sentences.

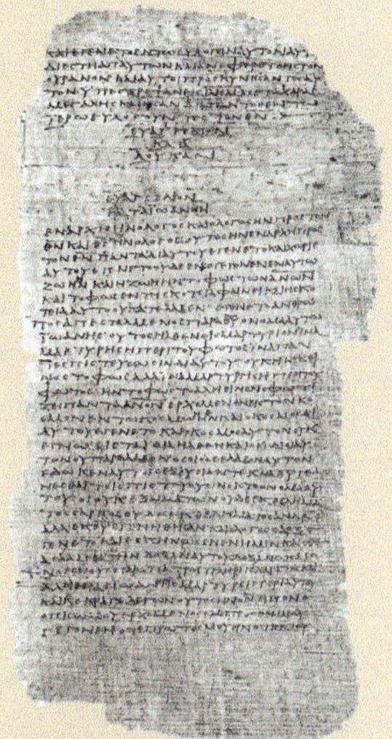

As with the Muratorian Canon, the second-century dating of the Anti-Marcionite Prologue to the Third Gospel has been questioned.[45] Some scholars have proposed a later fourth-century or early fifth-century date for this work, but such a later date may well apply to the final edited version we now possess without negating that the first version was written in Greek in the second century. The prologues to Mark and John are preserved only in Latin, but one manuscript does, in fact, preserve the Anti-Marcionite Prologue to Luke in Greek.[46]

---

45. See R. G. Heard, "The Old Gospel Prologues," *JTS* ns 6 (1955): 1–16, esp. p. 16; and Jürgen Regul, *Die antimarcionistischen Evangelienprologe*, VL 6 (Freiburg: Herder, 1969), esp. pp. 266–67.

46. See Joseph A. Fitzmyer, *Luke the Theologian: Aspects of His Teaching* (New York: Paulist, 1989), 9. Perhaps complicating this dating issue is the existence of another prologue statement similar to the anti-Marcionite Prologue. Known as the Monarchian Prologue, it is also difficult to date but likely comes from the fourth century (AD 330–350):

> Luke, Syrian by nationality, an Antiochene, physician by art, disciple of the apostles, later followed Paul up until his confession, serving God without fault. For, never having either a wife or sons, he died in Bithynia at seventy-four years of age, full of the holy spirit. When the gospels through Matthew in Judea, through Mark, however, in Italy, had already been written, he wrote this gospel at the instigation of the holy spirit in the regions of Achaea, he himself also signifying in the beginning that others had been written beforehand. . . . To this not immeritorious Luke was given the power in his ministry of writing also the acts of the apostles.

This English translation is that of Ben C. Smith, accessed February 13, 2024, at http://prenicea.net/doc2/29951-en-01.pdf (page 10). The Latin text of this Monarchian Prologue can be readily accessed in Aland, ed., *Synopsis Quattuor Evangeliorum*, 538–39.

Early Testimony to Luke as Author of the Third Gospel & Acts

Eusebius (ca. AD 260–340) served as bishop of Caesarea Maritima in the early fourth century and is thus referred to as Eusebius of Caesarea. He is sometimes referred to as the first historian of the Christian church—an ascription that seems to disregard the Acts of the Apostles.

Eusebius, *Ecclesiastical History*, 3.4.6–7 (ca. AD 323)

> Luke, who was by race an Antiochian and a physician by profession, was long a companion of Paul and had careful conversation with the other Apostles, and in two books left us examples of the medicine for souls which he had gained from them—the Gospel, which he testifies that he had planned according to the tradition received by him by those who were from the beginning eyewitnesses and ministers of the word, all of whom he says, moreover, he had followed from the beginning, and the Acts of the Apostles which he composed no longer on the evidence of hearing but of his own eyes. And they say that Paul was actually accustomed to quote from Luke's Gospel since when writing of some Gospel as his own he used to say, "According to my Gospel."
>
> (See also Eusebius, *Hist. eccl.* 3.4.1–11; 3.24.15; and 6.25.10.)

Dating to AD 175–225, the manuscript ***P***[75] (a.k.a. the ***Bodmer Papyrus XIV–XV***) is the oldest extant Greek manuscript of the Third Gospel. It has the first occurrence of the title Gospel According to Luke interestingly placed at the end of the book. Such titles were not original to any of the gospels but seem to have become more common in manuscripts toward the end of the second century, perhaps reflecting that the traditional authorship views were already commonly held positions by that time.[47]

Early church fathers are those Christian leaders from the first few centuries after Christ (the title "apostolic fathers" is given to the church fathers of the first two centuries who might have known some of the original twelve apostles). Among these early Christian leaders, several have written works that identify Luke as author of both the Third Gospel and the book of Acts.[48] These include several apostolic church fathers such as Irenaeus (ca. AD 130–200), Clement of Alexandria (ca. AD 150–215), Tertullian (ca. AD 155–240), and Origen (ca. AD 184–254).

---

47. Fitzmyer, *Luke*, 1:36.

48. For a convenient collection of many of these texts—with both transcriptions of the original language and an English translation—see Henry Joel Cadbury, "The Tradition," in *The Beginnings of Christianity*, part 1: *The Acts of the Apostles*, ed. Frederick John Foakes-Jackson and Kirsopp Lake, 5 vols. (London: Macmillan, 1920–33; repr., Grand Rapids: Baker, 1979), 2:209–64, esp. 212–45.

The Teachings of Church Tradition

We use the word *tradition* to refer to the handing down of Christian faith—both its teachings and practices—from one generation to another in the church. This term is sometimes viewed with suspicion, and rightly so when human preferences in tradition are given precedence over and against the clear teaching of Scripture. Jesus warned against this (Matt 15:1-9; Mark 7:1-13), as did Paul (see Gal 1:13-14; Col 2:8). Nevertheless, we must recognize that handing down true Christian teaching from one generation to another is God's design: it was God's intention for OT Israel (e.g., Deut 6:4-9; Jer 6:16) and is seen at work in the New Testament (e.g., 1 Cor 11:2, 23; 15:3-8; 2 Thess 2:15; 3:6; 2 Tim 2:2). Such careful and faithful handing down of truth is, in fact, how Luke describes his own writing (Luke 1:1-4). So in this way some sense of "tradition" is good and even unavoidable. It can be a helpful tool—even viewed as God's provision—that, rightly utilized, can fill voids where literary and archaeological evidence is lacking. But tradition is not inerrant and must always be submissive to Scripture. As Anthony Lane notes, "Valuable as tradition may be, it is not infallible and must be tested by Scripture. Scripture is well suited to this normative role since it remains fixed, while tradition is constantly changing. . . . [T]he authority of both church and tradition . . . is real but limited, in that both are subject to the word of God in Scripture. They are open to be reformed and corrected, while Scripture is not."*

*Anthony N. S. Lane, "Tradition," *DTIB*, 812 (cf. 809-12).

Writings of later church fathers that continue to attribute the Third Gospel and Acts to Luke include *The Teaching of the Apostles* (ca. AD 230), Pamphilus of Caesarea (died AD 309), Jerome (ca. AD 347–420), *Apostolic Constitutions* (ca. AD 375–380), Epiphanius of Salamis (ca. 310/320–403), Chromatius, bishop of Aquileia (ca. AD 345–407), John Chrysostom, bishop of Antioch (ca. AD 349–407), and Pseudo-Athanasius (ca. fifth century?). Of particular note is Eusebius (ca. AD 260–340), the fourth-century bishop of Caesarea Maritima. Eusebius was a historian who is sometimes dubbed the father of church history (although some scholars think that moniker should go to Luke![49]). He regularly refers to Luke as the author of the Third Gospel and of Acts (see the sample in the sidebar). Given this lineup of testimonies by early church fathers, we can confidently conclude that, by the close of the second

49. See, for example, Martin Dibelius, *The Book of Acts: Form, Style, and Theology*, ed. K. C. Hanson, Fortress Classics in Biblical Studies (Minneapolis: Fortress, 2004), 5; F. F. Bruce, "The First Church Historian," in *Church, Word, and Spirit: Historical and Theological Essays in Honor of Geoffrey W. Bromiley*, ed. J. E. Bradley and R. A. Miller (Grand Rapids: Eerdmans, 1987), 1–14; and Daniel Marguerat, *The First Christian Historian: Writing the 'Acts of the Apostles,'* trans. Ken McKinney, Gregory J. Laughery, and Richard Bauckham, SNTSMS 121 (Cambridge: Cambridge University Press, 2002).

century, Christians widely held Luke to be the author of both the Third Gospel and Acts and that the two books were consequently titled accordingly.[50]

1.1.9 Conclusions on the Author of Acts

How much does knowing the precise identity of the author of Acts matter? It should not matter more to us than it did to the author himself—who has left both of his books unsigned. From his prologue to the Gospel of Luke and reflected in his prologue to Acts, we see that the author's primary concern was to confirm for his audience the truth of historical events about Jesus and his followers. This concern for accuracy and assurance outweighed any desire to reveal his identity. Nevertheless, some readers find further reassurance in seeing how the evidence stacks up for the author having close connections to the original eyewitnesses to the life and ministry of Jesus and to the apostle Paul.

Overall, the internal evidence fits well with the tradition that the first-century physician Luke, the sometimes companion of Paul, wrote the book of Acts. It seems clear enough that the author of Acts was likely the same as the author of the Third Gospel, an educated person who was a fellow traveler with Paul on several missionary journeys. There is little reason to doubt the early church tradition that identifies Luke—an otherwise seemingly insignificant person—as the author of both the Third Gospel and Acts. While these deductions may be less than conclusive to some, I nevertheless find them compelling enough to accept (at least tentatively) the traditional view, and I regularly refer to the author of the Third Gospel and Acts as Luke.

1.2 THE RECIPIENTS OF ACTS: WHO IS THEOPHILUS, AND WHAT ABOUT US?

Both the Gospel of Luke and Acts are directly addressed to one ***Theophilus***. These are the only uses of this name in the New Testament. Various theories have been proposed regarding this especially named recipient of Luke's writings.

1.2.1 A Symbolic Address?

Some have suggested that Luke used "Theophilus" as a catchy moniker for any reader who is a "God lover" or "beloved by God" or "friend of God," as the name most woodenly might connote (*theos* for "God" + *philos* for "friend"). That Luke was addressing any "friend of God" is an ancient suggestion. Origen (ca. AD 184–254) remarked, "Someone might think that Luke addressed the Gospel to a specific man named Theophilus. But, if you are the sort of people God can love, then all of you

50. Similarly, Strelan, *Luke the Priest*, 78.

who hear us speaking are Theophiluses, and the Gospel is addressed to you."[51] Some modern scholars have been attracted to this thought.[52]

Nevertheless, such symbolic dedications to books were not common in ancient writing.[53] While the "friend of God" adjective is used frequently by the first-century Jewish writers Philo (over sixty times) and Josephus (twelve times) as a descriptor of a person's character, it never occurs as a form of direct address.[54] Furthermore, the name Theophilus is found for real people in the ancient world, particularly among Jews outside Israel.[55] Thus, there is no compelling reason to suspect that Luke's use of the name Theophilus is merely symbolic.[56]

1.2.2 An Actual Individual

Despite the attractiveness of the symbolic address theory, Theophilus is an actual name evidenced as early as the third century BC in papyri and inscriptions, including among first-century Jews.[57] Furthermore, Theophilus being addressed as "most excellent" (*kratiste*; Luke 1:3) implies that the named recipient of Luke's writings was a real person known to Luke or someone of sufficient reputation that Luke could address him in this way. For example, the second-century letter from the Christian Mathetes to the non-Christian Diognetus also opens by addressing its recipient as "most excellent" (*kratiste*). Even as Felix the governor of Judea (Acts 23:26; 24:3) and his successor Festus (Acts 26:25) are addressed in this fashion, perhaps Theophilus was a person of some notable rank or office.[58]

Nevertheless, it seems unlikely that a Roman official in the first century would go by "Theophilus" in public. But if he were a public figure of some kind, perhaps this name served as a pseudonym or alias for him; it might even have been an adopted

---

51. Origen, *Homilies on Luke, Fragments on Luke*, trans. Joseph T. Lienhard, FC 94 (Washington, DC: Catholic University of America Press, 1996), 1.6. See also Ambrose, *Exp. Luc.*, 1.12.

52. E.g., Barbara Shellard, *New Light on Luke: Its Purpose, Sources, and Literary Context*, JSNTSup 215 (Sheffield: Sheffield Academic Press, 2002), 51n69; cf. the playfulness of Mikeal C. Parsons, *Acts*, Paideia Commentaries on the New Testament (Grand Rapids: Baker Academic, 2008), 26–27: "To imitate the authorial audience of Acts, the real reader must assume the posture of Theophilus, a 'lover of God.'"

53. Alexander, *The Preface to Luke's Gospel*, 188.

54. For example, Philo uses the *theophil-* adjective to describe as "dear to God" such people as Noah (*Abraham* 5 §27), Abraham (*Abraham* 19 §89), Jacob (*Joseph* 28 §167 and 33 §200), Moses (*Alleg. Interp.* 1.24 §76; 2.23 §90; *Moses* 2.13 §67; et al.), and the Israelites (*Migration* 20 §114); and Josephus uses the adjective for Isaac (*Ant.* 1.22.1 §346), David (*Ant.* 6.13.2 §280), Elisha (*Ant.* 19.8.6 §183), Daniel (*Ant.* 10.11.7 §264), the Israelites (*J.W.* 5.9.4 §382); and even Herod the Great (*Ant.* 14.15.11 §455; *J.W.* 1.17.4 §331).

55. Christopher Francis Evans, *Saint Luke*, TPINTC (London: SCM, 1990; Philadelphia: Trinity Press International, 1990), 134.

56. See Fitzmyer, *Luke*, 1:299–300; Alexander, *The Preface to Luke's Gospel*, 187–88.

57. See Richard Anderson, "Theophilus: A Proposal," *EvQ* 69 (1997): 195–215.

58. See Kuhn, *The Kingdom according to Luke and Acts*, 60; and Martin Hengel, *The Four Gospels and the One Gospel of Jesus Christ* (Harrisburg, PA: Trinity Press International, 2000), 102. It is possible to use the address "most excellent" (*kratiste*) in a less formal and more friendly manner; see Alexander, *The Preface to Luke's Gospel*, 188–90.

(or baptismal) name among Christians.[59] Even apart from such proposals, R. Robert Creech has argued that a real person—whatever his true identity—lies behind the name Theophilus as the actual first reader of Luke and Acts. From clues in Luke's storytelling, Creech's summary portrait is that Theophilus was an educated, Greek-speaking gentile familiar with Rome and a God-fearer knowing a Hellenistic Judaism (having never traveled to Palestine) but interested in Christianity's offer for gentiles to be included in God's people.[60] Over the years various suggestions have been made for the true identity of Theophilus (see sidebar).[61]

1.2.3 A Dedication Statement

Without denying that Theophilus was a real person, most scholars suggest that Luke's naming of him serves as an honorary dedication statement. In this way, Theophilus would be an individual recipient of Luke's writings who nevertheless serves as a surrogate for, or representative of, a wider audience.[62] It was not at all uncommon to have a larger audience in mind for a book and yet to dedicate it to an individual person, especially if that person was paying for the book's publication. Given this kind of patronage practice among many ancient authors, the idea that Theophilus might have been Luke's "publisher" is quite common among Lukan scholars.[63]

A commonly noted parallel to Luke's two-part dedication to Theophilus in Luke and Acts is found in the two-volume first-century work by Josephus known as *Against Apion*. Josephus dedicates these to "most excellent Epaphroditus" in volume 1 (*Ag. Ap.* 1.1 §1) and "my most esteemed Epaphroditus" in volume 2 (*Ag. Ap.* 2.1 §1).[64]

59. Arthur M. Ross, "Theophilus," *ZEB* 5:830; cf. Hengel, *The Four Gospels*, 102; Werner G. Marx, "A New Theophilus," *EvQ* 52 (1980): 18; contra, Craig S. Keener, *Acts: An Exegetical Commentary*, 4 vols. (Grand Rapids: Baker Academic, 2012–2015), 1:657; David G. Peterson, *The Acts of the Apostles*, Pillar New Testament Commentary (Grand Rapids: Eerdmans, 2009), 102.

60. R. Robert Creech, "The Most Excellent Narratee: The Significance of Theophilus in Luke-Acts," in *With Steadfast Purpose: Essays on Acts in Honor of Henry Jackson Flanders, Jr.*, ed. Naymond H. Keathley (Waco: Baylor University Press, 1990), 107–26, esp. 122–23.

61. My list of suggestions for the true identity of Theophilus is inspired by that of Marx, "A New Theophilus," 18–19; Marx argues at length for Theophilus to be identified as King Herod Agrippa II.

62. See Paul S. Minear, "Dear Theo: The Kerygmatic Intention and Claim of the Book of Acts," *Int* 27 (1973): 131–50.

63. See, for example, Edgar J. Goodspeed, "Some Greek Notes: I. Was Theophilus Luke's Publisher?" *JBL* 73 (1954): 84; Dibelius, *The Book of Acts: Form, Style, and Theology*, 25 and 54–56; Ernst Haenchen, *The Acts of the Apostles: A Commentary*, trans. and ed. Bernard Noble, Gerald Shinn, Hugh Anderson, and R. McLeod Wilson (Philadelphia: Westminster, 1971), 136n3, cf. n4; I. Howard Marshall, *Luke: Historian and Theologian*, 3rd ed. (Carlisle: Paternoster, 1988; repr., New Testament Profiles, Downers Grove, IL: InterVarsity Press, 1998), 38; Harry Y. Gamble, *Books and Readers in the Early Church: A History of Early Christian Texts* (New Haven, CT: Yale University Press, 1995), 102; Ben Witherington III, *The Acts of the Apostles: A Socio-Rhetorical Commentary* (Grand Rapids: Eerdmans, 1998; Carlisle: Paternoster, 1998), 13–14; Peterson, *Acts*, 102; Keener, *Acts*, 1:656; Eckhard J. Schnabel, *Acts*, ZECNT (Grand Rapids: Zondervan, 2012), 70; and Carl R. Holladay, *Acts: A Commentary*, NTL (Louisville: Westminster John Knox, 2016), 73.

64. For other reiterated prefaces in ancient works, see Philo's *Moses* 2.1.1; and *Spec. Laws* 2.1.1.

Suggestions for the Identity of Theophilus

- Theophilus, the Jewish high priest in AD 37–41 and brother-in-law to Caiaphas, fits Luke's first-century time period as well as the name itself (see Josephus, *Ant.* 18.5.3 §123; 19.6.2 §297).
- Theophilus, an official in Athens, was convicted of perjury by the Areopagus council. This suggestion seems to fit with a tradition that claims Luke wrote while in Achaia and Boeotia (see Tacitus, *Ann.* 2.55; and Jerome, *Comm. Matt.*, preface).
- The Roman official Sergius Paulus, proconsul of Cyprus, could have been given the name Theophilus by Luke as a protective pseudonym after he became a believer (see Acts 13:7–12).
- Lucius Junius Annaeus Gallio, the brother of Seneca, is another Roman official mentioned in Acts, but he shows little interest in Christianity (see Acts 18:12–17).
- Theophilus, a bishop of Antioch, died around AD 183–85. While this fits with the tradition that Luke was from Antioch, he is at least one hundred years too late for Luke's named reader.
- Titus Flavius Clemens, nephew of Roman Emperor Vespasian and heir apparent of Emperor Domitian, may have been executed in Rome (in AD 95 just prior to the assassination of Domitian in AD 96) because of his apparent interests in Christianity, for his wife Domitilla was a Christian.
- Philo Judaeus, the famed first-century Jewish writer who lived in Alexandria, Egypt, has the Hebrew name *Yadîdyâ*, which is roughly equivalent to "Theophilus."
- King Herod Agrippa II (Marcus Julius Agrippa) is mentioned at some length in Acts, and Luke shows him to be knowledgeable about (although resistant to) Christianity (Acts 25–26).
- Of course, Theophilus could also have been someone otherwise unknown in recorded history.

But this does not mean that Luke or Josephus intended their books to be read by just one person. In fact, Josephus closes his second volume of *Against Apion* with a reiterated dedication to Epaphroditus that explicitly expresses his intention for a wider audience: "To you, Epaphroditus, who are a devoted lover of truth, and for your sake to any who, like you, may wish to know the facts about our race, I beg to dedicate this and the preceding book" (*Ag. Ap.* 2.41 §296). Similarly, Luke can certainly dedicate his work to Theophilus precisely because he intends to address Theophilus's questions and leave him an accurate record of the Jesus tradition, all of which he also intends to be useful to a wider audience. By writing for the specific person Theophilus, Luke writes for any others who have questions and concerns similar to those of Theophilus.[65]

1.2.4 A Christian or a Non-Christian?

Scholars are divided as to whether Theophilus was already a Christian when Luke wrote to him. Given the evangelistic nature of the Gospel of Luke, which is structured in such a way as to bring the reader to faith in Jesus as the Christ, it makes sense to understand Theophilus as an inquiring unbeliever at the receipt of Luke's first book. The book of Acts is certainly unambiguous about the gospel message regarding Jesus as the Christ, but its emphasis seems to be more on encouraging the church to continue its mission of spreading that gospel message. Intriguingly, the greeting in the preface to Acts reiterates the name Theophilus without repeating the honorary title "most excellent" that was utilized in the gospel prologue. Could it be that Theophilus—a respected Roman official of some kind—was not a believer when the Gospel of Luke was written but had become a friend and even a fellow Christian when the book of Acts was penned?[66] Given the nuanced emphases of Luke's two books and this slight change in the preface addresses, this is an attractive proposition.

1.2.5 An Intended Gentile Readership?

It is often remarked that the Gospel of Luke was written for gentiles. Certainly, Luke's inclusion of several stories about ministry to non-Jewish audiences by Jesus in the gospel and by the early church in Acts, as well as other themes, demonstrates his concern for gentiles (see sidebar). And his explanation of who the Pharisees and Sadducees were (e.g., Acts 23:6–8; cf. Luke 20:27) is evidence that Luke is concerned to be understood by a gentile readership.

Nevertheless, a close examination of Luke's writing shows that he also has a deep interest in communicating with Jewish readers (see sidebar). He utilizes the Hebrew Scriptures and is respectful of the Jewish way of life. For all his interest in making known that the gospel message is intended to be inclusive of gentiles, Luke is just as clear that this gospel message is tied to the Hebrew Scriptures. Even the dedication statement to someone with the Greek name Theophilus does not prove that he was writing to a gentile audience, as this name (and other Greek names) were regularly taken by Jewish people in the first century.

---

65. On this dedication idea, see the nuanced and even contrary discussions of Roman Garrison, *The Significance of Theophilus as Luke's Reader*, Studies in the Bible and Early Christianity 62 (Lewiston, NY: Mellen, 2004), esp. 22–28; Strelan, *Luke the Priest*, 36, cf. 55–56; and Marx, "A New Theophilus," 17.

66. Ross, "Theophilus," *ZEB* 5:830. Ross suggests also the possibility that Theophilus might have given up his Roman office or even been forced out upon giving a profession of Christian faith. Keener (*Acts*, 1:65) remarks, "Theophilus was almost certainly a Christian."

Evidence of Luke's Interest in Gentiles

The following features of Luke-Acts suggest that Luke writes with an interest in gentile readers.

- Luke uses various phrases that indicate a universal interest: e.g., "all the people" (Luke 2:10, 31); "all people" (lit. "flesh"; Luke 3:6; Acts 2:17); "all nations" (Luke 24:47; Acts 14:16; 17:26); "ends of the earth" (Luke 11:31; Acts 1:8; 13:47).
- At his infancy, the salvation Jesus was to bring was recognized as "a light for revelation to the Gentiles" (Luke 2:30–32).
- Luke alone extends the citation of Isaiah 40:3–5 all the way to include the phrase "And all people will see God's salvation" (Luke 3:4–6; cf. Matt 3:3; Mark 1:3; John 1:23).
- In Jesus's Nazareth sermon, only Luke recounts the references to the OT ministries that Elijah and Elisha had with gentiles (Luke 4:16–30; cf. Matt 13:53–58; Mark 6:1–6).
- Luke is more affirming of ministry to gentiles even during the ministry of Jesus (e.g., Luke 7:1–10; cf. Matt 8:5–13).
- Luke includes a number of positive stories about Samaritans (e.g., Luke 9:52–56; 10:33; 17:16; Acts 8:25).
- Much of the narrative of Acts shows gentiles believing in Jesus (e.g., Acts 8:4–17; 10:1–48; 11:19–26; 16:11–34; 17:1–4, 34; 21:19–25) and makes explicit argument for the inclusion of gentiles in the church (e.g., Acts 11:1–18; 15:1–35).

Thus, we should be cautious about turning all such observations into overstatements about Luke's intentions. While both the Gospel of Luke and Acts show particular interest in the expansion of the gospel message to include all nations, the author also incorporates a number of Jewish elements in both of his volumes. Conversely, arguments against a gentile audience for Luke-Acts due to the author's constant use of Hebrew Scriptures seem to miss that gentile Christians—by virtue of coming to faith in Jesus as the Messiah foretold in the Hebrew Scriptures—would also quickly recognize them as authoritative texts for their Christian faith. The NT message is greatly indebted to Judaism and the Hebrew Scriptures. This Jewishness is not at all lost on Luke, the most prolific gentile contributor to the New Testament. In the end, we might best say that Luke is sensitive to a gentile audience without intending to limit his works to a gentile audience. It should be evident that Luke-Acts appeals to both Jews and gentiles. And as our study unfolds, we will see that the subject matter of Acts demonstrates Luke's interest in community audiences and not merely individual readers.

Evidence of Luke's Interest in Jews

The following features of Luke-Acts suggest that Luke writes with an interest in Jewish readers.

- As is immediately evident in Luke 1–2, Luke's presentation of Jesus as the Messiah is the most Jewish such presentation in all the New Testament.
- Rather than the word "church" (*ekklēsia*), Luke prefers to use the word "people" (*laos*) for the church. This is a Jewish way of referring to the people of God.
- Luke notes that the promises of salvation are given to Israel and those belonging to the people of God; while some within Israel reject salvation, the promises are never taken away from the people. Luke recounts several mass conversions of Jews and some of individual God-fearers, but he reports none of large crowds of gentiles.
- As it does for Jews, the law of God has full validity for Luke (e.g., Luke 16:16–17; Acts 24:14–16; 25:8; 28:23; cf. 10:43; 17:2–3; 18:28). Fulfilling the law of Moses never brings remission of sins and salvation—which is not a Jewish concept either (e.g., Acts 13:38–39); but keeping God's law is what God's people find themselves doing.
- While Luke occasionally explains a Jewish concept or custom, most often he does not; yet he includes many such Jewish words, conceptions, and customs throughout Luke-Acts.
- Luke presents Paul as very Jewish, as the Pharisee par excellence and not as an ex-Pharisee. The charges against Paul in Acts 22–28 are about his Jewish beliefs in Scripture and the resurrection—noticeably difficult ideas for the gentiles within the story.
- While capable of writing classical Greek (evident in Luke 1:1–4), Luke writes in a biblical Greek style reflective of the Septuagint (LXX), a Greek translation of the Hebrew Scriptures.

This list is an adaptation from Jacob Jervell, "Retrospect and Prospect in Luke-Acts Interpretation," in *The Society of Biblical Literature 1991 Seminar Papers*, ed. Eugene H. Lovering Jr., SBLSP 30 (Chico, CA: Scholars Press, 1991), 384–86.

1.3 THE CHARACTERS OF ACTS: WHO IS THE STORY OF ACTS ABOUT?

In both the Gospel of Luke and the book of Acts, Luke seldom introduces any individual to whom he does not give a name.[67] This might complicate the answer to the question, Who is the story of Acts about? Nevertheless, I think this question can be addressed with some brevity.

1.3.1 The Apostles

At the close of the Gospel of Luke, the twelve ***apostles*** had been reduced in number to only eleven. While Luke occasionally refers to the apostles as "the Twelve" before the crucifixion (e.g., Luke 8:1; 9:1, 12; 18:31; 22:3, 47), after the defection of Judas Iscariot

67. So observes Green-Armytage, *A Portrait of St. Luke*, 61.

(Luke 22:47) he refers to them as "***the Eleven***" (Luke 24:9, 33). In the opening chapter of his second volume, Luke is careful to report that the Twelve are restored to their full number with the selection of Matthias (Acts 1:12–26). But remarkably, Matthias is never mentioned again in Acts, or even in the rest of the New Testament. And apart from Acts naming the Eleven in the opening chapter (Acts 1:13), while the apostles as a group are occasionally mentioned in Acts (e.g., Acts 1:26, 2:37, 42–46; 4:33–5:12; 5:17–42; 6:6; 9:27; 11:1; 15:1–16:4), most of the book does not read like an account of what the apostles have accomplished. Indeed, it is patently obvious that the first half of Acts features primarily ***Peter*** as the main apostle (with brief mentions of John in Acts 3:1, 3, 11, 4:13, 19; 8:14 and James in Acts 12:2), and the second half of Acts features ***Paul***, who was not one of the original Twelve apostles. For this reason, some have proposed that the title of Luke's second volume should not be the Acts of the Apostles.

Fresco of the twelve apostles by Enrico Reffo (1914), Chiesa di San Dalmazzo church, Italy.
sedmak/iStock.com

1.3.2 God, Holy Spirit, or Jesus

Rather than the apostles being in the full name of the book of Acts, some have suggested that the volume be named after one of its true key characters: the Acts of God, the Acts of the Holy Spirit, or the [Continued] Acts of Jesus Christ. Naturally, preference for one such title depends on the particular features of the story that are emphasized. Because Luke writes the story of Acts with clear indication that God is sovereign over everything and that the story is ultimately his, perhaps it could be called the Acts of God.[68]

68. Cf. George Sweeting and Donald W. Sweeting, *The Acts of God* (Chicago: Moody, 1986).

Then again, because the book of Acts has a particular focus on the Holy Spirit—who intervenes, guides, and empowers the story and characterizes the main people of the story—the Acts of the Holy Spirit seems a fitting title.[69] And yet again, it is unmistakable that the story of Jesus and a call to faith in him as Lord of all is the central aim of the story of Acts. As Luke records it, Jesus takes a personal interest in the events of Acts and even makes several appearances in the story (e.g., Acts 7:55–60; 9:4–6). Furthermore, Acts begins with a description of the Gospel of Luke as the book about "all that Jesus *began* to do and to teach" (Acts 1:1, emphasis added), and so it is that the book of Acts might be dubbed the [Continued] Acts of Jesus Christ.[70]

Of course, there is no real reason for us to settle on one of these monikers as if there is a need to change the name of the book of Acts. As far as we know, the title the Acts of the Apostles is not Luke's name for the book and does not appear as a title for the volume until the second century when Irenaeus refers to the book by this name.[71] We can be satisfied that the author of Acts wrote about events of world-impacting significance in a volume dedicated to one man but intended for many. The story of Acts—a story directed by God according to his plan, a story empowered by the Holy Spirit now present in believers, a story about the continued work of Jesus through his people—draws us in and invites us to consider where we fit in this story.

1.4 CONCLUDING REMARKS

The book of Acts is clearly a narrative that tells a story. There is more to say about the kind of narrative Acts is and Luke's intentions for telling the story as he does (see chapter 2). But it is noteworthy that Acts is not merely a chronicle of events that we can use in reconstructing the history of early Christianity.[72] Luke is concerned with recording accurate history but also with communicating theological truth, and he utilizes narrative to accomplish his goals.[73] Luke writes history in such a way so as to invite personal consideration and corporate reflection for the church. And so we find that identifying with characters in the story of Acts can lead to both conviction and

69. Cf. Lloyd J. Ogilvie, *Acts of the Holy Spirit: God's Power for Living* (Wheaton, IL: Shaw, 1999); and C. Peter Wagner, *The Acts of the Holy Spirit*, rev. ed. (Ventura, CA: Regal, 2000; revised as, *The Book of Acts: A Commentary*; Ventura: Regal, 2009).

70. Cf. Alan J. Thompson, *The Acts of the Risen Lord Jesus: Luke's Accounts of God's Unfolding Plan*, NSBT 27 (Downers Grove, IL: InterVarsity Press, 2012).

71. *Haer.*, 3.13.3; Christopher R. Matthews, "Acts of the Apostles," *OEBB* 1:12; Matthews remarks, "It is uncertain whether Irenaeus inherited this title from the tradition that preceded him or whether he coined it himself. What does seem clear is that the author of Acts not only refused to identify himself but also declined to provide a title for his composition."

72. Bauer, *The Book of Acts as Story*, 2.

73. Luke's dual concerns for recording accurate history and true theology led to the title of Marshall's helpful book, *Luke: Historian and Theologian*.

encouragement. How do I factor the teaching of Scripture into my decision-making processes (e.g., Acts 1:12–26)? What is my sense of community with other believers (e.g., Acts 2:42–47)? Do I have the courage of Peter and John in the face of intimidation (e.g., Acts 4:13)? What motivates my interactions with others (e.g., Acts 4:36–5:11)?

If we are open to it, such self-examination might come easily when reading Acts, where we find characters with somewhat mixed descriptions. For example, some of the people in the early church had questionable motives for their church involvements (Acts 4:36–5:11), some had trouble with fair food distribution (6:1–2), some were at first unreceptive of Saul after his conversion (9:26), some displayed racial discrimination (11:1–4; 15:1–2), and some were susceptible to hearsay (21:20–22). Even Paul and Barnabas, admirable champions of church unity (15:1–35), have a sharp disagreement and part ways (15:36–41). The realism with which Luke records events in the early church—including various hardships, momentary failures, and struggles to find solutions—helps us to identify analogous issues in our own day and to receive Luke's instruction and encouragement for a life of faith.[74]

The author of Acts—whom I gladly refer to as Luke—was a real person who lived in a less-than-perfect world. He believed passionately that God had acted in Jesus Christ to rescue humanity from its sinfulness and that God was still at work in the world through Jesus's followers now empowered by the Holy Spirit. This author was concerned that the people of the church would continue to play their proper role in the continuing story. So he wrote to Theophilus—and for all of us—to proclaim God's ongoing work and to encourage and challenge us. You do not need to be one of the original twelve apostles to have a legitimate ministry for the Lord in this continuing story. And thus, Luke invites us all to find our place in the continuing story of Jesus.

1.5 Key People, Places, and Terms

- Anti-Marcionite Prologues
- Antioch of Syria
- apostle
- Bodmer Papyrus XIV–XV
- codex
- early church fathers
- gentile
- Greek, classical
- Greek, *Koine*
- *inclusio*
- Jew
- Luke
- Muratorian Canon
- P^{75}
- papyrus
- Paul
- Peter
- priests
- *scripta continua*
- Septuagint
- the Eleven
- Theophilus
- "we sections"

74. Kuhn, *The Kingdom according to Luke and Acts*, 190.

1.6 Questions for Review and Discussion

1. On a scale of one to ten, how convinced are you of the tradition that the writer of Acts was the physician and Paul's sometimes coworker Luke? How much does knowing the name of the author matter to you?
2. Whatever the name of the author of Acts, how would you describe him from what you know from his written work?
3. What do you make of Theophilus being named at the beginning of the Gospel of Luke and the book of Acts?
4. Who appears to be the intended readership of Acts and how does this impact your reading of it in your own context?
5. Given the main players in the story of Acts, who or what would you say it is all about?
6. What impact do you think the story of Acts is meant to have on its readers?

1.7 Optional Assignments

1. **Text Reflection Project**—*Relating the concepts discussed in this chapter to another biblical text.* Examine the NT texts discussed in this chapter related to the identity of Luke (i.e., Col 4:10–14; 2 Tim 4:9–13; Phlm 23–24), and write up your thoughts about the connection of the author of Acts with one of the missionary colleagues of the apostle Paul.
2. **Interview Project**—*Inquiring of others their views concerning the concepts discussed in this chapter.* Arrange an interview with your pastor (or some other respected Christian leader) and ask him or her the following questions:
    - Who do you think wrote the NT book of Acts? Of what relative importance is the identity of the author?
    - Why is the book of Acts called the Acts of the Apostles and not the Acts of God or the Acts of the Holy Spirit?
3. **Service-Learning Project**—*Applying the concepts discussed in this chapter in some form of service to others outside the class.* If the suggestion of tradition is correct and the author of Acts is Luke the physician who sometimes served with Paul, it is no surprise that Paul is well-portrayed in Acts. Furthermore, it is reasonable to expect that some of Paul's teaching would be reflected in Luke's writing. Investigate the possibility of serving with some ministry that you respect or with someone whose teaching represents convictions similar to your own.
4. **Prayer Project**—*Talking with God about the concepts discussed in this chapter.* Write a prayer of gratitude to the Lord about the generations of people who have gone before you and passed on the gospel message—including people like Luke—so that you could eventually hear the truth of the gospel.

5. **Testimony Project**—*Telling others about the concepts discussed in this chapter.* As noted in this chapter, Luke researched the foundational events of the Christian faith and recorded them for Theophilus (and for us). Arrange to share what you have learned in this chapter with a Bible study group, Sunday school class, or other gathering.

1.8 Bibliography for Going Further

1.8.1 The Identity of Luke

Green-Armytage, A. H. N. *A Portrait of St. Luke*. London: Burns and Oates, 1955; Chicago: Henry Regnery, 1955.

Harnack, Adolf von. *Luke the Physician: The Author of the Third Gospel and the Acts of the Apostles*. Translated by J. R. Wilkinson. New Testament Studies I. London: Williams and Norgate, 1908; New York: Putnam, 1909. Repr., Eugene, OR: Wipf & Stock, 2009.

Kuhn, Karl Allen. *Luke: The Elite Evangelist*. Paul's Social Network: Brothers and Sisters in Faith. Collegeville, MN: Liturgical Press, 2010.

Marshall, I. Howard. *Luke: Historian and Theologian*. 3rd ed. Carlisle: Paternoster, 1988. Repr., New Testament Profiles. Downers Grove, IL: InterVarsity Press, 1998.

Marguerat, Daniel. *The First Christian Historian: Writing the 'Acts of the Apostles.'* Translated by Ken McKinney, Gregory J. Laughery and Richard Bauckham. SNTSMS 121. Cambridge: Cambridge University Press, 2002.

Marx, Werner G. "Luke, the Physician, Re-examined." *ExpTim* 91 (1980): 168–71.

McLachlan, Herbert. *St. Luke, the Man and His Work*. Publications of the University of Manchester, Theology Series 3. Manchester: Manchester University Press, 1920; New York: Longmans/Green, 1920.

Parsons, Mikeal C. *Luke: Storyteller, Interpreter, Evangelist*. Peabody, MA: Hendrickson, 2007.

Reece, Steve. *The Formal Education of the Author of Luke-Acts*. LNTS 669. New York: T&T Clark, 2022.

Strelan, Rick. *Luke the Priest: The Authority of the Author of the Third Gospel*. Burlington, VT: Ashgate, 2008. Repr., New York: Routledge, 2016.

Wenham, John. "The Identification of Luke." *EvQ* 63 (1991): 3–44.

1.8.2 The Identity of Theophilus

Anderson, Richard. "Theophilus: A Proposal." *EvQ* 69 (1997): 195–215.

Creech, R. Robert, "The Most Excellent Narratee: The Significance of Theophilus in Luke-Acts." Pages 107–26 in *With Steadfast Purpose: Essays on Acts in Honor of Henry Jackson Flanders, Jr.* Edited by Naymond H. Keathley. Waco: Baylor University Press, 1990.

Garrison, Roman. *The Significance of Theophilus as Luke's Reader*. Studies in the Bible and Early Christianity 62. Lewiston, NY: Mellen, 2004.

Goodspeed, Edgar J. "Some Greek Notes: I. Was Theophilus Luke's Publisher?" *JBL* 73 (1954): 84.

Marx, Werner G. "A New Theophilus." *EvQ* 52.1 (1980): 17–26.

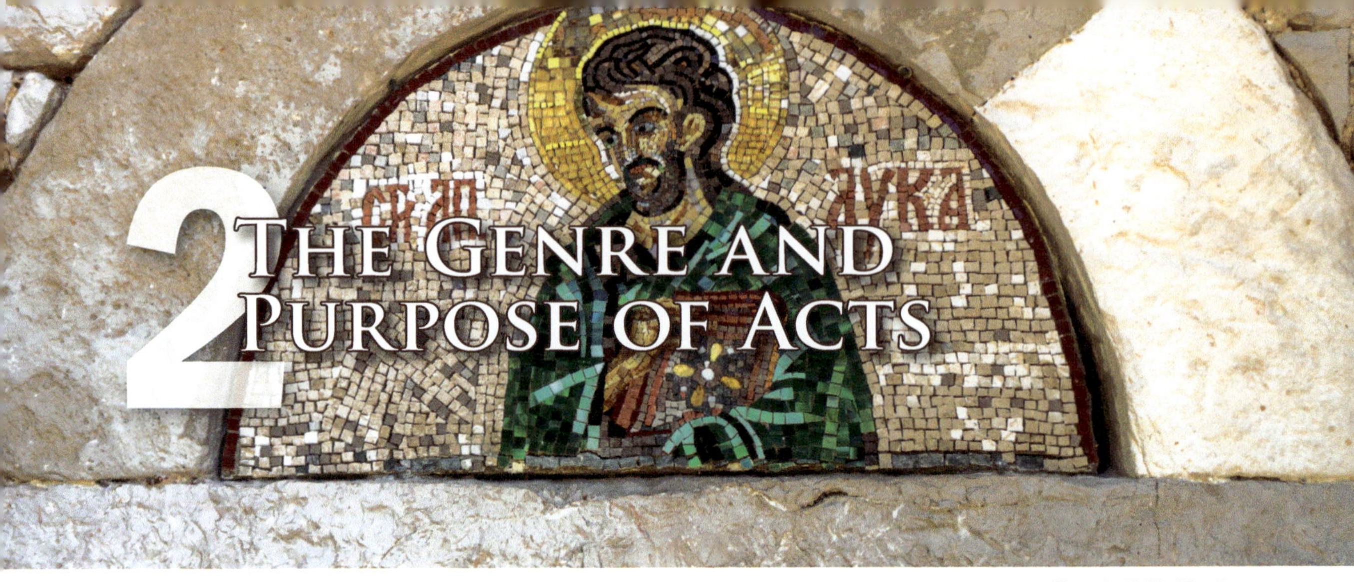

2 The Genre and Purpose of Acts

Blazenka Babic/iStock.com

Chapter Goals

After reading this chapter, you should be able to:

- Describe the place of genre in the interpretation process.
- Describe the relationship of the Acts of the Apostles to the Gospel of Luke.
- Explain why Acts might be viewed as a biographical historical monograph.
- Outline some of the possible purposes for Luke's writing of Acts.
- Appreciate the historical trustworthiness of Acts and recognize the value and demands of its message on the life of a believer and in the life of the church.

Chapter Overview

2.1 Understanding "Genre": What Role Does Genre Play?
2.2 Acts as Sequel: Are Luke and Acts One Book or Two?
2.3 Luke-Acts and Genre: What Is the Genre of Acts?
2.4 Luke's Goals: What Are Luke's Purposes for Acts?
2.5 Historicity: How Trustworthy Is Acts?
2.6 Concluding Remarks
2.7 Key People, Places, and Terms
2.8 Questions for Review and Discussion
2.9 Optional Assignments
2.10 Bibliography for Going Further

Key Verses

Many have undertaken to draw up an account of the things that have been fulfilled among us, just as they were handed down to us by those who from the first were eyewitnesses and servants of the word. With this in mind, since I myself have carefully investigated everything from the beginning, I too decided to write an orderly account for you, most excellent Theophilus, so that you may know the certainty of the things you have been taught. (Luke 1:1–4)

In my former book, Theophilus, I wrote about all that Jesus began to do and to teach until the day he was taken up to heaven, after giving instructions through the Holy Spirit to the apostles he had chosen. (Acts 1:1–2)

INTRODUCTION

An author utilizes a particular genre for his or her story as a fitting means for communicating the intended message(s) of the story. This chapter examines the kind of literature that Acts represents and how understanding its categorization affects our understanding of the author's intentions.

2.1 UNDERSTANDING "GENRE": WHAT ROLE DOES GENRE PLAY?

The word ***genre*** is used to describe the kind of literature category a particular work is best slotted under. Thus, we easily think of genres like detective novels, romance stories, fantasy, biography, and the like. This term has been adopted in other realms—like television, film, and music—to describe their various groupings (e.g., dramas, situation comedies, news programs, Westerns, action-adventures, romantic comedies, anthems, ballads, operas, etc.). The various genres of the NT documents are sometimes accounted for in familiar terms: the four gospels, the twenty-one epistles (thirteen ascribed to Paul and eight "general letters"), one apocalypse, and one book of "acts." I will return to the question of the genre of the book of Acts in section 2.3. But first let us briefly address the role that genre plays in understanding a particular piece of literature.

2.1.1 Genre and Expectations

Understanding the genre of a particular book is important for following the story being told. When reading a science fiction novel, the audience is not surprised when space travel is a regular event and characters from other planets are regular parts of the storyline. With the modern genre of science fiction, readers would be disappointed in a story that does not contain such items. Likewise, with fantasy genres readers expect the storyline to contain some involvement of magical spells and some level of interaction with mythical figures (e.g., dragons, elves, unicorns, etc.). On the other hand, when reading one of the leading newspapers, audiences expect a high level of accuracy and truthful correspondence to actual events in the real world. The same is expected of biographical works and history books. To be sure, the first-century world in which Luke was writing did not have precisely the same genre options popular in our twenty-first-century setting, nor did particular genres always envisage the same expectations as their modern counterpart. Nevertheless, in the world of literature, knowing something about the genre of a work helps the audience adjust their expectations for what they will discover in it.

2.1.2 Genre and the Intended Message

But even more than expectations, knowing the genre of a work helps the reader understand the author's intended messages carried in the work. Literary genre is not a mere matter of packaging convenience for an author's written work. Rather, a genre provides something of a social agreement between the author and the audience within which they consent to communicate meaning. That is, a given text has a particular significance for the author and the audience as outlined by the genre.[1] An author selects to write in a particular genre because she desires to utilize that genre's various conventions to communicate her message to her readers. Thus, a responsible author is trusted to be clear enough in unveiling the genre for the responsible reader to correctly understand the intended message.

As noted in chapter 1, Luke has given his readers hints about his intentions for his two works that we find in the New Testament: they are written as historical documents of some kind.[2] Thus, whether or not they ultimately choose to believe him, Luke's audience will expect to find in his works his accounts of actual events. Luke has intentions for his audience, and he has selected history-related genre(s) to bear his intentions. Luke writes as he does because he thinks the story he is telling has meaning for his readers, and the readers will understand that meaning from the way he tells the story.[3]

---

1. David E. Aune, *The New Testament in Its Literary Environment*, LEC 8 (Philadelphia: Westminster, 1987), 13.

2. Barrett likewise observes, "Beyond question, Luke was a historian of some kind; but of what kind?"; Charles Kingsley Barrett, *Luke the Historian in Recent Study*, A. S. Peake Memorial Lecture (London: Epworth, 1961), 12. Aune suggests five Hellenistic history-related genres and that the "history" genre itself has three subgenres; Aune, *The New Testament in Its Literary Environment*, 84–89.

3. As Donald Juel states it, "Luke sought to help his audience make sense of their lives by telling them a story. He provided a framework in which they could locate themselves and in which they could find meaning"; Donald Juel, *Luke-Acts: The Promise of History* (Atlanta: John Knox, 1983), 121.

2.2 ACTS AS SEQUEL: ARE LUKE AND ACTS ONE BOOK OR TWO?

The discussion of a literary genre category for Acts necessarily asks the same question for Luke's other sizable contribution to the New Testament, the Gospel of Luke. Since the work of Henry J. Cadbury in the 1920s, scholars have regularly referred to the authorial corpus of the Third Gospel and the Acts of the Apostles with the hyphenated label Luke-Acts. Some scholars use this label as a convenient way to reference the literary body of work by this one author. Some, however, have gone further to argue that this material is actually one literary work presented in two parts. In this view they follow Cadbury's own suggestion that Luke intentionally authored one long book in two parts.[4] For these scholars, Luke's two volumes are each one half of one book; the separation of the book into two volumes is merely a pragmatic matter of each volume being able to fill one scroll of standard length.[5] Thus, for some Luke-Acts is one book and not merely a corpus.

The Narrative Unity of Luke and Acts

The question of whether the Gospel of Luke and the Acts of the Apostles form one book or two actually has three basic options. I argue for the second of these three options.

a. One Book Telling One Long Story: Luke-Acts is one book written across two volumes.

The Gospel of Luke | The Acts of the Apostles

b. Two Books Telling One Long Story: The Gospel of Luke is a prequel volume in the story, and the book of Acts is a sequel volume in the same story.

The Gospel of Luke | The Acts of the Apostles

c. Two Books Telling Two Stories: The Gospel of Luke tells a biographical story about Jesus, and the book of Acts tells a historical story about the church.

The Gospel of Luke | The Acts of the Apostles

4. Henry J. Cadbury, *The Making of Luke-Acts*, 2nd ed. (London: SPCK, 1958. Repr., Peabody, MA: Hendrickson, 1999), 8–9; cf. pp. 8–11.

5. E.g., Joel B. Green, *The Gospel of Luke*, NICNT (Grand Rapids: Eerdmans, 1997), 8–10; Robert C. Tannehill, *The Narrative Unity of Luke-Acts: A Literary Interpretation*, 2 vols., FF (Minneapolis: Fortress, 1986/1990), esp. 1:1–12 and 2:1–8; cf. Craig S. Keener, *Acts: An Exegetical Commentary*, 4 vols. (Grand Rapids: Baker Academic, 2012–2015), 1:550–81.

2.2.1 The Extent of Unity

In the century since the practice of hyphenating Luke-Acts began, Lukan scholars have reflected much upon the multifaceted question of the unity of Luke and Acts (or is it the unity of Luke-Acts?). A specific concern here, then, is whether these two NT books have generic unity, i.e., if they are written in the same genre.

Comparing the prefaces to the Gospel of Luke and to the book of Acts (i.e., Luke 1:1–4 and Acts 1:1–2) makes it plain enough for most that the two books are related to one another by sharing not only an author and intended readership (see chapter 1) but also a general subject matter and purpose. Indeed, the narrative overlap between Luke 24 and Acts 1 betrays the common storyline between the two works. The unity of the Gospel of Luke and the book of Acts seems easily demonstrable in these, and other, ways.[6]

But, contrary to the argument of some, these kinds of demonstrable unity are hardly enough to demand that the works are two halves of one book. If this were the case and the Gospel of Luke is only half a book, then such an argument would seem to conclude that the gospels of Matthew, Mark, and John are each only half a book. So it seems far better to understand Acts as the intended sequel to the Gospel of Luke. As I. Howard Marshall has expressed it, it is proper to consider Acts separately from the Gospel of Luke but not in isolation from it.[7]

2.2.2 Sequel Is Enough Unity

Reaching this conclusion grants us all the freedom necessary to see the unity of these two NT documents without forcing us to search for some genre category that might adequately explain the complexity of Luke-Acts as a single book.[8] Whatever their specific classifications, both Luke and Acts are historical narratives punctuated with speeches by their main characters. This is sufficient for Acts to be the sequel to the Gospel of Luke, without feeling the need to press either book into the precise genre category of the other.

---

6. The last few decades have seen a sizable discussion of the unity of Luke and Acts. Most noteworthy are these contributions: Mikeal C. Parsons and Richard I. Pervo, *Rethinking the Unity of Luke and Acts* (Minneapolis: Fortress, 1993); Robert F. O'Toole, *The Unity of Luke's Theology: An Analysis of Luke-Acts* (Wilmington: Michael Glazier, 1984); Tannehill, *Narrative Unity of Luke-Acts*; Joseph Verheyden, ed., *The Unity of Luke-Acts*, BETL 142 (Leuven: Leuven University Press, 1999); Andrew F. Gregory and C. Kavin Rowe, eds., *Rethinking the Unity and Reception of Luke and Acts* (Columbia, SC: University of South Carolina Press, 2010). See also Patrick E. Spencer, "The Unity of Luke-Acts: A Four-Bolted Hermeneutical Hinge," *CurBR* 5 (2007): 341–66.

7. I. Howard Marshall, "How Does One Write on the Theology of Acts?," pp. 3–16 in *Witness to the Gospel: The Theology of Acts*, ed. I. Howard Marshall and David Peterson (Grand Rapids: Eerdmans, 1998), 16. It may be worth noting here that there is no definitive manuscript evidence that Luke and Acts were ever presented together as one book; on this, see Bruce M. Metzger, "Appendix II: Variations in the Sequence of the Books of the New Testament," pp. 295–300 in *The Canon of the New Testament: Its Origin, Development, and Significance* (Oxford: Clarendon, 1987), 297; cf. 311.

8. Examples of straining for a single genre for Luke-Acts can be found in Aune, *The New Testament in Its Literary Environment*, 77–115 and 139–41; Cadbury, *The Making of Luke-Acts*, 132; and Richard A. Burridge, "The Genre of Acts—Revisited," in *Reading Acts Today: Essays in Honour of Loveday C. A. Alexander*, ed. Steve Walton, Thomas E. Phillips, Lloyd Keith Pietersen, and F. Scott Spencer, LNTS 427 (New York: T&T Clark, 2011), 3–28. Judging Acts to be a sequel rather than the second half of a single book helps avoid this difficulty.

Acts as the Intended Sequel to the Gospel of Luke

In response to overconfident commitments to the idea that Luke-Acts was written as a single book, C. K. Barrett offered an oft-referenced reply. Barrett argued instead that the preface to the Gospel of Luke (Luke 1:1–4) was, indeed, intended to serve both the gospel and Acts, but that Acts was intended to be a sequel and not the second half of the gospel.

> We speak of Luke's "two-volume work" as if it were certain that he intended from the beginning to produce a book in two parts. It may be that he did not. Many an author has written a book which he intended to stand on its own, but then decided, on grounds historical or literary—sometimes economic—, to produce a sequel. It may have been so with Luke; at least, we cannot a priori exclude the possibility. . . . [I]t would be ludicrous to suggest that Luke thought the story of Jesus to be a mere preliminary, useful only to lead up to the more important words and deeds of Peter and Paul: the words and deeds of Peter and Paul as Luke presents them make this inconceivable. It is clear that the gospel, standing as one member of the four-gospel canon, can be, and very often has been, read independently, and taken on its own it makes the same good sense as Matthew, Mark, and John. But this does not in itself mean that it was not intended to serve the additional purpose of introducing a second volume which from the beginning was part of the author's plan.

From C. K. Barrett, "The Third Gospel as a Preface to Acts? Some Reflections," pp. 2:1452–66 in *The Four Gospels 1992: Festscrift Frans Neirynck*, ed. F. Van Segbroeck et al., 3 vols., BETL 100 (Leuven: Leuven University Press, 1992), 2:1453.

2.3 LUKE-ACTS AND GENRE: WHAT IS THE GENRE OF ACTS?

Scholars have made several suggestions for the genre category for Acts, which I outline here. Some of these suggestions are broad classifications, and some are more specific subcategories within those broader classifications. As indicated previously, some of the scholars representative of these classifications put the Gospel of Luke and Acts in the same category.[9]

9. The work of Sean Adams has been particularly helpful for this survey of genre positions; Sean A. Adams, "The Genre of Luke and Acts: The State of the Question," in *Issues in Luke-Acts: Selected Essays*, ed. Sean A. Adams and Michael Pahl, Gorgias Handbooks 26 (Piscataway, NJ: Gorgias, 2012), 97–120; and idem, *The Genre of Acts and Collected Biography*, SNTSMS 156 (Cambridge: Cambridge University Press, 2013). See also Todd C. Penner, "Madness in the Method? The Acts of the Apostles in Current Study," *CurBR* 2 (2004): 223–93; and Thomas E. Phillips, "The Genre of Acts: Moving Towards a Consensus?" *CurBR* 4 (2006): 365–96.

2.3.1 *PRAXEIS* ("ACTS") LITERATURE

The common title for Luke's second volume, the Acts of the Apostles, was not Luke's title for it but became attached to the book by the middle of the second century AD (e.g., Muratorian Canon, Irenaeus, Tertullian, Clement). Several other ancient books bear the title "Acts of . . ." (the Greek term is ***praxeis***, for "deeds" or "achievements"). While some have suggested this to be an established genre (or a title that betrays a particular genre), the term is flexibly applied to narratives in a wide variety of genres. That is to say, the term *praxeis* is not a proper label for a literary genre; rather, it is a nontechnical term used descriptively of a variety of ancient works that narrated the deeds or achievements of notable figures—sometimes historical, sometimes fictional, sometimes mythical.[10] Thus, with some irony I suggest that the Acts of the Apostles is not in an "acts" genre.

2.3.2 FICTION

Questions about Luke's reliability as a historian of first-century events have led some scholars to favor genre categories for Acts that are outside historiography.[11] Most notable are suggestions that Acts is intended to be entertaining fiction in the form of an ancient novel[12] and that Acts is an epic in the style of Homeric poems.[13] While others have taken up those suggestions, by and large they have not met with much acceptance, especially given Luke's blatant statements of intending to record historical events with accuracy (see Luke 1:1–4 and Acts 1:1–2) and the renewed scholarly support Luke has been receiving as a reliable historian. Any similarities Acts has to ancient novels and epics are not enough to convince us that Luke wrote the book as a work of fiction.[14]

---

10. Aune, *The New Testament in Its Literary Environment*, 78; contra Joseph A. Fitzmyer, *The Acts of the Apostles*, AB 31 (New York: Doubleday, 1998), 47–49, who views the title of Acts as an indication that the book belongs to the historical monograph genre.

11. Even apart from the genre question, a study of ancient fiction can have some benefit for understanding the New Testament; see Ronald F. Hock, J. Bradley Chance, and Judith Perkins, eds., *Ancient Fiction and Early Christian Narrative*, SBLSymS 6 (Atlanta: Scholars Press, 1998).

12. E.g., Saundra Schwartz, "The Trial Scene in the Greek Novels and in Acts," in *Contextualizing Acts: Lukan Narrative and Greco-Roman Discourse*, ed. Todd C. Penner and Caroline Vander Stichele, SBLSymS 20 (Atlanta: Scholars Press, 2003; Leiden: Brill, 2003), 105–38. For more on ancient novels and how Acts compares with them, see Loveday C. A. Alexander, "Fact, Fiction and the Genre of Acts," in *Acts in Its Ancient Literary Context: A Classicist Looks at the Acts of the Apostles*, LNTS 298 (London: T&T Clark, 2005), 133–63; and Keener, *Acts*, 1:62–83.

13. E.g., Dennis R. MacDonald, *Does the New Testament Imitate Homer?: Four Cases from the Acts of the Apostles* (New Haven, CT: Yale University Press, 2003); idem, *Luke and the Politics of Homeric Imitation: Luke-Acts as Rival to the Aenid* (Lanham, MD: Fortress Academic, 2018); and Marianne Palmer Bonz, *The Past as Legacy: Luke-Acts and Ancient Epic* (Minneapolis: Fortress, 2000), who suggests viewing Luke's work as analogous to ancient Latin epic rather than Greek epic.

14. For a detailed critique of the novel proposal, see David L. Balch, "The Genre of Luke-Acts: Individual Biography, Adventure Novel, or Political History," *SwJT* 33 (1990): 5–19, esp. 7–11. For nuanced critiques of the *epic* proposal, see Loveday C. A. Alexander, "New Testament Narrative and Ancient Epic," in *Acts in Its Ancient Literary Context*, 165–82; and Keener, *Acts*, 1:83–87.

2.3.3 Defense Document

Noting the positive presentation of the Roman government in Acts and the central role of Paul's defense before Roman rulers, some scholars have argued that Luke wrote the book to defend Christianity as a legitimate religion in the Roman Empire.[15] Others have suggested that Luke-Acts is an apologetic work written as a defense of the gospel.[16] Still others have suggested that it was intended to serve as a defense document for Paul in his trial before Nero, perhaps even something of a legal brief compiled for the benefit of the Roman investigator preparing for Paul's trial.[17] In the end, however, defense document proposals have not met with general acceptance because they deal too selectively with the content of Acts and render too much of the material irrelevant to the genre. If Acts had been written as a defense document for the trial of Paul (or any other Christian or Christianity in general) before Caesar, it is difficult to imagine that the emperor would have the patience to read through the many pages of material that he would deem irrelevant to such a trial in a Roman court.[18] While the defense document (a.k.a. *apologia*) genre classification has been largely rejected, several apologetic purposes for Acts have been incorporated into other genre suggestions. These suggestions for Luke's defense purposes for writing—and not a defense document genre—are examined in section 2.4.

2.3.4 Demonstration

Josep Rius-Camps and Jenny Read-Heimerdinger have suggested a unique proposal regarding the genre of Acts. They are adamant that the Third Gospel and Acts are two halves of one work: "neither is complete without the other." And observing the shared authorship and purpose, they conclude, "Both books thus share the same genre, which is neither gospel nor historical chronicle or biography."[19]

---

15. E.g., Burton Scott Easton, *Early Christianity: The Purpose of Acts and Other Papers*, ed. Frederick C. Grant (London: SPCK, 1955), 41–56. Of course, many scholars see a defense making *purpose* for Luke's writing without defining Acts as a defense document; e.g., see Ernst Haenchen, *The Acts of the Apostles: A Commentary*, trans. and ed. Bernard Noble, Gerald Shinn, Hugh Anderson, and R. McLeod Wilson (Philadelphia: Westminster, 1971), 98–103, 630–31, and 691–94; see section 2.4.

16. E.g., Alexandru Neagoe, *The Trial of the Gospel: An Apologetic Reading of Luke's Trial Narratives*, SNTSMS 116 (Cambridge: Cambridge University Press, 2002), esp. 219–24; cf. 17, 21–22.

17. E.g., John W. Mauck, *Paul on Trial: The Book of Acts as a Defense of Christianity* (Nashville: Nelson, 2001). See also a series of articles by Andrew J. Mattill Jr., "The Purpose of Acts: Schneckenburger Reconsidered," pp. 108–22 in *Apostolic History and the Gospel: Biblical and Historical Essays Presented to F. F. Bruce on his 60th Birthday*, ed. W. Ward Gasque and Ralph P. Martin (Grand Rapids: Eerdmans, 1970; Exeter: Paternoster, 1970), 108–22; idem, "*Naherwartung, Fernerwartung,* and the Purpose of Luke-Acts: Weymouth Reconsidered," *CBQ* 34 (1972): 276–93; idem, "The Jesus-Paul Parallels and Purpose of Luke-Acts: H. H. Evans Reconsidered," *NovT* 17 (1975): 15–46; and idem, "The Date and Purpose of Luke-Acts: Rackham Reconsidered," *CBQ* 40 (1978): 335–50.

18. Barrett, *Luke the Historian in Recent Study*, 63.

19. Josep Rius-Camps and Jenny Read-Heimerdinger, *The Message of Acts in Codex Bezae: A Comparison with the Alexandrian Tradition*, 4 vols.; JSNTSup/LNTS 257, 302, 366, 415 (New York: T&T Clark, 2004, 2006, 2007, 2009), 3:2; cf. 1:27. They offer a more detailed argument in Jenny Read-Heimerdinger and Josep Rius-Camps, *Luke's Demonstration to Theophilus: The Gospel and the Acts of the Apostles According to Codex Bezae* (New York: Bloomsbury, 2013), xxvii–xxviii.

The genre category they suggest is that of demonstration, or to use the Greek term, *epideixis*. Luke-Acts is a demonstration of the truth to Theophilus based on Luke's research. Although well intended, as with the "defense document" proposals for the genre of Acts, the Rius-Camps and Read-Heimerdinger proposal seems to confuse the concepts of purpose and genre. And the proposed demonstration genre does this in such a way that, in the end, it does not do justice to the works of the other gospels nor to Luke and Acts.

2.3.5 Biography

If the Gospel of Luke belongs in the genre of biography—although it is perhaps best to think of gospel as a subcategory of ***biography***[20]—those desiring to recognize Luke-Acts as a single work in two parts are understandably attracted to slotting Acts in the biography genre as well. Charles H. Talbert has been a leader of this view, and several have followed his approach.[21] There are also scholars who see Acts as a separate book that is the sequel to the Gospel of Luke who nevertheless likewise assign the sequel to some form of biography. In particular, even as gospel may be a subcategory of biography, perhaps Acts also falls into a biography subcategory, one that traces the life of a particular group of people or movement.[22] Thus, some form of biography subcategory has become an attractive proposal for Acts.

2.3.6 History

Luke's expressed interest in recording the history of the beginnings of the Christian faith has led many (if not most) scholars to suggest some kind of historical writing as the genre classification for Acts. Believing Luke-Acts to be one literary work, Cadbury made his influential argument in the 1920s to place the work in the expansive categorization of ***history***: "No doubt Luke's work is nearer to history

---

20. Ancient biographies would record the life a hero and celebrate that hero's virtues, teachings, and/or deeds. The canonical gospels do this with Jesus, but they seem to be more than mere biographies, for they also proclaim the good news of salvation through Jesus and call the reader to respond with faith in Jesus as Lord and Savior. Thus, the genre classification of gospel is best considered a subcategory of biography; see esp. Richard A. Burridge, *What Are the Gospels? A Comparison with Graeco-Roman Biography*, 3rd ed. (Waco, TX: Baylor University Press, 2018).

21. See Charles H. Talbert, *Literary Patterns, Theological Themes and the Genre of Luke-Acts*, SBLMS 20 (Missoula: Scholars Press, 1974); idem, "The Acts of the Apostles: Monograph or *Bios*?" in *History, Literature and Society in the Book of Acts*, ed. Ben Witherington III (Cambridge: Cambridge University Press, 1996), 58–72; and idem, *What Is a Gospel?: The Genre of the Canonical Gospels* (Minneapolis: Fortress, 1977). Much more cautious are David L. Barr and Judith L. Wentling, "The Conventions of Classical Biography and the Genre of Luke-Acts: A Preliminary Study," in *Luke-Acts: New Perspectives from the Society of Biblical Literature Seminar*, ed. Charles H. Talbert (New York: Crossroad, 1984), 63–88.

22. See F. F. Bruce, *The Acts of the Apostles: The Greek Text with Introduction and Commentary*, 3rd ed. (Grand Rapids: Eerdmans, 1990; Leicester: Apollos, 1990), 30; Stanley E. Porter, "The Genre of Acts and the Ethics of Discourse," pp. 1–15 in *Acts and Ethics*, ed. Thomas E. Phillips, New Testament Monographs 8 (Sheffield: Sheffield Phoenix Press, 2005), esp. 9–15; and Loveday C. A. Alexander, "Acts and Ancient Intellectual Biography," in *Acts in Its Ancient Literary Context*, 43–68.

than to any other familiar classification."[23] David Aune has offered a more detailed argument for categorizing all of Luke-Acts together as general history.[24] On the other hand, while viewing Luke and Acts as two separate works of differing genres by the same author, Martin Dibelius also categorizes Acts as history.[25] Many scholars have followed in this trend and defined the genre of Acts broadly as Hellenistic historiography,[26] Jewish historiography,[27] and even biblical history[28] or typological history[29] or historical hagiography.[30] Others have suggested the still somewhat vague but narrower category of historical monograph.[31] Recognizing that Luke-Acts fits neither formal history or biography, Cadbury ventured the more narrow history-related suggestion of a kind of popular folk literature.[32] Even more specific history-related subcategories have been proffered, including the suggestions of theological history,[33] kerygmatic history,[34] apologetic historiography,[35] rhetorical history,[36] institutional

23. Cadbury, *The Making of Luke-Acts*, 132–35 (the quote is from p. 133).

24. Aune, *The New Testament in Its Literary Environment*, 77–115 and 139–41.

25. Martin Dibelius, *The Book of Acts: Form, Style, and Theology*, ed. K. C. Hanson, Fortress Classics in Biblical Studies (Minneapolis: Fortress, 2004), 5; cf. pp. 14–26 where Dibelius dubs Luke "the first Christian historian."

26. E.g., Willem C. Van Unnik, "Luke's Second Book and the Rules of Hellenistic Historiography," in *Les Actes des Apôtres: Traditions, rédaction, théologie*, ed. Jacob Kremer, BETL 48 (Gembloux: Duculot, 1979; Leuven: Leuven University Press, 1979), 37–60; and Daryl D. Schmidt, "Rhetorical Influences and Genre: Luke's Preface and the Rhetoric of Hellenistic Historiography," in *Jesus and the Heritage of Israel: Luke's Narrative Claim upon Israel's Legacy*, ed. David P. Moessner, Luke the Interpreter of Israel, vol. 1 (Harrisburg: Trinity Press International, 1999), 27–60.

27. E.g., Samson Uytanlet, *Luke-Acts and Jewish Historiography: A Study on the Theology, Literature, and Ideology of Luke-Acts*, WUNT 2:366 (Tübingen: Mohr Siebeck, 2014), esp. 257–60.

28. E.g., Brian S. Rosner, "Acts and Biblical History," in *The Book of Acts in its Ancient Literary Setting*, ed. Bruce W. Winter and Andrew D. Clarke, BAFCS 1 (Grand Rapids: Eerdmans, 1993; Carlisle: Paternoster, 1993), 65–82.

29. E.g., Michael D. Goulder, *Type and History in Acts* (London: SPCK, 1964), 34; and Rebecca. I. Denova, *The Things Accomplished among Us: Prophetic Tradition in the Structural Pattern of Luke-Acts*, JSNTSup 141 (Sheffield: Sheffield Academic Press, 1997), 103–4.

30. E.g., Craig A. Evans, "Luke and the Rewritten Bible: Aspects of Lukan Hagiography," pp. 170–201 in *The Pseudepigrapha and Early Biblical Interpretation*, ed. J. H. Charlesworth and C. A. Evans, JSPSup 14 (Sheffield: Sheffield Academic Press, 1993), esp. 175 and 200–201.

31. E.g., Hans. Conzelmann, *Acts of the Apostles: A Commentary on the Acts of the Apostles*, trans. James Limburg, A. Thomas Kraabel, and Donald H. Juel, ed. Eldon Jay Epp with Christopher R. Matthews, Hermeneia (Philadelphia: Fortress, 1987), xl; Martin Hengel, *Acts and the History of Earliest Christianity*, trans. John Bowden (Philadelphia: Fortress, 1980), 14 and 36–37; and Darryl W. Palmer, "Acts and the Ancient Historical Monograph," in Winter and Clarke, *The Book of Acts in its Ancient Literary Setting*, 1–29.

32. E.g., Cadbury, *The Making of Luke-Acts*, 134; and James M. Dawsey, "Characteristics of Folk-Epic in Acts," in *SBL 1989 Seminar Papers*, SBLSP 28 (Atlanta: Scholars Press, 1989), 317–25.

33. E.g., Robert L. Maddox, *The Purpose of Luke-Acts*, FRLANT (Göttingen: Vandenhoeck & Ruprecht, 1982; repr., ed. John Riches, SNTW, Edinburgh: T&T Clark, 1985), 16.

34. E.g., Fearghus Ó Fearghail, *The Introduction to Luke-Acts: A Study of the Role of Luke 1:1–4:44 in the Composition of Luke's Two-Volume Work*, AnBib 126 (Rome: Biblical Institute Press, 1991), 165–80. See also Hengel, *Acts and the History of Earliest Christianity*, 34 and 47–49.

35. E.g., Gregory E. Sterling, *Historiography and Self-Definition: Josephos, Luke-Acts and Apologetic Historiography*, NovTSup 64 (Leiden: Brill, 1992), esp. 1–19 and 386–89; and Daniel Marguerat, *The First Christian Historian: Writing the 'Acts of the Apostles,'* trans. Ken McKinney, Gregory J. Laughery, and Richard Bauckham, SNTSMS 121 (Cambridge: Cambridge University Press, 2002), 34.

36. E.g., Kota Yamada, "A Rhetorical History: The Literary Genre of the Acts of the Apostles," in *Rhetoric, Scripture and Theology: Essays from the 1994 Pretoria Conference*, ed. Stanley E. Porter and Thomas H. Olbricht,

history,[37] political history,[38] and oral history.[39] One wonders if the specific subcategory suggestions are not so much differences in genre (i.e., related to formal structures and presentation features) as they are differences in the intended purpose(s) for the document (i.e., related to specific content and kind of argument). Nevertheless, the plethora of scholarly searches for a genre label within the broader history classification demonstrates the weight of evidence that Luke's work provides for a history-related categorization. Furthermore, the wide variety of more specific suggestions within this category demonstrates that genre labels are not self-contained, mutually exclusive classifications. I say more on this in the sidebar entitled "The Overlap of Genre Categories."

2.3.7 Biographical Historical Monograph

Regarding a genre category for the Gospel of Luke, the work of Richard A. Burridge has done much to move scholars toward a general consensus of slotting Luke into a specialized gospel subcategory of the Greco-Roman genre of biography.[40] Understanding Acts as the sequel to the Gospel of Luke does not, however, demand that it be in the same genre classification. Genres—in ancient times as well as in our current day (e.g., for music and film as well as books)—are classifications with blurred and permeable borders. The blending of cultures that occurred in the first century led to literary ingenuity and experimentation such that genre categories were flexible and somewhat fluid and even overlapping.[41] All that is needed for a work to be a sequel is for it to be in an area of genre overlap with its prequel so that it can continue the story in some sense. Like the Gospel of Luke, the book of Acts treats a historical subject matter via narrative with interspersed speeches. Thus, the genre label given to Acts must be fitting to these similarities, but it need not be limited to the identical genre label used for Luke's Gospel.[42]

JSNTSup 131 (Sheffield: Sheffield Academic Press, 1996), 230–50; idem, "The Preface to the Lukan Writings and Rhetorical Historiography," in *The Rhetorical Interpretation of Scripture: Essays from the 1996 Malibu Conference*, ed. Stanley E. Porter and Dennis L. Stamps, JSNTSup 180 (Sheffield: Sheffield Academic Press, 1999), 154–72; and Clare K. Rothschild, *Luke-Acts and the Rhetoric of History: An Investigation of Early Christian Historiography*, WUNT 2:175 (Tübingen: Mohr Siebeck, 2004), esp. 291–96.

37. E.g., Hubert Cancik, "The History of Culture, Religion, and Institutions in Ancient Historiography: Philological Observations Concerning Luke's History," *JBL* 116 (1997): 673–95.

38. E.g., David L. Balch, "ΜΕΤΑΒΟΛΗ ΠΟΛΙΤΕΙΩΝ—Jesus as Founder of the Church in Luke-Acts: Form and Function," in Penner and Vander Stichele, *Contextualizing Acts*, 139–88.

39. E.g., Samuel Byrskog, "History or Story in Acts—A Middle Way? The 'We' Passages, Historical Intertexture, and Oral History," in Penner and Vander Stichele, *Contextualizing Acts*, 257–83.

40. See Burridge, *What Are the Gospels?* Cf. esp. I.53–66, 237–39, 275–79, 341–66 regarding the genre of Acts.

41. Adams, "The Genre of Luke and Acts: The State of the Question," 98. Burridge discusses the overlap of genres, commenting esp. on the proximity of the history and biography genres among others; see Burridge, *What Are the Gospels?*, 62–67. Marguerat remarks that "the boundary between historiography and ancient biography is not always clear"; Marguerat, *The First Christian Historian*, 32.

42. For another argument that the narrative unity of Luke and Acts does not necessitate that the two books belong to the same genre, see Marguerat, *The First Christian Historian*, 43–64.

Burridge has made a rigorous application of genre theory to Acts, including the generic characteristics of opening features, subject matter, external features, and internal features.[43] His detailed analysis suggests that Acts fits somewhat among historical monographs and as well as with ancient biographies. Burridge notes, "Where biography and history overlap in monographs, it is extremely difficult to distinguish them," so it is unsurprising that he clearly places Acts in the overlapping region of these two genres, so much so that he prefers a combined label for the genre classification of Acts: "biographical monograph."[44] Following the lead of Burridge and emphasizing the location of Acts in the place where the two leading genre proposals overlap, I find it most useful to utilize both the biographical and the historical labels: ***biographical historical monograph***.

The Overlap of Genre Categories

Genres are not self-contained, mutually exclusive classifications. Genre categories are somewhat fluid and even overlap. Given its various features and fit with some of the genre categories, Acts most likely belongs in the place where the genres of biography and history overlap—a biographical historical monograph.

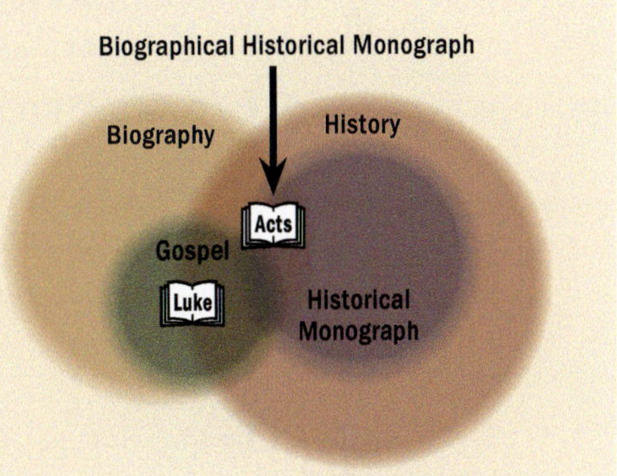

2.3.8 Not *Sui Generis* (Unique Genre) but *Polygeneris* (Influenced by Several Genres)

We could throw up our hands on the genre decision, were it not for the fact that we must decide what it is that Luke would expect of his readers to intuitively understand in order to make sense of his literary work. But this is the point of noting that Luke and Acts display elements of the genres of history and biography. Indeed, authors sometimes write at the overlapping edges of the genre categories and not always in their distinct centers. For Luke, his subject matter factored heavily into his genre selection, and he adapted extant genres at his disposal to portray the story of Jesus and his followers. To be a sequel to the Gospel of Luke, the book of Acts need not be written in exactly the same gospel subcategory of ancient biography but need

43. Burridge, "The Genre of Acts—Revisited," 3–28, reprinted in Burridge, *What Are the Gospels?* 341–66.
44. Ibid., 28.

only to be written in a similar history-recording genre. Thus, rather than being a unique genre (***sui generis***), perhaps Acts is best viewed as influenced by several genres (***polygeneris***). This is the benefit of the suggested biographical historical monograph genre classification for Acts.

Genre Proposals for the Acts of the Apostles

A variety of genres have been proposed for the NT book of Acts. Given its content, style, prologue, and connection to the Gospel of Luke, Acts most likely belongs in the place where the genres of biography and historical monograph overlap—a biographical historical monograph (option 7 on this list).

1. *Praxeis* ("Acts") literature—not really a genre.
2. Fiction—not how Luke describes his writing.
3. Defense document—Acts is so much more than this.
4. Demonstration—confuses genre with purpose.
5. Biography—Gospels are a sub-category of biography.
6. History—the most common genre suggestion for Acts.
7. Biographical historical monograph—where biography and historical monograph overlap.
8. Not *sui generis* (unique genre) but *polygeneris* (influenced by several genres).

The question of genre is a helpful interpretation tool. As indicated earlier, genre functions as a social agreement between an author and his audience; even if this bond is unconscious, it establishes certain communication expectations in a kind of contract between them.[45] Nevertheless, proper interpretation of a text can actually be impeded by an overly strict separation of genre classifications, a separation that ignores not only the possible overlap of categories but also the mix of shared literary devices. So while there is hardly unanimity on this question, scholars involved in the discussion seem to be moving toward general agreement that Acts resides in the area of overlapping genres. Understanding the flexible overlap of the various history-related genres, we can return to where we began this genre discussion. The narrative(s) of Luke's two books shares historical and theological concerns and is intended to instruct, challenge, and encourage the readers. With no danger to the unity of the message, Acts can be a sequel for the Gospel of Luke without sharing its precise genre classification.

45. Burridge, *What Are the Gospels?* 66.

On Luke as Ancient Historiographer with Literary Flair

In the world of academic historical studies, more and more scholars are readily recognizing Luke's skill as an ancient historian and writer.

> Luke is the finest historical writer in the Bible, and that for many reasons, but one is his literary ability. . . .
>
> All attempts to turn Luke into an ancient novelist or epicist or anything other than a historiographer fail against both the plain texts of his own writing and also their corroboration from contextual evidence in the ancient world. Using the same tools as Hellenistic historians in the secular world, Luke delivers records that may be of sacred significance, to be sure, but are not, on that account, unreliable. Call him an evangelist, a Gospel writer, a missionary, and a dedicated Christian, but clearly he was also a Hellenistic historian. His qualifications for historiography, his methodology, use of sources, attempted objectivity, literary ability, and accuracy not only run parallel to those of the most important Greco-Roman historians of his day, but often exceed them.

From Paul L. Maier, "Luke as a Hellenistic Historian," pp. 413–34 in *Early Christianity in Its Hellenistic Context*, vol. 1: *Christian Origins and Greco-Roman Culture: Social and Literary Contexts for the New Testament*, ed. Stanley E. Porter and Andrew W. Pitts, TENTS 9 (Leiden: Brill, 2013), 424, 434.

2.4 LUKE'S GOALS: WHAT ARE LUKE'S PURPOSES FOR ACTS?

Even as the genre question has been difficult for scholars, so also has been the related question of the purpose for Acts. Walter Liefeld has suggested, "It is probable that more theories exist as to the purpose of Acts than for any other New Testament book." Liefeld outlines six factors to consider when proposing a purpose for the writing of Acts: the introduction of the work, the historical or implied reader, the narrative plot, the book's conclusion, the literary characteristics, and the dominant themes.[46] Like many others, Liefeld notes that no one purpose for the writing of Acts is readily given in the book itself, nor is any one proposed purpose for Acts broad enough to cover the complex evidence of its content. Rather, even if we are able to suggest one primary purpose, it seems best to acknowledge several overlapping areas of purpose.[47] Others have offered various

46. Walter L. Liefeld, *Interpreting the Book of Acts*, Guides to New Testament Exegesis (Grand Rapids: Baker, 1995), 22–30 (the quote is from p. 21).

47. See Robert F. O'Toole, "Why Did Luke Write Acts (Lk-Acts)?" *BTB* 7 (1977): 66–76.

outlines of potential purposes for (Luke-)Acts.[48] The list of categories of potential purposes for Acts outlined here allows that, within each category, various nuanced versions might be noted. While not denying the possibility that Luke had any or all of these kinds of purposes in mind for Acts, the following survey of suggestions begins with those that seem most ancillary and ends with those that are most convincing given the evidence we have at hand (particularly with, as noted in chapter 1, Luke's prologue in Luke 1:1–4 indicating his desire to confirm the truth about Jesus and his followers).

2.4.1 Entertainment

Some scholars have suggested that Acts is something of a first-century novel or adventure story. About the genre question discussed previously, we could summarize here quite simply that Acts is best thought of as a historical work. Nevertheless, we must refuse the temptation to think of entertainment as meaning "fiction" and of history as meaning "not entertaining." Ancient historical works were written with more complex purposes than merely communicating factual information for information's sake.[49] Could it be that Luke wanted to accurately record historical events, in part, so that his audience could enjoy the adventures that Peter and Paul and others had experienced?

2.4.2 Mediation

Acts shows Christianity as a united effort. The church struggled against the dangers of splits along the Jewish-Samaritan and the Jewish-gentile lines, and it came through these struggles as a somewhat united group. This seems to be something Luke wants to emphasize by noting parallel kinds of ministry between Peter and Paul, but also in the ministries of Philip, Stephen, and Jesus. Luke observed and recorded the struggle for the harmony between Jewish and gentile believers and provided evidence for the unity of the Christian movement.

2.4.3 Paradigmatic Model

While many in the church today will want to look to the book of Acts as a model for how to "do church," nothing within Acts itself indicates that Luke's primary purpose in writing was to provide a precise paradigm for Christian evangelism or church life. It may not be a "how to" manual, but this does not mean that Luke's story lacks helpful principles or good models to follow. We find several of these in reading Acts. Nevertheless, rather than methodological models, if the main goal of Acts was to

48. See Maddox, *The Purpose of Luke-Acts*, 19–23; Joel B. Green, "Acts of the Apostles," *DLNT*, 7–24 (esp. p. 17); Mark L. Strauss, "The Purpose of Luke-Acts: Reaching a Consensus," pp. 135–50 in *New Testament Theology in Light of the Church's Mission: Essays in Honor of I. Howard Marshall*, ed. Jon Laansma, Grant R. Osborne, and Ray Van Neste (Eugene, OR: Cascade, 2011), 135; Liefeld, *Interpreting the Book of Acts*, 30–33; and Bruce, *Acts: Greek Text*, 21–27.

49. Keener, *Acts*, 1:436. Thus, the variety of different kinds of history writing surveyed in section 2.3.6.

provide the church with a paradigm of some kind, it would be for the church's goal of getting the gospel message to the ends of the earth by the power of the Spirit.[50]

2.4.4 Biographical Intent

Acts is not primarily a biographical writing, but it does seem purposely to illustrate the work of God in the lives of some of the earliest of Christian believers. While the lives and ministries of Peter and Paul get more coverage, Acts includes some significant stories of several other, nonapostle believers. So while the Gospel of Luke is unmistakably biographical in some regard concerning the life of Jesus, the way Luke tells the continuation of the story in Acts indicates that his primary focus goes beyond biography to events that God has been orchestrating. Luke-Acts is biographical and historical, but the author's intentions seem to go much further.

2.4.5 Doctrinal Intent

Even as a narrative, in some ways Acts teaches theological truths. Since the mid-twentieth century, when viewing the NT gospel writers as theologians became a more serious consideration, recognizing Luke as a theologian in his own right, and not merely as a historian, has gathered much momentum. This was particularly spurred on by the work of Hans Conzelmann in the 1950s and preceded a decade earlier by Ned Stonehouse.[51] Many theological truths are taught, supported, and illustrated in Luke's writings. This has become clear, and Luke's theological concerns have become a much-discussed topic (see chapter 3). But just as recognizable is that Luke is not merely a theologian; if that were his primary purpose, he might have selected a different genre (e.g., an epistle or a treatise like that of Hebrews).

2.4.6 Historical Account

If Luke was writing in a history-related genre as discussed previously, it makes sense that he would have some historical purpose(s) for the book of Acts. Many scholars can agree to this broad statement while disagreeing on his more precise historical purposes. Nevertheless, it is easy to recognize that Luke does in fact have a sense of history about him and that he desired for believers to likewise appreciate God's work in human history. I have already suggested that Luke writes Luke-Acts (in both his writing style and content) as a continuation of the biblical history of the Hebrew Scriptures.

---

50. Liefeld, *Interpreting the Book of Acts*, 32.

51. Hans Conzelmann, *Die Mitte der Zeit* (Tübingen: Mohr Siebeck, 1954); English trans.: *The Theology of St. Luke*, trans. Geoffrey Buswell (New York: Harper & Row, 1960; repr., Philadelphia: Fortress, 1982). Ned Stonehouse took a comparable, albeit more conservative, approach earlier; see Ned Bernard Stonehouse, *The Witness of Matthew and Mark to Christ* (Philadelphia, The Presbyterian Guardian, 1944); and idem, *The Witness of Luke to Christ* (Grand Rapids: Eerdmans, 1951); the two volumes were published together as idem, *The Witness of the Synoptic Gospels to Christ* (Grand Rapids: Baker, 1979). See esp. I. Howard Marshall, *Luke: Historian and Theologian*, 3rd ed. (Carlisle: Paternoster, 1988; repr., New Testament Profiles, Downers Grove, IL: InterVarsity Press, 1998).

The Gospel of Luke shows what Jesus "began to do and to teach" (Acts 1:1); Acts is the sequel with the purpose of showing the continuation of the story of Jesus and of Jesus's ministry via believers empowered by the Holy Spirit.

2.4.7 Apologetic Intent

As already mentioned in the discussion of genre, some rather specific apologetic purposes for Acts have been proposed, even to the extent that some scholars have argued that Acts belongs in the genre category of defense document. Some have suggested that Acts was intended to serve as something of a legal brief for Paul or for Christianity in general in the world of Roman citizenry; conversely, others suggest that Acts may have been written to defend Roman citizenship itself to Christians.[52] But such politically oriented apologetic proposals fail to account adequately for all the material in Luke-Acts. Rejecting the theory that Acts was written in the defense document genre, however, does not prevent us from recognizing that Luke has ideas he wants to defend. Indeed, F. F. Bruce has quite famously quipped, "The author of Acts has a right to . . . be recognized as the first Christian apologist."[53]

More likely is the idea that Acts defends Christianity as nonpolitical—neither for nor against Rome. This idea can also be turned on its head, for certainly Acts "defends" the idea that supposedly political persons (e.g., Roman centurions) can be believers. In a broad sense, Acts defends Christianity as the proper outgrowth of the OT faith and shows Christians as godly people who believe in the God of the Hebrew Scriptures, who has kept his promises in sending a Savior for all humanity.

Nevertheless, discussions of Luke's apologetic purposes usually center on Luke's political views. Steve Walton has nicely surveyed five disparate proposals for Luke's politics:[54] (a) Luke-Acts defends Christianity to Rome as a legitimate religion;[55] (b) Luke-Acts defends Rome to the church;[56] (c) Luke-Acts is about legitimation of Christian identity;[57]

---

52. Even if it is not a defense document per se, this sort of political purpose for Acts has been variously argued by scholars like Paul Walaskay, *"And So We Came to Rome": The Political Perspective of St. Luke*, SNTSMS 49 (Cambridge: Cambridge University Press, 1983), esp. 64–67; cf. Maddox, *The Purpose of Luke-Acts*, esp. 91–99.

53. Bruce, *Acts: Greek Text*, 22. Conversely, see the argument against apologetic purposes for Acts in Richard J. Cassidy, *Society and Politics in the Acts of the Apostles*, 2nd ed. (Eugene, OR: Wipf & Stock, 2014), esp. 145–57.

54. Steve Walton, "The State They Were In: Luke's View of the Roman Empire," pp. 42–66 in *Rome in the Bible and the Early Church*, ed. Peter Oakes (Grand Rapids: Baker, 2002), 1–41.

55. E.g., Easton, *Early Christianity*, 41–56; Cadbury, *The Making of Luke-Acts*, 308–15; Conzelmann, *The Theology of St. Luke*, 137–49; F. F. Bruce, *The Book of Acts*, 2nd ed., NICNT (Grand Rapids: Eerdmans, 1988), 8–13; Harry W. Tajra, *The Trial of St. Paul: A Juridical Exegesis of the Second Half of the Acts of the Apostles*, WUNT 2:35 (Tübingen: Mohr Siebeck, 1989), 199; and Robert F. O'Toole, "Luke's Position on Politics and Society in Luke-Acts," pp. 1–17 in *Political Issues in Luke-Acts*, ed. Richard J. Cassidy and Philip J. Sharper (Maryknoll: Orbis, 1983), 4–8.

56. E.g., Maddox, *The Purpose of Luke-Acts*; Walaskay, *"And So We Came to Rome"*; and Vernon K. Robbins, "Luke-Acts: A Mixed Population Seeks a Home in the Roman Empire," in *Images of Empire*, ed. Loveday Alexander, JSOTSup 122 (Sheffield: JSOT Press, 1991), 202–21.

57. E.g., Philip Francis Esler, *Community and Gospel in Luke-Acts: The Social and Political Motivations of Lucan Theology*, SNTSMS 57 (Cambridge: Cambridge University Press, 1987).

Coordinating Proposals for Luke's Political Apologetic

Lukan scholars have suggested a variety of proposals—even diametrically opposed proposals—for Luke's potential political purposes in writing Acts. On one extreme, some suggest Luke was defending Christianity against Rome; on the other extreme, some suggest Luke was defending Rome to Christians. In Luke's world, was Rome thinking Christianity was either good or bad? In Luke's church, were Christians thinking Rome was either good or bad? It is quite possible that various people in the first-century world could be found in all four corners of the diametrically opposed options. But could it be that, to the extent Luke had politically involved apologetic concerns, he was intending Christians to think about these matters in a completely different way? I propose here that Luke was in a kind of middle way between the extreme alternatives held by people in the first-century world.

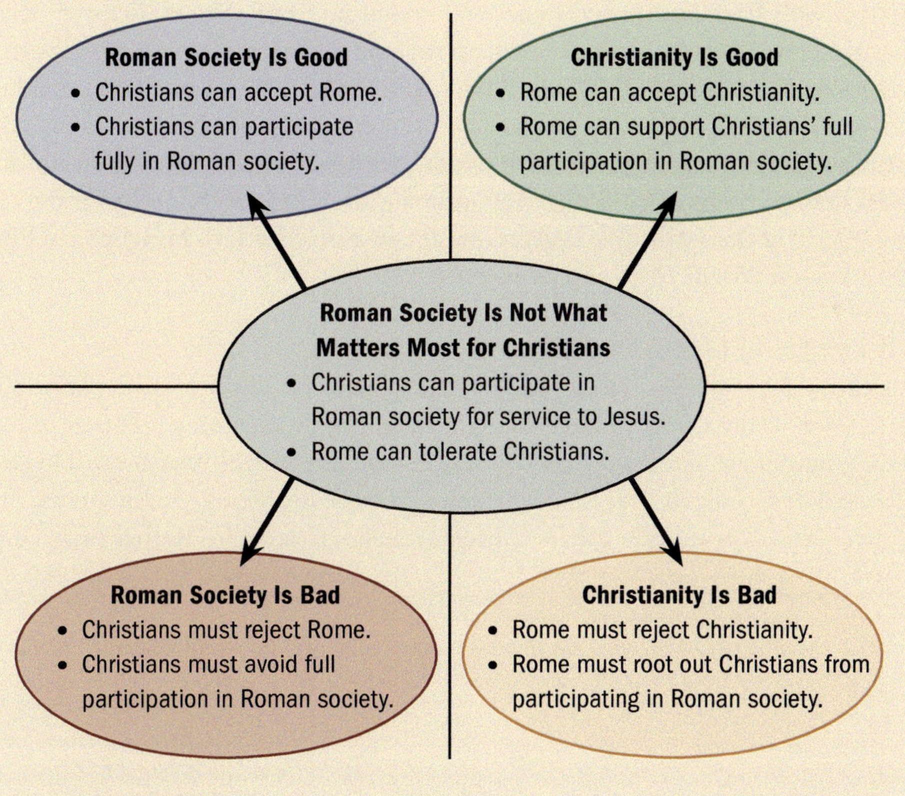

Of course, while many in the Roman world held the "Christianity is bad" position, it is patently *not* Luke's view and no one suggests it to be; it is on the chart merely to complete the logic of the diagram.

(d) Luke-Acts intends to equip Christians to interact with a political world;[58] and (e) Luke-Acts expresses no interest in politics.[59] Even apart from Luke's overall purposes for Acts, when it comes to Luke's political views, the trend among NT scholars is to understand Acts as favoring the political possibility of peaceful coexistence between Rome and early Christianity.[60] A surface reading of Acts reveals, on the one hand, statements about the innocence of Christians in the Greco-Roman political environment and, on the other hand, statements about Christians spreading a message that will change the Greco-Roman world. Interpreters are tempted to favor one set of Luke's statements over against the other set, but certainly there is a middle way between the various alternatives. Luke's interest was not so much to be supportive of Rome for Rome's sake nor was it to be antagonistic against Rome. Being a Christian means thinking about things a bit differently (see sidebar).

C. Kavin Rowe has similarly challenged both those who understand Luke to be compliant with Roman rule and those who understand Luke to conflict with Rome. Jesus's universal lordship requires neither a definite defense of Rome nor an outright opposition to Rome. Rather, "the way of the Lord" (Acts 18:25) is something completely other. Acts portrays Christianity not as a governmental takeover but as God's gracious act of reculturation, rescuing the world out of darkness.[61] In Luke-Acts (and the other gospels), Jesus is both resistant to giving ultimate allegiance to Rome and at the same time innocent of the anti-Rome charges that the first-century Jews bring against him.[62] Jesus calls his followers to go and do likewise.

2.4.8 Evangelistic Intent

Clearly, Luke believes that Jesus is the Savior, and his desire is that people follow Jesus as Lord. Many stories in Luke-Acts are about people becoming followers of Jesus, and these stories are written affirmations of conversion to faith in Christ. This leads many scholars to suggest that Luke's primary purpose in writing—even among other purposes—was to evangelize others to become believers as well.[63] Rather than a broad

58. E.g., Cassidy, *Society and Politics in the Acts*, esp. 158–70; cf. Richard J. Cassidy, *Jesus, Politics and Society: A Study of Luke's Gospel* (Maryknoll: Orbis, 1978).

59. E.g., Jervell, *The Theology of the Acts of the Apostles*, esp. pp. 15–16, 86–88, 100–106; and Eric Franklin, *Christ the Lord: A Study in the Purpose and Theology of Luke-Acts* (London: SPCK, 1975), esp. 134–39.

60. C. Kavin Rowe, *World Upside Down: Reading Acts in the Graeco-Roman Age* (New York: Oxford University Press, 2009), 53.

61. Ibid., 136.

62. See Yong-Sung Ahn, *The Reign of God and Rome in Luke's Passion Narrative: An East Asian Global Perspective*, BibInt 80 (Leiden: Brill, 2006), 192; John T. Carroll, *Luke: A Commentary*, NTL (Louisville: Westminster John Knox, 2012), 398–404; and Amanda C. Miller, *Rumors of Resistance: Status Reversals and Hidden Transcripts in the Gospel of Luke*, Emerging Scholars (Minneapolis: Fortress, 2014), 255; cf. Rowe, *World Upside Down*, 149–51.

63. E.g., Bruce, *Book of Acts*, 6–13; idem, *Acts: Greek Text*, 21–27; and David Wenham, "The Purpose of Luke-Acts: Israel's Story in the Context of the Roman Empire," pp. 79–103 in *Reading Luke: Interpretation, Reflection, Formation*, ed. Craig G. Bartholomew, Joel B. Green, and Anthony C. Thiselton, Scripture and Hermeneutics 6 (Grand Rapids: Zondervan, 2005), 79–103, esp. p. 101.

evangelistic appeal, some scholars have suggested that Luke had a narrow audience in mind, be that educated pagans,[64] God-fearing gentiles,[65] or privileged members of society's elite.[66] While some people in the story of Acts can reject the gospel, nothing and no one can stop its spread.

The sovereign plan of God seems to be more of a theme in Luke-Acts than even the very important witness theme. Looking at all the conversion stories in Luke-Acts makes some scholars think that Luke's primary motive was not about evangelizing his readers per se (although he is certainly in favor of their conversion); rather, Luke seems concerned to point out that God is at work in the Christian movement drawing Jews and gentiles alike into the people of God. So while the conversion accounts in Acts are fine models for unbelievers to follow, more importantly they serve as confirming evidence that the good news of Messiah Jesus is taking over the world and that his followers—both Jews and gentiles—are the true people of God.[67] This confirmation purpose (a.k.a. legitimization) is a distinct concern of the author of Luke-Acts.

2.4.9 Confirmation

Robert Maddox argues that Luke wrote to reassure the faith of his readers, i.e., "to confirm the gospel": it is "in every way a book devoted to clarifying the Christian self-understanding."[68] The early Christian faith faced several obstacles, and the all-too-surprising rejection of Christianity by the Jewish community that should have been receptive of their long-awaited Messiah provided opportunities to second-guess the legitimacy of faith in Jesus as the Christ. So Luke found it necessary to reassure his readers that the Christian church of believing Jews and gentiles was indeed moving in the correct direction.[69] This confirming (a.k.a. legitimatizing) purpose is congruent with Luke's own preface to his writing. The explicit statement in Luke 1:4 seems to apply to Acts as well: "so that you may know the certainty of the things you have been taught."

So many Lukan scholars have rallied around this idea as the primary purpose of Luke-Acts that Mark Strauss has ventured to call it a consensus. Luke wants to assure his audience that God's great plan of salvation for all peoples, heralded through OT

---

64. E.g., John Cochrane O'Neill, *The Theology of Acts in Its Historical Setting*, 2nd ed. (London: SPCK, 1970), 172–85.

65. E.g., John Nolland, *Luke*, 3 vols., WBC 35a, 35b, 35c (Dallas: Word, 1990, 1993), 1:xxxii.

66. E.g., Karl Allen Kuhn, *The Kingdom according to Luke and Acts: A Social, Literary, and Theological Introduction* (Grand Rapids: Baker Academic, 2015), 255.

67. Strauss, "The Purpose of Luke-Acts: Reaching a Consensus," 140.

68. Maddox, *The Purpose of Luke-Acts*, 181.

69. See also I. Howard Marshall, "Luke and His 'Gospel,'" pp. 289–308 in *Das Evangelium und die Evangelien: Vorträge vom Tübinger Symposium 1982*, ed. Peter Stuhlmacher, WUNT 28 (Tübingen: Mohr Siebeck, 1983), 302; Strauss, "The Purpose of Luke-Acts: Reaching a Consensus," 140–41; and J. Andrew Cowan, *The Writings of Luke and the Jewish Roots of the Christian Way: An Examination of the Aims of the First Christian Historian in the Light of Ancient Politics, Ethnography, and Historiography*, LNTS 599 (London: Bloomsbury, 2019).

Israel and preached now by the expanding Christian church, has reached its climactic revelation in the life, death, resurrection, and exaltation of Jesus.[70] This legitimization of the church as God's people gives legitimacy to the church's evangelistic mission as well.

Possible Purposes for Luke Writing Luke-Acts

Listed here are ten suggestions for why Luke wrote Luke and Acts. It is unlikely that Luke had one and only one purpose for the complex story traced in his two books. But the reasons listed here are somewhat in order of increasing conviction.

- Entertainment—for readers to enjoy some adventures.
- Biographical—to show readers God's work in and through certain people.
- Mediation—to show readers that Christianity is a united work.
- Paradigmatic—to portray for readers methods for evangelism and church life.
- Doctrinal—to portray for readers key beliefs and their corresponding behaviors.
- Historical—to provide for readers a record of actual historical events.
- Apologetic—to defend key ideas (and people) to readers.
- Evangelistic—to persuade the reader to believe the truth of the gospel.
- Confirmational (or legitimatizing)—to confirm for readers the truth of Christianity.
- Combined purposes—several of these purposes fit with what Luke has written.

2.4.10 Combination of Purposes

After all this discussion of possible motives for Luke to have written Acts, it may be good for us to step back and acknowledge that Luke may well have written with less definition than we would want him to have. As noted at the beginning of this section, Luke may well have had multiple purposes for writing Luke and Acts. Transparently, he has stated his instructive intentions in the opening statement of the gospel (Luke 1:1–4). But while that may be understood as his primary purpose, it need not be understood as his sole purpose. Indeed, some scholars suggest that Luke's purpose (singular) has more than one facet. For example, Strauss says it quite baldly: "Luke's purpose in his two-volume work centers around legitimation and apologetic."[71] Thus, Luke seems to have a combination of purposes for his historical work.

---

70. Strauss, "The Purpose of Luke-Acts: Reaching a Consensus," 143.

71. Ibid. On this combination apologetic/legitimization purpose for Luke-Acts, see also N. T. Wright and Michael F. Bird, *The New Testament in Its World* (Grand Rapids: Zondervan Academic, 2019), 616: "Thus, while Luke-Acts has several utilities, didactic, polemical, and evangelistic, it is principally an apologetic work. . . . Luke engages in a form of ethnic reasoning that legitimates the multi-ethnic churches as God's new-covenant people. . . . There is more to Acts than this, but not less." Cf. Barrett, *Luke the Historian in Recent Study*, 52–53.

2.5 HISTORICITY: HOW TRUSTWORTHY IS ACTS?

As noted, regardless of the precise genre category for each of Luke's books, both of his contributions to the New Testament are decidedly historical in nature. This naturally raises the question of how trustworthy Luke is in reporting historical events. I address this question first by looking at Luke's intentions to write history, then by examining two areas of historical concern in studying Acts (i.e., the speeches and the life of Paul), and finally by making some summary observations about the historicity of Acts.

2.5.1 The Historiographical Intentions of Acts

To understand Luke properly, we should respect his intentions even if we don't agree with what he says. A casual reading of Luke-Acts makes it readily recognizable that Luke intended his writings to be understood as historical works. Luke wrote about historical events in historical places that many of his first-century readers would have been able to verify. Ancient historiographers wrote about the standard of historical accuracy expected of competent historians (see sidebar). Ancient historians regularly made claims about conducting careful research, having eyewitness experience, traveling to involved locations, and reporting things fairly and accurately.[72] The preface to Luke's Gospel (Luke 1:1–4) and his other documentary devices (e.g., naming historical figures and events and places, referencing crowds of witnesses, etc.) fit these standards nicely, and Luke's written work measures up well according to the rules of Hellenistic historiography (see sidebar).[73]

As Paul Ricoeur discusses it, the issue of historiography can be better addressed by distinguishing between documentary history, explicative history, and poetic history.[74]

---

72. Paul L. Maier, "Luke as a Hellenistic Historian," pp. 413–34 in *Early Christianity in Its Hellenistic Context*, vol. 1: *Christian Origins and Greco-Roman Culture: Social and Literary Contexts for the New Testament*, ed. Stanley E. Porter and Andrew W. Pitts, TENTS 9 (Leiden: Brill, 2013), 416. For an extended discussion of Acts and ancient historiography, see Keener, *Acts*, 1:90–165.

73. While Van Unnik proposes that Luke scores well on ten measures of accuracy for Hellenistic historiography (Van Unnik, "Luke's Second Book and the Rules of Hellenistic Historiography," 37–60; see sidebar), some like Daniel Marguerat suggest that Luke departs from the Hellenistic history writing rules regarding a noble subject matter and impartiality in reporting. But Marguerat himself notes that this may be due to Luke's observance of Jewish historiography in pointing to the acts of God in history and calling for faith and worship; see Marguerat, *The First Christian Historian*, 1–25. Indeed, on this point Darrell Bock suggests that Luke's subject matter is noble precisely because it is about divine acts in history and that Luke's perspective is not impartial only to the extent that he calls attention to the significance of those divine acts; Darrell L. Bock, "Apologetics Commentary on the Acts of the Apostles," pp. 635–764 in *The Holman Apologetics Commentary on the Bible: The Gospels and Acts*, ed. Jeremy Royal Howard (Nashville: B&H, 2013), 641.

74. See Paul Ricoeur, "Philosophies critiques de l'histoire: recherche, explication, écriture," in *Philosophical Problems Today*, ed. G. Floistad (Dordrecht: Kluwer, 1994), 1:139–201; see also idem, *La critique et la conviction* (Paris: Calmann-Lévy, 1995), 131–32. Brief summaries are available in Marguerat, *The First Christian Historian*, 8–9; and Darrell L. Bock, *A Theology of Luke and Acts: God's Promised Program, Realized for All Nations*, Biblical Theology of the New Testament (Grand Rapids: Zondervan, 2012), 48–51. For an ancient expression of these historiographical intentions, see Diodorus Siculus, *The Library of History* 30.15 (ca. 80–20 BC).

Historians do not usually produce mere lists of historical events (documentary history); they also seek to explain the historical events with a narrative of how those events came about (explicative history) and sometimes even use the story to call their readers to believe and act in certain ways (poetic history). Whatever their specific genre classifications, the Gospel of Luke and Acts—and the other canonical gospels—make evident that their writers share all three historiographical concerns (see the explicit statements in Luke 1:1–4; Acts 1:1–3; 4:12; John 20:30–31; 21:24–25).

Accuracy Standards among Ancient Historiographers

Several ancient historians made remarks on their craft of writing history (i.e., historiography) and expressed a concern that historians write accurately about events for the sake of remembering the truth. Some contrasted the work of good historians against writers who had motives other than accurate reporting. Some even commented that historical accuracy is more important than their friendships or their commitments against sworn enemies. Here is a remark by Dio Cassius as one example, and following is a list of other such comments.

Dio Cassius, *Roman History*, 1.1.2–3 (ca. AD 230)

> Although I have read pretty nearly everything about them that has been written by anybody, I have not included it all in my history, but only what I have seen fit to select. I trust, moreover, that if I have used a fine style, so far as the subject matter permitted, no one will on this account question the truthfulness of the narrative, as has happened in the case of some writers; for I have endeavoured to be equally exact in both these respects, so far as possible. I will begin at the point where I have obtained the clearest accounts of what is reported to have taken place in this land which we inhabit.

Other Ancient Statements on Historiography

- Herodotus (ca. 484–430 BC) in *Histories* (a.k.a. *The Persian Wars*) 1.1
- Thucydides (ca. 460–395 BC) in *History of the Peloponnesian War* 1.21–22
- Polybius (ca. 200–118 BC) in *The Histories* 1.14.4–8
- Cicero (ca. 106–43 BC) in *De oratore* 2.15 §§62–64
- Diodorus Siculus (ca. 80–20 BC) in *The Library of History* 30.15
- Dionysius of Halicarnassus (ca. 60–7 BC) in *De Thucydide* 8
- Livy (ca. 59 BC–AD 17) in *History of Rome* 1.Preface
- Josephus (ca. AD 37–100) in *Jewish Antiquities* 20.12.1 §§261–63
- Plutarch (ca. AD 46–120) in *Theseus* 1.1 and *Galba* 2.3

Acts and Ten Rules of Hellenistic Historiography

Outlining ten basic rules held by ancient Hellenistic history writers, Willem C. van Unnik observes that Acts scores well on all ten measures. These ten basic rules are summarized here, and a statement or two on each is provided from the works of ancient historiographers Dionysius of Halicarnassus (ca. 60–7 BC) and Lucian of Samosata (ca. AD 120–190). See Van Unnik, "Luke's Second Book and the Rules of Hellenistic Historiography," 37–60.

1. Choice of a Noble Subject

Dionysius of Halicarnassus, *Letter to Gnaeus Pompeius* 3.2

> The first, and one might say the most necessary task for writers of any kind of history is to select a noble subject which will please their readers.

2. A Subject That Will Be Useful to Readers

Dionysius of Halicarnassus, *Roman Antiquities* 1.1.2

> For I am convinced that all . . . those who write histories, in which we have the right to assume that Truth, the source of both prudence and wisdom, is enshrined, ought first of all, to make choice of noble and lofty subjects and such as will be of great utility to their readers. . . .

Lucian of Samosata, *How to Write History* 53

> He will omit the appeal for a favourable hearing and give his audience what will interest and instruct them. For they will give him their attention if he shows that what he is going to say will be important, essential, personal, or useful.

3. Impartial Reporting of Facts

Dionysius of Halicarnassus, *Letter to Gnaeus Pompeius* 4.2

> The moral qualities which he shows are those of piety, justice, perseverance and affability—a character, in short, which is adorned with all the virtues. Such, then, is his manner in the treatment of subject-matter.

Lucian of Samosata, *How to Write History* 58

> That, then, is the sort of man the historian should be: fearless, incorruptible, free, a friend of free expression and the truth, intent, as the comic poet says, on calling a fig a fig and a trough a trough, giving nothing to hatred or to friendship, sparing no one, showing neither pity nor shame nor obsequiousness, an impartial judge, well disposed to all men up to the point of not giving one side more than its due, in his books a stranger and a man

without a country, independent, subject to no sovereign, not reckoning what this or that man will think, but stating the facts.

4. Proper Narrative Construction with a Good Beginning and a Good Ending

Dionysius of Halicarnassus, *Letter to Gnaeus Pompeius* 4.2

But it is not only for his subjects, which he chose . . . [that he] deserves to be praised, but also for his arrangement of his material. Everywhere he has begun at the most appropriate place, and he has concluded each episode at the most suitable point.

5. Adequate Collection of Source Materials

Dionysius of Halicarnassus, *Roman Antiquities* 1.1.2

For I am convinced that all . . . those who write histories, [ought] . . . with great care and pains, to provide themselves with the proper equipment for the treatment of their subject.

6. For Ease of Reading, a Variety of Included Materials

Dionysius of Halicarnassus, *Letter to Gnaeus Pompeius* 3.4

[Another] question which a historian must consider is which events he should include in his work, and which he should omit. . . . that any narrative that proceeds to a great length has a pleasant effect on the minds of its hearers provided that it contains a number of pauses, . . . that change is a pleasant quality in an historical work, and gives it variety.

Lucian of Samosata, *How to Write History* 56

Rapidity is everywhere useful, especially if there is no lack of material; and one must look to the subject matter to provide this rather than to the words and phrases—I mean, if you run quickly over small and less essential things, while giving adequate treatment to matters of importance; indeed, a great deal should even be omitted.

7. Sequential and Thematic Ordering of the Material

Dionysius of Halicarnassus, *Letter to Gnaeus Pompeius* 3.5

The historian's next function is to distribute the material of his account and arrange each item in its proper place . . . [so that it] does not break the continuity of the narrative.

Lucian of Samosata, *How to Write History* 55

For all the body of the history is simply a long narrative. So let it be adorned with the virtues proper to narrative, progressing smoothly, evenly and consistently, free from humps and hollows. Then let its clarity be limpid, achieved, as I have said, both by diction and the interweaving of the matter. For he will make everything distinct and complete, and when he has finished the first topic he will introduce the second, fastened to it and linked with it like a chain, to avoid breaks and a multiplicity of disjointed narratives; no, always the first and second topics must not merely be neighbours but have common matter and overlap.

8. A Vividness to the Narration

Dionysius of Halicarnassus, *De Lysia* 7

Vividness is a quality which the style of Lysias has in abundance. This consists in a certain power he has of conveying the things he is describing to the senses of his audience, and it arises out of his grasp of circumstantial detail. Nobody who applies his mind to the speeches of Lysias will be so obtuse, insensitive or slow-witted that he will not feel that he can see the actions which are being described going on and that he is meeting face-to-face the characters in the orator's story. And he will require no further evidence of the likely actions, feelings, thoughts or words of the different persons.

Lucian of Samosata, *How to Write History* 50–51

In brief, we must consider that the writer of history should be like Phidias or Praxiteles or Alcamenes or one of the other sculptors . . . and their art lay in handling their material properly.

The task of the historian is similar: to give a fine arrangement to events and illuminate them as vividly as possible. And when a man who has heard him thinks thereafter that he is actually seeing what is being described and then praises him—then it is that the work of our Phidias of history is perfect and has received its proper praise.

9. Moderation in the Use of Topographical Details

Lucian of Samosata, *How to Write History* 58

You need especial discretion in descriptions of mountains, fortifications, and rivers, to avoid the appearance of a tasteless display of your word-power and of indulging your own interests at the expense of the history; you will touch on them lightly for the sake of expediency or clarity, then change the subject.

10. Speeches Must Be Fitting to the Speaker and the Narrative Situation

Lucian of Samosata, *How to Write History* 58

If a person has to be introduced to make a speech, above all let his language suit his person and his subject, and next let these also be as clear as possible. It is then, however, that you can play the orator and show your eloquence.

An Author's Historiography Intentions

There are three basic kinds of history writing that an author may intend for his work:

I. **Documentary history** (recording historical facts for the readers)—see Luke 1:1-2; Acts 1:3; John 21:24-25.
II. **Explicative history** (using narrative to explain history to the readers)—see Luke 1:3-4; Acts 1:1-2.
III. **Poetic history** (making an ideological or theological appeal to the readers through the story)—see Acts 4:12; John 20:30-31.

The Gospels and Acts involve **all three** kinds of historiography.

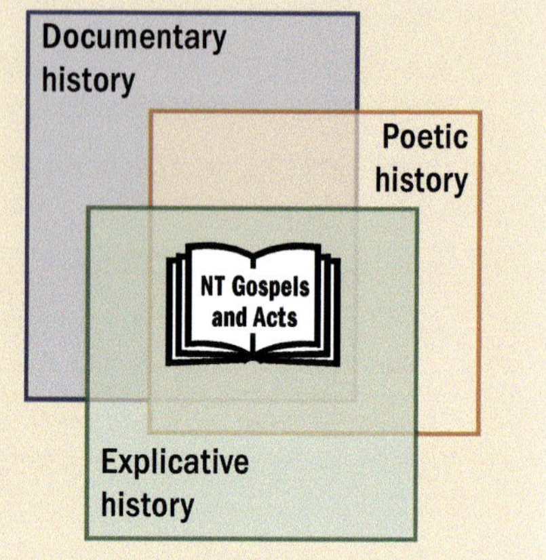

2.5.2 Speech Expectations

One area of particular concern in thinking about the trustworthiness of Luke's historical record is the speeches in Acts. A number of scholars have suggested that the similarities among the speeches in Acts betray that Luke has simply imagined them all. Others, however, have argued that Luke has not invented the speeches but that he provides accurate summaries of what was spoken on those occasions. There are two things to consider here.

First, like all historians, Luke is selective. With Acts covering about thirty years' worth of events, Luke had to be judicious about what to include in such a short book (only three hours of reading). When providing a record of a speech, ancient authors like Luke had no electronic recording equipment capable of catching every word, vocal inflection, and facial expression. They necessarily had to summarize what was spoken—whether it was a speech they had heard themselves or one that had been summarized for them—using an informal summary system like we use in everyday reporting of what our friends have told us. His selectivity, then, should encourage us to attend more carefully to what Luke has recorded and summarized for us in Acts, knowing that his (necessary) selectivity is designed to serve the message he is trying to communicate.

Second, just as we expect accuracy in our informal conversations, ancient historians likewise expected accuracy in their accounts of speeches. In addition to the ancient written expectations of truthfulness for reporting events, we have several statements by ancient historians regarding accuracy in reporting speeches (e.g., Thucydides and Polybius; see sidebar).[75] In the second century AD, Lucian indicated that, even in a

75. Cf. Sean A. Adams, "On Sources and Speeches: Methodological Discussions in Ancient Prose Works and Luke-Acts," in Porter and Pitts, *Christian Origins and Greco-Roman Culture*, 389–411. There has been some debate

Ancient Historians' Expectations Regarding Speech Records

Without the formal system of quotation used in modern research (and lacking any audio or video recording equipment), the ancients used an informal system of quotation (like we do in casual conversation). Nevertheless, they expected a responsible level of accuracy when reporting speeches.

Thucydides, *History of the Peloponnesian War* 1.22.1 (ca. 431–411 BC)

With reference to the speeches in this history, some were delivered before the war began, others while it was going on; some I heard myself, others I got from various quarters; it was in all cases difficult to carry them word for word in one's memory, so my habit has been to make the speakers say what was in my opinion demanded of them by the various occasions, of course adhering as closely as possible to the general sense of what they really said.

Polybius, *The Histories* 12.25.A–B (ca. 146–118 BC)

The peculiar function of history is to discover, in the first place, the words actually spoken, whatever they were, and next to ascertain the reason why what was done or spoken led to failure or success. . . . But a writer who passes over in silence the speeches made and the causes of events and in their place introduces false rhetorical exercises and discursive speeches, destroys the peculiar virtue of history.

(See also Polybius, *The Histories* 2.56.10-12 and 36.1.6-7.)

Lucian of Samosata, *How to Write History* 58 (ca. 120-190 AD)

If a person has to be introduced to make a speech, above all let his language suit his person and his subject, and next let these also be as clear as possible. It is then, however, that you can play the orator and show your eloquence.

mere summary of what was said, an account of a speech was to be historically accurate. Given what we know of Luke's interest in history, there is little reason to think Luke did anything different when reporting speeches.

---

regarding how best to understand the writings of Thucydides and the extent to which he argues for historical accuracy in speeches; see particularly Stanley E. Porter, "Thucydides 1.22.1 and Speeches in Acts: Is There a Thucydidean View?" *NovT* 32 (1990): 121–42. I understand Thucydides to be arguing for the need of historians (including himself) to write in a trustworthy manner about the content of speeches even as they need to do so in reporting events; for Thucydides to be saying otherwise is for him to be telling his readers not to trust him. See also the ancient authors who complain about Thucydides's historical standards as too restrictive for other literary fields: for rhetoric, see Cicero, *Brut.* 287 (ca. 106–43 BC); and for entertaining engagement, see Dionysius of Halicarnassus, *Pomp.* 3.8 (ca. 60–7 BC).

2.5.3 The Paul in Acts versus the Paul of the Epistles

Another special area of concern regarding Luke's historical accuracy has to do with his description of Paul in Acts, especially compared to Paul's own self descriptions in his epistles. As might be expected, Paul provides information about his own life that Luke does not report; and conversely, Luke mentions things that Paul does not report. But the issue of the two authors including different things in their reports is quite different from the problem of finding apparent conflicts between reports. In this regard, scholars discuss five areas, with critics proposing that Luke differs too much in his descriptions of Paul: (1) Paul's letter writing is not mentioned in Acts; (2) Acts does not vigorously argue for Paul's apostleship; (3) Paul keeps the Jewish law in Acts but argues against the need to keep it in his letters; (4) Paul is a worker of miracles in Acts but not so much in his letters; and (5) the number of trips Paul makes to Jerusalem appears to differ between Acts and Paul's letters.[76]

Fresco of St. Paul (ca. end of 19th century) by Friedrich Stummel and Karl Wenzel, Sacred Heart Church, Berlin.
Renáta Sedmáková/ stock.adobe.com

In the face of these observations, however, we must recall that the two writers, Luke and Paul, writing for different purposes to different audiences, have each chosen to include certain things and not to include other things. Such historical selectivity only renders them as selectors of facts (as all writers must be) and need not render either of them as falsifiers of the facts. No author of historical events can record absolutely everything that happened; therefore writers are necessarily selective of what they record and do so in accordance with their chosen themes. So there may be differences in emphases between the writings of Luke and Paul in what they record about Paul's life, but there are no necessary contradictions. Indeed, it is unsurprising that a person's incidental self-description in comments found in various letters will differ somewhat from a third-party description of the person by even one of his close friends. In reality, the points of agreement between Acts and the Pauline epistles are quite numerous, so numerous that some scholars have proposed that, without mentioning them directly, Luke actually used some of Paul's letters as research

76. See A. J. Mattill Jr. "The Value of Acts as a Source for the Study of Paul," in *Perspectives on Luke-Acts*, ed. Charles H. Talbert, Perspectives in Religious Studies 5 (Danville, VA: Association of Baptist Professors of Religion, 1978), 76–98; and Stanley E. Porter, *The Paul of Acts: Essays in Literary Criticism, Rhetoric, and Theology* (Tübingen: Mohr Siebeck, 1999; repr., *Paul in Acts*, Library of Pauline Studies, Peabody, MA: Hendrickson, 2001), 187–206.

sources for the writing of Acts.[77] These points of connection corroborate a consistency between the Paul of Acts and the Paul of the Epistles.[78]

In the end, then, the discrepancies detected in these areas are only apparent, and the portrait of Paul in Acts conforms with what we learn about Paul from the Epistles. The noncontradictory differences are precisely the kinds expected from two different authors writing with different purposes in different literary genres.[79] While reading carefully for the intended meaning of the authors, readers do not have to choose between trusting Paul or trusting Luke; both can be viewed as trustworthy writers.

2.5.4 The Historical Accuracy of Acts

Intending to write history accurately does not guarantee that one will, and some scholars have doubted Luke's accuracy as a historian, if not also his intentions. In the 1800s and first half of the 1900s, scholars highly questioned the historicity of Acts (and, of course, some still question it today).[80] But more and more scholars in a variety of historical disciplines have been accepting Luke's trustworthiness with fewer hesitancies. On this I want to note two things.

First, Luke is remarkably accurate in small, measurable details. An example of Luke's detailed accuracy is his use of correct political titles in a variety of settings. Instances include "Caesar Augustus" ruling over the entire Roman world (Luke 2:1; see also Tiberius in Luke 3:1 and Claudius in Acts 11:28); "tetrarch" for Herod Antipas (Luke 3:1, 19; 9:7), but "king" for Herod the Great, Herod Agrippa I, and Herod Agrippa II (Luke 1:5; Acts 12:1; 25:13); "proconsul" in Cyprus (Acts 13:7); "magistrates" in the Roman colony of Philippi (Acts 16:20); "city officials" (lit. "politarchs") in Thessalonica (Acts 17:6); "officials" (lit. "asiarchs"), "city clerk," and "proconsuls" in Ephesus (Acts 19:31, 35, 38); and "the chief official" in Malta (Acts 28:7). Given the vast geographic and chronological coverage of his gospel and Acts, to get every single title correct would have been very difficult in Luke's day. It would have been much easier—and acceptable to us all—for Luke to use terms that were more generic in nature, like "leader." Yet there is no known place where Luke is incorrect or out-of-date in his use of these specific titles. This level of accuracy on these detailed points may well incline us to trust Luke's accuracy on other points. If he is this careful in

---

77. I will discuss the similarities between Acts and Paul's letters in more detail in the discussion of Luke's sources in chapter 4.

78. On these biographical connections between the writings of Luke and Paul, see F. F. Bruce, "The First Church Historian," pp. 1–14 in *Church, Word, and Spirit: Historical and Theological Essays in Honor of Geoffrey W. Bromiley*, ed. J. E. Bradley and R. A. Miller (Grand Rapids: Eerdmans, 1987), 11–13.

79. Porter, *Paul in Acts*, 199.

80. In the most recent seven decades, see particularly Dibelius, *The Book of Acts: Form, Style, and Theology*; Haenchen, *Acts*; and Gerd Lüdemann, *Early Christianity According to the Traditions in Acts: A Commentary*, trans. John Bowden (Minneapolis: Fortress, 1989).

such small details that we can measure, we should expect him to be similarly careful in the main points of his story and with details that are not as easy for us to measure.[81]

Second, theology and history can fit together, and Luke's theological interests do not necessarily falsify his historical reporting. Some scholars have suggested that historical accuracy is necessarily compromised when one's theological agenda is introduced

In Support of the Historical Accuracy of Luke-Acts

The following are examples of experts in a variety of history-related fields who, over the course of the past century and a half, have been uncovering evidence and making arguments in support of the historical accuracy of Luke's reports in the Gospel of Luke and the book of Acts.

Archaeology and Geography of the Ancient Middle East

Sir William M. Ramsay, *St. Paul the Traveller and the Roman Citizen*, 11th ed. (London: Hodder & Stoughton, 1895), 14; and idem, *The Bearing of Recent Discovery on the Trustworthiness of the New Testament*, 4th ed. (London: Hodder & Stoughton, 1920), 89.

Roman Law

A. N. Sherwin-White, *Roman Society and Roman Law in the New Testament* (Oxford: Oxford University Press, 1963; repr., Grand Rapids: Baker, 1992), 189.

Ancient Sea Voyages

James J. Smith, *The Voyage and Shipwreck of St. Paul*, 4th ed., ed. Walter E. Smith (London: Longmans/Green, 1880), 20–21.

Hellenistic Historiography

Colin J. Hemer, *The Book of Acts in the Setting of Hellenistic History*, ed. Conrad H. Gempf, WUNT 49 (Tübingen: Mohr Siebeck, 1989; repr., Winona Lake, IN: Eisenbrauns, 1990), 412.

The Speeches in the Acts of the Apostles

F. F. Bruce, *The Speeches in the Acts of the Apostles*, Tyndale Monographs 1 (London: Tyndale, 1942), 8, 27.

The History of Early Christianity

Martin Hengel, *Acts and the History of Earliest Christianity*, trans. John Bowden (Philadelphia: Fortress, 1980), 60–61.

The Life and Teaching of Paul in Acts versus Paul in His Letters

Stanley E. Porter, *The Paul of Acts: Essays in Literary Criticism, Rhetoric, and Theology* (Tübingen: Mohr Siebeck, 1999; repr., *Paul in Acts*, Library of Pauline Studies, Peabody, MA: Hendrickson, 2001), 6–7, 206.

Luke as Trustworthy Historian and Theologian

I. Howard Marshall, *Luke: Historian and Theologian*, 3rd ed. (Carlisle: Paternoster, 1988; repr., New Testament Profiles, Downers Grove, IL: InterVarsity Press, 1998), 18–19, 85.

Luke among Other Ancient Historians

Craig S. Keener, *Acts: An Exegetical Commentary*, 4 vols. (Grand Rapids: Baker Academic, 2012–2015), 1:220.

81. Douglas S. Huffman, "The Gospel of Luke," pp. 80–101 in *What the New Testament Authors Really Cared About: A Survey of Their Writings*, ed. Kenneth Berding and Matt Williams, 2nd ed. (Grand Rapids: Kregel, 2015), 81–83; cf. Henry Joel Cadbury, *The Book of Acts in History* (New York: Harper & Brothers, 1955), 40–43.

(which is an interesting claim with its own theological agenda!). In recent decades, however, there has been a renewed respect for Luke's historical accuracy. For example, long ago Sir William Ramsay began his archaeological studies related to Acts with the assumption that Luke was inaccurate in his descriptions but concluded in favor of the book's historicity.[82] Since then, experts in diverse fields have investigated other aspects of Luke's work and have concluded that Luke is an accurate historian (see sidebar).

In his contribution to the New Testament, Luke has shown that Christianity is based on real historical events because—especially for Christians—an accurate understanding of theology is based on an accurate understanding of history. Thus, Luke sought to write with accuracy for the assurance of his reader (see again Luke 1:1–4). The real historical events Luke records were part of a greater unfolding series of events orchestrated by God.

Stylus similar to what Luke might have used to write Acts of the Apostles.
Public domain, Metropolitan Museum of Art.

2.6 CONCLUDING REMARKS

Even if we are satisfied with the truth of what Luke records in the historical accounts he relays to us in history-based genres, we must ask why Luke chooses to record the story as he does. Certainly, he could have related the historical facts just as accurately in some other fashion, with some other selection of terms, with some different set of emphases. Rather than reading Acts (and any other part of Scripture) with our own agendas and by our own definitions of successful living, we should seek out Luke's agenda and try to understand his definition of a successful life. To help us properly understand Luke's story on Luke's terms, we look at Luke's storytelling techniques in chapter 3.

2.7 Key People, Places, and Terms

- ancient historiographer standards
- apologetic purpose
- biographical historical monograph
- biographical purpose
- biography
- combined purposes
- confirmational purpose
- defense document
- demonstration
- doctrinal purpose
- entertainment purpose
- evangelistic purpose
- fiction
- genre
- historical purpose
- historian selectivity
- historicity
- history
- Luke-Acts
- mediation purpose
- paradigmatic purpose
- Paul of Acts versus Paul's letters
- *polygeneris*
- *praxeis*
- sequel
- speech expectations
- *sui generis*
- theology and history

82. Ramsay, Sir William M., *St. Paul the Traveller and the Roman Citizen*, 11th ed. (London: Hodder & Stoughton, 1895), 7–8.

2.8 Questions for Review and Discussion

1. What is "genre"? What role does it have in the interpretation process?
2. How would you describe the relationship between the NT books of the Gospel of Luke and the Acts of the Apostles?
3. What would you say is the genre of Acts, and how should that influence our interpretation of the book?
4. For what purposes do you think Luke wrote the book of Acts, especially given that he is the only gospel writer with a sequel volume?
5. How does Luke's writing measure up to the standards of ancient historiography?
6. What factors favor the historical trustworthiness of Acts, and in what way(s) does the trustworthiness of Acts matter for its message to your church?

2.9 Optional Assignments

1. **Text Reflection Project**—*Relating the concepts discussed in this chapter to another biblical text.* This chapter suggests that the canonical gospels and Acts involve all three kinds of historiographical writing: documentary history (recording historical facts for the readers), explicative history (using narrative to explain history to the readers), and poetic history (making an ideological or theological appeal to the readers through the story). Examine the purpose statements of Luke and John (Luke 1:1–4; Acts 1:1–3; 4:12; John 20:30–31; 21:24–25) regarding their contributions to the New Testament, and assess the strength of the suggestion that they involve all three kinds of historiographical writing. Do Matthew or Mark make any similar claims?
2. **Interview Project**—*Inquiring of others their views concerning the concepts discussed in this chapter.* In an interview with your pastor (or some other respected Christian leader), ask the following questions:
   - What would you say is the genre of Acts, and how should that influence our interpretation of the book?
   - For what purposes do you think Luke wrote the book of Acts, especially given that he is the only gospel writer with a sequel volume?
3. **Service-Learning Project**—*Applying the concepts discussed in this chapter in some form of service to others outside the class.* Given Luke's gifted writing ability and opportunities to research the historical events, it is no surprise that his service to the church has taken on a literary form. Assess your own interests and giftedness and, in light of that assessment, make arrangements to serve the church—either a local church body or some parachurch organization that represents God's people.
4. **Prayer Project**—*Talking with God about the concepts discussed in this chapter.* Write a prayer of praise and gratitude to the Lord for the historical trustworthiness of Luke's record in Acts, expressing some of the specific implications this trustworthiness has for your life.

5. **Testimony Project**—*Telling others about the concepts discussed in this chapter.* Write up a one-page summary of why we should respect the historicity (i.e., the historical trustworthiness) of Acts and arrange to share that information with someone. How did they respond to the summary of data you pulled together?

2.10 Bibliography for Going Further

2.10.1 The Unity of Luke-Acts

Cadbury, Henry J. *The Making of Luke-Acts*. 2nd ed. London: SPCK, 1958. Repr., Peabody, MA: Hendrickson, 1999.

Gregory, Andrew F., and C. Kavin Rowe, eds. *Rethinking the Unity and Reception of Luke and Acts*. Columbia, SC: University of South Carolina Press, 2010.

Menoud, Philippe H. "Jesus and His Witnesses: Observations on the Unity of the Work of Luke." Pages 149–66 in *Jesus Christ and the Faith: A Collection of Studies*. Translated by Eunice M. Paul. PTMS 18. Pittsburgh: Pickwick, 1978.

Parsons, Mikeal, and Richard I. Pervo. *Rethinking the Unity of Luke and Acts*. Minneapolis: Fortress, 1993.

Verheyden, Joseph, ed. *The Unity of Luke-Acts*. BETL 142. Leuven: Leuven University Press, 1999.

2.10.2 The Genre(s) of Luke and Acts

Adams, Sean A. "The Genre of Luke and Acts: The State of the Question." Pages 97–120 in *Issues in Luke-Acts: Selected Essays*. Edited by Sean A. Adams and Michael Pahl. Gorgias Handbooks 26. Piscataway, NJ: Gorgias, 2012.

———. *The Genre of Acts and Collected Biography*. SNTSMS 156. Cambridge: Cambridge University Press, 2013.

Alexander, Loveday C. A. *Acts in Its Ancient Literary Context: A Classicist Looks at the Acts of the Apostles*. LNTS 298. London: T&T Clark, 2005.

Bale, Alan J. *Genre and Narrative Coherence in the Acts of the Apostles*. LNTS 514. New York: Bloomsbury T&T Clark, 2015.

Burridge, Richard A. "The Genre of Acts—Revisited." Pages 3–28 in *Reading Acts Today: Essays in Honour of Loveday C. A. Alexander*. Edited by Steve Walton, Thomas E. Phillips, Lloyd Keith Pietersen, and F. Scott Spencer. LNTS 427. New York: T&T Clark, 2011.

Penner, Todd. "Madness in the Method? The Acts of the Apostles in Current Study." *CurBR* 2 (2004): 223–93.

Phillips, Thomas E. "The Genre of Acts: Moving Towards a Consensus?" *CurBR* 4 (2006): 365–96.

2.10.3 The Purpose(s) of Luke-Acts

Franklin, Eric. *Christ the Lord: A Study in the Purpose and Theology of Luke-Acts*. London: SPCK, 1975.

Maddox, Robert L. *The Purpose of Luke-Acts*. FRLANT. Göttingen: Vandenhoeck & Ruprecht, 1982. Repr., edited by John Riches. SNTW. Edinburgh: T&T Clark, 1985.

Peterson, David. "The Motif of Fulfillment and the Purpose of Luke-Acts." Pages 83–104 in *The Book of Acts in its Ancient Literary Setting*. Edited by Bruce W. Winter and Andrew D. Clarke. BAFCS 1. Grand Rapids: Eerdmans, 1993; Carlisle: Paternoster, 1993.

Strauss, Mark L. "The Purpose of Luke-Acts: Reaching a Consensus." Pages 135–50 in *New Testament Theology in Light of the Church's Mission: Essays in Honor of I. Howard Marshall*. Edited by Jon Laansma, Grant R. Osborne, and Ray Van Neste. Eugene, OR: Cascade, 2011.

2.10.4 The Historicity of Acts

Bruce, F. F., "The First Church Historian." Pages 1–14 in *Church, Word, and Spirit: Historical and Theological Essays in Honor of Geoffrey W. Bromiley*. Edited by J. E. Bradley and R. A. Miller. Grand Rapids: Eerdmans, 1987.

Gasque, W. Ward. "The Book of Acts and History." Pages 54–72 in *Unity and Diversity in New Testament Theology*. Edited by Robert A. Guelich. Grand Rapids: Eerdmans, 1978.

Hemer, Colin J. *The Book of Acts in the Setting of Hellenistic History*. Edited by Conrad H. Gempf. WUNT 49. Tübingen: Mohr Siebeck, 1989. Repr., Winona Lake, IN: Eisenbrauns, 1990.

Hengel, Martin, *Acts and the History of Earliest Christianity*. Translated by J. Bowden. London: SCM/Philadelphia: Fortress, 1979.

Jervell, Jacob. "Paul in the Acts of the Apostles: Tradition, History, Theology." Pages 297–306 in *Les Actes des Apôtres: Traditions, rédaction, théologie*. Edited by Jacob Kremer. BETL 48. Gembloux: Duculot, 1979; Leuven: Leuven University Press, 1979.

Marshall, I. Howard. *Luke: Historian and Theologian*. 3rd ed. Carlisle: Paternoster, 1988. Repr., New Testament Profiles. Downers Grove, IL: InterVarsity Press, 1998.

McKnight, Scot, and Matthew C. Williams. "Luke." Pages 39–57 in *Historians of the Christian Tradition: Their Methodologies and Influence on Western Thought*. Edited by Michael Bauman and Martin I. Klauber. Nashville: Broadman & Holman, 1995.

Porter, Stanley E. *The Paul of Acts: Essays in Literary Criticism, Rhetoric, and Theology*. Tübingen: Mohr Siebeck, 1999. Repr., *Paul in Acts*. Library of Pauline Studies. Peabody, MA: Hendrickson, 2001.

3 Storytelling in Acts

The Ascension of Jesus by S. G. Rudl (1900), Svatého Václava, Prague.
Renáta Sedmáková/stock.adobe.com

Chapter Goals

After reading this chapter, you should be able to:

- Give an outline for the Acts of the Apostles.
- Describe Luke's storytelling techniques in Acts.
- Discuss some of Luke's most emphasized themes in Acts.
- Outline some of the basic elements of the gospel message as described in Acts.

Chapter Overview

3.1 The Structure of Acts: How Might We Outline Acts?
3.2 Telling the Story of Acts: What Are Luke's Storytelling Techniques?
3.3 Themes in Acts: What Are Some of the Key Ideas in Acts?
3.4 The Jesus Story in Acts: How Do People Tell the Gospel in Acts?
3.5 Concluding Remarks
3.6 Key People, Places, and Terms
3.7 Questions for Review and Discussion
3.8 Optional Assignments
3.9 Bibliography for Going Further

Key Verses

You will receive power when the Holy Spirit comes on you; and you will be my witnesses in Jerusalem, and in all Judea and Samaria, and to the ends of the earth. (Acts 1:8)

Salvation is found in no one else, for there is no other name under heaven given to mankind by which we must be saved. (Acts 4:12)

I now realize how true it is that God does not show favoritism but accepts from every nation the one who fears him and does what is right. You know the message God sent to the people of Israel, announcing the good news of peace through Jesus Christ, who is Lord of all. (Acts 10:34–36)

INTRODUCTION

In telling his story so as to communicate his concerns to his readers, Luke outlines his material in an orderly fashion and utilizes several storytelling techniques. Scholars have proposed various ways to organize Acts and have likewise suggested various outlines of Luke's key theological themes in Acts. This chapter examines these storytelling matters of structure, techniques, and themes in Acts. Lastly, the message about Jesus is unquestionably one of Luke's concerns, so we briefly address some of the basic elements of the gospel message as described in Acts.

3.1 THE STRUCTURE OF ACTS: HOW MIGHT WE OUTLINE ACTS?

Developing an outline for the flow of thought in a document is a helpful way to approach the study of any book of Scripture. Of course, to develop an outline for studying a book, one must study the book![1] Not surprisingly, in studying Acts, scholars have varied in their suggestions for outlining the book. There may be more differing proposals for the structure of Acts than for any other narrative of the New Testament.[2] I survey here four kinds of outlines for Acts before proposing a fifth as more helpful.

1. This is not as circular as it might sound, for the idea is to maintain a willingness to learn and keep on learning as one studies.

2. See Bruce W. Longenecker, *Rhetoric at the Boundaries: The Art and Theology of the New Testament Chain-Link Transitions* (Waco, TX: Baylor University Press, 2005), 227.

3.1.1 An Ethnogeographic Witness Outline for Acts

Some utilize an ethnogeographic witness outline based on the sections of Acts that appear to follow the spread of the gospel message as described by Jesus in Acts 1:8: "You will be my witnesses in Jerusalem, and in all Judea and Samaria, and to the ends of the earth." Although readers of Acts may differ as to the precise boundaries of each of the main sections for this outline, this is a common way to approach the book of Acts. With the three groupings of place names (i.e., Jerusalem, Judea and Samaria, the ends of the earth), some suggest that the author is indicating his work is to be understood structurally according to this geographic layout. But the ancient use of the Greek phrase for "to the ends of the earth" (*heōs eschatou tēs gēs*) indicates that it is more likely a reference to gentile people groups rather than merely to physical territories.[3] And this makes good sense of Luke's report in Acts: the gospel goes to the people of these territories and not merely to the physical places.

An Ethnogeographic Outline for Acts

For a use of this type of outline, see I. Howard Marshall, *The Acts of the Apostles*, NTG (Sheffield: Sheffield Academic, 1992), 29.

The Acts of the Apostles

- I. Witnesses in Jerusalem—Acts 1:1–5:42
    - A. The beginning of the church (1:1–2:47)
    - B. The church and the Jewish authorities (3:1–5:42)
- II. Witnesses in Judea and Samaria—Acts 6:1–11:18
    - A. The church begins to expand (6:1–9:31)
    - B. The beginning of the gentile mission (9:32–11:18)
- III. Witnesses to the Ends of the Earth—Acts 11:19–28:31
    - A. The mission from Antioch to Asia Minor (11:19–14:28)
    - B. The discussion concerning the gentiles in the church (15:1–35)
    - C. Paul's missionary campaign in Macedonia and Achaia (15:36–18:17)
    - D. Paul's missionary campaign in Asia Minor (18:18–20:38)
    - E. Paul's arrest and imprisonment (21:1–28:31)

3. See esp. David W. Pao, "Jesus's Ascension and the Lukan Account of the Restoration of Israel," pp. 137–55 in *Ascent into Heaven in Luke-Acts: New Explorations of Luke's Narrative Hinge*, ed. David K. Bryan and David W. Pao (Minneapolis: Fortress, 2016), 144–45.

A Biographical Outline for Acts

For a use of this type of outline, see Walter L. Liefeld, *Interpreting the Book of Acts*, Guides to New Testament Exegesis (Grand Rapids: Baker, 1995), 39.

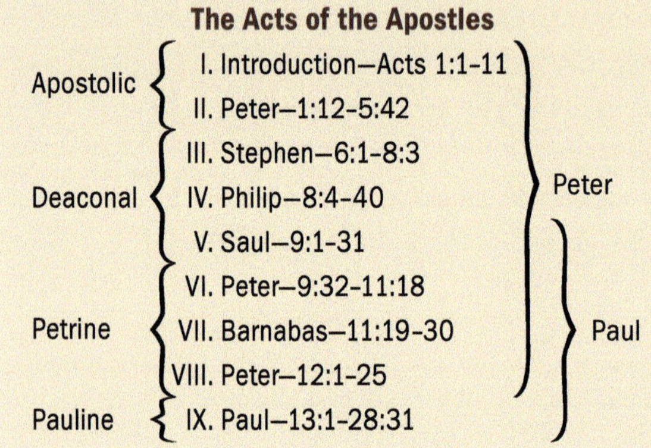

An Ecclesiological Outline for Acts

For a use of this type of outline, see Simon J. Kistemaker, *Exposition of the Acts of the Apostles*, New Testament Commentary (Grand Rapids: Baker, 1990), 36.

The Acts of the Apostles

I. Before Pentecost–Acts 1:1-26
II. The Church in Jerusalem–2:1-8:1a
III. The Church in Palestine–8:1b-11:18
IV. The Church in Antioch–11:19-13:3
V. The First Missionary Journey–13:4-14:28
VI. The Council at Jerusalem–15:1-35
VII. The Second Missionary Journey–15:36-18:22
VIII. The Third Missionary Journey–18:23-21:16
IX. In Jerusalem and Caesarea–21:17-26:32
X. Voyage to and Stay in Rome–27:1-28:31

3.1.2 A Biographical Outline for Acts

Because the book of Acts traces the ministries of several key figures, some scholars prefer a biographical outline for the book. As already noted, while this NT book is known as The Acts of the Apostles, it ironically has major stories about only one of the original twelve (i.e., Peter) and then even more stories about one who is not one of the original twelve (i.e., Paul). Thus, such biographical outlines tend to stress Peter in the first half of Acts (Acts 1–12) and Paul in the last half (Acts 13–28). Nevertheless, within these two halves of Acts, other significant characters have smaller sections devoted to stories about their lives and ministries. As the gospel expands among the people groups of the world, the number of gospel witnesses—beyond the original twelve—expands as well.

3.1.3 An Ecclesiological Outline for Acts

Because the book of Acts traces the growth and expansion of the early church, some scholars prefer an ecclesiological outline, charting church-growth activities and locations. Such outlines treat Acts as the first work of church history and focus on the way the stories of Acts are grouped around the churches of certain geographic localities, including those developed during Paul's missionary travels.

3.1.4 A Panels of Progress Outline for Acts

Similar to an ecclesiological outline is the more literary "panels" outline, offered by Cuthbert Hamilton Turner. Rather than its divisions being based on geographic localities of the churches, however, this outline takes its cues from summary statements on the gospel's progress that Luke inserts at six places in the story.[4] Because it focuses on the progress of the church as portrayed in the book's summary statements, this literary outline has been popularized in a nuanced form by Richard Longenecker as a "panels of progress" outline (see sidebar).[5] While laudable for its attempt to discover Luke's organization by attending to the summary statements, there are two drawbacks to Longenecker's panels of progress outline. First, this outline bypasses several other progress summary statements in Acts (see sidebar "Progress Summary Statements"). Second, some of the selected summary statements occur in places that seem to disrupt the storyline if taken as major breaks rather than as minor breaks. This is most notable in the second half of Acts where the progress summaries interrupt the reports of the missionary journeys.[6]

A Panels of Progress Outline for Acts

For a use of this type of outline, see Longenecker, "Acts," 696.

The Acts of the Apostles

Introduction—Acts 1:1-2:41

Part I: The Christian Mission to Jewish World (Acts 2:42-12:24)

- Panel 1: Earliest Days of the Church—2:42-6:7
- Panel 2: Events in the Lives of Three Pivotal Figures—6:8-9:31
- Panel 3: Advances of the Gospel in Palestine-Syria—9:32-12:24

Part II: The Christian Mission to Gentile World (Acts 12:25-28:31)

- Panel 4: Missionary Journey #1 and Jerusalem Council—12:25-16:5
- Panel 5: Missionary Journeys #2 and #3—16:6-19:20
- Panel 6: To Jerusalem and Thence to Rome—19:21-28:31

4. Cuthbert Hamilton Turner, "Chronology of the New Testament" pp. 403–25 in *A Dictionary of the Bible*, ed. James Hastings (Edinburgh: T&T Clark, 1898; repr., Peabody, MA: Hendrickson, 1988), 1:421. Turner's article is referenced and discussed in Floyd V. Filson, "Live Issues in the Acts," *BR* 9 (1964): 26–37, esp. 26–29.

5. Richard N. Longenecker, "Acts," pp. 663–1102 in *Luke-Acts*, vol. 10 of *The Expositor's Bible Commentary*, ed. Tremper Longman III and David E. Garland, rev. ed. (Grand Rapids: Zondervan, 2007), 696; Longenecker separates out Acts 1:1–2:41 as an "Introduction" apart from the six panels identified by C. H. Turner.

6. Making a different set of literary observations, Bruce W. Longenecker has suggested a four-part outline of Acts; see Longenecker, *Rhetoric at the Boundaries*, 165–252. At three points in Acts, Longenecker suggests that Luke has utilized an interlocking method of storytelling to facilitate a literary transition from one section to another. For example, at the halfway point in Acts, rather than a clean break from the Peter stories in Acts 1–12 to the Paul stories in Acts 13–28, there is an interplay of anticipatory and retrospective stories with one final episode glancing back to Peter (12:1–24) amid the forward-looking report about Saul/Paul (11:27–30/12:25). Observing three such major "chain-link interlock" passages, Longenecker outlines Acts into four main sections (see esp. pp. 226–35):

Progress Summary Statements in Acts

At times Luke ceases from narrating events within the story to comment briefly on the events from a perspective outside the story. Here are some of the most significant summary statements in Acts reporting on the spreading gospel message and growth of the church.

Acts 2:41–Those who accepted his message were baptized, and about three thousand were added to their number that day.

Acts 2:47–The Lord added to their number daily those who were being saved.

Acts 4:4–Many who heard the message believed; so the number of men who believed grew to about five thousand.

Acts 5:14–Nevertheless, more and more men and women believed in the Lord and were added to their number.

Acts 6:7–The word of God spread. The number of disciples in Jerusalem increased rapidly, and a large number of priests became obedient to the faith.

Acts 8:4–Those who had been scattered preached the word wherever they went.

Acts 9:31–Then the church throughout Judea, Galilee and Samaria enjoyed a time of peace and was strengthened. Living in the fear of the Lord and encouraged by the Holy Spirit, it increased in numbers.

Acts 9:42–This became known all over Joppa, and many people believed in the Lord.

Acts 11:21–The Lord's hand was with them, and a great number of people believed and turned to the Lord.

Acts 12:24–The word of God continued to spread and flourish.

Acts 13:49–The word of the Lord spread through the whole region.

Acts 15:35–Paul and Barnabas remained in Antioch, where they and many others taught and preached the word of the Lord.

Acts 16:5–The churches were strengthened in the faith and grew daily in numbers.

Acts 19:10–This went on for two years, so that all the Jews and Greeks who lived in the province of Asia heard the word of the Lord.

Acts 19:20–In this way the word of the Lord spread widely and grew in power.

Acts 28:30-31–For two whole years Paul stayed there in his own rented house and welcomed all who came to see him. He proclaimed the kingdom of God and taught about the Lord Jesus Christ–with all boldness and without hindrance!

I. Early Christianity in Jerusalem (Acts 1:1–8:3; interlock transition at 8:1b–3)
II. Persecution and the Consequent Spread of Christianity (Acts 8:4–12:25; interlock transition at 11:27–12:25)
III. The Spread of Christianity through the Ministry of Paul (Acts 13:1–19:41; interlock transition at 19:21–41)
IV. The Spread of Christianity through Events that Take Paul from Jerusalem to Rome (Acts 20:1–28:31)

A Storytelling Outline for Acts

Each section of this outline for Acts closes with a summary statement of some kind. The summary statements in the first half of the outline are progress summaries about the expansion of the gospel message (e.g., Acts 2:41; 6:7; 9:31). The summary statements in the second half of the outline are travel summaries about the journeys and work of the missionaries (e.g., Acts 14:27-28; 15:35; 18:22; 21:17; 26:32). The summary statement in the middle of the outline (Acts 12:24-25) contains both a note about progress (v. 24) and a note about travel (v. 25), and each of the three missionary campaigns has a progress summary within the section rather than at the end with the travel summary (Acts 13:49; 16:5; and 19:10, 20). Finally, the summary statement at the end of the book (Acts 28:30-31) contains both a note about travel (28:30; Paul could not travel) and a note about progress (28:31; the gospel was unhindered).

The Acts of the Apostles

Part A: The Story of Jesus Reaching the Jewish World (Acts 1-12)

I. The Story of Jesus Continues—Acts 1:1-2:41
II. The Story of the Church in Its Earliest Days—2:42-6:7
III. Three Key Non-apostle Characters in the Story—6:8-9:31
IV. The Story Advances in Palestine—9:32-12:24-25

Part B: The Story of Jesus Reaching the Gentile World (Acts 13-28)

V. The Story of the First Missionary Campaign—13:1-14:27-28
VI. The Central Interlude in the Story: The Jerusalem Council—15:1-35
VII. The Story of the Second Missionary Campaign—15:36-18:22
VIII. The Story of the Third Missionary Campaign—18:23-21:17
IX. The Story Moves in Prison in Jerusalem and Caesarea—21:18-26:32
X. The Story in Rough Waters on the Way to Rome—27:1-28:30-31

3.1.5 A Storytelling Outline for Acts

The variations between these outlines for Acts illustrates that a detailed structure for the book is difficult to come by because Luke is a skillful storyteller who has intricately interlocked its various parts.[7] Given the strengths exhibited by the various kinds of outlines in their connections to the story as Luke tells it—i.e., the focus on Acts 1:8 of ethnogeographic outlines, the ministry focus of biographical outlines, the church focus of ecclesiological outlines, and the focus on summary statements of the panels of progress outline—I offer here an adaptation of the panels of progress outline

7. I. Howard Marshall, *The Acts of the Apostles*, NTG (Sheffield: Sheffield Academic Press, 1992), 29.

that uses elements of the other outlines to overcome some of its difficulties. I call it a storytelling outline, as it focuses on the narrative content of Acts.

Like the panels of progress outline, each section of the storytelling outline ends with a summary statement of some kind. Unlike the panels of progress outline, however, the summary statements in the second half of the storytelling outline are travel summaries at the close of a journey about the work of the missionaries at that time in the story (see the summarizing statements of Acts 14:27–28; 15:35; 18:22; 21:17; 26:32).[8] Notably, the summary statement in the middle of the outline—between the focus on the Jewish world in Acts 1–12 and the focus on the gentile world in Acts 13–28—contains both a progress summary (12:24) and a travel summary (12:25); and this might be said of the summary statement at the end of the book as well (Acts 28:30–31) with a (non)travel summary (28:30; Paul could not travel) and a progress summary (28:31; the gospel was unhindered). Also worthy of note (as already indicated) is that Luke offers a progress summary within each of the journey sections in the second half of Acts rather than at the end of each journey (see Acts 13:49 in the midst of the first missionary campaign, Acts 16:5 in the midst of the second missionary campaign, and Acts 19:10 and 20 in the midst of the third missionary campaign).[9]

Like other outlines for Acts, this storytelling outline is an expansion of the outline provided in Acts 1:8. That is to say, sections I and II address "in Jerusalem," sections III and IV address "in Judea and Samaria," and sections V–X cover "to the ends of the earth." Beginning in chapter 6, our study of the book of Acts follows this storytelling outline section by section.

3.2 TELLING THE STORY OF ACTS: WHAT ARE LUKE'S STORYTELLING TECHNIQUES?

Luke uses a variety of literary conventions in writing Luke-Acts; I list here some of the most notable of these techniques.[10] Some of these appear only in Luke's Gospel, but I mention them for a sense of completeness. Naturally, the point of being aware of Luke's storytelling methods is that they help us better understand his message.

8. Strictly speaking, Acts 26:32 is not a summary statement at the close of its particular captivity section of the book (Acts 21:18–26:32); it is not even a narrative aside, as it is actually a citation of one character addressing another within the story rather than a comment from the narrator about the story. Nevertheless, the statement made by King Agrippa II does summarize for the reader in an authoritative way the verdict already indicated in the hearings Paul has endured up to this point: he is innocent. Rather than summarize Paul's "journey" in prison, Acts 26:32 summarizes Paul's innocent condition in that he could have been set free (i.e., journeyed away) had he not appealed to Caesar. Thus, Acts 26:32 transitions the reader to the final section of Acts where Paul journeys to Rome.

9. For a nuanced and yet positive analysis of utilizing Paul's missionary travels for outlining segments of Acts, see Patrick Schreiner, "Evaluating the Validity of the 'Three Missionary Journeys' Structuring Motif in Acts," *JETS* 63 (2020): 505–516.

10. This discussion is stimulated by, and is an expanded adaptation of, the list of Luke's literary conventions discussed in Karl Allen Kuhn, *Luke: The Elite Evangelist*, Paul's Social Network: Brothers and Sisters in Faith (Collegeville, MN: Liturgical Press, 2010), 43–70; cf. idem, *The Kingdom according to Luke and Acts: A Social, Literary, and Theological Introduction* (Grand Rapids: Baker Academic, 2015), 78–91.

Luke's Storytelling Techniques in Luke-Acts

1. Prologues (a.k.a. prefaces: Luke 1:1-4; Acts 1:1-2)
2. Infancy Narratives (Luke 1-2)
3. Genealogies (Luke 3:23-38)
4. Travel narratives (e.g., Luke 9:51-19:44; Acts 12:25-21:16; 27:1-28:6)
5. Parallelisms (e.g., Peter-Paul; Jesus-Paul; Jesus-Stephen)
6. Use of Scripture (e.g., citations, allusions, reminiscences, and echoes)
7. Chiasms (e.g., A-B-C-B'-A')
8. Foreshadowing (from section to section as well as from Luke to Acts)
9. Summary statements (more than a dozen in Acts)
10. Embedded letters (Acts 15:23-29; 23:26-30)
11. Speeches (about 30 percent of Acts consists of speeches)
12. Hospitality notes (the names of people hosting other believers)
13. Rhetoric (Luke's use of language in the art of persuasion)
14. Repetition (e.g., similar words and themes between episodes and within episodes)
15. Space allocation (some episodes are much longer than others)

3.2.1 Prologues (Luke 1:1–4; Acts 1:1–2)

In the analysis of Luke's writings, much has been written about his use of an introductory ***prologue*** to each of his two books. Some scholars have convincingly argued that Luke's introductory remarks (a.k.a. prefaces) to his two books (Luke 1:1–4; Acts 1:1–2) are written with similarities to the ancient scientific or historiographical traditions.[11] This would indicate that Luke intended his material to be taken seriously as history and not as fiction.[12]

3.2.2 Infancy Narratives (Luke 1–2)

Of the four gospels in the New Testament, only Matthew and Luke record stories about Jesus's birth and infancy.[13] While recording several different episodes than

11. See esp. Loveday C. A. Alexander, *The Preface to Luke's Gospel: Literary Convention and Social Context in Luke 1.1–4 and Acts 1.1*, SNTSMS 78 (Cambridge: Cambridge University Press, 1993); cf. David E. Aune, "Luke 1:1–4: Historical or Scientific *Prooimon*?" in *Paul, Luke and the Graeco-Roman World: Essays in Honour of Alexander J. M. Wedderburn*, ed. Alf Christophersen, Carsten Claussen, Jörg Frey, and Bruce Longenecker, JSNTSup 217 (Sheffield: Sheffield Academic Press, 2002; repr., London: T&T Clark, 2003), 138–48; and Sean A. Adams, "Luke's Preface and Its Relationship to Greek Historiography: A Response to Loveday Alexander," *JGRChJ* 3 (2006): 177–91. Cf. François Bovon, *Luke 1: A Commentary on the Gospel of Luke 1:1–9:50*, trans. Christine M. Thomas, ed. Helmut Koester, Hermenia (Minneapolis: Fortress, 2002), 17–18.

12. In addition to the several works of Loveday C. A. Alexander (such as those mentioned in the previous note), see also Osvaldo Padilla, *The Acts of the Apostles: Interpretation, History and Theology* (Downers Grove, IL: InterVarsity Press, 2016), 76–88, where Padilla argues that the prologues give evidence to Luke's historical and theological intentions.

13. For a thorough analysis of these narratives, see the landmark work by Raymond E. Brown, *The Birth of the Messiah: A Commentary on the Infancy Narratives of Matthew and Luke*, 2nd ed. (New York: Doubleday, 1993).

Matthew, Luke also goes further to include stories of the birth and childhood of John the Baptist. Luke writes these ***infancy narratives*** in a parallel, almost formulaic, fashion. Each has an angelic birth announcement, a reflective statement by the mother, a narration of the births and responses by others, and a statement about the child's growth. Unsurprisingly, as the continuation of the story of Jesus, Acts has no infancy narratives of any of its figures.

3.2.3 Genealogies (Luke 3:23–38)

In a world where family relations were deemed highly significant, ***genealogies*** could be very important for tracking one's heritage. Luke has a long genealogy for Jesus (Luke 3:23–38); the only other gospel to give an extended genealogy is Matthew (Matt 1:1–17).[14] The book of Acts contains no genealogical lists, but it does have several mentions of Abrahamic ancestry (Acts 3:12–26; 7:2–53; 13:26–33). Furthermore, in Acts, Luke occasionally mentions family relationships, e.g., spouses (Acts 5:1; 18:2; 24:24), parents/children (Acts 12:12; 19:14; 21:5, 8–9), and more general household references (Acts 10:2, 24; 16:15, 29–34; 18:8).

3.2.4 Travel Narratives (Luke 9:51–19:44; Acts 12:25–21:16; 27:1–28:6)

The book of Acts is somewhat famous for its record of apostles traveling to spread the gospel message (e.g., Paul's missionary journeys), but the Gospel of Luke is also noted for its unique travel narrative of Jesus en route to Jerusalem (Luke 9:51–19:44). Scholars often remark that the Gospel of Luke has a travel narrative that moves *toward* Jerusalem while the book of Acts traces travel *out from* Jerusalem.

Male-Female Parallels in Luke-Acts

In both of his books, Luke is noted for pairing similar accounts of men and women in telling the story of Jesus and the early church. Here are some notable examples.

Event Descriptions	Man / Men	Woman / Women
Visited by the angel Gabriel	Luke 1:5-25 (Zechariah)	Luke 1:26-38 (Mary)
Singers of prophetic songs	Luke 1:57-80 (Zechariah)	Luke 1:46-56 (Mary)
Proclaimers of prophecy	Luke 2:22-35 (Simeon)	Luke 2:36-40 (Anna)
Household healings	Luke 7:1-10 (centurion's servant)	Luke 7:11-17 (widow's son)
Traveling disciples of Jesus	Luke 8:1 (the Twelve)	Luke 8:2-3 (named women)

14. For more on the genealogies of Jesus in the New Testament, see Douglas S. Huffman, "Genealogy," *DJG*[1], 253–59; and David R. Bauer, "Genealogy," *DJG*[2], 299–302.

Event Descriptions	Man / Men	Woman / Women
Household healings	Luke 8:40–56 (Jairus's daughter)	Luke 8:43–48 (unnamed woman)
Parable figures suffering loss	Luke 15:11–32 (father and sons)	Luke 15:8–10 (unnamed woman)
Parable figures with requests	Luke 18:9–14 (Pharisee and tax man)	Luke 18:1–8 (persistent widow)
Witnesses on crucifixion day	Luke 23:26 (Simon from Cyrene)	Luke 23:27–31 (group of women)
Participants in Jesus's burial	Luke 23:50–54 (Joseph of Arimathea)	Luke 23:55–56 (women of Galilee)
Witnesses to the resurrection	Luke 24:12–35 (Peter, Cleopas, others)	Luke 24:1–11 (Mary, Joanna, Mary, others)
Early gathering of believers	Acts 1:12–13 (named apostles)	Acts 1:14 (women and Mary, Jesus's mother)
Receivers of the Spirit	Acts 2:15–21 (sons, men)	Acts 2:15–21 (daughters, women)
Accountable for behavior	Acts 5:1–11 (Ananias)	Acts 5:1–11 (Sapphira)
Recipients of healing	Acts 9:32–35 (Aeneas)	Acts 9:36–42 (Tabitha/Dorcas)
Sources of persecution	Acts 13:50 (leading men of the city)	Acts 13:50 (women of high standing)
Respondents to the gospel	Acts 17:34 (Dionysius)	Acts 17:34 (Damaris)
Partners in ministry	Acts 18:1–28 (Aquila)	Acts 18:1–28 (Priscilla)
Ministry hosts	Acts 21:8 (Philip the evangelist)	Acts 21:9 (Philip's four daughters)
Leader and his spouse	Acts 24:24 (Felix)	Acts 24:24 (Drusilla)
Leader and his consort	Acts 25:13, 23 (Agrippa)	Acts 25:13, 23 (Bernice)

3.2.5 Parallelisms

As a storyteller, Luke uses several forms of ***parallelism*** where he pairs episodes with similar descriptions. For example, Luke is noted for pairing similar accounts of men and women in Luke-Acts. As the Luke-Acts story progresses, several parallels unfold between people like Jesus and Stephen and between Peter and Paul and between them and Jesus (see sidebars).[15] As Luke saw it, God was at work in history, and it is not

15. See esp. Charles H. Talbert, *Literary Patterns, Theological Themes and the Genre of Luke-Acts*, SBLMS 20 (Missoula: Scholars Press, 1974), 15–65. For Jesus-Paul parallels, see also A. J. Mattill Jr., "The Jesus-Paul Parallels and Purpose of Luke-Acts: H. H. Evans Reconsidered," *NovT* 17 (1975): 15–46; cf. idem, "The Purpose of Acts: Schneckenburger Reconsidered," in *Apostolic History and the Gospel: Biblical and Historical Essays Presented to*

surprising that God would work in similar ways in different parts of history.[16] And the parallels between Jesus and some of the key disciples in the story make sense in light of Luke's explicit comment, "The student is not above the teacher, but everyone who is fully trained will be like their teacher" (Luke 6:40).[17] While not equivalent in all their details, Luke's similar accounts of events in the lives of his principal characters evoke a sense of parallelism nonetheless.

Jesus-Paul Parallels between Luke and Acts

Luke writes a number of parallel descriptions between Jesus in Luke and Paul in Acts. Naturally, some of these are Jesus-Peter-Paul parallelisms too.

Parallel Descriptions	Jesus in Luke	Paul in Acts
Synagogue preaching	4:16 ("his custom")	17:1-2 ("his custom"; cf. 9:20; 13:5, 14; 14:1; 17:10, 17; 18:4; 19:8)
Jew-gentile table fellowship	4:25-27	11:25-30; 15:1-35; 27:33-38
Jews responding to gentile inclusion	4:28	13:46, 50; 22:21-22
Jews threating to kill him	4:29; 6:7, 11; 11:53-54; 22:1-2	14:5, 19; 20:3, 19; 23:12-22
Healing of a demonized person	4:33-35; 8:26-39; 9:37-42	16:16-18
Healing of a fevered person	4:38-39	28:8
Healing of many sick people	4:40	28:9
Healing of a disabled man	5:17-26	14:8-14
Raising the dead	7:11-17; 8:41-56	20:9-12
Healing by touch of clothing	8:43-48 (garment hem)	19:12 (kerchiefs and aprons)
Predicting trouble in Jerusalem	9:22, 44; 17:25; 18:31-34	20:23; 21:4, 10-14
Determined to travel to Jerusalem	9:51	19:21
Sending disciples ahead	9:52; 19:28-34	19:22
Going to Jerusalem with disciples	10:38; 19:28-44	20:4-6; 21:1-17
Declaring readiness to die	12:50; 22:19; 23:46	21:13
Determined to complete his mission	13:32-33	20:24

F. F. Bruce on his 60th Birthday, ed. W. Ward Gasque and Ralph P. Martin (Grand Rapids: Eerdmans, 1970; Exeter: Paternoster, 1970), 110–11. See also Susan Marie Praeder, "Jesus-Paul, Peter-Paul, and Jesus-Peter Parallelisms in Luke-Acts: A History of Reader Response," in *The Society of Biblical Literature 1984 Seminar Papers*, ed. K. H. Richards, SBLSP 23 (Chico, CA: Scholars Press, 1984), 23–39; and David P. Moessner, "'The Christ Must Suffer': New Light on the Jesus–Peter, Stephen, Paul Parallels in Luke-Acts," *NovT* 28 (1986): 220–56.

16. Cf. Robert F. O'Toole, "Parallels between Jesus and His Disciples in Luke-Acts: A Further Study," *BZ* 27 (1983): 195–212.

17. See James R. Edwards, "Parallels and Patterns between Luke and Acts," *BBR* 27 (2017): 485–501.

Parallel Descriptions	Jesus in Luke	Paul in Acts
Initially well received at Jerusalem	19:35-44	21:17-19
Going to the temple	19:45-46	21:20-26
Facing opponents at the temple	19:47-48	21:27-32
Final communal meal	22:14-23 (Last Supper)	27:34-36 (before the shipwreck)
Giving a farewell discourse	22:24-38	20:17-35
Kneeling to pray	22:40-46	20:36-38; 21:5
Submitting to God's will	22:42	21:13-14
Hearing before the Sanhedrin	22:54-71	22:30-23:10
Hearing 1 before a Roman prefect	23:1-5 (Pilate)	24:1-27 (Felix)
Hearing before a Herod	23:6-12 (Herod Antipas)	25:13-26:32 (Herod Agrippa II)
Hearing 2 before a Roman prefect	23:13-25 (Pilate)	25:1-12 (Festus)
A crowd shouting to get rid of him	23:18	21:33-36
Final words/final defense	24:44-48	26:22-23

Peter-Paul Parallels in Acts

Luke writes parallel descriptions of some of the key characters in Acts. For example, there are a number of such parallels between Peter and Paul.

Parallel Descriptions	Peter	Paul
Healing a disabled man	3:1-10 (at Jerusalem temple)	14:8-14 (near Zeus temple)
Healing by strange means	5:15 (shadow)	19:12 (kerchiefs and aprons)
Announcing divine punishment	5:1-11 (Ananias & Sapphira)	13:6-12 (Elymas)
Highly regarded	5:12-13 (with the apostles)	14:4, 14 (called "apostle")
Miraculous prison release	5:19-21; 12:6-11 (at Jerusalem)	16:23-34 (at Philippi)
Defended by Pharisees	5:34-40 (led by Gamaliel)	23:9 (esp. vs. Sadducees)
Spirit with laying on of hands	8:17 (at Samaria)	19:6 (at Ephesus)
Confronting sorcerers	8:18-23 (Simon Magus)	13:6-12 (Elymas)
Healing a sick man	9:32-35 (Aeneas)	28:8 (Publius's father)
Raising the dead	9:36-43 (Dorcas)	20:9-12 (Eutychus)
Kneeling to pray	9:40 (over Dorcas)	20:36-38; 21:5 (with believers)
Receiving a message in a trance	10:9-16; 11:4-10 (in Joppa)	22:17-21 (in Jerusalem)
Refusing to be worshipped	10:25-26 (from Cornelius)	14:13-15 (at Lystra)
Leading household conversions	10:27-48 (Cornelius)	16:14-15 (Lydia), 29-34 (jailer)

3.2.6 Use of Scripture

I have already commented on how Luke's general writing style mimics the way the Hebrew Scriptures are written. In Luke-Acts he gives many explicit citations of OT passages (often preferring the Old Greek translation commonly referred to as the Septuagint, abbreviated LXX). Sometimes Luke makes general references to OT stories without quoting them (e.g., Luke 24:25, 46; Acts 3:18, 24; 10:43; 17:3; 18:28; 24:14; 26:23), and other times he merely makes more subtle allusions to the OT by means of borrowed phrases, without explicit citation or even general reference. Twice in Acts he gives a general recital of Israelite history as found in the OT Scriptures (Acts 7:2–53; 13:17–25). I will have more to say about Luke's view of Scripture (in section 3.3.2) and his use of Scripture (in chapter 4).

3.2.7 Chiasms

Chiasms are sometimes referred to as "verbal bookends" or "narrative nestings." As a literary technique, a ***chiasm*** employs repetition of phrases or ideas in a particular pattern illustrated by a sequence of letters like A-B-C-C'-B'-A', that is, a sequence of ideas or phrases (A-B-C) is immediately repeated but in reverse order (C'-B'-A').[18] Sometimes the middle item has no parallel (e.g., A-B-C-B'-A'). Several chiasms of various size and structure occur in Luke-Acts.

A Sample Large-Scale Chiasm in Acts 11:19–13:3

A: Acts 11:19-26—Barnabas brings Saul to Antioch church
  B: Acts 11:27—Prophets in Antioch
    C: Acts 11:28-30—Famine relief plan
      D: Acts 12:1-2—Herod Agrippa I kills
        E: Acts 12:3-19—Peter rescued
      D': Acts 12:20-23—Herod Agrippa I is killed
    C': Acts 12:24-25—Famine relief accomplished
  B': Acts 13:1—Prophets in Antioch
A': Acts 13:2-3—Saul and Barnabas sent by Antioch church

18. Originally appearing in 1942, the classic study of chiastic structures in the NT is by Nils Wilhelm Lund, *Chiasmus in the New Testament: A Study in the Form and Function of Chiastic Structures* (Peabody, MA: Hendrickson, 1992); it has been reprinted yet again as *Chiasmus in the New Testament: A Study in Formgeschichte* (Chapel Hill, NC: University of North Carolina Press, 2013).

3.2.8 Foreshadowing

Like any good author, from time to time Luke mentions what appears to be a minor detail (like the name of a person or a city) that later becomes an important factor in Acts. Sometimes even big events have a foreshadowing effect in the story (e.g., in Acts 2 the gospel is preached in Jerusalem to visitors "from every nation under heaven," foreshadowing the worldwide spread of the gospel later in Acts). Luke's creative storytelling has a number of forward-looking hints to upcoming portions of the story.

3.2.9 Summary Statements

In the discussion about the outline for Acts, I have already noted a series of summary statements in Acts. In those statements Luke ceases from narrating events within the story to comment briefly from an external perspective on the progress of the expanding gospel message and sometimes to summarize some missionary travels (see the earlier sidebar on progress summaries).[19] Such narrative asides can be used for purposes beyond progress summaries and travel summaries. For example, Luke uses summary statements to emphasize what is important to learn from the story, to affirm particular actions, to reinforce the character of particular figures in the story, to credit God with orchestrating the events, to uphold the church as the group to be affiliated with, etc. This is particularly noticeable in Luke's church life summaries (e.g., Acts 1:12–14; 2:42–47; 4:32–35; 5:12–16; 6:7; 9:31; 12:24), which Eckhard Schnabel suggests serve as historical reports of real activity, literary markers of time, theological pointers to God's work in the church, ecclesiological outlines of characteristic activity, and missiological reports of continued growth.[20] While most noted in Acts, Luke also makes use of various kinds of summary statements in the Gospel of Luke (e.g., Luke 1:80; 2:19–20, 40, 52; 4:14, 37, 40–41; 5:15; 6:17–19; 7:17, 21; 9:6; 19:47; 24:53).

3.2.10 Embedded Letters (Acts 15:23–29; 23:26–30)

Luke gives the wording of two different letters: one composed by the apostles and elders of the Jerusalem church (Acts 15:23–29) and one composed by the Roman military commander Claudius Lysias (Acts 23:26–30). These letters make for interesting insight into the story of Acts, but they also excite our curiosity about Luke's sources. Without quoting them, Luke also mentions a letter of authorization for Saul (Acts 9:2; 22:5) and a letter of reference for Apollos (Acts 18:27), and he indicates that Festus was planning to write a letter to Caesar regarding the charges against Paul (Acts 25:26).

---

19. For an analysis of the summary statements in Acts, see Walter L. Liefeld, *Interpreting the Book of Acts*, Guides to New Testament Exegesis (Grand Rapids: Baker, 1995), 41–46. See also H. Alan Brehm, "The Significance of the Summaries for Interpreting Acts," *SwJT* 33 (1990): 29–40; and Benjamin R. Wilson, "The Depiction of Church Growth in Acts," *JETS* 60 (2017): 317–32.

20. Eckhard J. Schnabel, *Acts*, ZECNT (Grand Rapids: Zondervan, 2012), 174–75.

3.2.11 Speeches

The Gospel of Luke has several sermons by Jesus, and Luke has recorded many conversations and sermons in Acts. Thus, Luke's use of speeches in his writings (especially in Acts) has been the subject of much investigation.[21] Luke would have personally heard some of the speeches he records in Acts, particularly those of Paul when they were traveling together. Necessarily selective as to which speeches to report and at what length to report them, historians can use speeches to interpret the events of the story (to the audience within the story and for the readers as well), to emphasize particular points, and to demonstrate the livability of the worldview being presented in the story.[22]

The Major Speeches in Acts

I. Eight speeches by Peter: Acts 1, 2, 3, 4, 5, 10, 11, and 13
II. Two speeches by James: Acts 15 and 21
III. One speech by Stephen: Acts 7 (the longest single speech in Acts)
IV. Nine speeches by Paul: Acts 13, 14, 17, 20, 22, 24, 26, 27, and 28
V. Four speeches by non-Christians:
- Acts 5:35–39 by Gamaliel
- Acts 19:35–40 by the town clerk in Ephesus
- Acts 24:2–8 by Tertullus
- Acts 25:14–21, 24–27 by Festus

Adapted from Witherington and Myers, *New Testament Rhetoric*, 46.

3.2.12 Hospitality Notes

Middle Eastern culture stresses hospitality, centered in people's homes. The Gospel of Luke many times mentions people staying, ministering, or eating with others in their homes. In the book of Acts, Luke reports the names of several people who seem to be noted for little other reason than their hospitality to Christian ministers. These include

21. See esp. F. F. Bruce, *The Speeches in the Acts of the Apostles*, Tyndale Monographs 1 (London: Tyndale, 1942); Marion L. Soards, *The Speeches in Acts: Their Content, Context, and Concerns* (Louisville: Westminster John Knox, 1994); and Osvaldo Padilla, *The Speeches of Outsiders in Acts* (Cambridge: Cambridge University Press, 2008). For more recent and briefer treatments, see Ben Witherington III and Jason A. Myers, "Early Christian Homilies: The Rhetorical Speech Summaries in Acts," in *New Testament Rhetoric: An Introductory Guide to the Art of Persuasion in and of the New Testament*, 2nd ed. (Eugene, OR: Cascade, 2022), 42–81; Osvaldo Padilla, "The Speeches in Acts: Historicity, Theology, and Genre," in *Issues in Luke-Acts: Selected Essays*, ed. Sean A. Adams and Michael Pahl, Gorgias Handbooks 26 (Piscataway, NJ: Gorgias, 2012), 171–93; and idem, *The Acts of the Apostles: Interpretation, History and Theology*, 123–97. See also Janusz Kucicki, *The Function of the Speeches in the Acts of the Apostles: A Key to Interpretation of Luke's Use of Speeches in Acts*, Biblical Interpretation Series 158 (Leiden: Brill, 2017).

22. Kuhn, *The Kingdom according to Luke and Acts*, 128; cf. idem, *Luke: The Elite Evangelist*, 54–55.

Judas in Damascus (Acts 9:11); Simon the tanner in Joppa (Acts 9:43; 10:6); Mary in Jerusalem (Acts 12:12); Lydia in Philippi (Acts 16:14–15); Jason in Thessalonica (Acts 17:5–9); Titius Justus in Corinth (Acts 18:7); Philip the evangelist in Caesarea (Acts 21:8–9); and Mnason in Jerusalem (Acts 21:16). Some have suggested that Luke met these people and that the inclusion of these hospitality notes serve as his documentation for some of his information sources.[23]

3.2.13 Rhetoric

I have already commented on Luke's Greek language abilities and capable writing style. His storytelling techniques are such that Luke regularly "chooses the style which is suitable for the different periods, places, and persons he is describing."[24] Luke's careful crafting of his story is not merely for entertainment purposes; he is attempting to persuade his readers of the truthfulness of the Christian message. Because ***rhetoric*** is sometimes described as the art of persuasion, some will refer to this as Luke's rhetorical ability. While scholars debate the ways and degrees to which early Christian rhetoric corresponds to formal classical rhetoric, the New Testament clearly evidences a concern to be persuasive. Rhetoric in this sense is found in Acts in various defense speeches (e.g., Acts 4:8–12; 13:16–41; 22–26), in some of the commissioning speeches (e.g., Acts 1:4–8; 20:18–35), and in evangelizing sermons (e.g., Acts 2:14–40; 10:34–43). Thus, people in Acts utilize rhetoric, and by the way he organizes and reports these events, Luke himself employs rhetoric to persuade his readers.[25]

3.2.14 Repetition

It is perhaps commonplace to observe that important ideas get repeated. Stories believed to be important are repeated in communities. There may be variety and valuable variation in the repetition—as, again, is noticeable with the four gospels in the New Testament—but the repetition itself shows some community emphasis. So too for individual authors: highly valued ideas will be treated repeatedly by an author. An author of historical events cannot record everything that happens, so when he chooses

---

23. Cf. Ben Witherington III, *The Acts of the Apostles: A Socio-Rhetorical Commentary* (Grand Rapids: Eerdmans, 1998; Carlisle: Paternoster, 1998), 165–70; J. Bradley Chance, *Acts*, Smyth & Helwys Bible Commentary (Macon, GA: Smyth & Helwys, 2007), 6.

24. Talbert, *Literary Patterns*, 1.

25. For more on rhetoric in Luke-Acts, see Daniel Lynwood Smith, *The Rhetoric of Interruption: Speech-Making, Turn-Taking, and Rule-Breaking in Luke-Acts and Ancient Greek Narrative* (Berlin: de Gruyter, 2012); C. Clifton Black, *The Rhetoric of the Gospel: Theological Artistry in the Gospels and Acts*, 2nd ed. (Louisville: Westminster John Knox, 2013); Joseph B. Tyson, "From History to Rhetoric and Back: Assessing New Trends in Acts Studies," in *Contextualizing Acts: Lukan Narrative and Greco-Roman Discourse*, ed. Todd C. Penner and Caroline Vander Stichele, SBLSymS 20 (Atlanta: Scholars Press, 2003; Leiden: Brill, 2003), 23–42; and Blake Shipp, "George Kennedy's Influence on Rhetorical Interpretation of the Acts of the Apostles," in *Words Well Spoken: George Kennedy's Rhetoric of the New Testament*, ed. C. Clifton Black and Duane F. Watson, Studies in Rhetoric and Religion 8 (Waco: Baylor University Press, 2008), 107–23.

to keep recording similar events and focusing on similar details and themes between different events, the reader is right to suspect a purpose to the repetition. So it is for Luke in his writing. Among the most notable instances of repetition in Acts are the thrice-described conversion of Paul (Acts 9, 22, and 26), the lengthy and redundantly told story of Cornelius's conversion (Acts 10:1–48; 11:1–18; 15:7–11), and the thrice-mentioned decision of the Jerusalem Council (Acts 15:19–21, 28–29; 21:24). Curiously, all three of these repeated elements are related to the inclusion of the gentiles, which suggests the critical importance of this theme in Acts.[26]

The martyrdom of St. Stephen. Church of Saints Gervais and Protais, Paris.

lemélangedesgenres/ stock.adobe.com

3.2.15 Space Allocation

Similar to noticing the use of repetition as a means of recognizing what is important to an author, noticing an abundance of space allocated to a particular topic or story may well be an indication of something important. The longest speech in the book of Acts is by Stephen (Acts 7:2–53). Given that most of Stephen's speech is a rehearsal of the OT story of faith, this seems to support Luke's point that faith in Jesus is the proper continuation of the OT faith. And this speech being given by Stephen—not by Peter or Paul!—seems to support the idea that one need not be an apostle to be used by God in ministry. One fourth of Acts covers the hardships of Paul, which helps the reader recognize that suffering is a normal experience in the life of faith.

3.3 Themes in Acts: What Are Some of the Key Ideas in Acts?

Luke has dozens of interests identifiable in the way he tells the story of Acts. In chapter 2, I noted that Luke intended to write the historical account of early church activities because he had theological motives for doing so. Scholars have variably described (and, of course, argued about) the theology of Luke-Acts.[27] Some have chosen particular metaphors or thematic ways to discuss Luke's theology such as "salvation," or "kingdom," or "bridge building."[28]

26. Mel Storm, *Living Lord, Empowering Spirit, Testifying People: The Story of the Church in the Book of Acts* (Eugene, OR: Wipf & Stock, 2014), 5.

27. Among the most notable works on Luke's theology are books by I. Howard Marshall, Jacob Jervell, Dennis E. Johnson, Darrell L. Bock, and Karl Allen Kuhn (see the bibliography at the end of the chapter). For brief and readable summaries of Lukan theology, see Walter L. Liefeld, "Luke, Theology of," *EDT*², 713–17; Scot McKnight and Matthew C. Williams, "Luke," in *Historians of the Christian Tradition: Their Methodology and Influence on Western Thought*, ed. M. Bauman and M. I. Klauber (Nashville: Broadman & Holman, 1995), 39–57; J. Julius Scott Jr., "Luke-Acts, Theology of," *EDBT*, 496–500; and Darrell L. Bock, "Luke-Acts," *NDBT*, 129–32.

28. For Luke's theology, the organizing metaphor of "salvation" is used by I. Howard Marshall and J. Julius Scott Jr., "kingdom" is used by Karl Allen Kuhn, and "bridge building" is used by Dennis E. Johnson.

For our purposes here, the thematic interests of Luke as found in Acts can be clustered together into ten statements (see sidebar) that revolve around the primary purpose of confirmation (or legitimization) identified in chapter 2. As expected, some of Luke's most emphasized theological statements support his central purpose: to show that God is at work in the world according to the Scriptures and through his Holy Spirit to bring the salvation of Jesus Christ to all people.[29] These ten key themes recur in Acts: they are expressed, proclaimed, explained, defended, and rejoiced over. And while these themes are interrelated, it will be useful here to briefly treat each theme separately.

Ten Key Theological Themes in Acts

1. The sovereign creator God is at work in the world.
2. The authoritative Scriptures are being fulfilled, especially in Jesus.
3. Jesus is the promised Messiah, the risen Lord and King.
4. Faith in Jesus Christ results in forgiveness of sins for all who repent.
5. The good news about Jesus is God's provision of salvation for humanity.
6. God is concerned for all people, and all who follow Jesus are God's true people.
7. Jesus followers witness to the good news about him.
8. The Holy Spirit is God's empowering presence in all his people.
9. In spreading the good news, believers will face opposition but can overcome it.
10. Jesus rules now but will return to rule more fully in his kingship role.

3.3.1 The Sovereign Creator God Is at Work in the World

Obviously, Luke believes in the Creator God of ancient Israel. As a character in Luke's storytelling, God seems rarely to enter the story directly. Nevertheless, God is credited for much of the activity in Luke-Acts (see sidebar on verbs emphasizing the ***sovereignty of God***). God created everything that exists and is sovereign over it all, including humanity. God can intervene in miraculous ways and give divine guidance by a variety of means. A most significant divine intervention in history attested by Luke-Acts involves God's activity in providing for salvation through faith in Jesus Christ. And God is credited with the spread of the gospel message, especially to the gentiles (Acts 11:17–18; 14:27; 21:19).

29. See Mark L. Strauss, "The Purpose of Luke-Acts: Reaching a Consensus," pp. 135–50 in *New Testament Theology in Light of the Church's Mission: Essays in Honor of I. Howard Marshall*, ed. Jon Laansma, Grant R. Osborne, and Ray Van Neste (Eugene, OR: Cascade, 2011), 146–49, who identifies eight major theological themes in Luke-Acts.

Verbs in Luke-Acts Emphasizing God's Sovereignty

Luke uses the following verbs in ways that emphasize God's sovereign activity in the world. Noted here are the Greek terms, the number of times each is used in the NT compared with the number of times Luke uses them, and some key passages in Luke-Acts.

- God "fulfills" his word and his plan. *plēroō*: NT–87; Luke–9, Acts–16 (see esp. Luke 1:20; 4:21; 21:24; 22:16; 24:44; Acts 1:16; 3:18; cf. Acts 13:27; 14:26).
- God "determines" how things will be. *orizō*: NT–8; Luke–1, Acts–5 (Luke 22:22; Acts 2:23; 10:42; 17:26, 31; cf. Acts 11:29).
- God "sets" times and people for certain tasks. *tithēmi*: NT–100; Luke–16, Acts–23 (see esp. Luke 20:43; Acts 1:7; 2:35; 13:47; 20:28).
- God "appoints" people to eternal life and to ministry. *tassō*: NT–8; Luke–1, Acts–4 (Luke 7:8; Acts 13:48; 15:2; 22:10; 28:23).
- Something "is necessary" or "must be" when God has designed it to be so. *dei*: NT–101; Luke–18, Acts–22 (see esp. Luke 2:49; 24:7, 26; Acts 4:12; 27:24-26).

3.3.2 The Authoritative Scriptures Are Being Fulfilled, Especially in Jesus

The plan of the sovereign creator God (Acts 2:23; 4:27–28) as foretold in the Hebrew Scriptures is being fulfilled (Luke 24:25–27, 44–48; Acts 3:18–26; 8:35; 17:2–3; 18:28). Luke so regularly appeals to the Hebrew Scriptures in a variety of forms (e.g., citations, allusions, and recollections) that his respect for its authority is apparent (see sidebar).[30] Luke has a high view of Scripture as the Word of God that will come to pass and cannot be thwarted. In Acts, Luke takes opportunities to summarize the message of the Hebrew Scriptures, and for him it centers on the suffering and death of the Messiah (Luke 24:25–27, 44–49; Acts 3:18; 10:43; 17:3; 18:28; 26:22–23).[31] Scripture fulfillment takes place especially in the life, death, resurrection, and exaltation of Jesus.[32]

---

30. For more on the tally of his appeals to Scripture and other details of Luke's use of the Old Testament, see chapter 6 of Douglas S. Huffman, *Understanding the New Testament Use of the Old Testament: Forms, Features, Framings, and Functions* (Grand Rapids: Baker Academic, 2024).

31. Jacob Jervell, *The Theology of the Acts of the Apostles*, New Testament Theology (Cambridge: Cambridge University Press, 1996), 73.

32. See François C. Bovon, *Luke the Theologian: Fifty-five Years of Research (1950–2005)*, 2nd ed. (Waco: Baylor University Press, 2006), 95. Generally acknowledged as launching modern scholarship on this Lukan interest is Paul Schubert, "The Structure and Significance of Luke 24," pp. 165–86 in *Neutestamentliche Studien für Rudolf Bultmann zu seinem Siebzigsten Geburtstag am 20 August 1954*, ed. W. Eltester, BZNW 21 (Berlin: Töpelmann, 1954). See also Darrell L. Bock, *Proclamation from Prophecy and Pattern: Lucan Old Testament Christology*, JSNTSup 12 (Sheffield: Sheffield Academic Press, 1987); and Mark L. Strauss, *The Davidic Messiah in Luke-Acts: The Promise and Its Fulfillment in Lukan Christology*, JSNTSup 110 (Sheffield: Sheffield Academic Press, 1995).

A Tally of the Uses of the Hebrew Scriptures in Luke-Acts

Forms of OT Use	Luke's Gospel	Book of Acts	Luke-Acts
Citations:	***24***	***33***	***57***
Introduced quotations	8	14	22
Introduced paraphrases	12	19	31
Unintroduced quotations	1	0	1
Unintroduced paraphrases	3	0	3
Allusions and Recollections:	***433***	***399***	***832***
Scripture summaries	14	19	33
Historical reminiscences	18	36	54
Specific allusions	159	82	241
Thematic echoes	242	262	504
Totals:	***457***	***432***	***889***

3.3.3 Jesus Is the Promised Messiah, the Risen Lord and King

It is a blinding glimpse of the obvious to state that the message about Jesus is a central concern in Luke-Acts. As noted, Luke sees Jesus as the fulfillment of Scripture. And in the story of Jesus, his resurrection is the core event that changed the course of history. Luke pictures Jesus as exalted by God in the resurrection and ascension (Luke 1:52; 14:11; 18:14; Acts 2:32–33, 36; 5:30–32; 7:55–56). This exaltation of Jesus points to his rightful kingship: this king has conquered death. Luke ascribes a variety of titles to Jesus, including "Christ" (Greek for "anointed one" ≈ Hebrew for "***Messiah***"), which is taken to be equivalent to "***Son of God***" (cf. Luke 22:66–71; Acts 9:20–22). Jesus's favorite self-designation is "***Son of Man***" (twenty-five times in Luke; in Acts only at 7:56 in the mouth of Stephen), a title echoing a glorious redeemer figure in Dan 7:13–14. But perhaps more significant for contemplating Luke's view of Jesus is that the predominant title for Jesus in Acts is "***Lord***" (*kyrios*), used almost fifty times (see sidebar).[33] For Luke, Jesus Christ is Lord of all (Acts 10:36). And in the places where Luke ascribes to Jesus both the title of "Lord" and "Christ," the contexts reveal that he is stressing Jesus's salvation-historical significance.[34]

---

33. See James D. G. Dunn, "ΚΥΡΙΟΣ in Acts," pp. 241–53 in *The Christ and the Spirit: Collected Essays of James D. G. Dunn*, vol. 1: *Christology*, ed. James D. G. Dunn (Edinburgh: T&T Clark; Grand Rapids: Eerdmans, 1998); and Ling Cheng, *The Characterization of God in Acts: The Indirect Portrayal of an Invisible Character*, Paternoster Biblical Monographs (Waynesboro, GA: Paternoster, 2011; repr., Eugene, OR: Wipf & Stock, 2015), 237–39. Observing that "Lord" is Luke's favorite title for Jesus, Jacob Jervell comments, "In using the title of both God and Jesus, Luke in some sense regarded Jesus as on a level with God"; Jervell, *The Theology of the Acts of the Apostles*, 29.

34. Pao, "Jesus's Ascension and the Lukan Account of the Restoration of Israel," 149n51; cf. Strauss, *The Davidic Messiah in Luke-Acts*, 27.

The Most Prominent Title for Jesus in Acts: "Lord" (*kyrios*)
Distinguishing Its Use for God and for Jesus

Referents	Spoken by a Character in Acts	Introduced by Luke as Narrator
God (21 + 10 = 31 times)	1:24; 2:20*; 2:21*?; 2:25*; 2:34a*; 2:39; 3:20; 3:22*; 4:26*; 4:29; 5:9; 7:31; 7:33; 7:49*; 10:33; 12:11; 13:11; 13:47?; 15:17a; 15:17b*; 17:24	2:47?; 5:19; 8:26; 8:39; 11:21a; 12:7; 12:17; 12:23; 14:3; 19:20?
Jesus (28 + 20 = 48 times)	1:6; 1:21†; 2:34b*; 2:36; 7:59†; 7:60; 9:5; 9:10b; 9:13; 9:17; 10:36; 11:16; 11:17†; 15:11†; 15:26†; 16:15; 16:31†; 20:19; 20:21†; 20:24†; 20:35†; 21:13†; 22:8; 22:10a; 22:10b; 22:19; 26:15a; 26:15b	4:33†; 8:16†; 9:1; 9:10a; 9:11; 9:15; 9:27; 9:28; 9:42; 11:20†; 13:12; 14:23; 18:8; 18:9; 18:25; 19:5†; 19:13†; 19:17†; 23:11; 28:31†
Unclear: God or Jesus (5 + 18 = 23 times)	8:22; 8:24; 13:10; 10:14; 11:8	5:14; 8:25; 9:31; 9:35; 11:21b; 11:23; 11:24; 13:2; 13:44; 13:48; 13:49; 15:35; 15:36; 15:40; 16:14; 16:32; 19:10; 21:14
Humans (4 times)	16:30; 25:26	16:16; 16:19
Supernatural Being (1 time)	10:4	
TOTALS (107 times):	**57 times spoken by characters in Acts**	**50 times spoken by Luke as narrator**

**kyrios* occurs in an OT citation (9 times); †*kyrios* occurs with the name of Jesus (17 times); ?*kyrios* refers to God but Jesus could be in mind (4 times)

Adapted, simplified, and corrected from the data found in Ling Cheng, *The Characterization of God in Acts: The Indirect Portrayal of an Invisible Character*, Paternoster Biblical Monographs (Waynesboro, GA: Paternoster, 2011; repr., Eugene, OR: Wipf & Stock, 2015), 237–39.

3.3.4 Faith in Jesus Christ Results in Forgiveness of Sins for All Who Repent

Scholars use the term ***salvation history*** to refer to God's activities in history to bring about the salvation of his people. Humanity's fundamental problem—the reason we need salvation of any kind—is our persistence in sinning against God. As it is, we are enslaved to sin and unable to save ourselves from it. Thus, God has acted to provide salvation for us, and Luke unambiguously notes that this salvation comes about only through Jesus Christ (Acts 4:12). Luke uses various interrelated terms in various combinations to express the theme of repentance for the forgiveness of sin. Repentance involves a turning from sin and is part of the faith necessary for forgiveness. In receiving forgiveness, the term *repentance* is a label for the negative facet, i.e., "turning from sin," and the term *faith* is a label for the positive facet, i.e., "turning toward God." Faith is a condition for the forgiveness of sin and resulting salvation (Luke 7:48–50; Acts 10:43; 13:39; 15:7–11; 16:31). But Luke is clear that repentance and saving faith are not human efforts by which people somehow earn salvation. Rather, Luke speaks about repentance as a gift given to both Jews and gentiles (Acts 5:31; 11:18); it is God who turns people from their sin to save them (Acts 3:26). Jesus has authority to forgive sins (e.g., Luke 5:17–26; Acts 2:38; 5:31; 10:43; 13:38–39; 22:16), and Luke even describes Jesus's mission in terms of seeking out sinners and calling them to repentance (Luke 5:27–32; 7:36–50; 15:1–2; 19:1–10; Acts 2:38; 3:19; 5:31).

3.3.5 The Good News about Jesus Is God's Provision of Salvation for Humanity

Salvation comes through the work of Jesus Christ, especially in his death and resurrection, so that creation in general and humans in particular can enjoy the fullness of life God intended. Evident among Luke's concerns is that salvation entails forgiveness of human sin against God. Salvation for all people is found only in Jesus (Acts 4:12).

The Purpose and Results of Faith in Jesus Christ

Faith in Jesus Christ is sometimes described with too simplistic a sense of purpose. Words like *salvation*, *redemption*, *life*, and *freedom* are appropriately used for what results when a person puts her faith in Christ. Luke uses the "salvation" family of words several times in his NT writings to talk about faith in Christ (see sidebar "Salvation Terms in Luke-Acts"). But these descriptions of faith have more robust implications than we sometimes recognize. For example,

- Jesus came to save us from sin:
    - from the eternal consequences of sin (i.e., eternal separation from God after death),
    - from the current power of sin (i.e., our enslavement to sin and its current damage).
- Jesus came to give us life:
    - eternal life with him in the future,
    - more abundant life on this side of eternity (but not mere "happiness").
- Jesus came to give us freedom:
    - but this freedom from sin comes by means of submission to Jesus as Lord of all,
    - and this freedom from sin is not freedom from hardship.

Can you think of other, more robust ways to describe the purpose and results of faith in Christ?

Salvation Terms in Luke-Acts

Luke uses a variety of salvation related terms. Here are a few of them and the number of times they appear in the New Testament, Luke, and Acts:

- salvation (*sōtēria*): NT—46; Luke—4; Acts—6
- salvation (*sōtērion*): NT—4; Luke—2; Acts—1
- savior (*sōtēr*): NT—24; Luke-Acts—4: Luke 1:47; 2:11; Acts 5:31; 13:23
- to save (*sōzō*): NT—107; Luke—17; Acts—13
- redemption (*lytrōsis*): NT—3: Luke 1:68; 2:38; Heb 9:12
- redemption (*apolytrōsis*): NT—10; Luke-Acts—1: Luke 21:28
- to redeem (*lytroō*): NT—3: Luke 24:21; Titus 2:14; 1 Pet 1:18
- redeemer (*lytrōtēs*): NT—1: Acts 7:35

The Greek verb for "save" (*sōzō*) is flexible enough to be used to mean "heal" (e.g., Luke 8:47-50) and "save/rescue [from danger]" (e.g., Luke 23:35-39) as well as "save from sin" (e.g., Luke 13:23; 18:26-27). But Luke is the only synoptic gospel to use the nouns for "salvation" (*sōtēria*, Luke 1:69, 71, 77; 19:9; and *sōtērion*, Luke 2:30; 3:6) and for "Savior" (*sōtēr*, Luke 1:47 of God; Luke 2:11 of Jesus), and he uses them predominantly with reference to saving from sin. Other phrases for salvation include "redeem" (*lytroō*, Luke 24:21), "redemption" ([*apo*]*lytrōsis*, Luke 1:68; 2:38; 21:28), "deliverer" (*lytrōtēs*, Acts 7:35), "to inherit eternal life" (Luke 10:25; 18:18), and "to enter the kingdom of God" (Luke 18:24-25). Here are five notable observations about Jesus's mission of salvation in Luke-Acts:

1. The concept of salvation—even aside from the special vocabulary—blankets Luke's writings as an overarching theme: from the birth narrative (Luke 1:47, 69, 77; 2:11) to Jesus's ministry (Luke 19:10) to Jesus's ascension (cf. Acts 5:31) to the gentile mission (Acts 28:28).
2. Jesus not only brings the message of salvation (Luke 7:22) but he is the Savior (Luke 19:10) and he is the message of salvation itself (Acts 4:12).
3. Assurance of salvation is part of Luke's reason for writing (Luke 1:1-4), and he speaks of the evidence God has provided for such assurance (Luke 24:37-43; Acts 17:31).
4. Salvation is universally available (Acts 9:15; 15:7-19; 18:6; 20:19-21; 28:28).
5. Luke uses the verb "saved" for physical healing too (Luke 7:50; 8:47-50; 17:19; 18:42-43).

Given the amount of space Luke gives to demonstrating that Jesus's suffering and death were in accordance with God's will as outlined in the OT Scriptures (e.g., Luke 9:22, 44; 17:3, 25; 18:31–34; 22:22; 24:7, 26, 46; Acts 2:24; 3:18; 9:22; 13:28–30; 17:3; 22:37; 24:7, 26, 44), essential among Luke's concerns is assuring his readers that Jesus is indeed the saving Messiah. The salvation Jesus provides is for now and not merely the future. Salvation is God's deliverance of humans from the current power and effects of sin in their lives as well as God's securing of eternity for humans.

Jesus as God the Divine Savior

H. Douglas Buckwalter, "The Divine Saviour," pp. 107–23 in *Witness to the Gospel: The Theology of Acts*, ed. I. Howard Marshall and David Peterson (Grand Rapids: Eerdmans, 1998), 107.

> The pulse of Luke's Christology is that of the exalted Jesus as God's co-equal. In comparing Jesus' heavenly reign in Acts with Yahweh's in the Old Testament, the parallels are pervasive and deliberate. As with Yahweh, Jesus visibly demonstrates his absolute superiority by personally revealing himself to people through his Spirit and direct self-manifestations, and by bringing to pass what he has personally communicated to them. Luke enhances this portrait of divine Christology by showing that as supreme deity, Jesus, by nature, behaves toward his people as 'one who waits on tables'. The exalted Jesus never behaves beneficently for reasons of self-aggrandizement, but to minister to his people.

3.3.6 God Is Concerned for All People, So All Who Follow Jesus Are God's True People

It is universally recognized that Jesus's selection of twelve apostles was symbolic of the people of God. Intriguingly, Luke makes a point to note that Jesus had many disciples from among whom he selected the twelve he called apostles (see Luke 6:12–16; cf. Luke 10:1). In Luke's parlance, any follower of Jesus is called a "disciple" (cf. Acts 11:26). The story Luke records in Luke-Acts is one in which the people of the world are offered the gift of becoming part of God's true people. Gentiles are invited to be people of God directly, without becoming Jews. But Luke means to demonstrate that gentiles are included, not that Jews are excluded.[35] All are invited to recognize God's saving work through Jesus Christ and to enter into the community of God's chosen people through the work of the Holy Spirit.

All those devoted to Jesus in faith are now part of God's people. And when one is in the community of God's people, one's priorities are reordered. Luke recognizes that this calls people away from their former prejudices. In essence, faith in Jesus calls people to reorder their priories to fit the "culture" of the family of God, to place their former systems of allegiance in submission to a greater allegiance.[36] Following Jesus completely changes a person's life, including all relationships and all priorities.

35. See the comments of Robert Lawson Brawley, *Luke-Acts and the Jews: Conflict, Apology, and Conciliation*, SBLMS 33 (Atlanta: Scholars Press, 1987), 159; Rebecca. I. Denova, *The Things Accomplished among Us: Prophetic Tradition in the Structural Pattern of Luke-Acts*, JSNTSup 141 (Sheffield: Sheffield Academic Press, 1997), 20; Darrell L. Bock, *A Theology of Luke and Acts: God's Promised Program, Realized for All Nations*, Biblical Theology of the New Testament (Grand Rapids: Zondervan, 2012), 121; and Jervell, *The Theology of the Acts of the Apostles*, 40–41.

36. See Aaron Kuecker, *The Spirit and the 'Other': Social Identity, Ethnicity and Intergroup Reconciliation in Luke-Acts*, LNTS 444 (New York: T&T Clark, 2011), 230; and Kuhn, *The Kingdom according to Luke and Acts*, 221.

Salvation Available to All in Luke-Acts

From Mark Allan Powell, "Salvation in Luke-Acts," *WW* 12.1 (1992): 10.

> Salvation, according to Luke-Acts, is available to all. Salvation is broadly conceived in these writings as participation in the reign of God, and, thus, as a present experience of life as God intends. This salvation is available because God has granted the Lord Jesus Christ the right to bestow salvation on whomever he chooses. People who wish to participate in the reign of God and desire to live as God intends receive this salvation when, through God's grace, they respond to the proclaimed word about Jesus with faith.

3.3.7 Jesus Followers Witness to the Good News about Him

The spread of the gospel message ("the good news," "the word," etc.) about Jesus is unmistakably a central theme in the book.[37] It is proclaimed or defended in one way or another on almost every page of Acts.[38] For Luke, serving as witnesses to the truth of the gospel message "is not just the task of one person, or choice persons, but is the province of the entire Christian community."[39] Luke offers a variety of examples of evangelism in a variety of settings and with different kinds of audiences. The importance of the witness theme in Acts is demonstrated in the many summary statements about the progress of the message. Remarkably, in some of the summary statements about the progress of the gospel, "the word of God" seems to refer not simply to a verbal sharing of the gospel message but to the church itself or the whole Christian movement (e.g., Acts 6:7; 12:24; 19:20).

Followers of Jesus spread the word about following Jesus because Jesus is Lord of all, and the resurrection of Jesus is a proof of his lordship (see Acts 17:31). That is to say, if there really is only one Lord over all people everywhere, as proven by Jesus's resurrection, then certainly his people should be announcing that reality everywhere.[40] In this way, the church's mission to reach the rest of the world with the gospel is the natural and necessary response to Jesus Christ being Lord of all.[41] With the witness theme tied to the theme of Jesus as risen Lord, Luke centers the church's mission on the

---

37. See Daniel Marguerat, *The First Christian Historian: Writing the 'Acts of the Apostles,'* trans. Ken McKinney, Gregory J. Laughery, and Richard Bauckham, SNTSMS 121 (Cambridge: Cambridge University Press, 2002), 37; and Leo O'Reilly, *Word and Sign in the Acts of the Apostles: A Study in Lucan Theology*. AnGreg 243. Rome: Gregorian University Press, 1987), 11.

38. So Padilla, *The Acts of the Apostles: Interpretation, History and Theology*, 237.

39. Lora Angeline B. Embudo, "A Lukan Paradigm of Witness: Community as a Form of Witness, Parts I & II," *AJPS* 20 (2017): 35.

40. John Dickson, *The Best Kept Secret of Christian Mission* (Grand Rapids: Zondervan, 2010), 35.

41. C. Kavin Rowe, *World Upside Down: Reading Acts in the Graeco-Roman Age* (New York: Oxford University Press, 2009), 116; cf. 123.

The Significance of the Church's Mission in Luke-Acts

The church's mission is so fundamental to Luke's contribution to the New Testament that it might be inadequate to discuss it merely as a "theme" in Luke-Acts. Michael Goheen suggests, "Mission is not just one of the many things Luke talks about, but it undergirds and shapes the text so that to read Luke in a non-missional way is to misread Luke and misunderstand what God is saying."* Thus, to discuss "mission" adequately in Acts is to discuss the whole book all at once. In contemplating the magnitude of mission for Luke, C. Kavin Rowe remarks, "That this is so makes it difficult to discuss 'mission' in Acts in as much as to do it adequately one must discuss the entirety of the narrative. Obviously that is beyond the scope of this (or any) book."†

*Michael Goheen, "A Critical Examination of David Bosch's Missional Reading of Luke," pp. 230–64 in Bartholomew, Green, and Thiselton, *Reading Luke*, 229.

†Rowe, *World Upside Down*, 245n147.

resurrection of Jesus, which is regularly mentioned in the apostolic preaching (see Acts 2:23–36; 3:13–20; 4:10–12; 5:30–32; 10:39–43; 13:27–41; 17:2–3, 31; 26:22–23).[42] The resurrection of the Lord Jesus is explicitly what the disciples give witness to in Acts.

3.3.8 The Holy Spirit Is God's Empowering Presence in All His People

The Holy Spirit is mentioned often in Luke's writings, especially in Acts (Luke—17 times; Acts—56 times; sometimes simply "Spirit"). With emphatic repetition, in both the final episode of the Gospel of Luke and the first episode of the book of Acts, the Holy Spirit is promised for the empowering of the believers' ministry (esp. Luke 24:46–49; Acts 1:8). In both of these reports, before he ascends into heaven Jesus insists that the believers not leave Jerusalem until the Spirit is poured out on the church. In the OT era, the Spirit of God came upon select individuals for brief periods of time; but after Jesus's ascension, the outpouring of the Spirit on the day of Pentecost signaled a paradigm shift that was in keeping with OT prophecy (Acts 2:1–41 citing Joel 2:28–32). Receiving the Spirit at the time one believes in Jesus is the new normal experience (Acts 2:38–39; 10:44–48; 11:15–18; 19:2). Luke sees the empowerment of the Spirit as vital to the life and ministry of the church. The Holy Spirit is the ever-present and primary active agent in the narrative of Acts, and he is the guiding influence and empowerment for ministry in every believer.

42. Storm comments, "There is no more constant theme in Acts than the proclamation of the resurrection of Jesus. In every major apostolic speech in Acts, the resurrection of Jesus is not only mentioned but is usually the centerpiece of the remarks"; Storm, *Living Lord, Empowering Spirit, Testifying People*, 7–8; cf. Rowe, *World Upside Down*, 122. See now Brandon D. Crowe, *The Hope of Israel: The Resurrection of Christ in the Acts of the Apostles* (Grand Rapids: Baker Academic, 2020).

Roles of the Holy Spirit Expressed in Luke-Acts

The Holy Spirit in Luke's writings emerges in a new light compared to his appearances in the OT. Whereas the Spirit seemed to work "externally" in people's lives in the OT (cf. Luke 2:25), in the NT the Spirit has a new "internal" presence in people's lives.

Roles of the Holy Spirit	References in Luke-Acts
Extends Jesus's ministry to believers	Luke 3:16; Acts 1:5; 2:38–39; 8:14–17; 9:17; 10:44–48; 11:15–17; 15:8–9
Empowers people for ministry	General: Luke 1:15–17; 4:14–19; Acts 20:28 Prophecy: Luke 1:41, 67; 2:26–27; Acts 1:16; 2:18 Miracles: Acts 10:38 Witnessing/Preaching: Acts 1:8; 2:4; 4:8
Guides believers	Luke 4:1; Acts 13:2–4; 15:28–29; 16:6–10; 20:22–23; 21:4
Comforts believers	Acts 9:31

3.3.9 In Spreading the Good News, Believers Will Face Opposition but Can Overcome It

While things go somewhat smoothly for the new church in the beginning of Acts (e.g., Acts 2:47; cf. 5:13–14), it is difficult to ignore the opposition they soon face as they carry out their mission (see Acts 8:1 and note that the last 25 percent of Acts focuses on Paul wrongfully imprisoned). The story of Acts is filled with reports of opposition and suffering.[43] And with some irony, the mission of spreading the gospel is even advanced sometimes by means of opposition to it. Thus, faithful witnessing brings opposition to the gospel, and opposition leads to a further spreading of the gospel.[44]

Given that their Lord suffered, the church in Acts is unsurprised when they face difficulty as they spread the good news about him. Thus, the church's suffering is in keeping with the suffering of Jesus. And even as in the Gospel of Luke Jesus faced opposition from both humans and the demonic, so in Acts opposition to the supernaturally empowered witness of the church comes both from people and from the spiritual realm. In Acts, success in facing opposition does not always entail avoidance of hardship. This too is in keeping with the life of Jesus. Rather, as modeled by Jesus, successful confrontations entail prayer, wise endurance of ill treatment, and persistent faithfulness to God's calling.

43. John J. Kilgallen, "Persecution in the Acts of the Apostles," pp. 143–60 in *Luke and Acts*, ed. Gerald O'Collins and Gilberto Marconi, trans. Matthew J. O'Connell (New York: Paulist, 1991), 160. On the essential contribution made by suffering to the story of Acts, see Paul R. House, "Suffering and the Purpose of Acts," *JETS* 33 (1990): 317–30; cf. Scott Cunningham, *"Through Many Tribulations": The Theology of Persecution in Luke-Acts*, JSNTSup 142 (Sheffield: Sheffield Academic Press, 1997), esp. 287–327.

44. Joel B. Green, "Acts of the Apostles," *DLNT*, 22.

Opposition and Persecution in Luke-Acts

In Luke-Acts both Jesus and his followers experience various kinds of opposition—and even persecution. Again, with the literary use of parallels, Luke interestingly mirrors the experiences of believers in Acts with some of the experiences of Jesus in the Gospel of Luke. And because of Luke's interest in Jesus's prayer life, he similarly records the believers in Acts responding to opposition with prayer as well as rejoicing and persistence in the mission.

Kinds of Opposition	Example of Jesus	Examples of Believers
Degraded and belittled	Luke 11:15	Acts 13:45; 14:2; 17:13
Slandered and threatened	Luke 23:2-5	Acts 4:21; 21:27-29
Arrested/segregated	Luke 22:47-53	Acts 4:3; 5:18-42; 16:19-40
Physically hurt and killed	Luke 22:63-23:46	Acts 7:57-60; 26:9-11
Challenged by demons and sorcery	Luke 4:31-37, 41; 6:18; 7:21; 8:2, 26-39; 9:37-43; 11:14-26; 13:10-17, 32	Acts 8:9-24; 13:6-12; 16:16-40; 19:11-20

Believers' Responses to Opposition

1. Prayer for boldness to further the gospel message (e.g., Acts 4:23-31).
2. Prayer for the persecutors (e.g., Acts 7:59-60).
3. Prayer for those being persecuted (e.g., Acts 12:5).
4. Prayer and singing hymns to God (e.g., Acts 16:22-25).
5. Rejoicing for being counted worthy of suffering disgrace for the name of Jesus (e.g., Acts 5:41).
6. Continuing to teach and to proclaim the good news (e.g., Acts 5:42; 8:1-4; 11:19-21).

Unexpected Benefits from Extreme Opposition Expressed in Acts

- Jesus's death secured our salvation (Acts 20:28).
- The gospel spread with persecution (Acts 8:1-4; 11:19-21).

3.3.10 Jesus Rules Now but Will Return to Rule More Fully in His Kingship Role

Examining God's activities in history through Jesus Christ to bring about the salvation of his people (a.k.a. "salvation history") leads people to ask about God's future activities at the end of time in the return of Jesus Christ, the resurrection and final judgment of people, and assignments to the afterlife of heaven or hell (a.k.a. ***eschatology***).

Luke's view of salvation history and eschatology has been one of the most controversial issues in recent Lukan scholarship.[45] As Luke records it, Jesus was aware of his unique role in fulfilling Scripture (e.g., Luke 4:16–30; 7:22–23; 24:25–27, 44–47), and Luke presents Jesus as the height of salvation-historical events (e.g., Acts 3:12–26; 18:28; 28:23). While the Jesus event—that is, Jesus's earthly ministry, death, resurrection, and ascension—is the turning point in salvation history, introducing the last days, it has not yet reached the culmination point with a final victory over all evil. The new age has merely dawned; it has not come to its full expression just yet. What life is to be like between the introduction of the new age in the Jesus event and the ultimate consummation of this new age at the end of time is a major theme of Luke-Acts and the rest of the New Testament.[46] This is often labeled an ***inaugurated eschatology*** or the ***already/not yet kingdom***, for it has already begun in Jesus and is currently at work in the lives of his followers even though its fullest expression has not yet been realized.

The Mount of Olives, Jerusalem. lucky-photo/stock.adobe.com

With the second coming of Jesus still future and certain (see Acts 1:6–7, 11; 3:19–21; 10:42; 24:25), in Acts, Luke focuses more on how Jesus followers live in the present while waiting for Christ to return. All the way to and including the end of Acts, Luke affirms God's control over all of human history. Following Jesus is not merely about guaranteeing one's place in heaven in the afterlife; it is also about how we live in the present. Certain that Jesus will keep his promise to return and bring about ultimate justice, believers can be witnesses for him with greater confidence as they engage with the culture around them.[47]

These ten theological themes certainly overlap one another. Even while addressing one of these themes, Luke is likely to mention one or two of the other themes. A particular episode in Acts might focus on one of the themes but will also have implications for some of the others.

---

45. For more on Luke's view of eschatology, see A. J. Mattill Jr., *Luke and the Last Things: A Perspective for the Understanding of Lukan Thought* (Dillsboro: Western North Carolina Press, 1979); Beverly Roberts Gaventa, "The Eschatology of Luke-Acts Revisited," *Encounter* 43 (1982): 27–42; John T. Carroll, *Response to the End of History: Eschatology and Situation in Luke-Acts*, SBLDS 92 (Atlanta: Scholars Press, 1988); John Nolland, "Salvation-History and Eschatology," in *Witness to the Gospel: The Theology of Acts*, ed. I. Howard Marshall and David Peterson (Grand Rapids: Eerdmans, 1998), 63–81; and Kylie Crabbe, *Luke/Acts and the End of History*, BZNW 238 (Berlin: de Gruyter, 2019).

46. J. Julius Scott Jr., "Luke-Acts, Theology of," 498; cf. Kuhn, *The Kingdom according to Luke and Acts*, 243.

47. Gaventa, "The Eschatology of Luke-Acts Revisited," 42, borrowing a phrase from Rubem Alvers, *Tomorrow's Child: Imagination, Creativity, and the Rebirth of Culture* (New York: Harper & Row, 1972; repr., Eugene, OR: Wipf & Stock, 2011), 195.

The Second Coming of Christ as Described in Luke-Acts

Luke does not use the common Greek word *parousia* ("appearance; arrival"; NT—24 times) as a label for the second coming of Christ, but he does write about it.

Features	References in Luke-Acts
Delayed and unknown timing	Luke 12:35-48; Acts 1:6-7; 3:19-21
Preceded by persecution	Luke 21:5-36; cf. persecutions in Acts
Imminent and sudden	Luke 17:20-18:8
Inescapable	Luke 17:20-18:8
Will involve judgment	Luke 10:13-15; Acts 10:42; 24:25
Will resemble the ascension	Acts 1:11

3.4 THE JESUS STORY IN ACTS: HOW DO PEOPLE TELL THE GOSPEL IN ACTS?

Many NT scholars have agreed that Luke's expression of precisely how the death of Jesus brings about salvation is not as explicit as it might have been. What is more important for Luke is to establish that salvation is provided by God, that salvation comes through faith in the Savior, and that the Savior is Jesus.[48] Nevertheless, Luke's theology contains a ***substitutionary atonement*** view of Jesus's death and resurrection, i.e., that Jesus died in our place taking the penalty for our sins (see esp. Luke 22:19–20; Acts 5:30; 10:40; 13:29; 20:28).[49] The necessity of Jesus's death (e.g., Luke 9:22, 44; 17:3, 25; 18:31–34; 22:22; 24:7, 26, 46; Acts 2:24; 3:18; 9:22; 13:28–30; 17:3; 22:37; 24:7, 26, 44) and the availability of forgiveness of sins are frequently mentioned in Luke's writings (e.g., Luke 1:77; 3:3; 5:17–26; 7:36–50; 11:4; 24:46–47; Acts 2:38–39; 5:30–32; 10:43; 13:38–39; 26:15–18).

As Luke recounts the believers in Acts presenting the gospel message, he stresses their telling of Jesus's resurrection from the dead (e.g., Acts 2:23–36; 3:13–20; 4:10–12; 5:30–32; 10:39–43; 13:27–41; 17:2–3, 31; 26:22–23). And, of course, there would be no resurrection from the dead unless Jesus had died! As Acts makes evident, Jesus's resurrection is the proof of the effectiveness of Jesus's death, of Jesus's power over sin and death, and of his lordship over all. Without spelling out how the atonement works,[50] Luke nonetheless presents Jesus's death as an atonement, i.e., as the provision for the

48. Jervell, *The Theology of the Acts of the Apostles*, 94–95.

49. See I. Howard Marshall, "The Place of Acts 20.28 in Luke's Theology of the Cross," in Walton, Phillips, Pietersen, and Spencer, *Reading Acts Today*, 154–70.

50. For some NT statements on how the atonement works, see Rom 3:21–26; 5:8–21; Gal 3:13–14; Heb 9:11–28; 10:10–22; 1 Pet 2:24; 3:18; 1 John 4:9–10; cf. John 10:14–18.

forgiveness of human sin. Thus, any telling of the gospel message of Jesus's death for the forgiveness of the sins of the world should stress the resurrection of Jesus from the dead. For Luke, then, the forgiveness of sins, Jesus's death, and Jesus's resurrection are some of the most significant elements to mention in the sharing of the gospel.

3.5 CONCLUDING REMARKS

With an intentional outline, Luke has written his second volume, the Acts of the Apostles, using identifiable literary tools and techniques so as to communicate particular theological ideas to his readers. The theological themes in Acts are common to the ones found in his first volume, the Gospel of Luke. These themes focus on God's work in the world to bring about salvation from sin through the death and resurrection of Jesus Christ and the spreading news of that work through Jesus's followers empowered by the Holy Spirit; in keeping with the OT Scriptures, this message is intended to be received by all and is to be preached, despite opposition, until Jesus returns. Given this understanding of Luke's work, it might do us well to investigate more specifically how best to interpret and apply his writings to our own lives and communities. This is the focus of chapter 4.

3.6 Key People, Places, and Terms

- already/not yet kingdom
- chiasm
- eschatology
- genealogies
- inaugurated eschatology
- infancy narratives
- Lord
- Messiah
- parallelism
- prologue
- rhetoric
- salvation history
- Son of God
- Son of Man
- sovereignty of God
- substitutionary atonement

3.7 Questions for Review and Discussion

1. What is a simple outline of Acts that flows from the words of Jesus in Acts 1:8?
2. What do you appreciate about the other suggested outlines for Acts?
3. To what extent do you agree with the expansion of the simple outline of Acts 1:8 suggested in this chapter, i.e., the storytelling outline?
4. Describe some of Luke's storytelling techniques used in Acts.
5. What are some of Luke's most emphasized theological themes in Acts?
6. What are the basic elements of the gospel message as found in the preaching of the believers in Acts?

3.8 Optional Assignments

1. **Text Reflection Project**–*Relating the concepts discussed in this chapter to another biblical text.* For each of the ten key theological themes of Luke's writings discussed in this chapter, find one non-Lukan passage that shows Luke to be in concert with the theology expressed elsewhere in the New Testament.
2. **Interview Project**–*Inquiring of others their views concerning the concepts discussed in this chapter.* In an interview with your pastor (or some other respected Christian leader), ask about the key theological themes outlined in this chapter (bring a simple list of these themes):
   - Of these ten Lukan theological themes, which might you suggest is more emphasized in Luke-Acts than the others?
   - Are there any Lukan theological themes not included in this list of ten? How would you phrase those themes?
3. **Service-Learning Project**–*Applying the concepts discussed in this chapter in some form of service to others outside the class.* Which of the ten key theological themes of Luke's writings discussed in this chapter motivate Christians to serve other people? Identify a place of ministry where you can serve others in light of the kinds of theological concerns Luke expresses in Acts.
4. **Prayer Project**–*Talking with God about the concepts discussed in this chapter.* The instructional prayer that Jesus offers the apostles–often called the Lord's Prayer–briefly touches on several theological themes (e.g., the sovereignty of God, the dependence of humanity, the need for forgiveness, the existence of opposition). Look at that prayer (see Luke 11:2–4; cf. Matt 6:9–13), then write your own prayer using all ten of Luke's key theological ideas outlined in this chapter.
5. **Testimony Project**–*Telling others about the concepts discussed in this chapter.* In your own words, write out each of the ten key theological themes of Luke's writings discussed in this chapter. Be brief and write with terminology you could use in sharing these things with your roommate–and then share them with your roommate!

3.9 Bibliography for Going Further

3.9.1 Structure of Acts

Denova, Rebecca I. *The Things Accomplished Among Us: Prophetic Tradition in the Structural Pattern of Luke-Acts.* JSNTSup 141. Sheffield: Sheffield Academic, 1997.

Filson, Floyd V. "The Journey Motif in Luke-Acts." Pages 68–77 in *Apostolic History and the Gospel: Biblical and Historical Essays Presented to F. F. Bruce on his 60th Birthday.* Edited by W. Ward Gasque and Ralph P. Martin. Grand Rapids: Eerdmans, 1970; Exeter: Paternoster, 1970.

Morton, Andrew Queen, and George Hogarth Carnaby MacGregor. *The Structure of Luke and Acts.* New York: Harper & Row, 1964.

Thomas, John Christopher. "The Charismatic Structure of Acts." *JPT* 13.1 (2004): 19–30.

Wolfe, Kenneth R. "The Chiastic Structure of Luke-Acts and Some Implications for Worship." *SwJT* 22.2 (1980): 60–71.

3.9.2 Luke's Literary Artistry and Literary Approaches to Luke-Acts

Alexander, Loveday C. A. *Acts in Its Ancient Literary Context: A Classicist Looks at the Acts of the Apostles*. LNTS 298. London: T&T Clark, 2005.

Bauer, David R. *The Book of Acts as Story: A Narrative-Critical Study*. Grand Rapids: Baker Academic, 2021.

Cadbury, Henry J. *The Making of Luke-Acts*. 2nd ed. London: SPCK, 1958. Repr., Peabody, MA: Hendrickson, 1999.

Karris, Robert J. *Luke, Artist and Theologian: Luke's Passion Account as Literature*. Theological Inquiries. New York: Paulist, 1985.

Kurz, William S. *Reading Luke-Acts: Dynamics of Biblical Narrative*. Louisville: Westminster John Knox, 1993.

Müller, Mogens, and Jesper Tang Nielsen, eds. *Luke's Literary Creativity*. LNTS 550. London: Bloomsbury T&T Clark, 2016.

Sheeley, Steven M. *Narrative Asides in Luke-Acts*. JSNTSup 72. Sheffield: Sheffield Academic, 1992.

Talbert, Charles H. *Literary Patterns, Theological Themes and the Genre of Luke-Acts*. SBLMS 20. Missoula: Scholars Press, 1974.

Thompson, Richard P., and Thomas E. Phillips, eds. *Literary Studies in Luke-Acts: Essays in Honor of Joseph B. Tyson*. Macon: Mercer University Press, 1998.

Tuckett, Christopher M., ed. *Luke's Literary Achievement: Collected Essays*. JSNTSup 116. Sheffield: Sheffield Academic, 1995.

Winter, Bruce W., and Andrew D. Clarke, eds. *The Book of Acts in Its Ancient Literary Setting*. BAFCS 1. Grand Rapids: Eerdmans, 1993; Carlisle: Paternoster, 1993.

3.9.3 Lukan Theology

Bock, Darrell L. *A Theology of Luke and Acts: God's Promised Program, Realized for All Nations*. Biblical Theology of the New Testament. Grand Rapids: Zondervan, 2012.

Chrupcala, Leslaw Daniel. *Everyone Will See the Salvation of God: Studies in Lukan Theology*. SBFA 83. Milan: Edizioni Terra Santa, 2015.

Conzelmann, Hans. *The Theology of St. Luke*. Translated by Geoffrey Buswell. New York: Harper & Row, 1960. Repr., Philadelphia: Fortress, 1982.

Dibelius, Martin. *Studies in the Acts of the Apostles*. Edited by H. Greeven. Translated by M. Ling. London: SCM Press, 1956. Repr. (with the chapters differently ordered), *The Book of Acts: Form, Style, and Theology*. Edited by K. C. Hanson. Fortress Classics in Biblical Studies. Minneapolis: Fortress, 2004.

Esler, Philip Francis. *Community and Gospel in Luke-Acts: The Social and Political Motivations of Lucan Theology*. SNTSMS 57. Cambridge: Cambridge University Press, 1987.

Green, Joel B. *The Theology of the Gospel of Luke*. New Testament Theology. United Kingdom: Cambridge University Press, 1995.

Jervell, Jacob. *The Theology of the Acts of the Apostles*. New Testament Theology. Cambridge: Cambridge University Press, 1996.

Johnson, Dennis E. *The Message of Acts in the History of Redemption*. Phillipsburg: P&R, 1997.

Kuhn, Karl Allen. *The Kingdom according to Luke and Acts: A Social, Literary, and Theological Introduction*. Grand Rapids: Baker Academic, 2015.

Marshall, I. Howard. *Luke: Historian and Theologian*. 3rd ed. Carlisle: Paternoster, 1988. Repr., New Testament Profiles. Downers Grove, IL: InterVarsity Press, 1998.

Marshall, I. Howard, and David Peterson, eds. *Witness to the Gospel: The Theology of Acts*. Grand Rapids: Eerdmans, 1998.

O'Toole, Robert F. *The Unity of Luke's Theology: An Analysis of Luke-Acts*. Wilmington: Michael Glazier, 1984.

Schreiner, Patrick. *The Mission of the Triune God: A Theology of Acts*. Wheaton, IL: Crossway, 2022.

4 Interpreting and Applying Acts

Yale Papyrus Collection, Beinecke Rare Book and Manuscript Library

Chapter Goals

After reading this chapter, you should be able to:

- Outline the proposed dates for the composition of Acts.
- Explain some possible sources for Luke's writing of Acts.
- Describe the two versions of Acts represented in the extant manuscripts.
- Discuss Luke's use of the Hebrew Scriptures in Acts.
- Explain some of the interpretation issues for Acts.
- Describe a proper approach to interpreting Acts.

Chapter Overview

4.1 The Time Period for Acts: What Are the Dates for Acts?
4.2 The Sources for Acts: What Sources Did Luke Use in Writing Acts?
4.3 Two Versions of Acts: Which Is the Correct Version?
4.4 The Hebrew Scriptures and Acts: How are the Hebrew Scriptures Understood in Acts?
4.5 The Hermeneutics of Acts: How Does Luke Want Us to Understand Acts?
4.6 Concluding Remarks
4.7 Key People, Places, and Terms
4.8 Questions for Review and Discussion
4.9 Optional Assignments
4.10 Bibliography for Going Further

Key Verses

In the fifteenth year of the reign of Tiberius Caesar—when Pontius Pilate was governor of Judea, Herod tetrarch of Galilee, his brother Philip tetrarch of Iturea and Traconitis, and Lysanias tetrarch of Abilene—during the high-priesthood of Annas and Caiaphas, the word of God came to John son of Zechariah in the wilderness. (Luke 3:1–2)

In my former book, Theophilus, I wrote about all that Jesus began to do and to teach until the day he was taken up to heaven, after giving instructions through the Holy Spirit to the apostles he had chosen. (Acts 1:1–2)

I am saying nothing beyond what the prophets and Moses said would happen—that the Messiah would suffer and, as the first to rise from the dead, would bring the message of light to his own people and to the Gentiles. (Acts 26:22–23)

He witnessed to them from morning till evening, explaining about the kingdom of God, and from the Law of Moses and from the Prophets he tried to persuade them about Jesus. (Acts 28:23)

INTRODUCTION

Almost two thousand years separate us from the time when the book of Acts was written. Furthermore, Acts was written in a different language than most of us use (Greek, not English), and it was written long before the printing press was developed, which means that for hundreds of years handwritten copies were the only way Acts was disseminated to other readers and to the communities of those listening to it being read.[1] This chapter examines the interpretation matters related to the date and sources for the composition of Acts, the manuscript tradition for Acts, and some hermeneutical principles for properly interpreting and applying Acts in our lives and church communities in the twenty-first century. And as noted in an earlier chapter, because Luke writes with an intentional OT style, interpreting the story of Jesus in light of the Scriptures, I briefly examine his use of the Hebrew Scriptures in Acts.

1. As noted in chapter 1, far beyond the individual person named Theophilus to whom his books are dedicated, Luke writes with a concern for many people and for communities of people. Thus, even apart from the relatively low literacy rates in the first-century Roman world, which at best were around 10 percent for most communities in Palestine (see Catherine Hezser, *Jewish Literacy in Roman Palestine*, Texts and Studies in Ancient Palestine 81 [Tübingen: Mohr Siebeck, 2001], 496–504), Luke would expect his gospel and the book of Acts to be read aloud in communities of people invested in the Jesus story and its continuation in their own lives; see Harry Y. Gamble, *Books and Readers in the Early Church: A History of Early Christian Texts* (New Haven, CT: Yale University Press, 1995), 203–18; cf. Col 4:16; 1 Thess 5:27; 1 Tim 4:13; Rev 1:3.

4.1 THE TIME PERIOD FOR ACTS: WHAT ARE THE DATES FOR ACTS?

When we speak of the dates for Acts, at least two issues might be in mind. First, we might be concerned with the time period for when the events of Acts took place. Second, we might be concerned with when Luke composed the book we now call Acts. Let's consider both of these issues.

4.1.1 When Did the Events in Acts Occur?

The events that comprise the story in Luke-Acts take place at the turn of the eras from BC to AD. Luke begins his gospel account with the announcement that John the Baptist would soon be born and, soon afterward, the announcement that Jesus would be born. John was born about six months before Jesus, who was born in 6–4 BC (see sidebar). There is scholarly debate regarding the precise dates for the public ministries of John the Baptist and of Jesus (e.g., as to whether Jesus's crucifixion and resurrection are best dated to the year AD 30 or 33).[2] Nevertheless, by beginning with Jesus's ascension, the opening of Acts briefly overlaps with the ending of the Gospel of Luke (by about forty days; see Acts 1:3). Then Luke extends the story for almost three more decades before rather abruptly ending the story (or putting it on pause) with Paul as a prisoner for two years in Rome (Acts 28:30–31). So we can give the approximate dates for the events of Acts as between AD 30 and AD 62.

The Odd Claim of Saying Jesus Was Born in 6–4 BC

Jesus is the center of the modern BC/AD calendar system with BC ≈ Before Christ and AD ≈ *anno Domini* (Latin for "in the year of the Lord").* This dating notation system was constructed in the Middle Ages (in AD 525) by ***Dionysius Exiguus*** of Scythia Minor (a.k.a. Dionysius the Humble or Dennis the Short), but his system was not widely used until after AD 800. Unfortunately, Dionysius's system assumes that Jesus was born a few years after Herod the Great's death, which is dated to 4 BC. But Matthew 1-2 clearly indicates that Herod the Great was alive when Jesus was born, ordering children two years old and younger to be killed in an attempt to destroy Jesus. Thus—allowing for the same two-year window that Herod did—Jesus's birth is dated as occurring sometime from 6-4 BC. So, in following Dionysius's system, we come up short by three to five years (NB: there was no "year 0"). Sadly, the discovery of Dionysius's error was not made until the early 1600s, several centuries too late to correct the system. So we are left with the oddity of noting that Jesus was born 6-4 BC.

*Instead of describing calendar years with BC and AD, some prefer, respectively, BCE for "before the common era" and CE for "common era." The years referenced, however, remain the same.

2. For a brief but helpful discussion of these dating matters, see Mark L. Strauss, *Four Portraits, One Jesus: An Introduction to Jesus and the Gospels*, 2nd ed. (Grand Rapids: Zondervan Academic, 2020), 492–96.

A Basic Timeline of Events in Acts

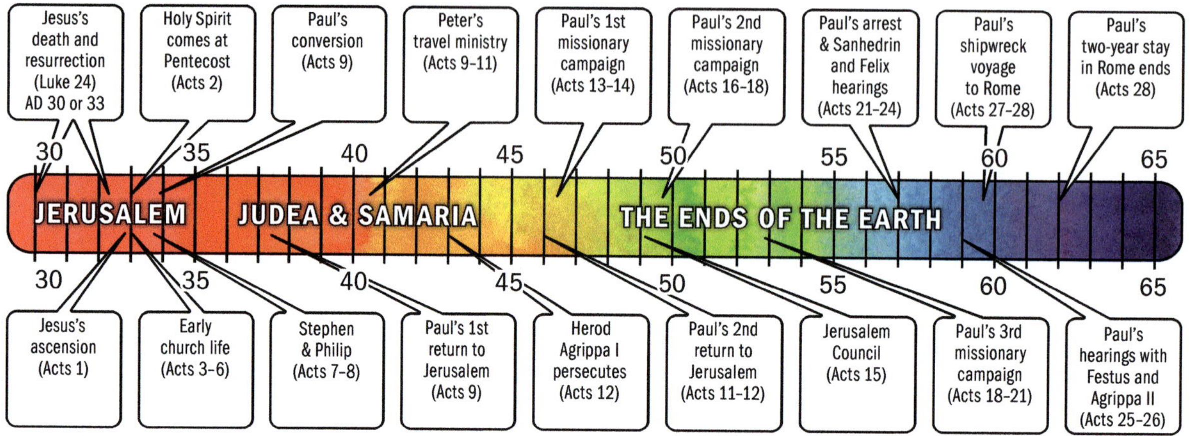

4.1.2 When Was the Book of Acts Written?

With the approximate dates of the events of Acts being between AD 30 and AD 62, Acts was written sometime after that. Furthermore, its prologue (Acts 1:1–2) implies that Acts was written after the Third Gospel, as its continuation or sequel.[3] If the events of Acts fit in history between the ascension of Jesus (ca. AD 30; Acts 1:1–11) and Paul's house arrest in Rome (ca. AD 60–62; Acts 28:16–31), this would put the date of Acts composition in the early to middle 60s at the earliest. But Luke could have written Acts several years, or even decades, after the events he chose to cover. Scholars tend to cluster around three general proposals for a date of the writing of Acts: an early date prior to AD 64, a midrange date of AD 70–85, and a late date in the second century AD. Of these three proposals, most scholars hold to the midrange date, and the smallest number of scholars hold to the late date. I present here arguments for all three views but argue for the earlier date and also offer my objections to the other proposals.

A. Early Date: Before AD 64

This early dating for Acts has at least seven supporting arguments.[4] The first three are admittedly arguments from silence, but they are worthy of mention nonetheless. The latter four arguments are more constructive and thus perhaps more convincing.

---

3. A few scholars have proposed that Acts was written before the Gospel of Luke: see Charles Stephen Conway Williams, "The Date of Luke-Acts," *ExpTim* 64 (1952–53): 283–84; Henry G. Russell, "Which Was Written First, Luke or Acts," *HTR* 48 (1955): 167–74; and Pierson Parker, "The 'Former Treatise' and the Date of Acts," *JBL* 84 (1965): 52–58; cf. A. H. N. Green-Armytage, *A Portrait of St. Luke* (London: Burns and Oates, 1955; Chicago Henry Regnery, 1955), 183–84.

4. For a similar line of reasoning, see Richard N. Longenecker, "Acts," pp. 663–1102 in *Luke-Acts*, vol. 10 of *The Expositor's Bible Commentary*, ed. Tremper Longman III and David E. Garland, rev. ed. (Grand Rapids: Zondervan, 2007), 699–701 (focusing on four features instead of seven).

(1) Acts makes no reference to important historical events after AD 64 (e.g., Nero's persecution of Christians beginning in AD 64, the Jewish revolt against Rome beginning in AD 66, the fall of Jerusalem in AD 70, or the deaths of significant people in the story of Acts like Peter and Paul in AD 64–68 or even Jesus's brother James in AD 62). The simplest and most natural way to explain Luke's silence about these noteworthy events is that they had not yet taken place.[5]

(2) The abrupt ending of Acts seems to indicate that, at the time of writing, Luke recorded all he knew and that Paul was still alive.[6] It is odd that he does not even mention Paul's trial before Caesar, much less his release from prison, a closing to the book that would seem more positive than the current mysterious ending (I say more on this in chapter 15).

(3) Luke's failure to mention Paul as having written letters hints that Luke wrote before the circulation of the Pauline Epistles.[7] The earlier the date of the writing of Acts, the more understandable it is that the letters are unmentioned.

(4) The Roman government is presented in Acts mostly as impartial toward believers, and this was not the case in the Roman world during the emperorships of Nero (AD 54–68) and Domitian (AD 81–96). Of course, the storyline of Acts does not cover the reigns of these two Roman emperors noted for persecuting Christians, so even if Luke wrote during one of their reigns, he may have accurately reported the apparent impartiality of the Roman government for the period he did cover in Acts.

(5) The primitive subject matter of the book suggests an early date for the writing of Acts. Much of Acts is concerned with specific subjects that were directly related only to the earliest period of Christianity (e.g., Christianity as a branch of Judaism, the Jew-gentile controversy, defending Paul).[8]

(6) Similarly, the primitive terminology of Acts also hints at an early date. With rather undeveloped terms, Luke refers to Jesus as "the Christ," the "servant" of God, "the Son of Man;" to believers as "disciples" (he uses "Christian" only twice: Acts 11:26; 26:28); to the Jewish nation as "the people;" and to Sunday as "the first day of the week." Furthermore, he refers to the Beautiful Gate (Acts 3:2, 10) and the Synagogue of the Freedmen (Acts 6:9) as if they are still current.[9]

---

5. Green-Armytage, *A Portrait of St. Luke*, 44.

6. See Blass's use of this argument for an early date of Acts in Friedrich Blass, *Philology of the Gospels* (London: Macmillan, 1898; repr., Chicago: Argonaut, 1969), 36–39.

7. Some suggest that the publication of Acts may well have induced the collecting together and publication of Paul's letters; see Edgar J. Goodspeed, *An Introduction to the New Testament* (Chicago: University of Chicago Press, 1937), 210–17; C. F. D. Moule, "The Problem of the Pastoral Epistles: A Reappraisal," *BJRL* 47 (1965): 452; cf. Robert C. Morgan, "Which Was the Fourth Gospel? The Order of the Gospels and the Unity of Scripture," *JSNT* 54 (1994): 27.

8. See Longenecker, "Acts," 699n96; F. F. Bruce, *The Acts of the Apostles: The Greek Text with Introduction and Commentary*, 3rd ed. (Grand Rapids: Eerdmans, 1990; Leicester: Apollos, 1990), 17–18; and Craig S. Keener, *Acts: An Exegetical Commentary*, 4 vols. (Grand Rapids: Baker Academic, 2012–2015), 1:223, 400–401.

9. Moreover, the dating schema used in Luke 3:1–2, with its particular territorial divisions, would have

(7) Perhaps the most interesting hint at an early date for Luke's writing of both the Gospel of Luke and the book of Acts is what Paul says in 1 Tim 5:18, citing two scriptural sayings: "For Scripture says, 'Do not muzzle an ox while it is treading out the grain,' and 'The worker deserves his wages.'" The first citation is from Deuteronomy 25:4, but the second is found only on the lips of Jesus as recorded in Luke 10:7. If Paul wrote the letter of 1 Timothy in the early 60s toward the end of his life and is quoting the Gospel of Luke as Scripture ("Scripture says, . . ."), then Luke must have written his gospel in the early 60s (or earlier), and the book of Acts may well have been written shortly after that.[10]

B. Midrange Date: Between AD 70 and 85

The midrange dating for the composition of Acts allows for the author of Acts to have been a companion of Paul but suggests that he wrote several years after Paul's death. This view utilizes four main arguments.

(1) If the Gospel of Mark was written in the late AD 60s, and if Luke wrote his gospel using Mark as a source (the usual presumption) and then wrote Acts, this midrange dating for Acts would seem necessary. But what if Mark wrote his gospel a decade earlier, or what if Luke acquired an early copy of it?

(2) Some argue that Mark 13:14 ("the abomination that causes desolation") is made much more specific in Luke 21:20 ("Jerusalem being surrounded by armies"), which means Luke had to be writing after the AD 70 fall of Jerusalem (see also the military implications of Luke 19:42–44 and Luke 23:28–30). But given the OT background to Mark's phrase (see Dan 9:27; 11:31; 12:11), it is entirely plausible that Jesus's prophetic comments recorded by Mark could be properly understood and communicated by Luke as having more specific military implications—even if Luke was writing before the event.[11] Furthermore, scholars actively debate Luke's view of Judaism, and the existence of the debate subtly supports that Luke was writing at a time when the distinctions between Christianity and Judaism were still being sorted out. For if Luke had been writing after the AD 70 fall of Jerusalem, he could have been more definitive in his presentation about the collapse of historic Judaism.[12]

---

disappeared in AD 66, never to be reformulated in the same way. Thus, this primitive dating formulation is evidence of an early writing period for Luke; so, H. S. Cronin, "Abilene, the Jewish Herods and St Luke," *JTS* 18 (1917): 147–51.

10. For a different approach to arguing for an early date for the writing of Luke-Acts (an approach that overlaps and dovetails with the evidence presented here), see A. J. Mattill Jr., "The Date and Purpose of Luke-Acts: Rackham Reconsidered," *CBQ* 40 (1978): 335–50. For the most recent and thoroughgoing arguments for an early date for the composition of Acts, see Karl Leslie Armstrong, *Dating Acts in Its Jewish and Greco-Roman Contexts*, LNTS 637 (New York: T&T Clark, 2021); and Jonathan Bernier, *Rethinking the Dates of the New Testament: The Evidence for Early Composition* (Grand Rapids: Baker Academic, 2022), esp. 3–84. See also David Seccombe, "Dating Luke-Acts: Further Arguments for an Early Date," *TynBul* 71 (2020): 207–27.

11. Some scholars have noted that, if writing after prophesied events, Luke could have been even more specific; e.g., David E. Aune, *Prophecy in Early Christianity and the Ancient Mediterranean World* (Grand Rapids: Eerdmans, 1983), 396–97n39; Green-Armytage, *A Portrait of St. Luke*, 45–46; cf. Blass, *Philology of the Gospels*, 39–48.

12. On the debate about Luke's view of Judaism, see Robert Lawson Brawley, *Luke-Acts and the Jews: Conflict,*

(3) Luke seems to hint at Paul's death (e.g., "Now I know that none of you . . . will ever see me again" and "What grieved them most was his statement that they would never see his face again" in Acts 20:25, 38; cf. Acts 21:11–14; 25:10–11), which did not take place until the mid-60s. Yet it is not at all unthinkable that Luke could record such statements before Paul's death.

(4) Luke seems to write as if he (and perhaps his audience) knew about Paul's trial before Caesar and what happened after it (see the angel's comment in Acts 27:24 and the note in Acts 28:30 that Paul's house arrest in Rome lasted for "two whole years").[13] Few doubt that Paul stood trial before Caesar; the question here is whether Luke was writing Acts before that trial or after it, and the remark about the two-year wait could simply bring the reader up to the time of the author's writing.

C. Late Date: Second Century (AD 110–130)

The late dating for Acts, with proponents coming primarily from the more liberal critical side of the scholarly spectrum, rules out the possibility that the book was written by Luke. It has had several approaches and lines of argument.

(1) Some have argued that Acts was an attempt to reconcile Petrine and Pauline factions of Christianity and that several decades had to pass for these proposed factions to have developed before needing reconciliation.[14] But contrary to this theory is that the New Testament itself shows that various factions had already developed in the opening decades of the early church; such divisions were not a mere second-century development (see 1 Cor 1:10–17). There is no need for the church to enter deep into the second century before the author of Acts could join in the concern for factions to be reconciled.

(2) To some, Luke seems to have consulted the first-century Jewish historian Josephus, and if so, Acts must come after ca. AD 94, the approximate date for Josephus's

---

Apology, and Conciliation, SBLMS 33 (Atlanta: Scholars Press, 1987). Jack T. Sanders, *The Jews in Luke-Acts* (Philadelphia: Fortress, 1987); Joseph B. Tyson, ed. *Luke-Acts and the Jewish People: Eight Critical Perspectives* (Minneapolis: Augsburg, 1988); idem, *Images of Judaism in Luke-Acts* (Columbia: University of South Carolina Press, 1992); idem, *Luke, Judaism, and the Scholars: Critical Approaches to Luke-Acts* (Columbia: University of South Carolina Press, 1999); and Robert C. Tannehill, *The Shape of Luke's Story: Essays on Luke-Acts* (Eugene, OR: Cascade, 2005), esp. pp. 105–65.

13. Keener, *Acts*, 1:386; cf. Ben Witherington III, *The Acts of the Apostles: A Socio-Rhetorical Commentary* (Grand Rapids: Eerdmans, 1998; Carlisle: Paternoster, 1998), 807.

14. For representative dating of Acts according to the Tübingen School following the teachings of nineteenth-century theologian F. C. Baur about Petrine vs. Pauline factions in the second century, see Franz C. Overbeck, "Introduction to the Acts of the Apostles," pp. 3–81 in Edward Zeller, *The Contents and Origin of the Acts of the Apostles Critically Investigated*, 2 vols., trans. Joseph Dare (London: Williams and Norgate, 1875; repr., Eugene, OR: Wipf & Stock, 2007), 1:69–73; cf. 2:267–83. While the Tübingen School is largely discounted today, some have nonetheless returned to a second-century dating of Acts; e.g., John T. Townsend, "The Date of Luke-Acts," in *Luke-Acts: New Perspectives from the Society of Biblical Literature Seminar*, ed. Charles H. Talbert (New York: Crossroad, 1984), 47–62; Mikeal C. Parsons, *Acts*, Paideia Commentaries on the New Testament (Grand Rapids: Baker Academic, 2008), 3, 16–17; and Joseph B. Tyson, *Marcion and Luke-Acts: A Defining Struggle* (Columbia: University of South Carolina, 2006), esp. 1–23, 119–20.

composition of *Jewish Antiquities*. But most of the information that Luke and Josephus have in common was widely known.[15] There is no need to assume that Luke wrote Acts late enough to have used Josephus's work as a source.[16]

(3) The earliest known and undisputed reference to Acts as a book is that of Irenaeus in his late second-century refutation of Marcion. But while clear attestation in a later source is testimony to the composition of Acts no later than that, it is hardly a fair criterion for determining the existence of Acts no earlier than that.[17]

(4) The theological viewpoints, philosophical imagery, and specific topic treatments found in Acts fit well with those found in second-century Christian writings.[18] As with comparing Acts to the writings of Josephus, however, this argument begs the question of historical order. In telling the story of the earliest decades of the church, Acts may very well represent an early version of such interests and arguments and need not be dated with them.[19] Some have observed in Acts reflections of a first-century setting that would have been odd had it been composed in the second century (e.g., failure to mention Paul's epistles or to stress some of Paul's theological interests; an apparent independence from the Gospel of Matthew, which was the most popular gospel in the second century; and other such features).[20]

Given these scholarly arguments, some may find it futile to try to discern a date for the composition of Acts. Why does it matter? For many, Luke's proximity to the events he describes in Acts lends credence to his reliability as a researcher.[21] But to this I suggest further that, while firmly establishing a precise date is not a most crucial factor in reading and understanding the book of Acts, establishing an approximate date for its composition is informative for its proper interpretation.

---

15. Adolf von Harnack, *Luke the Physician: The Author of the Third Gospel and the Acts of the Apostles*, trans. J. R. Wilkinson, New Testament Studies I (London: Williams and Norgate, 1908; New York: Putnam, 1909; repr., Eugene, OR: Wipf & Stock, 2009), 24–25n2; see also Frederick J. Foakes Jackson, *The Acts of the Apostles*, MNTC (New York: Harper, 1931), xiv–xv; Charles Stephen Conway Williams, *A Commentary on the Acts of the Apostles* (Edinburgh: Black, 1964; repr., HNTC, Peabody, MA: Hendrickson, 1988), 19–22; and Bruce, *Acts: Greek Text*, 43–44.

16. For more on the relationship of Josephus with Luke-Acts, see Steve Mason, *Josephus and the New Testament*, 2nd ed. (Peabody, MA: Hendrickson, 2003), 251–95; esp. 273–93 on dating.

17. Keener, *Acts*, 1:399; cf. Andrew Gregory, "Irenaeus and the Reception of Acts in the Second Century," pp. 47–65 in *Contemporary Studies in Acts*, ed. Thomas E. Phillips (Macon, GA: Mercer University Press, 2009), esp. 65: "As has often been noted, the absence of evidence is not evidence of absence."

18. E.g., John Cochrane O'Neill, *The Theology of Acts in Its Historical Setting*, 2nd ed. (London: SPCK, 1970), 5; and Rubén R. Dupertuis, "Bold Speech, Opposition, and Philosophical Imagery in the Acts of the Apostles," pp. 153–68 in *Engaging Early Christian History: Reading Acts in the Second Century*, ed. Rubén R. Dupertuis and Todd C. Penner, BibleWorld (Durham: Acumen, 2013), 166–67.

19. See Abraham J. Malherbe, *Paul and the Popular Philosophers* (Minneapolis: Fortress, 1989), esp. 147–50, 163.

20. Keener, *Acts*, 1:395–96; cf. Witherington, *Acts*, 61–62; Charles Kingsley Barrett, *A Critical and Exegetical Commentary on the Acts of the Apostles*, 2 vols., ICC (Edinburgh: T&T Clark, 1994/1998), 1:48.

21. And the authorship of Acts by a companion of Paul such as Luke becomes less possible with later date proposals. See Keener, *Acts*, 1:383–84.

Arguments for the Date of Composition for Acts

Early Date: Before AD 64

1. Acts makes no reference to important historical events after AD 64.
2. The abrupt ending of Acts seems to indicate that its story is up to date.
3. Acts does not mention Paul as having written letters.
4. The Roman government is presented in Acts mostly as impartial toward believers.
5. The primitive subject matter of the book suggests an early date of writing.
6. The primitive theological terminology of Acts also hints at an early date.
7. In 1 Tim 5:18 Paul seems to reference the Gospel of Luke as authoritative Scripture.

Midrange Date: Between AD 70 and 85

1. If Luke wrote his gospel using Mark, this midrange dating for Acts would seem necessary.
2. The specificity of Luke 21:20 compared to Mark 13:14 suggests a date after the AD 70 fall of Jerusalem.
3. Luke seems to hint at Paul's death (Acts 20:25 and 38), which did not take place until the mid-60s.
4. Luke seems to write as if Paul's trial before Caesar had already happened (Acts 27:24; 28:30).

Late Date: Second Century (AD 110–130):

1. The attempt to reconcile Petrine and Pauline factions with Acts necessitates a second-century setting.
2. Luke seems to have consulted Josephus's *Jewish Antiquities*, so Acts must come after ca. AD 94.
3. The earliest reference to Acts as a book is that of Irenaeus in his late second-century refutation of Marcion.
4. The theological viewpoints and specific treatments in Acts fit well with second-century Christian writings.

Thus, the evidence laid out here leads me to favor the earlier dating for the composition of Luke's writing: sometime before AD 64 (which is, of course, within a decade of the more common proposal of AD 70–85). And this conclusion leads me to recommend approaching the book of Acts as a first-century document written by a first-century author in a first-century setting. This does not, however, relegate the lessons of Acts to a first-century audience; rather, if we understand the book properly in its original context, we can hope to better apply the lessons of Acts to the analogous issues we face now in the twenty-first century.

4.2 THE SOURCES FOR ACTS: WHAT SOURCES DID LUKE USE IN WRITING ACTS?

If, as I have suggested, Luke was an educated author (chapter 1) with a concern to report historical events accurately (chapter 2) and utilizing recognizable authorial techniques (chapter 3), we naturally ask about the sources he might have used in composing Acts. The discussion of Luke's sources for Acts is a complex one and very different from the discussion of sources for the composition of the Gospel of Luke. While we possess the Gospels of Mark and of Matthew with which to make comparisons to the Gospel of Luke and to formulate source theories, we have only one book of Acts. Furthermore, the language and style of Luke's writing is so smooth that it is difficult to propose different sources for the various sections of Acts.

Nevertheless, as Luke himself reports, he had various sources available to him for writing the gospel and Acts. Some of these were written sources (e.g., Luke 1:1; the letters cited in Acts 15:23–29; 23:25–30), some were oral sources (e.g., Luke 1:2), and some were his own firsthand experiences (e.g., the places in Acts where Luke includes himself using the word "we").

4.2.1 FIRSTHAND EXPERIENCES: THEORIES ABOUT THE "WE SECTIONS" OF ACTS

There are four places in Acts where our author changes his pronominal point of view from third-person narration to first-person plural narration (Acts 16:10–17; 20:5–15; 21:1–18; 27:1–28:16). That is, he moves from reporting on Paul's travels with *he* and *they* pronouns (e.g., "they went there, . . . he said this, . . . ," etc.) to reporting the story with *we* statements (e.g., "we decided this, . . . , then we went there, . . . ," etc.). There are three standard explanations for the "we sections." First, the simplest and oldest explanation is that the "we sections" are intentional indications that the writer was a companion of Paul at those particular points in the story (e.g., Irenaeus, *Haer.* 3.1.1). The "we sections" exhibit the same basic writing style as the rest of Acts, but Luke's reporting seems more detailed and complete in the "we sections" of Acts than in the other sections, an observation suggesting the writer's presence.[22]

Second, some have suggested that the "we sections" are evidence that Luke copied sections of someone else's diary into the book of Acts. But the "we sections" are so thoroughly written in Luke's own style that we must wonder why he would rewrite someone else's travel notes and yet leave the pronominal references unchanged.[23] Furthermore, if the author of Acts were trying to look more authoritative by falsifying his presence

22. So Keener, *Acts*, 1:180.

23. See Joseph A. Fitzmyer, *Luke the Theologian: Aspects of His Teaching* (New York: Paulist, 1989), 16–22.

with insertions of "we" into the story,[24] it is odd that he does so infrequently and in places that are relatively bland and of little historical insignificance.[25]

Third, some have purported that the "we sections" of Acts are examples of an ancient literary convention, i.e., when an author wrote about sea voyages, he was expected to use first-person pronouns. Several extrabiblical accounts of sea travels seem to offer parallels that give some warrant to this theory.[26] But in the end, this theory is found to be straining at the evidence, for several sea voyages in Acts lack the use of first-person plural pronominal references (Acts 13:4, 13; 14:26; 17:14; 18:18, 21; 20:1–2); conversely, some portions of the "we sections" are not sea voyages at all (Acts 16:13–17; 20:7–8; 21:8–18); and the extrabiblical examples of ancient sea voyage literature are similarly not at all consistent. [27] Thus, the best proposal regarding the "***we sections***" in Acts is that these are intentional reflections of places where the author himself was present for the events being narrated, and this offers us a greater sense of Luke's reliability as a firsthand witness of these events.

4.2.2 Written Sources

Luke himself comments on the availability of written sources particularly for his composition of the Gospel of Luke (e.g., Luke 1:1), and studies of the Synoptic Gospels generally agree that the first three gospels have some kind of literary interdependence, with most suggesting that Luke used a copy of the Gospel of Mark as a source. The study of written sources used in the composition of Acts, however, has been less productive in formulating agreed-upon theories. Nevertheless, if Luke was a careful researcher and consulted literary sources for his first volume (the Gospel of Luke), it seems sensible that he would have continued that practice for his second volume (Acts). Indeed, the evidence suggests this to be the case.

First, at two places in Acts, Luke cites letters: one composed by the Jerusalem elders to believers who were part of churches with mixed Jew-gentile memberships (Acts 15:23–29) and another composed by the Roman army commander Claudius Lysias addressed to Governor Felix regarding Paul's arrest in Jerusalem (Acts 23:25–30). While some may suspect that Luke has fabricated these letters, there is little reason to accuse

---

24. Strelan suggests this possibility; Rick Strelan, *Luke the Priest: The Authority of the Author of the Third Gospel* (Burlington, VT: Ashgate, 2008; repr., New York: Routledge, 2016), 73; see also Overbeck, "Introduction to the Acts of the Apostles," pp. 1:31–54 in Zeller, *The Contents and Origin of the Acts of the Apostles Critically Investigated*; cf. Zeller's own comments in 2:257–60.

25. Ben Witherington III, *Invitation to the New Testament: First Things* (New York: Oxford University Press, 2013), 107.

26. See Vernon K. Robbins, "By Land and By Sea: The We-Passages and Ancient Sea Voyages," in *Perspectives on Luke-Acts*, ed. Charles H. Talbert, Perspectives in Religious Studies 5 (Danville, VA: Association of Baptist Professors of Religion, 1978), 215–42; and idem, *Sea Voyages and Beyond: Emerging Strategies in Socio-Rhetorical Interpretation*, Emory Studies in Early Christianity (Dorset, England: Deo, 2010).

27. See Fitzmyer, *Luke the Theologian*, 16–22.

him of such. The first letter was, in fact, intended to be circulated among the various churches in gentile territories (cf. Acts 15:30–31; 16:4; 21:25), so Luke would have had easy access to it. As for the second letter, if Luke were in the habit of creating such communications, it seems that he would have done so for the (arguably) more significant transfer of Paul to Rome, a letter he comments on but apparently has not read (Acts 25:24–27; so also the letters mentioned in Acts 9:2).

Second, a few scholars have proposed that Luke consulted the writings of the first-century Jewish historian Josephus.[28] Luke and Josephus were contemporaries, and there are, indeed, several parallels of information between Acts and Josephus's *Jewish Antiquities* (ca. AD 94). But they do not always agree with each other, and given that most of the information Luke and Josephus have in common was widely known anyway, the dependence of either writer upon the other is hardly a necessary conclusion.[29] In the end, then, it is highly unlikely that Luke was dependent on Josephus as a literary source.[30]

Flavius Josephus
Public domain

Third, it is noteworthy that Acts nowhere mentions any of the letters of Paul. This observation has been used as evidence for an early date of composition for Acts, i.e., before Paul's letters were gathered together as a valuable collection. Of course, it seems likely that if he is really the same Luke who was the sometimes companion of Paul in his travels, then the author of Acts would have known about Paul as a letter writer. But Luke clearly chose not to mention Paul's letters, perhaps not having direct access to any of them, not feeling a need to consult them, or not realizing how important the letters would eventually become to the Christian faith.[31] But even apart from the dating question, several scholars have argued that some small details in Acts do, in fact, betray the author's familiarity with the content of at least some of Paul's letters.[32] This is particularly noted in terms of events and chronol-

28. E.g., Barbara Shellard, *New Light on Luke: Its Purpose, Sources, and Literary Context*, JSNTSup 215 (Sheffield: Sheffield Academic Press, 2002), 31–34; and Mason, *Josephus and the New Testament*, 251–95. See a response to Mason's proposal in Witherington, *Acts*, 235–39.

29. See Bruce, *Acts: Greek Text*, 43–44; and Colin J. Hemer, *The Book of Acts in the Setting of Hellenistic History*, ed. Conrad H. Gempf, WUNT 49 (Tübingen: Mohr Siebeck, 1989; repr., Winona Lake, IN: Eisenbrauns, 1990), 94–99; cf. Conrad H. Gempf, "Public Speaking and Published Accounts," pp. 259–303 in *The Book of Acts in its Ancient Literary Setting*, ed. Bruce W. Winter and Andrew D. Clarke, BAFCS 1 (Grand Rapids: Eerdmans, 1993; Carlisle: Paternoster, 1993), 288.

30. Keener, *Acts*, 1:394.

31. For a discussion on Luke's access to Paul's letters, see Keener, *Acts*, 1:233–37; Keener remarks that "if Luke had enough to say about Paul without the letters, he had little reason to depend on them or consult them" (p. 235).

32. See esp. Morton S. Enslin, "'Luke' and Paul," *JAOS* 58 (1938): 81–91; idem, "Once Again, Luke and Paul," *ZNW* 61 (1970): 253–71; William O. Walker Jr., "Acts and the Pauline Corpus Reconsidered," *JSNT* 24 (1985): 3–23;

ogy, theological ideas, and what appears to be Pauline phraseology (see sidebar). But familiarity with events as well as Paul's theology and way of saying things could come from Luke's time traveling with Paul himself and not merely from reading his letters.[33] Thus, scholars are divided on whether Luke utilized Paul's letters while writing Acts.[34] In the end, in addition to the simple fact that the letters are never directly referenced in Acts, the differences in emphasis as well as the inclusion and exclusion of different details about Paul's life, ministry, and teaching seem to weigh in favor of Luke not being dependent on Paul's letters as sources of information, even if he was aware of them.[35]

Paul's Poetic Citations in Acts

In his speech before the Areopagus of Athens (Acts 17), rather than citing from Hebrew Scriptures, Paul cites from some poets with whom he thought his audience would be familiar.

> The God who made the world and everything in it is the Lord of heaven and earth and does not live in temples built by human hands. And he is not served by human hands, as if he needed anything. Rather, he himself gives everyone life and breath and everything else. From one man he made all the nations, that they should inhabit the whole earth; and he marked out their appointed times in history and the boundaries of their lands. God did this so that they would seek him and perhaps reach out for him and find him, though he is not far from any one of us. "For in him we live and move and have our being." As some of your own poets have said, "We are his offspring." (Acts 17:24–28)

- "For in him we live and move and have our being."
  –from the Cretan poet Epimenides in *Cretica* (ca. 600 BC)
- "We are his offspring."
  –from the Cilician poet Aratus in *Phaenomena* (ca. 315–240 BC) or from Cleanthes in *Hymn to Zeus* (ca. 331–233 BC)

---

and idem, "Acts and the Pauline Letter Corpus Revisited: Peter's Speech at the Jerusalem Conference," in *Literary Studies in Luke-Acts: Essays in Honor of Joseph B. Tyson*, ed. Richard P. Thompson and Thomas E. Phillips (Macon, GA: Mercer University Press, 1998), 77–86; cf. John Knox, "Acts and the Pauline Letter Corpus," in *Studies in Luke-Acts: Essays Presented in Honor of Paul Schubert*, ed. Leander E. Keck and Louis J. Martyn (Nashville: Abingdon, 1966; repr., Philadelphia: Fortress, 1980), 279–87.

33. Cf. Keener, *Acts*, 1:234–35; Stanley E. Porter, *The Paul of Acts: Essays in Literary Criticism, Rhetoric, and Theology* (Tübingen: Mohr Siebeck, 1999; repr., *Paul in Acts*, Library of Pauline Studies, Peabody, MA: Hendrickson, 2001), 206.

34. See the survey of William O. Walker Jr., "Acts and the Pauline Letters: A Select Bibliography with Introduction," *Forum* NS 5 (2002): 105–15, which lists scholarly works in three categories: those arguing that Luke did not know Paul's letters, those arguing that Luke knew some of Paul's letters but did not use them, and those arguing that Luke knew and used at least some of Paul's letters.

35. So Keener, *Acts*, 1:235–36.

Correspondences between Acts and Paul

Similarities	Pauline Letters	Acts
The apostles led the early church	Gal 1:17; 1 Cor 15:5	1:13; 6:2
The Lord's brothers as leaders	1 Cor 9:5	1:14
The Jerusalem church was large	1 Cor 15:6	1:15; 2:41; 4:4
Baptism in the name of Jesus was a church entrance ritual	Rom 6:3–4; Gal 3:27; 1 Cor 1:13–15	2:38, 41; 8:12-13; 10:47-48
The apostles did signs and wonders	2 Cor 12:11–12	2:43; 14:3
Peter and John were key apostles	Gal 2:9	3:1–4:23; 8:14–25
Peter as apostolic spokesperson	Gal 1:18; 1 Cor 15:5	2:37; cf. 1:15–22; 2:14–40; passim
Peter had an itinerant ministry	Gal 2:7–8, 11	9:32-43; 12:17
Paul from the tribe of Benjamin	Rom 11:1; Phil 3:5	9:1; cf. 13:21 (named Saul)
Paul "a Hebrew of Hebrews"	Phil 3:5; 2 Cor 11:22	21:40; 22:2–3 (Hebrew language)
Paul a Pharisee	Phil 3:5	23:6; 26:5
Paul a persecutor of the church	Gal 1:13; 1 Cor 15:9; Phil 3:6	8:3; 9:1; 22:4–5, 19–20; 26:9–11
Paul converted on a trip to Damascus	Gal 1:15–17	9:1–19; 22:6-16; 26:12–18
Paul saw the Lord	1 Cor 9:1, 17; 15:8	9:17; 22:14
Paul departed Damascus in a basket	2 Cor 11:32–33	9:23–25
Paul visited Jerusalem from Damascus	Gal 1:18–19	9:23-27; 22:17-21; 26:20
Paul preached in Jerusalem	Rom 15:19	9:28–29
Paul went next to Syria and Cilicia	Gal 1:21–23	9:28–30; 11:22–26
Barnabas ministered to/with Paul	Gal 2:1–10; 1 Cor 9:6	9:27; 11:22–30; 12:25; 13–14
Paul visited Jerusalem from Antioch	Gal 2:1–10	11:27–30
Paul gathered funds for Jerusalem from among gentile believers	Gal 2:10; 1 Cor 16:1–3; 2 Cor 8:1–4; 9:1–15; Rom 15:15–31	11:27–30; 24:17
The Lord's brother James as leader	1 Cor 15:7; Gal 2:9, 12	12:17; 15:13-21; 21:18
Paul visited Antioch, Iconium, Lystra	2 Tim 3:11	13–14
Paul as an "apostle"	Rom 1:1, 5; 1 Cor 1:1; 9:1–2; 15:8-10; 2 Cor 1:1; 11:5; passim	14:4, 14
Barnabas as an "apostle"	1 Cor 9:5–6	14:4, 14
Judean churches followed the law and had potential tension with Paul	Gal 2:12	15:1–5; 21:20–21
John Mark was connected to Barnabas	Col 4:10	15:37–39

Similarities	Pauline Letters	Acts
Paul ministered in Philippi	1 Thess 2:2; Phil 4:15	16:8-40
Paul ministered in Thessalonica	1 Thess 2:1-2; Phil 4:16	17:1-9
Paul visited Thessalonica and Corinth with Silvanus (Silas) and Timothy	1 Thess 1:1; 2 Thess 1:1; 2 Cor 1:19	15:22, 40; 16:1-18:22
Believers faced trouble in Thessalonica	1 Thess 1:6-7; 2:13-16	17:5-9
Paul ministered briefly in Athens	1 Thess 3:1-3	17:15-34
Paul began ministry in Corinth alone	1 Cor 2:1; 1 Thess 3:1, 6	18:1-4
Paul did not ask Corinthians for support	1 Cor 4:12; 9:6; 2 Cor 11:7-9	18:3
In Corinth Crispus became a believer	1 Cor 1:14	18:8
Paul visited Cenchreae	Rom 16:1-2	18:18
Apollos ministered in Corinth	1 Cor 1:12	18:24-19:1
Paul stayed a while in Ephesus	1 Cor 16:8-9	19:1-41; 20:31
Paul planned to visit Rome	Rom 15:23-29	19:21
Via Macedonia Paul visited Corinth again	1 Cor 16:5-9; 2 Cor 1:8-2:13; 9:4	20:1-3.
Paul expected trouble in Jerusalem	Rom 15:25-31	20:22-23; 21:10-14

Compiled and adapted from lists by Bruce, *Book of Acts*, 47-52; Michael D. Goulder, *Paul and the Competing Mission in Corinth*, Library of Pauline Studies (Peabody, MA: Hendrickson, 2001), 223; Keener, *Acts*, 1:237-50; and Adolf von Harnack, *The Acts of the Apostles*, trans. J. R. Wilkinson, Crown Theological Library 27 (New York: Putnam, 1909), 264-74.

Finally, there is little reason to think Luke did not make use of other written sources in his composition of Acts. Various scholars have suggested that Acts may contain evidence of Luke's use of classical Greek works.[36] Some of the most interesting evidence of external sources is found in Paul's speech in Acts 17:28, where two brief citations of extrabiblical poetry occur (see sidebar). Paul appears to quote Greek poets in his own writings (e.g., 1 Cor 15:33; Titus 1:12), so perhaps Luke is simply utilizing Paul's report of the event and not the written works of the poets. It is likely that written records were kept of Paul's official trials in Acts 24–26, including summaries of the speeches and proceedings, and Luke may well have had access to those records (in addition to being present at some of the hearings).[37] Nevertheless, in the end, the evidence that Luke used other written sources stops far short of demonstrable proof of any particular source.

36. This is particularly the case among scholars who think Acts is a work of fiction; see chapter 2.

37. See Bruce W. Winter, "Official Proceedings and the Forensic Speeches in Acts 24–26," pp. 305–36 in Winter and Clarke, *The Book of Acts in its Ancient Literary Setting*, 306–9; and idem, "The Importance of the *Captatio Benevolentiae* in the Speeches of Tertullus and Paul in Acts 24:1–21," *JTS* 42 (1991): 505–31, esp. 527–31; cf. Keener, *Acts*, 1:288; 4:3353; Eckhard J. Schnabel, *Acts*, ZECNT (Grand Rapids: Zondervan, 2012), 949.

On Luke's Use of Sources for the Speeches in Acts

From A. T. Robertson, *Luke the Historian in the Light of Research* (New York: Scribner, 1920), 220.

> If he consulted sources, written and oral, for the addresses of Jesus in the Gospel, as can be proven, it is natural to think that he pursued the same careful research in the Acts. He made selections from the material in the Gospel, as he apparently did in the Acts. His reports in the Acts vary in the degree of completeness, as in the Gospel. We know that Luke heard some of Paul's addresses, which he reports. He had abundant opportunity to consult those who heard others, as we have seen in the study of the sources of Acts. Luke was in touch personally with James and Paul. Philip and Paul heard Stephen. Mark and Philip and Manaen heard Peter.

4.2.3 Oral Sources

Luke's use of personal testimony from eyewitnesses as information sources would be just as applicable to Acts as it is to the Gospel of Luke (Luke 1:2). If the author of Acts is really the physician Luke who sometimes traveled with Paul (as I argue in chapter 1), then not only would he have his own experiences to draw upon, but also his interaction with other members of Paul's missionary teams and other church members would afford him trustworthy testimony regarding the events he wanted to record. Luke knew Mark among Paul's coworkers (Phlm 24; Col 4:10–14), and Luke includes several stories about Mark in Acts (esp. in Acts 12, 13, and 15). Mark may well have been a source of information for Luke about these events and perhaps other events as well.

Naturally, traveling with Paul on some of his journeys would have afforded Luke the opportunity to hear Paul reminisce about events that Luke himself did not experience (e.g., Acts 9, 11, 13–15, 17–19). In these travels, Luke also had opportunities to interview others about recent events. With "we sections" about Paul's final trip to Jerusalem where he was arrested (Acts 20:5–15; 21:1–18) and again two years later on Paul's trip to Rome for a trial before Caesar (Acts 27:1–28:16), Luke may well have had those two intervening years in Judea for gathering information from Christians in the area.[38]

Ancient writers did not use the same footnoting and bibliography protocols of modern researchers. Nevertheless, ancient historians did sometimes identify some of their written sources and even their oral sources.[39] Perhaps Luke's mentioning people and especially his insertion of "hospitality notes"—i.e., the names of people who hosted

38. Cf. Keener, *Acts*, 1:180.
39. Keener, *Acts*, 1:170–73.

Paul and his itinerant group—were ways of giving credit to individuals who served as sources of information for Luke's written account.[40]

In the end, we can only with great difficulty make guesses at the sources Luke used in composing Acts. At the very least, Luke makes claim to have access to some eyewitness accounts—his own experience and the testimony of others—as well as to written records of some kind.[41]

4.3 TWO VERSIONS OF ACTS: WHICH IS THE CORRECT VERSION?

Whatever dating one applies to the composition of Acts, Acts was written long before the invention of the printing press in the fifteenth century by Johannes Gutenberg (ca. 1450). Prior to the printing press, books were written by hand and "published" by having people make handwritten copies of the book. For centuries then, books were preserved and passed on to the next generation in hand-copied manuscripts, which were replaced as they wore out by new hand-copied manuscripts. As this was the process for producing any ancient book, all ancient writings must be reconstructed from the available surviving manuscripts—copies that may have differences between them due to such things as spelling errors, accidental exclusions of words or phrases, unintentional alterations of word order, and even intentional changes. This process of sorting through the variations between manuscripts, identifying transcription alterations, tracing the transmission of the texts, and reconstructing the original readings is known as ***textual criticism***.[42]

Papyrus 29 (Third Century AD)

This pair of images of the papyrus fragment known as P^{29} shows the Greek text of Acts 26:7-8 on one side and 26:20 on the other.

Papyrus 29 (third century AD)
The Bodleian Libraries, University of Oxford, MS. Gr. bib. g. 4 (P), recto and verso.

4.3.1 The New Testament and Textual Criticism

In comparison with other ancient texts, the New Testament has an embarrassingly large number of extant manuscripts to work with in reconstructing the original reading. Over 5,800 Greek manuscripts

40. See remarks on this in chapter 3.

41. See Jacques Dupont, *The Sources of Acts*, trans. Kathleen Pond (New York: Herder and Herder, 1964).

42. See one of the standard textbooks on textual criticism such as Bruce M. Metzger and Bart D. Ehrman, *The Text of the New Testament: Its Transmission, Corruption, and Restoration*, 4th ed. (New York: Oxford University Press, 2005); for briefer treatments, see Stanley E. Porter, "Textual Criticism," *DNTB*, 1210–14; and more recently, N. T. Wright and Michael F. Bird, *The New Testament in Its World* (Grand Rapids: Zondervan Academic, 2019), 850–65.

Papyrus 45 (ca. AD 250)

The heavily damaged P[45] (a.k.a. Chester Beatty Papyrus I) was at one time a papyrus codex of as many as 220 pages, of which only 30 survive, containing parts of the Gospels and Acts. There are 2 pages of Matthew, 6 pages of Mark, 7 pages of Luke, 2 pages of John, and 13 pages of Acts.

Papyrus 45 (ca. AD 250)

ART Collection / Alamy Stock Photo

Papyrus 50 (Fourth or Fifth Century AD)

This image from P[50] shows the Greek text of Acts 8:26–32.

Papyrus 50 (fourth or fifth century AD)

Yale Papyrus Collection, Beinecke Rare Book and Manuscript Library

Codex Sinaiticus (ca. AD 350)

Named for having been found at Saint Catherine's Monastery on Mount Sinai, Codex Sinaiticus (א, 01) is one of the oldest manuscripts containing all of the New Testament. The full-page image here is of Acts 11; the close-up image shows the text of Acts 11:20.

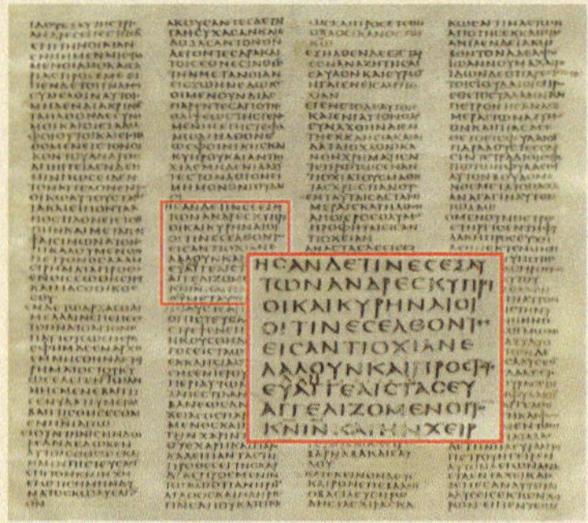

Codex Sinaiticus (ca. AD 350)

Codex Vaticanus (ca. AD 350)

In the Vatican library, Codex Vaticanus (B, 03) is another of the great fourth-century NT manuscripts.

Cadex Vaticanus (ca. AD 350)

Alexander Schick/bibelausstellung.de (courtesy of BiblePlaces.com)

Codex Bezae (Fifth Century AD)

Codex Bezae (D, 05) is one of the primary witnesses to the so-called Western text (a.k.a. D-text) of Acts, which is almost 10 percent longer than the standard text of Acts. The eleventh line from the bottom of the page in this image adds a flowery detail to Peter's escape from prison (at Acts 12:10): the angel and Peter "go down seven steps" into the street.

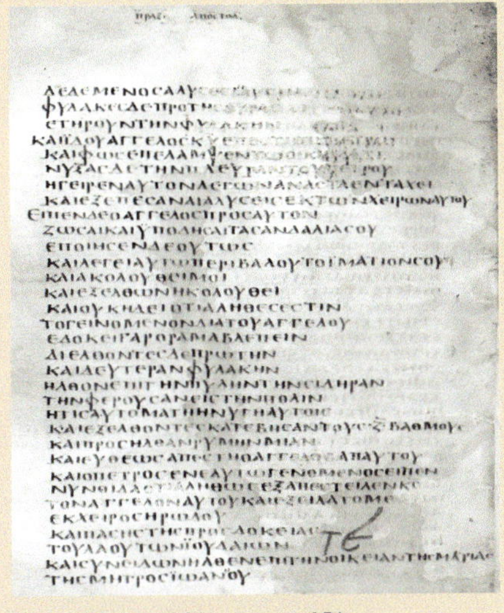

Codex Bezae (fifth century AD)
Cambridge University Library (MS Nn.2.41, fol. 463v)

Confidence in Reconstructing the Text

The NT versus Other Ancient Writings

From Daniel B. Wallace, "Has the New Testament Text Been Hopelessly Corrupted?" in *In Defense of the Bible: A Comprehensive Apologetic for the Authority of Scripture*, ed. Steven B. Cowan and Terry L. Wilder (Nashville: B&H Academic, 2013), 151.

> In terms of extant manuscripts, the New Testament textual critic is confronted with an embarrassment of riches. If we have doubts about what the autographic New Testament said, doubts would have to be multiplied at least a *hundred*-fold for the average classical author. And when we compare the New Testament manuscripts to the very *best* that the classical world has to offer, it still stands head and shoulders above the rest. The New Testament is far and away the best-attested work of Greek or Latin literature from the ancient world.

containing all or portions of the New Testament are extant, with additional various other ancient translations and quotations of portions of the New Testament found in the writings of early church fathers. Not only is the evidence plentiful, it is also quite old, with some copies of almost half of the verses of the New Testament dating to within 125 years of the ***autographs*** (i.e., the original physical documents penned by the NT writers themselves—the authors or their amanuenses).[43] Compared to all other ancient literature, the New Testament is the best attested (see sidebar).

43. Daniel B. Wallace, "Has the New Testament Text Been Hopelessly Corrupted?" in *In Defense of the Bible: A Comprehensive Apologetic for the Authority of Scripture*, ed. Steven B. Cowan and Terry L. Wilder (Nashville: B&H Academic, 2013), 147.

Manuscript Evidence for the Text of the New Testament

Over 5800 extant Greek manuscripts pertain to the New Testament. Many of these are written on parchment made from animal skins (a.k.a. vellum) and date to the fourth century AD and the centuries following (while some are loose leaf or fragmentary, others are bound in book form, called a "***codex***"). More than one hundred of the manuscripts are written on an ancient paper made from ***papyrus*** reeds (signified with a "P" in their identification codes) and contain fragments of various parts of the New Testament; half of these date to the first four centuries AD. Here are a few of the more famous manuscripts particularly relevant for Acts, with their identification insignia and approximate dates.

- Codex Sinaiticus (א, 01)—the whole NT, ca. AD 350.
- Codex Alexandrinus (A, 02)—the whole NT, ca. AD 400-440.
- Codex Vaticanus (B, 03)—much of the NT, ca. AD 350.
- Codex Ephraemi Rescriptus (C, 04)—most of the NT, ca. AD 450.
- Codex Bezae (D, 05)—the Gospels and Acts, fifth century AD.
- Codex Laudianus (E, 08)—portions of Acts, sixth or seventh century AD.
- P^{29} (Oxyrhynchus Papyrus 1597)—Acts 26:7-8 and 20, early third century AD.
- P^{38} (Michigan Papyrus 138)—Acts 18:27-19:6 and 12-16, early third century AD.
- P^{45} (Chester Beatty Papyrus I)—parts of the Gospels and Acts, ca. AD 250.
- P^{48}—portions of Acts 23:11-29, third century AD.
- P^{50}—Acts and the General Epistles, fourth or fifth century AD.
- P^{53}—Matt 26:29-40; Acts 9:33-10:1, third century AD.
- P^{75} (Bodmer Papyrus XIV-XV)—parts of Luke and John, ca. AD 175-225.
- P^{91}—Acts 2:30-37 and 2:46-3:2, mid third century AD.
- P^{112} (Oxyrhynchus Papyrus 4496)—portions of Acts and General Epistles, fifth century AD.
- P^{127} (Oxyrhynchus Papyrus 4968)—portions of Acts and General Epistles, fifth century AD.

4.3.2 Acts in Two Textual Versions

The confidence about the text of the New Testament as a whole extends to the book of Acts as well. One oddity with the book of Acts, however, is that the manuscript evidence divides into two old and somewhat different versions of the book. The version followed in edited Greek texts of the New Testament and most English translations is based on the preponderance of Greek manuscripts and some of the best representations of the extant manuscripts (like Codex Sinaiticus, Codex Alexandrinus, and Codex Vaticanus). This version comes from what is called the "Alexandrian text."

The second version follows another textual tradition—inaccurately dubbed the

"***Western text.***"[44] It is based largely on a very few, albeit old, Greek manuscripts (esp. Codex Bezae, a.k.a. manuscript D). The Western text (a.k.a. the D-text) is of particular interest in its treatment of Acts because of the amount of additional material found in Western manuscripts of Luke's second volume. Depending on how one chooses to measure it, the Western text of Acts is between 6 and 9 percent longer than the standard (i.e., the Alexandrian) text of Acts.[45] Notably, the extra length is not due to the Western text containing more stories. Rather, the Western text of Acts contains more flowery language and slight expansions of the stories in the standard text, and some of these editorial nuances seem to have particular ideological slants to them.[46] Scholars have identified four characteristics of the Western text: clarifications for smoothness, changes attempting to solve perceived points of internal inconsistency, long additions and paraphrases, and a few omissions of details contained in the Alexandrian text.[47] In addition to noting these literary features, scholars discuss the possibility that the Western text of Acts was an intentional revision of the book and that it evidences the particular ideological and theological tendencies of its reviser(s) (e.g., a heightened anti-Judaic attitude and an anti-woman tendency).[48]

Various theories have been proposed to explain the origin of the text of Acts in its two forms. The age of the Alexandrian text (a.k.a., the B-text)—especially the papyri bearing its textual characteristics—has convinced most scholars that it represents the more original version of Acts.[49] But age is not the only consideration. After all, if a very early manuscript had errors in it, then those mistakes could be reproduced in subsequent copies, even if those copies are also very old. Thus, comparisons of the previously mentioned themes or tendencies in the textual clusters have also factored into the discussion

44. The misnomer "Western text" comes from an early period in the history of textual criticism when manuscripts with these particular readings were first recognized as being in use by early western Christians. It was later recognized that such manuscripts were also in use in the east (e.g., Egypt, Syria, and among church father citations), but the title for this kind of manuscript was already in wide use and has been difficult to shed.

45. See W. A. Strange, *The Problem of the Text of Acts*, SNTSMS 71 (Cambridge: Cambridge University Press, 1992), 213n18.

46. See Charles S. C. Williams, *Alterations to the Text of the Synoptic Gospels and Acts* (Oxford: Blackwell, 1951), 54–82.

47. See Roger L. Omanson, *A Textual Guide to the Greek New Testament: An Adaptation of Bruce M. Metzger's* Textual Commentary *for the Needs of Translators* (Stuttgart: German Bible Society, 2006), 22* and 214.

48. E.g., Eldon Jay Epp, *The Theological Tendency of Codex Bezae Cantabrigiensis in Acts*, SNTSMS 3 (Cambridge: Cambridge University Press, 1966); and Ben Witherington III, "The Anti-Feminist Tendencies of the 'Western' Text in Acts," *JBL* 103 (1984): 82–84. Offering some correctives, however, are Max Wilcox, "Luke and the Bezan Text of Acts," pp. 447–55 in Kremer, *Les Actes des Apôtres*, 448; C. K. Barrett, "Is There a Theological Tendency in Codex Bezae?" pp. 15–27 in *Text and Interpretation: Studies in the New Testament Presented to Matthew Black*, ed. Ernest Best and R. McL. Wilson (Cambridge: Cambridge University Press, 1979), esp. 26–27; and Michael W. Holmes, "Women and the 'Western' Text of Acts," in *The Book of Acts as Church History: Text, Textual Traditions and Ancient Interpretations*, ed. Tobias Nicklas and Michael Tilly, BZNW 120 (Berlin: de Gruyter, 2003), 183–203.

49. See François Bovon, *Studies in Early Christianity* (Grand Rapids: Baker, 2005), 25; and Dieter R. Roth, "The Text of Luke and Acts: Witnesses, Features, and the Significance of the Textual Traditions," pp. 51–71 in Adams and Pahl, *Issues in Luke-Acts*, 65; cf. Christopher M. Tuckett, "The Early Text of Acts," in *The Early Text of the New Testament*, ed. Charles E. Hill and Michael J. Kruger (Oxford: Oxford University Press, 2012), 157–74.

Modifications of Acts in the Western Text

The following examples illustrate the kinds of modifications produced in the Western text of Acts. Some passages may exhibit more than one of the characteristic modifications. The English translations here for the standard (i.e., Alexandrian) text are from the NIV and for the Western text are dependent on the Greek of the Western text provided in Read-Heimerdinger and Rius-Camps, *Luke's Demonstration to Theophilus*.

Western Text Characteristic	Alexandrian Text	Western Text
Clarifications for smoothness of the reading—Here, an insertion clarifies the Sanhedrin's agreement.	Acts 4:18—Then they called them in again and commanded them not to speak or teach at all in the name of Jesus.	Acts 4:18—And being in agreement on their decision, they called them and commanded them not to speak or teach at all in the name of Jesus.
Attempts to solve perceived internal inconsistencies—Here, Paul's healing declaration is brought into closer conformity with those by Jesus (Luke 5:24; 7:14) and Peter (Acts 3:6).	Acts 14:9-10—Paul looked directly at him, saw that he had faith to be healed and called out, "Stand up on your feet!" At that, the man jumped up and began to walk.	Acts 14:9-10—But Paul looked directly at him, saw that he had faith to be healed and called out, "To you I say in the name of the Lord Jesus Christ: stand up on your feet and walk." And suddenly the man jumped up immediately and began to walk.
Long additions or paraphrases—In this example, Peter's arrival in Caesarea and exchange with Cornelius has more colorful detail.	Acts 10:24-26—The following day he arrived in Caesarea. Cornelius was expecting them and had called together his relatives and close friends. As Peter entered the house, Cornelius met him and fell at his feet in reverence. But Peter made him get up. "Stand up," he said, "I am only a man myself."	Acts 10:24-26—The following day, he arrived in Caesarea. Cornelius was anticipating them, and having called together his relatives and close friends, he was waiting. And when Peter was getting close to Caesarea, one of the servants ran ahead and reported that he had arrived. And Cornelius jumped up and as he met him, he fell at his feet and revered him. But Peter made him get up, saying, "What are you doing? I am a man, just like you also."
Omissions of detail—Here, the explanation for some Athenian responses to Paul's preaching is omitted.	Acts 17:18—Others remarked, "He seems to be advocating foreign gods." They said this because Paul was preaching the good news about Jesus and the resurrection.	Acts 17:18—Others remarked, "He seems to be advocating foreign gods."
Ideological/theological tendency of the reviser—Some suspect here (and in 17:4, 12; 18:26) an anti-woman motive for the revision.	Acts 17:34—Some of the people became followers of Paul and believed. Among them was Dionysius, a member of the Areopagus, also a woman named Damaris, and a number of others.	Acts 17:34—Some of the people became followers of Paul and believed. Among whom was Dionysius, a certain member of the Areopagus of high standing, and a number of others.

of which is closer to the original. Most understand the Western text readings as more likely to have arrived as alterations of the Alexandrian text rather than the other way around.[50] For such reasons as these, I join in the general consensus among NT scholars (and English Bible translations) favoring the Alexandrian text of Acts.[51] I suggest that the "Western" version of Acts is something of a paraphrased version of Luke's original story of Acts. All this is to say that even early on in the life of the church, readers of Acts found its story interesting and helpful, and they chose to pass it on in its original version as well as (at least for some readers) in a paraphrased version.

4.4 THE HEBREW SCRIPTURES AND ACTS: HOW ARE THE HEBREW SCRIPTURES UNDERSTOOD IN ACTS?

In discussing Luke's literary methods in chapter 3, we noted that he regularly cites the Hebrew Scriptures. In his recounting of the story of Jesus and his followers, Luke uses the Hebrew Scriptures in a variety of ways and for a variety of purposes. Sometimes his quotation (or paraphrase) of a particular OT passage has a formulaic introduction (e.g., "it is written"), and sometimes it is without such an introduction; in either case, I refer to these as citations. Sometimes he summarizes the teaching of Scripture in a simple statement (a Scripture summary); sometimes he alludes to a passage by means of a borrowed phrase (a specific allusion); sometimes he references a person or event in an OT passage without quoting it or borrowing its phrasing (a historical reminiscence); and sometimes the reference is so vague and mixed that it seems to come from a variety of OT passages rather than a single one (a thematic echo). (See the chart in chapter 3 for a tally of these forms in Luke-Acts).

Programmatic Motives for the Use of the OT in Luke-Acts

In addition to—or in coordination with—his particular theological truth claims, Luke aims to accomplish several things with his use of the Hebrew Scriptures in Luke-Acts.

1. Evangelizing people to faith in Jesus Christ, the fulfillment of Scripture.
2. Extolling God's sovereign plan for history.
3. Authenticating the faith heritage of Christianity.
4. Expanding the notion of God's people to include gentiles in the church.
5. Encouraging the interpretation of Scripture.

50. See esp. Peter M. Head, "Appendix: Acts and the Problem of Its Texts," in Winter and Clarke, *The Book of Acts in its Ancient Literary Setting*, 415–44.

51. Darrell L. Bock, *Acts*, BECNT (Grand Rapids: Baker Academic, 2007), 29.

A quick survey of Luke's use of the Hebrew Scriptures reveals that Luke utilizes Scripture to support several theological truth claims (several of these theological themes of particular interest to Luke were surveyed in chapter 3). Furthermore, Luke seems to have five larger overlapping programmatic motives for his references to Scripture; that is, Luke intends to *do* things by using Scripture in the whole of Luke-Acts.[52]

4.4.1 Evangelizing People to Faith in Jesus Christ, the Fulfillment of Scripture

In speaking about the fulfillment of Scripture, it is best to think of "fulfillment" as having several possible connotations. Arguably the most common understanding of Scripture "fulfillment" is when a prediction comes true in its one-and-only anticipated outcome (e.g., Deut 18:15 in Acts 3:22–23; 7:37). While this is certainly the case for some OT prophecies about Jesus, he "fulfills" Scripture in a different sense when an OT pattern or promise finds still another repeated realization in him (e.g., Joel 2:28–32 in Acts 2:17–21). In yet another sense, Jesus "fulfills" Scripture when a NT author notices that an OT person or event or institution serves as a kind of prefigurement that finds its completion in Jesus (e.g., Ps 16:8–11 in Acts 2:25–32 and 13:35). Thus, Jesus is the fulfillment—in many senses of the word—of the Hebrew Scriptures. This is set out early in Luke-Acts, with prophetic figures using scriptural words to speak about Jesus (i.e., Luke 2:22–40; esp. Isa 42:6; 49:6, 9 in v. 32) and with Jesus himself announcing his fulfillment of specific Scripture (i.e., Isa 61:1–2; 58:6 in Luke 4:16–21; and Isa 29:18; 35:5–6; 42:18; 26:19; and 61:1 in Luke 7:22–23) and even his fulfillment of all of Scripture (e.g., Luke 24:25–27, 44–47). Luke occasionally includes synopses of the message of the Hebrew Scriptures, which often center on the suffering and death of the Messiah (see esp. Luke 24:25–26, 27, 44, 46–47; Acts 3:18, 21; 10:43; 13:27, 29; 17:2–3). One of the primary purposes for Luke's use of Scripture is to proclaim Jesus as the Messiah for the whole world.

4.4.2 Extolling God's Sovereign Plan for History

Four Lukan texts describe quite clearly that God has a plan for history, and each of them references (or at least alludes to) the Hebrew Scriptures (see Luke 7:24–28; 16:16–17; Acts 10:42–43; 17:24–31). While Christianity may seem new, it has actually been God's plan all along. Luke has several more general statements and turns of phrase that also reflect his commitment to God's sovereign plan for history (see esp. Luke 7:30; Acts 2:23; 3:13–26; 4:28; 5:38–39; 10:38–41; 11:18; 13:23, 32–33, 36; 14:16–17, 27; 15:4, 12; 17:26, 30–31; 20:27; 21:19; 27:23–24). This plan of God has not yet reached its completion, but it will culminate in the future and still be centered on Jesus Christ.

---

52. What follows here summarizes my remarks in chapter 6 of Douglas S. Huffman, *Understanding the New Testament Use of the Old Testament: Forms, Features, Framings, and Functions* (Grand Rapids: Baker Academic, 2024).

4.4.3 Endorsing the Faith Heritage of Christianity

Luke's constant use of the Hebrew Scriptures is another way to stress that the story of the Christian church is the continuation of the Jesus story even as the Jesus story is the continuation of the story recorded in Israel's sacred writings. Luke is concerned to demonstrate that faith in Christ is the proper carrying forward of Israelite faith. Of the four gospels, it is Luke's that best displays an intentional and seamless continuity with OT Israel's storyline, and this continues in the book of Acts.[53] Faith in Jesus as the Messiah is not an attempt to break away from the ancient Israelite faith; it is a claim that the long-awaited promises of the ancient faith are now coming to pass.[54] Luke uses the Hebrew Scriptures to make this clear to his audience (e.g., Acts 18:28; 23:6; 24:14–15, 21; 26:6–8, 22–23; 28:20, 23).

4.4.4 Expanding the Notion of God's People to Include Gentiles

Luke appeals to the Hebrew Scriptures to encourage the expansion of God's people to include gentile believers. One need not become a Jew first to be a follower of Jesus. This is not a new idea; it has been part of God's plan from of old, and the Scriptures indicate it to have been thus. Luke often utilizes the words of Isaiah in addressing this particular concern (e.g., Isa 42:6; 49:6, 9 in Luke 2:32; Isa 40:3–5 in Luke 3:4–6; Isa 66:1–2 in Acts 7:49–50; Isa 49:6 in Acts 13:46–47; Isa 42:7, 16 in Acts 26:17–18; and Isa 6:9–10 in Acts 28:26–27). Faith heritage is not a matter of heredity but of response to God. Because Jesus is Lord of all by God's design, the gospel message is to go to all peoples. As displayed in the Scriptures, gentile involvement has always been part of God's plan and promise.[55]

4.4.5 Encouraging the Interpretation of Scripture

Most citations of the Hebrew Scriptures in Luke-Acts occur in speeches, primarily with Jesus speaking in the Gospel of Luke and with apostolic preaching in Acts. Bart Koet suggests that Luke puts citations in the mouths of characters in the story with the intention to portray Jesus and his followers as interpreters of Scripture.[56] Acts betrays a persistent christological reading of the Hebrew Scriptures by the characters in the story. Luke records these things in such a way as to encourage his readers to recognize that the OT Scriptures point to Jesus. This was Jesus's expectation (see esp. Luke 24:25–27, 32, 44–49); Luke likewise expects all believers to be able to interpret the Hebrew Scriptures in this same manner and so to forward the Scripture-based gospel message to the world.

---

53. Richard B. Hays, *Echoes of Scripture in the Gospels* (Waco, TX: Baylor University Press, 2016), 191.

54. Bock, *A Theology of Luke and Acts*, 416.

55. Ibid., 419.

56. Bart J. Koet, *Five Studies on Interpretation of Scripture in Luke-Acts*, SNTA 14 (Leuven: Leuven University Press, 1989), 149–50.

4.5 THE HERMENEUTICS OF ACTS: HOW DOES LUKE WANT US TO UNDERSTAND ACTS?

The word ***hermeneutics*** can be defined as the theory and method of interpretation. It is the scholarly label used especially in discussions of Scripture interpretation. When interpreting Scripture, people want to know not only what a text meant to the original audience and their churches but also how it applies now in the present to us in our churches. The question asked here, then, regards how we are to interpret and apply the book of Acts in our communities of faith.

4.5.1 Narrative versus Didactic Material

While the theory and method of interpretation is basically the same for understanding the message of a written work in any and all genres,[57] one of the most basic problematic issues in considering the interpretation of the book of Acts is that it is a narrative, a story. In contrast, while we still encounter some difficulties in reading the NT epistles, we usually find the questions of meaning and application less problematic in such ***didactic*** (i.e., instructional) ***material*** than we do in Luke's narrative material. When Paul writes, "Therefore each of you must put off falsehood and speak truthfully to your neighbor, for we are all members of one body" (Eph 4:25), few of us question what this means and how we should apply it to our lives. We conclude, "I should not tell lies, but I should tell the truth." This is what Paul meant when he wrote what he did; this is how Paul expects us to apply his instruction to our lives.

But how does Luke want us to understand his comment in Acts 1:12–13, "Then the apostles returned to Jerusalem from the hill called the Mount of Olives, a Sabbath day's walk from the city. When they arrived, they went upstairs to the room where they were staying"? It would seem odd for us to conclude that we must all go into an upper room in Jerusalem! What did Luke mean when he wrote what he did? How does Luke expect us to apply this passage to ourselves and our communities of faith today? This is one of the fundamental issues when reading historical narratives in Scripture, particularly when trying to apply Scripture's accounts of past events to one's own life and church in the present. Aside from an author reporting the facts of the events, any message intended in a narrative is usually conveyed implicitly rather than explicitly.[58] But this issue is not unique to the book of Acts, for narrative is the most common kind of literature in the Bible.

57. So Liefeld, *Interpreting the Book of Acts*, 113.

58. So Robert H. Stein, *A Basic Guide to Interpreting the Bible: Playing by the Rules*, 2nd ed. (Grand Rapids: Baker Academic, 2011), 87.

Scriptural Narratives

From Gordon D. Fee and Douglas Stuart, *How to Read the Bible for All Its Worth*, 4th ed. (Grand Rapids: Zondervan, 2014), 94.

> Narratives are stories—purposeful stories retelling the historical events of the past that are intended to give meaning and direction for a given people in the present. This has always been so for all peoples in all cultures; and in this regard the biblical narratives are no different from other such stories. Nonetheless, there is a crucial difference between the biblical narratives and all others because, inspired by the Holy Spirit as they are, the story they tell is not so much our story as it is God's story—and it becomes ours as he "writes" us into it. The biblical narratives thus tell the ultimate story—a story that, even though often complex, is altogether true and crucially important. Indeed, it is a magnificent story, grander than the greatest epic, richer in plot and more significant in its characters and descriptions than any humanly composed story could ever be.

4.5.2 Context! Context! Context!

When interpreting any written message—this includes such things as traffic signs, newspapers, and blog posts, as well as Scripture!—the interpreter's constant cheer is, "Context! Context! Context!" When it comes to interpreting the message of Acts (or any other book of Scripture), we do best to reckon with three levels of context: the context of the author's own work, the context of Scripture as God's Word, and the context of the world in which the author was writing.

First, regarding the context of the author's work, skilled writers are able to communicate their purposes. They utilize various literary methods within their selected literary genres to carry out their designs for their written works. This is no less true for writers of narratives than it is for writers of didactic material. In chapter 1, I recommended respecting Luke as a highly skilled literary artist. In chapter 2, I suggested that he purposely selected history-related genres for Luke-Acts because he wanted to report historical events and to comment on the significance of those events. And Luke's message in Acts is explicitly connected to the message in his gospel account (Acts 1:1–11), so to properly interpret Acts, we must take the Gospel of Luke as part of its context. In chapter 3, I pointed out several of the literary methods Luke uses in his writing and several possible ways to outline the book of Acts. By noting these features and methods of his work, we are more quickly able to understand Luke's message in the book of Acts.

Second, regarding the context of Scripture as God's Word, we might recall from chapter 1 the suggestion that Luke was purposely constructing his accounts of Jesus and the early church as a continuation of the storyline that had begun with the Hebrew Scriptures.

Because Luke writes with much reflection on the Hebrew Scriptures (e.g., using its language, referencing its themes, and directly citing it), it makes sense to read Acts in the context of his reflections on Scripture. As noted in chapter 3, Luke exhibits several theological themes in Luke-Acts. In particular, Luke argues that Jesus was not only living in and continuing the storyline of Scripture but also somehow bringing history to a climactic turning point that fulfilled Scripture, signaled God's faithfulness, and provided promise for the future for all who choose to live in the power of the Holy Spirit. If we want to understand the message of Acts properly, we should read it in this scriptural context.

Third, regarding the context of the ancient world, note that simply recognizing a book like Acts to be part of the Bible does not somehow make it thereby easy to understand. While the Bible speaks a timeless message, that message comes to us in a time-related form.[59] This is why I have discussed the date of Luke's act of writing: we need to recognize that he was a first-century writer using first-century methods for first-century audiences. Even recognizing Luke as an inspired writer of God's Word does not remove the importance of understanding Luke's work in the context of the ancient world. As I survey the book of Acts, I will make helpful suggestions about the light shed on Luke's meaning by understanding his ancient context, and chapter 5 will outline some broad concepts of the historical-political, religious, and sociocultural background to the NT era.

Context, Context, Context!

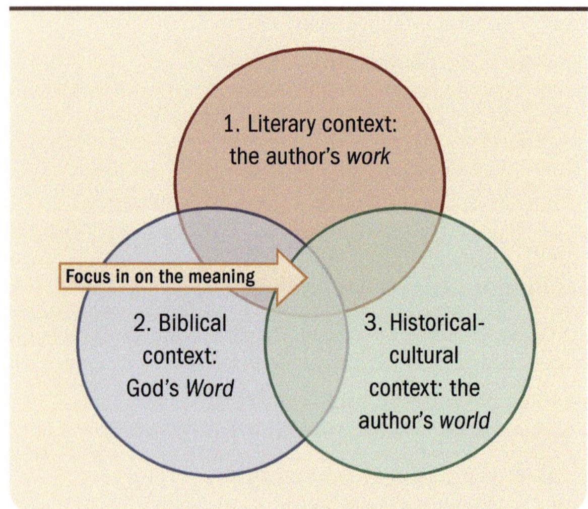

4.5.3 The Question of Historical Precedent: Description or Prescription?

In their bestselling book on interpretation, *How to Read the Bible for All Its Worth*, Gordon Fee and Douglas Stuart have a chapter devoted to instructions for reading and applying the book of Acts. It is entitled "Acts: The Question of Historical Precedent" precisely because Acts—more so than any other biblical narrative—is one that Christians often look to for instructions on how to live in the world after the resurrection and ascension of Jesus.[60] The concept of historical precedent has to do

59. Gary M. Burge and Gene L. Green, *The New Testament in Antiquity: A Survey of the New Testament within Its Cultural Contexts*, 2nd ed. (Grand Rapids: Zondervan Academic, 2020), 21.

60. Gordon D. Fee and Douglas Stuart, *How to Read the Bible for All Its Worth*, 4th ed. (Grand Rapids: Zondervan, 2014), 112–31.

with whether something done in the past is reason enough for it to be done again in the same way. Indeed, the book of Acts begins with the resurrection and ascension of Jesus and then describes the expansion of the gospel message and comments on the growth of the church. Acts tells the earliest history of the Christian church, and it seems rather natural, then, to assume that Acts serves as a normative model for the Christian church of all time periods. Thus, the way Christians lived in the book of Acts seems to set a precedent for how Christians should live now. And this brings on us perhaps the most serious set of questions for our interpretation and application of Acts: Because it happened in the history of the early church in Acts, is it proper for us to expect it to be happening that same way today? What should we emulate in the book of Acts, and conversely, what should we not emulate? How do we distinguish when what Luke reports in Acts is merely historical *description* and when it is universal *prescription*?

Chapter 3 comments on some of Luke's literary methods for writing Luke-Acts. Recognizing his methods can help us understand his intentions. Robert Stein suggests that paying attention to context, introductions and conclusions, authorial comments, authorial summaries, repetition, proportion, authoritative speakers, and dialogue or direct discourse will help us understand the author's intended message within a historical narrative.[61] Conversely, recognizing the lack of particular methods and patterns will help us refrain from concluding prescriptions for the church today where Luke intends none.

Suggested here are three kinds of behavior patterns to notice in Acts: regular past patterns, repeatable pragmatic patterns, and required prescriptive patterns. Each of these patterns has its place in appreciating the story Luke tells, and thus each has value for believers today. But when it comes to applying the book of Acts to our lives and in our faith communities, noting the differences in these patterns can offer some wisdom and direction in recognizing Luke's intentions for his original audience and for us.

A. Regular Past Patterns

Regular past patterns of behavior are simply the way things happened in the first century. A rather mundane example is the pattern we see in how missionaries travel in the book of Acts. That missionaries always travel by foot or by boat in Acts would hardly be thought today to have any restrictive implications for missionaries in the twenty-first century. Traveling by foot and by boat were simply two of the regular ways people traveled in the first century; no one imagines that Luke was intending to teach that these were to be the only means of missionary transportation in all times and in all places. Luke says nothing for or against travel by horse or beast-drawn cart—first-century modes of transportation available to those who could afford them.

61. Stein, *A Basic Guide to Interpreting the Bible*, 87–98.

B. Repeatable Pragmatic Patterns

Repeatable pragmatic patterns are patterns of behavior in Acts that are potentially more than mere historical descriptions and can be helpful even if they are not required behaviors. As pragmatic procedures, such patterns of behavior may prove as productive in parallel or analogous situations in the twenty-first century as they were in the first century. One example of such repeatable but not required patterns in Acts is the pattern Paul exhibited in visiting local synagogues first in his missionary travels (see Acts 17:1–2; cf. 9:20; 13:5, 14; 14:1; 17:10, 17; 18:4; 19:8). Does this mean that Christian ministers today should always first preach in a local synagogue before preaching the gospel anywhere else? Many would see this as merely a regular past pattern of Paul, and few (if any) would suggest that this is required prescriptive pattern for missionaries everywhere in all times. I suggest that this is a repeatable pragmatic pattern. What is noteworthy (and repeatable) is that, in a new setting, Paul first shares the gospel with people who are most likely to receive it. Given his shared background with Jewish worshipers studying Scripture in the synagogue and awaiting God's activity to bring about salvation, in Paul's world, these seemed like people who might be ready to receive the news that the Messiah promised in their Scriptures had indeed come.

Fourth century synagogue ruins at Capernaum

If these people, prepared by the study of Scripture, came to believe in Jesus, then Paul would have more coworkers ready to reach out to the rest of the people in that locale. It is noteworthy that Luke records Paul preaching the gospel in Philippi, a city that apparently had no synagogue, so he looked for "a place of prayer" to find people ready to receive the gospel (Acts 16:12–14). The repeatable pragmatic pattern for us in the twenty-first century is, when ministering in new territories, to share the gospel first with those most prepared to receive it.[62]

C. Required Prescriptive Patterns

Required prescriptive patterns display behaviors that Luke expects of all believers everywhere. For a pattern to have prescriptive weight, it must be related to the author's intent. Does Luke intend Christians of all time periods to persist in spreading the good news of salvation through Jesus Christ? The tenor of Luke's story in Acts assures us that the answer to this question is a resounding yes! If Luke walked into the room and we asked him whether he thought Christians should persist in spreading the gospel message even amid persecution, we would expect him to answer in the affirmative, and perhaps with an inquisitive expression of surprise: "Didn't you read my books?" Sometimes the author of a narrative conveys universal truths by reporting what a trustworthy character in the story says. So when Peter says, "Salvation is found in no one else, for there is no other name under heaven

Interpreting the Book of Acts

From the conclusion of Liefeld, *Interpreting the Book of Acts*, 127.

> The Book of Acts is unique in the New Testament. Its narratives and speeches help us to relive the experiences of the early Christians as they witnessed to their resurrected Lord and Savior. Luke no doubt had clear purposes in his mind as he wrote, and the Spirit of God has used this book in various ways over the centuries. Our responsibility is to seek ways to learn from it and apply it in our own circumstances, being careful not to violate its own integrity. The modern interpreter now has the privilege of understanding and teaching Acts for the good of the church and for the salvation of all who respond to the gospel it so vividly presents, becoming part of this ongoing interpretive tradition.

Patterns to Consider in Acts

I. **Regular past patterns**—simply the way things were done in the first century.
II. **Repeatable pragmatic patterns**—more than mere historical descriptions but patterns that can be helpful even if they are not required.
III. **Required prescriptive patterns**—expected of all believers everywhere at all times.

62. For some guidelines regarding the firmness one can have about some potentially repeatable patterns, see Fee and Stuart, *How to Read the Bible for All Its Worth*, 130–31, where they use as examples such things as (in order of strong-to-weak arguments) immersion as the mode of baptism, observance of the Lord's Supper each Sunday, and infant baptism. See also William W. Klein, Craig L. Blomberg, and Robert L. Hubbard Jr., *Introduction to Biblical Interpretation*, 3rd ed. (Grand Rapids: Zondervan, 2017), 539–41.

Herodian bottle of oil and lamp.
Alexander Schick/bibelausstellung.de (courtesy of Bible Places.com)

given to mankind by which we must be saved" (Acts 4:12), I take this as prescriptive. Conversely, I expect that Luke would want us to hold as suspect any narrative pattern that runs counter to his general message and counter to the clear teaching of Scripture elsewhere.

Indeed, if we've read and reread Luke's contributions to the New Testament, it is sometimes helpful to imagine such conversations with Luke about the application of a particular passage. If Luke is the competent literary artist I have suggested he is, then we can anticipate that a fair-minded familiarization with his work will help us distinguish between the regular past, repeatable pragmatic, and required prescriptive patterns he utilizes. Of course, we will run into a few difficult passages where identifying Luke's intended applications is more challenging, but that will be part of our adventure in the story of Acts.

4.6 CONCLUDING REMARKS

We seek to understand Luke as a competent first-century author of well-researched, historically reliable narrative material meant to portray for his readers particular theological truths that are in line with the OT Scriptures and that apply universally. With Luke living in the first century and writing specifically about first-century events, it will be helpful for us as twenty-first-century readers to be more familiar with first-century history and concerns. This is the subject of chapter 5.

4.7 Key People, Places, and Terms

- autographs
- codex
- didactic material
- Dionysius Exiguus
- hermeneutics
- papyrus
- textual criticism
- "we sections"
- Western text of Acts

4.8 Questions for Review and Discussion

1. Outline the three main options for the date of the composition of Acts. Which is most convincing to you, and why?
2. Explain some of the possible sources for Luke's writing of Acts.
3. Describe the two versions of Acts represented in the extant manuscripts.
4. What are some of the features of Luke's use of the Hebrew Scriptures in Acts?
5. What are some of the chief interpretation issues in reading Acts?
6. What is the recommended proper approach for interpreting Acts?

4.9 Optional Assignments

1. **Text Reflection Project**—*Relating the concepts discussed in this chapter to another biblical text.* People in the story of Acts (and Luke as the story's narrator) utilize the Hebrew Scriptures to evangelize people to have faith in Jesus Christ. Make a list of some OT Scriptures that are most useful in sharing the gospel message about Jesus. Describe how each passage is applicable to the gospel message.
2. **Interview Project**—*Inquiring of others their views concerning the concepts discussed in this chapter.* This chapter examines some of the interpretation issues for a historical narrative like the book of Acts. Ask your pastor (or some other respected Christian leader) about their view of how best to interpret and apply the narrative portions of Scripture to our lives.
3. **Service-Learning Project**—*Applying the concepts discussed in this chapter in some form of service to others outside the class.* This chapter discussed a number of possible sources Luke might have used to compile stories to include in Acts, and this included personal interactions (i.e., oral sources). Check with your local church to see if you could share Scripture orally. This might be as a Scripture reader for someone with eyesight trouble or confined to a hospital bed. Or it might be for children too young to read Scripture for themselves.
4. **Prayer Project**—*Talking with God about the concepts discussed in this chapter.* Viewing Acts as part of the NT Scriptures entails understanding it as God's Word to believers still today. Desiring to understand God's Word correctly, write a brief prayer you could pray before studying any portion of Scripture, asking God for wisdom and insight regarding the proper application of the Scriptures to your life.
5. **Testimony Project**—*Telling others about the concepts discussed in this chapter.* In a two-page paper, briefly explain what you see as the main interpretation issues for the book of Acts and describe a proper approach to interpreting and applying this NT narrative to our lives today. Share this paper with another person in the class and get their suggestions for improving the paper.

4.10 Bibliography for Going Further

4.10.1 Dating Acts

Armstrong, Karl Leslie. *Dating Acts in Its Jewish and Greco-Roman Contexts*. LNTS 637. New York: T&T Clark, 2021.

Bernier, Jonathan. "The Synoptic Gospels and Acts." Pages 3–84 (Part 1) of *Rethinking the Dates of the New Testament: The Evidence for Early Composition*. Grand Rapids: Baker Academic, 2022.

Freedman, David Noel, and Henry Innes MacAdam. "Acts 28:15–31: The Critical Witness to Early Dating of the Synoptic Gospels." *Scripta Judaica Cracoviensia* 6 (2008): 15–37.

Harnack, Adolf von. *The Date of the Acts and of the Synoptic Gospels*. Translated by J. R. Wilkinson. NT Studies 4/Crown Theo. Lib. 33. London: Williams and Norgate, 1911. Repr., Eugene, OR: Wipf & Stock, 2004.

Hemer, Colin J. "The Date of Acts." Pages 365–410 (chapter 9) in *The Book of Acts in the Setting of Hellenistic History*. Edited by Conrad H. Gempf. WUNT 49. Tübingen: Mohr Siebeck, 1989. Repr., Winona Lake, IN: Eisenbrauns, 1990.

Keener, Craig S. "Date." Pages 1:383–401 (chapter 10) in *Acts: An Exegetical Commentary*. 4 vols. Grand Rapids: Baker Academic, 2012–15.

Seccombe, David. "Dating Luke-Acts: Further Arguments for an Early Date." *TynBul* 71.2 (2020): 207–27.

Torrey, Charles Cutler. *The Composition and Date of Acts*. HTS 1. Cambridge: Harvard University Press, 1916. Repr., Eugene, OR: Wipf & Stock, 2005.

4.10.2 Sources of Acts

Dupont, Jacques. *The Sources of Acts: The Present Position*. Translated by Kathleen Pond. London: Darton, Longman, and Todd, 1964.

Hemer, Colin J. "Sources." Pages 335–64 (section of chapter 8) in *The Book of Acts in the Setting of Hellenistic History*. Edited by Conrad H. Gempf. WUNT 49. Tübingen: Mohr Siebeck, 1989. Repr., Winona Lake, IN: Eisenbrauns, 1990.

Keener, Craig S. "Approaching Acts as a Historical Source." Pages 1:166–220 (chapter 6) in *Acts: An Exegetical Commentary*. 4 vols. Grand Rapids: Baker Academic, 2012–15.

Smith, T. C. "The Sources of Acts." Pages 55–75 in *With Steadfast Purpose: Essays on Acts in Honor of Henry Jackson Flanders, Jr.* Edited by Naymond H. Keathley. Waco: Baylor University Press, 1990.

4.10.3 Text of Acts

Boismard, Marie-Émile. "The Texts of Acts: A Problem of Literary Criticism?" Pages 147–57 in *New Testament Textual Criticism: Its Significance for Exegesis*. Edited by Eldon J. Epp and Gordon D. Fee. Oxford: Clarendon, 1981.

Delobel, Joël. "The Text of Luke-Acts: A Confrontation of Recent Theories." Pages 83–107 in *The Unity of Luke-Acts*. Edited Joseph Verheyden. BETL 142. Leuven: Leuven University Press, 1999.

Head, Peter M. "Appendix: Acts and the Problem of Its Texts." Pages 415–44 in *The Book of Acts in its Ancient Literary Setting*. Edited by Bruce W. Winter and Andrew D. Clarke. BAFCS 1. Grand Rapids: Eerdmans, 1993; Carlisle: Paternoster, 1993.

Klijn, Albertus Frederik Johannes. "In Search of the Original Text of Acts." Pages 103–10 in *Studies in Luke-Acts: Essays Presented in Honor of Paul Schubert*. Edited by Leander E. Keck and Louis J. Martyn. Nashville: Abingdon, 1966. Repr., Philadelphia: Fortress, 1980.

Osburn, Carroll D. "The Search for the Original Text of Acts—The International Project on the Text of Acts." *JSNT* 44 (1991): 39–55.

Roth, Dieter R. "The Text of Luke and Acts: Witnesses, Features, and the Significance of the Textual Traditions." Pages 51–71 in *Issues in Luke-Acts: Selected Essays*. Edited by Sean A. Adams and Michael Pahl. Gorgias Handbooks 26. Piscataway, NJ: Gorgias, 2012.

Strange, W. A. *The Problem of the Text of Acts*. SNTSMS 71. Cambridge: Cambridge University Press, 1992.

Tuckett, Christopher M. "The Early Text of Acts." Pages 157–74 in *The Early Text of the New Testament*. Edited by Charles E. Hill and Michael J. Kruger. Oxford: Oxford University Press, 2012.

4.10.4 Use of the Hebrew Scriptures in Luke-Acts

Arnold, Bill T. "Luke's Characterizing Use of the Old Testament in the Book of Acts." Pages 300–323 in *History, Literature and Society in the Book of Acts*. Edited by Ben Witherington III. Cambridge: Cambridge University Press, 1996.

Bock, Darrell L. "Old Testament in Acts." *DLNT*, 823–26.

Evans, Craig A., and James A. Sanders. *Luke and Scripture: The Function of Sacred Scripture in Luke-Acts.* Minneapolis: Fortress, 1993.

Fitzmyer, Joseph A. "The Use of the Old Testament in Luke-Acts." Pages 295–313 (chapter 14) in *To Advance the Gospel: New Testament Studies.* 2nd ed. The Biblical Resource Series. Grand Rapids: Eerdmans, 1998; Livonia, MI: Dove, 1998.

Litwak, Kenneth Duncan. "The Use of the Old Testament in Luke-Acts: Luke's Scriptural Story of the 'Things Accomplished among Us.'" Pages 147–69 in *Issues in Luke-Acts: Selected Essays.* Edited by Sean A. Adams and Michael Pahl. Gorgias Handbooks 26. Piscataway, NJ: Gorgias, 2012.

O'Day, Gail R. "The Citation of Scripture as a Key to Characterization in Acts." Pages 207–21 in *Scripture and Traditions: Essays on Early Judaism and Christianity in Honor of Carl R. Holladay.* Edited by Patrick Gray and Gail R. O'Day. Leiden: Brill, 2008.

Peterson, David. "The Motif of Fulfillment and the Purpose of Luke-Acts." Pages 83–104 in *The Book of Acts in its Ancient Literary Setting.* Edited by Bruce W. Winter and Andrew D. Clarke. BAFCS 1. Grand Rapids: Eerdmans, 1993; Carlisle: Paternoster, 1993.

Porter, Stanley E. "Scripture Justifies Mission: The Use of the Old Testament in Luke-Acts." Pages 104–26 in *Hearing the Old Testament in the New Testament.* Edited by Stanley E. Porter. McMaster New Testament Studies. Grand Rapids: Eerdmans, 2006.

4.10.5 Interpreting Acts

Cook, David. *Introducing Act: A Book for Today.* PT Resources. London: Proclamation Trust Resources, 2012; Ross-shire, Scotland: Christian Focus, 2012.

Fee, Gordon D., and Douglas Stuart. *How to Read the Bible for All Its Worth.* 4th ed. Grand Rapids: Zondervan, 2014; esp. pp. 112–31.

Gasque, W. Ward. *A History of the Interpretation of the Acts of the Apostles.* 2nd ed. Peabody: Hendrickson, 1989.

Liefeld, Walter L. *Interpreting the Book of Acts.* Guides to New Testament Exegesis. Grand Rapids: Baker, 1995.

Marshall, I. Howard. *The Acts of the Apostles.* NTG. Sheffield: Sheffield Academic, 1992.

Matthews, Shelly. *The Acts of the Apostles: An Introduction and Study Guide: Taming the Tongues of Fire.* 2nd ed. T&T Clark's Study Guides to the New Testament. New York: Bloomsbury T&T Clark, 2017.

Turner, David L. *Interpreting the Gospels and Acts: An Exegetical Handbook.* Handbooks for New Testament Exegesis. Grand Rapids: Kregel, 2019.

5 The Setting of Acts

Chapter Goals

After reading this chapter, you should be able to:

- Trace the larger flow of the biblical storyline Acts falls into, from its roots in "Abraham and His Children" to when "The Romans Take Over," with approximate dates for each segment.
- Recognize the geopolitical setting of Acts on a map of the Mediterranean world.
- Discuss some of the key features of the religious setting of Acts.
- Describe some of the key religious figures in the world of Acts and how they factor into the story of Acts.
- Discuss some of the key features of the sociocultural world of Acts.
- Offer a description of the relationship of Christian faith with the sociopolitical-cultural world of Acts.

Chapter Overview

5.1 The Stories Everyone Knew: What Is the Historical-Political Setting of Acts?
5.2 What People Believed: What Is the Religious Setting of Acts?
5.3 How People Interacted: What Is the Sociocultural Setting of Acts?
5.4 Concluding Remarks
5.5 Key People, Places, and Terms
5.6 Questions for Review and Discussion
5.7 Optional Assignments
5.8 Bibliography for Going Further

Key Verses

In the fifteenth year of the reign of Tiberius Caesar—when Pontius Pilate was governor of Judea, Herod tetrarch of Galilee, his brother Philip tetrarch of Iturea and Traconitis, and Lysanias tetrarch of Abilene—during the high-priesthood of Annas and Caiaphas, the word of God came to John son of Zechariah in the wilderness. (Luke 3:1–2)

In my former book, Theophilus, I wrote about all that Jesus began to do and to teach until the day he was taken up to heaven, after giving instructions through the Holy Spirit to the apostles he had chosen. After his suffering, he presented himself to them and gave many convincing proofs that he was alive. He appeared to them over a period of forty days and spoke about the kingdom of God. (Acts 1:1–3)

For two whole years Paul stayed there in his own rented house and welcomed all who came to see him. He proclaimed the kingdom of God and taught about the Lord Jesus Christ—with all boldness and without hindrance! (Acts 28:30–31)

INTRODUCTION

If we understand the book of Acts to have been written in the first-century about a first-century story (chapter 4) in a history-related genre (chapter 2) by a first-century author to first-century readers (chapter 1) containing a message applicable to the first century and to the twenty-first century (chapter 3), it will be helpful to understand the first-century setting of Acts. Surveying the first-century context of Acts is the goal of this chapter.

To survey the complex setting of Acts, this material (albeit somewhat artificially) has been divided into three parts. This allows me to treat more succinctly the historical-political, religious, and sociocultural background material for understanding, appreciating, and applying Acts.

5.1 THE STORIES EVERYONE KNEW: WHAT IS THE HISTORICAL-POLITICAL SETTING OF ACTS?

We cannot fully understand the New Testament or any portion of it without some grasp of the historical and political forces that influenced the shape of its world and culture.[1]

1. Gary M. Burge and Gene L. Green, *The New Testament in Antiquity: A Survey of the New Testament within Its Cultural Contexts*, 2nd ed. (Grand Rapids: Zondervan Academic, 2020), 30; N. T. Wright and Michael F. Bird, *The New Testament in Its World* (Grand Rapids: Zondervan Academic, 2019), 86–87.

Luke wrote his two volumes in a first-century historical-political context in what we call today "the Middle East." As already noted, Luke writes Luke-Acts in such a way as to imply that it is a continuation of the biblical story of the Hebrew Scriptures. Writing in the first century for first-century readers, Luke would have naturally presumed some basic familiarity with the historical-cultural setting that he and his audience shared. Readers unaware of the historical-cultural context might miss some of the most basic allusions Luke intended. This section outlines the historical-political context of Luke's first-century world by tracing briefly the stories of history that everyone in his orbit would have known.[2] And I note particular passages in Luke-Acts that give evidence of Luke's awareness of, and appeal to, these historical events.

The Stories Everyone Knew: The Historical-Political Setting of Acts

Major Sections in the Storyline	Approximate Dates	*Key Characters &* Lasting Effects	Some Key OT Scriptures	Some Relevant Luke-Acts Passages Reflecting on the History of the Period
Beginnings in Palestine: Abraham and His Children	2100–1450 BC	*Abraham, Isaac, Jacob, Joseph* Dedication to Yahweh	Genesis 12-50	**Luke** 1:46–55, 67–79; 3:8; 13:16, 28; 16:19–31; 19:9; **Acts** 3:12–26; 7:2–53; 13:16–41; cf. 26:6–7
Exodus to Palestine: From Egypt to the Promised Land	1450–1050 BC	*Moses & Joshua;* Dedication to OT Law	Exodus-Deuteronomy	**Luke** 1:5–7; 2:22–40; 7:16, 39; 9:28–36; 16:14–18; 24:19; **Acts** 3:12–26; 7:37; 13:13–20, 38–39; 25:8; 26:22–23
Life Back in Palestine: Kings and Prophets	1050–722 BC	*Saul, David, kings & OT prophets* Organized self-governance	1–2 Samuel; 1–2 Kings; Isaiah; Minor Prophets; Wisdom Literature	**Luke** 1:30–33; 2:1–21, 25–32; 3:21–22; 6:1–5; 7:18–23, 36–50; 9:20, 28–36; 11:45–52; 18:35–43; 20:41–44; 24:25–27, 44–48; **Acts** 2:22–36; 3:12–26; 4:10–12; 5:29–32, 42; 7:45–52; 8:27–39; 9:19–22; 10:36, 43; 13:21–41; 17:2–3; 18:5, 28

2. Of course, "everyone" is a hyperbole (similar to what we find in places like Acts 21:28 and 22:15!), and by it we mean the usually informed audience—whether Jew or gentile—interested in what Luke had written in connection with the God of ancient Israel. The concept of "stories everybody knew" comes from David M. Hoffeditz, "Walking in the Sandals of a First-Century Jew," in *What the New Testament Authors Really Cared About: A Survey of Their Writings*, ed. Kenneth Berding and Matt Williams, 2nd ed. (Grand Rapids: Kregel, 2015), 17–35. In this section I am also somewhat dependent on Karl Allen Kuhn, *The Kingdom according to Luke and Acts: A Social, Literary, and Theological Introduction* (Grand Rapids: Baker Academic, 2015), 4–9; and Calvin J. Roetzel, *The World that Shaped the New Testament*, rev. ed. (Louisville, KY: Westminster John Knox, 2002), 2–36.

Major Sections in the Storyline	Approximate Dates	*Key Characters* & Lasting Effects	Some Key OT Scriptures	Some Relevant Luke-Acts Passages Reflecting on the History of the Period
Exile from Palestine: Conquered by Assyria (722 BC) and Babylon (586 BC)	722–539 BC	*Daniel, Shadrach, Meshach, Abednego, Jeremiah* Synagogue practice	Daniel; Jeremiah	**Luke** 4:14–30; 7:5; 9:51–56; 10:25–37; 11:43; 17:11–19; 20:46; **Acts** 9:20; 13:5, 14–48; 14:1; 15:21
Return to Palestine: The Persians End the Exile	539–334 BC	*Zerubbabel, Ezra Nehemiah* Aramaic language, rebuilt temple, and renewed worship	Esther; Ezra; Nehemiah; Ezekiel; Haggai; Zechariah; Malachi	**Acts** 21:40; 22:2; 26:14
"Exile" within Palestine: The Greeks Take Over	334–166 BC	*Alexander the Great, Ptolemy, Seleucus* Greek language and culture, and LXX		**Acts** 6:1; 9:29; 11:19–20
Independence in Palestine: The Hasmoneans Rule	166–63 BC	*The Hasmoneans* Jewish sense of independence		**Luke** 6:15; **Acts** 1:13; 21:38
Return to "Exile" within Palestine: The Romans Take Over	63 BC–AD 135	*Caesar, Herod the Great and other Roman rulers, Zealots* The peace of Rome		**Luke** 1:5; 2:1-7; 3:1-3, 19-20; 8:3; 9:7-9; 13:31-33; 23:1-25, 52; **Acts** 3:13; 4:27; 11:28; 12:1-23; 13:1, 28; 16:11-40; 21:30-40; 22:22-30; 23:12-26:32

5.1.1 The Story of Beginnings in Palestine: Abraham and His Children

The OT figure of ***Abraham*** is the father of the Jewish nation. This was not mere historical trivia, for Genesis 12 records that God himself selected Abraham (then known as Abram) for the establishment of the nation. This promise included a people, a place, and a purpose. The people would be a great nation of Abraham's descendants (eventually known by the name of his grandson, ***Israel***). The place would be the strip of land along the eastern edge of the Mediterranean Sea between the continents of Asia, Europe, and Africa: the geographic region between the Jordan River and the eastern coast of the Mediterranean generally referred to as ***Palestine*** that would eventually become known as the land of Israel.[3] And the purpose would be to serve as a blessing

3. Of course, use of the label "Palestine" for the land at the southeastern corner of the Mediterranean Sea is here in keeping with ancient geographic nomenclature; e.g., Herodotus in the fifth century BC is the first known historian to use the term of this territory; see his *Hist.* 3.91; 4.39; 7.89; et al. This region-oriented use of the label should not be connected with modern geopolitical discussions regarding a State of Palestine.

to all the peoples of the world, a blessing that would eventually come in the form of the Savior of humanity. This promise to Abraham was reaffirmed to him and to his descendants (Gen 22:11–18; 26:2–5; 28:10–16; 35:9–15). The story of Abraham and his children was thus foundational for the first-century world that Luke was addressing.

God's Promise to Abram

The LORD had said to Abram, "Go from your country, your people and your father's household to the land I will show you.

"I will make you into a great nation,
and I will bless you;
I will make your name great,
and you will be a blessing.
I will bless those who bless you,
and whoever curses you I will curse;
and all peoples on earth
will be blessed through you." (Gen 12:1-3)

Abraham is mentioned more in Luke's Gospel than in any other, and the people of God are clearly identified with the faith that Abraham expressed (e.g., Luke 3:8; 13:16, 28; 16:19–31; 19:9). In Acts, Peter likewise reflects on the promise to Abraham being brought to fruition in Jesus (Acts 3:12–26). The longest speech in the book of Acts (by Stephen in Acts 7:2–53) begins its historical testimony about Jesus with the call of Abraham. And Paul also connects the historical calling of the people of Israel with their eventual purpose of spreading the message of salvation in Christ (Acts 13:16–41; cf. 26:6–7).

Abraham's Migration to Palestine

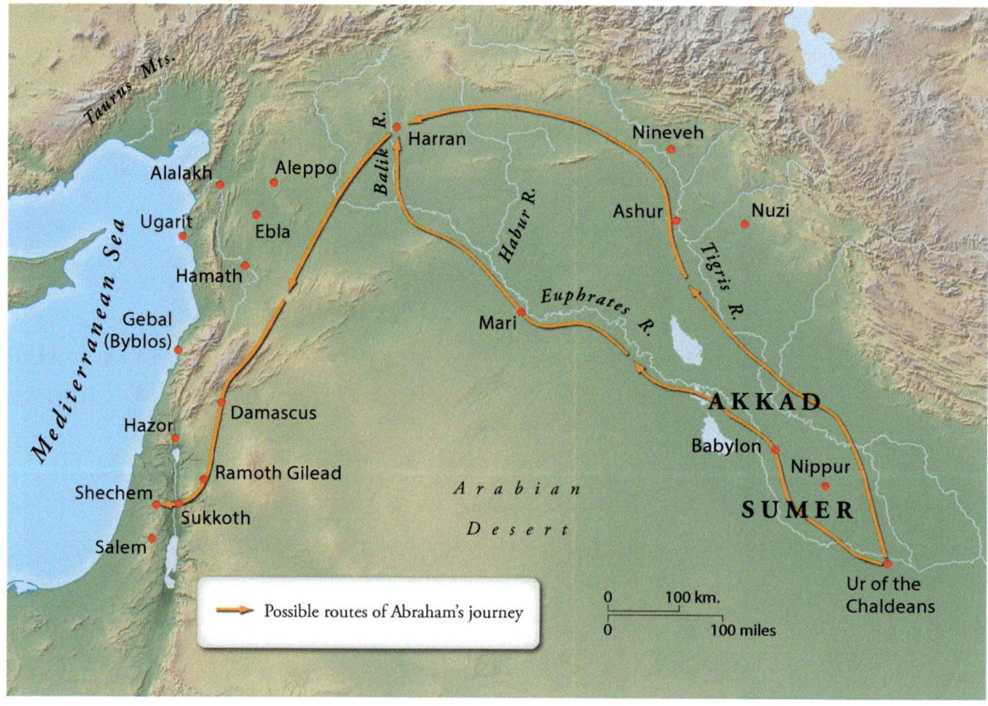

5.1.2 The Story of Exodus to Palestine: From Egypt to the Promised Land

The book of Genesis closes with the descendants of Abraham settled in the land of ***Egypt*** because God had rescued them from famine (Gen 37–50). Over the course of several centuries, the family grew into the promised nation of Israel (Exod 1:6–7). But the Egyptians enslaved the Israelites (Exod 1:8–14), so God rescued his people again. This time he selected an Israelite named ***Moses*** to lead the promised nation in an ***exodus*** out of slavery and back to the ***promised land*** of Palestine (Exod 3:1–4:16). God delivered the Israelites from Egypt (Exod 5–18) and miraculously led them through the desert to Mount Sinai, where he revealed to Moses the covenant he was making with his people (Exod 19–24). This covenant included the Ten Commandments but also other moral, civil, and ceremonial laws expected of the new nation.

While an important expression of faith, the law of God conveyed through Moses was not designed to be a means of salvation (see Gal 3:10–14; Heb 10:1–14). Israel's rebellious history—which led to forty years of wilderness wandering before entering the promised land (Num 14:1–38; Deut 1:19–40) and ultimately led to the nation being exiled (2 Kgs 24–25)—displays the law's failure to save and the need for a God-given Savior.

The positive characters of the story in Luke-Acts are those living in line with the law of God (e.g., Luke 1:5–7; 2:22–40; Acts 25:8; 26:22–23), and Jesus defends the truthfulness and applicability of the law (e.g., Luke 16:14–18). Indeed, Jesus is repeatedly referenced as the ***prophet like Moses*** whom Moses himself had foretold (Acts 3:12–26; 7:37; cf. Deut 18:15–19; Luke 7:16, 39; 24:19). But Luke alone among the gospel writers notes that Jesus is an exodus leader (Luke 9:28–36; the Greek word describing Jesus's "departure" is *exodos*). The OT law could never itself save humanity but could only point to Jesus as the provider of salvation (Acts 13:13–20, 38–39).

Jesus, the Prophet like Moses in Luke-Acts

Moses (Looking Ahead)

The Lord your God will raise up for you a prophet like me from among you, from your fellow Israelites. You must listen to him. (Deut 18:15)

Luke (On the Transfiguration)

Two men, Moses and Elijah, appeared in glorious splendor, talking with Jesus. They spoke about his departure [Greek: "exodus"], which he was about to bring to fulfillment at Jerusalem. (Luke 9:30–31)

Peter (About Jesus)

For Moses said, "The Lord your God will raise up for you a prophet like me from among your own people; you must listen to everything he tells you. Anyone who does not listen to him will be completely cut off from their people." (Acts 3:22–23)

Stephen (About Jesus)

This is the Moses who told the Israelites, "God will raise up for you a prophet like me from your own people." (Acts 7:37)

So even as the law served a timely purpose in the OT exodus, Luke seeks to show the law reaching its fulfillment in Jesus as the Christ with his greater exodus. This becomes a central concern in Acts.

5.1.3 The Story of Life Back in Palestine: Kings and Prophets

Not long after entering the promised land under the leadership of Joshua (which means "Yahweh is salvation"), the Israelites incurred God's judgment for breaking his covenant. They eventually sought the leadership of a king, but this was driven by comparison and not by a desire to obey God (1 Sam 8:1–22). After the failure of the first Israelite king (i.e., Saul), the Lord directed the selection of a new king, David. God established a covenant with David and his descendants, promising rulership over an eternal kingdom (2 Sam 7:8–16). During this era of the Israelite kings, various OT prophets ministered the word of God to the kings and the nation. The words of prophets like Isaiah, Jeremiah, the "minor" prophets, and others heightened the expectation that God would fulfill his promise to David through a Davidic descendant (e.g., Jer 33:14–26; Ezek 37:24–28; Amos 9:11; Zech 12:7–10; Ps 2). This work of God would involve a new covenant, one vastly different from the Mosaic covenant (Isa 42:5–9; 43:16–21; Jer 31:31–34).

Luke speaks freely of Jesus as fulfilling scriptural prophecy and sees him as the foretold Davidic king and Savior (e.g., Luke 1:30–33; 2:1–21, 25–32; 3:21–22; 9:20; 24:25–27, 44–48; Acts 2:32–36; 3:12–26; 4:10–12; 5:29–32, 42; 7:45–52; 8:27–39; 9:19–22; 10:36, 43; 13:21–41; 17:2–3; 18:5; 18:28). As such, Jesus is in fact greater than the OT prophets and David, and he has greater authority (Luke 6:1–5; 7:18–23, 36–50; 9:28–36; 11:45–52; 18:35–43; 20:41–44; Acts 2:22–36).

5.1.4 The Story of Exile from Palestine: Conquered by Assyria and Babylon

In the OT era of kings and prophets, the people of Israel had become lax in their commitment to God, and life in the promised land became presumed privilege and cultural compromise. The Israelite nation underwent civil war that resulted in a northern kingdom (called ***Israel***) and a southern kingdom (called ***Judah***). Despite prophetic warnings against their idolatrous behavior, the Israelites persisted in their rebellious activity and brought upon themselves the consequences of their sin against God. In 722 BC, ***Assyria*** conquered the northern kingdom of Israel, forcing their people to intermarry with foreigners (a possible explanation for the Samaritan people; see 2 Kgs 17:24–41; cf. Josephus, *Ant.* 11.7.1–7 §§297–347).[4] In the next century, ***Babylon*** conquered Judah and carried them into ***exile*** in waves of deportation: in 605 BC (2 Kgs 24:1–5), in 597 BC (2 Kgs 24:6–16), and in 586 BC, when Jerusalem was destroyed (2 Kgs 25:1–21).

---

4. See Ben Witherington III, *New Testament History: A Narrative Account* (Grand Rapids: Baker Academic, 2001), 189–91.

Israel and Judah Taken into Exile

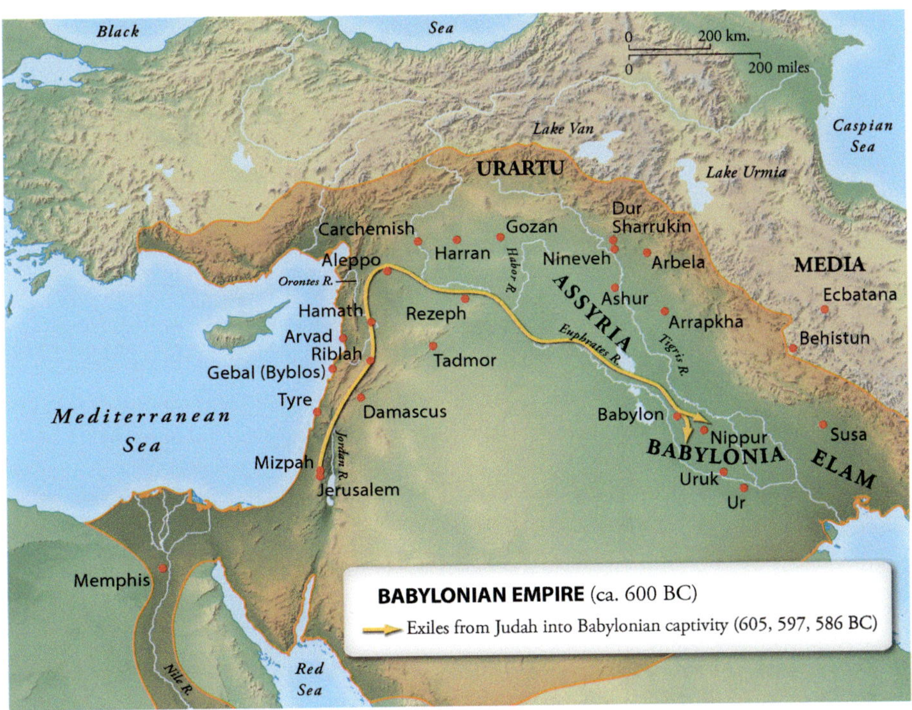

The loss of their prized homeland had its proper effect, and some of the Jewish people refocused their attention back to the law of God. The exile saw the development of gatherings of people for study of the law and for prayer, which may be the origins of Jewish synagogues—the Greek term (*sunagōgē*) means "brought together." By the time of Luke in the first century, buildings were intentionally constructed to serve as synagogue meeting places (e.g., Josephus, *J.W.* 2.14.4–5 §§285–91; 7.3.3 §§43–44; Luke 7:5; 11:43; 20:46; Acts 9:20; 13:5, 14, 42; 14:1; 15:21; etc.).[5]

5.1.5 The Story of Return to Palestine: The Persians End the Exile

When the kingdom of ***Persia*** defeated Babylon in 539 BC, the Persian monarch Cyrus the Great began permitting Babylon's captured and exiled groups to emigrate back to their homelands. The OT book of Esther recounts something of Jewish life in exile in this time period, and the books of Ezra and Nehemiah cover the story of Israel's return to Palestine. The first wave of Jewish returners with Zerubbabel, Sheshbazzar, and other leaders began rebuilding the temple in 537 BC, which was not completed until 516 BC (see Ezra 1–6). A second wave of returners came with Ezra in 458 BC (see Ezra 7–10), and another wave returned in 445 BC with Nehemiah, whose focus was on rebuilding the walls of Jerusalem (see Neh 1–6).

Scale model of the second temple, first century Jerusalem. Israel Museum. dimamoroz/stock.adobe.com

When the temple was completed, the Jewish temple sacrifices could be put back into practice: thus began what is now referred to as the ***Second Temple period***.[6] Nevertheless, the practice of gathering in local groups for prayer and study remained part of their faith expression back in their homeland. So too Aramaic, a cognate Semitic language with Hebrew that had been the *lingua franca* of the East, had become the common language of Israel (thus, when the New Testament mentions "the language of the Hebrews" or "the Hebrew dialect," it likely means Aramaic, not Hebrew; e.g., the ESV and NASB translations of Acts 21:40; 22:2; 26:14).[7]

5. See Roetzel, *The World that Shaped the New Testament*, 90–97; Witherington, *New Testament History*, 186–87; Kenneth D. Litwak, "Synagogue and Sanhedrin," in *The World of the New Testament: Cultural, Social, and Historical Contexts*, ed. Joel B. Green and Lee Martin McDonald (Grand Rapids: Baker Academic, 2013), 264–71; and Anders Runesson, "Synagogues," in *T&T Clark Encyclopedia of Second Temple Judaism*, ed. Daniel M. Gurtner and Loren T. Stuckenbruck, 2 vols. (New York: Bloomsbury T&T Clark, 2020), 2:766–72.

6. "Second Temple period" (covering 516 BC–AD 70) is arguably a more inclusive and more useful label than "Intertestamental period," which is used to describe the time between the writing of Malachi, the last OT book (ca. 430 BC) and the birth of Jesus in the New Testament (ca. 6–4 BC).

7. Burge and Green, *The New Testament in Antiquity*, 33.

With Persian Support the Jews Return to Palestine from Babylonian Exile

5.1.6 The Story of "Exile" within Palestine: The Greeks Take Over

With his classical Greek education (tutored by Aristotle), Alexander took over the Macedonian kingdom of his father Philip at age twenty in 336 BC. After a couple of years of securing his borders, Alexander crossed into Asia Minor (modern Turkey) in 334 BC and began to push on the borders of the world power of Persia. After subjugating the eastern coast of the Mediterranean Sea (333 BC) and Egypt (332 BC), he continued in the next few years to conquer the regions of the former Persian Empire all the way to the borders of India and the Indian Ocean. While not literally exiled into other countries, nations like that of Israel found themselves in subjection to a foreign power. By his death in 323 BC (just short of his thirty-third birthday), ***Alexander the Great*** had conquered most of the known world, and his influence was such that he had effectively made the international language and culture Greek, a process referred to now as ***Hellenization***.

This Greek (a.k.a. Hellenistic) culture was maintained into Luke's first-century time period. It is felt most plainly by the very fact that Luke, like all the New Testament writers, wrote in the Greek language common to that time (a.k.a. ***Koine Greek***, or Hellenistic Greek). In much of his storytelling, Luke was able to maintain a Hebrew tone similar to that of the Septuagint (abbreviated LXX; the Greek translation ca. 250 BC of the Hebrew Scriptures). And Luke's focus on cities in Acts gives a nod to Alexander's networking of urban centers across his empire.

Alexander the Great's Empire

5.1.7 The Story of Independence in Palestine: The Hasmoneans Rule

After Alexander the Great died, a series of conflicts ensued among his generals (and their families and friends) over control of the empire. Known as the Wars of the Diadochi ("successors"), the conflicts lasted from 322 to 281 BC. Eventually, the Jewish territory of Palestine was ruled first by the Ptolemaic dynasty until 198 BC, and then by the Seleucid dynasty after that. The Seleucid ruler Antiochus IV (a.k.a. Antiochus Epiphanes) came to power in 175 BC and sought to utilize Hellenistic culture to help him stabilize his regional rule against the growing pressures of Rome. The intrusive and Hellenizing efforts of Antiochus Epiphanes met with mixed reception among the Jews, and unrest in the nation was deep. When he replaced the altar in the Jewish temple with an altar to Zeus and sacrificed a pig on it in 167 BC (1 Macc 1:41–58; 2 Macc 6:3–9), this ultimate act of sacrilege eventuated in a revolt led by a country priest named Mattathias.

When Mattathias died in 166 BC, one of his five sons, ***Judas Maccabeus*** (sometimes referred to as "Judas the Hammer") led the movement to a victorious reclaiming of Jerusalem in 164 BC. The cleansing of the temple at this time has been commemorated ever since with the Jewish festival of Hanukkah. The Maccabean revolt was more like a time of civil war, but under the leadership of Simon, the last surviving brother of ***the Maccabees*** (142–134 BC), recognized political autonomy for Israel was finally achieved.

Palestine during Hasmonean Rule

The ruling ***Hasmonean dynasty*** that followed (named after a family ancestor, Hasmon) expanded the borders of the newly independent nation. In the fifth generation of Jewish independence fighters, internal power struggles eventuated in Rome taking over in 63 BC. Roman rule of Palestine was eventually solidified under Herod the Great in 37 BC.

The Hasmonean Dynasty Ruling Judea for 100 Years

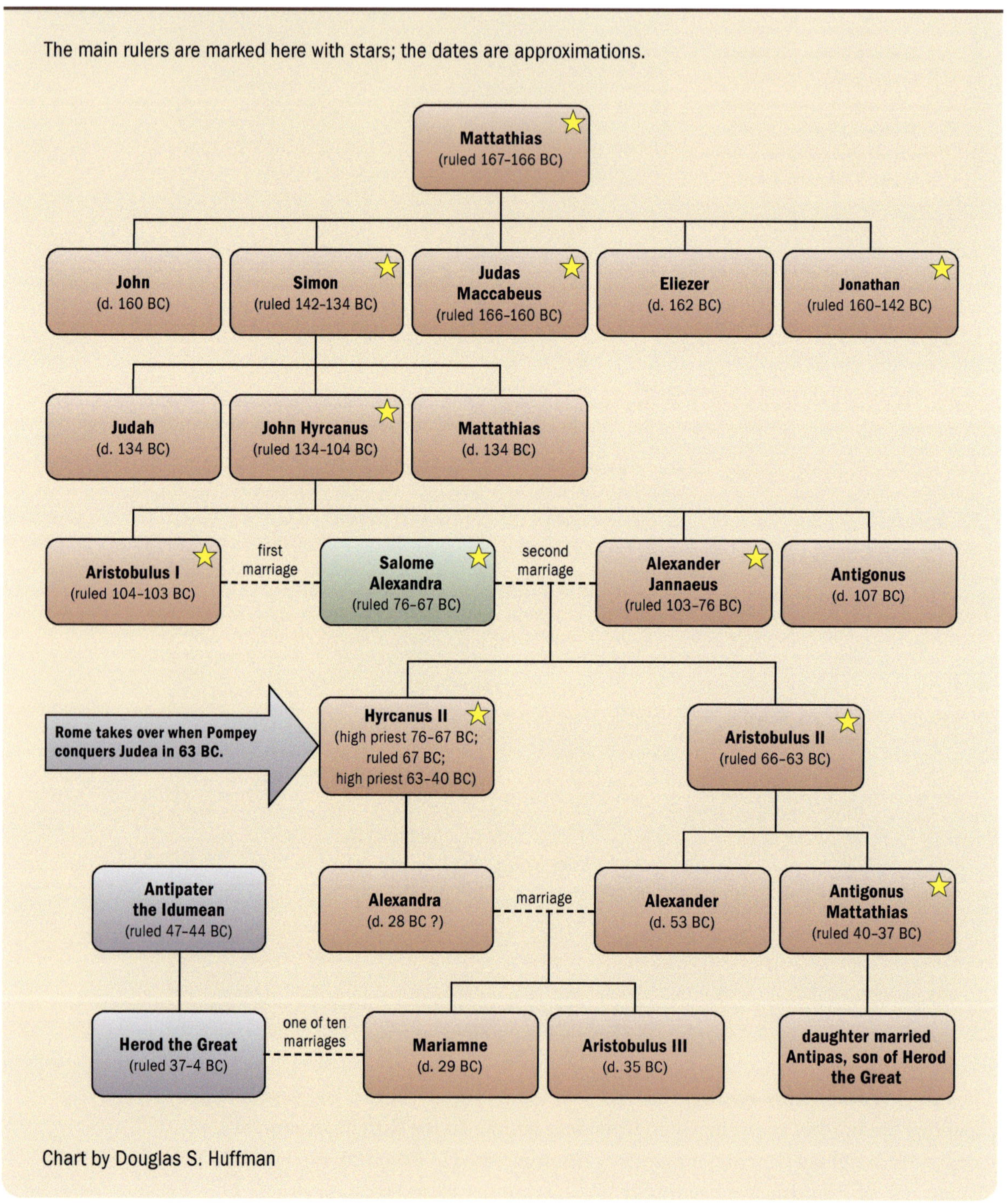

Chart by Douglas S. Huffman

The craving for national independence embodied by the Hasmonean movement lived on into the Roman period (see Zealots and Sicarii in 5.2.3). At the close of the NT era, the anti-Roman sentiment would reach the level of warring revolt (most notably the Great Revolt of AD 66–70 and the Bar Kokhba Revolt in AD 132–135). While the Hasmonean movement sought to bring Jewish independence so that they could more freely celebrate their religious convictions, ironically the cultural influence of Hellenism persisted and continued into the Roman period.

5.1.8 The Story of Return to "Exile" within Palestine: The Romans Take Over

Rome had been a republic for almost five hundred years and ruled by a senate of elite landowners and elected magistrates. As it expanded its influence throughout the known world in the last century BC, various Roman generals sought more control over Rome's interests. After several decades of struggles, by 31 BC Octavian had become the obvious sole leader. He assumed the name Caesar, took on the title of "Augustus," and by 27 BC had become Rome's first emperor, replacing the senatorial government. Here the Roman Republic became the Roman Empire, and in the simple phrase *Greco-Roman* used to describe the cultural setting of the first century, Caesar Augustus is to *Roman* what Alexander the Great is to *Greco*.

The Roman Empire of the First Century

For some in the first-century time of Acts, the Roman occupation of Palestine (since Pompey had overtaken those territories in the mid-60s BC) felt like being in exile, even though they were not carted off away from their homeland.[8] Things like Roman taxation, military presence, and forced servitude were burdensome. Nevertheless, Roman occupation did bring several advantages for everyday life, including safer trade and travel and better communication. Of note in Acts, these benefits greatly facilitated the movement of Christian missionaries around the Roman Empire.[9] Although never directly referenced in the New Testament, this beneficial burden of Roman rule is sometimes referred to as the ***Pax Romana***, or the "Roman peace," and extended from the beginning of the rule of Caesar Augustus (27 BC) to the death of Emperor Marcus Aurelius (AD 180).[10]

The Empire was divided into Roman provinces with senatorial provinces governed by senate-appointed ***proconsuls*** (e.g., Sergius Paulus of Cyprus in Acts 13:7–8 and Gallio of Achaia in Acts 18:12) and imperial provinces governed by emperor-appointed ***legates*** (e.g., Quirinius of Syria in Luke 2:2). Some smaller imperial provinces were

The First Two Centuries of Roman Emperors

With one brief exception (i.e., Galba, emperor in AD 68–69), the Roman emperors from Augustus to Commodus (the 218 years from January 16, 27 BC to December 31, AD 192) were all related to one another (albeit complexly and not merely in natural-born father-to-son successions).

- Augustus/Octavian (27 BC–AD 14)
- Tiberius (AD 14–37)
- Caligula (AD 37–41)
- Claudius (AD 41–54)
- Nero (AD 54–68)
- Galba (seven months in AD 68–69)
- Otho (three months in AD 69)
- Vitellius (eight months in AD 69)
- Vespasian (AD 69–79)
- Titus (AD 79–81)
- Domitian (AD 81–96)
- Nerva (sixteen months in AD 96–98)
- Trajan (AD 98–117)
- Hadrian (AD 117–138)
- Antoninus Pius (AD 138–161)
- Lucius Verus (AD 161–169; coemperor with Marcus Aurelius)
- Marcus Aurelius (AD 161–180)
- Commodus (AD 180–192; jointly with father Marcus Aurelius, AD 177–180)
- Pertinax (three months in AD 193)
- Didius Julianus (two months in AD 193)
- Septimius Severus (AD 193–211)
- Caracalla (AD 211–217)

8. On debates regarding how much first-century Jews considered themselves in exile under Roman rule, see Nicholas Perrin, "Exile," in Green and McDonald, *The World of the New Testament*, 25–37.

9. Burge and Green, *The New Testament in Antiquity*, 25.

10. See James E. Bowley, "Pax Romana," *DNTB*, 771–75.

governed by emperor-appointed ***prefects*** (military men to serve as governors; e.g., Pontius Pilate of Judea in Luke 22–23; Acts 3:13; 4:27; 13:28) or ***procurators*** (civilian fiscal governors; e.g., Felix of Judea in Acts 23–24 and Festus of Judea in Acts 25–26). The emperor sometimes ruled from afar through ***client kings***—local rulers Rome kept in power and supported as long as those rulers served the interests of Rome (e.g., Herod the Great of all Israel in Matt 2:1–23; Luke 1:5; and Herod Agrippa I of all Israel in Acts 12). More than any other NT writer, Luke mentions members of the Herod family in telling the story of Jesus and the church.

Roman Prefects (pre-Agrippa I) and Procurators (post-Agrippa I) of Judea

In the world of Roman provinces, the province of Judea (encompassing the geographic territory of Judea, Samaria, and Idumea) was a minor province in the shadow of the province of Syria until Herod Agrippa I. Generally speaking, a *prefect* was a military appointment and a *procurator* was a civilian appointment. The dates here are approximations.

Name	Date	Notable NT Events
Coponius	AD 6–9	First prefect after Archelaus (son of Herod the Great) was deposed.
Marcus Ambibulus	AD 9–12	
Annius Rufus (Rufinus)	AD 12–15	
Valerius Gratus	AD 15–26	Prefect for much of Jesus's life prior to his ministry.
Pontius Pilate	AD 26–36	Jesus was crucified under Pilate (Luke 3:1; 23:1).
Marcellus	AD 36–37	
Marullus	AD 37–41	
King Herod Agrippa I	AD 41–44	Ruled Judea and all Palestine, persecuted Christians (Acts 12).
Cuspius Fadus	AD 44–46	
Tiberius Julius Alexander	AD 46–48	
Ventidius Cumanus	AD 48–52	Procurator at the time of the Jerusalem Council.
Marcus Antonius Felix	AD 52–59	Paul had a hearing before Felix (Acts 24).
Porcius Festus	AD 59–62	Paul had a hearing before Festus (Acts 25).
Lucceius Albinus	AD 62–64	
Gessius Florus	AD 64–66	
Marcus Antonius Julianus	AD 66–70	Procurator when the Jews revolted against Rome.
Sextus Vettulenus Cerialis	AD 70–72	First Roman legate of Judea after the fall of Jerusalem.

Adapted from information in Clinton E. Arnold, "Acts," vol. 2B of *ZIBBCNT*, ed. Clinton E. Arnold (Grand Rapids: Zondervan, 2002), 233; and H. Wayne House, *Chronological and Background Charts of the New Testament*, 2nd ed., Zondervan Charts (Grand Rapids: Zondervan, 2009), 65. Some dates are disputed by scholars.

A Basic Timeline of the Rulers of Judean Palestine

539
331
323
198
167
142
63
30
60
PERSIANS
PTOLEMIES
SELEUCIDS
HASMONEANS
ROMANS
500 BC
400 BC
300 BC
200 BC
100 BC
1 AD
Alexander the Great
Maccabean Revolt
ACTS

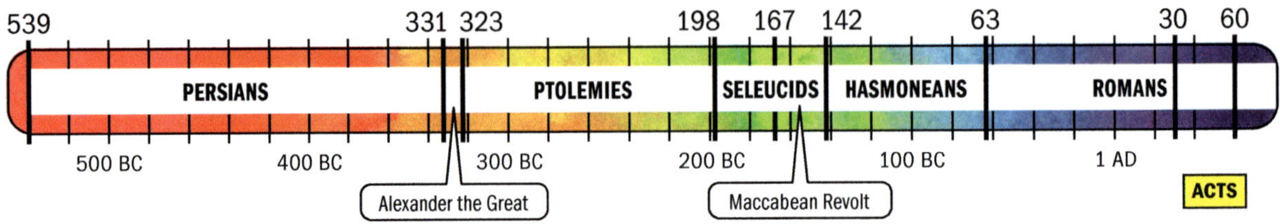

The Herodian Dynasty

In this partial family tree for Herod the Great and his ruling descendants, the dates for governing Israel (or regions of it) and for deaths are approximations. The circled numbers refer to the following notes.

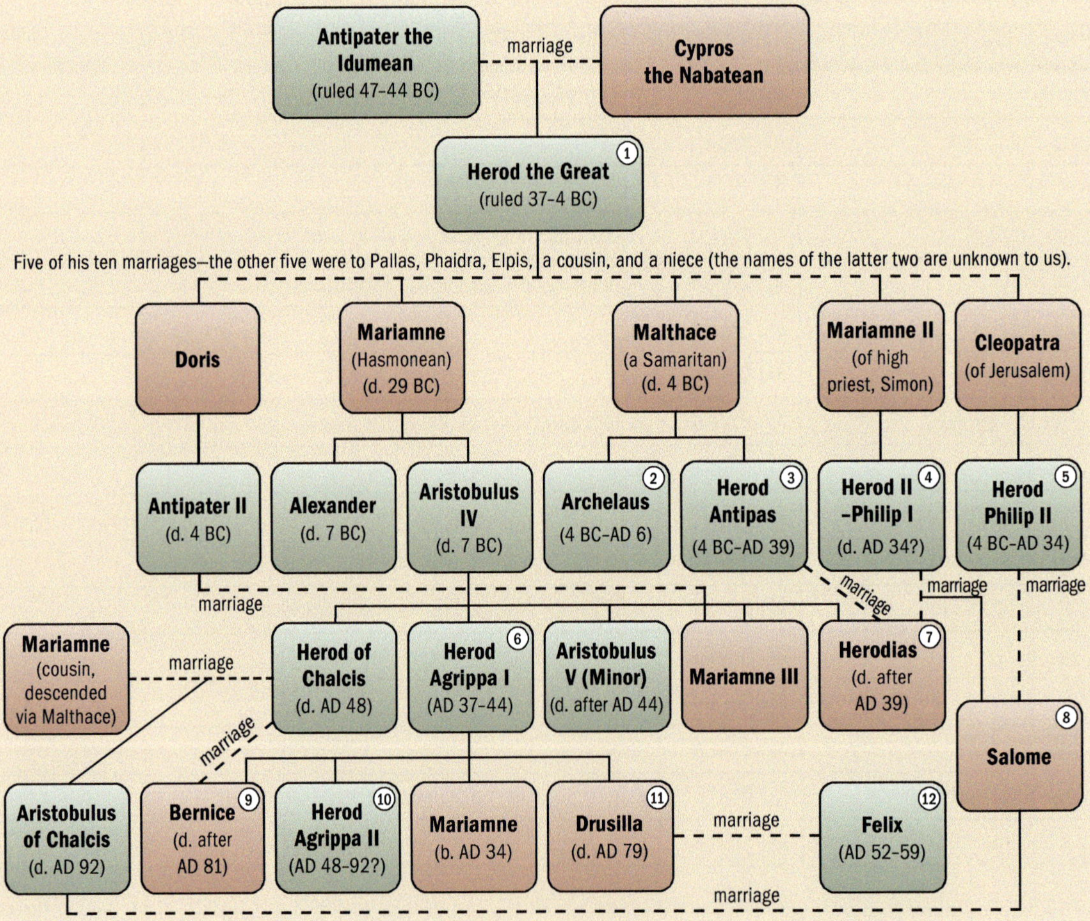

Antipater the Idumean (ruled 47-44 BC)
marriage
Cypros the Nabatean
1 Herod the Great (ruled 37-4 BC)
Five of his ten marriages—the other five were to Pallas, Phaidra, Elpis, a cousin, and a niece (the names of the latter two are unknown to us).
Doris
Mariamne (Hasmonean) (d. 29 BC)
Malthace (a Samaritan) (d. 4 BC)
Mariamne II (of high priest, Simon)
Cleopatra (of Jerusalem)
Antipater II (d. 4 BC)
Alexander (d. 7 BC)
Aristobulus IV (d. 7 BC)
2 Archelaus (4 BC-AD 6)
3 Herod Antipas (4 BC-AD 39)
4 Herod II -Philip I (d. AD 34?)
5 Herod Philip II (4 BC-AD 34)
marriage
marriage
marriage
marriage
Mariamne (cousin, descended via Malthace)
marriage
Herod of Chalcis (d. AD 48)
6 Herod Agrippa I (AD 37-44)
Aristobulus V (Minor) (d. after AD 44)
Mariamne III
7 Herodias (d. after AD 39)
8 Salome
marriage
Aristobulus of Chalcis (d. AD 92)
9 Bernice (d. after AD 81)
10 Herod Agrippa II (AD 48-92?)
Mariamne (b. AD 34)
11 Drusilla (d. AD 79)
marriage
12 Felix (AD 52-59)
marriage

Notes on Various Descendants of Herod the Great Who Are Mentioned in the New Testament

1. Met with the magi and then killed infants in Bethlehem because of Jesus's birth (Matt 2:1–20).
2. Ethnarch over Judea and Samaria (Matt 2:22); replaced by Roman governors like Pilate, Felix, Festus, et al.
3. Tetrarch over Galilee and Perea, killed John the Baptist, saw Jesus (Matt 14:1–12; Luke 3:19; 9:9; 23:6–12).
4. First husband of Herodias (Matt 14:1–4; Mark 6:17); dropped in his father's will from receiving a ruling role.
5. Tetrarch over Iturea, Traconitis, Gaulanitis, Auranitis, Batanea, and Paneas (Luke 3:1).
6. Appointed first as tetrarch in AD 37 over where his uncle Philip had ruled, then in AD 40 added the former tetrarchy of his uncle Antipas, and by AD 41 became king over most of his grandfather's (Herod the Great's) former territory including Judea and Samaria; killed James and imprisoned Peter (Acts 12:1–24).
7. Begrudged the confrontation of John the Baptist (Matt 14:4; Mark 6:17–19; Luke 3:19).
8. Requested the head of John the Baptist in return for dancing (Matt 14:6–12; Mark 6:21–29).
9. Married to her uncle but lived with her brother Herod Agrippa II (Acts 25:13).
10. Initially tetrarch over the Syrian territory of Chalcis in AD 48, but in AD 53 was given the title of king over what was formerly the tetrarchy of his great uncle Philip (i.e., Iturea, Traconitis, Gaulanitis, Auranitis, Batanea, and Paneas) and what was formerly the neighboring tetrarchy of Lysanias (i.e., Abilene); heard Paul's defense (Acts 25:13–24).
11. Mentioned with her husband (Acts 24:24); died on August 24, 79 in the eruption of Mount Vesuvius.
12. Procurator of Judea; heard Paul's defense (Acts 24:1–27).

The Anti-Family Paranoia of Herod the Great

Herod's suspicion and fear of conspiracy against his rule was so great that he was willing to execute family members to defend against (either real or suspected) treasonous opposition. Herod is reported to have executed a brother, a brother-in-law, two wives, a mother-in-law, three sons, and two grandsons. He killed his son Antipater II shortly before his own death in 4 BC, around the time he killed the babies in response to the news of Jesus's birth (Matt 2:1–23). The only ancient writer apart from Matthew to report Herod's paranoid slaughter of the infants in the Bethlehem area notes the following:

> On hearing that the son of Herod, king of the Jews, had been slain when Herod ordered that all boys in Syria under the age of two be killed, Augustus said, "It's better to be Herod's pig than his son." (Macrobius, Saturnalia 2.4.11)

With potential word play—although not so in Latin, in Greek the words for "pig" and "son" (*hus* and *huios*) sound similar—in making this comment, the Roman emperor Augustus assumes that Herod the Great, as king of the Jews, would not eat pork.

The clever, creative, and powerful ***Herod the Great*** could also be jealous, paranoid, and brutal. In his clever creativity, he wrested control over Judea away from the Hasmoneans and curried the favor of Rome. Among his many architectural achievements—which included not just official fortresses and personal palaces but also aqueducts and public buildings like theaters and stadiums—was his expansion of the Temple Mount in Jerusalem and a remodeling of the temple and its courtyards, a forty-year project resulting in the Second Temple outstripping the splendor of the First Temple, built by Solomon (see Luke 21:5). Nevertheless, his pursuit of Hellenistic and Roman culture brought disdain from the more conservative people of Judea, which fed his fear of conspiracy in the face of the history of Jewish strivings for political independence. Thus, fueled by jealous paranoia, Herod's brutality was evidenced by such cruelties as the slaughter of innocent two-year-olds (Matt 2:1–18) and the execution of his own family members when he suspected them of conspiring against him. After Herod's death, Rome assigned rule of Palestine to three of his sons (Archelaus, Herod Antipas, and Herod Philip II), and Luke mentions a grandson (Herod Agrippa I in Acts 12) and a great-grandson (Herod Agrippa II in Acts 25–26) as having roles in the story of the church. The ***Romans*** ruled the first-century world of Acts.

A Chronology of Important NT Events in Acts and Their Historical Contexts

Dates	Christian History (Acts)	Rulers and Events in Israel	Roman Emperors
ca. 6–4 BC †	Birth of Jesus	Herod the Great (37–4 BC)	Augustus (27 BC–AD 14)
4 BC		Herod Antipas, tetrarch (4 BC–AD 39) Herod Philip II, tetrarch (4 BC–AD 34) Archelaus, ethnarch (4 BC–AD 6)	
AD 14		Caiaphas, high priest (AD 18)	Tiberius (AD 14–37)
ca. AD 26/29*	Public ministry of John the Baptist	Pilate, prefect of Judea (26–36)	
27–30	Public ministry of Jesus		
30	Crucifixion, resurrection, ascension (Acts 1)		
30	Outpouring of Spirit at Pentecost (Acts 2)		
30	Peter & John before the Sanhedrin (Acts 3–4)		
31	Death of Ananias & Sapphira (Acts 5)		
31	Apostles before the Sanhedrin (Acts 5)		
32	Ministry and stoning of Stephen (Acts 6–7)		
32	Philip in Samaria (Acts 8)		
32	Paul converted (Acts 9)		
32–35	Paul in Damascus and Arabia (cf. Gal 1:17)		
35	Paul's 1st post-conversion Jerusalem visit	Marcellus, prefect of Judea (36–37)	

Dates	Christian History (Acts)	Rulers and Events in Israel	Roman Emperors
35	Paul goes to Tarsus in Cilicia (Acts 9)	Marullus, prefect of Judea (37–41)	Caligula (37–41)
40–41	Peter's itinerate ministry (Acts 9–11)	Herod Agrippa I, tetrarch (37–41)	
41	Barnabas & Paul in Syrian Antioch (Acts 11)	Agrippa I gets Herod the Great's territory (41–44)	
41	Herod Agrippa persecutes believers (Acts 12)		Claudius (41–54)
44	Herod Agrippa dies (Acts 12)		
ca. 44–46	Paul's 2nd Jerusalem (famine) visit (Acts 12)	Fadus, procurator of Judea (44–46)	
ca. 45	*James writes his epistle*	Tiberius Alexander procurator of Judea (46–48)	
47–48	1st missionary campaign (Cyprus & Galatia) (Acts 13–14)		
ca. 48	Peter at Antioch (cf. Gal 2:11–16)	Cumanus, procurator of Judea (48–52)	
ca. 48	*Paul's letter to the Galatians from Antioch*	Herod Agrippa II over various regions of Palestine (48–?)	
ca. 48/49	Paul's 3rd Jerusalem (Council) visit (Acts 15)		
49–50	2nd missionary campaign (part 1) (Asia Minor & Macedonia) (Acts 16–17)	Claudius (49) expels Jews from Rome	
ca. 50	*Paul's letters to the Thessalonians from Corinth*		
50–52	2nd missionary campaign (part 2) (Paul in Corinth) (Acts 18)	Gallio, proconsul of Achaia (51–52)	
Summer 52	Paul's 4th Jerusalem visit (Acts 18:22)	Felix, procurator of Judea (ca. 52–59)	
53–55	3rd missionary campaign (part 1) (Paul in Ephesus) (Acts 18–19)		Nero (54–68)
ca. 54–55	*Paul's letter to the Corinthians (1) from Ephesus*		
55–57	3rd missionary campaign (part 2) (Macedonia & Achaia) (Acts 20)		
ca. 54–56	*Paul's letter to the Corinthians (2) from Macedonia*		
ca. 57	*Paul's letter to the Romans from Corinth*		

(continued)

Dates	Christian History (Acts)	Rulers and Events in Israel	Roman Emperors
Spring 57	Paul's 5th Jerusalem visit, and his arrest (Acts 21)		
57	Paul's barracks steps testimony (Acts 22)		
57	Paul's hearing before the Sanhedrin (Acts 23)		
57–59	Paul imprisoned in Caesarea (Acts 24)		
57	Paul's hearing before Felix (Acts 24)		
59	Paul's hearing before Festus (Acts 25)	Festus, procurator of Judea (ca. 59–62)	
59	Paul's hearing before Agrippa II (Acts 25–26)		
Fall 59	Paul begins voyage to Rome (Acts 27)		
60–62	Paul under house arrest in Rome (Acts 28)		
ca. 60–62	*Paul's Prison Epistles (Ephesians, Colossians, Philemon, Philippians) from Rome*		
62	Martyrdom of James, Jesus's brother	Albinus, procurator of Judea (62–64)	
ca. 63–67	Paul in Spain, Crete, Macedonia, Asia Minor	Florus, procurator of Judea (64–66)	Rome burns and Nero blames Christians (64)
ca. 63–67	*Paul's Pastoral Epistles (1 Timothy from Macedonia, Titus from Ephesus, and finally 2 Timothy while imprisoned in Rome)*		
66	Jerusalem Christians flee east to Pella	Jewish revolt against Rome (66–70)	
ca. 67/68	Paul executed in Rome	Destruction of Jerusalem (70)	
70			Vespasian (69–79)

†The modern calendar system was developed in the Middle Ages presuming that Jesus was born after Herod the Great's death, which is dated to 4 BC. But Matthew 1–2 indicates that Herod the Great was alive when Jesus was born, ordering children up to two years old to be killed in an attempt to destroy Jesus. Thus, Jesus's birth is dated to 6–4 BC.

*Scholars debate the precise dates for the public ministries of John the Baptist and of Jesus, esp. as to whether Jesus's crucifixion and resurrection are best dated to the year AD 30 or 33. For a succinct argument favoring the earlier date—i.e., that Jesus was crucified on the Friday of Nisan 14 (April 7) AD 30—see Eckhard J. Schnabel, *Jesus in Jerusalem: The Last Days* (Grand Rapids: Eerdmans, 2018), 140, whom we follow here. For an argument favoring the latter date—i.e., that Jesus was crucified on the Friday of Nisan 14 (April 3) AD 33—see Harold W. Hoehner, *Chronological Aspects of the Life of Christ* (Grand Rapids: Zondervan, 1977), 95–114; cf. idem and Jeannine K. Brown, "Chronology," *DJG*[2], 137–38. Naturally, some dates on this chart are more approximate than others (thus the use of "ca." for "circa"); the italicized dates for the epistles are debated.

Sources: F. F. Bruce, *Paul: Apostle of the Heart Set Free* (Grand Rapids: Eerdmans, 1977), 475; Walter A. Elwell and Robert W. Yarbrough, *Encountering the New Testament*, Encountering Biblical Studies (Grand Rapids: Baker, 1998), 255; H. Wayne House, *Chronological and Background Charts of the New Testament*, 2nd ed., Zondervan Charts (Grand Rapids: Zondervan, 2009), 118–19, 127–31.

5.2 WHAT PEOPLE BELIEVED: WHAT IS THE RELIGIOUS SETTING OF ACTS?

The first-century reader of Acts would probably be confused by a discussion of the religious setting of Acts as though it were something separable from its historical-political setting (in the 5.1 section) and its sociocultural setting (in the 5.3 section). This would not make sense to most first-century readers because they recognized that all areas of life affect each other.[11] The intertwining of these life concerns is just as true today as it was two thousand years ago; first-century people were simply much better than we are at recognizing this. Their grasp on the necessary interconnectedness of all of life helps explain why some groups of people in Acts radically opposed the Christian missionaries. Those preaching the gospel were not calling for riotous insurrection, but they were introducing radical ideas that incited radical opposition. To recognize Jesus Christ as the most supreme power necessitated seeing all other authorities as lesser, even invalid, powers.[12]

Nevertheless, we still find it helpful to think specifically about religious matters in a focused manner, so this section quickly surveys some of the religious features of the first century that underlie the story of Acts. It focuses first on the belief system of first-century ***Judaism*** and then remarks on non-Jewish religious practice in Luke's world.[13]

5.2.1 CORE BELIEFS AND DIVERSE TRENDS IN FIRST-CENTURY JUDAISM

First-century Judaism can be characterized by three core beliefs: monotheism, covenant, and torah. ***Monotheism*** is the belief in one true God over the entire universe; nothing is outside his omniscience and omnipotence. Having only one true God—Yahweh, the God of Abraham, Isaac, and Jacob (e.g., Acts 3:13; 7:32)—means that all other gods are false and unworthy of worship.[14] This one true God of the universe established a ***covenant*** with Abraham, and as Abraham's descendants, the Jews believed they were in a unique relationship with God. God had established a unique saving relationship with Abraham that extended to the people of Israel. Not only had God initiated this covenant relationship (per the Abraham story recounted previously), but he also had given his law—the ***torah***—to his people (per the Exodus story recounted previously). In the law, God had outlined his standards and expectations for Israel,

11. See C. Kavin Rowe, *World Upside Down: Reading Acts in the Graeco-Roman Age* (New York: Oxford University Press, 2009), 7; and more fully, Brent Nongbri, *Before Religion: A History of a Modern Concept* (New Haven, CT: Yale University Press, 2013).

12. Rowe, *World Upside Down*, 26. Rowe notes that "what we think about God will determine what we think about everything else" (p. 17). See also Larry Hurtado, *Destroyer of the Gods: Early Christian Distinctiveness in the Roman World* (Waco, TX: Baylor University Press, 2016).

13. My discussion of first-century Judaism here is indebted to that of Mark L. Strauss, *Four Portraits, One Jesus: An Introduction to Jesus and the Gospels*, 2nd ed. (Grand Rapids: Zondervan Academic, 2020), 157–87.

14. See Nathan MacDonald, "Monotheism," in Green and McDonald, *The World of the New Testament*, 77–84.

and four practices marked the uniqueness of Judaism: (1) worship of Yahweh alone, (2) circumcision for all male children, (3) a weekly Sabbath rest day, and (4) dietary laws prohibiting certain ceremonially unclean foods.[15]

Two additional points are worthy of mention. First, observing torah, Israel sought to be faithful in their covenant relationship with the one God of the universe. It is important to see that, in its best expressions, this was a faith responding to God's loving selection; it was not a religion of earning salvation. Second, given the core beliefs of first-century Judaism, there were nevertheless a variety of expressions of the Jewish faith.[16] For example, some people had a narrower view of torah and some had a more expansive view of the law. Some had more ritual purity concerns and some had fewer (or perhaps, different) such concerns. Some had greater nationalistic expressions and some had less. One particular area of diversity has to do with messianic expectation.[17] Many were awaiting a David-like king (see Pss. Sol. 17:32; 4 Ezra 7:26–29; 12:31–34); some looked for a Moses-like deliverer (e.g., the Samaritans; cf. John 4:19–26); others anticipated a heavenly judge (see 1 Enoch 46–48); some were looking for dual messiahs, both kingly and priestly (e.g., the Qumran community; 1QS 9.10–11); and there were even those who expected no messiah at all, assuming the messianic age had begun during the Hasmonean period (e.g., the Sadducees). Fascinatingly, Luke presents Jesus as fulfilling aspects of all these various messianic expectations but only in nuanced—even unexpected—ways.

5.2.2 Main Institutions in First-Century Judaism

Readers of the New Testament are familiar with the two main institutions of first-century Judaism: the temple and the synagogue. The ***temple in Jerusalem*** had its roots in the portable tabernacle of the exodus; its leadership was the priesthood, and its primary expression of worship was its all-encompassing sacrifice system. Replacing the tabernacle, Solomon's Temple was built in Jerusalem as Israel's worship center but was destroyed in 586 BC when Babylon conquered Jerusalem. The temple was rebuilt by Zerubbabel in 516 BC when the Jews were returning to the promised land (thus, the phrase *Second Temple period* to describe the era that followed), and this second temple and its surrounding courtyards were extensively remodeled by Herod the Great only to be destroyed by the Romans in AD 70.[18]

---

15. Strauss, *Four Portraits, One Jesus*, 159–60.

16. On the variety of first-century Jewish faith expressions, see esp. D. A. Carson, Peter T. O'Brien, and Mark A. Seifrid, eds., *Justification and Variegated Nomism*, 2 vols. (Grand Rapids: Baker Academic, 2001).

17. See Jacob Neusner, William Scott Green, and Ernest S. Frerichs, eds., *Judaisms and Their Messiahs at the Turn of the Christian Era* (Cambridge: Cambridge University Press, 1987); Marianus de Jonge, "Messiah," *ABD* 4:777–87; Jakob Jocz, "Messiah," *ZEB* 4:216–28; cf. C. Warren Carter, *Seven Events the Shaped the New Testament World* (Grand Rapids: Baker Academic, 2013), 60–61.

18. For an extensive survey on the Jerusalem temple(s)—including history, significance, construction, and reconstructions—see, Harold G. Stigers, "Temple, Jerusalem," *ZEB* 5:716–52 (esp. relevant for Acts is the section on Herod's temple, pp. 742–50).

Order of Service in the Ancient Synagogue on Sabbath

This suggested order of service for the ancient synagogue utilizes some of "The Eighteen" prayers of blessing, or *Tefilat ha-Amidah* ("The Standing Prayer") found in rabbinic literature and dating back to the first century. These "Eighteen Benedictions," had a nineteenth (#12) added early on, and the nineteen prayers of blessing for use in daily prayers are not to be confused with other Jewish benedictions. The Sabbath synagogue service would typically utilize the first three (#1–3) and the last three (#17–19) of the prayers of blessing, interspersed with other statements of benediction, expressions of prayer, recitations and readings, and a sermon. This ancient pattern seems to fit the NT synagogue services described in Luke-Acts (i.e., in Luke 4 and Acts 13).

I. **Benediction 1**: (led by a cantor with congregational response).
II. **Benediction 2**: (led by a cantor with congregational response).
III. ***Shema***: recitation of Deuteronomy 6:4–9; 11:13–21; and Numbers 15:37–41.
IV. **Prayer.**
V. **Prayer of Blessing 1**: praising God as the God of the biblical patriarchs (led by a cantor with congregational response).
VI. **Prayer of Blessing 2**: praising God for his power and might (led by a cantor with congregational response).
VII. **Responses.**
VIII. **Prayer of Blessing 3**: praising God's holiness (led by a cantor with congregational response).
IX. **Other Prayers**: extemporaneous prayers might be added here.
X. **Prayer of Blessing 17**: asking God to be pleased with his people (led by a cantor with congregational response).
XI. **Prayer of Blessing 18**: thanking God for our lives and for God's miracles present in our everyday lives (led by a cantor with congregational response).
XII. **Priestly Benediction**: from Numbers 6:23–27 (i.e., Aaron and his sons blessing Israel).
XIII. **Prayer of Blessing 19**: asking God for peace, goodness, blessings, kindness, and compassion (led by a cantor with congregational response).
XIV. **Reading of the Law**: by seven readers, appointed from the congregation by the synagogue ruler and notified by the assistant; a translator interprets if necessary (cf. Acts 13:14–15a).
XV. **Reading of the Prophets**: by one reader, appointed from the congregation as above (Jesus serves as reader of the prophet Isaiah in Luke 4:16–20; cf. Acts 13:15b).
XVI. **Sermon**: by a congregational member (Jesus preaches in Luke 4:21–27 and Paul preaches in Acts 13:14–41).
XVII. **Benediction** (cf. Luke 4:28–30 and Acts 13:42–43).

Adapted from Ernest DeWitt Burton, "The Ancient Synagogue Service," *The Biblical World* 8.2 (1896): 143–48.

As mentioned previously, the second Jewish institution, the ***synagogue***, seems to have developed during the Babylonian exilic period—a time when the Jews were forced to practice their faith traditions without their temple. Even after the temple was rebuilt in 516 BC, Jews maintained the practice of meeting together in local communities for worship and education. Most of our detailed information about synagogues come from the rabbinic period several centuries after the NT era, and therefore must be used cautiously when reflecting on NT times. Nevertheless, the oldest known accounts of the structure of synagogue services are found in Luke's writings (Luke 4:14–30; Acts 13:14–48) (see sidebar). With a minimum of ten Jewish men and under scribal leadership, a local community could establish a synagogue gathering for the purposes of prayer and study of the law (see b. Meg. 23b; y. Meg. 4:4).[19]

5.2.3 Diverse Groups in First-Century Judaism

The diversity of people groups in Israel's religious setting is even more complex than its institutions. I've already mentioned the priesthood and scribal leadership related to the two institutions, and I can describe these here with a little more complexity along with some other first-century groups.

In Judaism's temple system, the ***Levites***—descendants from the Israelite tribe of Levi—served in various roles as assistants to the Jewish priesthood. The ***priests*** were themselves Levites from the specific branch of Aaron's descendants, and they led in the temple worship activities. Aaron, Moses's brother, had served as Israel's first ***high priest***, and this highest office in Judaism was perpetuated in the priest who oversaw all the other priests. The high priesthood was intended to be a lifelong, hereditary position, but especially during the Roman period political rulers sometimes interfered, deposing one high priest and appointing another.[20]

The role of scribe was not inherited (nor politically appointed); it was earned through education and ability. In first-century Judaism, ***scribes*** (a.k.a. "teachers of the law" and "lawyers") were experts at interpreting and teaching the law of Moses.

Possibly having roots in the Persian period (cf. Ezra 5:5, 9; Neh 2:16), in the New Testament, the ***Sanhedrin*** was the highest Jewish court and was made up of seventy-one lay leaders and priests and led by the high priest. After Herod the Great's death, the high priest and Sanhedrin regained influence in Jewish life. The coastal city of Caesarea became the seat of Roman governmental concerns over the territory, so the Jerusalem-based Sanhedrin exerted wide-ranging authority over matters of Jewish law and religion.[21]

---

19. For surveys on the synagogue, see William White Jr., "Synagogue," *ZEB* 5:648–59; and Runesson, "Synagogues." For more extensive investigations, see Anders Runesson, Donald D. Binder, and Birger Olsson, *The Ancient Synagogue from its Origins to 200 C.E.: A Source Book*, AJEC 72 (London: Brill, 2008); and Stephen K. Catto, *Reconstructing the First-Century Synagogue: A Critical Analysis of Current Research*, LNTS 363 (London: T&T Clark, 2007).

20. For an overarching article on Israel's Levites and priests in both the Hebrew Scriptures and the New Testament, see Charles L. Feinberg and Gordon D. Fee, "Priests and Levites," *ZEB* 4:963–85.

21. Strauss, *Four Portraits, One Jesus*, 164; cf. Donald A. Hagner, "Sanhedrin," *ZEB* 5:320–26; and Graham H. Twelftree, "Sanhedrin," *DNTB*, 1061–65.

The Jewish High Priests, AD 6–70

Despite the Jewish custom of lifetime service for a high priest, Rome often asserted control over the Jews by replacing the high priest with a man of their own choosing (those marked *). There are some vagaries (marked with ?).

Name	Date	Notable NT Events
*Annas, son of Seth	AD 6–15	Remained influential after removal (Luke 3; John 18).
*Ishmael, son of Fabus (I ?)	AD 15–16	
*Eleazar, son of Annas	AD 16–17	
*Simon, son of Camithus	AD 17–18	
*Joseph Caiaphas (son-in-law to Annas, son of Seth)	AD 18–36	In office during Jesus's ministry, death, and resurrection (John 18); for the arrests/hearings of the apostles (Acts 4–5); and for Saul's persecution of the church (Acts 7, 9).
Jonathan, son of Annas	AD 36–37	
*Theophilus, son of Annas	AD 37–41	
*Simon Kantheras, son of Boethus	AD 41–42	
*Matthias, son of Annas	AD 42–43	
*Elioenai, son of Kantheras	AD 43–44	
*Jonathan, son of Annas (restored)	AD 44	
*Joseph, son of Camydus	AD 44–46	
*Ananias, son of Nebedeus	AD 46–58	In office for Paul's arrest/hearing (Acts 23).
? Jonathan	AD 58	Felix arranged for this high priest to be killed.
*Ishmael, son of Fabus (II ?)	AD 58–62	In office when Festus was procurator.
*Joseph Cabi, son of Simon	AD 62–63	
*Ananus, son of Ananus	AD 63	Ordered the death of Jesus's brother James.
*Joshua, son of Damnaeus	AD 63	
*Joshua, son of Gamaliel	AD 63–65	
*Matthias, son of Theophilus	AD 65–67	High priest when Jews revolted against Rome.
Phinehas, son of Samuel of Habta	AD 67–70	In office when Jerusalem fell; the last high priest.

Adapted from information in Arnold, "Acts," 228, and House, *Chronological and Background Charts of the New Testament*, 69–70. Some dates are disputed.

While members could be Sadducees or Pharisees, in the NT era the Sadducees dominated the Sanhedrin (Acts 4:1–22; 5:17–27). In the New Testament, priests tended to be associated with the party of the ***Sadducees*** (Acts 5:17), and the Sadducees tended to be content with Roman rule. They had a kind of conservatism about them: they held the Pentateuch (the five books of Moses) to be the most authoritative Scripture and were not looking for a messianic figure to arise; and they denied life after death, physical resurrection, and spiritual beings (Matt 22:23; Mark 12:18; Luke 20:27; Acts 23:8).[22] Like the Sadducees, the ***Herodians***, although little is known about them, were apparently likewise supporters of Roman rule via the Herodian dynasty (Mark 3:6; 12:13; Matt 22:16).[23]

The ***Pharisees***, on the other hand, are often contrasted with the Sadducees. While the Sadducees were the party of the priestly aristocracy, the Pharisees were the party of the laypeople. The Pharisees were highly respected Bible believers: they held to the whole of the Hebrew Scriptures as God's Word and desired to maintain a life of purity by properly observing of the law, in both its written form and oral traditions about it. Unlike the Sadducees, the Pharisees affirmed life after death, physical resurrection, and spiritual beings (Acts 23:8). Pharisees were not professional religious leaders and were, thus, primarily connected with the local synagogues and held more influence with the common people. Habitually assuming that Pharisees were bad people, readers of the New Testament can be surprised to learn that the Pharisees were often well-intentioned good people interested in applying the Bible to their everyday lives. Thus, it is important to note that Jesus's complaint about the Pharisees was not so much about their goal of holy living but their hypocritical ways of favoring their own oral traditions over the actual intent of the written law (e.g., Matt 15:1–20; 23:1–36; Mark 7:1–23; Luke 11:37–54).[24]

Another first-century group similar to the Pharisees but not directly mentioned in the New Testament was the ***Essenes***. The Essenes tended to be more separatist than Pharisees, detaching even from the temple sacrificial system, which they regarded as corrupted by the errant priesthood of the day. Some have suggested that John the Baptist may have been raised in an Essene community (see Luke 1:80), but this is uncertain. Most scholars concur with the suggestion that a group of Essenes populated the Qumran community where the Dead Sea Scrolls were found.[25]

---

22. For a survey on the Sadducees, see Donald A. Hagner, "Sadducee," *ZEB* 5:253–59.

23. See D. Edmond Hiebert, "Herodians," *ZEB* 3:150–51.

24. For a survey on the Pharisees, see Steve Mason, "Pharisees," *DNTB*, 782–87; cf. Donald A. Hagner, "Pharisee," *ZEB* 4:842–52. More extensively, see John Bowker, *Jesus and the Pharisees* (New York: Cambridge University Press, 1973); Anthony J. Saldarini, *Pharisees, Scribes and Sadducees in Palestinian Society: A Sociological Approach*, The Biblical Resource Series (Grand Rapids: Eerdmans, 2001); and the many essays in Jacob Neusner and Bruce D. Chilton, eds., *In Quest of the Historical Pharisees* (Waco, TX: Baylor University Press, 2007) and in Joseph Sievers and Amy-Jill Levine, eds., *The Pharisees* (Grand Rapids: Eerdmans, 2021).

25. For discussions of the Essenes, see Todd S. Beall, "Essenes," *DNTB*, 342–48; and R. K. Harrison, "Essenes," *ZEB* 2:398–408. See also Michelle Lee-Barnewall, "Pharisees, Sadducees, and Essenes," in Green and McDonald, *The World of the New Testament*, 217–27.

A somewhat distinct group in first-century Judaism was the ***Samaritans***, who lived in the central part of the land of Israel, referred to as ***Samaria***. Because Samaritans were descendants of Israelites who intermarried with foreigners, NT Jews of untainted descent tended to look down on them (e.g., Luke 9:51–56; 10:25–37; 17:11–19). Thus, the Samaritans had their own religious worship center at Mount Gerizim, their own version of the Scriptures, and their own particular beliefs.[26]

The most extreme opposition to Roman rule over the Jews was demonstrated by various groups called the ***Zealots***, who were active Jewish nationalists willing to engage in a variety of activities to counter Roman oppression and to encourage Jewish freedom. Luke specifically describes one of Jesus's apostles as a Zealot (Luke 6:15; Acts 1:13). Luke later mentions some "terrorists" ("Assassins" in CSB, ESV, NASB, NET, NLT) referred to as the ***Sicarii*** (Acts 21:38; Greek: *sikarioi*), whose precise relation to the Zealots is debated. The Sicarii were assassins who utilized short daggers (Latin: *sicae*) to murder Roman sympathizers in broad daylight, especially during crowded festivals.[27]

Diverse Groups in First-Century Judaism

Leadership

1. Levites: Descendants of Levi; assistants to priests (e.g., Luke 10:32; John 1:19; Acts 4:36).
2. Priests: Levites descending from Aaron; leaders of temple worship (see Luke 1:5–9; 10:31; Acts 4:1; 6:7).
3. High priest: Highest office in Judaism; overseer of the priests (see Luke 3:2; Acts 4:6; 5:17–27; 7:1; 9:1; 22:5; 23:1–5; 24:1).
4. Chief priests (lit. "high priests"): Probably the wealthy, powerful priests (see Acts 4:23; 5:24; 9:14, 21; 22:30; 23:14; 25:2, 15; 26:10, 12).
5. Sanhedrin: The highest Jewish court, made up of lay leaders and priests (see Acts 4:15; 5:17–41; 6:12, 15; 7:54; 22:30; 23:1–20, 28; 24:20).
6. Scribes (a.k.a. "teachers of the law" and "lawyers"): Experts in interpretation and exposition of the Law of Moses (see Acts 4:5; 6:12; 23:9).

26. For more on Samaritans, see Lidija Novakovic, "Jews and Samaritans," in Green and McDonald, *The World of the New Testament*, 207–16; and more thoroughly, Robert T. Anderson and Terry Giles, *The Keepers: An Introduction to the History and Culture of the Samaritans* (Peabody, MA: Hendrickson, 2002).

27. For surveys of various Jewish conflicts with Rome, see William J. Heard and Craig A. Evans, "Revolutionary Movements, Jewish," *DNTB*, 936–47; cf. James D. G. Dunn, "Prophetic Movements and Zealots," in Green and McDonald, *The World of the New Testament*, 242–51; and J. Julius Scott Jr., "Zealot," *ZEB* 5:1201–4.

Religio-Political Groups

Pro-Rome

Anti-Rome

1. Herodians: Supporters of Roman rule via the Herodian dynasty (see Matt 22:16; Mark 3:6; 12:13).
2. Sadducees: Priestly party, dominating the Sanhedrin (see Matt 22:23; Mark 12:18; Luke 20:27; Acts 4:1; 5:17; 23:1–10).
3. Pharisees: Somewhat middle-class laypeople party, highly respected Bible believers (see Acts 15:5; 23:1–10; 26:5).
4. Essenes: More conservative separatists than Pharisees (not mentioned in the NT; cf. John the Baptist in Luke 1:80?).
5. Zealots: Various active nationalists (perhaps including the Sicarii) who wanted Israel free from Rome (see Mark 3:18; cf. 15:7; Acts 5:36; 21:38).
6. Samaritans: Descendants of Israelites intermarried with foreigners (see Luke 9:51–56; 10:25–37; 17:11–19; John 4:4–42; 8:48; Acts 8:25).
7. People of the Land: An OT phrase for average people living in the land of Israel.

5.2.4 Jewish Literature Relevant to the First Century

A variety of Jewish literature sheds light on the first-century world of Judaism. Some of this literature was available to Luke and his contemporaries in the early church (e.g., the Hebrew Scriptures, the Apocrypha, and some of the Pseudepigrapha); some of it is contemporaneous with Luke (e.g., Philo, Josephus, and some of the Dead Sea Scrolls); and some of it comes from later centuries but offers a window looking back at the first-century era (e.g., the rabbinic writings).[28]

The Hebrew Scriptures were the books of our Old Testament, called the Tanak. The name ***Tanak*** is actually an acronym from the Hebrew consonants (*T-N-K*) representing the three primary categories of the Hebrew Bible: the Law (i.e., Hebrew: *Torah*), the Prophets (i.e., Hebrew: *Nevi'im*), and the Writings (i.e., Hebrew: *Ketuvim*). Sometime in the second or third century BC, the Hebrew Scriptures were translated into Greek; this old Greek translation is commonly referred to as the ***Septuagint*** (abbreviated LXX).

In addition to the canonical Scriptures, there are two important collections of noncanonical Jewish writings from the Second Temple period helpful for study of the New Testament. One set of extrabiblical Greek books is commonly called the ***Apocrypha*** (meaning "hidden"). While not considered Hebrew Scriptures themselves,

---

28. For fuller surveys on the literature of Second Temple Judaism, see Larry R. Helyer, *Exploring Jewish Literature of the Second Temple Period: A Guide for New Testament Students* (Downers Grove, IL: InterVarsity Press, 2002); and George W. E. Nickelsburg, *Jewish Literature Between the Bible and the Mishnah: A Historical and Literary Introduction*, 2nd ed. (Minneapolis: Fortress, 2005).

Books of the Apocrypha

The number and identity of the books included in the Apocrypha have fluctuated over time. The first twelve of the following books are those commonly listed in the so-called OT Apocrypha by the Roman Catholic branch of Christianity (recognized as "deuterocanonical" books), albeit sometimes with different names and placed in varying locations in printings of the Bible that include the apocryphal books (e.g., the Prayer of Azariah and Song of the Three Young Men, Susanna, and Bel and the Dragon—the Additions to Daniel—are sometimes placed within Daniel rather than kept as separate books). Various parts of the Eastern Orthodox branch of Christianity sometimes include some of the next five books, and 4 Maccabees is found in an appendix to the Greek Bible.

- Tobit
- Judith
- Additions to Esther (a.k.a. Esther 10:4–16:24)
- Wisdom of Solomon (a.k.a. Wisdom)
- Ecclesiasticus (a.k.a. Wisdom of Jesus the Son of Sirach, or simply Sirach)
- Baruch (a.k.a. 1 Baruch in distinction from three like-named pseudepigraphic books)
- The Letter of Jeremiah (sometimes incorporated as Baruch chapter 6)
- The Prayer of Azariah and Song of the Three Young Men (a.k.a. Daniel 3:24–90)
- Susanna (a.k.a. Susanna and the Elders, or simply Daniel chapter 13)
- Bel and the Dragon (a.k.a. Daniel chapter 14)
- 1 Maccabees
- 2 Maccabees
- 1 Esdras (a.k.a. 3 Esdras, when Ezra and Nehemiah are respectively named 1 and 2)
- The Prayer of Manasseh
- Psalm 151
- 3 Maccabees
- 2 Esdras (a.k.a. 4 Esdras, when Ezra and Nehemiah are respectively named 1 and 2)
- 4 Maccabees

the apocryphal writings were sometimes nevertheless collected with the Scriptures (in varying numbers; see sidebar), and they provide valuable testimony regarding how at least some Jews sought to live out their scriptural faith in difficult times with hopes that God would vindicate his people.[29]

The second grouping of extrabiblical books of Jewish writing from the Second Temple period is commonly referred to today as the ***Pseudepigrapha*** (or sometimes more fully, the Old Testament Pseudepigrapha). This name, meaning "falsely attributed writings," refers to the fact that many of the books bear the names of biblical figures (such as Abraham, Moses, Baruch, and Enoch) as if those figures had authored these books or were otherwise somehow related to them. Also excluded from Hebrew

29. For a standard English translation of the Apocrypha, see Michael D. Coogan et al., eds., *The New Oxford Annotated Apocrypha: New Revised Standard Version*. 5th ed. (New York: Oxford University Press, 2018).

Books of the OT Pseudepigrapha in the Second Temple Period

The list of pseudepigraphic books fluctuates in scholarly discussions and particularly with additional discoveries; lists have ranged from thirteen to nearly eighty pseudepigraphic books. Some scholars include books composed after AD 70, which would then be, strictly speaking, outside the Second Temple period, and some place several of the books in the OT Apocrypha instead of the OT Pseudepigrapha. Furthermore, not all the books in the discussion are technically "falsely attributed," and some of the more expansive lists include documents authored (or edited) by Christians and even documents of pagan origin. Thus, the field of pseudepigraphic studies is expanding. Nevertheless, the following representative selection is a more restricted listing of the well-known books of the OT Pseudepigrapha from the more narrowly defined era of Second Temple Judaism. They are grouped here by genre (not by title or character) according to those given primary and secondary attention in Gurtner, *Introducing the Pseudepigrapha of Second Temple Judaism*.

Apocalypses	**Expansions of Biblical Narratives and Rewritten Scripture**
• 1 Enoch (a.k.a. Ethiopic Book of Enoch) • 4 Ezra • 2 Baruch • Apocalypse of Abraham • Sibylline Oracles 3–5 and 11 • 2 Enoch (a.k.a. Slavonic Book of Enoch) • 3 Baruch • Apocalypse of Zephaniah • Testament of Abraham • fragmentary apocalyptic DSS texts	• Jubilees • Biblical Antiquities • Genesis Apocryphon • Letter of Aristeas • Joseph and Aseneth • Life of Adam and Eve • 4 Baruch • Ezekiel the Tragedian • Book of Giants
Testaments	**Poetic Literature, Wisdom Literature, and Prayers**
• Testament (or Assumption) of Moses • Testament of Job • Aramaic Levi Document • Testament of Qahat • Visions of Amram • Testament of Solomon • Testaments of the Twelve Patriarchs • (Qumran) Testament of Naphtali • fragmentary testamentary DSS texts	• Psalms 151–155 • Psalms of Solomon • Pseudo-Phocylides • Hellenistic Synagogal Prayers • Prayer of Joseph • Prayer of Nabonidus (4Q242)

Scriptures and with debates about which books are to be included in the grouping (see sidebar), pseudepigraphic writings nevertheless reveal something about the faith expressions of many Jews in the Second Temple period.[30]

A third set of ancient Jewish writings from the Second Temple period was discovered in the last century in caves along the northwestern edge of the Dead Sea near ***Qumran***. This Jewish community was destroyed during the Jewish Revolt (AD 66–70), but their collection of documents was discovered in the 1940s. The ***Dead Sea Scrolls***, as they are called (abbreviated DSS), have been hailed as the most important archaeological discovery of the twentieth century. The documents (numbering around 950!) cover a variety of topics in varying formats, including community discipline manuals, worship liturgies, pseudepigraphic texts, and commentaries on the Hebrew Scriptures.[31]

Two Jewish writers contemporary with the NT era are worth noting here. The first was a Jewish scholar, author, and politician named Philo Judaeus (ca. 20 BC–AD 50), who lived in Alexandria, Egypt, and wrote some seventy or so works (of which about fifty have survived in whole or in part). The writings of this diaspora Jew, commonly referred to as ***Philo of Alexandria***, is another source of insight into how some Second Temple period Jews approached their faith, particularly dealing with the tensions of Judaism with the Hellenistic culture.[32] The other Jewish writer of the first century was Flavius Titus ***Josephus*** (ca. AD 37–100). Born to a wealthy priestly family, Josephus served as a general in the Jewish army in the fight against Rome in Galilee during the First Jewish Revolt (AD 66–70). When his troops were defeated, he recognized the futility of opposing Rome and served the Roman forces by attempting to convince other Jewish troops to surrender. When the revolt was put down, Josephus retired to Rome, where he wrote several important historical works, works that represent a significant source of historical information and offer something of a contemporary perspective to Luke's historical accounts in Luke-Acts, including references to Jesus.[33]

---

30. For a brief treatment on the Pseudepigrapha (and Apocrypha), see Daniel M. Gurtner, "Noncanonical Jewish Writings," in Green and McDonald, *The World of the New Testament*, 291–309. With a generous inclusion of pseudepigraphic books, a standard English collection and translation of texts is James H. Charlesworth, ed., *The Old Testament Pseudepigrapha*, 2 vols. (Garden City, NY: Doubleday, 1983–1985), recently even more generously supplemented with Richard J. Bauckham, James R. Davila, and Alexander Panayotov, eds., *Old Testament Pseudepigrapha: More Noncanonical Scriptures*, 2 vols. (Grand Rapids: Eerdmans, 2013). But see now Annette Yoshiko Reed, "Pseudepigrapha, 'Old Testament'," in *T&T Clark Encyclopedia of Second Temple Judaism*, ed. Daniel M. Gurtner and Loren T. Stuckenbruck, 2 vols. (New York: Bloomsbury T&T Clark, 2020), 2:634–37; and Daniel M. Gurtner, *Introducing the Pseudepigrapha of Second Temple Judaism: Message, Content, and Significance* (Grand Rapids: Baker Academic, 2020).

31. For a brief survey of the Dead Sea Scrolls, see R. K. Harrison and Martin G. Abegg Jr., "Dead Sea Scrolls," *ZEB* 2:60–73. For an English translation of the Dead Sea Scrolls, see Michael O. Wise, Martin G. Abegg Jr., and Edward M. Cook, trans. and eds., *The Dead Sea Scrolls: A New Translation*, 2nd ed. (New York: HarperCollins, 2005).

32. For a brief treatment on Philo, see Torrey Seland, "Philo and the New Testament," in Green and McDonald, *The World of the New Testament*, 405–12.

33. For a brief treatment on Josephus, see Michael F. Bird, "Josephus and the New Testament," in Green and McDonald *The World of the New Testament*, 398–404.

The Literature of Judaism

	Dates	Literature	Constituent Parts	Additional Notes
SCRIPTURE	ca. 1400–400 BC	*Tanak*	The Law: *Torah* The Prophets: *Nevi'im* The Writings: *Ketuvim*	Although outlined and numbered differently, the Hebrew Bible is the same material as the 39 books of the Protestant Old Testament.
SECOND TEMPLE LITERATURE	ca. 250 BC	Septuagint (LXX)	The Greek translation of the Hebrew Scriptures	Various "old Greek" versions of the Hebrew Bible are commonly all referred to as the LXX.
	ca. 250–50 BC	Apocrypha	A small collection of Second Temple books included in Roman Catholic and Eastern Orthodox Bibles	The term *apocrypha* means "hidden," referring to the cryptic nature of these books. Their secondary nature is noted in their being called "deuterocanonical" books.
	ca. 200 BC–AD 70	Pseudepigrapha	A diverse collection of works from the Second Temple period; most are later than the books of the Apocrypha.	The term *pseudepigrapha* means "written under an assumed (thus, 'false') name," which is descriptive of many (but not all) of these books.
	ca. 200 BC–AD 70	Dead Sea Scrolls	Of around 950 manuscripts, about a fourth are biblical texts, and the remainder represent a range of Jewish religious texts (including hymns, prayers, letters, exegetical texts, calendar texts, and about a fifth of the total number are sectarian texts).	Scholars debate the nature of the Qumran community where most of the Dead Sea Scrolls were found, with many (but not all) suggesting they were an Essene sect of Second Temple Judaism.
RABBINIC LITERATURE	ca. AD 200–220	Mishnah	Oral traditions of the rabbis' discussions of Torah that were finally written down	The term *mishnah* means "repetition," as this material primarily repeats the *halakah* (i.e., legal rulings) of rabbis.
	ca. AD 270	Tosefta	Additions to the Mishnah	The term *tosefta* means "additions."
	ca. AD 250–500	Gemara	Commentary on the Mishnah	The term *gemara* means "completion," and it contains both *halakah* and *haggadah* (i.e., illustrative material).
	ca. AD 200–1000	Midrashim	Interpretative expositions and commentaries on the biblical books	The term *midrash* means "exposition" or "interpretation."
	ca. AD 100–1000	Targums	Written Aramaic paraphrases of the Hebrew Bible	Aramaic superseded Hebrew as Second Temple Judaism's spoken language.
	4th century AD	Palestinian Talmud	Mishnah + Gemara	a.k.a. "Jerusalem Talmud."
	5th century AD	Babylonian Talmud	Mishnah + Gemara	The Babylonian Talmud is significantly longer than the Palestinian Talmud.

A final set of Jewish literature relevant to the first century, generally known as ***rabbinic writings***, did not actually take shape until a century or more later. After Rome conquered Jerusalem in AD 70 and destroyed the temple, Second Temple Judaism came to an end, and first-century Judaism needed to adapt for living in this new situation. The oral teachings of the first-century Jewish rabbis—said by some branches of Judaism to bear the authority of Moses (see m. Avot 1:1–18; b. Menah. 29b; b. Git. 60b; y. Meg. 4:1; cf. b. Tem. 14b)—were official applications of OT teaching to the current lives of the people. Around AD 200, the oral tradition that had been repeated from generation to generation (since ca. 50 BC) was written down in what is now called the ***Mishnah*** (meaning "repetition"). About fifty years after the Mishnah was produced, some supplemental statements were drafted; these are called the ***Tosefta*** (meaning "additions"). Succeeding generations of rabbis in the third through fifth centuries added commentary called the ***Gemara*** (meaning "completion") to bring the Mishnah to completion. The Mishnah and Gemara together are called the ***Talmud*** (meaning "learning" or "study"), the complete record of Jewish oral tradition. Other rabbinic writings developed in the first ten centuries, including ***midrashim*** (interpretative commentaries on the biblical books) and ***Targums*** (written Aramaic paraphrases of Hebrew Scripture). Thus, the field of rabbinic literature is a vast arena of study in its own right. While there are questions of continuity between the first century and the era when the rabbinic teachings were finally codified, cautious appeal to rabbinic writings remains informative, and at least illustrative, for study of the New Testament.[34]

5.2.5 Non-Jewish Religious Practices in the First Century

Many non-Jewish religious options were available for people interested in worship in the first-century world of Luke. And of course, "worship" was not always an altruistic endeavor motivating the religious activities of the variously enthused devotees.[35]

Polytheism was the norm in the broader world of the first century; people believed that many gods existed. Some of the gods were thought to be international (e.g., the Greek gods of Mount Olympus), but many were regional deities (and these were sometimes merged with the Olympian gods). The polytheism of the first century is perhaps most evident in Acts when Paul arrives in Athens and sees the many and various objects of worship in the public marketplace, i.e., "the city was full of idols" (Acts 17:16; cf. vv. 22–23). In the general polytheistic culture of the Roman Empire, it would be odd to insist on conversion from one kind of belief to another; people could simply

34. For a brief treatment on rabbinic literature, see Bruce Chilton, "Rabbinic Literature and the New Testament," in Green and McDonald, *The World of the New Testament*, 413–23.

35. For an overarching survey on religion in the Greco-Roman world, see David E. Aune, "Religion, Greco-Roman," *DNTB*, 917–26. For a more thorough examination, see Hans-Josef Klauck, *The Religious Context of Early Christianity: A Guide to Graeco-Roman Religions*, SNTW (Minneapolis: Fortress, 2003); cf., Gordon H. Clark, "Greek Religion and Philosophy," *ZEB* 2:878–93; and Edward M. Blaiklock, "Roman Religion," *ZEB* 5:174–78.

add another god to their polytheistic belief system. A positive spin-off of this general tolerance was a tolerance of Judaism, even if its insistence on one-and-only-one God was unique. Rome tolerated the ancient belief system of the Jews, which had Scriptures attesting to its centuries of existence. This explains the tolerance Rome seems to extend to Christians in the book of Acts, for Rome knew no distinction between Jews and Christians, particularly with people like Paul claiming Christianity to be the proper extension of the ancient Jewish faith (e.g., Acts 24:14–21; 26:4–7, 22–23; cf. 18:14–15).

Given the normalcy of polytheism, ***magic*** (along with divination and superstition) was also prevalent in the first century. Greco-Roman religious belief was not about having a personal relationship with the gods and interacting ethically as much as it was about figuring out how to gain blessings from the gods and avoiding their wrath.[36] This meant that religious practices could entail various activities meant to appease the gods, to build up good will with the gods, or even to manipulate the gods. The book of Acts reflects this broad culture (e.g., Acts 8:9–25; 13:4–12; 19:13–20). Related to the magic practices, the belief in demonic beings was something Jews and Christians had in common with the pagan religious systems in the broader culture. Of course, in pagan worldviews, demons tended to be treated as gods to be worshiped or appeased; for Jews and Christians, demons are spiritual beings to be avoided and opposed. This too is evident in Luke's writings (e.g., Luke 4:33–41; 7:21; 8:2, 26–39; 9:37–43; 11:14–26; 13:32; Acts 5:16; 16:16–24; 19:12).

The idea of the ***imperial cult***—that the Roman emperor was to be paid homage as if to a god—appears to have had a spontaneous beginning among zealous Roman citizens. The earliest Roman emperors, perhaps borrowing the practice from other ancient kingdoms (e.g., Egypt), accepted this adulation, and their successors promoted it as a useful political tool. Nevertheless, this concept should not be overstated. Paul in Acts confidently argues that he has lived a proper life as a Roman citizen and was willing to stand trial before Caesar himself (Acts 25:8–12); he was apparently unafraid of being accused of apostasy against Rome, despite his commitment to monotheism. Thus, while there was widespread encouragement of emperor worship, it was not mandatory for Roman citizens.[37] However, several later Roman persecutions of Christians demonstrate that use of the imperial cult as a political tool was no less threatening, even if it was more about political allegiance than religious submission—which, of course, were less distinct categories in antiquity. Declaring that the risen Jesus Christ was Lord and Savior of the universe could easily be construed by Rome as some kind of dissidence.[38]

---

36. See Moyer V. Hubbard, "Greek Religion," pp. 105–23 in Green and McDonald, *The World of the New Testament*, 105–6; cf. idem, *Christianity in the Greco-Roman World: A Narrative Introduction* (Peabody, MA: Hendrickson, 2010).

37. Carter, *Seven Events the Shaped the New Testament World*, 82; see also Edward M. Blaiklock, "Emperor Worship," *ZEB* 2:327–29.

38. See Nicholas Perrin, "The Imperial Cult," in Green and McDonald, *The World of the New Testament*, 124–34; cf. Hurtado, *Destroyer of the Gods*, 81–82.

Principal Greek and Roman Gods/Personifications

Greek Name	Roman Name	Primary Roles or Associations
Aphrodite	Venus	Goddess of beauty, sexual love, and fertility
Apollo	Phoebus	God of music, poetry, art, and sun
Ares	Mars	God of war
Artemis*	Diana	Goddess of fertility & chastity, wilderness, and hunting
Asklepios	Asclepius	God of healing
Athena	Minerva	Goddess of wisdom, arts and crafts, and war
Castor & Pollux*	Gemini	The twin (demi-)gods; patrons of sailors
Cronus	Saturn	God of time and agriculture; father of Zeus
Demeter	Ceres	Goddess of grain and the harvest
Dike*	Justitia	Goddess of justice
Dionysus/Liber	Bacchus	God of nature, wine, and merriment
Eros	Cupid	God of love
Gaia	Terra	Earth goddess, mother of the Titans
Hades	Pluto	God of the underworld and the dead
Helios	Sol	God of the sun
Hephaestus	Vulcan	God of fire, industry, and the forge
Hera	Juno	Goddess of the sky, marriage; wife of Zeus
Herakles	Hercules	God of strength, bravery, and victory
Hermes*	Mercury	God of trade and eloquence; messenger of the gods
Hestia	Vesta	Goddess of hearth and home and domestic virtues
Nike	Victoria	Goddess of victory
Pan	Faunus	God of shepherds
Persephone	Proserpine	Goddess of the underworld
Poseidon	Neptune	God of the sea and earthquakes
Rhea	Ops	Wife of Cronus; mother of Zeus
Selene	Luna	Goddess of the moon
Uranus	Uranus	Sky god; father of the Titans
Zeus*	Jupiter	God of the sky; ruler of the gods

*These gods are specifically mentioned in Acts: respectively in Acts 19:23–41; 28:11; 28:4; 14:12; and 14:12–13.

5.2.6 Non-Jewish Literature Particularly Relevant to the First Century

In addition to the Jewish literature mentioned previously, a variety of non-Jewish ancient literature is also informative regarding first-century life as it relates to Acts. These include the writings of such non-Jewish authors as ***Epictetus*** (ca. AD 55–135) a teacher of Stoic philosophy from Hierapolis, an ancient city in what is now modern Turkey; Publius Ovidius Naso, known more simply as ***Ovid*** (43 BC–ca. AD 17), a lawyer and poet born in Italy near Rome; Gaius Plinius Caecilius Secundus, better known simply as ***Pliny the Younger*** (ca. AD 61–113), the nephew and adopted son of a Roman government official and natural scientist known now as Pliny the Elder; Lucius Mestrius ***Plutarch*** (ca. AD 46–120), a native of Greece and teacher of Platonist philosophy; Lucius Annaeus ***Seneca*** (ca. 4 BC–AD 65), a Stoic philosopher who served as a tutor and then advisor to Nero; Gaius ***Suetonius*** Tranquillus (ca. AD 69–125), a Roman historian and friend of Pliny the Younger; and Publius (or Gaius) Cornelius ***Tacitus*** (ca. AD 56–120), a Roman official regarded as one of the greatest Roman historians.

Hierapolis is known for its hot springs.

5.3 How People Interacted: What Is the Sociocultural Setting of Acts?

Intertwined with their religious commitments and expressions, the people of the first century had a number of sociocultural values that are helpful to understand for a more productive reading of the story of Acts. Some of these key social values held by first-century people will be familiar to twenty-first-century readers, and this is well and good for our proper understanding and appreciation of the story of Acts. But some of the social values exhibited in Acts will seem exaggerated (or conversely, understated) or even strange to modern readers. While whole books have been written about these matters, this section will cover the significant social values in the NT era that will be most helpful in understanding Acts.[39]

5.3.1 Collectivism Mentality

A fundamental difference (still today) between Middle Eastern and Western social values has to do with the ***collectivism*** mentality of the Middle East versus the individualism of the West.[40] For the most part in the first-century world, people did not seek to become successful, influential, and famous as individuals. Rather, people sought to belong to a group and to be part of the success and influence of that group. Luke gives expression to this value in the early church, as they sought to care for each other (e.g., Acts 2:42–47; 4:32).

5.3.2 Extended Family

The high value of collectivism is reflected in the way first-century people thought about their families. It was the extended family that mattered far more, and each individual had a role to play in the support of the extended family, not the other way around. The plural Greek word for "brethren" (*adelphoi*) was a default for any mix of male and female relatives[41] but was also used for groups of people who had some close affinity with one another beyond being blood relatives.[42] Familial labels were even sometimes utilized within various voluntary associations like occupational guilds, special interest clubs, immigrant groups, and religious organizations.[43] Luke-Acts shows Jesus beginning to redefine what it means to be a member of the family of God, and it is an expansion that goes beyond blood relatives to emphasize obedience to God as Father (see Luke 2:48–49; 3:8; 8:19–21; 11:27–28; 14:25–27; 18:29–30) and entails relating to fellow believers as "brothers and sisters" (see Acts 1:16; 6:3; 11:29; 12:17; 15:23, 36;

---

39. Here I am influenced again by Strauss, *Four Portraits, One Jesus*, 189–210. See also Stephen C. Barton, "Social Values and Structure," *DNTB*, 1127–34; John E. Stambaugh and David L. Balch, *The New Testament in Its Social Environment*, LEC (Philadelphia: Westminster, 1986); and Dietmar Neufeld and Richard E. DeMaris, eds., *Understanding the Social World of the New Testament* (New York: Routledge, 2010).

40. Bruce J. Malina, "Collectivism in Mediterranean Culture," in *Understanding the Social World of the New Testament*, ed. Dietmar Neufeld and Richard E. DeMaris (New York: Routledge, 2010), 17–28.

41. See BDAG, s.v. ἀδελφός 1.

42. See BDAG, s.v. ἀδελφός 2, "one who shares beliefs."

43. See Philip A. Harland, "Familial Dimensions of Group Identity: 'Brothers' (ἀδελφοί) in Associations of the Greek East," *JBL* 124 (2005): 491–513; idem, "Familial Dimensions of Group Identity (II): 'Mothers' and 'Fathers' in Associations and Synagogues of the Greek World," *JSJ* 38 (2007): 57–79.

16:40; 18:18, 27; 21:7, 17; 28:14–15). Followers of Jesus have strong family-like ties with one another, a bond stronger than ancestral and national commitments.[44]

5.3.3 Honor and Shame

A societal emphasis on group identity and interaction raises the sense of ***honor and shame*** as a social value. This was the case in the first-century Greco-Roman world in which Luke lived. A person's honor was his own sense of value dependent on his social group's acknowledgment of it. And in a society that emphasizes the welfare of the group, the honor (or shame) given to an individual brings honor (or shame) to that individual's whole group. Thus, to gain and maintain respect and approval from one's group and for one's group was more important than wealth and power. This honor-and-shame concept sheds light on the nature of many of the public challenges Jesus received from Pharisees and Sadducees (e.g., Luke 13:10–17; 20:1–47) and some of the interactions in the book of Acts as well (e.g., Acts 16:35–40).[45]

5.3.4 Social and Economic Stratifications

Speaking of honor and shame naturally brings to mind the related concept of social status regarding a person's position and role in society relative to everyone else. Unlike modern Western cultures with their emphases on equality and democratic freedoms, the first-century world was more concerned with maintaining a properly ordered society with each individual fulfilling the role of his or her given position. In maintaining this order, Roman society in particular had a stratified system of social standings with a detailed delineation of the powerful elite at the top of the system and a general mix of the more dependent nonelite groups (see sidebar on stratification of the Roman elite).[46]

---

44. For more on the value of the extended family in the NT, see David A. deSilva, *Honor, Patronage, Kinship and Purity: Unlocking New Testament Culture*, 2nd ed. (Downers Grove, IL: InterVarsity Press, 2022). On Christian use of family metaphors like "brothers and sisters," see Stephen Finlan, *The Family Metaphor in Jesus' Teaching: Gospel Imagery and Application*, 2nd ed. (Eugene, OR: Cascade, 2013); Joseph H. Hellerman, *The Ancient Church as Family* (Minneapolis: Fortress, 2001); idem, *When the Church Was a Family: Recapturing Jesus' Vision for Authentic Christian Community* (Nashville: B&H Academic, 2009). More fully, see Paul Trebilco, *Self-Designations and Group Identity in the New Testament* (Cambridge: Cambridge University Press, 2012).

45. For brief introductions to honor and shame, see David A. deSilva, "Honor and Shame," *DNTB*, 518–22; and Bruce J. Malina and Jerome H. Neyrey, "Honor and Shame in Luke-Acts: Pivotal Values of the Mediterranean World," in *The Social World of Luke-Acts: Models for Interpretation*, ed. Jerome H. Neyrey (Peabody, MA: Hendrickson, 1991), 25–65.

46. For brief discussions of the stratification of Roman society see the somewhat dated Duane F. Watson, "Roman Social Classes," *DNTB*, 999–1004; and Everett Ferguson, *Backgrounds of Early Christianity*, 3rd ed. (Grand Rapids: Eerdmans, 2003), 55–63. While some have suggested more detailed layers for the nonelite, recent scholarship has questioned the extent to which Roman society was stratified in such layers; see John Kloppenborg, *Christ's Associations: Connecting and Belonging in the Ancient City* (New Haven, CT: Yale University Press, 2019), esp. 162–208; "In imagining ancient Roman society, we should not think of it as a series of horizontal layers defined by income levels but instead as vertically integrated pyramids with elite at the top, connected through patronage and benefaction to multiple associations of nonelite, including freeborn, freedmen and freedwomen, and slaves, citizens, resident aliens, and foreigners" (p. 35).

Such a stratified system had several potential advantages (e.g., ordered society and productive teamwork) but also had abuses and extreme disparities (e.g., significant social inequality and slavery). As evidenced in part by the variety of responses to Rome among the Jews in Palestine, the question of how thoroughly Roman sensibilities influenced a given local culture when Rome conquered them is a matter of debate. And as can be seen in Acts, local customs and social expectations also were in operation even within the broader Roman context of the first century.

Social Stratification of the Roman Elite

An adaptation of descriptions in Duane F. Watson, "Roman Social Classes," *DNTB*, 999–1004. For upper-class property value qualifications measured in denarii, one denarius ≈ one day's wage for a laborer.

Groupings		Descriptions
ROMAN EMPEROR		Ruler of the Roman Empire whose status was shared by the imperial household members and the officials of the central administration.
PATRICIANS The elite—*honestiores*—an extreme minority of the population.	**Senators**	The 600–900 top government office holders in the empire; freeborn citizens with a minimum of 250,000 denarii worth of property. This was less than .002% of the total population.
	Equestrians	Wealthy landowners (named as those who could afford to ride a horse to war); freeborn citizens with a minimum of 100,000 denarii worth of property. This was less than .1% of the total population.
	Decurions	Local administrators in the Roman provinces; freeborn citizens with a minimum of 25,000 denarii worth of property. This was less than 5% of the total population.
PLEBEIANS		The nonelite—*humiliores*—were the bulk of the population. Unlike the clearly defined horizontal layers of socioeconomic groupings for the elite as sketched above, the nonelite (or subelite) are better understood in overlapping and interdependent social connections via patronage and voluntary associations.
SLAVES		People born into slavery and those reduced to slavery by means of conquest or piracy.

Attempts to chart Roman society by socioeconomic stratifications have commonly suggested that 1 percent of the population was at the elite level, disproportionately controlling almost all the wealth, while 99 percent of the population lived at (or below) subsistence level.[47] But this binary stratification has been called into question, with evidence suggesting a substantial middle grouping (see sidebar on economic standings). Furthermore, while the members of a society might be graphed on a stratified social scale and then again on a stratified economic scale, the two scales

47. So, for example, Justin J. Meggitt, *Paul, Poverty and Survival*, SNTW (Edinburgh: T&T Clark, 1998), 99; and Watson, "Roman Social Classes," 1000.

are not necessarily the same. This is becoming clearer for our grasp of the first-century Roman world. It is a mistake to assume that social status always mapped onto economic status, with the rich always having higher social status and the poor always having lower social status.[48] For example, students of the New Testament readily recognize that Jews who became rich by serving as tax collectors for Rome were highly disregarded by their fellow Jews (see Luke 5:29–30; 7:34; 19:1–7). While wealth certainly mattered to people, wealth and social status likely came together only for those of the very highest levels of society; for most members of ancient honor/shame societies, one's social status was measured more by social connections than by wealth.[49] Relationships between an employer and his laborers, between a city official and the citizens, between a master and his servants, between a commander and his soldiers, and (in Acts) between church leaders and the membership—these social connections mattered greatly. Moreover, the relative social value of such connections could vary depending on who the employer, city official, master, commander, etc. was.

Economic Standings in the First-Century Roman World

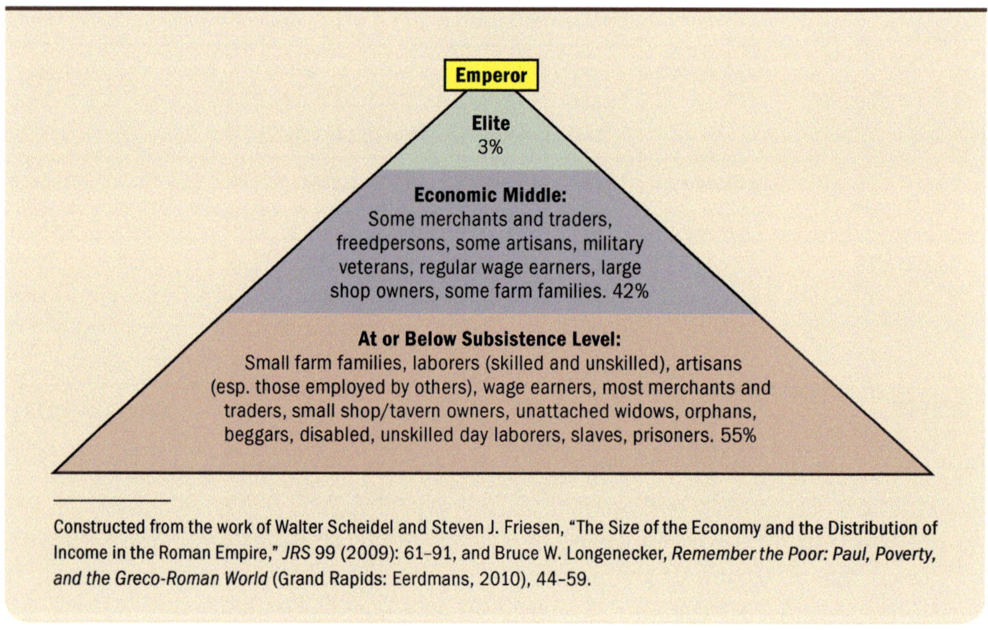

Constructed from the work of Walter Scheidel and Steven J. Friesen, "The Size of the Economy and the Distribution of Income in the Roman Empire," *JRS* 99 (2009): 61-91, and Bruce W. Longenecker, *Remember the Poor: Paul, Poverty, and the Greco-Roman World* (Grand Rapids: Eerdmans, 2010), 44-59.

48. Kloppenborg, *Christ's Associations*, 162.

49. Kloppenborg, *Christ's Associations*, 164, 201–8. On the differences between social stratifications and economic stratifications that have overlap primarily at the small upper ends of the scales, see Kloppenborg's explanation on pp. 164–68, where he leans on Géza Alföldy, *The Social History of Rome*, rev. ed., trans. David Braund and Frank Pollock, Ancient Society and History (Baltimore: Johns Hopkins University Press, 1988), 147–49.

For example, the servant of a powerful master could have more social clout than the freeborn laborer working for a lower-level farmer. A member of a guild of metal workers connected to a famous and highly revered goddess could have higher social standing than an independent shop owner lacking such connections (but how might it compare with the social standing of an independent teacher connected to local politicians? See Acts 19:24–41).[50]

This more complex picture suggests more fluidity for one's social status—i.e., gaining or losing status—even if one's economic status changed little.[51] For instance, quite apart from their economic status, with the healing of a disabled man in Lystra, Paul and Silas suddenly gained social status, for they were mistakenly thought to be connected with Zeus; but when that connection was dissolved, the social status in that immediate context quickly evaporated and their very lives were threatened (Acts 14:8–19). While this is perhaps a rather extreme example, we see that the relationships of social status came with certain expectations for maintaining those relationships (see also Luke 19:11–27). Nevertheless, Jesus sometimes challenged the rigidity of the various social systems by associating with people outside the normal lines of expected interaction (e.g., Luke 7:1–10, 34; 14:12–14; 15:1–2; 17:11–19). Jesus's followers in Acts are found emulating these kinds of countercultural behaviors even while, in some ways, the church appeared to operate as (at least) a kind of social organization within its cultural settings (e.g., Acts 2:42–47; 4:32–37).[52]

On Christianity's Appeal at Multiple Levels of Society

From Linford Stutzman, *With Paul at Sea: Learning from the Apostle Who Took the Gospel from Land to Sea* (Eugene, OR: Cascade, 2012), xii.

> Part of the attraction of the kingdom for those at the bottom is for immediate change to their life. The immediate life-changing physical and social benefits of joining the movement are evident in the very first chapters of Acts, and are verified in the attraction of the lower classes to the movement. The Christian movement is in the position to attract those from both extremes of the pyramid, and to bring them together into a radically different social entity than that of the empire.

---

50. See other such examples in Kloppenborg, *Christ's Associations*, 167.

51. For a brief overview of social mobility in first-century Roman society, see Watson, "Roman Social Classes," 1002–1003.

52. On the tension that Christianity maintains—and must maintain—between being relatable to its culture and yet distinct from it, see Hurtado, *Destroyer of the Gods*, 7–10.

5.3.5 Benefaction/Patronage and Voluntary Associations

The inequities of the stratification of the Roman society were offset by the ideals of benefaction or patronage. To function smoothly, society depended on its wealthier citizens to make donations to fund public works (civic benefaction/patronage), and individuals at the lower levels—perhaps as members of voluntary associations with others like themselves—depended on the generosity of specific higher-level citizens (personal benefaction/patronage). Indeed, as part of a collective group, a person might have access to an improved social standing and its benefits that would be unavailable to him as an individual.[53] Luke-Acts gives evidence of such benefaction/patronage relationships and volunteer associations, for example, a gentile centurion building a local Jewish synagogue (Luke 7:4–5), the wealthier believers helping the less fortunate (Acts 4:32–37), individuals using their homes as meeting places for Christians (e.g., Lydia in Acts 16:13–15, 40; Jason in Acts 17:5–9), the association of metal craftsmen in Ephesus (Acts 19:24–41), Paul's relationship with the Asiarchs of Ephesus (Acts 19:31), and the responses of healed persons (e.g., Acts 28:8–10).

Benefaction/patronage had expectations of reciprocity. That is, the benefactors sponsoring civic improvements or benefits such as libraries, stadiums, and public festivals expected public honor in return. Similarly, patrons assisted their individual clients with the expectation that the clients would reciprocate with such things as political support, public honor, or other services.[54] Thus, in a world that emphasized honor and shame, the interpersonal bonds of the patron-client relationship involved particularly important role expectations in the stratified Roman society.[55] But the Christian faith sometimes turned benefaction and its reciprocal expectations on its head (see Luke 14:1–24; 22:24–27).

5.3.6 Table Fellowship

The first-century world operated with an expectation regarding hospitality in general, and this brings to mind one final social value worth discussing here. Table fellowship in the first-century Middle East was of value not merely for the avoidance of loneliness but for the implications of eating together, i.e., sharing a meal was a celebration of what people held in common and communicated acceptance and belonging to one another as well as communicating this connection to those outside

---

53. Kloppenborg, *Christ's Associations*, 208.

54. Hubbard, *Christianity in the Greco-Roman World*, 146–48.

55. For more on benefaction and patronage, see Donald D. Walker, "Benefactor," *DNTB*, 157–59; David A. deSilva, "Patronage," *DNTB*, 766–71; and Keener, *Acts*, 3:2408–13. On voluntary associations in antiquity, see the brief overview by Michael S. Moore, "Civic and Voluntary Associations in the Greco-Roman World," in Green and McDonald, *The World of the New Testament*, 149–55; and more fully Kloppenborg, *Christ's Associations*, 23–54.

the group. Many of Judaism's annual festivals were celebrations of God's actions in their OT history, and their dietary restrictions served as important identity markers separating them as God's people who were to be different from the unbelievers around them. Thus, in recognizing Jesus as the fulfillment of the historic Jewish faith—a faith into which gentile peoples were to be invited—the first Jewish Christians struggled with the implications gentile inclusion had for their table fellowship practices. Luke makes clear in his gospel that Jesus challenged some of the Jewish table fellowship practices and assumptions (e.g., Luke 5:27–35; 7:34; 14:1–24; 15:1–2, 22–32; 19:1–10), and as the story continues in Acts, he shows the church finally recognizing the proper extension of table fellowship (e.g., Acts 10 and 15).[56]

A first-century feast was usually held at a triclinium table like this.
Public domain

5.4 CONCLUDING REMARKS

Understanding the history leading up to the NT era and knowing the religious and sociocultural values and practices of the first-century world gives us a better appreciation for how the story of Jesus and his followers started and for how Luke has reported that story to us in his gospel and in Acts. While Jesus and his followers are better understood

56. For more on table fellowship, see Mark Allan Powell, "Table Fellowship," *DJG*[2], 925–31; cf. Kloppenborg, *Christ's Associations*, 209–44.

within the first-century culture, interestingly Luke reports that they challenged the first-century culture to become other than what it was. We should not only watch for the various first-century cultural elements in our study of the book of Acts, but we should also evaluate our own culture. If we want to be followers of Jesus in the new "culture" he has established, we need to examine our own cultural settings. We need to see, on the one hand, where our current cultures properly support the message of the gospel and, on the other hand, where we need to live counterculturally to stay faithful to the gospel. And so we turn now to the book of Acts to examine these matters in the story Luke tells us there.

5.5 Key People, Places, and Terms

- Abraham
- Alexander the Great
- Apocrypha
- Assyria
- Babylon
- benefaction/patronage
- client kings
- collectivism
- covenant
- Dead Sea Scrolls
- Egypt
- Epictetus
- Essenes
- exile
- exodus
- Gemara
- Greek, *Koine*
- Hasmonean dynasty
- Hellenization
- Herod the Great
- Herodians
- high priest
- honor and shame
- imperial cult
- Israel
- Josephus, Flavius Titus
- Judah
- Judaism
- legates
- Levites
- Maccabees, the
- Maccabeus, Judas
- magic
- midrashim
- Mishnah
- monotheism
- Moses
- Ovid
- Palestine
- *Pax Romana*
- Persia
- Pharisees
- Philo of Alexandria
- Pliny the Younger
- Plutarch
- polytheism
- prefects
- priests
- proconsuls
- procurators
- promised land
- prophet like Moses
- Pseudepigrapha
- Qumran
- rabbinic writings
- Romans
- Sadducees
- Samaria
- Samaritans
- Sanhedrin
- scribes
- Second Temple period
- Seneca
- Septuagint
- Sicarii
- Suetonius
- synagogue
- Tacitus
- Talmud
- Tanak
- Targums
- temple in Jerusalem
- torah
- Tosefta
- Zealots

5.6 Questions for Review and Discussion

1. Trace the larger biblical storyline from which the story of Acts flows.
2. What geopolitical power was governing the world at the time of the events in Acts? How did this power influence the story of Acts?
3. What are some of the key features of the religious setting(s) of Acts?
4. Who were some of the key religious figures in the world of Acts, and how do they factor into the story of Acts?
5. What are some of the key features of the sociocultural world of Acts?
6. How would you describe the relationship of Christian faith with the socio-political-cultural world of Acts?

5.7 Optional Assignments

1. **Text Reflection Project**–*Relating the concepts discussed in this chapter to another biblical text.* Utilizing the texts mentioned in the table entitled "The Stories Everyone Knew: The Historical-Political Setting of the Story of Acts," explain one of Luke's primary interests in each of the eight time periods discussed in this chapter.
2. **Interview Project**–*Inquiring of others their views concerning the concepts discussed in this chapter.* This chapter argues that Luke sees an important connection of the story of Jesus and the church to the Hebrew Scriptures, to the point that Luke even wrote Luke-Acts as a kind of continuation of the story of Scripture. Ask your pastor (or some other respected Christian leader) about their view of how well today's church is connected with its place in the whole storyline of Scripture.
3. **Service-Learning Project**–*Applying the concepts discussed in this chapter in some form of service to others outside the class.* Reread the section of this chapter that describes the sociocultural values of the world of Acts (i.e., collectivism, extended family, honor/shame, social stratification, benefaction, and table fellowship), and evaluate the connections these values have (or don't have) with scriptural virtues. Then engage in some community service project (e.g., food distribution, clothing aid, volunteer health work) to more consciously apply the scriptural virtues that your reflections have uncovered.
4. **Prayer Project**–*Talking with God about the concepts discussed in this chapter.* Reflecting on how culture affects us and how we are to affect culture, write a prayer asking the Lord to grant you wisdom for distinguishing the righteous and unrighteous features of your current culture and requesting the courage to live counterculturally to stay faithful to his Word.
5. **Testimony Project**–*Telling others about the concepts discussed in this chapter.* Reflecting on the idea that the social values of the first century affected how Luke communicates in his writing, write a brief description of how the social values of the twenty-first century might affect how we communicate the gospel message today. Consciously distinguish between eternal truths and social values.

5.8 Bibliography for Going Further

5.8.1 English Translations of Primary Writings

Bauckham, Richard J., James R. Davila, and Alexander Panayotov, eds. *Old Testament Pseudepigrapha: More Noncanonical Scriptures*. 2 vols. Grand Rapids: Eerdmans, 2013.

Charlesworth, James H., ed. *The Old Testament Pseudepigrapha*. 2 vols. Garden City, NY: Doubleday, 1983–1985.

Coogan, Michael D., et al., eds. *The New Oxford Annotated Apocrypha: New Revised Standard Version*. 5th ed. New York: Oxford University Press, 2018.

Rabbinic Writings (e.g., Mishnah, Talmud, Tosefta): see www.sefaria.org/.

Wise, Michael O., Martin G. Abegg Jr., and Edward M. Cook, trans. and eds. *The Dead Sea Scrolls: A New Translation*. 2nd ed. New York: HarperCollins, 2005.

5.8.2 The Historical-Political Setting of Acts

Bruce, F. F. *New Testament History*. New York: Doubleday, 1972.

Carter, Warren. *Seven Events That Shaped the New Testament World*. Grand Rapids: Baker Academic, 2013.

House, H. Wayne. *Chronological and Background Charts of the New Testament*. 2nd ed. Zondervan Charts. Grand Rapids: Zondervan, 2009.

Kim, Seyoon. *Christ and Caesar: The Gospel and the Roman Empire in the Writings of Paul and Luke*. Grand Rapids: Eerdmans, 2008.

Roetzel, Calvin J. *The World that Shaped the New Testament*. Rev. ed. Louisville, KY: Westminster John Knox, 2002.

Sherwin-White, A. N. *Roman Society and Roman Law in the New Testament*. Oxford: Oxford University Press, 1963. Repr., Grand Rapids: Baker, 1992.

Witherington, Ben, III. *New Testament History: A Narrative Account*. Grand Rapids: Baker Academic, 2001.

Wright, N. T., and Michael F. Bird. *The New Testament in Its World*. Grand Rapids: Zondervan Academic, 2019.

5.8.3 The Religious and Sociocultural Setting of Acts

Burge, Gary M., and Gene L. Green. *The New Testament in Antiquity: A Survey of the New Testament within Its Cultural Contexts*. 2nd ed. Grand Rapids: Zondervan Academic, 2020.

Chapman, David W., and Andreas J. Köstenberger. "Jewish Intertestamental and Early Rabbinic Literature: An Annotated Bibliographic Resource." *JETS* 55.2 (2012): 235–72 (Part 1) and *JETS* 55.3 (2012): 457–88 (Part 2).

Cohen, Shaye J. D. *From the Maccabees to the Mishnah*. 3rd ed. Louisville: Westminster John Knox, 2014.

Evans, Craig A., and Stanley E. Porter, eds. *DNTB*.

Ferguson, Everett. *Backgrounds of Early Christianity*. 3rd ed. Grand Rapids: Eerdmans, 2003.

Green, Joel B., and Lee Martin McDonald, eds. *The World of the New Testament: Cultural, Social, and Historical Contexts*. Grand Rapids: Baker Academic, 2013.

Helyer, Larry R. *Exploring Jewish Literature of the Second Temple Period. A Guide for New Testament Students*. Christian Classics Bible Studies. Downers Grove, IL: InterVarsity Press, 2002.

Hubbard, Moyer V. *Christianity in the Greco-Roman World: A Narrative Introduction*. Peabody, MA: Hendrickson, 2010.

Klauck, Hans-Josef. *The Religious Context of Early Christianity. A Guide to Graeco-Roman Religions*. SNTW. Minneapolis: Fortress, 2003.

Nickelsburg, George W. E. *Jewish Literature Between the Bible and the Mishnah: A Historical and Literary Introduction*. 2nd ed. Minneapolis: Fortress, 2005.

Rowe, C. Kavin. *World Upside Down: Reading Acts in the Graeco-Roman Age*. New York: Oxford University Press, 2009.

Scott, J. Julius. *Jewish Backgrounds of the New Testament*. Grand Rapids: Baker, 2000.

PART 2

THE STORY OF JESUS REACHING THE JEWISH WORLD

Acts 1–12

The storytelling outline we are utilizing in this survey of Acts divides the book into two major halves. The first half of the book—Acts 1–12—focuses on the story of Jesus reaching the Jewish world. The second half of the book—Acts 13–28—focuses on the story of Jesus reaching the gentile world. This division is not wholesale, for there are hints of the gentile mission in the first half of the book and there are constant reflections of the Jewish mission in the second half of the book. Nevertheless, this twofold division is a helpful generalization that fits the way Luke tells the story.

In the first twelve chapters, Luke organizes his message around four major movements, with each utilizing a different organizational principle; so a chapter of this textbook is dedicated to each of these. First, Luke reports the beginning of the Christian community with the coming of the Holy Spirit (chapter 6, discussing Acts 1:1–2:41), overlapping the promise of the Holy Spirit and ascension story at the end of the Gospel of Luke with what he reports in the beginning of the book of Acts. Next, Luke gives a more detailed description of the life of the Christian community as it began in Jerusalem, examining in particular how it faced certain threats (chapter 7, discussing Acts 2:42–6:7). Then switching from a focus on the community to a focus on individuals, Luke tells the stories of three individuals and their gospel ministries: Stephen, Philip, and Saul (chapter 8, discussing Acts 6:8–9:31). And finally, organizing his comments around the spread of the gospel in different cities, Luke relays the story of the gospel spreading to cities further and further outside Jerusalem and Judea and Samaria (chapter 9, focusing on Acts 9:32–12:25). Each of these four major segments of the first half of Acts ends with a summary statement on the progress of the gospel in that region (i.e., Acts 2:41; 6:7; 9:31; and 12:24), and the final progress summary adds a travel summary (Acts 12:25).

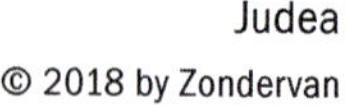

Judea
© 2018 by Zondervan

The Outline and Summary Statements of the First Half of Acts

Each section in the first half of Acts ("Part A" of my outline for the book) ends with a summary statement of some kind, identified and quoted here.

Part A: The Story of Jesus Reaching the Jewish World (Acts 1–12)

I. The Story of Jesus Continues—Acts 1:1–2:41

Progress Summary: "Those who accepted his message were baptized, and about three thousand were added to their number that day" (2:41).

II. The Story of the Church in Its Earliest Days—2:42–6:7

Progress Summary: "So the word of God spread. The number of disciples in Jerusalem increased rapidly, and a large number of priests became obedient to the faith" (6:7).

III. Three Key Non-Apostle Characters in the Story—6:8–9:31

Progress Summary: "Then the church throughout Judea, Galilee and Samaria enjoyed a time of peace and was strengthened. Living in the fear of the Lord and encouraged by the Holy Spirit, it increased in numbers" (9:31).

IV. The Story Advances in Palestine—9:32–12:24–25

Progress Summary: "But the word of God continued to spread and flourish" (12:24).

Travel Summary: "When Barnabas and Saul had finished their mission, they returned from Jerusalem, taking with them John, also called Mark" (12:25).

Samaria
Joshua Raif/
Shutterstock.com

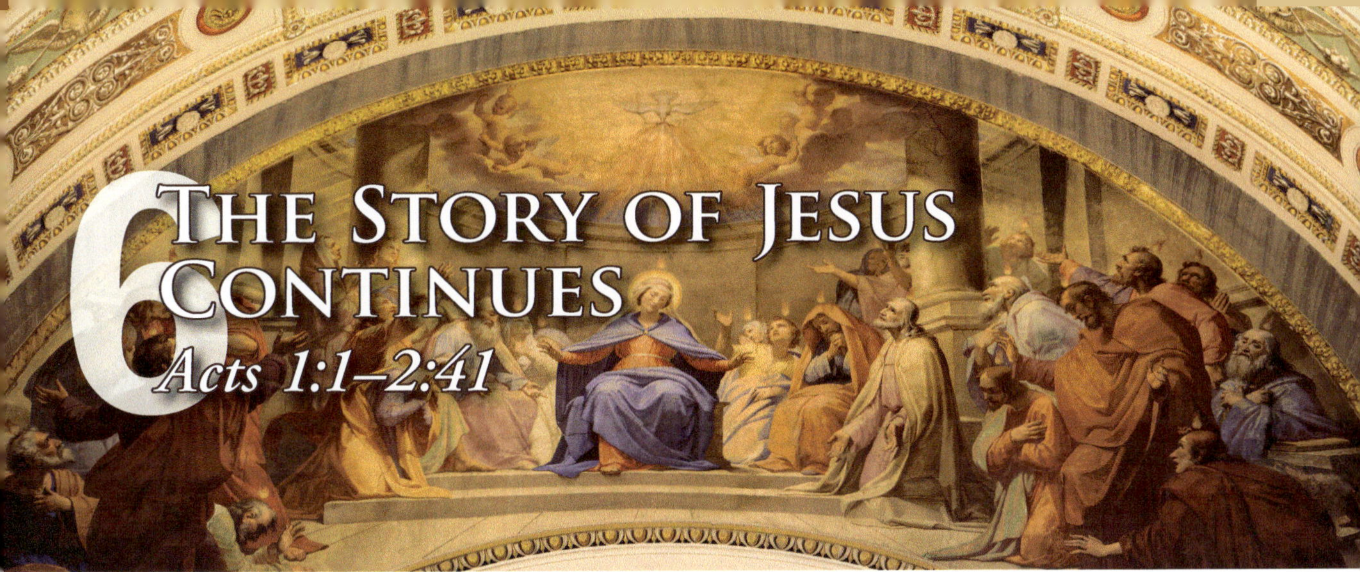

Renáta Sedmáková/stock.adobe.com

Chapter Goals

After reading this chapter, you should be able to:

- Recognize the literary overlap Acts has with the Gospel of Luke.
- Feel the impact of the Great Commission for you as an individual as well as for your community of believers.
- Gain a sense of the importance of the ascension.
- See the importance of joining the community of God's people.
- Reflect on proper decision-making.
- Discern the presence of the Holy Spirit in your own life and in the life of the community of believers.

Chapter Overview

6.1 A Reflective Prologue (Acts 1:1–2)
6.2 Instructions: The Great Commission (Acts 1:3–8)
6.3 The Ascension (Acts 1:9–11)
6.4 The Completion of the Twelve (Acts 1:12–26)
6.5 The Promised Spirit Is Poured Out for the Church (Acts 2:1–41)
6.6 Concluding Remarks
6.7 Key People, Places, and Terms
6.8 Questions for Review and Discussion
6.9 Optional Assignments
6.10 Bibliography for Going Further

Key Verses

In my former book, Theophilus, I wrote about all that Jesus began to do and to teach until the day he was taken up to heaven, after giving instructions through the Holy Spirit to the apostles he had chosen. (Acts 1:1–2)

But you will receive power when the Holy Spirit comes on you; and you will be my witnesses in Jerusalem, and in all Judea and Samaria, and to the ends of the earth. (Acts 1:8)

Repent and be baptized, every one of you, in the name of Jesus Christ for the forgiveness of your sins. And you will receive the gift of the Holy Spirit. The promise is for you and your children and for all who are far off—for all whom the Lord our God will call. (Acts 2:38–39)

Summary Statement

Those who accepted his message were baptized, and about three thousand were added to their number that day. (Acts 2:41)

Jesus appears to his disciples on the road to Emmaus in this mosaic on church facade, Berlin.

Renáta Sedmáková/stock.adobe.com

INTRODUCTION

The first major section of Acts consists of a brief preface (a.k.a. prologue) and four episodes (a.k.a. pericopes—***pericope*** is a scholarly term for a self-contained story unit). After the reflective prologue referencing his first volume (see sidebar), Luke also recounts, as a continuation of the story of Jesus, two pericopes that have an intentional overlap with the Gospel of Luke. Even as modern television serial programs regularly review significant and climactic events of the previous installment, Luke reiterates some of the events of Luke 24 in Acts 1 (see sidebar).[1] Then Luke continues the story with two new episodes about Jesus's followers remaining in Jerusalem as they were instructed until the Holy Spirit is poured out on them. This section ends with a summary statement on the young church's growth.

1. See also the comparison charts of J. Bradley Chance, *Acts*, Smyth & Helwys Bible Commentary (Macon, GA: Smyth & Helwys, 2007), 34; and Craig S. Keener, *Acts: An Exegetical Commentary*, 4 vols. (Grand Rapids: Baker Academic, 2012–2015), 1:648.

The Prologues of Luke and Acts

The prologues to the Gospel of Luke and the Acts of the Apostles evidence one author with historiographical intentions and demonstrate several connections between the books, including:

- the author of Acts refers to having written a "former book" (Acts 1:1),
- both books are dedicated to someone named "Theophilus" (Luke 1:3; Acts 1:1),
- the author of Acts summarizes the contents of his previous book as being about "all that Jesus began to do and to teach until he was taken up to heaven" (Acts 1:1–2), which is an apt summary of the Gospel of Luke,
- and the prologue to Acts fades into a narrative of events between Jesus's resurrection and his ascension, which fittingly overlaps with the ending of Luke's Gospel (Luke 24:44–53 and Acts 1:1–11).

Luke 1:1–4	Acts 1:1–4
Many have undertaken to draw up an account of the things that have been fulfilled among us, just as they were handed down to us by those who from the first were eyewitnesses and servants of the word. With this in mind, since I myself have carefully investigated everything from the beginning, I too decided to write an orderly account for you, most excellent Theophilus, so that you may know the certainty of the things you have been taught.	In my former book, Theophilus, I wrote about all that Jesus began to do and to teach until the day he was taken up to heaven, after giving instructions through the Holy Spirit to the apostles he had chosen. After his suffering, he presented himself to them and gave many convincing proofs that he was alive. He appeared to them over a period of forty days and spoke about the kingdom of God. On one occasion, . . .

The Overlap of Luke 24 and Acts 1

Luke overlaps his reporting of events in Luke 24 and Acts 1. These overlapping elements include:

- Jesus presenting himself and giving proofs that he was alive (Luke 24:36–40 and Acts 1:3),
- eating with the disciples (Luke 24:41–43 and Acts 1:4),
- the commissioning of the apostles (Luke 24:44–49 and Acts 1:2, 4–8),
- the command to stay in Jerusalem (Luke 24:49 and Acts 1:4),
- the promise that believers will receive "power" (Luke 24:49 and Acts 1:4–5, 7–8),
- word that believers will be "witnesses" for Jesus (Luke 24:46–48 and Acts 1:8),
- and the ascension (Luke 24:50–53 and Acts 1:9–11).

6.1 A REFLECTIVE PROLOGUE (ACTS 1:1–2)

As noted, Luke begins each of his two NT volumes with a prologue, which demonstrate Luke's intention that his reports be taken seriously as history and not as fiction.[2] Furthermore, comparing the prologue to Acts with the prologue to Luke clearly shows that Acts references the Gospel of Luke as its prequel.[3] Other ancient authors of historical works in multiple volumes also utilized reflective prologues like this (see sidebar).

The Prologues of Josephus's *Against Apion*

The first-century Jewish historian Josephus (ca. AD 37–100) wrote a two-volume work defending Judaism against the criticisms of someone named Apion. He dedicated each of the two volumes to a man named Epaphroditus, with the dedication of the second volume sounding similar to the prologue to the book of Acts (*Ag. Ap.* 1.1 §1 and 2.1 §§1–2).

Flavius Josephus, *Against Apion* 1.1 §1 (ca. AD 97)

> In my history of our Antiquities, most excellent Epaphroditus, I have, I think, made sufficiently clear to any who may peruse that work the extreme antiquity of our Jewish race, the purity of the original stock, and the manner in which it established itself in the country which we occupy to-day. That history embraces a period of five thousand years, and was written by me in Greek on the basis of our sacred books.

Flavius Josephus, *Against Apion* 2.1 §§1–2 (ca. AD 97)

> In the first volume of this work, my most esteemed Epaphroditus, I demonstrated the antiquity of our race, corroborating my statements by the writings of Phoenicians, Chaldaeans, and Egyptians, besides citing as witnesses numerous Greek historians; I also challenged the statements of Manetho, Chaeremon, and some others. I shall now proceed to refute the rest of the authors who have attacked us.

6.1.1 References to the Gospel of Luke

In the prologue to Acts, Luke references "my former book" (Acts 1:1a) and then describes it as what he "wrote about all that Jesus began to do and to teach until the day he was taken up to heaven" (1:1c–2a). Certainly, the Gospel of Luke is about what Jesus did and taught, but a most interesting delineation here is the notation of when the former book ends: "until the day he was taken up to heaven," a clear description of Jesus's

2. See chapters 2 and 3.

3. See the sidebar "The Prologues of Luke and Acts" and the fuller discussion in chapter 2.

ascension. Luke's Gospel is the only gospel that narrates the ascension, so the prologue to Acts is most likely referring to the Gospel of Luke as the author's former book.

6.1.2 A Change in Greeting Theophilus

As in the prologue to the Gospel of Luke, the prologue to Acts contains a dedication statement to someone named Theophilus (Luke 1:3c and Acts 1:1b). The dedication statement in the Gospel of Luke, however, is more formal ("most excellent Theophilus") than that in Acts ("Theophilus"). Various reasons can be offered for this change in greeting (e.g., the formality of the first greeting covers both books; or by the time of Acts, Luke and Theophilus know each other well enough for the formality to be dropped). One suggestion for the change in greeting has to do with the possible effects Luke's writing had on Theophilus. Perhaps Theophilus—a respected Roman official of some kind—had become a believer in Jesus by reading the Gospel of Luke and now, as a friend and fellow Christian, he is addressed more simply in Acts.[4] While it is difficult to ascertain this idea with any certainty, it is an attractive proposal regarding the dedicatee of Luke's two volumes.[5]

6.1.3 A Statement of Continuation

As prequel and sequel, Luke's two volumes tell one story and not two. It is not that the Gospel of Luke tells the story of Jesus and Acts tells the (separate) story of the church. Rather, Luke's first volume, his gospel, tells the story of Jesus's ministry in the body, and his second volume, the book of Acts, tells the story of Jesus's continued ministry in the Spirit through the church.[6]

The prologue to Acts supports this viewpoint. In describing his gospel account, Luke says it covers "all that Jesus began to do and to teach" (Acts 1:1c). In the first book, Luke tells his reader what Jesus *began* to do and to teach; now in the second book, Luke will report what Jesus *continues* to do and to teach. We should view Acts as a continuation of the story of Jesus.[7] Furthermore, Luke wants to convince his audience that the work of Jesus still continues beyond the book of Acts.[8]

---

4. Arthur M. Ross, "Theophilus," *ZEB* 5:830; see the discussion in chapter 1.

5. But see the cautions of F. F. Bruce, *The Book of Acts*, 2nd ed., NICNT (Grand Rapids: Eerdmans, 1988), 29; and John B. Polhill, *Acts*, NAC (Nashville: Broadman, 1992), 79n5.

6. Mel Storm, *Living Lord, Empowering Spirit, Testifying People: The Story of the Church in the Book of Acts* (Eugene, OR: Wipf & Stock, 2014), 14; cf. John R. W. Stott, *The Message of Acts: To the Ends of the Earth*, The Bible Speaks Today (Downers Grove, IL: InterVarsity, 1994), 32–34. The First Nations Version of the New Testament introduces the book of Acts with the descriptive moniker "The Good Story Continues"; *First Nations Version: An Indigenous Translation of the New Testament* (Downers Grove, IL: InterVarsity Press, 2021), 211.

7. See Bruce, *Book of Acts*, 30; Eckhard J. Schnabel, *Acts*, ZECNT (Grand Rapids: Zondervan, 2012), 70; David John Williams, *Acts*, NIBCNT 5 (Peabody: Hendrickson, 1990), 26; cf. Charles Kingsley Barrett, *A Critical and Exegetical Commentary on the Acts of the Apostles*, 2 vols., ICC (Edinburgh: T&T Clark, 1994/1998), 2:lxxxv. See the popular level introductory study of Acts by J. Ellsworth Kala, *The Story Continues: The Acts of the Apostles for Today* (Nashville: Abingdon, 2016).

8. Polhill, *Acts*, 79–80.

6.1.4 Fading into the Narrative

At the very beginning of his grand narrative about Jesus and the church, Luke offers a prologue that is a technically well-written statement in rather classical Greek style. In the original Greek, Luke 1:1–4 is an impressively balanced single sentence that linguists call a *periodic sentence* (or simply a *period*). In content as well as in style, it stands apart from the narration of the story in the Gospel of Luke. The reflective prologue to the book of Acts, however, is not so well defined. While it begins somewhat officially, the prologue to Acts quickly fades into the narrative. The second-person address to Theophilus and first-person reference to the author's former book (Acts 1:1ab) soon become a third-person description of the Gospel of Luke (1:1c–2), which turns into third-person narration (1:3–4a) that somehow slides midsentence into a quotation of Jesus (1:4b–5). While not as visible in English as it is in Greek, this fading away of the reflective prologue is another testimony to the fact that Acts is a sequel, the continuation of the story and not a new story all its own.

The fading Acts prologue has led to variations among English translations regarding the boundaries for the first paragraph in Acts (e.g., 1:1–2 in CEV or 1:1–3 in CSB and ESV or 1:1–5 in NIV and NASB). If the prologue to Acts is envisioned as encompassing only Acts 1:1–2 (a single sentence in the original Greek), it is noteworthy that verse 2 mentions four topics, each of which is discussed more fully in the remainder of this section of Acts (i.e., 1:3–2:41). Acts 1:2 reads, ". . . until the day he was taken up to heaven, after giving instructions through the Holy Spirit to the apostles he had chosen." And the topics discussed (albeit in a different order) are the ascension ("the day he was taken up to heaven"; see 1:9–11), Jesus's commissioning of the apostles ("giving instructions"; see 1:3–8), the coming of the Holy Spirit ("the Holy Spirit"; see 2:1–41), and the choice of Matthias as the twelfth apostle ("the apostles he had chosen"; see 1:12–26).

6.2 INSTRUCTIONS: THE GREAT COMMISSION (ACTS 1:3–8)

As the preface to Acts drifts into Luke's report of events, some of his report reviews what we know from the last chapter of the Gospel of Luke, but some new information is also included. For example, a cursory reading of Luke 24 might lead a reader to assume that the resurrection along with Jesus's various resurrection appearances (Luke 24:1–49) and his ascension (Luke 24:50–53) happened on the same day. Stanley Porter, however, offers a brief and effective critique of such hasty readings of Luke 24.[9] Scholars sometimes

9. Stanley E. Porter, "The Unity of Luke-Acts and the Ascension Narratives," pp. 111–36 in *Ascent into Heaven in Luke-Acts: New Explorations of Luke's Narrative Hinge*, ed. David K. Bryan and David W. Pao (Minneapolis: Fortress, 2016), 125–28; comments in the sidebar on telescoping reflect Porter's threefold observations of Luke 24.

refer to Luke's reporting style here (with vague time indications) as ***telescoping***, i.e., a closed telescope gives little indication of how far apart the lenses might be when the instrument is in use (see sidebar). Luke himself corrects shortsighted views by specifying in Acts that there were forty days between the resurrection and the ascension (Acts 1:3). And this forty-day period certainly fits with other reports of resurrection appearances involving travel between Jerusalem and Galilee (e.g., Matt 28:7–20; John 21:1–23).

This was forty days of instruction from Jesus, which help ensure that the apostles would be equipped to pass on the authentic teachings of Jesus. In briefly rehearsing Jesus's final instructions, Luke focuses on four things: resurrection proofs (1:3), the future coming of the Holy Spirit (1:4–5), the kingdom of God (1:6–7), and the mission the disciples would have: witnessing (1:8).

"Telescoping" in Reporting Events

When an author reports a series of events one right after another, readers sometimes wrongly assume that those events occurred one right after the other, perhaps even on the same day. In this way, some readers of Luke 24 assume that Jesus's resurrection (Luke 24:1-12) and his various resurrection appearances (Luke 24:13-43 and 44-49) occurred on the same day as his ascension (Luke 24:50-53). But just because the author does not explicitly indicate the exact amount of time passing between the events does not mean he thinks there was none. He may simply be "collapsing the telescope" of his report to cover the events more quickly.

A closer reading of Luke 24 shows that only the first two episodes include time indicators as having occurred on the same day. Furthermore, it would be odd for Jesus to command the disciples to remain in Jerusalem (Luke 24:49) only for him to take them immediately out of the city (Luke 24:50). And how would the disciples view the ascension if it occurred at night (Luke 24:29)? A careful reading of Luke 24 suggests a gap of time between Luke 24:49 and 24:50, and in Acts 1:3 Luke makes clear that there were indeed forty days between Jesus's resurrection and his ascension.

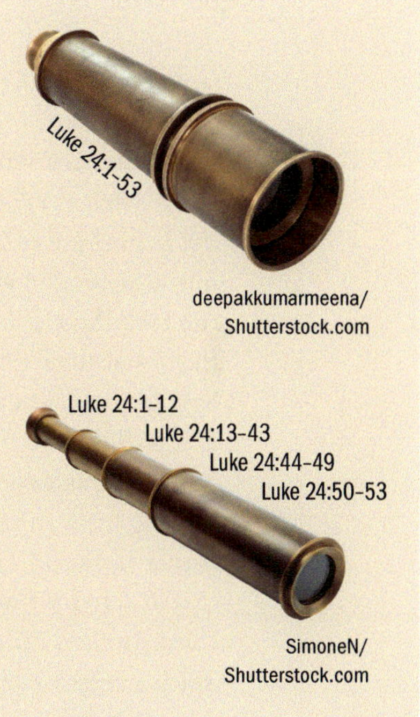

deepakkumarmeena/ Shutterstock.com

SimoneN/ Shutterstock.com

6.2.1 The Resurrection—Many Proofs

Still referring to what he had reported in his gospel (i.e., Luke 24:1–49), Luke summarizes here, "After his suffering, he presented himself to them and gave many convincing proofs that he was alive" (Acts 1:3). Jesus's resurrection, an important concept for Luke, comes up early in Acts and often (e.g., 1:3; 2:24, 32; 3:15, 26; 4:10; 5:30; 10:40; 13:30, 33–34, 37; 17:31). The historical event of the resurrection is paramount for Luke. This emphasis on a single event is unique in ancient historiography, for no other historian makes one particular event the central turning point of all history, looking both backward at the past and forward into the future, the way Luke does with Jesus's resurrection.[10]

For Luke, confirmation of the resurrection included not merely the circumstantial evidence of the empty tomb (Luke 24:1–3) and the empty grave clothes (Luke 24:12), and not merely the angelic announcement in keeping with Jesus's prediction (Luke 24:4–8). The evidence also included people individually and in groups seeing Jesus and interacting with him (Luke 24:13–35). The postresurrection appearances of Jesus included not only sensible exchanges of conversation but also sensate examinations of Jesus's hands and feet to prove he was not a ghost (Luke 24:36–40). Jesus even ate food to prove he was really alive (Luke 24:41–42). Luke wants us to be certain: the appearances were not mere dreams but infallible evidence that Jesus had risen from the dead.[11]

6.2.2 The Holy Spirit—Fulfillment of a Promise

The report of Luke 24:36–49 indicates Jesus eating with the disciples in a setting where he instructs them to stay in Jerusalem until they are empowered for ministry with "what my Father has promised" (Luke 24:49). Luke includes a similar report in the beginning of Acts, where over a meal Jesus commands, "Do not leave Jerusalem, but wait for the gift my Father promised, which you have heard me speak about . . . the Holy Spirit" (Acts 1:4–5). Acts makes more explicit than the Gospel of Luke does that what the Father has promised is in fact the Holy Spirit. Luke's interest in the Holy Spirit is evident early in Acts, with three anticipatory mentions of the Spirit (i.e., Acts 1:2, 5, 8) before his arrival in Acts 2.[12]

But this expectation of the Spirit's coming has a longer history in Luke-Acts. During his ministry, Jesus had instructed his followers to depend on the Spirit for wise words (Luke 11:13; 12:11–12; cf. 21:14–15). So it is no surprise that Jesus returns to this idea in his final instructions, commanding that the disciples wait for the arrival of this promised Spirit "in a few days" (Acts 1:5). Luke's emphasis on the necessity of the Spirit's empowerment—both in the conclusion of his gospel and at the beginning of Acts—reveals its centrality to his understanding of the church's mission.[13]

---

10. Scott Shauf, *The Divine in Acts and in Ancient Historiography* (Minneapolis: Fortress, 2015), 259–60. See also Brandon D. Crowe, *The Hope of Israel: The Resurrection of Christ in the Acts of the Apostles* (Grand Rapids: Baker Academic, 2020).

11. Ernst Haenchen, *The Acts of the Apostles: A Commentary*, trans. and ed. Bernard Noble, Gerald Shinn, Hugh Anderson, and R. McLeod Wilson (Philadelphia: Westminster, 1971), 140–41; Gervais T. D. Angel, "τεκμήριον," *NIDNTT* 3:571; cf. Gerald O'Collins, "Luke on the Closing of the Easter Appearances," pp. 161–66 in *Luke and Acts*, ed. Gerald O'Collins and Gilberto Marconi (New York: Paulist, 1993).

12. Regarding Luke's interest in the Holy Spirit, see chapter 3.

13. Keener, *Acts*, 1:675–76.

6.2.3 The Kingdom of God—Already/Not Yet

Having already mentioned that the forty days of instruction were about the ***kingdom of God*** (Acts 1:3), Luke now reports a specific conversation between the apostles and Jesus on this topic (1:6–7). Luke's chiastic mentions of the "kingdom"—i.e., twice in the opening of Acts and again twice at the end of Acts (1:3, 6; 28:23, 31)—suggest its importance. Indeed, Luke is in the good company of the other evangelists in referring to Jesus explicitly as "king" (six times: Luke 19:38; 23:2, 3, 37, 38; Acts 17:7; cf. Matthew: eight times; Mark: six times; John: twelve times). Many first-century Jews anticipated that God would fulfill his kingdom promises to Israel (e.g., Luke 1:68–79; 24:21; cf. Sir 48:10). And now, recognizing the resurrected Jesus as the true Lord and king, the disciples ask Jesus a question that shows their faithful longing for the kingdom of God to be restored to God's people: "Lord, are you at this time going to restore the kingdom to Israel?" (Acts 1:6).

Royal Language for Jesus in Luke-Acts

The metaphorical language about the "kingdom of God" includes royal references made with and without the expected words "king" (*basileus*), "kingdom" (*basileia*), or "reign" (*basileuō*). Even so, we can make the following cursory observations about Luke's royal presentation of Jesus:

- The angel Gabriel announces that Jesus will reign on the throne of David and that his kingdom will have no end (Luke 1:32-33; cf. Acts 2:30-32).
- Jesus preaches "the good news of the kingdom of God" (Luke 4:43; 8:1; 9:11; 16:16-17; cf. 13:18-21, 28-29; 14:15-24; 18:24-25, 29-30: 19:11; 21:31; Acts 1:3).
- Jesus claims to bring the kingdom of God, granting it to his faithful followers (Luke 6:20; 7:28; 8:10; 9:27, 62; 11:20; 12:32; 17:20-21; 18:16-17; 22:15-20, 29-30; 23:42-43; cf. Luke 23:51; Acts 1:6-8).
- Jesus sends his followers "to proclaim the kingdom of God" (Luke 9:2, 60; 10:9, 11; cf. Acts 8:12; 14:22; 19:8; 20:25; 28:23, 30-31)
- Jesus teaches his followers to pray for God's kingdom to come and to seek it (Luke 11:2; 12:31).
- Jesus is celebrated as a king (Luke 19:28-40; with "king" inserted into the citation of Ps 118:26).
- Jesus is accused of making a false claim to kingship (Luke 23:2).
- When directly asked by Pilate, "Are you the king of the Jews?" Jesus gives the cryptic reply, "You have said so" (Luke 23:3).
- Jesus is taunted at the crucifixion: "If you are the king of the Jews, save yourself." (Luke 23:37).
- Over Jesus's head on the cross is a sign that reads, "This is the king of the Jews" (Luke 23:38).
- His followers are accused of serving Jesus as king instead of Caesar (Acts 17:7).
- Jesus is described as enthroned at God's right hand (Luke 20:41-44; 22:69; Acts 5:31; 7:55-56).

In response to this inquiry, Jesus does not rebuke them for their faithful longing; he simply notes that human speculation about God's schedule for these things is unfruitful: "It is not for you to know the times or dates the Father has set by his own authority" (Acts 1:7).[14] This is another expression of the ***already/not yet kingdom*** or inaugurated eschatology. The kingdom of God has already begun in the hearts of the believers (cf. Luke 17:20–21) and will eventually come to climactic fulfillment with the return of Christ at some time yet unknown to us (cf. Acts 1:11; 3:19–21). Meanwhile, Jesus's followers have a mission on this side of eternity.

6.2.4 The Mission—Witnessing about Jesus

While waiting for the consummation of the kingdom of God, Jesus notes that believers will have the Spirit-empowered mission of witnessing about him to others (Acts 1:8).[15] ***The Great Commission*** is the oft-given label for the final instructions Jesus gives to his followers regarding their carrying the gospel message to the rest of the world. Arguably the most common version of the Great Commission is Matthew's summary of it (Matt 28:18–20). But John has a version of it (John 20:21) and Luke has two paraphrases of it (Luke 24:46–49; Acts 1:8). Furthermore, all four gospels have earlier hints preparing the disciples for this witnessing mission (see sidebar). But as Jesus departs, he notes that his followers must wait for the Spirit to come to empower this mission (Luke 24:46–49; Acts 1:4–5, 8).

As noted in chapter 3, the Great Commission as phrased in Acts 1:8 contains something of a broad outline for the book of Acts. Empowered by the Holy Spirit, Jesus's followers will witness about him in three ethnogeographic arenas (sometimes identified generically as city, region, and world). "Jerusalem" is where the believers begin ministry—right where they find themselves (in Acts 1–7). The surrounding regions of "Judea and Samaria" is where the gospel message goes next (in Acts 8–12). Finally, the last half of Acts traces the spread of the gospel beyond Palestine to the known world, "the ends of the earth" (Acts 13–28).

The exact Greek phrase for "to the ends of the earth" (*heōs eschatou tēs gēs*) occurs only five times in ancient Greek (in the LXX of Isa 8:9; 48:20; 49:6; and 62:11; and in Pss. Sol. 1:4—a first-century BC work influenced by Isaiah).[16] In the poetic parallelism of Isaiah 49:6 (explicitly cited in Acts 13:47), the line "that my salvation may reach to

14. Jesus had earlier needed to stall a similar, overly immediate expectation of the kingdom even before his death and resurrection; see Luke 19:11.

15. See Robert P. Menzies, *Empowered for Witness: The Spirit in Luke-Acts*, JPTSup 6 (Sheffield: Sheffield Academic Press, 1994); and James B. Shelton, *Mighty in Word and Deed: The Role of the Holy Spirit in Luke-Acts* (Peabody, MA: Hendrickson, 1991).

16. See also two less exact parallels in 1 Macc 3:9 and Pss. Sol. 8:15 and the discussions in Barrett, *Acts*, 1:80; Joseph A. Fitzmyer, *The Acts of the Apostles*, AB 31 (New York: Doubleday, 1998), 206–7; and Keener, *Acts*, 1:707.

The Great Commission(s)

Jesus may well have reiterated his commissioning statement in different forms on different occasions: e.g., the statements of Matthew and John are said to have occurred in Galilee, and those of Luke-Acts appear to have occurred in Judea. Regardless of how often it may have been repeated, the NT reports of the Great Commission are obviously cohesive:

Matthew 28:18–20—"All authority in heaven and on earth has been given to me. Therefore go and make disciples of all nations, baptizing them in the name of the Father and of the Son and of the Holy Spirit, and teaching them to obey everything I have commanded you. And surely I am with you always, to the very end of the age."

Mark 16:15–16—"Go into all the world and preach the gospel to all creation. Whoever believes and is baptized will be saved, but whoever does not believe will be condemned." [This statement is an addition to Mark's Gospel in some later manuscripts.]

Luke 24:46–49—"This is what is written: The Messiah will suffer and rise from the dead on the third day, and repentance for the forgiveness of sins will be preached in his name to all nations, beginning at Jerusalem. You are witnesses of these things. I am going to send you what my Father has promised; but stay in the city until you have been clothed with power from on high."

Acts 1:8—"But you will receive power when the Holy Spirit comes on you; and you will be my witnesses in Jerusalem, and in all Judea and Samaria, and to the ends of the earth."

John 20:21—"Peace be with you! As the Father has sent me, I am sending you."

Other Statements—Notice also several anticipations of the Great Commission earlier in the Gospels: Matthew 10:5–42; Mark 6:7–13; Luke 9:1–6; 10:1–20; John 17:18.

the ends of the earth" repeats the idea of the previous line, "I will also make you a light to the Gentiles." Thus, "the ends of the earth" is not merely a geographic reference but is also a synonym for "the gentiles." Luke has a similar kind of parallelism in his two accounts of Jesus's commissioning statements: believers are to preach the gospel "to all nations [Greek: *ethnoi*], beginning at Jerusalem" (Luke 24:47), which is parallel to the "Jerusalem . . . to the ends of the earth" summary (Acts 1:8). These observations help us see that "the ends of the earth" as the goal of the Great Commission is best taken with an emphasis on its ethnic sense rather than a mere geographic sense; it's a reference to participating in the expansion of the gospel to all peoples.[17]

17. David W. Pao, "Jesus's Ascension and the Lukan Account of the Restoration of Israel," pp. 137–55 in Bryan and Pao, *Ascent into Heaven in Luke-Acts*, 145n37.

In Luke's versions of the Great Commission, Jesus's command to remain in Jerusalem until the Spirit arrived (Luke 24:49; Acts 1:4–5) is clearly a descriptive report by Luke about an instruction intended only for the first disciples; that is, there is no need for all believers today to move to, and remain in, Jerusalem! After all, the thing for which the believers were to wait in Jerusalem, the Spirit, comes in Acts 2, and the deadline for remaining in Jerusalem soon passes. As the story unfolds, however, we see that the Great Commission is not merely a descriptive command for the first-century believers present at the ascension. Rather, the Great Commission challenges all believers to participate in the expansion of the gospel to all peoples of the world.

Witnessing and Scripture

From Christopher J. H. Wright, *The Mission of God's People: A Biblical Theology of the Church's Mission*, Biblical Theology for Life (Grand Rapids: Zondervan, 2010), 175.

> All our witness to the Lord Jesus Christ and the saving power of the gospel is dependent on the trustworthiness of the Bible. The Scriptures point to him. Indeed Jesus himself used the language of witness to speak of the Scriptures that we now call the Old Testament: "You study the Scriptures diligently because you think that in them you possess eternal life. These are the very Scriptures that testify about me" (John 5:39). The Old Testament bore its witness to the one who came to fulfill God's promise. The New Testament bears witness to him through those who were, as Peter put it, "witnesses whom God had already chosen—by us who ate and drank with him after he rose from the dead" (Acts 10:41).
>
> The mission of God's people, then, is a witnessing mission—bearing witness to the Lord Jesus Christ. But all our witnessing is authenticated by the witness of those who were God's own chosen eyewitnesses. And their testimony is in our hands—God's Word through their words—our Bible.

6.3 THE ASCENSION (ACTS 1:9–11)

After discussing Jesus's final instructions for the apostles, Luke takes up a second topic from the four items he had mentioned in Acts 1:2: the ***ascension*** of Jesus into heaven. As noted, this is Luke's second account of the ascension (see Luke 24:50–53). Other NT writers make reference to the fact or results of Jesus's ascension (e.g., John 6:62; 20:17; Rom 8:34; Eph 1:20–22; 4:7–13; Phil 2:9–11; Col 3:1; 1 Tim 3:16; Heb 1:3; 4:14; 8:1–6; 9:24; 10:12; 12:2; 1 Pet 3:21–22), as does Luke (Luke 9:51; Acts 1:2, 22; 2:33–34; 3:21; 5:31–32; 7:55–56; cf. Luke 9:31; 24:26); but Luke is the only NT writer to narrate an account of the event, and he does so twice.

Significances of the Ascension

Scholars have proposed a variety of theological or narrative significances for Luke's accounts of Jesus physically ascending into heaven in view of the apostles (Luke 24:50-53 and Acts 1:9-11). Here are some of the most prominent suggestions.

- Jesus's bodily ascension is another confirmation of his bodily resurrection.
- Jesus's bodily ascension demonstrates that his departure from the earth was not merely another death.
- His ascension into heaven is evidence that Jesus has accomplished salvation for humanity.
- His ascension into heaven is a demonstration that Jesus has been exalted to an elevated status above all others.
- Jesus's bodily ascension gives evidence that an afterlife awaits all humans who follow Jesus.
- Jesus's bodily ascension gives promise that he will return to earth in like manner.
- The ascension account provides a fitting division of the story into two periods and marks the shift from Jesus's earthly ministry to his continued work through his disciples.
- Jesus's departure to the Father in heaven helps the readers of Luke's story to anticipate the sending of the promised Spirit from the Father.

This event is important to Luke, and scholars have proposed a variety of significances for it (see sidebar). I focus here on three reasons for Luke's emphasis on the ascension.

6.3.1 The Ascension Was a True Historical Event

The ancient world passed along several rumors of ascensions into heaven by heroes of the past (e.g., Hercules, Romulus, Julius Caesar, and Augustus), but few of the ancient Greco-Roman writers understood these ascension stories as historical records; they were mere legends told to honor deceased leaders.[18] In his short account of Jesus's ascension in Acts 1:9–11, Luke draws on the OT background of Daniel 7:13–14, where, after suffering, the "son of man" figure rides a cloud to the exalted position next to "the Ancient of Days" (see sidebar).[19] But in contrast to the Greco-Roman legends and the poetic visionary language of Daniel, Luke has an almost alarming fivefold repetition of the fact that the disciples observed this event happening. Jesus "was taken up before

18. See James Buchanan Wallace, "Benefactor and Paradigm: Viewing Jesus's Ascension in Luke-Acts through Greco-Roman Ascension Traditions," in Bryan and Pao, *Ascent into Heaven in Luke-Acts*, 83–107.

19. N. T. Wright, *The Resurrection of the Son of God* (Minneapolis: Fortress, 2003), 655; and Pao, "Jesus's Ascension and the Lukan Account of the Restoration of Israel," 144.

their very eyes" (1:9a) and hidden from "their sight" (1:9b) as they "were looking intently up into the sky as he was going" (1:10a); then an angelic envoy queries why they are "looking into the sky" (1:11a) and promise that Jesus will return "in the same way you have seen him go into heaven" (1:11b). With this repetition, Luke records Jesus's ascension as an actual historical occurrence: it was an observable event that has become a matter of testimony. Jesus physically rose from the dead and physically ascended into heaven.

Echoes of Daniel 7:13–14 in the Ascension Account of Acts 1:9–11

Daniel 7:13–14—"In my vision at night I looked, and there before me was one like a son of man, coming with the clouds of heaven. He approached the Ancient of Days and was led into his presence. He was given authority, glory and sovereign power; all nations and peoples of every language worshiped him. His dominion is an everlasting dominion that will not pass away, and his kingdom is one that will never be destroyed."

Acts 1:9–11—"After he said this, he was taken up before their very eyes, and a cloud hid him from their sight.

They were looking intently up into the sky as he was going, when suddenly two men dressed in white stood beside them. 'Men of Galilee,' they said, 'why do you stand here looking into the sky? This same Jesus, who has been taken from you into heaven, will come back in the same way you have seen him go into heaven.'"

6.3.2 Jesus the Lord Now Works from Heaven

Another point of repetition in the short space of these verses is the quadrupled phrase "into heaven" (*eis ton ouranon*) in Acts 1:10–11 (NIV renders the phrase as "into the sky" the first two times and "into heaven" the second two times). This repetition draws attention to the fact that the real Jesus who was here on earth has now gone into heaven. Luke's dual recounting of the ascension and its repeated heavenly vocabulary emphasizes Jesus's already established authority as exalted Lord.[20] Jesus has conquered death and secured salvation for humanity by advocating for us in the courts of heaven; Jesus is Lord over all the world and has a position of authority in heaven; Jesus still works in the world from heaven and will return from there some day.

Luke's emphasis on Jesus as securely positioned in heaven has led scholars to debate whether Luke means to portray Jesus as absent from the story after the ascension.

---

20. David K. Bryan, "A Revised Cosmic Hierarchy Revealed: Apocalyptic Literature and Jesus's Ascent in Luke's Gospel," pp. 61–82 in Bryan and Pao, *Ascent into Heaven in Luke-Acts*.

A close reading of Acts, however, suggests that the universally authoritative Jesus is still present and active in the story. Jesus makes appearances on several occasions even after his ascension (Acts 7:55–60; 9:4–6, 10–17; 18:9–10; 22:17–21; 23:11; cf. 10:13–15 and 11:7–9). Thus, while in heaven, Jesus nevertheless remains fully engaged in the story of Acts as Lord of all.[21] So Acts is the continuation of the story of Jesus. He is still present and active in the story but simply in a different manner. Jesus has gone into heaven from whence he continues his ministry on earth through his Spirit-empowered followers.

6.3.3 The Ascension Has a Helpful Storyline Function

In addition to defending the lordship of Jesus, Luke's double reporting of the ascension functions to display the continuation of Jesus's ministry through his apostolic church. The ascension functions as a transitional "hand-off" episode that closes the first half of the story (i.e., the Gospel of Luke) and launches the second half of the story (i.e., the book of Acts) and shows that the ministry Jesus began in person is now turned over to Jesus's followers, who are charged with continuing Jesus's work until his return.[22]

Thus, the ascension of Jesus becomes an intentional turning point for the single, two-part story Luke is telling. With his reference to his "former book" (Acts 1:1), Luke wants his audience to recognize that, even if they are two different books, the Gospel of Luke and the book of Acts are in fact not two different stories. The story of the church is a continuation of the story of Jesus Christ, turned now in the direction in which the story was always intended to go. The apostles were the commissioned witnesses of the resurrected Christ who ascended into heaven. From heaven this same Jesus continues his work in the world through the church as it is empowered by the Holy Spirit, whom Jesus will soon send.

6.4 THE COMPLETION OF THE TWELVE (ACTS 1:12–26)

Imitating the style of the LXX version of Scripture, Luke writes the story of Jesus as a continuation of the biblical story. To the Jewish way of thinking, the twelve tribes of Israel (see Gen 35:22–26; Num 1:1–54) gave a symbolic value to the number twelve as representative of the people of God.[23] And the number twelve is sometimes considered

---

21. Steve Walton, "Jesus, Present and/or Absent? The Presence and Presentation of Jesus as a character in the Book of Acts," pp. 123–40 in *Characters and Characterization in Luke-Acts*, ed. Frank Dicken and Julia Snyder, LNTS 548 (London: T&T Clark, 2016): 128; cf. Matthew Sleeman, *Geography and the Ascension Narrative in Acts*, SNTSMS 146 (Cambridge: Cambridge University Press, 2009); and Arie W. Zwiep, *Christ, the Spirit and the Community of God: Essays on the Acts of the Apostles*, WUNT 2.293 (Tübingen: Mohr Siebeck, 2010), 66.

22. Porter, "The Unity of Luke-Acts and the Ascension Narratives,"134–35.

23. See Scot McKnight, "Jesus and the Twelve," in *Key Events in the Life of the Historical Jesus: A Collaborative Exploration of Context and Coherence*, ed. Darrell L. Bock and Robert L. Webb (Grand Rapids: Eerdmans, 2009), 181–214.

an indication of order and associated with God's elective purposes.[24] Thus, in calling the people of God together to embrace God's new covenant work, Jesus uncoincidentally selected twelve to serve as apostles (Luke 6:13; cf. Matt 19:28; Luke 22:30; see also Rev 21:14). In picturing the twelve tribes of Israel, the twelve apostles demonstrate the continuity between following Jesus and following the God of Israel.

But now in adjusting to life after the exaltation of Jesus, the community of believers recognizes that the defection of ***Judas Iscariot*** has depleted their foundation of twelve official witnesses to the life and ministry of Jesus. So the group decides to replace Judas, and with a lengthy report, Luke clarifies for his readers that this completion of the twelve apostles has been properly accomplished in a scriptural fashion.[25]

Luke's Lists of the Apostles

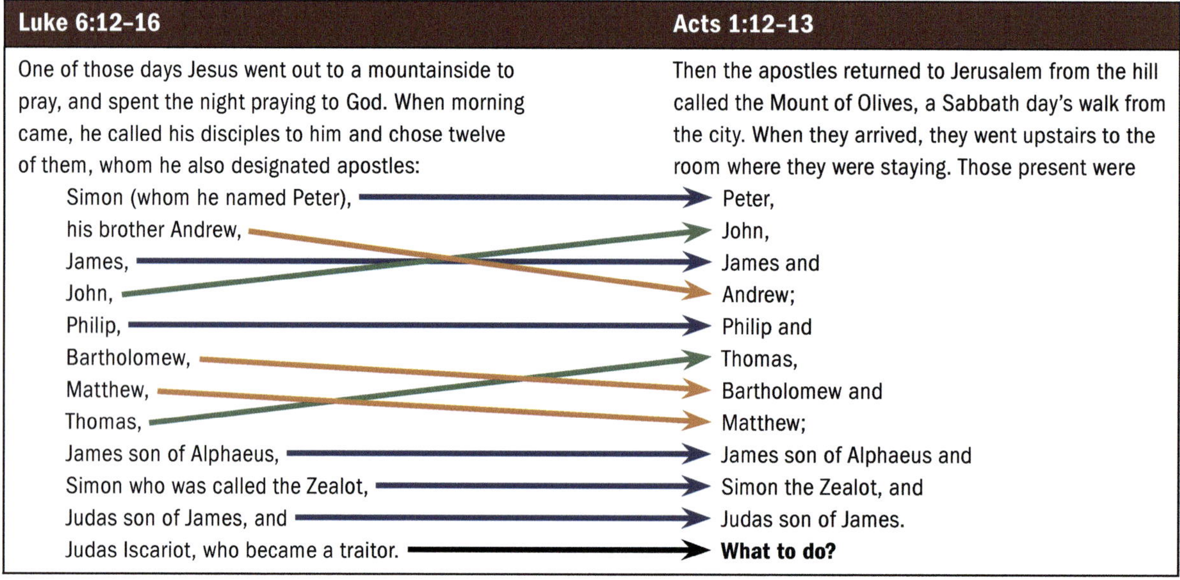

6.4.1 The Nascent Community

After watching the ascension on the ***Mount of Olives***, the believers return to Jerusalem in keeping with Jesus's command to wait in ***Jerusalem*** for the Spirit to come (Acts 1:12). Luke names some of the community members, people familiar to us from Luke's first volume, including the eleven apostles "along with the women and Mary the mother of Jesus, and with his brothers" (1:13–14). Obviously, this is not a complete listing of all the believers, which was a group of about 120 (1:15). Rather,

24. See Keith A. Burton, "Numbers," *EDB*, 973–74.
25. See Zwiep, *Christ, the Spirit and the Community of God*, 75–76.

Luke uses the list to note specifically the shortfall that is now felt in the apostolic band: with Judas defecting, there were only eleven apostles now (already noted in Luke 24:9). Having portrayed prayer as a regular activity in the life of Jesus (see Luke 3:21; 5:16; 6:12; 9:18, 28–29; 11:1–13; 22:32, 39–45), Luke shows prayer as a regular activity of the nascent community (Acts 1:14). And dealing with Judas's defection soon becomes a topic of prayer.

6.4.2 The Historical Occasion

Between the ascension of Jesus and the coming of the Holy Spirit ("in those days," Acts 1:15), Peter addresses the group of believers about the historical situation in which they now find themselves (Acts 1:16–22). Peter opens his address with a comment on the necessity of Scripture being fulfilled, noting that the Holy Spirit speaks through the writers of Scripture. When used with reference to Scripture, the term "fulfill" (*plēroō* in 1:16a) is frequently understood in an overly simplistic manner that assumes a specific forward-looking OT prediction is "fulfilled" when it meets its one-time anticipated NT outcome. This certainly happens sometimes, but completion of predictive prophecy is not the only way NT writers like Luke utilize the term "fulfill." Sometimes the term "fulfill" refers to promises kept not merely once but over and over again or to some other OT pattern that is still followed. And sometimes a writer uses "fulfill" in reference to a prefigurement of some kind (e.g., a person or an institution) that comes to light in some escalated form.[26]

With this more robust understanding of Scripture fulfillment, we can recognize that Peter finds a couple of psalms of David to be "concerning" (Greek: *peri*) Judas without necessitating that the psalms be predictive prophecies about Judas. Rather, Peter finds a pattern to be followed regarding how discovered enemies of the king were to be treated. Peter describes Judas as the one "who served as guide for those who arrested Jesus" (Acts 1:16b) even though he had been "one of our number and shared in our ministry" as a member of the twelve apostles (1:17). Earlier, Luke had noted that Judas, even though he was "one of the Twelve," was in league with Satan (Luke 22:3–6, 47–53) and that he would eventually be recognized as a "traitor" (Luke 6:16). Peter's suggestion will be that Judas needs to be replaced because he has been discovered to be a defector from following Jesus; he is not to be merely succeeded due to his untimely death.[27]

26. See particularly "πληρόω," *NIDNTTE* 3:784–93; and John Goldingay, *Reading Jesus's Bible: How the New Testament Helps Us Understand the Old Testament* (Grand Rapids: Eerdmans, 2017), 65–67.

27. There has been some scholarly debate regarding the eternal fate of Judas, esp. with reference to the Matthean account of his demise. Did Judas repentantly turn from his sinful betrayal of Jesus or merely remorsefully, yet hopelessly, acknowledge it? See now Catherine Sider Hamilton, "The Death of Judas in Matthew: Matthew 27:9 Reconsidered," *JBL* 137 (2018): 419–37.

The Death of Judas in Acts 1:18–19 and Matthew 27:3–10

Luke's account in Acts of the death of Judas Iscariot differs from that of Matthew in his gospel. There are three apparent contradictions between the accounts:

- Was it Judas who bought the field (Acts 1:18) or the chief priests who purchased it (Matt 27:6–7)?
- Was his death because he "fell headlong" (Acts 1:18) or "hanged himself" (Matt 27:5)?
- Was the field called "Field of Blood" because Judas died and was buried there (Acts 1:19) or because it was purchased with blood money (Matt 27:6–8)?

Possible Solutions

- The chief priests purchased the field using Judas's money (Matt 27:6–7), so Luke is correct in saying that Judas "acquired" the field ("acquired" is a proper translation for the Greek term rendered "bought" in Acts 1:18 NIV).
- Judas may have hung himself (Matt 27:5) such that the mechanism broke, causing him to fall headlong and burst open (Acts 1:18). Or after death, Judas's body may have been thrown and burst in the field.
- "Field of Blood" seems to be a doubly fitting label for a field purchased with blood money (Matt 27:6–8) and where the bloody dead bodies of strangers can be buried (Acts 1:19; Matt 27:7).

For those concerned to respect both Matthew and Luke as NT writers, knowing with certainty the actual resolutions to these difficulties is not necessary for affirming that solutions are possible.

Acts 1:18–19	Matt 27:3–10
[18] With the payment he received for his wickedness, Judas bought a field; there he fell headlong, his body burst open and all his intestines spilled out. [19] Everyone in Jerusalem heard about this, so they called that field in their language Akeldama, that is, Field of Blood.	[3] When Judas, who had betrayed him, saw that Jesus was condemned, he was seized with remorse and returned the thirty pieces of silver to the chief priests and the elders. [4] "I have sinned," he said, "for I have betrayed innocent blood." "What is that to us?" they replied. "That's your responsibility." [5] So Judas threw the money into the temple and left. Then he went away and hanged himself. [6] The chief priests picked up the coins and said, "It is against the law to put this into the treasury, since it is blood money." [7] So they decided to use the money to buy the potter's field as a burial place for foreigners. [8] That is why it has been called the Field of Blood to this day. [9] Then what was spoken by Jeremiah the prophet was fulfilled: "They took the thirty pieces of silver, the price set on him by the people of Israel, [10] and they used them to buy the potter's field, as the Lord commanded me."

Luke inserts here a parenthetical remark to inform the reader of the whereabouts of Judas. Intriguingly, Matthew has also provided a description of the death of Judas (Matt 27:3–10), but there are three apparent discrepancies between the two accounts. These questions, however, are not as problematic as some might imagine (see sidebar).

"Fulfillment" of Scripture

For the ways in which the New Testament utilizes the Hebrew Scriptures, it is best to see at least three possible implications for the "fulfillment" of Scripture. These three nuances of "fulfillment" can be at work separately or together in the New Testament's use of the Hebrew Scriptures.

I. ***Predictive Prophecy***—Scripture is "fulfilled" in this sense when a prediction comes true.

   Example: First-century Jews expected a specific fulfillment of Moses's prediction of a prophet like him coming to them (see Deut 18:15 used in Acts 3:22–23a; 7:37; cf. "the one who is to come" in Luke 7:18–35).

II. ***Promising Pattern***—Scripture is "fulfilled" in this sense when a promise is still kept or some other *pattern* is still followed.

   Example: The "day of the Lord" was the anticipated time of God's intervention in history to bring judgment on the unfaithful (e.g., Isa 2:1–22; 13:1–13; Joel 2:1–11; Amos 5:18–20) and blessing on the faithful (e.g., Isa 11:10–12; Joel 3:14–18; Amos 9:11–15). Initial fulfillments of this judgment and blessing came to OT Israel. The arrival of the Holy Spirit (see Acts 2:17–21 specifically citing Joel 2:28–32) and the spread of the gospel to the gentiles (see Acts 15:16b–17 specifically citing Amos 9:11–12) indicate a further "filling out" of this pattern. But a final eschatological fulfillment of this pattern is still anticipated (see Acts 3:19–21; 10:42; 24:25; 2 Pet 3:10–14).

III. ***Prefigurement (a.k.a. Typology)***—Scripture is "fulfilled" in this sense when a prefigured person, place, event, or institution reaches an escalated form of some kind.

   Example: David is a prefigurement (a "type") of the Messiah (the "antitype") (see the use of Ps 2 in Luke 3:22; 9:35; Acts 4:25–26; 13:33 comparing royal crises the king of Israel faced to those Jesus faced).

6.4.3 The Scriptural Warrant and Criteria for Replacing Judas

After his parenthetical description of the demise of Judas, Luke returns to his account of Peter's address where he quotes from Psalm 69:25 and Psalm 109:8. As indicated previously, Peter finds in these two psalms of David not predictive prophecies about Judas but a pattern to follow in a situation like this one concerning Judas. In their original settings, the two psalms that Peter cites describe how the enemies of God are to be treated when they reject God's purposes. Thus, Peter suggests that Judas fits into the pattern of how those who oppose God are to be treated.[28] If an enemy of the Israelite

28. Darrell L. Bock, *A Theology of Luke and Acts: God's Promised Program, Realized for All Nations*, Biblical Theology of the New Testament (Grand Rapids: Zondervan, 2012), 420.

king over God's people was to be replaced, then certainly an enemy of the ultimate King over God's people should be treated in similar fashion. Understanding Jesus to be the messianic Davidic king, Peter uses these psalms as a pattern to conclude that an enemy of the King, like Judas, should be removed from his office ("May his place be deserted") and that another should be named to the apostolic band ("let another take his place of leadership").

After giving this scriptural warrant for his suggestion, Peter closes his address with a suggestion of criteria for finding worthy candidates for the replacement (Acts 1:21–22a). Like the rest of the apostles, the disciple selected to take Judas's now vacant place should be someone who had been a follower of Jesus from the very beginning of Jesus's ministry (i.e., Jesus's baptism by John the Baptist) all the way to the very end of Jesus's ministry (i.e., the ascension). While Judas Iscariot may have been with Jesus from the beginning, he clearly did not remain with the group to the end of Jesus's ministry; Judas missed out on seeing Jesus's resurrection and ascension. To complete the symbolic foundation of the renewed people of God, the young community needs a twelfth person who has experienced the whole earthly ministry of Jesus. As Peter expresses it here, giving eyewitness testimony to Jesus's ministry and resurrection was the virtual job description for the apostolic band: "For one of these must become a witness with us of his resurrection" (1:22b).

6.4.4 The Decision-Making Process

Given Luke's earlier description of Jesus's selection of the apostles—i.e., that he had chosen twelve out of the "large crowd of his disciples" (see Luke 6:12–17)—it is perhaps no surprise that they can come up with more candidates than they need. They needed only one person, but they discover that two (otherwise unknown) men fit the criteria. In naming them, Luke tells us a little more about the first candidate—the one not selected: he is "Joseph called Barsabbas (also known as Justus)" (Acts 1:23). Perhaps he was related to Judas Barsabbas mentioned later in the story (15:22), and perhaps the nickname Justus is provided to distinguish him from other Josephs in the story (e.g., Joseph from Arimathea; Luke 23:50–51). The second candidate, Matthias, is simply named and is specifically mentioned only here in the New Testament (Acts 1:23, 26).

With the two candidates named, the community prays to the "Lord," by which Luke most likely means Jesus, as he was credited for choosing the apostles in the first place (1:2), and they are asking him now to "show us which of these two you have chosen" (1:24). Judas's defection is mentioned in the prayer in clear terms: they need a substitute "to take over this apostolic ministry, which Judas left to go where he belongs" (or "to his own place"; 1:25 ESV), which some scholars suggest as an indication of Judas's finalized apostasy. The point here is that the believers are communicating to the Lord about their decision based on what they know, and they are asking for his help, certain that he knows more than they do.

The final selection of Judas's replacement is conducted by casting lots (1:26). In several decision-making circumstances in the Hebrew Scriptures, people trusted God to reveal his will through their use of lots, as Proverbs 16:33 indicates: "The lot is cast into the lap, but its every decision is from the LORD." For example, priests and Levites received their duty assignments by use of lots (e.g., 1 Chr 24:5, 31; 25:8; 26:13–16; cf. Luke 1:8–9). Even so, we are unclear about exactly what ***casting lots*** (*didōmi klērous*) was in antiquity. It appears that they were small stones or pieces of wood (the OT Hebrew word originally meant "stone" or "pebble"), and they are always referred to as being thrown or shaken or cast in decision-making settings.[29] This description lends credence to the suggestions of throwing dice or drawing straws as modern parallels for randomized selections (cf. at 1:26 "drew names" CEV).

6.4.5 Decision-Making Today

Is casting lots the best way to make decisions today? Is the use of lots in Acts 1 a mere historical description or is it meant to somehow be prescriptive for Christian decision-making? Acts 1:26 is the last NT mention of casting lots; even in his accounts of the selection of other church leaders (e.g., 6:1–6; 14:23), Luke does not mention the use of lots. Had Luke intended to endorse the use of lots for all believers as a model for all their decision-making, it seems that his story would clarify this with more mentions of their use. Conversely, some commentators have suggested that even the decision to replace Judas with Matthias (both the method and the result) was wrong and that the new twelfth apostle should have been Paul.[30] Luke, however, gives no indication that the replacement of Judas with Matthias was a mistaken action. On the contrary, he portrays the group as well intentioned, utilizing Scripture, and seeking the Lord's guidance in prayer.[31] Without a hint of regret, Luke specifies that ***Matthias*** was added to the "eleven apostles" (1:26), and he comments later about the leadership of "***the Twelve***" (6:2), which obviously includes Matthias and not the as-of-yet unknown Paul.

Even among those who see the nascent church as correctly replacing Judas with Matthias, the opinion is often expressed that such chance methods are no longer

---

29. For examples of the use of lots in political decisions, see Cicero, *Verr.* 1.8.21; in military decisions, see Tacitus, *Hist.* 2.41 and *Ann.* 3.21; in legal decisions, see Quintilian, *Decl.* 250; and in pairing contestants in the ancient Olympic Games, see Lucian, *Hermot.* 39. See Julye Bidmead, "Lots," *EDB*, 825; cf. Floyd E. Hamilton, "Lots," *ZEB* 3:1110–111. For a very different view, see Jared M. August, "'Casting Lots'? An Alternative Reading of Acts 1:26," *BBR* 31 (2021): 356–67.

30. See the discussions in Richard N. Longenecker, "Acts," pp. 663–1102 in *Luke-Acts*, vol. 10 of *The Expositor's Bible Commentary*, ed. Tremper Longman III and David E. Garland, rev. ed. (Grand Rapids: Zondervan, 2007), 732; and Arie W. Zwiep, *Judas and the Choice of Matthias: A Study on Context and Concern of Acts 1:15–26*, WUNT 2.187 (Tübingen: Mohr Siebeck, 2004), 172–74.

31. See also Bock, *A Theology of Luke and Acts*, 420.

necessary or valid after the coming of the Holy Spirit.[32] While Luke never mentions lots again in Acts, on many occasions he notes that the believers are guided and empowered by the Holy Spirit. Obviously, being directed by the Spirit is Luke's intention for believers everywhere. But out of fairness to the believers in Acts 1, we should be clear that Luke does *not* portray their decision as one of mere blind chance. Rather, the believers found a pattern in Scripture that applied to their circumstances, crafted well-defined criteria for applying it, and then looked for candidates who plainly met the criteria. It was not until they reached the place of having more candidates than they needed (and what a great position to be in!), that they resorted to a randomized, tie-breaking mechanism over which God was in control (Prov 16:33). And even then, they did not move ahead without praying first.

When described in this way, the young church's decision-making process looks like a potentially helpful pattern for decision-making. Of course, with the selection of Matthias, the twelve apostolic witnesses to the resurrection are complete, and there is no more need for us to choose additional apostles today; even as the Twelve all eventually died (like the apostle James in Acts 12:2), the early church never replaced any of them. Thus, for us today the selection of an apostle in Acts is only descriptive of what occurred back then. On the other hand, we see the church in Acts selecting various other kinds of leaders and making other sorts of decisions as well (e.g., Acts 6:1–6; 13:1–3).

The Acts 1 Decision-Making Process

Contrary to what some people think, the decision-making process utilized in replacing Judas Iscariot was not completely by chance. The following steps were taken in the process:

I. Scriptural precedent was observed.
II. Sensible criteria were determined according to Jesus's life.
III. Selection of candidates who meet the criteria.
IV. Submissive prayer asking for the Lord's will to be accomplished.
V. Surrender to a tiebreaker when the options are truly equal.

Sometimes people want to skip down to steps IV and V. For example, "Dear Lord, make the next person who calls me be the person I should marry. Amen." But that would be poor and unbiblical decision-making!

32. E.g., Ajith Fernando, *Acts*, The NIV Application Commentary (Grand Rapids: Zondervan, 1998), 79; David G. Peterson, *The Acts of the Apostles*, Pillar New Testament Commentary (Grand Rapids: Eerdmans, 2009), 128–29; contra Longenecker, "Acts," 731; and Schnabel, *Acts* 103.

So the decision-making process observed in Acts 1 can prove helpful for us. If more individual believers and church groups made decisions by consulting Scripture, applying its patterns to their own circumstances, formulating sensible criteria, looking for qualified options that meet the criteria, and praying about the decision, even apart from randomized selection mechanisms, it seems that better decisions would most likely be the result, especially with the Spirit speaking in our hearts at every stage along the way.

6.5 THE PROMISED SPIRIT IS POURED OUT FOR THE CHURCH (ACTS 2:1–41)

In the forty days between his resurrection and ascension, Jesus talked with the disciples about several things, including the promise of the Spirit (Acts 1:4–5; cf. Luke 24:49). The Holy Spirit was to empower the ministry of Jesus's followers as they continued living out the Jesus story (Acts 1:8). Luke gets to this part of the story early in Acts. Jesus was crucified at Passover time (Luke 22:7) and after the resurrection appeared to the apostles over a forty-day period (Acts 1:3) before ascending into heaven. The Holy Spirit came during the Pentecost festival (Acts 2:1), which is fifty days after Passover, so that means that the "few days" until the coming of the Spirit (Acts 1:5) turns out to be about ten days after the ascension.

6.5.1 The Event on the Pentecost Holiday (2:1–13)

As one of the three annual Jewish pilgrimage holidays (see sidebar), the Festival of Weeks occurred seven weeks after Passover and also became known by the Greek word for "fiftieth," ***Pentecost***, for it was held the fiftieth day after Passover. It is a one-day harvest festival at the close of the early summer grain harvest (see Exod 23:16; 34:22; Lev 23:15–22; Num 28:26; Deut 16:9–12).[33] Eventually it became associated with the giving of the law at Mount Sinai. Philo describes the giving of the law in a manner similar to Luke's description of the giving of the Spirit in Acts 2 (see sidebar). There are several parallels here between the reception of the law and the reception of the Spirit, including miraculous sights and sounds and the leader (Moses/Jesus) going up into God's presence to bring God's provision for guidance to the people.[34] Interestingly, Luke uses a "fulfillment" word (Greek: *symplēroō*) to say the day of Pentecost "came" (Acts 2:1). "For Luke it may be more than ironic that the inauguration of the new

33. With a bit of insensitivity toward Pentecost being an annual Jewish holiday, Christians sometimes talk about the historic coming of the Holy Spirit in Acts 2 with the simple label of "Pentecost," as if Pentecost and the coming of the Holy Spirit are the same thing. But this misapplication of the word has been ensconced in popular parlance, even to the point of utilizing the adjectival form of the word—*Pentecostal*—for people and denominations who have a particular focus on an experience with the Holy Spirit.

34. See Zwiep, *Christ, the Spirit and the Community of God*, 130.

covenant through Jesus took place at the time when Israel celebrated the establishment of the first covenant."[35] Indeed, the arrival of the Holy Spirit at Pentecost accentuates the role of the Spirit in fulfilling and superseding the OT law.[36]

The Three Great Pilgrimage Festivals in First-Century Judaism

"Three times a year all your men must appear before the LORD your God at the place he will choose: at the Festival of Unleavened Bread, the Festival of Weeks and the Festival of Tabernacles" (Deut 16:16; cf. 2 Chr 8:13).

Festival of	OT Description	Luke-Acts Mention
Unleavened Bread (a.k.a. Passover)	Exod 12:1-20; Lev 23:5-8; Num 28:16-25; Deut 16:1-8	Luke 2:41; 22:1, 7-20; Acts 12:1-4
Weeks (a.k.a. Pentecost)	Lev 23:15-22; Num 28:26-31; Deut 16:9-12	Acts 2:1-4; 20:16
Tabernacles/Booths (a.k.a. Sukkoth)	Lev 23:33-43; Num 29:12-38; Deut 16:13-15	Luke 9:28-36

For more on Jewish festivals (or feasts), see Jack P. Lewis, "Feasts," *ZEB* 2:559-65.

The experience of the believers in Acts 2 includes several signs of the Spirit: the sound of wind (2:2), flames of fire (2:3), and speaking in other languages (2:4). It is somewhat playful of Luke to note that the sound of the blowing violent wind "filled" (Greek: *plēroō*) the whole house and then later that the believers were "filled" (Greek: *pimplēmi*) with the Holy Spirit. In the Hebrew Scriptures, the life-giving presence of God's Spirit is sometimes pictured by wind (e.g., 1 Kgs 19:11; Ezek 37:1–14; cf. John 3:8). A second sign was a visual one: "tongues of fire that separated and came to rest on each of them" (Acts 2:3). In the Hebrew Scriptures fire sometimes serves as a sign of God's presence (e.g., Exod 3:2–6; 13:21; 19:18; 1 Kgs 19:12) and pictures purification and judgment (e.g., Deut 32:22; Ezek 22:17–22). In his gospel Luke recounts John the Baptist's prediction that Jesus would "baptize you with the Holy Spirit and fire" (Luke 3:16; cf. 12:49). With more word play, Luke describes the shape of the flames as "tongues" (Greek: *glōssa*) of fire (Acts 2:3), the same word he uses to describe the third sign: the speaking in other "tongues [languages]" (Greek: *glōssa*) that the Spirit enables (2:4).

The word for "tongue" (*glōssa*) is about as flexible in Greek as it is in English. That is, a "tongue" can be the muscular mouth organ, something in the shape of the muscular mouth organ, or a spoken language. While some want to define the verbal phenomenon

35. Storm, *Living Lord, Empowering Spirit, Testifying People*, 25–26.

36. Clinton E. Arnold, "Acts," vol. 2B of *ZIBBCNT*, ed. Clinton E. Arnold (Grand Rapids: Zondervan, 2002), 15.

in Acts 2 as ecstatic speech (i.e., unrecognizable utterances delivered in a state of ecstasy, a.k.a. glossolalia), Luke is unmistakable here that these were real human languages. Not only does he interchange the word "tongues" with the Greek term for "dialects" (*dialektos*; 2:6, 8—NIV has "language" and "native language," respectively), he also gives a list of the countries where the real human languages were spoken (2:9–11) (see sidebar).

The Countries and Languages Reflected in Acts 2:9–11

Countries	Local Dialects	What Is Known about Judaism There
1. Parthia 2. Media 3. Elam 4. Mesopotamia	Aramaic, Parthian, Iranian	This eastern region of the world (modern Iran and Iraq) is where the tribes of OT Israel were exiled under Assyria (722 BC) and later under Babylon (586 BC). Although they were permitted to return to Israel during the Persian Empire (5th cent. BC), many chose to stay. There may have been hundreds of thousands of Jews in this region in the NT era.
5. Judea	Aramaic, Hebrew	Jerusalem was in this Roman province. Jews from all the surrounding villages streamed to Jerusalem for the festivals.
6. Cappadocia 7. Pontus 8. Asia 9. Phrygia 10. Pamphylia	Numerous local dialects include Phrygian, Pisidian, Lydian, Carian, Lycian, Celtic, Lycaonian, et al.	These five countries were all ethnic territories or Roman provinces of Asia Minor (modern-day Turkey). There are numerous literary texts and archaeological evidences illustrating the extensive Jewish presence in Asia Minor from the second century BC. The earliest Jewish presence can be traced to the late sixth or fifth century BC.
11. Egypt	(pre-) Coptic	Egypt had one of the largest Jewish communities in the world in the NT era; Philo reports one million Jews in that country. The date of origin for the Coptic phase of the Egyptian language, however, is debated, and in the first century it may have still been in its late Demotic phase just prior to Coptic.
12. Libya (Cyrene)	Latin, Numidian	There is considerable evidence for Jewish presence in North Africa, especially in the city of Cyrene.
13. Rome	Latin	Jews established a colony in Rome during the second century BC. The Roman general Pompey brought a great number from Palestine to the city in 62 BC. By some estimates the Jewish population in Rome swelled to as high as fifty thousand by the first century AD.
14. Crete	Greek	First-century Jewish writer Philo (*Embassy*, 282) says the islands of Euboea, Cyprus, and Crete were "full of Jewish colonies."
15. Arabia	Nabatean (a branch of Aramaic), Aramaic, Arabic	This region of the Nabatean Arabs was to the east of the Jordan River and to the south of Palestine with Petra as its capital, about fifty miles south of the Dead Sea. There is ample evidence of Jewish presence in the key cities and in the territory.

Adapted and simplified from Arnold, "Acts," 17.

Philo's Description of the Giving of the Law

Philo Judaeus, a first-century Jewish writer from Alexandria, Egypt (ca. 20 BC–AD 50) describes the giving of the OT law in terms somewhat similar to Luke's description of the coming of the Holy Spirit in Acts 2.

Philo, *On the Decalogue* 11 §46 (ca. AD 40–49)

> Then from the midst of the fire that streamed from heaven there sounded forth to their utter amazement a voice, for the flame became articulate speech in the language familiar to the audience, and so clearly and distinctly were the words formed by it that they seemed to see rather than hear them.

It is worth noting that nothing in Acts 2 indicates that the Holy Spirit would never cause any other believers to speak in other unlearned human languages, but there is also nothing to indicate that all believers everywhere must so speak (cf. 1 Cor 12:29–30, where Paul notes that not all believers have the gift of speaking in tongues).

The different languages are useful as the Jewish holiday had attracted to Jerusalem a large number of "God-fearing Jews from every nation under heaven" (Acts 2:5). While most are amazed and perplexed at hearing the wonders of God being proclaimed in languages that Galilean fishermen do not learn (2:6–8, 12), some suggest that the believers are simply babbling as the result of being drunk with wine (2:13). Such comments as these lead Peter to address the crowd to dispense with wrong impressions and to answer their stated question, "What does this mean?" (2:12).

6.5.2 The Sermon by Peter (2:14–39)

Peter repeatedly addresses the gathered crowd as Jews (2:14, 22, 29, cf. v. 37), explaining that their OT Scriptures are being fulfilled right before their very eyes (and ears!). Indeed, Peter's sermon touches on three Scripture passages and makes the point that Jesus fulfills scriptural prophecy in ways that a faithful Jewish crowd should be able to recognize (see sidebar).

Peter first addresses the suggestion that the clamor of speaking is the result of being drunk with wine. The contrast offered here—distinguishing being filled with the Spirit (Acts 2:4) and being drunk with wine (2:13, 15)—may well bring to mind a similar contrast written by Paul: "Do not get drunk on wine, which leads to debauchery. Instead, be filled with the Spirit" (Eph 5:18). The liquid metaphor "to be filled" with a thing speaks of being directed, empowered, and characterized by that thing. Even as we do in our day-to-day interactions, Luke uses the "filled" metaphor with many concepts: wisdom (Luke 2:40); wrath or fury (4:28; 6:11 ESV); awe (5:26); joy

(Acts 2:28; 13:52); wonder and amazement (3:10); jealousy (5:17; 13:45); confusion (19:29 ESV); and even Satan (5:3). In all these matters, the person filled with a thing is directed, empowered, and characterized by that thing. Likewise, the Spirit-filled person is directed, empowered, and characterized by the Spirit. The result of being filled with the Holy Spirit in Luke-Acts is not always speaking in other languages. It variously results in speaking prophetically (Luke 1:67), defending the gospel (Acts 4:8), speaking with boldness (4:31), confronting opponents (13:9), or being joyful (13:52). The Spirit-filled person is guided, strengthened, and typified by the Spirit.

The Role of the Holy Spirit in Acts: Empowerment, Direction, and Characterization

From Timothy C. Tennent, *Invitation to World Missions: A Trinitarian Missiology for the Twenty-first Century* (Grand Rapids: Kregel, 2010), 412–13 (emphasis original).

There are three major themes that summarize the purpose and work of the Holy Spirit in the life of the early church.

First, *the Holy Spirit empowers the church for global mission. . . .*

Second, *the Holy Spirit endues the church with God's authority. . . .*

Third, *the Holy Spirit extends the inbreaking of the New Creation through the powerful manifestation of signs and wonders and holiness of life.*

Rather than drunkenness, Peter explains that the language phenomenon is the result of Scripture being fulfilled, and he highlights three passages. Peter first cites ***Joel*** 2:28–32 (Acts 2:16–21) to explain that the declaration of God's wonders in unlearned languages displays that the prophetic Spirit of the end times has come. The Spirit's arrival is evidence that the long-awaited new era has commenced, and salvation can be declared in the name of the Lord. If the people need more proof, they can simply recall the miraculous life and ministry of Jesus, including his resurrection (2:22–24). Then, having mentioned Jesus's resurrection, Peter cites Psalm 16:8–11 (Acts 2:25–28) to note more specifically that Jesus is David's promised heir, the long-awaited Messiah, proven by his rising from the dead (2:29–32). Finally, Peter notes that Jesus's pouring out of the Holy Spirit is proof that he has been exalted as the Messiah (2:33), an exaltation that is pictured in Psalm 110:1 (Acts 2:34–35). Thus, in pointing to Jesus, Peter delivers the punchline: "Therefore let all Israel be assured of this: God has made this Jesus, whom you crucified, both Lord and Messiah" (2:36).

Hearing about this fulfillment of Scripture, the people are convicted (i.e., "cut to the heart"; 2:37) and ask what they should do. Peter replies with an invitation to faith in Jesus as the Messiah (i.e., Christ): "Repent and be baptized, every one of you, in the name of Jesus Christ for the forgiveness of your sins. And you will receive the gift of the Holy Spirit" (2:38). Following Jesus as the Messiah and receiving the Holy Spirit was not merely for the twelve original apostles or for the 120 believers gathered on that day of Pentecost; it is for everyone. "The promise is for you and your children and for all who are far off—for all whom the Lord our God will call" (2:39). Repentance from sin and faith in Jesus is the avenue each of us must travel to arrive at forgiveness of sins and to become part of the people of God. And in doing so we receive the Holy Spirit as a gift, a gift that can direct, empower, and characterize our lives as individuals and as a community.

The Gospel Message in Summary

According to John R. W. Stott, the gospel message as found in Acts can be outlined in four parts, each part with two components. The following is a distillation and adaptation of Stott's summary from Stott, *Message of Acts*, 80–81.

1. **The Gospel Events**—actual happenings in history.
    i. *Jesus's death* serves as punishment for our sins.
    ii. *Jesus's resurrection* (and exaltation) secures forgiveness and life for all believers.
2. **The Gospel Witnesses**—those testifying to the truth of the gospel.
    i. The *OT Scriptures* prophesied about the gospel events.
    ii. The *apostles* were eyewitnesses to the historic gospel events fulfilling Scripture.
3. **The Gospel Promises**—good things offered to those who believe the gospel.
    i. The *forgiveness of our sins* is a cleaning up of our past.
    ii. The gift of *the Holy Spirit* makes us new people moving into the future.
4. **The Gospel Conditions**—because the gospel is not imposed on us.
    i. *Repentance* is a radical turning away from sin.
    ii. *Faith* is a radical turning to Jesus Christ as Savior and Lord.

Moses's Wish Finally Fulfilled

In the wilderness of Sinai, when the Lord distributed some of the power of the Spirit from Moses onto seventy of the Israelite elders (Num 11:16–30), Moses expressed this wish: "I wish that all the Lord's people were prophets and that the Lord would put his Spirit on them!" (Num 11:29). Now in Acts 2, Luke reports Peter's promise, which shows Moses's wish finally being fulfilled: "Repent and be baptized, every one of you, in the name of Jesus Christ for the forgiveness of your sins. And you will receive the gift of the Holy Spirit. The promise is for you and your children and for all who are far off—for all whom the Lord our God will call" (Acts 2:38–39).

Peter's Sermon on Pentecost (Acts 2:14–39)

1. **Introduction** (Acts 2:14–15).
2. **Joel 2:28–32**—The prophetic Spirit of the end times has arrived declaring God's wonders as proven in Jesus's life and ministry (Acts 2:16–24; cf. Luke 24:47–48).
3. **Psalm 16:8–11**—Jesus is David's promised heir who, although he suffered, is proven to be the long-awaited Messiah by Jesus's resurrection (Acts 2:25–32; cf. Luke 24:46).
4. **Psalm 110:1**—Jesus is exalted to God's throne as proven by Jesus's pouring out the Spirit (Acts 2:33–36; cf. Luke 24:49).
5. **Response**: "Repent and be baptized, every one of you, in the name of Jesus Christ for the forgiveness of your sins. And you will receive the gift of the Holy Spirit" (Acts 2:38; cf. vv. 37–39).

The Place of Baptism in Conversion

> Repent and be baptized, every one of you, in the name of Jesus Christ for the forgiveness of your sins. And you will receive the gift of the Holy Spirit. (Acts 2:38)

Peter's invitation in Acts 2:38 raises the question of how necessary baptism is for salvation and forgiveness of sins. The rite of baptism—immersing a believer under water and bringing her up again—symbolically pictures a death, burial, and resurrection. Baptism is not a means of salvation; rather, it is a demonstration that the person is trusting Jesus's action of death and resurrection as the means of salvation (see Col 2:12; Rom 6:3–4). Baptism does not save a person; rather, it announces that they have been saved already. Capitalizing on the identification purposes of baptism, Clint Arnold suggests that Peter's words in Acts 2:38 could be rephrased, "Repent and put your faith in Jesus Christ to be identified with him in his saving work so that your sins may be forgiven." Arnold goes on to explain that, in the early church's ritual of baptism, it occurred so closely to a person's profession of faith that it could be viewed as simply one part of a chain of events that happened at conversion.

See Clinton E. Arnold and Jeff Arnold, "Do I Need to Be Baptized to Go to Heaven? The Role of Baptism," pp. 343–48 in *Short Answers to Big Questions about God, the Bible, and Christianity* (Grand Rapids: Baker, 2015), 346.

6.5.3 The Result with a Summary Statement (2:40–41)

Peter closes with a final plea for them to believe (2:40). His sermon expresses the expectation that God-fearing Jews were to recognize the Spirit-induced phenomenon of the believers speaking in multiple languages as the fulfillment of the Scriptures and as a confirmation that Jesus is the anticipated Messiah. In a progress summary statement,

Luke notes that many do recognize this, declare their faith in Jesus Christ, and are added to the group of believers: "Those who accepted his message were baptized, and about three thousand were added to their number that day" (2:41). In God's timing, this expansive preaching of the gospel message was to people from around the known world, and the mention of multiple languages is reminiscent of the origin of multiple languages in the tower of Babel incident in Genesis 10–12; so in some sense the coming of the Holy Spirit represents a reversal of that event.[37] Thus, the expansion of the gospel "to the ends of the earth" (Acts 1:8) gets a head start right away in the story, an expansion we should continue to support.

Fresco of the Day of Pentecost by Pietro Gagliardi (ca. 19th century), Santo Spirito dei Napoletani, Rome. Renáta Sedmáková/stock.adobe.com

6.6 CONCLUDING REMARKS

The story of Jesus in the Gospel of Luke is about what Jesus began to do and to teach while he was on earth; the story of Jesus in the book of Acts is about what Jesus continues to do and to teach from heaven, particularly through his people empowered by the Holy Spirit. Merely knowing the facts of the Jesus story in the Gospel of Luke—as important as that is—is not Luke's goal. He makes this evident in the lengthy

37. See Michael D. Goulder, *Type and History in Acts* (London: SPCK, 1964), 158–59; and John H. Walton, "The Tower of Babel and the Covenant: Rhetorical Strategy in Genesis Based on Theological and Comparative Analysis," pp. 109–18 in *Evangelical Scholarship, Retrospects and Prospects: Essays in Honor of Stanley N. Gundry*, ed. Dirk R. Buursma, Katya Covrett, and Verlyn D. Verbrugge (Grand Rapids: Zondervan, 2017), 116–18.

(and almost humorous) episode near the end of his gospel with the two on the road to Emmaus (Luke 24:13–35). There Cleopas and his unnamed companion recount the facts of the Jesus story—they even report having heard about the resurrection—and yet they remain discouraged. It is not until they recognize the resurrected Lord that the facts make sense and they see their own place in the story. So it is with Acts as well. Knowing the facts of the Jesus story from the Gospel of Luke is one thing, but how do those facts affect your life and the way you interact with others? Have you responded as the three thousand listeners who heeded Peter's sermon on the day of Pentecost? After all, those of us living in the twenty-first century are among the "all who are far off" that Peter includes in the invitation: "Repent and be baptized, every one of you, in the name of Jesus Christ for the forgiveness of your sins. And you will receive the gift of the Holy Spirit. The promise is for you and your children and for all who are far off—for all whom the Lord our God will call" (Acts 2:38–39).

Traditional site of Jesus's baptism at Bethany on the other side of the Jordan.
Alatom/iStock.com

6.7 Key People, Places, and Terms

- already/not yet kingdom
- ascension
- casting lots
- Great Commission, the
- Jerusalem
- Joel
- Judas Iscariot
- kingdom of God
- Matthias
- Mount of Olives
- Pentecost
- pericope
- telescoping
- Twelve, the

6.8 Questions for Review and Discussion

1. Describe how the beginning of the story of Acts overlaps with the ending of the Gospel of Luke.
2. Often Christians point to Matthew's version of the Great Commission (i.e., Matt 28:18–20), but Luke also has a version in his gospel and in Acts. How would you describe Luke's emphases in his version of the Great Commission?
3. Luke is the only NT writer to offer narrations of the ascension, and he tells the story twice. What is the significance of the ascension in Luke's thinking?

4. Describe the importance of participating in the community of God's people according to Acts.
5. What can we learn from Acts 1 about proper decision-making?
6. Describe the importance Luke puts on the presence of the Holy Spirit in the lives of individual believers, in their local church communities, and in the church at large.

6.9 Optional Assignments

1. **Text Reflection Project**—*Relating the concepts discussed in this chapter to another biblical text.* Compare and contrast the overlapping components of Luke's two books, i.e., Luke 24:44–53 and Acts 1:1–11. What are the similarities and differences between these accounts? How do they fit together? How do these two accounts inform each other?
2. **Interview Project**—*Inquiring of others their views concerning the concepts discussed in this chapter.* In an interview with your pastor (or some other respected Christian leader), ask, "What is the gospel message?" How does his or her answer compare to how the gospel message is defined in this chapter and as it is preached by Peter and the other apostles in Acts 2:14–41?
3. **Service-Learning Project**—*Applying the concepts discussed in this chapter in some form of service to others outside the class.* When Peter issued his invitation for the people to respond to the gospel message (Acts 2:38–40), Luke reports, "Those who accepted his message were baptized, and about three thousand were added to their number that day" (2:41). Managing that many baptisms in one day would certainly call for some organizational assistance! Check with your local church to see if you can assist in some way the next time they conduct a baptismal service.
4. **Prayer Project**—*Talking with God about the concepts discussed in this chapter.* The community of believers in Acts 1:12–26 faced an important decision and prayed about it. But first they consulted Scripture, drew up sensible criteria, and outlined a selection of options that met the criteria. Describe a decision you are facing right now, and (like the believers in Acts 1) describe what Scripture says about it, what the sensible criteria are in facing the decision, and what options meet that criteria. Then write a prayer about your situation, similar to the prayer in Acts 1:24–25.
5. **Testimony Project**—*Telling others about the concepts discussed in this chapter.* After hearing the gospel message from Peter and the other apostles in Acts 2, the listeners were convicted (i.e., "cut to the heart") and asked, "What shall we do?" (2:37). Peter's response was that they should repent and put their faith in Jesus Christ for the forgiveness of their sins and the gift of the Holy Spirit (2:38). He specifically mentions that the promise of salvation by faith was "for you and your children and for all who are far off" (2:39), which would include us in the twenty-first century! If you have responded to the gospel message with faith in Christ, write up a short summary of how you came to faith in Christ and arrange to share that story with a friend.

6.10 Bibliography for Going Further

6.10.1 The Preface(s) of Luke-Acts

Alexander, Loveday C. A. *The Preface to Luke's Gospel: Literary Convention and Social Context in Luke 1.1–4 and Acts 1.1*. SNTSMS 78. Cambridge: Cambridge University Press, 1993.

Brown, Schuyler. "The Role of the Prologues in Determining the Purpose of Luke-Acts." Pages 99–111 in *Perspectives on Luke-Acts*. Edited by Charles H. Talbert. Perspectives in Religious Studies 5. Danville, VA: Association of Baptist Professors of Religion, 1978.

Callan, Terrance. "The Preface of Luke-Acts and Historiography." *NTS* 31 (1985): 576–81.

Parsons, Mikeal C. "Christian Origins and Narrative Openings: The Sense of a Beginning in Acts 1:1–5." *RevExp* 87 (1990): 403–22.

6.10.2 The Resurrection

Anderson, Kevin L. *"But God Raised Him from the Dead": The Theology of Jesus's Resurrection in Luke-Acts*. Paternoster Biblical Monographs. Waynesboro, GA: Paternoster, 2006.

Crowe, Brandon D. *The Hope of Israel: The Resurrection of Christ in the Acts of the Apostles*. Grand Rapids: Baker Academic, 2020.

Habermas, Gary R., and Michael R. Licona. *The Case for the Resurrection of Jesus*. Grand Rapids: Kregel, 2004.

Horton, Dennis J. *Death & Resurrection: The Shape and Function of a Literary Motif in the Book of Acts*. Eugene, OR: Pickwick, 2009.

Licona, Michael R. *The Resurrection of Jesus: A New Historiographical Approach*. Downers Grove: IVP Academic, 2010.

McDowell, Josh. *The Resurrection Factor*. Milton Keynes, UK: Authentic Media, 2005.

6.10.3 The Kingdom of God in Luke-Acts

Buzzard, Anthony. "Acts 1:6 and the Eclipse of the Biblical Kingdom." *EvQ* 66.3 (1994): 197–215.

Cho, Youngmo. *Spirit and Kingdom in the Writings of Luke and Paul: An Attempt to Reconcile these Concepts*. Paternoster Biblical Monographs. Waynesboro, GA: Paternoster, 2005. Repr., Eugene, OR: Wipf & Stock, 2007.

Kuhn, Karl Allen. *The Kingdom according to Luke and Acts: A Social, Literary, and Theological Introduction*. Grand Rapids: Baker Academic, 2015.

McLean, J. A. "Did Jesus Correct the Disciples' View of the Kingdom?" *BSac* 151 (1994): 215–27.

Salmeier, Michael A. *Restoring the Kingdom: The Role of God as the "Ordainer of Times and Seasons" in the Acts of the Apostles*. PTMS. Eugene, OR: Pickwick, 2011.

Ziccardi, Costantino Antonio. *The Relationship of Jesus and the Kingdom of God according to Luke-Acts*. TGST 165. Rome: Gregorian University Press, 2008.

6.10.4 The Great Commission and Witnessing in Luke-Acts

Bolt, Peter G. "Mission and Witness." Pages 191–214 in *Witness to the Gospel: The Theology of Acts*. Edited by I. Howard Marshall and David Peterson. Grand Rapids: Eerdmans, 1998.

Embudo, Lora Angeline B. "A Lukan Paradigm of Witness: Community as a Form of Witness, Parts I & II." *AJPS* 20.1 (2017): 7–35.

Maynard-Reid, Pedrito U. *Complete Evangelism: The Luke-Acts Model*. Scottdale, PA: Herald, 1997.

Simpson, Albert Benjamin. *The Spirit-Filled Church in Action: The Dynamics of Evangelism from the Book of Acts.* Camp Hill, PA: Christian Publications, 1996.

Trites, Allison A. *New Testament Witness in Today's World.* Valley Forge, PA: Judson, 1983.

Turner, Max. *Power from on High: The Spirit in Israel's Restoration and Witness in Luke-Acts.* JPTSup 9. Sheffield: Sheffield Academic, 1996. Repr., Eugene, OR: Wipf & Stock, 2015.

Twelftree, Graham H. *People of the Spirit: Exploring Luke's View of the Church.* Grand Rapids: Baker Academic, 2009.

Zwiep, Arie W. "Church between Ideal and Reality: Some Comments on the Role of the Church in the Acts of the Apostles." Pages 120–38 in *Christ, the Spirit and the Community of God: Essays on the Acts of the Apostles.* WUNT 2.293. Tübingen: Mohr Siebeck, 2010.

6.10.5 The Ascension

Atkins, Peter. *Ascension Now: Implications of Christ's Ascension for Today's Church.* Collegeville, MN: Liturgical 2001.

Bryan, David K., and David W. Pao, eds. *Ascent into Heaven in Luke-Acts: New Explorations of Luke's Narrative Hinge.* Minneapolis: Fortress, 2016.

Dawson, Gerrit Scott. *Jesus Ascended: The Meaning of Christ's Continuing Incarnation.* Phillipsburg, NJ: P&R, 2004; New York: T&T Clark, 2004.

Maile, John F. "The Ascension in Luke-Acts." *TynBul* 37 (1986) 29–59.

Parsons, Mikeal C. *The Departure of Jesus in Luke-Acts: The Ascension Narratives in Context.* JSNTSup 21. Sheffield: JSOT, 1987.

Schreiner, Patrick. *The Ascension of Christ: Recovering a Neglected Doctrine.* Snapshots. Bellingham, WA: Lexham, 2020.

Walton, Steve. "Ascension of Jesus." *DJG*[2], 59–61.

Zwiep, Arie W. *The Ascension of the Messiah in Lukan Christology.* NovTSup 87. Leiden: Brill, 1997.

6.10.6 The Replacement of Judas with Matthias

Fuller, Reginald H. "The Choice of Matthias." *SE* VI (TU 112 [1973]): 140–46.

Soards, Marion L. "Peter's Speech and the Disciples' Prayer Prior to the Enrollment of Matthias." Pages 26–31 in *The Speeches in Acts: Their Content, Context, and Concerns.* Louisville: Westminster John Knox, 1994.

Wilcox, Max. "The Judas-Tradition in Acts 1:15–26." *NTS* 19.4 (1973): 438–52.

Zwiep, Arie W. *Judas and the Choice of Matthias: A Study on Context and Concern of Acts 1:15–26.* WUNT 2.187. Tübingen: Mohr Siebeck, 2004.

6.10.7 The Coming of the Holy Spirit

Haya-Prats, Gonzalo. *Empowered Believers: The Holy Spirit in the Book of Acts.* Edited by Paul Elbert. Translated by Scott A. Ellington. Eugene, OR: Cascade, 2011.

Hur, Ju. *A Dynamic Reading of the Holy Spirit in Luke-Acts.* JSNTSup 211. Sheffield: Sheffield Academic, 2001. Repr., New York: T&T Clark, 2004.

Keener, Craig S. "The Spirit and the Mission of the Church in Acts 1–2." *JETS* 62.1 (2019): 25–45.

Menzies, Robert P. *Empowered for Witness: The Spirit in Luke-Acts.* JPTSup 6. Sheffield: Sheffield Academic, 1994.

Shelton, James B. *Mighty in Word and Deed: The Role of the Holy Spirit in Luke-Acts.* Peabody, MA: Hendrickson, 1991.

Shepherd, William H., Jr. *The Narrative Function of the Holy Spirit as a Character in Luke-Acts.* SBLDS 147. Atlanta: Scholars Press, 1994.

Turner, Max. "The Work of the Holy Spirit in Luke-Acts." *WW* 23.2 (2003): 146–53.

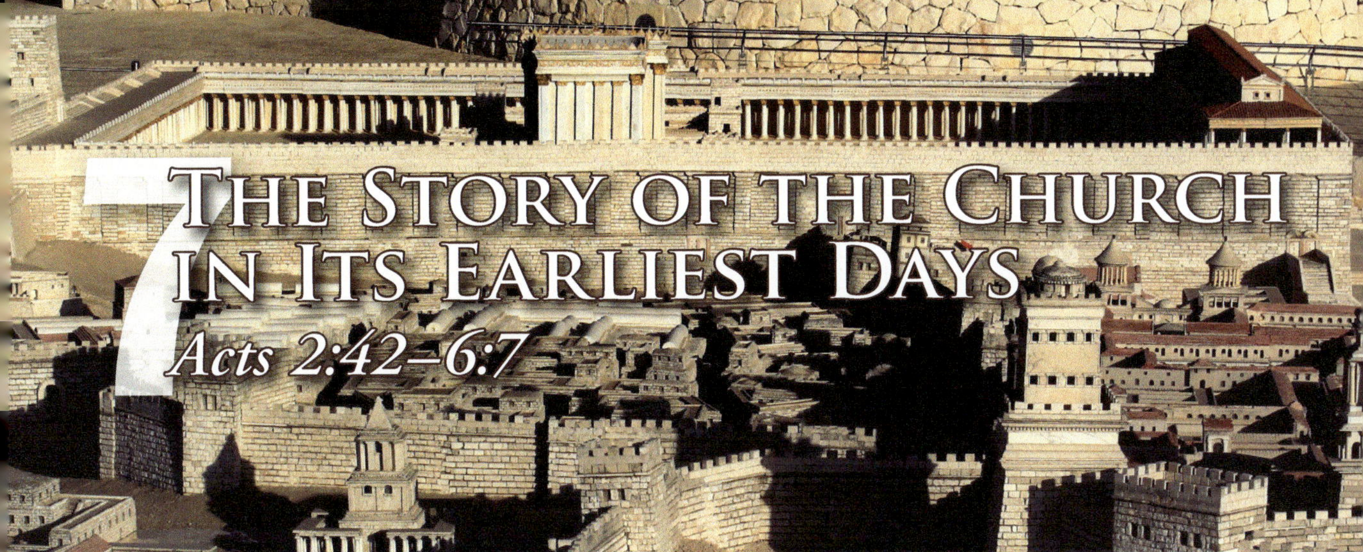

aquatarkus/stock.adobe.com

Chapter Goals

After reading this chapter, you should be able to:

- Describe the ideal features of life in the church as portrayed in Acts.
- Recognize four general threats to, or problems in, the life of the church as portrayed in Acts.
- Explain helpful responses observed in Acts to these general threats to, or problems in, the life of the church.

Chapter Overview

7.1 Overview of Church Life (Acts 2:42–47)
7.2 An External Challenge to Church Life: Intimidation (Acts 3:1–4:31)
7.3 An Internal Challenge to Church Life: Corruption (Acts 4:32–5:16)
7.4 An External Challenge to Church Life: Persecution (Acts 5:17–42)
7.5 An Internal Challenge to Church Life: Disruption (Acts 6:1–7)
7.6 Concluding Remarks
7.7 Key People, Places, and Terms
7.8 Questions for Review and Discussion
7.9 Optional Assignments
7.10 Bibliography for Going Further

Key Verses

They devoted themselves to the apostles' teaching and to fellowship, to the breaking of bread and to prayer. (Acts 2:42)

Salvation is found in no one else, for there is no other name under heaven given to mankind by which we must be saved. (Acts 4:12)

But Peter and John replied, "Which is right in God's eyes: to listen to you, or to him? You be the judges! As for us, we cannot help speaking about what we have seen and heard." (Acts 4:19–20)

Summary Statement

So the word of God spread. The number of disciples in Jerusalem increased rapidly, and a large number of priests became obedient to the faith. (Acts 6:7)

INTRODUCTION

In the first major section of Acts (Acts 1:1–2:41), Luke recounts the Great Commission, Jesus's ascension, the completion of the Twelve, and the coming of the Spirit, which many suggest was the birth of the church. Now in the second major section of Acts (2:42–6:7), Luke focuses on the life of the Jerusalem church in its infancy. Jesus had sketched a vision of the Spirit-empowered church reaching the world (1:8), and now in this next major section of Acts, Luke addresses the question of the church's self-understanding. While he might have addressed the question with theological propositions or missional goal statements, Luke chooses instead to tell some stories of how the people of the church lived, how they interacted with other believers, and how they interacted with people who were not (or not yet) followers of Jesus. These episodes illustrate for us something of the church's self-understanding, and I am suggesting that Luke casts this vision of the church for all Jesus followers.

First century synagogue ruins, Magdala.
dudlajzov/stock.adobe.com

This section of Acts opens with a summary overview on the life of the church (2:42–47) followed by four other subsections that alternate between external challenges (3:1–4:31; 5:17–42) and internal challenges (4:32–5:16; 6:1–7) to the life of the church. Each subsection recounts how the church responded to those challenges. Then the whole section closes with Luke's summary of the spread of the gospel message to that point (6:7).

7.1 OVERVIEW OF CHURCH LIFE (ACTS 2:42–47)

The short paragraph of 2:42–47 gives a summary overview of what life was like for the church in Jerusalem after the arrival of the Holy Spirit.[1] Luke repeats such church life summary statements describing how Jesus followers live, and this repetition is a way Luke encourages Christians to continue in unity (see 1:12–14; 2:42–47; 4:32–35; 5:12–16; 6:7; 9:31; 12:24). Eckhard Schnabel suggests several purposes behind Luke's use of these overview statements: (a) historically, they report what happened; (b) literarily, they indicate the passage of time in the story; (c) theologically, they point to God's presence and power in the community; (d) ecclesiologically, they outline the church's essential characteristics, and (e) missiologically, they record the church's growth and expansion (see sidebar).[2] The Acts 2 overview of church life specifies four activities to which the church "devoted themselves": the teaching of the apostles, fellowship, breaking of bread, and prayer (2:42). Luke immediately develops these four things in the following verses: miracles affirm the teaching (2:43), property is sold to care for others in fellowship (2:44–45), they meet in the temple (for prayer) (2:46a), and they break bread in each other's homes (2:46b).[3] This is all part of the life of a vibrant church (2:47).

Mosaic found in Tabgha where Jesus may have multiplied the loaves and fishes to feed the hungry.

Ella/stock.adobe.com

Luke's Purposes for Overview Summaries of Church Life in Acts

I. **Historical purpose:** The summaries report what happened in the early church.
II. **Literary purpose:** The summaries indicate the passage of time in the telling of the story.
III. **Theological purpose:** The summaries point to God's presence and power in the community.
IV. **Ecclesiological purpose:** The summaries outline the church's essential characteristics.
V. **Missiological purpose:** The summaries record the church's continued growth and expansion.

Adapted and simplified from Schnabel, *Acts*, 175.

1. John Stott refers to this short paragraph as "the effect of Pentecost"; John R. W. Stott, *The Message of Acts: To the Ends of the Earth*, The Bible Speaks Today (Downers Grove, IL: InterVarsity, 1994), 81.
2. Eckhard J. Schnabel, *Acts*, ZECNT (Grand Rapids: Zondervan, 2012), 174–75.
3. Mel Storm, *Living Lord, Empowering Spirit, Testifying People: The Story of the Church in the Book of Acts* (Eugene, OR: Wipf & Stock, 2014), 33.

7.1.1 Devoted to Four Things: Teaching, Fellowship, Breaking Bread, Prayer (2:42)

Acts 2:42 is a grand but simple statement naming the activities to which the church was devoted. The simplicity of this statement is captured in its brevity; the grandeur of this statement is seen in its ever-present applicability to the church everywhere else in Acts. Luke seems to think these are the things to which all churches everywhere should be devoted. And it is noteworthy that these four activities need not be separate and self-contained. That is, believers can pray and discuss the apostles' teaching while they break bread in fellowship with one another.[4] Nevertheless, for convenience, I will discuss each of these items separately here.

We saw the importance that Luke put on the completion of the twelve apostles (Acts 1:12–26), due particularly to the significance of the number twelve as symbolic of the people of God. While Jesus had many, many disciples (cf. Luke 6:17), he selected twelve of them to serve as apostles (cf. Luke 6:12–16), with whom he invested more time and effort during his earthly ministry, including instructions regarding the proper interpretation of Scripture (esp. Luke 24:25–27, 32, 44–47). Indeed, Luke specifically reports that, in the forty days between Jesus's resurrection and ascension, he instructed the apostles and taught them about the kingdom of God (Acts 1:2–3). Now in Acts 2 Luke notes that the apostles are passing this teaching on to the rest of the church. Fortunately, the teaching of the apostles has become embodied for us in the documents of the New Testament.[5] And as we will see in the sermons in Acts, apostolic teaching often reflects on the OT Scriptures. Thus, good churches today are still devoted to the apostles' teachings as found in both the New Testament and the Hebrew Scriptures.

The second item of the believers' devotion is fellowship. The Greek word for "fellowship"—*koinōnia*—has come into popular parlance in many churches today, often as the name of the informal gathering place in the church building: e.g., the "Koinonia Room" or the "Fellowship Hall." Thus, the idea of fellowship has come to mean the act of hanging out together, talking, and interacting informally. But more than informal interactions between Christians on Sundays in the church building, true Christian fellowship is broad-ranging and covers all areas of life, on any and every day of the week, and in any and all locations. Luke spells this out with greater detail

4. Witherington favors the idea that there are only two things mentioned here, teaching and fellowship, and that breaking bread and prayer are two things involved in (or resulting in) fellowship; Ben Witherington III, *The Acts of the Apostles: A Socio-Rhetorical Commentary* (Grand Rapids: Eerdmans, 1998; Carlisle: Paternoster, 1998), 160; so also F. F. Bruce, *The Book of Acts*, 2nd ed., NICNT (Grand Rapids: Eerdmans, 1988), 73. Barrett argues otherwise in Charles Kingsley Barrett, *A Critical and Exegetical Commentary on the Acts of the Apostles*, 2 vols., ICC (Edinburgh: T&T Clark, 1994/1998), 1:164.

5. See chapter 16 for a brief discussion of the NT canon and how Acts became a recognized part of it.

immediately after his overview summary. He mentions the believers being together and sharing everything (2:44), sacrificing to provide for one another's practical needs (2:45), and meeting in the temple courts as well as in each other's homes (2:46). The fellowship of the believers was very practical interdependence and accountability and not merely some ethereal sense of spiritual affinity.

"Fellowship" in the New Testament

The nineteen occurrences of the NT Greek term for "fellowship" (*koinōnia*) are found in two different contexts, sometimes referring to some kind of participatory gathering or partnership (the fifteen occurrences listed here) and sometimes referring more specifically to sharing contributions to aid the needy (see the four occurrences in Rom 15:26; 2 Cor 8:4; 9:13; Heb 13:16). With the context of Acts 2:44-46 and 4:32-35, Luke's one use of the term, in Acts 2:42, certainly makes a connection between the nuances of "participation" and "sharing."

Acts 2:42—"They devoted themselves to the apostles' teaching and to fellowship, to the breaking of bread and to prayer."

1 Corinthians 1:9—"God is faithful, who has called you into fellowship with his Son, Jesus Christ our Lord."

1 Corinthians 10:16—"Is not the cup of thanksgiving for which we give thanks a participation in the blood of Christ? And is not the bread that we break a participation in the body of Christ?"

2 Corinthians 6:14—"Do not be yoked together with unbelievers. For what do righteousness and wickedness have in common? Or what fellowship can light have with darkness?"

2 Corinthians 13:14—"May the grace of the Lord Jesus Christ, and the love of God, and the fellowship of the Holy Spirit be with you all."

Galatians 2:9—"James, Cephas and John, those esteemed as pillars, gave me and Barnabas the right hand of fellowship when they recognized the grace given to me. They agreed that we should go to the Gentiles, and they to the circumcised."

Philippians 1:4-5—"In all my prayers for all of you, I always pray with joy because of your partnership in the gospel from the first day until now."

Philippians 2:1-2—"Therefore if you have any encouragement from being united with Christ, if any comfort from his love, if any common sharing in the Spirit, if any tenderness and compassion, then make my joy complete by being like-minded, having the same love, being one in spirit and of one mind."

Philippians 3:10—"I want to know Christ—yes, to know the power of his resurrection and participation in his sufferings, becoming like him in his death."

Philemon 6—"I pray that your partnership with us in the faith may be effective in deepening your understanding of every good thing we share for the sake of Christ."

1 John 1:3—"We proclaim to you what we have seen and heard, so that you also may have fellowship with us. And our fellowship is with the Father and with his Son, Jesus Christ."

1 John 1:6-7—"If we claim to have fellowship with him and yet walk in the darkness, we lie and do not live out the truth. But if we walk in the light, as he is in the light, we have fellowship with one another, and the blood of Jesus, his Son, purifies us from all sin."

The phrase "breaking of bread" was a rudimentary way of referring to meals (cf. Luke 4:3–4; 7:33; 9:3; 11:3, 5; and 14:1, 15; 15:17 where "eat food" in NIV is "eat bread" in Greek), meals where bread was a common staple and in the first century was torn or broken apart instead of sliced.[6] But "breaking bread" also referenced what we call the Lord's Supper or Communion, the sharing of bread and wine to commemorate Jesus's sacrifice of his body and blood on our behalf, an observance that Jesus instituted on the night he was betrayed (Luke 22:14–22; 1 Cor 11:23–26; cf. 1 Cor 10:16–17; Acts 20:7). Some scholars have suggested that this third item of devotion in Acts 2:42 references only the sharing of ordinary meals;[7] others have suggested that Luke references only the observance of eucharistic communion services;[8] and still others have suggested that Luke intends both ordinary meals and communion services recalling the Lord's Supper.[9]

Ideal Characteristics of a Sound Church

Luke's description of the fledgling community of believers sets up his audience to expect certain features to be characteristic of any sound local church: "They devoted themselves to the apostles' teaching and to fellowship, to the breaking of bread and to prayer" (Acts 2:42). These four ideal features can be expressed in several ways for describing a healthy community of believers.

Teaching—a *radical obedience* to the **word** of God as taught by the apostles.
Fellowship—a *radical accountability* regarding the **work** of God in one another.
Breaking of bread—a *radical generosity* for the **welfare** of God's people.
Prayer—a *radical dependence* upon God expressed in the **worship** of him.

---

6. For descriptions of meals in antiquity, see esp. Dennis E. Smith, *From Symposium to Eucharist: The Banquet in the Early Christian World* (Minneapolis: Fortress, 2003). More specific to Luke-Acts, see now Matthias Klinghardt, "Meals in the Gospel of Luke," and Dennis E. Smith, "Meals as a Literary Motif in Acts of the Apostles," pp. 108–20 and 165–76 respectively in *T&T Clark Handbook to Early Christian Meals in the Greco-Roman World*, ed. Soham Al-Suadi and Peter-Ben Smit (New York: T&T Clark, 2019).

7. E.g., Hans. Conzelmann, *Acts of the Apostles: A Commentary on the Acts of the Apostles*, trans. James Limburg, A. Thomas Kraabel, and Donald H. Juel, ed. Eldon Jay Epp with Christopher R. Matthews, Hermeneia (Philadelphia: Fortress, 1987), 23; David G. Peterson, *The Acts of the Apostles*, Pillar New Testament Commentary (Grand Rapids: Eerdmans, 2009), 161; Darrell L. Bock, *Acts*, BECNT (Grand Rapids: Baker Academic, 2007), 150–51; J. Behm, *TDNT* 3:731.

8. E.g., Bruce, *Book of Acts*, 73; idem, *The Acts of the Apostles: The Greek Text with Introduction and Commentary*, 3rd ed. (Grand Rapids: Eerdmans, 1990; Leicester: Apollos, 1990), 73; Simon J. Kistemaker, *Exposition of the Acts of the Apostles*, New Testament Commentary (Grand Rapids: Baker, 1990), 111; Luke Timothy Johnson, *The Acts of the Apostles*, SP 5 (Collegeville: Liturgical for Michael Glazier, 1992), 58; Everett Falconer Harrison, *Interpreting Acts: The Expanding Church* (Chicago: Moody, 1975; repr., Grand Rapids: Zondervan, 1986), 74; Joseph A. Fitzmyer, *The Acts of the Apostles*, AB 31 (New York: Doubleday, 1998), 270–71; Dean Pinter, *Acts*, The Story of God Bible Commentary (Grand Rapids: Zondervan, 2019), 83–84.

9. E.g., Clinton E. Arnold, "Acts," vol. 2B of *ZIBBCNT*, ed. Clinton E. Arnold (Grand Rapids: Zondervan, 2002), 21; Stott, *The Message of Acts*, 85; Witherington, *Acts*, 160–61; idem, *Making a Meal of It: Rethinking the Theology of the Lord's Supper* (Waco, TX: Baylor University Press, 2015), 29–31; Barrett, *Acts*, 1:165; John Paul Heil, *The Meal Scenes in Luke-Acts: An Audience-Oriented Approach*, SBLMS 52 (Atlanta: Scholars Press, 1999), 243; Schnabel, *Acts*, 179; cf. Smith, *Symposium*, 175, 263, 285–87; Keener calls this the majority view; Craig S. Keener, *Acts: An Exegetical Commentary*, 4 vols. (Grand Rapids: Baker Academic, 2012–2015), 1:1003.

Devotion to Four Aspects of Church Life in Acts 2:42

My good friend Jeff Bradbury (who builds furniture as a hobby) has suggested that the four aspects of church life mentioned in Acts 2:42 are something akin to the four legs of a table. These four aspects of church life support the community of the believers. As with the legs of a table, if one aspect is too short—or missing altogether—the community of believers becomes wobbly and unstable. Thus, Luke would insist that believers even today remain devoted to all four aspects.

> They devoted themselves to the apostles' teaching and to fellowship, to the breaking of bread and to prayer. (Acts 2:42)

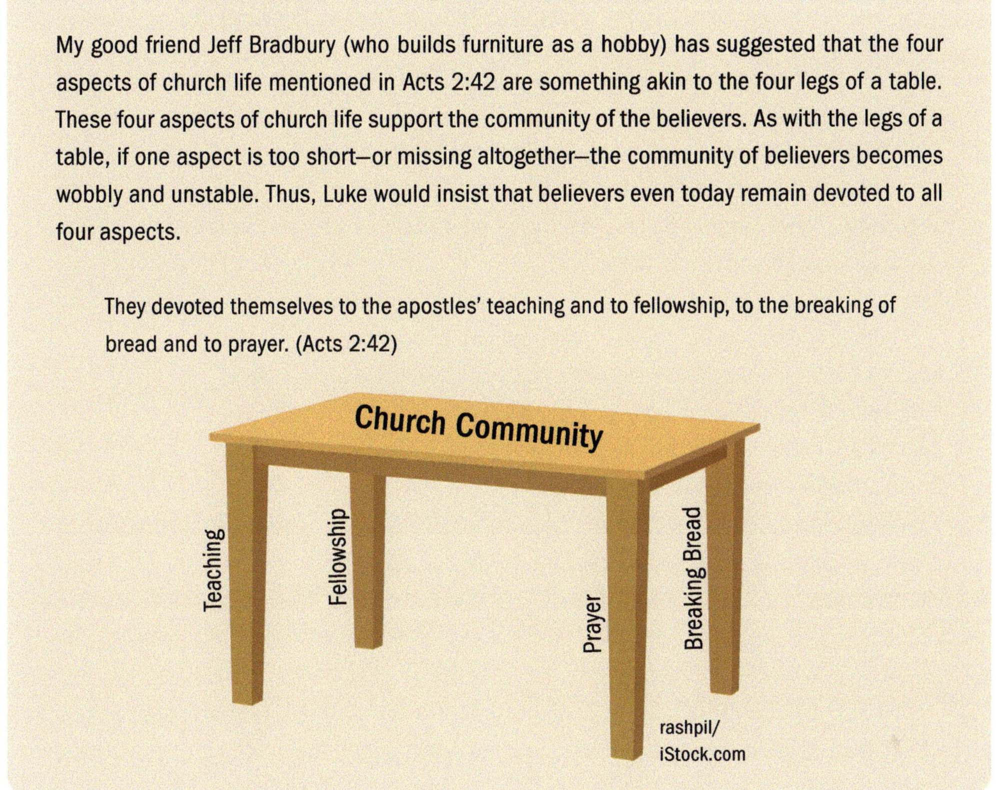

rashpil/
iStock.com

Even as the four major activities of the church need not be viewed as self-contained and separate from one another, so also their sacramental and ordinary functions need not be viewed as self-contained and separate from one another. In fact, this is perhaps the genius of Jesus's establishment of the communion commemoration of his death during his last meal before the crucifixion. That is, for a Christian, any meal is an opportunity to offer thanks not only for sustaining physical life but for the Lord's sacrifice that brings us eternal life (cf. Luke 24:30). So also, any meal for Christians gathered jointly is an opportunity to discuss the apostles' teachings, to support one another in fellowship, to recall God's provision of salvation as well as food, and to offer prayer to the Lord together.

The fourth item of the believers' devotion is "prayers" (Acts 2:42). The Greek here is literally "the prayers" and brings to mind the three regular times for prayer in the daily Jewish schedule (morning, afternoon, and sunset), which some of the early believers appear to have maintained (e.g., Acts 3:1; cf. 10:2–3, 30). But of course, Luke is clear that the believers also practiced prayer spontaneously as need arose (e.g., 6:6; 8:15; 9:40;

"Breaking Bread" in the New Testament

Matthew 26:26—"While they were eating, Jesus took bread, and when he had given thanks, he broke it and gave it to his disciples, saying, 'Take and eat; this is my body.'" (cf. Mark 14:22; Luke 22:19)

Luke 24:30—"When he was at the table with them, he took bread, gave thanks, broke it and began to give it to them." (cf. v. 35)

Acts 2:42—"They devoted themselves to the apostles' teaching and to fellowship, to the breaking of bread and to prayer."

Acts 2:46—"Every day they continued to meet together in the temple courts. They broke bread in their homes and ate together with glad and sincere hearts."

Acts 20:7—"On the first day of the week we came together to break bread."

Acts 20:11—"Then he went upstairs again and broke bread and ate."

Acts 27:35—"After he said this, he took some bread and gave thanks to God in front of them all. Then he broke it and began to eat."

1 Corinthians 10:16—"Is not the cup of thanksgiving for which we give thanks a participation in the blood of Christ? And is not the bread that we break a participation in the body of Christ?"

12:5, 12; 13:3; 14:23; 20:36; 21:5; 27:29; 28:8). Luke's particular interest in prayer has already appeared in his gospel, where he mentions prayer more than any of the other three gospel writers. Luke's interest in prayer continues in the book of Acts with the story of the life of the church.[10] In the Gospel of Luke, Jesus is found praying before every major event in his life, and similarly in the book of Acts, the apostles are found praying before any major decision.[11] Sometimes we hear the specific words of a prayer in Acts (e.g., 1:24–25; 4:24–31); sometimes we are simply told that people prayed for particular things without any summary of the words utilized (e.g., 6:6; 8:15, 22–24; 9:11, 40; 12:5; 13:3; 14:23; 27:29; 28:8); but most often we read about prayer in a more general way as a regular activity of believers (e.g., 1:14; 2:42; 3:1; 6:4; 10:2, 4, 9, 30, 31; 11:5; 12:12; 16:13, 16, 25; 20:36; 21:5; 22:17).[12]

---

10. Scott Shauf suggests Acts has "approximately twenty-five" prayer scenes; Scott Shauf, *The Divine in Acts and in Ancient Historiography* (Minneapolis: Fortress, 2015), 213; and Joel Green counts "over thirty"; Joel B. Green, "Persevering Together in Prayer: The Significance of Prayer in the Acts of the Apostles," pp. 183–202 in *Into God's Presence: Prayer in the New Testament*, ed. Richard N. Longenecker (Grand Rapids: Eerdmans, 2001), 184.

11. Mark G. Boyer, *Praying Your Way through Luke's Gospel and the Acts of the Apostles* (Eugene, OR: Wipf & Stock, 2015), xii.

12. See Shauf, *The Divine in Acts*, 214; and Geir Otto Holmås, *Prayer and Vindication in Luke-Acts: The Theme of Payer within the Context of the Legitimating and Edifying Objective of the Lukan Narrative*, LNTS 433 (New York: Bloomsbury T&T Clark, 2011), 59.

Luke's Theology of Prayer in Acts

From Steven F. Plymale, *The Prayer Texts of Luke-Acts*, AUSTR 118 (New York: Lang, 1991), 110–14.

1. Prayer is the appropriate means of preparing oneself for a life of service in God's salvific plan (see Acts 1:14).
2. Prayer is an expression of rejoicing at the evidence of God's saving activity in the world (see Acts 4:24-30).
3. Prayer is habitual, offered regularly at the established times and spontaneously at other moments (see Acts 3:1; 4:24-30; 8:24; 9:11, 40; 10:9; 16:11-16, 25; 22:17-21; 28:8).
4. Prayer is a proper aspect of commissioning and authorizing persons for roles in salvation history (see Acts 1:24; 6:6; 13:1-3; 14:21-23; 20:17, 36, 38).
5. Prayer frequently is offered before events that prove to be significant manifestations of God's saving activity (see Acts 2:1-41; 4:24-31; 9:40; 10:3-4, 9; 11:5; 16:25-34; 28:8).
6. Intercessory prayer distinguishes participants in the Kingdom of God (see Acts 8:14-17, 18-24; 12:5).
7. One prays to know, accept, and implement the will of God (see Acts 1:14, 24; 4:24-31; 6:4; 7:59-60; 22:17-21).
8. Since God answers prayer, one may pray with confidence (see Acts 4:24-31; 7:59-60; 9:11, 40-42; 28:7-9).

Joel Green summarizes the significance of prayer in Acts in two points: (1) prayer is a means for discerning God's purposes, and (2) prayer is the means by which people become aligned with what God is doing.[13] To these, Scott Shauf adds two more points: (3) prayer is a means for people to petition God, and (4) prayer provides opportunities for God's power and presence to be experienced. This is noteworthy because Acts portrays prayer as the time when divine manifestations often occur (e.g., Acts 4:31; 8:14–17; 10:2–4, 9, 30; 11:5; 16:25; 22:17; cf. Luke 3:21; 9:28–29).[14] Luke's account of Christianity's origins, punctuated as it is with prayer by Jesus and his followers, demonstrates the centrality of God's activity in the story.[15] It is evident then that any follower of Jesus should, like him, be involved in prayer.[16]

13. Green, "Persevering Together in Prayer," 194.

14. Shauf, *The Divine in Acts*, 215.

15. Holmås, *Prayer and Vindication in Luke-Acts*, 60–61; cf. Steven F. Plymale, "Luke's Theology of Prayer," pp. 529–51 in *SBL Seminar Papers, 1990*, ed. David J. Lull, SBLSP 29 (Atlanta: Scholars Press, 1990), 551; Peter T. O'Brien, "Prayer in Luke-Acts," *TynBul* 24 (1973): 127.

16. Cf. Boyer, *Praying Your Way through Luke's Gospel and the Acts of the Apostles*, xiii.

7.1.2 Signs and Wonders through the Apostles (2:43)

Acts 2:43 is something of a summary statement about the occurrence of the miraculous in the early church (cf. 5:12; 8:7; 19:11–12; 28:9), confirming the continuity of the apostolic message with the work of Jesus (cf. 2:22; 10:38). Luke's connection here of signs and wonders with the twelve apostles (cf. 2 Cor 12:12; Heb 2:3–4) has led some to assume that God performed miraculous deeds only through the apostles. This would seem to support a ***cessationist view*** of the miraculous gifts (i.e., that doing the miraculous was a gift of the Twelve that has ceased since the Twelve are no longer with us). The casual reader of Acts will notice, however, that in some miraculous interventions, God used other believers who were not members of the Twelve (e.g., Stephen in Acts 6:8; Philip in Acts 8:6–7, 13; Paul and Barnabas in Acts 14:3; 15:12; and Paul in Acts 19:11–12). There is, then, little in Luke's writing to suggest that God will not continue to intervene supernaturally in human events apart from the presence of members of the original twelve apostles—sometimes called a ***continuation view***. But also, nothing in Luke's writing indicates that all believers everywhere must be able to perform miracles (cf. 1 Cor 12:29–30, where Paul notes that not all believers have the gift of working miracles).[17]

Elsewhere in Acts, Luke seems to use the terms "wonders" and "signs" interchangeably along with the term "miracles" (e.g., Acts 2:22; 4:33; 6:8; 8:13; 19:11) all to refer to God's supernatural interventions in human events. Rather than three kinds of supernatural deeds, it is better to consider these somewhat interchangeable

Do Miracles Still Happen?

From Stott, *Message of Acts*, 104.

> If, then, we take Scripture as our guide, we will avoid opposite extremes. We will neither describe miracles as 'never happening', nor as 'everyday occurrences', neither as 'impossible' nor as 'normal'. Instead, we will be entirely open to the God who works both through nature and through miracle. And when a healing miracle is claimed, we will expect it to resemble those in the Gospels and the Acts and so to be the instantaneous and complete cure of an organic condition, without the use of medical or surgical means, inviting investigation and persuading even unbelievers.

17. For an introduction to the debate about supernatural gifts, see Wayne A. Grudem, ed., *Are Miraculous Gifts for Today? Four Views*, Counterpoints: Bible and Theology (Grand Rapids: Zondervan, 1996). For accessible whole book treatments, see Thomas R. Schreiner, *Spiritual Gifts: What They Are and Why They Matter* (Nashville: B&H Books, 2018) on the cessationist side of the spectrum; and see Sam Storms, *Practicing the Power: Welcoming the Gifts of the Holy Spirit in Your Life* (Grand Rapids: Zondervan, 2017) on the continuationist side of the spectrum.

terms as emphasizing three aspects of God's interventions, i.e., deeds that authenticate the gospel message ("signs"), arouse awe ("wonders"), and display God's power ("miracles").[18] Luke tends to give God credit for supernatural events; that these miraculous things were "performed by the apostles" (Acts 2:43 NIV) might be better rendered "were being done through the apostles" (ESV; Greek: *dia tōn apostolōn egineto*).

7.1.3 Communism or Common Life? (2:44–47)

In Acts 2:44–47 Luke expands on the concepts of fellowship and breaking of bread with a description of the church's radical generosity with one another: "All the believers were together and had everything in common" (2:44). Some have suspected Luke of describing a kind of Christian communism that entailed common living quarters and joint finances for everyone in the local church.[19] Some groups in first-century Judaism did practice versions of this kind of communal living (e.g., the Qumran community and the Essenes).[20] Is Luke suggesting that such communal living is prescriptive for believers? I don't think so. We read too much into Luke's remark if we think he meant all Christians sold everything and moved in with each other. Luke's comment here that the believers "broke bread in their homes" (v. 46) indicates that the people still had separate homes, and Peter's confrontational comments in Acts 5:3–4 clarifies that people still had private control of their finances.[21] Rather, Luke's comment alludes to a widespread proverbial saying in the Hellenistic world: "Friends have all things in common," which refers to friends freely sharing their possessions with one another such that common use—not common ownership—was the emphasis (see sidebar).[22]

"Friends Have All Things in Common"

Aristotle, *Politics* 2.2.5, §1263a34–39 (ca. 350 BC)

. . . for individuals while owning their property privately put their own possessions at the service of their friends and make use of their friends' possessions as common property. . . . It is clear therefore that it is better for possessions to be privately owned but to make them common property in use.

18. Murray J. Harris, *The Second Epistle to the Corinthians: A Commentary on the Greek Text*, NIGTC (Grand Rapids: Eerdmans, 2005), 875.

19. E.g., Brian J. Capper, "The Palestinian Cultural Context of the Earliest Christian Community of Goods," in *The Book of Acts in Its Palestinian Setting*, ed. Richard Bauckham, BAFCS 4 (Grand Rapids: Eerdmans, 1995; Carlisle: Paternoster, 1995), 323–56; cf. idem, "Essene Community Houses and Jesus' Early Community," in *Jesus and Archaeology*, ed. James H. Charlesworth (Grand Rapids: Eerdmans, 2006), 472–502.

20. See 1QS 1.11–13; 6.16–23; Josephus, *Ant.* 18.1.5 §§18–22; idem, *J.W.* 2.8.2–4 §§119–27; Philo, *Hypothetica* 11.1–18. Regarding the followers of Pythagoras, see Hippolytus of Rome, *Refutation of All Heresies*, trans. M. David Litwa, WGRW 40 (Atlanta: SBL Press, 2016), 21 (1.2.16); and Iamblichus, *The Life of Pythagoras*, trans. Thomas Taylor (Los Angeles: Theosophical Publishing House, 1918), 25 and 58 (§§30 and 90). See also Joshua Nobel, *Common Property, the Golden Age, and Empire in Acts 2:42–47 and 4:32–35*, LNTS 636 (London: T&T Clark, 2020).

21. See Christopher M. Hays, *Renouncing Everything: Money and Discipleship in Luke* (New York: Paulist, 2016), esp. pp. 53–65; and idem, *Luke's Wealth Ethics: A Study in Their Coherence and Character*, WUNT 2.275 (Tübingen: Mohr Siebeck, 2010), esp. pp. 189–211.

22. Hays, *Renouncing Everything*, 58–59.

Ancient Descriptions of Communal Living

Qumran Community

Rule of the Community (1QS) 1.11–13 and 6.16–22 (ca. 100–75 BC)

All who volunteer for His truth are to bring the full measure of their knowledge, strength, and wealth into the Yahad of God. Thus will they purify their knowledge in the verity of God's law, properly exercise their strength according to the perfection of his ways, and likewise their wealth by the canon of His righteous counsel. . . .

If he does proceed in joining the party of the Yahad, he must not touch the pure food of the general membership before they have examined him as to his spiritual fitness and works, and not before a full year has passed. Further, he must not yet admix his property with that of the general membership. When he has passed a full year in the Yahad, the general membership shall inquire into the details of his understanding and works of the Law. . . . They shall also take steps to incorporate his property, putting it under the authority of the Overseer together with that of the general membership, and keeping account of it—but it shall not yet be disbursed along with that of the general membership.

The initiate is not to touch the drink of the general membership prior to passing a second year among the men of the Yahad. When that second year has passed, the general membership shall review his case. If it be ordained for him to proceed to full membership in the Yahad, they shall enroll him at the appropriate rank among his brothers for discussion of the Law, jurisprudence, participation in pure meals, and admixture of property.

Essenes

Flavius Josephus, *Jewish Antiquities* 18.1.5 §§20–22 (ca. AD 94)

Moreover, they hold their possessions in common, and the wealthy man receives no more enjoyment from his property than the man who possesses nothing. . . . They live by themselves and perform menial tasks for one another. They elect by show of hands good men to receive their revenues and the produce of the earth and priests to prepare bread and other food.

Flavius Josephus, *Jewish War* 2.8.3 §§122–23 (ca. AD 94)

Riches they despise, and their community of goods is truly admirable; you will not find one among them distinguished by greater opulence than another. They have a law that new members on admission to the sect shall confiscate their property to the order, with the result that you will nowhere see either abject poverty or inordinate wealth; the individual's possessions join the common stock and all, like brothers, enjoy a single patrimony. . . . They elect officers to attend to the interests of the community, the special services of each officer being determined by the whole body.

Philo, *Hypothetica* 11.4–5 (ca. AD 40–49)

None of them allows himself to have any private property, either house or slave or estate or cattle or any of the other things which are amassed and abundantly procured by wealth, but they put everything together into the public stock and enjoy the benefit of them all in common. They live together formed into clubs, bands of comradeship with common meals, and never cease to conduct all their affairs to serve the general weal.

Pythagorians

Hippolytus of Rome, *Refutation of All Heresies* 1.2.16 (ca. AD 170–236)

Pythagoras had a custom that whenever someone came to him to be a student, the student sold his belongings and deposited his money, kept sealed, with Pythagoras.

Then the student would remain in silence sometimes for three, but sometimes for five years while learning. When permitted again to speak, he would mix with the others, remain as a student, and have a share at table. But if not, he would receive back his property and be expelled.

Iamblichus, *The Life of Pythagoras* §§30 and 90 (ca. AD 245–325)

For with his disciples, all things were common and the same to all and no one possessed any thing private. Those who approved of this community used all possessions in the most just way, but he who did not, received back his own property which he had brought into the common stock, with an addition and departed. . . .

. . . During this probationary period, the property of each was disposed of in common and was committed to the care of those appointed for this purpose. . . . Those of the probationers who proved themselves worthy to participate of his dogmas, after a silence of five years' duration, became Esoterics and both heard and saw Pythagoras himself, behind the veil. . . . If they were rejected they received double the wealth which they had brought and a tomb was raised to them, as if they were dead.

Nevertheless, we must be careful not to take the sting out of the "everything in common" (Acts 2:44) practice of the believers. Following Jesus is a radical thing with radical implications for every aspect of our lives, including personal property and finances. John the Baptist already referenced this (Luke 3:10–14; 9:57–62), and Jesus stated it quite bluntly when he remarked that "those of you who do not give up everything you have cannot be my disciples" (Luke 14:33; cf. 18:18–27). By declaring faith in Jesus Christ, individual believers have acknowledged that all they have belongs to God. Thus, while individual believers might maintain individual stewardship over the things God has granted them, a radical generosity—one that may appear strange but no less attractive to onlookers—is the expected norm for those following Jesus. The overall point here seems to be that the Jesus movement was not only a *growing* endeavor, but it was also a notably *united* endeavor. There was familial joy in this generous togetherness ("glad and sincere hearts, praising God"), and onlookers observed and appreciated this joyous existence ("enjoying the favor of all the people"; Acts 2:46–47).

Making bread in Nazareth Village, a first-century open-air museum.

After this brief overview summary of church life, Luke zooms in to recount four specific instances about how these matters were lived out practically. Each of the four specific episodes illustrates a challenge to the life of the church. These stories of challenge alternate between external challenges (3:1–4:31; 5:17–42) and internal challenges (4:32–5:16; 6:1–7), and each demonstrates a proper response to the issue being faced.

7.2 AN EXTERNAL CHALLENGE TO CHURCH LIFE: INTIMIDATION (ACTS 3:1–4:31)

Luke examines a first challenge to church life in a rather extensive episode that begins with Peter and John going to the temple courts, and this challenge involves an external threat. The episode consists of four basic parts: a miracle that takes place (3:1–10), a message Peter preaches (3:11–26), the reaction the Jewish leadership has to Peter's message (4:1–22), and the reflection that the young church has on all that transpires (4:23–31).

7.2.1 MIRACLE (3:1–10)

Beginning with a simple narration, the episode recounts a dramatic example of a miracle accomplished through the apostles: a disabled beggar is healed.[23] Rather than being given what he asked for (i.e., money; 3:2–5), the beggar was given what he really wanted and had never had (i.e., health; 3:7). This changed life became an opportunity for others to hear the life-changing message of the gospel (3:8–10). Interestingly, Luke repeats the location of this event, mentioning the ***temple in Jerusalem*** six times (3:1, 2 [twice], 3, 8, 10) and naming the particular gate twice (3:2, 10). With such points of repetition (see also "walk," "leap," "praise," "saw," "all the people") and other storytelling techniques for emphasis (see 4:14, 16, 22), Luke communicates clearly to his reader that a confirmed miraculous event had occurred.

7.2.2 MESSAGE (3:11–26)

The miracle took place on the steps to the temple at the Beautiful Gate (see sidebar).[24] As the crowd grows larger, Peter and John move out to the larger gentile courtyard. Perhaps continuing his concern to defend the historicity of the miracle, Luke identifies the location more precisely as Solomon's Colonnade, the portico along the eastern side of the outer temple courts.[25] With the healed man present, Peter sees an opportunity to address the Israelite crowd gathering in astonishment (3:11). Miracles in Luke-Acts seldom occur as if they were their own goal; that is, miracles are always about something else: more than to the person experiencing the miraculous intervention, miracles point to Jesus. For Peter this miracle is a conspicuous opportunity to direct people's attention to God and to Jesus.

In his message, Peter specifies that he and John are not responsible for the miracle (3:12); rather, the God of Israel did it through his servant Jesus (3:16). Luke's summary of Peter's message does not take long to get from preaching about God to preaching about Jesus, and he is not shy about describing the recent events of Jesus's life, death,

23. Stott, *Message of Acts*, 90.
24. See Howard G. Andersen, "Beautiful Gate," *ZEB* 1:534–35.
25. See J. Barton Payne, "Solomon's Colonnade (Porch)," *ZEB* 5:562.

The Beautiful Gate of the Temple

Herod the Great conducted an extensive remodeling project to expand the Jerusalem Temple Mount and to beautify the buildings and various courtyards around the temple. One of the gateways between two of the courtyards is dubbed in Acts—and only in Acts—The Beautiful Gate (Acts 3:2, 10). The precise identity of this gate is disputed, but the two most likely candidates are the Nicanor Gate (the gate at the top of a set of curved steps between the Court of the Women and the Court of the Israelites approaching the front of the temple) and the Corinthian Gate (the central gate utilized when moving from Solomon's Colonnade in the Court of the Gentiles straight into the Court of the Women). The Mishnah describes the bronze Nicanor Gate as one that gleamed like gold (*m. Middot* 2:3), and Josephus describes the Corinthian Gate as made of "Corinthian bronze, and far more valuable than those overlaid with silver plates and set in gold" (Josephus, *J.W.* 5.5.3 §§201-6).

Second Temple model

In the Name of Jesus

To do something "in the name of" another person is to do something the other person desires and authorizes. In the extended narrative of Acts 3-5, the word "name" (Greek: *onoma*) is mentioned twelve times in connection with Jesus (Acts 3:6, 16 [twice]; 4:7, 10, 12, 17, 18, 30; 5:28, 40, 41) pertaining to *preaching* the gospel of salvation, *healing* people, and *obeying* God.

and resurrection (3:13–15). Peter calls the Jews from their rejection of Jesus to repentance and faith in him because this miraculous event was accomplished by Jesus's name (3:16–20). In addition to referring to the "name" of Jesus (3:6, 16 [twice]), Peter uses a variety of descriptive titles for Jesus in this particular sermon, including "servant" (3:13, 26), "the Holy and Righteous One" (3:14), "the author of life" (3:15), and "Messiah" (3:18, 20), titles that would have significance for the Jewish listeners.

Proem ("Introduction") Sermon Framing

A Homiletical Format for Discussing Several Passages in One Sermon

From rabbinic Judaism (early fourth century AD), the sermonic format for this approach generally had the following outline:

I. An initial text for the day, usually from the Pentateuch.
II. A second text, the proem, as the "introduction" for the discourse.
III. The exposition, including supplementary quotations, parables, and other commentary, with verbal links to both the initial text and the final text.
IV. A final text, usually alluding to the initial text and sometimes adding a concluding application.

NT examples of this format regularly lack a secondary text, occasionally lack verbal links between the texts, and regularly have some eschatological orientation or application. Variations on proem framings are recognizable in Luke 20:9–19 (cf. the Synoptic parallels Matt 21:33–46 // Mark 12:1–12) and Acts 3:11–26; 7:2–53; 13:17–41.

In other ways Luke's summary of Peter's message points to the proper Jewishness of faith in Jesus. In particular, Peter argues that faith in Jesus has a scriptural basis in the OT prophets, utilizing several statements to summarize the teaching of the prophets (3:18, 21, 24) and offering paraphrases of several passages from the Pentateuch (Acts 3:22–23a cites Deut 18:15–19; Acts 3:23b cites Lev 23:29; and Acts 3:25 cites Gen 22:18; cf. 26:4). Thus, Peter begins with connecting the miracle to Jesus and then connects the gospel events about Jesus with the Hebrew Scriptures to call his listeners to respond to the gospel. Some see in Peter's sermon here a midrash homiletical format known as the proem (see sidebar).[26] The point here is that Peter is preaching the gospel

26. See esp. John W. Bowker, "The Speeches in Acts: A Study in Proem and Yelammedenu Form," *NTS* 14 (1967–1968): 96–111; cf. the caution of I. Howard Marshall, "Acts," pp. 513–606 in *Commentary on the New Testament Use of the Old Testament*, ed. G. K. Beale and D. A. Carson (Grand Rapids: Baker Academic, 2007), 521. See also E. Earle Ellis, *The Old Testament in Early Christianity: Canon and Interpretation in the Light of Modern Research*

to a Jewish audience, appealing to the Hebrew Scriptures in a Jewish sermon format, and addressing their need to accept the Jewish Messiah. The nation of Israel ought to recognize that God was working to fulfill his Scriptures through the message that Jesus is the long-awaited Messiah.

7.2.3 Reactive Pressure (4:1–22)

As Luke reports it, the reaction to Peter's message in Acts 3 is somewhat mixed. On the one hand, the religious leadership is disturbed about the messianic resurrection teaching regarding Jesus, and this led to the arrest of Peter and John and a night in jail (4:1–3). On the other hand, there is a sizable positive response, with the number of believers growing to about five thousand (4:4). Remarkably then, opposition to faith in Christ came from the Jewish religious leaders, not the general populace. At their hearing before the Jewish council of elders and rulers (Acts 4:5, a.k.a. the Sanhedrin in 4:15), Peter and John are asked, "By what power or what name did you do this?" (4:7; cf. Luke 20:1–2), which becomes another opportunity to share the gospel message.

Luke specifically notes that Peter is "filled with the Holy Spirit" (4:8; cf. Luke 12:11–12), and Peter astutely utilizes the somewhat vague question to connect the healing event directly to the gospel message (4:8–10). In so doing, he again connects the gospel to the Hebrew Scriptures identifying Jesus as the one "you builders rejected" (4:11; citing Ps 118:22), which marks the Jewish religious leaders as standing against the cornerstone of the Jewish faith. Stott observes that this is the third time Peter uses "the graphic formula 'you killed him, but God raised him'" (Acts 2:23–24; 3:15; 4:10).[27] Nevertheless, Peter finishes his testimony opportunity by explaining the truly unique benefit of faith in Jesus as the Christ: "Salvation is found in no one else, for there is no other name under heaven given to mankind by which we must be saved" (4:12).

Peter's bold proclamation of the gospel leaves the Sanhedrin with the distinct impression that "these men had been with Jesus" (4:13). Furthermore, with the undeniable evidence of the miracle literally standing before them, the Sanhedrin was in a quandary and felt it necessary to discuss the matter privately (4:14–15), where they eventually decide simply to warn Peter and John to stop speaking and teaching at all in the name of Jesus (4:16–18). Peter and John nonetheless insist that "we cannot help speaking about what we have seen and heard" (4:20). So, persisting in their resistant indecision, the Sanhedrin resorts to intimidation tactics, and with further threats they simply release Peter and John (4:21–22).

(Tübingen: Mohr Seibeck, 1991; repr., Eugene, OR: Wipf & Stock, 2003), 96–100; idem, "How the New Testament Uses the Old," pp. 199–219 in *New Testament Interpretation: Essays on Principles and Methods*, ed. I. Howard Marshall (Grand Rapids: Eerdmans, 1977), 203–5; and idem, *Prophecy & Hermeneutic in Early Christianity: New Testament Essays* (Grand Rapids: Eerdmans, 1978; repr., Eugene, OR: Wipf & Stock, 2003), 155–58.

27. Stott, *Message of Acts*, 97.

7.2.4 Reflective Prayer (4:23–31)

Released from custody, Peter and John report their experience with the Sanhedrin to the other Jesus followers, and the immediate response of the believers is to pray together about this opposition (4:23–30). Their prayer utilizes the words of Scripture in three forms. First, in addressing the Lord as sovereign, the believers echo an OT theme expressing faith in the ***sovereignty of God*** over everything: "you made the heavens and the earth and the sea, and everything in them" (Acts 4:24; cf. Exod 20:11; Ps 146:6; 2 Kgs 19:15; 2 Chr 2:12; Neh 9:6; Isa 37:16; 42:5). Second, the believers cite Psalm 2:1–2 in their prayer, finding another typological correlation between the treatment of the OT Israelite king David and the treatment of Jesus, the ultimate king (cf. Acts 1:15–26). In their prayer they draw out the parallels to explain that Herod (a "king"), Pilate (a "ruler"), gentiles ("nations"), and Jews ("people" of Israel) have all conspired against Jesus (Acts 4:25–27). A third occurrence of Scripture in their prayer is a subtle allusion to the OT belief in God's sovereign control even over bad things (4:28; cf. Isa 46:10). Thus, in their prayer these believers are expressing good theology and submission to the Lord in the face of intimidating circumstances.

When the believers finally reach their actual request for the sovereign Lord's intervention, they do not ask for the threatening intimidation to be stopped. Rather, in light of the threats, they ask the Lord to enable them to speak the gospel message with great boldness and to perform whatever miraculous signs might be helpful (Acts 4:29–30). Luke then concludes this episode with a brief report of their prayer being answered: "After they prayed, the place where they were meeting was shaken. And they were all filled with the Holy Spirit and spoke the word of God boldly" (4:31). Noteworthy here is that Luke again uses the "filled" metaphor to indicate that the believers were being empowered by the Holy Spirit—here not to speak in tongues but to speak with boldness. They had prayed for "boldness" to speak God's word (4:29) and the Lord empowered them so that they "spoke the word of God boldly (4:31).

7.2.5 Response to Intimidation: Pray for Boldness

So, in his examination of a first challenge to church life, Luke tells a lengthy story about a couple of dedicated believers who, while doing good and giving Jesus credit for it, find themselves in a threatening situation. While the believers persisted to represent the gospel message with courage and clarity, the opposition resorted to intimidating threats and the church responded to the intimidation with prayer—not prayer for the threats to stop, but prayer for boldness to face the challenges. This would be a good model for churches to follow today. This kind of prayer displays the radical dependence Jesus followers are to have on God.

7.3 AN INTERNAL CHALLENGE TO CHURCH LIFE: CORRUPTION (ACTS 4:32–5:16)

Various elements in 4:32–5:16 are reminiscent of Luke's earlier summary on the common life of the church in 2:42–47. So much so that some scholars have suggested Luke may have accidentally repeated himself (or mixed up his notes in writing the book).[28] But such a suggestion seems shortsighted and ignores Luke's larger context and purposes. His repetition is intentional and is not merely repetition but also expansion on church life. This is because the second challenge to church life that Luke examines comes not from an external threat but has its origins within the church itself. Thus, to explore this inside threat, Luke begins with a reiteration of the church's common life (4:32–35). Then he briefly describes a positive example (4:36–37), which serves as a foil for the negative example that proves to be a source of the internal challenge (5:1–11). Finally, once the threat is addressed, this episode concludes with yet another synopsis of church life (5:12–16).

7.3.1 COMMUNITY LIFE (AGAIN) (4:32–35)

In this recapitulation of the church's community life, Luke stresses their unity ("one in heart and mind"; 4:32a) and their radical generosity ("they shared everything they had"; 4:32b). Of the four aspects of community life in Acts 2:42, this applies to the "fellowship" feature of the church, which is the primary focus of this episode. God's grace was powerfully at work, Luke says, with the rather pragmatic result "that there were no needy persons among them" (4:33–34a). This was the effect of the believers' God-induced radical generosity, not from a militant socialist mandate. As Luke states it, from time to time wealthier believers would voluntarily liquidate assets to help others in need (4:34b–35); people were not required to sell off all their property at once when they became believers.[29] While some have speculated that the new church may have given too much away and that they squandered their resources to the point that they became poor and dependent on others,[30] Luke specifies that the poverty the Jerusalem believers suffered a little later in the story was due to a famine (11:27–30). Other NT writers also describe extreme benevolence among believers (e.g., John 15:12–13; Rom 12:13–21; Jas 1:27; 2:14–17; 1 John 3:16–18), which supports the claim that Luke is recounting instances of radical generosity in the early church as positive examples for all believers to emulate.

---

28. See the brief discussions in Ernst Haenchen, *The Acts of the Apostles: A Commentary*, trans. and ed. Bernard Noble, Gerald Shinn, Hugh Anderson, and R. McLeod Wilson (Philadelphia: Westminster, 1971), 193–96; and Fitzmyer, *Acts*, 312–13; contra, Keener, *Acts*, 2:1175.

29. Schnabel, *Acts*, 272; Keener, *Acts*, 2:1177.

30. E.g., J. A. Ziesler, *Christian Asceticism* (Grand Rapids: Eerdmans, 1974), 110; cf. David John Williams, *Acts*, NIBCNT 5 (Peabody: Hendrickson, 1990), 92–93; contra Ajith Fernando, *Acts*, The NIV Application Commentary (Grand Rapids: Zondervan, 1998), 182–82; Keener, *Acts*, 2:1176.

7.3.2 Positive Example (4:36–37)

Regarding the generous sharing among believers, Luke points to the positive example of "Joseph, a Levite from Cyprus, whom the apostles called ***Barnabas*** (which means 'son of encouragement'), sold a field he owned and brought the money and put it at the apostles' feet" (Acts 4:36–37). Barnabas's given name, Joseph, was perhaps so common that a nickname would be helpful to distinguish him from others of the same name.[31] Luke sometimes introduces readers to a character in some detail earlier in the story as a matter of foreshadowing to that character's role later in the story. This is the case with Barnabas, who will soon play several key roles in Acts. While Luke's comment on the nickname has been a bit baffling to scholars,[32] whatever its etymology, Luke's story bears out that the nickname "Barnabas" is attached to an agent of encouragement (cf. 9:27; 11:22–26; 13:15; 15:37–39) who speaks as a prophet of God's word (cf. 13:1, 5, 43, 46; 14:1, 3, 7, 14–18, 21, 25). At this first introduction, Barnabas is noted as being radically generous in his fellowship with other believers.

7.3.3 Negative Example (5:1–11)

After his brief description of Barnabas as a positive example (two verses), Luke embarks on a longer (and thus more emphatic) account of a negative example (eleven verses) seen in a husband-and-wife couple, ***Ananias*** and ***Sapphira***. This married couple sold some property and gave some of the proceeds to the church fund, but then they lied about it by claiming to have given all the proceeds (5:1–3). Perhaps there were good reasons to keep back some of the money, which Peter said would have been just fine; after all, there was no requirement for believers to sell their property or to give any of the proceeds (5:4). The problem here is the deliberate, premeditated deception that was sinfully planned, apparently to gain a name for godliness and good works—perhaps trying to look as generous as Barnabas.[33] But the dishonesty of Ananias and Sapphira was not merely to the members of the church: they also lied to the Holy Spirit (5:3), which is lying to God (5:4).

It is noteworthy that Peter asks, "Ananias, how is it that Satan has so filled your heart . . ." (5:3). "Filled" by Satan—i.e., Satan has directed, empowered, and characterized them—Ananias and Sapphira approached God with a wrong disposition, and the results here are reminiscent of OT stories where people brought offerings to God with wrong means or motivations (e.g., Lev 10:1–3; Num 3:4; 16:1–35; 26:61; 1 Sam 2:12–36

31. Keener, *Acts*, 2:1181.

32. See G. Adolf Deissmann, *Bible Studies: Contributions Chiefly from Papyri and Inscriptions to the History of the Language, the Literature, and the Religion of Hellenistic Judaism and Primitive Christianity*, trans. Alexander Grieve (Edinburgh: T&T Clark, 1901; repr. Peabody, MA: Hendrickson, 1988), 307–10; Barrett, *Acts*, 1:258–59; and Keener, *Acts*, 2:1180–81.

33. Stott suggests that Luke's term "kept back" (Greek: *nosphizomai*) might indicate that Ananias and Sapphira had contracted before the sale of their property to give all the proceeds to the church, which means their holding some of the proceeds back for themselves amounted to a kind of embezzlement; Stott, *Message of Acts*, 109, where he says further, "They were not so much misers as thieves and—above all—liars."

Stories of Divine Discipline in the Hebrew Scriptures

Several stories of God miraculously disciplining his people occur in the Hebrew Scriptures, usually the result of open defiance of the Lord or for profaning something sacred. Those in Luke's audience familiar with such stories would have been less concerned about the miraculous judgment of Ananias and Sapphira than many modern readers (see Keener, *Acts*, 2:1192–93). Here is a sampling of these OT stories.

Exodus 32:1–35—When the Israelites made a golden calf to worship at Mount Sinai, the Lord sent a plague.

Leviticus 10:1–3 (cf. 16:1–2)—Nadab and Abihu, sons of Aaron, presumptuously offered a sacrifice of unauthorized incense before the Lord, which resulted in their deaths by fire from the Lord.

Numbers 11:1–3—At Taberah, the Israelites complained about the misfortunes of their life in the wilderness, and fire from the Lord consumed some of them.

Numbers 11:4–35—At Kibroth Hattaavah, the Israelites complained about having nothing but manna to eat, so the Lord provided quail for their appetites and a plague for their punishment.

Numbers 14:36–38—Ten of the twelve men Moses sent to spy out the promised land died by means of a plague sent by the Lord because of their negative influence on the Israelites.

Numbers 16:1–35—Korah, Dathan, Abiram, their households, and companions (250 people) were swallowed up by the earth as a result of their opposition to the Lord's chosen leaders.

Numbers 16:36–50—In the wake of the Korah affair, many of the Israelites complained about God's judgment, and their speaking against Moses and Aaron led to a plague in which another 14,700 people died.

Numbers 21:4–9—Because of their speaking against God and against Moses, many Israelites died in a plague of fiery serpents sent by the Lord.

Numbers 25:1–9—When the Israelites participated in open idolatry to the pagan god Baal when living among the Midianites, a plague led to the deaths of 24,000 of the Israelites.

2 Samuel 6:1–15 (and 1 Chronicles 13:1–14)—Uzzah was struck dead for touching the ark of the covenant.

2 Kings 1:1–17—King Ahaziah participated in idolatry and sent disrespectful messengers to God's prophet Elijah; two groups of messengers died by the fire of God, and the king died.

2 Kings 2:23–24—The mocking of God's prophet Elisha resulted in violent death.

with 4:1–11). Luke does not address the question of whether Ananias and Sapphira were really believers.[34] He simply points out that Ananias's dishonest action was conspiratorial with Sapphira (Acts 5:1–2), that it was indicative of Satan's work and not God's (5:3–4), and that both were held equally responsible for their corrupt action (5:5–10).

34. The NT gives evidence of such a thing as false belief (e.g., Acts 20:30; 1 Cor 11:19; 1 John 2:19; John 17:12; Luke 8:11–15—see more on this in chapter 8), but it also suggests that true believers can unwisely open themselves to the work of Satan in their lives (e.g., Matt 16:23; Mark 8:33; 1 Cor 5:5; 7:5; Eph 4:27; 1 Tim 1:20; 3:6–7). While Luke does not directly address any question about the genuineness of the conversions of Ananias and Sapphira, he recounts this event—contrasting them with Barnabas—as if they were all part of the Jerusalem church.

The "Church" and Its Other Names in Acts

In Luke-Acts, the term *church* does not occur until (the rather serious circumstances of) Acts 5:11. But even before then, Luke expresses some sense of community for the group of Jesus followers. The vocabulary utilized in Acts for believers—in reference to the group as well as to individuals—can be informative regarding the community's own understanding of themselves.

Terms for the Group

church—(Greek: *ekklēsia*)—18 times for a local Christian assembly (e.g., Acts 5:11; 11:26; 20:17; 14:23); 1 time for a regional cluster of Christian assemblies (Acts 9:31); 3 times for a generic assembly of people (Acts 19:32, 39, 41); and 1 time for the OT assembly of God's people (Acts 7:38).

kingdom—(*basileia*)—8 times to refer to the reign or rule of God specifically through Jesus (Acts 1:3, 6; 8:12; 14:22; 19:8; 20:25; 28:33, 31).

the Way—(*hēhodos*)—6 times in reference to Christianity (Acts 9:2; 19:9, 23; 22:4; 24:14, 22).

multitude/company—(*plēthos*)—often for a "crowd" (e.g., Acts 2:6; 5:16) or a great "number" (e.g., Acts 5:14); 5 times for the company of believers in Jesus (Acts 4:32; 6:2, 5; 15:12, 30).

the people [of God]—(*ho laos*)—occasional uses for the OT Israelites (e.g., Acts 3:23; 7:34; 13:17; 23:5; 26:23); 2 times for the followers of Jesus as God's people (Acts 15:14; 18:10).

flock—(*poimnion*)—2 times as a metaphor for Jesus's followers (Acts 20:28, 29; cf. Luke 12:32).

the Nazarenes—(*hoi Nazōraioi*)—with Christ known as "Jesus of Nazareth" (Acts 2:22; 3:6; 4:10; 6:14; 22:8; 26:9; cf. 10:38), his followers are once reckoned as a Jewish "sect" or party dubbed "the Nazarenes" (Acts 24:5; cf. *hairesis* for "sect" also in 24:14; 28:22).

Terms for Individuals (or the Group When Plural)

the brothers and sisters—(*hoi adelphoi*)—a total of 57 times: 3 times for literal brothers (Acts 1:14; 7:13; 12:2); 21 times for fellow Israelites (e.g., Acts 2:29, 37; 3:17, 22; 7:2, 23, 25, 26, 37); and 33 times for fellow followers of Jesus (Acts 1:15, 16; 6:3; 9:30; 10:23; 11:1, 12, 29; 12:17; 14:2; 15:1, 3, 7, 13, 22, 23 [twice], 32, 33, 36, 40; 16:2, 40; 17:6, 10, 14; 18:18, 27; 21:7, 17, 20; 28:14, 15).

the disciples—(*hoi mathētoi*)—26 times for followers of Jesus (Acts 6:1, 2, 7; 9:1, 10, 19, 26 [twice], 38; 11:26, 29; 13:52; 14:20, 22, 28; 15:10; 16:1; 18:23, 27; 19:9, 30; 20:1, 30; 21:4, 16 [twice]).

the believers—(participle of *pisteuō*)—14 times for followers of Jesus, i.e., "those believing" in him (Acts 2:44; 4:32; 5:14; 10:43; 11:17, 21; 13:39; 15:5; 16:34; 18:27; 19:18; 21:20, 25; 22:19).

the holy ones (saints)—(*hoi hagioi*)—4 times for believers as "holy people" (Acts 9:13, 32, 41; 26:10; NIV sometimes uses "the Lord's people").

the servants/slaves [of God]—(*hoi douloi*)—3 times for followers of God/Jesus (Acts 2:18; 4:29; 16:17).

the sanctified—(passive participle of *hagiazō*)—2 times in Acts for people made holy by faith in Jesus (Acts 20:32; 26:18).

the Christians—(*hoi Christianoi*)—3 times in the whole NT (Acts 11:26; 26:28; 1 Pet 4:16).

What seems to be the focus of Luke's remarks here about corruption in the church is bound up in the repeated response of the church: "the whole church" and all who hear the news about Ananias and Sapphira respond with "great fear" (5:5, 11). Apparently, people should be afraid of the consequences of their dishonesty. Or said more positively, the fellowship of the church is important to God, and honesty is a fundamental and functional expectation in the community of believers.[35]

It is perhaps informative that Luke's first use of the term "church" (*ekklēsia*) is in this serious context of dishonesty (5:11; see the sidebar for Luke's terms for the church).[36] While the term is used in first-century Greek to refer to public gatherings and nonreligious assemblies (e.g., Acts 19:32, 39, 41), the Septuagint tends to utilize this term especially for the people of God. Thus, Peterson suggests that "reserving the use of such a significant term for this climactic moment in his narrative" is a way for Luke to characterize the group as God's designated people.[37] This episode is sometimes compared to the lie of Achan and his family in Joshua 7–8, where God's people are summoned to better living (Josh 8:34–35 LXX utilizes the term *ekklēsia*). Luke similarly challenges God's newly reformulated people to uncorrupted living.[38] Luke is getting his audience to face their need for radical accountability in their fellowship with one another.

7.3.4 Accountable Community Life (5:12–16)

Even though "great fear" came upon the whole church (5:11), Luke notes that they were still gathering "together" (5:12). The size of the group necessitated a large gathering place, and the temple courts provided such a space, even with some covering like that provided by ***Solomon's Colonnade***. With the power of God evidenced in the apostolic leadership (Acts 5:12, 15–16), unbelievers were reluctant to intrude on such meetings of the church, but they still held the believers in high esteem (5:13).[39] And as they became convinced of the serious truth of the gospel, more and more people became believers and joined the community (5:14).

---

35. See Witherington, *Acts*, 220; John B. Polhill, *Acts*, NAC (Nashville: Broadman, 1992), 161.

36. See Schnabel, *Acts*, 176; and Kendell H. Easley, "The Church in Acts and Revelation: New Testament Bookends," pp. 65–102 in *The Community of Jesus: A Theology of the Church*, ed. Kendell H. Easley and Christopher W. Morgan (Nashville: B&H Academic, 2013), esp. 65–82. The works of Schnabel and Easley have influenced the sidebar presentation of the vocabulary for the church in Acts.

37. Peterson, *Acts*, 213.

38. Storm, *Living Lord, Empowering Spirit, Testifying People*, 49. In addition to the OT parallel to the sin of Achan and his family as recounted in Joshua 7–8, Peterson speaks of the "original sin" of the church and compares the sin of Ananias and Sapphira in Acts 5 to that of Adam and Eve in Genesis 3; Peterson, *Acts*, 209.

39. D. Williams, *Acts*, 102–3.

Solomon's Colonnade

Built by Herod the Great as part of his remodeling of the Jerusalem Temple Mount, Solomon's Colonnade ("Porch" in CEV; "Portico" in ESV, NASB, NET) was a long, roofed porch lined with columns that ran along the outermost eastern edge of the temple courts. It may have gotten its name from a tradition (reported by Josephus, *J.W.* 5.5.1–2 §§184–93; cf. *Ant.* 8.3.9 §§95–98) that Solomon had built a similar structure on the eastern side of the grounds around the original temple. Jesus taught in Solomon's Colonnade (John 10:22–39, esp. v. 23), so it is unsurprising that the early Christians continued to meet there (Acts 3:11; 5:12).

aquatarkus/stock.adobe.com

Healed in Peter's Shadow

In Acts 5:15–16, Luke makes a somewhat strange comment about Peter's shadow. He remarks that "people brought the sick into the streets and laid them on beds and mats so that at least Peter's shadow might fall on some of them as he passed by. Crowds gathered also from the towns around Jerusalem, bringing their sick and those tormented by impure spirits, and all of them were healed." What is this about?

The term for "overshadow" (Greek: *episkiazō*) is used four other times in the New Testament (Matt 17:5; Mark 9:7; Luke 1:35; 9:34) and four times in the LXX (Exod 40:35; Pss 91:4; 140:7; Prov 18:11). Most of these usages are in reference to God's presence (the exception is Prov 18:11), so even the connection to being "overshadowed" by Peter's shadow in Acts 5:15 can be understood as giving God the credit for the miraculous.

7.3.5 Response to Corruption: Fellowship in Accountability

The second threat to the life of the church is the internal challenge of corruption. Not all the church's problems come from the outside. We should remind ourselves that there is no perfect church this side of eternity.[40] As the young church was exercising its generous fellowship, the problem of corrupt motives entered the community, which led to people lying. The proper response to such corruption is accountability. Accountability in the fellowship of the church can include confrontation, which has restoration as its goal (NB: Peter confronted the sin discovered in the church but did not suggest, much less carry out, capital punishment against Ananias and Sapphira when he made his confrontation). Indeed, we can imagine a more pleasant result for Ananias and Sapphira had either or both of them repented of their conspiracy rather than persist in the lie. But accountability in the fellowship of the church will help the work of the church to continue fittingly motivated, supportively encouraged, and with proper results. As a community of imperfect people saved by the Lord and empowered by his Spirit to make a difference in one another's lives and in the world around them—and very different from a mere social club—the church is to be a community of radical accountability.[41]

7.4 AN EXTERNAL CHALLENGE TO CHURCH LIFE: PERSECUTION (ACTS 5:17–42)

Now Luke switches from an internal challenge to address another external challenge to church life, and unsurprisingly there are some natural parallels with the previously discussed external challenge (3:1–4:31). The similarities between Luke's descriptions of the two external threats are such that some scholars have suggested that Luke has accidentally created a doublet here with the same event being recorded twice. While both episodes involve arrests at the instigation of the Jewish priesthood and recount hearings before the Sanhedrin where the apostles hold to their convictions, there are enough variances to be convincing that they are two different events. Acts 5:17–42 involves all the apostles (not merely Peter and John as in the earlier episode), a miraculous release from jail necessitating a secondary summons (not the case with Peter and John), and a physical beating of all the apostles (not merely an intimidating warning). Particularly noteworthy here is that the high priest specifically references the previous episode as a separate event that went unheeded and has escalated to this new confrontation (5:28). Thus, the two episodes are in fact two different events.

40. I playfully remind students, "If you find a perfect church, don't join it; it won't be perfect after you get there!"

41. See Michael S. Moore, "Civic and Voluntary Associations in the Greco-Roman World," in Green and McDonald, *The World of the New Testament*, 149–55; cf. Wayne A. Meeks, *The First Urban Christians: The Social World of the Apostle Paul*, 2nd ed. (New Haven, CT: Yale University Press, 2003), 75–84.

7.4.1 Arrest and Miraculous Release (5:17–26)

In Acts 4 Peter and John were arrested because the priesthood had been "greatly disturbed" at their preaching about the resurrection (4:1–2); in Acts 5 all the apostles are arrested because the priesthood is "filled with jealousy" at the impact they are having on the people of Jerusalem (5:17–18; cf. vv. 12–16). A significant difference between the two episodes is that in Acts 5 the apostles are miraculously released from the jail during the night and need to be reapprehended, and Luke offers a somewhat lengthy account of it (5:19–26). This is the first of several such miraculous escapes from custody in Acts.

7.4.2 Legal Hearing (5:27–33)

When the apostles are eventually brought in for a Sanhedrin hearing, the presiding high priest notes that the council's previous demand issued to Peter and John (cf. 4:18) was meant to apply to all of them: they were not to preach in the name of Jesus. Furthermore, the Sanhedrin did not appreciate the people being reminded that the Jewish authorities had a role in Jesus's death—after all, it does not look good for the Jewish religious leadership to be responsible for the death of the long-awaited Jewish Messiah (5:27–28).

Nevertheless, even as Peter and John had been undeterred in Acts 4, so also the apostles remain steadfast in Acts 5. Peter speaks for the group: "We must obey God rather than human beings!" (5:29), and his words are consistent with his earlier response (see sidebar). Whereas in the previous hearing the Sanhedrin was astonished (4:13) and threatening (4:21), things have escalated now, especially given that all the apostles have continued teaching in the name of Jesus. So Luke notes here that the Sanhedrin has reached a new emotive level: "When they heard this, they were furious and wanted to put them to death" (5:33).

Comparing Peter's Responses to the Sanhedrin

Acts 4:8–12, 19–20	Acts 5:29–32
Then Peter, filled with the Holy Spirit, said to them: "Rulers and elders of the people! If we are being called to account today for an act of kindness shown to a man who was lame and are being asked how he was healed, then know this, you and all the people of Israel: It is by the name of Jesus Christ of Nazareth, whom you crucified but whom God raised from the dead, that this man stands before you healed. Jesus is "'the stone you builders rejected, which has become the cornerstone.' Salvation is found in no one else, for there is no other name under heaven given to mankind by which we must be saved." . . . But Peter and John replied, "Which is right in God's eyes: to listen to you, or to him? You be the judges! As for us, we cannot help speaking about what we have seen and heard."	Peter and the other apostles replied: "We must obey God rather than human beings! The God of our ancestors raised Jesus from the dead—whom you killed by hanging him on a cross. God exalted him to his own right hand as Prince and Savior that he might bring Israel to repentance and forgive their sins. We are witnesses of these things, and so is the Holy Spirit, whom God has given to those who obey him."

7.4.3 Gamaliel's Advice (5:34–39)

As noted in chapter 5, the ***Sanhedrin*** ("the full assembly of the elders of Israel"; 5:21) consisted of Sadducees (5:17) and Pharisees (5:34). As the party of the priesthood, the Sadducees held more power in the Jewish council, but as the party of the common people, the Pharisees maintained some influence. A Pharisee named ***Gamaliel***, "a teacher of the law, who was honored by all the people" (5:34) and who we learn later was Paul's teacher (22:3), stood up and ordered that the apostles be temporarily removed from the proceedings so that the Sanhedrin could discuss its public relations problem privately. Gamaliel's advice to the council is that they proceed with caution. Even as other disrupters of society have come and gone without any intervention of the council (he notes two in particular: see the sidebar on ***Theudas and Judas***), the same could be the case with these Jesus enthusiasts (5:35–37). So he advises, "Leave these men alone! Let them go! For if their purpose or activity is of human origin, it will fail. But if it is from God, you will not be able to stop these men; you will only find yourselves fighting against God" (5:38–39). For Luke's informed readers, there is a certain irony in Gamaliel's counsel. For what Gamaliel expresses as a mere possibility to the Sanhedrin turns out to be the truth: when people oppose the followers of Jesus, they are actually opposing the work of God.

Theudas and Judas in Acts 5 versus Judas and Theudas in Josephus

In Acts 5:36–37, Luke records Gamaliel as referencing two failed revolutionary leaders: first Theudas and then ("after him") Judas the Galilean. Scholars note that Josephus likewise references two failed revolutionaries (among others) named Judas the Galilean and Theudas, but in the reverse order (Josephus, *Ant.* 17.10.4–5 §§269–72 recounts a Judas, and 20.5.1 §§97–99 recounts a Theudas; cf. *J.W.* 2.8.1 §118). Scholars have discussed this apparent discrepancy, wondering whether it is Luke or Josephus who is wrong about the order (or perhaps Gamaliel was wrong and Luke simply reported what Gamaliel wrongly said in Acts 5).

But another suggestion seems just as likely: they could all be correct if they are talking about two different men named Theudas. The Theudas mentioned in Acts 5 would have led a rebellion before ca. AD 6–7, when Judas the Galilean led his rebellion; but the Theudas whom Josephus mentioned actually dates to a rebellion in ca. AD 44–46, "when Fadus was procurator of Judea," which would be about a decade or more after Gamaliel gave his speech in Acts 5. Thus, Gamaliel must have been speaking of a different Theudas than Josephus. Furthermore, albeit with some overstatement, Josephus himself says that there were "continuous and countless disorders" (or as some translate him, "ten thousand other disorders"), so it would not be surprising if there was another rebel with the name Theudas.

Flavius Josephus, *Jewish Antiquities* 17.10.4–5 §§269–72 (ca. AD 94)

> Meanwhile continuous and countless new tumults filled Judaea, and in many quarters many men rose in arms either in hope of personal gain or out of hatred for the Jews. For

example, two thousand of the soldiers who had once campaigned with Herod and had been disbanded, now assembled in Judaea itself and fought against the king's troops. These were led against them by Achiab, a cousin of Herod, but he was forced out of the plains into higher country by the enemy, who were very experienced in warfare, and by retreating to an inaccessible position, he saved what he could.

Then there was Judas, the son of the brigand chief Ezekias, who had been a man of great power and had been captured by Herod only with great difficulty. This Judas got together a large number of desperate men at Sepphoris in Galilee and there made an assault on the royal palace, and having seized all the arms that were stored there, he armed every single one of his men and made off with all the property that had been seized there. He became an object of terror to all men by plundering those he came across in his desire for great possessions and his ambition for royal rank, a prize that he expected to obtain not through the practice of virtue but through excessive ill-treatment of others.

Flavius Josephus, *Jewish Antiquities* 20.5.1 §§97–99 (ca. AD 94)

During the period when Fadus was procurator of Judaea, a certain impostor named Theudas persuaded the majority of the masses to take up their possessions and to follow him to the Jordan River. He stated that he was a prophet and that at his command the river would be parted and would provide them an easy passage. With this talk he deceived many. Fadus, however, did not permit them to reap the fruit of their folly, but sent against them a squadron of cavalry. These fell upon them unexpectedly, slew many of them and took many prisoners. Theudas himself was captured, whereupon they cut off his head and brought it to Jerusalem. These, then, are the events that befell the Jews during the time that Cuspius Fadus was procurator.

Gamiliel (on right) as depicted in the Sarajevo Haggadah, a fourteenth century illuminated manuscript (ca. 1350).

The Picture Art Collection / Alamy Stock Photo

7.4.4 Conclusion of the Hearing (5:40–42)

Gamaliel's advice is persuasive to the rest of the Sanhedrin, and they determine to release the apostles. But merely releasing the apostles with nothing but a verbal warning might not achieve the immediate results the council members desire; this is how they had treated Peter and John in Acts 4, and it proved ineffective. So to emphasize their warning for the apostles to stop teaching in the name of Jesus, the Sanhedrin has them flogged, i.e., physically whipped (5:40). Thus, the external threat to the young church has escalated from mere verbal intimidation to physical persecution.

Of course, not recognizing Jesus as the Messiah, the persecutors probably thought they themselves were properly following the OT law; after all, the OT law allowed for the ***flogging*** of criminals (see sidebar).

The apostles' response to being flogged is one of rejoicing. Jesus had instructed them to rejoice when persecuted on his behalf (Luke 6:22–23). Now that the opposition has intensified to include physical suffering, the apostles sense in the suffering a kind of affirmation that they are on the right track. That is, they do not take pleasure in the pain; rather, given that their suffering is explicitly connected to their following of Jesus, Luke notes that they rejoiced "because they had been counted worthy of suffering disgrace for the Name" (Acts 5:41). And given this affirmation, they continue teaching and proclaiming the gospel message (5:42).

7.4.5 Response to Persecution: Teaching Continued

Luke's storytelling in this account emphasizes over and over again that the proper response to persecution is continued teaching of the truth. Intimidation had not been successful in stopping the praying church from carrying out their role as witnesses to the gospel; now persecution will not work against a church that is persistent at teaching the truth. Luke summarizes at the conclusion of the episode, "Day after day, in the temple courts and from house to house, they never stopped teaching and proclaiming the good news that Jesus is the Messiah" (5:42; cf. vv. 20, 21, 25, 28). In this way Luke emphasizes that persistence in apostolic teaching is the proper response to the external threat of ***persecution***, and the episode demonstrates the church's need for radical obedience to the Lord (which may call for civil disobedience to human authorities; see sidebar).[42]

The Hebrew Scriptures on Flogging Criminals

Deuteronomy 25:1–3

When people have a dispute, they are to take it to court and the judges will decide the case, acquitting the innocent and condemning the guilty. If the guilty person deserves to be beaten, the judge shall make them lie down and have them flogged in his presence with the number of lashes the crime deserves, but the judge must not impose more than forty lashes. If the guilty party is flogged more than that, your fellow Israelite will be degraded in your eyes.

Acts and the Importance of Teaching with Words

From N. T. Wright, *Acts: 26 Studies for Individuals and Groups*, N. T. Wright for Everyone Bible Study Guides (Downers Grove, IL: InterVarsity Press, 2010), 33.

> The angel told the apostles to go take their stand in the temple and speak (5:20). Wordless symbols, however powerful, remain open to a variety of explanations. From the very beginning, the apostolic faith has been something that demands to be explained, that needs to be taught. Without words to guide it, faith wanders in the dark and can easily fall over a cliff.

42. See the collection of essays on civil disobedience in Hannah Nation, ed., *Faithful Disobedience: Writings on Church and State from a Chinese House Church Movement* (Downers Grove, IL: IVP Academic, 2022).

Civil Disobedience and Acts 5:17–42

From Schnabel, *Acts*, 323.

> Following Jesus may lead to civil disobedience. The apostles continue to defy the ban on speaking that the highest court of the land had imposed. Peter insists that "we must obey God rather than human beings" (v. 29). Civil disobedience is never easy, but sometimes necessary. Some define civil disobedience as a deliberate, public, nonviolent action that is contrary to law (e.g., blocking a street) and that is designed to draw public attention to some policy of the government (e.g., abortion) in the hope that the policy will be changed. This is not in view here. The apostles do not mobilize the thousands of believers for a "march on the Sanhedrin" in order to pressure them to make faith in Jesus legal. But they do disobey the policy of the Sanhedrin that nobody may teach about Jesus as Israel's Messiah.
>
> If the alternative is between obeying God and obeying a government policy, disobedience to earthly authorities becomes a necessity. While Christians are citizens of an earthly state, they are also citizens of heaven, whose obligations they cannot ignore. Jesus said that we need to give to Caesar what is Caesar's but to give to God what is God's. And if there is a conflict, God's demands have priority. This happens when Christians are required to deny their faith in Jesus as Messiah and Savior, when they are required to commit sinful acts, and when they are required to act contrary to God's specific commands.

7.5 AN INTERNAL CHALLENGE TO CHURCH LIFE: DISRUPTION (ACTS 6:1–7)

Luke addresses one more threat to the life of the church, and this is another threat that originates from within the group of believers. Luke's readers may be surprised (and a little relieved) to find that this last threat is covered in only seven verses. It seems that Luke handles this significant threat to church life with a brevity that fits the pragmatics of the problem.

7.5.1 The Problem of Community Disruption (6:1–2)

Luke begins the description of the threat to church life with a reminder that the church was growing (6:1). Growth in the number of believers is a good thing, to be sure, but with such growth comes some complexities for life together, which can in turn introduce some problems. At this early stage in the church's history, the members of the Jerusalem church were all Jews, those who believed their long-awaited Messiah had come in the person of Jesus to save them from their sins (and not necessarily from Rome). But even sharing the same racial ethnicity as Jews would not necessitate that they all shared the same cultural/language background.[43] Since the time of Alexander the Great, Greek had become the international language, and Jews who had grown up in Greek-speaking territories away from Jerusalem would be unaccustomed with the language of the Hebrews. The ***Hebraic Jews*** were those speaking the first-century Hebrew language (i.e., Aramaic, a sister dialect to the OT Hebrew language), and the ***Hellenistic Jews*** were likely those who spoke Greek.[44] As Luke describes it, the Hellenistic Jews complained that their widows were being overlooked while the widows among the Hebraic Jews were being well-served by the Jerusalem church's system of caring for their poor.

Feading the hungry by Frederick Preedy (1868), Norfolk, England.

Holmes Garden Photos / Alamy Stock Photo

Whatever the detailed cause(s) for the difficulties—conspiracy, overt cultural discrimination, administrative oversight, etc.—this food distribution problem was disrupting the harmony of the church and threatening to be a distraction from its ministry of spreading the gospel message. The apostles, i.e., "the Twelve," recognize this disruption and are determined to have the church correct it: "It would not be right for us to neglect the ministry of the word of God in order to wait on tables" (6:2). Luke uses the same word "service, ministry" (Greek: *diakonia*) for both social work ("distribution" in 6:1) and for preaching the gospel message of the word of God ("ministry" in 6:4; cf. the related "ministry" verb in 6:2). These ministries fit together. The church is to pay attention to the community disruption with social ministry so as to avoid being distracted from the ministry of the word (cf. 1:8; 2:42; 4:2; 5:25, 42; 6:4). As Lesslie Newbigin has stated, "So words without deeds are empty, but deeds without words are dumb."[45] But what is to be done to properly attend to both concerns, healing the disruption and neutralizing the potential distraction?

7.5.2 The Solution of Shared Ministry (6:3–4)

In saying "a complaint arose" (Acts 6:1 in CSB, ESV, NET; "complained" in NIV, NLT), the noun for "complaint" (Greek: *goggusmos*) is a cognate term with the verb used in the LXX when some OT Israelites "complained" (*gogguzō*) about their hardships, which included the daily food rations of manna from heaven (Num 11:1–15, esp. v. 1).

43. Reta Halteman Finger, *Of Widows and Meals: Communal Meals in the Book of Acts*, (Grand Rapids: Eerdmans, 2007), 91–92, 253, 275; cf. Craig C. Hill, *Hellenists and Hebrews: Reappraising Division within the Earliest Church* (Minneapolis: Fortress, 1992); see esp. 11–17 and 193–97.

44. NLT has "Hebrew-speaking believers" and "Greek-speaking believers"; CEV has "the ones who spoke Aramaic" and "the ones who spoke Greek."

45. Lesslie Newbigin, *Mission in Christ's Way* (New York: Friendship, 1987), 11. Indeed, illustrating that words and deeds go together, Luke reports that the church selects seven new action-oriented ministers to attend to the disruption (Acts 6:1–6) and then soon discusses in more detail the speaking ministries of two of those seven (Stephen in 6:8–8:3; and Philip in 8:4–40).

A Solution That Follows a Scriptural Example

The apostles found it difficult to manage all the nuances of leadership over the expanding membership of the young church. Moses had faced similar difficulties in leading the people of God in the OT exodus (see Exod 18:13–26; Num 11:16–30). Luke does not report that the church intentionally emulated the OT Israelites, but the parallel is palpable. The Lord distributed some of Moses's duties to seventy of Israel's elders noted for their skills as leaders. It would similarly seem fitting for some of the leadership duties of the apostles to be distributed to qualified leaders over the growing needs of the church. And if seventy was the right number for the large nation of Israel (i.e., six hundred thousand men plus women and children; Num. 11:21; cf. Exod. 12:37; 38:25–26), then seven additional ministers should be sufficient at this early stage of the church's growth (i.e., five thousand men plus women and children; Acts 4:4).

Numbers 11:16–17	Acts 6:2–3
The Lord said to Moses: "Bring me seventy of Israel's elders who are known to you as leaders and officials among the people. Have them come to the tent of meeting, that they may stand there with you. I will come down and speak with you there, and I will take some of the power of the Spirit that is on you and put it on them. They will share the burden of the people with you so that you will not have to carry it alone."	So the Twelve gathered all the disciples together and said, "It would not be right for us to neglect the ministry of the word of God in order to wait on tables. Brothers and sisters, choose seven men from among you who are known to be full of the Spirit and wisdom. We will turn this responsibility over to them and will give our attention to prayer and the ministry of the word."

The apostles (and Luke, as he reports the event) may well be seeing a pattern here. It is instructive that the solution the apostles propose is similar to the solution that the Lord gave Moses: to appoint additional Spirit-empowered leaders who could share in the burden of ministry (see Num 11:16–17; cf. Exod 18:13–26).[46] In a similar way, the apostles suggest that the church "choose seven men from among you who are known to be full of the Spirit and wisdom" so that they can "turn this responsibility over to them" (Acts 6:3). These additional servants of the church would help the community address such pragmatic problems as the food distribution matter.

7.5.3 The New Ministers (6:5–6)

Addressing the problem of food distribution among the church's widows does not seem to define fully the duties of the newly selected leaders. Robert Price suggests

46. On the apostles emulating the example of Moses, see Keener, *Acts*, 2:1287; Schabel, *Acts*, 332.

several reasons that the Seven were not selected merely to wait on tables but to oversee such matters. First, Luke immediately tells stories of the speaking ministries of two of the Seven (Stephen and Philip in Acts 6–8). Second, the Seven were to be "known to be full of the Spirit and wisdom" (6:3), qualifications that imply ministry beyond simply distributing food. Third, the Twelve say that the Seven are to be given "this responsibility," that is, the responsibility of solving disputes and complaints, which would fit with the parallel of the ministers selected to help Moses in Numbers 11 (mentioned previously). The Seven were significant ministers and not merely food distributors.[47]

Luke provides the names of the Seven: "Stephen, a man full of faith and of the Holy Spirit; also Philip, Procorus, Nicanor, Timon, Parmenas, and Nicolas from Antioch, a convert to Judaism." (Acts 6:5). His expanded descriptions of the first and last on the list—i.e., Stephen and Nicholas—serve as narrative foreshadows of things yet to come in Acts. Stephen becomes a significant person in the next segment of the story as the first Christian martyr (6:8–8:1). And as the only one of the Seven whose hometown is mentioned, Nicholas "from Antioch" provides a narrative hint about a significant international place in the story (11:19–30), particularly for the sending of international missionaries (13:1–3).

Ordination of Stephen by St. Peter (other deacons in background) by Fra Angelico (ca. 1400-1455), Chapel of Nicholas V, Vatican Palace. World History Archive / Alamy Stock Photo

Not only were these new ministers selected by the church, they were also recognized by the apostles as legitimate ministers, and this recognition was demonstrated with the apostles praying for them and commissioning them with the physical gesture of laying their hands on them (Acts 6:6).[48] Luke does not give a title to this new administrative role; he simply calls them "the Seven" (Acts 21:8). While Luke's use of the generic noun for "service, ministry" (Greek: *diakonia*; Acts 6:4) leads some to refer to them with the related anglicized word ***deacons***, this passage in Acts does not really give definition to that role. Paul's letters indicate that some church leaders later had this title (see Phil 1:1; 1 Tim 3:8–13; cf. Rom 16:1), and the technical church offices of "deacon" and "deaconess" developed even later in church history.[49]

47. Robert M. Price, *The Widows Traditions in Luke-Acts: A Feminist-Critical Scrutiny*, SBLDS 155 (Atlanta: Scholars Press, 1997), 211–13.

48. For more on laying on of hands, see chapter 8 and the discussion of Philip's ministry in Acts 8:4–40.

49. See Jaroslav Pelikan, *Acts*, Brazos Theological Commentary on the Bible (Grand Rapids: Brazos, 2005), 91–93; Phillip W. Sell, "The Seven in Acts 6 as a Ministry Team," *BSac* 167 (2010): 58–67; and more generally, John Stam, "Deacon, Deaconess," *ZEB* 2:52–54.

Jewish Precedent for Selecting Seven Leaders

Several instances of shared leadership in the history of the Jews indicate something of a precedent for selecting seven as an ideal number of leaders for community tasks.

Joshua 6:4 (cf. vv. 8, 13)– "Have seven priests carry trumpets of rams' horns in front of the ark. On the seventh day, march around the city seven times, with the priests blowing the trumpets."

Jeremiah 52:25–"Of those still in the city, he took the officer in charge of the fighting men, and seven royal advisers."

Ezra 7:13–14–"Now I decree that any of the Israelites in my kingdom, including priests and Levites, who volunteer to go to Jerusalem with you, may go. You are sent by the king and his seven advisers to inquire about Judah and Jerusalem with regard to the Law of your God, which is in your hand."

Esther 2:9–"She pleased him and won his favor. Immediately he provided her with her beauty treatments and special food. He assigned to her seven female attendants selected from the king's palace and moved her and her attendants into the best place in the harem."

Josephus, *Jewish Antiquities* 4.8.14 §214–"As rulers let each city have seven men long exercised in virtue and in the pursuit of justice; and to each magistracy let there be assigned two subordinate officers of the tribe of Levi."

Josephus, *Jewish Antiquities* 4.8.38 §287–"But if, without any act of treachery, the depositary lose the deposit, let him come before the seven judges and swear by God that nothing had been lost through his own intention or malice, and that he had not appropriated any part of it to his own use, and so let him depart exempt from blame."

Josephus, *Jewish War* 2.20.5 §571–"He, therefore, selected from the nation seventy persons of mature years and the greatest discretion and appointed them magistrates of the whole of Galilee, and seven individuals in each city to adjudicate upon petty disputes, with instructions to refer more important matters and capital cases to himself and the seventy."

War Scroll (1QM) 7.13–14–"When the priests go out into the space between the battle lines, seven Levites shall go out with them. In their hands shall be seven trumpets of rams' horns."

Babylonian Talmud, Megillah 26a.17–26b.1–"Rava said: They taught that there is a limitation on what may be purchased with the proceeds of the sale of a synagogue only when the seven representatives of the town who were appointed to administer the town's affairs had not sold the synagogue in an assembly of the residents of the town. However, if the seven representatives of the town had sold it in an assembly of the residents of the town, then even to drink beer with the proceeds seems well and is permitted. The seven representatives have the authority to annul the sanctity of the synagogue, and therefore the proceeds of its sale do not retain any sanctity."

Jerusalem Talmud, Megillah 3:2.2–"Three from a synagogue act for the synagogue, seven from a town act for the town."

7.5.4 Response to Disruption: Breaking of Bread Improved by Increased Ministry Team

In the first-century world—without social security, unemployment benefits, hospitals, retirement centers, and other public services—widows (along with orphans) were typical examples of society's destitute and defenseless (and Luke shows particular interest in widows: Luke 7:11–15; 18:1–5; 20:45–47; 21:1–4; Acts 6:1–6; 9:36–42). So in light of Jesus's command to love one's neighbor as oneself (Luke 10:27), it is of little surprise that NT writers also encourage care for widows (e.g., 1 Tim 5:3–16; Jas 1:27). This particular episode in Acts 6 utilizes this commonplace concern as an example of how to handle the internal threat of community disruption. Disruptions can come in the form of something as basic as food distribution, but this social justice matter is merely one of many possibilities for interrupting community harmony and distracting from united ministry. The disruption of community here is addressed by means of distributed ministry leadership. In fact, this method is repeatedly drawn upon elsewhere in Acts (e.g., 11:19–26; 13:1–3; 14:23; 15:40; 16:1–3; 18:18; 20:4)—culminating with Paul's speech about church leadership (20:17–38)—such that we can conclude that Luke suggests expanded ministry leadership as a helpful pattern for addressing community disruptions of all kinds.[50] Rather than the apostles hoarding their ministry influence, there is a radical generosity not merely of bread but of ministry leadership. One need not be one of the original twelve apostles to have a legitimate gospel ministry.

Bread stamp from early Roman period, used to identify baker.
Kris Udd/BiblePlaces.com

7.5.5 Summary Statement (6:7)

The expansion of gospel ministers improved not merely the social services of the church but also the advancement of the gospel and the number of disciples. Luke reports this in the summary statement at the end of this section of Acts: "So the word of God spread. The number of disciples in Jerusalem increased rapidly" (Acts 6:7a).[51] When properly handling threats against its life, the church will discover that the gospel advances even among those who formerly had opposed Jesus: Luke specifically notes, "And a large number of priests became obedient to the faith" (Acts 6:7b).

50. See F. Scott Spencer, *The Portrait of Philip in Acts: A Study of Roles and Relations*, JSNTSup 67 (Sheffield: Sheffield Academic Press, 1992), 198–99.

51. As mentioned in chapter 3, Luke sometimes uses the phrase "the word of God" to refer not simply to a verbal sharing of the gospel message but also to the church itself or the whole Christian movement. This happens in the progress summary statement here in Acts 6:7, but see also 12:24 and 19:20.

7.6 CONCLUDING REMARKS

This second major section of Acts begins with a synopsis of church life noting that believers were devoted to four aspects of life together: the apostles' teaching, fellowship, the breaking of bread, and prayer. Then Luke describes how the church handled challenges to its life together, two from outside the church and two from within. While the summary description of the church is how the church should always function, each of the four challenges seems to be met by an emphasis on one of the four areas of the church's devotion. The threat of intimidation is addressed by prayer for boldness; the threat of corruption is addressed by accountable fellowship; the threat of persecution is addressed by continued teaching; and the threat of community disruption is addressed by improved ministry teams for things such as breaking of bread. Church life according to Luke is not without its difficulties on this side of eternity, but the ways to address those difficulties are in fact found in a scriptural living out of the life of the church. This includes a radical obedience to God's word, a radical accountability to one another, a radical generosity with others, and a radical dependence on the Lord.

7.7 Key People, Places, and Terms

- Ananias (of Jerusalem)
- Barnabas
- cessationist view
- continuation view
- deacons
- flogging
- Gamaliel
- Hebraic Jews
- Hellenistic Jews
- persecution
- Sanhedrin
- Sapphira
- Solomon's Colonnade
- sovereignty of God
- temple in Jerusalem
- Theudas and Judas

7.8 Questions for Review and Discussion

1. As Luke presents the earliest group of believers, what are the four ideal features of life in the church, i.e., the four things to which the believers are devoted?
2. Describe each of the ideal features of life in the church. What does it mean to be devoted to each of those things?
3. How would you define the four general threats to the church's community life as Luke describes it?
4. To what extent are these same general threats to the church still present for today's believers?
5. In Luke's portrayal, the four general threats to church life seem to be answered by the four ideal features of church life. How would you describe the connection between each threat and its corresponding ideal feature?

6. Which of the four ideal characteristics and which of the four threats is most poignant for you and your local church at this juncture?

7.9 Optional Assignments

1. **Text Reflection Project**—*Relating the concepts discussed in this chapter to another biblical text.* Compare Luke's various summary overviews of church life in the first half of Acts (see 1:12–14; 2:42–47; 4:32–35; 5:12–16; 6:7; 9:31; 12:24) and make a list of the things Luke seems to emphasize in those statements. What might we learn from this?
2. **Interview Project**—*Inquiring of others their views concerning the concepts discussed in this chapter.* Ask your pastor (or some other ministry leader) about the extent to which they agree with the table metaphor as illustrative of Acts 2:42, and what they think is the proper balance of teaching, fellowship, breaking of bread, and prayer for the church.
3. **Service-Learning Project**—*Applying the concepts discussed in this chapter in some form of service to others outside the class.* In Acts 6:1–6, the leadership of the Jerusalem church suggested that additional ministry workers be selected to help solve pragmatic ministry difficulties in the life of the church (e.g., the distribution of food to the poor widows). Inquire about the pragmatic ministry needs at your church and see how you can help.
4. **Prayer Project**—*Talking with God about the concepts discussed in this chapter.* What challenges are you or your church facing right now? Reflecting on the prayer of the believers in Acts 4:24–30, write such a prayer that is specific to your situation.
5. **Testimony Project**—*Telling others about the concepts discussed in this chapter.* Do you know a fellow believer caught up in some sin? Perhaps it is something obvious, or maybe it is something more subtle—like the sin of Ananias and Sapphira—and even appears socially acceptable. You may not have the authority of a leadership position to confront the situation like Peter did in Acts 5, but you can still lovingly intervene out of concern for their welfare. Considering Paul's counsel in Galatians 6:1–2, what might you do?

7.10 Bibliography for Going Further

7.10.1 Apostolic Preaching and Teaching

Chou, Abner. *The Hermeneutics of the Biblical Writers: Learning to Interpret Scripture from the Prophets and Apostles*. Grand Rapids: Kregel, 2018.

Dodd, C. H. *The Apostolic Preaching and Its Development*. London: Hodder & Stoughton, 1936.

Hengel, Martin. *Between Jesus and Paul: Studies in the Earliest History of Christianity*. Philadelphia: Fortress, 1983. Repr., Eugene, OR: Wipf & Stock, 2003.

Morris, Leon. *The Apostolic Preaching of the Cross*. 3rd ed. London: Tyndale, 1965. Repr., Grand Rapids: Eerdmans, 2000.

Polhill, John B. "Kerygma and Didache." *DLNT*, 626–29.

7.10.2 Church Life in Acts

Blue, Bradley. "Acts and the House Church." Pages 119–222 in *The Book of Acts in Its Graeco-Roman Setting*. Edited by David W. J. Gill and Conrad Gempf. BAFCS 2. Grand Rapids: Eerdmans, 1994; Carlisle: Paternoster, 1994.

Chambers, Andy. *Exemplary Life: A Theology of Church Life in Acts*. Nashville: B&H Academic, 2012.

Ijatuyi-Morphe, Randee O. *Community and Self-Definition in the Book of Acts: A Study of Early Christianity's Strategic Response to the World*. Dulles: Academica, 2003.

Thompson, Alan J. *One Lord, One People: The Unity of the Church in Acts in Its Literary Setting*. LNTS 359. New York: T&T Clark, 2008.

Twelftree, Graham H. *People of the Spirit: Exploring Luke's View of the Church*. Grand Rapids: Baker Academic, 2009.

7.10.3 The Lord's Supper

Armstrong, John H., ed. *Understanding Four Views on the Lord's Supper*. Counterpoints: Church Life. Grand Rapids: Zondervan, 2007.

LaVerdiere, Eugene. *The Breaking of the Bread: The Development of the Eucharist according to the Acts of the Apostles*. Chicago: Liturgy Training Publications, 1998.

Schreiner, Thomas R., and Matthew R. Crawford. *The Lord's Supper: Remembering and Proclaiming Christ Until He Comes*. NAC Studies in Bible & Theology. Nashville: B&H Academic, 2010.

Smith, Gordon T., ed. *The Lord's Supper: Five Views*. Counterpoints: Church Life. Downers Grove, IL: InterVarsity Press, 2008.

Wainwright, Geoffrey. "Lord's Supper, Love Feast." *DLNT*, 686–94.

7.10.4 Prayer in Luke-Acts

Crump, David M. *Jesus the Intercessor: Prayer and Christology in Luke-Acts*. WUNT 2.49. Tübingen: Mohr Siebeck, 1992. Repr., Biblical Studies Library. Grand Rapids: Baker, 1999.

Green, Joel B. "Persevering Together in Prayer: The Significance of Prayer in the Acts of the Apostles." Pages 183–202 in *Into God's Presence: Prayer in the New Testament*. Edited by Richard N. Longenecker. Grand Rapids: Eerdmans, 2001.

Holmås, Geir Otto. *Prayer and Vindication in Luke-Acts: The Theme of Payer within the Context of the Legitimating and Edifying Objective of the Lukan Narrative*. LNTS 433. New York: T&T Clark, 2011.

Jacob, Milton. *Prayer in Luke-Acts: A Study of Prayer in the Life of Jesus and in the History of the Early Church to Trace the Pedagogical Accent of Luke*. Nashville: Abingdon, 2001.

O'Brien, Peter T. "Prayer in Luke-Acts." *TynBul* 24 (1973): 111–27.

Plymale, Steven F. *The Prayer Texts of Luke-Acts*. AUSTR 118. New York: Lang, 1991.

Trites, Allison A. "The Prayer Motif in Luke-Acts." Pages 168–86 in *Perspectives on Luke-Acts*. Edited by Charles H. Talbert. Perspectives in Religious Studies 5. Danville, VA: Association of Baptist Professors of Religion, 1978.

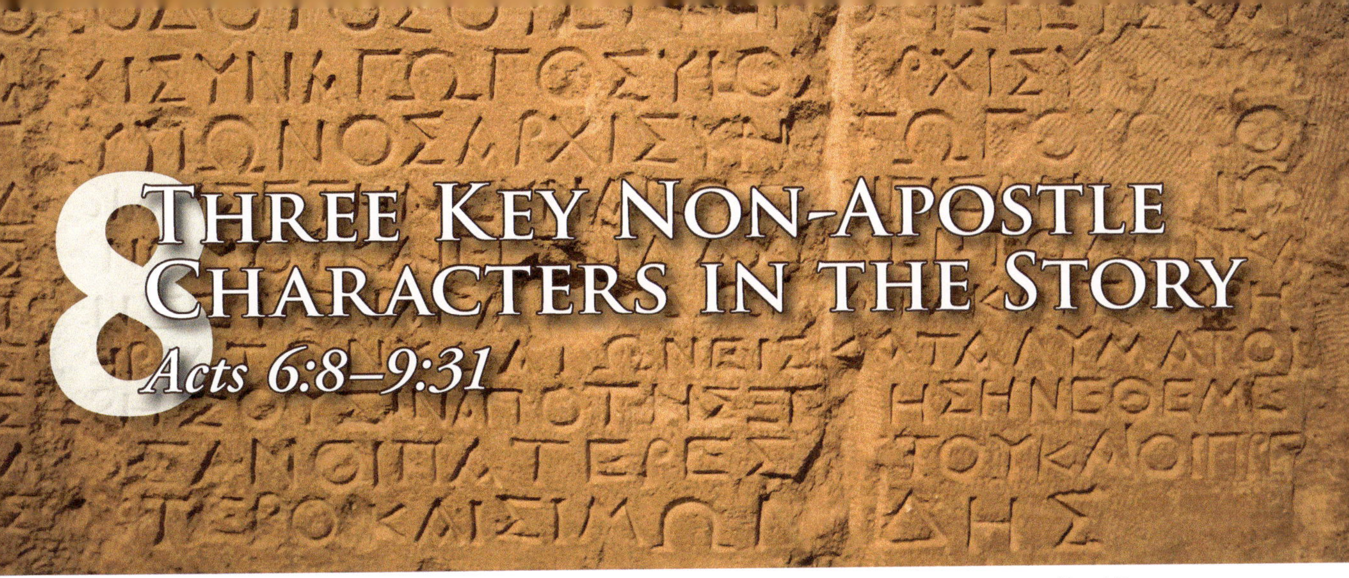

8 Three Key Non-Apostle Characters in the Story

Acts 6:8–9:31

Chapter Goals

After reading this chapter, you should be able to:

- Beyond the foretaste of its fulfillment with the coming of the Spirit on Pentecost (Acts 2:5–11), comment on the early development of the ethnographic and geographic spread of the gospel outward from Jerusalem in Acts 6–9 that was announced in Acts 1:8.
- Reflecting on the hardships faced in Acts 6–9, begin to recognize that God can still be at work even in difficult situations.
- Reflecting on the faith of various characters in Acts 6–9, examine the genuineness of your own faith in Jesus Christ.
- Explain that one need not be part of the original twelve apostles to be used by God in effective ministry.

Chapter Overview

8.1 The Story of Stephen (Acts 6:8–8:3)
8.2 The Story of Philip (Acts 8:4–40)
8.3 The Beginning of the Story of Saul/Paul (Acts 9:1–31)
8.4 Concluding Remarks
8.5 Key People, Places, and Terms
8.6 Questions for Review and Discussion
8.7 Optional Assignments
8.8 Bibliography for Going Further

Key Verses

Now Stephen, a man full of God's grace and power, performed great wonders and signs among the people. (Acts 6:8)

Then Philip began with that very passage of Scripture and told him the good news about Jesus. (Acts 8:35)

But Barnabas took him and brought him to the apostles. He told them how Saul on his journey had seen the Lord and that the Lord had spoken to him, and how in Damascus he had preached fearlessly in the name of Jesus. (Acts 9:27)

Summary Statement

Then the church throughout Judea, Galilee and Samaria enjoyed a time of peace and was strengthened. Living in the fear of the Lord and encouraged by the Holy Spirit, it increased in numbers. (Acts 9:31)

INTRODUCTION

The third major section of Acts treats the ministries of three pivotal characters in the expansion of the gospel: Stephen (6:8–8:3), Philip (8:4–40), and Saul (a.k.a. Paul; 9:1–31). One of the most notable things about these three characters is that none of them is among the original twelve apostles. And yet, empowering them with the Holy Spirit, God uses these three in influential ministry.

The first two of these three key people are members of the ministry team introduced in Acts 6:1–6. As already indicated in the discussion of that passage, those seven ministers were not limited to the social work of managing food supplies for widows. This is unmistakable now in the stories of Stephen and Philip: both of them are also sharing the gospel message with words. The third character, Saul, begins as a radical opponent of the gospel message—to the point of actively seeking out and persecuting Jesus followers—but he ends up himself being a persecuted follower of Jesus. It seems as though Luke has intentionally crafted this section to utilize the stories of Stephen and Philip to introduce his audience to the beginning of the story of Saul, a man of greater focus later in Acts and remembered more today by his other name: Paul.

8.1 THE STORY OF STEPHEN (ACTS 6:8–8:3)

In its earliest days, the church was growing and "enjoying the favor of all the people" (2:47). But the novelty of Christian teaching began to wear down, particularly when people realized that belief in Jesus made demands on their whole lives. The story of

Ananias and Sapphira was especially sobering: "Great fear seized the whole church and all who heard about these events" (5:11). For outsiders looking in, the fear was real and brought some caution to their admiration of the church, which nevertheless continued to grow (5:13–14).

Luke returns to the theme of the seriousness of following Jesus with the story of ***Stephen***, a man noted for being the first Christian martyr. In his account, Luke stresses Stephen's character and effectiveness, offers a sample of Stephen's speaking ministry, and demonstrates Stephen's commitment to Jesus. With his martyrdom, the story of Stephen marks something of a defining moment for the young church.

8.1.1 Stephen's Character and Effectiveness (6:8–15)

In the previous pericope, Luke has already commented on Stephen's character when he introduced him as a member of the Seven (6:1–6). All seven of the newly appointed ministers were men "known to be full of the Spirit and wisdom" (6:3). But with a touch of foreshadowing, Stephen alone gets an additional description as "a man full of faith and of the Holy Spirit" (6:5). That preview is now enlarged as Luke describes Stephen as "a man full of God's grace and power" (6:8) and a third time as "full of the Holy Spirit" (7:55). The repetition about Stephen as being directed, empowered, and characterized by the Holy Spirit helps us recognize that Stephen—someone who was not one of the original twelve apostles—was still used by God in legitimate and effective ministry. Furthermore, God used Stephen in speaking ministry and even in signs and wonders (6:8–10). Up to this point in the story, miraculous signs and wonders have been credited only to Jesus (e.g., 2:22) and the apostles (e.g., 2:43; 5:12). But now Stephen is an instrument of such miraculous deeds (6:8). Luke is clear enough that God can do the miraculous through whomever he so desires.[1] One need not be one of the Twelve to be used by God.

The effectiveness of any ministry is put to the test when it faces opposition. Luke is quite blunt about Stephen facing opposition. Unlike the church's earlier opposition, which came from the priesthood centered in the institution of the temple, Stephen's opposition comes from the institution of the synagogue. Luke names a particular one called the "Synagogue of the Freedmen," which apparently had an international flavor with Jews from Cyrene, Alexandria, Cilicia, and Asia (6:9; see sidebar).

By the end of Acts 7, attentive readers of the Gospels will have begun to recognize that some of Luke's descriptions of Stephen sound vaguely familiar. Indeed, some of the phrases Luke uses of Stephen have been used to describe Jesus. These kinds of parallels include speaking effectiveness, charges of blasphemy, a hearing before the Sanhedrin, asking God to receive his spirit at death, and praying that God would forgive his killers.

1. John R. W. Stott, *The Message of Acts: To the Ends of the Earth*, The Bible Speaks Today (Downers Grove, IL: InterVarsity, 1994), 126.

The Theodotus Synagogue Inscription

A dedicatory inscription carved into a limestone slab measuring 28 x 17 inches hung in a first-century synagogue of Jerusalem. A translation of the Greek reads, "Theodotus son of Vettenus, a priest and synagogue leader, son of a synagogue leader, grandson of a synagogue leader, built the synagogue for the reading of the Law and the teaching of the commandments, the guesthouse and the rooms and the water installation as a lodging place for those who have need from abroad. His forefathers established it with the elders and Simonides." Its use of Greek rather than Hebrew and its mention of hosting Jews "from abroad" suggest that this synagogue was similar to the Synagogue of the Freedmen in Acts 6:9, which served as a home away from home for Jews from Cyrene, Alexandria, Cilicia, and Asia.

© 2018 by Zondervan, courtesy of Israel Museum

And most of the parallel descriptions of Jesus are found in Luke's Gospel (see sidebar). Among the parallel descriptions is Luke's remark that the Sanhedrin saw Stephen's face to be "like the face of an angel" (6:15), which is reminiscent of Jesus's glowing face at the transfiguration (Luke 9:29). Given that Stephen has been accused of opposing the law of Moses, this facial radiance recalls the radiance of Moses's face when he received the law (Exod 34:29–35). With a bit of irony, God was showing that Stephen's interpretation of the law of Moses is correct.[2]

2. Ibid., 129.

Parallels between Jesus in the Gospels and Stephen in Acts

Jesus in the Gospels				Description	Stephen in Acts
Matthew	Mark	Luke	John		
		20:39–40 24:19		Spoke with wisdom and effectiveness	6:10
26:65	14:64			Charged with speaking blasphemy	6:11
26:57–59	14:53	22:54	18:13, 24	Hearing before the Jewish high priest and Sanhedrin	6:12; 7:1
26:60–61	14:56–57			False witnesses testified against him	6:13
26:61	14:58			Destruction of the temple is mentioned	6:14
17:2	9:2–3	9:29		Transfigured in the presence of witnesses	6:15
26:63	14:61	[22:66–67]	18:19	Asked to give a defense	7:1
	14:58			Temple/houses made by human hands are mentioned	7:48
26:64	14:62	22:69		Son of Man at the right hand of God	7:56
		23:46	[19:30]	Called out for his spirit to be received by God	7:59
27:46, 50	15:34, 37	23:46		Called out with a loud voice just before dying	7:60
		23:34		Prayed that God would forgive his killers	7:60

See the similar but less extensive listing of comparative features in Ben Witherington III, *The Acts of the Apostles: A Socio-Rhetorical Commentary* (Grand Rapids: Eerdmans, 1998; Carlisle: Paternoster, 1998), 253.

Stephen's speaking ministry is such an effective representation of the gospel that others have difficulty responding (6:10) and people resort to making false charges against him, which result in a hearing with the Sanhedrin (6:11–15). Stephen is accused of speaking against the law and against the temple and thus charged with ***blasphemy*** (i.e., utterly offensive speech or action that conveys contempt for God and his authority).[3] It is not too difficult to note that the charges against Stephen find their roots in what Jesus had taught: in particular Jesus had remarked that he would somehow be a replacement of the temple (e.g., Matt 12:6; 26:61; 27:40; Mark 14:58; 15:29; John 2:19–22) and that he would fulfill the law (e.g., Matt 5:17–18; cf. Luke 16:16–17; 24:44). Because the people had misunderstood Jesus and rustled up false witnesses against him, it is no surprise that Stephen suffers the same treatment and is asked to give a defense of himself.

3. My comparison of the charges against Stephen is dependent on Stott, *Message of Acts*, 128.

8.1.2 A Sample of Stephen's Speaking Ministry (7:1–53)

Luke's summary of Stephen's defense speech before the Sanhedrin in Acts 7 is the longest recorded speech in all of Acts, fifty-two verses (Acts 7:2–53). Some have noted a classical quality to Stephen's speech that betrays a quality education, particularly regarding ***rhetoric*** (see sidebar). And with the speech filled with OT citations and allusions—including at least twenty-two passages from Genesis, Exodus, Deuteronomy, Isaiah, and Amos—Luke portrays Stephen as quite knowledgeable about the Scriptures and Moses.

Stephen begins answering the charges against him by telling the story of the nation of Israel, focusing on God's work in Israelite history to bring about the salvation of his people. Some might say Stephen engages in ***narrative theology*** by recounting ***salvation history*** (see sidebar). He briefly covers Abraham moving from Mesopotamia to Palestine (7:2b–8) and Joseph moving from Palestine to Egypt (7:9–16), but centers most of his comments on a three-part rehearsal of the life of Moses moving the people of Israel from Egypt in the exodus (7:17–44). This makes sense, given that the false charges against Stephen were that he was against the law of Moses and the temple (6:13). Later in the speech, Stephen also touches on the OT heroes of the Israelite monarchy, David and Solomon (7:45–50). Noteworthy to all four of these OT stories is that God's presence with the people is never limited to one location.

A Rhetorical Outline for Stephen's Speech in Acts 7:2–53

Some have noted that Stephen's speech in Acts 7 has a rather classical quality that betrays a good education. Here is one such outline for his speech as Luke has summarized it.

***Exordium* (7:2a)**

The introductory call to listen.

***Narratio* (7:2b–34)**

The story of Abraham (vv. 2b–8).

The story of Joseph (vv. 9–16).

The story of Moses (vv. 17–34).

***Propositio* (7:35)**

The main proposition: God's deliverer has been rejected by God's people.

***Argumentatio* (7:36–50)**

The main argument: Obeying God is the central issue, not the worship location.

***Peroratio* (7:51–53)**

The emotional appeal: "You are just as disobedient as your ancestors!"

See the suggestion for this outline in Witherington, *Acts*, 260; Witherington references Jacques Dupont, "La structure oratoire du discours d'Etienne (Actes 7)," *Bib* 66 (1985): 153–67.

The God of Scripture is living and active, and whenever he calls his people into action, he accompanies them and gives them direction.[4]

Transitioning from his narration of OT history, Stephen comments on how the Israelites responded to Moses, observing that those claiming to be God's people ultimately rejected the deliverer that God had provided for them (7:35). Using Scripture, he argues his point further that obeying God is far more important than observing rituals in a particular physical place of worship (7:36–50). Here Stephen makes his primary point: his listeners are just like their ancestors in rejecting God's provided deliverer. Moses had told the Israelites, "God will raise up for you a prophet like me from your own people" (7:37 citing Deut 18:15), and that deliverer is the Righteous One—Jesus—whom the Jews of Stephen's day were now rejecting. Thus, it turns out that Stephen is not the one against obedience to God's law and proper worship; rather, it is the Jewish religious system that is being disobedient. "You are just like your ancestors!" (Acts 7:51–53). By rejecting Jesus, the Jewish religious leaders were rejecting God's deliverer. Christians like Stephen were simply declaring that God's law was being fulfilled and God's people should recognize this.

8.1.3 Stephen's Martyrdom (7:54–8:3)

The climactic application point of his remarks brings Stephen's defense speech to a conclusion. While he might have wanted to say more, his listeners were done listening. Luke remarks that when the Sanhedrin heard Stephen's indictment of them as disobedient to the law, they gnashed their teeth at him (7:54). The grinding of one's teeth was an expression of anger; in the Hebrew Scriptures, the wicked are said to gnash their teeth against the righteous (Pss 35:16; 37:12; 112:10; Lam 2:16), and in the

Stephen's Speech and Salvation History

Salvation history can be defined as God's activity in the course of human history to bring about the salvation of his people. God is, and always has been, in control. God has orchestrated history and is fulfilling his plan, which is the same plan the Jews had been (haphazardly) following through OT history. That plan—pictured in the Jewish heroes of people like Abraham, Joseph, Moses, and David—is being fulfilled in Jesus Christ. Stephen in Acts 7, just like the apostles and other earlier followers of Jesus, presents Christianity as the proper continuation of the OT faith, suggesting that Judaism has now come to a point where it must decide (again, as it reached such decision points in the past) whether it will follow God's plan. Stephen suggests that his listeners have chosen to reject their own salvation history and to step away from God's plan.

Israel's Pattern of Rejecting God's Deliverer

From Mel Storm, *Living Lord, Empowering Spirit, Testifying People: The Story of the Church in the Book of Acts* (Eugene, OR: Wipf & Stock, 2014), 60.

> The figures of Joseph and Moses serve as precursors to Jesus, the one who was rejected by his own people and yet through whom these same people could find deliverance.

4. Stott, *Message of Acts*, 130–31.

New Testament, the gnashing of teeth is associated with the future place of punishment as a continued expression of one's rage-filled refusal to repent (Matt 8:12; 13:42, 50; 22:13; 24:51; 25:30; Luke 13:28).[5]

The rage of the Sanhedrin toward Stephen boils over when he reports that he sees into the throne room of heaven (Acts 7:55–56). Both Luke (narrating in v. 55) and Stephen (speaking in v. 56) report this experience as a genuine sighting of Jesus in the opened heavens (where Luke had reported Jesus physically ascending; Acts 1:9–11) and not a mere dream.[6] Various proposals have been made for why Jesus is standing at God's right hand rather than the usual references to being seated at God's right hand (see Ps 110:1; Luke 20:41–44; 22:69; Acts 2:34–35; Heb 10:12). Other than Jesus himself, Stephen is the only NT person to use the title "Son of Man" in direct reference to Jesus, and this could be a nod to the messianic vision of Daniel (Dan 7:13–14). But rather than a picture of Jesus's reception of the kingdom, his posture of standing may have more to do with his advocacy for, and welcoming of, Stephen as he becomes the first Christian martyr. Reflecting on Jesus's promise that "whoever publicly acknowledges me before others, the Son of Man will also acknowledge before the angels of God" (Luke 12:8), some suggest that Jesus stands up as a witness to Stephen's innocence or as an advocate in Stephen's defense.[7] The report of this vision is too much for the hard-hearted, stiff-necked members of the Sanhedrin. Hearing what they deem to be further blasphemy (i.e., that the crucified Jesus could be Messiah and that Stephen could see into heaven), they cover their ears, yell at the top of their voices, and rush Stephen so as to drag him off for capital punishment (Acts 7:57–58).

A wood engraving of the stoning of Stephen (1890). ZU_09/iStock.com

As evidenced by the Hebrew Scriptures, first-century Judaism had a long history with the practice of stoning as the most common method of capital punishment. ***Stoning*** was accomplished outside the city and carried out by throwing stones at and on the convicted person until that person died. Scripture outlined the proper use of stoning in the OT Israelite society (see Lev 20:2;

5. See "Gnashing of Teeth," *BIBD*, 673–74.

6. Craig S. Keener, *Acts: An Exegetical Commentary*, 4 vols. (Grand Rapids: Baker Academic, 2012–2015), 2:1436; Keener notes that Paul (Acts 9:3; 22:6; 26:19) and Peter (Acts 10:11–16; 11:5–10) would soon have such visionary experiences. Paul converses with explicitly "Jesus"; Peter converses with "a voice" from heaven whom Peter calls "Lord."

7. So F. F. Bruce, *The Book of Acts*, 2nd ed., NICNT (Grand Rapids: Eerdmans, 1988), 156.

24:14–16; Num 15:32–36; Deut 13:1–11; 17:2–7; 21:18–21; 22:23–24). Extending beyond first-century Judaism, the post-NT rabbinic literature likewise appeals to the Hebrew Scriptures for guidance on proper stoning (see sidebar). Nevertheless, because Rome reserved the right to administer capital punishment in the territories it ruled (see John 18:31), some commentators suggest that Stephen was illegally lynched by mob action, perhaps conveniently facilitated during the change of Roman prefects in Judea in AD 36/37. But Josephus's account of the changeover of power between prefects that year does not leave any room for such vigilantism (see Josephus, *Ant.* 18.4.2 §89 where, instead of a gap in leadership, Josephus describes Marcellus arriving to serve as the new Roman prefect *before* Pilate departed). Rather, as evidenced elsewhere in Josephus's writings, Rome allowed the Jewish authorities to carry out traditional capital punishment for offenses against the temple (see Josephus, *J.W.* 6.2.4 §§124–28).[8] Thus, even though carried out with spontaneous rage and based on false charges of blasphemy against the law and the temple, Stephen's death can be viewed as a formal execution carried out by the Sanhedrin with proper witnesses (Acts 7:58).

Rabbinic Regulations for Stoning

Mishnah, *Sanhedrin* 6:1–4

Once the verdict is reached, they bring him out to stone him. The stoning area was outside the courthouse, as it says, [Leviticus 24:14] "Bring out he who has cursed." . . .

[Once the accused] was about ten cubits from the stoning area, they say to him, "Confess," for such is the way of those sentenced to death to confess, for all who confess have a share in the World to Come. . . .

[Once] he was four cubits from the stoning area, they remove his clothing. [If it is] a man, his front is covered; [if it is] a woman, her front and her back are covered, according to Rabbi Yehudah. But the Sages say, a man is stoned naked, but a woman is not stoned naked.

The stoning area's height was that of two men. One of the witnesses pushes him on his loins. If he is turned on his heart, they turn him [over,] on his loins. If he dies from this, [the court] has discharged [its obligation]. If not, the second [witness] picks up the stone and puts it on his heart. If he dies from this, [the court] has discharged [its obligation]. If not, he is pelted with stones by all of Israel, as it says, [Deuteronomy 17:7] "The hand of the witnesses shall be first upon him to put him to death, and afterward the hand of all the people."

As Stephen is dying, he prays with an echo of Jesus's prayer on the cross. Both Jesus and Stephen ask God to forgive their murderers (Luke 23:34 and Acts 7:60),

8. Cf. Acts 21:28 and the sidebar in chapter 14 quoting Josephus, *J.W.* 6.2.4 §§124–28.

St. Stephen's Basilica, just outside the walls of Jerusalem, was built over the traditional site of Stephen's stoning. Aleksandar Todorovic/stock.adobe.com

and both ask the Lord to receive their spirit (Luke 23:46 and Acts 7:59). A sometimes overlooked but significant difference between their prayers is that Jesus prayed to God the Father, but Stephen prays to Jesus. Jesus's ascension into heaven, where Stephen sees him now at God's right hand, means that believers can rightly pray to Jesus in requesting God's action.[9] Although unjustly judged and violently executed, Stephen dies calmly and seemingly peacefully. Luke even uses a euphemism for Stephen's death: "he fell asleep" (7:60; cf. 13:36; Luke 8:52).

In his account of Stephen's ***martyrdom***, as if verbally zooming in on the scene, Luke introduces a young man named Saul, who watches over the coats of the witnesses stoning Stephen (Acts 7:58). As Luke closes out this part of the story with the death of Stephen and his mournful burial by godly men (8:2), he intersperses two more comments about this Saul figure: Saul approved of the execution of Stephen (8:1), and Saul moved from being an observer of Christian opposition to an active participant seeking to destroy the church (8:3).[10] After this point in Acts, Christianity no longer enjoys the same level of popularity with the general Jewish population, and Saul took an active role in this persecution. This literary foreshadowing will make sense when we reach Acts 9, where Luke returns to the story of Saul. But first he breaks off from the Saul storyline to recount some other events in the ministry of one of Stephen's colleagues, Philip, another one of the seven ministers selected in Acts 6.

8.2 THE STORY OF PHILIP (ACTS 8:4–40)

Luke notes immediately that the martyrdom of Stephen launched not only a great ***persecution*** against the church (8:1) but also a great outreach by the church: "Those who had been scattered preached the word wherever they went" (8:4). Some of the expansion of the gospel occurs in group presentations (e.g., the several sermons already mentioned in Acts) and some of it in interactive conversations (e.g., Stephen's ministry in Acts 6:8–10). The story of Philip's ministry in the wake of Stephen's martyrdom provides good examples of both of these evangelistic experiences, and he is later dubbed ***Philip the evangelist*** (Acts 21:8).

9. Charles Anderson, "Lukan Cosmology and the Ascension," pp. 175–212 in *Ascent into Heaven in Luke-Acts: New Explorations of Luke's Narrative Hinge*, ed. David K. Bryan and David W. Pao (Minneapolis: Fortress, 2016), 191.

10. Peterson points out that laying their coats at Saul's feet could signify that the witnesses already recognized Saul as an authoritative leader in opposing Christianity (cf. Acts 4:35–37; 5:2); David G. Peterson, *The Acts of the Apostles*, Pillar New Testament Commentary (Grand Rapids: Eerdmans, 2009), 268. While Luke's comment that Saul was "a young man" (Greek: *neanias*, i.e., between eighteen and thirty years of age; see Eckhard J. Schnabel, *Acts*, ZECNT [Grand Rapids: Zondervan, 2012], 392; cf. Keener, *Acts*, 2:1447–49) might count against this suggestion, Luke is clear that Saul approved of Stephen's death (Acts 8:1) and soon afterward was a leader in persecuting the church (8:3; 9:1–2). For Paul's own remarks about his persecuting the followers of Jesus, see 1 Cor 15:9; Gal 1:13, 23; Phil 3:6; 1 Tim 1:13; cf. Acts 22:4–5; 26:10–11.

8.2.1 Philip's Cross-Cultural Ministry in Samaria (8:4–8)

Luke reports first about Philip traveling to ***Samaria***, the region just north of Jerusalem in Judea, and preaching the gospel there. The NT-era Jews of untainted descent tended to look down on Samaritans (e.g., Luke 9:51–56; 10:25–37; 17:11–19), which resulted in the Samaritans maintaining their own worship center and practices (see chapter 5). But Jesus had shown that Samaritans were not outside the reach of faith and should be presented with the message of salvation (e.g., Luke 10:25–37; 17:11–19), so Philip proclaims Jesus as Messiah to the ***Samaritans*** (Acts 8:5). Thus, we see in Philip an important step in the gospel moving out of strictly Jewish territory. Indeed, reflecting on the threefold description of Acts 1:8 (i.e., "Jerusalem—Judea and Samaria—ends of the earth"), the Spirit utilizes the persecution of the Jerusalem church to help spread the gospel to the next major stage of its expansion.

As with Stephen, Philip's ministry was not limited to social causes and administrative work. The Lord was using him to speak the gospel and to perform miraculous signs as well, resulting in many becoming believers (8:6–8, 13). So here Luke points out that Philip has a legitimate ministry that includes signs, healing, and preaching. A person need not be one of the original twelve apostles for God to use them in powerful gospel ministry. Luke has even pointed out that the apostles had not yet left Jerusalem and that the gospel message was being spread in Judea and Samaria by non-apostles (8:1). Nevertheless, as the story unfolds, we see that Philip continues to work in concert with the apostles and that they recognize his ministry.

Evangelism Involves an Invitation to Respond

From J. I. Packer, *Evangelism and the Sovereignty of God* (Chicago: Inter-Varsity Press, 1961), 50.

> Christians are sent to convert, and they should not allow themselves, as Christ's representatives in the world, to aim at anything less. Evangelizing, therefore, is not simply a matter of teaching, and instructing, and imparting information to the mind. There is more to it than that. Evangelizing includes the endeavour to elicit a response to the truth taught. It is communication with a view to conversion. It is a matter, not merely of informing, but also of inviting.

8.2.2 The Delay of the Holy Spirit Coming Upon the Samaritan Believers (8:9–17)

In Philip's ministry reaching the Samaritans, there is something different about their reception of the gospel: Luke notes that the Samaritan believers did not receive the Holy Spirit right away (8:14–16). The delay in the arrival of the Holy Spirit is odd, especially in light of Peter's comment in Acts 2:38–39: "Repent and be baptized, every one of you, in the name of Jesus Christ for the forgiveness of your sins. And you will receive the gift of the Holy Spirit. The promise is for you and your children and for all who are far off—for all whom the Lord our God will call." Some have suggested that since they had not received the Spirit, perhaps none of the Samaritans were true believers at that juncture. But this is not how Luke describes them: he states that they received the gospel and "believed" (8:12). Conversely, some have suggested that the Samaritan experience represents a pattern that believers must follow today. But this also does not fit with Luke's description, for after the pouring out of the Spirit at Pentecost, nowhere else in Acts is there a two-stage salvation experience where a person comes to faith in Christ without receiving the Spirit at the same time.

Rather, it is instructive that Luke writes about the delay in the Spirit's arrival as if he recognizes the oddity of it (8:14–17). Thus, Luke signals for the readers that the Samaritan experience is not the norm. The best explanation for the delayed arrival of the Holy Spirit on the first group of Samaritan believers is a salvation-historical one that understands God as doing something special in this particular historical event. Because this is the first strictly non-Jewish group of believers in Jesus, God waits until some Jewish believers are present before granting them the gift of the Holy Spirit. Peter and John arrive at the Samaritan village and recognize—as official witnesses to what God is doing—that the Samaritan believers are true believers in Jesus. It is then, in the presence of the apostolic witnesses, that God sends the Spirit on the Samaritans. In a very real sense, the delay in the Spirit's coming was not for the Samaritans but for the apostles: the apostles were the ones who needed the reassurance that the spread of the gospel to non-Jews was indeed God's plan.

In reflecting on the description versus prescription question (introduced in chapter 4), we can ask whether the delayed coming of the Spirit in Acts 8 was simply Luke's description of what happened in the first century or if he was prescribing an activity for all churches to follow. Here it seems easy enough to see that the church in the twenty-first century is now far beyond the need of a delayed sign of the Spirit's acceptance of non-Jewish believers. After all, the sign in Acts 8 should be sufficient, and none of the twelve original apostles are around to witness any further signs. Thus, Christians today should not expect to have a separate reception of the Holy Spirit apart from their conversion experience. And already in the New Testament, Paul noted this (see Rom 8:9; Eph 1:13–14). Moreover, believers do not control the coming of the Holy Spirit anyway; the assumption that people can somehow control the Spirit's coming is the error that Simon the Sorcerer makes.

8.2.3 Simon the Sorcerer (8:18–25)

One of the people of Samaria who profess faith in Christ during Philip's ministry there is a man named Simon, who was known as a wonder-worker. Commentators often refer to him as ***Simon the Sorcerer*** or even Simon Magus (from the Greek term *magos* for "magician, sorcerer"; cf. related terms in Acts 8:9, 11). Interestingly, Luke gives a somewhat extended description of Simon (8:9–11) such that parallels between him and Philip are noticeable (see sidebar). Luke at first describes Simon's profession of faith in Jesus as plainly as he describes that of others (8:13), but the authenticity of his profession is put to the test when Peter and John arrive in Samaria. Assuming he could somehow learn how to control the Holy Spirit, Simon attempts to buy from Peter the authority and power to impart the Holy Spirit with the laying on of hands (8:18–19; see sidebar).[11] As the story unfolds, clinging to his sorcery commitments and desiring to regain the attention he enjoyed in his previous lifestyle, Simon appears to have been motivated more by ambition than by a desire to follow Jesus.

Similar Descriptions of Philip and Simon the Sorcerer

Description by Luke	Philip the Evangelist	Simon the Sorcerer
Drew crowds	Acts 8:6-7	Acts 8:9-10
Worked wonders	Acts 8:6, 13	Acts 8:11
Heeded by listeners	Acts 8:6	Acts 8:10-11
Amazed people with great powers	Acts 8:13	Acts 8:9, 11

Laying on of Hands and Luke-Acts

Luke, like other writers of Scripture, uses the concept of laying hands on someone with literal and/or symbolic implications. (1) Literally, to take someone away, that is, to arrest them (e.g., Luke 20:19; 21:12; 22:53; Acts 4:3; 5:18; 12:1; 21:27). (2) Literally, to lay hands on a person so as to hurt or destroy them (e.g., Luke 22:53). (3) Symbolically, a gesture to illustrate the transfer of something from one person to another, like authority (e.g., Acts 6:6; 13:3), life and health (e.g., Acts 9:12; 28:8), or the Holy Spirit (e.g., Acts 8:17-19; 9:17; 19:6). That the gesture is symbolic rather than mystically causing the transfer by means of touch is evidenced by miracles credited to faith and not the accompanying touch (e.g., Luke 17:19; Acts 3:12-16; 14:9), by healings without any touch (e.g., Luke 17:11-19; Acts 5:15; 9:32-35, 40-41; 14:8-10; 16:18), by the Holy Spirit's arrival without touch (e.g., Acts 10:45-45), and by Peter's rebuke of Simon Magus for assuming the Spirit was dispensed by means of touch (Acts 8:17-24).

Adapted and simplified from "Laying on of Hands," *BIBD*, 1040-41.

11. The English language commemorates Simon Magus by giving the name "simony" to the practice of paying money to gain some church position or ministry or other spiritual benefit.

The Legend of Simon the Sorcerer as Founder of Gnosticism

The second-century Christian writers Justin Martyr and Irenaeus both recorded legends of Simon the Sorcerer as the founder of Christian heresy, a heresy later known as Gnosticism. Remarkably, the statue mentioned in Justin Martyr's account was recovered in the sixteenth century, but it is dedicated to "*Semoni Sancus*," a Sabine deity, and not to Simon the Sorcerer (i.e., the Latin *Semoni Sancus* ≠ *Simoni Deo Sancto*). The errant identification may have originated before Justin but was passed along as if it were true.

Justin Martyr, *First Apology* 26 (ca. AD 155–157)

There was a Samaritan, Simon, a native of the village called Gitto, who in the reign of Claudius Caesar, and in your royal city of Rome, did mighty acts of magic, by virtue of the art of the devils operating in him. He was considered a god, and as a god was honoured by you with a statue, which statue was erected on the river Tiber, between the two bridges, and bore this inscription, in the language of Rome: Simoni Deo Sancto ("To Simon the holy God"). And almost all the Samaritans, and a few even of other nations, worship him, and acknowledge him as the first god; and a woman, Helena, who went about with him at that time, and had formerly been a prostitute, they say is the first idea generated by him. And a man, Meander, also a Samaritan, of the town Capparetaea, a disciple of Simon, and inspired by devils, we know to have deceived many while he was in Antioch by his magical art. He persuaded those who adhered to him that they should never die, and even now there are some living who hold this opinion of his.

Irenaeus, *Against Heresies* 1.23.1–2 (ca. AD 175–185)

Simon the Samaritan was that magician of whom Luke, the disciple and follower of the apostles, says, "But there was a certain man, Simon by name, . . ." This Simon, then—who feigned faith, supposing that the apostles themselves performed their cures by the art of magic, and not by the power of God; . . . He, then, not putting faith in God a whit the more, set himself eagerly to contend against the apostles, in order that he himself might seem to be a wonderful being, and applied himself with still greater zeal to the study of the whole magic art, that he might the better bewilder and overpower multitudes of men. . . .

Now this Simon of Samaria, from whom all sorts of heresies derive their origin, formed his sect out of the following materials: Having redeemed from at Tyre, a city of Phoenicia, a certain woman named Helena, he was in the habit of carrying her about with him, declaring that this woman was the first conception of his mind, the mother of all.

Peter confronts Simon with a description of his heart that makes us suspect Simon to be outside of true faith: "Your heart is not right before God. . . . For I see that you are full of bitterness and captive to sin" (8:21, 23). While potentially sociologically influenced or even self-deceptive rather than maliciously dishonest, Simon's profession of faith ultimately appears to be a false profession of faith, i.e., he claimed to believe in Jesus but actually did not. The New Testament evidences this kind of false belief elsewhere (e.g., Luke 8:11–15; John 17:12; Acts 20:30; 1 Cor 11:19; 1 John 2:19), with Judas Iscariot as perhaps the most famous example (see Luke 6:16; 22:3).

Simon's response to Peter is not ideal. Luke does not report any recognition on Simon's part of the error in his thinking or any repentance of the evil in his heart. Luke's account records nothing more about Simon Magus (Acts 8:24–25). Early Christian literature offers some legends about him, suggesting that Simon persisted in his power interests and even became the founder of a heretical faith system known later as Gnosticism (see sidebar). Nevertheless, we must be careful to acknowledge that Scripture reports nothing about Simon Magus's ultimate fate. But even so, two observations here can be helpful. On the one hand, with Luke's record of such a person interacting with the first-century church, we must recognize the possibility that false faith can exist in our churches today, and like Peter, we must be willing to confront it. On the other hand, we must be willing to recognize that such people are to be invited to repent and that we must entrust them and their fate to God.

8.2.4 Philip's Cross-Cultural Ministry in a One-on-One Conversation (8:26–40)

It might seem a bit odd that Philip would leave the productive ministry in Samaria to meet with one person on a deserted road near the town of ***Gaza***, but this is precisely what the Spirit of the Lord directs him to do. As Luke tells the story, without informing Philip what is ahead, God simply communicates to Philip that he must leave Samaria. While the directions are somewhat specific—"Go south to the road—the desert road—that goes down from Jerusalem to Gaza" (8:26)—we might admit that, in Philip's place, we would want to ask for more information. If Philip has any such questions, Luke does not recount them. He simply notes that Philip goes. As he is traveling, Philip receives further guidance from God, now to approach a foreign traveler reading in his chariot. In whatever way it came, it was recognizable to Philip as God's direction and, even as he had taken steps to follow God to this point, he obeyed this next level of direction as well. Luke's presentation of Philip suggests that we should likewise be obedient to what we already know from God, trusting that he will provide more clear direction if and when we need it.

Among the uncertain things in this story is the background of the traveler in the chariot. Luke identifies him as "an Ethiopian eunuch, an important official in charge of all the treasury of the Kandake (which means 'queen of the Ethiopians')" (8:27a). In the first century, ***Ethiopia*** was the name of the territory of Nubia in the upper Nile region of Africa (a.k.a., Cush) that is now northern Sudan, and most scholars agree that the Nubian kingdom of Meroë is in view here.[12] But his ethnic/cultural background remains somewhat unclear. Because this man "had gone to Jerusalem to worship"

12. "Kandake," *BIBD*, 995; Keener, *Acts*, 2:1550–65.

The Jewish Diaspora

The Greek term *diaspora* (meaning "dispersion") is used to describe Jews who lived outside Palestine, a phenomenon assisted by the deportation of Jews from Israel by conquering enemies (e.g., the OT exile experiences) but also due to voluntary choices as well. By the first century AD, large concentrations of Jewish people could be found in places like Egypt, Mesopotamia, Syria, Asia Minor, Macedonia, Achaia (Greece), and Italy. Luke gives evidence of this in Acts. For example, in Acts 2:5 he observes, "Now there were staying in Jerusalem God-fearing Jews from every nation under heaven," and subsequently provides a list of some of the nations represented by Jews visiting Jerusalem for the Jewish holiday of Pentecost (2:9–11). The remains of Jewish synagogues have been discovered in several locations outside Palestine, and a variety of ancient sources—some by Jewish writers and some by non-Jewish writers—provide information on diaspora Judaism, but few can be considered exhaustive and systematic treatments. While some might suspect diaspora Jews to have been less devout than Jews living in Palestine, recent scholarship has come to recognize that levels of devotion to Jewish beliefs and practice were not uniformly tied to geographic locations; there were diverse levels of faith expression among Jews in Palestine as well as among Jews scattered across the known world. In the NT, on diaspora Jews in general, see John 7:35; on Jewish Christians living outside Palestine, see James 1:1; 1 Peter 1:1; cf. 2:11–12.

Select Bibliography

John J. Collins, *Between Athens and Jerusalem: Jewish Identity in the Hellenistic Diaspora*, 2nd ed. (Grand Rapids: Eerdmans, 2000; Livonia, MI: Dove Booksellers, 2000).

Huber L. Drumwright Jr., "Diaspora," *ZEB* 2:133–36.

Irina Levinskaya, *The Book of Acts in Its Diaspora Setting*, BAFCS 5 (Grand Rapids: Eerdmans, 1996; Carlisle: Paternoster, 1996).

Margaret Williams, *The Jews among the Greeks and Romans: A Diasporan Sourcebook* (Baltimore: The Johns Hopkins University Press, 1998).

(8:27b), scholars ask whether he was a God-fearing gentile of ancient Ethiopia, a full convert to the Jewish faith, or a ***diaspora*** Jew, i.e., a Jewish person living in another country (see sidebar).

Luke's first-century audience would understand the reference to "Ethiopian" to mean that the eunuch was a Black man. This expectation is clear enough from ancient texts (see sidebar).[13] So the Ethiopian eunuch of Acts 8 should be understood to be either a God-fearing gentile or a full convert to the Jewish faith. If he was truly a gentile, then perhaps he is to be credited as the first gentile convert to Christianity in Acts.[14]

---

13. See Keener, *Acts*, 2:1560–65; and Marcus Jerkins, *Black Lives Matter to Jesus: The Salvation of Black Life and All Life in Luke and Acts* (Minneapolis: Fortress, 2021), esp. 92.

14. Pao suggests that, while the Ethiopian eunuch can be considered the first gentile convert to faith in Christ, Luke highlights his social identity so as to represent the inclusion of outcasts in the people of God; David W. Pao, "Jesus's Ascension and the Lukan Account of the Restoration of Israel," pp. 137–55 in Bryan and Pao, *Ascent into Heaven in Luke-Acts*, 2016), 152n59.

Understanding "Ethiopian" as Implying Black Skin

In the first-century Mediterranean world, it would be natural for Luke's audience to understand the Ethiopian of Acts 8 to be Black. While we might not agree with their explanations of causation, the following sampling of ancient texts demonstrates that Ethiopians were assumed to be black skinned.

Herodotus, *Histories* (a.k.a. *The Persian Wars*) 3.101 (ca. 484–430 BC)

> These Indians of whom I speak . . . are all black-skinned, like the Ethiopians.

Aristotle, *Generation of Animals* 2.2.736a.11–14 (ca. 384–322 BC)

> Herodotus is incorrect when he says that the semen of Ethiopians is black, as though everything about a person with a black skin were bound to be black—and this too in spite of their teeth being white, as he could see for himself.

Pseudo-Aristotle, *Problems* 10.66 (ca. 384–322 BC)

> Why are the teeth of the Ethiopians white, and whiter than those of other people, but their nails are not? Are their nails (not white) because their skin is dark, and darker than that of other people, and the nails grow from the skin? But why are their teeth white? Is it because whatever the sun extracts moisture from, without dyeing it, becomes white, such as wax? Now it dyes the skin, whereas it does not dye the teeth, but the moisture is evaporated from them owning to the warmth.

Diodorus Siculus, *The Library of History* 3.8 (ca. 80–20 BC)

> But there are also a great many other tribes of the Ethiopians, some of them dwelling in the land lying on both banks of the Nile and on the islands in the river, others inhabiting the neighbouring country of Arabia, and still others residing in the interior of Libya. The majority of them, and especially those who dwell along the river, are black in colour and have flat noses and woolly hair.

Seneca, *Natural Questions* 4A.2.18 (ca. 4 BC–AD 65)

> First of all, the burnt colour of the people indicates that Ethiopia is very hot.

Ptolemy, *Tetrabiblos* 2.2 (ca. AD 100–178)

> The demarcation of national characteristics is established in part by entire parallels and angles, through their position relative to the ecliptic and the sun. For while the region which we inhabit is in one of the northern quarters, the people who live under the more southern parallels, that is, those from the equator to the summer tropic, since they have the sun over their heads and are burned by it, have black skins and thick, woolly hair, are contracted in form and shrunken in stature, are sanguine of nature, and in habits are for the most part savage because their homes are continually oppressed by heat; we call them by the general name Ethiopians. Not only do we see them in this condition, but we likewise observe that their climate and the animals and plants of their region plainly give evidence of this baking by the sun.

Lucian, *Hermotimus* 31 (ca. AD 120–190)

> Suppose an Ethiopian, a man who had never seen other men like us, because he had never been abroad at all, should state and assert in some assembly of the Ethiopians that nowhere in the world were there any men white or yellow or of any other colour than black, would he be believed by them?

But if he was a convert to Judaism, Luke's identification of him as a eunuch becomes a complicator, for Israelite law had restrictions about the participation of eunuchs in the Jewish community (Lev 21:16–23; Deut 23:1). It is possible, however, that the term ***eunuch*** (Greek: *eunouchos*) was not a description of his physical body but a description of his official role as a member of the queen's court, or perhaps both.[15]

Ethiopia as the Ends of the Earth

In ancient times Ethiopia—the region of Nubia or Cush south of Egypt—was thought to be the southern edge of civilization (cf. Esth 1:1; Ezek 29:10; Zeph 3:10). Several ancient authors reflect this idea. Thus, Luke's identification of the eunuch in Acts 8 as coming from Ethiopia (Acts 8:27) could be a subtle reference to the gospel going to the "ends of the earth" (Acts 1:8). With biblical Ethiopia lying far to the south of the land of Israel, perhaps Luke's comment in his gospel is also noteworthy here: "The Queen of the South will rise at the judgment with the people of this generation and condemn them, for she came from the ends of the earth to listen to Solomon's wisdom; and now something greater than Solomon is here" (Luke 11:31).

Homer, *Odyssey* 1.23 (ca. 735 BC)

> But now Poseidon had gone among the far-off Ethiopians—the Ethiopians who dwell divided in two, the farthermost of men, . . .

Herodotus, *Histories* (a.k.a. *The Persian Wars*) 3.114–15 (ca. 484–430 BC)

> Where south inclines westwards, the part of the world stretching farthest towards the sunset is Ethiopia; here is great plenty of gold, and abundances of elephants, and all woodland trees, and ebony; and the people are the tallest and fairest and longest-lived of all men.
>
> These then are the most distant parts of the world in Asia and Libya.

Strabo, *Geography* 1.2.27–28 (ca. 64 BC–AD 24)

> I maintain, I say, that just so, in accordance with the opinion of the ancient Greeks, all the countries in the south which lie on Oceanus were called "Ethiopia." . . .
>
> Ephorus, too, discloses the ancient belief in regard to Ethiopia, for in his treatise *On Europe* he says that if we divide the regions of the heavens and of the earth into four parts, the Indians will occupy that part from which Apeliotes blows [i.e., the southeast wind], the Ethiopians the part from which Notus blows [i.e., the south wind], the Celts the part on the west, and the Scythians the part from which the north wind blows. And he adds that Ethiopia and Scythia are the larger regions; for it is thought, he says, that the nation of the Ethiopians stretches from the winter sunrise to sunset [i.e., from the southeast horizon to the southwestern horizon], and that Scythia lies directly opposite in the north.

15. See F. Scott Spencer, *The Portrait of Philip in Acts: A Study of Roles and Relations*, JSNTSup 67 (Sheffield: Sheffield Academic Press, 1992), 166–67; William White Jr., "Ethiopian Eunuch," *ZEB* 2:447–48; and Terence C. Mitchell, "Eunuch," *ZEB* 2:449–50. On the complexity of the Ethiopian eunuch's identity, see Scott Shauf, "Locating the Eunuch: Characterization and Narrative Context in Acts 8:26–40," *CBQ* 71 (2009): 762–75. While acknowledging the ambiguity of the eunuch's identity but arguing for him to be understood as a black-skinned gentile who had become a God-fearer, see Jerkins, *Black Lives Matter to Jesus*, 90–93.

Perhaps the uncertainty of this man's background is its own encouraging lesson for us. God is so concerned for this person that he divinely breaks Philip away from a productive ministry in Samaria to travel into a deserted region to minister to this man. Readers of the story who have questions about their own backgrounds can be uplifted in knowing that their pasts do not prevent them from having more certain futures by responding to the gospel. William Larkin suggests that this indicates that God is not merely interested in the burgeoning *quantity* of evangelistic opportunities (e.g., in Samaria) but also in the *quality* of conversion prospects (e.g., to get the gospel to another people group).[16] This story also indicates that God is not merely interested in *groups* of people but also in *individuals*, even those at the "ends of the earth" (Acts 1:8; see sidebar). Thus, this episode with the Ethiopian eunuch signals a universality of the gospel not only in its reference to extent but also in its nebulous reference to ethnic identity and in its explicit reference to the inclusion of those who might otherwise feel marginalized.[17]

Homeward bound, the Ethiopian eunuch is reading on his chariot when he and Philip cross paths (see sidebar on literacy in the first century). Encouraged by the Spirit, Philip draws near and hears the eunuch reading from the book of Isaiah—which is easily recognized as ***Isaiah 53***:7–8. A messianic figure called the ***servant of the Lord*** appears repeatedly in Isaiah 40–55, and particularly in a suffering role (Isa 52:13–53:12) such that he is sometimes referred to as the ***suffering servant***. Philip asks the eunuch if he understands what he is reading, and when the eunuch asked him about the passage, "Philip began with that very passage of Scripture and told him the good news about Jesus" (8:35). Thus, Philip identifies the suffering servant of the Lord who offers himself as a sacrifice for the sins of God's people as descriptive of Jesus. This conversation leads to the eunuch coming to faith in Jesus. Throughout the book of Acts, believers share the good news of salvation through faith in Jesus Christ utilizing the OT Scriptures. This use of the Hebrew Scriptures is unsurprising, for Jesus himself had declared that all of the Scriptures were ultimately about him

Philip's Missionary Travels

The Chiasm of Acts 6:8–9:31

A: Acts 6:8–7:60—Saul is introduced at the end of the ministry of Stephen

B: Acts 8:1–3—Saul begins to persecute Jesus's followers

C: Acts 8:4–40—The ministry of Philip

B': Acts 9:1–2—Saul is still persecuting Jesus's followers

A': Acts 9:3–31—Saul is called and begins ministry in the name of Jesus

16. William J. Larkin Jr., *Acts*, The IVP New Testament Commentary Series (Downers Grove, IL: InterVarsity Press, 1995), 132.

17. For another biblical episode of an Ethiopian eunuch being included in the story of God's people, see Jer 38:7–13 and 39:15–18.

Literacy in the First-Century Roman World

In the first century BC the overall literacy rate was no greater than 10 percent, and there was only a slight increase, if any at all, in the first century AD. Examination of the papyri school texts that have survived from Hellenistic Egypt and investigations of ancient Greek and Roman writers on the topic of education confirm this estimation. Even for those societies dedicated to written communication (as were the first-century Jews in their dedication to Scripture), there was merely a necessary dependence upon the relatively small group of literate members of those societies. This has been the accepted conclusion for many years. To move the discussion of ancient literacy a bit further along, Michael O. Wise investigated the Bar Kokhba documents (from ca. AD 132–135) not so much for their content but as artifacts giving testimony to literacy skills. In the end, Wise concluded that between 5 percent and 10 percent of men in Roman Judea were literary literates (i.e., able to read and write) and that very few women were literate by any definition.

Select Bibliography

William V. Harris, *Ancient Literacy* (Cambridge: Harvard University Press, 1989).

Catherine Hezser, *Jewish Literacy in Roman Palestine*, Texts and Studies in Ancient Palestine 81 (Tübingen: Mohr Siebeck, 2001).

Martin S. Jaffee, *Torah in the Mouth: Writing and Oral Tradition in Palestinian Judaism, 200 BCE–400 CE* (New York: Oxford University Press, 2001),

Teresa Morgan, *Literacy Education in the Hellenistic and Roman Worlds*, Cambridge Classical Studies (Cambridge: Cambridge University Press, 1998).

H. Gregory Snyder, *Teachers and Texts in the Ancient World: Philosophers, Jews and Christians*, Religion in the First Christian Centuries (New York: Routledge, 2000).

Michael Owen Wise, *Language and Literacy in Roman Judaea: A Study of the Bar Kokhba Documents*, The Anchor Yale Bible Reference Library (New Haven, CT: Yale University Press, 2015).

(Luke 24:27, 44–48).[18] Also instructive for us is Philip's simple approach to sharing the gospel message about Jesus: he begins with what the eunuch is thinking about and takes the conversation on its natural path to Jesus.

The Ethiopian eunuch's confession of faith in Christ (Acts 8:36–39) was evidently God's intention for this little trip. For when he and Philip came out of the baptismal waters, God caught Philip away (some kind of teleportation!) and Philip found himself ("appeared") in the nearby town of ***Azotus***. Luke reports rather simply that Philip "traveled about, preaching the gospel in all the towns until he reached Caesarea" (8:40).

18. Furthermore, Larkin (*Acts*, 134) suggests that Philip's interpretation of Isaiah 53 as applying to Jesus goes back to Jesus himself in Luke 22:37; cf. Bruce, *Book of Acts*, 176. See also Darrell L. Bock, "Isaiah in Acts 8," pp. 133–44 in *The Gospel According to Isaiah 53: Encountering the Suffering Servant in Jewish and Christian Theology*, ed. Darrell L. Bock and Mitch Glazer (Grand Rapids: Kregel, 2012).

Where Is Acts 8:37?

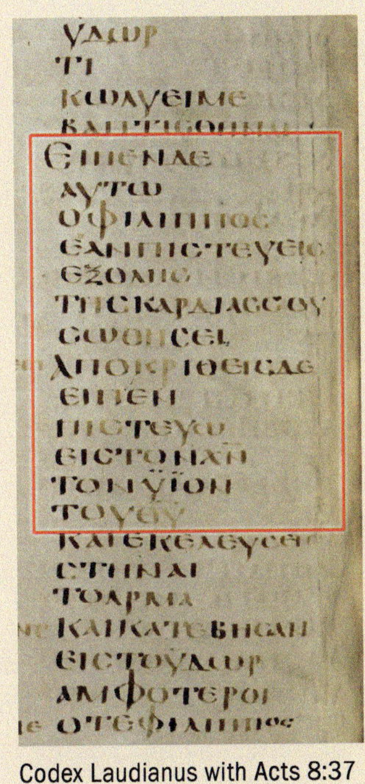

Codex Laudianus with Acts 8:37

The Bodleian Libraries, University of Oxford, MS. Laud Gr. 35, fol 70v

Most modern English translations of the New Testament do not have Acts 8:37. A few ancient manuscripts include this verse: "Philip said, 'If you believe with all your heart, you may.' The eunuch answered, 'I believe that Jesus Christ is the Son of God.'" This appears to be a late addition by a scribe involved in the manuscript hand-copying process, perhaps motivated by the desire to make clear what it takes to be baptized into the Christian church.

Codex Sinaiticus without Acts 8:37

This action of Philip is a helpful pattern of behavior: we can all be sharing the gospel message wherever we go. Luke wants his readers to notice that God is using the non-apostle Philip to conduct important, cutting-edge gospel ministry for the benefit of groups and individuals. God can likewise use any follower of Jesus who is willing to respond to his directions. Placing the story of Philip amid the story of Saul, Luke appears to use a chiastic structure so as to reassure his reader that God really can use any Jesus follower in ministry, even a former persecutor of the church (see sidebar). Saul is the next non-apostle on whom Luke focuses.

8.3 THE BEGINNING OF THE STORY OF SAUL/PAUL (ACTS 9:1–31)

Luke has briefly introduced his readers to the young man named ***Saul*** who quickly became a zealous persecutor of Jesus followers (Acts 7:58; 8:1–3). This vicious enemy of faith in Jesus will soon become a powerful advocate for the faith. But before Luke could report that change, he broke away to tell the story of Philip as a convincing piece of evidence that God can use a non-apostle to spread the gospel message powerfully. Even as Philip's ministry helps advance the gospel to the ends of the earth, Saul's ministry will do so in the last half of Acts, primarily under the name Paul. So here Luke takes up the story of Saul/Paul.

The story of Saul's conversion is very important to Luke, so important that he recounts it three times in Acts (9:1–19; 22:3–16; 26:9–18). Luke narrates the event for the reader here in Acts 9 and then has Saul/Paul recounting his experience later to a Jewish mob (Acts 22) and in a Roman legal hearing (Acts 26). Scholars discuss whether the Damascus road experience should be considered a conversion experience for Saul or a divine calling. This, of course, depends on how one defines the terms. If the word *conversion* is defined as a change of personal faith—i.e., to convert from having no faith in Jesus to having faith in Jesus—then clearly Saul/Paul undergoes that kind of life change in Acts 9. Saul's meeting of Jesus on the road to Damascus may well be the most famous conversion experience in all of church history.[19] Indeed, Luke's repetition of Paul's Damascus road experience in Acts 22 and Acts 26 shows Paul explaining it precisely as a personal change of life and furthermore as a way to encourage others to undergo the same kind of personal change. Rather than conversion versus calling, perhaps it is best to see Paul's Damascus road experience as both a conversion story and a calling story (see sidebar). The two go together, and there is no need to decide between them.[20]

Conversion versus Calling

While scholars debate whether Saul's Damascus road experience (Acts 9, 22, 26) was a *conversion* (i.e., a change of religions) or a *calling* (i.e., a change of personal mission), Luke presents it as something of both: it changed both his personal faith and his life mission; for Saul it was a *change of life*.

8.3.1 Saul's Damascus Road Experience (9:1–9)

Saul's conversion event happens while he is en route to Damascus to persecute Christians (Luke repeats the city name seven times; 9:2, 3, 8, 10, 19, 22, 27). The Syrian city of ***Damascus*** was a major stop on the international trade route between Egypt and Mesopotamia, so as followers of Jesus were scattering outside Judea, Damascus would be a key place for eastward-flowing traffic to bring the gospel message. This was apparently Saul's concern for wanting to chase down believers there. Luke describes Saul's zealous campaign as one of "breathing out murderous threats against the Lord's disciples" (9:1). Schnabel suggests that the text should be understood as "threats and murder" (Greek: *apeilēs kai phonou*), which better communicates Saul's desire not only to threaten Christians but to see them punished and even killed (cf. Acts 22:4,

19. Stott, *Message of Acts*, 165.

20. Storm, *Living Lord, Empowering Spirit, Testifying People*, 76.

Damascus

- Located on the Barada River about 150 miles northeast of Jerusalem on the edge of the desert in southern Syria.
- Situated on the primary north-south international trade route through Palestine.
- Had important political and economic roles at various times in its long history.
- Mentioned in the OT as being in existence in the time of Abram (Gen 14:15 and 15:2), as having been conquered by David (2 Sam 8:5–6); and as attaining independence during Solomon's reign (1 Kgs 11:23–25), which was the beginning of its prime years as the capital of the Aramean kingdom, a serious rival for the northern kingdom of Israel (e.g., 1 Kgs 15:16–21; 19:15; 20:1–34; 2 Kgs 14–16; Isa 7:1–8:18; 17:1–3).
- Had been Hellenized with Greek culture and was controlled by Rome in NT times, with Antioch on the Orontes River replacing it as the capital of the Roman province of Syria.
- Had a sizable Jewish population with ten to eighteen thousand Jews being killed there in the Jewish revolt of AD 66 (Josephus, *J.W.* 2.20.2 §§559–61; 7.6.7 §368).
- In modern times is again the Syrian capital and is sometimes reputed to be the world's oldest continually inhabited city.

Select Bibliography

Andrew Bowling, "Damascus," *ZEB* 2:9–12.

Martin Hengel and Anna Maria Schwemer, *Paul Between Damascus and Antioch: The Unknown Years*, trans. John Bowden (Louisville, KY: Westminster John Knox, 1997).

Wayne T. Pitard, "Damascus," *EDB*, 308–9.

Colin Thubron, *Mirror to Damascus* (London: Heinemann, 1967).

19–20; 26:9–11; 1 Cor 15:9; Gal 1:13, 23; Phil 3:6; 1 Tim 1:13).[21] This was an active persecution, with letters secured from the high priest (probably Caiaphas, high priest AD 18–36) authorizing Saul to arrest any Jews who belonged to "the Way," i.e., the Jesus way of belief (Acts 9:1–2).[22] Saul wanted to bring these people, as Jews, to trial in Jerusalem—the center of the Jewish faith—and have them punished there.

Saul's 150-mile trip to Damascus to carry out his search for Jesus followers is interrupted by Jesus himself when a light from heaven flashes around Saul and he falls to the ground (9:3–4). Luke reports elsewhere that this happens around noon (22:6; 26:13) and that those with Saul also fall to the ground (26:14). Saul hears a voice (addressing him in Aramaic; 26:14): "Saul, Saul, why do you persecute me?" (9:4), and so Saul finds himself engaged in conversation with Jesus. The experience is shocking

21. Schnabel, *Acts*, 441.

22. This is the first of six times that Luke refers to Jesus followers as members of "the Way" (Acts 9:2; 19:9, 23; 22:4; 24:14, 22; cf. 13:10; 18:25, 26).

enough to Saul's companions that they stand speechless, hearing the sound of the voice but not seeing anyone (9:7).

We might smile at Saul's responsive query in his position of conquered vulnerability.[23] A light has flashed upon him and a voice from heaven has called him by name asking him about the motive for his persecuting behavior, and to this Saul answers, "Who are you, Lord?" (9:5). A voice from heaven might well be addressed as "Lord" (i.e., God), but why then ask who it is? How could Saul have not asked himself something like, "Who am I persecuting that could address me like this from heaven?" At any rate, it is not long before his query about the identity of his confronter is confirmed: "I am Jesus, whom you are persecuting" (9:5).

The sudden meeting of Jesus as the risen Christ would certainly require Saul's reevaluation of his worldview. While Jesus's appearance to him on the road to Damascus is sudden and dramatic (9:3; 22:6), Saul's change of heart takes a bit longer: three days in the city in blind anticipation, not eating or drinking anything (9:6–9). Later in Acts, in one of Paul's own recountings of this event, he gives the further detail that Jesus confronted him using an agrarian proverb: "It is hard for you to kick against the goads" (26:14). The implication of such a proverb is that, even prior to the Damascus road experience, Saul had already been faced with evidence prompting him toward belief in Jesus (e.g., Saul had already heard the preaching of Stephen), and he had been fighting that prior evidence. This is often the case still today, where people fight against being convinced of the truth of the gospel. But by God's grace a final revelatory act of some kind occurs, and they have one last battle with indecision before they find themselves compelled to respond in genuine faith. This seems descriptive of Saul's experience in Acts 9.

Apart from the miraculous encounter with Jesus Christ risen from the dead(!), most interesting in the exchange between Jesus and Saul in Acts 9 is Jesus's identification with his followers. While Saul was taking action "against the Lord's disciples," persecuting men and women "who belonged to the Way" (9:1–2), Jesus identifies himself with them: "I am Jesus, whom you are persecuting" (9:5). Jesus explicitly identifies with his followers. Stott suggests that this identification added to Saul's trauma: if persecuting Jesus's followers was persecuting Jesus, and if Jesus stood before him now, then Jesus and his followers are in the right and Saul is wrong.[24] That Jesus so explicitly identifies with his followers and takes their persecution personally should be encouraging to all who face opposition for their faith in Jesus and be heartening to the church in the face of such trying times.

---

23. See Thomas Walker, *The Acts of the Apostles*, Indian Church Commentaries Series (London: SPCK, 1910; repr., Chicago: Moody, 1965), 207.

24. Stott, *Message of Acts*, 170.

8.3.2 Ananias of Damascus (9:10–19a)

Luke introduces the reader to a believer in Damascus named Ananias, who is distinct from the deceased man of the same name in Jerusalem (5:1–11). This name is repeated five times here (9:10 [twice], 13, 15, 17). In a visionary encounter with Jesus, ***Ananias*** is instructed to visit Saul, but he is understandably reluctant. It is difficult to believe that such a zealous persecutor of believers like Saul could himself become a believer (9:11–14; cf. 9:21, 26–28), but God can do such a thing. The Lord overcomes Ananias's reluctance by sharing the news that Saul will be a preacher of the name of Jesus and will himself be persecuted for the name of Jesus (9:15–16).

Convinced that the Lord will fulfill his word, Ananias obeys the Lord's command and goes to Saul. Luke does not provide all the details of their conversation, but it appears that shortly after Ananias's arrival, Saul's sight is restored—physically and spiritually—and Saul becomes a follower of Jesus, including reception of the Holy Spirit (9:17). And so, in keeping with Christian practice, Saul announces his newfound faith with baptism (9:18). As significant as Saul's conversion is, it is important to notice that the Lord used Ananias to bring Saul's conversion to fruition. Thus, Luke tells of another believer who is not one of the original twelve apostles but whom God still uses in significant ministry.

8.3.3 Saul in Damascus (9:19b–25)

Saul's purpose for visiting Damascus has been interrupted and inverted. Rather than chasing down believers to persecute them, Saul has become one of them himself. Nevertheless, even as Ananias had questioned the idea of Saul becoming a believer, others in Damascus were likewise incredulous about his conversion (9:21). But Saul's life is noticeably different after coming to faith in Jesus. Evidence of his conversion includes the cessation of his persecuting efforts, his baptism, his spending time with other believers, and his preaching that Jesus is the Son of God and Messiah (9:9b–22). He is even willing to undergo persecution. Meeting Jesus completely changes the direction and character of a person's life. Even if a person does not have a dramatic before-versus-after testimony of faith in Christ, they do have a dramatic change-of-direction story; they become something other than what they would have been without Christ directing their lives. In Saul's case, of course, there is a dramatically noticeable change in relatively short order in Damascus.

Luke's comments are not specific enough to reveal how long Saul was in Damascus. In his letter to the Galatians, Paul recounts that he left Damascus for a while and went to Arabia—apparently for as much as three years (Gal 1:15–18). Luke, however, does not mention this trip, but it may have occurred after the "several days" Saul spent with the Damascus disciples (Acts 9:19). After his time in Arabia, Saul returned to Damascus (Gal 1:17), where as a follower of Jesus he is targeted to be killed. The persecutor has become the persecuted. So after "many days" go by (9:23), it is time for Saul to leave

Damascus. The opposition has become so intensely focused on Saul in Damascus that other believers must sneak him out of the city by lowering him in a basket over the city wall (9:23–25; cf. 2 Cor 11:32–33; see sidebar).

Paul's Escape from Damascus

Luke's Account in Acts 9:23-25	Paul's Account in 2 Cor 11:32-33
After many days had gone by, there was a conspiracy among the Jews to kill him, but Saul learned of their plan. Day and night they kept close watch on the city gates in order to kill him. But his followers took him by night and lowered him in a basket through an opening in the wall.	In Damascus the governor under King Aretas had the city of the Damascenes guarded in order to arrest me. But I was lowered in a basket from a window in the wall and slipped through his hands.

8.3.4 Saul Visits Jerusalem (9:26–30)

Upon his escape from Damascus, Saul goes back to Jerusalem (9:26; cf. Gal 1:18–21; see sidebar). Just as in Damascus, Saul's reputation as a persecutor of Jesus followers causes people to doubt that he had experienced an authentic conversion. But ***Barnabas***—true to his nickname ("son of encouragement"; Acts 4:36–37)—introduces Saul as a genuine believer to the apostles. Luke narrates that Barnabas recounts for the apostles "how Saul on his journey had seen the Lord and that the Lord had spoken to him," and he also spoke of some of the evidence of Saul's conversion, specifically "how in Damascus he had preached fearlessly in the name of Jesus" (9:27). With Barnabas's encouragement, Saul is accepted in the Jerusalem community of believers.

Paul's First Post-Conversion Trip to Jerusalem

Luke's Account in Acts 9:26-30	Paul's Account in Gal 1:18-21
When he came to Jerusalem, he tried to join the disciples, but they were all afraid of him, not believing that he really was a disciple. But Barnabas took him and brought him to the apostles. He told them how Saul on his journey had seen the Lord and that the Lord had spoken to him, and how in Damascus he had preached fearlessly in the name of Jesus. So Saul stayed with them and moved about freely in Jerusalem, speaking boldly in the name of the Lord. He talked and debated with the Hellenistic Jews, but they tried to kill him. When the believers learned of this, they took him down to Caesarea and sent him off to Tarsus [in Cilicia].	Then after three years, I went up to Jerusalem to get acquainted with Cephas [Peter] and stayed with him fifteen days. I saw none of the other apostles—only James, the Lord's brother. I assure you before God that what I am writing you is no lie. Then I went to Syria and Cilicia.

Luke describes Saul's life in the Jerusalem community of believers much as it was in Damascus. In particular, Saul was "speaking boldly in the name of the Lord"

(9:28), including debates with Hellenistic Jews (9:29a; cf. Stephen in 6:9). Here too, Saul's exuberance for faith in Christ eventually brings him into the crosshairs of Jews who want to kill him. When the Jerusalem community of believers hear about this plan, they arrange for him to leave Jerusalem for the seaport city of ***Caesarea***, where they could put him on a ship to get him to his hometown of ***Tarsus*** in Cilicia (9:29b–30).

Saul's Travels in Acts 9

8.3.5 Summary Statement (9:31)

This section of Acts is focused on the contributions of three significant non-apostles to the work of the gospel, and Luke closes it by giving another summary of the church's growth: "Then the church throughout Judea, Galilee and Samaria enjoyed a time of peace and was strengthened. Living in the fear of the Lord and encouraged by the Holy Spirit, it increased in numbers" (9:31). In the face of the persecution that spurred on a new level gospel expansion, this summary statement shows that the church enjoyed a time of peace.

8.4 CONCLUDING REMARKS

The three key people of this section of Acts have some similarities (e.g., they are all devout Jewish men living in the Jerusalem area, and Stephen and Philip are both ministers in the Jerusalem church), and yet they have quite different stories. Stephen is found carrying on public debates in a local synagogue; Philip seems to be less flamboyant but is used by God to quietly cross ethno-social boundaries with the gospel; Saul is an outspoken enemy of faith in Jesus until Jesus himself confronts him on the road to Damascus. By the end of this section, Stephen has become the first Christian martyr, Philip is living in Caesarea (the Roman capital of the province of Judea), and Saul the persecutor has had such a radical change that he has become Saul the preacher. Working through this section of Acts should convince us that God can advance his purposes for spreading the gospel even amid difficult situations. Furthermore, God can use whomever he wants to do so. You do not need to be one of the original twelve apostles to be used by God to advance the gospel message.

8.5 Key People, Places, and Terms

- Ananias of Damascus
- Azotus
- Barnabas
- blasphemy
- Caesarea
- Damascus
- diaspora
- Ethiopia
- eunuch
- Gaza
- Isaiah 53
- martyrdom
- narrative theology
- persecution
- Philip the evangelist
- rhetoric
- salvation history
- Samaria
- Samaritans
- Saul
- servant of the Lord
- Simon the Sorcerer
- Stephen
- stoning
- suffering servant
- Tarsus

8.6 Questions for Review and Discussion

1. As Luke outlines it, who does God utilize to begin the ethnographic and geographic spread of the gospel outward from Jerusalem?
2. What are the implications of God utilizing non-apostles for the spread of the gospel?
3. While the church seemed to enjoy the favor of most people in their surrounding culture in the first six chapters of Acts, Luke indicates a persecution of believers breaking out after the stoning of Stephen (Acts 8:1). What does Acts 8:4 indicate about God's use of the adversity for the spread of the gospel in Acts? What are the implications of this for God's use of difficult situations in our lives today?
4. The story of Simon the Sorcerer in Acts 8 confronts us with the concept of false belief. What is the difference in Acts between true belief and false belief?
5. When he was persecuting Christians, Saul thought he was serving God properly (see Acts 22:3–5; 26:4–11; Gal 1:13–16; Phil 3:4–6). But when Jesus confronted him on the road to Damascus, Saul literally came face-to-face with the Truth, learned that he had been misinterpreting Scripture, and had to rearrange his thinking and way of life. Albeit with less drama, Luke had earlier pointed out that others with devotion to the Jewish religious system were coming to faith in Jesus ("a large number of priests became obedient to the faith"; Acts 6:7). From the stories Luke has shared so far, whether with great drama or very little, what does he want his readers to understand about conversion to faith in Jesus?
6. Given Saul's prior persecution of believers, people were suspicious of his conversion (see Acts 9:13–14, 21, 26). But through Saul's story, Luke's readers come to understand that belief in Jesus can produce radical change in a person's life, even in the life of one who had formerly been hostile against Jesus. What pattern of behavior does Luke want the church to continue to live by when it comes to accepting other believers?

8.7 Optional Assignments

1. **Text Reflection Project**—*Relating the concepts discussed in this chapter to another biblical text.* Compare Luke's account of Paul's conversion to faith in Christ (Acts 9:1–19) with Paul's own testimonies in his letters (1 Cor 9:1; 15:3–11; Gal 1:11–20; Phil 3:1–14; 1 Tim 1:12–14). How well do these accounts coordinate? Describe how these different accounts inform each other.
2. **Interview Project**—*Inquiring of others their views concerning the concepts discussed in this chapter.* Reflecting on the different ministries of Stephen, Philip, and eventually Saul, in an interview with your pastor (or some other respected Christian leader), inquire about how they do evangelism (e.g., in group settings, one-on-one settings, formal interactions, informal interactions, etc.). Also ask them how they face opposition when targeted for their faith in Jesus Christ.
3. **Service-Learning Project**—*Applying the concepts discussed in this chapter in some form of service to others outside the class.* Reflecting on Stephen's experience of persecution, find out about some Christian or group of Christians facing persecution for their faith in Jesus Christ (e.g., imprisoned, loss of job, rejection by family members) and then figure out some way to help or encourage them.
4. **Prayer Project**—*Talking with God about the concepts discussed in this chapter.* While a single prayer can have multiple facets to it (e.g., worship, thanksgiving, confession, commitment, request, intercession, etc.), prayers often have a more singular or primary purpose. Briefly compare and contrast the three prayers found in Acts 7:59–60; 8:14–17; and 9:11–12, and decide into which primary category you would place each of these prayers. Then write one of these kinds of prayers for yourself, making it specific to your current situation.
5. **Testimony Project**—*Telling others about the concepts discussed in this chapter.* In Acts 9, Luke reports Saul's/Paul's life-changing experience of meeting Jesus on the road to Damascus. In two short pages, write up the story of your experience of coming to belief in Jesus Christ. Your story may not be as dramatic as that of Paul (i.e., from persecuting Jesus followers to following Jesus), but that's all right; what matters is that it is your story of conversion. Then select someone to tell your story to. Afterward, write up a single-page reflection on the experience: describe why you selected the person, report what went well and what did not go so well, and reflect on how you might do it differently next time you have the opportunity to share your testimony.

8.8 Bibliography for Going Further

8.8.1 Stephen

Blackburn, Barry L. "Stephen." *DLNT,* 1123–26.

Dayton, Wilber T. "Stephen." *ZEB* 5:606–09.

Matthews, Shelly. *Perfect Martyr: The Stoning of Stephen and the Construction of Christian Identity.* Oxford: Oxford University Press, 2010.

Neudorfer, Heinz-Werner. "The Speech of Stephen." Pages 275–94 in *Witness to the Gospel: The Theology of Acts.* Edited by I. Howard Marshall and David Peterson. Grand Rapids: Eerdmans, 1998.

Penner, Todd C. *In Praise of Christian Origins: Stephen and the Hellenists in Lukan Apologetic Historiography.* ESEC 10. London: T&T Clark, 2004.
Watson, Alan. *The Trial of Stephen: The First Christian Martyr.* Athens: University of Georgia Press, 1996.

8.8.2 Persecution and Martyrdom

Bammel, Ernst. "Jewish Activity against Christians in Palestine according to Acts." Pages 357–64 in *The Book of Acts in Its Palestinian Setting.* Edited by Richard Bauckham. BAFCS 4. Grand Rapids: Eerdmans, 1995; Carlisle: Paternoster, 1995.
Cunningham, Scott. *"Through Many Tribulations": The Theology of Persecution in Luke-Acts.* JSNTSup 142. Sheffield: Sheffield Academic, 1997.
Kilgallen, John J. "Persecution in the Acts of the Apostles." Pages 143–60 in *Luke and Acts.* Edited by Gerald O'Collins and Gilberto Marconi. Translated by Matthew J. O'Connell. New York: Paulist, 1991.
Mittelstadt, Martin William. *The Spirit and Suffering in Luke-Acts: Implications for a Pentecostal Pneumatology.* JPTSup 26. London: T&T Clark, 2004.
Rapske, Brian M. "Opposition to the Plan of God and Persecution." Pages 235–56 in *Witness to the Gospel: The Theology of Acts.* Edited by I. Howard Marshall and David Peterson. Grand Rapids: Eerdmans, 1998.
Talbert, Charles H. "Martyrdom in Luke-Acts and the Lukan Social Ethic." Page 99–110 in *Political Issues in Luke-Acts.* Edited by Richard J. Cassidy and Philip J. Sharper. Maryknoll: Orbis, 1983.

8.8.3 Philip

Matthews, Christopher R. *Philip: Apostle and Evangelist: Configurations of a Tradition.* NovTSup 105. Leiden: Brill, 2002.
Samkutty, V. J. *The Samaritan Mission in Acts.* LNTS 328. New York: T&T Clark, 2006.
Spencer, F. Scott. *The Portrait of Philip in Acts: A Study of Roles and Relations.* JSNTSup 67. Sheffield: Sheffield Academic, 1992.
Thomas, Geoffrey. *Philip and the Revival in Samaria.* Edinburgh: Banner of Truth, 2005.

8.8.4 Simon Magus

Ferreiro, Alberto. *Simon Magus in Patristic, Medieval and Early Modern Traditions.* SHCT 125. Leiden: Brill, 2005.
Haar, Stephen. *Simon Magus: The First Gnostic?* BZNW 119. Berlin: de Gruyter, 2003.
Harris, B. F. "Simon Magus." *ZEB* 5:519–22.
Ludemann, Gerd. "The Acts of the Apostles and the Beginnings of Simonian Gnosis." *NTS* 33.3 (1987): 420–26.

8.8.5 Saul's/Paul's Conversion

Churchill, Timothy W. R. *Divine Initiative and the Christology of the Damascus Road Encounter.* Eugene, OR: Pickwick, 2010.
Hengel, Martin, and Anna Maria Schwemer. "Damascus and the Turning Point in Paul's Life." Pages 24–61 (chapter 2) in *Paul Between Damascus and Antioch: The Unknown Years.* Louisville: Westminster John Knox, 1997.
Kim, Seyoon. *The Origin of Paul's Gospel.* Tübingen: Mohr Siebeck, 1993. Repr., Eugene, OR: Wipf & Stock, 2007.
Légasse, Simon. "Paul's Pre-Christian Career according to Acts." Pages 365–90 in *The Book of Acts in Its Palestinian Setting.* Edited by Richard Bauckham. BAFCS 4. Grand Rapids: Eerdmans, 1995; Carlisle: Paternoster, 1995.
Lohfink, Gerhard. *The Conversion of St. Paul: Narrative and History in Acts.* Herald Scriptural Library. Chicago: Franciscan Herald, 1976.

9 The Story Advances in Palestine

Acts 9:32–12:25

Chapter Goals

After reading this chapter, you should:

- Be able to comment on the continued ethnographic and geographic spread of the gospel outward from Jerusalem as described in Acts.
- Recognize that God planned and initiated the inclusion of gentiles in the church.
- Begin appreciating and articulating the differences between the demands of faithful expressions of faith and personal preferences in cultural expressions of faith, even as the believers in Acts were learning to do.
- Articulate specifically the message that Luke has for the church when it is faced with opposition and difficult situations.

Chapter Overview

9.1 Peter's Itinerant Ministry in Lydda and Joppa (Acts 9:32–43)
9.2 The Conversion of Cornelius in Caesarea (Acts 10:1–11:18)
9.3 The Gospel Advances to Syrian Antioch (Acts 11:19–30)
9.4 Opposition to the Church Back in Jerusalem (Acts 12:1–25)
9.5 Concluding Remarks
9.6 Key People, Places, and Terms
9.7 Questions for Review and Discussion
9.8 Optional Assignments
9.9 Bibliography for Going Further

Key Verses

Do not call anything impure that God has made clean. (Acts 10:15 and 11:9)

I now realize how true it is that God does not show favoritism but accepts from every nation the one who fears him and does what is right. You know the message God sent to the people of Israel, announcing the good news of peace through Jesus Christ, who is Lord of all. (Acts 10:34–36)

So then, even to Gentiles God has granted repentance that leads to life. (Acts 11:18)

The disciples were called Christians first at Antioch. (Acts 11:26)

Summary Statement

But the word of God continued to spread and flourish. When Barnabas and Saul had finished their mission, they returned from Jerusalem, taking with them John, also called Mark. (Acts 12:24–25)

INTRODUCTION

While the previous section of Acts was organized around the lives of three key individuals, the fourth major section of Acts organizes the story around the gospel's movement in various cities. Luke focuses particularly on the spread of the gospel northward along the coast of the Mediterranean Sea, zooming in on events in Lydda and Joppa (Acts 9:32–43), Caesarea Maritima (10:1–11:18), and Syrian Antioch (11:19–30) before returning to Jerusalem (12:1–25). Here readers see that outreach beyond Jerusalem is a normal activity.

At the beginning of the persecution of the church, Luke comments that "all except the apostles were scattered throughout Judea and Samaria" (8:1). Even so, while Jerusalem remained their home base of operations in the early days, some of the apostles traveled about for ministry purposes (e.g., Peter and John; 8:4–25). Now in this section of Acts, we see more of Peter's ministerial travels outside Jerusalem (9:32–43), which includes a blatant welcoming of gentile converts into the faith (10:1–11:18). Here too we see the establishment of a local church outside Israel that behaves just like the Jerusalem church (11:19–30). And here we see that the Jerusalem church is still facing challenges (12:1–25), some of which apparently prompt further travels for Peter to parts undisclosed (12:17).

Looking toward Lydda from the south (ca. 1900). Public domain

9.1 PETER'S ITINERANT MINISTRY IN LYDDA AND JOPPA (ACTS 9:32–43)

Luke opens this section of Acts with a matter-of-fact statement: "As Peter traveled about the country . . ." (9:32). Jesus had a home base from which he had carried out an itinerant ministry for approximately three years (Capernaum; see Matt 9:1; Mark 2:1); so it is perhaps unremarkable that the apostles would utilize Jerusalem as a home base in carrying out itinerant ministry. Furthermore, given that Peter (and John) had traveled to Samaria following up on Philip's ministry there (Acts 8:4–25), we might be inclined to see Peter's travels here to Lydda and Joppa (and then later to Caesarea, 10:1–11:18) as a kind of follow-up ministry as well, recalling that Philip had traveled up the coastline from Azotus "preaching the gospel in all the towns until he reached Caesarea" (8:40), which would have included the cities of Lydda and Joppa.

Peter's Itinerant Follow-Up to Philip's Missionary Travels

Peter's ministry travels trace somewhat on top of Philip's ministry travels; in Samaria, Peter (and John) minister to those who had received the gospel via Philip's preaching (Acts 8:14–25), and in Lydda and Joppa, Peter visits the Lord's people and "disciples" in those towns (Acts 9:32–43).

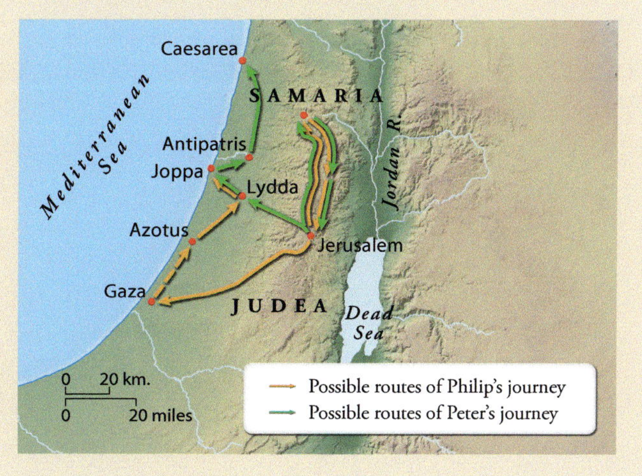

9.1.1 Aeneas Is Healed in Lydda (9:32–35)

Among the believers in ***Lydda*** is a man named Aeneas who has been bedridden for eight years (9:33). Briefly and explicitly Luke recounts that ***Aeneas*** is healed by Jesus Christ through Peter (9:34). Indeed, this miracle is reminiscent of Jesus's healing of the paralytic man in Capernaum (Luke 5:17–26) whom Jesus had instructed, "I tell you, get up, take your mat and go home" (Luke 5:24); here Peter similarly instructs Aeneas, "Get up and roll up your mat" (Acts 9:34). This miraculous healing of Aeneas leads many of that region to trust in the Lord Jesus (9:35), turning what may have begun as a follow-up ministry into an advancement of the gospel as well.

Lydda

- Located about twenty-four miles northwest of Jerusalem and about eleven miles southeast of Joppa in the fertile lowlands of the Shephelah.
- Was known as Lod in OT times and is said to have been founded by the Benjamite Shemed (1 Chr 8:12).
- At the intersection of the highway between Egypt and Babylon and the road between Jerusalem and its seaport at Joppa; had commercial and military significance and was often contested.
- Became known as Lydda during the Maccabean period and, after being transferred from Samaria's control, served as capital of one of Judea's eleven districts (1 Macc 11:34; Josephus, *J.W.* 3.3.5 §§54–58).
- Was known in the NT era for its cattle raising, textile and pottery industries, and academic pursuits.
- Became a noted center of rabbinical learning shortly after the AD 70 fall of Jerusalem to Rome.
- Became a Roman colony ca. AD 200 and was renamed Diospolis; Rabbinic Judaism lost influence then, but Christianity persisted.
- Crusaders renamed the city St. George, commemorating his martyrdom there in ca. AD 303.
- Possibly where the modern city of Lod is now located.

Select Bibliography

Robert A. Derrenbacker Jr. and Stephen Von Wyrick, "Lydda," *EDB*, 832.

"Lod," *BEB* 3:1345–46.

Joshua Schwartz, "Peter and Ben Stada in Lydda," in *The Book of Acts in Its Palestinian Setting*. Edited by Richard Bauckham. BAFCS 4. Grand Rapids: Eerdmans, 1995; Carlisle: Paternoster, 1995, 391–414.

9.1.2 Tabitha Is Raised in Joppa (9:36–43)

While Peter is in Lydda ("about that time," Acts 9:37), a believer (i.e., "disciple") who lived in the nearby town of ***Joppa*** becomes sick and dies. The woman's name is ***Tabitha*** or ***Dorcas*** (the respective Aramaic and Greek words for "gazelle"), and she was well known for her deeds of kindness (9:36, 39). Even though Tabitha is dead, when the disciples in Joppa hear that Peter is in Lydda, they send for him, perhaps hopeful of some miraculous intervention given the widespread news about the miraculous healing of Aeneas (9:38). This pairing of stories—one about a man and the other about a woman—is a common feature of Luke's storytelling.[1] In fact, this healing-resuscitation pairing is reminiscent of two such pairings in Jesus's ministry: healing a centurion's servant and raising a widow's son (Luke 7:1–17) and healing an unnamed woman and raising Jairus's daughter (Luke 8:40–56).

1. See chapter 3.

Joppa

- Having the only natural harbor on the coastline between Egypt and Ptolemais, in ancient times served as Jerusalem's seaport, located about thirty-five miles northwest of Jerusalem on the Mediterranean Sea.
- In OT times, known as Yapho, a name of Phoenician origins meaning "the beautiful"; Alexander the Great changed it to Joppa (in honor of the daughter of the Greek god of the winds).
- Received cedars from Lebanon for constructing Solomon's temple (2 Chr 2:16) and again for the temple's reconstruction (Ezra 3:7).
- Where Jonah boarded a ship bound for Tarshish in his effort to avoid ministry in Nineveh (Jonah 1:3).
- Control often changed hands in biblical times (e.g., the Philistines vs. David) and during the intertestamental period (e.g., Egyptians, Seleucids, Hasmoneans, etc.).
- Captured by Herod the Great in 37 BC, but the citizens' hatred for him led him to build Caesarea Maritima as a new, and much improved, seaport about forty miles north.
- Where the modern city of Jaffa is now located, in the southern Tel Aviv urban continuum.

Select Bibliography

Wayne C. Hensley, "Joppa," *BEB* 3:1209.
James L. Kelso, "Joppa," *ZEB* 3:778–79.
Jacob Kaplan et al., "Jaffa," *NEAEHL* 2:655–59 and 5:1791–92.
Samuel Tolkowsky, *The Gateway of Palestine: A History of Jaffa* (London: Routledge, 1924).

Peter's conduct in Joppa is helpful in recognizing the place of the miraculous. Rather than making a public show of power and reciting a magic formula, Peter dismisses the crowd from the room and prays. When the Lord responds by restoring Tabitha back to life, Peter restores her back to the community of believers (Acts 9:40–41). News of this miraculous restoration spreads and leads many to trust in the Lord Jesus (Acts 9:42). In both the Tabitha and Aeneas events, it was God's work among believers that unbelievers noticed. A pattern seems evident here: God can use testimonies about his work in our lives to attract others to himself.

Old city of Jaffa (Joppa) on the shore of the Mediterranean Sea.

Roman/adobe .stock.com

Luke closes the account of the Tabitha miracle by commenting on Peter remaining in Joppa "for some time" (9:43). As the story continues, we see that Peter's willingness to be summoned from Lydda to Joppa puts him in the place where he would again gain new direction from the Lord, for in the next episode, Peter is summoned from Joppa to take part in a significant movement of God in ***Caesarea*** (10:1–11:18). God's people should be faithful with what they already know and trust God to reveal to them any necessary next steps (cf. Luke 16:10–12).

Caesarea Maritima

- On the Mediterranean Sea about sixty-five miles from Jerusalem; constructed by Herod the Great (beginning in 22 BC and finishing in 10 BC) on the site of an older Phoenician (and then Greek) settlement named Strato's Tower.
- Named in honor of Caesar Augustus (as were many cities); this one is "by the sea" (thus Caesarea Maritima). The other notable NT city named in honor of a Caesar is Caesarea Philippi, north of the Sea of Galilee.
- Was supplied with fresh water by a high-level aqueduct (as much as twenty feet) from springs about six miles to the northeast of the city; later more aqueducts and tunnels were added and extended so as to deliver water from springs about thirteen miles away, south of the slopes of Mt. Carmel.
- Served as headquarters of the Roman government for the province of Judea in the first century, beginning AD 6.
- As seen in Acts, the major seaport city for first-century Palestine with a large artificial harbor engineered by Herod the Great—the first of its kind and utilizing a hydraulic concrete. The harbor was also specifically dedicated to Caesar Augustus as "Sebastos Harbor" (*sebastos* is Greek for "Augustus").
- Had a first-century population of over fifty thousand people.
- Prominent religions present in the NT era: Tyche (Fortuna), Ephesian Artemis (Diana), Apollo, Dionysius, Isis, Serapis, Demeter, Mithras, the ruler cult (Augustus and Roma), and Judaism.
- The location of the so-called Pilate stone, a damaged limestone block with a partially intact dedication inscription mentioning Pontius Pilate, the prefect of the Roman province of Judea in AD 26–36; this significant archaeological find was discovered in 1961.

Select Bibliography

Edward M. Blaiklock, "Caesarea," *ZEB* 1:702–703.
Kenneth G. Holum, "Caesarea," *OEANE* 1:399–404.
John R. McRay, "Caesarea Maritima," *DNTB*, 176–77.
Avner Raban, "Caesarea," *NEAEHL*, 1:270–91 and 5:1656–84.
Avner Raban and Kenneth G. Holum, eds., *Caesarea Maritima: A Retrospective after Two Millennia*, DMOA 21 (Leiden: Brill, 1996).

9.2 THE CONVERSION OF CORNELIUS IN CAESAREA (ACTS 10:1–11:18)

Acts 10:1–11:18 is one of the longest pericopes in Acts; because it is a key episode in the story, Luke allots a significant amount of space to it. Especially noteworthy is the amount of repetition Luke includes, for the repetitious elements evidence Luke's points of emphasis in the lengthy episode. In particular, Cornelius's vision is told four times (10:3–7, 22, 30–33; 11:13–14), Peter's vision is mentioned two times (10:9–16; 11:5–10), and the coming of the Spirit on the gentiles is mentioned five times (10:44, 45, 47; 11:15, 17; cf. 15:7–11).

This repetition stresses two things. First, just as Jews are brought back to being

God's people through faith in Jesus Christ, so also gentiles are to be included in God's people through faith in Jesus Christ. While Cornelius was perhaps not the first gentile convert (cf. the Ethiopian eunuch in 8:26–40), Luke features the conversion of the gentile Cornelius (and his family) as clear public testimony of God's inclusion of gentiles among the believers.[2] Second, Luke uses repetition in this pericope to emphasize that outreach to gentiles was God's idea and not anyone else's. Cornelius's and Peter's separate visions and the coming of the Spirit on the gentiles all took place at God's initiative. God's intention is to include the gentiles.

Repetitions in the Cornelius Episode

As one of the longest episodes in the book, Acts 10:1-11:18 utilizes several points of repetition to emphasize that gentile inclusion was at God's initiative and was not anyone else's idea.

Repeated Story Items	Texts and Contexts
Cornelius's vision:	Acts 10:3-7: narrated by Luke as it happens in the storyline Acts 10:22: reported by Cornelius's messengers to Peter Acts 10:30-33: reported by Cornelius himself to Peter Acts 11:13-14: reported by Peter to believers in Jerusalem
Peter's vision:	Acts 10:9-16: narrated by Luke as it happens in the storyline Acts 11:5-10: reported by Peter to believers in Jerusalem
The Holy Spirit comes on the gentiles:	Acts 10:44: "The Holy Spirit came on all who heard the message." Acts 10:45: "The gift of the Holy Spirit had been poured out even on Gentiles." Acts 10:47: "They have received the Holy Spirit just as we have." Acts 11:15: "The Holy Spirit came on them as he had come on us." Acts 11:17: "God gave them the same gift he gave us." cf. Acts 15:8: "God, who knows the heart, showed that he accepted them by giving the Holy Spirit to them, just as he did to us."

9.2.1 God Instructs the Roman Centurion Cornelius to Send for Peter (10:1–8)

This pericope begins with a Roman centurion in Caesarea. With Caesarea as the seat of government for the Roman province of Judea, it is no surprise that troops of Roman soldiers were stationed there along with their significant commanders, called centurions.[3]

2. Pao calls it "the paradigmatic conversion of a Gentile"; David W. Pao, "Jesus's Ascension and the Lukan Account of the Restoration of Israel," pp. 137–55 in *Ascent into Heaven in Luke-Acts: New Explorations of Luke's Narrative Hinge*, ed. David K. Bryan and David W. Pao (Minneapolis: Fortress, 2016), 152n59.

3. For a brief survey on the structure of the Roman military and the place of centurions as the most important tactical officers, see Glen L. Thompson, "Roman Military," *DNTB*, 991–95. For more on the soldiers and centurions in Caesarea, see Craig S. Keener, *Acts: An Exegetical Commentary*, 4 vols. (Grand Rapids: Baker Academic, 2012–2015), 2:1734–44.

More than any other NT author, Luke shows himself to have an interest in centurions; he has sixteen uses of ***centurion*** (Greek: *hekatontarchēs*: Luke 7:2, 6; 23:47; Acts 10:1, 22; 21:32; 22:25, 26; 23:17, 23; 24:23; 27:1, 6, 11, 31, 43), and Matthew has the only other four NT uses of this term (Matt 8:5, 8, 13; 27:54), with Mark using a plain synonym three times (Greek: *kenturiōn* in Mark 15:39, 44, 45). Centurions were people of authority and power in the first-century Roman military, and Luke's interest in centurions seems at least partially motivated by their sense of order and proper response to authority (see esp. Luke 7:1–10).

Unlike the unnamed centurion of Capernaum in Luke 7:1–10, the centurion of Caesarea in Acts 10 is introduced by name and regiment: "At Caesarea there was a man named Cornelius, a centurion in what was known as the Italian Regiment" (Acts 10:1). Similar to the Capernaum centurion, ***Cornelius*** is described as a monotheistic gentile worshiping the God of the Hebrew Scriptures, attending synagogue, observing the Sabbath, and practicing the main requirements of Jewish piety. While they were reluctant to become full-fledged ***proselytes*** to Judaism—thus remaining "unclean gentiles" in the eyes of Jews—such gentiles were sometimes called ***God-fearers*** (see sidebar).[4] Luke indicates that Cornelius along with "all his family were devout and God-fearing" and that "he gave generously to those in need and prayed to God regularly" (10:2; cf. Luke 7:4–5).

With great detail, Luke describes a vision that Cornelius experiences. At "about three in the afternoon" (Acts 10:3; more literally "about the ninth hour of the day," which started at sunrise or about 6:00 a.m.; see sidebar), Cornelius sees an angel of God addressing him, and in their interaction Cornelius is told that God wants him to hear something from Simon Peter, who is currently staying with Simon the tanner in Joppa (10:4–6). With Cornelius immediately doing precisely as he has been instructed, his response to the vision reinforces his character as someone determined to be obedient to God (10:7–8).

Some have suggested that the "more light" principle is at work in the story of Cornelius. That is, when a person responds faithfully to lower levels of illumination of the truth, then God grants more light by which they may be saved.[5] The means by which that additional knowledge comes to that person—whether through divine

4. Regarding the vast and varied literature discussing "God-fearers" in the NT, particularly helpful is Ben Witherington III, *The Acts of the Apostles: A Socio-Rhetorical Commentary* (Grand Rapids: Eerdmans, 1998; Carlisle: Paternoster, 1998), 341–44; more extensive is Irina Levinskaya, *The Book of Acts in Its Diaspora Setting*, BAFCS 5 (Grand Rapids: Eerdmans, 1996; Carlisle: Paternoster, 1996), esp. 1–126.

5. William J. Larkin Jr., *Acts*, The IVP New Testament Commentary Series (Downers Grove, IL: InterVarsity Press, 1995), 154–55; cf. Everett Falconer Harrison, *Interpreting Acts: The Expanding Church* (Chicago: Moody, 1975; repr., Grand Rapids: Zondervan, 1986), 176; and Dean Pinter, *Acts*, The Story of God Bible Commentary (Grand Rapids: Zondervan, 2019), 252.

direction or through circumstantial encounters—is of lesser importance than the reception of the truth itself. What Luke is emphasizing here is that God has taken the initiative to see to it that Cornelius and his family will hear the gospel message from Peter. It was not Peter's idea to preach in Caesarea, and Cornelius did not come up with the idea either. God supernaturally intervenes with a vision so the word of salvation will be brought to Cornelius and his family.

God-Fearers and the Aphrodisias Inscription (Third Century AD)

The existence of people known as "God-fearers" as described in the book of Acts (not a technical term but found in various Greek phrases, e.g., *sebomenoi ton theon*, *phoboumenoi ton theon*, cf. *theosebeis*) was a topic of some scholarly debate until the discovery of the Aphrodisias inscription. Even though the inscription dates to the third century, it acknowledges "God-fearer" as a recognized descriptor of particular people in antiquity.

Kenan T. Erim of NYU excavated the ancient Roman city of Aphrodisias (today in southwest Turkey) and found many stone-cut works of art, marble statues and a large public inscription written in Greek installed by the Jewish community at Aphrodisias.

This register of donors or founders inscribed in Greek on a doorjamb or pilaster from a third-century A.D. building at Aphrodisias provides incontrovertible evidence, says Louis Feldman, that a class of gentile "sympathizers" with Judaism called "God-fearers" did exist.

The six-foot-high marble pillar was part of a "memorial building" referred to in the inscription as having been built by the people whose names were listed there. Possibly this building was a community soup kitchen attached to a synagogue; neither building has been found.

The inscription, uncovered in 1976, includes two lists. The first is a register of common Jewish names, presumably, of *ktistai* (Greek for donors or founders). The second, shown here, lists Greek names under the phrase *kai hosoi theosebeis*, Greek for "and those who are God-fearers."

A second inscription (not seen here) from Aphrodisias's odeum, or theater, reads "the place of those who are complete Hebrews," and suggests that the citizens of the Anatolian city felt it necessary to differentiate between "full" Jews and pagan "half-converts" known as "God-fearers," who may have observed some, but not all, Jewish religious practices.

HolyLandPhotos.org

From a summary regarding an article by Louis H. Feldman, "The God-Fearers: Did They Exist? The Omnipresence of the God-Fearers," *BAR* 12.5 (1986); the summary is posted on the website for The Center for Online Judaic Studies and accessed on January 24, 2024, at https://cojs.org/aphrodisias_inscription-_3rd_century_ce/.

The Hours of the Day in First-Century Reckoning

Ancient timekeeping devices such as sundials and clepsydras ("water stealers," i.e., marked containers from which a liquid could drip out at a constant rate) could be utilized to track twenty-four equal hours of the day, but these were generally more precise than most people needed. Even with the seasonal variance of longer days in the summer and shorter days in the winter, approximate time measures were sufficient for the typical laborer.

The workday of the first-century Jewish world was the twelve hours from sunrise to sunset (see John 11:9), which can be generally reckoned in modern time parlance as from 6:00 a.m. until 6:00 p.m. This is nicely pictured in the parable of Matthew 20:1-12, where a vineyard owner hires laborers "early in the morning" (i.e., sunrise, about 6:00 a.m.; v. 1), again at "about nine in the morning" (literally "the third hour"; v. 3), again at "about noon" (literally "the sixth [hour]"; v. 5) and "about three in the afternoon" (literally "the ninth hour"; v. 5), and finally at "about five in the afternoon" (literally "the eleventh [hour]"; v. 6). Then "when evening came" (v. 8), the owner paid all the workers the same amount, even the eleventh-hour hires who had worked "only one hour" (i.e., until the end of the workday at about 6:00 p.m.; v. 12). This twelve-part reckoning of hours was similarly utilized for marking the evening hours from sunset to sunrise, roughly 6:00 p.m. until 6:00 a.m.

Thus, the literal hour-of-day phrases in the Greek of Luke-Acts are regularly rendered into modern English time reckonings as follows:

- Luke 23:44—"About the sixth hour" is rendered as "about noon" (NIV).
- Luke 23:44—"the ninth hour" is rendered as "three in the afternoon" (NIV).
- Acts 2:15—"The third hour of the day" is rendered as "nine in the morning" (NIV).
- Acts 3:1—"At the ninth hour" is rendered as "at three in the afternoon" (NIV).
- Acts 10:3—"About the ninth hour of the day" is rendered as "at about three in the afternoon" (NIV).
- Acts 10:9—"About the sixth hour" is rendered as "about noon" (NIV).
- Acts 10:30—"At the ninth hour" is rendered as "at three in the afternoon" (NIV).
- Acts 23:23—"The third hour of the night" is rendered as "nine tonight" (NIV).

The Romans used a different division of daily hours, with the day beginning at midnight rather than at sunrise. Some have proposed that NT authors sometimes utilized the Roman rather than the Jewish system of reference, which might explain an apparent incongruity between the Gospels of Mark and John. Mark 15:25 reports that Jesus was crucified at "nine in the morning" (literally "the third hour"), but John 19:14 reports Pilate presenting Jesus for crucifixion at "about noon" (literally "about the sixth hour"). This appears almost backward. But if John is reporting the Roman ruler Pilate's presentation of Jesus via Roman reckoning, i.e. "the sixth hour" would be 6:00 a.m., the discrepancy disappears. In this instance, however, given the imprecise time approximations of the first-century general populace, most scholars are content to recognize the crucifixion as beginning in the morning between 9:00 a.m. and noon, i.e., between Mark's "third hour" and John's "about the sixth hour," with John emphasizing that the proceedings were dragging on during the Jewish "Preparation of the Passover" when the Passover lamb would be sacrificed (John 19:14; cf. John 4:6 where "the sixth hour" is also most likely noon).

The hours of the night were also divided into

"watches." The Jews observed three watches of the night (Exod 14:24; Judg 7:19; 1 Sam 11:11; Lam 2:19); the first watch would be from sunset until 10:00 p.m., the middle watch from 10:00 p.m. until 2:00 a.m., and the morning watch from 2:00 a.m. until sunrise. The Romans utilized four watches of three hours each (cf. "four squads of soldiers" to guard Peter through the night in Acts 12:4). These four time periods of the night are pictured by the wording of Mark 13:35: "in the evening" (i.e., sunset until 9:00 p.m.), "at midnight" (i.e., 9:00 p.m. until midnight), "when the rooster crows" (i.e., midnight until 3:00 a.m.), or "at dawn" (i.e., 3:00 a.m. until sunrise). The Roman watches appear to be in mind in Matthew 14:25 and Mark 6:48 where the Greek for "the fourth watch of the night" is rendered as "shortly before dawn" (NIV; cf. Luke 12:38).

9.2.2 God Sends a Message to Peter (10:9–23a)

Peter also is the recipient of a supernatural vision, and Luke includes a lot of details in this part of the story as well, e.g., it happened at noon (i.e., the sixth hour), while Cornelius's messengers were en route, on a roof top, and during Peter's prayer time (10:9–10). Like Cornelius's vision, Peter's is one of interaction with a divine character, but just a voice rather than an angelic figure. The conversation is about the appearance of a sheet suspended by its four corners coming down from heaven and containing "all kinds of four-footed animals, as well as reptiles and birds" (10:12). Peter is instructed to kill and eat whatever he wants from this collection; but, as some of the animals were on the OT list of forbidden items (see sidebar), Peter emphatically refuses: "Surely not, Lord! . . . I have never eaten anything impure or unclean" (10:14; cf. Ezek 4:13–14). But the voice responds decisively to Peter's refusal: "Do not call anything impure that God has made clean" (10:15).

God himself had established the OT food laws (see Lev 11:1–47; 20:25–26; Deut 14:3–21), and now he himself was announcing a scheduled adjustment to those commands. Green-Armytage offers a two-part observation on the built-in obsolescence of the law: first, that it was honorable because it came from God, and second, that God designed it to become obsolete when its specific purposes were fulfilled.[6] The food laws for OT Israel had a specific purpose: to help in distinguishing faith in the true God from the surrounding pagan religions.[7] Given the whole Christ event, the specific purity laws had served their purpose well: to provide a community through which to bring the Messiah into the world. Thus, the OT food laws were not so much invalidated; rather, they had been fulfilled. The arrival of the Messiah was to bring about many intended changes, and loosening the restrictive food laws was one such intended change

6. A. H. N. Green-Armytage, *A Portrait of St. Luke* (London: Burns and Oates, 1955; Chicago Henry Regnery, 1955), 105–6.

7. See Walter J. Houston, "Foods, Clean and Unclean," *DOTPent*, 326–36; and Jack P. Lewis, "Food," *ZEB* 2:622–28.

Forbidden Food Items in the Hebrew Bible

The following list of "impure and unclean" (Greek: *koinon kai akatharton*; Acts 10:14) animals that were forbidden as food for the OT Israelites is constructed from Leviticus 11:1-47 and Deuteronomy 14:3-21 (LXX using "unclean" = *akatharton*; cf. 1 Macc 1:62 using "common, impure" = *koina*).

- camel
- hyrax
- rabbit
- pig
- eagle
- vulture
- black vulture
- red kite
- black kite
- falcon
- raven
- horned owl
- screech owl
- gull
- hawk
- little owl
- great owl
- white owl
- desert owl
- osprey
- cormorant
- stork
- heron
- hoopoe
- bat
- weasel
- rat
- great lizard
- gecko
- monitor lizard
- wall lizard
- skink
- chameleon
- any other creatures that move along the ground on their bellies
- sea creatures without fins and scales
- flying insects (apart from those with hopping legs, like locust, katydid, cricket, grasshopper)

(see Mark 7:14–19; Heb 9:10; cf. Rom 14:14, 17, 20; 1 Cor 10:25–26; 1 Tim 4:3–4; Titus 1:13–15). Once the Jewish culture had brought the Messiah for all humanity, that specialized culture was no longer to be viewed in the same way. For a determined Jew like Peter, this change in food restrictions was unanticipated and difficult to grasp. Luke notes that Peter's interactive vision occurred three times (Acts 10:16), an apparent point of emphasis to help him grasp this lesson.

While Peter is still pondering this visionary experience, the emissaries from Cornelius arrive at the house asking for him (10:17–18). The Holy Spirit communicates to Peter—whether via an inner voice or an audible voice, Luke does not say—that these men are sent by God (!) and that Peter should go with them (10:19–20). Peter greets the messengers and asks why they have come, and Luke repeats for his readers their message about Cornelius's person, character, and visionary experience (10:21–23a). Not immediately aware of the implications of his own visionary experience, Peter is nonetheless willing to act in obedience to what he does know. Eventually Peter will be able to recognize how a proper understanding of the vision—that gentiles are to be welcomed into the people of God—is confirmed by the Spirit coming upon believing gentiles, who are included in this fulfillment of Jesus's own words (11:1–18; esp. v. 16).[8]

8. Cf. Mark G. Boyer, *Praying Your Way through Luke's Gospel and the Acts of the Apostles* (Eugene, OR: Wipf & Stock, 2015), 61.

Visions in Acts

Luke includes reports of several vision experiences in Acts. He usually employs the term "vision" (Greek: *horama*) to refer to a visual, dreamlike experience. See his reports of the visions Ananias experienced in 9:10–16; Cornelius in 10:3–6; Peter in 10:9–20; cf. 11:4–10; and Saul/Paul in 9:12; 16:9–10; and 18:9–10. Conversely, when an angel was rescuing Peter from prison, Luke reports in 12:7–11 that Peter mistakenly assumed he was merely seeing a vision (*horama*), but it was happening in reality. Similarly, in his report of the appearance of Jesus to Saul/Paul on the road to Damascus (9:1–9), Luke does not use the term "vision" (*horama*) because this was a visitation of Jesus and not merely a dreamlike experience: Jesus was actually appearing on the road to Damascus. When Paul later describes this experience as a "vision" (26:19), Luke uses a different term (Greek: *optasia*), the same term used of the appearance of angels to the women on the morning of the resurrection of Jesus (Luke 24:23).

9.2.3 God Sends the Spirit as Peter Preaches to Cornelius and His Household (10:23b–48)

On the next day, Peter departs with Cornelius's messengers headed back to Caesarea along with six other Jewish believers from Joppa (10:23b; cf. 10:45; 11:12). Upon entering Cornelius's home, where a crowd of Cornelius's friends and relatives are gathered, Peter corrects Cornelius's attempt at reverential homage: "Stand up . . . I am only a man myself" (10:26). Commenting on the well-known Jewish concern for purity, he remarks that it is unlawful (Greek: *athemitos*) for a Jew to associate with or visit a gentile (10:28a)—an overstatement, given that there is no such OT law, but some of the strict Jewish customs assume that affiliation with gentiles would undoubtedly lead one to become ritually unclean (see sidebar). Nevertheless, Peter continues with a correction of such views, explaining that "God has shown me that I should not call anyone impure or unclean" (10:28b). Peter's threefold vision had been about food, but remarkably he applies it to fellowship with gentiles. What is the connection?

The high value on hospitality in Middle Eastern society meant that entering a person's home had the entailment of expecting to eat with them.[9] When Peter eventually reports on his Caesarea experience to the Jewish believers in Jerusalem, this is their concern: "You went into the house of uncircumcised men and ate with them" (11:3). Given the detailed OT food laws, it was easiest for the Jews simply to declare gentile homes off limits, for this would remove all concern about being defiled by any restricted food items.

9. See this expectation at work in Luke 11:5–8. For a brief discussion of hospitality in antiquity including both Gentile and Jewish valuations of it as well as its expectations and obligations, see Keener, *Acts*, 3:2414–20.

Jewish Concern over Association with Gentiles

Entering Cornelius's home, Peter comments on Jewish misgivings about doing so: "You are well aware that it is against our law for a Jew to associate with or visit a Gentile" (Acts 10:28). While there is no OT law forbidding such a visit, Jewish concerns about maintaining ritual purity described in Scripture led to the development of additional strict customs among some groups of Jews against close interaction and dining with gentiles. Here are some examples of this custom.

Jub 22:16—"Separate yourself from gentiles, and do not eat with them, and do not perform deeds like theirs. And do not become associates of theirs. Because their deeds are defiled, and all their ways are contaminated, and despicable, and abominable."

Tob 1:10–13—"Now when I was carried away captive to Nineveh, all my brethren and my relatives ate the food of the Gentiles; but I kept myself from eating it, because I remembered God with all my heart. Then the Most High gave me favor."

Jdt 12:1–2—"Then he commanded them to bring her in where his silver dishes were kept, and ordered them to set a table for her with some of his own food and to serve her with his own wine. But Judith said, 'I cannot eat it, lest it be an offense; but I will be provided from the things I have brought with me.'"

3 Macc 3:3–6—"The Jews, however, steadily maintained their good will toward the kings and their unwavering loyalty. But reverencing God and conducting themselves according to his Law, they kept themselves apart in the matter of food, and for this reason they appeared hateful to some. They adorned their community life with the excellent practice of righteousness and so established a good reputation among all men. But of this excellent practice, which was common talk everywhere regarding the Jewish nation, the foreigners took no account whatever."

Jos. Asen. 7:1—"And Joseph entered the house of Pentephres and sat upon the throne. And they washed his feet and set a table before him by itself, because Joseph never ate with the Egyptians, for this was an abomination to him."

This meant the label of "impure" was applied both to restricted foods and to gentiles who might serve such items. In this way, Peter is able to connect God's purification of formerly restricted food items with God's ability to purify people. The Messiah had come, and now the Jewish believers like Peter and those with him were slowly coming to understand the implications of this movement of God.

Emphasizing that God was taking the initiative here, Luke again repeats the story of Cornelius's angelic vision—this time in the mouth of Cornelius himself when Peter asks why Cornelius sent for him (10:29–33a). Cornelius closes his account with an overt invitation for Peter to address the crowd: "Now we are all here in the presence of God to listen to everything the Lord has commanded you to tell us" (10:33b). Peter takes up the invitation by repeating what he has been learning: "I now realize how true it is that God does not show favoritism but accepts from every nation the one who fears him and does what is right" (10:34–35). Peter is not denying his ancestral Jewish faith but is noting God's plan to invite people of other cultures to have faith in Messiah Jesus without completely leaving their own cultural context. Peter's next comment says this most directly: "You know the message God sent to the people of Israel, announcing the good news of peace through Jesus Christ, who is Lord of all" (10:36). Jesus Christ came to and through the people of Israel as God's provision of the way to peace with him, and Jesus is this solution for all people.

Interestingly, some English translations render the climactic comment in Acts 10:36—"Jesus Christ . . . is Lord of all"—as something of a parenthetical interruption in Peter's message (e.g., ESV, KJV, NASB, NET; see sidebar). C. Kavin Rowe, however, argues that this phrase is best understood as central to Peter's claim and decidedly not parenthetical.[10] The sentence leading up to this phrase introduces the gospel as the preaching of peace through Jesus Christ, and so this brief line expresses one of the main themes of this whole section (and all of Acts!): "Jesus Christ . . . is Lord of all."[11] So the NIV translation here better represents the message of Acts.

English Translations of Acts 10:36

Peter's remark about Jesus—"Jesus Christ . . . is Lord of all"—is rendered as a parenthetical comment in some English translations. But the NIV represents it as more central to the message, which fits the context of Peter's sermon (so also CEV, CSB, NLT).

NIV: "You know the message God sent to the people of Israel, announcing the good news of peace through Jesus Christ, who is Lord of all."

CEV: "This is the same message that God gave to the people of Israel, when he sent Jesus Christ, the Lord of all, to offer peace to them."

CSB: "He sent the message to the Israelites, proclaiming the good news of peace through Jesus Christ—he is Lord of all."

ESV: "As for the word that he sent to Israel, preaching good news of peace through Jesus Christ (he is Lord of all), . . ."

KJV: "The word which God sent unto the children of Israel, preaching peace by Jesus Christ: (he is Lord of all:) . . ."

NASB: "The word which He sent to the sons of Israel, preaching peace through Jesus Christ (He is Lord of all)—"

NET: "You know the message he sent to the people of Israel, proclaiming the good news of peace through Jesus Christ (he is Lord of all)—"

NLT: "This is the message of Good News for the people of Israel—that there is peace with God through Jesus Christ, who is Lord of all."

10. C. Kavin Rowe, *World Upside Down: Reading Acts in the Graeco-Roman Age* (New York: Oxford University Press, 2009), 105.

11. Ibid., 113.

Acts 10:36–43 and the Gospel of Luke

Luke's summary in Acts 10 of the message Peter shared with those gathered at Cornelius's house covers the basic content of the Gospel of Luke, with many elements of the life of Christ in the same order. Note that Jesus's death and resurrection appearances account for about half of Peter's sermon.

The Sermon in Acts 10	The Gospel of Luke
36 You know the message God sent to the people of Israel, announcing the good news of peace through Jesus Christ, who is Lord of all.	**Luke 1–2**—the announcements of the births of John the Baptist and of Jesus, esp. the angelic announcement of "good news" and "peace" in Luke 2:9–14
37 You know what has happened throughout the province of Judea, beginning in Galilee after the baptism that John preached—	**Luke 3:1–20**—the ministry of John the Baptist
38 how God anointed Jesus of Nazareth with the Holy Spirit and power,	**Luke 3:21–4:14**—Jesus's baptism and Spirit empowerment
and how he went around doing good and healing all who were under the power of the devil, because God was with him.	**Luke 4:15–6:11**—Jesus's Galilee ministry
39 "We are witnesses of everything he did in the country of the Jews and in Jerusalem.	**Luke 6:12–22:46**—the appointment of the apostles and Jesus's subsequent ministry
They killed him by hanging him on a cross,	**Luke 22:47–23:56**—the arrest and crucifixion of Jesus
40 but God raised him from the dead on the third day and caused him to be seen.	**Luke 24:1–35**—Jesus's resurrection and appearances
41 He was not seen by all the people, but by witnesses whom God had already chosen—by us who ate and drank with him after he rose from the dead.	**Luke 24:36–43**—Jesus's appearances to the apostles
42 He commanded us to preach to the people and to testify that he is the one whom God appointed as judge of the living and the dead. 43 All the prophets testify about him that everyone who believes in him receives forgiveness of sins through his name."	**Luke 24:44–53**—Jesus's teaching about his fulfillment of OT prophecy and his command to preach about forgiveness of sins through his name

After pointing to Jesus as Lord of all people everywhere, Peter asks his listeners to recall the historical facts that they already know about Jesus (10:37–43). In brief form the whole gospel is recounted: that Jesus lived a real life, that he died on a cross and verifiably rose again on the third day, and that those who believe in him are forgiven of their sins and thus ready for the coming judgment. Fascinatingly, the elements of Jesus's life, death, and resurrection recounted in Peter's sermon follow in broad terms the content of the Gospel of Luke (see sidebar).

In the midst of Peter's sharing the gospel message, his listeners become believers and receive the Holy Spirit. As noted, Luke is rather redundant about this fact (10:44, 45, 47; 11:15, 17; cf. 15:7–8). The manner in which Luke recounts the event at Cornelius's

"Baptism with the Holy Spirit"

The metaphor of "baptism in/with/by the Holy Spirit," an expression most often connected to John the Baptist, is used only seven times in the New Testament, and three of those are in Luke-Acts (Matt 3:11; Mark 1:8; Luke 3:16; John 1:33; Acts 1:5; 11:16; and 1 Cor 12:13). Metaphors are picturesque ways of expressing ideas, ideas that can be expressed more plainly. In Acts 10–11 Luke provides the plain expression as well as the colorful expression. And even as "pour out" means "give," we see that "baptism with the Holy Spirit" means to "receive the Holy Spirit," something that happens at conversion (Acts 2:38; cf. Acts 8:16).

Acts 10:44–47—"While Peter was still speaking these words, the Holy Spirit came on all who heard the message. The circumcised believers who had come with Peter were astonished that the gift of the Holy Spirit had been poured out even on Gentiles. For they heard them speaking in tongues and praising God.

"Then Peter said, 'Surely no one can stand in the way of their being baptized with water. They have received the Holy Spirit just as we have.'"

Acts 11:15–18—"'As I began to speak, the Holy Spirit came on them as he had come on us at the beginning. Then I remembered what the Lord had said: "John baptized with water, but you will be baptized with the Holy Spirit." So if God gave them the same gift he gave us who believed in the Lord Jesus Christ, who was I to think that I could stand in God's way?'

"When they heard this, they had no further objections and praised God, saying, 'So then, even to Gentiles God has granted repentance that leads to life.'"

house reveals that the Holy Spirit was more readily available than perhaps Peter and the other Jewish believers present realized (10:45–46). The gentiles heard the gospel, believed it, and immediately received the Holy Spirit. This is in keeping with Peter's earlier expression of the gospel promise of the Holy Spirit (2:38–39). Furthermore, the experience of these gentiles clearly calls into question any view that claims Spirit baptism must be an experience subsequent to conversion. ***Holy Spirit baptism***—to be "baptized with the Holy Spirit"—simply means to "receive the Holy Spirit" (see the sidebar). The gentiles received the Spirit when they believed and not at a later date.[12] Convinced of their faith, Peter commands that the new believers be baptized as followers of Jesus Christ (10:47–48).

12. See David G. Peterson, *The Acts of the Apostles*, Pillar New Testament Commentary (Grand Rapids: Eerdmans, 2009), 346–48.

Ironic Conversion Situations

Luke's descriptions in Acts of various conversions to faith in Jesus Christ might defy some assumptions about how one comes to faith. It is easy to assume that individuals who are close to the people of God have smooth conversions to faith in Christ and that those who are farther away from the people of God have more dramatic conversions to faith. But comparing the conversions of Paul and Cornelius shows that the converse can happen too. Thus, Luke seems to challenge his audience to be open to various patterns of conversion.

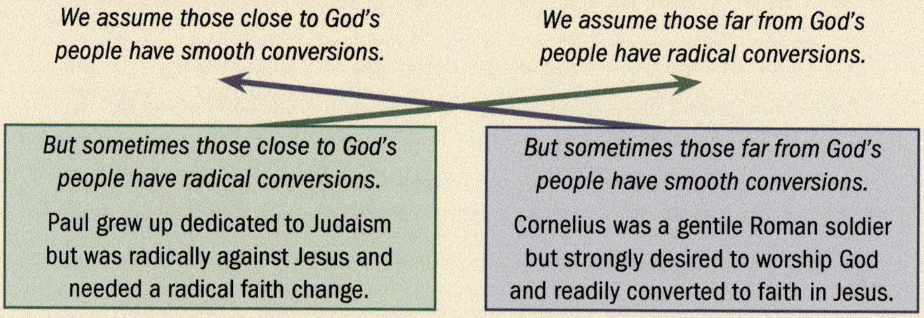

We assume those close to God's people have smooth conversions.

We assume those far from God's people have radical conversions.

But sometimes those close to God's people have radical conversions.

Paul grew up dedicated to Judaism but was radically against Jesus and needed a radical faith change.

But sometimes those far from God's people have smooth conversions.

Cornelius was a gentile Roman soldier but strongly desired to worship God and readily converted to faith in Jesus.

Have you come to faith in Jesus Christ? Where would you place your conversion experience on a scale of smooth to radical? How does your background and conversion experience compare with those of Paul and Cornelius?

9.2.4 Peter Credits God for the Outreach to Gentiles (11:1–18)

While Peter is staying with the new gentile believers in Caesarea for a few days (10:48), the news of their faith spreads (11:1). So when Peter returns to Jerusalem, the Jewish believers there want him to account for his involvement with the gentiles (11:2–3). The Jewish believers in Jerusalem were still assuming that to be a follower of Jesus the Jewish Messiah, one needed to be an observer of the Jewish cultural guidelines. While they may have made excuses for the Samaritans as partially Jewish, they were skeptical about the idea of the completely non-Jewish gentiles becoming believers in the Jewish Messiah without becoming (at least a little more) Jewish. Peter was a bit ahead of them in facing this Jew-gentile question, and now it fell to him to bring the others up to speed.

Regarding this Jew-gentile issue, Peter recounts for the Jerusalem believers the events of the recent days, including his own rooftop vision experience (11:4–10), the arrival of Cornelius's messengers in Joppa and the Spirit's instructions (11:11–12), the story of Cornelius's angelic vision (11:13–14), and finally the immediate coming of the Spirit upon the gentile believers (11:15). In his report Peter clarifies the connection of gentile believers receiving the Spirit with what Jesus had said earlier: "Then I remembered what the Lord had said: 'John baptized with water, but you will be baptized with the Holy Spirit'" (11:16; cf. 1:5 and Luke 3:16). And thus, Peter explains his sensible conclusion that "if God gave them the same gift he gave us who believed in the Lord Jesus Christ, who was I to think that I could stand in God's way?" (Acts 11:17). So the Jewish believers begin to realize more clearly that gentiles do not need to become Jews to be saved by the Jewish Messiah, and Luke closes his account with their proclamation: "So then, even to Gentiles God has granted repentance that leads to life" (11:18).[13] By recounting this episode as he does, Luke stresses to his readers that they should recognize God as the one who calls people to faith in Jesus Christ regardless of such things as race and culture.

The traditional site of Simon the Tanner's house where Peter stayed in Joppa. www.LifeintheHolyLand.com

9.3 THE GOSPEL ADVANCES TO SYRIAN ANTIOCH (ACTS 11:19–30)

This episode focuses on the gospel message taking root in the Syrian city of Antioch. ***Antioch of Syria*** was the third largest city in the first-century world, behind Rome and Alexandria (see Josephus, *J.W.* 3.2.4 §29). Antioch is mentioned six times in this pericope (11:19, 20, 22, 26 [twice], 27); perhaps Luke wants his readers to take special note of this place. Acts has shown us *Jewish believers within Israel's borders* (Acts 1) and *Jewish believers outside Israel's borders* (Acts 2 and Acts 9). Then we saw that it is possible to have *gentile believers within Israel's borders* (Cornelius, 10–11:18), and now with the establishment of a solid Christian church in Syrian Antioch (11:19–30), we see it is possible to have well-established *gentile believers outside Israel's borders.*[14] In this pericope Luke emphasizes that the church in Antioch is a real Christian church.

13. So Pao, "Jesus's Ascension and the Lukan Account of the Restoration of Israel," 152n59.

14. And in Acts 8 Luke had already anticipated insider/outsider issues regarding evangelism with his account of Philip's outreach ministry to Samaritans and to the Ethiopian eunuch.

Antioch of Syria

- One of sixteen cities in the ancient world named in honor of the Syrian emperor Antiochus.
- One of two cities in Acts with the name Antioch—the other being Pisidian Antioch.
- Located fifteen miles inland from the north-eastern shore of the Mediterranean Sea on the Orontes River, about three hundred miles north of Jerusalem.
- Was served by the seaport city of Seleucia Pieria at the mouth of the Orontes River.
- Third largest city in the first-century Roman Empire, with a population of five hundred thousand or more.
- Capital of the Roman province of Syria in the first century.
- Important crossroads city on trade routes between the ancient south, east, and northwest.
- Cultured cosmopolitan city, but had a reputation for poor morality.
- Had a large Jewish population between twenty-five thousand and sixty-five thousand.
- Christian church founded there ca. AD 36–37 (Acts 11:19–30).
- Believers were first called "Christians" there (Acts 11:26).
- In ca. AD 39–40, gentile hostility toward Jews resulted in the killing of many and the burning of their synagogues. The Jerusalem high priest Phineas sent an army of thirty thousand Jews to Antioch to retaliate by killing many gentiles. Emperor Caligula intervened by having Phineas beheaded.
- Christian Jew-gentile interaction was a significant issue here (Gal 2:11–14; Acts 15:1–35).
- Antiochene believers sent relief to Judean believers for the famine of ca. AD 45–47 (Acts 11:27–30).
- The main hub of early Christian missions (Acts 13:1–3; 14:24–28; 15:22–36; 18:22–23).

Select Bibliography

Jørgen Christensen-Ernst, *Antioch on the Orontes: A History and a Guide*. Lanham, MD: Hamilton, 2012.

Glanville Downey, *A History of Antioch in Syria from Seleucus to the Arab Conquest* (Princeton: Princeton University Press, 1961).

Edwin A. Judge, "Antioch of Syria," *ZEB* 1:210–13.

Lee M. McDonald, "Antioch (Syria)," *DNTB*, 34–37.

John R. McRay, "Antioch," *EDB*, 67–68.

9.3.1 Unnamed Ministers Take the Gospel to Antioch (11:19–21)

The pericope begins by reflecting back to the persecution that had erupted at the martyrdom of Stephen that caused believers to scatter, spreading the gospel as they went (11:19a; cf. 8:1–4). At first it was only to Jews, but some began spreading the good news to gentiles as well, and Luke notes this specifically in Antioch (11:19b–20). And he continues to mention that the gentile mission is properly a successful work of God: "The Lord's hand was with them, and a great number of people believed and turned to the Lord" (11:21).

9.3.2 Barnabas Endorses the Antioch Outreach (11:22–24)

Upon hearing the news of conversions in Antioch, the Jerusalem church sends ***Barnabas*** to investigate (11:22–24). The Jerusalem church had initiated other such follow-up investigations regarding the expansion of the gospel to new people groups (e.g., Peter and John in 8:14; perhaps Peter in 9:32–43; cf. 11:1–3). The difference here is that now it is Barnabas and not Peter doing the investigation. The Jerusalem church had already learned about the need to expand its ministry teams beyond the Twelve (6:1–6), and perhaps with Peter's testimony about gentile conversions (11:1–18) they do not view it as necessary to have one of the original twelve apostles directly involved.[15]

Arriving in Antioch and observing "what the grace of God had done," Barnabas continues in his usual work and "encouraged them all to remain true to the Lord with all their hearts" (11:23; cf. 4:36). Once again Luke offers a description of Barnabas's character as "a good man, full of the Holy Spirit and faith" (11:24; cf. 4:36–37; 9:27). Barnabas's competence in ministry is not ascribed to his education or his having a proper strategy and effective plan; rather, his integrity of character, his submission to the Spirit, and his faith are highlighted.[16] And the prior work of the Lord in Antioch continues to happen after Barnabas's arrival ("a great number of people were brought to the Lord"; 11:24).

9.3.3 Saul Joins the Christian Antioch Community (11:25–26)

The ministry in Syrian Antioch is so productive that Barnabas seeks additional help by recruiting Saul to come from Tarsus (11:25–26a). Barnabas knew that Saul, after his conversion, had become effective in gospel ministry in Hellenistic places (9:15–30), and Tarsus was just a few miles from Antioch. Saul agrees to join Barnabas in the Antioch ministry, where they work with the church for "a whole year" teaching "great numbers of people" (11:26b).

In a narrative aside at Acts 11:26c, Luke makes an thought-provoking comment: "The disciples were called Christians first at Antioch." The term ***Christian*** (*Christianos*) is used only three times in the New Testament (11:26; 26:28; 1 Pet 4:16). With this sparseness and its apparent use in the latter two instances by those who are hostile to the gospel, it seems likely to some scholars that this was intended as a derogatory label for followers of Jesus and that Luke is here simply giving its origin.[17] If this was so, believers soon overlooked its derisive origins and adopted the term as a self-designation. Even as

15. Note, however, Gal 2:11–14 indicates that Peter *did* visit Antioch at some time, a trip that Luke does not specifically mention in Acts; perhaps that visit occurred during the indefinite travels of Peter mentioned at Acts 12:17.

16. Eckhard J. Schnabel, *Acts*, ZECNT (Grand Rapids: Zondervan, 2012), 528.

17. Keener notes that the label *Christianos* is analogously formed like other Latin political terms and that it frequently shows up in extrabiblical documents as a legal charge against believers; Keener, *Acts*, 2:1847–50. Cf. Eckhard J. Schnabel, "The Persecution of Christians in the First Century," *JETS* 61 (2018): 530, "While the exact circumstances are unknown, it is plausible to assume that the encounter which required labelling the new Jewish movement and which involved the Roman magistrates was a hostile event." See also the discussion in Paul Trebilco, *Self-Designations*

Yankees, by some accounts, originated as a disdainful term that eventually became an accepted moniker, so also the people who were assigned the label *Christians* eventually embraced the name (perhaps even in keeping with Peter's encouragement in 1 Pet 4:16!). With a sizable Jewish population in first-century Antioch, it would be helpful to have such a label for distinguishing followers of the Jewish Messiah Jesus (in community with gentile believers) from the Jews who did not believe in Jesus. The eventual separation of Christianity and Judaism, as Judaism persisted in refusing to acknowledge Jesus as the long-awaited Messiah, took place slowly in the latter half of the first century and beyond, "so that what looks self-evident in hindsight was anything but evident in the first century."[18]

9.3.4 The Antioch Community Is Authenticated (11:27–30)

The group of Jewish believers in Jerusalem is called a "church" (11:22), and the group of believers of mixed ethnicities in Antioch is also called a "church" (11:26). The best explanation of what makes for a recognizable, healthy local church is from Acts 2:42: devotion to the apostles' teaching, fellowship, the breaking of bread, and prayer (see chapter 7). Luke has just commented on the Antioch believers being taught (11:26), and now he comments on their fellowship in that the believers of Antioch were sharing their possessions with other believers in need. When the disciples in Antioch hear (via the prophet Agabus; 11:27–28) that Judean believers will suffer during a coming famine, they send relief "as each one was able" (11:29–30), which reminds us of Luke's earlier descriptions of how believers voluntarily cared for each other (cf. 4:34–37). Luke offers a narrative aside to note that Agabus's prophetic prediction came to pass during the reign of Claudius (AD 41–54; confirmed by Suetonius and Josephus; see sidebar).[19]

The Antioch believers send their famine relief gift to the believers in Judea by way of Barnabas and Saul (11:30). This ***famine visit*** is Paul's second trip to Jerusalem after his conversion, the first being the trip to Jerusalem from Damascus (9:22–30). Although scholars debate how Paul's Jerusalem trips recorded in Acts match up with his own accounts in his letters, it seems likely that the famine relief visit in Acts 11 is the same as the second visit described in Galatians 2:1–10.[20] Both accounts mention

---

and Group Identity in the New Testament (Cambridge: Cambridge University Press, 2012), 272–98, where he argues that "Christian" was likely coined by gentile non-Christians, particular those in the Roman administration.

18. Bruce W. Longenecker and Todd D. Still, *Thinking through Paul: A Survey of His Life, Letters, and Theology* (Grand Rapids: Zondervan, 2014), 15. See James D. G. Dunn, *The Parting of the Ways: Between Christianity and Judaism and Their Significance for the Character of Christianity*, 2nd ed. (London: SCM, 2006).

19. See Colin J. Hemer, *The Book of Acts in the Setting of Hellenistic History*, ed. Conrad H. Gempf, WUNT 49 (Tübingen: Mohr Siebeck, 1989; repr., Winona Lake, IN: Eisenbrauns, 1990), 164–65; Bruce W. Winter, "Acts and Food Shortages," in *The Book of Acts in Its Graeco-Roman Setting*, ed. David W. J. Gill and Conrad Gempf, BAFCS 2 (Grand Rapids: Eerdmans, 1994; Carlisle: Paternoster, 1994), 59–78; Keener, *Acts*, 2:1856–58.

20. So also Clinton E. Arnold, "Acts," vol. 2B of *ZIBBCNT*, ed. Clinton E. Arnold (Grand Rapids: Zondervan, 2002), 142; Darrell L. Bock, *Acts*, BECNT (Grand Rapids: Baker Academic, 2007), 487–93; F. F. Bruce, *The Book of Acts*, 2nd ed., NICNT (Grand Rapids: Eerdmans, 1988), 231, 282–84; Ajith Fernando, *Acts*, The NIV Application Commentary (Grand Rapids: Zondervan, 1998), 414; Richard N. Longenecker, "Acts," pp. 663–1102 in *Luke-Acts*, vol. 10 of *The Expositor's Bible Commentary*, ed. Tremper Longman III and David E. Garland, rev. ed. (Grand Rapids:

Accounts of the Great Famine during the Reign of Claudius

In Acts 11:27–30, Luke recounts a prophetic announcement of a great famine and remarks that it took place during the reign of Emperor Claudius (AD 41–54). Other ancient historians also comment on this famine (ca. 45–46). Here are the accounts of the Roman historian Suetonius and the Jewish historian Josephus.

Suetonius, *Divus Claudius*, 18 (ca. AD 121)

When there was a scarcity of grain because of long-continued droughts, he [Claudius] was once stopped in the middle of the Forum by a mob and so pelted with abuse and at the same time with pieces of bread, that he was barely able to make his escape to the Palace by a back door; and after this experience he resorted to every possible means to bring grain to Rome, even in the winter season. To the merchants he held out the certainty of profit by assuming the expense of any loss that they might suffer from storms, and offered to those who would build merchant ships large bounties, adapted to the condition of each.

Flavius Josephus, *Jewish Antiquities* 20.2.5 §§49–53 (ca. AD 94)

Helena, the mother of the king [of Adiabene], saw that peace prevailed in the kingdom and that her son was prosperous and the object of admiration in all men's eyes, even those of foreigners, thanks to the prudence that God gave him. Now she had conceived a desire to go to the city of Jerusalem and to worship at the temple of God, which was famous throughout the world, and to make thank-offerings there. She consequently asked her son to give her leave. Izates was most enthusiastic in granting his mother's request, made great preparations for her journey, and gave her a large sum of money. He even escorted her for a considerable distance, and she completed her journey to the city of Jerusalem. Her arrival was very advantageous for the people of Jerusalem, for at that time the city was hard pressed by famine and many were perishing from want of money to purchase what they needed. Queen Helena sent some of her attendants to Alexandria to buy grain for large sums and others to Cyprus to bring back a cargo of dried figs. Her attendants speedily returned with these provisions, which she thereupon distributed among the needy. She has thus left a very great name that will be famous forever among our whole people for her benefaction. When her son Izates learned of the famine, he likewise sent a great sum of money to leaders of the Jerusalemites.

Barnabas on the trip, both describe a prophecy as the instigation of the trip, both describe a meeting with the Jerusalem leaders, and both reference gifts for the poor (see sidebar).

Zondervan, 2007), 939–42; I. Howard Marshall, *The Acts of the Apostles: An Introduction and Commentary*, TNTC (Grand Rapids: Eerdmans, 1980), 204–5, 244–47; Peterson, *Acts*, 420; Schnabel, *Acts*, 620–21; Stott, *Message of Acts*, 206, 241–44; Charles Stephen Conway Williams, *A Commentary on the Acts of the Apostles* (Edinburgh: Black, 1964; repr., HNTC, Peabody, MA: Hendrickson, 1988), 24–30; Witherington, *Acts*, 90–97, 375, 440–45. See more on this issue in chapter 11.

The Similarities between Acts 11 and Galatians 2

Scholars debate whether Paul's trip to Jerusalem described in Galatians 2 matches up best with the trip in Acts 11 or the trip in Acts 15. The suggestion here is that it matches best with the Acts 11 famine visit as both accounts are Paul's second trip to Jerusalem after his conversion (i.e., the first visit in Acts 9:22–30 ≈ the first visit in Gal 1:18–24) and both mention Barnabas on the trip, a prophecy as the instigation of the trip, a meeting with the Jerusalem leaders, and gifts for the poor.

Acts 11:27–30	Galatians 2:1–10
During this time some prophets came down from Jerusalem to Antioch. One of them, named Agabus, stood up and through the Spirit predicted that a severe famine would spread over the entire Roman world. (This happened during the reign of Claudius.) The disciples, as each one was able, decided to provide help for the brothers and sisters living in Judea. This they did, sending their gift to the elders by Barnabas and Saul.	Then after fourteen years, I went up again to Jerusalem, this time with Barnabas. I took Titus along also. I went in response to a revelation and, meeting privately with those esteemed as leaders, I presented to them the gospel that I preach among the Gentiles. I wanted to be sure I was not running and had not been running my race in vain. . . . . . . James, Cephas and John, those esteemed as pillars, gave me and Barnabas the right hand of fellowship when they recognized the grace given to me. They agreed that we should go to the Gentiles, and they to the circumcised. All they asked was that we should continue to remember the poor, the very thing I had been eager to do all along.

9.4 OPPOSITION TO THE CHURCH BACK IN JERUSALEM (ACTS 12:1–25)

Reporting the famine visit to Judea, Luke returns his attention to the church's foundational city in that province and offers a report on some of the activities of the Jerusalem church. In his literary artistry, it appears that Luke has written Acts 11:19–13:3 with a large scale chiasm that focuses on the rescue of Peter in Acts 12 (see sidebar). Furthermore, Luke has recorded the events of Acts 12 with several well calculated points of ***irony*** that betray an attentive author. Despite the somber subject matter of this part of the story—including death and imprisonment—if read carefully, Luke's writing will produce a wry smile. In this sense, Acts 12 may well be one of the most humorous chapters in the New Testament (see sidebar).

Twelve Ironic Elements of Luke's Account in Acts 12

Despite its somber subject matter of persecution and death, Acts 12 is perhaps the most ironic chapter in the New Testament. Here are twelve points of irony—places of somewhat surprising contrasts—in Luke's report of the events of Acts 12. Trusting in the Lord, can we describe life's difficulties with a proper sense of humor?

I. Herod's *violence* (12:1–2) is *pleasing* to the Jews (12:3).

II. At the celebration of *freedom* (the Festival of Unleavened Bread; 12:3), Peter is *imprisoned* (12:4–5).

III. Herod's *four* squads of *four* soldiers each (12:4) can't stop *one* angel of the Lord (12:6–10).
IV. Peter confuses *reality* (12:7–8) with a *vision* (12:9–11).
V. The prison gate *opens automatically* (12:10), but Rhoda *forgets to open* the door of the home (12:13–14).
VI. An *angel takes Peter* out of prison (12:7–11) and the church *mistakes Peter for an angel* (12:15).
VII. The church *prayed earnestly* for Peter to be rescued (12:5, 12) but was amazed that Peter was rescued in *answer to their prayer* (12:15–16).
VIII. The *apostle* Peter leaves *non-apostle* James in charge of the Jerusalem church (12:17).
IX. The *quiet* guards (12:6, 10) experience "*no small commotion*" (12:18, emphasis added).
X. Peter's *captors* (12:6) get Peter's *sentence* (12:19).
XI. Herod *feeds* others (12:20), but Herod *is eaten* by worms (12:21–23).
XII. In prison Peter is *"struck" by an angel and awakens* (12:7; Greek: *patassō*); on his throne Herod is *"struck" by an angel and dies* (12:23; Greek: *patassō*).

Jerusalem

- The primary city of ancient Israel, particularly after David established it as the nation's capital and the central city of Israel's worship practices.
- As with most ancient cities, the city's physical shape changed over the centuries. After David conquered the former Jebusite city, he extended its borders northward to encompass the hill that would eventually be the Temple Mount.
- Herod the Great made a number of physical improvements, especially on the Temple Mount.
- In subsequent centuries, the city borders were extended to encompass the hills immediately to the west. Herod Agrippa I (AD 41–44) began enclosing the northernmost quarter of the city within its walls but abandoned the project for fear that it might be misunderstood by the Romans as an act of rebellion.
- The population during Herod the Great's rule could have reached seventy thousand people.
- The Old City of Jerusalem today is marked out by walls reconstructed in the sixteenth century—and not precisely where they were in the first century. Nevertheless, the remains of many first-century locations, including evidence of Herod the Great's architectural genius, are readily visible inside and around the ancient city.

Select Bibliography

Joachim Jeremias, *Jerusalem in the Time of Jesus: An Investigation into Economic and Social Conditions during the New Testament Period*, trans. F. H. Cave and C. H. Cave (Philadelphia: Fortress, 1969).

Benjamin Mazar et al., "Jerusalem," *NEAEHL* 2:698–804 and 5:1801–37.

J. Barton Payne, "Jerusalem," *ZEB* 3:528–64.

Leen and Kathleen Ritmeyer, *Jerusalem at the Time of Jesus* (Nashville: Abingdon, 2009).

The Chiasm of Acts 11:19-13:3

A: Acts 11:19-26—Barnabas brings Saul to Antioch church
B: Acts 11:27—Prophets in Antioch
C: Acts 11:28-30—Famine relief plan
D: Acts 12:1-2—Herod Agrippa I puts James to death
E: Acts 12:3-19—Peter rescued
D': Acts 12:20-23—Herod Agrippa I dies
C': Acts 12:24-25—Famine relief accomplished
B': Acts 13:1—Prophets in Antioch
A': Acts 13:2-3—Saul and Barnabas sent by Antioch church

9.4.1 Herod Agrippa I Puts James to Death (12:1–2)

The Rome-installed ruler identified simply as "Herod" in Acts 12 is ***Herod Agrippa I***, the son of Aristobulus and the grandson of Herod the Great. In AD 37 Herod Agrippa I was appointed the tetrarch of a quadrant of the land of the Jews north and east of the Sea of Galilee that had formerly been ruled by Agrippa's uncle Philip (over the territories of Iturea, Traconitis, Gaulanitis, Auranitis, Batanea, and Paneas), and in AD 40 Agrippa received the tetrarchy of his uncle Antipas (over Galilee and Perea).

Four or Five Men Named James in the New Testament

James the son of Alphaeus, possibly the same as James the Lesser or Younger (see below)	One of the twelve apostles (Matt 10:3; Mark 3:18; Luke 6:15; Acts 1:13).
James the father of the apostle Judas (not Iscariot)	The father of Judas, who was one of the twelve apostles, but not Judas Iscariot (Luke 6:16; Acts 1:13); the son of this James was a.k.a. Thaddaeus (Matt 10:3; Mark 3:18).
James the brother of John, a son of Zebedee, referenced in tradition as James the Greater (in distinction from James the Lesser or Younger; see below)	One of the twelve apostles (Matt 10:2; Mark 3:17; Luke 6:14; Acts 1:13), a son of Zebedee (Matt 4:21; Mark 1:19; Luke 5:10), this James—along with his brother John and Peter—was in Jesus's inner circle of friends (e.g., Mark 5:37; Luke 8:51; Matt 17:1-8; Mark 9:2-8; Luke 9:28). He was killed by Herod Agrippa I (Acts 12:2).
James the brother of Jesus, whom second-century writer Hegesippus (according to Eusebius, *Hist. eccl.* 2.23) dubs James the Just	The son of Mary and Joseph, he was one of the half-brothers of Jesus (Matt 13:55; Jude 1) to whom the resurrected Lord made an appearance (1 Cor 15:7). This James became an important leader of the early church (Acts 12:17; 15:13; 21:18; Gal 1:19; 2:9, 12) and author of one of the NT letters (Jas 1:1).
James the Lesser or Younger, possibly the same as James the son of Alphaeus (see above)	The son of Mary (not Jesus's mother), one of the women who met the resurrected Jesus (Matt 27:56; 28:1; Mark 15:40; 16:1; Luke 24:10).

Agrippa I's Kingdom

Then in AD 41, after aiding in Claudius becoming emperor, Herod Agrippa I was granted the kingly rulership of basically the whole of Jewish territory that had once been ruled by his grandfather Herod the Great.[21] Thus, it can be reasoned that the events of Acts 12 take place in AD 41–44, when Herod Agrippa had been made king and perhaps began exercising his authority over his newly expanded territory, which now included Jerusalem. One of Agrippa's authoritative actions was to show aggression against the Jerusalem church, having ***James the apostle*** arrested and killed (12:1–2).

21. See Schnabel, "The Persecution of Christians in the First Century," 532.

9.4.2 Peter Is Imprisoned and Rescued (12:3–19)

Agrippa is encouraged by the Jews' positive response to his killing of James—suggesting his interest in making a good show of his recently expanded rulership—so he imprisons Peter, intending to kill him as well (12:3–4). The Jewish leaders had been afraid to harm the apostles early in Acts for fear of the people's response (cf. 5:26), but a change of the Jewish public opinion toward Christians occurred at the time of the martyrdom of Stephen (cf. 8:1). Perhaps the Jews were beginning to understand the significant change that the coming of Jesus makes if he indeed is Messiah; and reluctant to follow Jesus, they are more ready to actively oppose his followers. It is ironic that Agrippa's unjust and violent actions against the believers are pleasing to the Jews. But things go differently for Agrippa in Peter's case than they did with James.

Luke remarks that Peter was arrested and imprisoned during the Festival of Unleavened Bread. Apparently out of sensitivity to the Jewish holiday, Agrippa was waiting until after the Passover holiday to proceed with his action against Peter. If the suggestion is correct that this is the first year of Agrippa's rule over all Israel, this Passover would have occurred on April 5 AD 41.[22] There is irony in that the Passover holiday is a celebration of freedom, and yet this is when Peter is imprisoned (12:3–4). Nevertheless, the night before Herod intends to bring Peter to trial, the Lord sends an angel to rescue him. It is almost entertaining that Herod's four squads of four soldiers each (12:4) cannot stop one angel of the Lord; but there is not even a battle of any kind, for the soldiers are somehow oblivious to the rescue (12:6, 10). Also entertaining is that Peter confuses the reality of the rescue with a mere vision or dream about it (12:9–11). But he comes to himself and realizes that the Lord has intervened to save him from the evil intentions of Agrippa and the Jews supporting such opposition.

The home of Mary the mother of John Mark was apparently a place where believers gathered regularly enough for Peter to think of going there (see sidebar). Peter knocks at the door of Mary's house, which is answered by the servant girl Rhoda. But unlike the prison gate, which had opened automatically (12:10), Rhoda forgets to open the door, so overcome by joy at hearing Peter's voice that she goes off to announce his arrival (12:13–14). With further irony, the believers who had been praying for Peter refuse to believe that Peter is at the door. When Rhoda insists, they suggest what seems to them a more rational explanation: "It must be his angel" (12:15), reflecting the Jewish belief in a kind of guardian angel who could take on the appearance of their entrusted charge and who would accompany the righteous upon death to heaven (see Ps 91:11–12; Tob 5:1–16; cf. Matt 18:10; Heb 1:14).[23] So, ironically an angel takes Peter

---

22. See Rainer Riesner, *Paul's Early Period: Chronology, Mission Strategy, Theology*, trans. Doug Stott (Grand Rapids: Eerdmans, 1998), 118–22.

23. See Stephen F. Noll, *Angels of Light, Powers of Darkness: Thinking Biblically about Angels, Satan & Principalities* (Downers Grove, IL: InterVarsity Press, 1998), 170–72.

out of prison (Acts 12:7–11) and the church mistakes Peter for an angel (12:15). But a more challenging irony here for Luke's audience is that the church prayed earnestly for Peter to be rescued (12:5, 12) but was amazed that Peter was rescued in answer to their prayer (12:15–16). While we might laugh at this story, in our more honest reflections, most of us will confess to slipping into a similarly pessimistic expectation and that we likewise sometimes pray earnestly without really believing the Lord can positively answer our prayers. And so Luke challenges his audience to pray believing that the Lord can indeed intervene.

The House of Mary, the Mother of John Mark

The current day Syriac Orthodox Monastery of Saint Mark in the Old City of Jerusalem is thought to stand over the remains of the house of Mary, the mother of John Mark. As indicated in Acts 12:12-17, Mary's home was a gathering place for early Christians. Some claim this to be the location of the original "upper room" and the first organized Christian church. It is found on the winding streets a few blocks from the ruins of Herod's Jerusalem palace (including his jail facilities), the current site of a museum called the Tower of David. Some speculate that Peter was imprisoned not in Herod's jail but at the larger prison facilities at the Fortress of Antonia at the northwest corner of the Temple Mount.

Doorway to the Syriac Orthodox Monastery of Saint Mark
A. D. Riddle/BiblePlaces.com

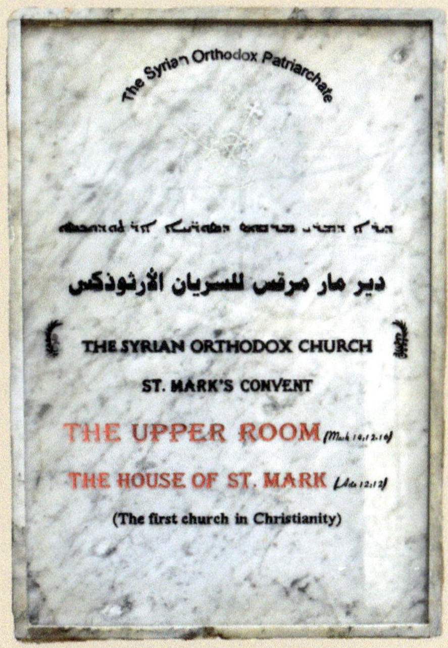

Close-up of the plaque at the entrance
Todd Bolen/BiblePlaces.com

When the believers finally open the door, they discover that their prayers for Peter have been answered. Peter quiets them and describes how the Lord brought him out of the prison. His instructions that they tell James and the other believers about this incident hints at other house-church gatherings in Jerusalem. Luke has recently reported the death of the apostle James (12:2), so the man mentioned here is the non-apostle ***James, Jesus's brother*** (Matt 13:55; cf. Jude 1). James had been among Jesus's skeptical family members (Mark 3:21; John 7:5), but a personal visit from the resurrected Jesus (1 Cor 15:7) may well have been a turning point in bringing him to faith. This non-apostle soon becomes a significant leader in the early church (Acts 12:17; 15:13; 21:18; Gal 1:19; 2:9, 12) and the author of a NT letter (Jas 1:1).

News of Peter's escape from prison was not joyous for all. Still with some irony Luke reports that the soldiers who had been mentioned but were rather inactive (Acts 12:6, 10) now experience "no small commotion" over Peter's whereabouts (12:18).[24]

The Code of Justinian

Justinian I, a Roman emperor in the sixth century AD, set out to reform the empire's legal system. He put together a team of experts to compile the laws of the empire, eliminating the unnecessary and obsolete items and making needed changes and updates. We find here a ruling from the fourth century—June 29, 371—that reflects the practice of jailers receiving the sentence of their escaped prisoners, as in Acts 12.

The Code of Justinian, 9.4.4 (ca. AD 528)

Emperors Valentinian, Valens, and Gratian Augusti to Probus, Praetorian Prefect.

The detention and care of persons taken into custody shall be the responsibility of the head warden (*commentariensis*). He shall not think that a lowly and base person is to be brought up on charges before a judge if a defendant has somehow escaped. For We wish that he himself be liable to a penalty of this kind, if it is shown that he was responsible for the escapee. If, indeed, the head warden is for some urgent reason away from his responsibilities, We order that his assistant shall exercise oversight with equal care, and lay down that the latter shall be constrained by the same statutory rigor.

Given June 29, at Contionacum, in the consulship of Gratian Augustus, for the second time, and Probus (371).

From *The Codex of Justinian: A New Annotated Translation, with Parallel Latin and Greek Text*, trans. Fred H. Blume, ed. Bruce W. Frier et al., 3 vols. (Cambridge: Cambridge University Press, 2016).

24. While not always specifically rendered in English translations, in Acts, Luke utilizes several of these litotes, a figure of speech that negates the smallness of a thing to emphasize its largeness: "no small commotion" (Acts 12:18 NIV); "not little time" (14:28 ESV); "no small dissension and debate" (15:2 ESV); "not a few of the leading women" (17:4 ESV); "not a few Greek women of high standing as well as men" (17:12 ESV); "no little disturbance" (19:23 ESV); "no little business" (19:24 ESV); and "no small storm" (27:20 NASB).

Indeed, it turns out that Peter's captors receive his death sentence (12:19), which is in keeping with the Code of Justinian, a sixth-century compilation of ancient Roman laws (see sidebar).[25]

9.4.3 Herod Is Killed (12:20–23)

After beginning his rule over the whole of Jewish Palestine with some violence in Jerusalem, as would be expected, Herod Agrippa I takes his seat in Caesarea Maritima, the Roman seaport city. In the year AD 44 he was in discussions about his country's food supplies for the people of Tyre and Sidon (perhaps the previously predicted famine was pending if not already in full swing; cf. 11:27–28). Luke's contemporary historian Josephus comments a bit more extensively about the interaction between Herod Agrippa and his audience, and both writers describe the meeting as formal, if not also flamboyant. During the apparently difficult negotiations, the delegates from Tyre and Sidon offer flattering words of praise, perhaps attempting to endear themselves to their neighboring ruler on whom they are dependent. Herod receives the worshipful praise of the people, the kind of praise that belongs to God alone. Josephus comments on Agrippa's culpability for receiving the people's luxurious praise: "The king did not rebuke them nor did he reject their flattery as pious." Even further, Josephus informs us that Herod himself recognized his guilt but nonetheless stubbornly luxuriated in his enviable lifestyle (Josephus, *Ant.* 19.8.2 §§346–48; see sidebar).

Both Luke and Josephus remark that Herod was immediately struck and began to die (Acts 12:23; Josephus, *Ant.* 19.8.2 §346), but Josephus discloses that Agrippa's condition took five days to have its full effect. While the details are too vague for a precise diagnosis, experts suggest that the fatal medical condition Herod Agrippa I suffered might have been due to peritonitis from a perforated appendix, an acute intestinal obstruction, a ruptured hydatid cyst, or even arsenic poisoning.[26] The irony here is that Herod had been giving life to others by feeding them (Acts 12:20) but now dies by being eaten by worms (12:21–23). We should note how Herod Agrippa's death is something of a fulfillment of Gamaliel's warning in Acts 5:38–39: "Leave these men alone! Let them go! For if their purpose or activity is of human origin, it will fail. But if it is from God, you will not be able to stop these men; you will only find yourselves fighting against God."

With perhaps an even greater ironic twist, Luke reports the judgment on Herod with the same turn of phrase that he reports the rescue of Peter: both men are "struck" (Greek: *patassō*) by an angel. In prison Peter is "struck" by an angel and awakens (12:7). On his throne Herod is "struck" by an angel and dies (12:23). Observing the twofold use of this term leads Luke's audience members to reflect on their own postures regarding the

25. While the Greek verb here (*apagō*; Acts 12:19) means the guards were "led away," Pinter notes that the clear implication is that they were led away for execution; Pinter, *Acts*, 289–90.

26. Bruce, *Book of Acts*, 242.

gospel message. Which pattern will they choose to follow? Like Peter, will they choose to advance the gospel even when it is difficult and dangerous, or like Herod, will they oppose it or obscure it somehow? Which "struck" are they setting themselves up for?

The Death of Herod Agrippa I (ca. AD 44)

Luke offers an abbreviated account of the death of Herod Agrippa I, emphasizing its divine causation because of Herod's sinfulness (Acts 12:20–23). Still allowing for the divine causation—and noting Herod's awareness of it!—Josephus offers a little more detail of the death.

Flavius Josephus, *Jewish Antiquities* 19.8.2 §§343–51 (ca. AD 94)

> After the completion of the third year of his reign over the whole of Judaea, Agrippa came to the city Caesarea, which had previously been called Strato's Tower. Here he celebrated spectacles in honour of Caesar, knowing that these had been instituted as a kind of festival on behalf of Caesar's well-being. For this occasion there were gathered a large number of men who held office or had advanced to some rank in the kingdom. On the second day of the spectacles, clad in a garment woven completely of silver so that its texture was indeed wondrous, he entered the theatre at daybreak. There the silver, illumined by the touch of the first rays of the sun, was wondrously radiant and by its glitter inspired fear and awe in those who gazed intently upon it. Straightway his flatterers raised their voices from various directions—though hardly for his good—addressing him as a god. "May you be propitious to us," they added, "and if we have hitherto feared you as a man, yet henceforth we agree that you are more than mortal in your being." The king did not rebuke them nor did he reject their flattery as pious. But shortly thereafter he looked up and saw an owl perched on a rope over his head. At once, recognizing this as a harbinger of woes just as it had once been of good tidings, he felt a stab of pain in his heart. He was also gripped in his stomach by an ache that he felt everywhere at once and that was intense from the start. Leaping up he said to his friends: "I, a god in your eyes, am now bidden to lay down my life, for fate brings immediate refutation of the lying words lately addressed to me. I, who was called immortal by you, am now under sentence of death. But I must accept my lot as God wills it. In fact I have lived in no ordinary fashion but in the grand style that is hailed as true bliss." Even as he was speaking these words, he was overcome by more intense pain. They hastened, therefore, to convey him to the palace; and the word flashed about to everyone that he was on the very verge of death. Straightway the populace, including the women and children, sat in sackcloth in accordance with their ancestral custom and made entreaty to God on behalf of the king. The sound of wailing and lamentations prevailed everywhere. The king, as he lay in his lofty bedchamber and looked down on the people as they fell prostrate, was not dry-eyed himself. Exhausted after five straight days by the pain in his abdomen, he departed this life in the fifty-fourth year of his life and the seventh of his reign.

In this part of the story of Acts, Luke challenges his audience to greater trust in God's complete control of things, even in the face of tremendous evil. An earthbound perspective on life's difficulties prevents us from knowing all of the present much less the future and how difficulties might turn out as we patiently await God's ultimate justice. Nevertheless, the story of Acts 12 helps us see that God is in control and the gospel is unstoppable.

9.4.4 Summary Statement (12:24–25)

This section closes with Luke's briefest progress summary on the spread of God's Word (12:24) and then a secondary note closing out the famine relief visit that Barnabas and Saul had accomplished (12:25): "But the word of God continued to spread and flourish. When Barnabas and Saul had finished their mission, they returned from Jerusalem, taking with them John, also called Mark." Thus, Luke closes the report on the Jerusalem church with a travel summary about Barnabas and Saul returning from there to Antioch and having John Mark with them. The inclusion of this travel summary, along with a progress summary, bears some foreshadowing of future ministry in which ***John Mark*** plays a role. It readies the reader for the new focus of the story in the second half of Acts, which begins back in Antioch. Recounted journeys that close with travel summaries will be a new organizational tool in the remainder of the book, but recurrent progress summaries remain as well.

St. Peter's Grotto (cave) Church is one of the oldest known Christian churches in Antioch.
David Padfield/ BiblePlaces.com

9.5 CONCLUDING REMARKS

The section of the story of Acts covered in 9:32–12:25 moves through four episodes focused on the progress of the gospel in different cities. The gospel work is tracked outward from Jerusalem to Lydda and Joppa (9:32–43), then northward to Caesarea (10:1–11:18), and then internationally to Antioch in Syria (11:19–30). But this section closes with a note on the continued experience of the church in Jerusalem (12:1–25). Three of these four episodes have Peter as one of the main characters, and one episode has Saul (along with Barnabas) as a central figure. This part of the story of Acts helps the reader transition with the gospel progress from Jerusalem to Judea and Samaria and to the ends of the earth (cf. 1:8) and helps the reader anticipate a transition from the story's focus on Peter in the first half of the book to a focus on Saul/Paul in the second half of the book. We have learned here to expect authentic churches in gentile territory: churches that teach the Word of God, that carry out the work of God, that care for the welfare of God's people, and that practice the worship of God (cf. 2:42). We have also learned that following Jesus brings potential hardship and persecution. This too is a theme that continues in the story in the second half of Acts.

9.6 Key People, Places, and Terms

- Aeneas
- Antioch of Syria
- Barnabas
- Caesarea Maritima
- centurion
- Christian
- Cornelius
- famine visit
- God-fearers
- Herod Agrippa I
- Holy Spirit baptism
- irony
- James the apostle
- James, Jesus's brother
- John Mark
- Joppa
- Lydda
- proselytes
- Tabitha (Dorcas)

9.7 Questions for Review and Discussion

1. What kinds of expansion of the gospel message are evidenced in Acts 9–12?
2. What evidence does Luke provide that God planned and initiated the inclusion of gentiles among the community of believers?
3. It was easy for first-century Jewish followers of Jesus to believe that anyone else who wanted to follow Jesus (their Jewish Messiah) should become Jewish as well. What evidence does Luke begin to give that the same specific cultural expressions of faith are not required of all who want to be faithful to the real gospel message?
4. In tracing the expansion of the gospel message, Luke makes specific mention of events in Syrian Antioch (e.g., Acts 11:19–30); what is the significance of this?
5. What do you make of Luke's approach to discussing the problem of evil and suffering in Acts, particularly in Acts 12?
6. In the scope of Luke's narration of events in the life of the early church—a narration that includes the church facing various hardships—what role does the episode of opposition from Herod Agrippa I serve? That is, what is it Luke wants to assure his audience of?

9.8 Optional Assignments

1. **Text Reflection Project**—*Relating the concepts discussed in this chapter to another biblical text.* One of the sidebars in this chapter suggests that Peter's sermon at Cornelius's home (Acts 10:36–43) follows

in order the general outline of the Gospel of Luke. Review each section of Peter's sermon and find a specific verse(s) in Luke's Gospel that reflects Peter's remarks.

2. **Interview Project**—*Inquiring of others their views concerning the concepts discussed in this chapter.* In Acts 9:32–12:25 the spread of the gospel message was followed up by Peter (in Joppa and Lydda) and Barnabas (in Syrian Antioch). In an interview with your pastor (or some other respected Christian leader), ask about the importance of follow-up ministries for the church today. To what extent do you agree with their answer?
3. **Service-Learning Project**—*Applying the concepts discussed in this chapter in some form of service to others outside the class.* In Acts 11, the young church in Syrian Antioch heard that the Judean church would suffer from a famine and decided to send them aid. Arrange to support the needs of a ministry that is suffering through a set of circumstances they cannot control, as the Judean church had to do.
4. **Prayer Project**—*Talking with God about the concepts discussed in this chapter.* In the city of Joppa, Peter faced a tragedy—the death of a beloved church member, Tabitha—and had the audacity to pray for a miracle. And God answered that prayer by raising Tabitha back to life (Acts 9:36–42)! Are you or someone you know facing a tragic situation? Write a prayer—submissive to God in his wise and loving sovereignty but audacious nonetheless—and see how God answers.
5. **Testimony Project**—*Telling others about the concepts discussed in this chapter.* When the church in Jerusalem heard about Peter preaching the gospel to the gentiles in Caesarea, they asked him to give an account of his actions (Acts 11:1–3). When Peter explained his ministry decisions, all was well (11:4–18). Is there someone in ministerial authority over you with whom you should be discussing your ministry decisions? Accountability is good for unity among believers; try it and see how it works out.

9.9 Bibliography for Going Further

9.9.1 Peter and His Ministry

Bockmuehl, Markus. *Simon Peter in Scripture and Memory: The New Testament Apostle in the Early Church.* Grand Rapids: Baker Academic, 2012.

Bond, Helen K., and Larry W. Hurtado, eds. *Peter in Early Christianity.* Grand Rapids: Eerdmans, 2015.

Cullmann, Oscar. *Peter: Disciple, Apostle, Martyr: A Historical and Theological Study.* 2nd ed. Philadelphia: Westminster, 1962.

Helyer, Larry R. *The Life and Witness of Peter.* Downers Grove, IL: InterVarsity Press, 2012.

Hengel, Martin. *Saint Peter: The Underestimated Apostle.* Translated by Thomas H. Trapp. Grand Rapids: Eerdmans, 2010.

9.9.2 Cornelius and the Roman Military in Luke-Acts

Brink, Laurie. *Soldiers in Luke-Acts: Engaging, Contradicting, and Transcending the Stereotypes.* WUNT 2.362. Tübingen: Mohr Siebeck, 2014.

Kyrychenko, Alexander. *The Roman Army and the Expansion of the Gospel: The Role of the Centurion in Luke-Acts*. BZNW 203. Berlin: de Gruyter, 2014.

Nguyen, vanThanh. *Peter and Cornelius: A Story of Conversion and Mission*. ASMS 15. Eugene, OR: Pickwick, 2012.

9.9.3 Barnabas and His Ministry

Hiebert, D. Edmond. "Barnabas." *ZEB* 1:508–509.

Kollmann, Bernd. *Joseph Barnabas: His Life and Legacy*. Translated by Miranda Henry. Collegeville, MN: Liturgical, 2004.

Robertson, C. K. *Barnabas vs. Paul: To Encourage or Confront?* Nashville: Abingdon, 2015.

9.9.4 The Antioch Christian Community

Crowe, Jerome. *From Jerusalem to Antioch: The Gospel Across Cultures*. Collegeville, MN: Liturgical, 1997.

Slee, Michelle. *The Church in Antioch in the First Century CE: Communion and Conflict*. JSNTSup 244. Sheffield: Sheffield Academic, 2003.

Wallace-Hadrill, D. S. *Christian Antioch: A Study of Early Christian Thought in the East*. New York: Cambridge University Press, 1982.

Zetterholm, Magnus. *The Formation of Christianity in Antioch: A Social-Scientific Approach to the Separation between Judaism and Christianity*. Routledge Early Church Monographs. New York: Routledge, 2003.

9.9.5 Herod Agrippa I

Allen, O. Wesley, Jr. *The Death of Herod: The Narrative and Theological Function of Retribution in Luke-Acts*. SBLDS 158. Atlanta: Scholars Press, 1997.

Busch, Fritz-Otto. "Herod Agrippa I." Pages 136–45 (chapter 4) in *The Five Herods*. Translated by E. W. Dickes. London: Robert Hale, 1958.

Chilton, Bruce. "Agrippa I." Pages 175–204 (chapter 7) in *The Herods: Murder, Politics, and the Art of Succession*. Minneapolis: Fortress, 2021.

Hoehner, Harold W. "Herod." *ZEB* 3:131–50.

Kokkinos, Nikos. *The Herodian Dynasty: Origins, Role in Society and Eclipse*. JSPSup 30. Sheffield: Sheffield Academic, 1998.

Schürer, Emil. *HJP* 1:442–54.

Schwartz, Daniel R. *Agrippa I: The Last King of Judaea*. TSAJ 23. Tübingen: Mohr Siebeck, 1990.

9.9.6 The Problem of Evil and Suffering

Dembski, William A. *The End of Christianity: Finding a Good God in an Evil World*. Nashville: B&H Academic, 2009.

Evans, Jeremy A. *The Problem of Evil: The Challenge to Essential Christian Beliefs*. B&H Studies in Christian Apologetics. Nashville: B&H Academic, 2013.

Peterman, Gerald W., and Andrew J. Schmutzer. *Between Pain & Grace: A Biblical Theology of Suffering*. Chicago: Moody, 2016.

Piper, John, and Justin Taylor, eds. *Suffering and the Sovereignty of God*. Wheaton, IL: Crossway, 2006.

Stackhouse, John G., Jr. *Can God Be Trusted? Faith and the Challenge of Evil*. 2nd ed. Downers Grove, IL: InterVarsity Press, 2009.

Part 3

THE STORY OF JESUS REACHING THE GENTILE WORLD

Acts 13–28

The first half of Acts (i.e., Acts 1–12) focuses on the Christian mission to the Jewish world in Palestine. Even so, several points in the first half of Acts foreshadow the gentile focus in the second half of Acts. For example, the risen Jesus indicates that his followers would be witnesses about him "in Jerusalem, and in all Judea and Samaria, and to the ends of the earth" (1:8). Then when the gospel is preached to "God-fearing Jews from every nation under heaven" who were in Jerusalem for the Jewish holiday of Pentecost (2:5)—Luke even names the countries and provinces these people were from (2:9–11)—this suggests that those who believe will bring the gospel with them back to those territories. We also have anticipations of ministry to non-Jewish audiences in the ministry of Philip (i.e., the Samaritans in 8:4–25 and the Ethiopian eunuch in 8:26–40), in the conversion of Cornelius and his family (10:1–11:18), and in the ministry to gentiles in Syrian Antioch (11:20–30). All these sections in the first half of Acts anticipate a further widening of the Christian mission.

The Baptism of the Eunuch (ca. 1626) by Rembrandt van Rijn.

The Baptism of the Eunuch (ca. 1626) by Rembrandt van Rijn.

Now, in the second half of Acts (i.e., Acts 13–28), Luke focuses on the Christian mission to the gentile world. Each of the major sections of the first half of Acts closes with a summary statement about the progress of the gospel. Intriguingly, the progress summary at the midpoint of the book is followed immediately by a travel summary about the trip Barnabas and Saul took from Antioch to Jerusalem (12:24–25). Like the first half, the second half of Acts can be divided into several sections by observing various progress summaries, but it can also be divided by travel summaries. The storyline of the second half of Acts focuses on Paul's well-known missionary campaigns, and each of these missionary campaigns closes with a travel summary statement. Notably, each of the three journey sections also contains a progress summary statement in the midst of, rather than at the end of, its narration. So, while noting the various progress summary statements, our storytelling outline of the second half of Acts is organized around the travel summaries that fit with the storyline of Paul's missionary journeys. It is also noteworthy that, even as there are hints of the gentile mission in the first half of the book, there are constant reflections of the Jewish mission in the second half of the book (e.g., Paul's regular practice in gentile territory is to preach first in the local Jewish synagogue) and Paul visits the church in Jerusalem after each of his missionary journeys.

Thus, following the pattern of Luke's storytelling, a chapter of this textbook has been dedicated to each of the following six sections of the story. First, Luke covers the initial missionary travels of Paul and Barnabas into Asia Minor (chapter 10, discussing Acts 13:1–14:28). This ministry in gentile territory begs for an official decision on the question of the gentile mission, which leads to the Jerusalem Council (chapter 11, discussing Acts 15:1–35). Next come Paul's second missionary campaign (chapter 12, discussing Acts 15:36–18:22) and his third missionary campaign (chapter 13, discussing Acts 18:23–21:17). And finally, Luke reports Paul's imprisonment in Jerusalem and Caesarea (chapter 14, discussing Acts 21:18–26:32) and his trip to Rome for a trial before Caesar (chapter 15, discussing Acts 27:1–28:31). Each of these six major segments closes with a storytelling travel summary statement of some kind (i.e., 14:27–28; 15:35; 18:22; 21:17; 26:32; and 28:30–31).

The Outline and Summary Statements of the Second Half of Acts

Each section in the second half of Acts ("Part B" of my outline for the book) ends with a travel summary statement of some kind, identified and quoted here. Luke also inserts progress summary statements in the midst of the missionary journey sections. And similar to the summary statement in the middle of Acts (i.e., Acts 12:24-25), he closes the book with a combined summary statement (28:30-31) that comments on both travel (v. 30) and the progress of the gospel (v. 31).

Part B: The Story of Jesus Reaching the Gentile World (Acts 13-28)

V. The Story of the First Missionary Campaign—Acts 13:1-14:28

Progress Summary: "The word of the Lord spread through the whole region" (13:49).

Travel Summary: "On arriving there, they gathered the church together and reported all that God had done through them and how he had opened a door of faith to the Gentiles. And they stayed there a long time with the disciples" (14:27-28).

VI. The Central Interlude in the Story: The Jerusalem Council—15:1-35

Travel Summary: "But Paul and Barnabas remained in Antioch, where they and many others taught and preached the word of the Lord" (15:35).

VII. The Story of the Second Missionary Campaign—15:36-18:22

Progress Summary: "So the churches were strengthened in the faith and grew daily in numbers" (16:5).

Travel Summary: "When he landed at Caesarea, he went up to Jerusalem and greeted the church and then went down to Antioch" (18:22).

VIII. The Story of the Third Missionary Campaign—18:23-21:17

Progress Summary: "This went on for two years, so that all the Jews and Greeks who lived in the province of Asia heard the word of the Lord" (19:10).

Progress Summary: "In this way the word of the Lord spread widely and grew in power" (19:20).

Travel Summary: "When we arrived at Jerusalem, the brothers and sisters received us warmly" (21:17).

IX. The Story Moves in Prison in Jerusalem and Caesarea—21:18-26:32

Travel Summary: "Agrippa said to Festus, 'This man could have been set free if he had not appealed to Caesar'" (26:32).

X. The Story in Rough Waters on the Way to Rome—27:1-28:31

Travel Summary: "For two whole years Paul stayed there in his own rented house and welcomed all who came to see him." (28:30).

Progress Summary: "He proclaimed the kingdom of God and taught about the Lord Jesus Christ—with all boldness and without hindrance!" (28:31).

Ruins at Caesarea showing the theater and Herod's palace along the shore of the Mediterranean Sea.

Bill Schlegel/ BiblePlaces.com

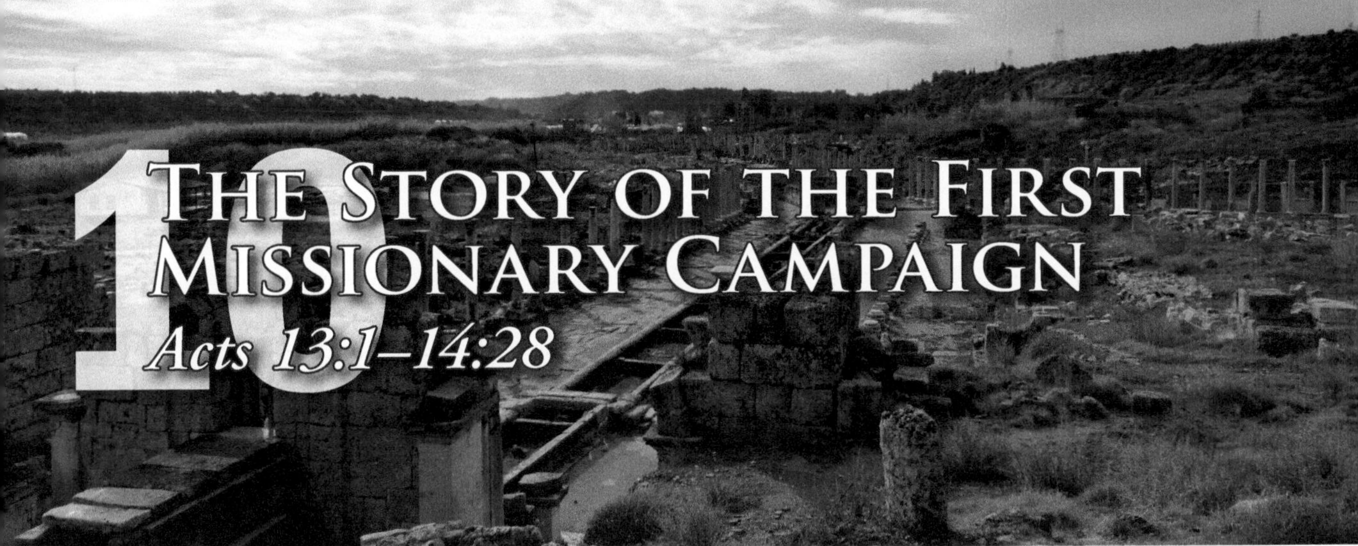

10 The Story of the First Missionary Campaign

Acts 13:1–14:28

Mark Bolen/BiblePlaces.com

Chapter Goals

After reading this chapter, you should be able to:

- Recognize that God initiated the church's intentional missionary activity.
- Explain God's plan for reaching the gentile world via Jewish faith in Jesus.
- Describe the typical experience Paul and Barnabas had in sharing the gospel.
- As exemplified in the ministry of Paul and Barnabas, distinguish different approaches to sharing the gospel message with different audiences—i.e., those familiar with Scripture and those who are not.
- In observing the missionary travels of Paul and Barnabas, describe what people mean when they speak about "follow-up ministry."

Chapter Overview

10.1 Barnabas and Saul Are Sent Out and Go to Cyprus (Acts 13:1–12)
10.2 Paul and Barnabas Minister at Pisidian Antioch (Acts 13:13–52)
10.3 Paul and Barnabas Minister at Iconium (Acts 14:1–7)
10.4 Paul and Barnabas Minister at Lystra and Derbe (Acts 14:8–20)
10.5 Paul and Barnabas Return to Syrian Antioch (Acts 14:21–28)
10.6 Concluding Remarks
10.7 Key People, Places, and Terms
10.8 Questions for Review and Discussion
10.9 Optional Assignments
10.10 Bibliography for Going Further

Key Verses

Therefore, my friends, I want you to know that through Jesus the forgiveness of sins is proclaimed to you. Through him everyone who believes is set free from every sin, a justification you were not able to obtain under the law of Moses. (Acts 13:38–39)

For this is what the Lord has commanded us:

> "I have made you a light for the Gentiles,
> that you may bring salvation to the ends of the earth."

When the Gentiles heard this, they were glad and honored the word of the Lord; and all who were appointed for eternal life believed. (Acts 13:47–48)

. . . strengthening the disciples and encouraging them to remain true to the faith. "We must go through many hardships to enter the kingdom of God," they said. (Acts 14:22)

Mid-Journey Progress Summary Statement

The word of the Lord spread through the whole region. (Acts 13:49)

Closing Travel Summary Statement

On arriving there, they gathered the church together and reported all that God had done through them and how he had opened a door of faith to the Gentiles. And they stayed there a long time with the disciples. (Acts 14:27–28)

Itinerary of Paul's First Missionary Journey, Acts 13:1–14:28 (ca. 47–48)

City	Province (Region)	Reference
Antioch	Syria	Acts 13:1–3
Seleucia	Syria	Acts 13:4
Salamis	Cyprus	Acts 13:5
Paphos	Cyprus	Acts 13:6–12
Perga	Lycia (Pamphylia)	Acts 13:13
Antioch	Galatia (Phrygia near Pisidia)	Acts 13:14–52
Iconium	Galatia (Lycaonia)	Acts 14:1–6a
Lystra	Galatia (Lycaonia)	Acts 14:6b–19

City	Province (Region)	Reference
Derbe	Galatia (Lycaonia)	Acts 14:6b–7, 20–21
Lystra	Galatia (Lycaonia)	Acts 14:21–23
Iconium	Galatia (Lycaonia)	Acts 14:21–23
Antioch	Galatia (Phrygia near Pisidia)	Acts 14:21–24a
Perga	Lycia (Pamphylia)	Acts 14:24b–25a
Attalia	Lycia (Pamphylia)	Acts 14:25b
Antioch	Syria	Acts 14:26–28

INTRODUCTION

In studies of Acts it is common practice to reference "Paul's three missionary journeys." As mentioned in chapter 3, on the one hand, such references are somewhat artificial, for Paul and his company of ministers did not necessarily live out of a suitcase on each of three separate short-term mission trips (à la ten-day church group experiences today). Paul actually lived for as long as three years in some of the places on these "journeys" (cf. Acts 18:11; 20:31), which seems to render them as "relocations" instead. On the other hand, in Luke's recounting of Paul's missionary activity, Paul seems determined to return periodically to Antioch or Jerusalem to report on God's work in the gentile territories (cf. 14:26–28; 18:21–22; 20:22–24), so there is something of a "journey" sense about his travels. While not completely abandoning the use of "journeys," reflections here regularly employ the labels "missionary travels" and "missionary campaigns" to capture the journeying idea while trying to avoid the misconception of his travels as short-term mission trips.[1] Regardless of the label assigned to it, the itinerant ministry of Barnabas and Saul in Acts 13–14 is recognized as the first such endeavor where the missionaries are intentionally sent out by a church (i.e., the church in Antioch) and return to report on their activities. It is on this circuitous mission that Luke switches from the use of "Saul" (his Hebrew name) to "Paul" (his Greco-Roman name) for the missionary who will become the main focal character for the remainder of the book of Acts.

10.1 BARNABAS AND SAUL ARE SENT OUT AND GO TO CYPRUS (ACTS 13:1–12)

As noted, Luke portrays God as the one initiating the spread of the gospel message. This was particularly noteworthy in the Cornelius episode, to which Luke dedicates much space in the story (10:1–11:18), but this divine initiative is seen elsewhere in Acts as well (e.g., 8:26–29; 9:1–19; 14:27; 16:6–10; 18:9–11; 21:19; 22:17–21). Here we see that God is credited with the intention for the church at Antioch to send out Barnabas and Saul on a new ministry endeavor.

10.1.1 Sending Out the Ministers (13:1–3)

In telling the story of Acts, Luke gives several lists of ministers and utilizes different organizational mechanisms. The listing of twelve apostles in Acts 1 begins with Peter (who becomes their main spokesperson) and ends with the selection of Matthias (who is

1. Of course, we must recognize that use of the term *campaign* suffers potential interference with undesirable political and military connotations!

never mentioned again) (1:14–26). The listing of seven church administrators in Acts 6 begins with Stephen, including a description of his character, and ends with Nicolas, including that he is from Antioch (6:5); these extended descriptions seem to serve as foreshadowing (i.e., Stephen soon has the longest speech in Acts, and Antioch becomes an important locale in the story). Luke's listing of five prophets and teachers in ***Antioch of Syria*** in Acts 13, however, has the converse organization as that in Acts 6. That is, the list of leaders in Acts 13 begins and ends with simple names (respectively Barnabas and Saul, who are soon to be the focus of attention in the story), but the three people on the list between them have longer descriptions. Luke provides Simeon's other name (Niger), Lucius's hometown (Cyrene), and something of Manaen's personal history (he had been brought up with Herod the tetrarch) (13:1). Perhaps this is a way Luke tries to acknowledge the importance of all, even while he plans to focus his story on only a few.[2]

Paul's First Missionary Journey (ca. AD 47–48)

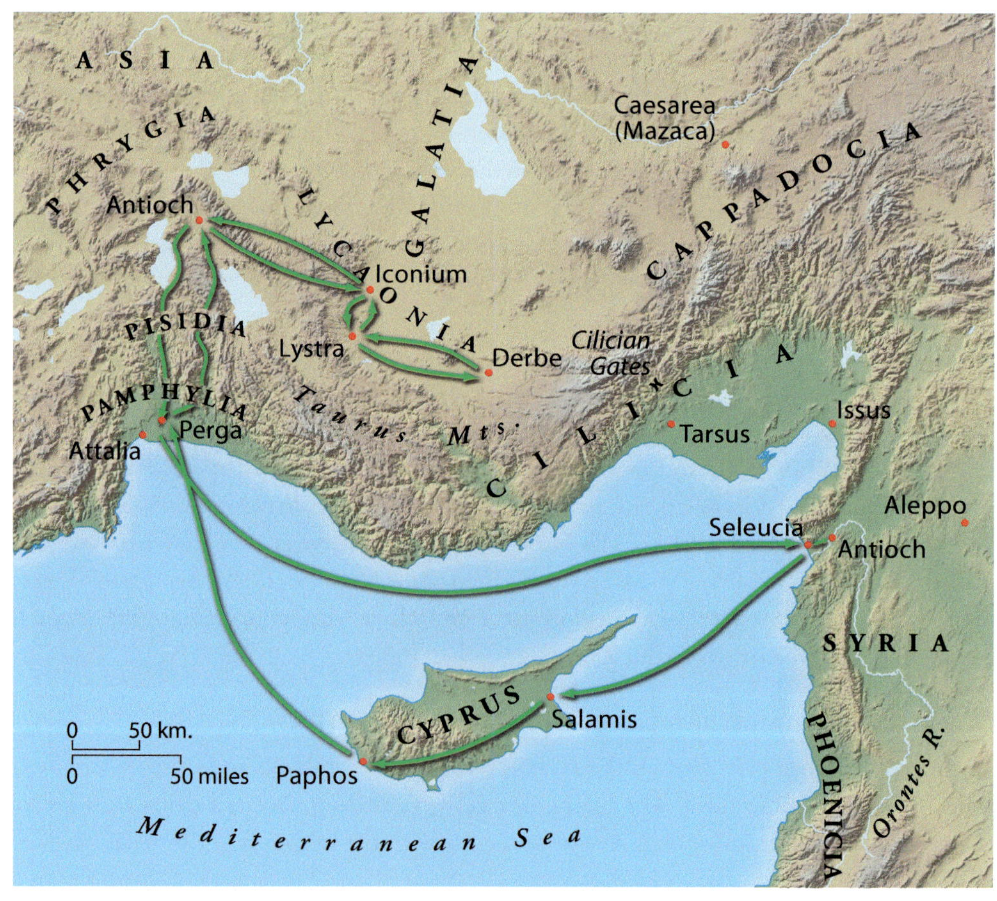

2. With 12 = 7 + 5, is it an accident that Luke's lists of Christian ministers contain twelve names, seven names, and five names?

While the Antioch church is worshiping the Lord and fasting, the Holy Spirit instructs them: "Set apart for me Barnabas and Saul for the work to which I have called them" (13:2). Once again Luke portrays God as the instigator of the new ministry. The divine initiative for this ministry is seen not only in that the Holy Spirit (somehow) communicates this message but also in that within the message itself the new ministry is divinely owned as "the work to which I have called them." The Antioch church demonstrates their recognition and support of the new ministry for ***Barnabas*** and ***Saul*** with the commissioning gesture of laying their hands on them (13:3). This is a common practice among Christian churches in sending out missionaries still today.[3]

10.1.2 Beginning at Cyprus (13:4–5)

In the northeastern part of the Mediterranean Sea just west of the coast of Syria and south of Cilicia, ***Cyprus*** was an island province under Roman control since 58 BC. Barnabas was a Jew from Cyprus (cf. 4:36), so in addition to its proximity to Syrian Antioch, his familiarity with the island makes it somewhat unsurprising that he and Saul would go there first. With Syrian Antioch located several miles inland from the Mediterranean on the Orontes River, the town of ***Seleucia,*** facing Cyprus, served as its seaport. Repeating the idea that Barnabas and Saul are "sent on their way by the Holy Spirit" (13:4), Luke notes that they sail from Seleucia to ***Salamis***, the eastern most seaport city of Cyprus (about 140 miles).

The Besikli Cave is a rock-hewn tomb dating to the first century AD in Seleucia, the seaport city for Syrian Antioch.
Czgur/iStock.com

3. For more on the laying on of hands practice, see chapter 8 and the discussion of Philip's ministry in Acts 8:4–40.

Cyprus

- A large island, about 140 miles long and 60 miles wide, in the northeast corner of the Mediterranean Sea, formed something like a misshapen stingray with its tail pointed toward Syrian Antioch.
- Has a long history of being ruled by various world powers through the centuries, including the Persians, Phoenicians, Alexander the Great, Ptolemaic Egypt, and then Rome beginning in 58 BC.
- In its early Roman period, was under the governorship of the territory of Cilicia in Asia Minor to the north, and in 51 BC the famous Roman orator Cicero was named governor of that province.
- With the reorganization of the Roman Empire under Caesar Augustus in 27 BC, became a separate Roman province—at first under Caesar's direct control (an "imperial" province) and then under the control of a proconsul (cf. Acts 13:7) (a "senatorial" province).
- An important source of copper, which was combined with tin from Cornwall to make the alloy bronze during the namesake Bronze Age (3300–1200 BC).
- Was an important center for the worship of the goddess Wanassa (Cypriot name) or Aphrodite (Greek name) or Venus (Roman name), said to have been birthed "from the foam" near the Cypriot city of Paphos.
- Luke mentions the island several times in Acts: where Barnabas was from (4:36), where some believers fleeing persecution went (11:19), home of some gospel preachers in Syrian Antioch (11:20), visited on Paul's first missionary journey (13:4–12), where Barnabas and Mark did follow-up ministry (15:39), a sailing landmark (21:3), and home of Mnason, "one of the early disciples" (21:16).

Select Bibliography

Edward M. Blaiklock, "Cyprus," *ZEB* 1:1120–23.

Pamela Gaber, "Cyprus," *EDB*, 303–5.

Vassos Karageorghis, *Cyprus: From the Stone Age to the Romans*, Ancient Peoples & Places 101 (London: Thames and Hudson, 1982).

Alanna Nobbs, "Cyprus," pp. 279–89 in *The Book of Acts in Its Graeco-Roman Setting*, ed. David W. J. Gill and Conrad Gempf, BAFCS 2 (Grand Rapids: Eerdmans, 1994; Carlisle: Paternoster, 1994).

Upon arriving at Salamis, Barnabas and Saul begin proclaiming the word of God in the Jewish synagogues there (13:5). Saul had been preaching the gospel of Jesus Christ in synagogues before (9:20), and Luke is adamant that preaching the gospel in a Jews-first ministry is Saul/Paul's usual approach (17:1–2; cf. 13:5, 14; 14:1; 17:10, 16–17; 18:4, 19; 19:8). Luke also notes here that ***John Mark*** travels with Barnabas and Saul to assist them, which makes sense of Luke's earlier foreshadowing comments about this young man (12:12, 25). We learn elsewhere that John Mark is a cousin of Barnabas (Col 4:10), so this may have added to his willingness to accompany the missionaries to Cyprus. John Mark's commitment to the mission, however, is short-lived as he deserts Barnabas and Saul at Perga (i.e., after leaving Cyprus) to return to Jerusalem (Acts 13:13).[4]

4. See Howard G. Anderson, "Mark, John," *ZEB* 4:96–97.

Ruins of Salamis on Cyprus
trabantos/iStock.com

10.1.3 Saul/Paul versus Elymas the Sorcerer at Paphos (13:6–12)

The town of Salamis lies at one end of Cyprus and the town of ***Paphos*** lies at the other (a distance of about ninety miles), making sense of Luke's comment that Barnabas and Saul "traveled through the whole island until they came to Paphos" (13:6). While Luke does not specify them preaching as they traveled, some suggest that the Greek terms for "traveled through" (*dierchomai*) and "whole" (*holos*) indicate a preaching tour of the island.[5] What Luke does specify about the ministry on Cyprus focuses on a confrontation with a sorcerer named Elymas and the subsequent conversion of the island's leader, the Roman proconsul Sergius Paulus. Luke first introduces Elymas as "a Jewish sorcerer and false prophet" with the name Bar-Jesus (13:6). Given that Judaism forbade sorcery, it is unsurprising that he would be dubbed a false prophet. Barnabas and Saul meet him because he is in some advisory role to the proconsul Sergius Paulus, who has called for them so that he can hear what they are preaching (13:7).

But Elymas is trying to turn the proconsul away from the faith (13:8), which prompts Saul/Paul to confront ***Elymas the sorcerer***, an encounter reminiscent of Peter's confrontation of Simon the sorcerer (8:18–24). Both Peter and Paul address the heart conditions of the sorcerers: Simon was "not right before God" and "full of bitterness and

5. E.g., Eckhard J. Schnabel, *Acts*, ZECNT (Grand Rapids: Zondervan, 2012), 556; Craig S. Keener, *Acts: An Exegetical Commentary*, 4 vols. (Grand Rapids: Baker Academic, 2012–2015), 2:2006; contra Ben Witherington III, *The Acts of the Apostles: A Socio-Rhetorical Commentary* (Grand Rapids: Eerdmans, 1998; Carlisle: Paternoster, 1998), 396.

Beach at Paphos, Cyprus
Balate Dorin/iStock.com

captive to sin" (8:21–23), and Elymas is "a child of the devil," "an enemy of everything that is right," and "full of all kinds of deceit and trickery" (13:10). Paul's confrontation closes with an announcement of the Lord's judgment on Elymas: "Now the hand of the Lord is against you. You are going to be blind for a time, not even able to see the light of the sun" (13:11), which immediately comes to pass. Luke's description of Elymas's blindness and his "seeking someone to lead him by the hand" (13:11) is reminiscent of Paul's own blindness when Jesus himself confronted him regarding his opposition to the faith (9:8–9).

In the midst of this report about Elymas, Luke switches from calling Saul by his Jewish name to calling him by his Roman name, Paul (13:9; see sidebar). As is evident elsewhere in Acts, Jews sometimes had both Hebrew and Greco-Roman names (e.g., Joseph Barsabbas in 1:23 and John Mark in 12:12, 25). Now that Luke is tracing missionary work in gentile territory, it seems fitting that he utilizes Saul's Roman name, Paul, which he uses for the rest of Acts. The fact that the proconsul of Cyprus has the similar name Sergius Paulus makes this a convenient time in the story for this referential change.[6]

6. See Rainer Riesner, *Paul's Early Period: Chronology, Mission Strategy, Theology*, trans. Doug Stott (Grand Rapids: Eerdmans, 1998), 137–46. On literary theories for Luke's use of "Saul" as Paul's name in the earliest parts of Acts, see now Michael Kochenash, "Better Call Paul 'Saul': Literary Models and a Lukan Innovation," *JBL* 138 (2019): 433–49.

Saul or Paul: What's in a Name?

The man known to us primarily as Paul in the New Testament is also known as Saul in the first part of Acts. The suggestion that he changed his name at the time of his conversion to faith in Jesus Christ is a mistake. It is several years after Paul's conversion experience (Acts 9) that Luke makes a referential change rather casually at Acts 13:9: "Then Saul, who was also called Paul . . ." How can this be?

Having both a Jewish name and a Roman name was not uncommon in the first century. Paul unashamedly describes himself as "an Israelite myself, a descendant of Abraham, from the tribe of Benjamin" (Rom 11:1) and "a Hebrew of Hebrews" from "the tribe of Benjamin" (Phil 3:5), showing his dedication to the Jewish law by being a member of the Jews' strictest sect, the Pharisees (Acts 26:5), a student of the well-respected Pharisee teacher named Gamaliel (Acts 22:3). It makes sense that someone with this Jewish pedigree would have a solid Hebrew name like Saul, the name of Israel's first king, who was also from the tribe of Benjamin (1 Sam 9:21). But Saul/Paul had been born outside Israel in the Roman town of Tarsus in Cilicia (Acts 21:39; 22:3; cf. 9:11, 30; 11:25), so it is no surprise that he also had a Roman name like Paul (which means "small"). After finding himself ministering primarily to people in non-Jewish territory, could it be that Saul himself decided to lean on his Roman name, Paul, not only in the story of Acts but also in his NT letters?

As a Roman province, Cyprus was ruled by a representative governor called a proconsul, and ***Sergius Paulus*** was proconsul there when Paul and Barnabas visited. Luke describes him as "an intelligent man" (13:7). In 1887, a boundary stone dating to the early part of Claudius's reign (AD 41–47) was discovered in Rome that mentions five men charged with managing the water levels of the Tiber River in the city, and "Lucius Sergius Paullus" is named as one of them. With Paul's trip to Cyprus dated about AD 47, Sergius Paulus would have served in Rome just prior to, or immediately after, his proconsulship in Cyprus (see sidebar).[7] Luke remarks that, as proconsul, Sergius Paulus "sent for Barnabas and Saul because he wanted to hear the word of God" (13:7), and without any apparent prior commitment to Judaism, he turns to faith in the Jewish Messiah. While Elymas had tried to turn him away from the faith, ironically it is the miraculous judgment against Elymas that confirms for Sergius Paulus the truth of the teaching about the Lord (13:12).

7. On various archaeological finds related to Sergius Paulus (and some purported to be about him), see esp. Alanna Nobbs, "Cyprus," in *The Book of Acts in Its Graeco-Roman Setting*, ed. David W. J. Gill and Conrad Gempf, BAFCS 2 (Grand Rapids: Eerdmans, 1994; Carlisle: Paternoster, 1994), 279–89.

Sergius Paulus: Cyprus, Rome, and Pisidian Antioch

Tiber River boundary marker

The Center for Epigraphical and Palaeographical Studies, The Ohio State University (CIL 6.31545)

Pisidian Antioch inscription

Todd Bolen/BiblePlaces.com

The text here is from Clinton E. Arnold, "Acts," vol. 2B of *ZIBBCNT*, ed. Clinton E. Arnold (Grand Rapids: Zondervan, 2002), 121–22; the images are added.

A Latin inscription discovered in Rome makes explicit mention of this man. His full name is given as "Lucius Sergius Paullus." He is listed along with four other men as a director of water management for the Tiber river in Rome. The men were responsible for managing the flow of the river to prevent the disastrous flooding that sometimes occurred in the city. The inscription explicitly mentions that he served in this capacity during the reign of Claudius. Since the title "censor" is not used in the inscription of Claudius (a title he gained in A.D. 47), the inscription can be dated to the early period of Claudius's reign, A.D. 41–47. The dating suggests that Sergius Paulus served as proconsul of Cyprus either just before his position in Rome or just after.

He and his son, who bare the same name, are mentioned on yet another inscription. In the 1912 excavation of the city of Pisidian Antioch, Sir William Ramsay discovered an inscription (dated in the period A.D. 60–100) that read: "To Lucius Sergius Paullus the younger, son of Lucius, one of the four commissioners in charge of the Roman streets, tribune of the soldiers of the sixth legion styled Ferrata, quaestor." Apparently the son of the proconsul of Cyprus became an important Roman official in Pisidian Antioch, the very place the apostle Paul and his companions travel to next. It is possible that the Sergii Paulli family, although ultimately of Italian origin, were native to Pisidian Antioch. The fact that the missionary team goes directly from Cyprus to Pisidian Antioch may have something to do with the proconsul's family connections in that city.

The Wrong Sergius

The Kythraia inscription (*IGR* 3.935) discovered in northern Cyprus and dated to the first century AD refers to a "Quintus Sergius" and one of the Julio-Claudian Caesars (in a damaged portion ". . . ius Caesar"). Some have thought this to be a reference to the Sergius Paulus of Acts 13, proposing that the damaged portion originally read "Claudius," who ruled during Paul's travels. But now most experts recognize the inscription to be naming Gaius (Caligula) as the Caesar, which would put the inscription earlier than Paul's time in Cyprus.

IGR 3.935: Kythraia inscription
Public domain, Metropolitan Museum of Art.

10.2 PAUL AND BARNABAS MINISTER AT PISIDIAN ANTIOCH (ACTS 13:13–52)

After reporting on the conversion of Sergius Paulus, the next thing Luke recounts is Paul and Barnabas traveling to the mainland en route to the city of Pisidian Antioch. Interestingly, in 1912 William Ramsay discovered a first-century inscription in Pisidian Antioch that mentions Sergius Paulus. The inscription is addressed to his son—who bears the same name—who apparently had a Roman government role in the city. Arnold suggests that the missionary team may have gone directly from Cyprus to Pisidian Antioch precisely because Sergius Paulus had family connections in that city.[8]

8. Clinton E. Arnold, "Acts," vol. 2B of *ZIBBCNT*, ed. Clinton E. Arnold (Grand Rapids: Zondervan, 2002), 121–22 (see sidebar). See also Eckhard J. Schnabel, *Early Christian Mission*, 2 vols. (Downers Grove, IL: InterVarsity Press, 2004), 2:1084–88.

Antioch Near Pisidia (a.k.a. Pisidian Antioch)

- One of sixteen cities in the ancient world named in honor of the Syrian emperor Antiochus.
- One of two cities in Acts with the name Antioch—the other being Syrian Antioch, a.k.a. Antioch on the Orontes (see chapter 8).
- Located in central Asia Minor (now modern Turkey), in the mountainous ancient territory of Phrygia but called "near Pisidia" to distinguish it from another Antioch in Phrygia; in the first century it was part of the Roman province of Galatia.
- One of the most important Roman colonies in the eastern Roman Empire.
- Physically laid out something like a miniature Rome.
- Home to indigenous Anatolians, Roman citizens, and a strong Jewish population.
- Prominent religions/deities present: Mên or Mên Askaênos (the moon god), Jupiter, Dionysius, Asklepios, the ruler cult (Augustus), and Judaism.
- Visited by Paul on the first missionary campaign in ca. AD 47–48 (Acts 13:13–52; 14:21).
- Likely visited by Paul on the second missionary campaign in ca. AD 49 (Acts 16:1–8).
- Likely visited by Paul on the third missionary campaign in ca. AD 53 (Acts 18:23; 19:1).

Select Bibliography

Arnold, "Acts," 125.

E. A. Judge, "Antioch of Pisidia," *ZEB* 1:209–10.

John McRay, "Antioch," *EDB*, 67–68.

Stephen Mitchell and Marc Waelkens, *Pisidian Antioch: The Site and Its Monuments* (London: Duckworth, 1998).

Brook W. R. Pearson, "Antioch (Pisidia)," *DNTB*, 31–34.

10.2.1 Getting to Pisidian Antioch (13:13–15)

Whatever their process for determining to go to Pisidian Antioch, the missionary team heads that direction. They sail from Paphos on Cyprus northward to the region of Pamphylia in southern Asia Minor (modern Turkey) where the city of Perga lay on the Kestros River. Without any explanation, Luke simply reports that John Mark departed from the missionary team at Perga "to return to Jerusalem" (13:13); indeed, with this mention of John Mark's departure, Luke foreshadows a significant event that will occur when John Mark reenters the story in Acts 15.[9] From Perga, Paul and Barnabas travel to the region of Phrygia in central Asia Minor. This trip would be made either by traveling northward across the rugged terrain of the Taurus Mountains and the region of Pisidia, or perhaps more likely, by traveling the *Via Sebaste*, a paved Roman roadway that circled westward from Perga through a lower-lying lake region and up to the city of Antioch (13:14). The Romans had constructed a vast network of roadways across the lands they ruled, and these highways were useful not only for commercial trade but

9. For a lengthier discussion of John Mark's departure from the missionary team, see John R. W. Stott, *The Message of Acts: To the Ends of the Earth*, The Bible Speaks Today (Downers Grove, IL: InterVarsity, 1994), 221–22. More is said about John Mark in chapter 11 when he reappears in Acts 15.

also for letter carriers and traveling missionaries.[10] This particular city in Phyrgia called Antioch was one of sixteen cities in the ancient world named in honor of the Syrian emperor Antiochus. Because Phrygia had another city named Antioch, this one was identified as the ***Antioch near Pisidia*** to distinguish it. In the first century, Pisidian Antioch was an administrative center for the Roman province of Galatia to the east of it.

Ruins of Ancient Perga
Mark Bolen/ BiblePlaces.com

Pisidian Antioch had a strong representation of Jews, so it is no surprise that Paul and his company find there a synagogue to attend on the Sabbath (13:14). The partial description found in Acts 13 helps inform our scant knowledge about the order of ancient ***synagogue*** services: a reading from the OT Law (13:15a), a reading from the Prophets (13:15a), a sermon by a congregation member (13:15b–41), and a benediction (13:42–43).[11] That Paul and Barnabas are still viewed as Jews is evident from the invitation they receive to address the people in the Sabbath service: "Brothers, if you have a word of exhortation for the people, please speak" (13:15b). Luke's summary of Paul's sermon shows that Paul views himself as a member of the Israelite faith, a faith coming to a climactic point with the arrival of the Messiah.

10. David French, "Acts and the Roman Roads of Asia Minor," pp. 49–58 in Gill and Gempf, The Book of Acts in Its Graeco-Roman Setting, 50–53; and G. Walter Hansen, "Galatia," pp. 377–95 in Gill and Gempf, *The Book of Acts in Its Graeco-Roman Setting*, 384. See now Mark W. Wilson, "The Route of Paul's First Journey to Pisidian Antioch," *NTS* 55 (2009): 471–83.

11. For more on first-century synagogues and their services, see chapter 5.

Ruins in Pisidian Antioch
Izabela Miszczak/ Shutterstock.com

10.2.2 Paul's Synagogue Sermon in Pisidian Antioch (13:16–41)

Standing and motioning to the crowd—a mixed audience of Jews and gentile God-fearers (13:16; cf. v. 26)—Paul delivers "a word of exhortation for the people" as the synagogue leaders had requested (13:15). For this audience Paul takes a Scripture-oriented approach, and his sermon can be outlined in three parts, each beginning with an invitation for the people to listen (13:16, 26, 38). In the first part of the sermon, Paul outlines the work of God in history from the Israelite patriarchs to King David to John the Baptist (13:16–25). God caused the Israelites to prosper in Egypt, led them out of Egypt to the land of Canaan as their intended territory, and provided them with leadership, the most honored of whom was King David (13:17–22). Paul explains that God used David's family line to bring to Israel the promised Savior Jesus (13:23), who was preceded by John the Baptist calling all the people of Israel to be prepared for the coming of their Savior (13:24–25). The emphasis here is that God was initiating his salvific work through the OT people of Israel to bring the Savior of the world.

In the second section of the sermon, Paul calls the people to recognize that God's activities in history result in a message of salvation for which they are responsible recipients. The Jewish authorities in Jerusalem had Jesus undeservingly executed, but this too, Paul says, turns out to be part of God's salvific plan, for in their condemnation of Jesus, "they fulfilled the words of the prophets that are read every Sabbath" (13:27). Jesus's death was part of God's scriptural plan as verified by his resurrection (13:29–33). This climactic point of the message is punctuated with quotations of three passages of Scripture to show God's identification of Jesus as the ***Davidic Messiah*** by means of his death and resurrection: Psalm 2:7; Isaiah 55:3; and Psalm 16:10 (Acts 13:33–37; cf. 2 Sam 7:12–16).

The third and final section of the sermon has a third address to the crowd (cf. "Fellow Israelites and you Gentiles who worship God" in Acts 13:16, and "Fellow children of Abraham and you God-fearing Gentiles" in 13:26). But this address is briefer and more endearing: "Therefore, my friends, . . ." and is followed by an invitation to faith in Jesus: ". . . I want you to know that through Jesus the forgiveness of sins is proclaimed to you" (13:38). This forgiveness of sins by faith in Jesus fulfills Scripture, puts people right with God, and is unattainable under the law of Moses (13:39). Paul closes the sermon with a final Scripture citation (Hab 1:5), warning his listeners not to miss recognizing and receiving this work of God for their salvation (Acts 13:40–41).

10.2.3 The Results Are Mixed and the Missionaries Move On (13:42–52)

Paul's presentation of the gospel message at the synagogue in Pisidian Antioch has mixed results. That is, some of the listeners are receptive of the gospel, some are curious but noncommittal, and others are decidedly opposed to the gospel. In the days after the sermon, Paul and Barnabas have additional opportunities to interact with the listeners, and their responses continue to be mixed (13:42–43). Word spreads through the city during the week, and such a large crowd turns out to hear the gospel on the next Sabbath that the Jews are "filled with jealousy" (i.e., they are directed, empowered, and characterized by jealousy) and begin to contradict the gospel message (13:44–45). Because of this signature response, Luke begins more and more to use the term "the Jews" to refer to synagogue members everywhere who reject the gospel. We must remember that Paul and Barnabas themselves are Jews—in fact, Luke portrays Paul in the remainder of Acts as a Jew who keeps Jewish holidays. But Jewish Christians become so much more identifiable by their discipleship to Jesus that Luke can use "the Jews" as a shortcut way to reference people of the Jewish faith who reject Jesus.

Luke reports that Paul and Barnabas respond to the opposition of their message with boldness, and in Luke's description of their response to the Jews we hear something of their ministry strategy. Paul and Barnabas provide something of the theological and practical rationale for their usual custom of preaching first in the local synagogue of a city. "We had to speak the word of God to you first," they say, citing Isaiah 49:6: "I have made you a light for the Gentiles, that you may bring salvation to the ends of the earth" (Acts 13:46–47). God would use the Jews to bring blessing to the whole world (cf. Gen 12:2–3). Thus, salvation is *of the Jews only* (i.e., the only saving Messiah Jesus

Potential Confusion with Use of "The Jews"

In modern use, the label "Jew" and its adjective form "Jewish" can have several different, albeit closely related, connotations:

I. **Ethnically Jewish**—A person who descends from Jewish ancestors. Regardless of their personal religious beliefs or cultural practices, such a person is Jewish in ethnicity.
II. **Culturally Jewish**—A person who identifies with the Jewish people in lifestyle and political affinities even if they are not of Jewish ethnicity or of Jewish faith. Such a person might consider themselves Jewish in culture.
III. **Religiously Jewish**—A person who practices Judaism, including those who have converted to Judaism as well as those who have been members of a Jewish religious group since birth. Such a person is Jewish in religion.

This kind of subtle distinction becomes particularly important in the latter chapters of Acts. Without denying that Paul and Barnabas are themselves Jews in an ethnic sense, Luke begins using the label "the Jews" in a religious sense when talking about the people of Jewish faith who oppose faith in Jesus as the Christ.

came to the world as a Jew; cf. Acts 4:10–12), but salvation is *not for the Jews only* (i.e., the only saving Messiah Jesus came to save *all humanity*; cf. Acts 10:36). Paul himself writes about this theological strategy in Romans 1:16: "I am not ashamed of the gospel, because it is the power of God that brings salvation to everyone who believes: first to the Jew, then to the Gentile" (cf. Rom 2:9–10; 9:4–5). Because the Jews had God's word in Scripture, they should be the most prepared to recognize Jesus as the Savior, so it makes sense to go to them first. Once the Jews believe in Jesus as the Messiah for the world, then the gospel ministry to the world will be expanded greatly as they "bring salvation to the ends of the earth." Even as Paul and Barnabas apply the Isaiah passage to themselves—"This is what the Lord has commanded us" (Acts 13:47)—there is a challenge for each individual hearing the message to recognize their responsibility to receive the gospel and to participate in the Messiah's mission to reach the whole world.

Unsurprisingly, the gentiles rejoice to hear that they are included in God's gracious offer of eternal life, and they honor the word of the Lord. The Lord's sovereignty over salvation is highlighted in Luke's comment that "all who were appointed for eternal life believed" (13:48)—no one can take credit for saving themselves. After this blatant explanation that God's sovereign plan for salvation includes gentiles, Luke offers a brief summary statement about the progress of the gospel: "The word of the Lord spread through the whole region" (13:49). In the first half of Acts, such progress summary statements occur at the end of each section of the "storyteller's outline" (i.e., 2:41; 6:7; 9:31; and 12:24–25; see chapter 3). In the second half of Acts, however, the storytelling switches to a travel motif, with each section of the outline ending with a summary about the travels just reported. Nevertheless, within each travel section, Luke inserts a brief progress summary like this one about the spread of the gospel.

But the progress of this ministry does not please the leadership of the Jews opposing the gospel message, and they incite the influential gentile God-fearers in the city—both women and men who have been favorable toward Jewish belief—to help them in their opposition toward the gospel. This opposition escalates from verbal intimidation to physical persecution in that Paul and Barnabas are expelled from the region (13:50). Western readers might find odd Luke's remark about the action Paul and Barnabas take in shaking the dust off their feet as a warning to them (13:51), but this ***dust-shaking gesture*** was customary in the first century (see sidebar).[12] Paul and Barnabas had explained the gospel message, and the Jews had expressed their insistent rejection of the message—to the point of persecution and expulsion—so Paul and Barnabas agree to depart but don't want their departure to be misunderstood as acquiescence. The gospel is the truth, and Paul and Barnabas want the opposition to remember it even if they don't accept it. Nevertheless, the new followers of Jesus—whom Luke persistently labels "disciples" no matter where they are located—are characterized (i.e., "filled") by joy and by the Holy Spirit (13:52).

Dusty Gestures

In Acts 13:51, Paul and Barnabas perform a gesture of separation that seems a bit strange to Westerners: "they shook the dust off their feet as a warning." When Jesus had sent out his disciples on short-term mission outings, he had given them instructions about using this gesture with anyone rejecting the proclamation of the good news: "Leave that place and shake the dust off your feet as a testimony against them" (Mark 6:11; cf. Matt 10:14; Luke 9:5; 10:11). This sort of expression of separation had been customary for the Jews for centuries and is evidenced in Nehemiah 5:13: "I also shook out the folds of my robe and said, 'In this way may God shake out of their house and possessions anyone who does not keep this promise. So may such a person be shaken out and emptied!'" When listeners rejected the truth, the messenger was to depart and symbolically demonstrate that the listeners have chosen to be shaken out and separated from the truth, preferring instead to receive the judgment that will come upon them because of their refusal. Thus, in Acts 13:51, Paul and Barnabas issue a dusty gesture to the Jews of Pisidian Antioch who are rejecting the gospel and expelling the missionaries from the region. Paul will utilize this kind of Jewish gesture again when he leaves the abusive synagogue of Corinth to preach the gospel to the gentiles there (Acts 18:6).

12. For later rabbinic teaching regarding the impurity one attains from walking in gentile territory, see m. 'Ohal. 18:6–7; and m. Tehar. 4:5. For rabbinic teaching about removing dust from one's feet before enter the temple, see b. Ber. 54a; and b. Yebam. 6b.

10.3 PAUL AND BARNABAS MINISTER AT ICONIUM (ACTS 14:1–7)

From their ministry with mixed results at Pisidian Antioch, Paul and Barnabas move on the *Via Sebaste* eastward to the city of ***Iconium*** in the southern part of the province of Galatia. By the Lord's enablement, they have a relatively long and productive ministry there, which nonetheless also turns out to be one of mixed results.

Stone Monuments at Iconium

Modern day Konya, Turkey, is the site of ancient Iconium. While Iconium has not yet been extensively excavated, Konya has an archaeological museum with articles of interest. Pertaining particularly to Paul's missionary travels, the museum contains several inscribed stone monuments. One mentions Derbe, one mentions Iconium, and one mentions Lystra (pictured here).

David Padfield/BiblePlaces.com

10.3.1 A Usual Ministry (14:1–3)

Paul and Barnabas take their usual approach to ministry in Iconium. Luke himself uses that phrase—"as usual" (Greek: *kata to auto*)—noting that they begin in the Jewish synagogue (14:1). As noted, it makes both theological and practical sense to begin sharing the gospel message with those who are familiar with Scripture and who might be expecting God to act for their salvation. Good theology always ends up being practical too.

Iconium

- About ninety miles to the southeast of Pisidian Antioch.
- Of uncertain origin, it appears that the people of the region of Phrygia settled here as some ancients refer to it as a Phrygian city and inscriptional evidence shows the lasting use of the Phrygian language here.
- The first-century chief town of Lycaonia, the southern region of the Roman province of Galatia.
- A prosperous city of agriculture and commercial interests, lying on the major trade route of the *Via Sebaste* (a Roman highway) in a well-watered, fertile plain with moderate climate.
- Persisted as a Greek city in tone and culture, resisting Roman influence even in its Roman era.
- Visited by Paul on his first missionary journey (Acts 14:1–6, 21–23 with Barnabas), on his second missionary journey (Acts 16:2 with Silas), and perhaps on his third missionary journey as well (cf. Acts 18:23).
- Where the second-century apocryphal book, the Acts of Paul, reports a legend about Paul and Thecla as having happened.
- Now the modern city of Konya, Turkey.

Select Bibliography

Edward M. Blaiklock, "Iconium," *ZEB* 3:268–69.
Paul Anthony Hartog, "Iconium," *EDB*, 624–25.

As with the other locations of their ministry, at Iconium, Paul and Barnabas face opposition, and as usual it comes from the unexpected source of the religiously minded people. Luke's description of the opposition is somewhat ominous: the unbelieving Jews "stirred up the other Gentiles and poisoned their minds against the brothers" (14:2). Nevertheless, Paul and Barnabas are "speaking boldly" (14:3; cf. 9:27, 28; 13:46; 18:26; 19:8; 26:26) at Iconium. We should not be surprised that Christian witness today still needs to be exercised with boldness in the face of opposition, which is a common experience for those sharing the gospel message.

As elsewhere, in their ministry at Iconium, the Lord enables Paul and Barnabas to perform signs and wonders. Luke elsewhere uses this same phrase, "signs and wonders" (Greek: *sēmeia kai terata*; e.g., 5:12; 6:8; 14:3; 15:12), or simply "signs" (e.g., 8:6). It is important to note here that miracles in ministry are performed by the Lord's enablement and serve the purpose of "confirm[ing] the message of his grace" (14:3). According to William Larkin's count, about half of the incidents of effective gospel preaching in Acts are accompanied by miracles of some kind. He suggests then, on the one hand, that the role of the miraculous in giving credence to the spoken word should not be despised, and yet on the other hand, that preaching accompanied by the miraculous should not be assumed as somehow superior. We have already seen in Acts that false belief can be centered on miraculous deeds, which can actually become a hindrance to genuine faith (e.g., Simon Magus in Acts 8). Saving faith rests on the truth of the message of Christ and not on any miracles, however great they might be, which serve as pointers to the truth.[13] Thus, when miracles do occur in Acts, they are most often connected to a confirmation of the gospel message and not merely a display of power (see sidebar).[14]

Miracles in Acts and the Message of Faith in Christ

About half the gospel presentations recounted in Acts are accompanied by miraculous events.

Passage	Miracle(s) Accompanying the Message	Speaker(s) of the Message
2:1-41	Speaking in tongues (v. 4)	Peter (vv. 14-41)
2:43-47	Many signs and wonders (v. 43)	Apostles (v. 47)
3:1-26	Disabled beggar healed (vv. 1-10)	Peter (vv. 12-26)
4:29-33	House shaken after prayer for miracles (vv. 29-31)	The believers and apostles (v. 33)
5:12-16	Many signs and wonders (vv. 12-16)	Apostles (v. 14)
5:17-42	Angelic release from prison (vv. 19-20)	Apostles (vv. 21, 29-32, 42)
6:8-8:2	Great wonders and signs (6:8)	Stephen (7:1-53)
8:5-25	Signs, exorcisms, and healings (vv. 6-7, 13)	Philip (v. 5)
9:1-19	Divine visitation and vision (vv. 3-7, 10-16)	Ananias (vv. 17-18)
9:32-35	Paralyzed man healed (v. 34)	Peter (v. 35)
9:36-43	Dead woman raised to life (vv. 40-41)	Peter (v. 42)
10:1-11:18	Divine visions and tongues (10:3-6, 9-16, 46)	Peter (vv. 34-48)
13:6-12	Elymas the sorcerer is struck blind (vv. 10-11)	Paul (v. 12)
14:1-5	Signs and wonders (v. 3)	Paul and Barnabas (v. 3)
14:6-20	Disabled man healed in Lystra (vv. 8-10)	Paul and Barnabas (vv. 15-17)
16:6-15	Divine vision about going to Macedonia (vv. 9-10)	Paul and Silas (vv. 11-15)
16:16-40	Exorcism and miraculous prison rescue (vv. 18, 26)	Paul and Silas (vv. 27-34)
19:1-7	Speaking in tongues (v. 6)	Paul (vv. 4-5)
19:8-12	Extraordinary miracles (vv. 11-12)	Paul (vv. 8-10)

13. William J. Larkin Jr., *Acts*, The IVP New Testament Commentary Series (Downers Grove, IL: InterVarsity Press, 1995), 151.

14. The few miracles in Acts not explicitly accompanied by reports of gospel preaching include Peter's release from prison (Acts 12:7–11), the death of Herod Agrippa I (12:22–23), Paul's survival of the viper bite (28:1–6), and the healings on Malta (28:7–9); although it seems that gospel preaching would be implied in the latter two instances.

Passage	Reports of the Message Shared with No Mention of Miracles
6:7	Believers spread the word of God, and many priests become believers (v. 7)
8:4	Scattered believers preach wherever they go (v. 4)
8:26–40	Philip shares the gospel with the Ethiopian eunuch (vv. 35–38)
8:40	Philip preaches along the coast to Caesarea (v. 40)
9:19–22	Saul preaches in Damascus (vv. 20, 22)
9:26–30	Saul preaches in Jerusalem (vv. 28–29)
11:19–21	Believers scattered by persecution preach wherever they go (vv. 19–20)
11:22–24	Barnabas preaches in Syrian Antioch (v. 24)
13:4–6	Barnabas and Saul preach in Cyprus (v. 5)
13:13–52	Paul and Barnabas preach in Pisidian Antioch (vv. 16–41, 46–49)
14:20–21	Paul and Barnabas preach in Derbe (v. 21)
14:24–25	Paul and Barnabas preach in Perga (v. 25)
17:1–9	Paul and Silas preach in Thessalonica (vv. 2–4)
17:10–15	Paul and Silas preach in Berea (vv. 10–12)
17:16–34	Paul preaches in Athens (vv. 17–18, 22–34)
18:1–18	Paul preaches in Corinth (vv. 4–8)
18:18–21	Paul preaches in Ephesus (v. 19)
18:24–26	Priscilla and Aquila explain the gospel to Apollos in Ephesus (v. 26)
18:27–28	Apollos preaches in Achaia (v. 28)
21:26–22:29	Paul preaches from the steps of Antonio Fortress in Jerusalem (22:1–21)
24:1–23	Paul shares before Felix (24:10–21)
24:24–26	Paul shares with Felix and Drusilla (v. 24)
25:13–26:32	Paul shares before Festus, Agrippa II, and Bernice (26:1–29)
28:17–31	Paul shares with the Jewish leaders in Rome (28:23–31)

10.3.2 The Results Are Mixed and the Missionaries Move On (14:4–7)

Even as the ministry of Paul and Barnabas at Iconium can be described as having their usual approach, so also the results of their ministry can be described as usual too: the results are mixed, in that some receive the gospel message and others reject it. Luke even says it rather plainly: "The people of the city were divided; some sided with the Jews, others with the apostles" (14:4). As seen throughout Acts, this was the usual experience, and it should be no surprise today to see the gospel message still received in this mixed way. Early in the life of the church, Luke had noted that opposition to the gospel could escalate from intimidation (3:1–4:31) to outright persecution (5:17–42) (see chapter 7). The escalation of opposition that Paul and Barnabas experience in Iconium could thus be considered "usual" as well. A plot to mistreat and even to stone Paul and Barnabas was developing among the gentiles and Jews who were opposed to the gospel (14:5). When the plot is discovered, the missionaries move on from Iconium to the neighboring cities of Lystra and Derbe, where despite the threats of persecution, Paul and Barnabas "continued to preach the gospel" (14:7; cf. 5:42).

Faithful Ministry and Mixed Results

From Bruce Riley Ashford and Heath A. Thomas, *The Gospel of Our King: Bible, Worldview, and the Mission of Every Christian* (Grand Rapids: Baker Academic, 2019), 142–43.

> In 1 Peter 3:15, Peter does not instruct us to preach to every person we meet. Neither does he say that he expects us to successfully persuade every person with whom we share the gospel. But he does expect us to be ready. And if Christ is our hope, then the Spirit will enable us to articulate why we have that hope. Neither our naturally introverted personalities, nor our fears and insecurities, nor our lack of theological training should keep us from engaging in spiritual conversations. It is no burden to speak about what we love. Just as we might speak in a relaxed and natural manner about our families or friends, we can engage in conversation about the one we love the most—the Lord Jesus Christ.

Remarkably, Luke uses the label "apostles" for Paul and Barnabas (14:4). He had carefully explained in Acts 1 how, after the defection of Judas Iscariot, the number of apostles had been restored to its proper allotment of twelve with the selection of Matthias.[15] But none of the Twelve are on this missionary trip with Paul and Barnabas, so seeing that label used here is surprising. But the term "apostle" (Greek: *apostolos*) basically means "sent one" (see esp. John 13:16; cf. Luke 11:49). Thus, "apostle" is a fitting term not only for the original Twelve whom Jesus personally chose to send out (see Luke 6:12–16 and Acts 1:2, 12–26) but also in a more general sense for commissioned emissaries like Paul and Barnabas (Acts 14:4 and 14), Andronicus and Junias (Rom 16:7), Epaphroditus (Phil 2:25), and Titus and others (2 Cor 8:23, where

15. See in chapter 6.

"representatives" is the Greek term *apostolos*) who were sent by churches.[16] Even Jesus is referred to as an "apostle" (Heb 3:1), which is fitting given that he was sent by God to be the Savior of the world.[17] To be sure, Paul offers in his letters arguments for why he can be called an apostle; and he particularly notes that, like the original Twelve, he had been personally chosen by Jesus and sent out by him (e.g., 1 Cor 9:1; Gal 1:1, 11–12; Eph 1:1; Col 1:1; 2 Tim 1:1, 11). Nonetheless, Paul recognizes the uniqueness of the apostleship of the Twelve and the difference he has from them (1 Cor 15:7–10). In its more general sense, this label is used both here and again in Acts 14:14: "The apostles Barnabas and Paul . . ." And for us today, while the original Twelve apostles are no longer present, with the examples noted previously, the New Testament indicates a proper broader use of the label "apostles" for people sent out by churches to share the gospel with other people groups, even though "missionaries" is now the far more common term.

10.4 PAUL AND BARNABAS MINISTER AT LYSTRA AND DERBE (ACTS 14:8–20)

Paul and Barnabas flee eastward to the Galatian cities of ***Lystra*** and ***Derbe***, which Luke describes as Lycaonian (Acts 14:6). The Roman province of Galatia (in the central region of Asia Minor, i.e., modern Turkey) had shifting borders, particularly with various occasional annexations of smaller regions. Regions sometimes encompassed by Galatia included Pamphylia (on the shores of the Mediterranean Sea), Phyrgia (more centrally located in Asia Minor), Pisidia (near the border of which the Phyrgian city of Pisidian Antioch was found), and Lycaonia (in the southern and eastern part of Galatia).[18] The region of Lycaonia was largely a grazing land for sheep and goats whose people were described as vigorous and militaristic enough to have maintained their independence in much of ancient times. The territory had become part of the Roman province of Galatia in 25 BC, but the people maintained their own regional language (cf. 14:11). Lystra (on the *Via Sebaste* Roman highway) and Derbe were two of the leading cities of Lycaonian culture.[19]

16. There has been some scholarly discussion about the mention of Andronicus and Junia(s) as "outstanding among the apostles" (Rom 16:7 NIV). The consensus among most scholars is that Paul hereby labels Andronicus and Junias as "apostles" in the general sense described previously; e.g., Douglas J. Moo, *Romans*, NICNT (Grand Rapids: Eerdmans, 1996), 923–24; and Thomas R. Schreiner, *Romans*, BECNT (Grand Rapids: Baker, 1998), 796–97. But some suggest that the phrase "outstanding among" (Greek: *episēmoi en*) implies only that they were "well known to" the apostles (see ESV); e.g., Michael H. Burer and Daniel B. Wallace, "Was Junia Really an Apostle? A Re-examination of Rom 16.7," *NTS* 47 (2001): 76–91.

17. On Heb 3:1, the one place in the NT where Jesus is called "apostle," see the brief but helpful discussion of William L. Lane, *Hebrews 1–8*, WBC 47A (Dallas: Word, 1991), 75–76.

18. On Galatia, see James M. Scott, "Galatia, Galatians," *DNTB*, 389–91; and Hansen, "Galatia," 377–95.

19. Robert C. Stone, "Lycaonia," *ZEB* 3:1138.

Lystra

- An out-of-the-way town in a secluded but fertile area about twenty-five miles south-southwest of Iconium in Lycaonia, the southern region of the Roman province of Galatia.
- Was designated a Roman colony in AD 6 along with Pisidian Antioch, so the two cities were connected by the Roman highway *Via Sebaste*, which also ran through Iconium.
- Had a garrison of Roman soldiers for defending the province of Galatia.
- Persisted in its local Lycaonian culture, with the Lycaonian language being used until the sixth century AD.
- On his first missionary journey, Paul was stoned here and left for dead (Acts 14:8–20) but survived and returned on his second missionary journey (Acts 16:1–4) and perhaps on his third missionary journey as well (cf. Acts 18:23).
- Home of Timothy, who may have become a believer during Paul's first visit there (cf. 2 Tim 3:10–11) and who joined Paul's ministry team on the second missionary journey (Acts 16:1–4).

Select Bibliography

Paul Anthony Hartog, "Lystra," *EDB*, 834.
Harold W. Hoehner, "Lystra," *ZEB* 3:1143–45.

Ancient Lystra
mozcann/iStock.com

10.4.1 A Crippled Man Healed in Lystra (14:8–10)

As elsewhere in Acts, the pairing of preaching and miracles occurs again for Paul and Barnabas when they get to Lystra. In Lystra, God uses Paul to heal a disabled man who was sitting and listening to Paul speak (14:8–9). Luke reports this miracle in a manner that resembles his report of a miracle in Peter's ministry (cf. 3:1–16). Among the parallels, both miracle accounts are healings of a man "lame from birth" (Greek:

chōlos ek koilias metros autou); say the apostle "looked straight/directly" (*atenisas*) at the man; involve "faith" (*pistis*); report that the man "jumped" up (a form of *hallomai*) "and began to walk" (*kai periepatei*); and result in amazement followed by opposition from some (see sidebar). These Peter-Paul parallels help Luke's audience recognize that God's use of Paul in gospel ministry has the same potential for power and effectiveness as God's use of Peter in gospel ministry.

Luke's Interest in People with Illnesses and Disabilities

The Gospel of Luke records more healing miracles than any other gospel account of Jesus's life and ministry, and the book of Acts has quite a few additional accounts involving the healing of people with disabilities, injuries, illnesses, diseases, and other conditions. Thus, Luke shows a particular interest in people suffering disorders that were not only unfortunate in themselves but also tended to make those people be marginalized in first-century society. With strong language, the Hebrew Scriptures emphasize the just treatment of people with disabilities (Lev 19:14; Deut 27:18), and their miraculous healing was to be considered an announcement of the arrival of the era of the Messiah (see Mic 4:6–7; Zeph 3:19–20; and esp. Luke 7:21–23, reflecting on such prophecies as Isa 26:19; 29:18–19; 35:5–6; 42:5–7; 61:1–2). Here are the stories of healings in Luke-Acts:

- general passages about people being healed (Luke 4:40–41; 7:21–23; 9:1–6; Acts 5:12–16; 19:11–12; 28:9)
- people healed of high fever (Luke 4:38–39; Acts 28:8)
- people cleansed from leprosy (Luke 5:12–14; 17:11–19)
- the paralyzed or lame being healed (Luke 5:17–26; 13:10–17; Acts 3:1–10; 8:6–7; 9:32–35; 14:8–10)
- a shriveled hand healed (Luke 6:6–11)
- an ill servant restored to health (Luke 7:1–10)
- demons exorcised (Luke 4:33–36; 8:26–39; 9:37–43; 10:17–20; 11:14–20; 16:16–18; Acts 8:6–7)
- a hemorrhaging woman healed (Luke 8:42–48)
- a man with abnormal swelling healed (Luke 14:1–6)
- a person healed of blindness (Luke 18:35–43)
- a severed ear restored (Luke 22:49–51)
- people raised from the dead (Luke 7:11–17; 8:49–56; Acts 9:36–42; 20:9–12)

Select Bibliography

Chad Hartsock, *Sight and Blindness in Luke-Acts: The Use of Physical Features in Characterization*, Biblical Interpretation 94 (Leiden: Brill. 2008).

Kathy McReynolds, "The Gospel of Luke: A Framework for a Theology of Disability," *CEJ*: Series 3, 13.1 (2016): 169–78.

Mikeal C. Parsons, *Body and Character in Luke and Acts: The Subversion of Physiognomy in Early Christianity* (Grand Rapids: Baker, 2006).

S. John Roth, *The Blind, the Lame and the Poor: Character Types in Luke-Acts*, JSNTSup 144 (Sheffield: Sheffield Academic, 1997).

Pamela Shellberg, *Cleansed Lepers, Cleansed Hearts: Purity and Healing in Luke-Acts*, Emerging Scholars (Minneapolis: Fortress, 2015).

David F. Watson, "Luke-Acts," in *The Bible and Disability: A Commentary*, ed. Sarah J. Melcher, Mikeal C. Parsons, and Amos Yong, Studies in Religion, Theology, and Disability (Waco, TX: Baylor University Press, 2017), 303–32.

Parallels in Peter and Paul Healing of Disabled Men

Peter in Acts 3–4	Paul in Acts 14
Ministering with John, Peter is the main speaker (3:1–4)	Ministering with Barnabas, Paul is the main speaker (14:8–12)
Healing a man "lame from birth" (3:2).	Healing a man "lame ... from birth" (14:8).
The apostle "looked straight" (3:4) at the man.	The apostle "looked directly" (14:9) at the man.
The miracle involves "faith" (3:16).	The miracle involves "faith" (14:9).
The healed man "jumped to his feet and began to walk" (3:8).	The healed man "jumped up and began to walk" (14:10).
The miracle resulted in amazement followed by opposition from some (3:9–10; 4:1–22).	The miracle resulted in amazement followed by opposition from some (14:11–20).
The gate (3:10; cf. v. 2) to the Jewish temple and its priests (4:1) are mentioned.	The gates to the city of Lystra and the priest (14:13) of Zeus are mentioned.
The miracle becomes an occasion for Peter to preach (3:12–26).	The miracle becomes an occasion for Paul to preach (14:14–18).

10.4.2 The People Attempt to Worship Paul and Barnabas as Gods (14:11–15a)

Luke reports the miracle as the Lycaonians would have understood it, i.e., "what Paul had done" (14:11), and the Lycaonians reach a hasty conclusion that they shout (in their own language): "The gods have come down to us in human form!" Luke explains that they began to refer to Barnabas as Zeus, the supreme god in Greek pagan religion (a.k.a. Jupiter in Roman worship), and to Paul as Hermes, the pagan messenger god (a.k.a. Mercury in Roman worship), because Paul was the main speaker of the two (14:12). As this word spread in the city, the priest of the local temple of Zeus brought items to offer in sacrificial worship of Paul and Barnabas (14:13).

This hasty and superstitious response by the people of Lystra is understandable in light of an ancient local legend that was recorded perhaps only fifty years earlier by the popular Latin poet Ovid. In one of the many stories of his fifteen-volume *Metamorphoses*, Ovid recounts the myth of Jupiter and Mercury (i.e., ***Zeus and Hermes***) visiting the Phrygian hill country near Lystra. Disguised as mere humans, Zeus and Hermes sought the hospitality of the local people but were turned away by all except one poor elderly couple. Despite their poverty, this poor couple were gladly willing to entertain the strangers as generously as they could. The myth reports that the gods rewarded the elderly couple for receiving them but destroyed the rest of the village. It seems reasonable to suppose that the people of Lystra knew this myth and would want to avoid the consequences meted out to their inhospitable Phrygian neighbors in the story (see sidebar).

The Legend of Zeus and Hermes Visiting Phrygia

Publius Ovidius Naso, a.k.a. Ovid (43 BC–ca. AD 17), was a popular Roman poet who lived during the reign of Augustus. Ovid's fifteen-volume *Metamorphoses*, a poetic narrative about "transformations" in the lives of Greek and Roman mythological characters, is an important source of classical mythology recounting almost 250 different myths. One particular myth—known in Paul's day—explains why the people of Lystra near Phrygia treated Barnabas and Paul as if they were Zeus and Hermes (see Acts 14:8–20).

Ovid, *Metamorphoses*, 8.611–724

> The power of heaven is indeed immeasurable and has no bounds, and whatever the gods decree is done. And, that you may believe it, there stand in the Phrygian hill-country an oak and a linden-tree side by side, surrounded by a low wall. . . . Not far from the place I speak of is a marsh, once a habitable land, but now water, the haunt of divers and coots. Hither came Jupiter [Zeus] in the guise of a mortal, and with his father came Atlas' grandson [Hermes], he that bears the caduceus, his wings laid aside. To a thousand homes they came, seeking a place for rest; a thousand homes were barred against them. Still one house received them, humble indeed, thatched with straw and reeds from the marsh; but pious old Baucis and Philemon, of equal age, were in that cottage wedded in their youth, and in that cottage had grown old together; there they made their poverty light by owning it, and by bearing it in a contended spirit. It was of no use to ask for masters or for servants in that house; they two were the whole household, together they served and ruled. And so when the heavenly ones came to this humble home and, stooping, entered in at the lowly door, the old man set out a bench and bade them rest their limbs, while over this bench busy Baucis threw a rough covering. Then she raked aside the warm ashes on the hearth and fanned yesterday's coals to life, which she fed with leaves and dry bark, blowing them into flame with the breath of her old body. Then she took down from the roof some fine-split wood and dry twigs, broke them up and placed them under the little copper kettle. . . . A moment and the hearth sent its steaming viands on, and wine of no great age was brought out, which was then pushed aside to give a small space for the second course. Here were nuts and figs, with dried dates, plums and fragrant apples in broad baskets, and purple grapes just picked from the vines; in the centre of the table was a comb of clear white honey. Besides all this, pleasant faces were at the board and lively and abounding goodwill.
>
> Meanwhile they saw that the mixing-bowl, as often as it was drained, kept filling of its own accord, and that the wine welled up of itself. The two old people saw this strange sight with amaze and fear, and with upturned hands they both uttered a prayer, Baucis and the trembling old Philemon, and they craved indulgence for their fare and meagre entertainment. They had one goose, the guardian of their tiny estate; and him the hosts were preparing to kill for their divine guests. But the goose was swift of wing, and quite wore the slow old people out in their efforts to catch him. He eluded their grasp for a long time, and finally seemed to flee for refuge to the gods themselves. Then the gods told them not

to kill the goose. "We are gods," they said, "and this wicked neighbourhood shall be punished as it deserves; but to you shall be given exemption from this punishment. Leave now your dwelling and come with us to that tall mountain yonder." They both obeyed and, propped on their staves, they struggled up the long slope. When they were a bowshot distant from the top, they looked back and saw the whole country-side covered with water, only their own house remaining. And, while they wondered at this, while they wept for the fate of their neighbours, that old house of theirs, which had been small even for its two occupants, was changed into a temple. Marble columns took the place of the forked wooden supports; the straw grew yellow and became a golden roof; there were gates richly carved, a marble pavement covered the ground . . .

Roman Inscription from Lystra

From the Konya Archaeological Museum in Konya, Turkey (the site of ancient Iconium), this stone inscription dates to the second century AD.

David Padfield/BiblePlaces.com

As the supreme god in pagan thought, Zeus was widely worshiped in Galatia. Carvings and inscriptions portraying Zeus accompanied by Hermes have been discovered in the territory of Lystra, including a stone altar dedicated to "The Hearer of Prayer [presumably Zeus] and Hermes." A later third-century inscription is the dedication to Zeus of a statue of Hermes by men with Lycaonian names, and another inscription mentions "priests of Zeus."[20]

When Paul and Barnabas distinguish what is happening (esp. with the arrival of bulls and wreaths as sacrificial items), they rush to prevent being the objects of worship. Tearing one's clothes was an ancient expression of grief and despair, and the use of this gesture by Paul and Barnabas would overcome any language barrier in communicating their distress (14:14). Addressing the crowd—presumably in the international language of Greek and establishing the avenue for clearer verbal communication—Paul and Barnabas declare, "Friends, why are you doing this? We too are only human, like you" (14:15a). This exclamation distinguishing the Christian missionaries from the ancient mythological gods is reminiscent of Peter's response to Cornelius bowing before him in Acts 10:26: "Stand up . . . I am only a man myself."

20. Hansen, "Galatia," 393; F. F. Bruce, *The Book of Acts*, 2nd ed., NICNT (Grand Rapids: Eerdmans, 1988), 274–75; idem, *The Acts of the Apostles: The Greek Text with Introduction and Commentary*, 3rd ed. (Grand Rapids: Eerdmans, 1990; Leicester: Apollos, 1990), 321–22; and Colin J. Hemer, *The Book of Acts in the Setting of Hellenistic History*, ed. Conrad H. Gempf, WUNT 49 (Tübingen: Mohr Siebeck, 1989; repr., Winona Lake, IN: Eisenbrauns, 1990), 111.

Found at Cnidus, Turkey, these bull and wreath motifs are evidence of the connection these items had in pagan worship contexts.
Thankful Photography/ iStock.com

A bull and wreath motif found on the altar of Domitian. Ephesus Archaeological Museum, Selçuk, Turkey.
Cheryl Dunn for Talbot Bible Lands

10.4.3 Paul's Sermon in Lystra (14:15b–18)

Paul addresses the would-be worshipers, but given the pagan audience at Lystra, Paul takes a different approach in his preaching than he had at the synagogue at Pisidian Antioch just a few days earlier. The synagogue audience was familiar with Scripture and could engage with Paul in his discussion of Jesus as the fulfillment of God's promises. In Lystra, however, with an audience less familiar with Scripture, Paul shows awareness of his contextual situation and takes a more general approach. Rather than the special revelation of Scripture (which his audience would not know), he begins with general revelation of creation (with which his audience is, of course, familiar) and moves more slowly toward the gospel message.

Paul's Preaching with Different Audiences

Luke gives summaries of two sermons by Paul on his first missionary journey (Acts 13-14). Comparing these, we see that Paul can preach the same gospel message but with two different approaches. With those familiar with the Hebrew Scriptures (i.e., a Jewish audience), Paul can take a Scripture approach and move more quickly to the gospel about Jesus Christ. With those unfamiliar with Scripture (i.e., a pagan audience), Paul takes a more general approach, beginning more broadly with the existence of a Creator God and moving more slowly to the gospel.

A Scripture Approach: Paul's Sermon to a Jewish Audience in Acts 13:16–41

1. God's acts in OT history: patriarchs to David to John the Baptist (vv. 16–25).
2. God identifies Jesus as the Davidic Savior via death and resurrection (vv. 26–37).
3. Invitation: receive forgiveness of sins by faith in Jesus—don't miss it! (vv. 38–41).

A General Approach: Paul's Sermon to a Pagan Audience in Acts 14:15–18

1. Good news about the one and only Creator God worthy of worship (v. 15).
2. God's past relationship with all the nations (v. 16).
3. In life this Creator God gives to everyone evidence of his kindness (v. 17).
4. [Paul's speech is interrupted] (v. 18).

After gently correcting the people of Lystra against their intention to worship the missionaries as gods (14:15a), Paul announces that they are, in fact, messengers bringing good news that will call them away from pagan worship. There is only one living God worthy of worship, the one and only Creator God, "who made the heavens and the earth and the sea and everything in them" (14:15b), a phrase that echoes a Scriptural theme (e.g., Exod 20:11; Ps 146:6; 2 Kgs 19:15; 2 Chr 2:12; Neh 9:6; Isa 37:16; 42:5). And again, rather than Paul expositing Scripture, Paul's word choices about "turning" to "the living God" echo Scripture (e.g., respectively, Deut 4:30; 30:2, 10; 2 Chr 19:4; Ps 85:8; Isa 55:7; Jer 3:12; 24:7; Hos 3:5; Joel 2:13 and Deut 4:33; 5:26; Josh 3:10; 1 Sam 17:36; 2 Kgs 19:4, 16; Ps 42:2; 84:2; Isa 37:4, 17; Hos 1:10). This one living Creator of all things everywhere is, naturally, to be the one God worshiped by all nations.

In times past, God allowed the nations to go their own way (Acts 14:16). And this has resulted in the people moving away from the truth and slipping into worthless worship. But lest his listeners think God had abandoned them, Paul quickly notes that the one living Creator God has, in fact, surrounded them with constant evidence of his existence and concern for them. God has been providing them with rain and crops and food and life's joys (14:17). All these things are testimony to the existence and character of God, and Paul is calling the citizens of Lystra to turn to this loving living God.

Paul's Seemingly Harsh Words in Acts 14:15–17

From Arnold, "Acts," 135.

> Paul's comments about other religions would solicit a hostile reaction today in the contemporary climate of pluralism. To infer that worshipers of other gods are devoted to "empty" things and neglect the living and true God would be viewed today as intolerant and inflammatory. It is important to realize that Paul was no angry man who said these things out of an unstable or uncharitable personality. He came to these people in love earnestly desiring for them to recognize and acknowledge the one true God. In Paul's understanding, there were not many paths that led to the same ultimate reality. There was one path and many deceptive counterfeits.

Unfortunately, it appears that Paul's speech is interrupted before he can get to an explicit declaration of the gospel message of Jesus's death and resurrection. As with other of Luke's speech summations in Acts, the impression is that more was said. But if Paul was able to declare at this time the specifics of God's most recent kindness in the gospel events, Luke does not report it here. Rather he comments only, "Even with these words, they had difficulty keeping the crowd from sacrificing to them" (14:18).

10.4.4 The Results Are Mixed and the Missionaries Move On (14:19–20)

While Paul has adjusted his approach to preaching the gospel so that it fits with the preparedness of his audience in Lystra, the result of the ministry there seems to be as mixed as it was in Pisidian Antioch and Iconium. It was with the influence of some Jews who came from Pisidian Antioch and Iconium that the crowds at Lystra are swayed to oppose the gospel. Here again Luke uses the simple term "the Jews" as a circumlocution to mean "the Jews who refused to believe." Somehow the unbelieving Jews are able to swing the Lystra people to the opposite extreme from where they had just been, i.e., from wanting to worship the missionaries to threatening their lives. Paul is even the victim of stoning and is dragged outside the city presumed dead (14:19; cf. 2 Cor 11:25).

While Luke does not report Paul's experience as one of miraculous resuscitation but only as an attempt on his life, more noteworthy here is that Luke reports that the "disciples" gathered around him (Acts 14:20a). The term "disciple" is one of Luke's favorite designations for followers of Jesus, so his use of the word here indicates that some had come to faith in Christ at Lystra. At Lystra, in a short span of time the missionaries had faced the extremes of flattery and persecution, but they were detoured by neither from their cause.[21] As before, in the face of opposition and after establishing a community of Jesus followers in this location, the missionaries move on to continue preaching elsewhere. From Lystra they set out for Derbe, a town about sixty miles away (14:20b).

Derbe

- Located about sixty miles southeast of Lystra in Lycaonia, the southern region of the Roman province of Galatia.
- Along with Lystra, a leading city for the local Lycaonian culture (note the pairing of Derbe and Lystra in Acts 14:6 and 16:1).
- Having been abandoned for centuries, its exact location was a matter of dispute for many years. But a dedicatory inscription honoring Roman Emperor Antoninus Pius in AD 157 by the people of Derbe was found in 1956 at a site called Kerti Hüyük. In 1962 a second inscription was discovered—a fourth-century Christian tombstone of one "most beloved of God, Michael, bishop of Derbe"—which has established this site as ancient Derbe's accepted location (a difference of thirty miles from previous guesses).
- Is briefly mentioned as a place of successful ministry on Paul's first missionary journey (Acts 14:20–21) and as a stop on his second missionary journey (Acts 16:1); it was perhaps visited on his third missionary journey as well (cf. Acts 18:23).
- Home of a believer named Gaius, a member of Paul's ministry team who accompanied him during his third missionary journey (Acts 20:1–5).

Select Bibliography

Edward M. Blaiklock, "Derbe," *ZEB* 2:107–8.

Clyde E. Fant and Mitchell G. Reddish, "Derbe," in *A Guide to Biblical Sites in Greece and Turkey* (Oxford: Oxford University Press, 2003), 174–77.

21. So Stott, *Message of Acts*, 233.

10.5 PAUL AND BARNABAS RETURN TO SYRIAN ANTIOCH (ACTS 14:21–28)

Luke is very brief about the ministry of Paul and Barnabas in Derbe: "They preached the gospel in that city and won a large number of disciples" (Acts 14:21). Again, Luke uses the term "disciples" for those who receive the gospel. With Derbe located at the eastern edge of the Roman province of Galatia, to travel further east at that point would mean entering a district of client kingdoms in the region of Cilicia.[22] Instead, the missionaries decide to return back through the towns where they had already been.

This tel is the possible location of ancient Derbe.
Todd Bolen/ BiblePlaces.com

10.5.1 Doing Follow-Up as They Return (14:21–23)

Ministers sometimes refer to working with new believers as "follow-up ministry." When a person becomes a believer in Jesus, a lot of questions can arise about how this new faith commitment impacts the rest of their life and decisions. So, after their ministry in Derbe, Paul and Barnabas turn back to visit the believers in Lystra, Iconium, and Pisidian Antioch. In their follow-up endeavors, the missionaries invest themselves in "strengthening the disciples and encouraging them to remain true to the faith" (14:22). The Greek terms Luke uses for "strengthening" (*epistērizō*) and "encouraging" (*parakaleō*) are found elsewhere in Acts in relation to the establishment of new believers into church communities (e.g., "strengthening" in 15:41; 18:23; "encouraging" in 2:40; 8:31; 9:38; 11:23; 16:40; 20:1, 2; and both terms in 14:22; 15:32). The new believers are encouraged to remain faithful to the Lord and to courageously trust the Lord in the face of opposition from the culture around them (cf. 13:43, where the missionaries "urged them to continue in the grace of God").

22. Edward M. Blaiklock, "Derbe," *ZEB* 2:107.

Paul's Final Teaching on Persecution

2 Timothy 3:10–17

You, however, know all about my teaching, my way of life, my purpose, faith, patience, love, endurance, persecutions, sufferings—what kinds of things happened to me in Antioch, Iconium and Lystra, the persecutions I endured. Yet the Lord rescued me from all of them. In fact, everyone who wants to live a godly life in Christ Jesus will be persecuted, while evildoers and impostors will go from bad to worse, deceiving and being deceived. But as for you, continue in what you have learned and have become convinced of, because you know those from whom you learned it, and how from infancy you have known the Holy Scriptures, which are able to make you wise for salvation through faith in Christ Jesus. All Scripture is God-breathed and is useful for teaching, rebuking, correcting and training in righteousness, so that the servant of God may be thoroughly equipped for every good work.

Perga

- Located on the plain of Pamphylia about eight miles inland from the northern shore of the Mediterranean Sea and about five miles west of the River Cestrus (the modern Aksu River) near the town of Murtana in southern Turkey.
- One of a series of Pamphylian cities, and from it ran several important trade routes, including a northward route across the rugged terrain of the Taurus Mountains and the region of Pisidia and the westward route of the *Via Sebaste*, a paved Roman highway.
- Its substantial architectural remains—including aqueducts, a 12,000-seat theater, a stadium, Roman baths, and a gymnasium—evidence its prosperity.
- Known for its local goddess, sometimes identified with Artemis.
- On Paul's first missionary journey, he and Barnabas sailed here from Paphos on Cyprus, at which point John Mark deserted the missionary team (Acts 13:13).
- During their return leg of the first missionary journey, Paul and Barnabas came back and preached here (Acts 14:25).
- The ruins of Christian church buildings dating to the fourth century AD have been found at the site of Perga.

Select Bibliography

Edward M. Blaiklock, "Perga," *ZEB* 4:789–91.

Clyde E. Fant and Mitchell G. Reddish, "Perga," in *A Guide to Biblical Sites in Greece and Turkey* (Oxford: Oxford University Press, 2003), 264–73.

Philip A. Harland, "Perga," *EDB*, 1029.

This follow-up ministry encouraging faithfulness to Jesus includes a warning, which is important enough for Luke to cite on the lips of the missionaries: "We must go through many hardships to enter the kingdom of God" (14:22). This warning harkens back to Jesus's teachings on the cost of discipleship. Jesus indicated that following him would involve adjustments to one's view of possessions (e.g., Luke 9:57–58; 18:18–30), one's view of family (Luke 9:59–62; 12:49–53; 14:26), one's view of social status (e.g., Luke 18:15–17), and one's view of life itself (e.g., Luke 9:23–27; 14:25–35). Paul and Barnabas were concerned that the new believers be ready for facing hardships, which naturally comes with following Jesus.

Working with the new believers won during their missionary travels, Paul and Barnabas "appointed elders for them in each church and, with prayer and fasting, committed them to the Lord, in whom they had put their trust" (Acts 14:23). Luke has shown a lot of attention to the appointment of ministers in Acts (e.g., Matthias in Acts 1; the seven administrators in 6:1–6; the five prophets and teachers of Syrian Antioch in 13:1; the missionaries in 13:2–3; and now ***elders*** of the new churches of Galatia in 14:23). Clearly, God can use in fruitful ministry those who are willing to serve.

10.5.2 Returning to the Sending Church (14:24–26)

From Derbe, the missionaries had retraced their steps back through Lystra, Iconium, and Pisidian Antioch (14:21). Now they travel through Pisidia down to the coastal region of Pamphylia (14:24) where they preach the word in ***Perga*** (14:25) before going to the seaport city of ***Attalia*** from where they sail back to Syrian Antioch (14:26),

The seaport city of Attalia

whence they had begun their missionary endeavors. There is no mention of appointing elders in the new church communities in Cyprus; perhaps the missionaries had already done that work before they left the island. While Luke does not take up this question at this juncture, later on Paul and Barnabas do desire to check up on the Cyprian churches and make plans to visit them (see on 15:36–41 in chapter 11).

Noteworthy here is Luke's comment that the missionaries "had been committed to the grace of God for the work they had now completed" (14:26). This comment at the end of the missionary travels matches Luke's description of the Syrian Antioch church's committal of the missionaries at the beginning: the missionaries were called and "sent on their way by the Holy Spirit." (13:4). That is to say, this missionary endeavor was God's idea to begin with, so the church knew they could entrust the missionaries to God's gracious care. God never asks his people to do something he does not also make all the provisions for its success.

10.5.3 Closing Travel Summary Statement (14:27–28)

The comment in Acts 14:26 about Paul and Barnabas returning to Antioch after "the work they had now completed" subtly echoes the summary statement of the previous section of Acts (i.e., 12:24–25). Both passages have Paul and Barnabas returning to Antioch after "completing" (i.e., "fulfilling"; Greek: *plēroō*) a ministry work they had been sent out to do. Having already given a progress summary in the middle of narrating this missionary campaign—i.e., "The word of the Lord spread through the whole region" (13:49)—Luke now gives a travel summary at the end of this campaign as the missionaries return to their home church in Antioch. "On arriving there, they gathered the church together and reported all that God had done through them and how he had opened a door of faith to the Gentiles. And they stayed there a long time with the disciples" (14:27–28).

With God being credited for initiating the missionary outreach, so also the missionaries report that God is to be credited with doing the work on the mission. To be sure, they note that God had accomplished this work "through them" (14:27), but it was nonetheless God who has invited gentiles into faith in Jesus Christ. Then Luke simply reports that Paul and Barnabas remain with the disciples in Antioch for "a long time" (14:28). This sets up the readers for the next segment of the story of Acts.

10.6 CONCLUDING REMARKS

This section of the story of Acts focuses on what is commonly called Paul's first missionary journey. As Luke tells the story, he clearly has a historical concern to report on the growth of the gospel. This is all well and good, but Luke seems also to have a concern to influence his audience with more than mere historical data: Luke wants his audience to be participants in the story of the gospel's expansion. From the experiences of Paul and Barnabas on this first-century outreach, we can see patterns of ministry that helpfully apply to ministry today.

A ship mosaic found in church ruins dating to the Byzantine period. Beth Loya, Israel.
rontav/Shutterstock.com

A Reflective Summary on the First Missionary Journey

From Robert C. Tannehill, *The Narrative Unity of Luke-Acts: A Literary Interpretation*, 2 vols., FF (Minneapolis: Fortress, 1986/1990), 2:182.

> Acts 13–14 presents a representative picture of Paul's mission and includes many themes that we will encounter again. He preaches first in the Jewish synagogue but turns to Gentiles when the synagogue preaching is no longer possible. He announces the one God to Gentiles who have had no contact with Jewish monotheism. He repeatedly encounters persecution and moves on when necessary, but he does not abandon his mission. He works signs and wonders. He strengthens the new churches. In this mission Paul is fulfilling the Lord's prophecy that he would "bear my name before Gentiles, and kings and sons of Israel" and "must suffer for my name" (9:15–16).

Furthermore, it is instructive that the missionaries were not members of the original twelve apostles and yet God could use them in effective ministry. Paul and Barnabas can still be "sent ones" (the basic meaning of the word "apostle"; cf. 14:4, 14) and share the gospel. The Holy Spirit works within a person to witness about Christ in ways that coordinate with how God has designed that person. We don't have to pretend to be someone else in order to witness. While every Christian is called on to share the gospel message with others, we don't all have the personality and skills to do so as gifted evangelists. And that is OK. We can be ourselves and be used by God in ministry to spread the gospel.[23]

10.7 Key People, Places, and Terms

- Antioch near Pisidia
- Antioch of Syria
- Attalia
- Barnabas
- Cyprus
- Davidic Messiah
- Derbe
- dust-shaking gesture
- elders
- Elymas the sorcerer
- Iconium
- John Mark
- Lystra
- Paphos
- Perga
- Salamis
- Saul/Paul
- Seleucia
- Sergius Paulus
- synagogue
- Zeus and Hermes

10.8 Questions for Review and Discussion

1. Why does Paul prefer to preach the gospel first in Jewish synagogues when he can (see Acts 13:46; Gen 12:2–3; Rom 1:16; 2:9)?
2. What are the most notable differences between Paul's approaches to witnessing to Jewish and to gentile audiences?
3. What is the helpful pattern in Paul's approaches with different audiences that we should consider applying to how we share the gospel with different audiences?
4. In Luke's summary description of the first missionary campaign (Acts 14:27–28), what does he emphasize that might be prescriptive for how we think about missionary endeavors today?
5. When Paul and Barnabas travel back through the cities of Lystra, Iconium, and Pisidian Antioch, they are involved in "strengthening the disciples and encouraging them to remain true to the faith" (Acts 14:22). How significant is this part of their ministry?
6. To what extent might Luke's descriptions of various follow-up ministries in Acts be intended for Luke's audience to understand as prescriptive behavior?

23. Bruce Riley Ashford and Heath A. Thomas, *The Gospel of Our King: Bible, Worldview, and the Mission of Every Christian* (Grand Rapids: Baker Academic, 2019), 144–45.

10.9 Optional Assignments

1. **Text Reflection Project**—*Relating the concepts discussed in this chapter to another biblical text.* In this section of Acts, Luke portrays God as the one taking initiative to send out missionaries to spread the gospel message. Luke has shown divine initiative elsewhere in Acts as well. Make a list (with brief descriptions) of all the places in Acts (or perhaps in all of Luke-Acts!) where Luke comments on God instigating outreach to the lost.
2. **Interview Project**—*Inquiring of others their views concerning the concepts discussed in this chapter.* The story of the first missionary campaign makes clear that ministers can expect to face hardship and opposition to the gospel. In encouraging the new Christians along the way, Paul and Barnabas say, "We must go through many hardships to enter the kingdom of God" (Acts 14:22). Ask your pastor (or some other respected Christian leader) about their view of how well today's church faces hardships.
3. **Service-Learning Project**—*Applying the concepts discussed in this chapter in some form of service to others outside the class.* On the first missionary journey in Acts, John Mark accompanied Barnabas and Paul to serve as their helper (Acts 13:1, 5, 13). Look for a venue where you might be able to serve as a helper to other ministers. But be careful to have a realistic grasp about this ministry commitment so that you can finish the agreed upon time and avoid deserting the ministry prematurely (Acts 13:13; cf. 15:37–38).
4. **Prayer Project**—*Talking with God about the concepts discussed in this chapter.* Prayer and fasting are mentioned a couple of times in this section of Acts, especially in connection with important decisions (see Acts 13:3 and 14:23). Fasting is a short-term denying of oneself something good (like meals) to focus on something better (like prayer); the longing for the fasted item (like a rumbling stomach!) is a reminder to focus on the Lord. Skip a meal to spend more time praying about an important decision you have to make this week. Write a brief reflection on this experience.
5. **Testimony Project**—*Telling others about the concepts discussed in this chapter.* In this section of Acts, Paul takes two approaches to talking with people about the gospel: one with people familiar with Scripture (i.e., in the Jewish synagogue of Pisidian Antioch; Acts 13:16–41) and another with people less familiar with Scripture (i.e., in the city of Lystra; Acts 14:15–18). Without changing the content of the gospel message itself, how might you adjust your approach to sharing the gospel when talking to different kinds of audiences? Think of two different audiences who need to hear the gospel, and write out different explanations of the gospel fitting to those two audiences.

10.10 Bibliography for Going Further

10.10.1 The Life and Ministry of Paul

Bruce, F. F. *Paul: Apostle of the Heart Set Free.* Grand Rapids: Eerdmans, 1977.

Jervell, Jacob. *The Unknown Paul: Essays on Luke-Acts and Early Christian History.* Minneapolis: Augsburg, 1984.

Lentz, John Clayton, Jr. *Luke's Portrait of Paul*. SNTSMS 77. Cambridge: Cambridge University Press, 1993.
Marguerat, Daniel. *Paul in Acts and Paul in His Letters*. Tübingen: Mohr Siebeck, 2013.
Mount, Christopher N. *Pauline Christianity: Luke-Acts and the Legacy of Paul*. NovTSup 104. Leiden: Brill, 2002.
Phillips, Thomas E. *Paul, His Letters, and Acts*. Library of Pauline Studies. Peabody, MA: Hendrickson, 2009.
Porter, Stanley E. *The Paul of Acts: Essays in Literary Criticism, Rhetoric, and Theology*. Tübingen: Mohr Siebeck, 1999. Repr., *Paul in Acts*. Library of Pauline Studies. Peabody, MA: Hendrickson, 2001.
Rosenblatt, Marie-Eloise. *Paul the Accused: His Portrait in the Acts of the Apostles*. Zacchaeus Studies. Collegeville, MN: Liturgical, 1995.
Schnabel, Eckhard J. *Paul the Missionary: Realities, Strategies and Methods*. Downers Grove, IL: InterVarsity Press, 2008.
Spell, David. *Peter and Paul in Acts: A Comparison of Their Ministries*. Eugene, OR: Wipf & Stock, 2006.

10.10.2 Paul's First Missionary Journey

Béchard, Dean Phillip. *Paul Outside the Walls: A Study of Luke's Socio-Geographical Universalism in Acts 14:8–20*. AnBib 143. Rome: Pontifical Biblical Institute, 2000.
Fournier, Marianne. *The Episode at Lystra: A Rhetorical and Semiotic Analysis of Acts 14:7–20a*. New York: Lang, 1997.
Greenway, Roger S. "Success in the City: Paul's Urban Mission Strategy: Acts 14:1–28." Pages 183–95 in *Mission in Acts: Ancient Narratives in Contemporary Context*. Edited by Robert L. Gallagher and Paul Hertig. ASMS 34. Maryknoll: Orbis, 2004.
Morgan-Wynne, John Eifion. *Paul's Pisidian Antioch Speech (Acts 13)*. Eugene, OR: Pickwick, 2014.
Nelson, Edwin S. *Paul's First Missionary Journey as Paradigm: A Literary-Critical Assessment of Acts 13, 14*. Boston: Boston University Press, 1984.
Pillai, C. A. Joachim. *Early Mission Preaching: A Study of Luke's Report in Acts 13*. Hicksville, NY: Exposition, 1979.
Rieser, Rainer. *Paul's Early Period: Chronology, Mission Strategy, Theology*. Translated by Douglas W. Stott. Grand Rapids: Eerdmans, 1998.
White, Jefferson. "The First Journey (47–49 AD)." Pages 9–17 (chapter 1) in *Evidence & Paul's Journeys: An Historical Investigation into the Travels of the Apostle Paul*. Hilliard, OH: Parsagard, 2001.
Wilson, Mark W. "The Route of Paul's First Journey to Pisidian Antioch." *NTS* 55.4 (2009): 471–83.
Zhang, Wenxi. *Paul among Jews: A Study of the Meaning and Significance of Paul's Inaugural Sermon in the Synagogue of Antioch in Pisidia (Acts 13:16–41) for His Missionary Work among the Jews*. Eugene, OR: Wipf & Stock, 2011.

Renáta Sedmáková/stock.adobe.com

Chapter Goals

After reading this chapter, you should be able to:

- Recognize the significance of the Jew-gentile issue faced at the Jerusalem Council.
- Outline the approach the Jerusalem Council took to address the Jew-gentile controversy.
- Offer an explanation for the church's use of the Hebrew Scriptures to address the Jew-gentile question of the first century.
- Draw out from Luke's description of the Jerusalem Council and the apostolic decree the principles he intends to be prescriptive in the life of the church today.
- Extract from observing the resolution of matters at the Jerusalem Council some prescriptive guidelines for how Christians can have more productive disagreements and work toward better solutions.

Chapter Overview

11.1 The Issue (Acts 15:1–4)
11.2 The Jerusalem Council Proceedings (Acts 15:5–21)
11.3 The Letter with the Apostolic Decree (Acts 15:22–35)
11.4 Concluding Remarks
11.5 Key People, Places, and Terms
11.6 Questions for Review and Discussion
11.7 Optional Assignments
11.8 Bibliography for Going Further

Key Verses

The apostles and elders met to consider this question. After much discussion, Peter got up and addressed them: "Brothers, you know that some time ago God made a choice among you that the Gentiles might hear from my lips the message of the gospel and believe. God, who knows the heart, showed that he accepted them by giving the Holy Spirit to them, just as he did to us. He did not discriminate between us and them, for he purified their hearts by faith. Now then, why do you try to test God by putting on the necks of Gentiles a yoke that neither we nor our ancestors have been able to bear? No! We believe it is through the grace of our Lord Jesus that we are saved, just as they are." (Acts 15:6–11)

It is my judgment, therefore, that we should not make it difficult for the Gentiles who are turning to God. Instead we should write to them, telling them to abstain from food polluted by idols, from sexual immorality, from the meat of strangled animals and from blood. For the law of Moses has been preached in every city from the earliest times and is read in the synagogues on every Sabbath. (Acts 15:19–21)

Summary Statement

But Paul and Barnabas remained in Antioch, where they and many others taught and preached the word of the Lord. (Acts 15:35)

INTRODUCTION

The second section in the second half of Acts recounts a significant meeting in Jerusalem to discuss the legitimacy of the gentile mission. The two primary questions about reaching out to gentiles with the gospel had persisted: (a) what does it take for gentiles to become followers of Jesus and (b) how are Jews and gentiles to interact in the church? So Luke recounts in Acts 15 a meeting of church leaders to discuss, and to reach final conclusions on, these matters.

In the two thousand years of church history, there have been over twenty ***church councils***, i.e., international meetings of church leaders to address problematic issues. While some of the councils dealt with governance matters, one of the primary significances of these gatherings was to clarify proper understandings of scriptural teaching and to sort out matters of practice for the church. Of the many such councils, the first seven gatherings between AD 325 and AD 787 are often referred to as "ecumenical councils" because all branches of Christianity recognize them today in some way or another, whether Catholic, Protestant, or Orthodox. In the opening centuries of the church's history, some of Christianity's most difficult questions regarding the nature of Christ and the salvation he provides were addressed in council meetings.[1]

1. See esp. Justin S. Holcomb, *Know the Creeds and Councils*, Know Series (Grand Rapids: Zondervan, 2014).

Curiously, the meeting of the early church leaders in Jerusalem recorded in Acts 15 is rarely included in lists of official church councils. This exclusion is not because the so-called Jerusalem Council was unimportant; rather, it is more likely because it took place when the church was so new that it hardly seemed organized and widespread enough to be able to conduct an ecumenical council (as evidenced by many of the later councils being convened by ruling emperors). Nonetheless, like the ecumenical councils, the Jerusalem meeting of Acts 15 covered a significant doctrinal matter in the crucial early years of the church and discussed its pragmatic implications for believers.

Scholars comment on the importance of the ***Jerusalem Council*** in the story of Acts. Marshall suggests that Luke's account of the Jerusalem Council forms the theological center as well as the structural center of the book of Acts.[2] Similarly, Witherington proposes that Acts 15 "is the most crucial chapter in the whole book."[3] The Jerusalem Council was successful in addressing the questions of gentile salvation and involvement in the church, and in the rest of Acts the gospel continues to flourish in gentile territory borne by the increasing number of Christian witnesses.

11.1 THE ISSUE (ACTS 15:1–4)

Questions about gentiles following the Jewish Messiah Jesus had already come up earlier in the life of the fledgling church, especially about the reception of the gospel by Samaritans (Acts 8) and the God-fearing gentile Cornelius and his family (Acts 10). Since that time, the gospel had spread among gentiles in Syrian Antioch (Acts 11:19–21), which had led to some investigative follow-up from the church in Jerusalem (11:22)—and the multicultural church in Antioch appears to have exhibited all the signs of a healthy and faithful church (11:23–30; 13:1–3). But now that Paul and Barnabas have returned from successfully bringing the gospel to both Jews and gentiles on Cyprus and in Asia Minor (Acts 13–14), questions about gentile salvation and church involvement arise again, and the discussion escalates to the point of inviting a more definitive and official response.[4]

Paul speaking to the Jerusalem Council
Renáta Sedmáková/stock.adobe.com

2. I. Howard Marshall, *The Acts of the Apostles: An Introduction and Commentary*, TNTC (Grand Rapids: Eerdmans, 1980), 242.

3. Ben Witherington III, *The Acts of the Apostles: A Socio-Rhetorical Commentary* (Grand Rapids: Eerdmans, 1998; Carlisle: Paternoster, 1998), 439.

4. So also John A. Wood, "The Ethics of the Jerusalem Council," pp. 239–58 in *With Steadfast Purpose: Essays on Acts in Honor of Henry Jackson Flanders, Jr.*, ed. Naymond H. Keathley (Waco: Baylor University Press, 1990), 256.

11.1.1 The Catalyst—Judaizers Preaching Jewish Proselyte Christianity (15:1)

As Luke reports it, "certain people came down from Judea" and show up in ***Antioch of Syria*** teaching that gentiles must become Jews to have Jesus as their Messiah. He offers a summary of their teaching: "Unless you are circumcised, according to the custom taught by Moses, you cannot be saved" (15:1). These people were teaching that gentiles had to become converts to Judaism before coming to faith in Christ in order to benefit from God's provision of salvation. While not used in Acts 15, the term for ***proselytes*** (Greek: *prosēlytos*) is sometimes used in the New Testament of gentiles who converted from some other religion to Judaism (2:11; 6:5; cf. Matt 23:15; Acts 13:43). As evidenced in the Scriptures, converting to Judaism meant ascribing to the teachings and practices of OT Israel, including circumcision (e.g., Exod 12:48–49), and thus gentiles could be accepted into Israel as those under God's protection (e.g., Ps 146:9; Ezek 14:7; Zech 7:9–10; Mal 3:5).[5] Gentiles who wanted to worship the God of Israel without fully converting to Judaism were sometimes dubbed "God-fearers" (e.g., Cornelius in Acts 10:1–2, 22; cf. 13:16, 26, 50; 17:4, 17; 18:7).[6]

It is noteworthy that the people coming down from Judea and encouraging gentiles to become Jews were themselves Christians. Luke does not indicate that these people were preaching against Jesus; rather, they were teaching that the Jewish Messiah Jesus came to be Savior of the Jews and anyone desiring to be saved by Jesus should likewise become a Jew.[7] While Luke does not call these ethnocentric believers ***Judaizers***, this label is derived from a remark Paul makes in Galatians 2:14 about Christians who insisted that all followers of Jesus "judaize" (Greek: *Ioudaizein*), i.e., live as Jews in accordance with Jewish customs. While Galatians 2:14 is the only NT occurrence of the term "judaize," ("to follow Jewish customs" in NIV; "to live like Jews" in CEV, CSB, ESV, NASB, NET) its use there makes *Judaizers* a common label among scholars for referring to those insisting that all believers live in accordance with Jewish customs (a.k.a., "the circumcision group" in Acts 11:2; Gal 2:12; Titus 1:10).[8]

---

5. For more detail on the term "proselyte," its nuanced usages in the OT, and its change in meaning in the NT era and beyond, see Charles L. Feinberg, "Proselyte," *ZEB* 4:1030–37. Witherington offers a brief and helpful discussion on the NT uses of "proselyte" and "God-fearer" as nontechnical terms; Witherington, *Acts*, 341–44.

6. On this use of "God-fearers" in the NT in distinction from "proselytes," see the brief discussion in chapter 9 and, more extensively, Scot McKnight, "Proselytism and Godfearers," *DNTB*, 835–47.

7. As noted in chapter 10 in the discussion of Acts 13:46, such believers were correct to emphasize that God's salvation comes "only *from* the Jews" (as Jesus himself had said in John 4:22, emphasis added; cf. Acts 4:12), but they were incorrect to claim that God's salvation is "only *for* the Jews."

8. See William S. Campbell, "Judaizers," *DPL*, 512–16. For more on circumcision in first-century Judaism and its discussion by early Christians, see Matthew Thiessen, *Contesting Conversion: Genealogy, Circumcision, and Identity in Ancient Judaism and Christianity* (New York: Oxford University Press, 2011); idem, *Paul and the Gentile Problem* (New York: Oxford University Press, 2016); and more briefly idem, "Circumcision" and "Conversion and Proselytism," in *T&T Clark Encyclopedia of Second Temple Judaism*, ed. Daniel M. Gurtner and Loren T. Stuckenbruck, 2 vols. (New York: Bloomsbury T&T Clark, 2020), 2:146–48 and 2:163–64, respectively.

The Controversy about Circumcision as a Symbol of Faith

From Gary E. Farley, "Circumcision," *ZEB* 1:905-906.

Among the Jews circumcision was a mark of distinction. The uncircumcised were viewed with contempt. This ethnocentric attitude lay behind the controversy about circumcision in the early church. This ethnocentrism also blinded many to the real meaning of the rite. It became a form of external religious practice lacking spiritual content. As such it was condemned by the prophets. Jeremiah attempted to get at its real meaning by the concept of a circumcised heart (Jer. 4:4, alluding to Deut. 10:16; 30:6). Jeremiah's contemporaries believed that God was on their side. Not so, cried Jeremiah. Religion must be internalized. Symbols must not be emptied of their meaning and allowed to stand alone. Circumcision was meant to symbolize a commitment of oneself to God's will forever. It is an outward sign of a heart, the inner core of one's personality, dedicated to doing the will of God. Paul picks up this train of thought in Rom. 4:9-13, where he contends that circumcision is not the cause of God's promise to Abraham, rather it is an act of faith symbolizing Abraham's confidence in God's ability to do what he has promised. . . .

The first generation of Christians were Jews. In general, they continued to frequent the synagogues and temple (Acts 5:42; 6:7). They saw themselves as a reform movement within Judaism, not a new religion. The central issue in the early chapters of Acts is whether or not Jesus was the Messiah. . . .

However, as converts among the Gentiles began to multiply, a great controversy arose. Essentially the issue was this: since circumcision is the mark of the people of the covenant, and since Christ brought and is bringing the fulfillment of the covenant promises, is it not necessary for one to be circumcised (be a proselyte Jew) to participate in these promises? Or phrased another way: Does one need to become a Jew before he can be a follower of Christ? At Jerusalem a "circumcision party" was formed. Countering this group were Paul and his followers.

This controversy led to the first church council, an account of which is given in Acts 15. . . . Here Paul won the support of the church leaders. Circumcision was dropped as a prerequisite for being recognized as a member of the Christian fellowship. The only requirements were a turning from pagan worship and refraining from immorality (Acts 15:19-21).

11.1.2 The Conflict—Dispute with Paul and Barnabas (15:2a)

With years of productive gospel ministry among gentiles, Paul and Barnabas take strong issue with the Judaizers who have come to Antioch. The NIV has "sharp dispute and debate" where Luke utilizes a litote (i.e., a figure of speech that negates the smallness of a thing to emphasize its largeness): "no small dissension and debate"

(15:2 ESV).[9] Questions about gentile inclusion were not small matters for Paul and Barnabas, they were significant matters.

As noted, Paul's letter to the Galatians treats the topic of Christian Jew-gentile expectations. If the "certain people [coming] down from Judea" (Acts 15:1) are to be understood as the same as the "certain men . . . from James" (Gal 2:12), then it is interesting that Luke does not give more detail on Barnabas's behavior. In his letter to the Galatians, Paul notes that Barnabas (along with Peter) had been temporarily distracted into withdrawing from proper fellowship with the gentile Christians (Gal 2:11–13). Luke says nothing of this, but neither does he deny that Barnabas had this failing. Paul writes as if his confrontation of Peter and the rest was effective in restoring right thinking and behavior (Gal 2:14–21). So rather than be distracted by the details of Barnabas's temporary weakness, Luke simply moves the story along in the light of Barnabas's restoration.

11.1.3 The Proposal—Discussion with the Apostles and Elders in Jerusalem (15:2b–4)

Phoenician perfume flask (ca. 800-600 BC). A.D. Riddle/ BiblePlaces.com

Reminiscent of the Jerusalem church acting as a community to address their culture-induced food distribution problem (Acts 6:1–6), the Antioch church here acts as a community to address their culture-induced fellowship problem. They appoint ***Paul*** and ***Barnabas***, "along with some other believers," to go up to Jerusalem to discuss this matter with the apostles and elders (15:2b). Even in his report of the representatives' trip to Jerusalem, Luke hints at the outcome. He specifies that they travel through the gentile territory of Phoenicia and the less-than-Jewish region of Samaria, reporting "how the Gentiles had been converted" and that this news was received with rejoicing by "all the believers" (15:3). Whatever the results of the meeting in Jerusalem will be, Luke unabashedly pictures gentile inclusion in Christian faith as a good thing.

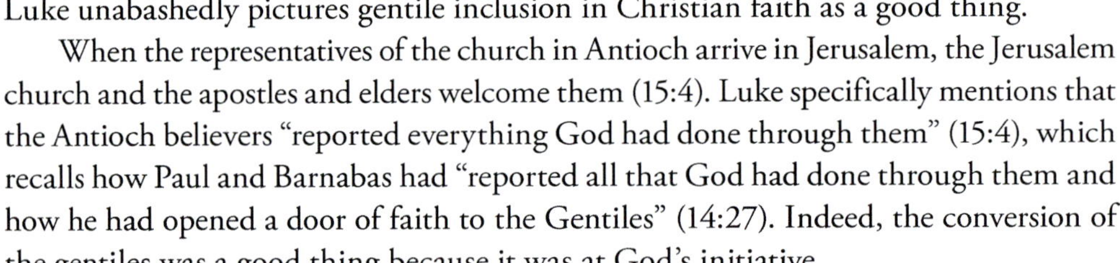

When the representatives of the church in Antioch arrive in Jerusalem, the Jerusalem church and the apostles and elders welcome them (15:4). Luke specifically mentions that the Antioch believers "reported everything God had done through them" (15:4), which recalls how Paul and Barnabas had "reported all that God had done through them and how he had opened a door of faith to the Gentiles" (14:27). Indeed, the conversion of the gentiles was a good thing because it was at God's initiative.

11.1.4 The Coordination with the Letter to the Galatians

As mentioned, it is commonplace to discuss the events of Acts 15 in coordination with Paul's letter to the Galatians.[10] Even a surface reading of Galatians reveals that it

9. While not always specifically rendered in English translations, Luke utilizes litotes in Acts 12:18; 14:28; 15:2; 17:4, 12; 19:23, 24; and 27:20. See footnote 24 in chapter 9.

10. For a chart suggesting where all of Paul's letters might fit into the narrative of Acts, see "A Chronology of Important NT Events in Acts and Their Historical Context" in chapter 5.

treats the subject of how much Jewish culture gentile Christians are required to adopt. Both Paul in Galatians and the Jerusalem Council in Acts 15 conclude that people don't need to be Jewish to follow Jesus. This conclusion is no surprise to the reader of Acts who has already seen the decisive story of gentile conversions in Acts 10 and read the conclusion in Acts 11:18: "So then, even to Gentiles God has granted repentance that leads to life." But the Jerusalem Council both firms up this observation and spells out some details regarding how this is to be lived out. And what Acts 15 spells out in narrative literature, Paul's letter to the Galatians spells out in didactic literature.

In Galatians 1–2 Paul describes taking no more than two trips to Jerusalem after his Damascus road conversion experience (Gal 1:11–17 ≈ Acts 9:1–22) and before writing to the Galatians. Because Acts describes Paul taking no less than five postconversion trips to Jerusalem, scholars discuss how these might coordinate with the record of Galatians.[11] There is general agreement about the identity of Paul's first postconversion trip (Gal 1:18–24 ≈ Acts 9:23–30), but the second journey—described in Galatians 2:1–10—has been the subject of much debate. Among various theories, the two biggest contenders for matching Paul's second postconversion trip in Galatians with the material in Acts are the trips described in Acts 11:27–30 and 12:25 (a.k.a. "the famine visit") and in Acts 15:1–35 (a.k.a. "the Jerusalem Council visit"). Assessment of the evidence in Acts and Galatians pertaining to this issue—i.e., whether Galatians 2 ≈ Acts 11 or Galatians 2 ≈ Acts 15 (see sidebar)—leads many to identify the trip in Galatians 2:1–10 with the famine visit trip of Acts 11:27–30 and 12:25.[12]

The conclusion that Paul's Jerusalem trips in Galatians 1 and 2 are equivalent to the trips in Acts 9 and 11, respectively, says nothing about further trips after the writing of Galatians. At the time of his writing to the Galatians, Paul had made only two postconversion trips to Jerusalem, but he could have intended more. Indeed, the "certain people [coming] down from Judea" (Acts 15:1) can be understood as the same as the "certain men . . . from James" (Gal 2:12), with Paul writing Galatians at Acts 15:2 just prior to his third trip to Jerusalem, the Jerusalem Council visit. Notice also that, if the letter to the Galatians was written after the Jerusalem Council, it is particularly odd that Paul does not mention the conclusion of the Jerusalem Council, the "apostolic decree," which would support his argument in Galatians. Thus, the suggestion that Galatians was written on the eve of the Jerusalem Council fits the evidence and respects the historical narrations of both Paul and Luke as accurate.[13]

---

11. Paul's five post-conversion trips to Jerusalem in Acts are: (1) his return from Damascus; Acts 9:26–30; (2) the famine visit; Acts 11:27–30; 12:25; (3) the Jerusalem Council visit; Acts 15:1–35; (4) at the end of his second missionary journey; Acts 18:22; and (5) at the end of his third missionary journey; Acts 21:15–19.

12. For a brief survey of issues involved in integrating Paul's letters with Acts, see Paul Trebilco, "Itineraries, Travel Plans, Journey, Apostolic Parousia," *DPL*, 446–56, esp. pp. 451–55 on coordinating the Galatians/Acts trips.

13. The phrase "the eve of the Jerusalem meeting" is from F. F. Bruce, "Galatian Problems 4: The Date of the Epistle," *BJRL* 54 (1972): 266; idem, *The Epistle to the Galatians*, NIGTC (Grand Rapids: Eerdmans, 1982), 55.

Paul's Jerusalem Trip in Galatians 2 and the Evidence in Acts

A majority of NT scholars suggest that Gal 2:1–10 ≈ Acts 15:1–35 (a.k.a. "the Jerusalem Council visit"), but a growing number argue that Gal 2:1–10 ≈ Acts 11:27–30 and 12:25 (a.k.a. "the famine visit"). The assessment of the evidence portrayed in the following chart—with ↔ showing matching evidence and ⇎ showing mismatching evidence—demonstrates that it might be best to identify Galatians 2:1–10 with Acts 11:27–30 and 12:25.

Acts 11:27–30 and 12:25		Galatians 2:1–10		Acts 15:1–35
Not described as being chiefly about the Jew-gentile issue.	⇎	Clearly described as dealing with the Jew-gentile issue.	↔	Clearly described as dealing with the Jew-gentile issue.
Begins with visitors from Jerusalem to Antioch.	↔	Begins with visitors from Jerusalem to Antioch.	↔	Begins with visitors from Jerusalem to Antioch.
Paul's second Jerusalem visit in the story of Acts.	↔	Paul's second Jerusalem visit in the account of Galatians.	⇎	Paul's third Jerusalem visit in the story of Acts.
Described as a private meeting.	↔	Described as a private meeting.	⇎	Described as a public meeting.
Paul goes in response to an explicit prophecy.	↔	Paul goes "in response to a revelation."	⇎	Paul goes as appointed by the Antioch church.
Near Peter's struggle with gentile belief (Acts 10–11).	↔	Evidences Peter's struggle with gentile belief (2:11–21).	⇎	Shows Peter expressly defend acceptance of gentile belief.
Primarily about famine relief for the poor.	↔	Ends expecting Paul to "continue to remember the poor."	⇎	Ends with a letter of expectations for the gentiles.

Special Studies Arguing for Gal 2:1–10 ≈ Acts 11:27–30 and 12:25

Richard J. Bauckham, "James, Peter, and the Gentiles," pp. 91–142 in *The Missions of James, Peter, and Paul: Tensions in Early Christianity*, ed. Bruce D. Chilton and Craig A. Evans, NovTSup 115 (Leiden: Brill, 2005), 135–39.

Colin J. Hemer, "Galatia and Galatians," (chapter 7) in *The Book of Acts in the Setting of Hellenistic History*, ed. Conrad H. Gempf, WUNT 49 (Tübingen: Mohr Siebeck, 1989; repr., Winona Lake, IN: Eisenbrauns, 1990), 277–307.

Robert G. Hoerber, "Galatians 2:1–10 and the Acts of the Apostles," *CTM* 31.8 (1960): 482–91.

Wilfred L. Knox, *The Acts of the Apostles* (Cambridge: University of Cambridge Press, 1948), 40–53.

Joe Morgado Jr., "Paul in Jerusalem: A Comparison of His Visits in Acts and Galatians," *JETS* 37.1 (1994): 55–68.

Eckhard J. Schnabel, *Early Christian Mission*, 2 vols. (Downers Grove, IL: InterVarsity Press, 2004), 2:987–1006.

Paul Trebilco, "Itineraries, Travel Plans, Journey, Apostolic Parousia," *DPL*, 446–56, esp. pp. 451–55.

David Wenham, "Acts and the Pauline Corpus, II: The Evidence of Parallels," in *The Book of Acts in its Ancient Literary Setting*, ed. Bruce W. Winter and Andrew D. Clarke, BAFCS 1 (Grand Rapids: Eerdmans, 1993; Carlisle: Paternoster, 1993), 226–43.

Special Studies Arguing for Gal 2:1–10 ≈ Acts 15:1–35

James D. G. Dunn, *Beginning from Jerusalem*, Christianity in the Making 2 (Grand Rapids: Eerdmans, 2009), 446–69.

Russell Lester, "Galatians 2:1-10 and Acts: An Old Problem Revisited," in *With Steadfast Purpose: Essays on Acts in Honor of Henry Jackson Flanders, Jr.*, ed. Naymond H. Keathley (Waco: Baylor University Press, 1990), 217–38.

Robert H. Stein, "Jerusalem," *DPL*, 463–74, esp. pp. 465–68.

11.2 THE JERUSALEM COUNCIL PROCEEDINGS (ACTS 15:5–21)

Having briefly introduced the Jew-gentile issue as the subject of this segment of the story of Acts, Luke invests the bulk of the episode discussing the proceedings of the Jerusalem Council convened to address the matter. Luke's account of the proceedings portrays several interested parties making contributions to the discussion and then James, the brother of Jesus, wrapping up the meeting with reflections on Scripture and a recommended course of action.

11.2.1 THE JUDAIZERS STATE THEIR POSITION (15:5)

After the representatives of the Antioch church are welcomed to Jerusalem and report on what God has been doing among the gentiles, the Judaizers present their opinion on what should be required of gentile believers in Jesus. While Luke does not call these people "Judaizers," here in Jerusalem he notes that it is "some of the believers who belonged to the party of the Pharisees" (Acts 15:5). First-century Judaism had a variety of Pharisaic groups, but on the whole the general populace highly respected them as people devoted to the Scriptures; they were associated with the local synagogues, and their strictness was often marked with added human traditions to protect against accidentally transgressing scriptural guidelines.[14] It is no surprise, then, to find Judaizers in the party of the ***Pharisees.*** And in spelling out the Judaizers' strict opinion on gentile involvement in the church, Luke had earlier mentioned that they viewed ***circumcision*** as a necessary condition for salvation. Now he offers more detail heightening their view by reporting it (again) on the lips of the Judaizers themselves: "The Gentiles must be circumcised and required to keep the law of Moses" (15:5; cf. v. 1).

11.2.2 THE APOSTLES AND ELDERS CONVENE THE MEETING (15:6)

After hearing the Judaizers' opinion about requiring gentile believers to live like Jews, Luke offers the briefest of descriptions about what happened next: "The apostles

14. For more on the Pharisees, see the discussion in chapter 5.

and elders met to consider this question" (15:6) We know the twelve apostles were significant authorities in the community of believers (Acts 1), and Luke has already described the expansion of church leadership in Jerusalem beyond that of the apostles (Acts 6:1–6). Furthermore, given that first-century Jewish society operated with leaders referred to as ***elders*** (Greek: *presbuteros*; cf. 4:5, 8, 23; 6:12; 23:14; 24:1; 25:15; cf. 22:5), it made sense for the new church made up of Jewish believers in Jesus to operate in a similar fashion.[15] Indeed, the Antioch church had previously sent Paul and Barnabas as their emissaries to the elders of the Jerusalem church with famine relief aid (11:30), and Luke has provided a glimpse of apostles and elders working together in the leadership of the Jerusalem church when Peter asked that James, the brother of Jesus, be informed about his release from prison (12:17). As it turns out, the apostle Peter and the elder James have important roles in the Jerusalem Council.

With Paul and Barnabas and "some other believers" from Antioch (15:2), some of the believers from the party of the Pharisees (15:5), and the apostles and elders (15:6) meeting together, the Jerusalem Council appears to have been a sizable group (contra the Jerusalem visit of Galatians 2 that was held "privately," and thus seeming to fit the visit of Acts 11:30; cf. Gal 2:2). That the Jerusalem Council was a larger public meeting inclusive of the whole Jerusalem church becomes clear in Acts 15:22, where a decision is reached by "the apostles and elders, with the whole church" (cf. "whole assembly" in 15:12).

The Church of the Holy Sepulchre, dating from the fourth century, is located in the Christian Quarter of Jerusalem.

15. For more on elders in the NT, see Donald M. Lake, "Elder (NT)," *ZEB* 2:290–91; Roger T. Beckwith, *Elders in Every City: The Origin and Role of the Ordained Ministry* (Carlisle: Paternoster, 2003); and Benjamin L. Merkle, *The Elder and Overseer: One Office in the Early Church*, StBibLit 57 (New York: Lang, 2003).

11.2.3 Peter Testifies Regarding His Experience (15:7–11)

We are not told how long the Jerusalem Council meeting lasted; Luke simply indicates that there was "much discussion" (15:7). Peter then stands up to address the group in what turns out to be his last appearance in the story of Acts; and notably it is largely a rehearsal of his experience in a previous episode. Peter refers to the time when God had selected him to preach the gospel to gentiles, which Luke's readers immediately recall as the Cornelius episode of Acts 10:1–48. Peter's comment that "you know" about this prior event (15:7) harkens back to Acts 11:1–18, when he gave an account of the ***Cornelius*** episode to the Jerusalem church. As before, Peter continues to credit God with the inclusion of gentiles, offering as proof that God granted the Holy Spirit to gentile believers "just as he did to us" (15:8; cf. 10:44, 47; 11:15, 17). Peter's conclusion on God's salvation of the gentiles is: "He did not discriminate between us and them, for he purified their hearts by faith" (15:9).

After reflecting on the clarity of God's intention to include gentiles in the faith, Peter now switches to the issue of how the church is to behave going forward. He asks a sharp question: "Now then, why do you try to test God by putting on the necks of gentiles a yoke that neither we nor our ancestors have been able to bear?" (15:10). The phrase "why do you try to test God" may well recall for the Jerusalem church the time Peter had asked a similar question of Sapphira: "How could you conspire to test the Spirit of the Lord," a question followed by the Lord's sobering and swift act of punishment (5:9–11). Peter's final statement is an emphatic answer to his own question: "No! We believe it is through the grace of our Lord Jesus that we are saved, just as they are" (15:11). Answering one's own question in an argument was a known rhetorical device in ancient presentations and is a common feature in Paul's writing, especially on this topic (e.g., Gal 3:19; Rom 3:1–30; 6:1–4, 15–18; 7:7, 13; cf. Rom 8:31–39; 9:14).[16] In comparing Jewish and gentile salvation experiences, Peter's comment contains another rhetorical turn of phrase in that he appears to put the gentiles in the position of the standard to be measured against: "we are saved, just as they are."[17] Readers of Acts know Peter had himself struggled to accept this conclusion (see esp. Acts 10:9–16), and Paul indicates that Peter had struggled with applying this lesson to life (see Gal 2:11–13). But by the time of the Jerusalem Council, Peter is confirmed in his conviction that gentiles need not become full-fledged Jews to be considered full-fledged members of the church.[18]

16. See R. Dean Anderson Jr., *Glossary of Greek Rhetorical Terms Connected to Methods of Argumentation, Figures and Tropes from Anaximenes to Quintilian*, CBET 24 (Leuven: Peeters, 2000), 14, 33, 51.

17. On the rhetoric of Peter's comment, see Craig S. Keener, *Acts: An Exegetical Commentary*, 4 vols. (Grand Rapids: Baker Academic, 2012–2015), 3:2238.

18. If Paul's visit to Jerusalem recounted in Gal 2:1–10 is equated with the Jerusalem Council visit of Acts 15:1–35 (rather than the famine visit of Acts 11:30 as argued here), then the behavior of Peter (and Barnabas) relapsing against full fellowship with gentile believers (Gal 2:11–13) puts them at odds with the conclusion they had defended at the Jerusalem Council. The scenario sketched previously arguably makes better sense of all the data.

11.2.4 Barnabas and Paul Testify Regarding Their Experience (15:12)

After Peter's declaration, the large crowd falls silent and is listening to Barnabas and Paul reporting on their missionary travels in Cyprus and Asia Minor. Earlier Luke had explicitly stated that the Lord "confirmed the message of his grace by enabling them [Paul and Barnabas] to perform miraculous signs and wonders" (Acts 14:3), and now in Acts 15:12, describing their report at the Jerusalem Council, Luke uses the same two terms—"signs and wonders"—perhaps to stress the authenticating role of those supernatural events as confirmation of the need to fully include the gentiles. The reader already knows the position of Paul and Barnabas on the question at hand, and Luke does not recount their words; nonetheless, he mentions that they report on their experiences to those in Jerusalem.[19] Even as Peter's remarks were about his experience of God's direction and work through his ministry, so also Barnabas and Paul appear to focus on their experience of God's work "through them" (15:12).

11.2.5 James Calls Their Attention to Scripture (15:13–18)

When Barnabas and Paul finish their report, James speaks up. We had last heard about this half-brother of Jesus in Acts 12:17, where he already seems to have a position of leadership in the Jerusalem church. Though he was initially among Jesus's skeptical family members (Mark 3:21; John 7:5), a personal visit from the resurrected Lord (1 Cor 15:7) may well have secured his faith in Jesus as the Messiah. He had a reputation for living by Scripture—a reputation that earns him the nickname "***James the Just***" (see sidebar)—and was already the author of the earliest of the NT letters (Jas 1:1; ca. AD 44–48).[20] Scot McKnight notes that the style of James's speech in Acts 15 matches the style of the NT epistle of James (see sidebar).[21] It is not surprising that the Scripture-oriented James the Just moves the Council discussion from its focus on experiencing God's work in history to listening to God's word in Scripture.

With an appeal for the crowd to listen to him (15:13), James refers to Peter's experience with gentile conversions—and by implication, that of Barnabas and Paul as well—as God's caring intervention in the life of the church (15:14) and something Scripture had already anticipated: "The words of the prophets are in agreement with this" (15:15). Indeed, God's intention to include the gentiles (or "nations") in his people

---

19. On Luke's de-emphasis of Paul's part in the final decision of the Jerusalem Council, see Conrad Gempf, "Luke's Story of Paul's Reception in Rome," in *Rome in the Bible and the Early Church*, ed. Peter Oakes (Grand Rapids: Baker, 2002), 45.

20. Regarding the dating of the NT letter of James, see the brief discussion of Wilber T. Dayton, "James, Epistle of," *ZEB* 3:456–63, esp. p. 459; for a longer discussion favoring an early date, see Luke Timothy Johnson, *The Letter of James*, AB (New York: Doubleday, 1995), 118–21.

21. Scot McKnight, *The Letter of James*, NICNT (Grand Rapids: Eerdmans, 2011), 24.

Hegesippus (ca. AD 110–180) on "James the Just"

(quoted by Eusebius, *Hist. eccl.* 2.23.3–18, ca. AD 323)

The charge of the Church passed to James the brother of the Lord, together with the Apostles. He was called the "Just" by all men from the Lord's time to ours, since many are called James, but he was holy from his mother's womb. He drank no wine or strong drink, nor did he eat flesh; no razor went upon his head; he did not anoint himself with oil, and he did not go to the baths. He alone was allowed to enter into the sanctuary, for he did not wear wool but linen, and he used to enter alone into the temple and be found kneeling and praying for forgiveness for the people, so that his knees grew hard like a camel's because of his constant worship of God, kneeling and asking forgiveness for the people. So from his excessive righteousness he was called the Just and Oblias, that is in Greek, "Rampart of the people and righteousness," as the prophets declare concerning him. Thus some of the seven sects among the people, who were described before by me (in the Commentaries), inquired of him what was the "gate of Jesus," and he said that he was the Saviour. Owing to this some believed that Jesus was the Christ. . . . So the Scribes and Pharisees . . . went up and threw down the Just, and they said to one another, "Let us stone James the Just," and they began to stone him since the fall had not killed him, but he turned and knelt saying, "I beseech thee, O Lord, God and Father, forgive them, for they know not what they do." And while they were thus stoning him one of the priests of the sons of Rechab, the son of Rechabim, to whom Jeremiah the prophet bore witness, cried out saying, "Stop! what are you doing? The Just is praying for you." And a certain man among them, one of the laundrymen, took the club with which he used to beat out the clothes, and hit the Just on the head, and so he suffered martyrdom. And they buried him on the spot by the temple, and his gravestone still remains by the temple. He became a true witness both to Jews and to Greeks that Jesus is the Christ.

is an oft-repeated theme in the Hebrew Scriptures (see sidebar). As a sample of such a prophecy, James offers a paraphrase of Amos 9:11–12 (see sidebar). This passage anticipates the restoration of David's kingdom, and when that happens, gentiles were to be more directly included in the people of God. Jesus, as the Davidic Messiah (cf. Acts 2:29–36; 13:22–23), has inaugurated this anticipated restoration of the Davidic kingdom, so the extension of the kingdom to include gentiles—as gentiles and not by becoming Jewish first—is now underway.[22] Gentiles join the restored kingdom the same way the Jews do: by putting their faith in Jesus the King.

22. See Jostein Ådna, "James' Position at the Summit Meeting of the Apostles and the Elders in Jerusalem (Acts 15)," *The Mission of the Early Church to Jews and Gentiles*, ed. Jostein Ådna and Hans Kvalbein, WUNT 127 (Tübingen: Mohr Siebeck, 2000), 125–61.

James's use of Amos 9:11–12 (in Acts 15:16–18) has been the object of much scholarly discussion, particularly because it noticeably follows the ***LXX*** translation of the Hebrew Scriptures and contains lines from other prophets. While his citation centers on the words of Amos, to his credit James introduces his citation with the plural "prophets" (15:15), and his introductory "After this I will return" (15:16; cf. Jer 12:15), and his concluding "things known from long ago" (Acts 15:18; cf. Isa 45:21) come from

Similarities between James in Acts 15 and the Epistle of James

1. **James in Acts 15 and the Epistle of James each connects "listen" to "brothers" [Greek: *akousate* and *adelphoi*]:**
   - James 2:5—Listen, my dear brothers . . .
   - Acts 15:13—Brothers, listen to me.
2. **James in Acts 15 and the Epistle of James each use "care for" [Greek: *episkeptomai*] pastorally:**
   - James 1:27— . . . to look after orphans and widows in their distress . . .
   - Acts 15:14— . . . how God first intervened to choose a people for his name from the Gentiles.
3. **James in Acts 15 and the Epistle of James each refer to the "name invoked" [Greek: *to onoma* + *epikaleō*] upon believers:**
   - James 2:7—Are they not the ones who are blaspheming the noble name of him to whom you belong?
   - Acts 15:17— . . . that the rest of mankind may seek the Lord, even all the Gentiles who bear my name, says the Lord, who does these things.
4. **James in Acts 15 and the Epistle of James each use "turn; return" [Greek: *epistrephō*] for coming to the Lord:**
   - James 5:19-20—My brothers and sisters, if one of you should wander from the truth and someone should bring that person back, remember this: Whoever turns a sinner from the error of their way will save them from death and cover over a multitude of sins.
   - Acts 15:19—It is my judgment, therefore, that we should not make it difficult for the Gentiles who are turning to God.
5. **The Acts 15 letter and the Epistle of James have similar beginnings [Greek: *chairein* and *adelphoi*]:**
   - James 1:1-2—James, a servant of God and of the Lord Jesus Christ, To the twelve tribes scattered among the nations: Greetings. Consider it pure joy, my brothers . . .
   - Acts 15:23—The apostles and elders, your brothers, To the Gentile believers in Antioch, Syria and Cilicia: Greetings.
6. **The Acts 15 letter and the Epistle of James each express the need for believers to "avoid" [Greek: *(dia)tēreō*] sins:**
   - James 1:27— . . . to keep oneself from being polluted by the world.
   - Acts 15:29—You are to abstain from food sacrificed to idols, from blood, from meat of strangled animals and from sexual immorality. You will do well to avoid these things.

Adapted and expanded from information in Scot McKnight, *The Letter of James*, NICNT (Grand Rapids: Eerdmans, 2011), 24.

prophetic passages on this same subject (see sidebar). This is perhaps not unlike our everyday conflated citations of Scripture passages introduced generically with "The Bible says, . . ." Furthermore, suggesting that the Hebrew and LXX texts of the Israelite Scriptures were both used in the Jerusalem Council discussion, W. Edward Glenny argues that James's citation of Amos 9:11–12 from the LXX in Acts 15 is conflated with Jeremiah 12:16 and Zechariah 2:10–11 and that it is the Hebrew text of these latter

A Sampling of OT Prophecies on Inclusion of the Gentiles

Isaiah 2:2-3—"In the last days the mountain of the LORD's temple will be established as the highest of the mountains; it will be exalted above the hills, and all nations will stream to it."

Isaiah 14:1—"The LORD will have compassion on Jacob; once again he will choose Israel and will settle them in their own land. Foreigners will join them and unite with the descendants of Jacob."

Isaiah 45:21-23—"Who foretold this long ago, who declared it from the distant past? Was it not I, the LORD? And there is no God apart from me, a righteous God and a Savior; there is none but me. Turn to me and be saved, all you ends of the earth; for I am God, and there is no other. . . . Before me every knee will bow; by me every tongue will swear."

Isaiah 49:6—"I will also make you a light for the Gentiles, that my salvation may reach to the ends of the earth." (cf. Acts 13:47)

Isaiah 56:6-7—"And foreigners who bind themselves to the LORD to minister to him, to love the name of the LORD, and to be his servants, all who keep the Sabbath without desecrating it and who hold fast to my covenant—these I will bring to my holy mountain and give them joy in my house of prayer."

Isaiah 66:18-19—"And I, because of what they have planned and done, am about to come and gather the people of all nations and languages, and they will come and see my glory. . . . They will proclaim my glory among the nations."

Jeremiah 3:17—"At that time they will call Jerusalem The Throne of the LORD, and all nations will gather in Jerusalem to honor the name of the LORD. No longer will they follow the stubbornness of their evil hearts."

Jeremiah 12:15-16—"But after I uproot them, I will again have compassion and will bring each of them back to their own inheritance and their own country. And if they learn well the ways of my people and swear by my name, saying, "As surely as the LORD lives"—even as they once taught my people to swear by Baal—then they will be established among my people."

Amos 9:11-12—"'In that day I will restore David's fallen shelter—I will repair its broken walls and restore its ruins—and will rebuild it as it used to be, so that they may possess the remnant of Edom and all the nations that bear my name,' declares the LORD, who will do these things."

Zechariah 2:11—"Many nations will be joined with the LORD in that day and will become my people. I will live among you and you will know that the LORD Almighty has sent me to you."

Zechariah 14:16—"Then the survivors from all the nations that have attacked Jerusalem will go up year after year to worship the King, the LORD Almighty, and to celebrate the Festival of Tabernacles."

James's Paraphrase of Amos 9:11–12

Rather than following the original Hebrew text (MT) of Amos 9:11–12, James's paraphrase is closer to the old Greek translation from the third century BC, commonly called the Septuagint (LXX). The English renderings of each of these passages are sufficient for noticing these differences.

Amos 9:11–12 NIV

"In that day
    I will restore David's fallen shelter—
        I will repair its broken walls
        and restore its ruins—
        and will rebuild it as it used to be,
    so that they may possess the remnant of Edom
        and all the nations that bear my name,"
            declares the LORD, who will do these things.

James's Paraphrase of Amos 9:11–12 (Acts 15:16–18 NIV)

"'After this I will return
    and rebuild David's fallen tent.
Its ruins I will rebuild,
    and I will restore it,
that the rest of mankind may seek the Lord,
    even all the Gentiles who bear my name,'
says the Lord, who does these things"—
    things known from long ago.

Septuagint of Amos 9:11–12

"In that day
    I will restore David's fallen tent,
and I will rebuild the fallen parts of it,
    and its ruins I will restore,
    and I will rebuild it as the days of old,
that the rest of mankind may seek [me]
    even all the Gentiles who bear my name,"
says the Lord God, who does these things.

passages that connect with Leviticus 17–18 from whence the apostolic decree takes its cue.[23] The connection to Leviticus will be addressed shortly.

It must be emphasized here that James is pointing the Jerusalem Council back to Scripture. Sometimes people allow their cultural prejudices or personal preferences to misguide their interpretation and application of Scripture. This seems to have been the problem for the Judaizers in their insistence that gentiles must become adherents to Judaism before coming to faith in Jesus. The Judaizers needed to be pointed back to Scripture to have their ideals recalibrated with the truth.

The Messianic View of Amos 9:11 at Qumran

The first-century Jewish community at Qumran is where the famous Dead Sea Scrolls were found in the 1940s. Among their hundreds of documents are various community writings and commentaries on OT Scriptures. As a separatist group that was eschatologically oriented, they viewed themselves as God's divinely appointed people to usher in the new age. As the following excerpts show, they too were looking forward to the fulfillment of prophecies like Amos 9:11 and worked on connecting it with other prophetic passages.

Damascus Document (CD) 7:13–21

> All who backslid were handed over to the sword, but all who held fast escaped to the land of the north, as it says, "I will exile the tents of your king and the foundation of your images beyond the tents of Damascus" [Amos 5:27]. The books of the Law are the tents of the king, as it says, "I will re-erect the fallen tent of David" [Amos 9:11]. The "king" is the congregation and the "foundation of your images" is the books of the prophets whose words Israel despised. The star is the Interpreter of the Law who comes to Damascus, as it is written, "A star has left Jacob, a staff has risen from Israel" [Num 24:17]. The latter is the Leader of the whole nation; when he appears, "he will shatter all the sons of Sheth" [Num 24:17].

DSS 4Q174 (a.k.a. 4QFlor) 3:10–13

> "Moreover the Lord declares to you that He will make you a house," and that "I will raise up your offspring after you, and establish the throne of his kingdom forever. I will be a father to him, and he will be My son" [2 Sam 7:11c, 12b, 13b–14a]. This passage refers to the Shoot of David, who is to arise with the Interpreter of the Law, and who will arise in Zion in the Last Days, as it is written, "And I shall raise up the booth of David that is fallen" [Amos 9:11]. This passage describes the fallen Branch of David, whom He shall raise up to deliver Israel.

23. See W. Edward Glenny, "The Septuagint and Apostolic Hermeneutics: Amos 9 in Acts 15," *BBR* 22 (2012): 1–26; see further Charles Haddon Savelle Jr., "James's Use of Amos 9:11–12 in Acts 15," *BBR* 31 (2021): 54–71.

11.2.6 The Conclusion and the Apostolic Decree (15:19–21)

After referencing the teaching of Scripture on the question at hand, James draws a sensible conclusion. As James traces it, the logic of the Jerusalem Council notes two premises that lead to his deduction: (a) via the testimonies of Simon Peter and Barnabas and Paul, we can see God's work in the world to include gentiles among his renewed people (Acts 15:14; cf. vv. 7–13); and (b) via the prophets like Amos, we can see in Scripture that God's intentions have always been to include gentiles among his renewed people (15:15–18); therefore (c) Jews are to accept believing gentiles as full-fledged members of God's renewed people, the church, without requiring them to become Jews first (15:19). In good team-building fashion, James professes this deduction as his own: "It is my judgment" (15:19), but he is confident that the logic is clear to the rest of the group.

The Logic of the Jerusalem Council Decision

A. **Premise 1:** Via the testimonies of Simon Peter and Barnabas and Paul, we can see God's work in the world to include gentiles among his renewed people (Acts 15:14; cf. vv. 7-13).

B. **Premise 2:** Via the prophets like Amos, we can see in Scripture that God's intentions have always been to include gentiles among his renewed people (Acts 15:15-18).

C. **Conclusion:** Jews are to accept believing gentiles as full-fledged members of God's renewed people, the church, without requiring them to become Jews first (Acts 15:19).

As a leader of the church, James knows there will be some pragmatic issues to work out for the application of a decision even if it is an abundantly clear conclusion. So he immediately offers a way forward for applying the decision in the communities of the local churches. The Jews must support Christian community by not placing undue expectations on the gentile believers, but what then should believing gentiles do to support Christian community? James has a ready list of four things that he suggests should be put into writing: "Instead we should write to them, telling them to abstain from food polluted by idols, from sexual immorality, from the meat of strangled animals and from blood" (15:20). This list is approved by the apostolic leadership and the whole church (15:22) and becomes known as the "apostolic decree" (cf. 16:4 where the NIV has "the decisions" for the Greek *ta dogmata*, which is rendered "the decrees" in KJV and NET). Before trying to sort these out, it is helpful to look at the rationale James offers for the pragmatic guidelines he is suggesting.

James does not at all suggest that the reason believing gentiles must refrain from these four things—no matter how they might be defined—is so that they might secure their salvation; the gentiles under consideration are already believers who have turned to God (cf. 15:19) and who are saved "through the grace of our Lord Jesus" and not through their own deeds (cf. 15:11). Rather, James offers a pragmatic reason for this particular list of guidelines: "For the law of Moses has been preached in every city from the earliest times and is read in the synagogues on every Sabbath" (15:21)—something other first-century Jewish writers also note (see sidebar). That is, because Jews have been far-flung all over the world in the diaspora, their scrupulous OT lifestyle concerns are easily known among gentiles everywhere. Thus, the prohibitions being suggested are nothing new or burdensome to the gentiles who come to faith in Christ.[24]

The Law of Moses Preached in Every City

In addressing the Jerusalem Council, James notes, "For the law of Moses has been preached in every city from the earliest times and is read in the synagogues on every Sabbath" (Acts 15:21). This observation was made by other first-century Jews as well.

Philo, *The Special Laws*, 2.62–64 (ca. AD 40–49)

> For the law bids us take the time for studying philosophy and thereby improve the soul and the dominant mind. So each seventh day there stand wide open in every city thousands of schools of good sense, temperance, courage, justice and the other virtues. . . . These things shew clearly that Moses does not allow any of those who use his sacred instruction to remain inactive at any season.

Flavius Josephus, *Jewish Antiquities* 16.2.3 §§43–45 (ca. AD 94)

> There is nothing hostile to mankind in our customs, but they are all pious and consecrated with saving righteousness. Nor do we make a secret of the precepts that we use as guides in religion and in human relations; we give every seventh day over to the study of our customs and law, for we think it necessary to occupy ourselves, as with any other study, so with these through which we can avoid committing sins. Now our customs are excellent in themselves, if one examines them carefully, and they are also ancient, even though some may not believe this, so that for those who have received them as sacred traditions and preserve them it is not easy to unlearn what has been hallowed by time.

Flavius Josephus, *Against Apion* 2.17 §175 (ca. AD 97)

> For ignorance he left no pretext. He appointed all the Law to be the most excellent and necessary form of instruction, ordaining, not that it should be heard once for all or twice or on several occasions, but that every week men should desert their other occupations and assemble to listen to the Law and to obtain a thorough and accurate knowledge of it, a practice which all other legislators seem to have neglected.

24. Luke Timothy Johnson, *The Acts of the Apostles*, SP 5 (Collegeville: Liturgical for Michael Glazier, 1992), 273.

With this general knowledge and for the sake of community in the church, the believing gentiles should be prepared to be sensitive to these particular lifestyle scruples of their Jewish brothers and sisters in Christ. This list of expected behaviors in churches of mixed Jew and gentile memberships would serve a pragmatic purpose of helping to unify the believers in Christ. Promotion of this kind of deference in worship gatherings will display the new identity of all the Christian believers united together. The apostolic decree thus seems to be a pragmatic compromise in the best sense of that term. But as we will soon see, the apostolic decree is also Scripture-motivated.

11.3 THE LETTER WITH THE APOSTOLIC DECREE (ACTS 15:22–35)

The apostles and elders and the whole Jerusalem church agree with the conclusion James has reached, and they agree with his proposal to draft a letter to explain the expectations for church fellowship among the gentile territories where the gospel is expanding and taking root. The leadership notwithstanding, Luke seems to indicate that the Jerusalem Council was not an autocratic setting where the apostles and elders simply forced their will on the rest. While the apostles and elders take responsibility for having written the letter (cf. 21:18–25), Luke gives credit to "the whole church" for being involved in the decision (15:22a).

11.3.1 The Letter Bearers (15:22)

Luke also notes that there were other leaders among the believers at Jerusalem beyond those already mentioned, specifically introducing "Judas (called Barsabbas) and Silas, men who were leaders among the believers" (15:22b). This brief comment not only introduces Silas (who soon becomes a significant person in the story) but also communicates that the expanding church was expanding its leadership as well. These two Jerusalem church leaders became part of the letter-bearing envoy going to Antioch. Thus, even as the church at Antioch had sent Paul and Barnabas and a few others to Jerusalem to discuss the Jew-gentile issue, now the Council determines "to choose some of their own men" to send back to Antioch with the news of the Council's decision. The expanded emissary group will bear the written letter and give their personal verbal verification of the decision (cf. 15:27).

11.3.2 The Letter Content (15:23–29)

Scholars have long noted that the style of the apostolic letter differs from Luke's own writing style, which is evidence that he did not fabricate the letter himself.[25]

25. E.g., see Adolf von Harnack, *Luke the Physician: The Author of the Third Gospel and the Acts of the Apostles*, trans. J. R. Wilkinson, New Testament Studies I (London: Williams and Norgate, 1908; New York: Putnam, 1909;

The Letter with the Apostolic Decree

In Acts 15:23-29 Luke provides the wording of the apostolic letter. Because the letter was to be circulated among the churches, it is not surprising that Luke could obtain a copy.

> The apostles and elders, your brothers,
>
> To the Gentile believers in Antioch, Syria and Cilicia:
>
> Greetings.
>
> We have heard that some went out from us without our authorization and disturbed you, troubling your minds by what they said. So we all agreed to choose some men and send them to you with our dear friends Barnabas and Paul—men who have risked their lives for the name of our Lord Jesus Christ. Therefore we are sending Judas and Silas to confirm by word of mouth what we are writing. It seemed good to the Holy Spirit and to us not to burden you with anything beyond the following requirements: You are to abstain from food sacrificed to idols, from blood, from the meat of strangled animals and from sexual immorality. You will do well to avoid these things.
>
> Farewell.

Because the letter was to be circulated among the churches, Luke could easily obtain a copy to include in the story of Acts. If he was a resident of Syrian Antioch, as some traditions have it, Luke may well have seen the original copy of the letter.[26]

In keeping with ancient letter-writing custom, the letter begins with a "from" statement, a "to" statement, and a salutation statement. With the apostles and elders authoring the letter and identifying themselves as "brothers" of the gentile believers, the letter is both official and friendly. While the letter specifies the gentile believers in the city of Antioch as well as the territories of Syria and Cilicia (15:23), we learn later that the letter was also distributed to the churches in Southern Galatia (16:4) and that it is applicable for gentile believers everywhere (21:25; cf. "in every city" in 15:21). The body of the apostolic letter rehearses the background that led to the Jerusalem Council, and it explains that the Judaizers who had caused the controversy in Antioch went without the authorization of the Jerusalem leadership (15:24). The letter is complimentary of Barnabas and Paul (15:25–26) and introduces Judas and Silas as those sent "to confirm by word of mouth what we are writing" (15:27).

---

repr., Eugene, OR: Wipf & Stock, 2009), 219; Wilfred L. Knox, *The Acts of the Apostles* (Cambridge: University of Cambridge Press, 1948), 50; and Richard N. Longenecker, "Acts," pp. 663–1102 in *Luke-Acts*, vol. 10 of *The Expositor's Bible Commentary*, ed. Tremper Longman III and David E. Garland, rev. ed. (Grand Rapids: Zondervan, 2007), 951.

26. Herbert McLachlan, *St. Luke, the Man and His Work*, Publications of the University of Manchester, Theological Series 3 (Manchester: University of Manchester Press, 1920; New York: Longmans/Green, 1920), 163–64.

Most significantly, of course, the letter introduces the decision of the Jerusalem Council. Interestingly, the apostolic decree in the letter has a slight change in the order of the four prohibited items. In James's conversational comments the items were listed in one order (15:20), but when committing the items to writing, they are reordered (15:29; cf. 21:25 where the letter is referenced again). The order written in the letter is evidence that they come from the OT guidelines for gentiles residing among God's people. Such guidelines—in the same order as in the apostolic letter—are provided in Leviticus 17–18, a passage from Moses that is fitting to James's earlier rationale for these guidelines (15:21).[27] There the refrain of "any Israelite or any foreigner residing among them" is repeated often, reminiscent of James's comments about the nations and Israel being God's people together, citing the prophets.[28] This comparison of the apostolic decree in Acts 15 with Leviticus 17–18 also helps clarify the definitions of the items (see sidebar).[29]

The Content and Order of Elements in the Apostolic Decree

The decision at the Jerusalem Council in Acts 15 was that gentiles did not need to become Jews to come to faith in Christ. Rather, they were to be instructed to abstain from four practices affiliated with paganism. When he suggested this approach, James listed these items in one order (Acts 15:20); but when these items were written into the apostolic letter, they were listed in another order (Acts 15:29; cf. 21:25). The order of the items written in the letter is evidence that they come from the OT guidelines for gentiles residing among God's people written in Leviticus 17-18.

Acts 15:20—in James's Jerusalem Council address	Acts 15:29 & 21:25—in the Jerusalem Council letter	Leviticus 17-18—regarding foreigners residing in Israel
• food polluted by idols • sexual immorality • strangled things • blood	• food polluted by idols • blood • strangled things • sexual immorality	• idol sacrifices (Lev 17:7-9) • eating blood (Lev 17:10-12) • eating bloody meat (Lev 17:13-16) • sexual immorality (Lev 18:1-30)

27. See Richard J. Bauckham, "James and the Gentiles (Acts 15:13–21)," pp. 154–84 in *History, Literature and Society in the Book of Acts*, ed. Ben Witherington III (Cambridge: Cambridge University Press, 1996), 177–78; cf. Charles Kingsley Barrett, *A Critical and Exegetical Commentary on the Acts of the Apostles*, 2 vols., ICC (Edinburgh: T&T Clark, 1994/1998), 2:737–38; Johnson, *Acts*, 273.

28. Again, see Glenny, "The Septuagint and Apostolic Hermeneutics: Amos 9 in Acts 15," 1–26; cf. Richard J. Bauckham, "James and the Jerusalem Church," pp. 415–80 in *The Book of Acts in Its Palestinian Setting*, ed. Richard Bauckham, BAFCS 4 (Grand Rapids: Eerdmans, 1995; Carlisle: Paternoster, 1995), 458–62; idem, "James and the Gentiles," 172–78.

29. There are other background suggestions for the apostolic decree; see the helpful surveys of options in Eckhard J. Schnabel, *Acts*, ZECNT (Grand Rapids: Zondervan, 2012), 644–46 and in Keener, *Acts*, 3:2260–69. Various background explanations are not necessarily mutually exclusive; see the sidebar on the "noahic commandments."

The Apostolic Decree and the Noahic Commandments

Some scholars discuss the similarities of the four prohibitions of the apostolic decree of Acts 15:20 and 29 (i.e., food polluted by idols, blood, strangled things, sexual immorality; cf. 21:25) with the three human failings that led to the Noahic flood as outlined in the apocryphal Book of Jubilees (e.g., Jub. 7:23–31; i.e., fornication, uncleanness, and iniquity). Others point to the seven stipulations of what have come to be called the "Noahic commandments" outlined in later rabbinic literature as the prohibitions meant for all humanity (e.g., b. Sanh. 56a:24; i.e., injustice, blasphemy, idol worship, sexual immorality, bloodshed, robbery, and eating a portion of a live animal; cf. b. Sanh. 56b–57a; b. 'Abod. Zar. 64b). Still others note similarities to the three severe transgressions forbidden to all Jews as outlined by rabbinic authorities in Lydda ca. AD 120 (e.g., b. Yoma 9b; i.e., idolatry, sexual immorality, and murder; cf. b. Sanh. 74a:12). Even if there are no direct, interdependent connections between the apostolic decree of Acts 15 and the Noahic commandments as outlined in extrabiblical literature, there is a noticeable consistency of interest in respecting life and protecting oneself from immorality, impurity, and injustice.

See Eckhard J. Schnabel, *Early Christian Mission*, 2 vols. (Downers Grove, IL: InterVarsity Press, 2004), 2:1015–20.

This context to the apostolic decree clarifies its purpose. The inclusion of gentiles among God's people has always been part of God's plan. He had already provided guidelines for peaceful interaction of believers from different backgrounds in the era of OT Israel; thus, in renewing a people for himself through faith in the revealed Messiah, it is no surprise to see God interested in guiding those of different backgrounds into one united people. Taking their cue from Leviticus 17–18, the four guidelines of the apostolic decree serve that purpose. It establishes a compromise regarding ritual practices to facilitate harmony in churches consisting of Christians from mixed cultural backgrounds.[30] Gentile believers in Jesus were asked to follow the guidelines not to secure their salvation, not to prove themselves worthy, but for the sake of community. While Jewish believers must accept gentile believers into the fellowship of their local churches, gentile believers must be respectful of the scrupulous issues for Jewish believers. The focus of the apostolic decree was not to expand diversity but to enhance church unity through honorable deference. Certainly, such sensitivity to one another is a sign of the new identity that the believers have in being united in Christ. More than merely putting ethnic diversity on display, Luke presses his audience to recognize that the one true God is bringing together a united people in relationship with him.[31]

---

30. Schnabel, *Acts*, 645.
31. Witherington, *Acts*, 442.

11.3.3 Applying the Apostolic Decree (15:30–34)

Luke gives an account of the apostolic decree being delivered to the church at Antioch, where the fomenting controversy had called for the Jerusalem Council in the first place. When the Council emissaries arrive, "they gathered the church together and delivered the letter" (15:30). And Luke is redundantly expressive about the positive reception of the news: the people "were glad for its encouraging message" (15:31), Judas and Silas "said much to encourage and strengthen the believers" (15:32), and they sent the Jerusalem representatives back "with the blessing of peace" (15:33). This positive outcome of the Jerusalem Council reinforces the intended unity within not only the mixed community of the Antioch church but also the budding international church.

In both Acts and his letters, Paul displays an interest in church unity. An early date for Paul's writing of Galatians is suggested here in part because if Paul were directly describing the Jerusalem Council to his Galatian readers, it is odd that he would fail to mention the Council's official document that supports his argument in the Galatian letter. Even so, in his later letters Paul likewise never directly mentions the apostolic decree, even when he is addressing similar topics about the interrelation of people from mixed cultural backgrounds. Nevertheless, in several places Paul applies in his letters this same principled concern for sensitivity to other believers without explicitly mentioning the apostolic decree. This happens particularly in 1 Corinthians 8–10 and Romans 14. Honorable deference to one another—not legalistic observance of religious or cultural customs—is the focus in all the contexts. It seems apparent from Paul's letters that the principle of deference for the sake of unity—found in the apostolic decree—is the pattern to be followed still today.

Most churches today do not struggle with the presence of literal Judaizers insisting that all Christians must live according to Jewish customs. A moment's reflection, however, reveals that it is not at all uncommon for Christians to disagree about the proper expression of Christian faith (e.g., regarding such things as foods to eat, holidays to observe, forms of worship to utilize, forms of entertainment, clothing styles, etc.). Such disagreements over religious and cultural expressions bring the

A New Cross-Cultural Community in Christ

While struggling for centuries to live accordingly, the church has long recognized that faith in Christ calls all believers to have a change in their community allegiances. Luke is among the NT writers who argue for this. In the generation after Luke, Justin Martyr (ca. AD 100–165) gave his voice to this concern.

Justin Martyr, *First Apology* 14.4 (ca. AD 155–157)

> We who hated and destroyed one another, and on account of their different manners would not live with men of a different tribe, now, since the coming of Christ, live familiarly with them, and pray for our enemies, and endeavour to persuade those who hate us unjustly to live comformably to the good precepts of Christ, to the end that they may become partakers with us of the same joyful hope of a reward from God the ruler of all.

first-century disagreement prompting the Jerusalem Council right up to the twenty-first century. From Luke's first-century description we find he intends something universally prescriptive. For all such matters as these, we must follow the principle of deference demonstrated in the apostolic decree and taught in Paul's letters. This principled way of thinking is what both Luke and Paul stress; the principle of deference for the sake of unity is still ours to apply even if the particular areas of dispute are not.

Furthermore, Luke's record of the Jerusalem Council and the apostolic decree demonstrates a deference to living in accord with Scripture. Like the first-century church, the church today will sometimes need to question its potentially faulty interpretations of Scripture. This should caution us all to always interpret our experiences by Scripture and not to interpret Scripture by our experiences.

Engraving of Paul and Barnabas at Antioch (ca. 1880). benoitb/iStock.com

11.3.4 Summary Statement (15:35)

In his usual narrative fashion, Luke closes this significant episode with a summary statement. This episode starts in Syrian Antioch, moves to Jerusalem for the first important church council meeting, and then returns to Syrian Antioch. While this episode contains travel, it is not a missionary journey per se. Nevertheless, it turns out that this journey was crucial to the mission of the church. Luke remarks not only that "Paul and Barnabas remained in Antioch," from where they would once again soon embark on further missionary travels, but also that "they and many others taught and preached the word of the Lord" (15:35). Indeed, the teaching and preaching of the word of the Lord remains a core activity of God's people. This teaching and preaching of the word of the Lord is intended for Jew and gentile alike. Teaching and preaching of the word of the Lord spreads the gospel message and, as with the Jew-gentile controversy at the Jerusalem Council, addresses the pragmatic issues of life together.

11.4 CONCLUDING REMARKS

In God's overarching plan for the salvation of humanity, Israel was to serve as a kind of "missional magnet" by which God draws all people toward him.[32] Of course, Jesus is the facing edge and active core of that magnet, as Jesus himself said: "I, when I am lifted up from the earth, will draw all people to myself" (John 12:32; cf. 6:44). The point is that Israel was not chosen to be separate from the nations of the earth in order to be forever blessed apart from the nations of the earth. Rather, God chose Israel from the nations of the earth to use Israel as a means through which to bless all the other nations of the earth.[33]

Some Guidelines for Decisions about Disputable Matters

Christians often dispute behaviors that Scripture doesn't appear to address directly. This is understandable when we realize it is entirely possible for some apparently "morally neutral" behaviors to affect one believer negatively and another positively. Thus, the following decision-making questions are not foolproof tests for approving or disapproving all disputed matters in all settings for all believers. They are merely helpful guidelines for assessing such behaviors and the potential impact those behaviors could have on you and your relationships in your particular situation.

Personal Guidelines		
Applicable Scripture	***Negative Test Questions***	***Positive Test Questions***
1 Cor 10:13–14; Rom 13:14	1. Will it tempt me to be led into sin?	1. Will it lead me away from the danger of sin?
1 Cor 10:14–22	2. Will it subject me to demonic attack?	2. Will it help me avoid demonic attack?
1 Cor 10:30; 1 Thess 5:18	3. Will it prevent me from being able to thank God?	3. Will it enable me to give thanks to God?
1 Cor 6:12	4. Will it tempt me to become addicted?	4. Will it help me avoid addiction?
1 Cor 6:19–20	5. Will it harm my physical or emotional health?	5. Will it help my physical or emotional health?

32. I get the concept of "missional magnetism" from Christopher J. H. Wright, *The Mission of God's People: A Biblical Theology of the Church's Mission*, Biblical Theology for Life (Grand Rapids: Zondervan, 2010), 129.

33. See Bruce Riley Ashford and Heath A. Thomas, *The Gospel of Our King: Bible, Worldview, and the Mission of Every Christian* (Grand Rapids: Baker Academic, 2019), 184.

Relational Guidelines		
Applicable Scripture	***Negative Test Questions***	***Positive Test Questions***
1 Cor 8:9–13; 10:23–24, 32–33	1. Will it do spiritual damage to me or others?	1. Will it spiritually build up me or others?
1 Cor 10:27–29; Rom 14:16	2. Will it be discovered and condemned by another person's conscience?	2. Will it be encouraged by others?
1 Cor 10:31; Col 3:17	3. Will it bring dishonor to God?	3. Will it bring honor and glory to God?
1 Cor 11:1; Eph 5:1–2; Heb 13:7	4. Will it violate the pattern of a Christlike role model?	4. Will it provide a Christlike role model?
Rom 14:19–20; 15:2, 5–6	5. Will it bring dissension or disunity to the body of Christ?	5. Will it bring peace and unity to the body of Christ?

Adapted from John Wecks, *Free to Disagree: Moving beyond the Arguments over Christian Liberty* (Grand Rapids: Kregel Resources, 1996), 115–16. Used by permission of the author.

It was easy for the Jews to assume that this meant the nations would become Jewish, but the Jerusalem Council helped the young church realize this was not the case. Jews and gentiles alike were to lose their identities to the overwhelming draw of God in Jesus. After all, Jews and gentiles alike are saved in exactly the same way. As Peter says it, "We believe it is through the grace of our Lord Jesus that we are saved, just as they are" (Acts 15:11).

The Jerusalem Council was initially convened to address the question of what gentiles must do to be saved. When the answer was clarified—or merely reiterated and reinforced from the earlier answer in Acts—that Jews and gentiles are saved in the same manner by faith in Jesus Christ, a second question came to the fore: How should Jews and gentiles get along in the church? While the first question is seldom asked in the twenty-first century (few would suggest that gentiles need to become Jews before becoming Christians), the second question is reflected on often. How can people of different cultural backgrounds get along together in one church community? Pointing to Scripture, the Jerusalem Council affirmed that expanded fellowship was always God's plan, so those in the church need, on the one hand, to widen their sense of fellowship and, on the other hand, to be sensitive to

Church of All Nations, Jerusalem

Picturellarious/stock.adobe.com

the scruples of others. This is how we should think about the community of believers in today's church. We should follow the guidelines of Scripture, promoting the truth of God's designs as well as the honorable deference he desires in our worship gatherings so as to display the new identity of all the Christian believers united together in Christ.

11.5 Key People, Places, and Terms

- Antioch of Syria
- Barnabas
- church councils
- circumcision
- Cornelius
- elders
- James the Just
- Jerusalem Council
- Judaizers
- LXX
- Paul
- Pharisees
- proselytes

11.6 Questions for Review and Discussion

1. Explain why the Jew-gentile issue was important for the first-century church.
2. What kind of evidence did the Jerusalem Council examine as they analyzed the Jew-gentile controversy?
3. Explain how the church used the Hebrew Scriptures to address the Jew-gentile question of the first century.
4. In Acts 15 the Jerusalem church crafted a way for Jews and gentiles to respectfully get along with one another that was based on the scriptural precedent for Jews to accept gentiles into the community of God's people. What parallels might there be for some kind of apostolic decree in the life of the church today?
5. The Jerusalem Council in Acts 15 faced the issue of just how "Jewish" non-Jews needed to behave to be considered real Christians. While this is particularly descriptive of a first-century issue, what are some analogous issues in today's church to which Luke would want us to apply the same principle?

11.7 Optional Assignments

1. **Text Reflection Project**—*Relating the concepts discussed in this chapter to another biblical text.* Explore the relationship of Acts 15 to Paul's letter to the Galatians, a topic debated in scholarly circles. This chapter suggests that Galatians 2:1–10 reflects Paul's visit to Jerusalem with famine relief from the Antioch church (≈ Acts 11:27–30 and 12:25), but many scholars suggest that it reflects Paul's visit for the Jerusalem Council (≈ Acts 15:1–35). Write a short paper about your thoughts on this debate. What issues are of importance in this debate?

2. **Interview Project**—*Inquiring of others their views concerning the concepts discussed in this chapter.* Acts 15 discusses one of the most difficult issues the early church faced, the Jew-gentile controversy. The chapter demonstrates how the church pulled together to talk through the problematic issue, to seek God's scriptural answer, and to make a pragmatic application. Interview your pastor (or some other respected Christian leader) about one of the most difficult situations his or her ministry has faced, and write up an analysis of how well the church or ministry mirrored the actions of the church in Acts 15.
3. **Service-Learning Project**—*Applying the concepts discussed in this chapter in some form of service to others outside the class.* If your church is facing a particularly difficult controversy, is there a role you are prepared to play in working toward a solution? Can you serve as an emissary for the views of some church members? Write a short paper about this possible role.
4. **Prayer Project**—*Talking with God about the concepts discussed in this chapter.* Circumcision was a God-given and historic symbol of the Israelite faith looking forward to the coming of the Messiah and his provision of the Holy Spirit to make "circumcised hearts" possible (Jer 4:4; cf. Deut 10:16; 30:6). Many of the Jewish believers in Jesus as the Messiah wanted gentiles to embrace this historic symbol with their same Israelite passion, and they had difficulty learning that this was not God's design for the church. Is there an analogous issue in your church—or in your own life—where people are improperly holding on to an old symbol of faith, one that might have lost its meaning? Write a prayer about this matter, asking the Lord to change hearts to be aligned with his purposes for his people.
5. **Testimony Project**—*Telling others about the concepts discussed in this chapter.* Similar to the Service-Learning Project suggestion, are you involved in a local community of believers—a church, Christian college, Bible study group, etc.—that is struggling because of a strong difference of opinion on some significant issue? Can you investigate the concerns on all sides to see how they measure up to Scripture, and perhaps in dialog with some wise leaders in the group, can you craft a way to address the matter so as to remain firmly aligned with Scripture and at the same time to address the most pressing pragmatic parts of the issue? Write a short paper about this potential way forward, and seek a fitting audience to whom you can present your ideas.

11.8 Bibliography for Going Further

11.8.1 The Church Councils in History

Bellitto, Christopher M. *The General Councils: A History of the Twenty-One Church Councils from Nicaea to Vatican II.* New York: Paulist, 2002.

Davis, Leo Donald. *The First Seven Ecumenical Councils (325–787): Their History and Theology.* Wilmington, DE: Glazier, 1983. Repr., Collegeville, MN: Liturgical, 1990.

Holcomb, Justin S. *Know the Creeds and Councils.* Know Series. Grand Rapids: Zondervan, 2014.

MacMullen, Ramsay. *Voting about God in Early Church Councils.* New Haven, CT: Yale University Press, 2006.

11.8.2 Paul's Trips to Jerusalem

Hemer, Colin J. *The Book of Acts in the Setting of Hellenistic History*. Edited by Conrad H. Gempf. WUNT 49. Tübingen: Mohr Siebeck, 1989. Repr., Winona Lake, IN: Eisenbrauns, 1990.

Huffman, Douglas S. "Galatians Reconciled with Acts: How Do They Do It? The Attempts of Hans Dieter Betz, F. F. Bruce, and George Howard." MA thesis, Wheaton, IL: Wheaton College Graduate School, 1985.

Morgado, Joe, Jr. "Paul in Jerusalem: A Comparison of His Visits in Acts and Galatians." *JETS* 37.1 (1994): 55–68.

Talbert, Charles H. "Again: Paul's Visits to Jerusalem." *NovT* 9.1 (1967): 26–40.

Trebilco, Paul. "Itineraries, Travel Plans, Journey, Apostolic Parousia." *DPL*, 446–56.

11.8.3 The Jerusalem Council and the Jew-Gentile Issue in Acts

Achtemeier, Paul J. *The Quest for Unity in the New Testament Church: A Study in Paul and Acts*. Philadelphia: Fortress, 1987.

Callan, Terrance. "The Background of the Apostolic Decree (Acts 15:20, 29; 21:25)." *CBQ* 55.2 (1993): 284–97.

Carter, Charles W. "Council of Jerusalem." *ZEB* 1:1045–47.

Glenny, W. Edward. "The Septuagint and Apostolic Hermeneutics: Amos 9 in Acts 15." *BBR* 22.1 (2012): 1–26.

Nolland, John. "Acts 15: Discerning the Will of God in Changing Circumstances." *Crux* 27.1 (1991): 30–34.

Strong, David K. "The Jerusalem Council: Some Implications for Contextualization: Acts 15:1–35." Pages 196–208 in *Mission in Acts: Ancient Narratives in Contemporary Context*. Edited by Robert L. Gallagher and Paul Hertig. ASMS 34. Maryknoll, NY: Orbis, 2004.

van de Sandt, Huub. "An Explanation of Acts 15.6–21 in the Light of Deuteronomy 4.29–35 (LXX)." *JSNT* 46 (1992): 73–97.

Wiarda, Timothy. "The Jerusalem Council and the Theological Task." *JETS* 46.2 (2003): 233–48.

11.8.4 Christian Liberty

Dunn, James D. G. *Christian Liberty: A New Testament Perspective*. Grand Rapids: Eerdmans, 1993.

McCracken, Brett. *Gray Matters: Navigating the Space between Legalism & Liberty*. Grand Rapids: Baker, 2013.

Naselli, Andrew David, and J. D. Crowley. *Conscience: What It Is, How to Train It, and Loving Those Who Differ*. Wheaton, IL: Crossway, 2016.

Rogers, Rex M. *Christian Liberty: Living for God in a Changing Culture*. Grand Rapids: Baker, 2003.

Wecks, John. *Free to Disagree: Moving beyond the Arguments over Christian Liberty*. Grand Rapids: Kregel, 1996.

11.8.5 James the Brother of Jesus

Ådna, Jostein. "James' Position at the Summit Meeting of the Apostles and the Elders in Jerusalem (Acts 15)." Pages 125–61 in *The Mission of the Early Church to Jews and Gentiles*. Edited by Jostein Ådna and Hans Kvalbein. WUNT 127. Tübingen: Mohr Siebeck, 2000.

Bauckham, Richard J. "James and the Gentiles (Acts 15:13–21)." Pages 154–84 in *History, Literature and Society in the Book of Acts*. Edited by Ben Witherington III. Cambridge: Cambridge University Press, 1996.

———. "James and the Jerusalem Church." Pages 415–80 in *The Book of Acts in Its Palestinian Setting*. Edited by Richard Bauckham. BAFCS 4. Grand Rapids: Eerdmans, 1995; Carlisle: Paternoster, 1995.

Chilton, Bruce D., and Craig A. Evans, eds. *James the Just and Christian Origins*. NovTSup 98. Leiden: Brill, 1999.

Chilton, Bruce D., and Jacob Neusner, eds. *The Brother of Jesus: James the Just and His Mission*. Louisville: Westminster John Knox, 2001.

Saxby, Alan. *James, Brother of Jesus, and the Jerusalem Church: A Radical Exploration of Christian Origin*. Eugene, OR: Wipf & Stock, 2015.

12 The Story of the Second Missionary Campaign

Acts 15:36–18:22

Theastock/stock.adobe.com

Chapter Goals

After reading this chapter, you should be able to:

- Recognize the value in Acts placed on follow-up ministry with new Christians.
- Recognize the continued typical experience Paul and his ministry team had in sharing the gospel.
- Appreciate Paul's persistence in preaching the gospel to Jews first (as the fulfillment of Scripture) and then to gentiles (as was always God's intention).
- Explain how Paul moved from observing expressions of desire for God in the culture around him to sharing the gospel message.
- From your study of Acts so far, offer an explanation of Luke's view of how a believer's citizenship in the church might relate to that believer's citizenship in a particular city, state, or government.

Chapter Overview

12.1 Debating and Deciding Who Should Go Where (Acts 15:36–16:10)
12.2 The Mission in Philippi (Acts 16:11–40)
12.3 The Mission in Thessalonica and Berea (Acts 17:1–15)
12.4 The Mission in Athens (Acts 17:16–34)
12.5 The Mission in Corinth (Acts 18:1–22)
12.6 Concluding Remarks
12.7 Key People, Places, and Terms
12.8 Questions for Review and Discussion
12.9 Optional Assignments
12.10 Bibliography for Going Further

Key Verses

Some time later Paul said to Barnabas, "Let us go back and visit the believers in all the towns where we preached the word of the Lord and see how they are doing." (Acts 15:36)

He then brought them out and asked, "Sirs, what must I do to be saved?" They replied, "Believe in the Lord Jesus, and you will be saved—you and your household." (Acts 16:30–31)

Therefore since we are God's offspring, we should not think that the divine being is like gold or silver or stone—an image made by human design and skill. In the past God overlooked such ignorance, but now he commands all people everywhere to repent. For he has set a day when he will judge the world with justice by the man he has appointed. He has given proof of this to everyone by raising him from the dead. (Acts 17:29–31)

Mid-Journey Progress Summary Statement

So the churches were strengthened in the faith and grew daily in numbers. (Acts 16:5)

Closing Travel Summary Statement

When he landed at Caesarea, he went up to Jerusalem and greeted the church and then went down to Antioch. (Acts 18:22)

Itinerary of Paul's Second Missionary Journey, Acts 15:36–18:22 (ca. 49–52)

City	Province (Region)	Reference
Antioch	Syria	Acts 15:35
	Cilicia	Acts 15:41
Derbe	Galatia (Lycaonia)	Acts 16:1
Lystra	Galatia (Lycaonia)	Acts 16:1–5
	Asia (Phrygia)	Acts 16:6
	Galatia	Acts 16:6
Troas	Asia (Mysia)	Acts 16:7–10
Samothrace	Thrace	Acts 16:11
Neapolis	Macedonia	Acts 16:11
Philippi	Macedonia	Acts 16:12–40
Amphipolis	Macedonia	Acts 17:1

City	Province (Region)	Reference
Apollonia	Macedonia	Acts 17:1
Thessalonica	Macedonia	Acts 17:1–9
Berea	Macedonia	Acts 17:10–14
Athens	Achaia	Acts 17:15–32
Corinth	Achaia	Acts 18:1–17
Cenchreae	Achaia	Acts 18:18
Ephesus	Asia	Acts 18:19–21
Caesarea	Judea (Palestine)	Acts 18:22a
Jerusalem	Judea (Palestine)	Acts 18:22b
Antioch	Syria	Acts 18:22c

INTRODUCTION

This section of Acts traces what is commonly referred to as Paul's second missionary journey (Acts 15:36–18:22). After a discussion of who should go where, this second missionary campaign begins with follow-up ministry in the southern part of the Roman province of Galatia, territory Paul and Barnabas had evangelized on the first missionary journey. Luke's narrative focuses on the expansion of missionary activity to three additional Roman provinces: Macedonia (i.e., northern Greece), Achaia (i.e., southern Greece), and Asia (i.e., western Turkey). Stott notes that the missionary team establishes churches in the capital city of each of these provinces—Thessalonica in Macedonia, Corinth in Achaia, and Ephesus in Asia—and that Paul would later write letters to each of these churches.[1]

Paul's Second Missionary Journey (ca. AD 49–52)

1. John R. W. Stott, *The Message of Acts: To the Ends of the Earth*, The Bible Speaks Today (Downers Grove, IL: InterVarsity, 1994), 258. For a chart suggesting where all of Paul's letters might fit into the narrative of Acts, see "A Chronology of Important NT Events in Acts and Their Historical Context" in chapter 5.

Luke narrates missionary activity in several other significant cities of Macedonia (i.e., Philippi and Berea) and Achaia (i.e., Athens). But he says only a little about what happens in Asia regarding the spread of the gospel there; Ephesus and its province of Asia will be of greater significance in Paul's third missionary campaign.

12.1 DEBATING AND DECIDING WHO SHOULD GO WHERE (ACTS 15:36–16:10)

Having just completed the pivotal episode of the story of Acts regarding different segments of the church learning to get along together (15:1–35), Luke ironically reports next the occurrence of a serious dispute. Even more ironic is that the debate is between Paul and Barnabas, two heroes of unity in previous episodes. Using a powerful term for this "sharp disagreement" (Greek: *paroxusmos*; 15:39), Luke reports that it is about a strategic matter regarding who to bring with them on a follow-up trip to visit the new believers in the places Paul and Barnabas had traveled during their first missionary journey. And the second journey will entail other decisions as well.

12.1.1 Planning a Follow-Up Ministry (15:36)

Paul initiates this second missionary campaign "some time later," when wondering about the believers in the churches established during the first missionary endeavor. He suggests to Barnabas, "Let us go back and visit the believers in all the towns where we preached the word of the Lord and see how they are doing" (15:36). Paul uses the Greek word for "brethren" (*adelphoi*) to describe the fellow "believers" (so NIV, NLT). These fellow believers in Jesus—those who entered the family of God during the prior missionary trip—are the people with whom Paul suggests he and Barnabas follow up.[2]

12.1.2 The Debate about John Mark (15:37–38)

In agreement with Paul's idea, ***Barnabas*** suggests that they once again take ***John Mark*** on the journey (15:37; cf. 13:5). But the idea of bringing John Mark again does not find favor with Paul because Mark had abandoned them on the prior trip (15:38; cf. 13:13). Paul does not think Mark is ready yet to return to traveling missionary work, and he stands strongly against Barnabas's suggestion. People have strong disagreements about all kinds of things, and resolving them depends somewhat on the nature of the disagreements. By "the nature of the disagreement," I am referring to whether the disagreement involves scriptural issues, scrupulous issues, or strategic issues (see sidebar). Of course, a disagreement can involve more than one issue, but even then,

2. See the discussion of extended family in chapter 5.

it is helpful to reflect on a disagreement's various components and to address each part of the conflict accordingly. In the sharp disagreement between Paul and Barnabas over John Mark's readiness for a second missionary journey, it is easy to see that their disagreement is not so much about a Scripture issue or even a scrupulous matter; rather, they are concerned with a strategic issue.

Three Kinds of Disagreements for Believers

Kinds	Scriptural Issues	Scrupulous Issues	Strategy Issues
Key Questions	What is the truth about what to believe and how to behave?	What behaviors negatively affect one's relationship with God?	What is the best approach for doing a particular ministry?
Key Term Distinctions	"Beliefs" are about facts, things that are either true or false in the real world for all people everywhere.	"Disputable matters" are things that might harm one person's relationship with God but be harmless to another's faith.	"Nonmoral preferences" are about people's opinions on how to do things most effectively and efficiently.
Examples in Acts	Gentiles do not need to become Jews before they can become Christians (Acts 15:13–19).	Gentile Christians should be sensitive to the Jewish Christian scruples (Acts 15:20–32; cf. Rom 14).	When (and where) John Mark would be ready for another missionary trip (Acts 15:36–41).
Might there be another kind of disagreement between believers? For example, regarding a particular issue, Christians may well disagree on which of the three categories to place it in!			

12.1.3 The Strategic Compromise (15:39–41)

It is instructive that Luke does not indicate that either Paul or Barnabas "wins" the disagreement. He simply comments that they parted company (15:39). Could it be that both Paul and Barnabas have accurate assessments of John Mark at this juncture? Barnabas could be correct in his suggestion that Mark is ready to do follow-up work, especially in familiar territory on the island of Cyprus (13:1–12). Likewise, Paul could be correct in his suggestion that Mark is not ready for missionary work in new territory. Interestingly, this assessment is reflected in the strategic compromise they settle on: Barnabas takes Mark to do follow-up work with the churches on Cyprus (15:39; i.e., where Mark had traveled before), and Paul takes Silas to do follow-up work with the churches on the mainland of Asia Minor (15:40–16:2; i.e., where Mark had not traveled before).

While Paul is adamant about not taking John Mark with him into new territory at this juncture, we learn later from Paul's letters of a much improved opinion about a more mature John Mark, who is to be welcomed (Col 4:10) as one of his "fellow workers" (Phlm 24) and as one who "is helpful to me in my ministry" (2 Tim 4:11). Furthermore, as these letters are written by Paul to believers in Asia Minor, clearly he later recognized Mark's growth and preparedness for missionary work in that geographical territory. Paul's assessment of Mark in Acts 15 was not a permanent judgment about his usefulness in ministry; it was merely a matter of preparedness.[3]

In dividing up the follow-up ministry territories, Paul needs a new travel partner and selects ***Silas***, one of the Jerusalem believers who accompanied Paul and Barnabas back to Syrian Antioch after the Jerusalem Council (Acts 15:22, 27). Thus, Luke's earlier and informative introduction of Silas—as a prophet who was effective in encouraging and strengthening others (15:32)—turns out to be literary foreshadowing of Paul's new travel partner (15:40–41).[4]

12.1.4 A New Team Member and Delivering the Apostolic Letter (16:1–5)

Luke reports that Paul and Silas visit the cities of southern Galatia, specifically naming Derbe, Lystra, and Iconium. There they meet a young believer named ***Timothy*** (Acts 16:1), who may have come to faith when Paul and Barnabas had earlier visited southern Galatia. Timothy has a good reputation among the other believers (16:2), and Paul asks him to join the missionary team, which continues Luke's theme regarding the expansion of gospel ministers.

Given that the Jerusalem Council of Acts 15 declares that gentiles need not be circumcised to be true Christians, it seems odd that Paul has Timothy circumcised to join the ministry team (16:3). Some suggest that Paul was behaving inconsistently (or even rebelliously). But Luke carefully explains Timothy's Jewish background (16:1–3; even though his father was Greek, with a Jewish mother, Timothy would be considered Jewish) and immediately mentions the apostolic decree (16:4), so this all fit together just as fine for Luke as it apparently did for Paul (and for Timothy). Paul is not being inconsistent. His circumcision of Timothy was not a requirement for the Jewish Christian; it was an exercise in cultural sensitivity for the sake of practical ministry objectives.[5] Even as the Jerusalem Council was asking gentiles to be sensitive to Jewish scruples, so Paul is asking Timothy as a Jewish man to be sensitive to Jewish scruples. Rather than a contradiction of the Jerusalem Council decision about salvation, this action was in keeping with the Council's decision about sensitivity for the sake of unity. With this unity reminder, Luke offers a brief mid-journey summary statement about the progress of the gospel: "So the churches were strengthened in the faith and grew daily in numbers" (16:5).

---

3. See Howard G. Anderson, "Mark, John," *ZEB* 4:96–97.

4. Interestingly, while he is always called "Silas" in Acts, the name "Silvanus" is used in the NT epistles (e.g., 1 Thess 1:1; 2 Thess 1:1; 2 Cor 1:19; 1 Pet 5:12; note: NIV uses the name "Silas" everywhere). See Arthur M. Ross, "Silas," *ZEB* 5:511–12.

5. Craig L. Blomberg, "The Law in Luke-Acts," *JSNT* 22 (1984): 66. Blomberg adds, "Regardless of Paul's preferences, an uncircumcised 'right hand man', who was regarded as a Jew by Jews, would have made Paul's work in the Jewish synagogues impossible."

12.1.5 Mysterious Guidance of the Spirit (16:6–10)

With his expanded ministry team, Paul attempts to go westward across the province of Asia, most likely from Pisidian Antioch to get to the capital city of Ephesus on its western shore.[6] God has other plans for him, however, and Paul and his team must travel northward "throughout the region of Phrygia and Galatia" (16:6), i.e., through the heart of modern Turkey. Being prevented from going further northward into Bithynia, the Roman province on the southern shore of the Black Sea (16:7), the travelers must head west, passing Mysia (an old name for the northwestern region of Asia Minor), and arrive at the coastal town of ***Troas*** (16:8).

Troas

- A seaport city on the Aegean coast of western Asia Minor near the mouth of the Dardanelles (the natural strait between the Aegean Sea and the Sea of Marmara).
- (Re)founded ca. 310 BC by Antigonus, a successor to Alexander the Great, on a site previously called Sigeia. Lysimachus renamed it Alexandria Troas in 301 BC in memory of Alexander the Great.
- One of the more important and sizable cities of the Roman Empire.
- On his second missionary journey, Paul (with Silas and Timothy) arrived here after being directed circuitously by the Spirit from southern Galatia (Acts 16:6–8).
- Here Paul had a vision of a man calling him to preach the gospel in Macedonia (Acts 16:9–10).
- Here Luke joined Paul's missionary team and traveled with them to Philippi (Acts 16:10–12).
- Paul passed through here on his third missionary journey en route to Macedonia (2 Cor 2:12).
- On the return half of the third missionary journey, while Paul was preaching there one night, a young man named Eutychus fell out of a window and died; but God used Paul to raise him from the dead (Acts 20:5–12).
- Paul left some personal items here (2 Tim 4:13).

Select Bibliography

Richard S. Ascough, "Troas," *EDB*, 1337.
Edward M. Blaiklock, "Troas," *ZEB* 5:943–44.
Colin J. Hemer, "Alexandria Troas," *TynBul* 26 (1975): 79–112.

Without being precise about the route the missionaries take,[7] Luke includes some mysterious comments about how the Spirit guided the group in this part of their travels. The group's (apparently unrequested) divine guidance might have been through an

6. See Craig S. Keener, *Acts: An Exegetical Commentary*, 4 vols. (Grand Rapids: Baker Academic, 2012–2015), 3:2328.

7. Johnson observes, "Although endless scholarly discussion has been devoted to determining the precise route Paul took . . . it is in fact unsolvable"; Luke Timothy Johnson, *The Acts of the Apostles*, SP 5 (Collegeville: Liturgical for Michael Glazier, 1992), 285. For a recent and cautious, but nonetheless convincing, argument for the most likely route the group traveled from Pisidian Antioch to Troas, see Glen L. Thompson and Mark Wilson, "The Route of Paul's Second Journey in Asia Minor: In the Steps of Robert Jewett and Beyond," *TynBul* 67 (2016): 217–46.

audible communication or some other miraculous intervention, or it might have been through some seemingly natural circumstances the Spirit utilized.[8] By Luke's description, however, it was largely God's preventative guidance that gets the group to Troas (16:6–8). Having traveled from the province's southeastern corner to its northwestern corner by a circuitous route, the missionaries must have been perplexed about God's purposes for them, especially given that the guidance they had received so far seems to have been primarily negative.[9]

Ruins of an ancient bath house in Troas

But in Troas divine guidance becomes more positive and specific in that Paul has a vision in the night of a man begging him, "Come over to Macedonia and help us" (16:9). The group decides this is God's direction on where to preach the gospel next (16:10). Perhaps this "positive" guidance regarding where to go next shed some light on the earlier "negative" guidance from the Spirit regarding where not to go. It might be suggested more strongly that God's "negative" guidance prepares his people to be more open to subsequent "positive" guidance. And clearly for Paul and his group, the direction of the Lord—both negative and positive—brought them to the place where they launched into an unforeseen ministry of evangelizing Europe.[10]

In reporting the group's decision to go to Macedonia, Luke switches from narrating the story in third person pronouns (e.g., *he* and *they*) to narrating in first person pronouns (e.g., *we* and *us*): "After Paul had seen the vision, we got ready at once to leave for Macedonia, concluding that God had called us to preach the gospel to them" (16:10).

---

8. For a full-length study on supernatural guidance in Luke-Acts, see John B. F. Miller, *Convinced that God Had Called Us: Dreams, Visions and the Perception of God's Will in Luke-Acts* (Leiden: Brill, 2007).

9. Stott, *Message of Acts*, 260.

10. Eckhard J. Schnabel, *Acts*, ZECNT (Grand Rapids: Zondervan, 2012), 669; cf. Keener, *Acts*, 3:2342.

This begins the first of four ***"we sections"*** (i.e., 16:10–17; 20:5–15; 21:1–18; 27:1–28:16) indicating Luke's presence on Paul's ministry team at these points in the story.[11]

12.2 THE MISSION IN PHILIPPI (ACTS 16:11–40)

Now accompanying Paul, Luke is more detailed in his narrative of the journey from Troas to Macedonia, mentioning an overnight stop on the island of Samothrace and landing at the Macedonian seaport of Neapolis (16:11). Walking about ten miles northwest on the *Via Egnatia* (a second-century BC Roman highway), brings the group to ***Philippi***, a leading city of Macedonia (16:12). Luke's presence with the missionary team at this point makes sense of the amount of space given to reporting events in Philippi.[12]

Samothrace

- An island in the northeast Aegean Sea, about twenty miles off the coast of Thrace in northern Greece.
- Very mountainous, and its 5,300-foot central peak, Mount Fengari, is the most prominent feature of the North Aegean landscape.
- Paul and his companions anchored here for a night on their way from Troas to Neapolis on Paul's second missionary journey (Acts 16:11).
- The mystery cult of Cabeiri and the fertility cult of Cybele both flourished here.
- When the cultic rites were abolished in the fourth century, the island lost its importance.
- A statue of the winged goddess Nike, (a.k.a. Winged Victory of Samothrace) dating to ca. 190 BC, was discovered here in the nineteenth century and is on display in the Louvre in Paris.

Winged goddess Nike
Todd Bolen/BiblePlaces.com, courtesy Louvre Museum

Select Bibliography

Arthur A. Rupprecht, "Samothrace," *ZEB* 5:295.
John Rea, "Samothrace" *WBD*, 1512–13.

11. See the more extended discussion of the "we sections" in chapter 4.
12. Scholars have variously suggested that Luke's focus on Philippi betrays a kind of hometown pride because Luke and/or perhaps Theophilus hailed from there (or at least had lived there for some time); e.g., see Richard G. Fellows, "Name Giving by Paul and the Destination of Acts," *TynBul* 67 (2016): 249–51.

12.2.1 Meeting a Woman Named Lydia (16:11–15)

We have noted Paul's usual practice of Jews-first ministry, preaching first in the local synagogue, but Philippi lacked such a meeting place. So on a Sabbath day the missionary team (i.e., "we") goes to the river where they were hoping "to find a place of prayer"—a place where others would be worshiping the God of the Jews on the Sabbath (16:13). If one were looking for a gathering of worshipful Jews ready to hear about the fulfillment of Scripture in Jesus, the nearness of water would be helpful because of its use in Jewish ceremonial washings.[13] Finding a group of women gathered at the river might explain the lack of a synagogue in Philippi, for a group of ten Jewish men was required for establishing a synagogue (see b. Meg. 23b; y. Meg. 4:4). One particular woman with whom the missionaries speak is ***Lydia*** from Thyatira, a city that was, interestingly, in the Lydian region of Asia Minor.[14] Thyatiran artisans are credited with perfecting the process for making purple dye from the madder root (more cost-effective than the dye from the shellfish murex).[15] And Lydia was "a dealer in purple cloth" (16:14a), from which can be inferred that she was a person of some wealth.[16]

The ruins of ancient Philippi
Todd Bolen/ BiblePlaces.com

13. Stott, *Message of Acts*, 263.

14. It is possible that the woman in Acts 16:14 had taken on the name of her place of origin; this was a common practice for slaves who achieved freed status, but we cannot be certain this was the case for Lydia. Conversely, some suggest that Luke's reference to her might be an adjective, i.e., "the Lydian [woman]," rather than her name; see D. Edmond Hiebert, "Lydia (person)," *ZEB* 3:1140; and JoAnn Ford Watson, "Lydia (person)," *EDB*, 832.

15. See Gary M. Burge, "Thyatira," *EDB*, 1307; and Edward M. Blaiklock, "Thyatira," *ZEB* 5:853–55. Thyatira is one of "the seven cities of the apocalypse" of Revelation, addressed specifically in Rev 2:18–29.

16. See Richard S. Ascough, *Lydia: Paul's Cosmopolitan Hostess*, Paul's Social Network: Brothers and Sisters in Faith (Collegeville, MN: Liturgical, 2009).

Philippi

- Located in eastern Macedonia on the plain east of Mount Pangaion between the Struma and Nestos Rivers.
- First settled in the sixth century BC and originally called Krenides ("the springs") but was renamed ca. 358 BC by Philip II of Macedon, the father of Alexander the Great.
- Was significant for its command over the regional fertile plain, the nearby prosperous gold mines, and its strategic location on a prominent Roman highway, the *Via Egnatia*.
- Came under Roman control in 167 BC when the Romans conquered the Macedonians.
- Was the site of a series of significant Roman civil war battles in 42 BC when Mark Antony and Octavian (who later became Caesar Augustus) defeated the assassins of Julius Caesar: Cassius and Brutus.
- Made a Roman colony by Augustus, who settled many veterans of the civil wars there. Roman colonists were granted special privileges (e.g., tax exemptions and property rights).
- Where a God-fearer named Lydia became a believer and hosted the ministry team on Paul's second missionary journey (Acts 16:13–15).
- Where Paul and Silas were imprisoned, which led to the jailor and his family coming to faith in Christ. Paul and Silas appeal to their Roman citizenship for better treatment of believers (Acts 16:16–40).
- Location of a famous school of medicine connected with a physicians guild that sent members throughout the Hellenistic world.
- Where Luke, a physician, spent time between Paul's second and third missionary journeys, arriving with Paul on his second missionary journey (Acts 16:10–12) and departing with him when Paul came through Philippi on his third missionary journey (Acts 20:5–6).
- Known for its generosity, the church at Philippi received the epistle of Philippians from Paul, expressing his thanks and encouraging them to value their citizenship in heaven.

Select Bibliography

John McRay, *Archaeology and the New Testament* (Grand Rapids: Baker, 1991), 283–92.

Arthur A. Rupprecht, "Philippi," *ZEB* 4:860–62.

Richard A. Spencer, "Philippi," *EDB*, 1048–49.

Eduard Verhoef, *Philippi: How Christianity Began in Europe* (New York: Bloomsbury T&T Clark, 2013).

Howard F. Vos, "Philippi," *WBD*, 1330–31.

Similar to his description of the gentile Cornelius, the "God-fearing" man (10:2, 22) whom Peter led to faith in Jesus, Luke reports that Lydia is "a worshiper of God" and "the Lord opened her heart to respond" to the gospel (16:14b). As in the story of Cornelius, Lydia "and the members of her household" express their newfound faith in Jesus with the Christian ceremony of water baptism (16:15a; see sidebar). And with this Lydia insists on hosting the missionary team in her home (16:15b). From the beginning of the church with its devotion to breaking bread together (cf. 2:42; 4:32–35), Luke continues to narrate a radical generosity as a consistent practice of those with faith in Jesus Christ.

Water Baptism in Luke-Acts

Role of Baptism: The rite of water baptism is a symbolic practice by which a person identifies with a group of people with whom they share a common worldview or faith system (e.g., John's "baptism of repentance" in Luke 3:3; cf. 7:29–30; Acts 10:37; 13:24; 18:25; 19:3–4; Christian baptism in Acts 2:38, 41; 8:38; 9:18; 10:47–48; 16:15, 33; 18:8; 19:5; 22:16).

The Practice of Baptism

1. Luke never requires water baptism for salvation but regularly records believers expressing their faith via baptism. The potentially problematic wording of Acts 2:38, where baptism is mentioned before forgiveness ("Repent and be baptized . . . for the forgiveness of your sins"), should be understood in light of passages such as Acts 16:30–34 ("Believe in the Lord Jesus, and you will be saved," after which the believers were baptized). Baptism should be a natural expression of repentance and faith but is not the effecting agent of salvation.
2. Repentance and faith are the regular prerequisites for Christian baptism; even instances of whole households being baptized indicate belief on the part of those in the household (e.g., Acts 10:44–48; 16:30–34; 18:8).
3. Even though baptism is a community rite for people to identify with others of the same faith, it is possible for people to participate in it under false pretenses (e.g., Simon Magus in Acts 8:13; cf. 8:18–24).

12.2.2 Meeting a Demonized Slave Girl (16:16–18)

The persisting "we section" here indicates Luke's firsthand witness to the events in Philippi. And one day the group ("we") meets a demonized slave girl who earns money for her owners by predicting the future (16:16). She follows the missionary team, shouting, "These men are servants of the Most High God, who are telling you the way to be saved" (16:17; cf. some of Jesus's encounters with demonized people, e.g., Luke 4:33–34, 41; 8:27–28). On the face of it, what the slave girl was announcing seems true enough. But rather than supporting faith in Jesus as the one-and-only way to be saved, her announcement has a pluralistic bent to it: she is announcing that the missionaries had *a* way to be saved (Greek: *hodon sōtērias*). Thus, her prophetic announcement has a deceptive half-truth feature that the people of that pluralistic society might have missed.

It may seem odd that Luke reports the demonized slave girl keeping up her shouting "for many days" before Paul does something about it (16:18). Demonic activity, however, then as now, is not always accompanied by overtly strange manifestations, and given the deceptive nature of her announcement, the slave girl's demon trouble may have been difficult to notice. Indeed, if it cannot draw attention away from the gospel, demonic activity aims at distorting the truth of the gospel. Eventually, however, Paul is not only aware of but annoyed by the distracting deceptive declarations, and he speaks authoritatively to the spirit: "In the name of Jesus Christ I command you to come out of her!" (16:18). Paul does not appeal to his own authority but to the authority of Jesus as Messiah (i.e., Christ), and the spirit leaves the slave girl immediately.

12.2.3 Meeting the Roman Jailer (16:19–40)

Because the slave girl's freedom from demonic influence had negative financial ramifications for her owners, they seize Paul and Silas and take them before the Philippian magistrates. Concealing their financial motives, they press exaggerated charges against the leaders of the missionary team: "These men are Jews, and are throwing our city into an uproar by advocating customs unlawful for us Romans to accept or practice" (16:20–21). The half-truths of their (now formerly demonized) slave girl have given way to them speaking their own half-truths. The missionaries are indeed Jews, but Judaism was tolerated in the first-century Roman world (see sidebar), and they were hardly causing an uproar. Ironically, the slave owners are the instigators of the trouble, with the crowd joining their attack on Paul and Silas.[17] To quiet the situation, the magistrates have Paul and Silas beaten and thrown into prison under the watchful eye of a jailer (16:22–23), who secures them in the jail (16:24).

Roman Religious Tolerance

From A. N. Sherwin-White, *Roman Society and Roman Law in the New Testament* (Oxford: Oxford University Press, 1963; repr., Grand Rapids: Baker, 1992), 79–80.

> All Roman historians are aware of the dualism that typifies Roman policy in this matter. Officially the Roman citizen may not practice any alien cult that has not received the public sanction of the State, but customarily he might do so as long as his cult did not otherwise offend against the laws and usages of Roman life, i.e. so long as it did not involve political and social crimes. The Julio-Claudian period was characterized by general laxity towards foreign cults, which spread freely in Italy and Rome. But this laxity is occasionally interrupted by a sharp reversal of policy when the extravagances of a particular sect call down a temporary and ill-enforced ban upon its activities. . . . The grounds of such bans, however, are found, not in the general principle of excluding alien cults as such, but in the criminal by-products of the cults. . . . This is the general picture of the age, with which no historian seriously disagrees.

17. See Richard N. Longenecker, "Acts," pp. 663–1102 in *Luke-Acts*, vol. 10 of *The Expositor's Bible Commentary*, ed. Tremper Longman III and David E. Garland, rev. ed. (Grand Rapids: Zondervan, 2007), 968.

Paul's prison in ancient Philippi

A prison cell interior

But this unjust treatment becomes for Paul and Silas an opportunity for spreading the gospel message: while they pray and sing hymns to God in their prison cell, the other prisoners listen (16:25). Then, about midnight, an earthquake shakes the prison to its foundations such that "all the prison doors flew open, and everyone's chains came loose" (16:26). This miraculous prison release is not encouraging to the jailer. Reminiscent of Peter's miraculous prison rescue when his jailers were held accountable by Roman law for the loss of their prisoner (cf. 12:19), seeing the prison doors open, the Philippian jailer assumes his prisoners have escaped and that he will be severely punished. So rather than await a disgraceful end, the jailer draws his own sword to kill himself, but Paul shouts out to stop him (16:27–28).

Hearing that the prisoners had not escaped, the jailer's initial despair subsides, and he soon feels a greater sense of accountability to a power higher than that of the city magistrates. Rushing to bring Paul and Silas out, he asks them, "Sirs, what must I do to be saved?" (16:30). Their answer is no surprise to Luke's readers: "Believe in the Lord Jesus, and you will be saved" (16:31). Then they share the gospel

The *Didache* on Baptism

The *Didache* is a short anonymous book on early church teachings (ca. AD 70-110). One whole section—chapter 7—treats some practical matters of carrying out the Christian initiation ceremony of baptism.

Didache 7.1–4 (ca. AD 70–110)

But with respect to baptism, baptize as follows: Having said all these things in advance, baptize in the name of the Father and of the Son and of the Holy Spirit, in running water.

But if you do not have running water, baptize in some other water. And if you cannot baptize in cold water, use warm.

But if you have neither, pour water on the head three times in the name of Father and Son and Holy Spirit.

But both the one baptizing and the one being baptized should fast before the baptism, along with some others if they can. But command the one being baptized to fast one or two days in advance.

message with the jailer and "all the others in his house" (16:32), and as an expression of their faith in Jesus, the jailer and all his household are baptized (16:33–34).

The next day when the city magistrates send word for Paul and Silas to be released (16:35–36), Paul is affronted by this quiet dismissal and refuses to leave the prison. He says to the officers, "They beat us publicly without a trial, even though we are Roman citizens, and threw us into prison. And now do they want to get rid of us quietly? No! Let them come themselves and escort us out" (16:37). Because Roman law prohibited punishment of Roman citizens without a trial (see sidebar), the magistrates are alarmed to learn of their mistake in hastily punishing the missionaries (16:38–39).[18] Paul's insistence on the magistrates publicly admitting their error in mistreating the missionaries will do little for Paul and Silas as they move on from Philippi, but it will do much for the believers who remain in Philippi. Paul forces the magistrates to admit that Christians cannot be punished on false charges and that there is nothing inherently illegal about believing in Jesus.

Roman Law against Beating Roman Citizens without Trial

Roman law had a long history of prohibiting punishment of Roman citizens without first putting them through a proper trial. The first-century Roman historian Livy comments on this Roman legal posture, particularly the Porcian laws from ca. 299 BC, which expanded on the earlier Valerian laws that date to ca. 509 BC. Later a second-century Roman legal authority named Ulpian—whose writings were later collected into a compendium of legal works call the *Digest* by order of the sixth-century Byzantine emperor Justinian—likewise comments on the similar rule in Julian law (first century BC). Cf. Cicero, *Verr.* 2.5.66 §§169-70.

Livy, *History of Rome* 10.9.4 (ca. 27-9 BC)

> Yet the Porcian law alone seems to have been passed to protect the persons of the citizens, imposing, as it did, a heavy penalty if anyone should scourge or put to death a Roman citizen.

Ulpian (ca. AD 170-223), *Digest* 48.6.7

> Anyone who is invested with authority or power, and subjects a Roman citizen to death or scourging, or orders this to be done, or attaches anything to his neck for the purpose of torturing him, without permitting him to appeal, is liable under the Julian Law relating to Public Violence. This also applies to deputies and orators, and their attendants, where anyone is proved to have beaten them, or caused them any injury.

18. See more on Roman citizenship in chapter 14.

Thus, Paul's demand for just treatment is not in his own interest as much as it is a preventative measure against the improper treatment of believers living in Philippi.[19] In fact, after leaving the prison, Paul and Silas go to Lydia's home and encourage the Philippian believers. After this, Luke reports simply, "Then they left" (16:40), a third-person statement that seems to indicate that Luke remained in Philippi until a future time.

12.3 THE MISSION IN THESSALONICA AND BEREA (ACTS 17:1–15)

Paul and his missionary team, albeit without Luke now, move westward on the *Via Egnatia*, ministering in other Macedonian cities. Luke mentions other towns (e.g., Amphipolis and Apollonia; 17:1) but focuses on Paul's ministry in Thessalonica (about ninety miles from Philippi on the highway) and then in Berea (southwest off the highway). Thessalonica and Berea both have Jewish synagogues, so Paul can utilize his usual approach of preaching the gospel there first. In both cities Paul's preaching is met with mixed results.

Amphipolis

- A Macedonian city near the northern coast of the Aegean Sea and located about thirty miles from Philippi on the *Via Egnatia*.
- The name Amphipolis ("around the city") may stem from its location on the Struma River, which curved around the city on three sides.
- Conquered by the Romans in 168 BC and a year later made the capital of the first district of Macedonia until Thessalonica was made the provincial capital of Macedonia.
- Economically important because of crops in the region's fertile soil, the fine wool produced in the area, and the silver and gold mined there.
- Strategically located with control of the Struma River waterway and a bridge for the *Via Egnatia* to cross the river, and it was only about three miles from the seaport city of Eion on the Aegean Sea.
- Visited by Paul on his way to Thessalonica from Philippi (Acts 17:1).

Select Bibliography

Richard S. Ascough, "Amphipolis," *EDB*, 57.
Arthur A. Rupprecht, "Amphipolis," *ZEB* 1:173.
E. Jerry Vardaman, "Amphipolis," *WBD*, 62–63.

19. See Darrell L. Bock, *Acts*, BECNT (Grand Rapids: Baker Academic, 2007), 545; cf. the nuanced discussion of Paul's use of his Roman citizenship in Ben Witherington III, *The Acts of the Apostles: A Socio-Rhetorical Commentary* (Grand Rapids: Eerdmans, 1998; Carlisle: Paternoster, 1998), 499–502.

Apollonia

- A town in eastern Macedonia, toward the middle of the *Via Egnatia*, about thirty miles from Amphipolis to its east-northeast and about thirty-eight miles from Thessalonica to its west.
- One of several towns in antiquity with this name and less famous than the Apollonia of Illyria near the western end of the *Via Egnatia*.
- Identified by some with modern Pollino.
- Visited by Paul and Silas on the second missionary journey while traveling from Philippi to Thessalonica (Acts 17:1).

Select Bibliography

Richard S. Ascough, "Apollonia," *EDB*, 77.
Edward M. Blaiklock, "Apollonia," *ZEB* 1:244.
E. Jerry Vardaman, "Apollonia," *WBD*, 112–13.

12.3.1 In Thessalonica (17:1–9)

The city of ***Thessalonica*** was the capital of first-century Macedonia. It had a large enough Jewish population to have a synagogue, where Paul preaches the gospel for three Sabbath days ("As was his custom"; 17:2). While the synagogue audience might be more prepared to hear the good news of the Hebrew Scriptures being fulfilled in Jesus Christ, for the Jewish mindset, however, a crucified Messiah was oxymoronic and difficult to accept. After all, the Scriptures declare that one hung on a cross was cursed by God (Deut 21:22–23; cf. 1 Cor 1:23). Thus, Paul must reason from the Scriptures to prove that the Messiah had to suffer, taking God's curse upon himself in our place, before rising from the dead victorious over death (Acts 17:2–3; cf. 9:20–22). And in his letters, we see Paul's fuller explanation that all sinners fall under God's curse for their disobedience, but it was Jesus who took that curse upon himself in the place of sinners to redeem them (see sidebar on Gal 3:13–14).

Paul's defense of Jesus as Messiah is somewhat effective, persuading "some of the Jews," "a large number of God-fearing Greeks," and "quite a few prominent women" (Acts 17:4). Nevertheless, some Jews are resistant to the gospel message and jealous over those who had become believers in Jesus (17:5). Thus, as persistently evident on the first missionary campaign, the ministry in Thessalonica has mixed results. As noted, even while many believers in Jesus remain Jewish in their ethnicity, Luke has begun using the label "the Jews" to reference people of Jewish religious convictions who reject Jesus. Thus, the Jewish religion takes on an identity of its own in distinction from the Jewish Messiah Jesus.

Thessalonica

- Founded in 315 BC by Cassander, a Macedonian general who named it after his wife, the daughter of Phillip and stepsister of Alexander the Great.
- Strategically located on important trade routes for both land and sea, with a magnificent harbor on the Thermaic Gulf as well as being on the Roman highway known as the *Via Egnatia*.
- In the Roman era, the capital of the second of the four districts of Macedonia, and then the capital of all of Macedonia when it was reorganized into one Roman province.
- Rewarded with the status of a free city for remaining loyal to Antony and Octavian in the second civil war between Caesar and Pompey (42 BC).
- As a free city, could appoint its own city magistrates, who were unusually titled "politarchs," a name Luke uses (Acts 17:6, 8; "city officials" in NIV) and that is attested in several first-century AD inscriptions found in the area.
- Visited by Paul on his second missionary journey (Acts 17:1–9; 1 Thess 2:1–2) and likely on his third missionary journey as well (cf. Acts 20:1–6; Phil 4:15–16).
- In the centuries that followed, the Thessalonian church remained one of the major strongholds of Christianity and was even dubbed "The Orthodox City."
- Home of some named NT Christians, including Jason (Acts 17:5), Secundus and Aristarchus (Acts 20:4), and possibly Demas (2 Tim 4:10).

Select Bibliography

Richard S. Ascough, "Thessalonica," *EDB*, 1300–01.
Leon Morris, "Thessalonica," *WBD*, 1698–99.
Robert H. Mounce, "Thessalonica," *BEB*, 4:2056–57.
Arthur A. Rupprecht, "Thessalonica," *ZEB* 5:837–39.

The Jews rejecting the gospel in Thessalonica form a mob and start a riot against the believers (17:5). Unable to find Paul and Silas at Jason's home, where the missionaries had been staying, the mob drags Jason and some other believers before the local authorities, whom Luke calls "politarchs" (17:6, 8; "city officials" in NIV), a label attested in archeological findings (see sidebar).[20] The charges against the believers are somewhat telling regarding the progress of the gospel: "These men who have caused trouble all over the world have now come here. . . . They are all defying Caesar's decrees, saying that there is another king, one called Jesus" (17:6–7). With some exaggeration, the believers are thus charged with disturbing the peace and with sedition.[21] Of course, ironically, even the unbelieving Jews view God as a greater authority than Caesar, but they are utilizing rhetoric in an attempt to get the Christians in trouble.[22] Before being released,

20. See G. H. R. Horsley, "The Politarchs," in *The Book of Acts in Its Graeco-Roman Setting*, ed. David W. J. Gill and Conrad Gempf, BAFCS 2 (Grand Rapids: Eerdmans, 1994; Carlisle: Paternoster, 1994), 419–31.

21. Bock, *Acts*, 552; Witherington, *Acts*, 507; cf. Joseph A. Fitzmyer, *The Acts of the Apostles*, AB 31 (New York: Doubleday, 1998), 596, who divides the second charge into two and suggests three charges: disturbing the peace, inciting against Caesar, and proclaiming a new king.

22. For a detailed discussion of how to interpret the charges brought against Paul and Silas in Thessalonica,

Why the Messiah Had to Die

Galatians 3:13–14 (citing Deut 21:23)

Christ redeemed us from the curse of the law by becoming a curse for us, for it is written: "Cursed is everyone who is hung on a pole." He redeemed us in order that the blessing given to Abraham might come to the Gentiles through Christ Jesus, so that by faith we might receive the promise of the Spirit.

Ruins of ancient Thessalonica
Andrei Nekrassov/Shutterstock.com

the Christians are made to post bond (17:9), i.e., promising to send the missionaries away quietly and not having them return for the term of the ruling.[23] Stott suggests that this legal ban is what blocked Paul from returning to Thessalonica as he wished later in the second missionary journey (a blockage Paul credits to Satan; 1 Thess 2:18).[24] Participation in gospel ministry can be dangerous and costly.

---

see Jeffrey A. D. Weima, "The Political Charges against Paul and Silas in Acts 17:6–7: Roman Benefaction in Thessalonica," in *Stones, Bones, and the Sacred: Essays on Material Culture and Ancient Religion in Honor of Dennis E. Smith*, ed. Alan H. Cadwallader, ECL 21 (Atlanta: SBL Press, 2016), 241–68.

23. Witherington, *Acts*, 509; cf. A. N. Sherwin-White, *Roman Society and Roman Law in the New Testament* (Oxford: Oxford University Press, 1963; repr., Grand Rapids: Baker, 1992), 95–96.

24. Stott, *Message of Acts*, 273.

Politarch Inscription

Located in the British Museum, this is one of many inscriptions that use the term *politarchs* (as indicated) to refer to the chief magistrates of Macedonian cities. This stone was removed from a gateway into Thessalonica and thus confirms Luke's use of the term in Acts 17:6 and 8 with reference to the rulers of that city.

HolyLandPhotos.org

12.3.2 In Berea (17:10–15)

The Thessalonian opposition to the gospel resulted in the local believers whisking the missionaries away under cover of darkness to the nearby town of ***Berea***. As expected, they go first to the Berean synagogue (Acts 17:10), but unexpectedly Luke notes, "Now the Berean Jews were of more noble character than those in Thessalonica, for they received the message with great eagerness and examined the Scriptures every day to see if what Paul said was true" (17:11). There is nobility in eager listeners investigating the truth on their own, and one result at Berea is that many of them believe, including "a number of prominent Greek women and many Greek men" (17:12). So as at Thessalonica, the gospel goes to both Jews and non-Jews.

Nevertheless, some unbelieving Jews of Thessalonica come to thwart Paul's preaching in Berea (17:13). So again, the preaching of the gospel has mixed results, with some believing and some rejecting the message. Furthermore, Paul's effectiveness is such that the opponents can tolerate it no longer, and so they resort to violence. The opposition directed specifically to Paul's preaching alarms the Berean believers such that they hurry him away to Athens and then return with his request that Silas and Timothy join him there soon (17:14–15).

Berea

- A city in southwestern Macedonia, about forty miles west of Thessalonica.
- Mention of the city by Thucydides (*History of the Peloponnesian War,* 1.61.4) evidences its existence by the end of the fifth century BC.
- Not on the *Via Egnatia,* which passed it by several miles to the north.
- The first Macedonian city to surrender to Rome. It was placed in the third of four Macedonian districts, prior to Macedonia being reorganized into a Roman province.
- Became one of the most populous first-century centers of Macedonia.
- Where Paul and his companions found refuge after the Jews cause them trouble in Thessalonica. The Berean Jews were more open to Paul's teaching and double-checked what he said against Scripture (Acts 17:10–15).
- Described by Cicero as a town off the beaten track where a Roman governor named Piso hid from complaints experienced in Thessalonica in a manner similar to Paul (see Cicero, *Pis.* 36 §89).
- Home of Sopater son of Pyrrhus, who was on Paul's ministry team during the third missionary journey (Acts 20:4).

Select Bibliography

Richard S. Ascough, "Beroea," *EDB*, 167–68.
Edward M. Blaiklock, "Berea," *ZEB* 1:558.

12.4 THE MISSION IN ATHENS (ACTS 17:16–34)

The golden era for ***Athens*** had been in the fifth and fourth centuries BC, and its political and commercial importance in the first century AD had long been surpassed by Corinth. While it could still glory in its great past, by the first century Athens had shrunk to a quiet little city of about five thousand residents.[25] Even so, in terms of education, philosophy, art, and architecture, Athens remained an important culture center in the first-century world.[26] It is no surprise, then, that Luke wants to give a little more story space to Paul's ministry here (i.e., nineteen verses compared to nine verses for Thessalonica and six verses for Berea).

25. Ernst Haenchen, *The Acts of the Apostles: A Commentary,* trans. and ed. Bernard Noble, Gerald Shinn, Hugh Anderson, and R. McLeod Wilson (Philadelphia: Westminster, 1971), 517.

26. John B. Polhill, *Acts,* NAC (Nashville: Broadman, 1992), 365–66. Conzelmann suggests that Athens served as "the museum of classical culture for the Hellenistic world"; Hans Conzelmann, "The Address of Paul on the Aeropagus," pp. 217–30 in *Studies in Luke-Acts: Essays Presented in Honor of Paul Schubert,* ed. Leander E. Keck and Louis J. Martyn (Nashville: Abingdon, 1966; repr., Philadelphia: Fortress, 1980), 217.

The Cultural Influence of Ancient Athens

From F. F. Bruce, *The Acts of the Apostles: The Greek Text with Introduction and Commentary*, 3rd ed. (Grand Rapids: Eerdmans, 1990; Leicester: Apollos, 1990), 375–76.

> Athens, the cradle of democracy, attained the foremost place among the Greek city-states early in the fifth century B.C. by reason of the lead she took in resisting the Persian invasions. She was at the height of her power between 478 and 431 B.C., and after her defeat by Sparta in the Peloponnesian War (431–404 B.C.) was not long in regaining much of her earlier influence. In the fourth century she again took the lead in resistance to Philip's aggression, and after his victory at Chaeronea (338 B.C.) was generously treated by him and allowed to retain much of her ancient freedom, which she enjoyed until the Roman conquest of Greece in 146 B.C. The Romans, too, in consideration of her glorious past, left her to carry on her own institutions as a free and allied city (*ciuitas libera et foederati*) within the empire. The sculpture, literature, and oratory of Athens in the fifth and fourth centuries B.C. remain unsurpassed. In philosophy, too, she took the leading place, being the native city of Socrates and Plato and the adopted home of Aristotle, Epicurus, and Zeno. Her cultural influence in the Greek world is also seen in the fact that it was the Attic dialect of Gk., spoken at first over a very restricted area as compared with Ionic and Doric, that formed the base of the later Hellenistic speech (Koinē). It was at this time a leading center of learning; in modern idiom we might describe it as a great university city (although the university analogy is overdone by [some]).

Ruins of ancient Athens
Lambros Kazan/ Shutterstock.com

Athens

- The capital of modern Greece and the chief city of the ancient city-state of Attica.
- Named for the Greek goddess of wisdom: Athena.
- About five miles from the Aegean Sea on the narrow plain between Mount Parnes, Mount Pentelicus, and Mount Hymettus.
- Its location was good for olive groves and vineyards; nearby clay beds were resources for pottery making; silver, lead, and marble were also mined in the region.
- Rose to prominence from its role in the Persian War, and its most glorious days were in the mid-fifth century BC. It became a democracy and grew in its encouragement of the arts and the study of philosophy, rhetoric, and science.
- The Peloponnesian War of the late-fifth century BC brought the city into a period of repeated subjugation from which it struggled to regain some sense of successful independence, ultimately being conquered by Rome.
- Enclosed by fortification walls through most of its history; another wall went around the Acropolis in the south-central area of the city.
- The steep hill of the acropolis remains the city's dominant feature. It is home to the Parthenon (the large shrine dedicated to Athena) and the ruins of several other shrines (e.g., to Athena Nike, to Erechtheus and Poseidon, to Roma and Augustus).
- Overshadowed by the political and commercial power of Corinth (only fifty miles away) in the first century; it had become a small town but nevertheless remained a cultural and educational center.
- Paul's preaching on Jesus and the resurrection led to his being summoned by the Areopagus, the civic body responsible for the city's religious and moral life (Acts 17:16–34).
- Of the several nearby harbor villages, the once fortified Piraeus is a likely candidate for the one utilized in Paul's travels.

Select Bibliography

Conrad Gempf, "Athens, Paul at," *DPL*, 51–54.

John McRay, *Archaeology and the New Testament* (Grand Rapids: Baker, 1991), 298–310.

Scott Nash, "Athens," *EDB*, 126–27.

Arthur A. Rupprecht "Athens," *ZEB* 1:431–34.

12.4.1 Paul's First Few Days in Athens (17:16–18)

Waiting in Athens for Silas and Timothy to catch up with him, Paul tours the city and becomes "greatly distressed to see that the city was full of idols" (Acts 17:16).[27] Luke's term for "greatly distressed" (Greek: *paroxunomai*) is utilized in the LXX to reference God being "provoked" to anger by idolatry (e.g., Deut 9:18; 32:16–19; Ps 106:29; Isa 65:3; Hos 8:5). Paul's response is to reason with the Athenian Jews and God-fearers in the synagogue (Acts 17:17a), where he would naturally find people likewise distressed about the city's idolatry.[28] But Luke adds that Paul also reasons with people

27. Charles Kingsley Barrett, *A Critical and Exegetical Commentary on the Acts of the Apostles*, 2 vols., ICC (Edinburgh: T&T Clark, 1994/1998), 2:828. For a survey of the Athenian statues, temples, and monuments as Paul might have seen them, see Oscar T. Broneer, "Athens: 'City of Idol Worship,'" *BA* 21 (1958): 2–28.

28. David G. Peterson, *The Acts of the Apostles*, Pillar New Testament Commentary (Grand Rapids: Eerdmans, 2009), 489.

in the marketplace (17:17b), which was a center of public life and interaction as well as commerce. The word for Paul's reasoning (Greek: *dialegomai*) relates to discourse more than preaching (Luke uses the term only in the latter half of Acts where gentile engagement is more prominent: 17:2, 17; 18:4, 19; 19:8, 9; 20:7, 9; 24:12, 25).[29] This recalls the classic philosophical figure of Socrates, notorious for public discussions in Athens, and Luke may well be intending to draw an analogy between Paul and Athens's most famous citizen.[30] What is unmistakable from Luke's report is that the widespread idolatry in Athens moved Paul to make a broad and energetic response.

As is well known, from ancient times Athens had been a chief center of philosophical thought, especially for four particular groups of philosophers: Epicureans, Stoics, Platonists, and Peripatetics.[31] Luke specifies that Paul debates with members of the first two groups, which were the most influential schools of thought.[32] ***Epicureanism*** might be compared to modern deistic thinking: "God exists but is not here, so try to find your own way through pain and live for whatever pleasure you can find." ***Stoicism***, on the other hand, might be compared to modern pantheistic thinking: "God is in all, so it is up to you to do your duty and to be self-sufficient." Thus, with admitted oversimplification, Stott suggests that Epicureans would emphasize chance, escapement from pain, and the enjoyment of pleasure, while the Stoics would emphasize fatalism, submission to circumstances, and the endurance of pain.[33] As different as these two philosophies are, they share a tendency toward materialism that could lead to dissatisfaction with life's apparent meaninglessness. Because they tended to live as if the world operated either by impersonal chance (Epicureans) or by inevitable fate (Stoics), Paul's preaching about a loving Ruler, personal Creator, and life-sustaining God could sound like good news to them.[34]

From the philosophers, Paul receives two derogatory responses. Some ask, "What is this babbler trying to say?" Others remark, "He seems to be advocating foreign gods" (17:18a). The Greek term for "babbler" (*spermologos*) pictures a person as a seed-picking bird scavenging for ideas that he could patch together and pass off as his own. Thus, some ancients used this label as an insult for people they perceived to be posing as philosophers by using borrowed jargon and trading in secondhand ideas.[35]

---

29. See Schnabel, *Acts*, 723–24.

30. Barrett, *Acts*, 2:828; cf. 829–30; see also Peterson, *Acts*, 490.

31. Cf. the second-century rhetorician Lucian, *The Eunuch* 3.

32. Keener, *Acts*, 3:2582.

33. Stott, *Message of Acts*, 281. See detailed excurses on the two philosophies in Keener, *Acts*, 3:2584–95.

34. William J. Larkin Jr., *Acts*, The IVP New Testament Commentary Series (Downers Grove, IL: InterVarsity Press, 1995), 257; cf. Keener, *Acts*, 3:2636–67 for a more extensive analysis of the philosophers' potential responses to Paul's description of God.

35. E.g., Demosthenes, *Cor.* 127; Philostratus, *Vit. Apoll.* 5.20.3; cf. Plutarch, *Busybody* 2, *Mor.* 516C. See the discussion in Keener, *Acts*, 3:2596. Thus, Peterson suggests that the Athenians were accusing Paul of ignorant plagiarism and being a religious charlatan; Peterson, *Acts*, 490.

The Philosophies of Stoicism and Epicureanism Compared

Area of Belief	Stoicism (founder: Zeno)	Epicureanism (founder: Epicurus)
Creation	The world has been created out of fire, the foundational element. From fire came air, from air water, and from water earth. The *logos*, the impersonal forces that create and hold together, keep the elements in balance.	The world developed out of a collection of atoms in space that operate according to natural laws. An essentially materialist worldview, Epicureanism has no room for divine creation, even though believing in gods.
God	Holding to pantheistic materialism, Stoics understand god as in everything. They equate the supreme god with fate, nature, *logos*, and the "world soul" (with the universe understood as a living organism), even though they may refer to him simply as Zeus. The gods of the popular religions exist, but such mythologies are only crude expressions of the truth.	Gods exist and are worthy of worship and honor, but they live outside the world in interstellar spaces. They do not intervene in human affairs, so there is not place for providence or prayer. Nor is there any reason to fear them. Because so little attention is paid to the gods, the Epicureans are called "atheists" by their contemporaries.
Soul	The soul is corporeal, similar to the human body. Its closest comparison is to the warm breath of a human.	The soul is corporeal and, like the human body, is composed of atoms. It cannot exist apart from the body.
Sin	There is no concept of sin or offending the will of a holy, righteous God. Error is nothing more than failing to attain the ideal, or acting contrary to the laws of nature.	There is no concept of sin or offending the will of a holy, righteous God. The avoidance of actions and chance happenings that produce pain is a major objective of Epicureans.
Ethics	All live in the grip of the relentless pull of fate. Although people have no control over destiny, they do have the power to control themselves and their wills. The pursuit of virtue is the primary good. To be virtuous is to live in harmony with reason (*logos*) and to be at one with nature.	The chief goal of human existence is to live in accord with nature and the physical laws of the universe. Pleasure is aligned with nature and instructs one how to live in harmony with her. Pleasure represents the absence of pain. Friendship in community is a primary source of pleasure.
Afterlife	There is a limited survival after death, but not in the sense of a personal, individual existence. Individual human souls will ultimately be absorbed into the basic elements in periodic cosmic conflagrations. There is no underworld or place of afterlife torment.	There is no life after death. When the body dies, the soul also disintegrates. There will be no bodily resurrection, and there is no underworld or place of afterlife torment.

Created with information from Clinton E. Arnold, "Acts," *ZIBBCNT*, 2B:172–73. See Diogenes Laertius, *Lives*, 7.1 §§1–160 on Zeno and the Stoics and *Lives*, 10 §§1–21 on Epicurus and the Epicureans.

More than simply accusing Paul of merely gossiping the ideas of others, the second response could imply that Paul might be dangerous.[36] Advocating "foreign gods" is the charge that led to the death of Socrates in Athens.[37] Perhaps some in the audience misunderstood Paul to be speaking about two new deities—Jesus and Anastasia (the Greek word for "resurrection"; 17:18b)—especially because the idea of rising from the dead would be so novel to Athenian thinking.[38] Given the differing worldviews of Paul's audience, the presence of some misunderstanding is understandable. But the resurrection of Jesus is the centerpiece of the gospel message, so Paul will return to that idea in addressing the Areopagus.

12.4.2 Paul Addresses the Areopagus (17:19–31)

Paul is taken to a meeting of the ***Areopagus***, the leading council of Athens (17:19). The tension in Luke's report does not necessarily indicate a legal proceeding against Paul.[39] Among its duties, the Areopagus council traditionally examined would-be public teachers so as to grant them approval for spreading their doctrine in the city, particularly those proclaiming a new deity. Thus, rather than conducting a court case, the Athenians were seeking to ascertain what official recognition should be given to the new divinity (or divinities) Paul was presenting (e.g., statues, feast days, etc.).[40] This also illuminates Paul's blatantly corrective comments that his God is not a new one, that his God does not need a temple and holiday meals, and that his God is offended by idols. In all of this, our author maintains a sense of humor in his report, for those who charged Paul as a "babbler" Luke now describes them as such: "All the Athenians and the foreigners who lived there spent their time doing nothing but talking about and listening to the latest ideas" (17:21).[41] Paul's remarks to the Areopagus can be outlined in four strategic elements (17:22–31; see sidebar).

Paul starts with the observable situation of his audience: "I see that in every way you are very religious" (17:22). It seems that Paul is straining to make a compliment out of the phenomenon that had been provoking him. Scholars are divided as to Paul's intentions for the term "very religious" (Greek: *deisidaimonesteros*), which could be

---

36. So Witherington, *Acts*, 515; cf. Schnabel, *Acts*, 727.

37. Plato, *Apol.* 24b–c; Xenophon, *Mem.* 1.1.1; for "foreign gods," Luke uses the same Greek word: *daimonion*.

38. E.g., Haenchen, *Acts*, 518; F. F. Bruce, *The Book of Acts*, 2nd ed., NICNT (Grand Rapids: Eerdmans, 1988), 331; Simon J. Kistemaker, *Exposition of the Acts of the Apostles*, New Testament Commentary (Grand Rapids: Baker, 1990), 627; Witherington, *Acts*, 515; Longenecker, "Acts," 981; Peterson, *Acts*, 491; Schnabel, *Acts*, 726; Johnson, *Acts*, 313–14; contra, Barrett, *Acts*, 2:830–31; cf. Bock, *Acts*, 562.

39. Scholars do not agree on the nature of this scene; see Haenchen, *Acts*, 527; and Bock, *Acts*, 562–63.

40. Bruce W. Winter, "Introducing the Athenians to God: Paul's Failed Apologetic in Acts 17?" in *A Graced Horizon: Essays in Gospel, Culture and Church in Honor of the Rev Dr Choong Chee Pang*, ed. Roland Chia and Mark Chan (Singapore: Genesis, 2005), 68 and 71. See the similar view of Polhill, *Acts*, 367–68; and the somewhat related view of Bertil E. Gärtner, *The Areopagus Speech and Natural Revelation*, trans. Carolyn Hannay King, ASNU 21 (Lund: Gleerup, 1955), 52–65; cf. Longenecker, "Acts," 891.

41. See Bock, *Acts*, 563; and C. Kavin Rowe, *World Upside Down: Reading Acts in the Graeco-Roman Age* (New York: Oxford University Press, 2009), 33.

Paul's Approach in His Aeropagus Address (Acts 17:22–31)

1. Start with the observable situation of the audience (vv. 22–23).
2. Appeal to human intellect where it agrees with biblical ideals (vv. 24–28).
   i. God is the creator of the universe (v. 24).
   ii. God is the sustainer of all life (v. 25).
   iii. God is the ruler of humanity (vv. 26–28a).
   iv. God is the source of human personality (v. 28b).
3. Draw a reasonable deduction: idolatry must be illegitimate (v. 29).
4. Summon the audience to repent in view of God's special revelation in Jesus (vv. 30–31).

understood as positive (i.e., "devoutly religious") or as negative (i.e., "very superstitious").[42] Perhaps it is best to let the tension stand and to understand the vagueness of the term to be intentional irony: a positive criticism or a negative compliment.[43] Among the many objects of worship in Athens, Paul focuses on one particular inscription, one "to an unknown god" (17:23).[44] The Athenians' open admission to this ignorance becomes Paul's opportunity for introducing them to the creator God of the universe who has provided for their salvation.

Appealing to the Athenians' intellect where it agrees with biblical ideals, the main body of Paul's remarks can be described as ***natural theology*** or philosophical theology, i.e., what can be learned about God from the use of human reason in observing the natural world (all created by God). Paul makes such arguments in his own writings (e.g., Rom 1:18–23), so it is no surprise to find Luke narrating Paul's use of this approach (cf. Acts 14:14–18). Paul makes four basic points.[45] First, God is the creator of the universe, so it is ridiculous to presume that he could be confined to human-made buildings (17:24).[46] Second, God is the sustainer of life, so it is absurd to assume that he is somehow dependent on humans (17:25). Third, God is the ruler of all humanity, so while able to rebel against him, humans would be silly to attempt conducting their affairs apart from him, especially when he wants to be in relationship with them (17:26–28a).

42. E.g., as a positive compliment, see Bruce, *Book of Acts*, 335; Johnson, *Acts*, 520; as a negative criticism, see Witherington, *Acts*, 520.

43. Cf. Peterson, *Acts*, 494; Bock, *Acts*, 564; Rowe, *World Upside Down*, 34; Polhill, *Acts*, 371. See also Flavien Pardigon, *Paul against the Idols: A Contextual Reading of the Areopagus Speech* (Eugene, OR: Pickwick, 2019), 141–43.

44. See Eckhard J. Schnabel, *Early Christian Mission*, 2 vols. (Downers Grove, IL: InterVarsity Press, 2004), 2:1176–77.

45. Following Stott, *Message of Acts*, 285–87.

46. Connecting the gospel to the Creator God, Paul deflects the charge of preaching a new foreign god. "Bluntly put, it can scarcely get older than this: the God about whom Paul speaks created the world in which Athens exists"; Rowe, *World Upside Down*, 34.

Altars to Unknown Gods

No altars to an unknown God have been found among the ruins at Athens. But other ancient writers refer to such altars in Athens and elsewhere in the ancient world, usually in the plural, e.g., "To Unknown Gods" (e.g., Pausanias, *Description of Greece*, 1.1.4; Philostratus, *Vit. Apoll.* 6.3.5). Diogenes Laertius speaks of "anonymous altars" (Greek: *bōmous anōnumous*) in the vicinity of Athens (*Lives*, 1.10 §110). Altars to unknown, or unnamed, or anonymous gods have been discovered in Palmyra, Pergamum, and Rome.

Found at Palatine Hill in Rome
Sailko/CC BY 3.0

Found at Palmyra
Todd Bolen/BiblePlaces.com, courtesy Louvre Museum

Fourth, God is the source of humanity, so if personhood stems from him, it is bizarre to believe God would be something less than personal, like a clump of mineral or stone (17:28b–29).

Using natural theology, Paul quotes some known intellectuals where they touch on biblical ideals, including an aphorism credited to the Cretan poet Epimenides (ca. 600 BC): "For in him we live and move and have our being"[47] and the third-century BC Stoic author Aratus: "We are his offspring."[48] In both of these citations, Paul uses

47. See the ground-breaking work of James Rendel Harris, "The Cretans Always Liars." *Expositor* 7.2.4 (Oct. 1906): 305–17; idem. "A Further Note on the Cretans." *Expositor* 7.3.4 (April 1907): 332–37; idem. "St. Paul and Epimenides." *Expositor* 8.4.4 (Oct. 1912): 348–53. On the difficulties of definitively identifying the source of the citation commonly attributed to Epimenides, see I. Howard Marshall, *The Acts of the Apostles: An Introduction and Commentary*, TNTC (Grand Rapids: Eerdmans, 1980), 288–89; and Pardigon, *Paul against the Idols*, 187–89.

48. It is worth noting that Paul is also found quoting intellectuals in his letters: Menander in 1 Cor 15:33 and Epimenides (again) in Titus 1:12.

Areopagus Etiquette

Lucian, *Anacharsis* 19 (Second century AD)

As long as they speak about the case, the court tolerates them and listens in silence; but if anyone prefaces his speech with an introduction in order to make the court more favourable, or brings emotion or exaggeration into the case—tricks that are often devised by the disciples of rhetoric to influence the judges,—then the crier appears and silences them at once, preventing them from talking nonsense to the court and from tricking the case out in words, in order that the Areopagites may see the facts bare.

Paul's Poetic Citations in Acts 17

In his speech before the Areopagus of Athens (Acts 17), rather than citing from Hebrew Scriptures, Paul cites from some poets with whom he thought his audience would be familiar. The lines Paul cites are in bold.

From Epimenides, *Cretica* (ca. 600 BC)

They fashioned a tomb for you, holy and high one,
Cretans, always liars, evil beasts, idle bellies.
But you are not dead: you live and abide forever,
For in you we live and move and have our being.

From Aratus, *Phaenomena*, 1–7 (ca. 275 BC)

From Zeus let us begin; him do we mortals never leave unnamed; full of Zeus are all the streets and all the market-places of men; full is the sea and the havens thereof; always we all have need of Zeus. **For we are also his offspring**; and he in his kindness unto men giveth favourable signs and wakeneth the people to work, reminding them of livelihood.

recognizable equivocation; the pagan intellectuals are correct, but only up to a certain point. Paul's acknowledgment that God is near to each of us is not due to any supposed agreement he might have with Stoic pantheism but because the transcendent God is personal and immanent. In a creational sense, all of humanity is the offspring of God; but in a redemption sense, God is Father only of those who have faith in Christ.

Paul is not quoting these poets out of context, nor is he assenting to everything in their philosophies about God. He is simply noting where these intellectuals have said things that touch on the truth. Indeed, while perhaps somewhat limited, comments that are ultimately against the message of Christianity can still be acknowledged for

Acts 17: A Model for Interacting with Unbelievers

From Winter, "Introducing the Athenians to God," 83.

> The strategies Paul adopted in Acts 17 provide the paradigm for contemporary Christian interactions with the minds of non-Christians. Connecting with the hearers, correcting their misconceptions, conversing with the theological or ideological framework, convicting them of their compromises with their consciences in the light of their own intellectual commitment are critical steps. It is also necessary to confront them with their need of repentance towards God and faith in the Lord Jesus Christ because of the coming day of judgment. These are all the essential features of a dialogue that is distinctly Christian and biblical.

whatever ways they do apprehend revealed truth.[49] It might even be observed that Paul now turns away from doing natural theology with general revelation to point to the need for God's special revelation.[50] The God of the universe cannot be contained as if a created thing, cannot be dependent on others, cannot be pushed away as if ruled by humans, and cannot be reduced to some inanimate object. If these things are true, then all idolatry is inexcusable and people need the special revelation of God (17:29).[51]

Creation of Sun, Moon, and Planets by Michelangelo (ca. 1512). Sistine Chapel, Rome.
Public domain

Despite its illogic, idolatry has been the persistent distraction of human ignorance, and God has been tolerant of this rebellion (cf. 14:16; Rom 3:25). But God's forbearance is not to be presumed upon, and Paul declares, "Now he commands all people everywhere to repent" (Acts 17:30). The summons to repentance is universal because the coming judgment will be universal (17:31a). And it will be a just judgment by a known agent of justice, the one whom God has raised from the dead (17:31b; cf. 1 Thess 1:9–10). So there is an ironic twist here, for Paul's God is not seeking authorization from the Areopagus; rather, Paul's God is seeking the repentance of all people everywhere.[52]

49. Ned B. Stonehouse, *Paul before the Areopagus and Other New Testament Studies* (Grand Rapids: Eerdmans, 1957), 30; cf. Winter, "Introducing the Athenians to God," 82.

50. See esp. Gärtner, *The Areopagus Speech*, 166–67; and Pardigon, *Paul against the Idols*, 185–86.

51. See Stott, *Message of Acts*, 287.

52. Winter, "Introducing the Athenians to God," 73.

Mars Hill and the Areopagus

Paul meets with the Areopagus in Acts 17. The term *Areopagus* could be a reference to (a) the physical location of the meeting, with the Greek meaning "Mars Hill" (pictured to the right), or (b) the ruling council of Athens that often met at Mars Hill and so was named after it, or (c) both (i.e., the council at the hill). Sometimes, however, the council held their meetings in Athens' ancient agora marketplace (seen in the following pictures from the top of Mars Hill). The context of Acts 17 shows that Paul is speaking before the Areopagus council, but it is not clear as to the specific location for this meeting.

Mars Hill
Theastock/stock.adobe.com

Temple of Hephaestus in the agora
CoinUp/stock.adobe.com

Athens' ancient agora
BreizhAtao/stock.adobe.com

12.4.3 The Results Are Mixed and the Missionaries Move On (17:32–34)

While structured to share the gospel with a pagan audience, Paul's Areopagus address has an overarching biblical-theological structure with a basic creation-fall-redemption-consummation pattern[53] and many biblical allusions (see sidebar). As Paul reaches the climax of this address (i.e., Jesus's resurrection), his listeners have a mixed reaction.

53. Pardigon, *Paul against the Idols*, 225.

Biblical Allusions in Paul's Areopagus Address

Lines in Acts 17:22–31	OT Passages [and other ancient authors]
"The God who made the world and everything in it" (v. 24a)	Exod 20:11; Ps 146:6 (LXX 145:6); 2 Kgs 19:15; 2 Chr 2:12; Neh 9:6; Isa 37:16; 42:5; Wis 9:9; cf. 2 Macc 7:23; 13:14; 4 Macc 5:25; Acts 4:24b
"the Lord of heaven and earth" (v. 24b)	Gen 24:3; Deut 10:14; Ps 115:15–16 (LXX 113:23–24); Tob 7:17
"[God] does not live in temples built by human hands" (v. 24c)	1 Kgs 8:27; 2 Chr 2:6 (LXX 2:5); Isa 66:1–2; cf. Isa 16:12 (LXX); Acts 7:48; 2 Cor 5:1
"And he is not served by human hands, as if he needed anything" (v.25a)	1 Chr 29:14–16; Job 22:2; Ps 50:8–13 (LXX 49:8–13); Mic 6:6–8
"He himself gives everyone life and breath and everything else" (v. 25b)	Gen 2:7; 7:22; Job 12:10; 27:3; 33:4; Ps 104:29–30 (LXX 103:29–30); Eccl 12:7; Isa 42:5; 57:15–16; Zech 12:1
"From one man he made all the nations, that they should inhabit the whole earth" (v. 26a)	Gen 9:18–11:8
"and he marked out their appointed times in history and the boundaries of their lands" (v. 26b)	Gen 1:14; Deut 32:8; Job 12:23; 14:5; Ps 74:17 (LXX 73:17); Wis 7:18
"God did this so that they would seek him and perhaps reach out for him and find him" (v. 27a)	Deut 4:29; Job 23:3–10; Ps 14:2; Prov 8:17; Isa 55:6; 65:1; Jer 29:13–14 (LXX 36:13–14); Amos 5:4; Wis 13:6
"though he is not far from any one of us" (v. 27b)	Deut 4:7; Ps 145:18 (LXX 144:18); Jer 23:23–24
"'For in him we live and move and have our being'" (v. 28a)	[Epimenides, *Cretica* (ca. 600 BC); cf. Titus 1:12]
"As some of your own poets have said, 'We are his offspring'" (v. 28b)	[Aratus, *Phaenomena* (ca. 315–240 BC)]
"Therefore since we are God's offspring" (v. 29a)	Gen 1:26–27; Ps 8:5–6 (LXX 8:6–7); Mal 2:10
"we should not think that the divine being is like gold or silver or stone—an image made by human design and skill" (v. 29b)	Deut 4:28; 5:8; Ps 115:2–8 (LXX 113:10–16); Isa 37:19; 40:18–25; 44:9–20; 46:5–7; Wis 13:10–19
"In the past God overlooked such ignorance" (v. 30a)	2 Kgs 17:29–41; cf. Ps 81:12 (LXX 80:13); Mic 4:5; Sir 28:7; Rom 3:25
"but now he commands all people everywhere to repent" (v. 30b)	Isa 59:20; Jer 15:19; Ezek 14:6; 18:30–32; cf. Matt 3:2; 4:17; Acts 2:38; 3:19
"For he has set a day when he will judge the world with justice by the man he has appointed. He has given proof of this to everyone by raising him from the dead" (v. 31)	Pss 9:7–8 (LXX 9:8–9); 96:13 (LXX 95:13); 98:9 (LXX 97:9); Isa 66:16; Jer 25:31; cf. Matt 11:22–24; 12:36; John 5:22–30

Adapted and expanded from Arnold, "Acts," 175.

Some of the Athenians laugh at the idea of someone coming back from the dead (Acts 17:32a);[54] others have their interest piqued and request to hear more at a later time (17:32b). While a few scholars have suggested that Paul's witness in Athens was an outright failure,[55] Luke himself gives no hint of disappointment. On the contrary, Luke remarks, "Some of the people became followers of Paul and believed" (17:34a), and he even identifies some of the converts—including an Areopagus member named Dionysius and a woman named Damaris—and adds further that there were "a number of others" as well (17:34b).[56] So with three responses—some mocking, some stalling, and some believing—this is a truly mixed reception.[57] That Paul is able simply to leave the Areopagus at the close of his speech with no report of any official action (17:33) is further indication that this was not a legal hearing as much as it was a formal lecture. As elsewhere in Acts, after a mixed reception and lacking encouragement to stay, Paul and his missionary team move on to a new location.

12.5 THE MISSION IN CORINTH (ACTS 18:1–22)

Paul goes from Athens to ***Corinth*** (18:1), the first-century capital of the Roman province of Achaia, which at about one hundred thousand in population, was twenty times the size of Athens.[58] Its location on the isthmus of land connecting the large land mass of Achaia to the northeast (where Athens is) to the Peloponnesian Peninsula to the southwest (where Olympia and Sparta are) gave Corinth a strategic position on the land routes across the province. Furthermore, being positioned at the isthmus gave Corinth access to harbors facing east (leading to the Aegean Sea) and facing west (on the southern Adriatic Sea; the section of the Adriatic Sea south of Italy is today

---

54. In his seminal work on the subject, N. T. Wright comments on "the universal pagan disbelief in resurrection"; *The Resurrection of the Son of God*, Christian Origins and the Question of God 3 (Minneapolis: Fortress, 2003), 500. See also Kevin L. Anderson, *'But God Raised Him from the Dead': The Theology of Jesus' Resurrection in Luke-Acts*, Paternoster Biblical Monographs (Waynesboro, GA: Paternoster, 2006), 92–117. For examples of the denial of resurrection in the ancient literature, see Homer, *Il.* 24.549–51 and 754–56; Aeschylus, *Eum.* 647–48; idem, *Ag.* 565–69, 1019–24, and 1360–61; Sophocles, *El.* 137–43; Euripides, *Hel.* 1285–87; Herodas, *Mimes* 1.41–46; Herodotus, *Hist.* 3.62; Pliny the Elder, *Nat.* 2.5 §27 and 7.55 §190. For Epicurean denials of resurrection, see Lucretius, *De Rerum Natura* 3.526–47, 624–33, 830–31, 842–62; and Diogenes Laertius, *Lives* 10 Epicurus (63–67, 124–27, 139). While specific Stoic views regarding resurrection are more difficult to define, see Diogenes Laertius *Lives* 7.1 Zeno (156–57).

55. E.g., F. F. Bruce, *Paul: Apostle of the Heart Set Free* (Grand Rapids: Eerdmans, 1977), 246; Eric Franklin, *Luke: Interpreter of Paul, Critic of Matthew*, JSNTSup 92 (Sheffield: Sheffield Academic Press, 1994), 85–86.

56. For a convincing defense of the Areopagus speech as successful, see Stonehouse, *Paul before the Areopagus*, 33–36. Cf. Stott, *Message of Acts*, 289–90; and Winter, "Introducing the Athenians to God," 65–84.

57. David Thomas labels the three responses at Athens as "derisive incredulity," "procrastinating resolve," and "practical faith"; David Thomas, *Acts of the Apostles: Expository and Homiletical Commentary* (Grand Rapids: Kregel, 1980), 286–87.

58. David W. J. Gill, "In Search of the Social Élite in the Corinthian Church," *TynBul* 44 (1993), 333–34; cf. Longenecker, "Acts," 989.

called the Ionian Sea). This location made Corinth an important commercial center of the first-century Mediterranean world. And if Corinth was strategically located for commercial trade, certainly it could be a significant center for the spread of the gospel.[59]

Corinth

- Located on a plateau overlooking the Isthmus of Corinth (the four-mile-wide land bridge connecting the mainland of Greece to the Peloponnesian Peninsula) and at the foot of Acrocorinth (a 1,886-foot acropolis).
- One of the ancient world's most strategically positioned cities, with influence over both land and sea traffic.
- Two miles away, Lechaeum was its west-facing seaport on the Gulf of Corinth leading to the southern Adriatic Sea (the section of the Adriatic Sea south of Italy is today called the Ionian Sea); five miles away, Cenchreae was its east-facing seaport on the Saronic Gulf of the Aegean Sea.
- Rose to its peak of prosperity and power under the house of Cypselus, who ruled ca. 657–627 BC.
- Had an important role in unifying the Greek city-states into the worldwide empire of Philip of Macedon and his son Alexander the Great.
- A center of commerce and of commercialized pleasure. In 146 BC, however, the city was severely damaged as punishment for its resistance to Roman expansion and lay in ruins for a hundred years until Julius Caesar decreed in 46 BC that it should be rebuilt.
- Became the capital of the Roman province of Achaia in 27 BC, and its commercial and political influence were restored.
- Industries included pottery and brass work (including brass mirrors).
- Gained a reputation for wealth and indulgence in Roman times. To "act as a Corinthian" meant to practice sexual immorality, and a thousand sacred prostitutes dedicated to Aphrodite supposedly roamed the city.
- At its height in the seventh century BC had a population of about two hundred thousand citizens and five hundred thousand slaves.
- Among the many gods worshiped here were Apollo, Aphrodite (with a temple atop the Acrocorinth), Poseidon, Asclepius and his daughter goddess Hygeia, and Demeter and Kore, along with various Egyptian deities.
- Nearby at Isthmia, the Isthmian Games (music and athletics) were held biennially in honor of Poseidon (games second only to the Olympic Games held every four years at Delphi).
- Paul lived and ministered here for one and a half years during his second missionary campaign (Acts 18:1–18); he likely visited here with a three-month stay on his third missionary journey as well (Acts 20:1–6; cf. 2 Cor 12:14; 13:1–10).

Select Bibliography

John McRay, *Archaeology and the New Testament* (Grand Rapids: Baker, 1991), 311–38.

Jerome Murphy-O'Connor, *St. Paul's Corinth: Texts and Archaeology*, 3rd ed. (Collegeville, MN: Liturgical, 2002).

Arthur A. Rupprecht "Corinth," *ZEB* 1:1007–1011.

Wendell Willis, "Corinth," *EDB*, 279–81.

59. Stott, *Message of Acts*, 294; cf. Larkin, *Acts*, 262.

Agora (marketplace) ruins, Corinth

© 2012 by Zondervan

Among other things (e.g., architecture, athletic contests), Corinth was famed for its immorality. In classical times, the name of the city was turned into a verb meaning "to practice sexual immorality" (Greek: *Korinthiazomai*; "to Corinthianize"), and "Corinthian companions" (*Korinthiai hetairai*) or "Corinthian girls" (*Korinthiai korai*) were prostitutes.[60] According to first-century historian Strabo, the temple of Aphrodite (a.k.a. Venus) on the acropolis of Corinth owned one thousand such prostitutes (see sidebar). Understanding this sexual licentiousness explains some of Paul's explicit clarification of sexual conduct for believers in his Corinthian letters (e.g., 1 Cor 5:1–13; 6:9–20; 2 Cor 12:21).[61]

On Temple Prostitutes in Corinth

Strabo, *Geography* 8.6.20 (ca. 64 BC–AD 24)

And the temple of Aphrodite was so rich that it owned more than a thousand temple-slaves, courtesans, whom both men and women had dedicated to the goddess. And therefore it was also on account of these women that the city was crowded with people and grew rich; for instance, the ship-captains freely squandered their money, and hence the proverb, "Not for every man is the voyage to Corinth."

60. Bruce, *Book of Acts*, 346n4.

61. See John McRay, *Archaeology and the New Testament* (Grand Rapids: Baker, 1991), 315–17.

12.5.1 Meeting Aquila and Priscilla (18:1–3)

Coming to Corinth, Paul meets Aquila and Priscilla, a married Jewish couple who were also recent arrivals to Corinth. They had come from Rome when emperor Claudius ordered that Jews must leave the imperial city (18:1–2). According to Suetonius, Claudius's edict of expulsion was due to some disruptions among the Jews "at the instigation of Chrestus" (see sidebar).[62] With Christianity understood as a version of the Jewish religion, the Roman authorities would see disputes over preaching about "Christ" (similar to "Chrestus" in pronunciation) as a Jewish matter and seek to solve it by dismissing particularly the leaders involved in the disputes. This suggests that Aquila and Priscilla were already believers in Jesus, and even Christian leaders, before meeting Paul.[63] They share another thing in common with Paul: the career of tentmaking (which may well have included leather work of any kind and working with other related fabrics).[64] Supporting his ministry work with his own labor was a regular activity for Paul (cf. 20:34), so perhaps he got connected with Aquila and Priscilla in looking for work (18:2–3; see sidebar on career expectations for Jewish rabbis).[65] Murphy-O'Connor suggests that with the Isthmian Games held in Corinth in the spring of AD 51, the additional demand for tents would have kept them quite busy.[66]

Career Expectations for Jewish Rabbis

Rabbi Gamaliel III in m. Pirkei Avot, 2.2

Rabban Gamaliel the son of Rabbi Judah Hanasi said: excellent is the study of the Torah when combined with a worldly occupation, for toil in them both keeps sin out of one's mind; But [study of the] Torah which is not combined with a worldly occupation, in the end comes to be neglected and becomes the cause of sin.

---

62. Luke reports that Claudius "had ordered" all Jews to leave Rome, but this does not mean all 30,000–50,000 of the Jews in first-century Rome actually left the city. Claudius had been a proponent of the rights of Jews earlier in his reign (see Josephus, *Ant.* 19.5.2–3 §§280–91). Thus, more likely is the suggestion that, rather than a systematically enforced edict for "all Jews" to leave Rome, Claudius merely desired to make a political show of addressing the problem involving the city's Jewish population; see Erich S. Gruen, *Diaspora: Jews amidst Greeks and Romans* (Cambridge: Harvard University Press, 2002), 37–41. The silence of several ancient historians regarding this edict (e.g., Josephus and Tacitus) further suggests that it was not a full-scale expulsion; cf. the extensive discussion in Keener, *Acts*, 3:2697–2711.

63. See A. Andrew Das, *Solving the Romans Debate* (Minneapolis: Fortress, 2007), 150–58; cf. Keener, *Acts*, 3:2703–11.

64. See Paul W. Barnett, "Tentmaking," *DPL*, 925–27; and Jerome Murphy-O'Connor, "Prisca and Aquila: Traveling Tentmakers and Church Builders," *Brev* 8.6 (1992): 40–51, 62.

65. So Longenecker, "Acts," 989.

66. Jerome Murphy-O'Connor, "The Corinth that Paul Saw," *BA* 47 (1984): 147–59; esp. p. 149.

On Claudius against the Jews in Rome

At the beginning of his reign in AD 41, Emperor Claudius was protective of Jewish rights across the Roman Empire (see Josephus, *Ant.* 19.5.2-3 §§280-91). When he became wary about Jews and their religion, according to Roman historian Dio Cassius, Claudius was hesitant to expel them from Rome and sought merely to restrict their gatherings. Nevertheless, by AD 49, Claudius issued an order for the Jews to leave the city of Rome, an edict that may have simply been political posturing to demonstrate his willingness to address a problem. According to Suetonius, this expulsion from Rome was due to some disruptions among the Jews "at the instigation of Chrestus," which is likely referencing responses to preaching about Jesus Christ. And this would fit with Luke's report of the expulsion that brought the Jews Aquila and Priscilla from Rome to Corinth (Acts 18:1-2).

Dio Cassius, *Roman History* 60.6.6 (ca. AD 230)

> As for the Jews, who had again increased so greatly that by reason of their multitude it would have been hard without raising a tumult to bar them from the city, he did not drive them out, but ordered them, while continuing their traditional mode of life, not to hold meetings.

Suetonius, *Divus Claudius* 25 (ca. AD 121)

> Since the Jews constantly made disturbances at the instigation of Chrestus, he expelled them from Rome.

12.5.2 Preaching to Jews First (18:4–6)

While working as a tentmaker, Paul also "reasoned" in the synagogue every Sabbath (18:4; cf. 17:17), attempting to "persuade" both Jews and Greeks (cf. 14:19; 17:4; 26:28; 28:23). Paul had been whisked suddenly from Berea to Athens, where he had asked Silas and Timothy to meet him (cf. 17:13–16), but it seems as if they don't catch up to him until now in Corinth (18:5a; cf. 1 Thess 3:1, 6). Their arrival frees Paul up to devote himself "exclusively to preaching" (Acts 18:5b), perhaps because they arrive with financial support (cf. 2 Cor 11:9; Phil 4:14–16).

Paul on His Ministry in Corinth

1 Corinthians 2:1–5

And so it was with me, brothers and sisters. When I came to you, I did not come with eloquence or human wisdom as I proclaimed to you the testimony about God. For I resolved to know nothing while I was with you except Jesus Christ and him crucified. I came to you in weakness with great fear and trembling. My message and my preaching were not with wise and persuasive words, but with a demonstration of the Spirit's power, so that your faith might not rest on human wisdom, but on God's power.

2 Corinthians 1:19

For the Son of God, Jesus Christ, who was preached among you by us—by me and Silas and Timothy—was not "Yes" and "No," but in him it has always been "Yes."

Nevertheless, as elsewhere, Paul's gospel preaching is largely rejected by the formal Jewish community in Corinth. This prompts Paul to carry out a gesture of separation, shaking out his clothes in protest against the Jews of Corinth who are rejecting the gospel (18:6a; cf. 13:51; Neh 5:13). The Messiah is Jesus, and Paul wants the Jews to remember that message—and their own responsibility for it—even if they don't accept the gospel. "Your blood be on your own heads! I am innocent of it," Paul declares using further biblical phrasing (Acts 18:6b; cf. Josh 2:19; 2 Sam 1:16; 1 Kgs 2:37; Ezek 33:2–9). And if they won't join him in evangelizing the gentiles, then Paul and his ministry team will need to take the gospel to the gentiles without them (Acts 18:6c).

Archaeological Evidence of Jews in Corinth

Several inscriptions have been discovered in Corinth that give evidence of Jews there, some in Hebrew and some depicting Jewish menorahs (i.e., the signature Jewish seven-branched candlestick). One inscription dating to the first or second century AD is a block of marble that likely served as a doorway lintel on which is inscribed "The Synagogue of the Hebrews."

Douglas S. Huffman

Douglas S. Huffman

Ruins of Ancient Corinth

The Acrocorinth

Leather-workers' shops

Douglas S. Huffman

Waterworks

Douglas S. Huffman

Temple of Apollo

Douglas S. Huffman

Paved plaza with Erastus inscription (at the top)

Douglas S. Huffman

Judgment seat (*bēma*) of Gallio

Douglas S. Huffman

12.5.3 Preaching to the Gentiles (18:7–11)

Paul's move from a Jewish audience to a gentile audience is not far: "Paul left the synagogue and went next door to the house of Titius Justus, a worshiper of God" (18:7; cf. 16:14). This broadening of Paul's ministry to include gentiles was not a wholesale exclusion of Jewish listeners. Interestingly, among the first Corinthian converts to faith in Christ was the Jewish synagogue leader Crispus and his entire household (18:8a). So Jews and gentiles were receiving the gospel message: "Many of the Corinthians who heard Paul believed and were baptized" (18:8b). A further confirmation of Paul's ministry comes when the Lord encourages him one night in a vision. Jesus commands Paul to keep preaching, promises Paul's safety, and explains, "I have many people in this city" (18:9–10). Paul's response to this powerful and personal encouragement is to remain in Corinth for a year and six months, continuing to teach the word of God (18:11). Thus, the Corinthian church becomes established.

12.5.4 Roman Legal Hearing before Gallio (18:12–17)

Jesus's promise of Paul's safety does not mean there would be no opposition, which becomes evident when the Jews of Corinth organize an attack on Paul. As the capital of Achaia, Corinth was home for the ruling proconsul, ***Gallio***, who we learn from extrabiblical sources served as the leader of Achaia for one year: summer of AD 51 to spring of AD 52 (see sidebar).[67] Desiring to capitalize on the attentiveness of a new leader, the Jews may well have brought their charges against Paul as Gallio was taking office in AD 51.[68] Luke's mention of "the place of judgment" in Corinth gives the air of a formal legal hearing (18:12). In their charges against Paul—"This man . . . is persuading the people to worship God in ways contrary to the law" (18:13)—the term "law" (*nomos*) is somewhat vague. In addressing a Roman leader, the Jews more likely would refer to Roman law instead of Jewish custom.[69] But perhaps they were being intentionally vague about which law was being broken, grasping at anything that might get Paul in trouble and stop the spread of the gospel.[70]

---

67. See Bruce W. Winter, "Gallio's Ruling on the Legal Status of Early Christianity (Acts 18:14–15)," *TynBul* 50 (1999): 213–24; Colin J. Hemer, "Observations on Pauline Chronology," pp. 3–18 in *Pauline Studies: Essays Presented to Professor F. F. Bruce on His 70th Birthday*, ed. Donald A. Hagner and Murray J. Harris (Exeter: Paternoster, 1980; Grand Rapids: Eerdmans, 1980), 6–9; Klaus Haacker, "Gallio," *ABD* 2:901–903.

68. So Hemer, "Observations on Pauline Chronology," 8.

69. For understanding it as Roman law, see esp. Longenecker, "Acts," 995; and Marshall, *Acts*, 297–98. For understanding it as a complaint that Paul was disrupting the quiet practice of Jewish customs legally tolerated by Rome, see Sherwin-White, *Roman Society and Roman Law*, 102–3.

70. See Winter, "Gallio's Ruling," 217–18; and Harry W. Tajra, *The Trial of St. Paul: A Juridical Exegesis of the Second Half of the Acts of the Apostles*, WUNT 2:35 (Tübingen: Mohr Siebeck, 1989), 56.

The Delphi (or Gallio) Inscription

The Delphi inscription—sometimes referred to as the Gallio inscription—is a collection of nine fragments of a message from Roman emperor Claudius ca. AD 52. The inscription mentions the proconsul Gallio ("ΓΑΛΛΙΩΝ"), who served in Corinth for one year, so this helps us narrow Paul's time in Corinth to overlap with that year (Acts 18:12–17).

> Tiber[ius Claudius Cae]sar Augustus Ge[rmanicus, invested with tribunician po]wer [for the 12th time, acclaimed Imperator for t]he 26th time, F[ather of the Fa]ther[land . . . sends greetings to . . .]. For a l[ong time have I been not onl]y [well-disposed toward t]he ci[ty] of Delpl[i, but also solicitous for its pro]sperity, and I have always guard[ed th]e cul[t of t]he [Pythian] Apol[lo. But] now [since] it is said to be desti[tu]te of [citi] zens, as [L. Jun]ius Gallio, my fri[end] an[d procon]sul, [recently reported to me, and being desirous that Delphi] should retain [inta]ct its for[mer rank, I] ord[er you (pl.) to in]vite well-born people also from [ot]her cities [to Delphi as new inhabitants, and to] all[ow] them [and their children to have all the] privy[leges of the Del]phians as being citi[zens on equal and like (basis)]. For i[f] so[me . . .] were to trans[fer as citi]zens [to these regions. . . .]

See "ΓΑΛΛΙΩΝ" in the middle of this photo.
Todd Bolen/BiblePlaces.com, courtesy Delphi Museum

The reconstructed translation here—with brackets marking estimations of the text in damaged portions—is from Jerome Murphy-O'Connor, *St. Paul's Corinth: Tests and Archaeology*, 3rd ed. (Collegeville, MN: Liturgical, 2002), 161.

Gallio, Proconsul of Achaia

From Tajra, *The Trial of St. Paul*, 51.

> Lucius Junius Gallio (born Marcus Annaeus Novatus) was a well-known historical figure. He was the son of Seneca the Elder, the brother of Seneca, the Philosopher and tutor of the future Emperor Nero, and the uncle of the poet Lucan. At this point in his career, he was Proconsul of Achaia. Pliny the Elder says that he also had a Consulship, but does not specify the date. Paul's appearance before the Proconsul Gallio was an important step in the apostle's judicial history for he was appearing before a man intimately linked to the Imperial court and the governing class at Rome.

As Paul opens his mouth to begin his defense, he is quickly cut off by Gallio himself, who simply dismisses the case. Rather than a violation of any Roman law, Gallio recognizes that Paul's preaching is of particular concern to the Jews and not really something for Roman judgment (18:14–15). So firm is his decision to dismiss the Jews' charge against Paul that, as Luke expresses it, Gallio "drove them off" from the court (18:16). As the session closes, "the crowd" (Greek: *pantes* for simply "all") turns on the Jewish synagogue leader Sosthenes and beats him in front of the court (18:17). While this could be gentile onlookers expressing their anti-Semitism,[71] it seems better to understand the "all" as the Jews who were beating a Jewish leader in front of Gallio, who lets them handle their own matters.[72] But whether it is gentiles doing injustice to a Jew, or Jews doing injustice to one of their own leaders, or simply a mixed mob behaving badly[73]—whoever is doing it for whatever reasons, in any case, Sosthenes gets a beating and Gallio ignores it.[74]

12.5.5 Paul Stops by Ephesus (18:18–21)

After staying in Corinth "for some time" beyond the scene in front of Gallio, Paul sets out to return to Syria, from where the Antioch church had sent him (18:18a; cf. 15:40). To sail east, Paul and his team, including Priscilla and Aquila, would depart from Corinth's eastern seaport city of ***Cenchreae***, where Luke notes that Paul has his hair cut off "because of a vow he had taken" (18:18b). While debated by scholars, this personal vow showing one's devotion to God appears to be similar to a Nazirite vow (see

---

71. So Longenecker, "Acts," 995; F. F. Bruce, *The Acts of the Apostles: The Greek Text with Introduction and Commentary*, 3rd ed. (Grand Rapids: Eerdmans, 1990; Leicester: Apollos, 1990), 397; Beverly Roberts Gaventa, *Acts*, ANTC (Nashville: Abingdon, 2003), 260; Everett Falconer Harrison, *Interpreting Acts: The Expanding Church* (Chicago: Moody, 1975; repr., Grand Rapids: Zondervan, 1986), 296–97; Johnson, *Acts*, 329; Peterson, *Acts*, 518; Haacker, "Gallio," 2:902.

72. See Fitzmyer, *Acts*, 630–31; cf. Larkin, *Acts*, 267; F. Scott Spencer, *Acts*, Readings: A New Biblical Commentary (Sheffield: Sheffield Academic Press, 1997), 180; and esp. Tajra, *The Trial of St. Paul*, 58–60.

73. See esp. Moyer V. Hubbard, "Urban Uprisings in the Roman World: The Social Setting of the Mobbing of Sosthenes," *NTS*, 51 (2005): 416–28; cf. Barrett, *Acts*, 2:875.

74. In attempts to clarify Luke's bare "all" in Acts 18:17, the scribes of some ancient handwritten manuscripts of Acts have inserted "Greeks" (e.g., the Western text and the Byzantine text) and others have inserted "Jews" (e.g., minuscules 36, 307, 453, 610, and 1678).

Num 6:1–21; m. Naz. 1:1–9:5; Josephus, *J.W.* 2.15.1 §§313–14), during which one's hair is allowed to grow long and after which the supplicant offers his hair to God with sacrifices in Jerusalem. As a ceremony to celebrate God's recent work in one's life, perhaps the vow was one of gratitude for Paul's experience of the safety that Jesus had promised in Corinth (cf. Acts 18:9–10).[75] Keeping this Jewish custom demonstrates that Paul was still a Jew (cf. 2 Cor 11:22; Phil 3:5), albeit one who was rejoicing that the Jewish Messiah Jesus had come to offer salvation to all.[76]

The sailing trip back to Palestine entails a stop at the city of ***Ephesus*** in western Asia Minor. Naturally, Paul goes to the synagogue to reason with the Jews (Acts 18:19), but when they ask him to spend more time with them, he declines (18:20), perhaps because of his plans to complete his vow in Jerusalem and to report back to the church in Syrian Antioch. As he departs, he promises to come back to Ephesus "if it is God's will" (18:21), a reference to God's direction at the end of the second missionary campaign that echoes the decision-making at the beginning of this journey (cf. 16:6–10). As indicated in much of the rest of the New Testament, the city of Ephesus does indeed become a significant location for the early church and the expansion of the gospel message.[77] Priscilla and Aquila are left in Ephesus (18:19), which foreshadows a significant ministry they will have there even apart from Paul (18:24–28; cf. 1 Cor 16:19). And, as the readers of the story will soon find out, it would be God's will for Paul to return to Ephesus (Acts 19:1–41).

Ruins at the harbor of ancient Cenchreae
Douglas S. Huffman

75. See Longenecker, "Acts," 998; Marshall, *Acts*, 300; and the more detailed discussion in Keener, *Acts*, 3:2781–87.

76. On the rhetorical value of Luke recounting stories of Paul's Jewish lifestyle along with his outreach to non-Jews, see Keener, *Acts*, 3:2783–85.

77. Besides the book of Acts and Paul's letter to the Ephesians, the city of Ephesus is mentioned in 1 Corinthians, 1 Timothy, 2 Timothy, and Revelation; furthermore, church tradition has the apostle John pastoring a church in Ephesus with which the NT letters of 1 John, 2 John, and 3 John are sometimes associated.

Cenchreae

- Corinth's seaport on the Saronic Gulf of the Aegean Sea, about five miles east of Corinth.
- Named after Cenchrias, a child of Poseidon (the Greek god of the sea and earthquakes).
- Where Paul got his hair cut off in compliance with a vow just prior to sailing to Jerusalem (by way of Ephesus) at the end of his second missionary campaign (Acts 18:18).
- Apparently home to Phoebe, who served the church there (Rom 16:1).

Select Bibliography

Richard E. Oster Jr., "Cenchreae," *EBD*, 227.
Arthur A. Rupprecht "Cenchrea," *ZEB* 1:802–803.

12.5.6 Closing Travel Summary Statement (18:22)

Luke closes Paul's second missionary campaign with one of the simplest of the travel summaries: "When he landed at Caesarea, he went up to Jerusalem and greeted the church and then went down to Antioch" (18:22). Rather than detailing the completion of Paul's vow in Jerusalem, it is more important to Luke that he mention Paul's connection to the Jerusalem church before returning to Syrian Antioch. Thus, Paul's second missionary campaign simply comes to a close.

12.6 CONCLUDING REMARKS

At first envisioned as a follow-up trip to check on the churches established on the first missionary campaign, the second missionary campaign soon finds Paul and his expanding team of ministers moving into new territory. They do so with the Lord's guidance, empowerment, and encouragement despite regular opposition to the gospel from unbelieving Jews, gentiles, and even the demonic.

One of the regular themes of the second missionary campaign is the relationship between the Christian faith and the ruling political powers. Paul appeals to his proper Roman citizenship in Philippi, faces political charges in Thessalonica, addresses the philosophically minded Athenian Areopagus, and sees the well-known Roman proconsul Gallio dismiss the charges against his preaching in Corinth. Lukan scholars have suggested a variety of (sometimes diametrically opposed) proposals for Luke's political purposes in writing Acts.[78] The manner in which Luke reports Paul's ministry—particularly in the second missionary campaign—seems to locate Luke in a kind of middle way between the extreme alternatives. The Gospel of Luke (as well as the other

78. See the discussion in chapter 2.

gospels) portrays Jesus as both resistant to giving ultimate allegiance to Rome and at the same time innocent of the anti-Rome charges that the Israelites bring against him.[79] It is no surprise, then, that in his second volume, Luke's hero Paul is portrayed as taking the same view. As Amanda Miller discusses it, Luke's complex relationship with the Roman Empire was "neither entirely resistant nor entirely complicit and conciliatory."[80] Luke encourages his readers not so much to be supportive of Rome for Rome's sake nor to be antagonistic against Rome. Christians can participate in civil society for service to Jesus and, as they are good citizens, secular governments can tolerate Christians. But citizenship in secular society is not what matters most for Christians; the spread of the gospel is far more important. Being a Christian means thinking about things a bit differently.[81]

Coin with portrait of Julius Caesar on front (44 BC).
Todd Bolen/BiblePlaces.com, courtesy British Museum

12.7 Key People, Places, and Terms

- Areopagus
- Athens
- Barnabas
- Berea
- Cenchreae
- Corinth
- Ephesus
- Epicureanism
- Gallio
- John Mark
- Lydia
- natural theology
- Philippi
- Silas
- Stoicism
- Thessalonica
- Timothy
- Troas
- "we sections"

12.8 Questions for Review and Discussion

1. Paul and Barnabas had a rather extreme disagreement about a strategy issue. What does this disagreement indicate about the value placed on follow-up ministry with new Christians in Acts?
2. In recounting Paul's second missionary journey, Luke makes several comments on how the Lord guided Paul's decision-making. Distinguish between the "negative" and "positive" guidance he received as well as the vague and more specific kinds of guidance provided to him.

79. See Yong-Sung Ahn, *The Reign of God and Rome in Luke's Passion Narrative: An East Asian Global Perspective*, BibInt 80 (Leiden: Brill, 2006), 192; and John T. Carroll, *Luke: A Commentary*, NTL (Louisville: Westminster John Knox, 2012), 398–404.

80. See Amanda C. Miller, *Rumors of Resistance: Status Reversals and Hidden Transcripts in the Gospel of Luke*, Emerging Scholars (Minneapolis: Fortress, 2014), 255; cf. Rowe, *World Upside Down*, 149–51.

81. See the sidebar on "Coordinating Proposals for Luke's Political Apologetic" in chapter 2.

3. Describe the potential advantages of Paul's usual approach to sharing the gospel as he traveled from city to city. How persistent was he in taking this approach?
4. What was the typical experience Paul and his ministry team had in sharing the gospel?
5. Amid the idolatry of Athens, Paul noted cultural expressions that betrayed a desire for God. And even though he was provoked by those things, he used them as an opportunity to talk about the gospel. How would you describe his approach to sharing the gospel with the Athenians?
6. As presented by Luke, how would you describe Paul's ways of interacting with various groups of people, including those with religious, financial, or political motives?

12.9 Optional Assignments

1. **Text Reflection Project**—*Relating the concepts discussed in this chapter to another biblical text.* Compare what Paul has to say in his letters (esp. 1 Thess 2:13–3:10; 2 Cor 11:9; and Phil 4:14–16) with the material in the story of Acts (esp. Acts 17:1–18:17) to find points of connection. Write a short explanation of how these passages coordinate and inform each other.
2. **Interview Project**—*Inquiring of others their views concerning the concepts discussed in this chapter.* Talk with your pastor (or some other respected Christian leader) about his or her views concerning Paul's speech before the Areopagus. Particularly inquire about Paul's use of general revelation and his references to things in Athenian culture (their interest in worship, the altar to an unknown god, and his citations of poets). What might be some appropriate analogous approaches that we can take in our current culture? What might be examples of unwise (or even illegitimate) approaches in our modern culture? Write up a summary of their perspective.
3. **Service-Learning Project**—*Applying the concepts discussed in this chapter in some form of service to others outside the class.* Paul's work making tents with Priscilla and Aquila to support his own ministry efforts has become a label for modern missionaries who earn a living in a secular job so that they can have funds to do ministry in some foreign country. They are dubbed "tentmaking missionaries" even when their jobs are in other businesses, medicine, education, communication, etc. Make a list of service options available to you right now, and describe how each can give you opportunities to share the gospel.
4. **Prayer Project**—*Talking with God about the concepts discussed in this chapter.* When was your last big disagreement with a Christian friend? What category of disagreement seems to fit it best (scriptural, scrupulous, or strategic)? To what extent did it get resolved? Spend some time praying about this situation. Perhaps you will thank God for how the conflict got resolved, but perhaps you will discover in prayer that there is more you must do to work toward a better resolution. Write up a brief reflection on this prayer experience and the conflict resolution coming from it.
5. **Testimony Project**—*Telling others about the concepts discussed in this chapter.* Reflecting on the Jerusalem Council (Acts 15:1–35, discussed in chapter 11) and the conflict between Paul and Barnabas

about John Mark (Acts 15:36–41), develop a short list of some principles for addressing conflict resolution. Which of these principles do you find easiest to apply and which do you find more difficult? Write up a brief discussion of these principles in a format you can share with a small group of friends.

12.10 Bibliography for Going Further

12.10.1 Follow-Up Ministry

Chan, Francis, with Mark Beuving. *Multiply: Disciples Making Disciples*. Colorado Springs: Cook, 2012.

Hull, Bill. *The Complete Book of Discipleship: On Being and Making Followers of Christ*. The Navigators Reference Library 1. Colorado Springs: NavPress, 2006.

Johnston, Thomas P. *Follow-Up, Discipleship, and the Local Church*. Vol. 3 of *Evangelizology: Standard Topics in the Study of Evangelizing*. 4th ed. Liberty, MO: Evangelism Unlimited, 2019.

Putnam, Jim, and Bobby Harrington, with Robert Coleman. *DiscipleShift: Five Steps That Help Your Church to Make Disciples Who Make Disciples*. Exponential Series. Grand Rapids: Zondervan, 2013.

12.10.2 Paul's Second Missionary Journey

Jewett, Robert. "Investigating the Route of Paul's 'Second Missionary Journey' from Pisidian Antioch to Troas." Pages 93–96 in *Acts du 1er Congres International sur Antioche de Pisidie*. Edited by Thomas Drew-Bear, Mehmet Taşhalan, and Christine M. Thomas. Paris: Université Lumière-Lyon, 2002.

———. "Mapping the Route of Paul's 'Second Missionary Journey' from Dorylaeum to Troas." *TynBul* 48.1 (1997): 1–22.

———. "Paul and the Caravanners: A Proposal on the Mode of 'Passing through Mysia.'" Pages 74–90 in *Text and Artifact in the Religions of Mediterranean Antiquity: Essays in Honor of Peter Richardson*. Edited by Stephen G. Wilson and Michel Desjardins. Waterloo, Ontario: Wilfred Laurier University Press, 2000.

Thompson, Glen L., and Mark Wilson. "The Route of Paul's Second Journey in Asia Minor: In the Steps of Robert Jewett and Beyond." *TynBul* 67.2 (2016): 217–46.

White, Jefferson. "The Second Journey (49–52 AD)." Pages 18–35 (chapter 2) in *Evidence & Paul's Journeys: An Historical Investigation into the Travels of the Apostle Paul*. Hilliard, OH: Parsagard, 2001.

12.10.3 Divine Guidance and Decision Making

Huffman, Douglas S., ed. *How Then Should We Choose? Three Views on God's Will and Decision Making*. Grand Rapids: Kregel, 2009.

Miller, John B. F. *Convinced that God had Called Us: Dreams, Visions and the Perception of God's Will in Luke-Acts*. Leiden: Brill, 2007.

Pilch, John J. *Visions and Healing in the Acts of the Apostles: How the Early Believers Experienced God*. Collegeville, MN: Liturgical, 2004.

12.10.4 Paul in Macedonia

Ascough, Richard S. *Lydia: Paul's Cosmopolitan Hostess*. Paul's Social Network: Brothers and Sisters in Faith. Collegeville, MN: Liturgical, 2009.

Barreto, Eric D. *Ethnic Negotiations: The Function of Race and Ethnicity in Acts 16*. WUNT 2.294. Tübingen: Mohr Siebeck, 2010.

Gruca-Macaulay, Alexandra. *Lydia as a Rhetorical Construct in Acts*. ESEC 18. Atlanta: SBL Press, 2016.

Verhoef, Eduard. *Philippi: How Christianity Began in Europe*. New York: Bloomsbury T&T Clark, 2013.

Weima, Jeffrey A. D. "The Political Charges against Paul and Silas in Acts 17:6–7: Roman Benefaction in Thessalonica." Pages 241–68 in *Stones, Bones, and the Sacred: Essays on Material Culture and Ancient Religion in Honor of Dennis E. Smith*. Edited by Alan H. Cadwallader. ECL 21. Atlanta: SBL Press, 2016.

12.10.5 Paul in Athens and His Areopagus Address

Conzelmann, Hans. "The Address of Paul on the Areopagus." Pages 217–30 in *Studies in Luke-Acts: Essays Presented in Honor of Paul Schubert*. Edited by Leander E. Keck and Louis J. Martyn. Nashville: Abingdon, 1966. Repr., Philadelphia: Fortress, 1980.

Gärtner, Bertil E. *The Areopagus Speech and Natural Revelation*. Translated by Carolyn Hannay King. ASNU 21. Lund: Gleerup, 1955.

Gempf, Conrad. "Athens, Paul at." *DPL*, 51–54.

Pardigon, Flavien. *Paul against the Idols: A Contextual Reading of the Areopagus Speech*. Eugene, OR: Pickwick, 2019.

Stonehouse, Ned B. *Paul before the Areopagus and Other New Testament Studies*. London: Tyndale, 1957.

12.10.6 Paul in Corinth

Adams, Edward, and David G. Horrell, eds. *Christianity at Corinth: The Quest for the Pauline Church*. Louisville: Westminster John Knox, 2004.

Engels, Donald. *Roman Corinth: An Alternative Model for the Classical City*. Chicago: University of Chicago Press, 1990.

Marshall, Peter. *Enmity in Corinth: Social Conventions in Paul's Relations with the Corinthians*. WUNT 2.23. Tübingen: Mohr Siebeck, 1987.

Murphy-O'Connor, Jerome. *St. Paul's Corinth: Texts and Archaeology*. 3rd ed. Collegeville, MN: Liturgical, 2002.

Theissen, Gerd. *The Social Setting of Pauline Christianity: Essays on Corinth*. Philadelphia: Fortress, 1982. Repr., Eugene, OR: Wipf & Stock, 2004.

13 The Story of the Third Missionary Campaign

Acts 18:23–21:17

Chapter Goals

After reading this chapter, you should be able to:

- Understand the significance of Paul's ministry in the city of Ephesus, as it was a central city in the geographical region of Asia Minor and the capital city of the Roman province of Asia.
- Think about the plurality of legitimate ministries and the variety of spiritual gifts and ministry roles.
- Examine your own life regarding things that need to be given up in following Jesus.
- Decide how to interact with the outside world when the Christian faith clashes with the surrounding culture, even facing the idea of suffering willingly for one's faith.
- Contemplate the importance of Christian fellowship and being part of a healthy church.

Chapter Overview

13.1 Beginning with a Story in Ephesus (Acts 18:23-28)
13.2 Paul's Ministry in Ephesus (Acts 19:1–41)
13.3 Follow-Up Ministry in Greece and Asia Minor (Acts 20:1–16)
13.4 Paul Addresses the Ephesian Elders at Miletus (Acts 20:17–38)
13.5 Journey to Jerusalem (Acts 21:1–17)
13.6 Concluding Remarks
13.7 Key People, Places, and Terms
13.8 Questions for Review and Discussion
13.9 Optional Assignments
13.10 Bibliography for Going Further

Key Verses

After spending some time in Antioch, Paul set out from there and traveled from place to place throughout the region of Galatia and Phrygia, strengthening all the disciples. (Acts 18:23)

After all this had happened, Paul decided to go to Jerusalem, passing through Macedonia and Achaia. "After I have been there," he said, "I must visit Rome also." (Acts 19:21)

And now, compelled by the Spirit, I am going to Jerusalem, not knowing what will happen to me there. I only know that in every city the Holy Spirit warns me that prison and hardships are facing me. However, I consider my life worth nothing to me; my only aim is to finish the race and complete the task the Lord Jesus has given me—the task of testifying to the good news of God's grace. (Acts 20:22–24)

Mid-Journey Progress Summary Statements

This went on for two years, so that all the Jews and Greeks who lived in the province of Asia heard the word of the Lord. (Acts 19:10)

In this way the word of the Lord spread widely and grew in power. (Acts 19:20)

Closing Travel Summary Statement

When we arrived at Jerusalem, the brothers and sisters received us warmly. (Acts 21:17)

Itinerary of Paul's Third Missionary Journey, Acts 18:23–21:17 (ca. 53–57)

City	Province (Region)	Reference
Antioch	Syria	Acts 18:23a
	Galatia	Acts 18:23b
	Asia (Phrygia)	Acts 18:23c
Ephesus	Asia	Acts 19:1–40
	Macedonia	Acts 20:1–2a
Corinth ?	Achaia	Acts 20:2b–3a
Cenchreae ?	Achaia	Acts 20:3b
	Macedonia	Acts 20:3b
Philippi	Macedonia	Acts 20:6a
Troas	Asia (Mysia)	Acts 20:6b–12
Assos	Asia	Acts 20:13–14a

City	Province (Region)	Reference
Mitylene	Asia	Acts 20:14b
Chios	Asia	Acts 20:15a
Samos	Asia	Acts 20:15b
Miletus	Asia	Acts 20:15c–38
Kos	Asia	Acts 21:1a
Rhodes	Rhodes	Acts 21:1b
Patara	Lycia	Acts 21:1c
Tyre	Syria	Acts 21:3–6
Ptolemais	Syria	Acts 21:7
Caesarea	Judea (Palestine)	Acts 21:8–14
Jerusalem	Judea (Palestine)	Acts 21:15–17

INTRODUCTION

This chapter discusses Paul's third missionary campaign as reported in Acts 18:23–21:17. As Luke recounts it, Paul's third missionary campaign begins much like his second: "After spending some time in Antioch, Paul set out from there and traveled from place to place throughout the region of Galatia and Phrygia, strengthening all the disciples" (Acts 18:23; cf. 15:36). After this simple sweeping overview of Paul's work in Galatia, Luke quickly jumps to the ministry of Priscilla and Aquila in Ephesus (18:24–28). On the second missionary campaign, Ephesus had been divinely bypassed at the beginning, and only briefly visited at the end. On the third missionary journey, however, Ephesus is visited at length at the beginning and almost skipped entirely at the end. Indeed, not much "journeying" is reported while Paul ministers for three years in Ephesus before quickly visiting the churches of the neighboring provinces and revisiting Jerusalem again.

Paul's Third Missionary Journey (ca. AD 53–57)

13.1 BEGINNING WITH A STORY IN EPHESUS (ACTS 18:23–28)

Paul left Priscilla and Aquila in Ephesus as he was headed for Jerusalem toward the close of the second missionary journey, saying, "I will come back if it is God's will" (18:21). That bit of foreshadowing soon meets is fulfillment as Luke returns to report on events in Ephesus. First, he reports on the ministry of Priscilla and Aquila in Ephesus (18:24–28) before reporting on Paul's return to the city (19:1–41).

13.1.1 FOLLOW-UP IN ASIA MINOR (18:23)

Once again, launching out from ***Antioch of Syria***, Paul does follow-up ministry "throughout the region of Galatia and Phrygia," i.e., presumably in cities where he had preached the gospel in his earlier travels: Derbe, Lystra, Iconium, and Pisidian Antioch. Because he doubled back on the route in the first missionary journey, this would mark Paul's fourth time visiting three of these cities. His "strengthening all the disciples" on this trip is a familiar theme in Acts (18:23; cf. 9:31; 14:22; 15:32, 41; 16:5) and is reminiscent of Paul's own comments regarding his concern for the churches (e.g., 2 Cor 11:28). But Luke interrupts his narration of Paul's travels to jump ahead to Ephesus to report on the ministry of Priscilla and Aquila.

The Ministry of Aquila and Priscilla (or Is It Priscilla and Aquila?)

Aquila was a Jew from Pontus who lived in Rome with his wife, Priscilla, until Emperor Claudius ordered all Jews to leave. We are not told exactly when they became Christians (but perhaps before they left Rome; see the sidebar about Claudius in chapter 12). Paul met this couple in Corinth and worked with them in their profession as tentmakers (Acts 18:1-3). The first time we are introduced to this couple, the husband is mentioned first (Acts 18:2), but each time afterward, the wife is given first mention (Acts 18:18, 26). This is also true when Paul writes of the couple in his letters: Aquila is mentioned first once (1 Cor 16:19), but in Paul's later letters Priscilla is mentioned first (Rom 16:3; 2 Tim 4:19). What, if anything, should we make of this? Was Priscilla of higher social status or the one with more leadership and teaching ability? We are not told why she gets mentioned first most often. Paul does indicate that this married couple hosted churches in their home in Ephesus (1 Cor 16:19) and again in Rome (Rom 16:3-5).

13.1.2 PRISCILLA AND AQUILA MINISTER TO APOLLOS IN EPHESUS (18:24–28)

In reporting on ***Priscilla and Aquila*** in Ephesus, Luke tells of the arrival of ***Apollos***, a Jew from ***Alexandria, Egypt***. The second largest city in the first century and known for education, Alexandria had a large Jewish population, so it is no surprise that a Jew from Alexandria would be well-educated "with a thorough knowledge of the Scriptures" (Acts 18:24). Apollos's knowledge of the Scriptures was such that he knew about "the way of the Lord" (18:25), a phrase used to describe John the Baptist's ministry of preparation for the coming of Jesus in fulfillment of OT prophecy (e.g., Luke 1:76; 3:4; cf. Isa 40:3). Nevertheless, Apollos's knowledge of the gospel message was incomplete, for while he "taught about Jesus accurately"—a phrase better rendered "he taught accurately about the things concerning Jesus" (Greek: *edidasken akribōs ta peri tou Iēsou*)—Luke adds that Apollos "knew only the baptism of John" (18:25). John's baptism had been a baptism of repentance, calling people to watch for the coming of the promised Messiah (cf. Luke 3:3, 8, 16; Acts 10:37; 13:24–25). Apparently, Apollos had benefited from the early teaching of John the Baptist (i.e., from John's disciples) but had not yet heard the news that John's preaching had been fulfilled

Fresco of Aquila and Priscilla with Saint Paul, Rome.
zatletic/stock.adobe.com

The Itinerant Ministry of Apollos

The name of the itinerant Apollos occurs ten times in the New Testament. In Acts 18:24 we learn he is a Jew from Alexandria, Egypt, who has traveled to Ephesus, where he learns the complete gospel message. In Acts 18:27–19:1 Apollos moves from Ephesus to preach the gospel effectively in Corinth.

Paul references Apollos several times in his letter to the Corinthians. Perhaps because of his effective ministry in Corinth, Apollos is named in 1 Corinthians 1:12 and 3:4 as one of the heroes of a faction within the church. In a rather extensive argument against such fracturing of the church, Paul teaches that various ministers like himself and Apollos have differing assignments serving the same Lord (3:5); neither he nor Apollos can take credit for the growth of the gospel (3:6); boasting about particular teachers like Paul, or Apollos, or Cephas (Peter) is foolishness (3:22); and this lesson against pride in following a particular teacher such as himself or Apollos over against another is an important lesson pointing to the priority of Scripture (4:6).

Paul wrote the letter we call 1 Corinthians from Ephesus, and it seems that Apollos had returned to Ephesus and wanted to stay there for a little longer (1 Cor 16:12). A few years later Apollos was traveling again and may have carried Paul's letter to Titus on the island of Crete (Titus 3:13).

in the person of Jesus when he died and rose again from the grave. So Priscilla and Aquila explain "the way of God more adequately," and Apollos hears the rest of the gospel message (18:26). Then armed with the complete good news, Apollos moves on to Achaia, where he has an effective ministry, proving from the Scriptures that the Messiah is Jesus (18:28). Thus, Luke gives an example of a successful wife-husband team in gospel ministry.[1]

Alexandria, Egypt

- Among the many cities that bore his name, Alexander the Great himself selected the site for this city in 331 BC and entrusted the planning of the city to Dinocrates, the architect of the temple of Artemis in Ephesus.
- Served as the capital of Egypt in the Hellenistic era and into the Roman era.
- Situated in the Nile delta on a strip of land between the Mediterranean Sea and Lake Mareotis.
- An important commercial port of call with several harbors.
- On the island of Pharos before the Alexandrian harbors stood the 330-foot Pharos lighthouse, named on some of the lists of the seven wonders of the ancient world.
- The point of departure for Egyptian grain shipments to Rome; an Alexandrian grain ship brought Paul part of the way to Rome (Acts 27:6, 38; cf. 28:11). Other commercial endeavors included papyrus and books, linen and tapestries, perfumes and cosmetics, and articles of glass, ivory, wood, and precious metals.
- A significant city of cultural influence known for its widely varying architecture and generously supported academic research. It had one of the first great universities of the world, a museum (emphasizing the collection of scientific and literary research more than the collection of objects), and a famous library reaching more than one million volumes (now lost).
- Representative religions included the worship of Serapis, Poseidon, Caesar, and the God of the Jews.
- Estimated population between five hundred thousand and a million by the time of Christ. In addition to its large African population, many Greeks, Persians, and Jews emigrated to Alexandria. Philo Judaeus (ca. 20 BC–AD 50) is one of its most famous Jewish scholars.
- Where Jewish scholars produced a Greek translation of the Hebrew Scriptures called the Septuagint (LXX) in about the third century BC.
- Home of the Jewish speaker Apollos who became a Christian in Ephesus (Acts 18:24–28).

Select Bibliography

J. Harold Ellens, "Alexandria," *EDB*, 1337.
Edward M. Blaiklock, "Alexandria," *ZEB* 1:116–19.
Birger A. Pearson, "Alexandria," *OEANE* 1:65–69.

1. Luke's positive report of the successful ministry of Priscilla and Aquila contrasts with his negative report of the only other married couple to which he gives extensive coverage, i.e., Ananias and Sapphira in Acts 5:1–11.

Ephesus

- A walled city with several gated entrances, nestled between and around Mounts Pion and Koressos on the west coast of Asia Minor (modern Turkey).
- Its harbor connected to the Cayster River, which was navigable by ships as it emptied into the Aegean Sea. This made it an important maritime hub for the region.
- Had a first-century population around 250,000 people.
- A bustling center of commerce as well as the capital of the Roman province of Asia. It ranked among the other great cities of the Roman Empire such as Egyptian Alexandria, Syrian Antioch, Corinth, and Rome itself.
- By some estimates (ancient and modern), the leading city of the richest region of the Roman Empire.
- The home reference point of many Roman milestone markers in Asia Minor.
- Dependent on the waters of the Cayster River, its port experienced many troubles. The requirements to maintain the harbor—sometimes botched by the ancient engineers—became too burdensome, and it eventually turned into a silt-laden marshland, which led to economic decline, and the city turned to focus more on the tourist trade.
- Ephesus is now six or seven miles inland from the Mediterranean Sea.
- As reflected in Acts 19, the most important deity in first-century Ephesus was Artemis (a.k.a. Diana), and her temple there ranked as one of the seven wonders of the ancient world.
- Evidence of other deities worshiped point to Agathe Tyche, Aphrodite, Apollo, Asclepius, Athena, the Cabiri, Concord, Cybele, Demeter, Dionysus, Enedra, Hecate, Hephaestus, Heracles, Hestia Boulaia, Isis, Kore, Nemesis, Pan, Pion, Pluto, Poseidon, Serapis, Theos Hypsistos, Tyche Soteira, Zeus, and the Roman emperor.
- Here Christianity flourished for a number of centuries. Many NT books have a relationship with the city (Acts, Ephesians, 1 Corinthians, 1 and 2 Timothy, Revelation, and the gospel and letters of John).
- Host to the Third Ecumenical Council in AD 431.
- Largely destroyed by earthquakes in the fourth and seventh centuries; eventually was only a small village that was abandoned by the fifteenth century.
- In addition to the impressive extant archaeological remains of the ancient city, some 3,500 inscriptions have been found here. Some of the remains and inscriptions go back to the NT era, and some are from subsequent centuries.

Select Bibliography

Clinton E. Arnold, "Ephesus," *DPL*, 249–53.

Anton Bammer, "Ephesus," *OEANE* 2:252–55.

Edward M. Blaiklock, "Ephesus," *ZEB* 2:352–57.

John McRay, *Archaeology and the New Testament* (Grand Rapids: Baker, 1991), 250–61.

Richard E. Oster Jr., "Ephesus," *ABD*, 2:542–49.

Ruins of Ancient Ephesus

Interior of the terraced housing complex, which displays some of the area's ancient opulence
Douglas S. Huffman

Library of Celsus (built in the early second century AD)
Douglas S. Huffman

Harbor Street from the grand theater to the harbor
© 2012 by Zondervan

13.2 PAUL'S MINISTRY IN EPHESUS (ACTS 19:1–41)

After discussing the ministries of Priscilla and Aquila and Apollos, Luke reports on Paul's return to the large and regionally significant city of ***Ephesus*** and his ministry there, including with a small group of twelve (19:1–7), with the greater regional population (19:8–12), in the wake of some false ministers (19:13–20), and leading up to a riot aimed at him (19:21–41). As Priscilla and Aquila did with Apollos, all these ministries involve moving people in Ephesus toward greater accuracy in their understanding of the gospel message.

13.2.1 Paul Ministers to Some Disciples of John the Baptist (19:1–7)

Paul comes to Ephesus via "the road through the interior" of Asia Minor, and there he meets some "disciples" (a term Luke regularly uses for believers; 19:1). Something leads Paul to ask them, "Did you receive the Holy Spirit when you believed?" (19:2). Peter had declared that all who believed in Jesus for the forgiveness of their sins would receive the promised Holy Spirit (2:38–39), and this was Paul's own experience (9:17–19), so reception of the Spirit is the expected norm (cf. Gal 3:1–3; Rom 8:9–11). But when these "disciples" respond by saying they had "not even heard that there is a Holy Spirit" (Acts 19:2), Paul inquires further about whose disciples they are, and they respond that they had been baptized to identify with the teachings of John the Baptist (19:3; note that John the Baptist had "disciples"; Luke 5:33–34; 7:18; 11:1). Well, that explains it. They had not heard the rest of the story, and as Priscilla and Aquila had done with Apollos, now Paul makes the final connections for them.

"John's baptism was a baptism of repentance. He told the people to believe in the one coming after him," Paul explains, "that is, in Jesus" (Acts 19:4). Upon hearing the rest of the gospel story, these men place their trust in Jesus as the Messiah they had been awaiting, and when they do, they receive the Holy Spirit, which is evidenced with speaking in tongues and prophesying (19:5–6).

13.2.2 Paul's Typical Ministry Strategy (19:8–12)

A familiar pattern in Paul's ministry is played out in Ephesus. He first shares the gospel in the Jewish synagogue, where he speaks "boldly" (19:8a; cf. 4:31; 9:28; 13:46; 14:3; 28:31), "arguing persuasively" (19:8b; cf. 17:4; 18:4, 13; 26:28) about the kingdom of God for three months. As has been common, Paul's preaching has mixed results, with some of the Jews becoming "disciples" and some of them refusing to believe (19:9). So he moves to minister directly to a gentile audience with as many Jewish believers as will join him, and this they do in the lecture hall of Tyrannus with daily discussions for some two years (19:9–10). In addition to these usual elements, Luke's report of Paul's ministry in Ephesus has several more specific parallels with his description of Paul's ministry in Corinth, the central city of Achaia (see sidebar). Now after almost three years (see sidebar),

Paul's Three Years in Ephesus

three months in the synagogue (Acts 19:8)
\+ two years in the lecture hall of Tyrannus (Acts 19:9-10)
\+ "in the province of Asia a little longer" (Acts 19:22)
≈ three years among the Ephesians (Acts 20:31)

Ruins of Ancient Ephesus

Curetes Street from the upper city to the lower city
Douglas S. Huffman

The Eternal Destiny of Disciples of John the Baptist

What would have happened to the disciples of John the Baptist in Acts 19:1-7 had they died before hearing the full gospel message from Paul? We should expect the same to have happened to them as happened to John the Baptist. With his forward-looking faith, John the Baptist was like any other OT believer among the twelve tribes of Israel who had to trust God to provide someday for the salvation of his people. The twelve Ephesian men were among God's people with forward-looking faith, and Paul simply had to inform these believers of the rest of the story. Unlike John the Baptist, who died before Jesus was crucified and resurrected, these twelve Ephesians, like people today, can now have a backward-looking faith to the historical events whereby God has secured in Christ our salvation.

Paul's extensive ministry in the central city of the Roman province of Asia is such that Luke can report with a progress summary statement "that all the Jews and Greeks who lived in the province of Asia heard the word of the Lord" (19:10).

Paul's ministry in Ephesus is publicly supernaturally confirmed with "extraordinary miracles," for which Luke specifically credits God as doing through Paul (19:11). These miracles include the healing of illnesses and the exorcism of evil spirits by means of handkerchiefs and aprons Paul had touched (19:12), which are reminiscent of other odd healings, e.g., from Peter's shadow (5:15) and from touching the hem of Jesus's garment (Luke 8:43–48).

Comparing Paul's Ministries in Corinth and Ephesus

Given the regularity of Paul's approach to ministry seen throughout Acts, it is perhaps unsurprising to find similarities between the ministries Paul had in Corinth (Acts 18:1-18) and in Ephesus (Acts 19:1-41). Nevertheless, it is interesting to note the many likenesses in Luke's descriptions of Paul's ministries in these two cities.

Paul in Corinth in Acts 18	Paul in Ephesus in Acts 19
Enters the capital city of its province, Achaia (18:1).	Enters the capital city of its province, Asia (19:1).
Begins in the synagogue, trying to "persuade" Jews to believe the gospel (18:4-5).	Begins in the synagogue, trying to "persuade" Jews to believe the gospel (19:8).
Experiences mixed results: some Jews believing the gospel and others rejecting it (18:6-8)	Experiences mixed results: some Jews believing the gospel and others rejecting it (19:9)
Moves to a gentile venue, the house of Titius Justus (18:6-7).	Moves to a gentile venue, the lecture hall of Tyrannus (19:9).
Sees many believe the gospel (18:8).	Sees many believe the gospel (19:10).
Is supernaturally confirmed by means of a vision in the night (18:9-10).	Is supernaturally confirmed by means of strange miracles (19:11-12).
Is vindicated before his opponents when they are dismissed by Roman authorities (18:12-17).	Is vindicated before his opponents when they are dismissed by Roman authorities (19:12-17).
Stays in the city for a long time, 1.5 years (18:11).	Stays in the city for a long time, 3 years (19:8-10, 22; 20:31).

This comparison in an expansion of a similar five-part comparison in Stott, *Message of Acts*, 294-95.

13.2.3 A Power Encounter for the Seven Sons of Sceva (19:13–20)

Ancient Ephesus was well known for its magical practices, including magic words and amulets (see sidebars). While magic was a widespread phenomenon in the Hellenistic world, as the empire's third largest city in the heart of the empire, Ephesus was most welcoming to all sorts of magicians and sorcerers.[2] Unsurprisingly then, Luke

2. Bruce M. Metzger, "St. Paul and the Magicians," *PSB* 38 (1944): 27.

includes an account of some magical practices in Ephesus. A particular group of Jews there—identified as the seven ***sons of Sceva***—try to carry out an exorcism by invoking "the name of the Jesus whom Paul preaches" (19:13) as a kind of magic formula, but they fail miserably and are severely beaten by the demonized man. Clint Arnold makes a helpful distinction between the occurrence of religious miracles and the practice of ***magic***: "In religion one prays and requests from the gods; in magic one commands the gods and therefore expects guaranteed results."[3] Thus, on the one hand, those with faithful dependence on the authority of God pray for miracles, but on the other hand, those with a worldview of magic attempt to manipulate spiritual powers to get desired results.[4] So despite their religious heritage, the sons of Sceva were practicing magic and appealing to other powers rather than praying to God for miracles.[5] Luke's account makes clear that the name of Jesus cannot be reduced to a magic formula for manipulative power.

Magic and the Occult in Ephesus

From Clinton E. Arnold, "Acts," vol. 2B of *ZIBBCNT*, ed. Clinton E. Arnold (Grand Rapids: Zondervan, 2002), 195.

> Ephesus was renown as being something of a center for magical practices in the Mediterranean world. The practice of magic was everywhere—it was part of the fabric of common "folk belief"—but Ephesus acquired a significant reputation for it.
>
> This reputation was perpetuated in part, by the so-called "Ephesian Letters" (*Ephesia Grammata*). These were actually six names—*askion, kataskion, lix, tetrax, damnameneus,* and *aisia*—thought to be laden with protective power for warding off evil demons. One ancient writer says that the "magi" instructed people possessed by evil spirits to repeat to themselves the magic words in order to drive the demons out. There was a story that circulated about an Ephesian wrestler who traveled to Olympia to compete in the games. This wrestler wore the "Ephesian Letters" on an ankle bracelet while he competed and was winning every match. Finally an opponent from Miletus discovered the bracelet and protested, whereupon the item was removed by the officials. The Ephesian wrestler then fell to three successive defeats by his Milesian opponent.
>
> No magical papyri have been discovered in Ephesus. But this has more to do with the fact that the climate of this area is not conducive to the preservation of papyri. Nevertheless, a variety of magical amulets, gems, and inscriptions have been discovered in the city.

3. Clinton E. Arnold, *Power and Magic: The Concept of Power in Ephesians* (Grand Rapids: Baker, 1989), 19.

4. Cf. Howard Clark Kee, *Medicine, Miracle and Magic in New Testament Times*, SNTSMS 55 (Cambridge: Cambridge University Press, 1986), 127.

5. For more on Jewish magic practices, particularly in Asia Minor, see esp. Arnold, *Power and Magic*, 29–33; cf. David E. Aune, "Magic and Early Christianity," *ANRW* II.23.2 (1980): 1507–57, reprinted in David E. Aune, *Apocalypticism, Prophecy, and Magic in Early Christianity: Collected Essays* (Grand Rapids: Baker Academic, 2008), 368–420.

Ephesian Magic Related Archaeological Finds

Ephesia grammata were magic words that were thought to have magical powers in pronouncing them. This amulet—the only known occurrence of the *Ephesia grammata* stamped in gold—also invokes the god Phoebus Apollo.

Invocation to the god Phoebus Apollo
The Schøyen Collection MS 5236, Oslo and London.

Tokens like these were struck in lead or bronze, and their function is debated. Some scholars suggest the tokens were inscribed with magical formulas or served as magical charms, and others suggesting they served merely as advertisements.

Ephesian tessera
ZRadovan/BibleLandsPictures.com

While decidedly in favor of miracles and power over the demonic (e.g., Luke 4:31–36, 41; 8:26–39; 9:37–43; 10:17–18; 11:14; 13:32; Acts 5:12–16; 8:7; 16:16–18; 19:11–12), Luke offers here a clear warning against ***syncretism***, i.e., compromises regarding cultural practices in the lives of true believers. As news of the failed magical exorcism spreads, the news that Jesus is the true Lord is likewise heard such that "the name of the Lord Jesus was held in high honor" rather than utilized as a mere magical formula (19:17). Moreover, this experience also causes Ephesian believers in Jesus to confront their own lingering attachments to magic such that they openly repent of their practices and even bring their magical scrolls to be burned (19:18–19). Luke estimates that the burned documents were valued at fifty thousand drachmas (about fifty thousand days of wages).[6]

Paul on His Ministry in Ephesus

A statement toward the end of 1 Corinthians gives evidence that Paul wrote this letter while serving in Ephesus in the midst of opposition.

1 Corinthians 16:8-9

But I will stay on at Ephesus until Pentecost, because a great door for effective work has opened to me, and there are many who oppose me.

6. Clinton E. Arnold, "Acts," vol. 2B of *ZIBBCNT*, ed. Clinton E. Arnold (Grand Rapids: Zondervan, 2002), 195, remarks, "Another way of looking at this is that it would require over 150 people working a full year to equal the financial value of these scrolls."

Thus, many Christians were repenting of their evil practices, and the burning of the scrolls shows the permanent intent of their repentance.[7]

This progress in the lives of the Ephesian believers prompts Luke to offer another mid-journey progress summary (19:20). Like previous progress summary statements in Acts, this summary statement reflects on the progress made to this point (i.e., "In this way the word of the Lord spread widely . . ."; 19:20a). But this summary also anticipates an expanding influence (i.e., ". . . and grew in power"; 19:20b).

Erastus, One of Paul's Helpers in Acts 19:22

At one point, Erastus (Acts 19:22) held a public office at Corinth (Rom 16:23 where the Greek *oikonomos* is rendered "director of public works" in NIV but "treasurer" in CEV, CSB, ESV, NASB, NET, NLT ; cf. 2 Tim 4:20). As such, he may well be the same person who donated some pavement to a public square in Corinth. In the plaza just east of the Corinthian theater is a Latin inscription with seven-inch-tall lettering that is translated "Erastus in return for his aedileship laid [the pavement] at his own expense."

Todd Bolen/BiblePlaces.com

Todd Bolen/BiblePlaces.com

7. Cf. C. Kavin Rowe, *World Upside Down: Reading Acts in the Graeco-Roman Age* (New York: Oxford University Press, 2009), 43.

The Church of Ephesus, the NT, and the Early Church

The city of Ephesus is connected to at least six of the books of the New Testament (Acts, Ephesians, 1 Corinthians, 1 and 2 Timothy, and Revelation). Furthermore, with the apostle John having lived at Ephesus after his exile on the island of Patmos (where he wrote Revelation), his four other NT books may have been produced there (the Gospel of John and his letters 1, 2, and 3 John). Also, the early church father Ignatius wrote a letter to the Ephesian church early in the second century AD. So Ephesus was very influential in the life of early church.

Acts: In Acts, we learn about the ministries of several people in Ephesus, including Priscilla and Aquila, Apollos, and Paul (see esp. Acts 18:19–19:41; 20:16–38)

Ephesians: The church at Ephesus is the named recipient of this Pauline letter.

1 Corinthians: Our best guess is that Paul wrote 1 Corinthians from the city of Ephesus not long after his eighteen-month ministry in Corinth (cf. Acts 18:1–18).

1 Timothy: Paul's first letter to Timothy reveals that Paul, while continuing on to Macedonia, had left Timothy in charge of the Ephesian church (see esp. 1 Tim 1:3–7).

2 Timothy: Paul's second letter to Timothy was also sent to him at Ephesus, apparently carried by Tychicus (4:12), and recalls the ministry at Ephesus (1:18).

Revelation: The first note among the letters to the seven churches of Revelation is specifically addressed to the church at Ephesus (Rev 2:1–7).

The Gospel of John and the Epistles of 1, 2, 3 John: While these other NT writings of the apostle John do not mention Ephesus, John may well have written these while living there.

Ignatius: This early church father was bishop of Antioch in Syria and wrote a brief letter to the Ephesian church ca. AD 107 as he was on his way to Rome, where he was martyred.

13.2.4 A Riot in the Theater at Ephesus (19:21–41)

At this point Paul begins planning to travel through Macedonia and Achaia on his way to Jerusalem and even sends some helpers ahead of him (Acts 19:21–22; cf. Jesus's travel plans to go to Jerusalem in Luke 9:51–52). About then "a great disturbance about the Way" arises, prompted by a silversmith named ***Demetrius*** (Acts 19:23–24).[8] Note that this disturbance in Ephesus was *concerning* Christianity but *not caused* by Christianity. From Luke's telling of the story, some of the core issues in this culture clash include apprehension over financial stability (19:25), concern about people being deceived (19:26a), distress about their religious practices (19:26b), fear of losing professional reputation (19:27a), and nervousness about the religious reputation of ***Artemis*** (19:27b).[9]

8. The Christian movement is referred to as "the Way" six times in Acts (Acts 9:2; 19:9, 23; 22:4; 24:14, 22); see the sidebar on "The 'Church' and Its Other Names in Acts" in chapter 7.

9. Archaeological finds at Ephesus confirm the historical reliability of Luke's account. See esp. James R. Edwards, "Archaeology Gives New Reality to Paul's Ephesus Riot," *BAR* 42.4 (2016): 62 (cf. pp. 24–32, 62).

The Seven Wonders of the Ancient World

Antipater of Sidon provides the most famous list of the seven wonders of the ancient world (underlined in the following text), but most other lists replace the wall of Babylon with the lighthouse of Alexandria. Lists that preceded the construction of the Colossus of the Sun at Rhodes (ca. 280 BC) have the Ishtar Gate as the seventh wonder. The Colossus fell in a 226 BC earthquake (with ruins visible until AD 654), so Antipater's seven wonders existed together for less than sixty years. Only the pyramids remain today. For Antipater, the temple of Artemis at Ephesus was the greatest of all these ancient wonders.

Antipater of Sidon, *Greek Anthology*, 9.58 (ca. 140 BC)

> I have set eyes on the wall of lofty Babylon on which is a road for chariots, and the statue of Zeus by the Alpheus, and the hanging gardens, and the Colossus of the Sun, and the huge labour of the high pyramids, and the vast tomb of Mausolus; but when I saw the house of Artemis that mounted to the clouds, those other marvels lost their brilliancy, and I said, "Lo, apart from Olympus, the Sun never looked on aught so grand."

The Temple of Artemis at Ephesus

Outside the walls of Ephesus, the temple of Artemis was on the list of the seven wonders of the ancient world. It was the largest religious building in the Hellenistic world (ca. 425 ft. x 220 ft.), about four times the size of the Parthenon in Athens, and the first to be constructed entirely of marble. In addition to being a worship center, the temple functioned as a refuge of government inscriptions. The Goths burned the temple in AD 263, and it was destroyed in the sixth century. Of its 127 drum-style columns, one has been reassembled, giving a sense of the temple's sixty-foot height. An artist's model of it gives some idea of the massively impressive construction in contrast to its current condition.

Model of the temple of Artemis
Serg Zastavkin/Shutterstock.com

Temple of Artemis ruins in Ephesus
Goldika/Shutterstock.com

Thus, we see that not every opposition to Christian faith will be promulgated simply on whether the gospel is true; sometimes other motives are at work. When popular cultural assumptions and habits are brought under suspicion by the message of the gospel, those defending the gospel will meet with opposition.[10]

Statues of Artemis

Described as the Greek goddess of hunting, the wilderness, wild animals, the moon, childbirth, protecting childhood, and chastity, Artemis is sometimes portrayed with bow and arrows and accompanied by wild animals. Other statuary portrayals present her as abundantly fruitful. The goddess Diana is her equivalent in the Roman pantheon of gods.

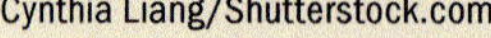

Cynthia Liang/Shutterstock.com

Douglas S. Huffman

The purported threat to the goddess Artemis and the Ephesians' city incites fury and exclamations of the reputations of both: "Great is Artemis of the Ephesians!" (19:28). Soon "the whole city" is in an uproar (19:29a). Apparently unable to seize Paul, the people grab two of Paul's team members—Gaius and Aristarchus—and bring them into the theater (19:29b). When Paul hears what is going on, he wants to go to the

10. Cf. Rowe, *World Upside Down*, 49.

theater himself to address the crowd, but the believers do not allow him to do so (19:30). Some of his friends who are officials of the Asian province (i.e., some "Asiarchs") send him a message begging him not to go (19:31).[11] Paul's friendship with these Roman leaders suggests that Rome did not have a policy of hostility toward Christianity at this time and that Paul's ministry was welcomed among the wealthy and educated of Ephesus and was not exclusively aimed at the poor and uneducated.[12] On the riotous nature of the people assembled in the theater, Luke comments, "The assembly was in confusion: Some were shouting one thing, some another. Most of the people did not even know why they were there" (19:32).[13] The Jews in the crowd push forward a man named Alexander, who attempts to make a defense before the people; but he is shouted down when the crowd realizes he is a Jew, and the shouting goes on for two hours (19:33–34).[14]

Gladiator relief found at Ephesus.
Clinton E. Arnold

The Ephesian city clerk interrupts the riot and, without any governmental favoritism toward Christianity, simply explains that the non-Christians were the ones behaving illegally. While clearly defending the honor of Ephesus as the "guardian of the temple of the great Artemis and of her image" (19:35), he nevertheless points out that Paul and the Christians have done no harm in word or deed (19:35–37) and instructs Demetrius and his fellow craftsmen to utilize the established court system to file any legitimate complaints (19:38–39). He concludes that the crowd is actually in danger of being brought up on legal charges for starting a riot without legitimate reason, and he dismisses them from the theater (19:40–41). Luke thus indicates that Paul and the Christian faith are free of any responsibility for the civil disturbance.

11. G. H. R. Horsley explains that more than 200 people with the title "*Asiarch*" or "*archiereis Asiae*" (or both) are known from inscriptional and numismatic (coin) sources—with 106 of them connected to Ephesus, the capital of the province; G. H. R. Horsley, "The Inscriptions of Ephesos and the New Testament," *NovT* 34 (1992): 137–38 (cf. pp. 105–68). Of course, not all Asiarchs were friends of Paul, and their "friendship" with Paul does not necessarily mean they were committed Christians; see also Craig S. Keener, "Paul's 'Friends' the Asiarchs (Acts 19.31)," *JGRChJ* 3 (2006): 134–41; cf. Craig S. Keener, *Acts: An Exegetical Commentary*, 4 vols. (Grand Rapids: Baker Academic, 2012–2015), 3:2908–18.

12. John McRay, *Archaeology and the New Testament* (Grand Rapids: Baker, 1991), 255–56; cf. F. F. Bruce, *The Book of Acts*, 2nd ed., NICNT (Grand Rapids: Eerdmans, 1988), 376–77.

13. On the normalcy of urban uprisings in the first-century Roman world, see Moyer V. Hubbard, "Urban Uprisings in the Roman World: The Social Setting of the Mobbing of Sosthenes," *NTS*, 51 (2005): 416–28.

14. Alexander may have been trying to distinguish between Judaism and Christianity, but Paul's explanation of Jesus as the true Jewish Messiah would make the two monotheistic faith systems somewhat indistinguishable to the Ephesian pagans. Might this be "Alexander the coppersmith" who did Paul "great harm" in Ephesus (2 Tim 4:14; cf. 1 Tim 1:20)?

The Great Theater at Ancient Ephesus

Seating an estimated twenty-four thousand people (and with standing room for another one thousand), the great theater in ancient Ephesus is the largest in Asia Minor and perhaps in the ancient world. First constructed in the third century BC, it was expanded in the Roman era from about AD 40 into the second century. It has sixty-six rows of stone seats divided into three horizontal sections by two walkways. Seats in the lowest section had marble backs and were likely used for reserved seating. In addition to theatrical and musical productions, the theater was also home to political, philosophical, religious, and even gladiator events. Here is where Demetrius and other craftsmen rioted in response to Paul's preaching of the gospel (Acts 19:23–41).

Todd Bolen/BiblePlaces.com

13.3 FOLLOW-UP MINISTRY IN GREECE AND ASIA MINOR (ACTS 20:1–16)

Paul's typical concern for the believers under his care is seen in his gathering of the disciples at Ephesus and encouraging them immediately after the riotous uproar ends (20:1). Then he embarks on his planned tour of Macedonia and Achaia (i.e., Greece) before heading for Jerusalem and then back to Syrian Antioch (cf. 19:21).

13.3.1 The Route in Greece (20:1–3).

Luke is rather vague about the details of this trip, perhaps because he expects his readers to understand that Paul's tour through Macedonia and Greece was to revisit the churches he had planted on his second missionary campaign.[15] What Luke does report is that, as Paul carries out his plan, he is "speaking many words of encouragement to the people" (20:2). When he arrives in Greece—presumably Corinth, where he had previously lived for one and a half years—Paul stays for three months (20:3a) before determing finally to head back to Syria.[16] But discovering a plot against him "just as he was about to sail for Syria" (20:3b, presumably at the Corinthian seaport of Cenchreae), rather than be trapped on a ship with such oppenents, Paul changes his route and decides to travel by land back through Macedonia (20:3c).

13.3.2 The Ministry Team (20:4–6)

At this point in narrating these travels, Luke lists Paul's co-ministers. Even as Paul's ministry had been prosperous in attracting people to faith in Christ, so also it was prosperous in expanding the ministry team (20:4). Luke himself rejoins the group, with the second "we section" beginning as the missionary team comes back to ***Philippi***, where Luke had presumably invested the intervening years (20:5; cf. 16:10–17, 40).[17] From Philippi, the previously named coworkers "went on ahead and waited for us at Troas. But we sailed from Philippi after the Festival of Unleavened Bread, and five days later joined the others at Troas, where we stayed seven days" (20:5–6). The trip from Philippi to Troas taking five days suggests strong head winds or delayed stops at such places as Samothrace, for the earlier journey in the other direction had taken only two days (cf. 16:11–12).

13.3.3 Raising Eutychus in Troas (20:7–12)

At ***Troas*** Luke reports that the believers came together "to break bread" (cf. 2:42) on "the first day of the week" (20:7), i.e., on Sunday. This is the earliest text we have indicating that Sunday had become a regular day of worship for Christians.[18] At this Sunday gathering, Paul speaks late into the evening (20:7). With the detail of one in attendance (cf. "we" in 20:7–8), Luke notes that the warmth of the upstairs meeting room and the late-night long-winded speaker created an unfortunate setting for a young man named ***Eutychus*** seated in an open window. He sinks into a sound sleep, falls from the third story, and is picked up dead (20:8–9).[19] Reminiscent of the OT miracle stories involving Elijah (1 Kgs 17:17–24) and Elisha (2 Kgs 4:18–37) and of God's use

15. For a few more details about this portion of Paul's third missionary journey, see 2 Cor 2:12–13; 7:5–7, 13; which seem to indicate that 2 Corinthians was written from Macedonia.

16. Paul's letter to the Romans seems to have been written from Corinth and mentions, along with future goals, Paul's immediate plan to deliver for the poor in Jerusalem the contributions he received from believers in Macedonia and Achaia (Rom 15:23–29; cf. Acts 24:17).

17. Some have suggested that Luke might be the person Paul calls "my true companion" in Phil 4:3; e.g., F. F. Bruce, *Philippians*, Understanding the Bible Commentary Series (Grand Rapids: Baker, 2011), 138.

18. Bruce, *Book of Acts*, 384; cf. 1 Cor 16:2 and Rev 1:10.

19. Green-Armytage dubs Eutychus "the patron saint of the defenestrated"; A. H. N. Green-Armytage, *A Portrait of St. Luke* (London: Burns and Oates, 1955; Chicago Henry Regnery, 1955), 61.

of Peter to restore the life of Tabitha (Acts 9:36–41), Paul goes down and embraces the dead young man, and Eutychus is brought back to life (20:10). While the people understandably rejoice over the miraculous raising of Eutychus from death (20:12), Luke's first comment is to mention that Paul goes back upstairs again, gets something to eat, and then continues his sermon "until daylight" (20:11). Luke does not portray Eutychus's fall as a rebuke for Paul's wordy message.[20] Rather, as seen elsewhere in Acts (and the rest of Scripture), miracles in ministry may be supportive and encouraging, but the message of God's word to humanity is central. Miracles are not the focus of ministry.

13.3.4 Sailing to Miletus (20:13–16)

The ministry team leaves Troas by ship, sailing southward along the Aegean coastline about twenty miles to Assos, where they take Paul onboard (20:13). Luke does not comment on why Paul wanted to travel apart from the team by foot to Assos, but the reunited group continues southward sailing to Mitylene (20:14). From Mitylene, they sail in successive days to Chios, to Samos, and to Miletus (20:15). The summer winds along this stretch of the Aegean Sea usually blow from the north early in the morning but die away in the afternoon, so sailing southward in short bursts and anchoring each evening was not unexpected.[21] In his hurry to reach Jerusalem, Paul decides to bypass Ephesus, lest he be distracted into spending a lot more time in Asia than he had room in his calendar (20:16; cf. 18:19–22).[22]

13.4 Paul Addresses the Ephesian Elders at Miletus (Acts 20:17–38)

Despite his desire to avoid spending time in Ephesus, Paul takes time to summon the ***elders*** of the Ephesian church to ***Miletus*** (20:17), which was about thirty miles south of Ephesus (perhaps a three-day round trip). When they arrive, Paul addresses them in what turns out to be the only lengthy address in Acts made to Christians (20:18–35). Interestingly, Luke's summary of the speech has a style much like Paul's letters.[23] Of the speech's many thematic parallels with Paul's letters (see sidebar), Witherington specifies that most of them come from letters Paul would have written in AD 56–58,

20. Richard N. Longenecker, "Acts," pp. 663–1102 in *Luke-Acts*, vol. 10 of *The Expositor's Bible Commentary*, ed. Tremper Longman III and David E. Garland, rev. ed. (Grand Rapids: Zondervan, 2007), 1024.

21. Dean Pinter, *Acts*, The Story of God Bible Commentary (Grand Rapids: Zondervan, 2019), 463.

22. See possible expanded rationale in Keener, "Paul's 'Friends' the Asiarchs," 140; cf. Barrett's suggestion that Paul avoided Ephesus out of concern for his safety, C. K. Barrett, "Paul's Address to the Ephesian Elders," pp. 107–21 in *God's Christ and His People: Studies in Honour of Nils Alstrup Dahl*, ed. Jacob Jervell and Wayne A. Meeks (Oslo: Universitetforlaget, 1977), 108.

23. George A. Kennedy, *New Testament Interpretation through Rhetorical Criticism*, Studies in Religion (Chapel Hill, NC: University of North Carolina Press, 1984), 139; cf. C. F. D. Moule, "The Christology of Acts," pp. 159–85 in *Studies in Luke-Acts: Essays Presented in Honor of Paul Schubert*, ed. Leander E. Keck and Louis J. Martyn (Nashville: Abingdon, 1966; repr., Philadelphia: Fortress, 1980), 171; and Barrett, "Paul's Address to the Ephesian Elders," 116–17.

The Pauline Language of the Speech in Acts 20

Luke's record of Paul's speech in Acts 20 reflects some of the style, terms, and concepts found in Paul's NT letters, and most of these parallels come from letters written prior to the event of the Acts 20 speech. These observations give testimony to Luke's accurate portrayal of Paul's actual address.

Term/Concept	Acts 20	Paul's Letters
Reminder of how he lived when with the audience	vv. 17-18	1 Thess 2:1–2; Phil 4:15
Paul's work called "serving the Lord"	v. 19	Rom 1:1; 12:11; Phil 2:22
On refusing to claim anything for self	v. 19	2 Cor 10:1; 11:7; 1 Thess 2:6
On his fears/showing personal concern	v. 19	Rom 9:2; 2 Cor 2:4; Phil 3:18
Jewish persecution	v. 19	2 Cor 11:24–26; 1 Thess 2:14–16
Taught from house to house	v. 20	Rom 16:5; Col 4:15; Phlm 21
Helpful/profitable teaching	v. 20	Gal 4:16; 2 Cor 4:2
Preaching to both Jew and Greek	v. 21	Rom 1:16; 1 Cor 9:20
Faith in our Lord Jesus	v. 21	Rom 10:9–13
Paul's uncertainty about his future	v. 22	Rom 15:30–32
Lack of attempt to preserve his own life	v. 24	2 Cor 4:7–5:10; 6:4–10; Phil 1:19–26; 2:17; 3:8
Desire to "finish the race"	v. 24	2 Tim 4:7
Paul's task—preach the gospel of grace	v. 24	Gal 1:15–16; 2 Cor 6:1
Being innocent of convert's blood	v. 26	1 Thess 2:10
Salvation by the blood of Jesus	v. 28	Rom 8:31
Discussion about invaders from without and predators within	vv. 29-30	2 Cor 10–13; Phil 3:2–6; Rom 16:17–20

Adapted and expanded from Witherington and Myers, *New Testament Rhetoric*, 65; cf. Ben Witherington III, *The Acts of the Apostles: A Socio-Rhetorical Commentary* (Grand Rapids: Eerdmans, 1998; Carlisle: Paternoster, 1998), 610.

i.e., prior to the Acts 20 event.[24] Given the remarkable Pauline language, style, and content, Green-Armytage suggests that it is impossible to attribute the speech to Luke's imaginative invention. Instead, the only reasonable conclusion from this evidence is that Luke has provided an accurate report of Paul's actual speech to the Ephesian elders.[25] Because this event is part of a "we section," we can understand Luke to be present and able to recount the event accurately.[26] As we have it, Luke's synopsis of the speech is

24. Ben Witherington III and Jason A. Myers, "Early Christian Homilies: The Rhetorical Speech Summaries in Acts," pp. 42–81 in *New Testament Rhetoric: An Introductory Guide to the Art of Persuasion in and of the New Testament*, 2nd ed. (Eugene, OR: Cascade, 2022), 65.

25. Green-Armytage, *A Portrait of St. Luke*, 66–67.

26. Ibid., 67.

largely a defense of Paul's ministry (20:18–24) and a collection of principles for good church leadership (20:25–35).

13.4.1 A Defense of Paul's Ministry (20:18–24)

Reviewing his past ministry among the Ephesians, Paul calls on the elders to remember his consistent personal life (20:18), his committed personal investment in ministry (20:19), and his constancy in teaching (20:20–21). Moving from his past with the Ephesians, Paul then talks about his future apart from them, a future certain to involve suffering for the gospel. Paul is "compelled by the Spirit" to go to Jerusalem (20:22) and at the same time is being prepared by the Spirit for the difficulties he will face there (20:23). But advanced knowledge of hardships is not the same thing as instruction to change plans. So Paul's plans for the future show a consistency with his past at Ephesus: he continues in his willingness to live sacrificially so as to complete "the task of testifying to the good news of God's grace" (20:24). Upon the moral authority of his lifestyle, Paul makes his appeal for the Ephesian elders to be good leaders.

13.4.2 Principles of Good Church Leadership (20:25–35)

Having begun his address to the Ephesian elders with "You know . . ." (20:18), Paul's remarks now change direction with "I know . . ." (20:25), and several leadership principles become evident (see sidebar). As part of his final goodbye to them, Paul wants to be clear that he has done them no wrong (20:26) and has kept back nothing in his teaching (20:27). On this basis, he challenges them in their role of church leadership, using shepherding metaphors: the leaders as "shepherds" (20:28), the church members as the "flock" (20:28–29), and false teachers as "savage wolves" (20:29).

Principles of Good Church Leadership from Paul's Address to the Ephesian Elders (Acts 20:18–35)

Collegial: Using good teamwork, as leadership is always in the plural (v. 26).

Courageous: Not shrinking back from declaring God's whole truth (v. 27).

Careful: Paying careful attention to yourselves in the Spirit-granted oversight of God's church obtained by the blood of his own Son (v. 28).

Cautious: Being aware that opponents will arise from outside and within to deceive (vv. 29–30).

Caring: Emotionally concerned for the people's welfare (v. 31).

Commending: Entrusting the people to God and his Word (v. 32).

Conscientious: Industriously working without coveting (vv. 33–34).

Compassionate: Helping the weak and giving to others (v. 35).

With various labels—e.g., "elders" (20:17), "overseers" (20:28a), and "shepherds" (20:28b)—the plurality of leaders in the Ephesian church is a healthy model still today for its provision of shared wisdom, skills, and accountability. Paul encourages these leaders to be courageous but at the same time to be careful; after all, for the church God had sacrificed "the blood of his own [Son]" (20:28).[27] He instructs them to be cautious regarding deceptive opponents who will arise from outside and within the church (20:29–30). They are to care for the welfare of God's people (20:31), entrusting them to God and his Word (20:32), conscientiously working without coveting (20:33–34), and always compassionate in giving to others (20:35). Paul closes with another nod to his ministry among them (20:34–35a) and a quotation of Jesus that we have nowhere else: ". . . remembering the words the Lord Jesus himself said: 'It is more blessed to give than to receive'" (20:35b).[28] These leadership principles fit with Luke's ongoing presentation of the Christian community that began back in Acts 2:42. And with his portrayal of Paul as a reliable teacher of truth, and with the closure of the speech referencing Jesus's own teaching, we can readily understand Luke to be championing the leadership principles of Paul's address as not mere first-century description but as ongoing prescription for churches still today.

Jesus's Note to the Church at Ephesus

The book of Revelation opens with notes to seven churches in Asia Minor (Rev 2:1–3:22). The church at Ephesus is the first mentioned, and perhaps not without reason. According to Luke, Paul's several years of ministry in Ephesus influenced the whole province (see Acts 19:10 and 26). Following is Jesus's note to the church at Ephesus.

Revelation 2:1–7

To the angel of the church in Ephesus write:

These are the words of him who holds the seven stars in his right hand and walks among the seven golden lampstands. I know your deeds, your hard work and your perseverance. I know that you cannot tolerate wicked people, that you have tested those who claim to be apostles but are not, and have found them false. You have persevered and have endured hardships for my name, and have not grown weary.

Yet I hold this against you: You have forsaken the love you had at first. Consider how far you have fallen! Repent and do the things you did at first. If you do not repent, I will come to you and remove your lampstand from its place. But you have this in your favor: You hate the practices of the Nicolaitans, which I also hate.

Whoever has ears, let them hear what the Spirit says to the churches. To the one who is victorious, I will give the right to eat from the tree of life, which is in the paradise of God.

27. While the NIV has "which he bought with his own blood" (Acts 20:28), the Greek (*hēn periepoiēsato dia tou haimatos tou idiou*) might be better rendered "which he bought with the blood of his own," i.e., God's own Son, Jesus (see NIV margin note); CEV and NET have "the blood of his own Son."

28. See Joachim Jeremias, *Unknown Sayings of Jesus*, trans. Reginald H. Fuller (New York: Macmillan, 1957; repr., Eugene, OR: Wipf & Stock, 2008), esp. 77–81.

13.4.3 Paul's Departure (20:36–38)

At the conclusion of his remarks to the Ephesian elders, Paul kneels with them to pray (20:36). Their tearful departure (20:37) is primarily due to Paul's statement that they would never see his face again (20:38a; cf. v. 25), which some scholars speculate is an indication that Luke is writing Acts after Paul's death.[29] This, of course, is unconvincing and unnecessary, as Luke may well be merely reporting what the living Paul had said. Furthermore, it is quite possible that Paul was released from his Roman captivity at the close of the book of Acts and that he was able to go on to Spain (cf. Rom 15:23–29) and return to visit the church of Ephesus before his final imprisonment in Rome (see esp. 2 Tim 4:9–22).[30] What is significant here is simply that Paul and the Ephesian elders share an emotional goodbye at the prospect of never seeing one another again. Then they accompany him to the ship, and Paul continues on his journey to Jerusalem (Acts 20:38).

13.5 Journey to Jerusalem (Acts 21:1–17)

Luke appears to share in the emotional departure from the Ephesians, writing, "After we had torn ourselves away from them . . ." (21:1a). Luke's narration of this final journey to Jerusalem is considered the third "we section" of Acts (21:1–18), although it can be thought of as a continuation of the second "we section" (20:5–15), being interrupted in the story merely by Paul's address to the Ephesian elders.

13.5.1 Christian Hospitality from Miletus to Tyre (21:1–6)

As already observed, extra details in the story continue to betray Luke's presence on the journey, including more explicit sailing and travel itinerary notes (21:1–3). But his teammates are not Paul's only connections with other Christians. When they reach the seaport of ***Tyre***, the missionary team seeks out other believers, and they end up staying with them for a week while their ship engages in cargo transfers (21:3–4). The week's stay is enough to establish some meaningful relationships such that, when it is time for the group to leave, all the Christians of Tyre, "including wives and children,"

29. E.g., Martin Dibelius, *The Book of Acts: Form, Style, and Theology*, ed. K. C. Hanson, Fortress Classics in Biblical Studies (Minneapolis: Fortress, 2004), 176n46; Ernst Haenchen, *The Acts of the Apostles: A Commentary*, trans. and ed. Bernard Noble, Gerald Shinn, Hugh Anderson, and R. McLeod Wilson (Philadelphia: Westminster, 1971), 595; Hans. Conzelmann, *Acts of the Apostles: A Commentary on the Acts of the Apostles*, trans. James Limburg, A. Thomas Kraabel, and Donald H. Juel, ed. Eldon Jay Epp with Christopher R. Matthews, Hermeneia (Philadelphia: Fortress, 1987), 174 and 176.

30. On this idea, see esp. Bruce W. Longenecker and Todd D. Still, *Thinking through Paul: A Survey of His Life, Letters, and Theology* (Grand Rapids: Zondervan, 2014), 45–47; F. F. Bruce, *Paul: Apostle of the Heart Set Free* (Grand Rapids: Eerdmans, 1977), 441–55; Eckhard J. Schnabel, *Early Christian Mission*, 2 vols. (Downers Grove, IL: InterVarsity Press, 2004), 2:1270–92; idem, *Paul the Missionary: Realities, Strategies, and Methods* (Downers Grove, IL: InterVarsity Press, 2008), 115–22.

accompany them out of the city and pray with them on the beach (21:5–6). Thus, Luke continues to stress the importance of generous Christian fellowship as a mark of church health, and Christians today often experience quickly formed friendships with strangers when they discover they are fellow believers.

Before leaving, however, the believers in Tyre warn Paul against going to Jerusalem. As Luke says it, "Through the Spirit they urged Paul not to go on to Jerusalem" (21:4). This phrasing sounds strange in light of Paul's earlier comment about being "compelled by the Spirit" to go to Jerusalem (20:22). Rather than suggesting that the Spirit has suddenly changed his mind and that Paul is now being disobedient by continuing toward Jerusalem, it makes most sense that the Tyre believers are mistaking the Spirit's warning about hardships as a warning not to go. But (as any hardworking student, musician, or athlete knows) knowledge of difficulty is not the same thing as direction to avoid it. The Tyre believers are correct in their understanding of the Spirit's warning that hardships await Paul in Jerusalem—this fits with what the Spirit has been telling Paul all along his journey (cf. 20:23). But their application of the Spirit-given knowledge—their conclusion that Paul should not go to Jerusalem—is incorrect. And so, compelled by the Spirit and given advanced warning of hardships, Paul continues toward Jerusalem.

Paul's Plans and Expectations of Hardship in Jerusalem

Romans 15:23–33

But now that there is no more place for me to work in these regions, and since I have been longing for many years to visit you, I plan to do so when I go to Spain. I hope to see you while passing through and to have you assist me on my journey there, after I have enjoyed your company for a while. Now, however, I am on my way to Jerusalem in the service of the Lord's people there. For Macedonia and Achaia were pleased to make a contribution for the poor among the Lord's people in Jerusalem. They were pleased to do it, and indeed they owe it to them. For if the Gentiles have shared in the Jews' spiritual blessings, they owe it to the Jews to share with them their material blessings. So after I have completed this task and have made sure that they have received this contribution, I will go to Spain and visit you on the way. I know that when I come to you, I will come in the full measure of the blessing of Christ.

I urge you, brothers and sisters, by our Lord Jesus Christ and by the love of the Spirit, to join me in my struggle by praying to God for me. Pray that I may be kept safe from the unbelievers in Judea and that the contribution I take to Jerusalem may be favorably received by the Lord's people there, so that I may come to you with joy, by God's will, and in your company be refreshed. The God of peace be with you all. Amen.

13.5.2 Christian Hospitality from Tyre to Caesarea to Jerusalem (21:7–16)

Continuing his first-person account of the group's travel southward, Luke reports a stop at Ptolemais (about twenty-five miles from Tyre; 21:7) and another on the next day at Caesarea, the NT seaport city for Jerusalem (about thirty miles from Ptolemais; 21:8). In both cities the group stays with fellow believers, but in ***Caesarea*** Luke names their host as "Philip the evangelist, one of the Seven," who "had four unmarried daughters who prophesied" (21:8–9). Luke likely uses this descriptive phrase to distinguish ***Philip the evangelist*** (cf. 6:6) from the apostle Philip (cf. 1:13).[31] Besides differentiating the Philips, these added details may well serve to acknowledge one of Luke's information sources. In this case, the specifics of Philip's ministries in Samaria, Gaza, and the coastal towns up to Caesarea (i.e., the episodes in 8:4–40) can be traced to Luke's interaction with Philip at this point in the story, where Luke reports spending "a number of days" there (21:10).

The Office of Evangelist in the Early Church

Luke's reference to "Philip the evangelist" (Greek: *euangelistēs*; Acts 21:8) not only helps distinguish this person as different from Philip the apostle (Acts 1:13), it also draws attention to one of his primary acts of service in the early church. With the noun *evangelion* a reference to "good news," the verb *euangelizō* represents "proclaiming the good news," something Philip is reported as doing (Acts 8:12, 35, 40). Paul's letters also reference people in the early church who served as "evangelists":

Ephesians 4:11–12—"So Christ himself gave the apostles, the prophets, the evangelists, the pastors and teachers, to equip his people for works of service, so that the body of Christ may be built up."

2 Timothy 4:5—"But you, keep your head in all situations, endure hardship, do the work of an evangelist, discharge all the duties of your ministry."

Thus, it appears that an evangelist is one who is particularly skilled at heralding the good news of the gospel but is not necessarily in possession of the authoritative leadership skills of apostles or the mentoring skills of pastors. See the discussion in F. Scott Spencer, *The Portrait of Philip in Acts: A Study of Roles and Relations*, JSNTSup 67 (Sheffield: Sheffield Academic, 1992), 262–70.

31. See the brief discussion of this matter in chapter 16.

During the missionary team's stay with Philip, the prophet ***Agabus*** comes from Judea (21:10; cf. 11:27–30) and offers an object lesson to Paul and the group by tying himself up with Paul's belt and announcing, "The Holy Spirit says, 'In this way the Jewish leaders in Jerusalem will bind the owner of this belt and will hand him over to the Gentiles'" (21:11). Many of the OT prophets acted out prophetic messages in various performances (e.g., 1 Kgs 11:29–40; 2 Kgs 2:19–22; Isa 20:1–6; Ezek 4:1–17).[32] While Agabus does not deduce the prophetic message to be a warning against going to Jerusalem, Luke and the believers at Caesarea (as those at Tyre had) plead with Paul not to go up to Jerusalem (Acts 21:12). But again, Paul demonstrates that this explicit prophecy is preparing him for the trouble he is meant to face in Jerusalem; it is not warning him against going there. "Why are you weeping and breaking my heart?" Paul answers their protests, "I am ready not only to be bound, but also to die in Jerusalem for the name of the Lord Jesus" (21:13). Luke and the other believers are eventually persuaded, recognizing Paul's resolve on what the prophecy is all about: "When he would not be dissuaded, we gave up and said, 'The Lord's will be done'" (21:14).

The Prophet Agabus predicting to Saint Paul his sufferings in Jerusalem by Louis Cheron (1687). Paris. © Pascal Lemaitre. All rights reserved 2024 / Bridgeman Images

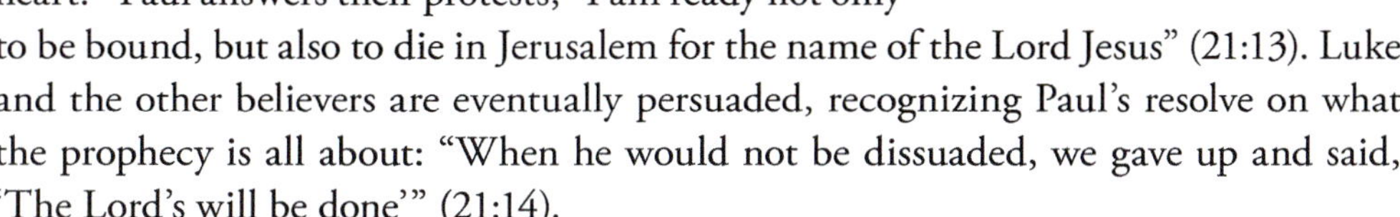

As the missionaries move on from Caesarea to Jerusalem (about sixty-five miles away), Luke includes another of his hospitality notes. Some Caesarean believers escort Paul and the missionary team to the home of Mnason where they would stay (21:15–16).[33] In addition to giving credit to another of his information sources,[34] Luke describes Mnason as "a man from Cyprus and one of the early disciples" (21:16b), reminding us that Cypriot natives like Barnabas had become Christians early in the story of Acts (4:36) and that some were instrumental in bringing the gospel to Greeks as well as to Jews (11:19–21). So perhaps Luke's point here is that an early Cypriot Christian in the staunchly Jewish region of Jerusalem might be more prepared to host the missionary team of people with various ethnic and cultural backgrounds.[35]

---

32. On various kinds of performance prophecies, see Terry Giles, "Performance Criticism," *DOTProph*, 578–83.

33. Luke is not clear on whether Mnason's home was in Jerusalem or in a village between Caesarea and Jerusalem, which is what the Western text indicates.

34. Bruce, *Book of Acts*, 403, mentions Ramsay's particular suggestion that Mnason was Luke's source for the stories about Peter's ministry with Aeneas and Dorcas in Acts 9:32–43; against this overly-specific suggestion, see Colin J. Hemer, *The Book of Acts in the Setting of Hellenistic History*, ed. Conrad H. Gempf, WUNT 49 (Tübingen: Mohr Siebeck, 1989; repr., Winona Lake, IN: Eisenbrauns, 1990), 199n76.

35. So Bruce, *Book of Acts*, 402–3.

Peter and Paul on Their Readiness to Die

Peter: "Lord, I am ready to go with you to prison and to death" (Luke 22:33).

Paul: "I am ready not only to be bound, but also to die in Jerusalem for the name of the Lord Jesus" (Acts 21:13).

13.5.3 Closing Travel Summary Statement (21:17)

As with his accounts of Paul's previous travels, Luke gives a brief storytelling summary at the end of this third missionary campaign. Unlike the first two journeys, however, which end with Paul back in Syrian Antioch, the summary statement at the end of the third missionary campaign is about Paul and his team—including Luke as part of the "we"—arriving in Jerusalem: "When we arrived at Jerusalem, the brothers and sisters received us warmly" (21:17). The reader will soon learn that Paul does not have the opportunity to return to Antioch, as he is arrested in Jerusalem. But before narrating Paul's fully anticipated troubles from the unbelieving Jews of the city, Luke explicitly remarks that the Christians of Jerusalem warmly receive him and his missionary team.

13.6 CONCLUDING REMARKS

Paul's third missionary campaign includes an extensive ministry during a three-year stay in Ephesus as well as journeying through Macedonia and Achaia, following up on the churches that had been established in earlier travels. Then in a hurry to get to Jerusalem, Paul bypasses Ephesus and addresses the elders of the Ephesian church in the city of Miletus. In all of this, as Luke's readers have come to expect, Paul's ministry faces a variety of oppositions as well as successful receptions of the gospel message. Rejections of the gospel are rarely made solely on the truth claims of the gospel itself and usually also involve other motives and values. Paul's experience in Acts, as well as the record of subsequent church history, shows that other factors competing with the gospel can include such things as cultural, social, political, national, economic, and personal desires.[36] These observations match with Paul's other missionary journeys.

What is noticeably different about Paul's third missionary campaign is the repeated words of warning that Paul receives regarding his aim of going to Jerusalem. Although some of the believers misunderstand these prophecies as warnings not to proceed with his travel plans, Paul knows that the Holy Spirit is encouraging him to go to Jerusalem

36. Thomas P. Schirrmacher, "Persecution," pp. 286–89 in *Dictionary of Mission Theology,* ed. John Corrie (Downers Grove, IL: InterVarsity Press, 2007), 289.

Persecution of Christians Today

From A. Scott Moreau, "Persecution," pp. 746–47 in *Evangelical Dictionary of World Missions*, ed. A. Scott Moreau (Grand Rapids: Baker, 2000), 747.

> Far from being only a thing of the past, persecution today continues to be a reality faced by many Christians, particularly those in militant religious states. It is estimated that more Christians have lost their lives through persecution in this century than all other centuries combined, though generally there has been little publicity of this in the secular press of free countries.

and at the same time preparing him for facing hardships there. This is, in fact, quite fitting with the encouragement Paul and Barnabas gave new believers on the first missionary campaign, saying, "We must go through many hardships to enter the kingdom of God" (14:22).

Despite such hardships, Paul sought to be of service in the expansion of the gospel of the kingdom of God. Indeed, hardships are not to be taken as sure signs of defeat. God's disciples are called to faithfulness, not to success. If a ministry is measured to be "successful," it should be because of the Lord's blessing of his followers' faithfulness. Christians are to live in obedience to Christ, submitting to his lordship over every aspect of life and humbly applying themselves to bring the gospel and its renewal to the world around them. Thus, rather than operating out of pride aimed at success by way of coercion, Christians should operate out of humility aimed at persuasive faithfulness, a faithfulness that is willing to sacrifice and even suffer for the sake of the gospel.[37]

13.7 Key People, Places, and Terms

- Agabus
- Alexandria, Egypt
- Antioch of Syria
- Apollos
- Artemis
- Caesarea
- Demetrius
- elders
- Ephesus
- Eutychus
- magic
- Miletus
- Philip the evangelist
- Philippi
- Priscilla and Aquila
- sons of Sceva
- syncretism
- Troas
- Tyre

37. Bruce Riley Ashford and Heath A. Thomas, *The Gospel of Our King: Bible, Worldview, and the Mission of Every Christian* (Grand Rapids: Baker Academic, 2019), 165.

13.8 Questions for Review and Discussion

1. What is your understanding of the variety of spiritual gifts and ministry roles, and how does Luke seem to exhibit that variety in the story of Acts?
2. Given how Luke seems to deal with it in Acts 18–19, how would you describe the way that the gospel fits with the faith God's people exhibit in the OT time period?
3. How would you describe the significance(s) of Paul's three-year ministry in the city of Ephesus, as it was a central city in the first-century region of Asia Minor?
4. The believers at Ephesus in Acts 19 had been hanging on to magic practices (somewhat famous in Ephesus). What made them eventually realize they needed to give up those practices?
5. What implications might be drawn from Luke's report that Paul had friends among the regional political leaders in Ephesus (Acts 19:30–31)?
6. Paul was willing to go to Jerusalem as planned, despite predictions of hardship awaiting him there (Acts 21:10–14). How does Luke depict Paul's decision to face those difficulties?

13.9 Optional Assignments

1. **Text Reflection Project**—*Relating the concepts discussed in this chapter to another biblical text.* On his third missionary campaign, Paul is "strengthening all the disciples" in churches he had previously visited (Acts 18:23). Examine this familiar theme in Acts (see 9:31; 14:22; 15:32, 41; 16:5), and take note of Paul's instruction to the elders of the Ephesian church in Acts 20:17–38. How does this theme in Acts inform Paul's own comments regarding his concern for the churches in 2 Corinthians 11:28? How does it compare to Peter's comments in 1 Peter 5:2–4?
2. **Interview Project**—*Inquiring of others their views concerning the concepts discussed in this chapter.* Talk with your pastor (or some other respected Christian leader) about how to negotiate ministry with other Christians, particularly with those who have different views on such things as the use of spiritual gifts and gender roles in ministry. What crucial things should believers agree on for strong ministry partnerships? What things are of lesser significance for those partnerships? Write up a summary of their advice on this matter.
3. **Service-Learning Project**—*Applying the concepts discussed in this chapter in some form of service to others outside the class.* We learn in Acts 19 that Paul had friends among the officials of the Roman province of Asia. Furthermore, one of the missionary team members with Paul in Ephesus was Erastus (Acts 19:22), who apparently served as a city officer in Corinth for a while (see Rom 16:23). Find a non-ministry related service opportunity with a local civic or regional governing organization, and volunteer to work with them for a few hours (e.g., working at the clean-up day for a public park, painting at a public school, ushering at a civic concert event, serving as a polling official in a public election). Write up a summary of what you did and some reflections about the people with whom you interacted during this service project. How might you pray for those people?

4. **Prayer Project**—*Talking with God about the concepts discussed in this chapter.* The story about the failed attempt at a magical exorcism by the sons of Sceva (19:13–19) brought to the attention of the people in Ephesus the power of Jesus as the true Lord (19:17). But it also caused Ephesian believers to confront their attachment to sinful practices from their past (19:18) and got them to turn from those evil ways (19:19). Write a prayer to the Lord about any evils you are struggling to give up, perhaps former habits or cultural vices from your past. Identify someone with whom you can share your prayer so as to gain their counsel and prayer support.
5. **Testimony Project**—*Telling others about the concepts discussed in this chapter.* Acts 20 contains Paul's farewell speech to the elders of the Ephesian church, where he reflects on his ministry time among them and offers his counsel about their own faith and ministry in the future. Read through Luke's synopsis of that speech (Acts 20:18–35). Then, reflecting on your time as a student and anticipating moving on after graduation, write your own farewell speech offering advice about the Christian life and ministry to the students you will leave behind.

13.10 Bibliography for Going Further

13.10.1 Paul's Third Missionary Journey

White, Jefferson. "The Third Journey (52–57 AD)." Pages 36–45 (chapter 3) in *Evidence & Paul's Journeys: An Historical Investigation into the Travels of the Apostle Paul.* Hilliard, OH: Parsagard, 2001.

Wilson, Mark, and Glen L. Thompson. "Paul's Walk to Assos: A Hodological Inquiry into Its Geography, Archaeology, and Purpose." Pages 269–314 in *Stones, Bones, and the Sacred: Essays on Material Culture and Ancient Religion in Honor of Dennis E. Smith.* Edited by Alan H. Cadwallader. ECL 21. Atlanta: SBL Press, 2016.

13.10.2 Paul in Ephesus

Immendörfer, Michael. *Ephesians and Artemis: The Cult of the Great Goddess of Ephesus as the Epistle's Context.* WUNT 2.436. Tübingen: Mohr Siebeck, 2017.

Pereira, Francis. *Ephesus: Climax of Universalism in Luke-Acts. A Redaction-Critical Study of Paul's Ephesian Ministry (Acts 18:23–20:1).* Jesuit Theological Forum Studies 10.1. Anand, India: Gujarat Sahitya Prakash, 1983.

Shauf, Scott. *Theology as History, History as Theology: Paul in Ephesus in Acts 19.* BZNW 133. Berlin: de Gruyter, 2005.

Strelan, Rick. *Paul, Artemis, and the Jews in Ephesus.* BZNW 80. Berlin: de Gruyter, 1996.

Trebilco, Paul. *The Early Christians in Ephesus from Paul to Ignatius.* Grand Rapids: Eerdmans, 2007.

13.10.3 Magic and the Demonic in Luke-Acts

Arnold, Clinton E. *Power and Magic: The Concept of Power in Ephesians.* Grand Rapids: Baker, 1989. Repr., Eugene, OR: Wipf & Stock, 1997.

Garrett, Susan R. *The Demise of the Devil: Magic and the Demonic in Luke's Writings.* Minneapolis: Fortress, 1989.

Klauck, Hans-Josef. *Magic and Paganism in Early Christianity: The World of the Acts of the Apostles.* Translated by Brian McNeil. Edinburgh: T&T Clark, 2000.

Klutz, Todd. *The Exorcism Stories in Luke-Acts: A Sociostylistic Reading*. SNTSMS 129. Cambridge: Cambridge University Press, 2004.

Reimer, Andy Melford. *Miracle and Magic: A Study in the Acts of the Apostles and the Life of Apolloniius of Tyana*. JSNTSup 235. Sheffield: Sheffield Academic, 2002. Repr., New York: Continuum, 2003.

13.10.4 Christianity and Culture

Carson, D. A. *Christ and Culture Revisited*. Grand Rapids: Eerdmans, 2008.

Crouch, Andy. *Culture Making: Recovering Our Creative Calling*. Downers Grove, IL: InterVarsity Press, 2008.

Hunter, James Davison. *To Change the World: The Irony, Tragedy, and Possibility of Christianity in the Late Modern World*. New York: Oxford University Press, 2010.

Platt, David. *Counter Culture: Following Christ in an Anti-Christian Age*. 2nd ed. Carol Stream, IL: Tyndale House, 2017.

Schmidt, Alvin J. *How Christianity Changed the World*. 2nd ed. Grand Rapids: Zondervan, 2004.

VanDrunen, David. *Living in God's Two Kingdoms: A Biblical Vision for Christianity and Culture*. Wheaton, IL: Crossway, 2010.

13.10.5 Paul's Farewell Speech

Kurz, William S. *Farewell Addresses in the New Testament*. Zacchaeus Studies: New Testament. Collegeville, MN: Liturgical, 1990 (esp. pp. 33–51).

Nielsen, Anders E. *Until It Is Fulfilled: Lukan Eschatology According to Luke 22 and Acts 20*. WUNT 2.126. Tübingen: Mohr Siebeck, 2000.

Walton, Steve. *Leadership and Lifestyle: The Portrait of Paul in the Miletus Speech and 1 Thessalonians*. SNTSMS 108. Cambridge: Cambridge University Press, 2000.

14 The Story Moves in Prison in Jerusalem and Caesarea

Acts 21:18–26:32

Chapter Goals

After reading this chapter, you should be able to:

- Describe Paul's responses to false rumors and false assumptions about his identity and actions.
- Explain why Luke would include three different tellings of Paul's conversion experience on the road to Damascus (Acts 9, 22, and 26).
- Account for the differences between the three reports of Paul's conversion experience on the road to Damascus (Acts 9, 22, and 26).
- Explain the difficult religious and political complications of Paul's situation for the Roman procurators hearing his case.
- Distinguish different approaches Paul takes for sharing the one-and-the-same gospel message.
- Reflect on Paul's confident persistence in sharing the gospel, even with people who know the message and persist in rejecting it.

Chapter Overview

14.1 Paul's Arrest and Hearing before the Sanhedrin (Acts 21:18–23:11)
14.2 Paul's Deliverance from a Jewish Plot (Acts 23:12–35)
14.3 Paul's Hearing before Felix (Acts 24:1–27)
14.4 Paul's Hearing before Festus (Acts 25:1–22)
14.5 Paul's Hearing before Herod Agrippa II (Acts 25:23–26:32)
14.6 Concluding Remarks
14.7 Key People, Places, and Terms
14.8 Questions for Review and Discussion
14.9 Optional Assignments
14.10 Bibliography for Going Further

Key Verses

Then Paul, knowing that some of them were Sadducees and the others Pharisees, called out in the Sanhedrin, "My brothers, I am a Pharisee, descended from Pharisees. I stand on trial because of the hope of the resurrection of the dead." (Acts 23:6)

The following night the Lord stood near Paul and said, "Take courage! As you have testified about me in Jerusalem, so you must also testify in Rome." (Acts 23:11)

When two years had passed, Felix was succeeded by Porcius Festus, but because Felix wanted to grant a favor to the Jews, he left Paul in prison. (Acts 24:27)

Paul answered: "I am now standing before Caesar's court, where I ought to be tried. I have not done any wrong to the Jews, as you yourself know very well. If, however, I am guilty of doing anything deserving death, I do not refuse to die. But if the charges brought against me by these Jews are not true, no one has the right to hand me over to them. I appeal to Caesar!" (Acts 25:10–11)

Summary Statement

Agrippa said to Festus, "This man could have been set free if he had not appealed to Caesar." (Acts 26:32)

INTRODUCTION

This chapter discusses the (mis)adventures of Paul in Roman custody as told in Acts 21:18–26:32. Paul had set a goal to return to Jerusalem (Acts 19:21), wanting to arrive in time for Pentecost (20:16) and concerned to deliver some relief funds (24:17; cf. Rom 15:25–28; 1 Cor 16:1–9; 2 Cor 8:1–9:15). Rather than celebration, however, the Holy Spirit had been preparing him for some kind of trouble in ***Jerusalem*** (e.g., Acts 21:10–14), and not long after his arrival Paul ends up in the custody of the Romans, where he remains for the rest of Acts. But being in Roman custody does not discontinue his ministry. Instead, after eight chapters of Paul's itinerant ministry (Acts 13–20), Luke shifts here to reporting eight chapters of Paul's prison ministry (Acts 21–28). In four different hearings in Acts 21–26 (one before the Jewish Sanhedrin, two before Roman procurators, and one before a descendant of Herod the Great), Paul is found innocent of breaking the law but continues to be held in custody nonetheless. Noteworthy in all this is Paul's audience sensitivity in sharing the gospel.

Paul was likely imprisoned at Antonia Fortress in Jerusalem (seen here in model of first-century Jerusalem).
© 2018 by Zondervan, courtesy Israel Museum

14.1 PAUL'S ARREST AND HEARING BEFORE THE SANHEDRIN (ACTS 21:18–23:11)

After Paul and his group were warmly received by the Jerusalem believers (21:17), the story takes a bit of a turn when Paul is informed about a rumor regarding his gospel ministry in other parts of the world. Ironically, while Paul is addressing this problematic rumor with great amenableness, another false claim about him leads to Paul's arrest. But these circumstances become opportunities to declare the gospel message before an unbelieving Jewish mob (21:37–22:22) and before the Sanhedrin (22:30–23:11).

14.1.1 A Plan for Maintaining Unity (21:18–26)

In meeting with the leaders of the Jerusalem church, Paul reports "in detail what God had done among the Gentiles through his ministry" (21:18–19). As with earlier such reports, the result is a sense of rejoicing and praise for God's expansion of the gospel to gentiles (21:20a; cf. 14:27; 15:3–4, 12). While the church had struggled with incorporating gentile believers into the community of God's people (climaxing in Acts 15), Luke's account here now demonstrates that this trouble had been definitively addressed; the church leaders even reiterate the apostolic decree that was crafted in Acts 15 for the sake of unity (21:25).

But the pendulum of unity concerns has swung a bit to the other side in that some of the Jewish believers were now feeling marginalized, for allegations had come to Jerusalem that Paul was preaching against Jewish expressions of Christian faith (21:20b–21). But the Jerusalem church leaders know the rumors are false: Paul is not against Jewish expressions of faith in Jesus. So they suggest that by joining with and even financially sponsoring four Jewish believers in keeping a Jewish vow, the indictments can be squelched and Paul can demonstrate the legitimacy of faithful Jewish expressions of trusting Jesus (21:22–24). Paul himself had previously been to Jerusalem to keep a Jewish vow (cf. 18:18–22), so it is no surprise that he agrees to this plan (21:26). Being a Christian is not a racial or ethnic issue; it is a matter of faithful expression of trust in Jesus Christ as one's Savior and Lord. So pertaining to false claims about Paul's supposed racial discrimination, Luke shows the believers taking specific steps to maintain the unity that should mark the church.

14.1.2 Paul Is Attacked and Arrested (21:27–36)

Luke does not specify the type of vow that the four men are taking and that Paul is sponsoring, but mention of haircuts, seven days of purification, and sponsorship all fit the parameters of a ***Nazarite vow*** (21:24–27; see sidebar).[1] Ironically, Paul is

1. Because of expectations of a thirty-day duration for Nazarite vows (see m. Naz. 6:3; cf. Josephus, *J.W.* 2.15.1 §§313–14), some suggest that Paul may have only been sponsoring the four men in the vow rather than fully participating

participating in a Jewish custom in accordance with Jewish law when he is attacked and accused of breaking Jewish law. Furthermore, Paul's support of a virtuous oath here will soon contrast with the immoral oath of his enemies in Acts 23:12.[2] Interestingly, rather than Jewish Christians from Jerusalem causing trouble for Paul (as the Jerusalem church leaders had feared), it is unbelieving Jews from out of town—"Jews from the province of Asia"—who instigate a riot against him while he is in the temple courts (21:27).[3] They publicly accuse Paul of countering Jewish law and defiling the temple (21:28),[4] and Luke quickly explains the false accusations as stemming from wrong assumptions (21:29).

Given the strict Jewish laws limiting gentile access to the Jewish temple courts—laws that permitted Jews to carry out capital punishment (see sidebars)—the charge of defiling the ***temple*** was serious and caused immediate panic among the Jewish worshipers. Rather than an organized legal proceeding, the Jewish crowd is incited to mob action. With typical hyperbolic expression, Luke says "the whole city" was aroused (21:30; cf. 2:47; 5:11; 9:42; 10:22, 37; 11:28; 13:49; 15:22; 19:27; 21:31).[5] Paul is dragged from the inner temple courts to its outer courts, where they attempt to beat him to death (21:31–32; cf. 4 Macc 4:11).

News of this riotous activity reaches the commander of the Roman troops in the ***Fortress Antonia***, which was adjacent to the temple and had a stairway that descended into the temple's outer courtyard.[6] The commander and some officers and soldiers rush to arrest and bind Paul (21:33), effectively moving Paul from Jewish custody to gentile custody (cf. Agabus's prophecy; 21:10–11). In the commotion of the mob's violence, the soldiers have to physically carry Paul off in an ironic "rescue" of sorts (21:34–35).[7]

---

in the vow himself. In keeping with other examples of ritual purifications (e.g., Num. 8:21; 19:12; 31:19), Paul's own purification (Acts 21:24, 26; 24:18) may have had to do with ritual cleansing from travel in foreign lands (see m. 'Ohal. 2:3; 17:5; 18:6–7) so as to accompany the men into the temple (see Num 6:13–21; cf. John 11:55). For scholarly discussions of the vow here, see esp. Ernst Haenchen, *The Acts of the Apostles: A Commentary*, trans. and ed. Bernard Noble, Gerald Shinn, Hugh Anderson, and R. McLeod Wilson (Philadelphia: Westminster, 1971), 611–12; Stanley E. Porter, *The Paul of Acts: Essays in Literary Criticism, Rhetoric, and Theology* (Tübingen: Mohr Siebeck, 1999; repr., *Paul in Acts*, Library of Pauline Studies, Peabody, MA: Hendrickson, 2001), 179–82; Craig S. Keener, *Acts: An Exegetical Commentary*, 4 vols. (Grand Rapids: Baker Academic, 2012–2015), 3:3135–39; Ben Witherington III, *The Acts of the Apostles: A Socio-Rhetorical Commentary* (Grand Rapids: Eerdmans, 1998; Carlisle: Paternoster, 1998), 648–51; and Clinton E. Arnold, "Acts," vol. 2B of *ZIBBCNT*, ed. Clinton E. Arnold (Grand Rapids: Zondervan, 2002), 217–18.

2. Keener, *Acts*, 3:3136.

3. See Keener's suggestion for why the Asian Jews (i.e., from Ephesus; cf. Acts 19:8–9, 33–34) were so angry with Paul; Keener, *Acts*, 3:3144–45.

4. Interestingly, these were precisely the charges brought against Stephen when Paul/Saul had begun his campaign against faith in Christ; Acts 6:12–14.

5. On the use of hyperbole in Scripture, see G. B. Caird, *The Language and Imagery of the Bible* (London: Duckworth, 1980), 110–17, 133.

6. For brief descriptions of the Fortress Antonia and its relation to the temple, see Brian Rapske, *The Book of Acts and Paul in Roman Custody*, BAFCS 3 (Grand Rapids: Eerdmans, 1994; Carlisle: Paternoster, 1994), 137–38; and James L. Kelso, "Antonia, Tower of," *ZEB* 1:220–21.

7. So Joseph A. Fitzmyer, *The Acts of the Apostles*, AB 31 (New York: Doubleday, 1998), 699; William J. Larkin Jr., *Acts*, The IVP New Testament Commentary Series (Downers Grove, IL: InterVarsity Press, 1995), 314–15;

Another Possible Example of a Nazarite Vow

Earlier in Acts, Luke reported the Christian Paul keeping a Jewish vow involving a haircut (Acts 18:18–22), which scholars suspect to be a Nazarite vow (see Num 6:1–21; m. Naz. 1:1–9:5; Josephus, *J.W.* 2.15.1 §§313–14). In Acts 21, James suggests that Paul sponsor some Jewish Christians in their observance of a Jewish vow, and in so doing, Paul could demonstrate that he is not against Jewish Christians living according to Jewish customs. The vow of the four men in Acts 21:23–27 also involves haircuts, and the idea of sponsorship for Nazarite vows is attested in the Mishnah tractate of Nazir, which is entirely dedicated to Nazarite vows (see m. Naz. 2:5–6), as well in Josephus (*Ant.* 19.6.1 §294 has Agrippa I sponsoring Nazarite haircuts). These observations, along with Luke's specification of a seven-day purification period (Acts 21:27; cf. Num 6:9–10), seem to support the theory that the four men were keeping a Nazarite vow, even if Paul was merely sponsoring them in it rather than fully joining in the vow himself.

m. Nazir 2:5–6

If one says: I am hereby a nazirite and it is incumbent upon me to shave a nazirite, meaning he will also pay for the offerings that a nazirite brings when he cuts his hair; and another heard and said: And I too am a nazirite and it is incumbent upon me to shave a nazirite, the other is also a nazirite and is obligated to pay for the offerings of a nazirite. If they were perspicacious and wish to limit their expenses, they shave each other. They may each pay for the other's offerings, so that their additional vows will not cost them anything. And if not, if this arrangement did not occur to them and each brought his own offerings, they shave other nazirites, i.e., they must pay for the offerings of other nazirites.

If one says: It is incumbent upon me to shave half a nazirite, i.e., he is vowing to pay half the costs of a nazirite's offerings, and another heard and said: And I, it is incumbent upon me to shave half a nazirite, this one shaves a whole nazirite and that one shaves a whole nazirite, i.e., each pays the full cost of a nazirite's offerings; this is the statement of Rabbi Meir, since there is no such entity as half a nazirite. And the Rabbis say: This one shaves half a nazirite and that one shaves half a nazirite; they may join together to pay for the offerings of one nazirite.

Flavius Josephus, *Jewish Antiquities* 19.6.1 §294 (ca. AD 94)

Agrippa naturally, since he was to go back with improved fortunes, turned quickly homewards. On entering Jerusalem, he offered sacrifices of thanksgiving, omitting none of the ritual enjoined by our law. Accordingly he also arranged for a very considerable number of Nazirites to be shorn.

Following the squad to the fortress stairway, the crowd keeps shouting, "Get rid of him!" (Greek: *aire auton*; 21:36), which is not unlike what the Jerusalem crowd had yelled about Jesus: "Away with this man!" (*aire touton*; Luke 23:18).

---

cf. Darrell L. Bock, *Acts*, BECNT (Grand Rapids: Baker Academic, 2007), 652–53; Witherington, *Acts*, 657; Mikeal C. Parsons, *Acts*, Paideia Commentaries on the New Testament (Grand Rapids: Baker Academic, 2008), 305–6.

Temple Warning Inscription

ΜΗΘΕΝΑ ΑΛΛΟΓΕΝΗ ΕΙΣΠΟ-
ΡΕΥΕΣΘΑΙ ΕΝΤΟΣ ΤΟΥ ΠΕ-
ΡΙ ΤΟ ΙΕΡΟΝ ΤΡΥΦΑΚΤΟΥ ΚΑΙ
ΠΕΡΙΒΟΛΟΥ. ΟΣ Δ ΑΝ ΛΗ-
ΦΘΗ, ΕΑΥΤΩΙ ΑΙΤΙΟΣ ΕΣ-
ΤΑΙ ΔΙΑ ΤΟ ΕΧΑΚΟΛΟΥ-
ΘΕΙΝ ΘΑΝΑΤΟΝ.

NOT ONE FOREIGNER IS TO
ENTER INSIDE THE AROUND
THE SANCTUARY BARRIER AND
EMBANKMENT. HE WHO IS
SEIZED, HIMSELF RESPONSIBLE
IS FOR THE FOLLOWING
DEATH PENALTY.

Currently housed in the Archaeological Museum of Istanbul, Turkey, this stone sign was found in Jerusalem in 1871 and measures 13¼" x 8¾" x 5¾". Its wording shows that it was a sign to warn gentiles against entering the temple precincts reserved for Jewish worshipers. The translation provided here is by Arnold vander Nat.

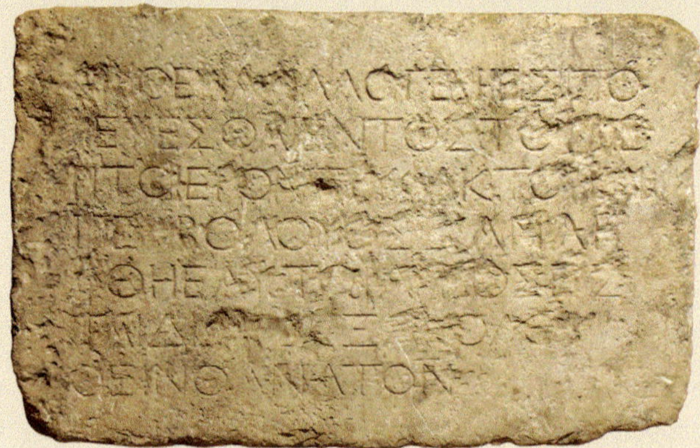

Todd Bolen/BiblePlaces.com, courtesy Istanbul Archaeological Museum

Jerusalem Temple Area

This photograph of a model of Herod's Temple in first-century Jerusalem is labeled with some of the basic regions of the Temple Mount as it existed during the time of Acts.

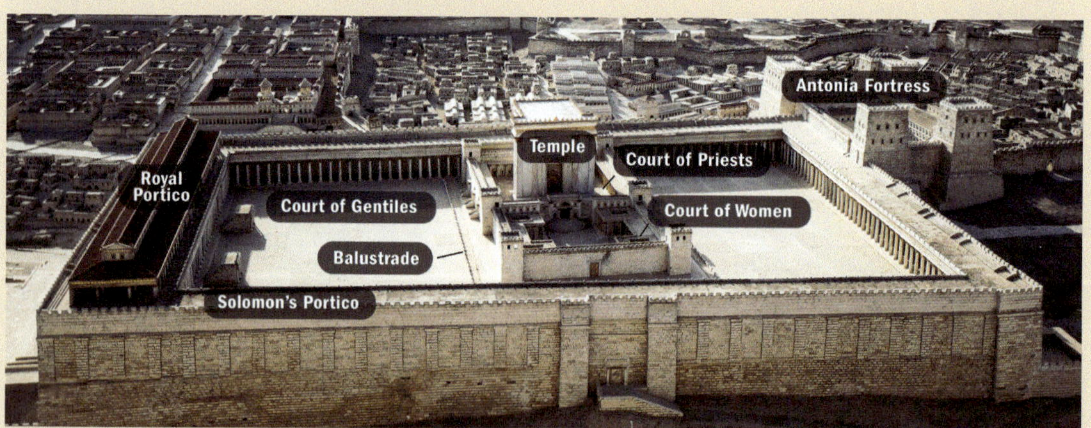

A Roman Concession for Jews to Carry Out Capital Punishment

Josephus reports a speech given by the Roman commander Titus to the Jews defending the temple during the Roman siege of Jerusalem in AD 70. In these remarks, Titus mentions a concession in Roman law that allowed the Jews to carry out the death penalty on those who defiled the Jerusalem temple. He even comments on the balustrade around the temple marking the boundary that gentiles could not cross and the warning signs that were posted.

Flavius Josephus, *Jewish War* 6.2.4 §§124–28 (cf. 5.5.2 §§193–94) (ca. AD 75)

> Titus, yet more deeply distressed, again upbraided John and his friends. "Was it not you," he said, "most abominable wretches, who placed this balustrade before your sanctuary? Was it not you that ranged along it those slabs, engraved in Greek characters and in our own, proclaiming that none may pass the barrier? And did we not permit you to put to death any who passed it, even were he a Roman? Why then, you miscreants, do you now actually trample corpses underfoot within it? Why do you defile your temple with the blood of foreigner and native? I call the gods of my fathers to witness and any deity that once watched over this place—for now I believe that there is none—I call my army, the Jews within my lines, and you yourselves to witness that it is not I who force you to pollute these precincts. Exchange the arena of conflict for another and not a Roman shall approach or insult your holy places; nay, I will preserve the temple for you, even against your will."

14.1.3 Paul's Defense before the Jewish Mob (21:37–22:22)

Paul shows himself to be quite patient with the Jewish mob, and rather than being happily whisked out of harm's way, he asks the commander if he can address the violent crowd. The commander is surprised to hear Paul speaking in Greek because, as Luke divulges, he had assumed that Paul was an agitator of Egyptian origins who had recently caused a rebellion in Jerusalem (Acts 21:37–38; see sidebar). The Roman commander had surmised that Paul was this leader of the "***terrorists***" (NIV) or "***Assassins***" (ESV) (see sidebar on the ***Sicarii***),[8] but Paul quickly dispels this new false assumption, explaining that he is a Jew and citizen of ***Tarsus***, "no ordinary city" (21:39; see sidebar). After Paul is granted permission to speak (21:40), several features of his defense assist in appealing to the agitated Jewish mob: addressing them as fellow Jews, "Brothers and fathers" (22:1); using their language (22:2);[9] recounting his own Jewish upbringing, Pharisaic education, and comparable zeal (22:3; cf. Gamaliel in 5:34–40);

---

8. Cf. Douglas S. Huffman, "Assassins," *EDB*, 117.

9. Regarding the term "Aramaic" at Acts 21:40 and 22:2, a margin note in the NIV says, "or possibly Hebrew." Many scholars think that Aramaic (a sister language to Hebrew) was the commonly spoken dialect of first-century people of Hebrew descent; see Michael Owen Wise, *Language and Literacy in Roman Judaea: A Study of the Bar Kokhba Documents*, The Anchor Yale Bible Reference Library (New Haven, CT: Yale University Press, 2015), esp. 7–20; Michael W. Graves, "Languages of Palestine," *DJG*², 484–92; Keener, *Acts*, 3:3191–95.

Josephus Describes the Egyptian Rebel

Writing in ca. AD 75, Josephus includes in his *Jewish War* a description of the Egyptian rebel that Luke mentions in Acts 21. Regarding the number of the Egyptian rebel's followers, scholars tend to think of Luke's figure (four thousand) as more reliable than Josephus's (thirty thousand), as Josephus is known to exaggerate numbers. For the Roman commander who referred to this incident while arresting Paul (Acts 21:38 in AD 57), this would have been a recent event in the procuratorship of Felix (ca. AD 52–59).

Flavius Josephus, *Jewish War* 2.13.5 §§261–63 (ca. AD 75)

> A still worse blow was dealt at the Jews by the Egyptian false prophet. A charlatan, who had gained for himself the reputation of a prophet, this man appeared in the country, collected a following of about thirty thousand dupes, and led them by a circuitous route from the desert to the mount called the mount of Olives. From there he proposed to force an entrance into Jerusalem and, after overpowering the Roman garrison, to set himself up as tyrant of the people, employing those who poured in with him as his bodyguard. His attack was anticipated by Felix, who went to meet him with the Roman heavy infantry, the whole population joining him in the defence. The outcome of the ensuing engagement was that the Egyptian escaped with a few of his followers; most of his force were killed or taken prisoners; the remainder dispersed and stealthily escaped to their several homes.

Josephus Describes the Sicarii

When arrested in Jerusalem, Paul was at first mistaken for the leader of a group of "assassins" or "terrorists." The Greek word Luke uses is a Latin loanword (*sicarius*) from the Latin word for "dagger" (*sica*). In ca. AD 75, Josephus commented on how these "dagger men" operated.

Flavius Josephus, *Jewish War* 2.13.3 §§254–57 (ca. AD 75)

> A new species of banditti was springing up in Jerusalem, the so-called sicarii, who committed murders in broad daylight in the heart of the city. The festivals were their special seasons, when they would mingle with the crowd, carrying short daggers concealed under their clothing, with which they stabbed their enemies. Then, when they fell, the murderers joined in the cries of indignation and, through this plausible behavior, were never discovered. The first to be assassinated by them was Jonathan the high-priest; after his death there were numerous daily murders. The panic created was more alarming than the calamity itself; every one, as on the battlefield, hourly expecting death. Men kept watch at a distance on their enemies and would not trust even their friends when they approached. Yet, even while their suspicions were aroused and they were on their guard, they fell; so swift were the conspirators and so crafty in eluding detection.

Tarsus

- The principal city of the first-century Roman province of Cilicia in southeast Asia Minor near the northeastern corner of the Mediterranean Sea; the modern city is called Tersous.
- On the Cydnus River and about twelve miles from the Mediterranean coast, it could function as a port city for ships able to navigate up the river to the lake of Rhegma just downstream from the city.
- About twenty-five miles south of the high and rugged Taurus mountain range and on the route of the only viable mountain pass, which was known as the Cilician Gates.
- A significant commerce center located between Asia Minor, Syria, and the Mediterranean Sea.
- An important culture and education center for rhetoric and Stoic philosophy, known for producing many notable scholars.
- Had a textile industry where the hair of the province's goats was woven into a rough linen known as "cilicium" that could be used in making tents, sails, and leggings.
- Incorporated into the Roman province of Cilicia by Pompey in 67 BC, it was declared a free city (exempt from Roman taxes) in 42 BC by Mark Antony for its support of Caesar against Pompey. Here in 41 BC Mark Antony met Cleopatra when her barge sailed up the Cydnus River.
- At its peak size in the first century AD had a population of about five hundred thousand people.

Select Bibliography

Edward M. Blaiklock, "Tarsus," *ZEB* 5:696–99.

Richard A. Spencer, "Tarsus," *EBD*, 1276–77.

Willem C. van Unnik, *Tarsus, or Jerusalem: The City of Paul's Youth*, trans. George Ogg (London: Epworth, 1962; repr. Eugene, OR: Wipf & Stock, 2009).

A Roman Road near Tarsus
David Padfield/ BiblePlaces.com

and reporting his own previous actions against Christians (22:4–5). All this brings Paul to the place where he can narrate the events that led to his drastic change from persecuting Christians to being one of them himself. Various scholars have suggested rhetorical outlines for this defense speech (see sidebar).

A Rhetorical Outline for Paul's Defense Speech in Acts 22:1–21

Some have suggested that Paul's speech in Acts 22 demonstrates his classical education in rhetorical speechmaking. Unfortunately, the address is interrupted before he can lay out the main proofs of his innocence. Here is one such outline for his speech as Luke has summarized it.

***Exordium* (22:1–2)**

The introductory call to listen.

***Narratio* (22:3–21)**

The story of Paul's life demonstrating his truly Jewish devotion:

- devout upbringing and life (22:3–5)
- encounter with Jesus (22:6–11)
- call/conversion/commissioning (22:12–16)
- continued devotion to Judaism via obedience to Jesus (22:17–21)

***Probatio* (—)**

The main proofs:

Missing because the speech is interrupted, but perhaps hinted at in the basic points of the preceding narrative section.

***Refutatio* (—)**

The rebuttal of the opponent's case:

Missing because the speech is interrupted.

***Peroratio* (—)**

The conclusion and appeal for action:

Missing because the speech is interrupted.

Adapted and expanded from Witherington, *Acts*, 668–75; and Larkin, *Acts*, 317–23; cf. Eckhard J. Schnabel, *Acts*, ZECNT (Grand Rapids: Zondervan, 2012), 887–88.

Unsurprisingly, Paul's own account here of his Damascus road experience is much like Luke's original narration of the event (cf. 9:1–19).[10] Moreover, it is also unsurprising that Luke's original narration contains details that are passed over in Paul's recounting of the event here in Acts 22 (and later in Acts 26).[11] Conversely, the latter two accounts contain details that were not reported in the original narration of Acts 9. None of this is problematic in principle, especially if previously unmentioned details might be of particular interest to the audience at hand. Following good narrative technique, Luke has varied the lengths of his multiple accounts of the event and has deliberately reserved

10. As Witherington notes, "It cannot be stressed enough that these accounts are *summaries* and Luke has written them up in his own style and way"; Witherington, *Acts*, 309–10.

11. Hedrick remarks that "Acts 22 is composed with the assumption of facts given only in Acts 9"; Charles W. Hedrick, "Paul's Conversion/Call: A Comparative Analysis of the Three Reports in Acts," *JBL* 100 (1981): 426.

some of the details for his later two reports of it.[12] Nonetheless, all three accounts include the same basic facts:

- Saul was authorized to oppose Christians and was en route to do so in Damascus.
- While nearing Damascus, Saul saw a light, fell to the ground, and heard a voice.
- The voice said, "Saul, Saul, why do you persecute me?"
- Saul asked for the identity of the speaker.
- The voice said, "I am Jesus, whom you are persecuting."
- Others were present with Saul and experienced at least some parts of this event.

Thus, all three reports of the event confirm that Jesus confronted Saul on the road to Damascus, conversed with him in the context of a bright light with others present, and ultimately turned Saul from disbelief and opposition to Christian belief.[13]

There are, however, a few places where differences in the details seem troublesome. The most difficult difference is between the Acts 9 and Acts 22 accounts regarding the experience of Saul's travel companions: Is it that they heard the voice (9:7) or did not hear it (22:9)? But two close observations can help clear up this apparent discrepancy. First, Luke uses different case spellings for the Greek word for "voice" in these two accounts. In classical times this spelling distinction for the word "voice" with the "hearing" verb would imply that Paul's companions did hear the sound of the voice (genitive: *tēs phōnēs*; 9:7) but did not understand the words of the voice (accusative: *tēn phōnēn*; 22:9).[14] Second, Acts 22:9 qualifies the unheard voice as that "of him who was speaking to me." In other words, the traveling companions did hear the sound of someone talking with Paul (9:7) but did not hear what was being said by the one talking to Paul (22:9).[15] By either or both of these observations, the NIV accounts for this difference in wording by translating the phrase in Acts 22:9 more simply as "they did not understand the voice" (so also ESV, NASB, NLT).[16]

---

12. Witherington, *Acts*, 311n27; cf. Hedrick, "Paul's Conversion/Call," 415–32.

13. Witherington, *Acts*, 310.

14. See, for example, Hedrick, "Paul's Conversion/Call," 428–29. It is instructive to notice that we sometimes utilize a similar distinction in modern conversational English emphasizing the preposition "of" (≈ genitive case): e.g., "I have heard *of* the story, but I have not heard the story." For an argument (complete with counter examples) that Luke was not here using this classical distinction between the accusative and genitive cases, see Daniel B. Wallace, *Greek Grammar Beyond the Basics* (Grand Rapids: Zondervan, 1996), 133–34.

15. See Ben Witherington III, "Editing the Good News: Some Synoptic Lessons for the Study of Acts," pp. 324–47 in *History, Literature, and Society in the Book of Acts*, ed. Ben Witherington III (Cambridge: Cambridge University Press, 1996): 342–43; John B. Polhill, *Acts*, NAC (Nashville: Broadman, 1992), 235n15; cf. Witherington, *Acts*, 313; and Eckhard J. Schnabel, *Acts*, ZECNT (Grand Rapids: Zondervan, 2012), 903.

16. Another biblical example of this phenomenon is seen in John 12:27–29 where people hear merely the sound of God speaking to Jesus without understanding what is said; some mistake the sound for thunder.

Comparing the Reports of Paul's Conversion Experience on the Road to Damascus

Luke's Narration in Acts 9:1–19

1 Meanwhile, Saul was still breathing out murderous threats against the Lord's disciples. He went to the high priest 2 and asked him for letters to the synagogues in Damascus, so that if he found any there who belonged to the Way, whether men or women, he might take them as prisoners to Jerusalem. 3 As he neared Damascus on his journey, suddenly a light from heaven flashed around him. 4 He fell to the ground and heard a voice say to him, "Saul, Saul, why do you persecute me?"

5 "Who are you, Lord?" Saul asked.

"I am Jesus, whom you are persecuting," he replied. 6 "Now get up and go into the city, and you will be told what you must do."

7 The men traveling with Saul stood there speechless; they heard the sound but did not see anyone. 8 Saul got up from the ground, but when he opened his eyes he could see nothing. So they led him by the hand into Damascus. 9 For three days he was blind, and did not eat or drink anything.

10 In Damascus there was a disciple named Ananias. The Lord called to him in a vision, "Ananias!"

"Yes, Lord," he answered.

11 The Lord told him, "Go to the house of Judas on Straight Street and ask for a man from Tarsus named Saul, for he is praying. 12 In a vision he has seen a man named Ananias come and place his hands on him to restore his sight."

13 "Lord," Ananias answered, "I have heard many reports about this man and all the harm he has done to your holy people in Jerusalem. 14 And he has come here with authority from the chief priests to arrest all who call on your name."

15 But the Lord said to Ananias, "Go! This man is my chosen instrument to proclaim my name to the Gentiles and their kings and to the people of Israel. 16 I will show him how much he must suffer for my name."

17 Then Ananias went to the house and entered it. Placing his hands on Saul, he said, "Brother Saul, the Lord—Jesus, who appeared to you on the road as you were coming here—has sent me so that you may see again and be filled with the Holy Spirit." 18 Immediately, something like scales fell from Saul's eyes, and he could see again. He got up and was baptized, 19 and after taking some food, he regained his strength.

Saul spent several days with the disciples in Damascus.

Paul's Testimony in Acts 22:1–22

1 "Brothers and fathers, listen now to my defense."

2 When they heard him speak to them in Aramaic, they became very quiet.

Then Paul said: 3 "I am a Jew, born in Tarsus of Cilicia, but brought up in this city. I studied under Gamaliel and was thoroughly trained in the law of our ancestors. I was just as zealous for God as any of you are today. 4 I persecuted the followers of this Way to their death, arresting both men and women and throwing them into prison, 5 as the high priest and all the Council can themselves testify. I even obtained letters from them to their associates in Damascus, and went there to bring these people as prisoners to Jerusalem to be punished.

6 "About noon as I came near Damascus, suddenly a bright light from heaven flashed around me. 7 I fell to the ground and heard a voice say to me, 'Saul! Saul! Why do you persecute me?'

8 "'Who are you, Lord?' I asked.

"'I am Jesus of Nazareth, whom you are persecuting,' he replied. 9 My companions saw the light, but they did not understand the voice of him who was speaking to me.

10 "'What shall I do, Lord?' I asked.

"'Get up,' the Lord said, 'and go into Damascus. There you will be told all that you have been assigned to do.' 11 My companions led me by the hand into Damascus, because the brilliance of the light had blinded me.

12 "A man named Ananias came to see me. He was a devout observer of the law and highly respected by all the Jews living there. 13 He stood beside me and said, 'Brother

Saul, receive your sight!' And at that very moment I was able to see him.

14 "Then he said: 'The God of our ancestors has chosen you to know his will and to see the Righteous One and to hear words from his mouth. 15 You will be his witness to all people of what you have seen and heard. 16 And now what are you waiting for? Get up, be baptized and wash your sins away, calling on his name.'

17 "When I returned to Jerusalem and was praying at the temple, I fell into a trance 18 and saw the Lord speaking to me. 'Quick!' he said. 'Leave Jerusalem immediately, because the people here will not accept your testimony about me.'

19 "'Lord,' I replied, 'these people know that I went from one synagogue to another to imprison and beat those who believe in you. 20 And when the blood of your martyr Stephen was shed, I stood there giving my approval and guarding the clothes of those who were killing him.'

21 "Then the Lord said to me, 'Go; I will send you far away to the Gentiles.'"

22 The crowd listened to Paul until he said this. Then they raised their voices and shouted, "Rid the earth of him! He's not fit to live!"

Paul's Testimony in Acts 26:2–23

2 "King Agrippa, I consider myself fortunate to stand before you today as I make my defense against all the accusations of the Jews, 3 and especially so because you are well acquainted with all the Jewish customs and controversies. Therefore, I beg you to listen to me patiently.

4 "The Jewish people all know the way I have lived ever since I was a child, from the beginning of my life in my own country, and also in Jerusalem. 5 They have known me for a long time and can testify, if they are willing, that I conformed to the strictest sect of our religion, living as a Pharisee. 6 And now it is because of my hope in what God has promised our ancestors that I am on trial today. 7 This is the promise our twelve tribes are hoping to see fulfilled as they earnestly serve God day and night. King Agrippa, it is because of this hope that these Jews are accusing me. 8 Why should any of you consider it incredible that God raises the dead?

9 "I too was convinced that I ought to do all that was possible to oppose the name of Jesus of Nazareth. 10 And that is just what I did in Jerusalem. On the authority of the chief priests I put many of the Lord's people in prison, and when they were put to death, I cast my vote against them. 11 Many a time I went from one synagogue to another to have them punished, and I tried to force them to blaspheme. I was so obsessed with persecuting them that I even hunted them down in foreign cities.

12 "On one of these journeys I was going to Damascus with the authority and commission of the chief priests. 13 About noon, King Agrippa, as I was on the road, I saw a light from heaven, brighter than the sun, blazing around me and my companions. 14 We all fell to the ground, and I heard a voice saying to me in Aramaic, 'Saul, Saul, why do you persecute me? It is hard for you to kick against the goads.'

15 "Then I asked, 'Who are you, Lord?'

"'I am Jesus, whom you are persecuting,' the Lord replied. 16 'Now get up and stand on your feet. I have appeared to you to appoint you as a servant and as a witness of what you have seen and will see of me. 17 I will rescue you from your own people and from the Gentiles. I am sending you to them 18 to open their eyes and turn them from darkness to light, and from the power of Satan to God, so that they may receive forgiveness of sins and a place among those who are sanctified by faith in me.'

19 "So then, King Agrippa, I was not disobedient to the vision from heaven. 20 First to those in Damascus, then to those in Jerusalem and in all Judea, and then to the Gentiles, I preached that they should repent and turn to God and demonstrate their repentance by their deeds. 21 That is why some Jews seized me in the temple courts and tried to kill me. 22 But God has helped me to this very day; so I stand here and testify to small and great alike. I am saying nothing beyond what the prophets and Moses said would happen— 23 that the Messiah would suffer and, as the first to rise from the dead, would bring the message of light to his own people and to the Gentiles."

As Paul continues narrating his experience for the Jewish mob, he mentions hearing another word from God in the temple (22:17–21). But the idea that the Lord would say to Paul, "Go; I will send you far away to the Gentiles" (22:21) reverts the quieted crowd back to their death-threatening chants: "Rid the earth of him! He's not fit to live!" (22:22). Apparently, these zealous Jews had forgotten the many OT passages that proclaim the Lord's intentions to include the gentiles in salvation.[17]

Flogging
ArtMari/Shutterstock.com

Flagrum whip
UtCon Collection / Alamy Stock Photo

14.1.4 Paul Is Protected by Roman Law (22:23–29)

When the mob's unruliness escalates, the Roman commander orders that Paul be taken into the fortress, where he sets out to interrogate him regarding the uproar (22:23–24). Ancient interrogation methods included torture and punishment practices such as flogging, which is what he orders for Paul (22:24b; cf. Matt 27:26; Acts 5:40; 16:23).[18] ***Flogging*** involved whipping the prisoner, often with a multiple-stranded *flagrum* that had weighted and even sharply barbed lashes (see sidebar). As the Roman soldiers prepare to flog him, Paul coyly asks the centurion standing nearby, "Is it legal for you to flog a Roman citizen who hasn't even been found guilty?" (22:25). Because such a step was indeed out of order (see sidebar), the centurion consults with the commander, who in turn questions Paul directly about his insinuated claim to Roman citizenship (22:26–27).

Those not born with ***Roman citizenship*** could be given the status as a reward for service (military or other), and a slave might receive citizenship by manumission.[19] As the commander indicates of himself to Paul, however, bribery was another method for obtaining Roman citizenship, a widespread practice during the reign of emperor Claudius (AD 41–54) (see sidebar). But Paul plainly states that his own Roman citizenship was not gained in any secondary fashion: "I was born a citizen" (22:28).[20] In some cases, Roman citizenship could be proved

17. See chapter 11.

18. Rapske, *Paul in Roman Custody*, 139.

19. See Everett Ferguson, *Backgrounds of Early Christianity*, 3rd ed. (Grand Rapids: Eerdmans, 2003), 62–63; Brian M. Rapske, "Citizenship, Roman," *DNTB*, 215–18; Keener, *Acts*, 3:3255; Sean A. Adams, "Paul the Roman Citizen: Roman Citizenship in the Ancient World and Its Importance for Understanding Acts 22:22–29," pp. 309–26 in *Paul: Jew, Greek, and Roman*, ed. Stanley E. Porter, Pauline Studies 5 (Leiden: Brill, 2008), 309–10; cf. A. N. Sherwin-White, *The Roman Citizenship*, 2nd ed. (Oxford: Clarendon, 1973), 225–50.

20. Given Paul's clear Jewish ethnicity, the implication is that one of Paul's ancestors (e.g., father or grandfather) had been awarded Roman citizenship for some outstanding service rendered or for their potential influence, or (alternatively) Paul's ancestors had been enslaved prisoners and the family was eventually emancipated and offered citizenship; see Arnold, "Acts," 226; and Adams, "Paul the Roman Citizen," 318–20; cf. 321–23 on Paul having dual citizenship with Rome and Tarsus.

by presentation of a certificate in the form of a small diptych (hinged tablet). False claims to Roman citizenship could result in punishment.[21] Whatever evidence Paul might have provided, clearly the soldiers are convinced enough to immediately withdraw from their interrogation approach and the commander himself is alarmed even about having put a natural-born Roman citizen in chains (22:29).

The Abomination of Beating a Roman Citizen without Trial

In the first century BC, Cicero wrote castigating Verres for having crucified a man named Gavius, a supposed spy, even though he had repeatedly cried out that he was a Roman citizen.

Cicero, *The Verrine Orations* 2.5.66 §§169–70 (ca. 70 BC)

> But I need say no more about Gavius. It was not Gavius against whom your hate was then displayed: you declared war upon the whole principle of the rights of the Roman citizen body. You were the enemy, I say again, not of that individual man, but of the common liberties of us all. . . . To bind a Roman citizen is a crime, to flog him is an abomination, to slay him is almost an act of murder: to crucify him is—what? There is no fitting word that can possibly describe so horrible a deed.

See also Livy, *History of Rome* 10.9.4 and Ulpian, *Digest* 48.6.7 (both cited in chapter 12).

Jews as Roman Citizens

From Arnold, "Acts," 226.

> It was not always necessary for Roman citizens to show their devotion to the emperor by engaging in emperor worship, worship of the goddess Roma, or by participating in the worship of any of the official Roman cults. Philo reports that the majority of Jews living in Rome were Roman citizens and yet were not compelled to compromise their ancestral laws [*Embassy*, 155–57]. Even Philo himself, as a wealthy Roman citizen living in Egypt, was never forced to worship the emperor or other gods.

---

21. See A. N. Sherwin-White, *Roman Society and Roman Law in the New Testament* (Oxford: Oxford University Press, 1963; repr., Grand Rapids: Baker, 1992), 148–49. On false claims to citizenship, the ancient writer Suetonius remarks of emperor Claudius, "Those who usurped the privileges of Roman citizenship he executed . . ."; Suetonius, *Claud.* 25.3.

Achieving Roman Citizenship through Bribery

The practice of obtaining Roman citizenship through bribery described by Roman historian Dio Cassius (ca. AD 155–235) gives evidence that bribing one's way into Roman citizenship was a widespread practice during the reign of Emperor Claudius (AD 41–54), at first at a high price and then later at low prices. The first-century Roman historian Tacitus gives examples of Emperor Nero taking action to halt this corruption during his reign (AD 54–68).

Dio Cassius, *Roman History* 60.17.5–7 (ca. AD 230)

> For inasmuch as Romans had the advantage over foreigners in practically all respects, many sought the franchise by personal application to the emperor, and many bought it from Messalina and the imperial freedmen. For this reason, though the privilege was at first sold only for large sums, it became so cheapened by the facility with which it could be obtained that it came to be a common saying, that a man could become a citizen by giving the right person some bits of broken glass.

Tacitus, *Annals* 14.50 (ca. AD 117)

> Fabricius Veiento succumbed to the not dissimilar charge of composing a series of libels on the senate and priests in the books to which he had given the title of his Will. The accuser, Tullius Geminus, also maintained that he had consistently sold the imperial bounty and the right to official promotion. This last count decided Nero to take the case into his own hands. He convicted Veiento, relegated him from Italy, and ordered his books to be burned.

14.1.5 Paul's Defense before the Jerusalem Sanhedrin (22:30–23:11)

Finding himself in the awkward position of investigating Jewish accusations against a Jewish man who is also a Roman citizen, the commander releases Paul from official custody but requires him to appear before the Jewish Sanhedrin (22:30). Facing the ***Sanhedrin***, Paul confidently claims, "My brothers, I have fulfilled my duty to God in all good conscience to this day" (23:1). Upon hearing this claim, the ***high priest*** Ananias (as Sanhedrin president) orders that Paul be struck on the mouth (23:2), at which Paul retorts, "God will strike you, you whitewashed wall! You sit there to judge me according to the law, yet you yourself violate the law by commanding that I be struck!" (23:3; cf. Lev 19:15). Those standing by, however, reprove Paul for insulting the high priest (23:4), and Paul immediately offers an apology for his rudeness and includes a Scripture citation: "Brothers, I did not realize that he was the high priest; for it is written: 'Do not speak evil about the ruler of your people'" (23:5 citing Exod 22:28).

While some understand Paul's retort as sarcasm—something like, "Given his unscriptural behavior, I could not recognize him as the high priest!"[22]—if that were

22. So I. Howard Marshall, *The Acts of the Apostles: An Introduction and Commentary*, TNTC (Grand Rapids:

Paul's intention, it seems that Luke could have made this more evident. Rather, it seems better to understand Paul as speaking sincerely here. Having been away from Jerusalem for several years, Paul may not have heard about Ananias becoming the next high priest (serving AD 46–58).[23] Or perhaps Paul was simply explaining his reactionary comment, intending something like, "I spoke without considering the person's position as high priest."[24] At any rate, when confronted with his error, Paul repents of his disrespectful behavior. Nonetheless, the episode betrays Ananias's true character, and the ironic contrast is acute. In a setting aimed at scriptural justice, the ruling high priest behaves unjustly by violating the law he is to uphold, while the accused Paul proves to be a model of Scripture-quoting piety.[25]

The shortage of principles in the Sanhedrin's leadership seems to convince Paul that he will not have a proper hearing before them.[26] So he simply identifies himself as a Pharisee of some long-standing who is being tried for believing in the resurrection of the dead—a claim that leads to a divided Sanhedrin (23:6–7). Luke inserts a reminder that the Sanhedrin consisted of representatives from two very different Jewish schools of thought—***Sadducees*** and ***Pharisees***[27]—and explains in brief that, unlike the Sadducees, the Pharisees affirmed life after death, physical resurrection, and spiritual beings (23:8). Paul is not merely siding with the Pharisees but is pointing to the Christian claim of Jesus's resurrection as being true to Jewish faith. Paul appeals to the Pharisees' cherished hope of resurrection as the hope of Israel and connects it directly to the resurrection of Christ (cf. 13:32–39).[28] Paul is willing to stand trial and even die for this principal claim of Christianity (cf. 1 Cor 15:12–28).[29] The result of Paul's claim is a dispute in the council that brings the hearing to such a violent impasse that the Roman commander once again feels the need to intervene, and he forcefully has Paul returned to the safety of the Fortress Antonia (Acts 23:9–10).

Eerdmans, 1980), 364; Luke Timothy Johnson, *The Acts of the Apostles*, SP 5 (Collegeville: Liturgical for Michael Glazier, 1992), 397; F. Scott Spencer, *Acts*, Readings: A New Biblical Commentary (Sheffield: Sheffield Academic Press, 1997), 212.

23. So Fitzmyer, *Acts*, 717; David G. Peterson, *The Acts of the Apostles*, Pillar New Testament Commentary (Grand Rapids: Eerdmans, 2009), 614–15; Arnold, "Acts," 228. Furthermore, some suspect that Paul's eyesight problem contributed to his lack of recognizing the high priest; see Gal 4:15; 6:11.

24. So Polhill, *Acts*, 469; Simon J. Kistemaker, *Exposition of the Acts of the Apostles*, New Testament Commentary (Grand Rapids: Baker, 1990), 810–11.

25. Keener, *Acts*, 3:3259; on the various nuanced interpretations of Paul's conflict with the high priest, see Keener, *Acts*, 3:3265–81.

26. Schnabel, *Acts*, 927–28; cf. Haenchen, *Acts*, 642.

27. See chapter 5.

28. F. F. Bruce, *The Acts of the Apostles: The Greek Text with Introduction and Commentary*, 3rd ed. (Grand Rapids: Eerdmans, 1990; Leicester: Apollos, 1990), 465. On resurrection hope in early Judaism, see Casey D. Elledge, *Resurrection of the Dead in Early Judaism, 200 BCE–CE 200* (Oxford: Oxford University Press, 2017).

29. See Robert J. Kepple, "The Hope of Israel, the Resurrection of the Dead, and Jesus: A Study of Their Relationship in Acts with Particular Regard to the Understanding of Paul's Trial Defense," *JETS* 20 (1977): 231–41; and Brandon D. Crowe, *The Hope of Israel: The Resurrection of Christ in the Acts of the Apostles* (Grand Rapids: Baker Academic, 2020).

Lest we assume that all this trouble has had no emotional effect on Paul, Luke inserts a note that the Lord appears to Paul and encourages him: "Take courage! As you have testified about me in Jerusalem, so you must also testify in Rome" (23:11). What God has personally communicated to Paul has always come to pass, so Paul can be confident that he will testify about Jesus in Rome. And Luke's readers will expect this in the story of Acts as well.

14.2 PAUL'S DELIVERANCE FROM A JEWISH PLOT (ACTS 23:12–35)

Jesus's promise to Paul is followed immediately by a meticulous description of a Jewish plot against Paul's life. The level of detail reassures us of Luke's continued presence at this point in the story of Acts, and this report also fits the continued trend of religious resistance to faith in Jesus. Of course, none of this shakes the reader's confidence that Paul will survive this threat as he has all the others he's faced.

14.2.1 The Plot Planned (23:12–15)

While official Jewish opposition to Paul and the gospel has been persistent, what is new here is that the fervency of the opposition is quantifiable in number and intensity: more than forty Jewish men take an oath not to eat or drink until they have killed Paul (23:12–13). Furthermore, the conspirators are rather open with the Jewish religious leaders about their plot against Paul and even ask the Sanhedrin to participate by petitioning the Roman commander to bring Paul out of the fortress—on the pretext of gaining more information—so that the conspirators can assassinate Paul (23:14–15). Given what we know about the high priest Ananias (see Josephus, *Ant.* 20.9.2 §§204–7), this level of corruption among the Jewish religious leaders may be disappointing, but it is unsurprising.

14.2.2 The Plot Discovered (23:16–22)

Meanwhile, Paul remains in protective Roman custody in the Fortress Antonia, but even there secrets can become known. While Luke says little of Paul's family status,[30] we learn here that Paul's sister had a son in Jerusalem who hears about the plot against his uncle and acts to intervene (23:16). Depending on the terms of confinement, family and friends could be allowed to visit those held in custody, and Paul is apparently afforded visitors.[31] When his nephew discloses the plot against him, not knowing how widespread

30. See Bruce W. Longenecker and Todd D. Still, *Thinking through Paul: A Survey of His Life, Letters, and Theology* (Grand Rapids: Zondervan, 2014), 26–27.

31. For discussions of people helping Paul during his various imprisonments see Rapske, *Paul in Roman Custody*, 369–92; and the earlier Brian M. Rapske, "The Importance of Helpers to the Imprisoned Paul in the Book of Acts," *TynBul* 42 (1991): 3–30.

and far-reaching the plot might be, Paul requests that the young man be taken to the commander, for "he has something to tell him" (23:17). Paul's experience with the Roman commander so far reassures him that the official wants to do things correctly, so Paul intends for the conspiracy to be exposed directly in the commander's hearing (23:18–21). The commander can also imagine the complexities of a widespread conspiracy and warns Paul's nephew not to tell anyone else about having disclosed this plot (23:22).

14.2.3 The Plot Foiled (23:23–35)

The Roman commander, ***Claudius Lysias*** by name (23:26), moves quickly to intervene in the life-threatening circumstances of his Roman citizen detainee. He assigns two of his centurions to prepare a detachment of scores of soldiers to begin relocating Paul to the Judean Roman capital, ***Caesarea***, at nine o'clock that night (literally "at the third hour of the night," with night starting at sunset, around 6:00 p.m.).[32] And he specifies that horses be utilized for the transfer (23:23–24).[33] To introduce the prisoner Paul to ***Felix***, the procurator of Judea (ca. AD 52–59), Claudius Lysias writes a letter for which Luke provides a transcript (23:26–30; see sidebar). The content of this letter reviews what we already know from Luke's narration of events, with the caveat that Lysias takes liberty with the truth in claiming to know of Paul's Roman citizenship before rescuing him from the Jewish mob (23:27; cf. 21:30–39 and 22:23–29).

Claudius Lysias's Letter to Felix

Acts 23:26-30

Claudius Lysias,

To His Excellency, Governor Felix:

Greetings.

This man was seized by the Jews and they were about to kill him, but I came with my troops and rescued him, for I had learned that he is a Roman citizen. I wanted to know why they were accusing him, so I brought him to their Sanhedrin. I found that the accusation had to do with questions about their law, but there was no charge against him that deserved death or imprisonment. When I was informed of a plot to be carried out against the man, I sent him to you at once. I also ordered his accusers to present to you their case against him.

---

32. See the sidebar on the hours of the day in chapter 9.

33. The need to transfer Paul from Jerusalem to Caesarea could well be attached to other (unmentioned) reasons for moving soldiers between the cities. See the discussions in Brian M. Rapske, "Acts, Travel and Shipwreck," pp. 1–47 in *The Book of Acts in Its Graeco-Roman Setting*, ed. David W. J. Gill and Conrad Gempf, BAFCS 2 (Grand Rapids: Eerdmans, 1994; Carlisle: Paternoster, 1994), 11–14; and Keener, *Acts*, 3:3339–45.

Continuing with eyewitness specifics, Luke reports that the soldiers carry out the commander's orders, taking Paul that night as far as the city of Antipatris, somewhere between thirty-five and forty-five miles toward Caesarea from Jerusalem (23:31).[34] The next day, once the entourage is out of the more dangerous Jewish foothills, the foot soldiers have the cavalry move Paul the rest of the way across the open country to Caesarea (23:32–33). Upon reading Lysias's letter and ascertaining that Paul is from the Roman province of Cilicia (23:34), Felix promises, "I will hear your case when your accusers get here" (23:35; see sidebar).[35] After this, he orders that Paul be kept under guard in Herod's palace in Caesarea.[36]

On Roman Law Requiring Accuser to Face the Accused

Appian, *Civil Wars* 3.54 (second century AD)

Then Piso said: "Our law, Senators, requires that the accused shall himself hear the charge preferred against him and shall be judged after he has made his own defence; and for the truth of this I appeal to Cicero, our greatest orator. . . ."

Marcian, *The Digest of Justinian* 48.17.1 (fifth century AD)

The deified Severus and Antoninus the Great wrote in a rescript that no one should be punished in his absence; and we apply this rule, that absent persons should not be condemned; for the argument of justice does not permit of a person's being condemned without his case being heard. . . . But the absent one should be searched for and registered [among the accused] so that he may take the opportunity [of defending] himself.

From Appian, *Civil Wars* in LCL, and *The Digest of Justinian*, trans. Alan Watson, 4 vols., rev. English-language ed. (Philadelphia: University of Pennsylvania Press, 1998).

14.3 PAUL'S HEARING BEFORE FELIX (ACTS 24:1–27)

Despite his wicked reputation (see sidebar), Felix appears at first to be somewhat respectful toward Paul and intent on hearing his case. In the very next verse, Luke reports, "Five days later the high priest Ananias went down to Caesarea with some of the elders and a lawyer named Tertullus, and they brought their charges against Paul before the governor" (24:1). But this potentially positive impression is short-lived for Luke's readers.[37]

34. See Charles Kingsley Barrett, *A Critical and Exegetical Commentary on the Acts of the Apostles*, 2 vols., ICC (Edinburgh: T&T Clark, 1994/1998), 2:1085–86; Keener, *Acts*, 3:3343–44.

35. Cf. Ferguson, *Backgrounds of Early Christianity*, 65.

36. Luke uses the term praetorium (Greek: *praitōrion*) for Herod's residence. Keener remarks, "The praetorium would be a more pleasant place of detention than others; Paul is a prisoner of high status, and such prisoners received better 'custodial arrangements' than those of lower status"; Keener, *Acts*, 3:3347; cf. Brian M. Rapske, "Prison, Prisoner," *DNTB*, 827–30.

37. So Spencer, *Acts*, 220–21; Parsons, *Acts*, 329.

Ancient Descriptions of Procurator Antonius Felix

A former slave, Antonius Felix is the first known freedman to be appointed to a Roman procuratorship. Felix's years as the procurator of Judea (ca. AD 52–59) fueled the tensions between the Jews and the Romans and led to outbreaks of rebellion that got Felix in trouble with Rome. The following remarks of ancient writers paint an unflattering portrait of the leader before whom Paul has a hearing in Acts 24. Married three times, two of his wives were named Drusilla.

Tacitus, *Histories* 5.9 (ca. AD 105)

> Claudius made Judea a province and entrusted it to Roman knights or to freedmen; one of the latter, Antonius Felix, practised every kind of cruelty and lust, wielding the power of king with all the instincts of a slave; he had married Drusilla, the granddaughter of Cleopatra and Antony, and so was Antony's grandson-in-law, while Claudius was Antony's grandson.

Suetonius, *Divus Claudius* 28 (ca. AD 121)

> Of his freedmen he [Claudius] . . . was equally fond of Felix, giving him the command of cohorts and of troops of horse, as well as of the province of Judaea; and he became the husband of three queens.

Flavius Josephus, *Jewish Antiquities* 20.7.1–2 §§137–44 (ca. AD 94)

> Not long afterwards Drusilla's marriage to Azizus was dissolved under the impact of the following circumstances. At the time when Felix was procurator of Judaea, he beheld her; and, inasmuch as she surpassed all other women in beauty, he conceived a passion for the lady. He sent to her one of his friends, a Cyprian Jew named Atomus, who pretended to be a magician, in an effort to persuade her to leave her husband and to marry Felix. Felix promised to make her supremely happy if she did not disdain him. She, being unhappy and wishing to escape the malice of her sister Berenice—for Drusilla was exceedingly abused by her because of her beauty—, was persuaded to transgress the ancestral laws and to marry Felix. By him she gave birth to a son whom she named Agrippa. How this youth and his wife disappeared at the time of the eruption of Mount Vesuvius in the times of Titus Caesar, I shall describe later.

Flavius Josephus, *Jewish Antiquities* 20.8.5 §§160–63 (ca. AD 94)

> Felix also bore a grudge against Jonathan the high priest because of his frequent admonition to improve the administration of the affairs of Judaea. For Jonathan feared that he himself might incur the censure of the multitude in that he had requested Caesar to dispatch Felix as procurator of Judaea. Felix accordingly devised a pretext that would remove from his presence one who was a constant nuisance to him; for incessant rebukes are annoying to those who choose to do wrong. It was such reasons that moved Felix to bribe Jonathan's most trusted friend, a native of Jerusalem named Doras, with a promise to pay a great sum, to bring in brigands to attack Jonathan and kill him.

14.3.1 Tertullus Presents the Charges (24:1–9)

The term for "lawyer" in Acts 24:1 (Greek: *rhētōr*) is found only here in the New Testament and, meaning "orator" or "rhetorician," is used for advocates in legal cases, not experts in Jewish law.[38] The orator ***Tertullus*** begins his presentation of the Jews' case against Paul with a flowery opening that flatters Felix and a promise to be brief (24:2–4). Attempts to win the goodwill of the judge with flattery and promises of brevity were typical in ancient court rooms.[39] The "long period of peace under you" (24:2) may imply Felix's recent restoration of order in defeating an Egyptian rebel (for whom Paul was mistaken by Lysias; 21:38), and this introductory reference subtly aligns Paul with such disturbers of the peace in hopes that Felix will treat Paul in like manner.[40]

Where Is Acts 24:7?

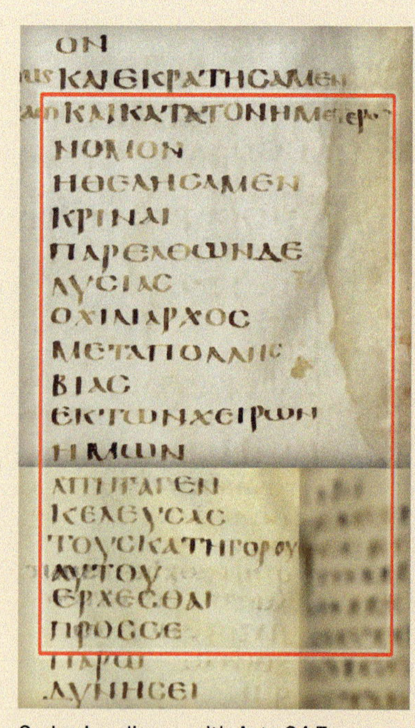

Codex Laudianus with Acts 24:7

The Bodleian Libraries, University of Oxford, MS. Laud Gr. 35, f 206r & 206v

While most modern English translations have no Acts 24:7, a few ancient manuscripts have a different reading for Acts 24:6–8. Some modern translations note this in a footnote with a comment such as this: "Some manuscripts include here *him, and we would have judged him in accordance with our law. [7] But the commander Lysias came and took him from us with much violence, [8] ordering his accusers to come before you*" (NIV footnote). This appears to be a late addition by a scribe involved in the manuscript hand-copying process, perhaps motivated by the desire to clarify how Paul got into the custody of the Romans.

Codex Sinaiticus without Acts 24:7

38. See Barrett, *Acts*, 2:1093; Ferguson, *Backgrounds of Early Christianity*, 65; Keener, *Acts*, 4:3357.

39. Keener, *Acts*, 4:3361–70; Harry W. Tajra, *The Trial of St. Paul: A Juridical Exegesis of the Second Half of the Acts of the Apostles*, WUNT 2:35 (Tübingen: Mohr Siebeck, 1989), 120.

40. Bruce W. Winter, "The Importance of the *Captatio Benevolentiae* in the Speeches of Tertullus and Paul in Acts 24:1–21," *JTS* 42 (1991): 505–31, esp. 516, 519.

Tertullus outlines the charges against Paul in three points. First, Paul is called a "troublemaker" guilty of "stirring up riots among the Jews all over the world" (24:5a), placing Paul at odds with Rome's interest in maintaining peace and order in the land. Second, Paul is labeled a "ringleader of the Nazarene sect" (24:5b), connecting Christianity with Jesus of Nazareth, whom the Romans had crucified just a few years earlier. Third, Paul is said to have "tried to desecrate the temple" (24:6), suggesting he is a disrupter of religious practices tolerated by Rome. Luke's readers can recognize where each of these charges gets its origins and yet how each falls short of expressing the truth. Trouble has certainly followed Paul in Acts, but he is hardly the one making the trouble. Paul is most certainly a follower of Jesus of Nazareth, but "ringleader" is unnecessarily pejorative. And finally, the charge of desecrating the temple is known to be false. Nevertheless, Tertullus claims with (over)confidence that Felix "will be able to learn the truth about all these charges" (24:8), and the other Jews present uphold Tertullus's claims (24:9).

14.3.2 Paul's Defense before Felix (24:10–21)

After a brief introduction (24:10a) and a simple, verifiable narrative about going to Jerusalem to worship (24:11–13), Paul outlines his remarks in a sort of doubled response to each of the charges laid out by Tertullus. First, as for being a ringleader of the Nazarene sect, Paul (A) admits to worshiping the God of the Jewish ancestors, following "the Way" that the Jews have dubbed a "sect," (24:14a) and (B) declares his devotion to the whole Jewish Law and the Prophets and to the Jewish hope of the resurrection (24:14b–15). Second, as for being a troublemaker among the Jews, Paul (A) says that he strives to live with a clear conscience before God and others (24:16) and (B) notes that he brought relief for the poor of Jerusalem, thus seeking to help others, not to stir up trouble (24:17). Third, as for desecrating the temple, Paul (A) notes that he was behaving properly (and was even ceremonially clean) when his accusers found him in the temple (24:18a) and (B) states that he was not rustling up a crowd or creating any kind of disturbance (24:18b).

Paul concludes his ***rhetoric***-laden defense by putting the burden of proof back on his Jewish accusers, those from Asia as well as those from Jerusalem (24:19–20). He notes that his only "crime" was to declare his Jewish belief in the resurrection of the dead (24:21). How odd, then, for the Jews to accuse him of being a troublemaker for simply being as Jewish as they claim to be. With this explanation, Paul skillfully turns the intended political charges into one theological charge: belief in the resurrection, a long-held Jewish belief that Paul readily embraces.[41] Rather than in terms of Roman law,

41. Bruce W. Winter, "Official Proceedings and the Forensic Speeches in Acts 24–26," pp. 305–36 in *The Book of Acts in its Ancient Literary Setting*, ed. Bruce W. Winter and Andrew D. Clarke. BAFCS 1 (Grand Rapids: Eerdmans, 1993; Carlisle: Paternoster, 1993), 326–27.

Rhetorical Outlines for Tertullus and Paul's Exchange in Acts 24

Scholars often comment on how the exchange of remarks by Tertullus and Paul in the hearing before Felix (Acts 24) match well with the expectations of ancient handbooks on rhetoric. Here is one such outline for their remarks.

Outline of Tertullus's Charges against Paul in Acts 24:2–8

***Exordium* (24:2b–4)**

The introductory call to listen, including a *captatio benevolentiae* (an attempt to win the goodwill of the judge) and a promise of brevity.

***Narratio* (24:5–6)**

A narrative of the defendant's infractions:

- A troublemaker among the Jews all over the world (v. 5a).
- A ringleader of the Nazarene sect (v. 5b).
- A desecrater of the temple—perhaps intended to serve as confirmation (*confirmatio*) or proof (*probatio*) of the charges (v. 6).

***Peroratio* (24:8)**

The conclusion and appeal for action.

Outline of Paul's Defense Speech in Acts 24:10–21

***Exordium* (24:10b)**

An introduction, including a gracious *captatio benevolentiae*.

***Narratio* (24:11)**

Paul was worshiping, not causing trouble, in the temple.

***Confirmatio* or *Probatio* (24:12–13)**

The accusers have no evidence to the contrary.

***Refutatio* (24:14–18)**

A rebuttal of the charges in three pairs of statements:

In response to the ringleader charge:

- Paul admits to worshiping the God of the Jewish ancestors, following "the Way" that the Jews have dubbed a "sect" (v. 14a).
- Paul holds to the whole Jewish Law and the Prophets and to the Jewish hope of the resurrection (vv. 14b–15).

In response to the troublemaker charge:

- Paul strives to live with a clear conscience before God and others (v. 16).
- Paul brought relief for the poor of Jerusalem and was there to present offerings (v. 17).

In response to the desecration charge:

- Paul was behaving properly in the temple (v. 18a).
- Paul was not rustling up a crowd or a disturbance (v. 18b).

***Peroratio* (24:19–21)**

The conclusion and appeal for action: the Jews—either from Asia or from Jerusalem—ought to state the crime they have against him (v. 19). Paul's only "riotous" act was to declare his (Jewish) belief in the resurrection of the dead (vv. 20–21).

Adapted and expanded from Witherington, *Acts*, 704–705; Bruce W. Winter, "The Importance of the *Captatio Benevolentiae* in the Speeches of Tertullus and Paul in Acts 24:1–21," *JTS* 42.2 (1991): 505–31; and Marion L. Soards, *The Speeches in Acts: Their Content, Context, and Concerns* (Louisville: Westminster John Knox, 1994), 117–19; cf. Schnabel, *Acts*, 949–50.

Paul reframes the trial in terms of Jewish theology because, after all, the dispute here centers on the Christian claim that Jesus's resurrection demonstrates that he is the Jewish Messiah.[42]

14.3.3 Felix's Non-Decision (24:22–27)

At this juncture, Luke notes that Felix is "well acquainted with the Way" of Christianity (24:22). Despite its thousands of followers, Christianity is not a political threat to the stability of his province.[43] Nevertheless, Felix is not in a hurry to make any decisions. Meanwhile, he will keep Paul under guard, allowing him some freedoms and permitting his friends to care for his needs, as was often the case for prisoners (24:23).[44] Despite his procrastination, Felix and his Jewish wife, ***Drusilla***,[45] do show some interest in—and fear of—what Paul has to say about faith in Christ Jesus. But even as the procrastination continues, Felix keeps bringing Paul back for frequent discussions, hoping for a bribe from him (24:24–26). Thus, Felix would like to benefit from Paul, but not spiritually.

This legal and spiritual procrastination goes on for two years(!), at which time Felix is removed from the procurator office and simply leaves Paul in prison (24:27). Now that Rome is recalling him because of his mismanagement of Jewish concerns with nearby Syria, Felix needs to avoid further upsetting the Jews by releasing Paul.[46] Moreover, he also needs to avoid being charged with punishing an innocent Roman citizen.[47] Deciding not to decide seems like an expedient option. All this demonstrates that it is entirely possible for a person to understand the gospel and still choose to put off deciding about it, which is simply another way of rejecting it.

14.4 PAUL'S HEARING BEFORE FESTUS (ACTS 25:1–22)

Three days after arriving as the new procurator of the Roman province of Judea (ca. AD 59), ***Festus*** travels from Caesarea to Jerusalem, perhaps out of sensitivity to the Jewish tensions exacerbated by Felix.[48] There the chief priests and the Jewish leaders present to him the charges they have against Paul (25:1–2).[49] The unbelieving Jews of

42. C. Kavin Rowe, *World Upside Down: Reading Acts in the Graeco-Roman Age* (New York: Oxford University Press, 2009), 78.

43. Keener, *Acts*, 4:3422.

44. See Keener, *Acts*, 3:3348 and 4:3427–29; cf. Rapske, *Paul in Roman Custody*, 195–225, esp. 209–16.

45. See Douglas S. Huffman, "Drusilla," *EDB*, 358; David C. Braund, "Drusilla," *ABD* 2:238–39.

46. Many commentators note this; e.g., Kistemaker, *Acts*, 853; Schnabel, *Acts*, 968; Peterson, *Acts*, 643n82.

47. Keener, *Acts*, 4:3442–44.

48. Tajra, *The Trial of St. Paul*, 135.

49. On prisoners' cases being lost in the bureaucratic shuffle during the change of rulers, see Rapske, *Paul in Roman Custody*," 321.

Jerusalem are still quite passionately opposed to Paul and his message of the gospel, despite the two-year passage of time. Upon learning about their complaints against Paul, Festus decides he will do something with this case when he returns to Caesarea. Festus has a more likeable reputation than his predecessor Felix (see sidebar on Festus).[50] Nevertheless, as things turn out, he is susceptible to manipulation.[51] So, like Paul, Luke's readers maintain their wariness.

Josephus's Descriptions of Procurator Porcius Festus

Appointed as procurator of Judea by emperor Nero, Porcius Festus inherited from his predecessor Felix a troubled set of tensions between the Jews and Romans. His was a short term as procurator (ca. AD 59–62), as he died in office. Apart from Luke's brief account of him in Acts 25–26, we know about Festus only from the writings of Josephus.

Flavius Josephus, *Jewish Antiquities* 20.8.9–11 §§182–96 (ca. AD 94)

When Porcius Festus was sent by Nero as successor to Felix, . . .

When Festus arrived in Judaea, it happened that Judaea was being devastated by the brigands, for the villages one and all were being set on fire and plundered. . . . Festus also sent a force of cavalry and infantry against the dupes of a certain impostor who had promised them salvation and rest from troubles, if they chose to follow him into the wilderness. The force which Festus dispatched destroyed both the deceiver himself and those who had followed him.

Flavius Josephus, *Jewish War* 2.14.1 §§271–75 (ca. AD 75)

Festus, who succeeded Felix as procurator, proceeded to attack the principal plague of the country: he captured large numbers of the brigands and put not a few to death.

14.4.1 Festus Decides to Examine Paul's Case (25:1–5)

Perhaps anxious to begin his procuratorship well, Festus is responsive to reasonable requests, but he balks at the request of the chief priests and Jewish leaders to have Paul transferred from Caesarea to Jerusalem. Luke explains that the Jews were still planning to assassinate Paul (25:3) without mentioning how suspicious Festus might be. Rather, Festus answers that he will hear the long-delayed case in Caesarea, where Paul is being held, and the Jewish leaders will need to press their charges against Paul there (25:4–5).

50. Ehrhardt calls Festus "the one honourable governor Rome ever sent to Judaea"; Arnold Ehrhardt, *The Acts of the Apostles: Ten Lectures* (Manchester: Manchester University Press, 1969), 117; cf. Witherington, *Acts*, 717.

51. Brian M. Rapske, "Roman Governors of Palestine," *DNTB*, 983–84.

14.4.2 Paul's Defense before Festus (25:6–12)

After spending eight or ten days in Jerusalem, Festus goes to Caesarea, and true to his word, he convenes a hearing the next day to examine Paul's case (25:6). The Jews who had come to Caesarea bring "serious charges against him" but are unable to prove any of their accusations (25:7). With the case about two years old now, it is not surprising that they have a difficult time being convincing.[52] Continuing in summary fashion, but now offering some dialog, Luke presents a single-sentence summary of Paul's defense: "I have done nothing wrong against the Jewish law or against the temple or against Caesar" (25:8). Luke similarly offers a single-sentence summary of Festus's remarks at the hearing. Still in his first month as procurator of Judea and desiring to curry favor with the general populace—and acquiescing to the earlier request of the Jews—Festus asks Paul if he is willing to be tried by him in Jerusalem regarding these charges (25:9).

After the single-sentence summaries of their exchange, Luke gives a more extensive recounting of Paul's answer to Festus (25:10–11). There is repetition here recalling Paul's Roman citizenship, reinforcing Paul's innocence, and revealing Paul's awareness of the Jewish plot against him. Paul sees through the time-wasting ruse of a change of location and answers Festus, "I am now standing before Caesar's court, where I ought to be tried" (25:10). Paul's patience with the Roman leadership has worn thin, especially in light of this potential threat to be handed over to those who want to murder him.[53] So Paul appeals to have his case reviewed by none other than ***Caesar*** (25:11). Festus confers with his council and delivers the closing statement of this hearing: "You have appealed to Caesar. To Caesar you will go!" (25:12).

14.4.3 Festus Seeks Advice from Agrippa II (25:13–22)

As was Felix before him, Festus is faced with a tricky situation as procurator of Judea. Keeping the peace in his assigned territory is of particular importance to Rome, but the Jews here are troubled by this Paul character, who, as far as Festus can tell, is not guilty. So, on the one hand, if he were to acquit and release Paul, the Jews would be displeased with their newly appointed governor. And yet, on the other hand, if he were to convict and execute an innocent Roman citizen, Rome could eventually second-guess his appointment. But Festus is able to avoid both of these difficult scenarios by simply allowing Paul's appeal to Caesar.[54] But his great sigh of relief is cut short when Festus recognizes another difficulty with this case: he is referring a case to Caesar that he does not understand.[55] So when King Herod Agrippa II and his sister Bernice come to pay

52. Marshall, *Acts*, 383–84.

53. Cf. F. F. Bruce, *The Book of Acts*, 2nd ed., NICNT (Grand Rapids: Eerdmans, 1988), 453.

54. Cf. Rowe, *World Upside Down*, 83.

55. Ibid.

their respects to the newly appointed neighboring official, Festus recruits the help of this "king of the Jews."[56]

Under Roman rule, the region of Palestine was divided into several provinces and governmental areas, with procurators like Festus over the province of Judea and rulers like Marcus Julius Agrippa II over nearby territories. As a descendant of Herod the Great, ***Herod Agrippa II*** was himself of Semitic heritage and had been ruling various parts of Palestine on behalf of Rome for more than a decade (since AD 48). Certainly, this Roman ruler—with the Herodian title of "king" and the authority from Rome to appoint Jewish high priests—would be able to give guidance regarding disputes with the Jewish elite.[57] So Festus explains his dilemma to King Agrippa II.

Luke is particularly detailed in his account, including repetition of quite a bit of the story in the mouth of Festus, "telling the story as it would appear from the Roman point of view."[58] As Festus's explanation goes on, it becomes apparent that he is willing to bend the truth to present himself in a more favorable light (25:14–20).[59] Even his report of Paul's appeal to Caesar is slanted and sounds like Festus was responsibly granting Paul's request to be held in protective custody (25:21).[60] Despite his slanted portrayal, Festus does seem to grasp—in at least a limited way—what the core issue is in Paul's case: it centers on a dispute "about a dead man named Jesus who Paul claimed was alive" (25:19). Indeed, by this point the unproven charge that Paul had desecrated the temple has been replaced by the dispute regarding Paul's insistence on the resurrection of Jesus (cf. 23:6; 24:21).[61] Herod Agrippa II is intrigued by what he has heard about Paul and wants to meet him (25:22).

14.5 PAUL'S HEARING BEFORE HEROD AGRIPPA II (ACTS 25:23–26:32)

Because Paul has not been charged with any crimes within the reach of Agrippa's jurisdiction, Paul's hearing before him is not a formal court defense.[62] Rather, Festus's request for advice becomes an opportunity for the curious Agrippa to hear Paul directly

56. Greek inscriptions refer to Agrippa II as "great king Agrippa, friend of Caesar, devout, and friend of the Romans"; *OGIS* §419; cf. Fitzmyer, *Acts*, 749.

57. For an account of Agrippa II sorting through difficulties with the Jews in cases that might involve appeals to Caesar, see Josephus, *Ant.* 20.8.11 §§189–96; cf. Rowe, *World Upside Down*, 83; Witherington, *Acts*, 718–19.

58. Marshall, *Acts*, 387. Ehrhardt suggests that "Luke fashioned this speech of Festus upon the official report to the Emperor, to which he probably had access on the journey to Rome"; Ehrhardt, *Acts Lectures*, 120. Witherington remarks, "I would not rule out a court informant"; Witherington, *Acts*, 728n397; cf. David John Williams, *Acts*, NIBCNT 5 (Peabody: Hendrickson, 1990), *Acts*, 410; Larkin, *Acts*, 348–49.

59. So also Richard J. Cassidy, *Society and Politics in the Acts of the Apostles*, 2nd ed. (Eugene, OR: Wipf & Stock, 2014), 110; cf. Witherington, *Acts*, 728–31.

60. Marshall, *Acts*, 389; Polhill, *Acts*, 493.

61. Marshall, *Acts*, 388.

62. Witherington, *Acts*, 734.

himself.[63] Moreover, it becomes an opportunity for Paul to share the gospel message with yet another audience (including a king, cf. 9:15). And for Luke, this becomes an opportunity to once again focus on the conversion story of Paul, decidedly a significant event in Luke's view of things.

The Territory Ruled for Rome by King Herod Agrippa II

Under Roman rule, the region of Palestine was divided into several provinces and governmental areas. With increasing responsibility as the years went by, Herod Agrippa II ruled as a client king for Rome over several of these territories.

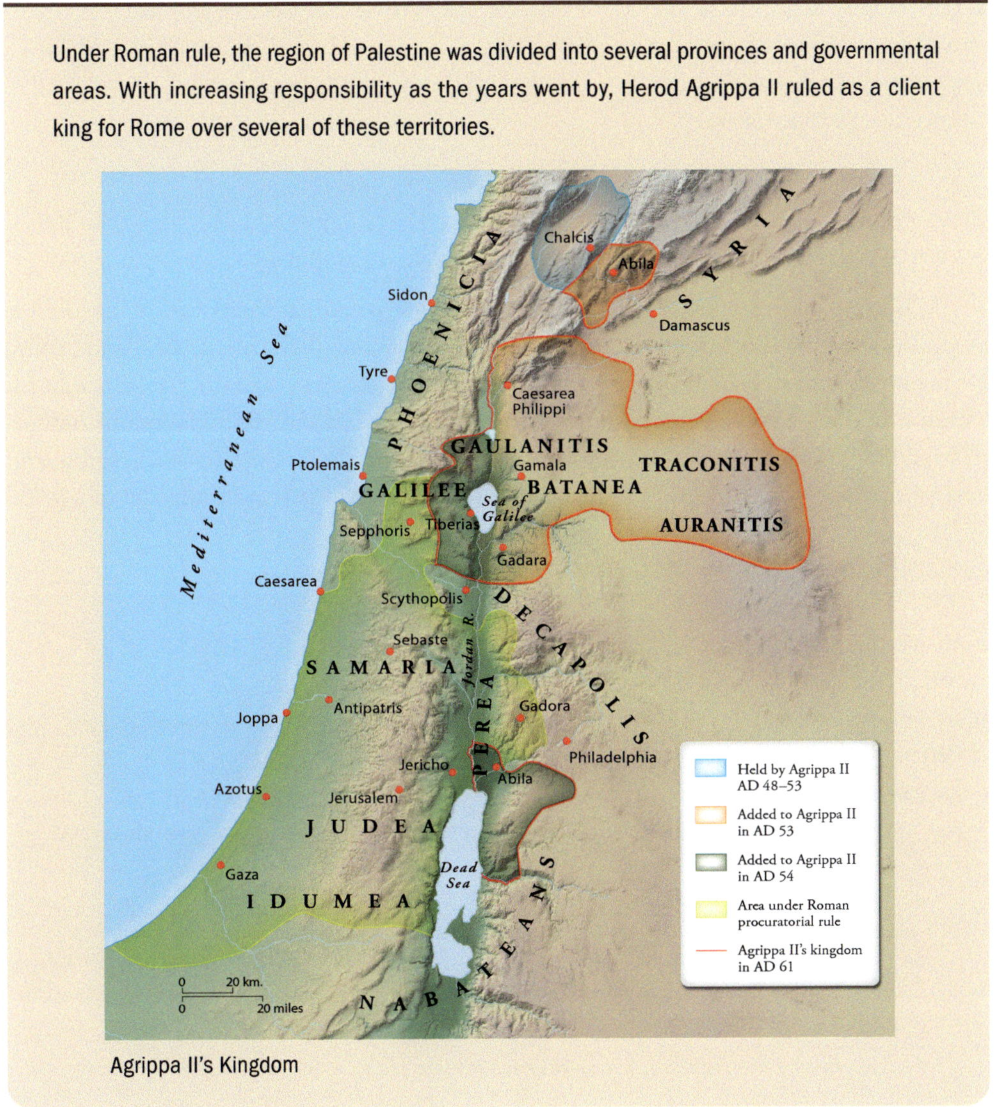

Agrippa II's Kingdom

63. David Williams suggests of Paul's hearing before Agrippa II that "above all, perhaps, it was an entertainment"; D. Williams, *Acts*, 415; cf. Ehrhardt comments about it being "a gala performance of Roman justice"; Ehrhardt, *Acts Lectures*, 120.

Jesus's Words Fulfilled in Paul's Experience

Luke 21:12–15

But before all this, they will seize you and persecute you. They will hand you over to synagogues and put you in prison, and you will be brought before kings and governors, and all on account of my name. And so you will bear testimony to me. But make up your mind not to worry beforehand how you will defend yourselves. For I will give you words and wisdom that none of your adversaries will be able to resist or contradict.

Acts 9:15–16

But the Lord said to Ananias, "Go! This man [Saul/Paul] is my chosen instrument to proclaim my name to the Gentiles and their kings and to the people of Israel. I will show him how much he must suffer for my name."

14.5.1 Festus Introduces the Case (25:23–27)

While not a formal trial, the meeting where Agrippa and ***Bernice*** hear Paul speak is treated as a formal affair of state.[64] After all, a nearby political ally would be a good thing for the novice procurator. So Festus treats his guests with pomp and circumstance fit for a king, complete with high-ranking military officers and prominent citizens of Caesarea in attendance (25:23). At Festus's command, Paul is brought into the audience room, and Festus introduces the case in much the way he had to Agrippa privately the day prior.

Roman Law on Appeals Including Letters of Report

In his *Digest*, the sixth century Justinian had collected and categorized various laws enacted in the Roman Empire over the previous centuries. Much of Book 49 contains laws related to judicial appeals and how to handle them. Marcian had recorded the requirements of "letters of report"—a.k.a. *apostoli*—that were to accompany those who made appeals to a higher court.

Marcian, *The Digest of Justinian* 49.6.1 (fifth century AD)

> After the lodging of the appeal, [the judge] from whom the appeal is made must send letters to the person who is to hear the appeal, whether the emperor or someone else; these letters are called letters of report or apostoli.

From *The Digest of Justinian*, trans. Alan Watson, 4 vols., rev. English-language ed. (Philadelphia: University of Pennsylvania Press, 1998).

---

64. Luke does not give a royal title to Agrippa's sister Bernice, but some ancient writers and inscriptions refer to her as "queen" (Josephus, *J.W.* 2.15.1 §§309–12; Suetonius, *Tit.* 7; Tacitus, *Hist.* 2.2; *CIG* 361). While she had been in several distinguished or royal marriages, upon the death of or separation from a husband, Bernice returned to live with her brother Agrippa II, which kept alive rumors of an incestuous relationship between them; see Douglas S. Huffman, "Bernice," *EDB*, 167; David C. Braund, "Bernice," *ABD* 1:677–78.

Now with a much larger audience, Festus briefly re-explains the situation, and once again his explanation seems a bit self-aggrandizing (25:24–25). What is new here is Festus's explicit rationale for consulting with Agrippa. Roman law required Festus to submit a report to Rome to accompany any prisoner who made an appeal to Caesar (see sidebar). In need of writing such an introduction to send with Paul to Caesar, Festus wants to get Agrippa's help understanding this confusing case (25:26–27). Thus, even if not a formal hearing, the meeting is official business.

14.5.2 Paul's Defense before Agrippa II (26:1–23)

After Festus's introduction of the issue at hand, Agrippa takes his cue and grants Paul permission to speak (26:1). With a respectful acknowledgment of Agrippa as a king acquainted with the concerns of Jewish living (26:2–3), Paul notes his own well-known Jewish commitments (26:4–5) and summarizes for Agrippa that he is on trial for his dedication to "what God has promised our ancestors" (26:6), a "hope" (three times in 26:6–7) that is the belief that God can raise the dead (26:8). He reveals that Jews are charging him as one who proclaims exactly what all Jews should believe in: the resurrection. He will return to this summary of the situation at the close of his defense.

"It Is Hard for You to Kick against the Goads" (Acts 26:14)

This Greek idiom refers to an instrument sometimes called a cattle prod, a stick with a sharp point used to make oxen (or other animals) move by poking them. The person with the goad can continue to poke the animal until it finally obeys. A metaphorical reference to the vanity of kicking against goads is used to mean something like *it is useless to fight against what you cannot change*. Metaphorical references to goads are also known to us in several ancient Greek writers. Here are three such examples.

Pindar, *Pythian Odes* 2.93–96 (ca. 470 BC)

> It helps to bear lightly the yoke one has taken upon one's neck, and kicking against the goad, you know, becomes a slippery path.

Aeschylus, *Agamemnon* 1623–24 (ca. 458 BC)

> You have eyes, and yet you don't see that? Don't kick against the goad, in case you hit it and get hurt.

Euripides, *Bacchae* 795 (ca. 405 BC)

> I would sacrifice to him rather than kick angrily against the goad, man against god.

But first Paul readily admits to having previously opposed this message himself. In his prior zeal he thoroughly persecuted followers of Jesus (26:9–11) until meeting the resurrected Jesus himself. And here we get a third account of Paul's Damascus road experience (26:12–23). Unsurprisingly, it is much like the other two accounts (Acts 9 and 22; see the sidebar earlier in this chapter with all three accounts side by side, and see the sidebar here contrasting the three accounts), with a few details left out (e.g., Paul's blindness and Ananias of Damascus) and a few new details revealed (e.g., in 26:14 that Paul was not alone in falling to the ground and the inclusion of a Greek idiom; see sidebar). As mentioned, there is thus no real conflict here between the accounts. The inclusion of new details in recounting the story—particularly details that might be of helpful interest to the new audience—is precisely how we recount events today as well.

Contrasting the Three Accounts of Paul's Conversion

Areas of Contrast	Acts 9:1-19	Acts 22:1-21	Acts 26:2-23
Perspective	third person	first person	first person
Language	narrated in Greek	given in Aramaic, recorded in Greek	given in Greek, recorded in Greek
Source	Luke learned from Paul	Luke learned from Paul	Luke present to hear
Audience	Theophilus (and Luke's other readers)	The Jewish mob in the temple	Herod Agrippa II and other Roman authorities
Paul's Prior Life	Summary: vv. 1-2	More detail: vv. 3-5	Most detail: vv. 4-11
Time of Event	–	noon	midday
Mention of Falling	Paul fell	Paul fell	Paul and companions fell
Others Hearing the Voice	companions hear the sound of the voice	companions don't understand the voice	the voice speaks in Aramaic
Jesus's Words	Saul, Saul, . . . – . . . I am Jesus	Saul, Saul, . . . – . . . I am Jesus	Saul, Saul, . . . Greek aphorism . . . I am Jesus
Instructions	Rise and enter the city	Rise and enter the city	Rise [city not mentioned]
Paul's Blindness	Paul is blinded and led by the hand into the city	Paul is blinded and led by the hand into the city	–
Ananias of Damascus	Ananias has a vision Ananias visits Saul Saul is healed	– Ananias visits Saul Saul is healed	– – –
Paul's Commission	Ananias references Paul's commission	Ananias references Paul's commission	Jesus's commissioning of Paul is explicitly recalled
Jerusalem Vision	–	Paul's vision in the temple	–
Account's Focus	***Confrontation of Paul***	***Change of Paul's life***	***Commission of Paul***
Exclusion of a detail is not the same thing as denying that detail. Thus, none of the differences of emphases or details included in the three accounts of Paul's conversion makes for necessary conflicting data between the accounts.			

One significant new feature in the story is the detail of Jesus commissioning Paul to be an ambassador of the gospel. In a sense, Luke has been keeping his readers in suspense on this. In the accounts of Paul's conversion in Acts 9 and 22 there is no specific mention of Jesus commissioning Paul on the Damascus road; that momentous detail is withheld until Acts 26.[65] This extra detail is fitting here, as the focus of Paul's testimony before Agrippa is his commissioning to testify to the resurrection. "So then, King Agrippa, I was not disobedient to the vision from heaven," says Paul, noting his continual preaching of the gospel (26:19–20). This continual preaching of the gospel with God's help is why some Jews have been upset with Paul (26:21–22a; i.e., not for breaking any Roman law). Then, returning to where he had begun his defense, Paul notes that the gospel is entirely in line with Jewish law: "I am saying nothing beyond what the prophets and Moses said would happen—that the Messiah would suffer and, as the first to rise from the dead, would bring the message of light to his own people and to the Gentiles" (26:22b–23).

A Rhetorical Outline for Paul's Defense Speech in Acts 26:2-29

As with Paul's other defense speeches, scholars suggest that Paul's speech in Acts 26 follows the general guidelines of ancient rhetorical handbooks. Here is one such outline for his speech in Acts 26 as Luke has summarized it.

***Exordium* (26:2-3)**

The introductory call to listen.

***Narratio* (26:4-18)**

The story of Paul's prior life and his call and commissioning by Jesus:

- devout upbringing and life (26:4-5)
- devotion to the Jewish hope of the resurrection (26:6-8)
- prior commitment to opposing the name of Jesus (26:9-11)
- encounter with Jesus (26:12-15)
- commissioning by Jesus (26:16-18)

***Probatio* or *Confirmatio* (26:19-28)**

The main proofs/confirmations (with interruptive dialog at vv. 24 and 28):

- Paul's changed way of life and ministry (26:19-20)
- Paul's willingness to suffer (26:21)
- God's help (26:22a)
- Paul's persistence in preaching the scriptural Messiah (26:22b-23)
- King Agrippa's knowledge of the prophets (26:25-27)

***Peroratio* (26:29)**

The conclusion and appeal for action.

Adapted and expanded from Jerome H. Neyrey, "The Forensic Defense Speech and Paul's Trial Speeches in Acts 22-26: Form and Function," in *Luke-Acts: New Perspectives from the Society of Biblical Literature Seminar*, ed. Charles H. Talbert (New York: Crossroad, 1984), 210-24; Witherington, *Acts*, 737-38; Schnabel, *Acts*, 985; cf. Robert F. O'Toole, *Acts 26: The Christological Climax of Paul's Defense (Ac 22:1-26:32)*, AnBib 78 (Rome: Biblical Institute Press, 1978), 27-34.

---

65. Hedrick, "Paul's Conversion/Call," 427; see also Larkin, *Acts*, 360; Witherington, *Acts*, 743–44; Bock, *Acts*, 717; and Schnabel, *Acts*, 1009. Alternatively, some scholars suggest that Ananias was the emissary of Paul's commissioning and that Acts 26 simply telescopes the report of the event; so Marshall, *Acts*, 395–96; Fitzmyer, *Acts*, 759; Peterson, *Acts*, 666.

From Witherington, *Acts*, 303, 309–10.

Without question, the story of Saul's "conversion" is one of the most important events, if not the most important event, that Luke records in Acts. . . . The importance of Saul's conversion in Luke's mind is shown by the fact that Luke gives the story no less than three full treatments, from three slightly different angles, with the later narratives in Acts 22 and 26 supplementing the basic third-person account in Acts 9. . . .

It cannot be stressed enough that these accounts are summaries and Luke has written them up in his own style and way. The accounts especially in Acts 22 and 26 appear to be condensations from speeches made by Paul himself. Paul would be presenting his story to two very different audiences here and wishing to convey some different aspects of the account to these two groups, but Luke is only summarizing these presentations at most.

. . . All three of these accounts go immediately back to Luke, who wrote them up, but in the case of Acts 9 and 22 ultimately they can go back to Paul, while Acts 26 is Luke's own firsthand account in all likelihood.

14.5.3 Paul and Festus and Agrippa II Interact (26:24–31)

Roman shackles. Todd Bolen/ BiblePlaces.com

At the climax of Paul's defense, mention of a suffering Messiah who rises from the dead leads Festus to interrupt with a declaration about Paul's mental stability (26:24). The claims that a messiah must suffer and die and that someone could rise from the dead would both be ludicrous to the Roman leader, so Festus concludes that Paul is raving mad.[66] Without ignoring it, Paul is undeterred by Festus's interruption. Politely denying the accusation—"I am not insane, most excellent Festus" (26:25a)—Paul presses the discussion back to the main issue of the truth of the gospel: "What I am saying is true and reasonable" (26:25b). Christian faith is not a matter of mere opinion; it is a matter of facts in history that can be grasped by reason.

Turning to Agrippa, Paul calls upon the king's expertise in these matters (the very reason Festus had asked for Agrippa's help!). Ruling in Palestine for more than a decade would put Agrippa in position to know quite a bit about the explosive growth of Christianity there (26:26).[67] From Agrippa's historical knowledge of Christian faith, Paul then moves to asking directly about Agrippa's own acknowledgement of scriptural teaching about the Messiah: "King Agrippa, do you believe the prophets? I know you do" (26:27). Agrippa is now in a theological dilemma analogous to Festus's political dilemma. That is, on the one hand, if Agrippa affirms belief in the Jewish prophets, he would feel pressure to declare faith in Jesus; but on the other hand, if Agrippa denies belief in the Jewish prophets, he could be denounced as a

66. Arnold, "Acts," 250.
67. Marshall, *Acts*, 399.

Declarations of Jesus's and Paul's Innocence

In Luke-Acts both Jesus and Paul are declared innocent several times by various people: Jesus four times and Paul five times. Some of the people rendering these judgments have similar roles in the stories of Jesus and Paul, so some scholars note a certain, albeit incomplete, parallelism.

Luke does not falsify the historical events by changing the order of the hearings (or the opinions in the Sanhedrin) to make the parallelism more consistent, but he does report the events that make for some kind of noticeable comparison.

Announced by	Jesus in Luke	Paul in Acts
Sanhedrin members	[found guilty in 22:66–71]	Pharisees in 23:9
Roman soldier	A centurion in 23:47	Claudius Lysias in 23:29
Roman governor	Pilate in 23:4	Felix in 25:18–19
Roman governor	Pilate again in 23:22	Festus in 25:25
Herodian ruler	Herod Antipas in 23:14–15	Herod Agrippa II in 26:32

disloyal Jew.[68] So Agrippa simply replies defensively with a deflecting rhetorical question: "Do you think that in such a short time you can persuade me to be a Christian?" (26:28). This judicial setting for the pejorative use of the label *Christian* (cf. 11:26) aligns with the earliest non-Christian uses of the term in the writings of Pliny, Tacitus, and Suetonius (see sidebar).[69] While we don't know what ultimately becomes of Agrippa II, here again we see that knowing about Christianity is not the same thing as becoming a believer.[70]

Wood engraving of Paul speaking to Festus King Agrippa II (1886).
benoitb/iStock.com

Even as he had transformed Festus's exclamation of insanity into a reasonable discussion about Scripture and evidence, now Paul transforms Agrippa's defensive retort into an opportunity to extend to the whole audience the invitation to believe in Jesus Christ. He is unembarrassed by his faith in Jesus and invites others to become a convert like him, "except for these chains" (26:29). Some have suggested that his remark about his chains

68. Ibid.

69. Christopher Mount, "Constructing Paul as a Christian in the Acts of the Apostles," pp. 141–52 in *Engaging Early Christian History: Reading Acts in the Second Century*, ed. Rubén R. Dupertuis and Todd C. Penner, BibleWorld (Durham: Acumen, 2013), 143.

70. Werner Marx has made an extended argument that Herod Agrippa II may have eventually become a Christian after a longer period of convincing, and then may have taken on the nickname Theophilus and become the dedicatee of Luke's NT writings (!); see Werner G. Marx, "A New Theophilus," *EvQ* 52 (1980): 17–26.

might have been said with some irony or even humor.[71] But Paul may be hoping his situation will become a test case of Christian innocence and protect other believers from such unnecessary ill treatment.[72] Indeed, when the hearing ends, the honored guests leave conversing with one another about Paul's innocence: "This man is not doing anything that deserves death or imprisonment" (26:31).

Ancient Non-Christian Authors Using the Term *Christian*

Several ancient authors use the term *Christian* in such a way that lends credence to the idea that the label was originally used as something of a pejorative term of disregard to distinguish followers of Jesus from other branches of belief in the God of the Jews.

Pliny the Younger, *Letters* 10.96–97 (ca. AD 112)

I have never been present at an examination of Christians. Consequently, I do not know the nature or the extent of the punishments usually meted out to them, nor the grounds for starting an investigation and how far it should be pressed. Nor am I at all sure whether any distinction should be made between them on the grounds of age, or if young people and adults should be treated alike; whether a pardon ought to be granted to anyone retracting his beliefs, or if he has once professed Christianity, he shall gain nothing by renouncing it; and whether it is the mere name of Christian which is punishable, even if innocent of crime, or rather the crimes associated with the name.

Tacitus, *Annals* 15.44 (ca. AD 117)

But neither human help, nor imperial munificence, nor all the modes of placating Heaven, could stifle scandal or dispel the belief that the fire had taken place by order. Therefore, to scotch the rumour, Nero substituted as culprits, and punished with the utmost refinements of cruelty, a class of men, loathed for their vices, whom the crowd styled Christians. Christus, the founder of the name, had undergone the death penalty in the reign of Tiberius, by sentence of the procurator Pontius Pilatus, and the pernicious superstition was checked for a moment, only to break out once more, not merely in Judaea, the home of the disease, but in the capital itself, where all things horrible or shameful in the world collect and find a vogue.

Suetonius, *Nero* 16.2 (ca. AD 121)

During his reign many abuses were severely punished and put down, and no fewer new laws were made: . . . Punishment was inflicted on the Christians, a class of men given to a new and mischievous superstition.

---

71. E.g., Schnabel, *Acts*, 1017; Richard N. Longenecker, "Acts," pp. 663–1102 in *Luke-Acts*, vol. 10 of *The Expositor's Bible Commentary*, ed. Tremper Longman III and David E. Garland, rev. ed. (Grand Rapids: Zondervan, 2007), 1079; Charles Stephen Conway Williams, *A Commentary on the Acts of the Apostles* (Edinburgh: Black, 1964; repr., HNTC, Peabody, MA: Hendrickson, 1988), 266.

72. Polhill, *Acts*, 509. Rapske remarks that Paul "makes it very clear that he wishes for his hearers the same faith that he has come to have, excepting . . . the great loss in honour and dignity which he has had to endure"; Rapske, *Paul in Roman Custody*, 309.

14.5.4 Summary Statement (26:32)

After concluding that Paul is innocent, Agrippa remarks to Festus, "This man could have been set free if he had not appealed to Caesar" (Acts 26:32). While Festus was legally able to acquit Paul of the charges and release him, Agrippa realizes the situation is a bit more complicated for Festus as the new procurator. It is not so much a legal matter as it is a matter of Festus's relationship with Caesar. While Festus would be happy to be rid of Paul as a prisoner, to acquit Paul despite his appeal to Caesar would be an offense to the emperor and bring Festus's procuratorship into question.[73] So, while he concludes that Paul is innocent, Agrippa does not counsel Festus to do anything other than send Paul on to Caesar.

Jesus-Paul Parallels in Luke 23 and Acts 25–26

Common Elements	Luke 23:1–25	Acts 25–26
Introduction to the episode	23:1	25:1
Hearing before a Roman procurator	23:2-5	25:2-12
Reasons to appear before a Herodian ruler	23:6-7	25:13-27
Hearing before a Herodian ruler	23:8-12	26:1-23
Dialogue	23:13-23	26:24-29
Conclusion to the episode	23:24-25	26:30-32

Adapted and simplified from the discussion in Robert F. O'Toole, *Acts 26: The Christological Climax of Paul's Defense (Ac 22:1–26:32)*, AnBib 78 (Rome: Biblical Institute Press, 1978), 22–24; cf. Keener, Acts, 4:3448–49.

Agrippa's final remark about Paul closes this section of Acts, even though, strictly speaking, it is not a summary statement like those at the close of each of the other sections. It is not even a narrative aside (as are the other summary statements); instead, it is a citation of one character addressing another within the story. Nevertheless, the statement made by King Agrippa II does summarize for the reader—in an authoritative way—the verdict of Paul's innocence.[74] Rather than summarize Paul's "journey" in prison, Acts 26:32 notes that Paul could have been set free (i.e., journeyed away) had he not appealed to Caesar. In this way, Acts 26:32 transitions the reader to the final section of the story of Acts, in which the innocent Paul journeys to Rome.

73. Sherwin-White, *Roman Society and Roman Law*, 65.
74. Cf. Marshall, *Acts*, 386.

The ruins of Herod Agrippa II's palace in Caesarea Philippi.

icksanglee/stock .adobe.com

14.6 CONCLUDING REMARKS

As it turns out, a rather sizable part of the story of Acts traces the ministry of Paul in prison in Jerusalem and Caesarea: almost six chapters (Acts 21:18–26:32). But this does not prevent Paul from continuing in his gospel ministry. Rather, in Luke's telling of the story, we find Paul adjusting his ministry strategy to match the different audiences he addresses.

Paul's Differing Strategies in Acts 21–26

Audience	Strategy in Sharing the Gospel
A Jewish mob in the temple	Paul speaks their language and tells the story of how his life was changed by meeting Jesus.
The unjust Jewish Sanhedrin	Paul focuses on the resurrection as the primary claim of the Christian (and Jewish) faith.
The harsh procurator Felix	Before the sitting Roman governor of the province, Paul makes a formal, point-by-point defense.
The vacillating procurator Festus	Recognizing that his audience had divided loyalties, Paul makes an appeal for a different venue.
The well-informed King Agrippa II, Festus, and other officials	Paul tells the story of his commissioning to spread the gospel and even presses his audience toward a decision.
While the gospel message of salvation through faith in Jesus Christ remains the same, Luke's account is instructive in demonstrating Paul's use of different strategies for sharing the gospel with differing audiences. We should likewise have a sensitivity to our audiences when sharing our faith.	

When faced with an angry Jewish mob in the Jerusalem temple, Paul speaks their language and tells the story of how his life changed. In his hearing before the unjust Sanhedrin, Paul focuses on the resurrection as the primary claim of the Christian (and Jewish) faith. In a more formal hearing before the Judean procurator Felix, Paul makes a formal, point-by-point defense. After two years of delays, when the next Judean procurator Festus toys with putting him in danger of Jewish assassination, Paul makes an official appeal to Caesar. And in a formal meeting before King Herod Agrippa II—a Roman official informed of both the Jewish faith and Christianity—Paul tells the story of his commissioning to spread the gospel and even presses the king toward a decision.

While the gospel message never changes, how Paul shares the gospel message is adjusted to communicate more effectively with the audience at hand. We have seen such audience sensitivity throughout Paul's ministry in Acts, and this strategy has continued even in his time of imprisonment. This is reminiscent of Paul's own claim in 1 Corinthians 9:22: "I have become all things to all people so that by all possible means I might save some." As we will see, Paul remains in custody for the last two chapters of Acts en route to Rome. But even then, Paul continues to spread the gospel message.

14.7 Key People, Places, and Terms

- Bernice
- Caesar
- Caesarea
- Claudius Lysias
- Drusilla
- Felix
- Festus
- flogging
- Fortress Antonia
- Herod Agrippa II
- high priest
- Jerusalem
- Nazarite vow
- Pharisees
- rhetoric
- Roman citizenship
- Sadducees
- Sanhedrin
- Sicarii
- Tarsus
- temple in Jerusalem
- terrorists/Assassins
- Tertullus

14.8 Questions for Review and Discussion

1. What were the various false rumors and false assumptions about Paul's identity and actions in Acts 21–22? In what ways did Paul respond to those falsehoods?
2. What is the significance of Luke providing three accounts of Paul's conversion experience on the road to Damascus (Acts 9, 22, and 26)? How are the differences between the three accounts to be accounted for?
3. How would you describe Paul's determination to stand for faith in Jesus as the true Jewish Messiah and Savior of the world?

4. Explain the difficult religious and political complications of Paul's situation for the Roman procurators hearing his case.
5. Even though Felix and Agrippa II appear to have understood the gospel message as Paul preached it, what factors were keeping them from accepting the gospel?
6. While the gospel message never changes, how Paul shares the gospel message is adjusted to communicate more effectively with the audience at hand. Describe his different strategies with his different audiences in Acts 21-26.

14.9 Optional Assignments

1. **Text Reflection Project**—*Relating the concepts discussed in this chapter to another biblical text.* Luke reports the conversion/call of Paul in Acts 9, and then he reports two times when Paul himself recounts his life-changing experience of meeting Jesus on the road to Damascus (Acts 22 and 26). Write a short paper comparing these three accounts, noting the similarities and differences. Are there any troubling differences between accounts? How might these differences be harmonized and accounted for?
2. **Interview Project**—*Inquiring of others their views concerning the concepts discussed in this chapter.* Interview at least three people who are committed Christians and ask them how they became believers in Jesus. Analyze the strategies that were effective in bringing them to faith, e.g., who responded to stories of change, to single-issue testimony, to point-by-point arguments, to authoritative appeals, etc. What does this suggest about being sensitive to our audience when sharing the gospel?
3. **Service-Learning Project**—*Applying the concepts discussed in this chapter in some form of service to others outside the class.* When Paul and his missionary team arrive in Jerusalem, he works out a service plan to demonstrate the unity he has with the Jewish believers in the city (see Acts 21:18-26). Think of some service project you can do to demonstrate your unity with other believers. After participating in that service project, write a short reflection paper on how your participation could be seen as a demonstration of Christian unity.
4. **Prayer Project**—*Talking with God about the concepts discussed in this chapter.* Make a list of people you know who have not yet responded to the gospel message with faith in Jesus Christ. See if you can group them into people types comparable to the zealous Jewish mob, the unjust Sanhedrin, selfish Felix, confused Festus, conflicted Agrippa II (or perhaps other types). Write a short reflection on how your understanding of these people might change the way you can pray for them.
5. **Testimony Project**—*Telling others about the concepts discussed in this chapter.* Examining the two times Paul recounts his Damascus road conversion experience (Acts 22 and 26) reveals that Paul—while remaining truthful in both accounts—tailored the telling of his story to fit the particular audience he was addressing. Write two versions of your experience of coming to faith in Jesus Christ: one for an audience

of people familiar with Christianity and one for people less familiar with Christianity. Be truthful in both versions, but (like Paul) be sensitive about the vocabulary you use and the kinds of details you focus on. Select someone to tell your story to and utilize the version that best fits the audience that person is in. Afterward, write up a single-page reflection on the experience: describe which version of your story you used and why, report what went well and what did not go so well, and reflect on how you might do it differently next time you have the opportunity to share your testimony.

14.10 Bibliography for Going Further

14.10.1 Paul's Final Jerusalem Visit

Stagg, Frank. "Paul's Final Mission to Jerusalem." Pages 259–78 in *With Steadfast Purpose: Essays on Acts in Honor of Henry Jackson Flanders, Jr.* Edited by Naymond H. Keathley. Waco: Baylor University Press, 1990.

White, Jefferson. "Paul's Judean Arrest and Trial (57–59 AD)." Pages 46–65 (chapter 4) in *Evidence & Paul's Journeys: An Historical Investigation into the Travels of the Apostle Paul.* Hilliard, OH: Parsagard, 2001.

14.10.2 Paul's Hearings in Acts 21–26

Cassidy, Richard J. *Society and Politics in the Acts of the Apostles.* 2nd ed. Eugene, OR: Wipf & Stock, 2014.

Neyrey, Jerome H. "The Forensic Defense Speech and Paul's Trial Speeches in Acts 22–26: Form and Function." Pages 210–24 in *Luke-Acts: New Perspectives from the Society of Biblical Literature Seminar.* Edited by Charles H. Talbert. New York: Crossroad, 1984.

O'Toole, Robert F. *Acts 26: The Christological Climax of Paul's Defense (Ac 22:1–26:32).* AnBib 78. Rome: Biblical Institute Press, 1978.

Rapske, Brian. *The Book of Acts and Paul in Roman Custody.* BAFCS 3. Grand Rapids: Eerdmans, 1994; Carlisle: Paternoster, 1994.

Skinner, Matthew L. *Locating Paul: Places of Custody as Narrative Settings in Acts 21–28.* AcBib 13. Atlanta: SBL Press, 2003.

Tajra, Harry W. *The Trial of St. Paul: A Juridical Exegesis of the Second Half of the Acts of the Apostles.* WUNT 2:35. Tübingen: Mohr Siebeck, 1989.

Veltman, Fred. "The Defense Speeches of Paul in Acts." Pages 243–56 in *Perspectives on Luke-Acts.* Edited by Charles H. Talbert. Perspectives in Religious Studies 5. Danville, VA: Association of Baptist Professors of Religion, 1978.

Winter, Bruce W. "Official Proceedings and the Forensic Speeches in Acts 24–26." Pages 305–36 in *The Book of Acts in its Ancient Literary Setting.* Edited by Bruce W. Winter and Andrew D. Clarke. BAFCS 1. Grand Rapids: Eerdmans, 1993; Carlisle: Paternoster, 1993.

14.10.3 Three Accounts of Paul's Conversion

Hedrick, Charles W. "Paul's Conversion/Call: A Comparative Analysis of the Three Reports in Acts." *JBL* 100.3 (1981): 415–32.

Lilly, Joseph L. "The Conversion of Saint Paul: The Validity of His Testimony to the Resurrection of Jesus Christ." *CBQ* 6.2 (1944): 180–204.

Marguerat, Daniel. "Saul's Conversion (Acts 9; 22; 26)." Pages 179–204 (chapter 9) in *The First Christian Historian: Writing the 'Acts of the Apostles.'* Translated by Ken McKinney, Gregory J. Laughery and Richard Bauckham. SNTSMS 121. Cambridge: Cambridge University Press, 2002.

Stanley, David Michael. "Paul's Conversion in Acts: Why Three Accounts?" *CBQ* 15.3 (1953): 315–38.

14.10.4 Roman Citizenship and Paul

Adams, Sean A. "Paul the Roman Citizen: Roman Citizenship in the Ancient World and Its Importance for Understanding Acts 22:22–29." Pages 309–26 in *Paul: Jew, Greek, and Roman*. Edited by Stanley E. Porter. Pauline Studies 5. Leiden: Brill, 2008.

Rapske, Brian M. "Citizenship, Roman." *DNTB*, 215–18.

Reasoner, Mark. "Citizenship, Roman and Heavenly." *DPL*, 139–41.

Sherwin-White, A. N. *The Roman Citizenship*. 2nd ed. Oxford: Clarendon, 1973.

———. *Roman Society and Roman Law in the New Testament*. Oxford: Oxford University Press, 1963. Repr., Grand Rapids: Baker, 1992.

14.10.5 Felix

Blaiklock, Edward M. "Felix." *ZEB* 2:565–66.

Braund, David C. "Felix." *ABD* 2:783.

Rapske, Brian M. "Roman Governors of Palestine." *DNTB*, 978–84.

Schürer, Emil. *HJP* 1:459–66.

14.10.6 Festus

Blaiklock, Edward M. "Festus, Porcius." *ZEB* 2:570–71.

Green, Joel B. "Festus, Porcius." *ABD* 2:794–95.

Schürer, Emil. *HJP* 1:465–68.

14.10.7 Herod Agrippa II

Busch, Fritz-Otto. "Herod Agrippa II." Pages 146–54 (chapter 5) in *The Five Herods*. Translated by E. W. Dickes. London: Robert Hale, 1958.

Chilton, Bruce. "Bereniké and Agrippa II." Pages 205–34 (chapter 8) in *The Herods: Murder, Politics, and the Art of Succession*. Minneapolis: Fortress, 2021.

Hoehner, Harold. W. "Herod." *ZEB* 3:131–50.

Jacobson, David. *Agrippa II: The Last of the Herods*. Routledge Ancient Biographies. New York: Routledge, 2019.

Kokkinos, Nikos. *The Herodian Dynasty: Origins, Role in Society and Eclipse*. JSPSup 30. Sheffield: Sheffield Academic, 1998.

Perowne, Stewart H. *The Later Herods: The Political Background of the New Testament*. London: Hodder & Stoughton, 1958; New York: Abingdon, 1958.

renato/stock.adobe.com

Chapter Goals

After reading this chapter, you should be able to:

- Offer an explanation for Luke's extended focus on Paul's journey to Rome.
- Identify evidence of the sovereign God at work in the midst of the various difficult circumstances of Paul's life.
- Evaluate Paul's interventions during the hardships faced on the journey.
- Offer an explanation for the abruptness of how Acts ends.
- Explain the inclusiveness of the gospel message that sees salvation exclusively through faith in Jesus Christ.

Chapter Overview

15.1 The Journey to Rome Begins (Acts 27:1–12)
15.2 Storm at Sea (Acts 27:13–38)
15.3 Shipwreck on Malta and Finally Getting to Rome (Acts 27:39–28:15)
15.4 Paul Ministers Under House Arrest in Rome (Acts 28:16–31)
15.5 Concluding Remarks
15.6 Key People, Places, and Terms
15.7 Questions for Review and Discussion
15.8 Optional Assignments
15.9 Bibliography for Going Further

Key Verses

When it was decided that we would sail for Italy, Paul and some other prisoners were handed over to a centurion named Julius, who belonged to the Imperial Regiment. We boarded a ship from Adramyttium about to sail for ports along the coast of the province of Asia, and we put out to sea. (Acts 27:1–2)

Men, you should have taken my advice not to sail from Crete; then you would have spared yourselves this damage and loss. But now I urge you to keep up your courage, because not one of you will be lost; only the ship will be destroyed. Last night an angel of the God to whom I belong and whom I serve stood beside me and said, "Do not be afraid, Paul. You must stand trial before Caesar; and God has graciously given you the lives of all who sail with you." So keep up your courage, men, for I have faith in God that it will happen just as he told me. Nevertheless, we must run aground on some island. (Acts 27:21–26)

My brothers, although I have done nothing against our people or against the customs of our ancestors, I was arrested in Jerusalem and handed over to the Romans. They examined me and wanted to release me, because I was not guilty of any crime deserving death. The Jews objected, so I was compelled to make an appeal to Caesar. I certainly did not intend to bring any charge against my own people. For this reason I have asked to see you and talk with you. It is because of the hope of Israel that I am bound with this chain. (Acts 28:17–20)

Therefore I want you to know that God's salvation has been sent to the Gentiles, and they will listen! (Acts 28:28)

Closing Summary Statement

For two whole years Paul stayed there in his own rented house and welcomed all who came to see him. He proclaimed the kingdom of God and taught about the Lord Jesus Christ—with all boldness and without hindrance! (Acts 28:30–31)

Itinerary of Paul's Trip to Rome, Acts 27:1–28:31 (ca. 59–60)

City [Place]	Province (Region)	Reference
Caesarea	Judea (Palestine)	Acts 27:1
Sidon	Phoenicia	Acts 27:3
Myra	Lycia	Acts 27:5
[off Cnidus]	Asia	Acts 27:7a
[lee of Crete]	Crete	Acts 27:7b
Fair Havens	Crete	Acts 27:8
[lee of Cauda]	Crete	Acts 27:16
[open sea]	[Mediterranean Sea]	Acts 27:17–26

City [Place]	Province (Region)	Reference
[beach]	Malta	Acts 27:27–28:1
Syracuse	Sicily	Acts 28:12
Rhegium	Lucania	Acts 28:13a
Puteoli	Latium	Acts 28:13b
Forum of Appius	Latium	Acts 28:15a
Three Taverns	Latium	Acts 28:15b
Rome	Latium	Acts 28:16

INTRODUCTION

Paul has been desiring to go to Rome for some time. As he was preparing to leave Ephesus to go to Jerusalem by way of Macedonia and Achaia, he said, "After I have been there, . . . I must visit Rome also" (Acts 19:21; cf. Rom 15:23–28). Furthermore, Jesus has assured Paul that he would make it to Rome: "Take courage! As you have testified about me in Jerusalem, so you must also testify in Rome" (Acts 23:11). Of course, going to Rome as a prisoner was likely not Paul's original plan. Nevertheless, it turns out that Paul's appeal to Caesar would be the means God uses to bring him to Rome.

Paul's Journey to Rome (ca. AD 59–60)

Luke's narration of Paul's journey to Rome is surprisingly long and detailed (and even uses nautical language). Scholars have proposed various rationales for this prolonged attention to the voyage: following ancient literary customs for sea voyage accounts,[1] offering readers some "narrative space" to relax between Paul's courtroom dramas and the anticipated drama in Rome,[2] drawing readers into experiencing the suspense of the story,[3] and paralleling Paul's suffering with Jesus's suffering at the end of the Gospel of Luke.[4] We cannot entirely dismiss the insights of such literary theories, but we must remember that Luke's literary artistry serves his historical and theological interests. Thus, it seems best to understand the space given to the voyage to Rome as Luke's way of emphasizing the historical realities of Paul's role as one of God's instruments in spreading the gospel. The details of the extended narrative demonstrate God's sovereign and gracious control for the fulfillment of his promises.[5] So, too, as he closes the story of Acts, Luke would have his readers consider their service to the gospel in their life voyages.

On Luke's Descriptions of Sailing in Acts

From Linford Stutzman, *With Paul at Sea: Learning from the Apostle Who Took the Gospel from Land to Sea* (Eugene, OR: Cascade, 2012), xii.

> In Scripture, indeed among sacred texts of any kind, Acts is unique. Acts is probably the only ancient sacred text that provides adequate information for voyage planning. It is, I discovered, one of the best descriptive documents in existence of sailing in the Mediterranean during the first century. Unlike Homer's *Odyssey*, real ports, thirty-seven in all, are named in Acts. The conditions of weather and descriptions of sailing are precise. Names and dates match the archaeological and historical evidence. Acts is a useful text, not only for preparing a sermon, but for planning a voyage on the Mediterranean.

In 2004–2005 Linford Stutzman and his wife, Janet, spent fifteen months sailing the Mediterranean on a thirty-three-foot sailboat visiting all the cities and harbors to which Paul had traveled as mentioned in Acts. Their adventures are described in Linford Stutzman, *Sailing Acts: Following an Ancient Voyage* (Intercourse, PA: Good Books, 2006).

1. E.g., Martin Dibelius, *The Book of Acts: Form, Style, and Theology*, ed. K. C. Hanson, Fortress Classics in Biblical Studies (Minneapolis: Fortress, 2004), 13; Ernst Haenchen, *The Acts of the Apostles: A Commentary*, trans. and ed. Bernard Noble, Gerald Shinn, Hugh Anderson, and R. McLeod Wilson (Philadelphia: Westminster, 1971), 710–11. But see the corrective of Susan Marie Praeder, "Acts 27:1–28:16: Sea Voyages in Ancient Literature and the Theology of Luke-Acts," *CBQ* 46 (1984): 694; cf. Troy M. Troftgruben, "Slow Sailing in Acts: Suspense in the Final Sea Journey (Acts 27:1–28:15)," *JBL* 136 (2017): 949–68, esp. 958–59.

2. E.g., Luke Timothy Johnson, *The Acts of the Apostles*, SP 5 (Collegeville: Liturgical for Michael Glazier, 1992), 458.

3. E.g., Troftgruben, "Slow Sailing in Acts: Suspense in the Final Sea Journey," 949–68.

4. E.g., Michael D. Goulder, *Type and History in Acts* (London: SPCK, 1964), 34–41.

5. Eckhard J. Schnabel, *Acts*, ZECNT (Grand Rapids: Zondervan, 2012), 1031; cf. Johnson, *Acts*, 458; I. Howard Marshall, *The Acts of the Apostles: An Introduction and Commentary*, TNTC (Grand Rapids: Eerdmans, 1980), 401–3; David G. Peterson, *The Acts of the Apostles*, Pillar New Testament Commentary (Grand Rapids: Eerdmans, 2009), 678.

15.1 THE JOURNEY TO ROME BEGINS (ACTS 27:1–12)

In Paul's trip to Rome, Luke's presence on the voyage becomes more noticeable with the reappearance of the pronoun "we" and the last of the ***"we sections"*** (27:1–28:16). Luke has been nearby ever since the missionary team arrived in Jerusalem at the close of the third missionary journey (cf. 21:17–18), but he had not been arrested with Paul. Now that Paul is being transported to Rome on a nongovernment ship, however, Luke and others from the missionary team can join in the journey. The detail with which Luke recounts the voyage gives further testimony to his presence.[6]

15.1.1 SAILING FROM CAESAREA TO MYRA (27:1–5)

Besides himself with "we," Luke specifically mentions "***Aristarchus***, a Macedonian from Thessalonica" traveling with the group (27:2b, emphasis added; cf. 19:29; 20:4).[7] The Roman centurion in charge of bringing Paul and other prisoners to Rome is also named: "***Julius***, who belonged to the Imperial Regiment" (27:1, emphasis added; see sidebar on Roman military structure). The specificity of the centurion's name and cohort anticipates the significance of Julius to the story. Julius would have the authority to requisition transit on a ship for himself and his party as well as provisions.[8] The ancient world did not have passenger ships,[9] so Julius secures passage on a commercial vessel from ***Adramyttium***, a seaport in the northwest of Asia Minor (27:2a). Because ships like this had the primary purpose of transporting cargo, passengers needed to provide their own food and amenities.[10] Paul's friends were likely allowed to accompany him at their own expense to care for his practical needs, and this would be a relief to the soldiers in charge of Paul.[11]

The day after leaving ***Caesarea***, the ship lands at Sidon, a large seaport for Phoenicia just to the north, and the Roman centurion allows Paul to visit friends there who can care for his needs (27:3).[12] This kindness of Julius reflects his deference to Paul's higher

6. A. H. N. Green-Armytage, *A Portrait of St. Luke* (London: Burns and Oates, 1955; Chicago Henry Regnery, 1955), 61. See also Colin J. Hemer, "First Person Narrative in Acts 27–28," *TynBul* 36 (1985): 79–109.

7. Interestingly, Luke and Aristarchus are mentioned together twice in Paul's letters (Col 4:10–14; Phlm 24).

8. Brian M. Rapske, "Acts, Travel, and Shipwreck," pp. 1–47 in *The Book of Acts in Its Graeco-Roman Setting*, ed. David W. J. Gill and Conrad Gempf. BAFCS 2 (Grand Rapids: Eerdmans, 1994; Carlisle: Paternoster, 1994), 28.

9. Lionel Casson, *The Ancient Mariners: Seafarers and Sea Fighters of the Mediterranean in Ancient Times*, 2nd ed. (Princeton: Princeton University Press, 1991), 209.

10. John E. Stambaugh and David L. Balch, *The New Testament in Its Social Environment*, LEC (Philadelphia: Westminster, 1986), 39.

11. Craig S. Keener, *Acts: An Exegetical Commentary*, 4 vols. (Grand Rapids: Baker Academic, 2012–2015), 4:3574; cf. Brian Rapske, *The Book of Acts and Paul in Roman Custody*, BAFCS 3 (Grand Rapids: Eerdmans, 1994; Carlisle: Paternoster, 1994), 272–73, 378; Ben Witherington III, *The Acts of the Apostles: A Socio-Rhetorical Commentary* (Grand Rapids: Eerdmans, 1998; Carlisle: Paternoster, 1998), 760–61.

12. The "friends" of Paul in Sidon are probably Christians, as Paul had ministered in Phoenicia in Acts 15:3 and may have passed through there on his earlier trip to Jerusalem in 11:29–30 and 12:25. On friendship in ancient contexts, see Craig S. Keener, "Friendship," *DNTB*, 380–88; and the essays in John T. Fitzgerald, ed., *Greco-Roman Perspectives on Friendship*, SBLRBS 34 (Atlanta: Scholars Press, 1997).

Imperial Roman Military Structure

Military Unit	Standard Number of Soldiers	Expanded Number of Soldiers
Contubernium	8	N/A
Century	80 (ten contubernia)	160 (twenty contubernia)
Cohort (or regiment)	480 (six centuries)	960 (six doubled centuries = a doubled cohort)
Legion	4,800 (ten cohorts)	5,280 (a doubled "first cohort" + nine standard cohorts)

Select Bibliography

John Brian Campbell, *The Roman Army, 31 BC–AD 337: A Source Book* (London: Routledge, 1994).

Jonathan Roth, "The Size and Organization of the Roman Imperial Legion," *Historia* 43.3 (1994): 346–62.

Pat Southern, *The Roman Army: A Social and Institutional History* (New York: Oxford University Press, 2007).

Glen L. Thompson, "Roman Military," *DNTB*, 991–95.

Adramyttium

Greek coins found at Adramyttium

ZRadovan/BibleLandPictures.com

- An ancient seaport city in the gulf of the same name in the region of Mysia in the northwest of Asia Minor at the base of Mount Ida.
- May have been founded as early as the sixth century BC.
- The importance of its harbor is evidenced by ancient coinage from the East discovered there.
- The worship of Castor and Pollux originated at Adramyttium.
- Home of the orator Xenocles, the tutor of Cicero.
- Abandoned ca. AD 1100 after it was plundered by Turkish pirates.

Select Bibliography

"Adramyttium," *EDB*, 22.

Howard G. Andersen, "Adramyttium," *ZEB* 1:74.

John D. Wineland, "Adramyttium," *ABD* 1:80.

status as a Roman citizen, perhaps even a recognition that Paul was not yet convicted of any crimes (unlike the other prisoners on the trip).[13] Continuing northward, even in the best of summer weather, it was usual for Rome-bound ships to sail around Cyprus before turning west to sail along the southern coast of Asia Minor to Rhodes (27:4).[14] Of the stops along the coast, Luke names only ***Myra***, a seaport of the province of Lycia (27:5), reachable in two weeks' time.[15]

Sidon

- A famous harbor city of Phoenicia (modern Lebanon) to the north of Israel.
- Its double harbor had small islands as breakwaters and included an island anchorage as well.
- The first biblical mention of this locale is Genesis 10:19.
- Mentioned in Egyptian, Hittite, Ugaritic, and Assyrian records dating back to the fourteenth century BC.
- Significant industries in ancient times included cedar lumber and the production of a purple dye made from murex shells.
- In the New Testament, often paired with the nearby Phoenician coastal city of Tyre, twenty-five miles to the south (e.g., Matt 11:21–22; 15:21; Mark 3:8; 7:31; Luke 6:17; 10:13–14; Acts 12:20).

Select Bibliography

Isam Ali Khalifeh, "Sidon," *OEANE* 5:38–41.
Bastiaan Van Elderen, "Sidon," *ZEB* 5:505–506.

Myra

- A metropolitan city in the southwest of Asia Minor (modern Turkey).
- The capital of the Roman province of Lycia.
- Located about three miles from the Mediterranean Sea, it had a port city called Andriace and was an important trading center.
- Of the city's products, it is most famed for rue, an evergreen shrub from which an oil was pressed and a wine flavoring extracted.
- Nicolaus, a Christian bishop in Myra in the early fourth century AD, was later declared a saint; he was the patron saint of children, sailors, and merchants, and of Greece and of Russia before becoming revered as Santa Claus.

Select Bibliography

Douglas Low, "Myra," *EDB*, 930.
Robert C. Stone, "Myra," *ZEB* 4:357.
Edwin M. Yamauchi, "Myra," *ABD* 4:939–40.

13. Witherington, *Acts*, 759; cf. John Clayton Lentz Jr., *Luke's Portrait of Paul*, SNTSMS 77 (Cambridge: Cambridge University Press, 1993), 15, 115; cf. Keener, *Acts*, 4:3577–78; Rapske, *Paul in Roman Custody*, 378.

14. Casson, *The Ancient Mariners*, 208–9.

15. The Western text of Acts 27:5 inserts "for fifteen days"; see Roger L. Omanson, *A Textual Guide to the Greek New Testament: An Adaptation of Bruce M. Metzger's* Textual Commentary *for the Needs of Translators* (Stuttgart: German Bible Society, 2006), 287; cf. Witherington, *Acts*, 761n39; David John Williams, *Acts*, NIBCNT 5 (Peabody: Hendrickson, 1990), 428; Clinton E. Arnold, "Acts," vol. 2B of *ZIBBCNT*, ed. Clinton E. Arnold (Grand Rapids: Zondervan, 2002), 253.

15.1.2 Slow Going from Myra to Crete (27:6–12)

When the Adramyttian ship arrives at the metropolis of Myra (perhaps headed northward toward its home port rather than any further toward Rome), Julius finds an Alexandrian ship headed for Italy and moves the group to that vessel (27:6; cf. 27:38) (see sidebar on grain ships). The Alexandria-Rome grain fleet was known for its speedy efficiency and serviceability for would-be passengers, and Myra was a regular stop for such ships.[16] Nevertheless, moving westward at this time of year made it difficult for the ship to reach Cnidus, a seaport at the western end of a forty-mile peninsula jutting out into the Mediterranean Sea between the islands of Kos and Rhodes. Here westbound ships were forced to detour south around the island of ***Crete***, where they could gain some shielding from the autumn northwestern winds (27:7).[17] Sailing slowly along the southern coast of Crete, the ship eventually comes to the port of Fair Havens near the town of Lasea (27:8). In good weather, eastward sailing from Rome to Alexandria could be accomplished in less than two weeks; with contrary winds, however, the westward voyage from Alexandria to Rome could take up to forty-five days.[18] Luke's repeated comments on the various hardships of the travel up to this point—"slow headway for many days" (27:7a), "had difficulty" (27:7b), "with difficulty" (27:8), and "become dangerous" (27:9)—bring readers to expect further difficulties as the story unfolds.[19]

The Ancient Navigational Year on the Mediterranean Sea

Approximate Dates	General Travel Expectations
May 27-September 14	Optimal sea travel
September 14-November 11	Risky sea travel
November 11-March 10	Extremely dangerous sea travel
March 10-May 26	Risky sea travel

Adapted from information in Rapske, "Acts, Travel, and Shipwreck," 22; cf. Lionel Casson, *Ships and Seamanship in the Ancient World* (Princeton: Princeton University Press, 1971), 270–73.

16. Lionel Casson, *Travel in the Ancient World* (London: George Allen & Unwin, 1974; Baltimore: Johns Hopkins University Press, 1996), 158; idem, *The Ancient Mariners*, 209; and Colin J. Hemer, *The Book of Acts in the Setting of Hellenistic History*, ed. Conrad H. Gempf, WUNT 49 (Tübingen: Mohr Siebeck, 1989; repr., Winona Lake, IN: Eisenbrauns, 1990), 134.

17. Mark J. Olson, "Cnidus," *ABD* 1:1066–67; cf. Casson, *The Ancient Mariners*, 211.

18. See Casson, *The Ancient Mariners*, 207–8; and Rainer Riesner, *Paul's Early Period: Chronology, Mission Strategy, Theology*, trans. Doug Stott (Grand Rapids: Eerdmans, 1998), 315; cf. Stambaugh and Balch, *The New Testament in Its Social Environment*, 39.

19. Praeder, "Acts 27:1–28:16: Sea Voyages," 683–706, esp. 686.

Crete

- The largest of the Greek islands, about 170 miles southeast of Athens and forms the southern boundary of the Aegean Sea.
- About 160 miles long and varies between 7 and 35 miles wide.
- Mountainous, fertile, and forested in the first century but today is mostly rocky and barren.
- Evidences Neolithic agrarian society in its eastern plains, developed the influential Minoan civilization in ca. 3000 BC, was rather quiet during the classical Greek period but a source of mercenary soldiers, and became part of the Roman Empire in 67 BC.
- Jews from Crete were in Jerusalem during the Pentecost holiday when the Spirit was poured out (Acts 2:11).
- The Alexandrian grain ship taking Paul to Rome sailed along its southern coast (Acts 27:7–8).
- It may have been during his Acts 27 visit that Paul appointed Titus (unmentioned in Acts) to oversee the Cretan church (Titus 1:5); but this may have occurred on a later trip after Paul's release from his first Roman imprisonment (i.e., after Acts).
- Cretans had a reputation in ancient times for being depraved people: Paul quotes the poet Epimenides (ca. 600 BC): "Cretans are always liars, evil brutes, lazy gluttons" (Titus 1:12).

Select Bibliography

Jane E. Francis and Anna Kouremenos, eds., *Roman Crete: New Perspectives* (Philadelphia: Oxbow, 2016).
Chris Moore, *A History of Crete* (London: Haus, 2019).
Arthur A. Rupprecht, "Crete," *ZEB* 1:1092.

Grain Ships Sailing from Egypt to Italy

At Myra, Paul, Aristarchus, and Luke board a grain ship sailing from Alexandria to Italy (Acts 27:6, 38). The second-century writer Lucian describes a huge Roman ship *Isis*, which transported grain from Egypt to Italy during the Roman Empire of his day. It could hold about twelve thousand tons of grain.

Lucian, *The Ship, or the Wishes* 5–6 (ca. AD 170–179)

> Incidentally, what a huge ship! A hundred and twenty cubits long [180 feet], the ship-wright said, and well over a quarter as wide, and from deck to bottom, where it is deepest, in the bilge, twenty-nine [44 feet]. Then, what a tall mast, what a yard to carry! What a fore-stay to hold it up! How gently the poop curves up, with a little golden goose below! And correspondingly at the opposite end, the prow juts right out in front, with figures of the goddess, Isis, after whom the ship is named, on either side. And the other decorations, the paintings and the topsail blazing like fire, anchors in front of them, and capstans and windlasses, and the cabins on the poop—all very wonderful to me. You could put the number of sailors at an army of soldiers. She was said to carry corn enough to feed all Attica for a year. And all this a little old man, a wee fellow, has kept from harm by turning the huge rudders with a tiny tiller.

Warning a Friend about Sea Voyages

In a letter dated November 27 of 50 BC, Cicero warns his friend Tiro about the dangers of sea travel with sailors who might take undesirable risks to increase their profits.

Cicero, *Letters to Friends* 16.9.4 §127

> The only other thing is to ask and beg you not to take ship without proper care. Sailors with their money to make are apt to be in a hurry. Take no chances, my dear Tiro. You have a long, difficult voyage ahead. If possible, go with Mescinius—he is not one to take chances with the sea. If not, then with some man of position whom the skipper will respect. If you take every care about this and render yourself up to me safe and sound, I shall have all I ever want of you.

An Ancient Description of the Mediterranean Navigational Year

Publius (or Flavius) Vegetius Renatus, known simply as Vegetius, was a late fourth-century or early fifth-century Latin writer of the later Roman Empire. Little is known of him except for what he reveals of himself in his two extant works. One of these books, *Epitoma rei militaris* (i.e., *Epitome of Military Science*), gives a description of the months in which it is safe to sail on the Mediterranean Sea.

Vegetius, *Epitoma rei militaris*, 4.39

> For the violence and roughness of the sea do not permit navigation all the year round, but some months are very suitable, some are doubtful, and the rest are impossible for fleets by a law of nature. When Pachon has run its course, that is, after the rising of the Pleiades, from six days before the Kalends of June (i.e., 27th May) until the rising of Arcturus, that is, eighteen days before the Kalends of October (i.e., 14th September), navigation is deemed safe, because thanks to the summer the roughness of the sea is lessened. After this date until three days before the Ides of November (i.e., 11th November) navigation is doubtful and more exposed to danger, . . . So from three days before the Ides of November (i.e., 11th November) until six days before the Ides of March (i.e., 10th March) the seas are closed. The minimal daylight and long nights, dense cloud-cover, foggy air, and violence of winds doubled by rain and snow not only keep fleets from the sea but also traffic from making journeys by land. But after the birthday, so to speak, of navigation which is celebrated with annual games and public spectacles in many cities, it is still perilous to venture upon the sea right up to the Ides of May (i.e., 15th May) by reason of very many stars and the season of the year itself—not that the activities of merchants cease, but greater caution should be shown when an army takes to the sea in warships than when the enterprising are in a hurry for their private profits.

From Flavius Vegetius Renatus, *Vegetius: Epitome of Military Science*, trans. and ed. N. P. Milner (Liverpool: Liverpool University Press, 1996), 146–47.

Evidence of Paul's Sailing Experience

Some have calculated that Paul's ten or more sea voyages in Acts covered about three thousand miles over three decades of ministry (e.g., Witherington, *Acts*, 754; Haenchen, *Acts*, 702-703). By Paul's own admission, some of his experiences were unpleasant. His letters also indicate his awareness of the need to spend winters in safe places rather than risk sea travel (1 Cor 16:6; Titus 3:12; 2 Tim 4:21; cf. Acts 20:2-3).

1 Corinthians 16:5-6—"After I go through Macedonia, I will come to you—for I will be going through Macedonia. Perhaps I will stay with you for a while, or even spend the winter, so that you can help me on my journey, wherever I go."

2 Corinthians 11:25-26—"Three times I was beaten with rods, once I was pelted with stones, three times I was shipwrecked, I spent a night and a day in the open sea, I have been constantly on the move."

Titus 3:12—"As soon as I send Artemas or Tychicus to you, do your best to come to me at Nicopolis, because I have decided to winter there."

2 Timothy 4:21—"Do your best to get here before winter."

Fair Havens

- A bay near the town of Lasea on the southern coast of the Mediterranean island of Crete, where the ship carrying Paul en route to Rome docked temporarily (Acts 27:8).
- Now identified with Kalous Limionas, a bay east of the modern Cape Littinos.
- The harbor opens toward the east with two small islands to the southwest.
- Despite its name, not an ideal place for a ship to be docked for the winter due to strong winds from the east and southeast (Acts 27:12-15).

Select Bibliography

Arthur A. Rupprecht, "Fair Havens," *ZEB* 2:514.
John D. Wineland, "Fair Havens," *ABD* 2:744.

Because of this problematic progress, the ship has arrived at Fair Havens after the Day of Atonement (i.e., "the Fast") and the storm season has already begun (27:9). The Day of Atonement fell late in AD 59: October 5.[20] So if Paul's trip to Rome occurred that year, departing from Fair Havens when even the Fast was already past put the travelers deep into the dangerous fall season of the ***navigation year*** (see sidebars). As an experienced traveler, and perhaps with his respected status as a Roman citizen, Paul offers a warning about continued travel at this late date (27:10).[21] His advice is not

20. Hemer, *The Book of Acts in the Setting of Hellenistic History*, 138n109; F. F. Bruce, *The Book of Acts*, 2nd ed., NICNT (Grand Rapids: Eerdmans, 1988), 481; cf. the discussions of this dating in Robert Jewett, *A Chronology of Paul's Life* (Philadelphia: Fortress, 1979), 50–52; and Keener, *Acts*, 4:3597.

21. Luke does not mention the Feast of Booths, which was only five days after the Day of Atonement, suggesting that the date of the Acts 27:9–12 discussion was between October 5 and 10 of AD 59; so Schnabel, *Acts*, 1037. On Paul's ability to offer sailing advice, see Keener, *Acts*, 4:3591–92.

heeded, however, and the views of the pilot and ship owner carry more weight with the centurion's decision to keep his prisoners with the ship (27:11).[22] Despite its name, the small settlement of ***Fair Havens*** was not an ideal place for wintering a ship or its sailors,[23] so those in charge decide to move it to the more suitable winter harbor of Phoenix, a Cretan port about forty miles to the west (27:12).

15.2 STORM AT SEA (ACTS 27:13–38)

When the winds temporarily change to a gentle breeze from the south, the sailors enact their plan and begin sailing westward along the shoreline of Crete toward Phoenix (27:13). Unfortunately, the winds soon switch direction, and a gale of hurricane force, called the "***Northeaster***" (27:14), sweeps down from the island and prevents their progress. Unable to proceed as planned, they soon acquiesce to the storm, allowing it to push them farther to the south of Crete (27:15). This is the beginning of two weeks of harrowing trouble at sea.

15.2.1 WEARYING WEATHER (27:13–20)

Blown away from the coast of Crete (27:13–15), the ship finds a momentary windbreak from the small island of Cauda, about twenty-five miles south. This gives the sailors an opportunity to ready the ship for the tempest they are now facing. In the words of a nonsailor, Luke describes some rather technical duties the sailors perform, which include securing the lifeboat (which was being towed by the ship; 27:16), firming up the ship's hull with ropes (a procedure today called ***frapping***; 27:17a), and lowering a sea anchor (for fear of running aground on the sandbars of ***Syrtis***; 27:17b; see sidebar).[24] Regarding this last action, a sea anchor was like a sail functioning as a parachute in the water so as to slow the speed of the ship, but another interpretation here is that the sailors lowered any superfluous sails and rigging.[25] With such preparations, they let the ship be driven along by the winds of the storm, hoping to move more west than south.

Subsequent days bring more drastic measures, including throwing overboard some of the cargo (27:18) and even the ship's tackle (i.e., gear like ropes and pullies; 27:19) to make the vessel float higher in the water so as to clear submerged rocks and sandbars.

---

22. Egyptian ships generally were owned or financed by citizens of a higher status rather than by the ship captains; see Naphtali Lewis, *Life in Egypt under Roman Rule* (Oxford: Clarendon, 1983), 143; cf. Rapske, "Acts, Travel, and Shipwreck," 27–28; Schnabel, *Acts*, 1038.

23. John D. Wineland, "Fair Havens," *ABD* 2:744; Keener, *Acts*, 4:3590.

24. Noted for their changing sandbar features, the "Greater Syrtis" of ancient times is the modern Gulf of Sidra (or Sirte) off the coast of Libya and the "Lesser Syrtis" is the modern Gulf of Gabes to the northwest off the coast of Tunisia; Mark J. Olson, "Syrtis," *ABD* 6:286.

25. So Schnabel, *Acts*, 1040. On the interpretation of the vague Greek term *skeuos*—e.g., "sea anchor" in NIV; "gear" in ESV; or "sail" in CEV—see esp. F. F. Bruce, *The Acts of the Apostles: The Greek Text with Introduction and Commentary*, 3rd ed. (Grand Rapids: Eerdmans, 1990; Leicester: Apollos, 1990), 520.

With neither sun nor stars being visible for many days (27:20a), navigation would be hampered, and unable to determine the location of the ship, the crew and passengers give up all hope of being saved (27:20b).

The Dangers of the Syrtis

The ancient Greek author Apollonius of Rhodes (third century BC) mentions the dangers of sailing in the Gulf of Sidra (or Sirte) off the coast of Libya in his epic poem about Jason and the Argonauts on their quest for the golden fleece.

Apollonius Rhodius, *Argonautica*, 4.1231–44

> The land of Pelops was just coming into view, when at that moment a deadly blast of the north wind seized them in mid-course and carried them toward the Libyan sea for nine whole nights and as many days, until they came far into Syrtis, where there is no getting back out again for ships, once they are forced to enter that gulf. For everywhere are shallows, everywhere thickets of seaweed from the depths, and over them silently washes the foam of the water. Sand stretches along to the horizon, and no land animal or bird travels there. Here it was that a flood tide—for frequently indeed does this tide recede from the mainland and then, rushing back again, violently disgorge itself on the beach—suddenly drove them to the innermost part of the shore, and very little of their keel was left in the water.

15.2.2 Paul Intervenes with Encouragement—*Keep Courage* (27:21–26)

In the midst of the storm and at the depths of despair, tensions are high and appetites are low. At this point, Paul speaks up with words of encouragement, the first of Paul's interventions in this episode. While he begins with what sounds like little more than an I-told-you-so, the real message here is that Paul tells the truth: he had been right in his earlier advice, and he is right in what he is about to say (27:21).[26] A speech by the main character at the height of a storm is common in ancient sea voyage stories.[27] But unlike such speeches, which usually increase the sense of doom, Paul's address intends the converse purpose—increasing hope in the dreadful situation.[28] They will not be lost (27:22).

And rather than advice based on his travel experience, Paul's message of encouragement now is based on a visit from an angel of the Lord the previous night. Being neither ashamed nor obnoxious about his personal faith, Paul describes the messenger

26. John B. Polhill, *Acts*, NAC (Nashville: Broadman, 1992), 523.
27. Praeder, "Acts 27:1–28:16: Sea Voyages," 696.
28. Polhill, *Acts*, 523.

as "an angel of the God to whom I belong and whom I serve" (27:23). The angel gave Paul two promises that have implications worth sharing: first, "You must stand trial before Caesar" (27:24a), and second, "God has graciously given you the lives of all who sail with you" (27:24b). Paul reasons with his listeners that they must keep up their courage because of the trustworthiness of his God: "For I have faith in God that it will happen just as he told me" (27:25). Paul's encouragement includes some foreshadowing realism about the ship running aground on an island (27:26), but they can keep courage nonetheless because even this great fear will not threaten their survival.

15.2.3 Paul Intervenes as Land Is Near—*Keep Together* (27:27–32)

Despite the words of encouragement, the storm continues. But on the fourteenth night since the ship left Crete, the sailors sense that they are approaching land (27:27). Being pushed along by the storm some forty miles a day would bring the ship across the 550 miles of the southern Adriatic Sea (which is today called the Ionian Sea) from Cauda to Malta in that two-week time period.[29] Whatever their reasons for sensing land (e.g., the

Sounding the Depth of the Sea

The modern use of sonar technology makes better sense of the metaphor of "sounding" the depth of water. In ancient times, however, determining the depth of the sea was accomplished with a cord that had interval measurements and a lead weight. Thus, the Greek term for taking soundings (*bolizō*) literally means "to heave lead." The lead weight had a hollow spot on the underside filled with sticky tallow or grease to retrieve a sample of the sea bottom. The fifth-century BC historian Herodotus indicates this kind of sounding instrument. The following diagram from the sixteenth century shows a sailor taking a sounding from the bow of a ship (note also the lifeboat and anchor) and a man on shore doing the same.

Herodotus, *Histories* (a.k.a. *The Persian Wars*) 2.5

For this is the nature of the land of Egypt: firstly, when you approach to it from the sea and are yet a day's run from land, if you then let down a sounding line you will bring up mud and find a depth of eleven fathoms. This shows that the deposit from the land reaches thus far.

Sounding the depth of the sea
Public domain

29. Luke calls this the "Adriatic Sea" (27:27), a name that correctly applied to the waters well south of Italy in his day (see NIV margin note); e.g., second-century AD scientist and geographer Ptolemy identifies the waters between Sicily and Crete as the "Adriatic Sea"; Ptolemy, *Geography*, 3.4.1 and 3.15.1; cf. 3.14.1. In modern times, "Adriatic Sea" applies to the waters east of Italy, and the waters south of Italy are called the "Ionian Sea."

Desperation among Sailors at Sea

The theme of sailors abandoning ship by means of the lifeboat—to the peril of the passengers—is found in ancient literature. Here is an example from a novel by the second-century AD author Achilles Tatius from Alexandria.

Achilles Tatius, *Leucippe and Clitophon*, 3.3

> At length the helmsman threw up his task. He dropped the steering oars from his hands and left the ship to the mercy of the sea; he then had the jolly-boat got ready, and bidding the sailors follow him, was the first to descend the ladder and enter her. They jumped in close after him, and then was confusion worse confounded and a hand-to-hand fight ensued. They who were already in the boat began to cut the rope which held her to the ship, while all the passengers made preparations to jump where they saw the helmsman holding on to the rope; the boat's crew objected to this, and, being armed with axes and swords, threatened to attack any who leaped in; many, on the other hand, of those still on the ship armed themselves as best they might, one picking up a piece of an old oar, another taking a fragment of one of the ship's benches, and so began to defend themselves. At sea might is right, and there now followed a novel kind of sea-fight; those already in the jolly-boat, fearing she would be swamped by the number of those desiring to enter her, struck at them as they jumped with their axes and swords, while the passengers returned the blows as they jumped with planks and oars. Some of them merely touched the edge of the boat and slipped into the sea; some effected their entry and were now struggling with the crew already there. Every law of friendship and pity disappeared, and each man, regarding only his own safety, utterly disregarded all feelings of kindliness towards his neighbours. Great dangers do away with all bonds, even the most dear.

sight or sound of waves crashing on rocks),[30] the sailors begin measuring the depth of the water (27:28), which would be accomplished by means of a cord with interval measurements and a lead weight (see sidebar on sounding sea depth).[31] As these measurements prove the water is becoming shallower, the sailors drop four anchors from the stern of the ship to brake its speed and to keep its bow pointed toward the fast approaching shore (27:29).[32]

Fearing for their lives, the sailors attempt to escape from the ship by letting down the lifeboat at the front of the ship, pretending to attend to further anchoring procedures (27:30).[33] Paul again intervenes in this desperation with greater wisdom that

30. So J. Michael Gilchrist, "The Historicity of Paul's Shipwreck," *JSNT* 61 (1996): 50; cf. Hemer, *The Book of Acts in the Setting of Hellenistic History*, 146n130.

31. Lionel Casson, *Ships and Seamanship in the Ancient World* (Princeton: Princeton University Press, 1971), 246.

32. Bruce, *Acts: Greek Text*, 523.

33. Anchoring a ship from the bow in these circumstances might best be accomplished using a small boat; see Marshall, *Acts*, 412; cf. Hemer, *The Book of Acts in the Setting of Hellenistic History*, 148; Charles Kingsley Barrett, *A Critical and Exegetical Commentary on the Acts of the Apostles*, 2 vols., ICC (Edinburgh: T&T Clark, 1994/1998), 2:1205.

everyone must keep together. By informing the military of a condition for the promise of safety, Paul foils any attempt of some to abandon ship prematurely: "Unless these men stay with the ship, you cannot be saved" (27:31). By now recognizing the wisdom of Paul, the soldiers jump into action. Perhaps with their own sense of desperation, however, they take the unfortunately drastic action of cutting the lifeboat lose so that it drifts away (27:32). The lifeboat would have been beneficial in the coming shipwreck disaster; nevertheless, the promise of Paul's God will prove true by other means. Paul's second word of intervention here has kept the sailors on board the ship—i.e., those who will know best how to beach the ship when it comes time to do so—and thus Paul's warning has served as a means for God's plan to save all on board.

15.2.4 Paul Intervenes with a Last Meal—*Keep Strong* (27:33–38)

Just prior to dawn, Paul speaks up for a third time. Because those aboard had been going without food for the storm's fourteen-day duration (27:33), Paul's third word of intervention in the storm is a practical one: "Now I urge you to take some food. You need it to survive. Not one of you will lose a single hair from his head" (27:34). The heavenly promise of safety does not preclude the pragmatics of the people maintaining their health to keep strong for the challenge ahead. So, after giving this word of encouragement to eat, Paul takes the lead and models his instruction by eating "in front of them all" (27:35–36).

This turns out to be their last meal on board the ship, which some scholars note is stylized by Luke with verbal nods to the Christian ordinance of the Lord's Supper.[34]

Jesus-Paul Scriptural Language Parallels

Paul's words of encouragement in Acts 27:34 are phrased much like Jesus's words of assurance in Luke 21:18, which utilize an aphorism found elsewhere in Scripture.

1 Samuel 14:45—"As surely as the Lord lives, not a hair of his head will fall to the ground, for he did this today with God's help."

2 Samuel 14:11—"As surely as the Lord lives, . . . not one hair of your son's head will fall to the ground."

1 Kings 1:52—"If he shows himself to be worthy, not a hair of his head will fall to the ground; but if evil is found in him, he will die."

Matthew 10:30—"And even the very hairs of your head are all numbered."

Luke 12:7—"Indeed, the very hairs of your head are all numbered."

Luke 21:18—"But not a hair of your head will perish."

Acts 27:34—"Not one of you will lose a single hair from his head."

34. See Praeder, "Acts 27:1–28:16: Sea Voyages," 699.

As fully described, however, the mixed company of believers and unbelievers does not share this meal in a worship setting, so it need not be considered anything more than an ordinary meal.[35] At this point Luke discloses that 276 people are on board the ship (he uses the Greek term *psychē for "souls"*; 27:37). Given God's earlier promise that not one of them would be lost (cf. 27:22 where he also uses *psychē* for "soul"), the size of the miracle about to take place seems to be Luke's emphasis. When this sizable group had eaten their fill, they lightened the ship by throwing the excess grain overboard, enabling the vessel to get closer to land before running aground (27:38).

15.3 SHIPWRECK ON MALTA AND FINALLY GETTING TO ROME (ACTS 27:39–28:15)

Thrice persuaded by Paul to keep courage, to keep together, and to keep strong, when daylight comes the stormed-tossed shipmates have the disposition and the means and the energy to face the final hardship of this horrific escapade. In the dawn they can see land but do not recognize it. At this juncture, however, they are satisfied to see a sandy beach where they might try to run the lightened ship aground and so escape the dangers of the sea (27:39). Rather than haul the four anchors back aboard, they merely cut the anchor ropes and simultaneously free the rudders so they can steer the ship (27:40a). Then to gain a little speed and maneuverability, they hoist one sail and aim for the beach (27:40b).

Josephus Shipwrecked En Route to Rome

Josephus writes about traveling to Rome in the year AD 64 aboard a large ship with about six hundred passengers. When shipwrecked in the Adriatic Sea, Josephus was among a group of about eighty survivors rescued by another ship, which eventually got him to the Italian seaport of Puteoli. In Paul's shipwreck experience on the Adriatic Sea five years earlier, all 276 passengers were saved (Acts 27:37, 44), and Paul too had eventually landed in Puteoli on his way to Rome (Acts 28:13).

Flavius Josephus, *Life* 3 §15 (ca. AD 99)

I reached Rome after being in great jeopardy at sea. For our ship foundered in the midst of the sea of Adria, and our company of some six hundred souls had to swim all that night. About daybreak, through God's good providence, we sighted a ship of Cyrene, and I and certain others, about eighty in all, outstripped the others and were taken on board. Landing safely at Dicaearchia, which the Italians call Puteoli, I formed a friendship with Aliturus, an actor who was a special favourite of Nero and of Jewish origin.

35. Marshall, *Acts*, 413–14; see also Witherington, *Acts*, 772–73.

15.3.1 Getting Ashore (27:39–44)

Unfortunately, the draft of the ship is still too deep to avoid all submerged obstructions, and the vessel runs aground on a sandbar before reaching the beach (27:41a). Now the ship is stuck, and the waves battering the stern of the ship are breaking it apart (27:41b). This complicates things for the travelers getting safely ashore. The previous night, the sailors had a plan to escape the ship to reach shore alone, a plan foiled by Paul and the soldiers. Now the soldiers hatch a plan to kill their prisoners to prevent them from reaching shore alone and escaping (27:42; cf. 12:19, where guards are held responsible for lost prisoners). But desiring to spare Paul's life, Julius prevents the soldiers from carrying out their rather normal course of action (27:43a). Instead, he orders all to make their way to shore by either swimming or floating on debris (27:43b–44a). The centurion's plan works, and "in this way everyone reached land safely" (27:44b).

15.3.2 A Bonfire (28:1–6)

Re-emphasizing their safe arrival on shore, Luke identifies their location: "Once safely on shore, we found out that the island was called Malta" (28:1). The term Luke uses for the "islanders" of ***Malta*** is actually the word "barbarians" (Greek: *barbaros*; Acts 28:2, 4), but it was not necessarily pejorative and was often used as a linguistic identifier to distinguish between Greek speakers and non-Greek speakers. Linguistically, the "bar- bar-" label is thought merely to describe phonetically something of how all non-Greek languages sounded.[36] That all of humanity might be divided into the two categories of Greeks and barbarians is evidenced by several ancient writers.[37] And while Jews typically divided humanity into either Jew or gentile, even the Jewish historian Josephus acknowledges the Greek or barbarian categorization.[38] The Maltese islanders greet the shipwrecked travelers with welcoming hospitality (Acts 28:2a), and Luke's term here (Greek: *philanthrōpia*) is one for a virtue highly prized and much praised in the Greek moral literature.[39] This term thus confirms that the use of "barbarians" here has a neutral linguistic connotation.[40] So as the two weeks of stormy weather continues, Luke notes that the kind islanders build a fire to welcome them ashore (28:2b).

In gathering up some brushwood to feed the fire, Paul shows himself to be interested in serving others. As he puts it on the fire, out from the pile comes a snake that

36. Arnold, "Acts," 262; Arnold suggests the term is onomatopoetic, i.e., the term's sound is its meaning.

37. E.g., Athenaeus, *Deipn.*, 10.457f; 11.461b; 14.628c; Dionysius of Halicarnassus, *Ant. Rom.*, 1.3.5; 1.5.3; 1.28.4; 2.24.2; 2.64.3; 4.79.3; 7.3.3; 7.13.4; 8.83.2; Lucian, *Salt.*, 64–67; *Demon.*, 34; *Hist.*, 54; Thucydides, *History of the Peloponnesian War*, 1.3.3; 1.5.1; 1.82.1; 6.33.5. See the discussion of ancient authors on this topic in Keener, *Acts*, 4:3665–67.

38. E.g., Josephus, *Ag. Ap.* 1.22 §§201–2; 2.14 §148; 2.39 §282; *J.W.* 5.1.3 §17; 6.3.3 §200; *Ant.* 1.3.9 §107; 4.2.1 §12; 8.11.3 §284; 11.7.1 §300; 15.5.3 §136; 16.6.8 §177; 18.1.5 §20.

39. See Mikeal C. Parsons, *Acts*, Paideia Commentaries on the New Testament (Grand Rapids: Baker Academic, 2008), 367–68; Johnson, *Acts*, 445.

40. So Schnabel, *Acts*, 1050.

Malta

- At about eighteen miles long and eight miles wide, the largest of the Maltese islands; about sixty miles south of Sicily.
- Called Melita in ancient times.
- Inhabited prior to 2000 BC but colonized by Phoenicians ca. 1000 BC and controlled by Carthaginians in the sixth to third centuries BC until Rome took over in 218 BC.
- Mostly rather barren and arid, but the eastern half had some commodities such as olive oil, wood, and lapdogs.
- Strategically located for control of the Mediterranean narrows, with excellent and sizable harbor facilities.
- Mentioned only once in the New Testament, naming where Paul was shipwrecked en route to Rome (Acts 28:1).
- A first-century inscription confirms that the leader of the island was called the "chief official" (Greek: *prōtos*; Acts 28:7).
- A place called St. Paul's Bay, about eight miles northwest of modern Valletta, marks the traditional landing spot of the shipwrecked survivors of Acts 27–28.

Select Bibliography

Colin J. Hemer, "Euraquilo and Melita," *JTS* ns 26 (1975): 100–11.

Uwe Jens Rudolf, *Historical Dictionary of Malta*, 3rd ed. (Lanham, MD: Rowman & Littlefield, 2018).

Robert C. Stone, "Malta," *ZEB* 4:58–59.

David H. Trump, "Malta," *OEANE* 3:402–405.

fastens to Paul's hand. The islanders immediately understand the snake biting Paul as an omen of his doom, assuming him to be guilty of some great crime for which the ***goddess Justice*** will not allow him to escape unpunished (28:4). This response of the Maltese betrays the deeply ingrained belief in ancient thought that "the misfortunes which befall the wicked are in reality punishments meted out by the gods for their crimes."[41] But when Paul merely shakes the snake off into the fire and suffers no ill effects, the islanders soon change their minds about him and conclude that he must be a god of some kind (28:5–6). While their new assessment is not quite correct(!), it is more correct than their previous opinion of Paul; Paul is not only to be declared innocent, but perhaps more importantly, he is to be recognized as a divinely appointed ambassador.[42] He is not to be identified as a deity, but Luke's readers know Paul to be a representative of the one true God and the one true Savior Jesus Christ.

41. Gary B. Miles and Garry Trompf, "Luke and Antiphon: The Theology of Acts 27–28 in the Light of Pagan Beliefs about Divine Retribution, Pollution, and Shipwreck," *HTR* 69 (1976): 260. Cadbury notes, "The murderer bitten in the hand would suggest to many readers the widespread idea of poetic justice that the member which sins is the part to receive punishment"; Henry Joel Cadbury, *The Book of Acts in History* (New York: Harper & Brothers, 1955), 24.

42. James D. G. Dunn, *The Acts of the Apostles*, Narrative Commentaries (Valley Forge: Trinity Press International, 1996), 347; cf. Joshua W. Jipp, *Divine Visitations and Hospitality to Strangers in Luke-Acts: An Interpretation of the Malta Episode in Acts 28:1–10*, NovTSup 153 (Leiden: Brill, 2013), 11–12.

Justice Finding Her Mark on Sea or Land

When the shipwrecked Paul was bitten by a viper on Malta, the islanders suspected him of being a murderer: "For though he escaped from the sea, the goddess Justice has not allowed him to live" (Acts 28:4). The idea that bad things happen to bad people was not odd in the first-century world, even among those who might not personify justice into a goddess figure. The poet Statyllius Flaccus wrote about a shipwrecked mariner who escaped death at sea only to die anyway of a snake bite.

Statyllius Flaccus, in *Greek Anthology*, 7.290 (ca. first century BC)

> The shipwrecked mariner had escaped the whirlwind and the fury of the deadly sea, and as he was lying on the Libyan sand not far from the beach, deep in his last sleep, naked and exhausted by the unhappy wreck, a baneful viper slew him. Why did he struggle with the waves in vain, escaping then the fate that was his lot on the land?

15.3.3 Hospitality and Healing (28:7–10)

The newfound respect of the Maltese for Paul results in his being welcomed into the home of ***Publius***, the island's leader, whose estate is not far from the beach where the shipwrecked travelers came ashore (28:7). Exactly who is included in the three days of generous hospitality is unclear, whether it is the entire band of 276 shipwrecked visitors,[43] only the most prominent of the group (e.g., the Roman military and Roman citizens like Paul),[44] or merely Paul and his Christian friends.[45] Whoever is included, the story reveals that Paul and Luke ("us") are among the guests in Publius's home. Interestingly, a first-century inscription discovered on Malta refers to the island's principal leader with the same term Luke uses for Publius: "***chief official***" (Greek: *prōtos*).[46] The missionary team becomes aware that Publius's father is ill, and Paul visits the man, prays for him, places his hands on him, and heals him (28:8). Luke may well intend the notable contrast between Paul surviving a snake bite on his hand and not dying and then the use of Paul's hands in healing someone else.[47]

---

43. So Joseph A. Fitzmyer, *The Acts of the Apostles*, AB 31 (New York: Doubleday, 1998), 783; Peterson, *Acts*, 701, appealing to Rapske, *Paul in Roman Custody*, 273.

44. So Arnold, "Acts," 263; Schnabel, *Acts*, 1052; Keener, *Acts*, 4:3683.

45. So Simon J. Kistemaker, *Exposition of the Acts of the Apostles*, New Testament Commentary (Grand Rapids: Baker, 1990), 951; Polhill, *Acts*, 533; Barrett, *Acts*, 2:1225.

46. See *IG* 14.601 = *IGR* 1.512; Barrett, *Acts*, 2:1224; Arnold, "Acts," 263; cf. Keener, *Acts*, 4:3682–83, who is a bit more cautious about this as a title for Publius. Compare a similar Latin inscription: *CIL* 10.7495 = *ILS* 5415; but see the caution of Hemer, "First Person Narrative in Acts 27–28," 100, followed by Bruce, *Acts: Greek Text*, 532–33 and others.

47. Annette Weissenrieder, *Images of Illness in the Gospel of Luke: Insights of Ancient Medical Texts*, WUNT 2.164 (Tübingen: Mohr Siebeck, 2003), 344–45.

Prayer is specifically mentioned here with the laying on of hands, perhaps to demonstrate Paul's reliance on God and so to differentiate him from traveling miracle workers in popular Greco-Roman literature.[48]

The healing of Publius's father from a fever encourages the Maltese to bring other sick citizens for healing. While this may have taken place over the three months they wintered on Malta (cf. 28:11), Luke simply reports in summary fashion that "the rest of the sick on the island came and were cured" (28:9), which is reminiscent of Luke's account of Jesus healing Simon Peter's mother-in-law from a fever and the subsequent healing of the crowds in Capernaum (Luke 4:38–41).[49] Although Luke does not specify Paul preaching here, even as miracles have elsewhere in Acts been an accompanying testimony to the truth of the gospel, Luke's readers would expect nothing less of the miraculous healings on Malta as well.[50] Paul found ways to share the gospel while imprisoned; it is unlikely he behaved any differently while in custody on the island of Malta for three months.[51]

Moving from the topic of healing back to the topic of hospitality, Luke seems to utilize a chiastic structure for this brief paragraph: hospitality—healing—healing—hospitality (see sidebar). Luke says the Maltese "honored us in many ways" (Acts 28:10a), and Luke's usual use of the noun for "honor" (Greek: *timē*) implies money or material gifts (4:34–35; 5:2–3; 7:16; 19:19) without precluding the sense of praise and respect.[52] This somewhat nebulous statement about honors, however, is given more specificity with the report that the Maltese supply the group with the provisions needed for the remainder of the voyage to Rome (28:10b). Given that radical generosity has been one evidence of conversion to faith in Christ (e.g., 2:42–47; 4:32–37; 11:25–30), this generosity of the Maltese islanders toward the shipwrecked travelers is further potential evidence that they have responded in faith to the gospel message.[53]

The Chiasm of Acts 28:7–10

A: Acts 28:7—Hospitality: an individual shows generous hospitality

B: Acts 28:8—Healing: an individual is healed

B': Acts 28:9—Healing: a mass of people is healed

A': Acts 28:10—Hospitality: a mass of people shows generous hospitality

---

48. Peterson, *Acts*, 702; cf. William J. Larkin Jr., *Acts*, The IVP New Testament Commentary Series (Downers Grove, IL: InterVarsity Press, 1995), 382; Schnabel, *Acts*, 1053.

49. See Praeder, "Acts 27:1–28:16: Sea Voyages," 702; Peterson, *Acts*, 702.

50. Cf. Schnabel, *Acts*, 1053; Johnson, *Acts*, 463.

51. The fourth-century church father John Chrysostom reasons that Paul's time on Malta resulted in a church there; Chrysostom, *Hom. Act.*, 54. Third- to sixth-century catacombs also testify to an early Christian presence on the island; Hansjörg Kalcyk and Hans Georg Niemeyer, "Melite (7)," *BNP* 8:638.

52. Keener, *Acts*, 4:3693; cf. Witherington, *Acts*, 780.

53. See Jipp, *Divine Visitations and Hospitality to Strangers in Luke-Acts*, esp. 251–53.

15.3.4 Finally Getting to Rome (28:11–16)

With the group supplied by the generous islanders so as to complete their journey, Luke notes that they set out for Rome after three months of wintering on Malta (28:11). If they had left Crete between October 5 and 10, AD 59 (cf. 27:9) and were pushed by the storm for fourteen days across the sea (cf. 27:27) and stayed on Malta for three months, then they are resuming their journey in late January or early February of AD 60.[54] While this would be much earlier than the more standard date of March 10 for the reopening of Mediterranean navigation, the first-century writer Pliny the Elder noted that the seas could reopen as early as February 8 if the west winds began to blow favorably.[55] Indeed, while standardized travel dates can be helpful for planning, the actual weather itself is not subjected to precise dates. All the group needed was a favorable wind that would allow them to sail the approximately sixty miles from Malta to Sicily, after which the remainder of the voyage would be easy sailing along coastlines.[56]

During the winter months, the centurion Julius negotiated travel arrangements for his party of soldiers and prisoners on an Alexandrian ship that had wintered in Malta.[57] This vessel, Luke notes, has "the figurehead of the twin gods Castor and Pollux" (28:11 NIV; a fulsome rendering for the more plain Greek term *Dioskouroi*; "sons of Zeus" or

The Dioscuri: Castor and Pollux

Bumann/stock.adobe.com

The vessel on which Paul and his party sail from Malta to Rome has "the figurehead of the twin gods Castor and Pollux" (28:11). The Greek Luke uses might be rendered more plainly as "sons of Zeus" (*Dioskouroi*). Known by various names in Greek mythology, these so-called divine twins were called upon in times of distress (particularly at sea) and were eventually associated with the Gemini constellation. Luke does not specify whether the images were statues posted in the bow of the ship or carved into the wood of the ship's prow or simply painted on the bow.

54. Luke's "after three months" (28:11) is a somewhat flexible phrase and may not include the first few days after the shipwreck along with the three days of hospitality at Publius's home (28:7); cf. Schnabel, *Acts*, 1054.

55. *Natural History*, 2.47 §122.

56. Bruce, *Acts: Greek Text*, 534.

57. Cf. Hemer, "First Person Narrative in Acts 27–28," 87, 94.

"divine twins"), pagan gods associated with sea voyages.[58] After the story of the living God saving people aboard a ship in a storm, there is certainly irony in Luke adding this note about a lifeless representation of powerless gods fixed on the front of a ship that is sailing safely in good weather.[59]

From Malta the Alexandrian ship sails north to the city of ***Syracuse*** on Sicily, where they stay for three days, perhaps for some cargo loading or unloading but more likely to wait for additional favorable winds (28:12).[60] From there, they sail about seventy miles to ***Rhegium***, a city on the toe of the Italian "boot" peninsula (28:13a). Favorable winds come up the next day, which enables them to arrive at the seaport city of Puteoli, about 180 miles farther north, another day later (28:13b). The well-structured harbor of ***Puteoli*** made it one of the more important seaports servicing first-century Rome, especially for Alexandrian grain ships.[61] Because the city was also a popular resort town, even when freight was intended for one of the ports closer to Rome, passengers usually disembarked at Puteoli.[62] With the centurion Julius needing a few days to

Syracuse

- A city on the eastern coast of Sicily, founded ca. 734 BC by the Corinthian Archias.
- The most important city of Sicily in ancient times.
- Referred to as the greatest and most beautiful of Greek cities by Cicero.
- Originally situated on the island of Ortygia but soon spread across the water to Sicily's mainland and the island was eventually joined to the mainland by a causeway.
- The Greek settlers are believed to have intermarried with the local indigenous people.
- Targeted for control by various tyrants—the Carthaginians, and the Greeks in the fifth and fourth centuries BC—but came firmly under Roman rule in 211 BC.
- The seat of the Roman province of Sicily and the home of its governor.
- Extensive catacombs provide evidence of a Christian community there.

Select Bibliography

Edward M. Blaiklock, "Syracuse," *ZEB* 5:659–60.

Dale Ellenburg, "Syracuse," *EDB*, 1263.

Jack Finegan, "Syracuse," in *The Archeology of the New Testament: The Mediterranean World of the Early Christian Apostles* (Boulder, CO: Westview; London: Croom Helm, 1981; repr., Routledge Library Editions: Archaeology; New York: Routledge, 2015), 205–8.

Gillian Shepherd, "Syracuse," *OEAGR* 6:413–15.

58. See Tanja Scheer and Anne Ley, "Dioscuri," *BNP* 4:518–21.

59. See Lynn Allan Kauppi, *Foreign but Familiar Gods: Greco-Romans Read Religion in Acts*, LNTS 277 (New York: T & T Clark, 2006), 116; cf. Keener, *Acts*, 4:3696n1432.

60. So Hemer, *The Book of Acts in the Setting of Hellenistic History*, 154.

61. Casson, *Travel in the Ancient World*, 129.

62. Johnson, *Acts*, 464; Hemer, "First Person Narrative in Acts 27–28," 93; idem, *The Book of Acts in the Setting of Hellenistic History*, 154–55.

Rhegium

- A notably Greek cultured city on the toe of the Italian "boot" peninsula across the Strait of Messina from Sicily.
- Ancient sources are divided on whether the name Rhegium stems from the Latin word for "royal" (*regius*) or from (more apparently) the Greek word for "to rend" (*rhēgnumi*) i.e., the place where Sicily was pulled away from Italy.
- Founded in the eighth century BC and is today called Reggio Calabria.
- Affiliated in Greek mythology with the navigational hazards of the rock outcropping Scylla and the whirlpool Charybdis.
- Its strategic location as a safe haven and guard post made the city a target for warring powers. The city became allied with Rome during the Punic Wars.
- Destroyed by an earthquake in 91 BC, it was rebuilt by Caesar Augustus early in the first century AD.
- Josephus notes that Gaius Caligula built places to receive Alexandrian grain ships in Sicily and Rhegium (Josephus, *Ant.* 19.2.5 §205).

Select Bibliography

Edward M. Blaiklock, "Rhegium," *ZEB* 5:125–26.
D. Larry Gregg, "Rhegium," *EDB*, 850.

Puteoli

- A seaport city on the western edge of Italy founded in the sixth century BC by Samian settlers and originally called Dicaearchia.
- When the Romans put a garrison there in 215 BC to protect against Hannibal's invading forces, the name was changed to Puteoli, due either to the "wells" there (Latin: *putei*) or to the foul, sulfurous odors there (Latin: *puteo*). A Roman colony was established there in 194 BC.
- The city's modern name is Pozzuoli.
- Located on the northern side of what is now known as the Gulf of Naples, in Roman times Puteoli was one of the most important seaport cities for bringing in goods for Rome, another 150 miles by road to the north.
- At 4,000+ feet in height, Mount Vesuvius would be visible from the deck of a ship approaching Puteoli.
- A naval base was established in the Gulf of Naples at the nearby Portus Julius in 37 BC.
- The region produced many metal works (e.g., military armor and farming implements), had access to a kind of cement mix of lime and volcanic ash (useful in constructing the extensive dock works of the harbor), and was also known for banking.
- Known for its crafts production and hot springs, it was a holiday destination for Roman aristocrats.
- Had a first-century population around one hundred thousand, and Josephus seems to indicate a sizable Jewish population (Josephus, *J.W.* 2.7.1 §§104–5; *Ant.* 17.12.1 §328; cf. 18.6.3 §160).

Select Bibliography

Edward M. Blaiklock, "Puteoli," *ZEB* 4:1106.
Maria Ida Gulletta and Dieter Steinbauer, "Puteoli," *BNP* 12:234–36.
Kent L. Yinger, "Puteoli," *EDB*, 1101.

make arrangements for the 150-mile overland trip to Rome, the group spends about a week in Puteoli before setting out.[63] Luke reports that they are hosted by some fellow Christians (i.e., "brothers and sisters"; 28:14a).[64]

In announcing how they finish the trip (i.e., "And so we came to Rome"; 28:14b),[65] Luke reports that word of their arrival in Italy had reached other believers in Rome (again "brothers and sisters"; 28:15a), some of whom take it upon themselves to travel to meet them on the road. They come as far as the Forum of Appius and the Three Taverns, which were about forty miles and thirty miles from Rome, respectively.

Watching Alexandrian Ships Arrive at Puteoli

The first-century Roman philosopher Seneca comments on the custom of crowds from the Italian province of Campania who would stand on the shoreline watching a fleet of grain ships from Alexandria, Egypt, come into harbor at Puteoli. The modern city of Pozzuoli (as it is called today) still has an important harbor.

Seneca, *Epistles* 77.1–2

> Suddenly there came into our view to-day the "Alexandrian" ships,—I mean those which are usually sent ahead to announce the coming of the fleet; they are called "mail-boats." The Campanians are glad to see them; all the rabble of Puteoli stand on the docks, and can recognize the "Alexandrian" boats, no matter how great the crowd of vessels, by the very trim of their sails. For they alone may keep spread their topsails, which all ships use when out at sea, because nothing sends a ship along so well as its upper canvas; that is where most of the speed is obtained. So when the breeze has stiffened and becomes stronger than is comfortable, they set their yards lower; for the wind has less force near the surface of the water. Accordingly, when they have made Capreae and the headland whence Tall Pallas watches on the stormy peak, all other vessels are bidden to be content with the mainsail, and the topsail stands out conspicuously on the "Alexandrian" mail-boats.

The harbor at Puteoli
Barry Beitzel/BiblePlaces.com

63. See Rapske, "Acts, Travel, and Shipwreck," 20–21.

64. Witherington notes that Luke's use of the term "brothers" in Acts 28:14–15 occurs in a "we section" and is most naturally understood to refer to fellow Christians, for it is doubtful that the gentile Luke would speak of Jews as "brothers" if they were not Christians; Witherington, *Acts*, 785.

65. See Schnabel, *Acts*, 1055; cf. Marshall, *Acts*, 419.

The trip to Rome from Puteoli would take as many as five days, requiring overnight resting places such as the Forum of Appius and the Three Taverns along the way.[66] The welcome parties of fellow believers at the rest stops are uplifting to Paul: Luke states it, "At the sight of these people Paul thanked God and was encouraged." (28:15b). Even the courageous need encouragement; and God is to be thanked in both difficult and easy circumstances (e.g., Acts 27:35; 28:15; cf. 1 Thess 5:18).

15.4 PAUL MINISTERS UNDER HOUSE ARREST IN ROME (ACTS 28:16–31)

Paul and his traveling party finally arrive in ***Rome*** (doubly announced in 28:14 and 16a), which marks the fulfillment of the Lord's statement to Paul in Acts 23:11: "Take courage! As you have testified about me in Jerusalem, so you must also testify in Rome."[67]

First-Century Rome

- Known to be the capital city of the Roman Republic, the Roman Empire, and of modern Italy.
- Officially founded in 753 BC on the lower Tiber River about fifteen miles inland in central Italy, the area shows signs of inhabitation back to the eleventh century BC.
- While sometimes referred to as the City of Seven Hills, counting the rises around the city makes the number seven seem somewhat arbitrary.
- The seat of the Roman government and the emperor's primary residence.
- Served by several seaport towns on the segment of the Mediterranean Sea known today as the Tyrrhenian Sea, including Puteoli and Ostia.
- Augustus (reigning 27 BC–AD 14) put the city through a major transformation and "so beautified it that he could justly boast that he found it built of brick and left it in marble" (Suetonius, *Aug.* 28.3).
- Became a multiethnic city with peoples from all over the world living there.
- The largest city in the first-century world, with a population of about one million people.
- The wealthiest city in the first-century world, but only a small number of its citizens had wealth.
- The most militarily powerful city in the first-century world.
- Religions included the whole pantheon of Roman gods, Greek deities, Asian gods, Persian gods, Egyptian gods, the goddess Roma, and the ruler cult.

Select Bibliography

David E. Aune, "Rome," *EDB*, 1138–42.

Edward M. Blaiklock, "Rome," *ZEB* 5:195–200.

Willem Jongman and Michael Heinzelmann, "Rome," *BNP* 12:669–725.

Rabun Taylor, "The City of Rome," *OEAGR* 6:172–85.

66. Rapske, *Paul in Roman Custody*, 206.

67. So Johnson, *Acts*, 464. Charles Puskas points out that Paul's arrival in Jerusalem also has a double announcement at Acts 21:15 and 17 paralleling the double announcement of his arrival in Rome at 28:14 and 16; Charles B. Puskas, *The Conclusion of Luke-Acts: The Significance of Acts 28:16–31* (Eugene, OR: Pickwick, 2009), 138n3.

Although arriving as a prisoner, instead of incarceration in a pubic prison, Paul is granted a lighter form of military custody in lodging that Paul rents himself (28:16b, 30).[68] And even though it is as a chained prisoner under house arrest and guarded by a Roman soldier, Paul (and his group of missionary friends) has arrived in Rome.

15.4.1 Discussion with the Jews of Rome (28:17–22)

In keeping with Luke's description of Paul's ministry everywhere else in Acts, Paul is concerned to meet first with the Jews of the city. The first of two such meetings Luke describes occurs three days after their arrival and at Paul's initiative (28:17a), and Paul addresses them with an explanation of how it is he has come to Rome as a prisoner (28:17b–20; cf. the earlier summaries of Paul's case in 23:26–30 and 25:14–21). His explanation has the tone of a defense speech in four statements: (a) he did nothing against the Jewish people or their ancestral customs (28:17b); (b) Roman investigations concluded that he could be released (28:18); (c) the Jerusalem Jews objected to the Roman ruling such that he felt the need to appeal to Caesar (28:19); and (d) he is a prisoner "because of the hope of Israel" (28:20). With "the hope of Israel" directly connected to the resurrection (cf. 23:6–8; 24:14–15; 26:6–8, 22–23), he has not been preaching against the historic faith of Jews but in keeping with their scriptural beliefs.

When Paul finishes his remarks, the Jewish leaders respond with four claims as well:[69] (a) they have not received any letters from the Judean Jews about Paul (28:21a); (b) none of the Jews coming to Rome from Jerusalem has reported or said anything bad about Paul (28:21b); (c) they want to hear more about Paul's views (28:22a); and (d) they have heard about Christianity as people everywhere are opposing it (28:22b). Thus, whatever the Jews at Rome had heard, they nevertheless still regarded Christianity as a branch (or "sect"; v. 22) within the Jewish faith even if Christianity had a particular interpretation of the Scriptures and distinctive ways to practice the Jewish faith.[70] With an apparently neutral posture, the Roman Jewish leaders would like to hear more about Christianity from Paul.[71]

15.4.2 Continued Discussion and Reaching Out to Gentiles (28:23–28)

Charles B. Puskas labels Paul's second interaction with the Roman Jews an "apologetic speech on the Gentile mission," as it has several parallels to Paul's earlier such apologetic speech in Acts 13. These similarities include formal, structural, and thematic

---

68. See Rapske, *Paul in Roman Custody*, 182.

69. Here I follow Schnabel, *Acts*, 1069–70.

70. Schnabel, *Acts*, 1070.

71. Luke's silence here about the (apparently ineffectual) influence of Christian Jews in Rome is a topic of much discussion.

features.[72] Guy Prentiss Waters has laid out these parallels in an even grander scheme that covers both of Paul's meetings with the Jews of Rome in Acts 28:17–28. Waters suggests Paul's interactions with the Roman Jews function as a closing *inclusio* (or "bookend") to Paul's first recounted missionary speech found in Acts 13:16b–41 (see sidebar).[73] Having explained his case to the Roman Jews in his earlier remarks, Paul's second address in Rome is more directly about the gospel message: "He witnessed to them from morning till evening, explaining about the kingdom of God, and from the Law of Moses and from the Prophets he tried to persuade them about Jesus" (28:23b). This is reminiscent of the report Luke gives about Jesus at the end of the Gospel of Luke: "And beginning with Moses and all the Prophets, he explained to them what was said in all the Scriptures concerning himself" (Luke 24:27; cf. 24:44–48). Despite Paul's scriptural preaching, the results are mixed: "Some were convinced by what he said, but others would not believe" (Acts 28:24).

Parallels between Paul's Speeches in Acts 13 and 28

Acts 13:14-48	Acts 28:17-28
Focus on Jews: Paul goes to the Pisidian Antioch synagogue (v. 14)	**Focus on Jews:** Paul invites the Roman synagogue to him (vv. 17, 23)
Double scene: 13:14-43 and 13:44-48 (in greater number, v. 44)	**Double scene:** 28:17-22 and 28:23-28 (in greater number, v. 23)
Pattern to Paul's words: preaching, resistance, and a parting declaration	**Pattern to Paul's words:** preaching, resistance, and a parting declaration
After the parting announcement: a turn to the gentiles is signaled (v. 46) with an appeal to Isaiah (v. 47 = Isa 49:6)	**After the parting announcement:** a turn to the gentiles is signaled (v. 28) with an appeal to Isaiah (vv. 26-27 = Isa 6:9-10)
Common phrase: "this message of salvation has been sent" (v. 26)	**Common phrase:** "God's salvation has been sent" (v. 28)

Adapted and simplified from the discussion in Guy Prentiss Waters, "With a Whimper or a Bang? Acts 28 and the Ending of Acts," *RTR* 74.1 (2015): 6-8.

Given this disagreement, Paul makes a final statement, which includes a citation of Isaiah 6:9–10 (Acts 28:25–27).[74] Thus, Paul appeals to the Jews of Rome by pointing to their Scripture and referencing their ancestors. For those who reject the gospel,

72. See Puskas, *The Conclusion of Luke-Acts*, 56–57, 113–14.

73. Guy Prentiss Waters, "With a Whimper or a Bang? Acts 28 and the Ending of Acts," *RTR* 74 (2015): 6–8.

74. See Craig A. Evans, *To See and Not Perceive: Isaiah 6:9–10 in Early Jewish and Christian Interpretation*, JSOTSup 64 (Sheffield: JSOT Press, 1989), who proposes that Isa 6:9–10 is "probably the single most important obduracy text in the Bible" (p. 7) and its citation in Acts 28 as "the single most important biblical witness to the early Church's experience of Jewish rejection and unbelief" (p. 127).

Paul says the word of Isaiah 6 applies to them as a predictive curse. What the Holy Spirit said to their ancestors through Isaiah the prophet regarding their stubborn refusal to hear God's word still applies to the Jews of Rome: *if you want to be excluded from God's salvation, you will be excluded from salvation.*[75] Persistently in Acts, Paul has conducted a Jews-first ministry, i.e., bringing the gospel message first to those who should be most ready to hear that God is fulfilling his scriptural promise of salvation.

Where Is Acts 28:29?

While most modern English translations have no Acts 28:29, a few ancient manuscripts have the extra sentence represented in the NIV footnote: "Some manuscripts include here *After he said this, the Jews left, arguing vigorously among themselves.*" This appears to be a late addition by a scribe involved in the manuscript hand-copying process, perhaps trying to wrap up the narration of Paul's interaction with the Jews before giving Luke's conclusion to the story of Acts.

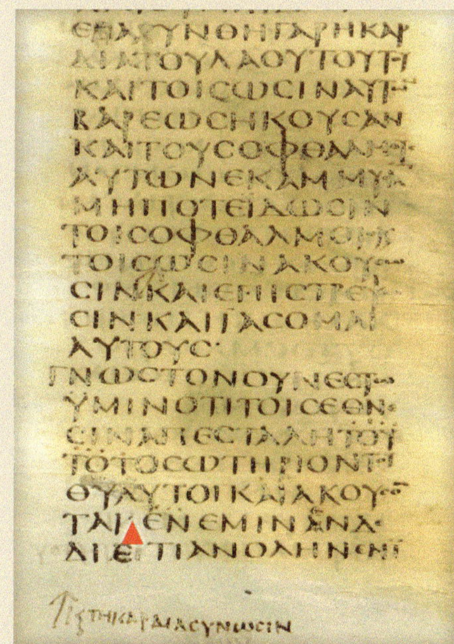

Codex Sinaiticus without Acts 28:29

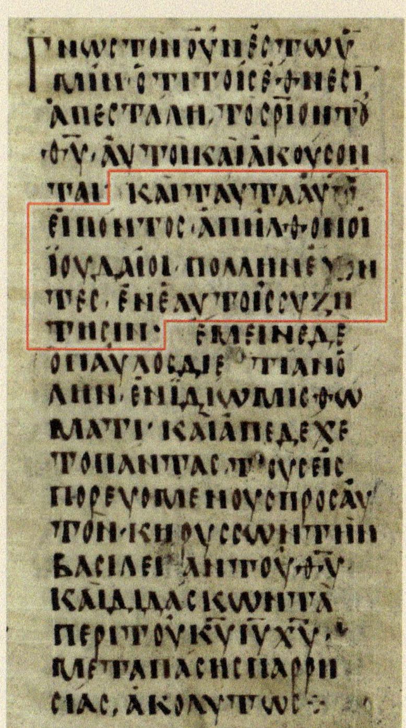

Codex Angelicus with Acts 28:29

Biblioteca Angelica, Rome Ang. gr. 39: page 42v

75. See Douglas S. Huffman, *Verbal Aspect Theory and the Prohibitions in the Greek New Testament*, SBG 16 (New York: Lang, 2104), 180–81n15, 275n30; cf. David Pao, *Acts and the Isaianic New Exodus*, WUNT 2.130 (Tübingen: Mohr Siebeck, 2000; repr., Grand Rapids: Baker Academic, 2000), 101–9; Barrett, *Acts*, 2:1245.

And just as persistently, while receptive Jews move with Paul to bring the gospel to gentiles, unreceptive Jews must be left behind (cf. 13:46–48; 18:5–7). So Paul concludes this conversation in Rome, "Therefore I want you to know that God's salvation has been sent to the Gentiles, and they will listen!" (Acts 28:28). Of course, Paul is not suggesting that Christianity is breaking away from Judaism, nor is he signaling an end to evangelism among Jewish people (none of Paul's similar statements in Acts have had such a significance).[76] On the contrary, Paul suggests that any Jews who reject the gospel are the ones thereby abandoning their beliefs. Faith in Jesus Christ is the fulfillment of the historic faith of Abraham, Moses, and David, and this faith was always meant to reach the world.[77]

Monument to Luke, Paul, and Peter. Santa Maria Church, Rome.

15.4.3 Summary Statement (28:30–31)

Luke's closing statement about Paul in the story of Acts is a final summary statement: "For two whole years Paul stayed there in his own rented house and welcomed all who came to see him. He proclaimed the kingdom of God and taught about the Lord Jesus Christ—with all boldness and without hindrance!" (28:30–31). Even as the summary statement in the middle of Acts contains a progress report and a travel

76. Note that after each of Paul's turnings to the gentiles, he is soon back preaching in a Jewish synagogue or to "all": Acts 13:46–48 and 14:1; 18:5–7 and 18:19; 28:28 and 28:30. See Darrell L. Bock, *Acts*, BECNT (Grand Rapids: Baker Academic, 2007), 756–57.

77. The context of Acts "reveals that the message is that Christianity has not rejected the Jews, although the Jews have rejected Christianity, but they have done so only after initially conceding that Christianity is a sect of Judaism"; Gempf, "Luke's Story of Paul's Reception in Rome," 60.

report (12:24 and 25, respectively), so also this final summary statement contains a travel summary (28:30; Paul could not travel) and a progress summary (28:31; the gospel is unhindered). But most notable here is the curtness of Luke's final summary. After extended accounts of Paul's two-year imprisonment (Acts 21–26) and his difficult voyage to Rome (Acts 27–28), Luke's culmination of the story seems so terse as to be potentially dissatisfying for Luke's readership.[78]

Scholars have proposed many various theories to explain Luke's abrupt ending to the story of Acts, and Schnabel has suggested three categories for helpfully organizing them (see sidebar).[79] Some of these theories are incompatible with one another; some seem far-fetched and unconvincing; but some are overlapping and could work together to explain the brusque ending of Acts. Some historical explanations suggest that Luke, writing ca. AD 62, is up to date in telling the story and has nothing more to record, or that the release of Paul would be presumed if after his two-year stay his accusers failed to appear in Rome, or Luke's audience would already otherwise know about Paul's release, or that Luke has come to the end of the papyrus roll and has no room for a fuller ending.[80] While such historical explanations for *why* Acts ends as it does might be helpful, they can divert us away from noting Luke's intentions for *how* Acts ends, which might be more important.[81]

Certainly, Luke's theological-programmatic intentions would affect how he ends the story of Acts. One of his goals has been attained in tracing the story of Acts to Rome as a representation of the gospel reaching the whole world.[82] His goal of providing an exemplar of gospel ministry climaxes with Paul able to preach the gospel freely in the very heart of the Roman Empire.[83] Paul's mission of the unhindered spread of the gospel everywhere is central to Luke's purposes, not the (potentially distracting) question of Paul's fate. At the end of Acts in Rome, Luke reaches the goal of distinguishing faith in Jesus—open to Jews and gentiles alike—from the misguided direction that the unbelieving Jews had chosen.[84]

78. Adolf von Harnack rather harshly opines that "the place where the narrative now breaks off is as unsuitable as it possibly can be. The readers are kept upon the rack"; Adolf von Harnack, *The Date of the Acts and of the Synoptic Gospels*, trans. J. R. Wilkinson, NT Studies 4/Crown Theological Library 33 (London: Williams and Norgate, 1911; repr., Eugene, OR: Wipf & Stock, 2004), 97n2.

79. Schnabel, *Acts*, 1062–63. For a different, but still helpful, four-part outline of theories, see Troy M. Troftgruben, *A Conclusion Unhindered: A Study of the Ending of the Acts within Its Literary Environment*, WUNT 2.280 (Tübingen: Mohr Siebeck, 2010), 8–28.

80. Regarding a supposed automatic release of prisoners after a two-year delay, see the discussion in Keener, *Acts*, 4:3763–64; as for the theory of the filled papyrus roll, see esp. the discussion of Hemer, *The Book of Acts in the Setting of Hellenistic History*, 386.

81. Troftgruben, *A Conclusion Unhindered*, 5 and 28. Troftgruben suggests that, without necessarily solving all the issues, "a gradual shift has occurred in the interpretation of the ending, from viewing it as inadvertent and abrupt, to viewing it as deliberate and even fitting" (p. 7).

82. Barrett, *Acts*, 1:80.

83. Steve Walton, "The State They Were In: Luke's View of the Roman Empire," pp. 1–41 in *Rome in the Bible and the Early Church*, ed. Peter Oakes (Grand Rapids: Baker, 2002), 29; cf. Bruce, *Book of Acts*, 511; Witherington, *Acts*, 808–809.

84. See Waters, "With a Whimper or a Bang?," 1–14; Brian S. Rosner, "The Progress of the Word," pp. 215–33 in *Witness to the Gospel: The Theology of Acts*, ed. I. Howard Marshall and David Peterson (Grand Rapids: Eerdmans, 1998), 229; cf. Peterson, *Acts*, 719.

Theories on the Ending of Acts

Scholars have proposed various theories to explain Luke's curt conclusion to the story of Acts. Some of these theories are incompatible with one another; some seem far-fetched and unconvincing; but some could work together. Schnabel (*Acts*, 1062–63) has suggested three broad categories for plotting the theories, and using his categories, I list here some of the most intriguing explanations for the abrupt ending of Acts.

Historical Explanations

1. Writing in ca. AD 62, Luke is up to date in telling the story and has nothing more to record.
2. Luke trusts that his readers already know about Paul's fate (his release or execution).
3. Luke comes to the end of the papyrus roll and has no more room for a fuller ending.
4. Luke does not want to jeopardize Paul's future missionary activity by publicizing his release.

Theological-Programmatic Explanations

5. With Paul reaching Rome, Luke attains his goal of distinguishing Christian faith per Acts 1:8.
6. Silence about Paul's fate avoids a disappointing and unedifying conclusion of the story.
7. Silence about Paul's fate avoids the appearance of glorifying martyrdom.
8. Silence about Paul's fate avoids a negative impression of Rome and/or the Roman church.

Literary-Rhetorical Explanations

9. Luke is more interested in Paul's mission as God's representative than in his personal fate.
10. Luke pulls readers into the story and challenges them to mimic Paul's unhindered testimony.
11. Even as the OT story appeared to end but did not, Acts too closes without ending the story.
12. Luke intended to write a third volume with a more satisfying conclusion (with some suggesting that the Pastoral Epistles of 1–2 Timothy and Titus form that "third volume").

Furthermore, as an excellent author with intentional literary strategy and technique, Luke would have a purposed closure for the story of Acts.[85] Even as his sea voyage account pulls his readers into the story with Paul, the manner in which Luke closes the book challenges readers to follow Paul's example by letting nothing hinder them from testifying to the truth of the gospel.[86] So it is that "the ending of Acts marks the end to the narrative, but not to the story it tells."[87] In this way readers are challenged to participate in the ongoing story of spreading the gospel.

---

85. See Daniel Marguerat, *The First Christian Historian: Writing the 'Acts of the Apostles,'* trans. Ken McKinney, Gregory J. Laughery, and Richard Bauckham, SNTSMS 121 (Cambridge: Cambridge University Press, 2002), 209; cf. 209–16.

86. See Marguerat, *The First Christian Historian*, 215–16, 230; Peterson, *Acts*, 724; cf. Rosner, "The Progress of the Word," 229–33; and Beverly Roberts Gaventa, *Acts*, ANTC (Nashville: Abingdon, 2003), 370.

87. Troftgruben, *A Conclusion Unhindered*, 181.

15.5 CONCLUDING REMARKS

The final section of Acts covers Paul's trip to Rome. Luke's remarkably detailed sea voyage account with dramatic and miraculous events emphasizes God's providential ability to keep his promises in any of life's storms. Almost oddly, however, Luke ends the story of Acts without reporting Paul's appearance before Caesar. Rather, he tersely summarizes Paul's continued ministry while under house arrest awaiting trial. This abrupt closing of Acts must be the authentic ending of the book with Luke's intentional exclamation point of the final word "unhindered" NASB (Greek: *akōlutōs; "without hindrance" in CSB, ESV, NIV*) epitomizing the basic message of both his books.[88] The suspense the reader experiences in the sea voyage account is meant to find relief in Paul reaching Rome, but Luke's intention is to draw his audience in so as to require them to think about their place in the story.[89] It seems that Paul, of all people, might have an understandable excuse not to be involved in ministry: he is under house arrest. And yet Luke is clear that Paul's testimony to the truth of the gospel is unhindered in his ministry at the end of Acts. Success in following Jesus is faithfulness to him. The victories of gospel expansion in Acts do not belong to those bearing the message, for they were regularly rejected, persecuted, imprisoned, and even killed. It is the gospel message itself that is triumphantly unbound.[90] Attentive readers see that their place in the story, like that of Paul, is to continue testifying to the truth of the gospel, a message that will go on unhindered.

15.6 Key People, Places, and Terms

- Adramyttium
- Aristarchus
- Caesarea
- chief official
- Crete
- Fair Havens
- frapping
- goddess Justice
- Julius
- Malta
- Myra
- navigation year
- Northeaster
- Publius
- Puteoli
- Rhegium
- Rome
- Syracuse
- Syrtis
- "we sections"

88. Frank Stagg, "The Unhindered Gospel," *RevExp* 71 (1974): 460. Stagg suggests that Luke's uses of the word "hinder" elsewhere in Acts (Greek *kōluō in* 8:36; 10:47; 11:17; 16:6; 24:23; 27:43) anticipate his ending for the book with the word "unhindered."

89. Cf. Troftgruben, "Slow Sailing in Acts: Suspense in the Final Sea Journey," 966.

90. Polhill, *Acts*, 547.

15.7 Questions for Review and Discussion

1. What are some possible reasons for Luke's extended focus on Paul's journey to Rome? Which are most convincing to you, and why?
2. Luke has shown that Jesus can calm a stormy sea to save the lives of his followers (see Luke 8:22–25). But in Luke's account of the trip to Rome (Acts 27–28), the Lord does not calm the stormy sea to save Paul. Nevertheless, what evidence do we see of God's sovereign work in the midst of the various difficulties Paul faced?
3. It appears that the Lord used the stormy seas at the end of Acts to put Paul in particular situations with ministry opportunities. Make a list of those ministry opportunities.
4. Three times Paul intervenes during the hardships faced on the journey to Rome. What descriptions might you give of Paul's intentions for speaking up in those situations?
5. There are many (sometimes overlapping) theories for why the story of Acts appears to end as abruptly as it does. Which theories are most convincing to you, and why?
6. As Luke has portrayed it and as Paul has preached it, how is it that salvation can be exclusively through faith in Jesus Christ and yet can be inclusively offered to all?

15.8 Optional Assignments

1. **Text Reflection Project**—*Relating the concepts discussed in this chapter to another biblical text.* It has been suggested that Luke's final report of Paul's ministry in Acts 27–28 is intentionally structured with parallels to his final report of Jesus's ministry in Luke 23–24. Create a chart of possible parallels between these two Lukan texts, and write a short paper about what might be learned by means of this comparison. Luke clearly does not think that Jesus's ministry stops after Luke 23–24; what might this mean for the possibility of Paul's continued ministry after Acts 27–28?
2. **Interview Project**—*Inquiring of others their views concerning the concepts discussed in this chapter.* Talk with your pastor (or some other respected Christian leader) about their understanding of the abruptness of the ending of Acts. If they have not put much thought into this matter before, perhaps you can share with them some of the options scholars have suggested and they can weigh in on their favored option(s) and why. Write up a summary of your discussion with this leader and describe the option or combination of options that you currently favor for explaining Luke's abrupt ending to Acts.
3. **Service-Learning Project**—*Applying the concepts discussed in this chapter in some form of service to others outside the class.* When Paul and his missionary team shipwreck on the island of Malta, he immediately begins serving others by gathering sticks for the fire. That service to others (after a snake bite!) turned into an opportunity to talk about spiritual things (i.e., the goddess Justice; Acts 28:4). Think of some "disaster relief" service project you can do, even if it is seemingly small. After participating in that service project, write a short reflection paper about your participation and what opportunities it occasioned.

4. **Prayer Project**—*Talking with God about the concepts discussed in this chapter.* In the midst of stormy seas, Paul prays and gives thanks to God (Acts 27:35); faced with a very ill man, Paul prays and is involved in a healing (Acts 28:8). Write a prayer about some "stormy seas" you are facing right now or some overwhelming circumstances in which you would like to see miraculous intervention. Don't forget to include gratitude in your prayer.
5. **Testimony Project**—*Telling others about the concepts discussed in this chapter.* Acts 27–28 recounts a perilous journey of several months that Paul (and Luke) took from Palestine to Rome. In a few short pages, recount a perilous time you faced in your life and how (as with Paul) the Lord Jesus provided you encouragement, brought you through the difficulties, and even used you to encourage others. As with Luke writing up the story of Paul and ending before reporting the final results, perhaps your story does not have a conclusive ending either. That is OK. But perhaps like Luke, you can conclude your write-up pointing in a hopeful direction with progress unhindered. Select someone to share this story with and then write up a single-page reflection on the experience: report what went well, what did not go so well, and how you might do it differently next time you have the opportunity to share this story.

15.9 Bibliography for Going Further

15.9.1 The Voyage to Rome

Hemer, Colin J. "First Person Narrative in Acts 27–28." *TynBul* 36 (1985): 79–109.

Gilchrist, J. Michael. "The Historicity of Paul's Shipwreck." *JSNT* 61 (1996): 29–51.

Jipp, Joshua W. *Divine Visitations and Hospitality to Strangers in Luke-Acts: An Interpretation of the Malta Episode in Acts 28:1–10*. NovTSup 153. Leiden: Brill, 2013.

Miles, Gary B., and Garry Trompf. "Luke and Antiphon: The Theology of Acts 27–28 in the Light of Pagan Beliefs about Divine Retribution, Pollution, and Shipwreck." *HTR* 69.3 (1976): 259–67.

Praeder, Susan Marie. "Acts 27:1–28:16: Sea Voyages in Ancient Literature and the Theology of Luke-Acts." *CBQ* 46.4 (1984): 683–706.

Rapske, Brian M. "Acts, Travel, and Shipwreck." Pages 1–47 in *The Book of Acts in Its Graeco-Roman Setting*. Edited by David W. J. Gill and Conrad Gempf. BAFCS 2. Grand Rapids: Eerdmans, 1994; Carlisle: Paternoster, 1994.

Troftgruben, Troy M. "Slow Sailing in Acts: Suspense in the Final Sea Journey (Acts 27:1–28:15)." *JBL* 136.4 (2017): 949–68.

White, Jefferson. "Paul's Voyage to Rome and Shipwreck (59–60 AD)." Pages 66–82 (chapter 5) in *Evidence & Paul's Journeys: An Historical Investigation into the Travels of the Apostle Paul*. Hilliard, OH: Parsagard, 2001.

15.9.2 The Conclusion to Acts

Cassidy, Richard J. "Paul's Proclamation of Lord Jesus as a Chained Prisoner in Rome: Luke's Ending Is in His Beginning." Pages 227–37 (added essay) in *Society and Politics in the Acts of the Apostles*. 2nd ed. Eugene, OR: Wipf & Stock, 2014.

Davies, Philip R. "The Ending of Acts." *ExpTim* 94.11 (1983): 334–35.

Marguerat, Daniel. "The Enigma of the End of Acts (28:16–31)." Pages 205–30 (chapter 10) in *The First Christian Historian: Writing the 'Acts of the Apostles.'* Translated by Ken McKinney, Gregory J. Laughery, and Richard Bauckham. SNTSMS 121. Cambridge: Cambridge University Press, 2002.

———. "On Why Luke Remains Silent about Paul's End (Acts 28:16–31)." Pages 305–32 in *The Last Years of Paul: Essays from the Tarragona Conference, June 2013.* Edited by Armand Puig i Tàrrech, John M. G. Barclay, and Jörg Frey. WUNT 352. Tübingen: Mohr Siebeck, 2015.

Puskas, Charles B. *The Conclusion of Luke-Acts: The Significance of Acts 28:16–31*. Eugene, OR: Pickwick, 2009.

Stagg, Frank. "The Unhindered Gospel." *RevExp* 71.4 (1974): 451–62.

Troftgruben, Troy M. *A Conclusion Unhindered: A Study of the Ending of the Acts Within Its Literary Environment.* WUNT 2.280. Tübingen: Mohr Siebeck, 2010.

Trompf, G. W. "On Why Luke Declined to Recount the Death of Paul: Acts 27–28 and Beyond." Pages 225–39 in *Luke-Acts: New Perspectives from the Society of Biblical Literature Seminar.* Edited by Charles H. Talbert. New York: Crossroad, 1984.

Waters, Guy Prentiss. "With a Whimper or a Bang? Acts 28 and the Ending of Acts." *RTR* 74.1 (2015): 1–14.

PART 4

THE STORY OF JESUS REACHING YOUR WORLD

T shooter/stock.adobe.com

16 Conclusion: Continuing the Story of Jesus Unhindered

Chapter Goals

After reading this chapter, you should be able to:

- Recount some of the traditions about the lives of the apostles after Acts as reflected in the extrabiblical literature of the early church.
- Describe how the book of Acts became recognized as Scripture.
- Explain how the message of Acts challenges you to participate in the spread of the gospel, in the community of other Jesus followers, so as to make your life story be about the gospel.

Chapter Overview

16.1 The Story after Acts for the Apostles: Dedicated Lives and Martyrdom
16.2 The Story after Acts for the Book of Acts: Acts as Scripture
16.3 The Story after Acts for Us: The Message, Encouragement, and Challenge of Acts
16.4 Concluding Remarks
16.5 Key People, Places, and Terms
16.6 Questions for Review and Discussion
16.7 Optional Assignments
16.8 Bibliography for Going Further

Key Verses

As for us, we cannot help speaking about what we have seen and heard. (Acts 4:20)

For two whole years Paul stayed there in his own rented house and welcomed all who came to see him. He proclaimed the kingdom of God and taught about the Lord Jesus Christ—with all boldness and without hindrance! (Acts 28:30–31)

I will make every effort to see that after my departure you will always be able to remember these things. For we did not follow cleverly devised stories when we told you about the coming of our Lord Jesus Christ in power, but we were eyewitnesses of his majesty. . . . We also have the prophetic message as something completely reliable, and you will do well to pay attention to it, as to a light shining in a dark place, until the day dawns and the morning star rises in your hearts. (2 Pet 1:15–16, 19)

The things you have heard me say in the presence of many witnesses entrust to reliable people who will also be qualified to teach others. (2 Tim 2:2)

INTRODUCTION

The abrupt ending of Acts has puzzled readers for centuries, but I have suggested that this fits Luke's intention to draw us into the story. Luke wants us to notice that, despite being under house arrest and awaiting trial before Caesar, Paul continued in ministry. If anyone had a good excuse not to be in ministry, it seems that Paul did at this juncture. Nevertheless, Luke closes the story noting that Paul remained bold and consistent in his sharing of the gospel: "He proclaimed the kingdom of God and taught about the Lord Jesus Christ—with all boldness and without hindrance!" (Acts 28:31).

16.1 THE STORY AFTER ACTS FOR THE APOSTLES: DEDICATED LIVES AND MARTYRDOM

After the abrupt ending of Acts, the spread of the gospel continued. Church tradition has recorded various legends about the ministries of the twelve apostles, the seven "deacons" of Acts 6, the apostle Paul, and others. These entertaining, intriguing, and sometimes confusing (and even conflicting) traditions have been recorded in various extrabiblical books.[1] These "apocryphal" works (meaning "hidden" or "kept private") were thought of as unauthoritative books meant for private reading rather than for official use in

1. See the sidebar on "The Teachings of Church Tradition" in chapter 1.

public church settings. They are of doubtful origin and are typically thought spurious rather than trusted as coming from the figures attached to the books.[2] Nevertheless, many of these apocryphal books have titles that borrow the term *acts* from the Acts of the Apostles. In so doing, they form a virtual (but not exact) subgenre of literature.[3]

Apocryphal Acts

The date ranges given here follow those suggested by Hans-Josef Klauck, *The Apocryphal Acts of the Apostles: An Introduction*, trans. Brian McNeil (Waco, TX: Baylor University Press, 2008).

The Five Major Apocryphal Acts

The Acts of John (ca. AD 150–160)
The Acts of Paul (ca. AD 170–180)
The Acts of Peter (ca. AD 190–200)
The Acts of Andrew (ca. AD 200–210)
The Acts of Thomas (ca. AD 220–240)

A Sampling of Other Apocryphal Acts

The Acts of Peter and Andrew (ca. AD 225–275)
The Acts of Peter and the Twelve Apostles (ca. AD 250–350)
The Acts of Simon and Jude (ca. AD 325–375)
The Acts of Philip (ca. AD 350–400)
The Acts of Andrew and Matthias (ca. AD 350–450)
The Acts of Timothy (ca. AD 350–550)
The Acts of Xanthippe, Polyxena, and Rebecca (ca. AD 350–550)
The Acts (or Passion) of Peter and Paul (ca. AD 400–450)
The Acts of Titus (ca. AD 450–550)
The Acts of Nereus and Achilleus (ca. AD 450–550)
The Acts and Martyrdom of Bartholomew (ca. AD 450–550)
The Acts of Barnabas (ca. AD 475–500)
The Acts and Martyrdom of Saint Matthew the Apostle (ca. AD 525–575)
The Acts of Mār Mārī (ca. AD 525–575)
The Acts of Thaddeus (ca. AD 550–950)

2. See the judgment of Eusebius, *Hist eccl.* 3.25.4–7 (in sidebar); cf. 3.3; 6.12. See also Jerome's remark on the extrabiblical works ascribed to Peter (including an Acts, a Gospel, a Preaching, and a Revelation) that they "are rejected as apocryphal"; Jerome, *Vir. Ill.*, 1.

3. Noting the use of the Greek term *praxeis* (for "deeds" or "achievements"), I briefly caution against identifying "acts" as a genre in chapter 2.

The Doubtful Authority of the Apocryphal Acts

Eusebius, *Ecclesiastical History* 3.25.4–7 (ca. AD 323)

Among the books which are not genuine must be reckoned the Acts of Paul, the work entitled the Shepherd, the Apocalypse of Peter, and in addition to them the letter called of Barnabas and the so-called Teachings of the Apostles. . . . These would all belong to the disputed books, but we have nevertheless been obliged to make a list of them, distinguishing between those writings which, according to the tradition of the Church, are true, genuine, and recognized, and those which differ from them in that they are not canonical but disputed, yet nevertheless are known to most of the writers of the Church, in order that we might know them and the writings which are put forward by heretics under the name of the apostles containing gospels such as those of Peter, and Thomas, and Matthias, and some others besides, or Acts such as those of Andrew and John and the other apostles. To none of these has any who belonged to the succession of the orthodox ever thought it right to refer in his writings. Moreover, the type of phraseology differs from apostolic style, and the opinion and tendency of their contents is widely dissonant from true orthodoxy and clearly shows that they are the forgeries of heretics. They ought, therefore, to be reckoned not even among spurious books but shunned as altogether wicked and impious.

Dating from the mid-second century into the sixth century, the ***apocryphal acts*** come later than the canonical Acts of the Apostles, and their titles often name particular individual apostles: e.g., the Acts of John, the Acts of Paul, the Acts of Peter, the Acts of Andrew, the Acts of Thomas.[4]

Out of a sense of curiosity—and perhaps piquing it further—we report here on some of the legends regarding the lives of the apostles after the book of Acts. Note that while sometimes focused on the individual apostles, the stories of believers are often not individual stories but stories of them in community. Similar to the biblical reports of the apostles serving in pairs (see Mark 6:7 and Luke 10:1), the extrabiblical stories

4. These five major apocryphal acts have been ascribed to Leucius Charinus, but it may be that he authored only the first, as he was a supposed disciple of the apostle John; Hans-Josef Klauck, *The Apocryphal Acts of the Apostles: An Introduction*, trans. Brian McNeil (Waco, TX: Baylor University Press, 2008), 5. English translations of the major apocryphal acts (and extracts and summary descriptions of many others) are available in *ANF* and J. K. Elliott, *The Apocryphal New Testament: A Collection of Apocryphal Christian Literature in an English Translation* (Oxford: Clarendon, 1993), esp. pp. 227–533; cf. Klauck, *The Apocryphal Acts of the Apostles*. For a brief but insightful comparison of the canonical Acts with the apocryphal acts, see François C. Bovon, "Canonical and Apocryphal Acts of the Apostles," in *New Testament and Christian Apocrypha: Collected Studies II*, WUNT 237 (Tübingen: Mohr Siebeck, 2009; repr. As *New Testament and Christian Apocrypha*, Grand Rapids: Baker Academic, 2011), 197–222; cf. J. Christopher Edwards, ed., *Early New Testament Apocrypha*, Ancient Literature for New Testament Studies 9 (Grand Rapids: Zondervan Academic, 2022), 195–339. For an imaginative proposal about the Acts of Paul, see Richard Bauckham, "The *Acts of Paul* as a Sequel to Acts," in *The Book of Acts in its Ancient Literary Setting*, ed. Bruce W. Winter and Andrew D. Clarke, BAFCS 1 (Grand Rapids: Eerdmans, 1993; Carlisle: Paternoster, 1993), 105–52.

report the apostles continuing to serve in pairs. Furthermore, these legendary traditions about the apostles have often influenced artistic representations of them.

16.1.1 Peter (a.k.a. Simon Peter, a.k.a. Cephas)

Simon—to whom Jesus gave the name ***Peter*** (Mark 3:16)—serves in Acts as the chief spokesperson among the apostles. Therefore he is often named first in the NT lists of apostles (Matt 10:1–4; Mark 3:13–19; Luke 6:12–16; Acts 1:13). While Acts focuses on Peter's ministry in Jerusalem (Acts 1–6) and in Judea and Samaria (Acts 8–11), Paul's letters inform us that he made a trip to Syrian Antioch (Gal 2:11–14 ≈ Acts 12:17?) and hint at a possible trip to Corinth (1 Cor 1:12; 3:22). Various extrabiblical traditions suggest that Peter did ministry in Syrian Antioch, and patristic claims of his preaching in the diverse territories and provinces of Pontus, Galatia, Cappadocia, Asia,

Some Extrabiblical Traditions about Simon Peter

Hippolytus of Rome, *On the Twelve Apostles* 1 (ca. AD 170–236)

Peter preached the Gospel in Pontus, and Galatia, and Cappadocia, and Betania, and Italy, and Asia, and was afterwards crucified by Nero in Rome with his head downward, as he had himself desired to suffer in that manner.

The Acts of Peter 7 (ca. AD 190–200)

Soon it became known among the scattered brethren of the city that Peter had come to Rome on account of Simon [Magus], to prove that he was a seducer and persecutor of the good. And the whole multitude came together to see the apostle of the Lord, confirming the congregation in Christ.

The Acts of Peter 36–40 (ca. AD 190–200)

While Peter was speaking the brethren wept and four soldiers arrested him and brought him to Agrippa. And being enraged he ordered that he be crucified for godlessness. . . .

And when he had come to the cross he began to say, "O name of the cross, hidden mystery; O unspeakable mercy, which is expressed in the name of the cross; . . . I seize you now I am standing at the end of my earthly career. . . . But the hour has come for you, Peter, to deliver your body to those who are taking it. Take it, whose business it is. Of you, executioners, I ask to crucify me with head downwards, and not otherwise. And the reason I shall explain to those who listen."

After they had hanged him up as he wished he began to speak again, "Men, whose calling it is to hear, listen to what I, being hanged, am about to tell you now. . . . The Word is this upright tree on which I am crucified; the sound, however, is the crossbeam, namely the nature of man; and the nail which holds the crossbeam to the upright in the middle is the conversion and repentance of man. . . . We now ask undefiled Jesus for that which you promised to give us; we praise you, we thank you, we confess you in glorifying you, though we are weak, because you alone are God and no other, to whom be glory now and for ever, Amen."

When the multitude surrounding him cried Amen, Peter, during this Amen, gave up his spirit to the Lord.

Eusebius, *Ecclesiastical History* 3.1.2 (ca. AD 323)

But Peter seems to have preached to the Jews of the Dispersion in Pontus and Galatia and Bithynia, Cappadocia, and Asia, and at the end he came to Rome and was crucified head downwards, for so he had demanded to suffer.

and Bithynia are supportive of the opening of his first epistle (see 1 Pet 1:1). In addition to Peter authoring the two NT letters that bear his name (with the help of Silas in the first letter; 1 Pet 5:12), patristic evidence suggests that he also influenced the writing of the Gospel of Mark.[5] Church tradition has Peter going to Rome to continue his opposition of Simon Magus (cf. Acts 8:9–24) and to serve as leader of the church and eventually being martyred for the Christian faith at the command of Nero. According to the apocryphal book called the Acts of Peter (§37), when Peter was to be crucified (ca. AD 64–68), he requested that it be upside down, as he did not consider himself worthy to die in the same manner as Jesus.

16.1.2 John, Son of Zebedee (a.k.a. the Beloved Disciple)

John the apostle is mentioned only briefly in Acts and always as a co-minister with Peter (Acts 3–4; 8:14), but his influence is clearly evidenced elsewhere in the New Testament. Recognized as "the disciple whom Jesus loved" (John 13:23; 19:26; 20:2; 21:7, 20), he is considered the author of five NT books: the Gospel of John; the letters of 1–3 John; and Revelation. John is the only named apostle present at Jesus's crucifixion, at which time Jesus assigned the care of his mother Mary to John (John 19:25–27). Church tradition reports that John was founder and leader of the church in Ephesus in the middle of the first century. After his exile on the nearby island of Patmos, where he had the visions of the book of Revelation, John returned to Ephesus.[6] Considered the youngest of Jesus's original apostles, John is also often thought to be the only one to die in old age rather than as a martyr.[7]

Some Extrabiblical Traditions about John

Clement of Alexandria, *Quis dives salvetur*, 42 (ca. AD 150–215)

And to give you confidence, when you have thus truly repented, that there remains for you a trustworthy hope of salvation, hear a story that is no mere story, but a true account of John the apostle that has been handed down and preserved in memory. When after the death of the tyrant [Domitian] he removed from the island of Patmos to Ephesus, he used to journey by request to the neighbouring districts of the Gentiles, in some places to appoint bishops, in others to regulate whole churches, in others to set among the clergy some one man, it may be, of those indicated by the Spirit.

The Acts of John 40–42 (ca. AD 150–160)

And [at the Temple of Artemis] John answered them, "If you do not wish to die, let me convince you of your idolatry. And why? So that you may desist from your old error.

5. E.g., Irenaeus, *Haer.* 3.1.1; Eusebius, *Hist eccl.* 2.15.1–2; 6.14.6–7; 6.25.5; John Chrysostom, *Hom. Matt.* 1.7.

6. E.g., Clement of Alexandria, *Quis div.* 42.

7. See esp. the sixth-century Ethiopic document by Abdias, *The Conflicts of the Holy Apostles*, trans. Solomon Caesar Malan (London: Nutt, 1871).

Be now converted by my God or I will die at the hands of your goddess. For I will pray in your presence to my God, and ask him to have mercy upon you."

After these words he prayed, "God, who are God above all so-called gods, who to this day have been despised at Ephesus, you induced me to come to this place, which I never had in view. You have abrogated every form of worship through conversion to you. In your name every idol, every demon, and every unclean spirit is banished. May the deity of this place, which has deceived so many, now also give way to your name, and thus show your mercy on this place! For they walk in error."

And with these words of John the altar of Artemis suddenly split into many parts, and the oblations put up in the temple suddenly fell to the ground, and its glory broke, and so did more than seven of the idols. And half of the temple fell down, so that when the roof came down, the priest also was killed at one stroke. And the people of the Ephesians cried, "There is only one God, that of John, only one God who has compassion for us; for you alone are God; now we have become converted, since we saw your miraculous deeds. Have mercy upon us, God, according to your will, and deliver us from our great error." And some of them lay on their faces and cried; others bent their knees and prayed; others rent their garments and lamented; still others tried to escape.

Abdias, *The Conflicts of the Holy Apostles* 9 (ca. late sixth century AD)

But after the Apostles had finished all their work, and had gone from this world, . . . every one of them, struggled with afflictions and many tribulations in the several countries whither they had gone to make disciples—John remained alive on earth many years, until the reign of Domitian, and continued for seventy years after our Lord's resurrection. He reached unto a very old age, and did not taste of death by the sword nor in any violent way, because our Lord loved him much for his innocence, as it is written in the Gospel.

Hippolytus of Rome, *On the Twelve Apostles* 3 (ca. AD 170–236)

John, again, in Asia, was banished by Domitian the king to the isle of Patmos, in which also he wrote his Gospel and say the apocalyptic vision; and in Trajan's time he fell asleep at Ephesus, where his remains were sought for, but could not be found.

The plain of Bethsaida looking towards the northern tip of the Sea of Galilee.

Todd Bolen/ BiblePlaces.com

16.1.3 James, Son of Zebedee (a.k.a. James the Greater)

James and his brother John were dubbed the "sons of thunder" by Jesus (Mark 3:17; perhaps for their harsh responses to opposition, see Mark 9:38; Luke 9:54). With two of the apostles named James, it is the son of Zebedee who is considered the "older" one or perhaps the "greater" one (because he was in the inner circle of Jesus's friends: Peter, James, and John). A medieval tradition suggests that ***James the Greater*** had a ministry in Spain, but this seems unlikely because his death occurred before persecution dispersed the apostles from Jerusalem (cf. Acts 8:1; 11:19).[8] According to Acts 12:1–3, he was the first of the apostles to die as a martyr for the gospel, being put to death by the sword at the command of Herod Agrippa I (ca. AD 41); a tradition reported by Clement of Alexandria as recorded by Eusebius is that the man escorting James to his death became a believer and was beheaded with him.[9]

Some Extrabiblical Traditions about James the Greater

John Chrysostom, *Commentary on Matthew* (ca. AD 349–407)

See how they all were imperfect: both these two [apostles John and James; cf. Matt 20:20–28] who wanted to be superior to the ten, and those ten who were envious of these two? But, as I have already said, Look at their subsequent life, and you shall see them free from all those passions. Listen how the same John who now comes to Jesus asking him to make him superior, later concedes the highest rank to Peter both in preaching and in miracles. . . . As far as James is concerned, although he didn't live too long, he was so on fire for God that he disregarded all things human, achieved unspeakable prowess and was immediately deemed worthy of martyrdom. They all became perfect in all virtues; but then, they were indignant.

Clement of Alexandria, *Hypotyposes* 7 (ca. AD 150–215) cited in Eusebius, *Hist. eccl.* 2.9.3 (ca. AD 323)

So they were both led away together, and on the way he asked for forgiveness for himself from James. And James looked at him for a moment and said, "Peace be to you," and kissed him. So both were beheaded at the same time.

16.1.4 Andrew, Brother of Simon Peter

Hailing from Bethsaida on the Sea of Galilee, ***Andrew*** had been a disciple of John the Baptist before deciding to follow Jesus, and he is credited with quickly recruiting his brother Simon Peter to follow Jesus as well (John 1:35–44; cf. Matt 4:18–20;

---

8. The twelfth-century, anonymously written chronicle *Historia Compostelana* connects James the Greater with Santiago de Compostela in northwestern Spain. For the unlikeliness of James traveling to Spain, see David Criswell, *The Apostles after Jesus: A History of the Apostles (Separating Tradition and History)* (Dallas: Fortress Adonai, 2013), 6–7, 37–39; contra William Steuart McBirnie, *The Search for the Twelve Apostles*, rev. ed. (Carol Stream, IL: Tyndale, 2004), 75–77. Alternatively, instead of traveling to Spain himself, James may have ministered to Spanish Jews who came to Jerusalem (cf. "Jews from every nation under heaven" in Acts 2:5).

9. Clement of Alexandria, *Hyp.* 7, cited in Eusebius, *Hist. eccl.* 2.9.3.

Some Extrabiblical Traditions about Andrew

Hippolytus of Rome, *On the Twelve Apostles* 2 (ca. AD 170–236)

Andrew preached to the Scythians and Thracians, and was crucified, suspended on an olive tree, at Patrae, a town of Achaia; and there too he was buried.

Abdias, *The Conflicts of the Holy Apostles* 9 (ca. late sixth century AD)

And when it was morning they brought Andrew out of the prison, they crucified him upon a wooden cross, and stoned him with stones until his martyrdom was accomplished, and he gave up his soul into the hands of God.

The Acts of Andrew and Matthias 19–21 (ca. AD 350–450)

Andrew went into the city along with his disciples, and no one beheld him. And when he came to the prison, he saw seven warders standing at the gate guarding, and he prayed within himself, and they fell down and expired; and he marked the gate with the sign of the cross, and it opened of its own accord. And having gone in with his disciples, he found Matthias sitting and singing; and seeing him, he stood up, and they saluted each other with a holy kiss; and he said to Matthias: Brother, how hast thou been found here? For yet three days, and they will bring thee out to be food for them. . . .

. . . And there were in all two hundred and seventy men and forty-nine women whom Andrew released from the prison. And the men went as the blessed Andrew said to them; and he made Matthias go along with his disciples out of the eastern gate of the city. And Andrew commanded a cloud, and the cloud took up Matthias and the disciples of Andrew; and the cloud set them down on the mountain where Peter was teaching, and they remained beside him.

The Acts of Andrew (ca. AD 200–210)

Then the proconsul Aegeates, being enraged, ordered the apostle of Christ to be afflicted by tortures. Being stretched out, therefore, by seven times three soldiers, and beaten with violence, he was lifted up and brought before the impious Aegeates. And he spoke to him thus: Listen to me, Andrew, and withdraw thy thoughts from the outpouring of thy blood; but if thou wilt not hearken to me, I shall cause thee to perish on the tree of the cross.

The holy Andrew said: I am a slave of the cross of Christ, and I ought rather to pray to attain to the trophy of the cross than to be afraid; but for thee is laid up eternal torment, which, however, thou mayst escape after thou hast tested my endurance, if thou wilt believe in my Christ. For I am afflicted about thy destruction, and I am not disturbed about my own suffering. For my suffering takes up a space of one day, or two at most; but thy torment for endless ages shall never come to a close. Wherefore henceforward cease from adding to thy miseries, and lighting up everlasting fire for thyself.

Aegeates then being enraged, ordered the blessed Andrew to be fastened to the cross.

Mark 1:16–17). Andrew is mentioned by name several times in the Gospels (Matt 10:2; Mark 1:29; 3:18; 13:3–4; Luke 6:14; John 6:8–9; 12:20–22) but only once in Acts (Acts 1:13). His ministry after Acts is said to have been in Achaia (Greece), Asia Minor (modern Turkey), and Macedonia, with a trip to Scythia (the region of modern Ukraine and Russia), where he was utilized to rescue Matthias from cannibals![10]

10. E.g., The Acts of Andrew and Matthias.

Hippolytus reports that Andrew was crucified on an olive tree at Patras, a town in Achaia.[11] A sixth-century Ethiopic document by Abdias reports further that Andrew was also stoned as well as crucified.[12] Andrew's bones were supposedly relocated in the fourth century to Scotland, and the eighth-century King Hungus of the Picts is said to have won a promised victory in battle under a "saltire" symbol in the sky. The saltire is an X-shaped cross associated with Andrew's crucifixion, and thus, Andrew has been the patron saint of Scotland ever since.[13]

16.1.5 Philip, the Apostle

Like Peter and Andrew, Philip was also from Bethsaida and an early follower of Jesus (Matt 10:3; Mark 3:18; Luke 6:14; John 1:43–44). He is noted for recruiting Nathanael (a.k.a. Bartholomew) to follow Jesus as well (see John 1:43–51). He is mentioned by name several times in the Gospel of John (6:5–7; 12:20–22; 14:6–10) but only once in Acts (Acts 1:13). Even from early times, ***Philip the apostle*** was confused with Philip the evangelist, one of the seven men selected by the Jerusalem church to assist the apostles by overseeing the food distribution ministry (6:1–6; 8:4–40; 21:8–9), and the legends about the two are often confused and conflated.[14] Some report that Philip founded a church in Athens, then traveled to Parthia (a region of modern Iran), and then preached with Bartholomew in Phrygia of Asia Minor (modern Turkey), where he was crucified upside down in Hierapolis, with Bartholomew similarly tortured but not to death.[15] Others report that Philip eventually ministered in northern Africa and was martyred there.[16]

Traditional site of Philip's tomb in Hierapolis.

Stephen/stock .adobe.com

11. Hippolytus, *On the Twelve Apostles* 2.

12. Abdias, *The Conflicts of the Holy Apostles*, 9.

13. See W. Brian Shelton, *Quest for the Historical Apostles: Tracing Their Lives and Legacies* (Grand Rapids: Baker Academic, 2018), 95–96. Sean McDowell concludes that "the tradition Andrew was crucified on an X-shaped cross is almost certainly false"; Sean McDowell, *The Fate of the Apostles: Examining the Martyrdom Accounts of the Closest Followers of Jesus* (New York: Routledge, 2015)185n46. See more fully Ursula Hall, *The Cross of St. Andrew* (Edinburgh: Birlinn, 2006).

14. Cf. Shelton, *Quest for the Historical Apostles*, 145–46. See the argument that the two Philips are actually one and the same person in Christopher R. Matthews, *Philip: Apostle and Evangelist: Configurations of a Tradition*, NovTSup 105 (Leiden: Brill, 2002); cf. Martin Hengel, *Saint Peter: The Underestimated Apostle*, trans. Thomas H. Trapp (Grand Rapids: Eerdmans, 2010), 116–20. Nevertheless, that Philip the apostle and Philip the evangelist are two distinct people seems plainly evident to me from the differentiation of their ministries (Acts 6:1–6); from the specification that the apostles initially stayed in Jerusalem (Acts 8:1–3) while other believers (like Philip the evangelist) dispersed (Acts 8:4–8; with Philip the evangelist ending up in Caesarea); and from Luke's clarifying the latter as "Philip the evangelist, one of the Seven" (vs. "one of the apostles"; Acts 21:8–9).

15. E.g., Hippolytus, *On the Twelve Apostles* 5, and The Acts of Philip; cf. the thirteenth-century collection of hagiographies, Jacobus de Voragine, *The Golden Legend*, trans. William Caxton, ed. F. S. Elllis, The Temple Classics (London: J. M. Dent, 1900), 3:156–57. See the various reports of Eusebius, *Hist. eccl.* 3.31.2–5; 3.39.9; 5.24.2, some of which seem to conflate Philip the apostle and Philip the evangelist.

16. E.g., Abdias, *The Conflicts of the Holy Apostles*, 8.

Some Extrabiblical Traditions about Philip

Hippolytus of Rome, *On the Twelve Apostles* 5 (ca. AD 170–236)

Philip preached in Phrygia, and was crucified in Hierapolis with his head downward in the time of Domitian, and was buried there.

Papias (ca. AD 110–140) cited in Eusebius, *Hist. eccl.* 6.14.6 (ca. AD 323)

But it is worth while to add to the words of Papias already given other sayings of his, in which he tells certain marvels and other details which apparently reached him by tradition. It has already been mentioned that Philip the Apostle lived at Hierapolis with his daughters, but it must now be shown how Papias was with them and received a wonderful story from the daughters of Philip; for he relates the resurrection of a corpse in his time and in another place another miracle connected with Justus surnamed Barsabas, for he drank poison but by the Lord's grace suffered no harm.

The Acts of Philip 13–15 (ca. AD 350–400)

About the time when the Emperor Trajan received the government of the Romans, . . . Philip the apostle, going through the cities and regions of Lydia and Asia, preached to all the Gospel of Christ.

And having come to the city of Ophioryma, which is called Hierapolis of Asia, he was entertained by a certain believer, Stachys by name. And there was with him also Bartholomew, one of the seventy disciples of the Lord, and his sister Mariamme, and his disciples that followed him. All the men of the city therefore, having left their work, ran to the house of Stachys, hearing about the works which Philip did. And many men and women having assembled in the house of Stachys, Philip along with Bartholomew taught them the things of Jesus. . . .

And the proconsul seeing them, gnashed his teeth, saying: Torture these deceivers that have deceived many women, and young men and girls, saying that they are worshippers of God, while they are an abomination. And he ordered thongs of raw hide to be brought, and Philip and Bartholomew and Mariamme to be beaten; and after they had been scourged with the thongs, he ordered their feet to be tied, and them to be dragged through the streets of the city as far as the gate of their temple. . . .

And he ordered Philip to be hanged, and his ankles to be pierced, and to bring also iron hooks, and his heels also to be driven through, and to be hanged head downwards, opposite the temple on a certain tree; and stretch out Bartholomew opposite Philip, having nailed his hands on the wall of the gate of the temple.

And both of them smiled, seeing each other, both Philip and Bartholomew; for they were as if they were not tortured: for their punishments were prizes and crowns.

Abdias, *The Conflicts of the Holy Apostles* 8 (ca. late sixth century AD)

It happened that Philip came to the city of Afrikia, and preached to the men of that city a new God, whom they knew not, and whose name was Jesus. . . .

But the great men of the city, when they saw what Philip did, and the wonders that God wrought by his hands, and how men were healed of all diseases; when they saw their beloved ones, their sons and their daughters and their brothers renounce their gods and come to believe in God through Philip's teaching, they that did not believe in his preaching gathered together, withdrew aside, and being assembled, plotted together to take him and to cast him into prison, and to put him to death. . . .

And one of them said: Let us kill him, that he may not deceive us; then their anger was kindled against him, and they took him and raised him upon a cross, with his head downwards and his feet upwards, and they tied him, so that he might not move his body; and they beat him with stripes, and ceased not to illtreat him, neither did they depart from him, beating him all the while, until he gave up the ghost on his Cross. Then they took him down, and said among themselves: Let us light a large fire, and burn his body in it, that no trace of him be found. But when they had lighted the fire and were about to cast Philip into it, God sent an angel who took Philip out of their hands.

Saint Thomas. Kerala, India.
Dinodia Photos / Alamy Stock Photo

16.1.6 Thomas (a.k.a. Didymus, a.k.a. Judas Thomas)

This apostle is perhaps most known for his reluctance to believe in the resurrection until gaining more evidence (see John 20:24–29). ***Thomas*** may have had a twin sibling ("Thomas" is the Anglicization of "twin" in Hebrew, and *didymus* is "twin" in Greek; cf. John 11:16), but some legends suggest that Thomas was a "twin" (in some sense or other) to Jesus, and a full name of Judas Thomas is sometimes used. While at first reluctant to go, Thomas is said to have traveled through Syria across Parthia and Bactria (regions of modern Iran and Afghanistan) to reach what is now India.[17] He sold himself into slavery as a carpenter in order to enter India. In spite of the widespread acceptance of his gospel preaching, he was martyred at the order of King Misdeus by being pierced through with pine spears. Conflicting stories of his martyrdom vary on the details of his torture and the location of his death in India.[18] Various legends report that Thomas's bones were moved to Edessa, Syria, and then several centuries later (to avoid destruction by Muslims) to Ortona, Italy.[19]

17. On his initial reluctance, see esp. the opening paragraph of The Acts of Thomas.

18. Eusebius (*Hist. eccl.* 3.1.1.) reports that Thomas was assigned Parthia; for Thomas's travels that eventually take him to India, see esp. The Acts of Thomas, and Abdias, *The Conflicts of the Holy Apostles*, 15; cf. the sweeping summary of Hippolytus, *On the Twelve Apostles* 8.

19. E.g., the sixth-century bishop and historian, Gregory of Tours writes, "According to the history of his suffering the apostle Thomas is said to have been martyred in India. Much later his blessed body was transferred to the city that the Syrians call Edessa, and there buried"; Gregory of Tours, *Glory of the Martyrs*, 31; translation by Raymond Van Dam, *Gregory of Tours: Glory of the Martyrs*, Translated Texts for Historians, Latin Series 3 (Liverpool: Liverpool University Press, 1988), 51. Similarly, the earlier account of the travels of the fourth-century Christian Etheria comments on "the church and memorial of saint Thomas" in Edessa being "very great, very beautiful and of new construction, well worthy to be the house of God"; translation from M. L. McClure and C. L. Feltoe, *The Pilgrimage of Etheria* (London: SPCK, 1919), 32.

Some Extrabiblical Traditions about Thomas

Hippolytus of Rome, *On the Twelve Apostles* 8 (ca. AD 170–236)

And Thomas preached to the Parthians, Medes, Persians, Hyrcanians, Bactrians, and Margians, and was thrust through in the four members of his body with a pine spear at Calamene, the city of India, and was buried there.

The Acts of Thomas (ca. AD 220–240)

By lot, then, India fell to Judas Thomas, also called Didymus. And he did not wish to go, saying that he was not able to go on account of the weakness of the flesh; and how can I, being an Hebrew man, go among the Indians to proclaim the truth? And while he was thus reasoning and speaking, the Saviour appeared to him through the night, and said to him: Fear not, Thomas; go away to India, and proclaim the word; for my grace shall be with thee. But he did not obey, saying: Wherever Thou wishest to send me, send me elsewhere; for to the Indians I am not going. . . .

And at dawn of the following day, the apostle having prayed and entreated the Lord, said: I go wherever Thou wishest, O Lord Jesus; Thy will be done.

Abdias, *The Conflicts of the Holy Apostles* 15 (ca. late sixth century AD)

But while he [Thomas] was saying these words to Peter, there came one of the king's body-guard, whose name was Cantacoros, king of India. And he looked at the Apostles, as they sat like wayfaring men, and said to them: Whence are ye, brethren? . . . I can only ask good questions of you; for I see you are very good men. I will then ask, may I buy one of you as a slave? . . .

Then that man looked upon Thomas and he liked him, because he was strong in body and powerful;. . . . Sell me this one. . . .

And Thomas girded his loins like a servant, and came to Peter and to Matthias and said to them: Remember me in your prayers. Then they saluted one another with a spiritual greeting, . . . and they gave thanks together with a spiritual farewell, and parted. And Thomas went with his master; but Peter and Matthias went on their journey.

And Thomas's master inquired what his calling was, when Thomas answered: I am a builder and an architect, and I am a physician. As regards laying out a construction, I correct the plans and ascertain the cost thereof, and choose the ground outside a land of thorns and briars, and anything else you mayest require.

The Acts of Thomas (ca. AD 220–240)

And while these things were saying, Misdeus was considering in what manner he should put him to death; for he was afraid of the multitude standing round, many, even some of the chief men, having believed in him. And he arose, and took Thomas outside of the city; and a few soldiers accompanied him with their arms. And the rest of the multitude thought that the king was wishing to learn something from him; and they stood and observed him closely. And when they had gone forth three stadia, he delivered him to four soldiers, and to one of the chief officers, and ordered them to take him up into the mountain and spear him; but he himself returned to the city. . . .

And when he [Thomas] had prayed, he said to the soldiers: Come and finish the work of him that sent you. And the four struck him at once, and killed him. And all the brethren wept, and wrapped him up in beautiful shawls, and many linen cloths, and laid him in the tomb in which of old the kings used to be buried.

16.1.7 Bartholomew (a.k.a. Nathanael)

The name ***Bartholomew*** appears in all the Synoptic lists of apostles (Matt 10:1–4; Mark 3:13–19; Luke 6:12–16; cf. Acts 1:13) but is not mentioned anywhere in the Gospel of John. ***Nathanael***, however, is named only in the Gospel of John, where he is included as one of the disciples (John 21:2). This leads to the conclusion that the one man had both names: Nathanael Bartholomew (as was common even among the twelve apostles: e.g., Simon Peter, Levi Matthew). While at first skeptical, Nathanael Bartholomew became a follower of Jesus because of Philip's persistent encouragement to investigate the possibility that Jesus might be the promised Messiah (John 1:43–51; notice that the synoptic lists of apostles always follow Philip with Bartholomew). After Acts, various traditions report that Bartholomew ministered in Asia Minor with Philip (not surprisingly), in Parthia (a region of modern Iran) with Andrew, in Egypt with Peter, and even as far as India.[20] A variety of traditions also report quite different means for Bartholomew's martyrdom: flayed alive, crucified, beaten to death, beheaded, or drowned in the sea.[21]

Some Extrabiblical Traditions about Bartholomew

Hippolytus of Rome, *On the Twelve Apostles* 6 (ca. AD 170–236)

Bartholomew, again, preached to the Indians, to whom he also gave the Gospel according to Matthew, and was crucified with his head downward, and was buried in Allanum, a town of the great Armenia.

The Acts and Martyrdom of Bartholomew (ca. AD 450–550)

Then the king [Polymius], and also the queen, with their two sons, and with all his people, and with all the multitude of the city, and every city round about, and country, and whatever land his kingdom ruled over, were saved, and believed, and were baptized in the name of the Father, and the Son, and the Holy Spirit. And the king laid aside his diadem, and followed Bartholomew the apostle of Christ.

And after these things the unbelievers of the Greeks, having come together to Astreges the king, who was the elder brother of the king who had been baptized, say to him: O king, thy brother Polymius has become disciple to a certain magician, who has taken down our temples, and broken our gods to pieces. . . . Then King Astreges in a rage sent a thousand armed men along with those priests, in order that, wherever they should find the apostle, they might bring him to him bound. And when they had done so, and found him, and brought him, he says to him: . . . As thou hast made my brother deny his gods, and believe in thy God, so I also will make you reject thy God and believe in my gods. The apostle says to

20. E.g., The Acts of Philip; The Acts and Martyrdom of Bartholomew; Abdias, *The Conflicts of the Holy Apostles*, 5–6; and Hippolytus, *On the Twelve Apostles* 6; cf. Jerome, *Vir. Ill.*, 36; and Eusebius, *Hist. eccl.* 5.10.3.

21. Examples of the varying traditions include these: Hippolytus reports Bartholomew as dying by crucifixion; The Acts and Martyrdom of Bartholomew reports him as being beaten and beheaded; the sixth-century Ethiopic document of Abdias reports his death by means of being drowned; and *The Golden Legend* (5:37) attempts to assuage some of the tension by suggesting a combination of crucifixion, removal from the cross to be flayed, and finally killed by beheading. A brief remark by Moses of Chorene in his *History of Armenia* (AD 480) simply notes that Bartholomew "suffered martyrdom among us in the town of Arepan."

him: If I have bound and kept in subjection the god which thy brother worshipped, and at my order the idols were broken in pieces, if thou also art able to do the same to my God, thou canst persuade me also to sacrifice to thy gods; but if thou canst do nothing to my God, I will break all thy gods in pieces; but do thou believe in my God.

And when he had thus spoken, the king was informed that this god Baldad and all the other idols had fallen down, and were broken in pieces. Then the king rent the purple in which he was clothed, and ordered the holy apostle Bartholomew to be beaten with rods; and after having been thus scourged, to be beheaded.

Abdias, *The Conflicts of the Holy Apostles* 6 (ca. late sixth century AD)

But the king was very wroth, and swore great oaths that he would not hearken unto their voice; and commanded that he should be put to the most painful death, and allowed not one word to be said in answer.

But Bartholomew, as he went about the country preached the Holy Gospel, and taught congregations in the name of the Lord Jesus. . . .

The king hearing this, was very wroth, and sent the second time for officers from among the great men of his army, and many went with them to look for Bartholomew. And he commanded that when they found him, they should bind his hands and feet and sink him into the sea with stones, that he should not be found.

Then when the officers were gone they found Bartholomew casting a devil out of a man in whom it had been a long time; and teaching the people, telling them to believe in God. . . . And he went with them to king Acarpus, who, when he saw Bartholomew said to him: Art thou he that troubles the city, and all the borders thereof . . . ?

And the holy Apostle answered and said to him: I am not he that troubles the city, . . .; but it is God in whom they believe with their whole heart, . . . And thou, O Acarpus, if thou hear my word, thou shalt save thyself, and inherit the Kingdom of heaven.

But when Acarpus heard this, he was very wroth indeed; . . . And he commanded his soldiers to fill a sack with sand, to put the Apostle upon it, and sink him into the sea.

They did as the king commanded them; and Bartholomew entered his rest on the 17th of Senne [June]. Afterwards the sea cast him upon the shore; and on the morrow, faithful men who had believed through him, took him and wound him up in cotton cloths and placed him in a good resting place.

16.1.8 Matthew (a.k.a. Levi)

The Synoptic Gospels recall the same episode of Jesus recruiting a tax collector to follow him, but one Gospel refers to the man as ***Matthew*** (Matt 9:9; cf. 10:3), and the others refer to him as ***Levi*** (Mark 2:14 and Luke 5:27–29; cf. "Matthew" in their lists of apostles: Mark 3:18; Luke 6:15; Acts 1:13).[22] Tradition assigns to Matthew the first gospel in the NT lineup and suggests that he lived in Judea and wrote in Hebrew.[23]

---

22. Richard Baukham argues that the names Matthew and Levi refer to two different people; Richard Baukham, *Jesus and the Eyewitnesses: The Gospels as Eyewitness Testimony*, 2nd ed. (Grand Rapids: Eerdmans, 2017), 108–12; for ancient evidence favoring this conclusion, see esp. Clement of Alexandria, *Strom.* 4.9; and *Quis div.* 13. See, however, the brief discussions in Shelton, *Quest for the Historical Apostles*, 189–90; and McDowell, *The Fate of the Apostles*, 27.

23. Irenaeus, *Haer.* 3.1.1; Jerome, *Vir. Ill.*, 3; and Eusebius, *Hist. eccl.* 6.25.4–7 (on Origen's Commentary on Matthew); cf. Jerome, *Vir. Ill.*, 36; and Eusebius, *Hist. eccl.* 3.24.5–6, 13; 3.39.15; 5.8.2; 5.10.3.

He then is said to have ministered in "Ethiopia," which could be either in East Africa or in the region of modern Georgia near the Caspian Sea (part of ancient Parthia).[24] While the means of his martyrdom are variously reported, it is generally agreed that Matthew died in Parthia by order of a king—either by beheading and quartering him or by nailing him to the ground and covering him with fuel to burn him alive.[25]

Some Extrabiblical Traditions about Matthew

Hippolytus of Rome, *On the Twelve Apostles* 7 (ca. AD 170–236)

And Matthew wrote the Gospel in the Hebrew tongue, and published it at Jerusalem, and fell asleep at Hierees, a town of Parthia.

Jerome, *De viris illustribus* 3 (ca. AD 347–420)

Matthew, also called Levi, apostle and aforetimes publican, composed a gospel of Christ at first published in Judea in Hebrew for the sake of those of the circumcision who believed, but this was afterwards translated into Greek though by what author is uncertain.

Abdias, *The Conflicts of the Holy Apostles* 7 (ca. late sixth century AD)

And it came to pass afterwards that Matthew came to Jerusalem and to Judea, he wrote his gospel in the Hebrew tongue. And he went to the Apayanno and preached unto them Christ, confirmed them in the right faith.

Then, when he knew that the faithfulness and the true faith of all the inhabitants of that city and of the country round, were strengthened, he went from among them, rejoicing and full of joy that God had vouchsafed unto them to be faithful; and went into the country of Parthia, where he preached the life-giving Word of the true God. . . .

And . . . there came a wicked man, who cried with a loud voice, saying: Hear, O ye men of Rome, I will tell you the disturbance which has taken place in this city; there is a man, a stranger, who preaches on the road a new God, whose name is Jesus of Nazareth; and if thou let him [do so], O judge Augustus, he will ruin the city and all them that dwell therein. Then Augustus, the judge, brought this saying to the king. And when the king heard it he was very wroth, and said to the officers of his army: Go ye in haste to where that man is, and as soon as ye find him cut off his head, and cast his body abroad on the ground as food for the birds of the heaven.

Then these officers went to Matthew and did as the king had commanded them; and cut up the body of the saint and cast it upon the ground.

16.1.9 James, Son of Alphaeus (a.k.a. James the Lesser)

As the second of the two apostles named James, ***James, son of Alphaeus***, is consistently named as such in the lists of apostles (i.e., Matt 10:3; Mark 3:18; Luke 6:15; Acts 1:13) but otherwise is seldom mentioned in the New Testament. He is often considered

24. See the fifth-century church historian Socrates, *Ecclesiastical History*, 1.19; cf. the comments of S. C. Malan in his translation of Abdias, *The Conflicts of the Holy Apostles*, 7 (pp. 43–44n2).

25. See The Acts and Martyrdom of St. Matthew the Apostle; Abdias, *The Conflicts of the Holy Apostles*, 7; and Hippolytus, *On the Twelve Apostles* 7.

identical with "James the younger" (Mark 15:40) and thus has the moniker "the lesser" as opposed to "the greater" James among the apostles (cf. the mothers of these two men named James are distinguished in Matt 27:56). Extrabiblical traditions sometimes confuse this particular James not with the son of Zebedee by that name but with Jesus's half-brother James (the influential church leader in Acts who is more fully identified as "James the Just" in extrabiblical tradition).[26] Conflating ***James the Lesser*** with Jesus's half-brother James, the Armenian Patriarchate of Jerusalem (a.k.a. the Armenian Patriarchate of Saint James) in the Old City of Jerusalem is said to have held his remains after his death by stoning, which were then later moved to Constantinople and later still to the Church of the Holy Apostles in Rome.[27] Other familial relationships have been suggested for James the son of Alphaeus with other NT figures—e.g., a cousin to Jesus (a view made popular by Jerome), a brother of Levi Matthew (whose father was also named Alphaeus; Mark 2:14), and a brother of Judas Thaddaeus (as deduced from remarks by Papias in the second-century AD)—but none is clearly evident.[28] In the midst of these confusions and conflations, one tradition suggests that James had a ministry with Armenian people and was martyred among them in Parthia (the region of modern Iran).[29] But another tradition suggests that, after travels in Eleutheropolis, Gaza, and Tyre, among other places, Egypt was his place of ministry and ultimate martyrdom by crucifixion.[30] That James the Lesser was martyred seems evident, but the traditions disagree widely about where and how. Thus, among all the apostles, James the Lesser is one of those about whom we know the least with any degree of confidence.

Inside the Armenian Patriarchate of Jerusalem. Tradition states that James the Lesser's remains were stored here.

Library of Congress, LC-matpc-00854/ www.LifeintheHolyLand.com

26. See Eusebius, *Hist. eccl.* 2.1.2–5; 2.23.1–25; and Jerome, *Vir. Ill.*, 2; both cite Hegesippus as noting, "Many indeed are called James." Examples of this confusion are seen in *The Golden Legend*, 3:158–59; and in the use of the martyrdom story of James the Just for that of James the Lesser in Abdias, *The Conflicts of the Holy Apostles*, 11.

27. See the explanation of this confusion in McBirnie, *The Search for the Twelve Apostles*, 143–49.

28. See Criswell's "tentative conclusion" that James the son of Alphaeus is the same person as both James the Lesser and James the Just (with Jesus's "brother" meaning "cousin"); Criswell, *The Apostles After Jesus*, 110–16. Cf. Jerome, *On the Perpetual Virginity of the Blessed Mary* 15; and Papias, *Exposition of the Sayings of the Lord*, fragment 10.

29. The fifth-century Hieronymian Martyrology marks the location of his death as "in Persia [for] James the son of Alphaeus the apostle"; see the Latin text in Hugh Jackson Lawlor, ed., *The Psalter and Martyrology of Ricemarch*, 2 vols., Henry Bradshaw Society 47–48 (London: Harrison and Sons, 1914), 1:17.

30. The tenth-century writer Nicetas David the Paphlagonian, in his *Oratio octava*, describes James the Lesser's traveling ministry ultimately ending in crucifixion in Ostracine, a city of Lower Egypt; see the brief discussions in McDowell, *The Fate of the Apostles*, 233; and Shelton, *Quest for the Historical Apostles*, 207. The work ascribed to the fourth-century Pseudo-Dorotheus, *List of the Apostles and Disciples*, refers to James the Lesser as "Simon, who was called Judas," and also reports the Egyptian ministry, crucifixion, and burial in Ostracine; see English translation by Tony Burke, "List of the Apostles and Disciples, by Pseudo-Dorotheus of Tyre," *e-Clavis: Christian Apocrypha*, accessed February 20, 2023 at https://www.nasscal.com/e-clavis-christian-apocrypha/list-of-the-apostles-and-disciples-by-pseudo-dorotheus-of-tyre/.

Some Extrabiblical Traditions about James the Lesser

Hippolytus of Rome, *On the Twelve Apostles* 9 (ca. AD 170–236)
And James the son of Alphaeus, when preaching in Jerusalem, was stoned to death by the Jews, and was buried there beside the temple.

Jerome, *On the Perpetual Virginity of the Blessed Mary* 15 (ca. AD 347–420)
No one doubts that there were two apostles called by the name James, James the son of Zebedee, and James the son of Alphaeus. Do you intend the comparatively unknown James the less, who is called in Scripture the son of Mary, not however of Mary the mother of our Lord, to be an apostle, or not? If he is an apostle, he must be the son of Alphaeus and a believer in Jesus, "For neither did his brethren believe in him." . . . The only conclusion is that the Mary who is described as the mother of James the less was the wife of Alpheaus and sister of Mary the Lord's mother, the one who is called by John the Evangelist "Mary of Clopas."

Pseudo-Dorotheus, *List of the Apostles and Disciples* 10 (ca. fourth century AD)
Simon, who was called Judas [i.e., James the Lesser], after preaching in Eleutheropolis and from Gaza as far as Egypt, having been crucified by Emperor Trajan was buried in the city of Ostracine of Egypt.

Bone handle of a woman in Roman dress (first-second century AD), Parthia.
A.D. Riddle/ BiblePlaces.com

16.1.10 Simon the Zealot (a.k.a. Simon the Cananaean)

The second of the apostles with the name Simon is distinguished from Simon Peter not by adding a second name but by adding a note about his political leanings, i.e., his affiliation with the Zealots (Luke 6:15; Acts 1:13). The Zealots were part of an anti-Roman movement among first-century Jews; *Cananaean* is a transliteration of the Aramaic word for Zealot (*Kananaios*; the KJV confusingly used the geographic label "Canaanite" instead of the transliteration term in Matt 10:4 and Mark 3:18). Little is known about this apostle, and the various traditions about him sometimes confuse and conflate him with stories about Jesus's brother named Simeon (as also occurs with the disciples who share the names of Jesus's brothers James and Judas; cf. Matt 13:55 and Mark 6:3) and with Simon the son of Clopas (cf. John 19:25).[31] Tradition records ***Simon the Zealot*** as having a ministry in Parthia (the region of ancient Persia and modern Iran), parts of which were in partnership with Judas Thaddaeus, a.k.a. Jude.[32] While legendary reports often pair various apostles in ministry and suffering, Simon the Zealot and Judas Thaddaeus are the only two apostles reported to die together.[33]

31. E.g., Hippolytus, *On the Twelve Apostles* 11; Abdias, *The Conflicts of the Holy Apostles* 6; and the seventh- or eighth-century *Breviary of the Apostles*; see English translation by Tony Burke, "Breviary of the Apostles (*Breviarum apostolorum*)," *e-Clavis: Christian Apocrypha*. Accessed February 20, 2023 at https://www.nasscal.com/e-clavis-christian-apocrypha/breviary-of-the-apostles-breviarium-apostolorum/.

32. See esp. The Acts of Simon and Jude. A brief remark by Moses of Chorene in his *History of Armenia* (AD 480) also places Simon the Zealot in Persia.

33. Shelton, *Quest for the Historical Apostles*, 230. See the account in The Acts of Simon and Jude, 21–22, as rendered in Elliott, *The Apocryphal New Testament*, 529–30.

Simon is thought to have also borne the gospel to parts of Africa (e.g., Egypt, Libya, and Mauritania) and possibly even to Britain and then to have served as bishop of Jerusalem after James the Just (but this is likely a confusion with the person of Simeon, son of Clopas).[34] Variously represented in the traditions, he was martyred in Parthia by being beaten, crucified, or hacked to death.[35]

Some Extrabiblical Traditions about Simon the Zealot

Hippolytus of Rome, *On the Twelve Apostles* 11 (ca. AD 170–236)
Simon the Zealot, the son of Clopas, who is also called Jude, became bishop of Jerusalem after James the Just, and fell asleep and was buried there at the age of 120 years.

Pseudo-Dorotheus, *List of the Apostles and Disciples* 12 (ca. fourth century AD)
Simon, the Zealot, after preaching Christ to all Mauritania and going around the region of Aphron [Africa?], later also was crucified in Britain by them and being made perfect, he was buried there.

The Acts of Simon and Jude (ca. AD 325–375)
After travelling through all the twelve provinces the apostles came to Suanir and lodged with a chief citizen, Sennes. The priests and mob flocked thither, crying out, "Bring out the enemies of our gods." So they were taken to the temple of the sun. . . . The priests would now compel the apostles to sacrifice. Jude said to Simon, "I see the Lord calling us." Simon said, "I see him also among the angels; moreover, an angel has said to me, 'Go out hence and the temple shall fall,' but I said, 'No, for some here may be converted.'" As they spoke (in Hebrew) an angel came and said, "Choose either the death of all here or the palm of martyrdom." They chose the palm. . . . The priests and people attacked the apostles and slew them.

Moses of Chorene, *The History of Armenia* 9 (ca. AD 480)
There came then into Armenia the Apostle Bartholomew, who suffered martyrdom among us in the town of Arepan. As to Simon, who was sent unto Persia, I cannot relate with certainty what he did, nor where he suffered martyrdom. It is said that one Simon, an apostle, was martyred at Veriospore. Is this true, or why did the saint come to this place? I do not know.

16.1.11 Judas, Son of James (a.k.a. Thaddaeus)

The potential confusion of ***Judas, son of James***, with Judas Iscariot was evident from the beginning, as John found it important to introduce him as "Judas (not Judas Iscariot)" (John 14:22–23). Luke specifies "Judas son of James" (Luke 6:16; Acts 1:13), whereas Mark and Matthew both utilize his Greek name "***Thaddaeus***" (Mark 3:18;

34. See Pseudo-Dorotheus, *List of the Apostles and Disciples* 12; *Breviary of the Apostles*; and *The Golden Legend*, 6:75; cf. Eusebius, *Hist. eccl.* 3.32.1–8; and the brief comments in Klauck, *The Apocryphal Acts of the Apostles*, 246.

35. E.g., for crucifixion, see Pseudo-Dorotheus, *List of the Apostles and Disciples* 12 and *Breviary of the Apostles*; for crucifixion and beating, see Abdias, *The Conflicts of the Holy Apostles* 6; and for being hewn asunder rather than crucifixion, see *The Golden Legend*, 6:80–81.

Matt 10:3).[36] With the notoriety of Judas Iscariot (cf. Matt 10:4; Mark 3:19; Luke 6:16; John 6:70–71), it makes sense that the lesser-known Judas would receive name adjustments.[37] And such adjustment sometimes includes a shortening of the name to simply "Jude." Luke's flexible Greek phrasing for "Judas of James" can be used for various family relations including "son of" or "brother of." Thus, suggestions for Judas Thaddaeus's identity have included the son of the apostle James (i.e., that "James the Greater" was old enough to have adult children) or the brother of James the Just (i.e., another of Jesus's half-brothers mentioned in Matthew 13:55 and Mark 6:3; and the likely author of the NT letter of Jude).[38] The mention of the apostles in Jude 17, however, makes a distinction between the author of Jude and those numbered among the apostles.[39]

Some Extrabiblical Traditions about Judas, Son of James

The Teaching of the Apostles 9 (ca. AD 230)

Edessa, and all the countries round about it which were on all sides of it, and Zoba, and Arabia, and all the north, and the regions round about it, and the south, and all the regions on the borders of Mesopotamia, received the apostles' ordination to the priesthood from Addaeus the apostle, one of the seventy-two apostles, who himself made disciples there, and built a church there, and was priest and ministered there in his office of Guide which he held there.

Hippolytus of Rome, *On the Twelve Apostles* 10 (ca. AD 170–236)

Jude, who is also called Lebbaeus, preached to the people of Edessa, and to all Mesopotamia, and fell asleep at Berytus, and was buried there.

The Acts of Thaddaeus (ca. AD 550–950)

And Thaddaeus along with Abgarus [converted ruler of Edessa] destroyed idol-temples and built churches; ordained as bishop one of his disciples, and presbyters, and deacons, and gave them the rule of the psalmody and the holy liturgy. And having left them, he went to the city of Amis, great metropolis of the Mesechaldeans and Syrians, that is, of Mesopotamia-Syria, beside the river Tigris. . . .

Having therefore remained with them for five years, he built a church; and having appointed as bishop one of his disciples, and presbyters, and deacons, and prayed for them, he went away, going round the cities of Syria, and teaching, and healing all the sick; whence he brought many cities and countries to Christ through His teaching. Teaching, therefore, and evangelizing along with the disciples, and healing the sick, he went to Berytus, a city of Phoenicia by the sea; and there, having taught and enlightened many, he fell asleep on the twenty-first of the month of August.

---

36. See the discussion in McDowell, *The Fate of the Apostles*, 26–27. At Mark 3:18 and Matt 10:3 some manuscripts have the spelling "Lebbaeus" for Thaddaeus, and some combined the names: e.g., "Thaddaeus who was called Lebbaeus." Other early Christian writings also speak of the apostle "Addaeus."

37. Shelton, *Quest for the Historical Apostles*, 212.

38. See Jude 1; cf. McBirnie, *The Search for the Twelve Apostles*, 151; and Shelton, *Quest for the Historical Apostles*, 212.

39. Shelton, *Quest for the Historical Apostles*, 214.

Judas Thaddaeus is also suggested to have been one of the seventy (or seventy-two) disciples sent out for short-term ministry in Luke 10:1–24.[40] Whatever his precise identity, tradition suggests that the apostle Judas Thaddaeus ministered in Syria in the city of Edessa and along the Euphrates River and elsewhere (esp. Armenia and Mesopotamia).[41] He is said to have preached the gospel in the midst of pagan priests and to take part in exorcisms. He is paired with Simon the Zealot (as in the NT lists of apostles) as having a ministry in Parthia (the region of modern Iran). Stories of Thaddaeus's martyrdom include tales of being clubbed to death and hacked asunder in Parthia alongside Simon the Zealot, but some reports hint at a possible peaceful death by natural causes.[42]

16.1.12 Judas Iscariot

By the time the gospels were written, the character of this apostle was so well known that he is introduced in the accounts of Jesus's selection of him as "***Judas Iscariot***, who betrayed him" (Matt 10:4, emphasis added; Mark 3:19; Luke 6:16 uses the phrase "became a traitor"; cf. John 6:70–71). The distinguishing name Iscariot is apparently from this Judas's father, Simon Iscariot (John 6:71; 13:2). John notes that Judas was a thief helping himself to money from the apostles' general fund (John 12:1–6) and then specifically comments on how his betrayal of Jesus was prompted by the devil (John 13:2, 27). The Synoptic Gospels pay particular attention to his greed motivation in the betrayal (Matt 16:14–16; Mark 14:10–11; Luke 22:3–6). After betraying Jesus (Matt 26:47–50; Mark 14:43–46; Luke 22:47–48; John 18:2–5), Judas killed himself in a field that came to be called Akeldama, or Field of Blood (Acts 1:18–19) (ca. AD 30 or 33).

Judas Iscariot

Judas Iscariot (i.e., the son of Simon Iscariot; cf. John 6:71; 13:16) is mentioned last in the New Testament lists of apostles, and all four gospel writers identify him as an enemy: as Jesus's betrayer (Matt 10:4; Mark 3:19; John 6:71) and a "traitor" (Luke 6:16). During Jesus's ministry with the apostles, Judas apparently served as the treasurer for the group and pilfered some of the funds for himself (John 12:1-6). Money was also a factor in his agreement to betray Jesus (Matt 26:14-16; Mark 14:10-11; Luke 22:3-6). After the betrayal in the garden of Gethsemane (Matt 26:47-50; Mark 14:43-46; Luke 22:47-48; John 18:2-5), Judas killed himself (Matt 27:3-10; Acts 1:18-19) (ca. AD 30 or 33).

40. Eusebius, *Hist. eccl.* 1.12.3; cf. Eusebius's longer account of Thaddaeus in *Hist. eccl.* 1.13.1–22.
41. See *Breviary of the Apostles*; and Pseudo-Dorotheus, *List of the Apostles and Disciples* 9.
42. See esp. The Acts of Thaddaeus; The Acts of Simon and Jude; and *The Golden Legend*, 6:80.

Of the twelve Jesus originally selected to serve as apostles, the New Testament reports only the deaths of James (the son of Zebedee; Acts 12:1–3) and Judas Iscariot, with the most detail given to the death of Judas (Matt 27:1–10 and Acts 1:18–19). This increased attention is perhaps testimony to Judas being replaced as an apostle (by Matthias; Acts 1:12–26) not because he died but because he defected from following Jesus (NB: James was not replaced as an apostle when he died).

16.1.13 MATTHIAS

Even as extrabiblical legends about apostles confuse others with similar names, the little-known replacement apostle ***Matthias*** (in the NT mentioned only in Acts 1:12–26) is often confused with the apostle Matthew. Because Matthias met the criterion set out by Peter—i.e., to have been following Jesus from the time of John the Baptist's ministry until the resurrection of Jesus (Acts 1:21–22), some traditional material suggests that Matthias was one of the seventy (or seventy-two) disciples sent out in Luke 10.[43]

Some Extrabiblical Traditions about Matthias

Hippolytus of Rome, *On the Twelve Apostles* 12 (ca. AD 170–236)

And Matthias, who was one of the seventy, was numbered along with the eleven apostles, and preached in Jerusalem, and fell asleep and was buried there.

Pseudo-Dorotheus, *List of the Apostles and Disciples* 11 (ca. fourth century AD)

Matthias, who was numbered with the eleven apostles in place of Judas Iscariot, after preaching Christ in Ethiopia Prima, later he was crucified in Britain by them and being made perfect, he was buried there.

The Acts of Andrew and Matthias 2–3 (ca. AD 350–450)

Matthias then having come into the gate of their city, the men of that city laid hold of him, and thrust out his eyes; and after putting them out they made him drink the drug of their magical deception, and led him away to the prison, and put beside him grass to eat, and he ate it not. . . .

While Matthias was thus praying in the prison, a light shone, and there came forth out of the light a voice saying: Beloved Matthias, receive thy sight. And immediately he received his sight. And again there came forth a voice saying: Be of good courage, our Matthias, and be not dismayed; for I shall not by any means forsake thee, for I shall deliver thee from all danger; and not only thee, but also all thy brethren who are with thee: for I am with thee everywhere and at all times. But remain here twenty-seven days for the edification of many souls; and after that I shall send forth Andrew to thee, and he shall lead thee forth out of this prison; and not thee only, but also all who hear. Having said this, the Saviour said again to Matthias, Peace be to thee, our Matthias, and went into heaven. Then Matthias having beheld Him, said to the Lord: Let thy grace abide with me, O my Lord Jesus.

Then Matthias therefore sat down in the prison, and sang.

43. E.g., Hippolytus, *On the Twelve Apostles* 12; Eusebius, *Hist. eccl.* 1.12.3; *Breviary of the Apostles*; and *The Golden Legend*, 3:54.

Abdias, *The Conflicts of the Holy Apostles* 12 (ca. late sixth century AD)

After this the Lord made him come out of the fire, and they saw his flesh like that of a living man; and his face like that of children. And all who saw him said: This man is not an enchanter; yet he has been in the fire and his body is not consumed; but his is alive, and not a hair of his head [is singed]; no, not even his nails.

Then, at that moment, all the men of the city and of the districts around believed; and they cried aloud, saying: There is no God in heaven or in earth, except the Lord the God of Matthias, the Apostle of Jesus Christ who saves every one that puts his trust in Him; and all those that believe in His Holy Name.

Mention is made of some possible but now lost written work by Matthias.[44] He reportedly ministered among a cannibalistic people in Scythia (the region of modern Ukraine and Russia), where he was rescued from prison by the apostle Andrew.[45] Some legends have him ministering also in "Ethiopia," but again there is some confusion whether this is in East Africa or in the region of modern Georgia near the Caspian Sea (part of ancient Parthia). His death is variously reported as being in Judea or Ethiopia or Britain.[46] While some traditions suggest that his was a natural death rather than martyrdom, some claim he died as a martyr by stoning and/or beheading after failed attempts to burn him or crucify him.[47]

16.1.14 Paul

As we have seen, the book of Acts gives a lot of information about the life and ministry of the first-century Jewish man Saul, who is better known by his Greco-Roman name ***Paul***. Before becoming a Christian, Paul was a well-educated and zealous Pharisee (Acts 23:6; 26:4–5; Phil 3:5), so zealous for the Jewish law that he was in favor of hunting down and punishing any whom he thought were offenders of it (Acts 8:3; 9:1–3; 22:4–5; Gal 1:13–14; Phil 3:6). But his worldview and understanding of the law drastically changed when he met the risen Jesus Christ on the road to Damascus (Acts 9:1–22; cf. Acts 22:1–21; 26:1–32). After some years of learning in Arabia and Damascus (Acts 9:20–25; Gal 1:17–18), he visited the apostles in Jerusalem and then went to his original home city of Tarsus, the capital of the Roman province of Cilicia (a region in modern Turkey) (Acts 9:26–30). Barnabas recruited him from Tarsus to minister with the church in Syrian Antioch (Acts 11:25–26), from whence he became

44. See Eusebius, *Hist. eccl.* 3.25.4–7 cited in the sidebar entitled "The Doubtful Authority of the Apocryphal Acts."

45. See esp. The Acts of Andrew and Matthias.

46. See the discussion in McDowell, *The Fate of the Apostles*, 253–56.

47. See Pseudo-Dorotheus, *List of the Apostles and Disciples* 11; Abdias, *The Conflicts of the Holy Apostles* 12; and *The Golden Legend*, 3:59–60.

a famous (and infamous) itinerant minister (Acts 13–21). The former persecutor of the Christian church ended up persecuted himself for his faith in Christ, and he spent the last quarter of the book of Acts a prisoner (Acts 21–28). But, as already noted, Acts does not report when and how Paul met his end.

Some Extrabiblical Traditions about Paul

The Acts of Paul (ca. AD 170–180)

And turning toward the east, Paul lifted up his hands to heaven and prayed at length; and after having conversed in Hebrew with the fathers during prayer he bent his neck, without speaking any more. When the executioner cut off his head milk splashed on the tunic of the soldier. And the soldier and all who stood near by were astonished at this sight and glorified God who had thus honoured Paul. And they went away and reported everything to Caesar.

Hippolytus of Rome, *On the Twelve Apostles* 13 (ca. AD 170–236)

And Paul entered into the apostleship a year after the assumption of Christ; and beginning at Jerusalem, he advanced as far as Illyricum, and Italy, and Spain, preaching the Gospel for five-and-thirty years. And in the time of Nero he was beheaded at Rome, and was buried there.

Jerome, *De viris illustribus* 5 (ca. AD 347–420)

Paul, formerly called Saul, an apostle outside the number of the twelve apostles, was of the tribe of Benjamin and the town of Giscalis in Judea. When this was taken by the Romans he removed with his parents to Tarsus in Cilicia. Sent by them to Jerusalem to study law he was educated by Gamaliel a most learned man whom Luke mentions. But after he had been present at the death of the martyr Stephen and had received letters from the high priest of the temple for the persecution of those who believed in Christ, he proceeded to Damascus, where constrained to faith by a revelation, as it is written in the Acts of the apostles, he was transformed from a persecutor into an elect vessel. . . . It ought to be said that at the first defence, the power of Nero having not yet been confirmed, nor his wickedness broken forth to such a degree as the histories relate concerning him, Paul was dismissed by Nero, that the gospel of Christ might be preached also in the West. . . . He then, in the fourteenth year of Nero on the same day with Peter, was beheaded at Rome for Christ's sake and was buried in the Ostian way, the twenty-seventh year after our Lord's passion.

Abdias, *The Conflicts of the Holy Apostles* 2 (ca. late sixth century AD)

Then was Nero very wroth, and he sent a valiant man whom he always kept by him, to cut S. Paul's neck at once.

And when he was gone, and sword in hand, drew near, Paul bowed his holy neck and his head in silence. The executioner said nothing, but abode a long time with his neck bent, and his sword by his side, drawn out of the sheath. But his hands trembled as if they could not alight on Paul.

At last he took courage, and smote and cut off Paul's head, and it fell upon the ground.

And there came forth from his body blood and milk, so that the executioner gathered together his garments [lest they should be sprinkled over with it].

And all those who were there gathered around, marveled at the sight, and praised God who had given so great a grace unto his disciple Paul.

Then the executioner returned and told Nero all that had happened; so that Nero also marveled, and the princes who were with him trembled greatly.

The fourth-century historian Eusebius states that "Paul's martyrdom was not accomplished during the sojourn in Rome which Luke describes." Instead, tradition reports—literally: "word has it" (Greek: *logos echei*)—that Paul stood trial before Caesar, was released from his Roman house arrest, and went on to further ministry.[48] Such a trial would certainly be in keeping with the vision Paul had in Acts 27:24, and such a release from his Roman custody would be in keeping with Paul's anticipation expressed in Philippians 1:12–26 and Philemon 22.[49] This later ministry of Paul could be when he traveled to Spain, which would be in keeping with his goal expressed in Romans 15:23–29. The letter of 1 Clement (ca. AD 100) may well be referring to Spain when it reports that Paul had "reached the farthest limits of the west" (1 Clem. 5:5–7). The Muratorian Canon, a document dating to the second century AD, suggests Luke's abrupt ending of Acts is because of his recording "particular things which happened in his own presence," which did not include "the departure of Paul from the city [of Rome] as he proceeded to Spain."[50] Furthermore, this later ministry of Paul comports well with the Pastoral Epistles (i.e., the letters of 1 Timothy, 2 Timothy, and Titus), which contain personal information about Paul that is otherwise difficult to squeeze into Paul's ministry as reported in Acts.[51] The apocryphal Acts of Paul reports that Paul was arrested again and returned to Rome for trial under Emperor Nero; after being condemned, he was beheaded on the Ostian Road (ca. AD 64–68). Despite the book's many fantastical stories, the narrative of Paul's martyrdom in the Acts of Paul is often judged as having been based on a historically accurate report of the apostle's trial and execution.[52]

Statue of the apostle Paul. Girona Cathedral, Catalonia, Spain. luisfpizarro/stock .adobe.com

48. Eusebius, *Hist. eccl.* 2.22.1–8.

49. Witherington suggests that, according to standard procedure in first-century Roman law, Paul would have been released if his accusers did not come to Rome to pursue the charges against him. The absence of his accusers would explain Paul's anticipation of his release expressed in Phil 1:12–26. See Ben Witherington III, "The Case of the Imprisonment that Did Not Happen: Paul at Ephesus," *JETS*, 60 (2017): 528n8.

50. Muratorian Canon, lines 35–39, as rendered in Harry Y. Gamble, *The New Testament Canon: Its Making and Meaning*, GBS (Philadelphia: Fortress, 1985), 94.

51. So John B. Polhill, *Acts*, NAC (Nashville: Broadman, 1992), 548n107. Those suspecting that Paul did not write the Pastoral Epistles are unconcerned to fit those letters into a timeline of Pauline chronology; for a thorough introduction to the issues in the debate regarding the authorship of the Pastoral Epistles, see William D. Mounce, *Pastoral Epistles*, WBC 46 (Nashville: Thomas Nelson, 2000), xli–cxxix, esp. cxviii–cxxix. Some scholars have suggested that the Pastoral Epistles are Luke's third volume; e.g., Stephen G. Wilson, *Luke and the Pastoral Epistles* (London: SPCK, 1979), esp. 136–43; Jerome D. Quinn, "The Last Volume of Luke: The Relation of Luke-Acts to the Pastoral Epistles," in *Perspectives on Luke-Acts*, ed. Charles H. Talbert, Perspectives in Religious Studies 5 (Danville, VA: Association of Baptist Professors of Religion, 1978), 62–75; cf. the mediating view of C. F. D. Moule, "The Problem of the Pastoral Epistles: A Reappraisal," *BJRL* 47 (1965) 430–52, who suggests that Luke wrote (i.e., was the "framer" of) the Pastoral Epistles "during Paul's lifetime, at Paul's behest, and, in part (but only in part), at Paul's dictation" (p. 434; cf. 447).

52. E.g., Bryan Litfin, *After Acts: Exploring the Lives and Legends of the Apostles* (Chicago: Moody, 2015), 176.

A Physical Description of Paul

The Acts of Paul (ca. AD 170–180)

And he [Onesiphorus] went along the road to Lystra, and stood waiting for him, and kept looking at the passers by according to the description of Titus. And he saw Paul coming, a man small in size, bald-headed, bandy-legged, well-built, with eyebrows meeting, rather long-nosed, full of grace. For sometimes he seemed like a man, and sometimes he had the countenance of an angel.

This is a facial composite of Paul the apostle created in February 2008 by German law enforcement experts of *Landeskriminalamt* (LKA) in North Rhine-Westphalia (NRW) using historical sources; proposed by the Düsseldorf historian Michael Hesemann.

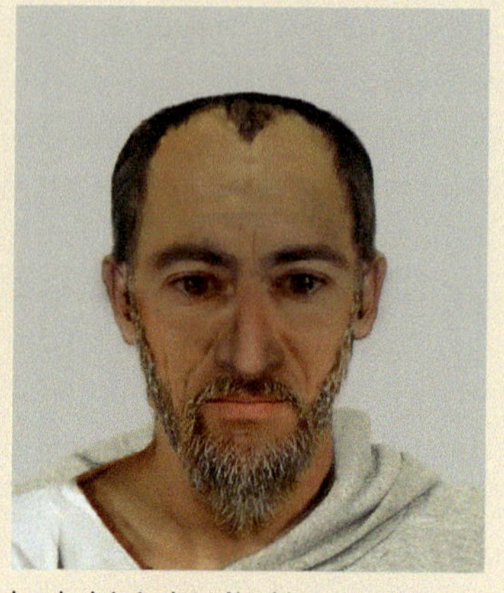

Landeskriminalamt Nordrhein-Westfalen

16.1.15 The Lives and Deaths of Other Believers after Acts

Legends report the stories of other NT figures after the abrupt ending of Acts. These include such people from the story of Acts as Barnabas, John Mark, Timothy, Priscilla, Aquila, Silas, and James the brother of Jesus (a.k.a. James the Just).[53] After lives of ministry for the sake of the gospel, many of these believers are said to have died as martyrs for their faith in Jesus Christ. As important as their personal stories might be, it is the story of the gospel that is the most important legacy here to remember. Beyond the legendary reports of their individual lives and ministries, the real legacy of the apostles and others among Jesus's first followers is their corporate testimony present in the ongoing life and ministry of the Christian church itself.[54] Thus, while the stories of the early followers of Jesus preaching the gospel and dying for its cause have been valued encouragements to Christian faith, the proper continuation of the story of Acts is not so much to write new chapters for the book or to craft additional sequels to Luke's work. The proper continuation of the story of Acts is to participate in the dissemination of the gospel message, the message it records spreading in the first century.

53. Mentioned by first-century historian Josephus (*Ant.* 20.9.1 §200) and by fourth-century historian Eusebius (*Hist. eccl.* 2.23, citing lost second-century works by Clement of Alexandria and by Hegesippus), James the Just has been the subject of significant scholarly treatments, particularly since the 2002 discovery of an ossuary (limestone bone box) bearing the inscription "James, son of Joseph, brother of Jesus," later proven to be a forgery. See Hershel Shanks and Ben Witherington III, *The Brother of Jesus: The Dramatic Story & Meaning of the First Archaeological Link to Jesus & His Family* (New York: HarperCollins, 2003); John Painter, *Just James: The Brother of Jesus in History and Tradition*, 2nd ed., Studies on Personalities of the New Testament (Columbia, SC: University of South Carolina Press, 2004); Alan Saxby, *James, Brother of Jesus, and the Jerusalem Church: A Radical Exploration of Christian Origins* (Eugene, OR: Wipf & Stock, 2015).

54. Shelton, *Quest for the Historical Apostles*, 276.

Josephus on the Death of James (ca. AD 62)

Flavius Josephus, *Jewish Antiquities* 20.9.1 §200 (ca. AD 94)

Possessed of such a character, Ananus thought that he had a favourable opportunity because Festus was dead and Albmus was still on the way. And so he convened the judges of the Sanhedrin and brought before them a man named James the brother of Jesus who was called the Christ, and certain others. He accused them of having transgressed the law and delivered them up to be stoned. Those of the inhabitants of the city who were considered the most fair-minded and who were strict in observance of the law were offended at this.

A Summary of the Apostles and Other Key Disciples after Acts

Apostle / Disciple	Ministry Locations (modern name)	Death and Approximate Year
Judas Iscariot	With Jesus until he betrayed him	Suicide at Jerusalem ca. AD 30 or 33 (see Matt 27:1–10; Acts 1:18–19)
Stephen	Judea	Stoned at Jerusalem ca. AD 34 (see Acts 6:1–8:4)
James the Greater	Judea	Executed by sword at Jerusalem ca. AD 44 (see Acts 12:1–3)
Barnabas	Syria, Cyprus, Asia Minor (Turkey)	Burned alive and/or stoned in Cyprus ca. AD 61
James the Just, brother of Jesus	Overseer of the Jerusalem church	Thrown from the temple parapet and stoned ca. AD 62
Matthias	Judea, Scythia (Ukraine and Russia), Ethiopia (East Africa or Georgia?)	Stoned and/or beheaded in Jerusalem ca. AD 64
Simon Peter	The greater Roman Empire	Crucified upside down in Rome under Nero ca. AD 64–68
Paul	The greater Roman Empire	Beheaded in Rome under Nero ca. AD 64–68
Andronicus	Hungary, Croatia, Bosnia, Serbia	Martyred under Nero ca. AD 65–68
Priscilla (a.k.a. Prisca)	Italy, Achaia (Greece), Macedonia, Asia Minor (Turkey)	Martyred under Nero ca. AD 65–68
Aquila	Italy, Achaia (Greece), Macedonia, Asia Minor (Turkey)	Martyred under Nero ca. AD 65–68
Aristarchus	Achaia (Greece), Italy, possibly Macedonia	Fed to lions under Nero ca. AD 65–68

(continued)

Apostle / Disciple	Ministry Locations (modern name)	Death and Approximate Year
Procorus	Asia Minor (Turkey)	Martyred under Nero ca. AD 65–68
Onesiphorus	Asia Minor (Turkey)	Dragged to death ca. AD 65–68
Silas/Silvanus	Asia Minor (Turkey), Macedonia, Achaia (Greece)	Martyred under Nero ca. AD 65–68
Philip the apostle	Parthia (Iran), Scythia (Ukraine and Russia), Northern Africa, Asia Minor (Turkey)	Crucified/hung upside down at Hierapolis ca. AD 66
John Mark	Cyprus, Asia Minor (Turkey), Italy, Egypt, possibly Achaia (Greece) and Albania	Beaten and burned to death at Alexandria ca. AD 67
Bartholomew	Armenia, Asia Minor (Turkey), Egypt, Parthia (Iran), Bactria (Afghanistan), India	Flayed alive, beheaded, or drowned at Albanopolis ca. AD 68
Andrew	Achaia (Greece), Macedonia, Asia Minor (Turkey), Scythia (Ukraine and Russia)	Crucified at Patras ca. AD 69
Levi Matthew	Parthia (Iran), Macedonia, Ethiopia (East Africa or Georgia?)	Beheaded or burned in Parthia ca. AD 70
James the Lesser, son of Alphaeus	Parthia (Iran), possibly Egypt	Crucified ca. AD 70
Simon the Zealot	Northern Africa, possibly Britain, Parthia (Iran)	Crucified, beaten, or hacked asunder in Parthia ca. AD 71
Judas Thaddaeus	Syria, Parthia (Iran), Mesopotamia, Egypt	Beaten or hacked asunder in Parthia ca. AD 71
Thomas	Parthia (Iran), Bactria (Afghanistan), India	Pierced with spears ca. AD 72
Timothy	Asia Minor (Turkey), Macedonia, Achaia (Greece)	Stoned to death at Ephesus ca. AD 80
Philip the evangelist	Asia Minor (Turkey)	Crucified upside down ca. AD 82
Luke	Asia Minor (Turkey), Macedonia, Italy, possibly Spain and Bulgaria	Natural death at age 84 at Thebes, or martyred by hanging ca. AD 85–100
Antipas	Asia Minor (Turkey)	Cooked alive ca. AD 95 (cf. Rev 2:13)
John	Asia Minor (Turkey)	Natural death in Ephesus ca. AD 103

Sources: David Criswell, *The Apostles after Jesus: A History of the Apostles* (Dallas: Fortress Adonai, 2013), 190–91; Thomas E. Schmidt, *The Apostles after Acts: A Sequel* (Eugene, OR: Cascade, 2013), 196–97; and McDowell, *The Fate of the Apostles*, passim. For ratings that estimate the levels of certainty for these traditions, see esp. Schmidt and also McDowell.

16.2 THE STORY AFTER ACTS FOR THE BOOK OF ACTS: ACTS AS SCRIPTURE

In chapter 4, we briefly examined the fact that the canonical book of Acts has come to us in two versions. The version followed in edited Greek texts and most English translations is based on the vast majority of Greek manuscripts and some of the best representations of those extant documents (like Codex Sinaiticus, Codex Alexandrinus, and Codex Vaticanus). The second version—inaccurately dubbed the "***Western text***"—is based largely on a very few, albeit old, Greek manuscripts (esp. Codex Bezae). Interestingly, while the Western text of Acts is 6–9 percent longer than the standard version, that is not due to the Western text containing more stories. Rather, the Western text of Acts contains more flowery language and slight expansions of the stories in the standard text, and some of these editorial nuances seem to have particular ideological slants to them.[55] For such reasons as these, I have suggested that the Western version of Acts is something of a paraphrased version of Luke's original story of Acts. All this is to say that, even early in the life of the church, readers of Acts found its story interesting and helpful, and they chose to pass it on in its original version as well as (at least for a few people) in a paraphrased version.[56]

Also noted in chapter 4 was that the approximate dates for the events in the story of Acts are between AD 30 and AD 62. In discussing the suggested dating for the writing of the story of Acts, I presented an argument for an early date: prior to AD 64. The abrupt ending of Acts—i.e., with Paul still under house arrest "for two years" in Rome awaiting his hearing before Caesar—is part of my reasoning for favoring an early composition date. Nevertheless, theories that fit the middle composition dating option of AD 70–85—and even those in the early second-century dating option of AD 115–125—still have the canonical book of the Acts of the Apostles predating the many various books among the apocryphal acts. But age is not the only consideration when addressing the matter of what makes a book worthy of inclusion as Scripture. So when and why did the book of Acts become recognized as Scripture?

55. See particularly Eldon Jay Epp, *The Theological Tendency of Codex Bezae Cantabrigiensis in Acts*, SNTSMS 3 (Cambridge: Cambridge University Press, 1966).

56. Scholars sometimes use the term *reception history* to refer to such examinations of how books are received by their original audiences and later generations. For the book of Acts, see particularly Andrew Gregory, *The Reception of Luke and Acts in the Period before Irenaeus: Looking for Luke in the Second Century*, WUNT 2.169 (Tübingen: Mohr Siebeck, 2003); for a commentary on Acts that focuses on its reception history, see Heidi J. Hornik and Mikeal Carl Parsons, *The Acts of the Apostles Through the Centuries* (Malden, MA: Wiley Blackwell, 2016); for a more general work organized on how the apostolic fathers received the NT documents, see Andrew F. Gregory and Christopher Tuckett, eds., *The Reception of the New Testament in the Apostolic Fathers*, The New Testament and the Apostolic Fathers (Oxford: Oxford University Press, 2007); and see also select essays in Andrew F. Gregory and C. Kavin Rowe, eds., *Rethinking the Unity and Reception of Luke and Acts* (Columbia, SC: University of South Carolina Press, 2010).

16.2.1 New Testament Canon Criteria and Date

We think of the ***NT canon*** as the list of books that the early church considered inspired by God such that those books were to be treated as Scripture alongside the OT books already recognized as God's Word.[57] Of the various overlapping ***canon criteria*** that appear to have been utilized in the process of recognition of books as inspired for the New Testament, the following are often acknowledged: the authority of Jesus and connection to the apostles, applicability and usage in the churches, and truth and orthodoxy in content.[58] On such measures, the apocryphal acts do not merit the same recognition as the canonical book of Acts.[59]

The actual date of the NT canon has seen much debate, especially in recent decades.[60] A festal letter written for Easter in AD 367 by ***Athanasius***, the bishop of Alexandria, is one of the earliest lists containing all twenty-seven books of our current New Testament; a poem attributed to ***Amphilochus***, bishop of Iconium in AD 394, lists the NT books in their current order; and three church councils—the ***Council of Hippo*** in AD 393, the ***Council of Carthage*** in AD 397, and the ***Council of Chalcedon*** in AD 451—are often credited as heralding a closing of the NT canon.[61] Many scholars look to the writings of the famed bishop of Lyons, ***Irenaeus*** (ca. AD 130–200), particularly his *Against Heresies* (ca. AD 180), as the firmest indicator of the first definitive idea of the NT canon.[62] Even though Irenaeus uses the terminology of "old covenant" and "new covenant," he does not associate any specific list of books with the latter term. Nonetheless, in addressing the heresies about which he is concerned, Irenaeus cites from twenty-one books of the New Testament (all but Philemon, Hebrews, James, 2 Peter,

57. In discussions of canon, it is arguably better to speak of a "recognition" or "authenticating" process rather than a "decision" or "determination" process. That is, the Christian church was not trying to determine its own books for itself as much as it was trying to discover what books had been provided to them by God. For an accessible and brief treatment of the NT canon, see N. T. Wright and Michael F. Bird, *The New Testament in Its World* (Grand Rapids: Zondervan Academic, 2019), 866–75; for a book-length discussion of this matter, see Michael J. Kruger, *Canon Revisited: Establishing the Origins and Authority of the New Testament Books* (Wheaton, IL: Crossway, 2012).

58. E.g., see Gamble, *The New Testament Canon*, 67–72; F. F. Bruce, *The Canon of Scripture* (Downers Grove, IL: InterVarsity Press, 1988), 255–69, 151–52; Arthur G. Patzia, *The Making of the New Testament: Origin, Collection, Text, and Canon*, 2nd ed. (Downers Grove, IL: InterVarsity Press, 2011), 166–76; and Wright and Bird, *The New Testament in Its World*, 873–74.

59. See, for example, the analysis of David E. Smith, *The Canonical Function of Acts: A Comparative Analysis* (Collegeville, MN: Liturgical Press, 2002), esp. 103–14.

60. E.g., Lee Martin McDonald and James A. Sanders, eds., *The Canon Debate: On the Origins and Formation of the Bible* (Peabody, MA: Hendrickson, 2002); and Craig A. Evans and Emanuel Tov, eds., *Exploring the Origins of the Bible: Canon Formation in Historical, Literary, and Theological Perspective*, Acadia Studies in Bible and Theology (Grand Rapids: Baker Academic, 2008). See also Lee Martin McDonald, *The Formation of the Biblical Canon*, 4th ed., 2 vols. (New York: Bloomsbury T&T Clark, 2017).

61. E.g., see Gamble, *The New Testament Canon*, 54–56; Bruce, *The Canon of Scripture*, 208–9, 232–33; Patzia, *The Making of the New Testament*, 98; and William Reuben Farmer, "A Study of the Development of the New Testament Canon," pp. 7–95 in *The Formation of the New Testament Canon: An Ecumenical Approach*, by William R. Farmer and Denis M. Farkasfalvy, Theological Inquiries (New York: Paulist, 1983), 9–10.

62. Others suggest that Marcion (to whom Irenaeus responds in *Haer.*) might be credited with the idea of a NT canon; e.g., Hans von Campenhausen, *The Formation of the Christian Bible*, 2nd ed., trans. J. A. Baker (Philadelphia: Fortress, 1977).

3 John, and Jude).[63] Thus, NT documents were used as having scriptural authority. And regarding the Acts of the Apostles specifically, arguments such as this led to the conclusion that Acts was accorded canonical status by the end of the second century at the latest.[64]

Recently, however, Michael Kruger has argued that this authoritative use of the New Testament as Scripture does not mean Irenaeus was the innovator of the NT canon. Indeed, Irenaeus's authoritative use of some of the NT documents demonstrates that they were already functioning authoritatively in the life of the church by the middle of the second century. To demonstrate that the NT canon was not merely a late second-century phenomenon, Kruger traces a scriptural respect for many of the NT documents among several contemporaries of, as well as predecessors to, Irenaeus.[65] Such authoritative recognition may well be pushed into the first century at least for some parts of the New Testament.

Some NT Evidence of Recognizing NT Scriptures

2 Peter 3:15–16—"Bear in mind that our Lord's patience means salvation, just as our dear brother Paul also wrote you with the wisdom that God gave him. He writes the same way in all his letters, speaking in them of these matters. His letters contain some things that are hard to understand, which ignorant and unstable people distort, as they do the other Scriptures, to their own destruction."

1 Timothy 5:18—"For Scripture says, 'Do not muzzle an ox while it is treading out the grain,' and 'The worker deserves his wages.'" (citing Deut 25:4 and Luke 10:7)

16.2.2 The Awareness of the New Testament Authors

At first glance, many assume that the NT authors were not writing with the immediate understanding or conviction that their own works would eventually be considered scriptural books. But upon closer examination, the NT documents reveal that their authors were often quite conscious of transmitting an authoritative apostolic message commissioned by Christ himself.[66] We have seen that Luke was purposely constructing his accounts of Jesus and the early church as a continuation of the storyline

63. See Bruce, *The Canon of Scripture*, 170–77; arguments might be put forward that Irenaeus refers to Hebrews, James, and 2 Peter, respectively, in *Haer.* 2.30.9; 4.16.2; and 5.28.3.

64. See Edmon L. Gallagher and John D. Meade, *The Biblical Canon Lists from Early Christianity* (New York: Oxford University Press, 2017), 49.

65. Kruger, *The Question of Canon*, esp. 155–203. See also François C. Bovon, "The Canonical Structure of Gospel and Apostle," chapter 12 in *Studies in Early Christianity* (Tübingen: Mohr Siebeck, 2003; repr., Grand Rapids: Baker Academic, 2005), 163–77; and the manuscript-driven argument for an early NT canon in David Trobisch, *The First Edition of the New Testament* (New York: Oxford University Press, 2000).

66. Kruger, *The Question of Canon*, 153; cf. 119–54.

that had begun with the Hebrew Scriptures, even using an identifiable biblical writing style.[67] Furthermore, Peter and Paul—two of the most prominent characters in the story of Acts—actually use the term "Scripture" (the Greek term used, *graphē*, means "writing") when referring to what we have in writing from other NT authors. Thus, Peter (in 2 Pet 3:15–16) and Paul (in 1 Tim 5:18) give evidence that the NT writers themselves began to recognize other NT works as "Scripture."[68]

The Intentions of Scripture versus Other Ancient Writings

Erich Auerbach has famously described Scripture in contrast to the ancient writings of Homer; see Erich Auerbach, *Mimesis: The Representation of Reality in Western Literature*, trans. Willard R. Trask (Princeton: Princeton University Press, 1953), 14–15.

> The world of the Scripture stories is not satisfied with claiming to be a historically true reality—it insists that it is the only real world, is destined for autocracy. All other scenes, issues, and ordinances have no right to appear independently of it, and it is promised that all of them, the history of all mankind, will be given their due place within its frame, will be subordinated to it. The Scripture stories do not, like Homer's, court our favor, they do not flatter us that they may please us and enchant us—they seek to subject us, and if we refuse to be subjected we are rebels.

Shauf (*The Divine in Acts*, 282) applies Auerbach's perspective directly to Acts.

The authority with which Luke writes Acts, the manner in which he portrays the story he records as the continuation of the biblical history, and the way in which the church has accepted Acts—all these things combine for us to recognize in Acts the scriptural aura that it has.[69] The story of Acts reads like Scripture. Regarding the uniqueness of Luke's project, Jacob Jervell suggests that Luke intentionally wrote in a scriptural fashion about God's fulfillment of his promises such that readers can recognize Acts as the continuation of the history presented in the Scriptures, a way of writing not seen elsewhere in Greco-Roman or even Jewish historiography.[70]

67. See chapter 1, particularly sections 1.1.1 and 1.1.6.

68. See the brief discussion of these NT texts in Kruger, *The Question of Canon*, 199–202.

69. Shauf concludes his volume comparing Acts and other ancient historiographies with this comment on Luke's view of history: "For Luke, a historical movement is one that carries out the divine plan—nothing else is worthy to be narrated as history. And in the history that Luke narrates, Luke sees not only the divine plan carried out in the time and place he covers, but the divine plan, and thus the history, laid out for all humanity and for all time"; Scott Shauf, *The Divine in Acts and in Ancient Historiography* (Minneapolis: Fortress, 2015), 300.

70. Jacob Jervell, "The Future of the Past: Luke's Vision of Salvation History and Its Bearing on His Writing of History," pp. 104–26 in *History, Literature and Society in the Book of Acts*, ed. Ben Witherington III (Cambridge:

16.2.3 The Place of Acts in the New Testament Canon

As it is, the Acts of the Apostles appears to have been recognized as NT Scripture only a little later than the gospels and many of the NT epistles, particularly those of Paul. This recognition adds to the argument that Acts is a sequel to the Gospel of Luke.[71] And while both Western and Eastern early church fathers cite Acts, like the Gospel of Luke it seems that its authorial link to the apostle Paul was a major contributor to the recognition of Acts as Scripture.[72] Given its position in the NT canon, as well as its unique genre among the documents of the New Testament, the Acts of the Apostles forms something of a bridge or hinge between the fourfold collection of the Gospels and the collection of the Pauline letters. Acts connects the authoritative records of Jesus's life, words, death, and resurrection to the authoritative teaching of Jesus's personally commissioned apostle to the gentiles.[73] This recognition has come to have an effect on those who believe in Jesus and seek to participate in his mission; in particular, they view Acts along with the other NT documents as inspired guides for living in today's world.[74]

The Position of Acts in the Bible

From Gordon D. Fee and Douglas Stuart, *How to Read the Bible Book by Book: A Guided Tour* (Grand Rapids: Zondervan, 2002), 299.

> A word about its placement in the canon. Luke understands his Gospel and Acts to be two parts of one story. It ended up in two books of about equal length (rather than one long book) because each would fit on one papyrus scroll. But in putting together the New Testament canon, the early church separated Luke from Acts (since both would have existed on separate scrolls, even when copied) through inspired insight. In the canon Luke now belongs to the fourfold Gospel, while Acts serves as a bridge between the Gospels and Paul. But in reading Acts, you need always to remember how it fits into Luke's inspired plan.

Cambridge University Press, 1996), 116; as examples of Jewish historiography, Jervell points specifically to 2 Macc 2.24–32; 3 Macc 1.1ff.; Josephus, *Ant* 1.1–2 §§1–9; *J.W.* 1.1–4 §§1–12.

71. See chapter 2, particularly section 2.2.

72. See Linda L. Belleville, "The Canon of the New Testament," pp. 374–95 in *Foundations for Biblical Interpretation: A Complete Library of Tools and Resources*, ed. David S. Dockery, Kenneth A. Mathews, and Robert B. Sloan (Nashville: B&H Academic, 1994), 388.

73. Bruce, *The Canon of Scripture*, 132–33, 151–52.

74. Some have taken this hermeneutical approach to greater extents; for advocates of such a canonical approach specifically to Acts, see Robert W. Wall, "The Acts of the Apostles in Canonical Context," pp. 110–28 in *The New Testament as Canon: A Reader in Canonical Criticism*, by Robert W. Wall and Eugene E. Lemcio, JSNTSup 76 (Sheffield: Sheffield Academic Press, 1992); and Gregory Goswell, "Reading Romans after the Book of Acts," *JETS* 62 (2019): 353–69.

Michael Graves notes a connection between "inspiration" and "interpretation" of the NT documents. If Scripture is inspired by God to instruct humanity in the ways of Jesus Christ, then humanity must interpret Scripture in such a way that people can encounter Jesus Christ and learn how to live in him.[75] That is how this survey has tried to approach the Acts of the Apostles. It has been recognized as authoritative Christian Scripture, and thus it has something meaningful for us to believe. And that meaningfulness is not mere intellectual truths for our minds but also encouraging perspectives for our hearts and effective skills for our lives. While I have addressed the issue of application in quite specific ways through the course of this survey of Acts, I want to discuss some points of application in a broader, summary fashion in the remainder of this chapter.

Entailments in Recognizing Something as Scripture

Among the twenty various entailments Michael Graves outlines when claiming a particular writing to be inspired Scripture, the following claims have to do with historicity, factuality, and truth in the Bible:

- Events narrated in the Bible actually happened.
- Scripture does not have any errors in its facts.
- Scripture is not in conflict with "pagan" learning.
- The original text of Scripture is authoritative.
- Scripture's teaching is internally consistent.
- Scripture does not deceive.
- Scripture's teaching agrees with a recognized external authority.
- Scripture's teaching must be worthy of God.

See Michael Graves, *The Inspiration and Interpretation of Scripture: What the Early Church Can Teach Us* (Grand Rapids: Eerdmans, 2014), esp. 81–130.

16.3 THE STORY AFTER ACTS FOR US: THE MESSAGE, ENCOURAGEMENT, AND CHALLENGE OF ACTS

In chapter 3 some of the most prevalent themes in the theology of Luke-Acts were introduced. In our study of Acts, we have seen these themes played out, emphasized, and repeated in a variety of situations as the story of Acts unfolded. From those themes

75. Michael Graves, *The Inspiration and Interpretation of Scripture: What the Early Church Can Teach Us* (Grand Rapids: Eerdmans, 2014), 12.

in the message of Acts, we have seen a variety of encouragements and challenges for ourselves and for our churches (and for other ministries and gatherings of believers). Let me here briefly spell out some of these truths from Acts and their accompanying encouragements as part of God's Word for us today and apply them as challenges to our own life stories.

16.3.1 The Sovereign Creator God Is at Work in the World

From the way Luke tells the story of Acts, we can see that the sovereign creator God is at work in the world. Even in what some might call the more "pagan" parts of the world (i.e., in cultures distracted by polytheism or set on ignoring the one creator God), Acts says God has been present and active (Acts 14:15–17; 17:24–31). God has not abandoned the world; indeed, one of the points of Acts is that God has chosen to be presently active in the world by working in it through human agency (e.g., Acts 2:23; 4:24–30). Do I trust God to work sovereignly in and through my life, in my life story? Can I notice God at work in the life of my church, in other local churches, and in the world at large?

16.3.2 The Authoritative Scriptures Are Being Fulfilled

As Luke tells the story of Acts, it is manifestly meant to be not only a continuation of the story of Jesus in the Gospel of Luke: it is also the continuation of the story of God's work in the world told in the Hebrew Scriptures. For Luke, the authoritative Scriptures are being fulfilled in the story of Jesus and his followers (e.g., Luke 24:25–27, 44–48; Acts 3:18–26; 8:35; 17:2–3; 18:28). While people had to wait for a long time, they learned that God is faithful; God keeps his promises, and his Word will come true. Luke is clear about this (e.g., Acts 7:5–7, 17; 13:23, 32–33). This should make us wonder about our view of the Bible—both the New Testament and the Hebrew Scriptures—and our use of it. Do I align myself with God's Word? How proficient is my local church (and other gatherings of believers with which I am involved) at paying attention to the whole Bible as the Word of God?

16.3.3 Jesus Is the Promised Messiah, the Risen Lord and King

Luke's use of God's Word and his presentation of the story of Jesus and his followers demonstrates that Jesus is the promised Messiah, the risen Lord and King. People in the story of Acts recognize Jesus as the Messiah (from the Hebrew term meaning "anointed one" ≈ Greek for "Christ"): his resurrection from the dead is proof of his ability to rescue people from their sins (e.g., Acts 13:32–39; cf. 17:31). For Israel in Luke's day, Yahweh was Lord and Savior (see Hab 3:18; Ps 24:6–7; Isa 12:2; Mic 7:7;

cf. Luke 1:46–47); but now Jesus is also called Savior (e.g., Luke 2:11; Acts 5:31; 13:23). Because he is more than a mere rescuer, the predominant title for Jesus in Acts is "Lord"—a term sometimes referring to the one God of Scripture (e.g., Acts 2:39, 47; 3:20, 22; 4:24), sometimes referring to Jesus (e.g., Acts 2:36; 4:33; 7:59–60; 9:1; 11:16–17) and sometimes used in places where we cannot tell the difference (e.g., Acts 11:20–21)! Thus, as Luke writes in a historical manner, he presents the historical person of Jesus as Lord and Christ (e.g., Luke 2:11, 26; 24:3; Acts 2:36; 4:26; 11:17; 15:26). And as God-in-the-flesh, Jesus can lay a kingly claim on us all. Do I recognize Jesus as the rightful Lord in all areas of my life? To what extent does my church conduct itself under the authority of Jesus?

16.3.4 Faith in Christ Results in Forgiveness of Sins for All Who Repent

And what does the Lord Jesus, in his authority, require of us? As Luke writes the story of Jesus and his followers, he specifies that Jesus calls all people to repentance (e.g., Luke 5:32; Acts 2:38; 3:19; 5:31; 17:30). Christians note that people respond to this call to repentance by "believing in Jesus," and this faith in Christ results in forgiveness of sins for all who repent. This is good news: Jesus died in our place on behalf of our sinfulness; was resurrected, proving his power over sin; and invites us to enjoy a forgiven life in relationship with him. Forgiveness is available to me. Have I repented of my sin and received the forgiveness he offers? Does this gospel message have a prominent place in the teaching of my church?

16.3.5 The Good News about Jesus Is God's Provision of Salvation for Humanity

Luke is clear that the gospel is not just for the Jews but for all nations (Acts 10:34–48; 20:21); Jesus is the Lord of all (Acts 10:36), not only Lord of the Jews. The good news about Jesus is God's provision of salvation for humanity, and this good news of salvation has reached me across centuries of time and across political and ethic borders. If I am trusting Jesus, then he is my salvation now and in eternity. Am I living the life of a saved person right now? How well is my church seeking to uphold God's provision of salvation and new life for all others?

16.3.6 All Who Follow Jesus Are God's True People

The position of being forgiven before God has become the measure of God's people. Some of the Jews in Luke's story had become accustomed to measuring their status with God by physical genetics: i.e., they assumed that all descendants of Abraham could lay claim to the title of "God's people" (e.g., Luke 3:8). But Jesus challenged this lazy assumption (Luke 6:43–49; 8:19–21; cf. John 8:31–47). While God clearly used the

Israelites as his own people to bring a Savior to the world, how one responds to God's provision of Jesus as that Savior is the measure of God's people (Acts 15:7–11; 26:17–18). The gospel message of faith in Jesus Christ forms a new center on which the people of God are united.[76] This means that all who follow Jesus are God's true people, even if they are not physical descendants of Abraham. As Luke recounts the beginning years of the church in Acts, this ethnocentrism was eventually overcome, albeit with some difficulty (see esp. Acts 10–11 and 15). But the encouragement here is that no matter my background, I can be one of God's true people. The invitation is open to me, and of course, the challenge is that I must decide to follow Jesus. But having accepted Jesus as my Savior, how well do I acknowledge him as the Savior of others, especially of those who are not like me? How proficient is my church at inviting those of different backgrounds into the community of God's people?

16.3.7 Jesus Followers Witness to the Good News about Him

We have indeed heard the good news of Jesus's death for our sins and his resurrection, and the reason we have heard this good news is because others have told us about it. The message that salvation is available through Jesus did not disappear into heaven with him at the ascension (Acts 1:9–11) precisely because the first Christians in Acts obeyed the command of Jesus to spread the good news (Acts 1:8; cf. 2:40; 14:3; 22:15; 26:16). Furthermore, after the book of Acts (for the past twenty centuries!), Jesus followers have continued to witness to the good news about him. Now, as a follower of Jesus myself in this century, do I find myself telling others about Jesus? Does my church have a passion for getting the good news to the ends of the earth? How am I participating with my church and other Christians in helping the good news reach the nations in my own era (and perhaps even in eras beyond my time)?

16.3.8 The Holy Spirit Is God's Empowering Presence in All His People

The idea of participating in the worldwide spread of the gospel can be overwhelming. But Luke has encouragement for us here too. Jesus's first followers were told rather plainly not to leave Jerusalem on their mission to reach the world until they receive God's provision for this mission (Luke 24:48–49; Acts 1:4–5, 8). Acts stipulates that the Holy Spirit is God's empowering presence in all his people for faithful living and for carrying out the gospel mission. The believers in Acts were

76. See Alan J. Thompson, *One Lord, One People: The Unity of the Church in Acts in Its Literary Setting*, LNTS 359 (London: T&T Clark, 2008); cf. Andrew C. Clark, *Parallel Lives: The Relation of Paul to the Apostles in the Lucan Perspective*, Paternoster Biblical and Theological Monographs (Carlisle: Paternoster, 2002), 29: "It is the issues of the identity and unity of the people of God which are Luke's main concern."

characterized, directed, and empowered by the Holy Spirit (e.g., Acts 2:1–33; 4:8–12; 6:3–10; 8:29, 39; 10:19; 11:12; 13:2–12; 16:6–7; 20:22–23). But Luke notes that the Holy Spirit is given to *all* who believe (Acts 2:38–39; 5:32), so if I am a Jesus follower, God's Spirit is part of my life (see also Paul's words on this in Romans 8:9–11 and Galatians 4:6; 5:16–25). So, how well do I tap the power of God's Spirit in my daily life? How attentive is my local church to the Holy Spirit's characteristic presence, direction, and empowerment?

16.3.9 Believers Will Face Opposition but Can Overcome It

The Spirit's presence in the lives of Christians is important; the empowerment of the Spirit is for spreading the gospel message but also for faithful living. After all, life on this mission has its hardships, and Acts is transparent about this (Acts 14:22). Thus, believers will face opposition but can overcome it by depending on the Lord's provision (cf. Luke 12:11–12; 21:14–15). While this notification of difficulties can be foreboding, there is a subtle encouragement here. When we face hardship as Christians, we can be reassured that such hardships are normal. Of course, there is a double challenge here: we are challenged to be grateful when life is going well, but we are also challenged to introspection when we don't experience hardship. That is, to what degree might we be acquiescing to the culture around us and ignoring our calling so as to avoid opposition? Am I or my church experiencing hardship as God's representatives in the world? What might I or my church do to be supportive of believers (near and far) who are faced with grave opposition on account of the gospel?

16.3.10 Jesus Rules Now but Will Return to Rule More Fully

Luke seems concerned that his readers live faithfully (e.g., Luke 3:8–14; 6:43–49; 8:19–21). When most characters in the story of Acts face difficult circumstances, we see them choosing to obey God rather than succumb to the human pressure to disobey (e.g., Acts 4:18–20; 5:27–32). God rescues some believers from their hardships (e.g., Acts 5:18–21; 12:3–19; 16:22–40), but others suffer to the bitter end of martyrdom (e.g., Acts 7:54–60; 12:1–2). This makes the current rule of Jesus as Lord and King appear only partial at this stage. Nevertheless, Luke encourages us to recognize that Jesus rules now but will return to rule more fully in his kingship role. When Jesus returns, he will bring about a final sense of justice and at long last set things in order (Luke 12:1–13:35; 17:20–18:8; 19:11–27; 21:5–36; 23:27–31; Acts 1:11; 10:42; 17:31; 24:25). Luke wants us to live faithfully now, boldly spreading the gospel, expecting Jesus to return. This is the message, encouragement, and challenge of Acts for all of us together in the community of believers.

The Message, Encouragement, and Challenge of Acts

Theological Truth	Encouragement	Application Challenge
1. The sovereign creator God is at work in the world.	God has not abandoned the world but is present.	How well do I trust God to work in and through my life? Can I notice God at work in the life of my church, in other local churches, and in the world at large?
2. The authoritative Scriptures are being fulfilled, especially in Jesus.	God keeps his promises, and his Word will come true.	How well do I align myself with God's Word? How proficient is my local church at paying attention to the whole Bible as the Word of God?
3. Jesus is the promised Messiah, the risen Lord and King.	This historical person Jesus is God in the flesh.	How well do I recognize Jesus as the rightful Lord of my life? To what extent does my church conduct itself under the authority of Jesus?
4. Faith in Christ results in forgiveness of sins for all who repent.	Forgiveness for our sins is available to us.	Have I repented of my sin and received God's forgiveness? Does this gospel message have a prominent place in the teaching of my church?
5. The good news about Jesus is God's provision of salvation for humanity.	Anyone trusting Jesus is saved now and in eternity.	How am I doing at living the life of a saved person right now? How well is my church seeking to uphold God's provision of salvation and new life for all others?
6. God is concerned for all people, so all who follow Jesus are God's true people.	No matter one's background, one can be part of God's true people.	How well do I acknowledge Jesus as Savior of others, esp. of those not like me? How proficient is my church at inviting those of different backgrounds into the community of God's people?
7. Jesus followers witness to the good news about him.	We have heard the good news because others have told us.	Does my church have a passion for getting the good news to the ends of the earth? How am I participating with my church and other Christians in that mission?
8. The Holy Spirit is God's empowering presence in all his people.	Every Jesus follower has God's Spirit in their lives.	How well do I tap the power of God's Spirit in my daily living? How attentive is my church to the Holy Spirit's characteristic presence, direction, and empowerment?
9. In spreading the good news, believers will face opposition but can overcome it.	When we face hardship as Christians, it is normal.	What does it mean if we don't experience hardship? What might I and my church do to be supportive of believers faced with grave opposition on account of the gospel?
10. Jesus rules now but will return to rule more fully.	Jesus is coming back some day to set things in proper order.	How am I and my church and Christian friends doing at expecting our Lord and King to return?

16.4 CONCLUDING REMARKS

The NT book of Acts reports the beginnings of the Christian church, telling what the first Jesus followers did in response to the gospel message after they received the Holy Spirit and while they waited for Jesus to return. We find ourselves in much the same position even now almost two thousand years later. Here, where we are now, we can be grateful that Luke recorded not only the story of Jesus in what we now call the

Gospel of Luke but also the continuation of the story of Jesus in what we now call the Acts of the Apostles.

Luke's second book lets us know something of how the gospel message reached us, and for this we can be grateful. But Acts has a not-so-subtle challenge for us to ask ourselves how we are participating in the continuation of the story. Modern biographies of Christians throughout the last two thousand years—historical figures and those from more recent years—tell the stories of people who have had significant impact on the world and who have helped forward the gospel in their times.[77] But there are thousands and thousands of others whose stories go unreported but who have nevertheless had an important impact on the spread of the kingdom of God. I am challenged to recognize that my life story is not really about me. My life story is to be about the story of the gospel message and the expanding kingdom of God.[78]

The kingdom of God, which has begun in some sense with Christ's first coming (e.g., Luke 9:27; 11:20; 17:20–21; cf.) and is expanding to this day (e.g., Luke 13:18–20), is still being anticipated to arrive more fully when Christ returns (as promised when he left in Acts 1:9–11; cf. Luke 10:8–15; 11:2; 19:11–27; 21:29–31; 23:51). In the meantime, we have lives to live faithfully and a message to bear boldly as we take up our role in the continuing story of the spread of the gospel. May God grant that we do so unhindered.

Fishing with nets on the Sea of Galilee.

Library of Congress, LC-matpc-22959/ www.LifeintheHolyLand.com

77. See the bibliography at the end of this chapter for some easy-to-read collections of biographical stories of Christians in history.

78. Helpful resources are available for reminding us about God's story and our place in it. See, for example, D. A. Carson, *The God Who Is There: Finding Your Place in God's Story* (Grand Rapids: Baker, 2010); Craig G. Bartholomew and Michael W. Goheen, *The True Story of the Whole World: Finding Your Place in the Biblical Drama* (Grand Rapids: Faith Alive Christian Resources, 2004); and Preben Vang and Terry G. Carter, *Telling God's Story: The Biblical Narrative from Beginning to End*, 2nd ed. (Nashville: B&H Academic, 2013).

16.5 Key People, Places, and Terms

- Amphilochus
- Andrew
- apocryphal acts
- Athanasius
- Bartholomew
- canon criteria
- Council of Carthage
- Council of Chalcedon
- Council of Hippo
- Irenaeus
- James, son of Alphaeus
- James the Greater
- James the Lesser
- John the apostle
- Judas Iscariot
- Judas, son of James
- Levi
- Matthew
- Matthias
- Nathanael
- NT canon
- Paul
- Peter
- Philip the apostle
- Simon the Zealot
- Thaddaeus
- Thomas
- Western text

16.6 Questions for Review and Discussion

1. What are the apocryphal acts?
2. What do the various legends and traditions from the first five centuries after the New Testament tell us about the lives of the apostles after the story of Acts?
3. Compared to the apocryphal acts, how does the Acts of the Apostles measure up as canonical Scripture?
4. As you reflect on the various encouragements and challenges of the message of Acts, which three would you say are the most significant for the Christian church today? Why?
5. Within your local community of believers, what might your role be for embracing the encouragements and challenges of the message of Acts (particularly the three you identified in question 4)?
6. If the story of the Christian church—and even your own life story—is really about Jesus and the gospel (rather than about ourselves), what are the implications of that idea for day-to-day living?

16.7 Optional Assignments

1. **Text Reflection Project**—*Relating the concepts discussed in this chapter to another biblical text.* I have commented on Luke's style of writing as being Scripture-like; some scholars suggest that he wrote with the intention of showing the story of Jesus as the continuation of the OT story. This chapter mentions how 2 Peter 3:15–16 and 1 Timothy 5:18 give evidence that the NT writers themselves began to recognize other NT works as "Scripture." Investigate these two non-Lukan passages and see if you think these writers show awareness in their own day of the NT Scriptures being written.
2. **Interview Project**—*Inquiring of others their views concerning the concepts discussed in this chapter.* Interview an elder Christian—someone who has been a follower of Jesus for many, many years (perhaps

your pastor can help you identify such a person)—and ask that person about his or her life of faith (e.g., their most challenging experiences, what they found most helpful to their faith, warnings they wish they would have heard and heeded at your age, sacrifices they made for the gospel, what helped them participate in the life of faith unhindered). Finally, ask what advice they might have for you.

3. **Service-Learning Project**—*Applying the concepts discussed in this chapter in some form of service to others outside the class.* If the story of Acts has encouraged and challenged you in the course of this study, perhaps you can serve others by passing some of this story on to them. Offer to teach a Sunday school lesson or youth group Bible study on some portion of Acts that you found particularly encouraging or challenging.
4. **Prayer Project**—*Talking with God about the concepts discussed in this chapter.* Write a prayer of gratitude to God about your study of the book of Acts and the two or three most impactful things you have learned. Then ask the Lord for wisdom and courage regarding how you will participate in the continuing story.
5. **Testimony Project**—*Telling others about the concepts discussed in this chapter.* Compose a letter to a person who influenced your faith journey. Use this opportunity to thank them for participating in the spread of the kingdom of God so that you could hear and respond to the gospel message.

16.8 Bibliography for Going Further

16.8.1 The Lives of the Apostles after Acts

Bruce, F. F. "The Last Days of Paul: History and Tradition." Pages 441–55 (chapter 37) in *Paul: Apostle of the Heart Set Free*. Grand Rapids: Eerdmans, 1977.

Criswell, David. *The Apostles After Jesus: A History of the Apostles (Separating Tradition and History)*. Dallas: Fortress Adonai, 2013.

Litfin, Bryan. *After Acts: Exploring the Lives and Legends of the Apostles*. Chicago: Moody, 2015.

McBirnie, William Steuart. *The Search for the Twelve Apostles*. Rev. ed. Carol Stream, IL: Tyndale, 2004.

McDowell, Sean. *The Fate of the Apostles: Examining the Martyrdom Accounts of the Closest Followers of Jesus*. New York: Routledge, 2015.

Puig i Tàrrech, Armand, John M. G. Barclay, and Jörg Frey, eds. *The Last Years of Paul: Essays from the Tarragona Conference, June 2013*. WUNT 352. Tübingen: Mohr Siebeck, 2015.

Quarles, Charles L. "Paul's Last Years." Pages 249–70 (chapter 9) in *Illustrated Life of Paul*. Nashville: B&H Academic, 2014.

Schmidt, Thomas E. *The Apostles after Acts: A Sequel*. Eugene, OR: Cascade, 2013.

Shelton, W. Brian. *Quest for the Historical Apostles: Tracing Their Lives and Legacies*. Grand Rapids: Baker Academic, 2018.

16.8.2 Apocryphal Acts and the New Testament Apocrypha

Bovon, François C. "Canonical and Apocryphal Acts of the Apostles." Pages 197–222 in *New Testament and Christian Apocrypha: Collected Studies II*. Edited by Glenn E. Snyder. WUNT 237. Tübingen: Mohr Siebeck, 2009. Repr., *New Testament and Christian Apocrypha*. Grand Rapids: Baker Academic, 2011.

Elliott, James Keith, ed. *The Apocryphal New Testament: A Collection of Apocryphal Christian Literature in an English Translation*. Oxford: Clarendon, 1993.

James, Montague Rhodes, ed. *The Apocryphal New Testament: Being the Apocryphal Gospels, Acts, Epistles, and Apocalypses, with Other Narratives and Fragments*. 2nd ed. Oxford: Clarendon, 1953.

Klauck, Hans-Josef. *The Apocryphal Acts of the Apostles: An Introduction*. Translated by Brian McNeil. Waco, TX: Baylor University Press, 2008.

Schneemelcher, Wilhelm, ed. *New Testament Apocrypha*. Vol. 2: *Writings Relating to the Apostles; Apocalypses and Related Subjects*. Translated by R. McL. Wilson. Cambridge: Clarke, 1992.

16.8.3 Acts and the Canon of the New Testament

Belleville, Linda L. "The Canon of the New Testament." Pages 374–95 in *Foundations for Biblical Interpretation: A Complete Library of Tools and Resources*. Edited by David S. Dockery, Kenneth A. Mathews, and Robert B. Sloan. Nashville: B&H Academic, 1994.

Berding, Kenneth. "New Testament Canon: Recognizing the Authoritative Writings." Pages 315–20 in *What the New Testament Authors Really Cared About: A Survey of Their Writings*. Edited by Kenneth Berding and Matt Williams. 2nd ed. Grand Rapids: Kregel, 2015.

Bruce, F. F. *The Canon of Scripture*. Downers Grove, IL: InterVarsity Press, 1988.

Ehrhardt, Arnold. "Time, Tradition, and Canonization of the Book of Acts." Pages 1–11 (chapter 1) in *The Acts of the Apostles: Ten Lectures*. Manchester: Manchester University Press, 1969.

Gallagher, Edmon L., and John D. Meade. *The Biblical Canon Lists from Early Christianity*. New York: Oxford University Press, 2017

Gregory, Andrew F. *The Reception of Luke and Acts in the Period before Irenaeus: Looking for Luke in the Second Century*. WUNT 2.169. Tübingen: Mohr Siebeck, 2003.

Kruger, Michael J. *Canon Revisited: Establishing the Origins and Authority of the New Testament Books*. Wheaton, IL: Crossway, 2012.

———. *The Question of Canon: Challenging the Status Quo in the New Testament Debate*. Downers Grove, IL: InterVarsity Press, 2013.

Metzger, Bruce M. *The Canon of the New Testament: Its Origin, Development, and Significance*. Oxford: Oxford University Press, 1987.

Patzia, Arthur G. *The Making of the New Testament: Origin, Collection, Text, and Canon*. 2nd ed. Downers Grove, IL: InterVarsity Press, 2011.

16.8.4 Collections of Short Biographies of Christians

DeRusha, Michelle. *50 Women Every Christian Should Know: Learning from Heroines of the Faith*. Grand Rapids: Baker, 2014.

Galli, Mark, and Ted Olsen, eds. *131 Christians Everyone Should Know*. Nashville: Broadman & Holman, 2000.

Metaxas, Eric. *Seven Men: And the Secret of Their Greatness*. Nashville: Nelson, 2013.

———. *Seven Women: And the Secret of Their Greatness*. Nashville: Nelson, 2015.

Noll, Mark A., and Carolyn Nystrom. *Clouds of Witnesses: Christian Voices from Africa and Asia*. Downers Grove, IL: InterVarsity Press, 2011.

Tucker, Ruth A. *Extraordinary Women of Christian History: What We Can Learn from Their Struggles and Triumphs*. Grand Rapids: Baker, 2016.

Wiersbe, Warren W. *50 People Every Christian Should Know: Learning from Spiritual Giants of the Faith*. Grand Rapids: Baker, 2009.

Woodbridge, John D., ed. *Ambassadors for Christ*. Chicago: Moody, 1994.

GLOSSARY

Abraham: The Hebrew patriarch (ca. 2100 BC) of the Jewish nation (see Gen 12:1–3).

Adramyttium: A seaport city in northwest Asia Minor and home of a ship transporting Paul from Caesarea to Myra (Acts 27:1–5).

Aeneas: A crippled man of Lydda healed through Peter (Acts 9:32–33).

Agabus: A Jerusalem prophet who predicted a Judean famine (Acts 11:27–30) and Paul's arrest (Acts 21:10–14).

Alexander the Great: The fourth-century BC Macedonian ruler whose military conquests of the Eastern Mediterranean and Middle East greatly advanced Hellenization.

Alexandria, Egypt: A major city founded in 332 BC by Alexander the Great and the traditional location where the Septuagint (LXX) Greek translation of the Hebrew Scriptures was made.

already/not yet kingdom: See "**inaugurated eschatology**."

Amphilochus: Bishop of Iconium in AD 394 and writer of a poem listing the twenty-seven NT books in their current order.

Ananias (of Damascus): The man the Lord used in bringing Saul (Paul) to faith (Acts 9).

Ananias (of Jerusalem): A Jerusalem church member who, with his wife Sapphira, died for lying about their offering (Acts 5:1–11).

Andrew: Brother of Simon Peter and one of the twelve apostles selected by Jesus after first being a disciple of John the Baptist.

Anti-Marcionite Prologues: Second-century introductory remarks (against Marcion's interpretations) to copies of the canonical gospels; they refer to the writer of the Third Gospel and Acts as Luke, a Syrian from Antioch, a physician by profession, a disciple of the apostles, and a follower of Paul.

Antioch near Pisidia: A.k.a. Pisidian Antioch, a city in the mountainous territory of Phrygia in central Asia Minor "near Pisidia" (to distinguish it from another Antioch in Phrygia); part of the Roman province of Galatia in the first century and visited by Paul.

Antioch of Syria: A.k.a. Syrian Antioch and Antioch on the Orontes, the third largest city in the first-century world, located near the northeastern shore of the Mediterranean Sea; a main hub of early Christian missions.

Apocrypha: A term meaning "hidden," the title of a collection of Jewish texts written after the OT period that were never part of the Hebrew Scriptures; rejected by Protestants as authoritative Scripture but accepted as secondary Scripture by Roman Catholics and Orthodox Christians. There are also apocryphal NT books.

apocryphal acts: Noncanonical writings from after the NT period (mid-second to sixth century) purporting to record the activities of various apostles.

Apollos: An itinerant Jewish preacher from Alexandria whom Priscilla and Aquila taught more accurately the way of God in Ephesus (Acts 18:24–28).

apostle: A term that basically means "sent one" or "messenger" (see esp. John 13:16; cf. Luke 11:49) and was used not only for the original Twelve who were personally chosen by Jesus as authoritative leaders of the church (see Luke 6:12–16; Acts 1:2, 12–26; 6:2) but also in a more general sense for commissioned emissaries like Paul and Barnabas (Acts 14:4 and 14), Andronicus and Junias (Rom 16:7), Epaphroditus (Phil 2:25), Titus and others (2 Cor 8:23) who were sent by churches.

Aquila and Priscilla: See "**Priscilla and Aquila**."

Areopagus: Literally "Mars Hill," referring to (a) the physical location just west of the acropolis in Athens, (b) the ruling council of Athens that often met at Mars Hill, or (c) both, i.e., the council at the hill (Acts 17).

Artemis: The Greek goddess (Roman: Diana) of hunting, the wilderness, wild animals, the moon, childbirth, protecting childhood, and chastity; the most important deity in first-century Ephesus where her temple was one of the seven wonders of the ancient world (Acts 19).

Aristarchus: One of Paul's coworkers from Thessalonica; accompanied Paul on his journey to Rome (Acts 19:29; 20:4; 27:2; cf. Col 4:10–14; Phlm 24).

ascension: The event of Jesus ascending into heaven forty days after his resurrection; only Luke narrates the event (Luke 24:50–53; Acts 1:9–11).

Assyria: The nation that conquered the northern kingdom of Israel in 722 BC.

Athanasius: Bishop of Alexandria whose festal letter for Easter in AD 367 contains one of the earliest lists of all twenty-seven books of the New Testament.

Athens: The historic Greek city whose glory days of the mid-fifth century BC had faded by the first century when Paul visited (Acts 17), but it remained a cultural and educational center in the Roman world.

Attalia: A first-century Mediterranean seaport city on the coast of Pamphylia visited by Paul and Barnabas on their first missionary journey.

autographs: The original physical NT documents penned by the NT writers themselves.

Azotus: The NT name for the OT Philistine city of Ashdod in southwestern Israel where Philip appeared after being swept away from the presence of the Ethiopian eunuch (Acts 8:40).

Babylon: The nation that carried the southern Israelite kingdom of Judah into exile in waves: 605 BC, 597 BC, and 586 BC, when Jerusalem was destroyed.

Bar-Jesus: See "**Elymas the sorcerer**."

Barnabas: A Levite from Cyprus and a radically generous member of the Jerusalem church who was instrumental in Saul being accepted among Jerusalem believers, in leading the Syrian Antioch church, and as a missionary with Saul/Paul.

Bartholomew: One of the twelve apostles (Matt 10:1–4; Mark 3:13–19; Luke 6:12–16; Acts 1:13), a.k.a. Nathanael (John 1:43–51; cf. John 21:2).

The Beloved disciple: See "**John the apostle**."

benefaction: A.k.a. patronage, the practice of individuals in the lower classes depending on the generosity of specific upper-class citizens as their patrons and offering in return their political support, public honor, or other services. Ancient societies could also practice such benefaction/patronage on the civic level, whereby a city depended on its wealthier citizens to make donations to fund such things as public works, libraries, stadiums, and festivals expecting public honor in return.

Berea: A small city in southwestern Macedonia visited by Paul after Thessalonica during his second missionary campaign and where the people were noted for being more noble as evidenced in their own study of Scripture (Acts 17:11).

Bernice: A daughter of Herod Agrippa I and sister to Herod Agrippa II, with whom she heard Paul's testimony in Acts 26.

biographical historical monograph: The genre category where the categories of biography and historical monograph overlap; see also "**biography**" and "**history**."

biography: The genre category for ancient literature that would record the life a hero and celebrate that hero's virtues, teachings, and/or deeds.

blasphemy: Utterly offensive speech or action that conveys contempt for God and his authority.

Bodmer Papyrus XIV–XV: A.k.a. P^{75} and dating to AD 175–225, the oldest extant Greek manuscript of the Third Gospel and has the first occurrence of the title "Gospel According to Luke," interestingly placed at the end of the book.

Caesar: The title used by Roman emperors.

Caesar Augustus: (63 BC–AD 14) At the close of the Roman Republic, August (a.k.a. Octavian) became the first true emperor of Rome and was ruling at the time of Jesus's birth (Luke 2:1–7).

Caesarea: A.k.a. Caesarea Maritima, the first-century headquarters city of the Roman government for the province of Judea and a major Mediterranean seaport city for Palestine, named in honor of Caesar Augustus. While unmentioned in Luke-Acts, the other notable NT city named in honor of a Caesar is Caesarea Philippi, north of the Sea of Galilee (Matt 16:13; Mark 8:27).

canon criteria: The standards by which a book measures up to be recognized as Scripture ("canon" means measure); the following are often acknowledged: the authority of Jesus and connection to the apostles, applicability and usage in the churches, and truth and orthodoxy in content.

casting lots: While unclear, it appears that lots were small stones or pieces of wood thrown or shaken or cast in decision-making settings.

Cenchreae: A seaport town five miles east of Corinth on the Saronic Gulf of the Aegean Sea (Acts 18:18).

centurion: A Roman officer in charge of approximately (not always precisely) one hundred troops (i.e., "a century").

cessationist view: The theological position that supernatural gifts of the Spirit ceased to operate after the apostolic era.

chiasm: When a sequence of ideas or phrases (A-B-C) is immediately repeated but in reverse order (C'-B'-A').

chief official: The title of the principal leader of the island of Malta in the first century (Acts 28:7).

Christian: First used in Syrian Antioch to distinguish followers of Jesus from adherents to Judaism, this term is used only three times in the New Testament (Acts 11:26; 26:28; 1 Pet 4:16) and may have originally developed as a term of derision.

church councils: International meetings of church leaders to address problematic issues; of the many church councils, the first seven (between AD 325 and AD 787) are often referred to as "ecumenical councils"; e.g., see "**Council of Carthage**," "**Council of Chalcedon**," and "**Council of Hippo**."

circumcision: Removal of the foreskin of the male genital organ; as a practice associated with the OT covenant of faith, the early church faced the question of whether it was to be required of Christians in their commitment to Jesus as the fulfillment of the OT faith.

Claudius Lysias: The commander of the Roman garrison in Jerusalem who took charge in arresting Paul and in transferring him to Caesarea (Acts 21–23).

client kings: Local rulers Rome kept in power and supported as long as those rulers served the interests of Rome; Herod the Great was a notorious example.

codex: An ancient manuscript text with pages bound in book form.

collectivism: The mentality of the Middle East—especially in ancient times—emphasizing the group; rather than be successful as individuals, people sought to belong to a group and to contribute to its success.

continuation view: The theological position that supernatural gifts of the Spirit have continued to operate in the current era.

Corinth: The first-century capital of the Roman province of Achaia (Greece), strategically positioned with influence over both land and sea traffic, and notorious as a place of wealth and indulgence; Paul stayed here for a year and a half during his second missionary journey.

Cornelius: A Roman centurion of the Italian Regiment who was stationed in Caesarea, where he heard the gospel from Peter and became a believer (Acts 10:1–11:18).

Council of Carthage: Held in AD 397, one of the seven ecumenical church councils; it is one of three (with that of Hippo and Chalcedon) that are often credited as heralding a closing of the NT canon.

Council of Chalcedon: Held in AD 451, one of the seven ecumenical church councils; it is one of three (with that of Hippo and Carthage) that are often credited as heralding a closing of the NT canon.

Council of Hippo: Held in AD 393, one of the seven ecumenical church councils; it is one of three (with that of Carthage and Chalcedon) that are often credited as heralding a closing of the NT canon.

covenant: A solemn binding agreement between two parties. Much of Scripture is structured around the covenant relationship God initiated with his people; salvation through faith in Jesus Christ is often referred to as the new covenant.

Crete: The fourth largest island in the Mediterranean Sea; the ship taking Paul to Rome sailed along its southern coast seeking a place to winter but was blown off course (Acts 27:7–15).

Cyprus: A large island in the northeast corner of the Mediterranean Sea; Barnabas was from Cyprus, and he and Paul began the first missionary journey with a visit to this island.

D-text: See "**Western text**."

Damascus: One of the world's oldest continually inhabited cities, situated on the primary ancient north-south international trade route through Palestine; Saul traveled there to persecute Christians but en route met the risen Jesus (Acts 9).

Davidic Messiah: Many branches of first-century Jewish faith expected a descendant of David to arise and serve as an end-times king ruling in righteousness and dispensing justice.

deacons: An office of leadership and service in the early church differentiated from that of "overseers" (see Phil 1:1; 1 Tim 3:1–13; cf. Rom 16:1). Because Luke uses a generic noun for "service, ministry" (Greek: *diakonia*) to describe the seven ministers selected in Acts 6:1–6, they are sometimes referred to as "deacons" (*diakonos*), but this suggestion for the origin of the church office is inconclusive.

Dead Sea Scrolls: A collection of around 950 ancient writings discovered in caves along the northwestern edge of the Dead Sea in the 1940s and associated with the first-century Jewish community at Qumran.

Demetrius: A silversmith in Ephesus who made and sold small silver shrines for worshiping the goddess Artemis; he was instrumental in a riot protesting Paul's gospel preaching (Acts 19:23–41).

Derbe: A Lycaonian town about sixty miles southeast of Lystra in southern Galatia. Gaius, a member of Paul's ministry team, was from Derbe.

Diana: See "**Artemis**."

diaspora: A term meaning "dispersion," referring to Jews living outside the land of Israel.

didactic material: Instructional material in literature (in contrast to "narrative material").

Dionysius Exiguus: A monk of Scythia Minor (a.k.a., "Dionysius the Humble" or "Dennis the Short") who, in AD 525, devised the modern BC/AD calendaring system (which was later discovered to be 4–6 years off).

disciple: A term meaning "learner," used of a devoted follower of some teacher; one of Luke's favorite terms for any follower of Jesus.

Dorcas: See "**Tabitha**."

Drusilla: A daughter of Herod Agrippa I and sister to Herod Agrippa II and Bernice; she left her husband to marry the Roman procurator Felix, with whom she heard the gospel from Paul (Acts 24:24).

dust-shaking gesture: Shaking the dust off one's feet or clothing as a symbol of separation; a gesture Paul and Barnabas perform to warn the Jews of Pisidian Antioch (Acts 13:51; cf. 18:6).

early church fathers: Christian leaders from the first few centuries after Christ.

Egypt: The country in northeast Africa where the descendants of Israel grew into a nation and from which God rescued the Israelites through Moses in the exodus.

elders: Leaders in faith communities; Jewish society operated with elders, so the new church did in Jerusalem (Acts 15:2), and Paul and Barnabas appointed elders in the churches they had established (Acts 14:23).

Eleven, the: A nickname for the Twelve apostles after the defection of Judas Iscariot (Luke 24:9, 33) until Matthias fills out their number (Acts 1:26; 6:2).

Elymas the sorcerer: A.k.a. Bar-Jesus, a Jewish sorcerer and false prophet confronted by Paul and stricken blind when he tried to turn the proconsul of Cyprus away from faith (Acts 13:4–12).

Ephesus: A city on the western coast of Asia Minor (modern Turkey) and the first-century center of the Roman Empire's richest region; where Paul ministered for three years on his third missionary campaign (Acts 19:8–10).

Epictetus: (ca. AD 55–135) a teacher of Stoic philosophy and known for a collection of his lectures and a handbook of his teachings put together by one of his students.

Epicureanism: A philosophical school of thought dedicated to the teaching of Epicurus, emphasizing chance and enjoyment of pleasure; comparable to deism, which denies God's involvement in human life.

eschatology: Study of God's future activities at the end of history in the return of Jesus Christ, the resurrection and final judgment of people, and assignments to the afterlife of heaven or hell.

Essenes: A Jewish sect more conservative and separatist than the Pharisees, rigorously keeping Jewish law and often living in monastic communities; they are not mentioned in the New Testament.

Ethiopia: Ancient name for the territory of Nubia in the upper Nile region of Africa (a.k.a., Cush) that is now northern Sudan; not to be confused with the modern country of this same name.

eunuch: A physical description (for a castrated man) and/or a role description (for ancient government servant positions).

Eutychus: A young man in Troas who died from a fall but was raised from the dead through Paul (Acts 20:7–12).

exile: Being carried away from one's homeland; the southern Israelite kingdom of Judah was carried off into exile by the Babylonians in waves (605, 597, and 586 BC).

exodus: The great saving event when God used Moses to lead the OT Israelites out of enslavement in Egypt to the promised land of Palestine (see Exod 1–18).

exorcism: Driving a demon or evil spirit out of a person.

Fair Havens: A seaport in southern Crete near the city of Lasea; the ship taking Paul to Rome stopped briefly here (Acts 27:8).

famine visit: Barnabas and Paul's delivery of famine relief funds from Antioch believers to the Jerusalem believers (Acts 11:27–30; cf. Gal 2:1–10).

Fate: See "**goddess Justice**."

Felix: The Roman procurator of Judea (ca. AD 52–59) who received the prisoner Paul in Caesarea but delayed making a ruling (Acts 23–24); Felix and his wife Drusilla heard the gospel from Paul but delayed making any response (Acts 24:24–27).

Festus: The Roman procurator of Judea (ca. AD 59–62) who succeeded Felix and quickly heard Paul's case but found nothing wrong, so he consulted with Herod Agrippa II (Acts 25–26).

flogging: An ancient method of torture/punishment whereby the victim is whipped or beaten (cf. Deut 25:2–3).

Fortress Antonia: A fortress for Roman soldiers built adjacent to the temple in Jerusalem, with a stairway that descended into the temple's outer courtyard.

frapping: The practice of passing ropes under and around a ship to hold it together more firmly against ravaging waves (Acts 27:17).

Galatia: A Roman province in the middle of Asia Minor (modern Turkey) where Paul visited on his missionary travels.

Gallio: The proconsul of the Roman province of Achaia (Greece) briefly stationed in Corinth (summer AD 51 to spring AD 52) and who dismissed the complaint against Paul there (Acts 18:12–17).

Gamaliel: A highly respected Pharisee who was Paul's teacher (Acts 22:3) and who cautioned the Sanhedrin against opposition to the church (Acts 5:33–39).

Gaza: One of the chief OT Philistine cities, a seaport on the Mediterranean Sea in southwestern Israel; Philip met an Ethiopian eunuch on the road toward Gaza (Acts 8:26–40).

Gemara: A word meaning "completion," used as the title for rabbinic writings of the third through fifth centuries adding commentary on the Mishnah.

genealogies: Tables or lists showing a person's line of descent from earlier ancestors.

genre: The classification of literature according to its particular features, forms, content, and function.

gentile: A person who is not a Jew.

God-fearers: Monotheistic gentiles who worshiped the God of the Hebrew Scriptures and observed some of the OT Jewish laws and customs but without becoming full-fledged proselytes to Judaism; e.g., Cornelius and Lydia; see also "**proselytes**."

goddess Justice: A.k.a. "**Fate**," a pagan goddess thought to assure that criminals would eventually be punished (cf. Acts 28:4).

Great Commission: Jesus's final instructions for his followers to take the gospel to the rest of the world (Matt 28:18–20; Mark 16:15–16; Luke 24:46–49; John 20:21; Acts 1:8).

Greek, classical: The Greek language (with its distinctive vocabulary and style) as utilized in approximately 500–330 BC.

Greek, Koine: The Greek language utilized as the "common" (Greek: *koinē*) international language throughout the Roman Empire in the NT era; sometimes called Hellenistic Greek or postclassical Greek and assigned to 330 BC–AD 330.

Hasmonean dynasty: The Jewish dynasty established by Judas Maccabeus and his brothers who led Israel in their struggle to establish Jewish independence from foreign rule, 167–63 BC.

Hebraic Jews: Jews who were more insistent on first-century Hebrew cultural practices and language (i.e., Aramaic) and resistant toward Hellenization.

Hellenistic Jews: Jews who were in support of Hellenization.

Hellenization: The spread and adoption of Greek culture and language into other nations of the world, whether by coercion, persuasion, or natural appeal.

hermeneutics: The theory and methodology of interpretation.

Herod Agrippa I: Ruler of increasing portions of Palestine on Rome's behalf, first as tetrarch in AD 37 where his uncle Philip had ruled, then in AD 40 added the former tetrarchy of his uncle Antipas, and by AD 41 became king over most of his grandfather's (Herod the Great's) former territory; put the apostle James to death and imprisoned Peter (Acts 12:1–3); died AD 44 (Acts 12:19–23).

Herod Agrippa II: A son of Herod Agrippa I and great-grandson of Herod the Great; initially tetrarch for Rome over the Syrian territory of Chalcis in AD 48, but in AD 53 was given the title of king over what was formerly the tetrarchy of his great uncle Philip (i.e., Iturea, Traconitis, Gaulanitis, Auranitis, Batanea, and Paneas) and what was formerly the neighboring tetrarchy of Lysanias (i.e., Abilene); heard Paul's testimony of faith in Christ (Acts 25:13–26:32).

Herod the Great: A clever, creative, and powerful Roman client king of Idumean (Edomite) descent who gained rulership of Israel 37–4 BC.

Herodians: Supporters of Roman rule via the Herodian dynasty (Matt 22:16; Mark 3:6; 12:13).

high priest: The highest religious office in Judaism, overseeing the religious life of the Jews; president of the Sanhedrin.

historiography: The philosophy of history and the expectations for the writing of history.

history: The genre category for ancient literature that would recount and interpret significant events that happened in the past.

Holy Spirit baptism: A metaphor for "receive the Holy Spirit" (cf. Acts 10:44–48 with 11:15–18), which is something that happens at conversion (Acts 2:38).

honor and shame: Significant values in first-century Greco-Roman culture related to gaining or losing status and esteem from others in the community.

Iconium: The first-century chief town of Lycaonia in southern Galatia; one of the towns Paul visited on his first, second, and possibly third missionary journeys.

imperial cult: The idea that the Roman emperor was to be paid homage as if to a god; while not mandatory for Roman citizens, emperor worship was still useful for some Roman rulers as a tool for demonstration of political allegiance.

inaugurated eschatology: The idea that the new age at the end of history has begun but without reaching its full expression just yet (a.k.a. the "already/not yet kingdom").

***inclusio*:** A literary device where an author states a particular idea or theme at both the beginning and the end of a section; also called bookending or bracketing or framing or an envelope structure.

infancy narratives: Only Matthew and Luke record stories about Jesus's birth and infancy; Luke also included stories about the birth and childhood of John the Baptist.

Irenaeus: The famed bishop of Lyons, whose book *Against Heresies* (ca. AD 180) offers perhaps the first definitive idea of the NT canon.

irony: A rhetorical device where the apparent, face-value meaning is contrary to the intended meaning (e.g., Acts 12 contains a number of ironic points).

Isaiah 53: The prophetic OT passage about the suffering servant of the Lord; read by the Ethiopian eunuch when Philip met him (Acts 8:32–33); see also "**servant of the Lord**" and "**suffering servant.**"

Israel: The nation descending from Abraham (named after his grandson); during the OT period of civil war, the northern kingdom had this name and the southern kingdom was called Judah.

James, Jesus's brother: Coming to faith in Jesus sometime after the resurrection (cf. John 7:5), he became a leader in the Jerusalem church (e.g., Acts 12:17; 15:13–21) and authored the NT letter of James; dubbed "James the Just" according to the second-century writer Hegesippus.

James, son of Alphaeus: One of the twelve apostles; dubbed "James the Lesser" to distinguish him from James the son of Zebedee.

James the apostle: A son of Zebedee and the brother of the apostle John; the first of the apostles to be martyred (Acts 12:1–2); dubbed "James the Greater" to distinguish him from James the son of Alphaeus.

James the Greater: See "**James the apostle**."

James the Just: See "**James, Jesus's brother**."

James the Lesser: See "**James, son of Alphaeus**."

Jerusalem: The primary city of ancient Israel, the location of the Jewish temple, the center of Jewish faith, and where the early church began (Acts 1–2).

Jerusalem Council: The meeting of the early church leaders to address the Jew-gentile issue (Acts 15).

Jew: A decedent of Abraham through Jacob/Israel, the genealogical line through which God sent Jesus to be the Savior for all humanity.

Jewish revolt of AD 66–70: A.k.a. Jewish War, the Jewish revolution against Rome that resulted in the destruction of Jerusalem and the temple in AD 70.

Jewish War: See "**Jewish revolt of AD 66–70**."

Joel: The OT prophet whose words were fulfilled by the outpouring of the Spirit on the day of Pentecost (Acts 2:1–41; cf. Joel 2:28–32).

John Mark: A young Jerusalem believer who accompanied Barnabas and Paul on the first missionary journey but deserted them to return to Jerusalem (Acts 13:5, 13); he accompanied Barnabas doing follow-up ministry on Cyprus (Acts 15:36–39) and was later a valuable co-minister with Paul (Col 4:10; Phlm 24; 2 Tim 4:11); author of the Gospel of Mark.

John the apostle: One of the twelve apostles; a son of Zebedee and brother of the apostle James; author of the Gospel of John, the letters of 1–3 John, and Revelation.

John the Baptist: The last of the OT-style prophets announcing the soon-to-come Messiah.

Joppa: A town on the Mediterranean Sea about thirty-five miles northwest of Jerusalem;

where Tabitha was raised back to life (Acts 9:36–43) and where Peter had a vision about gentile outreach (Acts 10:9–20).

Josephus, Flavius Titus: A first-century Jewish historian (ca. AD 37–100) whose works are arguably the most important extrabiblical source for the history and culture of first-century Judaism.

Judah: The name of the southern kingdom of the Israelites during the OT period of civil war when the northern kingdom was called Israel.

Judaism: The monotheistic faith of the descendants of Abraham through his son Isaac embodied in the religious and cultural traditions of the Jewish people and based on the Hebrew Scriptures.

Judaizers: Those insisting that all Christian believers must live in accordance with Jewish customs.

Judas Iscariot: One of the original twelve apostles, most known for his betrayal of Jesus; having deserted his place among the apostles, he was replaced by Matthias (Acts 1).

Judas, son of James: A.k.a. Thaddaeus, the second of the twelve apostles named Judas, distinguished from Judas Iscariot with his father's name.

Julius: The Roman centurion of the Imperial Regiment responsible for taking Paul to Rome (Acts 27:1).

kingdom of God: God's sovereign reign and authority over all things; the central theme of Jesus's preaching; already begun in the hearts of the believers and yet to climax with the return of Christ.

legates: Roman emperor-appointed rulers of larger imperial provinces; of a higher rank than a prefect or procurator; e.g., Quirinius (Luke 2:2); see also "**prefects**," "**proconsuls**," and "**procurators**."

Levi: See "**Matthew**."

Levites: Descendants of Jacob's son Levi, who were dedicated as a tribe to serve God by assisting the priests.

Lord: The predominant title for Jesus in Acts; used throughout the Septuagint (LXX) as a translation for Yahweh, Israel's covenant name for God.

Luke: A physician and Paul's devoted friend and coworker (Col 4:14; Phlm 24; 2 Tim 4:11) who authored the Third Gospel and the Acts of the Apostles.

LXX: See "**Septuagint**."

Lydda: The OT city of Lod, located about twenty-four miles northwest of Jerusalem and eleven miles southeast of Joppa; where Aeneas was healed (Acts 9:32–35).

Lydia: A Thyatira believer in the textile business in Philippi, where she hosted Paul's missionary team on his second missionary campaign (Acts 16:14–40).

Lystra: A city about twenty-five miles south-southwest of Iconium in south Galatia; where Paul was stoned during his first missionary journey but survived and returned in subsequent travels.

Maccabees, the: The name given to the second-century BC Jewish leader Judas and his brothers, who liberated Israel from Seleucid rule; see also "**Hasmonean dynasty**."

Maccabeus, Judas: Son of Mattathias and the first great leader of the Maccabean revolt against Seleucid rule; his family became known as the Hasmoneans.

magic: Various activities meant to appease, to build up good will with, or even to manipulate the gods; contrasted with "miracles."

Malta: The island about sixty miles south of Sicily on which Paul was shipwrecked while en route to Rome (Acts 28:1).

martyrdom: Being killed for holding to one's beliefs.

Matthew: A.k.a. Levi, a tax collector selected to be one of the twelve apostles.

Matthias: A follower of Jesus since the days of John the Baptist and selected to be the twelfth apostle after Judas Iscariot defected (Acts 1:12–26).

Messiah: From a Hebrew term meaning "anointed one" and translated into Greek with the word rendered as "Christ"; the redeemer of Israel's hopes; God's end-times Savior sent to deliver his people.

midrashim: Rabbinic writings providing interpretative commentaries on biblical books.

Miletus: A city on the Mediterranean Sea about thirty miles south of Ephesus where Paul stopped at the end of his third missionary campaign and addressed the Ephesian church elders (Acts 20:16–38).

Mishnah: The earliest of the rabbinic writings from about AD 200 codifying the rabbinic oral traditions on the application of torah to everyday life.

monotheism: Belief in only one true God.

Moses: The Israelite chosen by God to lead the people in an exodus out of slavery in Egypt (see esp. Exodus 1–18).

Mount of Olives: A hill located a Sabbath-day's walk from Jerusalem where the ascension took place.

Muratorian Canon: From the latter part of the second century (ca. AD 170–180), a list of books belonging in the New Testament and attributing both the Third Gospel and Acts to Luke.

Myra: A metropolitan seaport on the southern coast of Asia Minor and regular stop for Alexandrian grain ships traveling to Rome.

narrative theology: Proclaiming theological truths by recounting God's saving acts in history.

Nathanael: See "**Bartholomew**."

natural theology: Pointing to what can be learned about God from observing the natural world and human reason, all created by him (e.g., Acts 14:14–18; 17:24–28).

navigation year: The weather conditions on the ancient Mediterranean Sea made the summer months (May 15–September 15) the optimal travel season; virtually no sea travel was possible in the winter months (November 11–March 10).

Nazarite vow: A pledge to demonstrate one's devotion to the Lord that involved shaving the head and culminated in a sacrifice (see Num 6:1–21; cf. Acts 18:18–22; 21:18–26).

Northeaster: A wind of hurricane force that swept down from the island of Crete and blew off course the ship Paul was on (Acts 27:14).

NT canon: The list of books that measure up to be recognized as God's authoritative word about Jesus; all branches of Christianity agree on the twenty-seven NT books.

Ovid: Publius Ovidius Naso (43 BC–ca. AD 17) was born in Sulmona, Italy, near Rome and educated to be a lawyer, but he is most known for his amorous poetry.

P^{75}: See "**Bodmer Papyrus**."

Palestine: A label for the geographic region along the eastern shore of the Mediterranean Sea, particularly between the Jordan River and the sea, that became known as the land of Israel; see also "**promised land**."

Paphos: A city on the southwest coast of Cyprus where Saul/Paul and Barnabas confronted Elymas the sorcerer and saw the conversion of the Roman proconsul Sergius Paulus (Acts 13); here Luke begins to identify Saul by his Greco-Roman name Paul.

papyrus: An ancient paper made from overlapping strips of the papyrus reed; NT manuscripts written on papyrus are given code numbers with the letter *P* (e.g., P^{75}).

parallelism: The pairing of similar episodes, events, or characters by means of how they are described; Luke-Acts is noted for several forms of parallelism (e.g., pairs of similar accounts of men and women, descriptions of Jesus and Stephen, the ministries of Peter and Paul, etc.).

patronage: see "**benefaction**."

Paul: The Greco-Roman name of a Jew known as Saul early in Acts who is hostile toward Christians until converted in an encounter with Jesus and becomes one of the greatest missionaries in the early church as reflected in the last half of Acts.

***Pax Romana*:** A.k.a. *Pax Augusta* (for its founder), a Latin term meaning "Roman peace," referring to the period of relative stability established by Caesar Augustus (27 BC) and extending to the death of Emperor Marcus Aurelius (AD 180).

Pentecost: An annual Jewish holiday fifty days after Passover; celebrated by Christians for the historic outpouring of the Holy Spirit (Acts 2).

Perga: A city about eight miles inland from the Mediterranean Sea on the plain of Pamphylia visited by Paul and Barnabas on the first missionary journey (Acts 13–14).

pericope: A self-contained story unit in the Gospels or the book of Acts.

persecution: An external challenge to the life of the church whereby outside people apply physical pressure to force Christians to abandon or alter their mission; this calls for radical obedience to God in constant devotion to gospel teaching.

Persia: The Middle Eastern empire that defeated the Babylonians in 539 BC and allowed the exiled people groups (like the Jews) to return to their homelands.

Peter: A.k.a. Simon Peter and Cephas, one of the original twelve apostles; Peter functions in Acts as the main apostolic spokesperson; was instrumental in the church recognizing God's desire to include the gentiles (Acts 10–11 and 15).

Pharisees: The religious/political party in first-century Judaism strictly adhering to both the written law and oral tradition; the general populace highly respected them as people devoted to the Scriptures.

Philip the apostle: One of the twelve apostles; noted for recruiting Nathanael to follow Jesus.

Philip the evangelist: Distinct from Philip the apostle; one of the seven chosen to oversee food distribution for the poor Christian widows in Jerusalem (Acts 6:5); effective in group ministry (8:4–25), one-on-one ministry (8:26–39), itinerate ministry (8:40), and hospitality ministry (21:8–9).

Philippi: A Roman colony in eastern Macedonia with a famous school of medicine; where Luke, a physician, spent several years, arriving on Paul's second missionary journey (Acts 16:10–12) and departing with him when Paul returned on his third journey (Acts 20:5–6).

Philo of Alexandria: A first-century Jewish philosopher (ca. 20 BC–AD 50) living in Alexandria, Egypt, whose written works help us understand Hellenized Judaism.

Pliny the Younger: Gaius Plinius Caecilius Secundus (ca. AD 61–113); a lawyer who became governor of Bithynia in AD 110; a prolific letter writer with more than two hundred extant letters; adopted son of his uncle, a Roman official and natural scientist known as Pliny the Elder.

Plutarch: Lucius Mestrius Plutarch (ca. AD 46–120), a native of Chaeronea, Greece, and a teacher of Platonist philosophy best known for his biographical writings and his collection of philosophical essays and speeches.

***Polygeneris*:** A term meaning "influenced by several genres," which is a good way to view Acts.

polytheism: The belief that many gods exist.

***Praxeis*:** The grouping of ancient literature that utilizes the term *Acts* in their titles; the variety of writings under such titles, however, suggests this is not really a genre category.

prefects: A Roman emperor-appointed ruler (usually a military man) of a smaller imperial province; a lower rank than a proconsul or legate; e.g., Pontius Pilate (Luke 23); see also "**legates**," "**proconsuls**," and "**procurators**."

priests: Levites descending from Aaron who served as leaders of temple worship at Jerusalem.

Priscilla and Aquila: The wife and husband team who were coworkers with Paul—in making tents and in ministry—in Corinth (Acts 18:1–4), in Ephesus (Acts 18:18–19, 24–28; 1 Cor 16:19; 2 Tim 4:19), and in Rome (Rom 16:3).

proconsuls: A senate-appointed ruler of a Roman senatorial province; e.g., Sergius Paulus of Cyprus (Acts 13:7–8) and Gallio of Achaia (Acts 18:12); see also "**legates**," "**prefects**," and "**procurators**."

procurators: A Roman emperor-appointed ruler (usually a civilian) of a smaller imperial province; a lower rank than a proconsul or legate; e.g., Felix (Acts 23–24) and Festus (Acts 25–26); see also "**legates**," "**prefects**," and "**proconsuls**."

prologue: A.k.a. preface, introductory remarks to a book; Luke's prologues (Luke 1:1–4 and Acts 1:1–2) reflect the ancient scientific and historiographical traditions.

promised land: The strip of land along the eastern edge of the Mediterranean Sea between the continents of Asia, Europe, and Africa that God had promised to Abraham and his descendants; the land of the nation of Israel; see also "**Palestine**."

prophet like Moses: Drawn from a prediction made my Moses himself (Deut 18:15), an important appellation made of Jesus (Acts 3:22–23; 7:37).

proselytes: People who completely convert from one religion to another; thus, Jewish proselytes are gentiles who give themselves over wholly to observing all of Jewish law and are distinguished from God-fearers, who wanted to affiliate with Judaism and worship the God of the Hebrew Scriptures without observing all of the Jewish law; see "**God-fearers**."

Pseudepigrapha: A large body of ancient Jewish writings in a variety of genres and dating between 300 BC and AD 300; the name—meaning "falsely attributed writings"—refers to the fact that many of the books bear the names of biblical figures (such as Abraham, Moses, Baruch, and Enoch) as if those figures had authored these books or were otherwise somehow related to them.

Publius: The principal leader of the island of Malta, where the ship carrying Paul to Rome shipwrecked (Acts 28:7–8); see also "**chief official**."

Puteoli: One of the more important seaports for Rome, especially for Alexandrian grain ships; where Paul landed on his trip to Italy (Acts 28:13–15); also a popular resort town in Roman times.

Qumran: A Jewish community along the northwestern shore of the Dead Sea that likely produced and/or stored the Dead Sea Scrolls; most scholars believe the Qumran community was made up of Essenes who thought they were living in the end times.

rabbinic writings: Discussions and interpretations of the Jewish law produced by rabbis in the centuries after the destruction of Jerusalem and eventually committed to writing, beginning with the Mishnah (ca. AD 200), with others following in subsequent centuries; see "**Mishnah**," "**Tosefta**," "**Gemara**," "**Talmud**," "**midrashim**," and "**Targums**."

Rhegium: A notably Greek cultured city on the toe of the Italian "boot" peninsula across the Strait of Messina from Sicily (Acts 28:13).

rhetoric: The persuasive manner in which a story is told so as to achieve the desired response; a regular field of Greco-Roman study.

Roman citizenship: A privileged legal status—with rights and responsibilities—granted to select individuals in the Roman Empire.

Romans: The political and military world power centered in Italy that had been a republic until the first century BC when it was expanding its worldwide influence; the Romans were the dominant world power during the NT period.

Rome: The well-known capital city of the Roman Republic, the Roman Empire, and of modern Italy. As the seat of the Roman government, Rome was the emperor's primary residence and where Paul needed to go to appear before Caesar.

Sadducees: A religious/political party in first-century Judaism consisting primarily of the priestly leadership and aristocracy; they often dominated the Sanhedrin.

Salamis: The eastern most seaport city of Cyprus where Saul and Barnabas began their first missionary journey by preaching in the Jewish synagogues there (Acts 13:5).

salvation history: The activities of God in history to bring about the salvation of his people.

Samaria: The region of the land of Israel between Galilee in the north and Judea in the south; the home of the Samaritan people; see also "**Samaritans**."

Samaritans: Descendants of Israelites intermarried with foreigners, living in the first century in the Israelite region of Samaria; typically despised by Jews.

Sanhedrin: The highest Jewish court, consisting of lay leaders and priests.

Sapphira: A Jerusalem church member who, with her husband Ananias, died for lying about their offering (Acts 5:1–11).

Saul: The Jewish name for the man better known as Paul; see "**Paul**."

scribes: A.k.a. "teachers of the law" and "lawyers," experts in interpretation and exposition of the law of Moses; some were affiliated with the priesthood and some with Pharisees.

scripta continua: The writing style of many ancient manuscripts wherein there are no spaces or markings between the words and sentences.

Second Temple period: The time from the completion of the second Jewish temple in 516 BC until its destruction in AD 70.

Seleucia: The first-century seaport for Syrian Antioch on the eastern coast of the Mediterranean Sea (Acts 13:4).

Seneca: Lucius Annaeus Seneca (ca. 4 BC–AD 65), son of a famous teacher with the same name; a Stoic philosopher known for his moral essays, letters, and tragic plays; tutor and then advisor for Nero.

Septuagint: The ca. 250 BC Greek translation of the OT Hebrew Scriptures; abbreviated LXX.

Sergius Paulus: The Roman proconsul of Cyprus who became a believer in Jesus due to the ministry of Paul and Barnabas (Acts 13:6–12).

servant of the Lord: A messianic figure who appears repeatedly in Isaiah 40–55 and particularly in a suffering role (Isa 52:13–53:12); Philip identifies this figure as descriptive of Jesus (Acts 8:26–40); see also "**suffering servant.**"

Sicarii: First-century Jewish assassins using short daggers (Latin: *sicae*) to murder Roman sympathizers (Acts 21:38).

Silas: A.k.a. Silvanus, a Jerusalem prophet who accompanied Paul and Barnabas back to Syrian Antioch after the Jerusalem Council and became Paul's teammate for the second missionary campaign (Acts 15).

Simon Magus: See "**Simon the Sorcerer.**"

Simon Peter: See "**Peter.**"

Simon the Sorcerer: A.k.a. Simon Magus, a magician in Samaria who professed faith in Jesus but whose heart was not right before God (Acts 8:9–24).

Simon the Zealot: A.k.a. Simon the Cananaean, one of the twelve apostles; distinguished from Simon Peter by noting his anti-Roman affiliation with Zealots.

Solomon's Colonnade: The portico along the eastern side of the outer courts of the Jerusalem temple where the early church would sometimes gather (Acts 5:12).

Son of David: A traditional messianic title in first-century Judaism reflecting the expectation that the Messiah would be a descendant of David, Israel's greatest king.

Son of God: A title used in Judaism for the Messiah and indicating a unique relationship with God the Father.

Son of Man: Jesus's most common self-designation in the Gospels; drawn from Daniel 7:13–14, referring not merely to Jesus's humanity but also to his role as glorious redeemer.

sons of Sceva: A group of Jewish exorcists who fail miserably when invoking "the name of the Jesus whom Paul preaches" as if it were a magic formula (Acts 19:13–16).

sovereignty of God: God's absolute control over all things.

Stephen: One of the seven people chosen to oversee food distribution for the poor Christian widows in Jerusalem (Acts 6:5); had an effective speaking ministry with wonders and signs (6:8–10), giving the longest speech in Acts (7:2–53); the first Christian martyr (7:54–8:3).

Stoicism: A philosophical school of thought dedicated to the teaching of Zeno, emphasizing fatalism and the endurance of pain; comparable to pantheism, suggesting that people must serve as their own authorities.

stoning: A form of capital punishment carried out by throwing stones at the convicted person.

substitutionary atonement: The view that Jesus died in our place, taking the penalty for our sins.

Suetonius: Gaius Suetonius Tranquillus (ca. AD 69–125), a Roman historian and friend of Pliny the Younger and Tacitus; served in secretarial roles for Roman emperors; best known for his biographical essays.

suffering servant: A messianic figure described in Isaiah 52:12–53:13 as offering himself as a sacrifice for the sins of God's people. NT writers identify this figure as descriptive of Jesus; see also "**Servant of the Lord**."

***sui generis*:** A term meaning "unique genre"; unhelpful as a classification for knowing how to approach Acts.

synagogue: A local gathering of Jews for worship, study, assemblies, and social events; eventually the name was attached to the buildings where such gatherings took place.

syncretism: The merging of different (even conflicting) religious and cultural ideas into a new system.

Syracuse: A seaport city on the eastern coast of Sicily where the ship taking Paul from Malta to Rome stopped for three days (Acts 28:12).

Syrtis: The large gulfs in the Mediterranean Sea off the coast of northern Africa noted for their changing sandbar features where ships could run aground.

Tabitha: A.k.a. Dorcas, a woman who was raised back to life in Joppa (Acts 9:36–43).

Tacitus: Publius (or Gaius) Cornelius Tacitus (ca. AD 56–120), a Roman official and friend of Pliny the Younger and Suetonius, was one of the greatest Roman historians; wrote two major Latin works and a variety of other literary items.

Talmud: The complete body of Jewish oral traditions in writing, including the Mishnah and the Gemara; of its two editions, the Babylonian (late fifth century) is considered more authoritative than the Palestinian (late fourth or early fifth century).

Tanak: The acronymic name of the Hebrew Scriptures (≈ Old Testament) from the Hebrew consonants (T-N-K) representing its three sections: Law (*Torah*), Prophets (Nevi'im), and Writings (Ketuvim).

Targums: Aramaic paraphrases and expansions of Hebrew Scriptures.

Tarsus: The principal city of the first-century Roman province of Cilicia in southeast Asia Minor near the northeastern corner of the Mediterranean Sea; an important center for commerce, culture, and education; Paul's hometown.

telescoping: When an author simply recounts a series of events one right after another without indicating how much time may have occurred between them.

temple in Jerusalem: The central place of worship for first-century Jews and the only place where sacrifices were to be made (Deut 12:5–14); various courtyards around the temple served as meeting places for religious, educational, and social gatherings.

terrorists/Assassins: See "**Sicarii**."

Tertullus: An orator or rhetorician representing the Jews in their claim against Paul in his hearing before Felix (Acts 24:1–9).

textual criticism: Reconstructing the original reading of an ancient literary work via sorting through the variations of its surviving manuscripts.

Thaddaeus: See "**Judas, son of James.**"

Theophilus: The addressee in both Luke and Acts; probably the patron who sponsored the publication of Luke's writings.

Thessalonica: A capital city in Macedonia during the Roman era; visited by Paul in his travels (Acts 17:1–9; 1 Thess 2:1–2).

Theudas and Judas: Two disrupters of first-century Jewish society referenced by Gamaliel in his caution against overreacting to the Christian movement (Acts 5:33–40).

Thomas: A.k.a. Didymus ("Twin") and Judas Thomas, one of the twelve apostles; most known for his reluctance to believe in the resurrection until gaining more evidence (John 20:24–29).

Timothy: A young believer from Lystra joining Paul's team on the second missionary campaign (Acts 16:1–3).

torah: A term meaning "the law" used for the first five books of the Hebrew Bible or for the Hebrew Scriptures broadly.

Tosefta: Additional rabbinic writings drafted about fifty years after the Mishnah as supplements.

Troas: A seaport city on the western coast of Asia Minor where Paul had a vision about traveling to Macedonia (Acts 16:8–10) and where Eutychus was raised back to life (20:6–12).

Twelve, the: A nickname for Jesus's twelve apostles (Luke 6:12–16; Acts 6:2); echoing the twelve tribes of Israel, this number symbolized the re-establishment of God's people.

Tyre: The southernmost seaport of Phoenicia on the eastern shore of the Mediterranean Sea.

"we sections": Four places in Acts where the narration changes from third-person to first-person point of view (Acts 16:10–17; 20:5–15; 21:1–18; 27:1–28:16); best explained as indicating the author's presence in those portions of the story.

Western text: A.k.a. the D-text; a text tradition with a paraphrase of the book of Acts about 6–9 percent longer than the standard text due to more flowery and expansive language.

Zealots: Various Jewish nationalists engaged in revolutionary activities against Roman authorities.

Zeus and Hermes: Two Greek gods (Roman: Jupiter and Mercury) with whom Barnabas and Paul were mistaken at Lystra (Acts 14:8–18).

Scripture Index

GENESIS

1:14 436
1:26–27 436
2:7 436
3. 249
7:22 436
9:18–11:8 436
10–12. 222
10:19 533
12. 145
12:1–3 . . . . 146, 609
12:2–3 . . . . 349, 372
14:15 287
15:2 287
22:11–18 146
22:18 242
24:3 436
26:2–5 146
26:4 242
28:10–16 146
35:9–15 146
35:22–26 207
37–50. 147

EXODUS

1–18. . . . . 615, 620
1:6–7 147
1:8–14 147
3:1–4:16. 147
3:2–6. 216
5–18. 147
12:1–20 216
12:37 258
12:48–49. 378
13:21 216
14:24 305
18:13–26 258
19–24. 147
19:18 216
20:11 . . . . . . 244, 364, 436
22:28 500
23:16 215
32:1–35 247
34:22 215
34:29–35 268
38:25–26 258
40:35 [LXX] 250

LEVITICUS

10:1–3 . . . . 246, 247
11:1–47 . . . . 305, 306
16:1–2 247
17–18. . . . . . 391, 396, 397
17:7–9 396
17:10–12 396
17:13–16 396
18:1–30 396
19:14 359
19:15 500
20:2 272
20:25–26 305
21:16–23 282
23:5–8. 216
23:15–22 . . . . .215, 216
23:29 242
23:33–43. 216
24:14 273
24:14–16 273

NUMBERS

1:1–54 207
3:4 246
4:1–11 247
6:1–21 . . . . . .447, 489, 621
6:9–10 489
6:13–21 488
6:23–27. 165
8:21 488
11. 259
11:1 257
11:1–3 247
11:1–15. 257
11:4–35 247
11:16–17 258
11:16–30 . . . . 220, 258
11:21 258
11:29 220
14:1–38 147
14:36–38 247
15:32–36 273
15:37–41 165
16:1–35 . . . . 246, 247
16:36–50 247
19:12 488
21:4–9 247
24:17 391
25:1–9 247
26:61 246
28:16–25 216
28:26. 215
28:26–31 216
29:12–38 216
31:19 488

DEUTERONOMY

1:19–40 147
3:13–14 423
4:7 436
4:28a 436
4:29 436
4:30 365
4:33 365
5:8 436
5:26 365
6:4–9. . . . . 25, 165
9:18 [LXX] 427
10:14 436
10:16 . . . . 379, 403
11:13–21 165
12:5–14 626
13:1–11 273
14:3–21 . . . . 305, 306
16:1–8 216
16:9–12 . . . . .215, 216

DEUTERONOMY (*continued*)

16:13–15 216
16:16 216
17:2–7 273
17:7 273
18:15 . . . . . . 130, 147, 211, 271, 623
18:15–19 . . . . 147, 242
21:18–21 273
21:22–23 421
21:23 423
22:23–24 273
23:1 282
25:1–3 255
25:2–3 615
25:4 . . . . 112, 595
27:18 359
30:2 365
30:6 . . . . 379, 403
30:10 365
32:8 436
32:16–19 [LXX] 427
32:22 216

JOSHUA

2:19 442
3:10 365
6:4, 8, 13 260
7–8 249
8:34–35 [LXX] 249

JUDGES

7:19 305

1 SAMUEL

2:12–36 246
8:1–22 148
9:21 343
11:11 305
14:45 542
17:36 365

2 SAMUEL

1:16 442
6:1–15 247
7:8–16 148
7:11c. 391
7:12–16 349
7:12b, 13b–14a. 391
8:5–6. 287
14:11 542

1 KINGS

1:52 542
2:23–24. 247
2:37 442
8:27 436
11:23–25 287
11:29–40 479
15:16–21 287
17:17–24 471
19:11 216
19:12 216
19:15 287
20:1–34 287

2 KINGS

1:1–17 247
2:19–22 479
4:18–37 471
14–16. 287
17:24–41 148
17:29–41 436
19:4 365
19:15 . . . . . . 244, 364, 436
19:16 365
24–25 147
24:1–5 148
24:6–16. 148
25:1–21 148

1 CHRONICLES

8:12 298
13:1–14 247
24:5, 31 213
25:8 213
26:13–16 213
29:14–16 436

2 CHRONICLES

2:6 [LXX 2:5] 436
2:12 . . . . 244, 364, 436
2:16 299
8:13 216
19:4 365

EZRA

1–6 150
3:7 299
5:5, 9 166
7–10. 150
7:1–10 7
7:13–14 260

NEHEMIAH

1–6 150
2:16 166
5:13 . . . . 351, 442
9:6 . . . . 244, 364, 436

ESTHER

1:1 282
2:9 260

JOB

12:10 436
12:23 436
14:5 436
22:2 436
23:3–10 436
27:3 436
33:4 436

PSALMS

2. 211
2:7 349
8:5–6 [LXX 8:6–7] . . . 436
9:7–8 [LXX 9:8–9] . . . 436
14:2 436
16:8–11 . . . . .130, 219, 221
16:10 349
24:6–7. 599
35:16 271
37:12 271
42:2 365
50:8–13 [LXX 49:8–13]. . . . 436
69:25 211
74:17 [LXX 73:17] 436
81:12 [LXX 80:13]. . . . 436
84:2 365
85:8 365
91:4 [LXX] 250
91:11–12 322
96:13 [LXX 95:13]. . . . 436
98:9 [LXX 97:9] 436
104:29–30 [LXX 103:29–30]. . 436
106:29 [LXX] 427
109:8 211
110:1 . . . . . . .219, 221, 272
112:10 271
115:2–8 [LXX 113:10–16] . . 436
115:15–16 [LXX 113:23–24]. . 436
118:22 243
118:26 201
140:7 [LXX] 250
145:18 [LXX 144:18] . . 436
146:6 . . . . 244, 364
146:6 [LXX 145:6] . . . 436
146:9 378

PROVERBS

8:17 436
16:33 . . . . 213, 214
18:11 [LXX] 250

ECCLESIASTES

12:7 436

ISAIAH

2:1–22 211

2:2–3 389
6. 555
6:9–10 . . . . 131, 554
7:1–8:18. 287
8:9 [LXX] 202
11:10–12 211
12:2 599
13:1–13 211
14:1 389
16:12 [LXX] 436
17:1–3 287
20:1–6 479
26:19 . . . . 130, 359
29:18 130
29:18–19 359
35:5–6 . . . . 130, 359
37:4 365
37:16 . . . . . . 244, 364, 436
37:17 365
37:19 436
40–55 . . . . 283, 625
40–55:18–25 436
40:3 457
40:3–5 . . . . 31, 131
42:5 . . . . 244, 364, 436
42:5–7 359
42:5–9 148
42:6 . . . . 130, 131
42:7, 16 131
42:18 130
43:16–21 148
44:9–20 436
45:21 388
45:21–23 389
46:5–7 436
46:10 244
48:20 [LXX] 202
49:6 . . . . 130, 131, 349, 389, 554
49:6 [LXX] 202
49:9 . . . . 130, 131
52:12–53:13. 626
52:13–53:12. . . . . 283, 625
53. 284
53:7–8 283
55:3 349
55:6 436
55:7 365
56:6–7 389
57:15–16 436
58:6 130
59:20 436
61:1 130
61:1–2 . . . . 130, 359
62:11 [LXX] 202
65:1 436
65:3 [LXX] 427
66:1–2 . . . . 131, 436
66:16 436
66:18–19 389

JEREMIAH

3:12 365
3:17 389
4:4 . . . . 379, 403
6:16 25
12:15 388
12:15–16 389
12:16 389
15:19 436
23:23–24 436
24:7 365
25:31 436
29:13–14 [LXX 36:13–14] . . . 436
31:31–34 148
33:14–26 148
38:7–13 283
39:15–18 283
52:25 260

LAMENTATIONS

2:16 271
2:19 305

EZEKIEL

4:1–17 479
4:13–14 305
14:6 436
14:7 378
18:30–32 436
22:17–22 216
29:10 282
33:2–9 442
37–50:1–14 216
37–50:24–28 148

DANIEL

7:13–14 . . . . .93, 205, 206, 272, 625
9:27 112
11:31 112
12:11 112

HOSEA

1:10 365
3:5 365
8:5 [LXX] 427

JOEL

2:1–11 211
2:13 365
2:28–32 . . . . . 99, 130, 211, 219, 221, 618
3:14–18 211

AMOS

5:4 436
5:18–20 211
5:27 391
9:11 391
9:11–12 . . . . 211, 387, 388, 389, 390
9:11–15 211

JONAH

1:3 299

MICAH

4:5 436
4:6–7 359
6:6–8 436
7:7 600

HABAKKUK

1:5 349
3:18 599

ZEPHANIAH

3:10 282
3:19–20 359

ZECHARIAH

2:10–11 389
2:11 389
7:9–10 378
12:1 436
14:16 389

MALACHI

2:10 436
3:5 378

MATTHEW

1–2. . . . . 109, 162
1:1–17 82
2:1–18 160
2:1–20 159
2:1–23 . . . . .157, 159
2:22 159
3:2 436
3:3 31
3:11 311
4:17 436
4:18–20 572
4:21 320
5:17–18 269
6:9–13 105
8:5 302
8:5–13 31
8:8 302
8:12 272
8:13 302
9:1 297
9:9 579
10:1–4 . . . . . .569, 578, 611

MATTHEW (*continued*)
10:2 . . . . 320, 573
10:3 . . . . 320, 574, 579, 580, 584
10:4 . . . . 582, 584, 585
10:5–42 203
10:14 351
10:30 542
11:21–22 533
11:22–24 436
12:6 269
12:36 436
13:42, 50 272
13:53–58 31
13:55 . . 320, 324, 582, 584
14:1–4 159
14:1–12 159
14:4 159
14:6–12 159
14:25 305
15:1–9 25
15:1–20 168
15:21 533
16:13 612
16:14–16 585
16:23 247
17:1–8 320
17:2 269
17:5 250
18:10 322
19:28 208
20:1 304
20:1–12 304
20:3 304
20:5 304
20:6 304
20:8 304
20:12 304
20:20–28 572
21:33–46 242
22:13 272
22:16 . . . . . . .168, 170, 617
22:23 . . . . 168, 170
23:1–36 168
23:15 378
24:51 272
25:30 272
26:14–16 585
26:26 234
26:29–40 126
26:47–50 585
26:57–59 269
26:60–61 269
26:61 269
26:63 269
26:64 269
26:65 269
27:1–10 . . . . 586, 591
27:3–10 . . . . 210, 585
27:5 210
27:6–7 210
27:6–8 210
27:7 210
27:26 498
27:40 269
27:46, 50 269
27:54 302
27:56 . . . . 320, 581
28:1 320
28:7–20 199
28:18–20 . . . . . . .202, 203, 223, 616

MARK
1:3 31
1:8 311
1:16–17 573
1:19 320
1:29 573
2:1 297
2:14 . . . . 579, 581
3:6 . . . . .168, 170, 617
3:8 533
3:13–19 . . . . .569, 578, 611
3:16 569
3:17 . . . . 320, 572
3:18 . . . 170, 320, 573, 574, 579, 580, 582, 583, 584
3:19 . . . . 584, 585
3:21 . . . . 324, 386
5:37 320
6:1–6 31
6:3 . . . . 582, 584
6:7 568
6:7–13 203
6:11 351
6:17 159
6:17–19 159
6:21–29 159
6:48 305
7:1–13 25
7:1–23 168
7:14–19 306
7:31 533
8:27 612
8:33 247
9:2–3 269
9:2–8 320
9:7 250
9:38 572
12:1–12 242
12:13 . . . . . .168, 170, 617
12:18 . . . . 168, 170
13:3–4 573
13:14 . . . . .112, 115
13:35 305
14:10–11 585
14:22 234
14:43–46 585
14:53 269
14:56–57 269
14:58 269
14:61 269
14:62 269
14:64 269
15:7 170
15:25 304
15:29 269
15:34, 37 269
15:39 302
15:40 . . . . 320, 581
15:44, 45 302
16:1 320
16:15–16 . . . . 203, 616

LUKE
1–2. . . . . 32, 81, 310
1:1 . . . . .116, 117
1:1–2 64
1:1–4 . . . . 4, 14, 15, 25, 32, 39, 42, 43, 44, 52, 58, 59, 60, 69, 70, 81, 96, 195, 198, 623
1:2 . . . .12, 14, 15, 116, 122
1:3 . . . . 27, 195
1:3–4 64
1:3c 197
1:4 57
1:5 . . . . .67, 145, 157
1:5–7 . . . . 144, 147
1:5–9 169
1:5–25 82
1:8–9 213
1:15–17 100
1:20 92
1:26–38 82
1:30–33 . . . . 144, 148
1:32–33 201
1:35 250
1:41 100
1:46–47 600
1:46–55 144
1:46–56 82
1:47 96
1:52 93
1:57–80 82
1:67 . . . . 100, 219
1:67–79 144
1:68 96
1:68–79 201
1:69, 71 96
1:76 457
1:77 . . . . 96, 103
1:80 . . . . .87, 168, 170
2:1 67
2:1–7 . . . . .145, 611

2:1–21 . . . . 144, 148
2:2 . . . . .156, 619
2:10 31
2:11 . . . . 96, 600
2:19–20 87
2:22–35 82
2:22–40. . . . 130, 144, 147
2:25–32 . . . . 144, 148
2:26–27. 100
2:30 96
2:30–32 31
2:31 31
2:32 . . . . 130, 131
2:36–40. 82
2:38 96
2:40 . . . . .87, 218
2:41 216
2:48–49. 179
2:49 92
2:52 87
3. 167
3:1 . . . . 67, 157, 159
3:1–2 . . . . . . .108, 111, 143
3:1–3 145
3:1–20 310
3:2 169
3:3 . . . . .103, 416, 457
3:4 457
3:4–6. . . . . 31, 131
3:6 . . . . 31, 96
3:8 . . . . 144, 146, 179, 457, 600
3:8–14 602
3:10–14 239
3:16 . . . . 100, 216, 311, 313, 457
3:19 . . . . .67, 159
3:19–20 145
3:21 . . . . 209, 235
3:21–22 . . . . 144, 148
3:21–4:14. 310
3:22 211
3:23–38. . . . . 81, 82
4. 165
4:3–4. 232
4:14 87
4:14–19 100
4:14–30 . . . . 145, 166
4:15–6:11. 310
4:16 84
4:16–20 165
4:16–21 130
4:16–30 . . . . 31, 102
4:21 92
4:21–27 165
4:25–27 84
4:28 . . . . 84, 218
4:28–30. 165
4:29 84
4:31–36 464
4:31–37 101
4:33–35 84
4:33–36. 359
4:33–41 176
4:35 8
4:37 87
4:38–39. . . . . 84, 359
4:38–41 547
4:40 84
4:40–41 . . . . 87, 359
4:41 . . . . 101, 464
4:43 201
5:10 320
5:11 218
5:12–14 359
5:15 87
5:16 209
5:17–26 . . . . . .84, 95, 103, 297, 359
5:18 8
5:24 . . . . 128, 297
5:26 218
5:27–29 579
5:27–32 95
5:27–35 185
5:29–30. 182
5:33–34. 460
6:1–5 . . . . 144, 148
6:6–11 359
6:7, 11 84
6:12 209
6:12–16 . . . . .97, 208, 230, 356, 569, 578, 610, 611, 627
6:12–17 212
6:12–22:46 310
6:13 208
6:14 . . . . 320, 573, 574
6:15 . . . 145, 169, 320, 579, 580, 582
6:16 . . . 209, 279, 320, 583, 584, 585
6:17 . . . . 230, 533
6:17–19 87
6:18 101
6:20. 201
6:22–23. 255
6:40. 84
6:43–49. . . . . 600, 602
7:1–10 . . . . 31, 82, 183, 302, 359
7:1–17 298
7:2 302
7:4–5 . . . . 184, 302
7:5 . . . . .145, 150
7:6 302
7:8 92
7:11–15. 261
7:11–17. . . . . . . 82, 84, 359
7:14 128
7:16 . . . . 144, 147
7:17 87
7:18 460
7:18–23 . . . . 144, 148
7:18–35 211
7:21 . . . . .87, 101, 176
7:21–23 359
7:22 96
7:22–23 . . . . 102, 130
7:24–28 130
7:28 201
7:29–30 416
7:30 130
7:33 232
7:34 . . . . .182, 183, 185
7:36–50 . . . . .95, 103, 144, 148
7:39 . . . . 144, 147
7:48–50 95
7:50 96
8:1 . . . . 32, 82, 201
8:2 . . . . .101, 176
8:2–3 82
8:3 145
8:10 201
8:11–15 . . . . 247, 279
8:19–21 . . . . 179, 600, 602
8:22–25 560
8:26–39 . . . . . 84, 101, 176, 359, 464
8:40–56 . . . . 83, 298
8:41–56 84
8:42–48 359
8:43–48. . . . . . 83, 84, 462
8:47–50 96
8:49–56 359
8:51 320
8:52 274
9:1 32
9:1–6 . . . . 203, 359
9:2 201
9:3 232
9:5 351
9:6 87
9:7 67
9:7–9 145
9:9 159
9:11 201
9:12 32
9:18 209
9:20 . . . . 144, 148
9:22 . . . . 84, 96, 103
9:23–27 369
9:27 . . . . 201, 604
9:28 320
9:28–29 . . . . 209, 235

LUKE (*continued*)

9:28–36 . . . . 144, 147, 148, 216
9:29 . . . . 268, 269
9:30–31 147
9:31 204
9:34 250
9:35 211
9:37–42 84
9:37–43 . . . . 101, 176, 359, 464
9:38–39 8
9:44 . . . . 84, 96, 103
9:51 . . . . 84, 204
9:51–52 466
9:51–56 . . . . 145, 169, 170, 275
9:51–19:44 . . . . 81, 82
9:52 84
9:52–56 31
9:54 572
9:57–58 369
9:57–62 239
9:59–62 369
9:60 201
9:62 201
10. . . . . 10, 586
10:1 . . . . 97, 568
10:1–20 203
10:1–24 585
10:7 . . . . 112, 595
10:8–15 604
10:9 201
10:11 . . . . 201, 351
10:13–14 533
10:13–15 103
10:17–18 464
10:17–20 359
10:25 96
10:25–37 . . . . 145, 169, 170, 275
10:27 261
10:30–35 8
10:31 169
10:32 169
10:33 31
11:1 460
11:1–13 209
11:2 . . . . 201, 604
11:2–4 105
11:3 232
11:4 103
11:5 232
11:5–8 307
11:13 200
11:14 464
11:14–20 359
11:14–26 . . . . .101, 176
11:15 101
11:20 . . . . 201, 604
11:27–28 179
11:31 . . . . 31, 282
11:37–54 168
11:43 . . . . .145, 150
11:45–52 . . . . 144, 148
11:49 . . . . 356, 610
11:53–54 84
12:1–13:35. 602
12:7 542
12:8 272
12:11–12 . . . 200, 243, 602
12:31 201
12:32 . . . . 201, 248
12:35–48 103
12:38 305
12:49 216
12:49–53 369
12:50 84
13:10–17 . . . .101, 180, 359
13:16 . . . . 144, 146
13:18–20 604
13:18–21 201
13:23 96
13:28 . . . . . 144, 146, 272
13:28–29 201
13:31–33 145
13:32 . . . . . . 101, 176, 464
13:32–33 84
14:1 232
14:1–6 359
14:1–24 . . . . 184, 185
14:11 93
14:12–14 183
14:15 232
14:15–24 201
14:25–27 179
14:25–35 369
14:26 369
14:33 239
15:1–2 . . . . . . 95, 183, 185
15:8–10 83
15:11–32 83
15:17 232
15:22–32 185
16:10–12 299
16:14–18 . . . . 144, 147
16:16–17 . . . . .32, 130, 201, 269
16:16–18 359
16:19–31 . . . . 144, 146
17:3 . . . . 96, 103
17:11–19. . . . 145, 169, 170, 183, 275, 277, 359
17:16 31
17:19 . . . . 96, 277
17:20–21 . . . 201, 202, 604
17:20–18:8. . . . . . 103, 602
17:25 . . . . 84, 96, 103
18:1–5 261
18:1–8 83
18:9–14 83
18:14 93
18:15–17 369
18:16–17 201
18:18 96
18:18–27 239
18:18–30 369
18:24–25 . . . . 96, 201
18:25 8
18:26–27 96
18:29–30 . . . . 179, 201
18:31 32
18:31–34 . . . . . 84, 96, 103
18:35–43 . . . 144, 148, 359
18:42–43 96
19:1–7 182
19:1–10 . . . . 95, 185
19:9 . . . . 96, 144, 146
19:10 96
19:11 . . . . 201, 202
19:11–27 . . . 183, 602, 604
19:28–34 84
19:28–40 201
19:35–44 85
19:38 201
19:42–44 112
19:45–46 85
19:47 87
19:47–48 85
20:1–2 243
20:1–47 180
20:19 277
20:27 . . . . 30, 168, 170
20:39–40 269
20:41–44 . . . . . . .144, 148, 201, 272
20:43 92
20:45–47 261
20:46 . . . . .145, 150
21:1–4 261
21:5 160
21:5–36 . . . . 103, 602
21:12 277
21:12–15 514
21:14–15 . . . . 200, 602
21:18 542
21:20 . . . . .112, 115
21:24 92
21:28 96
21:29–31 604
21:31 201
22–23 157
22:1 216
22:1–2 84
22:3 . . . . 32, 279
22:3–6. . . . . 209, 585

22:7 215
22:7–20 216
22:14–22 232
22:14–23 85
22:15–20 201
22:16 92
22:19 . . . . 84, 234
22:19–20 103
22:22 . . . . 92, 96, 103
22:24–38 85
22:29–30 201
22:30 208
22:32 209
22:33 480
22:37 284
22:39–45 209
22:40–46. 85
22:42 85
22:47 . . . . 32, 33
22:47–48 585
22:47–53 . . . . 101, 209
22:47–23:56. 310
22:49–51 359
22:53 277
22:54 269
22:54–71 85
22:63–23:46 101
22:66–67. 269
22:66–71 . . . . 93, 519
22:69 . . . . . . 201, 269, 272
23. . . . . 521, 622
23–24 560
23:1 . . . . .157, 521
23:1–5 85
23:1–25 . . . . .145, 521
23:2 201
23:2–5 . . . . .101, 521
23:3 201
23:4 519
23:6–7 521
23:6–12 . . . . 85, 159
23:8–12 521
23:13–23 521
23:13–25 85
23:14–15 519
23:18 . . . . 85, 489
23:22 519
23:24–25 521
23:26 83
23:27–31 . . . . 83, 602
23:28–30. 112
23:34 . . . . 269, 273
23:35–39 96
23:37 201
23:38 201
23:42–43. 201
23:44 304
23:46 . . . . 84, 269, 274
23:47 . . . . 302, 519
23:50–51 212
23:50–54 83
23:51 . . . . 201, 604
23:52 145
23:55–56 83
24. . . . . . . 10, 42, 110, 194, 198, 199
24:1–3 200
24:1–11 83
24:1–12 199
24:1–35 310
24:1–49 . . . . 198, 199
24:1–53 199
24:4–8 200
24:7 . . . . 92, 96, 103
24:9 . . . . 33, 209, 614
24:10 320
24:12 200
24:12–35 83
24:13–35 . . . . 200, 223
24:13–43 199
24:19 . . . . . . .144, 147, 269
24:21 . . . . 96, 201
24:23 307
24:25 86
24:25–26 130
24:25–27 . . . .92, 102, 130, 131, 144, 148, 230, 599
24:26 . . . . 92, 96, 103, 204
24:27 . . . . . . 130, 284, 554
24:29 199
24:30 . . . . 233, 234
24:32 131
24:32–33 230
24:33 . . . . 33, 614
24:35 234
24:36–40. . . . . . . 195, 200
24:36–43. 310
24:36–49. 200
24:37–43 96
24:41–42 200
24:41–43 195
24:44 . . . . 92, 130, 269
24:44–47 . . . 102, 130, 230
24:44–48. . . . .85, 92, 144, 148, 284, 554, 599
24:44–49. . . . . . . .92, 131, 195, 199
24:44–53 . . . 195, 224, 310
24:46 . . . . 86, 96, 103, 221
24:46–47. . . . . . 103, 130
24:46–48. 195
24:46–49. . . . . . . .99, 202, 203, 616
24:47 . . . . 31, 203
24:47–48 221
24:48 14
24:48–49. 601
24:49 . . 195, 199, 200, 204, 215, 221
24:50 199
24:50–53 . . . .xxi, 195, 198, 199, 204, 205, 610
24:53 87

JOHN

1:19 169
1:23 31
1:33 311
1:35–44. 572
1:43–44. 574
1:43–51 . . . . .574, 578, 611
2:19–22 269
3:8 216
4:4–42. 170
4:6 304
4:19–26 164
4:22 378
5:22–30. 436
5:39 204
6:5–7 574
6:8–9 573
6:44 400
6:62 204
6:70–71 . . . . 584, 585
6:71 585
7:5 . . . . 324, 386, 618
7:35 280
8:31–47 600
8:48 170
10:14–18 103
10:22–39 250
10:23 250
11:9 304
11:16 576
11:55 488
12:1–6 585
12:20–22 . . . . 573, 574
12:32 400
13:2 585
13:16 . . . . . . 356, 585, 610
13:23 570
13:27 585
14:6–10 574
14:22–23 583
15:12–13 245
17:12 . . . . 247, 279
17:18 203
18. 167
18:2–5 585
18:13 269
18:19 269
18:24 269
19:14 304
19:25 582
19:25–27 570
19:26 570

JOHN (*continued*)
19:30 269
20:2 570
20:17 204
20:21 . . . . . . 202, 203, 616
20:24–29 . . . . 576, 627
20:30–31 . . . . . . 60, 64, 70
21:1–23 199
21:2 . . . . 578, 611
21:7, 20 570
21:24–25 . . . . . . 60, 64, 70

ACTS
1. . . . . 42, 88, 110, 160, 194, 213, 214, 215, 224, 313, 337, 369, 384, 619
1–2. 618
1–6 569
1–7. 202
1–12. . . . 13, 76, 77, 79, 80, 189, 190, 191, 332
1:1 . . . . xxi, 6, 34, 54, 195, 207
1:1–2 . . . . .4, 6, 39, 42, 44, 64, 81, 108, 110, 193, 194, 195, 196, 198, 623
1:1–3 . . . . 60, 70, 143, 198
1:1–4 . . . . 6, 195
1:1–5 198
1:1–11 . . . . . . 76, 110, 133, 195, 224
1:1–26 76
1:1–2:41 . . . . . . 77, 79, 190, 191, 193, 228
1:1–2:47. 75
1:1–5:42. 75
1:1–8:3. 78
1:1a 196
1:1ab 198
1:1b 197
1:1c 197
1:1c–2 198
1:1c–2a. 196
1:2 . . . .195, 198, 200, 204, 212, 356, 610
1:2–3 230
1:3 . . . . . 64, 109, 195, 199, 201, 215, 248
1:3–4a 198
1:3–8. . . . . 193, 198
1:3–2:41. 198
1:4 195
1:4–5 . . 195, 199, 200, 202, 204, 215, 601
1:4–8. . . . . 89, 195
1:4b–5 198
1:5 . . . . 100, 200, 215, 311, 313
1:6 . . . . 94, 201, 248
1:6–7 . . .102, 103, 199, 201
1:6–8. 201
1:7 . . . . 92, 202
1:7–8 195
1:8 . . 31, 74, 75, 79, 80, 99, 100, 104, 194, 195, 199, 200, 202, 203, 215, 222, 257, 265, 275, 282, 283, 327, 332, 558, 601, 616
1:9–11 . .xxi, 193, 195, 198, 204, 205, 206, 272, 601, 604, 610
1:9a 206
1:9b 206
1:10–11 206
1:10a 206
1:11 . . . 102, 103, 202, 602
1:11a. 206
1:11b 206
1:12 208
1:12–13 . . . . . 83, 132, 208
1:12–14 . . . . . 87, 229, 263
1:12–26 . . 33, 35, 193, 198, 207, 224, 230, 356, 586, 610, 620
1:12–5:42. 76
1:13 . . . . 33, 120, 145, 169, 320, 478, 569, 573, 574, 578, 579, 580, 582, 583, 611
1:13–14 208
1:13–15 13
1:14 . . . .83, 120, 209, 234, 235, 248
1:14–26 338
1:15 . . . 120, 208, 209, 248
1:15–22 120
1:15–26 244
1:16 . . . . 100, 179, 248
1:16–22 209
1:16a 209
1:16b 209
1:17 209
1:18 . . . . 210, 466
1:18–19 . . . . .210, 585, 586, 591
1:19 . . . . 10, 210
1:21 94
1:21–22 586
1:21–22a 212
1:22 . . . . 15, 204
1:22b 212
1:23 . . . . 212, 342
1:24 . . . . 94, 212, 235
1:24–25 . . . . 224, 234
1:25 212
1:26 . . . . .33, 212, 213, 614
2. . . . 87, 88, 110, 160, 200, 204, 215, 216, 217, 218, 220, 224, 229, 313, 621
2:1 215
2:1–4 216
2:1–13 215
2:1–33 602
2:1–41 . . 99, 193, 198, 215, 235, 354, 618
2:1–8:1a 76
2:2 216
2:3 216
2:4 . . . . .216, 218, 354
2:5 . . . . 218, 280, 332, 572
2:5–11 265
2:6 . . . . .217, 248
2:6–8. 218
2:8 217
2:9–11 . . . . . .217, 280, 332
2:11 . . . . 378, 535
2:11–21 382
2:12 218
2:13 218
2:14 218
2:14–15 221
2:14–39 . . . . 218, 221
2:14–40 . . . . 89, 120
2:14–41 . . . . 224, 354
2:15 . . . . 218, 304
2:15–21 83
2:16–21 219
2:16–24 221
2:17 31
2:17–21 . . . . 130, 211
2:17–38 472
2:18 . . . . 100, 248
2:20 94
2:21 94
2:22 . . . 218, 236, 248, 267
2:22–24 219
2:22–36 . . . . 144, 148
2:23 . . . . 92, 130, 599
2:23–24 243
2:23–36 . . . . 99, 103
2:24 . . . . 96, 103, 199
2:25 94
2:25–28 219
2:25–32 . . . . 130, 221
2:28 219
2:29 . . . . 218, 248
2:29–32 219
2:29–36 387
2:30–32 201
2:30–37 126
2:32 199
2:32–33 93
2:32–36 148
2:32–37 183
2:33 219
2:33–34 204
2:33–36 221

2:34–35 . . . . 219, 272
2:34a 94
2:34b 94
2:35 92
2:36 . . . . . 93, 94, 219, 600
2:37 . . . . 33, 120, 218, 219, 224, 248
2:37–39 221
2:38 . . . . 95, 120, 220, 221, 224, 311, 416, 436, 600, 617
2:38–39 . . . . . 99, 100, 103, 194, 220, 223, 275, 311, 460, 602
2:38–40 224
2:39 . . . . 94, 220, 224, 600
2:40 . . . . 221, 367, 601
2:40–41 221
2:41 . . . . . 78, 79, 120, 190, 191, 194, 222, 224, 351, 416
2:42 . . . 228, 229, 230, 231, 232, 233, 234, 245, 257, 263, 316, 328, 415, 471, 475
2:42–46. 33
2:42–47 . . . . . . 35, 87, 179, 183, 227, 228, 229, 245, 263, 547
2:42–6:7 . . . . . 77, 79, 190, 191, 227, 228
2:42–12:24 77
2:43 . . . 120, 229, 236, 237, 267, 354
2:43–47 354
2:44 . . . . 231, 237, 239, 248
2:44–45 229
2:44–46. 231
2:44–47 237
2:45 231
2:46 . . . . 231, 234, 237
2:46–47 239
2:46–3:2 126
2:46a 229
2:46b 229
2:47 . . . . . 78, 94, 100, 229, 266, 354, 488, 600
3. . . . . 88, 243
3–4 . . . . 160, 360, 570
3–5 241
3–6 110
3:1 . . . . . 33, 233, 234, 235, 240, 304
3:1–4 360
3:1–10 . . 85, 240, 354, 359
3:1–11 13
3:1–16 358
3:1–26 354
3:1–4:23 120
3:1–4:31. . . . 227, 228, 239, 240, 251, 356
3:1–5:42. 75
3:2 . . . . . 111, 240, 241, 360
3:2–5 240
3:3 . . . . 33, 240
3:4 360
3:6 . . . . 128, 241, 242, 248
3:7 240
3:7–8 8
3:8 . . . . 240, 360
3:8–10 240
3:9–10 360
3:10 . . . . 111, 219, 240, 241, 360
3:11 . . . . 240, 250
3:11–26 . . . . 240, 242
3:12 240
3:12–16 277
3:12–26 . . . . . 82, 102, 144, 146, 147, 148, 354, 360
3:13 . . . . 145, 157, 163, 242
3:13–15 242
3:13–20 . . . . 99, 103
3:13–26 130
3:14 242
3:15 . . . . 199, 242, 243
3:16 . . . 240, 241, 242, 360
3:16–20 242
3:17 248
3:18 . . . . . . 86, 92, 96, 103, 130, 242
3:18–26 . . . . 92, 599
3:19 . . . . 95, 436, 600
3:19–21 . . . . 102, 103, 202, 211
3:20 . . . . 94, 242, 600
3:21 . . . . 130, 204, 242
3:22 . . . . 94, 248, 600
3:22–23 . . . . . 130, 147, 623
3:22–23a 211, 242
3:23 248
3:23b 242
3:24 . . . . 86, 242
3:25 242
3:26 . . . . 95, 199, 242
4. . . . . 88, 252, 254
4–5 167
4:1 . . . . 169, 170, 360
4:1–2 252
4:1–3 243
4:1–22 . . . . 168, 240, 243, 360
4:2 257
4:3 . . . . 101, 277
4:4 . . . . 78, 120, 243
4:5 . . . . 169, 243, 384
4:6 . . . . 13, 169
4:7 . . . . 241, 243
4:8 . . . . 219, 243, 384
4:8–10 243
4:8–12 . . . . . . 89, 252, 602
4:10 . . . 199, 241, 243, 248
4:10–12 . . . . . 99, 103, 144, 148, 350
4:11 243
4:12 . . . . 60, 64, 70, 74, 92, 94, 95, 96, 138, 228, 241, 243, 378, 466
4:13 . . 13, 33, 35, 243, 252
4:14 240
4:14–15 243
4:15 . . . . 169, 243
4:16 240
4:16–18 243
4:17 241
4:18 . . . . 128, 241, 252
4:18–20 602
4:19 . . . . 13, 33
4:19–20 . . . . 228, 252
4:20 . . . . 243, 566
4:21 . . . . 101, 252
4:21–22 243
4:22 240
4:23 . . . . 169, 384
4:23–30 244
4:23–31 . . . . 101, 240, 244
4:24 . . . . 244, 600
4:24–30 . . . . 235, 263, 599
4:24–31 . . . . 234, 235
4:24b 436
4:25–26 211
4:26 94
4:27 . . . . 145, 157
4:27–28 92
4:28 130
4:29 . . . . 94, 244, 248
4:29–30 244
4:29–31 354
4:29–33 354
4:30 241
4:31 . . . . 219, 235, 244, 461
4:32 . . . . 179, 248
4:32–35 . . . . . 87, 229, 231, 245, 263, 415
4:32–37 . . . . 184, 547
4:32–5:16. . . . . . . 227, 228, 239, 245
4:32a 245
4:32b 245
4:33 . . . . 94, 236, 354, 600
4:33–34 416
4:33–34a 245
4:33–5:12. 33
4:34–35 547
4:34–37 316
4:34b–35 245

ACTS (*continued*)

4:35–37 274
4:36 . . . . 169, 315, 339, 340, 479
4:36–37 . . . . .245, 246, 290, 315
4:36–5:11. 35
4:41 416
5. . . . . . . .88, 160, 249, 252, 253, 263
5:1 82
5:1–2 247
5:1–3 246
5:1–11 . . .83, 85, 245, 246, 289, 458, 609, 624
5:2 274
5:2–3 547
5:3 . . . . 219, 246
5:3–4. . . . . 237, 247
5:4 246
5:5 249
5:5–10 247
5:9 94
5:9–11 385
5:11 . . . 248, 249, 267, 488
5:12 . . . . . . .236, 249, 250, 267, 353, 625
5:12–13 85
5:12–16 . . . . . 87, 229, 245, 249, 252, 263, 354, 359, 464
5:13 249
5:13–14 . . . . 100, 267
5:14 . . . . .78, 94, 248, 249, 354
5:15 . . . . 85, 250, 277, 462
5:15–16 . . . . 249, 250
5:16 . . . . 176, 248
5:17 . . . .168, 170, 219, 253
5:17–18 252
5:17–26 252
5:17–27 . . . . 168, 169
5:17–41 169
5:17–42 . . . . .33, 228, 239, 251, 256, 354, 356
5:18 277
5:18–21 602
5:18–42 101
5:19 94
5:19–21 85
5:19–20 354
5:19–26 252
5:20 255
5:21 . . . . 253, 255, 354
5:24 169
5:25 . . . . 255, 257
5:26 322
5:27–28 252
5:27–32 602
5:27–33 252
5:28 . . . . .241, 251, 255
5:29 252
5:29–32 . . . . .144, 148, 252, 354
5:30 . . . . 103, 199
5:30–32 . . . . . . 93, 99, 103
5:31 . . . . . 95, 96, 201, 600
5:31–32 204
5:32 602
5:33 252
5:33–39 616
5:33–40. 627
5:34 253
5:34–39. 253
5:34–40. . . . . 85, 491
5:35–37 253
5:35–39 88
5:36 170
5:36–37 253
5:38–39 . . . . 130, 253, 325
5:40 . . . . 241, 254, 498
5:40–42. 254
5:41 . . . . .101, 241, 255
5:42 . . . 101, 144, 148, 255, 257, 354, 356, 379
6. . . . . . 261, 274, 338, 566
6–7 160
6–8 259
6–9 265
6:1 . . . . 145, 248, 256, 257
6:1–2 . . . . 35, 256
6:1–6 . . 213, 214, 257, 261, 263, 266, 267, 315, 369, 380, 384, 574, 613
6:1–7 . . 227, 228, 239, 256
6:1–8:3. 76
6:1–8:4. 591
6:1–9:31. 75
6:1–11:18 75
6:2 . . . . 120, 213, 248, 257, 610, 614, 627
6:2–3 258
6:3 . . . . 179, 248, 258, 259, 267
6:3–4. 257
6:3–10 602
6:4 . . . . . .15, 234, 257, 259
6:5 . . 9, 248, 259, 267, 338, 378, 622, 625
6:5–6. 258
6:6 . . . . .33, 233, 234, 235, 259, 277, 478
6:7 . . . . 78, 79, 87, 98, 169, 190, 191, 228, 229, 248, 261, 263, 292, 351, 355, 379
6:7a 261
6:7b 261
6:8 . . . . .236, 266, 267, 353, 354
6:8–10 . . . . . .267, 274, 625
6:8–15 267
6:8–7:60 283
6:8–8:1 259
6:8–8:2 354
6:8–8:3 . . . . 257, 265, 266
6:8–9:31 . . . . . 77, 79, 190, 191, 265, 283
6:9 . . . . .111, 267, 268, 291
6:10 269
6:11 269
6:11–15 269
6:12 . . . . 169, 269, 384
6:12–14 488
6:13 . . . . 269, 270
6:14 . . . . 248, 269
6:15 . . . . 169, 268, 269
7. . . .88, 167, 267, 270, 271
7–8 110
7:1 . . . . 169, 269
7:1–53 . . . . 270, 354
7:2 248
7:2–53 . . . .82, 86, 90, 144, 146, 242, 270, 625
7:2a 270
7:2b–8 270
7:2b–34 270
7:5–7 599
7:9–16 270
7:13 248
7:16 547
7:17 599
7:17–34 270
7:17–44 270
7:23, 25, 26 248
7:31 94
7:32 163
7:33 94
7:34 248
7:35 . . . . 96, 270, 271
7:36–50 . . . . 270, 271
7:37 . . . 130, 144, 147, 211, 248, 271, 623
7:38 248
7:45–50 270
7:45–52 . . . . 144, 148
7:48 . . . . 269, 436
7:49 94
7:49–50 131
7:51–53 . . . . 270, 271
7:54 . . . . 169, 271
7:54–60 602
7:54–8:3 . . . . 271, 625
7:55 . . . . 267, 272
7:55–56 . 93, 201, 204, 272
7:55–59 xxi
7:55–60 . . . . 34, 207

7:56 . . . . 93, 269, 272
7:57–58 272
7:57–60 101
7:58 . . . . 273, 274, 285
7:59 . . . . 94, 269, 274
7:59–60 . . . . 101, 235, 293, 600
7:60 . . . . 94, 269, 273, 274
8. . . . . . 160, 276, 281, 282, 292, 313, 353, 377
8–11. 569
8–12 202
8:1 . . . . 100, 274, 275, 292, 296, 322, 572
8:1–3 . . . . . . 283, 285, 574
8:1–4 . . . . .101, 314
8:1b–3 78
8:1b–11:18 76
8:2 274
8:3 . . . . 120, 274, 587
8:4 . . . . . 78, 274, 292, 355
8:4–8 . . . . 275, 574
8:4–17 31
8:4–25 . . . . . 296, 297, 332
8:4–40 . . . . . . 76, 257, 259, 265, 266, 274, 283, 339, 478, 574
8:4–25 622
8:4–12:25. 78
8:5 . . . . 275, 354
8:5–25 354
8:6 . . . . 277, 353
8:6–7 . . 236, 277, 354, 359
8:6–8 275
8:7 . . . . 236, 464
8:9 . . . . 276, 277
8:9–10 277
8:9–11 276
8:9–17 275
8:9–24 . . . . . .101, 570, 625
8:9–25 176
8:10–11 277
8:11 . . . . 276, 277
8:12 . . . 201, 248, 276, 478
8:12–13 120
8:13 . . . . . . .236, 275, 277, 354, 416
8:14 . . . . . .13, 33, 315, 570
8:14–16 275
8:14–17 . . . . .100, 235, 276, 293
8:14–25 . . . . 120, 297
8:15 . . . . 233, 234
8:16 . . . . 94, 311
8:17 85
8:17–24 277
8:18–19 277
8:18–23 85
8:18–24 . . . . .235, 341, 416
8:18–25 276
8:21 278
8:21–23 342
8:22 94
8:22–24 234
8:23 278
8:24 . . . . 94, 235
8:24–25 279
8:25 . . . . 31, 94, 170
8:26 . . . . 94, 279
8:26–29 337
8:26–32 124
8:26–39 622
8:26–40. . . . 279, 301, 332, 355, 616, 625
8:27 282
8:27–28 416
8:27–39 . . . . 144, 148
8:27a 279
8:27b 280
8:29 602
8:31 367
8:32–33 618
8:35 . . . . .92, 266, 283, 478, 599
8:35–38 355
8:36 559
8:36–39 284
8:37 285
8:38 416
8:39 . . . . 94, 602
8:40 . . . . 297, 355, 478, 611, 622
9. . . .90, 110, 122, 160, 161
9–11. . . . . .110, 161
9. . . . . . 167, 274, 286, 288, 293, 313, 343, 381, 485, 494, 495, 517, 518, 523, 609, 613
9–12. 328
9:1 . . . . . 94, 120, 169, 248, 286, 600
9:1–2 . . . . . . 274, 283, 287, 288, 516
9:1–3 587
9:1–9 . . . . 286, 307
9:1–19 . . . . . 120, 286, 337, 354, 494, 496, 516
9:1–22 . . . . 381, 587
9:1–31 . . 76, 265, 266, 285
9:2 . . . . . 87, 118, 248, 286, 287, 466
9:3 . . . . 272, 286, 288
9:3–4 287
9:3–6 xxi
9:3–7 354
9:3–31 283
9:4 287
9:4–6 . . . . 34, 207
9:5 . . . . 94, 288
9:6–9 288
9:7 . . . . 288, 495
9:8 286
9:8–9 342
9:9b–22 289
9:10 . . . . 248, 286, 289
9:10–16 . . . . 307, 354
9:10–17 207
9:10a 94
9:10b 94
9:11 . . . . .89, 94, 234, 235, 343
9:11–12 293
9:11–14 289
9:12 . . . . 277, 307
9:13 . . . . 94, 248, 289
9:13–14 292
9:14 169
9:15 . . . . . 94, 96, 289, 513
9:15–16 . . . . .289, 371, 514
9:15–30 315
9:17 . . . . 94, 100, 120, 289
9:17–18 354
9:17–19 460
9:18 . . . . 289, 416
9:19 . . . . 248, 286, 289
9:19–22 . . . . 144, 148, 355
9:19b–25 289
9:20 . . . . 84, 136, 145, 150, 340, 355
9:20–22 . . . . 93, 421
9:20–25 587
9:21 . . . . 169, 289, 292
9:22 . . . . 96, 103, 286, 355
9:22–30 318
9:23 289
9:23–25 . . . . 120, 290
9:23–27 120
9:23–30 381
9:26 . . . . 35, 248, 290, 292
9:26–28 289
9:26–30 . . . . .290, 355, 381, 587
9:27 . . 13, 33, 94, 120, 246, 266, 286, 290, 315, 353
9:28 . . . . .94, 291, 353, 461
9:28–29 . . . . 120, 355
9:28–30 120
9:29 145
9:29a 291
9:29b–30 291
9:30 . . . . 248, 343
9:31 . . . 78, 79, 87, 94, 100, 190, 191, 229, 248, 263, 266, 291, 351, 456, 482
9:32 . . . . 248, 297
9:32–33 609

ACTS (*continued*)

9:32–35 . . 83, 85, 277, 297, 354, 359, 619
9:32–43 . . . . 120, 295, 296, 297, 315, 327, 479
9:32–11:18 . . . . 75, 76
9:32–12:24 77
9:32–12:25 . . . 79, 190, 191, 295, 327, 329
9:33 . . . . 8, 297
9:33–10:1 126
9:34 . . . . xxi, 297, 354
9:35 . . . . 94, 297, 354
9:36 298
9:36–41 472
9:36–42 . . 83, 261, 329, 359
9:36–43 . . . . . 85, 298, 354, 619, 626
9:37 298
9:38 . . . . 248, 298, 367
9:39 298
9:40 . . . . 85, 233, 234, 235
9:40–41 . . . . 277, 299, 354
9:40–42 235
9:41 248
9:42 . . . . 78, 94, 299, 354, 488
9:43 . . . . 89, 299
10 . . . 88, 185, 310, 377, 381
10–11 . . . 311, 382, 601, 622
10:1 302
10:1–2 378
10:1–8 301
10:1–48 . . . . . . 31, 90, 385
10:1–11:18 . . 295, 296, 297, 299, 300, 301, 313, 327, 332, 337, 354, 613
10:2 . . . . 82, 234, 302, 415
10:2–3 233
10:2–4 235
10:3 . . . . 302, 304
10:3–4 235
10:3–6 . . . . 307, 354
10:3–7 . . . . 300, 301
10:4 . . . . 94, 234
10:4–6 302
10:6 89
10:7–8 302
10:9 . . . . 234, 235, 304
10:9–10 305
10:9–16 . . . . . 85, 300, 301, 354, 385
10:9–20 . . . . 307, 619
10:9–23a 305
10:11–16 272
10:12 305
10:13–15 207
10:14 . . . . 94, 305, 306
10:15 . . . . 296, 305
10:17–18 306
10:19 602
10:19–20 306
10:21–23a 306
10:22 . . . . . . 300, 301, 302, 378, 415, 488
10:23 248
10:23b 307
10:23b–48 307
10:24 82
10:24–26 128
10:25–26 85
10:26 . . . . 307, 362
10:27–48 85
10:28 308
10:28a 307
10:28b 307
10:29–33a 308
10:30 . . 233, 234, 235, 304
10:30–33 . . . . 300, 301
10:31 234
10:33 94
10:33b 308
10:34–35 309
10:34–36 . . . . 74, 296
10:34–43 89
10:34–48 . . . . 354, 600
10:36 . . . . 93, 94, 144, 148, 309, 350, 600
10:36–43 . . . . . 15, 310, 328
10:37 . . . . 416, 457, 488
10:37–43 310
10:38 . . . . . . 100, 236, 248
10:38–41 130
10:39–43 . . . . 99, 103
10:40 . . . . 103, 199
10:41 204
10:42 . . . . 92, 102, 103, 211, 602
10:42–43 130
10:43 . . 32, 86, 92, 95, 103, 130, 144, 148, 248
10:44 . . 300, 301, 310, 385
10:44–47 311
10:44–48 . . . . 99, 100, 416, 617
10:45 . . . 300, 301, 307, 310
10:45–46 311
10:46 354
10:47 . . . . . . 300, 301, 310, 385, 559
10:47–48 . . . . 120, 311, 416
10:48 312
11 . . 88, 122, 161, 316, 318, 329, 381
11–12 110
11:1 . . . . 33, 248, 312
11:1–3 . . . . 315, 329
11:1–4 35
11:1–18 . . 31, 90, 306, 312, 315, 385
11:2 378
11:2–3 312
11:3 307
11:4–10 . . . . . . 85, 307, 312
11:4–18 329
11:5 . . . . 234, 235
11:5–10 . . . . 272, 300, 301
11:7–9 207
11:8 94
11:9 296
11:11–12 312
11:12 . . . . . . 248, 307, 602
11:13–14 . . . 300, 301, 312
11:15 . . . . . . 300, 301, 310, 313, 385
11:15–17 100
11:15–18 . . . . . 99, 311, 617
11:16 . . . 94, 306, 311, 313
11:16–17 600
11:17 . . . 94, 248, 300, 301, 310, 313, 385, 559
11:17–18 91
11:18 . . . . 95, 130, 296, 313, 381
11:19 . . . . . . 313, 340, 572
11:19–20 . . . . 145, 355
11:19–21 . . . 101, 314, 355, 377, 479
11:19–26 . . . . 31, 86, 261, 320
11:19–30 . . 9, 76, 259, 295, 296, 313, 314, 327, 328
11:19–13:3 . . . . 76, 86, 318, 320
11:19–14:28 75
11:19–28:31 75
11:19a 314
11:19b–20 314
11:20 . . . 94, 124, 313, 340
11:20–21 600
11:20–30 332
11:21 . . . . 78, 248, 314
11:21a 94
11:21b 94
11:22 . . . . 13, 313, 316, 377
11:22–24 . . . . 315, 355
11:22–26 . . . . 120, 246
11:22–30 120
11:23 . . . . 94, 315, 367
11:23–30 377
11:24 . . . . 94, 315, 355
11:25 343
11:25–26 . . . . 315, 587
11:25–26a 315
11:25–30 . . . . 84, 547
11:26 . . . 97, 111, 248, 296, 313, 314, 315, 316, 519, 612
11:26b 315

11:27 . . . . 86, 313, 320
11:27–28 316
11:27–30 . . . . 77, 120, 245, 314, 316, 317, 318, 381, 382, 402, 479, 609, 615
11:27–38 325
11:27–12:25 78
11:28 . . . . 9, 145, 488
11:28–30 . . . . 86, 320
11:29 . . . . 92, 179, 248
11:29–30 . . . . 316, 531
11:30 . . . 13, 316, 384, 385
12. .110, 122, 157, 160, 161, 318, 320, 321, 324, 327, 328, 617
12:1 . . . . 67, 277
12:1–2 . . . . . . 86, 318, 320, 321, 618
12:1–3 . .572, 586, 591, 617
12:1–4 216
12:1–21 602
12:1–23 145
12:1–24 . . . . .77, 159
12:1–25 . . . . .76, 295, 296, 318, 327
12:2 . . . . . 13, 33, 214, 248, 320, 324
12:3 318
12:3–4 322
12:3–19 . . . . .86, 320, 322, 602
12:4 . . . . 305, 319, 322
12:4–5 318
12:5 . . . . 101, 234, 235, 319, 323
12:6 . . . . 319, 322, 324
12:6–10 319
12:6–11 85
12:7 . . . . .94, 319, 325
12:7–8 319
12:7–11 .307, 319, 323, 354
12:9–11 . . . . 319, 322
12:10 . . .125, 319, 322, 324
12:11 94
12:12 . . 13, 18, 82, 89, 234, 319, 323, 340, 342
12:12–17 323
12:13–14 . . . . 319, 322
12:15 . . . . . . 319, 322, 323
12:15–16 . . . . 319, 323
12:17 . . . . 13, 94, 120, 179, 248, 296, 319, 320, 324, 384, 386, 569, 618
12:18 . . . . . . 319, 324, 380
12:19 . . .319, 325, 418, 544
12:19–23 617
12:20 . . . . . . .319, 325, 533
12:20–23 . . . . .86, 320, 325, 326
12:21–23 . . . . .319, 325
12:22–23 354
12:23 . . . . .94, 319, 325
12:24 . . . 78, 79, 80, 87, 98, 190, 191, 229, 261, 263, 327, 557
12:24–25 . . . . .79, 86, 296, 320, 327, 332, 333, 351
12:25 . . 13, 77, 79, 80, 120, 190, 191, 327, 340, 342, 381, 382, 402, 531, 557
12:25–15:38. 13
12:25–16:5. 77
12:25–21:16. . . . . . . 81, 82
12:25–28:31. 77
13. . 88, 122, 165, 338, 553, 554, 621
13–14: 110, 120, 161, 337, 364, 371, 377, 621
13–15. 122
13–20 486
13–21. 588
13–28 . . . . . 76, 77, 79, 80, 190, 202, 331, 332, 333
13:1 . . 10, 13, 86, 145, 246, 320, 338, 369, 373
13:1–3 . . . 9, 214, 235, 259, 261, 314, 336, 337, 377
13:1–12 . . . . .335, 337, 409
13:1–14:28. . . . . . .79, 333, 335, 336
13:1–19:41 78
13:1–28:31 76
13:2 . . . . 94, 339
13:2–3 . . . . . . 86, 320, 369
13:2–4 100
13:2–12 602
13:3 . . . 234, 277, 339, 373
13:4 . . . . 117, 336, 339, 370, 624
13:4–5 339
13:4–6 355
13:4–12 . . . . 176, 340, 614
13:4–14:28. 76
13:5 . . . . . 13, 84, 136, 145, 150, 246, 336, 340, 355, 373, 408, 618
13:6 341
13:6–12 . . . . . 85, 101, 336, 341, 354, 625
13:7 . . . . 67, 340, 341, 343
13:7–8 . . . . 156, 623
13:7–12 29
13:8 341
13:9 . . . . 219, 342, 343
13:10 . . . . 94, 287, 342
13:10–11 354
13:11 . . . . 8, 94, 342
13:12 . . . . 94, 343, 354
13:13 . . . 13, 117, 336, 340, 346, 368, 373, 408, 618
13:13–15 346
13:13–20 . . . . 144, 147
13:13–52 . . . . . . .335, 345, 346, 355
13:14 . . .84, 136, 150, 340, 346, 347, 554
13:14–15a. 165
13:14–41 165
13:14–43 554
13:14–48 . . . 145, 166, 554
13:14–52 336
13:15 . . . . .246, 348
13:15a 347
13:15b 165, 347
13:15b–41 347
13:16 . . . . . . 348, 349, 378
13:16–25 . . . . 348, 364
13:16–41 . . . . 89, 144, 146, 348, 355, 364, 373
13:16b–41 554
13:17 248
13:17–22 348
13:17–25 86
13:17–41 242
13:21 120
13:21–41 . . . . 144, 148
13:22–23 387
13:23 . . . . . . .96, 130, 348, 599, 600
13:24 416
13:24–25 . . . . 348, 457
13:26 . . 348, 349, 378, 554
13:26–33 82
13:26–37 364
13:27 . . . . 92, 130, 349
13:27–41 . . . . 99, 103
13:28 . . . . .145, 157
13:28–30 . . . . 96, 103
13:29 . . . . 103, 130
13:29–33 349
13:30 199
13:32–33 . . . . 130, 599
13:32–39 . . . . 501, 599
13:33 211
13:33–34 199
13:33–37 349
13:35 130
13:36 . . . . 130, 274
13:37 199
13:38 . . . . 348, 349
13:38–39 . . . . .32, 95, 103, 144, 147, 336
13:38–41 364
13:39 . . . . 95, 248, 349
13:40–41 349
13:42 150

ACTS (*continued*)

13:42–43 . . . .165, 347, 349
13:42–52 349
13:43 . . . . . . 246, 367, 378
13:44 . . . . 94, 554
13:44–45 349
13:44–48 554
13:45 . . . . .101, 219
13:46 . . .84, 246, 353, 372, 378, 461, 554
13:46–47 . . . . 131, 349
13:46–48 556
13:46–49 355
13:47 . . . . .31, 92, 94, 202, 350, 554
13:47–48 336
13:48 . . . . 92, 94, 350
13:49 . . 78, 79, 80, 94, 333, 336, 350, 370, 488
13:50 . . . . 83, 84, 351, 378
13:51 . . . . . . .351, 442, 614
13:52 . . . . . . .219, 248, 351
14 . . . . 88, 360
14:1 . . . . 84, 136, 145, 150, 246, 340, 352, 556
14:1–3 352
14:1–5 354
14:1–6 353
14:1–6a 336
14:1–7 . . . . 335, 352
14:2 . . . . 101, 248, 353
14:3 . . . .94, 120, 236, 246, 353, 354, 386, 461, 601
14:4 . . . . .85, 120, 356, 372, 610
14:4–7 355
14:5 . . . . 84, 356
14:6 . . . . 357, 366
14:6–20 354
14:6b–7 336
14:6b–19 336
14:7 . . . . 246, 356
14:8 . . . . 8, 360
14:8–9 358
14:8–10 . . . . 277, 354, 358, 359
14:8–12 360
14:8–14 . . . . 84, 85
14:8–18 627
14:8–19 183
14:8–20 . . . . 335, 357, 358, 361
14:9 . . . . 277, 360
14:9–10 128
14:10 360
14:11 . . . . 357, 360
14:11–15a 360
14:11–20 360
14:12 . . . . 177, 360
14:12–13 177
14:13 360
14:13–15 85
14:14 . . . 85, 120, 356, 357, 362, 372, 610
14:14–18 . . . . . . .246, 360, 431, 620
14:15 . . . . 355, 364
14:15–17 . . . 354, 365, 599
14:15–18 . . . . 364, 373
14:15a 362, 364
14:15b 364
14:15b–18 364
14:16 . . . 31, 364, 365, 434
14:16–17 130
14:17 . . . . 364, 365
14:18 . . . . 364, 365
14:19 . . . . 84, 366, 441
14:19–20 365
14:20 248
14:20–21 . . . 336, 355, 366
14:20a 366
14:20b 366
14:21 . . . . . .246, 346, 355, 367, 369
14:21–23 . . . . . . .235, 336, 353, 367
14:21–24a 336
14:21–28 . . . . 335, 367
14:22 . . . . . .201, 248, 336, 367, 369, 372, 373, 456, 481, 482, 602
14:23 . . .94, 213, 234, 248, 261, 369, 373, 614
14:24 369
14:24–25 . . . . 355, 370
14:24–26 369
14:24–28 314
14:24b–25a 336
14:25 . . . . . . 246, 368, 369
14:25b 336
14:26 . . . .92, 117, 369, 370
14:26–28 . . . . . 9, 336, 337
14:27 . . . 91, 130, 337, 370, 380, 487
14:27–28 . . . . .79, 80, 333, 336, 370, 372
14:28 . . 248, 324, 370, 380
15 . . 88, 110, 122, 161, 185, 318, 346, 376, 377, 378, 379, 380, 381, 386, 388, 389, 396, 397, 402, 403, 410, 487, 601, 618, 622, 625
15:1 . . . . . . .248, 378, 380, 381, 383
15:1–2 35
15:1–4 . . . . 375, 377
15:1–5 120
15:1–16:4 33
15:1–35 . . . . 31, 35, 75, 76, 79, 84, 314, 333, 375, 381, 382, 383, 385, 402, 408, 450
15:2 . . . .92, 324, 380, 381, 384, 614
15:2a 379
15:2b 380
15:2b–4 380
15:3 . . . . 248, 380, 531
15:3–4 487
15:4 . . . . 130, 380
15:5 . . . 170, 248, 383, 384
15:5–21 . . . . 375, 383
15:6 . . . . 383, 384
15:6–11 376
15:7 . . . . 248, 385
15:7–8 310
15:7–11 . . .13, 90, 95, 300, 385, 601
15:7–13 392
15:7–19 96
15:8 . . . . 301, 385
15:8–9 100
15:9 385
15:10 . . . . 248, 385
15:11 . . . 94, 385, 393, 401
15:12 . . 130, 236, 248, 353, 384, 386, 487
15:13 . . .13, 248, 320, 324, 386, 388
15:13–18 386
15:13–19 409
15:13–21 . . . . 120, 618
15:14 . . 248, 386, 388, 392
15:15 . . . . 386, 388
15:15–18 392
15:16 388
15:16–18 . . . . 388, 390
15:16b–17 211
15:17 388
15:17a 94
15:17b 94
15:18 388
15:19 . . . . . . 388, 392, 393
15:19–21 . . . . .90, 376, 379, 392
15:20 . . . . . . 392, 396, 397
15:20–32 409
15:21 . . 145, 150, 393, 395, 396
15:22 . . 121, 212, 248, 384, 392, 394, 410, 488
15:22–35 . . . . 375, 394
15:22–36 314
15:22–18:5 13
15:22a 394
15:22b 394

15:23 . . 179, 248, 388, 395
15:23–29 . . 81, 87, 116, 117, 394, 395
15:24 395
15:25–26 395
15:26 . . . . 94, 600
15:27 . . . . . . 394, 395, 410
15:28–29 . . . . 90, 100
15:29 . . . . . . 388, 396, 397
15:30 . . . . 248, 398
15:30–31 118
15:30–34 398
15:31 398
15:32 . . 248, 367, 398, 410, 456, 482
15:33 . . . . 248, 398
15:35 . . 78, 79, 80, 94, 333, 376, 399, 400, 406
15:35–40 9
15:36 . . . . 94, 248, 406, 408, 455
15:36–39 618
15:36–41 . . . . 35, 370, 409, 451
15:36–16:10 . . . . . 405, 408
15:36–18:17 75
15:36–18:22 . . . 76, 79, 333, 405, 406, 407
15:37 408
15:37–38 . . . . 373, 408
15:37–39 . . . . 13, 120, 246
15:38 408
15:39 . . . . . . 340, 408, 409
15:39–41 409
15:40 . . . . 94, 121, 248, 261, 446
15:40–41 410
15:40–16:2 409
15:41 . . 367, 406, 456, 482
16–17 161
16–18 110
16:1 . . . . 13, 248, 366, 406, 410
16:1–3 . . . . . 261, 410, 627
16:1–4 358
16:1–5 . . . . 406, 410
16:1–8 346
16:1–18:22 121
16:2 . . . . 353, 410
16:3 410
16:4 . . . . 118, 392, 395, 410
16:5 . . . . . 78, 79, 333, 406, 410, 456, 482
16:6 . . . . 406, 411, 559
16:6–7 602
16:6–8 . . . . 411, 412
16:6–10 . . . . 100, 337, 411, 447
16:6–15 354
16:6–19:20 77
16:7 . . . . xxi, 411
16:7–10 406
16:8 411
16:8–10 627
16:8–40 121
16:9 412
16:9–10 . . . . 307, 354, 411
16:10 412
16:10–12 . . . . 411, 415, 622
16:10–17 . . 11, 12, 15, 116, 413, 471, 627
16:11 . . . . 406, 413
16:11–12 471
16:11–15 . . . . 354, 414
16:11–16 235
16:11–34 31
16:11–40 . . . . 145, 405, 413
16:12 413
16:12–14 137
16:12–40 406
16:13 . . . . 234, 414
16:13–15 . . . . 184, 415
16:13–17 117
16:14 . . . . 94, 414, 444
16:14–15 . . . . 85, 89
16:14–40 619
16:14a 414
16:14b 415
16:15 . . . . 82, 94, 416
16:15a 415
16:15b 415
16:16 . . . . 94, 234, 416
16:16–18 . . . . 84, 416, 464
16:16–24 176
16:16–40 . . . . 101, 354, 415
16:17 . . . . 248, 416
16:18 . . . 277, 354, 416, 417
16:19 . . . . 12, 94
16:19–40 . . . . 101, 417
16:20 67
16:20–21 417
16:22–23 417
16:22–25 101
16:22–40 602
16:23 498
16:23–34 85
16:24 417
16:25 . . . . . . 234, 235, 418
16:25–34 235
16:26 . . . . 354, 418
16:27–28 418
16:27–34 354
16:29–34 . . . . 82, 85
16:30 . . . . 94, 418
16:30–31 406
16:30–34 416
16:31 . . . . 94, 95, 418
16:32 . . . . 94, 419
16:33 416
16:33–34 419
16:34 248
16:35–36 419
16:35–40 180
16:37 419
16:38–39 419
16:40 . . . . . . 179, 184, 367, 420, 471
17 . . . . . . 88, 119, 433, 434, 435, 610
17–19 122
17:1 . . . . 406, 420, 421
17:1–2 . . . . . . 84, 136, 340
17:1–4 31
17:1–9 . . . . . 121, 355, 406, 421, 422, 627
17:1–15 . . . . 405, 420
17:1–18:17 450
17:2 . . . . 421, 428
17:2–3 . . . . 32, 92, 99, 103, 130, 144, 148, 421, 599
17:2–4 355
17:3 . . . . . . 86, 92, 96, 103
17:4 . . . 128, 324, 378, 380, 421, 441, 461
17:5 . . . . 421, 422, 422
17:5–9 . . . . 13, 89, 121, 184
17:6 . . . . 67, 248, 422, 424
17:6–7 422
17:7 201
17:8 . . . . 422, 424
17:9 423
17:10 . . . . 84, 136, 248, 340, 424
17:10–12 355
17:10–14 406
17:10–15 . . . 355, 424, 425
17:11 . . . . 424, 611
17:12 . . 128, 324, 380, 424
17:13 . . . . 101, 424
17:13–16 441
17:14 . . . . 117, 248
17:14–15 . . . . 13, 424
17:15–32 406
17:15–34 121
17:16 175
17:16–17 340
17:16–18 427
17:16–34 . . . . 355, 405, 425, 427
17:17 . . . . 84, 136, 378, 428, 441
17:17–18 355
17:17a 427
17:17b 428
17:18 128
17:18a 428

ACTS (*continued*)

17:18b 430
17:19 430
17:19–31 430
17:21 430
17:22 430
17:22–23 . . . . 175, 431
17:22–31 . . . 430, 431, 436
17:22–34 355
17:23 431
17:24 . . . . 94, 431
17:24–28 . . . .119, 431, 620
17:24–31 . . . . 130, 599
17:24a 436
17:24b 436
17:24c 436
17:25 431
17:25a 436
17:25b 436
17:26 . . . . 31, 92, 130
17:26–28a 431
17:26a 436
17:26b 436
17:27a. 436
17:27b 436
17:28 121
17:28a 436
17:28b 431, 436
17:28b–29 432
17:29 . . . . 431, 434
17:29–31 406
17:29a 436
17:29b 436
17:30 . . . . 434, 600
17:30–31 . . . . 130, 431
17:30a 436
17:30b 436
17:31 . .92, 96, 98, 99, 103, 199, 436, 599, 602
17:31a. 434
17:31b 434
17:32–34 435
17:32a 437
17:32b 437
17:33 437
17:34 . . . . 31, 83, 128
17:34a 437
17:34b 437
18. . . . . 161, 462
18–19. . . . . 161, 482
18–21. 110
18:1 . . . . 437, 462
18:1–2 . . . . 440, 441
18:1–3 . . . . 440, 456
18:1–4 . . . . 121, 622
18:1–17 406
18:1–18 . . . . 355, 438, 466
18:1–22 . . . . 405, 437
18:1–28 83
18:2 . . . . 13, 82, 456
18:2–3 440
18:3 121
18:4 . . . 84, 136, 340, 428, 441, 461
18:4–5 462
18:4–6. 441
18:4–8. 355
18:5 . . . . 13, 144, 148
18:5–7 556
18:5a 441
18:5b 441
18:6 . . . . .96, 351, 614
18:6–7 462
18:6–8. 462
18:6a 442
18:6b 442
18:6c 442
18:7 . . . . 89, 378, 444
18:7–11 444
18:8 . . . . . . 13, 82, 94, 121, 416, 462
18:8a 444
18:8b 444
18:9 94
18:9–10 . . . . .xxi, 207, 307, 444, 447, 462
18:9–11 337
18:10 248
18:11 . . . . . . 337, 444, 462
18:12 . . . . . . 156, 444, 623
18:12–17 . . . .29, 444, 445, 462, 616
18:13 . . . . 444, 461
18:14–15 . . . . 176, 446
18:16 446
18:17 . . . . 13, 446
18:18 . . . .13, 117, 121, 179, 248, 261, 406, 448, 456, 612
18:18–19 622
18:18–20:38. 75
18:18–21 . . . . 355, 446
18:18–22 . . . 487, 489, 621
18:18a 446
18:18b 446
18:19 . . . . . .340, 355, 428, 447, 556
18:19–21 406
18:19–22 472
18:19–19:41 466
18:20 447
18:21 . . . . . . .117, 447, 456
18:21–22 337
18:22 . . . . 79, 80, 161, 333, 381, 406, 448
18:22–23 . . . . 9, 314
18:22a 406
18:22b 406
18:22c 406
18:23 . .248, 346, 353, 358, 366, 367, 454, 455, 456
18:23–28 . . . . 453, 456
18:23–21:16. 76
18:23–21:17 . . 79, 333, 334, 453, 454, 455
18:23a 454
18:23b 454
18:23c 454
18:24 . . . . 13, 457
18:24–26 355
18:24–28 . . . 447, 455, 456, 458, 610, 622
18:24–19:1. 121
18:25 . . . . .56, 94, 287, 416, 458
18:26 . . . 13, 128, 287, 353, 355, 456, 457
18:27 . . . . .13, 87, 179, 248
18:27–28 355
18:27–19:1 457
18:27–19:6. 126
18:28 . . . . .32, 86, 92, 102, 131, 144, 148, 355, 458, 599
19. . . . . 459, 462, 482, 610
19–20. 287
19:1 . . . . 13, 346, 460, 462
19:1–7 . . . . . 354, 460, 461
19:1–40 454
19:1–41 . . . . 121, 447, 453, 456, 460
19:2 . . . . 99, 460
19:3 460
19:3–4. 416
19:4 461
19:4–5 354
19:5 . . . . 94, 416
19:5–6. 461
19:6 . . . . 85, 354
19:8 . . . .84, 136, 201, 248, 340, 353, 428, 461, 462
19:8–9. 488
19:8–10 . . . . 354, 462, 614
19:8–12 . . . . 354, 460, 461
19:8a 461
19:8b 461
19:9 . . . 248, 287, 428, 461, 462, 466
19:9–10 461
19:10 . .78, 79, 80, 94, 334, 454, 462, 475
19:11 . . . . 236, 462
19:11–12 . . .236, 354, 359, 462, 464
19:11–20 101
19:12 . . . . 84, 85, 176, 462
19:12–17 462

19:13 . . . . 94, 463
19:13–16 625
19:13–19 483
19:13–20 . . . 176, 460, 462
19:14 82
19:17 . . . . 94, 464, 483
19:18 . . . . 248, 483
19:18–19 464
19:19 . . . . 483, 547
19:20 . . .78, 79, 80, 94, 98, 261, 334, 454, 465
19:20a 465
19:20b 465
19:21 . . . 84, 121, 454, 470, 486, 529
19:21–22 466
19:21–41 . . . . 78, 460, 466
19:21–28:31 77
19:22 . . . . 13, 84, 461, 462, 465, 482
19:23 . . . . . .248, 287, 324, 380, 466
19:23–24 466
19:23–41 . . . .177, 470, 614
19:24 . . . . 324, 380
19:24–41 . . . . 183, 184
19:25 466
19:26 475
19:26a 466
19:26b 466
19:27 488
19:27a 466
19:27b 466
19:28 468
19:29 . . . . 13, 219, 531, 610
19:29a 468
19:29b 468
19:30 . . . . 248, 469
19:30–31 482
19:31 . . . . 67, 184, 469
19:32 . . . . . . 248, 249, 469
19:33–34 . . . . 469, 488
19:35 . . . . 67, 469
19:35–37 469
19:35–40 88
19:38 67
19:38–39 469
19:39 . . . . 248, 249
19:40–41 469
19:41 . . . . 248, 249
20 . . . . . .88, 161, 473, 483
20:1 . . . . 248, 367, 470
20:1–2 117
20:1–2a 454
20:1–3 . . . . 121, 470
20:1–5 366
20:1–6 . . . . 422, 438
20:1–16 . . . . 453, 470
20:1–28:31 78
20:2 . . . . 367, 471
20:2–3 537
20:2b–3a 454
20:3 84
20:3a 471
20:3b 454, 471
20:3c 471
20:4 . . . . 13, 261, 425, 471, 531, 610
20:4–5 12
20:4–6 . . . . 84, 471
20:5 471
20:5–6 . . . . . .415, 471, 622
20:5–12 411
20:5–15 . . 11, 15, 116, 122, 413, 476, 627
20:6–12 627
20:6a 454
20:6b–12 454
20:7 . . . 232, 234, 428, 471
20:7–8 . . . . .117, 471
20:7–12 . . . . .471, 615
20:8–9 471
20:9 428
20:9–12 . . . . . . 84, 85, 359
20:10 472
20:11 . . . . 234, 472
20:12 472
20:13 472
20:13–14a 454
20:13–16 472
20:14 472
20:14b 454
20:15 472
20:15a 454
20:15b 454
20:15c–38 454
20:16 . . . . . . 216, 472, 486
20:16–38 . . . . 466, 620
20:17 . . 235, 248, 472, 475
20:17–18 473
20:17–35 85
20:17–38 . . . 261, 453, 482
20:18 474
20:18–24 474
20:18–35 . .89, 472, 474, 483
20:19 . . . . 84, 94, 473
20:19–21 96
20:20 473
20:20–21 474
20:21 . . . . 94, 473, 600
20:22 . . . . . . 473, 474, 477
20:22–23 . . . 100, 121, 602
20:22–24 . . . . 337, 454
20:23 . . . . 84, 474, 477
20:24 . . . . 84, 94, 473, 474
20:25 . . 113, 115, 201, 248, 474, 476
20:25–35 474
20:26 . . . . 473, 474
20:27 . . . . 130, 474
20:28 . . . 92, 100, 101, 103, 248, 473, 474, 475
20:28–29 474
20:28a 475
20:28b 475
20:29 . . . . 248, 474
20:29–30 . . . 473, 474, 475
20:30 . . . . . . 247, 248, 279
20:31 . . 121, 337, 461, 462, 474, 475
20:32 . . . . . . 248, 474, 475
20:33–34 . . . . 474, 475
20:34 440
20:34–35a 475
20:35 . . . . 94, 474, 475
20:35b 475
20:36 . . . . . . 234, 235, 476
20:36–38 . . . . 85, 476
20:37 476
20:38 . . . 113, 115, 235, 476
20:38a 476
21 . . . . . . 88, 162, 489, 492
21–22 523
21–23 612
21–24 110
21–26 . . . . . .486, 522, 523, 524, 557
21–28 . . . . 486, 588
21:1–3 476
21:1–6 476
21:1–17 . . . . . 84, 453, 476
21:1–18 . . 11, 15, 116, 122, 413, 476, 627
21:1–28:16 122
21:1–28:31 75
21:1a 454, 476
21:1b 454
21:1c. 454
21:3 340
21:3–4 476
21:3–6 454
21:4 . . . . 84, 100, 248, 477
21:5 . . . . 82, 85, 234
21:5–6 477
21:7 . . . 179, 248, 454, 478
21:7–16 478
21:8 . . . . .83, 259, 274, 478
21:8–9 . . . . . . .82, 89, 478, 574, 622
21:8–14 454
21:8–18 117
21:9 83
21:10 . . . . 478, 479
21:10–11 488
21:10–14 . . . .84, 121, 482, 486, 609

ACTS (*continued*)

21:11 479
21:11–14. 113
21:12 479
21:13 . . . . 84, 94, 479, 480
21:13–14 85
21:14 . . . . 94, 479
21:15–16 479
21:15–17 454
21:15–19 381
21:16 . . . . 89, 248, 340
21:16b 479
21:17 . . . . 79, 80, 179, 248, 333, 334, 454, 480, 487
21:17–18. 531
21:17–19. 85
21:17–26:32 76
21:1813, 120, 320, 324, 542
21:18–19 487
21:18–25 394
21:18–26 . . . 487, 524, 621
21:18–23:11 . . . . . 485, 487
21:18–26:32 . . . 79, 80, 333, 334, 485, 486, 522
21:19 . . . . 91, 130, 337
21:19–25 31
21:20 248
21:20–21 120
21:20–22 35
21:20–26 85
21:20a 487
21:20b–21 487
21:22–24 487
21:23–27 489
21:24 . . . . 90, 488
21:24–27 487
21:25 . . 118, 248, 395, 396, 397, 487
21:26 . . . . 487, 488
21:26–22:29 355
21:27 . . . . . . 277, 488, 489
21:27–32 85
21:27–36 487
21:27–29 101
21:28 . . . . . . 144, 273, 488
21:29 . . . . 13, 488
21:30 488
21:30–39 503
21:30–40 145
21:31 488
21:31–32 488
21:32 302
21:33 488
21:33–36 85
21:34–35 488
21:36 489
21:37–38 491
21:37–22:22. . . . . 487, 491
21:38 . . 145, 169, 170, 492, 506, 625
21:39 . . . . 343, 491
21:40 . . . 120, 145, 150, 491
22 . . . . . 88, 90, 162, 286, 485, 494, 495, 517, 518, 523, 524
22–26 89
22–28 32
22:1 491
22:1–2 494
22:1–21 . . . . 355, 494, 516, 587
22:1–22 496
22:2 . . . . 145, 150, 491
22:2–3 120
22:3 . . . . 253, 343, 491, 616
22:3–5 . . . . . 292, 494, 516
22:3–16 286
22:3–21 494
22:4 . . . 248, 286, 287, 466
22:4–5 . 120, 274, 494, 587
22:5 . . . . 87, 169, 384
22:6 . . . . 272, 287, 288
22:6–11 494
22:6–16 120
22:8 . . . . 94, 248
22:9 495
22:10 92
22:10a 94
22:10b 94
22:12–16 494
22:14 120
22:15 . . . . 144, 601
22:16 . . . . 95, 416
22:17 . . . . 234, 235
22:17–21 . . . . 85, 120, 207, 235, 337, 494, 498
22:19 . . . . 94, 248
22:19–20 120
22:21 498
22:21–22 84
22:22 498
22:22–30 145
22:23–29 498
22:23–24 498
22:23–29 503
22:24–27 184
22:24b 498
22:25 . . . . 302, 498
22:26 302
22:26–27 498
22:28 498
22:29 499
22:30 . . . . 169, 500
22:30–23:10. 85
22:30–23:11. . . . . 487, 500
22:37 . . . . 96, 103
23. . . . . 162, 167
23–24 . . . . . . 157, 615, 623
23:1 500
23:1–5 169
23:1–10 170
23:1–20 169
23:2 500
23:3 500
23:4 500
23:5 . . . . 248, 500
23:6 . . . . 120, 131, 486, 512, 587
23:6–7 501
23:6–8 . . . . 30, 553
23:8 . . . . 168, 501
23:9 . . . . 85, 169, 519
23:9–10 501
23:11 . . . xxi, 94, 207, 486, 502, 529, 552
23:11–29 126
23:12 488
23:12–13 502
23:12–15 502
23:12–22 84
23:12–35 . . . . 485, 502
23:12–26:32. 145
23:14 . . . . 169, 384
23:14–15 502
23:16 502
23:16–22 502
23:17 . . . . 302, 503
23:18–21 503
23:22 503
23:23 . . . . 302, 304
23:23–24 503
23:23–35 503
23:25–30 . . . . 116, 117
23:26 . . . . 27, 503
23:26–30 . . 81, 87, 503, 553
23:27 503
23:28 169
23:29 519
23:31 504
23:32–33 504
23:34 504
23:35 504
24. . . 88, 157, 162, 505, 508
24–26 121
24:1 . . . 169, 384, 504, 506
24:1–9 . . . . 506, 626
24:1–23 355
24:1–27 . . 85, 159, 485, 504
24:2 506
24:2–4 506
24:2–8 . . . . 88, 508
24:2b–4 508
24:3 27
24:5 248
24:5–6 508
24:5a 507, 508
24:5b 507, 508

24:6 . . . . 507, 508
24:6–8 506
24:7 . . . . 96, 506
24:8 . . . . 507, 508
24:9 507
24:10–21 . . . .355, 507, 508
24:10a 507
24:10b 508
24:11 508
24:11–13 507
24:12 428
24:12–13 508
24:14 . . . 86, 248, 287, 466
24:14–15 . . . . .131, 553
24:14–16 32
24:14–18 508
24:14–21 176
24:14a 507, 508
24:14b–15 . . . . . . 507, 508
24:16 . . . . 507, 508
24:17 . . . . . .120, 471, 486, 507, 508
24:18 488
24:18a 507, 508
24:18b 507, 508
24:19 508
24:19–20 507
24:19–21 508
24:20 169
24:20–21 508
24:21 . . . . . . .131, 507, 512
24:22 . . 248, 287, 466, 509
24:22–27 509
24:23 . . . . . . 302, 509, 559
24:24 . . . . 82, 83, 159, 355, 614
24:24–26 . . . . 355, 509
24:24–27 615
24:25 . . . . . . 102, 103, 211, 428, 602
24:26 96
24:27 . . . . 486, 509
24:44 . . . . 96, 103
25 . . . . .157, 162
25–26 . . 29, 110, 157, 160, 162, 510, 521, 615, 623
25:1 521
25:1–2 509
25:1–5 510
25:1–12 85
25:1–22 . . . . 485, 509
25:2 169
25:2–12 521
25:3 510
25:4–5 510
25:6 511
25:6–12 511
25:7 511
25:8 . . . . .32, 144, 147, 511
25:8–12 176
25:9 511
25:10 511
25:10–11 . . . .113, 486, 511
25:11 511
25:12 511
25:13 . . . . .67, 83, 159
25:13–22 511
25:13–24 159
25:13–27 521
25:13–26:32. . .85, 355, 617
25:14–20 512
25:14–21 . . . . 88, 553
25:15 . . . . 169, 384
25:18–19 519
25:19 512
25:21 512
25:22 512
25:23 . . . . 83, 514
25:23–27 514
25:23–26:32 . . . . 485, 512
25:24–25 515
25:24–27 . . . . 88, 118
25:25 519
25:26 . . . . 87, 94
25:26–27 515
26 . .88, 90, 286, 485, 494, 517, 518, 523, 524, 611
26:1 515
26:1–23 . . . . .515, 521
26:1–29 355
26:1–32 587
26:2–3 . . . . .515, 517
26:2–23 . . . . .497, 516
26:2–29 517
26:4–5 . . . . . . 515, 517, 587
26:4–7 176
26:4–11 . . . . 292, 516
26:4–18 517
26:5 . . . . 120, 170, 343
26:6 515
26:6–7 . . . . . .144, 146, 515
26:6–8 . . . . . . 131, 517, 553
26:7–8 . . . . 123, 126
26:8 515
26:9 248
26:9–11 . . . . 101, 120, 287, 517
26:9–18 286
26:10 . . . . 169, 248
26:10–11 274
26:12 169
26:12–15 517
26:12–18 120
26:13 287
26:14 . . . . . . 145, 150, 287, 288, 515
26:15–18 103
26:15a 94
26:15b 94
26:16 . . . . 15, 601
26:16–18 517
26:17–18 . . . . 131, 601
26:18 248
26:19 . . . . 272, 307
26:19–20 517
26:19–28 517
26:20 . . . . . . 120, 123, 126
26:21 517
26:21–22a 517
26:22–23 . . 85, 92, 99, 103, 108, 131, 144, 147, 176, 553
26:22a 517
26:22b–23 517
26:23 . . . . 86, 248
26:24 . . . . 517, 518
26:24–29 521
26:24–31 518
26:25 27
26:25–27 517
26:25a 518
26:25b 518
26:26 . . . . .353, 518
26:27 518
26:28 . . 111, 248, 315, 441, 461, 517, 519, 612
26:29 . . . . 517, 519
26:30–32 521
26:31 520
26:32 . . . .79, 80, 333, 334, 486, 519, 521
27 . . . . 88, 162, 535
27–28 . . . . . . 110, 545, 557, 560, 561
27:1 . . . .302, 528, 531, 619
27:1–2 528
27:1–5 . . . . 531, 609
27:1–12 . . . . .527, 531
27:1–28:6 . . . . 81, 82
27:1–28:16 . . . . 11, 15, 116, 413, 531, 627
27:1–28:31 . . . . 76, 79, 333, 334, 527
27:2 . . . . .11, 13, 610
27:2a 531
27:2b 531
27:3 . . . . 528, 531
27:4 533
27:5 528
27:6 . . . 302, 458, 534, 535
27:6–12 534
27:7 534
27:7–8 535
27:7–15 613
27:7a 528, 534
27:7b 528, 534

ACTS (*continued*)

27:8 . . . . 528, 534, 537, 615
27:9 . . . . 534, 537, 548
27:9–12 537
27:10 537
27:11 . . . . 302, 538
27:12 538
27:12–15 537
27:13 538
27:13–15 538
27:13–20 538
27:13–38 . . . . 527, 538
27:14 . . . . 538, 621
27:15 538
27:16 . . . . 528, 538
27:17 615
27:17–26 528
27:17a. 538
27:17b 538
27:18 538
27:19 538
27:20 . . . . 324, 380
27:20a 539
27:20b 539
27:21 539
27:21–26 . . . . 528, 539
27:22 . . . . 539, 543
27:23 540
27:23–24 130
27:24 . . . . 113, 115, 589
27:24–26 92
27:24a 540
27:24b 540
27:25 540
27:26 540
27:27 . . . . 540, 548
27:27–32 540
27:27–28:1 528
27:28 541
27:29 . . . . 234, 541
27:30 541
27:31 . . . . 302, 542
27:32 542
27:33 542
27:33–38 . . . . 84, 542
27:34 542
27:34–36 85
27:35 . . . . . . 234, 552, 561
27:35–36 542
27:37 543
27:38 . . 458, 534, 535, 543
27:39 543
27:39–44 544
27:39–28:15. . . . . 527, 543
27:40a 543
27:40b 543
27:41a 544
27:41b 544
27:42 544
27:43 . . . . 302, 559
27:43a 544
27:43b–44a 544
27:44 543
27:44b 544
28. . . . . . 88, 110, 162, 554
28:1 . . . . 544, 545, 620
28:1–6 . . . . 354, 544
28:2 544
28:2a 544
28:2b 544
28:4 . . . 177, 544, 545, 546, 560, 616
28:5–6 545
28:7 . . . . 67, 545, 546, 547, 548, 612
28:7–8 623
28:7–9 . . . . 235, 354
28:7–10 . . . . 546, 547
28:8 . . . . . 84, 85, 234, 235, 277, 359, 546, 547, 561
28:8–9 8
28:8–10 184
28:9 . . . . 84, 236, 359, 547
28:10 547
28:10a 547
28:10b 547
28:11 . . . 177, 458, 547, 548
28:11–16 548
28:12 . . . . . . 528, 549, 626
28:13 . . . . 543, 623
28:13–15 623
28:13a 528, 549
28:13b 528, 549
28:14 . . . . 248, 552
28:14–15 179
28:14a 551
28:14b 551
28:15 . . . . 248, 552
28:15a 528, 551
28:15b 528, 552
28:16 528
28:16–31 . . . . 110, 527
28:16b 553
28:17 554
28:17–20 528
28:17–22 . . . . 553, 554
28:17–28 554
28:17–31 355
28:17a 553
28:17b 553
28:17b–20 553
28:18 553
28:19 553
28:20 . . . . .131, 553
28:21a 553
28:21b 553
28:22 . . . . 248, 553
28:22a 553
28:22b 553
28:23 . . . .32, 92, 102, 108, 131, 201, 441, 554
28:23–28 . . . . 553, 554
28:23–31 355
28:23b 554
28:24 554
28:25–27 554
28:26–27 . . . . 131, 554
28:28 . . . 96, 528, 554, 556
28:29 555
28:30 . . . . 79, 80, 113, 115, 333, 334, 553, 556, 557
28:30–31 . . 78, 79, 80, 109, 143, 201, 333, 528, 556, 566
28:31 . . . . . 79, 80, 94, 201, 248, 333, 334, 461, 557, 566
28:33 248

ROMANS

1:1 . . . . 120, 473
1:5 120
1:16 . . . . 372, 473
1:18–23 431
2:9 372
2:9–20 350
3:1–30 385
3:21–26 103
3:25 434
4:9–13 379
5:8–21 103
6:1–4 385
6:3–4. . . . . 120, 221
6:15–18 385
7:7, 13 385
8:9 276
8:9–11 . . . . 460, 602
8:31 473
8:31–39 385
8:34 204
9:2 473
9:4–5 350
9:14 385
10:9–13 473
11:1 . . . . 120, 343
12:11 473
12:13–21 245
13:14 400
14. . . . . 398, 409
14:14 306
14:16 401
14:17 306
14:19–20 401
14:20 306
15:2, 5–6. 401

15:15–31 120
15:19 120
15:23–28 529
15:23–29 . . . . 121, 471, 476, 589
15:23–33 477
15:25–28 486
15:25–31 121
15:26 231
15:30–32 473
16:1 . . . . 14, 259, 448, 613
16:1–2 121
16:3 . . . . 456, 622
16:3–5 456
16:3–6 13
16:5 473
16:6 14
16:7 . . . . . 14, 356, 357, 610
16:9 14
16:12 14
16:17–20 473
16:21 . . . . 11, 13
16:22 14
16:23 . . 11, 13, 14, 465, 482

1 CORINTHIANS

1:1 . . . . 11, 13, 120
1:8 231
1:10–17 113
1:12 . . . . . 13, 121, 457, 569
1:13–15 120
1:14 . . . . 11, 13, 121
1:16 14
1:23 421
2:1 121
2:1–5 441
3:4 457
3:4–6 13
3:5 457
3:6 457
3:22 . . . . 13, 457, 569
4:6 . . . . 13, 457
4:12 121
4:17 13
5:1–13 439
5:5 247
6:9–20 439
6:12 400
6:19–20 400
7:5 247
8–10. 398
8:9–13 401
9:1 . . . . 120, 293, 357
9:1–2 120
9:5 . . . . 13, 120
9:6 . . . . 13, 120, 121
9:17 120
9:20 473
9:22 523
10:13–14 400
10:14–22 400
10:16 . . . . 231, 234
10:16–17 232
10:23–24 401
10:25–26 306
10:27–29 401
10:30 400
10:31 401
10:32–33 401
11:1 401
11:2 . . . . 15, 25
11:19 . . . . 247, 279
11:23 . . . . 15, 25
11:23–26 232
12:13 311
12:29–30 . . . . 218, 236
15:3 15
15:3–8 25
15:3–11 293
15:5 . . . . 13, 120
15:6 120
15:7 . . . . 13, 120, 320, 324, 386
15:7–10 357
15:8–10 120
15:9 . . . . 120, 274, 287
15:12–28 501
15:18 120
15:33 . . . . 121, 432
16:1–3 120
16:1–9 486
16:2 471
16:5–6 537
16:5–9 121
16:6 537
16:8–9 . . . . 121, 464
16:10 13
16:12 . . . . 13, 457
16:15 14
16:17 14
16:19 . . . 13, 447, 456, 622

2 CORINTHIANS

1:1 . . . . 13, 120
1:8–2:13. 121
1:19 . . 11, 13, 121, 410, 441
2:4 473
2:12 411
2:12–13 471
2:13 14
4:2 473
4:7–5:10. 473
5:1 436
6:1 473
6:4–10 473
6:14 231
7:5–7 471
7:6–16 14
7:13 471
8:1–4 120
8:1–9:15. 486
8:4 231
8:6 14
8:16–24 14
8:18–19 10
8:23 . . . . 11, 356, 610
9:1–15 120
9:4 121
9:13 231
10–13. 473
11:5 120
11:7–9 121
11:9 . . . . 441, 450
11:22 . . . . 120, 447
11:24–26 473
11:25 366
11:25–26 537
11:28 . . . . 456, 482
11:32–33 . . . . 120, 290
12:7–10 7
12:11–12 120
12:12 236
12:14 438
12:18 14
12:21 439
13:1–10 438
13:14 231

GALATIANS

1. 381
1–2. 381
1:1 357
1:11–12 357
1:11–17 381
1:11–20 293
1:13 . . . . 120, 274, 287
1:13–14 . . . . 25, 587
1:13–16 292
1:15–16 473
1:15–17 120
1:15–18 289
1:17 . . . . 120, 160, 289
1:17–18 587
1:18 . . . . 13, 120
1:18–19 120
1:18–21 290
1:18–24 . . . . 318, 381
1:19 . . . . 13, 320, 324
1:21–23 120
1:23 . . . . 274, 287
2. . . . . 318, 381, 382
2:1 . . . . 11, 13
2:1–3 14
2:1–10 . . . . . 120, 316, 318, 381, 382, 383, 385, 402, 615

GALATIANS (*continued*)
2:2 384
2:7–8 120
2:7–11 13
2:9 . . . . 13, 120, 231, 320, 324
2:10 120
2:11 120
2:11–13 . . . . 380, 385
2:11–14 . . . . .314, 315, 569
2:11–16 161
2:12 . . . . 13, 120, 320, 324, 378, 380, 381
2:13 13
2:14 . . . . 13, 378
2:14–21 380
3:1–3 460
3:10–14 147
3:13–14 . . . . 103, 421
3:19 385
3:27 120
4:6 602
4:13–15 7
4:15 501
4:16 473
5:16–25 602
6:1–2 263
6:11 501

EPHESIANS
1:1 357
1:13–14 276
1:20–22 204
4:7–13 204
4:11–12 478
4:25 132
4:27 247
5:1–2 401
5:18 218
6:21 . . . . 11, 13

PHILIPPIANS
1:1 . . . . . . .11, 13, 259, 613
1:4–5 231
1:12–26 589
1:19–26 473
2:1–2 231
2:9–11 204
2:17 473
2:19–23 13
2:22 473
2:25 . . . . . .11, 14, 356, 610
3:1–14 293
3:2–6 473
3:4–6 292
3:5 . . . . 120, 343, 447, 587
3:6 . . . . 120, 274, 287, 587
3:8 473
3:10 231
3:18 473
4:2 14
4:3 . . . . 14, 471
4:14–16 . . . . 441, 450
4:15 . . . . 121, 473
4:15–16 422
4:16 121
4:18 . . . . 11, 14

COLOSSIANS
1:1 . . . . .11, 13, 357
1:7 . . . . 11, 14
2:8 25
2:12 221
3:1 204
3:17 401
4:7 . . . . 11, 13
4:9 14
4:10 . .11, 13, 120, 409, 618
4:10–14 . . . . .4, 10, 11, 36, 122, 610
4:11 . . . . 11, 14
4:12 . . . . 11, 14
4:12–14 11
4:14 . . . 5, 7, 10, 11, 14, 619
4:15 473
4:16 108
4:17 14

1 THESSALONIANS
1:1 . . . . . . .11, 13, 121, 410
1:6–7 121
1:9–10 434
2:1–2 . . 121, 422, 473, 627
2:2 121
2:10 473
2:13–16 121
2:13–3:10 450
2:14–16 473
2:18 423
3:1 . . . . 121, 441
3:1–3 121
3:6 . . . . 121, 441
5:18 . . . . 400, 552
5:27 108

2 THESSALONIANS
1:1 . . . . . . .11, 13, 121, 410
2:15 . . . . 15, 25
3:6 . . . . 15, 25

1 TIMOTHY
1:3–7 466
1:12–14 293
1:13 . . . . 274, 287
1:20 . . . . 247, 469
3:1–13 613
3:6–7 247
3:8–13 259
3:16 204
4:3–4 306
4:13 108
5:3–16 261
5:18 . . . . . . 112, 115, 595, 596, 605

2 TIMOTHY
1:1, 11 357
2:2 . . . . 25, 566
3:10–11 358
3:10–17 368
3:11 120
4:5 478
4:7 473
4:9–13 . . . . 4, 36
4:9–22 476
4:10 . . . . . . 11, 12, 14, 422
4:11 . . . . . 5, 10, 11, 13, 14, 409, 618, 619
4:12 . . . . 11, 13
4:13 411
4:14 469
4:19 . . . . 13, 456, 622
4:20 . . . . 11, 13
4:21 . . . . 14, 537

TITUS
1:4 14
1:5 535
1:10 378
1:12 . . . 121, 432, 436, 535
1:13–15 306
2:14 96
3:12 . . . . . . .11, 13, 14, 537
3:13 . . . . 13, 14, 457

PHILEMON
1 . . . . 11, 14
2 14
6 231
10 14
21 473
22 589
23 . . . . 11, 14
23–24 . . . . 4, 36
24 . . . 5, 10, 11, 13, 14, 122, 409, 610, 618, 619

HEBREWS
1:3 204
1:14 322
2:3–4 236
3:1 357
4:14 204
8:1–6 204
9:10 306

9:11–28 103
9:12 96
9:24 204
10:1–14 147
10:10–22 103
10:12 . . . . 204, 272
12:2 204
13:7 401
13:16 231

JAMES

1:1 . . . . 280, 320, 324, 386
1:1–2 388
1:27 . . . . 245, 261, 388
2:5 388
2:7 388
2:14–17 245
5:19–20 388

1 PETER

1:1 . . . . 280, 570
1:18 96
2:11–12 280
2:24 103
3:15 356
3:18 103
3:21–22 204
4:16 . . . .248, 315, 316, 612
5:2–4 482
5:12 . . . . 410, 570

2 PETER

1:15–16, 19 566
3:10–14 211
3:15–16 . . . . 595, 596, 605

1 JOHN

1:3 231
1:6–7 231
2:19 . . . . 247, 279
3:16–18 245
4:9–10 103

JUDE

1. . . . . 320, 324
3. 15
17. 584

REVELATION

1–3. 455
1:3 108
1:10 471
2:1–7 . . . . 466, 475
2:1–3:22. 475
2:13 592
2:18–29 414
21:14 208

Extrabiblical Sources Index

SEPTUAGINT, APOCRYPHA, AND PSEUDEPIGRAPHIC WORKS

1 Clement 5:5–7 589
1 Enoch 46–48 164
1 Maccabees 1:41–58 152
1 Maccabees 1:62 306
1 Maccabees 3:9 202
1 Maccabees 11:34 298
2 Maccabees 2:24–32 597
2 Maccabees 6:3–9 152
2 Maccabees 7:23 436
2 Maccabees 13:14 436
3 Maccabees 1:1ff. 597
3 Maccabees 3:3–6 308
4 Maccabees 4:11 488
4 Maccabees 5:25 436
4 Ezra 7:26–29; 12:31–34 164
Baruch 6 171
Esther 10:4–16:24 171
Joseph and Aseneth 7:1 308
Jubilees 7:23–31 397
Jubilees 22:16 308
Judith 12:1–2 308
Psalms of Solomon 1:4 202
Psalms of Solomon 8:15 202
Psalms of Solomon 17:32 164
Sirach 28:7 436
Sirach 48:10 201
Tobit 1:10–13 308
Tobit 5:1–16 322
Tobit 7:17 436
Wisdom 7:18 436
Wisdom 9:9 436
Wisdom 13:6 436
Wisdom 13:10–19 436

DEAD SEA SCROLLS AND RELATED TEXTS

1QM 7.13–14 260
1QS 1.11–13 . . . . 237, 238
1QS 6.16–22 238
1QS 6.16–23 237
1QS 9.10–11 164
4Q174 (4QFlor) 3:10–13 391

MISHNAH, TALMUD, AND RELATED LITERATURE

Babylonian Talmud, ʿAbodah Zarah 64b 397
Babylonian Talmud, Berakot 54a 351
Babylonian Talmud, Gittin 60b 175
Babylonian Talmud, Megillah 23b 166, 414
Babylonian Talmud, Megillah 26a.17–26b.1 260
Babylonian Talmud, Menahot 29b 175
Babylonian Talmud, Sanhedrin 56a:24 397
Babylonian Talmud, Sanhedrin 56b–57a 397
Babylonian Talmud, Sanhedrin 74a:12 397
Babylonian Talmud, Temurah 14b 175

MISHNAH, TALMUD, AND RELATED LITERATURE *(continued)*

Babylonian Talmud, Yebamot 6b 351
Babylonian Talmud, Yoma 9b 397
Jerusalem Talmud, Megillah 3:2.2 260
Jerusalem Talmud, Megillah 4:1 175
Jerusalem Talmud, Megillah 4:4 . . . . 166, 414
Mishnah, Avot 1:1–18 175
Mishnah, Middot 2:3 241
Mishnah, Nazir 1:1–9:5 . . . . 447, 489
Mishnah, Nazir 2:5–6 489
Mishnah, Nazir 6:3 487
Mishnah, 'Ohalot 2:3; 17:5 488
Mishnah, 'Ohalot 18:6–7 . . . . 351, 488
Mishnah, Pirkei Avot 2.2 440
Mishnah, Sanhedrin 6:1–4 273
Mishnah, Teharot 4:5 351

OTHER ANCIENT TEXTS

Abdias, *The Conflicts of the Holy Apostles* 2 588
Abdias, *The Conflicts of the Holy Apostles* 5–6 578
Abdias, *The Conflicts of the Holy Apostles* 6 . . 579, 582, 583
Abdias, *The Conflicts of the Holy Apostles* 7 580
Abdias, *The Conflicts of the Holy Apostles* 9 . . 571, 573, 574
Abdias, *The Conflicts of the Holy Apostles* 11 581
Abdias, *The Conflicts of the Holy Apostles* 12 587
Abdias, *The Conflicts of the Holy Apostles* 15 . . . . . . 576, 577
Achilles Tatius, *Leucippe and Clitophon* 3.3 541
Acts and Martyrdom of Bartholomew, the 578
Acts and Martyrdom of St. Matthew the Apostle, the . . 580
Acts of Andrew, the 573
Acts of Andrew and Matthias, the 587
Acts of Andrew and Matthias, the 2–3 586
Acts of Andrew and Matthias, the 19–21 573
Acts of John, the 40–42 570
Acts of Paul, the 588, 590
Acts of Peter, the 7 569
Acts of Peter, the 36–40 569
Acts of Peter, the 37 570
Acts of Philip, the 578
Acts of Philip, the 13–15 575
Acts of Simon and Jude, the 582, 583
Acts of Simon and Jude, the 21–22 . . . . 582, 585
Acts of Thaddaeus, the 584, 585
Acts of Thomas, the 576, 577
Aeschylus, *Agamemnon* 565–69, 1019–24, 1360–61 . . . 437
Aeschylus, *Agamemnon* 1623–24 515
Aeschylus, *Eumenides* 647–48 437
Ambrose, *Expositio evangelii secundum Lucan* 1.12 27
Antipater of Sidon, *Greek Anthology* 9.58 467
Apollonius Rhodius, *Argonautica* 4.1231–44 539
Appian, *Civil Wars* 3.54 504
Aratus, *Phaenomena* 436
Aratus, *Phaenomena* 1–7 433
Aristotle, *Generation of Animals* 2.2.736a.11–14 281
Aristotle, *Politics* 2.2.5 §1263a34–39 237
Athenaeus, *Deipnosophistae* (a.k.a. *Learned Banqueters*) 10.457f; 11.461b; 14.628c 544
Breviary of the Apostles 582, 583, 585, 586
Chrysostom, *Homiliae in Acta apostolorum* (a.k.a. *Commentary on Acts*) 54 547
Chrysostom, *Homiliae in Matthaeum* (a.k.a. *Commentary on Matthew*) 1.7 570
Cicero, *Brutus* (a.k.a. *De Claris oratoribus*) 287 65
Cicero, *De oratore* 2.15 §§62–64 60
Cicero, *In Pisonem* 36 §89 425
Cicero, *In Verrem* (a.k.a. *The Verrine Orations*) 1.8.21 213
Cicero, *In Verrem* (a.k.a. *The Verrine Orations*) 2.5.66 §§169–70 . . . . 419, 499
Cicero, *Letters to Friends* 16.9.4 §127 536
Clement of Alexandria, *Hypotyposes* 7 572
Clement of Alexandria, *Quis dives salvetur* 13 579
Clement of Alexandria, *Quis dives salvetur* 42 570
Clement of Alexandria, *Stromateis* (a.k.a. *Miscellanies*) 4.9 579
Code of Justinian 9.4.4 324
Damascus Document 7:13–21 391
Demosthenes, *De Corona* (a.k.a. *On the Crown*) 127 . . . 428
Didache 7.1–4 418
Dio Cassius, *Roman History* 1.1.2–3 60
Dio Cassius, *Roman History* 60.6.6 441
Dio Cassius, *Roman History* 60.17.5–7 500
Diodorus Siculus, *The Library of History* 3.8 281
Diodorus Siculus, *The Library of History* 30.15 . . . . . 59, 60
Diogenes Laertius, *Lives* 1.10 §110 432
Diogenes Laertius, *Lives* 7.1 §§1–160 429
Diogenes Laertius, *Lives* 7.1 §§156–57 437

Diogenes Laertius, *Lives* 10 437
Diogenes Laertius, *Lives* 10 §§1–21 429
Dionysius of Halicarnassus, *Antiquitates romanae* (a.k.a. *Roman Antiquities*)1.3.5; 1.5.3; 1.28.4; 2.24.2; 2.64.3; 4.79.3; 7.3.3; 7.13.4; 8.83.2 544
Dionysius of Halicarnassus, *De Lysia* 7 63
Dionysius of Halicarnassus, *De Thucydide* 8 . . . . 60, 65
Dionysius of Halicarnassus, Epistula ad Pompeium Germinum (a.k.a. *Letter to Gnaeus Pompeius*) 3.2 . . . 61
Dionysius of Halicarnassus, Epistula ad Pompeium Germinum (a.k.a. *Letter to Gnaeus Pompeius*) 3.4 . . . 62
Dionysius of Halicarnassus, Epistula ad Pompeium Germinum (a.k.a. *Letter to Gnaeus Pompeius*) 3.5 . . . 62
Dionysius of Halicarnassus, Epistula ad Pompeium Germinum (a.k.a. *Letter to Gnaeus Pompeius*) 3.8 . . . 65
Dionysius of Halicarnassus, Epistula ad Pompeium Germinum (a.k.a. *Letter to Gnaeus Pompeius*) 4.2 . . . . 61, 62
Dionysius of Halicarnassus, *Roman Antiquities* 1.1.2 . . . . 61, 62
Epimenides, *Cretica* 433, 436
Epiphanius of Salamis, *Panarion* 51.11.6–7. 10
Euripides, *Bacchae* 795 515
Euripides, *Helen* 1285–87 437
Eusebius, *Ecclesiastical History* 1.12.3. . . . . 585, 586
Eusebius, *Ecclesiastical History* 1.13.1–22. 585
Eusebius, *Ecclesiastical History* 2.1.2–5 581
Eusebius, *Ecclesiastical History* 2.9.3. 572
Eusebius, *Ecclesiastical History* 2.15.1–2. 570
Eusebius, *Ecclesiastical History* 2.22.1–8 589
Eusebius, *Ecclesiastical History* 2.22.6 9
Eusebius, *Ecclesiastical History* 2.23 320
Eusebius, *Ecclesiastical History* 2.23.1–25. 581
Eusebius, *Ecclesiastical History* 2.23.3–18 387
Eusebius, *Ecclesiastical History* 3.1.1 576
Eusebius, *Ecclesiastical History* 3.1.2. 569
Eusebius, *Ecclesiastical History* 3.3 567
Eusebius, *Ecclesiastical History* 3.4.1–11 24
Eusebius, *Ecclesiastical History* 3.4.6–7 24
Eusebius, *Ecclesiastical History* 3.4.7. 9
Eusebius, *Ecclesiastical History* 3.24.5–6, 13 579
Eusebius, *Ecclesiastical History* 3.24.15. 24
Eusebius, *Ecclesiastical History* 3.25.4–7 . . . . 567, 568, 587
Eusebius, *Ecclesiastical History* 3.31.2–5. 574
Eusebius, *Ecclesiastical History* 3.32.1–8 583
Eusebius, *Ecclesiastical History* 3.39.3. 574
Eusebius, *Ecclesiastical History* 3.39.15. 579
Eusebius, *Ecclesiastical History* 5.8.2 579
Eusebius, *Ecclesiastical History* 5.10.3. . . . . 578, 579
Eusebius, *Ecclesiastical History* 5.24.2 574
Eusebius, *Ecclesiastical History* 6.12 567
Eusebius, *Ecclesiastical History* 6.14.6. 575
Eusebius, *Ecclesiastical History* 6.14.6–7 570
Eusebius, *Ecclesiastical History* 6.25.4–7 579
Eusebius, *Ecclesiastical History* 6.25.5. 570
Herodas, *Mimes* 1.41–46. 437
Herodotus, *Histories* (a.k.a. *The Persian Wars*) 1.1 60
Herodotus, *Histories* (a.k.a. *The Persian Wars*) 2.5. 540
Herodotus, *Histories* (a.k.a. *The Persian Wars*) 3.62. . . . 437
Herodotus, *Histories* (a.k.a. *The Persian Wars*) 3.91; 4.39; 7.89. 145
Herodotus, *Histories* (a.k.a. *The Persian Wars*) 3.101 . . . 281
Herodotus, *Histories* (a.k.a. *The Persian Wars*) 3.114–15. 282
Hippolytus, *On the Seventy Apostles* 15 10
Hippolytus, *On the Twelve Apostles* 1. 569
Hippolytus, *On the Twelve Apostles* 2. . . . . 573, 574
Hippolytus, *On the Twelve Apostles* 3. 571
Hippolytus, *On the Twelve Apostles* 5. . . . . 574, 575
Hippolytus, *On the Twelve Apostles* 6. 578
Hippolytus, *On the Twelve Apostles* 7. 580
Hippolytus, *On the Twelve Apostles* 8. . . . . 576, 577
Hippolytus, *On the Twelve Apostles* 9. 582
Hippolytus, *On the Twelve Apostles* 10. 584
Hippolytus, *On the Twelve Apostles* 11 . . . . 582, 583
Hippolytus, *On the Twelve Apostles* 12. 586
Hippolytus, *On the Twelve Apostles* 13. 588
Hippolytus, *Refutation of All Heresies* 1.2.16 . . . . . 237, 238
Homer, *Illiad* 24.549–51, 24.754–56 437
Homer, *Odyssey* 1.23 282
Iamblichus, *The Life of Pythagorus* §§30, 90 . . . . . 237, 239
Irenaeus, *Adversus haereses* 1.23.1–2. 278
Irenaeus, *Adversus haereses* 2.30.9 595
Irenaeus, *Adversus haereses* 3.1.. . . . . 1, 116, 570, 579
Irenaeus, *Adversus haereses* 3.3.3 9
Irenaeus, *Adversus haereses* 3.13.3. 34
Irenaeus, *Adversus haereses* 3.14.1. 9
Irenaeus, *Adversus haereses* 4.16.2; 5.28.3. 595

OTHER ANCIENT TEXTS (*continued*)

Jacobus de Voragine, *The Golden Legend* 3:54 586
Jacobus de Voragine, *The Golden Legend* 3:59–60 587
Jacobus de Voragine, *The Golden Legend* 3:156–57 574
Jacobus de Voragine, *The Golden Legend* 3:158–59 581
Jacobus de Voragine, *The Golden Legend* 5:37 578
Jacobus de Voragine, *The Golden Legend* 6:75 583
Jacobus de Voragine, *The Golden Legend* 6:80 585
Jacobus de Voragine, *The Golden Legend* 6:80–81 583
Jerome, *De viris illustribus* 1 567
Jerome, *De viris illustribus* 2 581
Jerome, *De viris illustribus* 3 . . . . 579, 580
Jerome, *De viris illustribus* 5 588
Jerome, *De viris illustribus* 7 9
Jerome, *De viris illustribus* 36 579
Jerome, *Epistulae* 53.9 9
Jerome, *On the Perpetual Virginity of the Blessed Mary* 15 . . . . 581, 582
Josephus, *Against Apion* 1.1 §1 . . . . 28, 196
Josephus, *Against Apion* 1.22 §§201–2 544
Josephus, *Against Apion* 2.1 §1 28
Josephus, *Against Apion* 2.1 §§1–2 196
Josephus, *Against Apion* 2.4 §39 10
Josephus, *Against Apion* 2.14 §148 544
Josephus, *Against Apion* 2.17 §175 393
Josephus, *Against Apion* 2.39 §282 544
Josephus, *Against Apion* 2.41 §296 29
Josephus, *Jewish Antiquities* 1.1–2 §§1–9 597
Josephus, *Jewish Antiquities* 1.3.9 §107 544
Josephus, *Jewish Antiquities* 1.22.1 §346 27
Josephus, *Jewish Antiquities* 4.2.1 §12 544
Josephus, *Jewish Antiquities* 4.8.14 §214 260
Josephus, *Jewish Antiquities* 4.8.38 §287 260
Josephus, *Jewish Antiquities* 6.13.2 §280 27
Josephus, *Jewish Antiquities* 8.3.9 §§95–98 250
Josephus, *Jewish Antiquities* 8.11.3 §284 544
Josephus, *Jewish Antiquities* 10.11.7 §264 27
Josephus, *Jewish Antiquities* 11.7.1 §300 544
Josephus, *Jewish Antiquities* 11.7.1–7 §§297–347 148
Josephus, *Jewish Antiquities* 12.3.1 §§119–24 10
Josephus, *Jewish Antiquities* 14.15.11 §455 27
Josephus, *Jewish Antiquities* 15.5.3 §136 544
Josephus, *Jewish Antiquities* 16.2.3 §§43–45 393
Josephus, *Jewish Antiquities* 16.6.8 §177 544
Josephus, *Jewish Antiquities* 17.10.4–5 §§269–72 253
Josephus, *Jewish Antiquities* 17.12.1 §328 550
Josephus, *Jewish Antiquities* 18.1.5 §§18–22 237
Josephus, *Jewish Antiquities* 18.1.5 §20 544
Josephus, *Jewish Antiquities* 18.1.5 §§20–22 238
Josephus, *Jewish Antiquities* 18.4.2 §89 273
Josephus, *Jewish Antiquities* 18.5.3 §123 29
Josephus, *Jewish Antiquities* 18.6.3 §160 550
Josephus, *Jewish Antiquities* 19.2.5 §205 550
Josephus, *Jewish Antiquities* 19.5.2–3 §§280–91 440
Josephus, *Jewish Antiquities* 19.6.1 §294 489
Josephus, *Jewish Antiquities* 19.6.2 §297 29
Josephus, Jewish Antiquities 19.8.2 §§343–51 326
Josephus, *Jewish Antiquities* 19.8.2 §346 325
Josephus, *Jewish Antiquities* 19.8.2 §§346–48 325
Josephus, *Jewish Antiquities* 19.8.6 §183 27
Josephus, *Jewish Antiquities* 20.2.5 §§49–53 317
Josephus, *Jewish Antiquities* 20.5.1 §§97–99 . . . . . 253, 254
Josephus, *Jewish Antiquities* 20.7.1–2 §§137–44 505
Josephus, *Jewish Antiquities* 20.8.5 §§160–63 505
Josephus, *Jewish Antiquities* 20.8.9–11 §§182–96 510
Josephus, *Jewish Antiquities* 20.8.11 §§189–96 512
Josephus, *Jewish Antiquities* 20.9.1 §200 . . . . 590, 591
Josephus, *Jewish Antiquities* 20.9.2 §§204–7 502
Josephus, *Jewish Antiquities* 20.12.1 §§261–63 60
Josephus, *Jewish War* 1.1–4 §§1–12 597
Josephus, *Jewish War* 1.17.4 §331 27
Josephus, *Jewish War* 2.7.1 §§104–5 550
Josephus, *Jewish War* 2.8.1 §118 253
Josephus, *Jewish War* 2.8.2–4 §§119–27 237
Josephus, *Jewish War* 2.8.3 §§122–23 238
Josephus, *Jewish War* 2.13.3 §§254–57 492
Josephus, *Jewish War* 2.13.5 §§261–63 492
Josephus, *Jewish War* 2.14.1 §§271–75 510
Josephus, *Jewish War* 2.14.4–5 §571 260
Josephus, *Jewish War* 2.15.1 §§309–12 514
Josephus, *Jewish War* 2.15.1 §§313–14 . . . . . . 447, 487, 489
Josephus, *Jewish War* 2.20.2 §§559–61 287
Josephus, *Jewish War* 2.20.5 §§285–91 150
Josephus, *Jewish War* 3.2.4 §29 . . . . 9, 313
Josephus, *Jewish War* 3.3.5 §§54–58 298
Josephus, *Jewish War* 5.1.3 §17 544
Josephus, *Jewish War* 5.5.1–2 §§184–93 250
Josephus, *Jewish War* 5.5.2 §§193–94 491

Josephus, *Jewish War* 5.5.3 §§201–6 241
Josephus, *Jewish War* 5.9.4 §382 27
Josephus, *Jewish War* 6.2.4 §§124–28 . . . . 273, 491
Josephus, *Jewish War* 6.3.3 §200 544
Josephus, *Jewish War* 7.3.3 §§43–44 150
Josephus, *Jewish War* 7.6.7 §368 287
Josephus, *Life* 3 §15 543
Justin Martyr, *First Apology* 14.4 398
Justin Martyr, *First Apology* 26 278
Livy, *History of Rome* 1.Preface 60
Livy, *History of Rome* 10.9.4 . . . . 419, 499
Lucian of Samosata, *Anacharsis* 19 433
Lucian of Samosata, *De saltatione* (a.k.a. *The Dance*) 64–67 544
Lucian of Samosata, *Demonax* 34 544
Lucian of Samosata, *The Eunuch* 3 428
Lucian of Samosata, *Hermotimus* (a.k.a. *Concerning Sects*) 31 281
Lucian of Samosata, *Hermotimus* (a.k.a. *Concerning Sects*) 39 213
Lucian of Samosata, *How to Write History* 50–51 63
Lucian of Samosata, *How to Write History* 53 61
Lucian of Samosata, *How to Write History* 55 62
Lucian of Samosata, *How to Write History* 56 62
Lucian of Samosata, *How to Write History* 58 . . . 61, 63, 65
Lucian of Samosata, *The Ship, or the Wishes* 5–6 535
Lucretius, *De Rerum Natura* 3.526–47, 624–33, 830–31, 842–62 437
Macrobius, *Saturnalia* 2.4.11 159
Marcian, *The Digest of Justinian* 48.17.1 504
Marcian, *The Digest of Justinian* 49.6.1 514
Moses of Chorene, *History of Armenia* 578, 582
Moses of Chorene, *History of Armenia* 9 583
Origen, *Homilies on Luke, Fragments on Luke* FC 94 27
Ovid, *Metamorphoses* 8.611–724 361
Papias, *Exposition of the Sayings of the Lord*, fragment 10 581
Pausanias, *Description of Greece* 1.1.4 432
Philo, *Allegorical Interpretation* 1.24 §76 27
Philo, *Allegorical Interpretation* 2.23 §90 27
Philo, *Hypothetica* 11.1–18 237
Philo, *Hypothetica* 11.4–5 238
Philo, *On the Decalogue* 11§46 218
Philo, *On the Life of Abraham* 5 §27 27
Philo, *On the Life of Abraham* 19 §89 27
Philo, *On the Life of Joseph* 28 §167 27
Philo, *On the Life of Joseph* 33 §200 27
Philo, *On the Life of Moses* 2.1.1 27
Philo, *On the Life of Moses* 2.13 §67 27
Philo, *On the Migration of Abraham* 20 §114 27
Philo, *On the Special Laws* 2.1.1 28
Philo, *On the Special Laws* 2.62–64 393
Philostratus, *Vita Apollonii* (a.k.a. *The Life of Apollonius of Tyana*) 5.20.3 428
Philostratus, *Vita Apollonii* (a.k.a. *The Life of Apollonius of Tyana*) 6.3.5 432
Pindar, *Pythian Odes* 2.93–96 515
Plato, *Apology* 24b–c 430
Pliny the Elder, *Natural History* 2.5 §27 437
Pliny the Elder, *Natural History* 2.47 §122 548
Pliny the Elder, *Natural History* 7.55 §190 437
Pliny the Younger, *Letters* 10.96–97 520
Plutarch, *Busybody* 2 428
Plutarch, *Moralia* 516C 428
Plutarch, *Galba* 2.3 60
Plutarch, *Theseus* 1.1 60
Polybius, *The Histories* 1.14.4–8 60
Polybius, *The Histories* 2.56.10–12 65
Polybius, *The Histories* 12.25.A–B 65
Polybius, *The Histories* 36.1.6–7 65
Pseudo-Aristotle, *Problems* 10.66 281
Pseudo-Dorotheus, *List of the Apostles and Disciples* 581
Pseudo-Dorotheus, *List of the Apostles and Disciples* 9 . . 585
Pseudo-Dorotheus, *List of the Apostles and Disciples* 10 582
Pseudo-Dorotheus, *List of the Apostles and Disciples* 11 . . . . 586, 587
Pseudo-Dorotheus, *List of the Apostles and Disciples* 12 583
Ptolemy, *Geography* 3.4.1 540
Ptolemy, *Geography* 3.14.1 540
Ptolemy, *Geography* 3.15.1 540
Ptolemy, *Tetrabiblos* 2.2 281
Quintilian, *Declamationes* 250 213
Seneca, *Epistles* 77.1–2 551
Seneca, *Natural Questions* 4A.2.18 281
Socrates, *Ecclesiastical History* 1.19 580
Sophocles, *Electra* 137–43 437

OTHER ANCIENT TEXTS (*continued*)

Statyllius Flaccus, *Greek Anthology* 7.290 546
Strabo, *Geography* 1.2.27–28 282
Strabo, *Geography* 8.6.20 439
Suetonius, *Divus Augustus* 28.3 552
Suetonius, *Divus Claudius* 18 317
Suetonius, *Divus Claudius* 25 441
Suetonius, *Divus Claudius* 25.3 499
Suetonius, *Divus Claudius* 28 505
Suetonius, *Divus Titus* 7 514
Suetonius, *Nero* 16.2 520
Tacitus, *Annals* 2.55 29
Tacitus, *Annals* 3.21 213
Tacitus, *Annals* 14.50 500
Tacitus, *Annals* 15.44 520
Tacitus, *Histories* 2.2 514
Tacitus, *Histories* 2.41 213
Tacitus, *Histories* 5.9 505
Teaching of the Apostles 9 584
Thucydides, *History of the Peloponnesian War* 1.3.3; 1.5.1 544
Thucydides, *History of the Peloponnesian War* 1.21–22 60
Thucydides, *History of the Peloponnesian War* 1.22.1 65
Thucydides, *History of the Peloponnesian War* 1.61.4 . . . 425
Thucydides, *History of the Peloponnesian War* 1.82.1; 6.33.5 544
Ulpian, *Digest* 48.6.7 . . . . 419, 499
Vegetius, *Epitoma rei militaris* 4.39 536
Xenophon, *Memorabilia* 1.1.1 430

Subject Index

Aaron, 166
Abraham, 145–46, 163, 270
Achan, 249, 249n. 38
acts, apocryphal, 567–69, 568n. 4
Acts of the Apostles
apologetic intent of, 54–56, 58
author of, xxii, 5, 26, 112
behavior patterns in, 135–38
as biographical historical monograph, 48–49, 50
as biography, 46, 46n. 20, 50, 53, 58
central aim of, 34
characters of, 32–34
chiasms in, 81, 86, 283, 285, 318, 320, 547
commonalities of with letters of Paul, 12, 120–21
as confirmation, 57–58, 91
as continuation of the story of Jesus, xxi, 54, 194–98, 207, 595–96, 599
coordination of with Paul's letter to the Galatians, 380–83
date of writing of, 110–15, 593
dating of events in, 109–10, 593
as defense document, 45, 50, 54
as demonstration, 45–46, 50
doctrinal intent of, 53, 58
embedded letters in, 81, 87
ending of, 556–57
as entertainment, 52, 58
evangelistic intent of, 56–57, 58
as fiction, 44, 50
foreshadowing in. *See* foreshadowing, in Acts
genre of, 43–51
hermeneutics of, 132–38
historical accuracy of, 59n. 73, 67–69
historical-political setting of, 143–62
as history, 46–48, 50, 53–54, 58, 59–60, 195
hospitality notes in, 81, 88–89, 122–23
inclusios in, 14, 15, 554
intended readers of, 29–31
as intended to be read aloud, 108n. 1
irony in, 318–19, 322–24, 325
litotes in, 324n. 24, 379, 380n. 9
male-female parallels in, 82–83
as mediation, 52, 58
messages of, 598–603
original language of, 6, 108, 151–52
outlines for, 74–80
as paradigmatic model, 52–53, 58
parallelisms in, 81, 82–85, 203
place of in New Testament canon, 597–98
poetic citations in, 119, 121, 432, 433
point of overlap of with the Gospel of Luke, 194, 195
as polygeneris, 49–50
prologues in, 81, 110, 195–98
purposes of, 51–59
recipients of, 26–32
relationship of to the gospel of Luke, 41–43, 45, 110, 194–98, 207, 597
religious setting of, 163–78
repetition in, 81, 89–90, 300, 301
rhetoric in, 81, 89
sailing description in, 530
as Scripture, 593–98
similarities of with the Gospel of Luke, 310
sociocultural setting of, 178–85
sources for, 116–23
space allocation in, 81, 90, 96, 100
speeches in. *See* speeches
storytelling techniques in, 80–90
summary statements in. *See* summary statements
telescoping in, 199
themes of. *See* themes, in Acts
title of as added later, 5, 23, 24, 34, 44
travel narratives in, 81, 82
use of Scripture in, 81, 86, 93, 129–30
versions of, 123–29, 593
visions in. *See* visions
"we sections" in. *See* "we sections"
witness theme of, 14, 57, 98

Adramyttium, 531, 532
Adriatic Sea, the, 540, 540n. 29
Aeneas, healing of, 197
Agabus, 316, 318, 479, 488
Alexander the Great, 151–52
Alexandria, Egypt, 456, 458
Alexandrian text, the, 126–29
already/not yet kingdom, the, 102, 202
alters to unknown gods, 432
Amphilochus, 594
Amphipolis, 420
Ananias, 160, 246–48, 246n. 33, 249n. 38, 251, 267, 458n.1
Ananias (high priest), 500–501, 502, 504
Ananias of Damascus, 289
Andrew, brother of Simon Peter, 572–74, 587, 591
Andronicus, 356, 357n. 16, 591
angels
  appearance of in visions, 255, 302, 528, 539–40, 583
  Gabriel, 82, 201
  at Herod's death, 319, 325
  rescuing Peter from prison, 125, 307, 319, 322, 325
  taking up Philip after his death, 576
Anti-Marcionite Prologues, the, 9, 22, 23
Antioch of Syria
  expansion of Christian church to, 313–18
  fellowship of Christian community in, 314, 316
  geographical and historical details of, 9, 313, 314
  Jewish community in, 10, 314, 316
  Luke as possible resident of, 9–10
  ministry of Barnabas in, 315, 332, 355
  ministry of Paul in, 315–16, 332
  Peter visit to, 315n. 15
Antiochus IV (Antiochus Epiphanes), 152
Antipas, 591
Antipater II, 159
Antipatris, 504
Apocrypha, the, 170–71, 174
Apollonia, 420, 421
Apollos, 13, 456–57, 458
apostles, the
  arrest and miraculous release of, 251, 252
  calling of by Jesus, 208, 212
  as characters in Acts, 32–33
  choice of Matthias as twelfth, 32, 198
  commissioning of, 195, 202–4, 207
  and commissioning of ministers to the Christian community, 257, 259
  compulsion of to witness, 228, 243, 252, 586
  flogging of, 251, 254
  hearing of before the Sanhedrin, 160, 251–55
  importance of twelve as number of, 207–8, 230
  and the Jerusalem Council, 383–84
  members of, 208
  Peter as spokesman of, 32, 569
  prayer of, 234
  replacement of Judas as member of, 208–9
  response of to persecution, 244, 255, 256
  serving the Word, 15, 257
  signs and wonders by, 236–37, 240, 250, 267, 297–99, 354, 359–60, 462
  teaching of, 229, 230
  use of term, 356–57
  as witnesses, 14–15, 199, 202–4, 207, 212
apostolic decree, the
  applicability of to all gentile believers everywhere, 395
  applying, 398–99, 401
  bearers of, 394
  content of, 392, 394–97
  as method of promoting church unity, 394, 397, 398
  and the Noahic commandments, 397
  reiteration of, 487
apostolicity, 12
Aquila
  as companion of Luke and Paul, 13, 446
  death of, 591
  in Ephesus, 447, 455–57
  first meeting with Paul, 440, 456
  ministry of, 456–57, 458n. 1, 591
  move of to Corinth, 440, 441, 456
Aramaic, 150
Archelaus, 158, 159, 160
Areopagus
  etiquette of, 433
  location of, 435
  Paul's address to, 430–37
Aristarchus, 11, 12, 13, 468, 531, 535, 591
Artemis
  as Greek goddess of fertility, chastity, wilderness, and hunting, 177, 468
  statues of, 468
  temple of, 458, 459, 467, 570–71
ascension, of Jesus
  accounts of in Scripture, 204, 206
  dating of, 110, 160, 199
  location of, 208
  significances of, 93, 102, 205
  storyline function of, 207
  as true historical event, 205–6
Asiarchs, 469, 469n. 11
Assyrian empire, 148, 149
Athanasius, 594
Athens
  cultural influence of, 426, 428
  debates of Paul with Epicureans and Stoics in, 427–29

geographical and historical details of, 425, 426, 427
idolatry in, 427, 428
Paul missionary visit to, 408, 425, 427–37, 448
Attalia, 369
autographs, 125

Babylonian empire, 148, 149, 150, 151
Babylonian Talmud, the, 174
baptism
as expression of faith, 416, 419
lack of necessity of for salvation, 221, 416
prerequisites for, 416
process for, 418
water, 415, 416
with the Holy Spirit, 311, 313
Bar Kokhba Revolt, the, 155
barbarians, 544
Barnabas
as apostle, 120, 356, 357, 372
appointing elders in the new churches, 369
bold response of to opposition, 349, 353
as champion of church unity, 35, 408
as companion of Luke and Paul, 13, 78, 86, 120, 181, 296, 315, 318
death of, 591
disagreement of with Paul, 35, 408–9
filled with the Spirit, 315
follow-up ministry of, 409
and inclusion of gentiles in Christian community, 378–79
and John Mark, 120, 191, 296, 327
as mediator between Paul and the apostles, 266, 290
ministry of after Acts, 591
ministry of in Antioch, 78, 86, 181, 315, 332, 355
ministry of in Cyprus, 339–43, 355, 409, 591
ministry of in Derbe, 355, 357, 366, 367
ministry of in Iconium, 352–53, 355–56, 367, 369
ministry of in Lystra, 357–60, 362, 364, 365–66, 367, 369
ministry of in Perga, 355, 369
ministry of in Pisidian Antioch, 345–51, 365, 367, 369
persecution of, 350, 356
as positive example of radical generosity, 246
signs and wonders by, 236, 386
as son of encouragement, 290
Barsabbas. *See* Joseph called Barsabbas (Justus)
Bartholomew, 574, 575, 578–79, 578n. 21, 591
Beautiful Gate, the, 111, 240, 241
behaviors, disputable, guidelines for assessing, 400, 401
benefaction, 184
Berea, 424, 425
Bernice, 158, 159, 511, 514, 514n. 64
blasphemy, 267, 269
Bodmer Papyrus XIV–XV, the, 23, 24
breaking bread, 229, 232, 234

Caesar Augustus, 155, 156, 422
Caesarea Maritima, 299, 300, 478–79
Caligula, 314
canon, New Testament
Acts as part of, 593–98
criteria for inclusion in, 594–55, 594n. 57
date of closing of, 594, 595
capital punishment, among Jews, 491
casting lots, 213
Cauda, 538
Cenchreae, 121, 406, 438, 446, 448, 454, 471
centurions, in Luke-Acts, 302
Cephas. *See* Peter
chiasms, in Acts, 81, 86, 283, 285, 318, 320, 547
Christian, use of term, 314, 315–16, 315n. 17, 519, 520
Christian community
accountability in, 251
all are invited to enter into, 97, 203, 283, 308–9, 313
appeal of to multiple levels of society, 183
appointment of additional ministers within, 258–59
breaking of bread of, 229, 232, 234, 415
as brothers and sisters, 179, 248, 551, 551n. 64
as Christians, 314, 315–16, 315n. 17
as the church, 248, 249
communal living within, 237, 238
conflict between Hebraic and Hellenistic Jews within, 257–61
as disciples, 97, 111, 248, 351, 366, 367, 460
external challenges to life of, 240–44, 251–55
fellowship in, 229, 230–31, 244, 477
filled with the Holy Spirit, 351
gentile membership in, 97, 131, 185, 203, 296, 301, 306, 350, 392
as God's true people, 91, 97, 249
growth of, 243, 249, 256, 261, 266–67, 291, 327, 410
as held in high esteem, 249
ideal characteristics of, 232, 233, 316, 327–28, 477
increased ministry leadership as solution to disruptions within, 261
internal challenges to life of, 245–51, 256–61
joy of, 351
meeting of in the temple, 229, 231

Christian community (*continued*)
mission of, 98–99
names used for, 248, 249
lack of necessity of following Jewish law for membership in, 97, 131, 313, 377–81, 383, 392, 396, 410
as nonpolitical, 54
number of, 208, 222, 243
opposition to and persecution of in Acts, 100–101, 243, 254, 320–27
prayer in, 209, 212, 214, 229, 233–34, 244, 321–22
precedent for selection of seven ministers to, 260
priests as converts to, 261
principles of good leadership in, 474–75
requirements for gentile membership in, 379, 392–97
responses of to opposition, 101, 244, 255, 256
sharing of resources in, 229, 231, 237, 239, 244, 415, 477, 547
table fellowship practices in, 185
to the ends of the earth, 202
unity of, 52, 58, 239, 245, 394, 397, 398, 487
as the Way, 466, 466n. 8, 507, 508, 509
as witnesses to Jesus, 91, 98–99, 104, 195, 202–4, 601, 603
women as members of, 208
as the word of God, 98, 261, 261n. 51
church, the. *See* Christian community
church councils, 376
church fathers, 24
Cicero, 340
circumcision
lack of necessity of for salvation among Gentiles, 379, 383, 410
as a symbol of faith, 379
as tenet of Judaism, 164, 378
of Timothy, 410
Claudius, Emperor, 317, 440, 440n. 62, 441, 445, 456
Claudius Lysias, 87, 117, 503,519
Cleopas, 223
client kings, 157
Cnidus, 534
Code of Justinian, the, 324, 325
codex, 23, 126
Codex Alexandrinus, 126, 593
Codex Bezae, 125, 126, 127, 593
Codex Sinaiticus, 124, 126, 593
Codex Vaticanus, 124, 126, 593
collectivism, 178–79
Communion, 232
conversion
as aim of evangelism, 275
baptism in, 221
irony in situations of, 312
of Jews (mass), 32
of Cornelius, 85, 90, 300–303, 305–11, 332, 415
of Crispus, 444
of Paul, 90, 110, 160, 286–89, 494–97, 516–18, 587
of the Roman Jailer, 417–19
of Sergius Paulus, 341
reception of Holy Spirit at, 276, 311
versus calling, 286
Corinth
archaeological evidence of Jews in, 442
geographical and historical details of, 437–38
Paul's missionary visit to, 407, 437–42, 444–46, 448, 454, 471
ruins of, 443
sexual immorality of, 438, 439
Cornelius
conversion of, 90, 300–303, 305–11, 332, 415
as God-fearer, 302, 415
intervention of God in conversion of, 303, 308–9
similarities of Peter's message at conversion of with Gospel of Luke, 310
vision of, 300, 301, 302, 303, 307, 308, 312
Council of Carthage, 594
Council of Chalcedon, 593
Council of Hippo, 594
Crescens, 4, 11, 14
Crete, 534, 535
Crispus, 13, 444
Cyprus
Barnabas and Saul ministry in, 336, 339–43, 355
geographical and historical details of, 339, 340
significance of in Acts, 340
Cyrus the Great, 150

Damascus, 286, 287, 355
David, 148, 211,219, 221, 270, 348
day of the Lord, the, 211
deacons, 259
Dead Sea Scrolls, the, 173, 174
death, of Jesus
as atonement, 103–4
dating of, 109, 110, 160, 162
as fulfillment of Scripture, 92, 96
necessity of, 96, 103, 348–49, 421, 423
salvation through, 95, 101, 103–4
defense document, 45
deference, principle of, 398–99, 401
Delphi inscription, the, 445
Demas, 11, 12
Demetrius, 466, 469
demons, 176
Derbe
geographical and historical details of, 357, 366
ministry of Barnabas and Paul in, 355, 357, 366, 367, 456
Diadochi, Wars of the, 152
didactic material, 132
Didymus. *See* Thomas the apostle
Dionysius Exiguus, 109
Dioscuri, the, 548

disagreements, types of, 409
disciples, 97, 111, 248, 351, 366, 367
divine discipline, 247
divine initiative, 301, 308–9, 313, 314, 337, 339
documentary history, 59, 60, 64
Domitian, 111
Dorcas. *See* Tabitha
Drusilla, 158, 159, 505, 509
dust-shaking gesture, 351, 442

Elijah, 31, 471
Elisha, 31, 471
Elymas the sorcerer, 341–42, 343, 354
embedded letters, in Acts, 81, 87
ends of the earth, to the, 202–4, 222, 282, 332, 350
Epaphras, 11
Epaphroditus, 11, 196, 356
"Ephesian Letters," the, 463, 464
Ephesus
- geographical and historical details of, 459
- great theater at, 470
- influence of on early church, 466
- Jesus's note to the church at, 475
- ministry of Paul in, 407–8, 446–47, 455, 460–62, 464, 466–69, 480
- occult practices in, 462–64
- Paul's address to elders of at Miletus, 472–76, 480
- riot in theater at, 466–69
- ruins of, 460, 461
- signs and wonders in, 462
- temple of Artemis at, 467

Epictetus, 178
Epicureanism, 428, 429
Erastus, 13, 465
eschatology, 101–2
Essenes, the, 168, 170, 237, 238
Ethiopia, 279, 282
Ethiopian eunuch
- cultural background of, 279–82
- encounter with Philip of, 279–80, 283–84, 300, 332, 355
- skin color of, 280, 281–84

Eusebius of Caesarea, 24, 25
Eutychus, 411, 471–72
evangelism, as requiring a response, 275
evangelist, office of, 478
explicative history, 59, 60, 64
Ezra, 7, 150, 151

Fair Havens, 534, 537, 538
faith
- circumcision as a symbol of, 379
- forgiveness as result of, 91, 94–95, 220, 349, 364, 600, 603
- in Jesus as proper continuation of Old Testament faith, 90, 130, 131, 146, 176, 242, 271, 556
- miracles credited to, 128, 277, 359, 360
- as necessary for salvation, 91, 95, 103, 243, 367, 401
- purpose and results of, 95
- suffering as part of, 90
- as turning toward God, 95, 220

family, extended, importance of, 179
Felix
- address of, 27
- defeat of Egyptian rebel, 506
- hearing of Paul before, 159, 162, 504, 506–9, 519
- and Herodian dynasty, 158
- letter of Claudius Lysias to, 503
- as procurator of Judea, 157, 159, 486, 505

Festival of Tabernacles/Booths, the (Sukkoth), 216
Festival of Unleavened Bread, the (Passover), 216, 318, 322
Festival of Weeks, the (Pentecost), 215, 216
Festus
- address of, 27
- hearing of Paul before, 110, 157, 162, 509–12, 519
- and hearing of Paul before Herod Agrippa II, 514–15, 518, 521
- letter to Caesar of, 87
- as procurator of Judea, 157, 486, 510
- speech of, 88, 514–15

Field of Blood, the, 210, 585
fire, as sign of Holy Spirit, 216
first missionary journey, of Paul
- itinerary of, 336
- map of, 338
- ministry of in Cyprus, 339–43, 355
- ministry of in Derbe, 355, 357, 366, 367, 410, 456
- ministry of in Iconium, 352–53, 355–56, 367, 369, 410, 456
- ministry of in Lystra, 357–60, 362, 364, 365–66, 367, 369, 410, 456
- ministry of in Perga, 355, 369
- ministry of in Pisidian Antioch, 345–51, 355, 365, 367, 369, 456
- mixed results of, 349, 352, 355–56, 365

flagrum, 498
flogging, 254, 255, 498
follow-up ministry, 367, 369, 407, 408
food laws, Old Testament, 305–6
foreshadowing, in Acts
- characters, 246, 259, 267, 274, 327, 338, 340, 346, 410
- narrative, 332, 540
- places, 259, 338, 447, 456
- technique of, 81, 87

Fortress Antonia, the, 408
frapping, 538
friend of God, 26–27

Gaius, 12, 13, 366, 468
Gaius Plinius Caecilius Secundus. *See* Pliny the Younger
Gaius Suetonius Tranquillus. *See* Suetonius

Galatians, the, Paul's letter to
  coordination of with Acts 15, 380–82, 385n. 18
  timing of writing of, 161, 381, 398
Gallio, 156, 444, 445, 446, 448
Gamaliel, 85, 88, 253, 254, 325
Gemara, the, 174, 175
genre
  and expectations, 39–40
  fluidity of, 48, 49
  and intended message, 40
  of Acts, 43–51
genealogies, in Luke-Acts, 81, 82
gentiles
  coming of the Holy Spirit on, 300, 301, 306, 310–11, 312–13
  ends of the earth as synonym for, 203
  God as driver of inclusion of in People of God, 301, 308–9, 337, 339, 380, 385–87, 392, 397
  gospel message as inclusive of, 30, 31
  inclusion of in Christian community, 97, 131, 185, 203, 296, 301, 306, 350, 392
  Jewish concern over association with, 307–8, 312
  lack of necessity of following Jewish law to be saved, 97, 131, 313, 377–81, 383, 392, 396, 410
  Luke's interest in, 9, 30–31
  Old Testament prophecies on the inclusion of in the People of God, 389
  requirements for membership of in Christian community, 379, 392–97
glossolalia. *See* tongues, speaking in
gnashing of teeth, 271–72
Gnosticism, 278, 279
God
  active in the world, 91–92, 104, 599, 603
  already/not yet kingdom of, 102, 201–2
  control of human history of, 102, 271, 348
  covenant of with Abraham, 145–46, 163
  discipline by, 247
  as driver of inclusion of gentiles in people of, 301, 308–9, 337, 339, 380, 385–87, 392, 397
  obedience to, 179, 270, 271
  presence of with the people not limited to one location, 270, 271
  as sovereign, 33, 91–92, 244, 599
  sovereign plan of, 57, 130, 348
  true people of, 600–601
  use of non-apostles in effective ministry, 266, 267, 275, 285–86, 289, 291, 372
  use of testimonies about his work to draw others to Him, 299
God-fearers, 11, 302, 303, 348, 350, 378
gods, Greek and Roman, 177
grain ships, Egypt to Italy, 535
great famine, 314, 317, 318
Great Commission, the, 202–4
Great Revolt, the, 155
Greek
  Attic dialect, 426
  classical, 6, 32
  Koine, 6, 23, 151–52, 426

Hanukkah, 152
Hasmoneans
  dynasty of, 153, 154
  map of Palestine under rule of, 153
  rule of Palestine, 152–55
healings
  by Jesus, 297, 462, 547
  by Paul, 183, 358–60, 462, 546–47
  by Peter, 240, 250, 297, 359–60, 462
Hellenization, 151
hermeneutics, 132
Herod Agrippa I
  as client king, 157, 159, 160, 161
  death of, 325, 326, 354n. 14
  and death of James the apostle, 159, 321, 572
  and the Herodian dynasty, 158
  and imprisonment of Peter, 159
  kingdom of, 320–21
  persecution of Christian church in Jerusalem, 321, 322
Herod Agrippa II
  as client king, 159, 160, 161
  as a possible Christian, 29, 519, 519n. 70
  consultation of Festus with, 511–12, 514–15
  hearing of Paul before, 159, 512–21
  and the Herodian dynasty, 158
  territory ruled by, 159, 513
Herod Antipas, 158, 159, 160, 519
Herod-Philip II, 158, 159, 160
Herod II-Philip I, 158, 159
Herod the Great
  attempt of to kill Jesus, 109, 158, 159, 162
  and building of Caesarea Maritima, 299, 300
  as client king, 157
  death of, 109, 162
  paranoia of, 159, 160
  as ruler of Palestine, 153, 154, 157, 158, 159–60
  and the Second Temple, 159–60, 164, 240, 250, 319
Herodian dynasty, the, 158–59, 168, 170
Herodias, 158, 159
historical precedent, 134–35
historical reminiscence, 129
history
  accuracy standards for writing, 60
  Acts as, 46–48, 50, 53–54, 58, 59–60

documentary, 59, 60, 64
expectations regarding speech records in, 65
explicative, 59, 60, 64
Hellenistic rules for writing, 61–63
poetic, 59, 60, 64
Holy Spirit, the
baptism with, 311, 313
and Barnabas's and Saul's missionary trip, 339
as comforter, 100
coming of at baptism, 275, 276
coming of at Pentecost, 99, 110, 160, 200
coming of on the gentiles, 300, 301, 310–11, 312–13
delay of in coming upon Samaritan believers, 275–76
as empowering believers, 54, 91, 99–100, 104, 214, 219, 244, 601–3
filling by, 218–19
as fulfilling and superseding Old Testament law, 216
gifts of, 219
as guide, 99, 100, 214, 219, 411
as internal presence, 100
necessity of empowerment of, 200
and preparation of Paul for trouble, 474, 479, 480–81, 486
as prominent focus in Acts, 34
as providing wise words, 200
roles of in Luke-Acts, 100, 219
signs of, 216
honor and shame, 179
hospitality notes, in Acts, 81, 88–89, 122–23, 479
hours of the day, first century, 304–5
house of Mary, mother of John Mark, 322, 323

Iconium
Barnabas and Paul ministry in, 352–53, 355–56, 367, 369, 456
geographical and historical details of, 353
signs and wonders at, 353, 354
stone monuments at, 352
Ignatius, 466
imperial cult, 176
imprisonment, of Paul
house arrest of in Rome, 9, 110, 113, 162, 553
in Caesarea, 9, 333, 504, 504n. 36, 509, 522
in Jerusalem, 333, 488, 498, 501, 502, 522
in Philippi, 417
inaugurated eschatology, 102, 201–2inclusio, 14, 15, 554
infancy narratives, in Luke-Acts, 81–82
Irenaeus, 594, 595
Isaiah, 148
Israel
language of, 150
as means through which to bless all nations of the earth, 400–401
name of, 145, 148

James, brother of Jesus
death of, 387, 591
forged ossuary of, 590n. 53
as James the Just, 320, 386, 387, 581
at the Jerusalem Council, 88, 383, 384, 386–93
as leader in early church, 320, 387, 591
and Peter's release from prison, 324
writing of epistle by, 161, 320, 386
James, son of Alphaeus. *See* James the Lesser or Younger
James the apostle
as companion of Luke and Paul, 13
death of, 111, 159, 162, 321, 572, 586, 591
extrabiblical traditions about, 572
as James the Greater, 320, 572
James the Lesser or Younger, 320, 580–82, 581n. 29, 581n. 30, 591
Jason, 11, 13, 89, 422
Jeremiah, 148
Jerusalem
destruction of, 162
geographical and historical details of city of, 319
Egyptian rebel in, 491, 492, 506
fall of, 111, 112, 148, 164
opposition to Christian community in, 100–101, 243, 254, 320–27
rebuilding of temple within, 150, 159–60, 164
Jerusalem Council, the
application of decision of, 392
catalyst for, 333, 378
final conclusions of, 381, 392
as large public meeting, 384
logic of decision of, 392–94
proceedings of, 383–91
repeated mentions of in Acts, 90
significance of in the book of Acts, 377
timing of, 110
Jerusalem Talmud, the. *See* Palestinian Talmud, the
Jesus
as active from heaven, 206–7
as apostle, 357
ascension of. *See* ascension, of Jesus
as the author of life, 242
authority of, 148, 206–7
baptizing with the Holy Spirit, 216
birth of, 109, 160, 162
calling of apostles by, 97, 208, 212
call to faith in as central aim of Acts, 34
as Christ, 93, 111, 148
David as prefigurement of, 211, 219, 221, 348
death of. *See* death, of Jesus
declarations of innocence of, 519

Jesus (*continued*)
drawing people to himself, 400–401
exaltation of, 92, 93, 219, 221
as exodus leader, 147–48
faith in as proper continuation of Old Testament faith, 90, 130, 131, 146, 176, 242, 271, 556
followers of as witnesses to, 91, 98–99
as forgiving sins, 95, 348
as fulfillment of God's promise to Abraham, 146
as fulfillment of Scripture, xxii, 91–93, 96, 130, 148, 218, 599, 603
future return of, 101–3, 202, 206, 602
healings by, 297, 462, 547
as the Holy and Righteous One, 242
as king, 201, 212, 244, 599, 602, 603
as Lord, 93–94, 98, 206, 599–600, 602, 603
as Messiah, xxii, 32, 93, 96, 130, 219, 242–43, 289, 458, 599, 603
mission of, 95
note of to the church at Ephesus, 475
opposition to and persecution of in Luke, 101
parallels with Paul, 521, 542
parallels with Stephen, 267–68, 269, 274
postresurrection appearances of, 200
pouring out the Holy Spirit, 219, 221
prayer of, 100, 208, 209, 234, 235
prayer to, 212, 274
promise of the Spirit of, 195, 200, 204, 215
as prophet like Moses, 147, 211, 271
public ministry of, 160, 162
rejection of, 271
as replacement of the temple, 269
resurrection of. *See* resurrection, of Jesus
at the right hand of God, 201, 272
as servant, 97, 111, 242
as Son of God, 93, 289
as Son of Man, 93, 111, 272
as source of salvation, 91, 94–98, 103, 137–38, 147, 206, 243, 600
suffering of, 92, 96, 100, 101, 130, 518
as the suffering servant, 283
at the transfiguration, 268
Jewish Revolt, the, 173
Jews, the
capital punishment among, 491
differing connotations of the term, 350
expulsion of from Rome, 440, 440n. 62, 441, 456
as Roman citizens, 499
as synagogue members who reject the gospel, 349, 350, 366, 421
John
as author of New Testament books, 570
as companion of Luke and Paul, 13
as companion of Peter, 570
contributions of to the New Testament, 5
death of, 570, 571, 591
as the disciple whom Jesus loved, 570
in Ephesus, 466, 570–71, 591
extrabiblical traditions about, 570–71
and falling of the Holy Spirit on the Samaritans, 276
hearing of before the Sanhedrin, 160
ministry of after Acts, 570–71, 591
ministry of in Samaria, 276, 297
role of in Acts, 33
John Mark
as companion of Luke and Paul, 13, 340, 408, 409
death of, 591
follow-up ministry of, 409
ministry of after Acts, 591
mission to Antioch, 327
mission to Cyprus of, 340, 346, 368, 409
name of, 342
John the Baptist
baptism of repentance by, 457, 461
dates of public ministry of, 160, 162
death of, 159
disciples of, 460
as Essene, 168
as preparing the people for the coming of Jesus, 348, 457
Jonah, 299
Joppa, 299
Joseph, 270
Joseph called Barsabbas, 212, 342
Josephus, Flavius Titus, 7, 28–29, 113–14, 118, 173, 196, 543
Joshua, 148
Judah, 148
Judaism, first century
beliefs on salvation, 164
core beliefs and practices of, 163–64
diverse groups in, 166–70
literature of, 170–75
main institutions in, 164–66
and messianic expectation, 164
Judaizers, 378, 383, 391, 395
Judas, son of James, 582, 583–85, 591
Judas (Barsabbas), 394, 395, 398
Judas (in Damascus), 89
Judas Iscariot
criteria for replacement of, 212, 214
death of, 210, 585, 586, 591
eternal fate of, 209n. 27
false belief of, 278–79

need for replacement of as apostle, 208, 209, 211–12, 214, 586
process for replacement of, 212–13, 214
as thief, 585
as traitor, 209, 212, 585, 591
Judas Maccabeus, 152, 154
Judas Thaddaeus. *See* Judas, son of James
Judas the Galilean, 253, 254
Judas Thomas. *See* Thomas the apostle
Jude. *See* Judas, son of James
Julius, 531, 534, 544, 548, 549
Junias, 356, 357n. 16
Justinian I, 324
Justus, 11
Justus. *See* Joseph called Barsabbas (Justus)

kicking against the goad, metaphor of, 515
kingdom of God, already/not yet, 102, 201–2

law, the
giving of the, 215, 218
lack of necessity of Gentiles following, 97, 131, 313, 377–81, 383, 392, 396, 410
preached in every city, 393
laying on of hands, 259, 277, 338, 546–47
leadership, church, principles of good, 474–75
legates, Roman, 156
Levi. *See* Matthew
Levites, the, 166, 169
literacy, in first-century Roman world, 284
Lord's Supper, the, 232
Lucius,11, 13
Lucius Junius Annaeus Gallio, 29
Lucius the Cyrene, 10, 338
Luke
apostolicity of, 12
as artist, 17–20
as author of the Book of Acts, xxii, 5, 20–26
authority of, 14, 15
contributions of to the New Testament, 5
death of, 591
educational background and career of, 7–9, 11
ethnic background of, 9–11
interest of in gentiles, 9, 30–31
interest of in Jews, 30, 32
interest of in people with illnesses and disabilities, 359
as ministry companion of Paul, 11–12, 411, 416, 471, 476, 480, 502, 531
ministry of after Acts, 591
as one of the seventy-two disciples, 10
as part of second generation of Jesus followers, 12, 15
place of residence of, 9, 29
relationship to Mark, 122
relationship with Roman Empire, 447–48
social location of, 12–16
writing style of, xxii, xxiii, 6–7, 14, 17, 32
written works of, 5–7
Luke-Acts, 41, 42
Lycaonia, 357
Lydda, 298
Lydia, 89, 414–15
Lystra
Barnabas and Paul ministry in, 357–60, 362, 364, 365–66, 367, 369, 456
geographical and historical details of, 357, 358
healing in, 358–59
Paul's sermon in, 364–65
magic, 176
Malta
early Christian church on, 547, 547n. 51
geographic and historic details of, 545
shipwreck on, 543–48
Manaen, 338
Marcellus, 273
Marcion, 594n. 62
Marcus Aurelius, 156
Mark, 11, 122
Mary, mother of Jesus, 208
Mattathias, 152, 154
Matthew, 579–80, 591
Matthias
death of, 586, 591
ministry of after Acts, 586–87
as replacement for Judas Iscariot, 33, 212, 213, 337–38, 356, 369
rescue of from cannibals, 573, 587
messianic expectation, 164
Midrashim, the, 174, 175
Miletus, 472
miracles. *See* signs and wonders
Mishnah, the, 174, 175
Mnason, 89, 340, 479, 479n. 33
Monarchian Prologue, the, 23n. 46
monotheism, 163
"more light" principle, 302–3
Moses, 147, 211, 215, 220, 258, 268, 270–71
Muratorian Canon, the, 20, 20n. 42, 21, 23
Myra, 533, 534

Nathanael. *See* Bartholomew
natural theology, 431
navigational year, Mediterranean Sea, 534, 536
Nazarite vows, 487, 487n. 1, 489
Nehemiah, 150, 151
Nero, 111, 162, 500, 570
Nicanor, 259

Nicholas from Antioch, 259, 338
Noahic commandments, the, 397
Northeaster, 538

Octavian. *See* Caesar Augustus
Onesiphorus, 592
opposition. *See* persecution
outlines, for Acts
biographical outline, 76
ecclesiological outline, 76
ethnogeogrraphic witness outline, 75
panels of progress outline, 76–77
storytelling outline, 79–80
Ovid, 178, 360, 361

Palestine
Abraham's migration to, 146, 270
beginnings of the nation of Israel in, 145–46
civil war in, 148
exile of Israelites from, 148–50
Exodus to, 147–48
Greek rule of, 151–52
Hasmonean rule of, 152–55
location of, 145
return of Israelites to, 150–51
Roman rule of, 154, 155–60
timeline of rulers of, 158
Palestinian Talmud, the, 174
Paphos, 341
Papyrus 29, 123, 126
Papyrus 45, 124, 126
Papyrus 50, 124, 126
parallelisms, 81, 82–85, 101
Parmenas, 259
patronage, 184
Paul/Saul
accuracy of description of in Acts, 66–67
address of to the Areopagus, 430–37
address of to the Ephesian elders at Miletus, 472–76, 480
as apostle, 356, 357, 372
appointing elders in the new churches, 369
arrest of, 487, 488
audience sensitivity of, 486, 522
baptism of, 289
barracks steps testimony of, 162
beating of, 488
bold response of to opposition, 349, 353
as champion of church unity, 35, 408
commissioning of, 15, 517
contributions of to the New Testament, 5
conversion of, 90, 110, 160, 286–89, 494–97, 516–18, 587
and conversion of the Roman jailer, 417–19
cutting of hair of, 446–47, 448, 489
death of, 111, 113, 115, 162, 588, 589, 591
declarations of innocence of, 519, 520, 521
defense of ministry of, 474
differing ministry strategies of, 522
disagreement of with Barnabas, 35, 408–9
exorcisms by, 416–17
extrabiblical traditions about, 587–80
first missionary journey of. *See* first missionary journey, of Paul
God's encouragement of, 444, 448, 480, 502, 552
healings by, 183, 236, 358–60, 462, 546–47
health issues of, 7
hearing of before Felix, 504, 506–9, 522
hearing of before Festus, 509–12, 522
hearing of before Gallio, 444, 446, 448
hearing of before Herod Agrippa II, 512–21, 522
hearing of before the Sanhedrin, 162, 486, 500–501, 522
imprisonment of. *See* imprisonment, of Paul
and inclusion of Gentiles in Christian community, 379–81
Jewish mission of, 332–33
Jewish plot against life of, 502–4
Jews-first ministry of, 340, 349–50, 352, 414, 421, 441, 461, 555
Luke's relationship to, 11–12, 411, 416, 471, 476, 480, 502, 531
map of travels of, 291
martyrdom of, 588–89
ministry companions of, 11, 13, 14. *See also* Aquila; Barnabas; John Mark; Luke; Silas; Timothy
ministry of after Acts, 589, 591
ministry of in Rome, 553–56, 566
ministry of in Syrian Antioch, 315–16, 332
name change of, 337, 342, 343
parallels between Corinthian and Ephesian ministries of,461, 462
parallels between speeches of, 553–54
parallels of with Jesus, 521, 542
persecution of, 289–91, 356, 366, 368, 424, 444, 488–89
persecution of Christians by, 274, 274n. 10, 285, 286–87, 288, 495, 516
as Pharisee, 32, 343, 486, 501, 587
and Philip the evangelist, 478–79
physical description of, 590
preparation of by the Holy Spirit for persecution, 474, 479, 480–81, 486
and principles of good church leadership, 474–75
and Priscilla and Aquila, 440
prominence of in Acts, 33

purification of, 487–88n. 1
raisings by, 411, 471–72
role of at Stephen's stoning, 274, 274n. 10
Roman citizenship of, 498–99, 498n. 20, 533
sailing experience of, 537
second missionary journey of. *See* second missionary journey, Paul
self-defense of before mob in Jerusalem, 491, 494–95, 498, 522
sermon of at Pisidian Antioch synagogue, 348–49, 364
sermon of in Lystra, 364–65
signs and wonders by, 66, 236, 353, 386. *See also* Paul: exorcisms by; Paul: healings by; Paul: raisings by
snake biting, 545, 546
and sponsorship of four Jewish men, 487, 489
stoning of, 358, 366
suffering of, 90, 474, 477, 514
support of missionary work by his own labor, 440, 441
third missionary journey of. *See* third missionary journey, Paul
trial of before Caesar, 111, 113, 115, 122, 333
and unity of the church, 398
visions of, 411, 444, 502, 589
visit of to Tarsus, 161, 291, 587
visits of to Damascus and Arabia, 160, 289–90, 355, 587
visits of to Jerusalem (first), 160, 290–91, 316, 318, 355, 381, 381n. 11, 587
visits of to Jerusalem (second, third, fourth), 161, 316–17, 318, 381, 381n. 11
visits of to Jerusalem (fifth), 162, 381n. 11, 477
voyage of to Rome. *See* voyage to Rome, Paul
willingness of to live sacrificially for the sake of the gospel, 474, 477, 479, 480, 481, 501
writings of, 112, 161, 162
Pax Romana, 156
People of the Land, 170
Pentecost
countries and languages represented at Pentecost, 217
as harvest festival, 215, 215n. 33
sermon by Peter at, 218–21
signs and wonders at, 216–17
timing of, 215
Perga, 355, 368, 369
pericopes, 194
periodic sentence (period), 198
persecution
believers' responses to, 101, 244, 255, 256
of the Christian community, 100–101, 243, 254, 320–27
current day, 481
as means of advancing the mission of the Christian community, 100, 101
of Paul, 289–91, 356, 366, 368, 424, 444, 488–89
Paul's final teaching on, 368
as reflection of suffering of Jesus, 100, 101
rejoicing in, 101
Persia, defeat of Babylon by, 150, 151
Peter
call of to repentance and faith in Jesus, 219–20
as companion of Luke and Paul, 13
comparison of Corinthian and Ephesian ministries of, 462
and conversion of Cornelius, 305–11, 385
death of, 111, 569–70, 591
empowerment of by the Holy Spirit, 243
extrabiblical traditions about, 569–70
and falling of the Holy Spirit on the Samaritans, 276
healings by, 240, 250, 297, 359–60, 462
hearing of before the Sanhedrin, 160, 243
imprisonment of, 159, 243, 318, 322
and inclusion of Gentiles in Christian community, 380, 382, 384, 385
and the Jerusalem Council, 384, 385
map of travels of, 297
ministry of after Acts, 569, 591
ministry of in Lydda and Joppa, 110, 297–99
ministry of in Samaria, 110, 276, 297, 569
prayer of, 299
raising of Tabitha by, 298–99, 472
rescue from prison of, 319, 320, 322, 354n. 14, 418
responses of to the Sanhedrin, 243, 252
sermon of at Pentecost, 218–21
speech at the Beautiful Gate, 240, 242–43
speech at Cornelius's conversion 308–10
speech of before the Sanhedrin, 243
as spokesman of the apostles, 32, 569
vision of, 300, 301, 305–6, 307, 312
willingness of to die for the gospel, 480
Pharisees, the, 168, 170, 180, 253, 383, 501
Philip the apostle, 574–76, 574n. 14, 578
Philip the evangelist
caught up by God, 284
dating of ministry of, 110
death of, 591

Philip the evangelist (*continued*)
encounter of with Ethiopian eunuch, 279–80, 282–83, 332, 355
hospitality notes and, 89
map of missionary travels of, 283, 297
as minister to Christian community, 259, 274, 574
ministry of after Acts, 591
ministry of in Samaria, 160, 275, 297, 332, 354, 574n. 14
signs and wonders by, 236, 275
similarities to Simon the Sorcerer, 276–77
visit of Paul to, 478–79
Philippi
geographical and historical details of, 415
lack of synagogue in, 414
Luke visit to, 415
Paul and Silas imprisonment in, 415
Paul's ministry in, 137, 408, 413, 414–20, 448, 454
Philo Judaeus, 29, 173, 218, 458, 499
Philo of Alexandria. *See* Philo Judaeus
philosophical theology, 431
Phineas, 314
Phoebe, 448
Pisidian Antioch
Barnabas and Paul ministry in, 345–51, 355, 365, 367, 369, 456
geographical and historical details of, 346, 347
Paul's synagogue sermon in, 348–49, 364
Pliny the Elder, 178
Pliny the Younger, 178
Plutarch, Lucius Mestrius, 178
poetic history, 59, 60, 64
politarchs, 422, 424
polygeneris, 49–50
polytheism, 175–76
Pompey, 154, 156, 217, 422
Pontius Pilate, 157, 273, 519
praxeis literature, 4
prayer
of the apostles, 234
for boldness, 244
of the Christian Community, 209, 212, 214, 229, 233–34, 244
of Jesus, 100, 208, 209, 234, 235
in overcoming opposition, 100, 101
of Peter, 299
purposes of, 235
prefects, Roman, 157
priests
chief, 169
high, 166, 167, 169
as Levites, 166, 169
Priscilla
as companion of Luke and Paul, 13, 446
death of, 591
in Ephesus, 447, 455–57
first meeting with Paul, 440, 456
ministry of, 456–57, 458n. 1, 591
move of to Corinth, 440, 441, 456
proconsuls, Roman, 156
Procorus, 259, 591
procurators, Roman, 157
proem sermon framing, 242
prologues, in Luke-Acts, 81
proselytes, 378
Pseudepigrapha, the, 171–73, 174
Ptolemais, 478
Publius (Maltese leader), 546
Publius Ovidius Naso. *See* Ovid
Puteoli, 528, 543, 549, 550, 551
Pythatogians, 238–39

Quirinius, 156
Qumran community, 173, 236, 237, 238, 391

rabbinic writings, the, 174, 175
rabbis, career expectations for, 440
regular past patterns, 135, 137
religious tolerance, Roman, 417
repeatable pragmatic patterns, 136, 137
repetition, in Acts, 81, 89–90
repentance
forgiveness as result of, 600, 603
as gift given to Jews and gentiles, 95
as turning from sin, 94, 220
resurrection, of Jesus
dating of, 109, 110, 160, 162
as fulfillment of Scripture, 92, 93
as proof of Jesus's lordship, 93, 98–99, 103, 219, 349, 509, 599
proofs of, 199–200
as turning point in salvation history, 102
required prescriptive patterns, 137
Rhegium, 528, 549, 550
rhetoric, in Acts, 81, 89
Rhoda, 319, 322
Roman jailer, conversion of, 417–19
Rome
benefaction/patronage in, 184
burning of, 162
citizenship of, 498–99, 499n. 21, 500
economic stratification in, 181–82
emperors of, 156
expulsion of Jews from, 440, 440n. 62, 441, 456
first-century historical details of, 552
formation of Empire, 155
Jewish revolt against, 162
Jews as citizens of, 499
law against punishing citizens without trial, 419–20, 499
laws of on judicial appeals, 514, 515
map of, 155
military structure of, 532
Paul's voyage to. *See* voyage to Rome, Paul
religious tolerance of, 417
requirement of accuser facing the accused in, 504
rule over Palestine, 154, 155–60

stratified social system in, 180–83, 180n. 46
tolerance of to Christianity, 176
volunteer associations in, 184

Sadducees, the, 168, 170, 180, 253, 501
Salamis, 339, 341
Salome, 158, 159
salvation
available to all, 96, 98, 349–50, 600, 603
current as well as future, 95, 96, 98
faith as necessary for, 91, 95, 103, 243, 367, 401
first-century Judaic beliefs on, 164
history, 94, 101, 270, 271
Jesus as source of, 91, 94–98, 103, 137–38, 147, 206, 243, 600
lack of necessity of baptism for, 221, 416
provided by God, 103
terms for in Luke-Acts, 96
Samaritans, the, 169, 170
Samothrace, geographical and historical details of, 413
Sanhedrin, the
as disobedient to God, 271
hearing of the apostles before, 160, 251–55
hearing of Paul before, 162, 486, 500–501
hearing of Peter and John before, 160, 243
influence of, 166
makeup of, 166, 168, 169, 170, 253, 501
Saphira, 160, 246–49, 246n. 33, 249n. 38, 251, 267, 385, 458n. 1
Saul. *See* Paul/Saul
scribes, 166, 169
scripta continua, 23
Scripture
Acts accepted as, 593–98
awareness of New Testament authors of their own works as, 595–96
citation of New Testament in New Testament, 595
criteria for New Testament canon, 594–95, 594n. 57
date of closing of New Testament canon, 594, 595
entailments in recognizing something as, 598
as God's word, 133–34
intention of, 596
Jesus as fulfillment of, xxii, 91–93, 96, 130, 148, 218, 599, 603
narratives in, 133
Septuagint, the, 86, 170, 174
summary, 129
Tanak, the, 170, 174
use of in Acts, 81, 86, 93, 129–30
second missionary journey, Paul
divine guidance in, 411–12, 444
follow-up ministry during, 346, 353, 358, 366, 407, 408, 409
itinerary of, 406
map of, 407
mixed results of, 420–21, 424, 435–37
opposition during, 446
visit to Athens, 406, 408, 425, 427–28, 429–37, 448
visit to Berea, 406, 408, 424–25
visit to Corinth, 406, 407, 437–42, 444–46, 448
visit to Ephesus, 406, 407, 408, 446–47, 455
visit to Philippi, 137, 406, 408, 413, 414–20, 448
visit to Thessalonica, 406, 407, 421–23, 448
visit to Troas, 406, 411
Second Temple, the, 159–60, 164
Second Temple Period, the, 150, 150n. 6, 164
Secundus, 12
sea anchor, 538, 541
sea voyages, dangers of, 536
Seleucia, 339
Seneca, Lucius Annaeus, 178
Septuagint, the, 86, 170, 174
Sergius Paulus, 29, 156, 341, 342, 343, 344, 345
Sheshbazzar, 150, 151
shipwrecks
Josephus, 543
Paul, 543–48
Sicarii, the, 169, 491, 492
Sidon, 531, 533
signs and wonders
as affirming the teaching of the apostles, 229, 353, 354
after Chistian community's prayer for boldness, 244
by Barnabas, 353, 354, 386
cessationist view of, 236
at the coming of the Holy Spirit in Ephesus, 461
continuation view, 236
earthquake, 418
exorcisms, 354, 416–17, 462
healings, 183, 236, 240, 250, 277, 354, 358–60, 462, 546–47
by Jesus, 267, 462, 547
in the name of Jesus, 241, 242, 417
not the focus of ministry, 472
by Paul. *See* Paul: signs and wonders by
at Pentecost, 216–17
by Peter, 240, 250, 297, 359–60, 462
by Philip, 236, 275, 354
as pointing to Jesus, 240
resurrections, 354, 359, 411, 471–72, 575
by Silas, 354
speaking in tongues. *See* tongues, speaking in
by Stephen, 236, 267, 354

signs and wonders (*continued*)
through the apostles, 236–37, 240, 250, 267, 297–99, 354, 359–60, 462
vs. magic, 463
Silas
as bearer of the apostolic decree, 394, 395, 398, 410
follow-up ministry of, 410
imprisonment of, 12, 417
as ministry companion of Paul, 11, 13, 183, 409, 410, 441
as Silvanus, 410n. 4
Silvanus. *See* Silas
Simeon, 582
Simon Peter. *See* Peter
Simon the Cananaean. *See* Simon the Zealot
Simon the Sorcerer (Simon Magus)
false belief of, 276–79, 341–42, 353, 416
as founder of Gnosticism, 278, 279
similarities to Philip the evangelist, 276–77
Simon the Tanner, 89
Simon the Zealot, 582–83, 585, 591
simony, 277n. 11
Socrates, 428, 430
Solomon, 160, 170
Solomon's Colonnade, 240, 249, 250
Solomon's Temple. *See* temple, Jerusalem: Solomon's
sons of Sceva, the, 463
Sopater/Sosipater, 11, 12, 13, 425
Sosthenes, 11, 13, 446
sounding, 540, 541
space allocation, in Acts, 81, 90
speeches
ancient historians' expectations regarding records of, 64–65, 64–65n. 75
commissioning, 89
defense, 89
historical accuracy of, 64–65
of James, 88, 386–93
Luke's sources for, 122
of Paul, 162, 348–49, 364–65, 430–47, 472–76, 480
as percentage of Acts, 81
of Peter, 88, 218–21, 240, 242–43, 308–10
of Stephen, 88, 90, 110, 146, 270–71, 338
St. Paul's Bay, 545
Stephen
as minister to Christian community, 259, 267, 338
character of, 267
charges against, 267, 269, 488n. 4
death of, 160, 259, 267, 271–74, 291, 591
and launch of outreach by the church, 274
ministry of, 160
parallels with Jesus of, 267–68, 269, 274
prayer of, 267, 269, 274
signs and wonders by, 236, 267
speech by, 88, 90, 110, 146, 270–71, 338
vision of Jesus of, 272
stoicism, 428, 429
stoning, 272–73
substitutionary atonement, 103
Suetonius, 178
suffering servant, the, 283
sui generis, 49–50
summary statements
closing, 520, 556
first half of Acts, 191, 194, 221–22, 261, 266, 291, 296, 327
importance of, 87
Jerusalem Council, 333, 376, 399–400
Paul's first missionary journey, 333, 336, 350–51, 370
Paul's second missionary journey, 333, 406, 410, 448
Paul's third missionary journey, 334, 454, 462, 480
prison ministry, 334, 486, 521, 528, 556
progress, 77–78, 80, 98, 191, 332, 333–34, 336, 350–51, 406, 454, 462
travel, 80, 191, 332, 333–34, 336, 351, 370, 406, 448, 454, 480
Sunday, as day of worship, 471
syncretism, warning against, 464
synagogue
of the Freedmen, 111, 267, 268
minimum requirements for establishment of, 166
order of service in ancient, 165, 166, 347
origin of, 150, 165–66
Syracuse, 528, 549
Syrtis, 538, 538n. 24, 538

Tabitha, raising of, 298–99, 472
table fellowship, 184–85
Tacitus, Publius Cornelius, 178
Talmud, the, 174, 175
Tanak, the, 170, 174
Targums, the, 174, 175
Tarsus, 493
Teacher of Righteousness, the, 7
telescoping, 199
temple, Jerusalem
building of, 299
Beautiful Gate of, 111, 240, 241
Christian community meeting in, 229, 231
destruction of, 164, 175
layout of, 490
leadership of, 164
rebuilding of, 150, 159–60, 164, 299
restrictions against gentiles entering, 488, 490, 491
sacrifices in, 164
Second, 159–60, 164
Solomon's, 164

Solomon's Colonnade of, 240, 249, 250
temple, Samaritan, 169
Tertullus, 88, 504, 506–7
textual criticism, 123
thematic echo, 129
themes, in Acts
Christians as God's true people, 91, 97
Christians as witnesses to Jesus, 91, 98–99
Christians will face opposition but can overcome it, 91, 100–101
forgiveness as result of faith and repentance, 91, 94–95
Holy Spirit as empowering God's people, 91, 99–100
Jesus as fulfillment of Scriptures, 91, 92–93
Jesus as Messiah, risen Lord and King, 91, 93–94
Jesus as ruling now and returning in the future, 91, 101–3
Jesus as source of salvation, 91, 95–97
sovereign God at work in the world, 91–92
Theophilus
Christian vs. non-Christian, 30, 197
identity of, 27–28, 29
naming of as dedication statement, 28, 195
as symbolic of readers, 26–27
Thessalonica
geographical and historical details of, 422
Paul's missionary visit to, 407, 421–23, 448
Theudas, 253, 254
third missionary journey, Paul
follow-up ministry during, 346, 353, 358, 366, 456, 470–71, 480
itinerary of, 454
map of, 455
ministry team for, 471
mixed results of, 461, 462
signs and wonders in, 462
visit to Athens, 438
visit to Caesarea, 478–79
visit to Ephesus, 455, 460–62, 464, 466–69, 480
visit to Miletus, 472–76
visit to Thessalonica, 422
visit to Troas, 471–72
visit to Tyre, 476–77
Thomas the apostle, 576–77, 576n. 18, 576n. 19, 591
Timon, 259
Timothy
circumcision of, 410
death of, 591
home of, 358
in charge of the Ephesian church, 466
as ministry companion of Paul, 11, 12, 13, 358, 410, 441
ministry of after Acts, 591
Titius Justus, 89
Titus, 11, 12, 535
Titus Flavius Clemens, 29
tongues, speaking in
at the coming of the Spirit in Ephesus, 461
at the coming of the Spirit at Pentecost, 216–17, 219, 354
as fulfillment of Scripture, 219, 221
as proof that Jesus is the Messiah, 221
at the giving of the law at Mt. Sinai, 218
as gift not possessed by all believers, 218
Torah, the, 163–64, 174
Tosefta, the, 174, 175
tradition, church, 25
travel narratives, in Luke-Acts, 81 82
Troas, 411, 471–72
Trophimus, 11, 12, 13
Tychicus, 11, 12, 13
Tyre, 476–77, 533

upper room, the, 323

Via Egnatia, the, 413, 415, 420, 421, 422, 425, 455
Via Sebaste, the, 346, 352, 353, 357, 358, 368
visions
of Ananias of Damascus, 289, 307
of Cornelius, 300, 301, 302, 303, 307, 308, 312
of Paul, 411, 444
of Peter, 300, 301, 305–6, 307, 312
of Stephen, 272
vs. visitations, 307
voyage to Rome, Paul
Caesarea to Myra, 531, 533
itinerary of, 528
Jesus's prediction of, 529
Luke's narration of, 529–30
Malta to Rome, 548–52
map of, 529
Myra to Crete, 534, 537–38
shipwreck on Malta during, 543–48
storm at sea during, 538–43

Wars of the Diadochi, 152
"we sections"
as indicating Luke's presence, 11, 12, 15, 116–17, 122
specific instances of in Acts, 412–13, 416, 471, 476, 531
Western text, the, 126–29, 127n. 44, 593
wind, as sign of Holy Spirit, 216
witnesses, apostles as, 14–15, 199, 202–4, 207, 212
wonders of the ancient world, the, 458, 459, 467
word of God, the, 98

Zealots, the, 169, 170, 582
Zerubbabel, 150, 151, 164

Author Index

Abegg, Martin G., Jr., 173
Abdias, 570
Adams, Sean A., 43, 48, 64, 81, 498
Ådna, Jostein, 387
Ahn, Yong-Sung, 56, 449
Aland, Kurt, 20, 23
Alexander, Loveday C. A., 8, 27, 44, 46, 81
Alföldy, Géza, 182
Alvers, Rubem, 102
Anderson, Charles, 274
Anderson, Howard G., 240, 340, 410
Anderson, Kevin L., 437
Anderson, R. Dean, Jr., 385
Anderson, Richard, 27
Anderson, Robert T., 169
Angel, Gervais T. D., 200
Armstron, Karl Leslie, 112
Arnold, Clinton E., 157, 167, 216, 217, 221, 232, 316, 344, 345, 365, 429, 436, 463, 464, 488, 498, 499, 501, 518, 533, 544, 546
Arnold, Jeff, 221
Ascough, Richard S., 414
Ashford, Bruce Riley, 356, 372, 400, 481
Auerbach, Erich, 596
August, Jared M., 213
Aune, David E., 40, 42, 44, 47, 81, 112, 175, 463
Bacci, Michele, 17
Balch, David L., 44, 48, 178, 531, 534
Barnett, Paul W., 440
Barr, David L., 46
Barrett, Charles Kingsley, 40, 43, 45, 58, 114, 127, 197, 202, 230, 232, 246, 396, 427, 428, 430, 446, 472, 504, 506, 541, 546, 555, 557
Bartholomew, Craig G., 604
Barton, Stephen C., 178
Bauckham, Richard J., 173, 396, 568, 579
Bauer, David R., xxiii, 34, 82
Baur, F. C., 113
Beall, Todd S., 168
Beckwith, Roger T., 384
Behm, J., 232
Belleville, Linda L., 597
Berding, Kenneth, 14
Bernier, Jonathan, 112
Bidmead, Julye, 213
Binder, Donald D., 166
Bird, Michael F., 58, 123 143, 173, 594
Black, C. Clifton, 89
Blaiklock, Edward M., 175, 176, 367, 414
Blass, Friedrich, 9, 111, 112
Blomberg, Craig L., 137, 410
Bock, Darrell L., 10, 59, 90, 92, 97, 129, 131, 211, 213, 232, 284, 316, 420, 422, 430, 431, 489, 517, 556
Bonz, Marianne Palmer, 44
Bovon, François C., 81, 92, 127, 568, 595
Bowker, John W., 168, 242
Bowley, James E., 156
Boyer, Mark G., 234, 235, 306
Braund, David C., 509, 514
Brawley, Robert Lawson, 97, 112
Brehm, H. Alan, 87
Broneer, Oscar T., 427
Brown, Jeannine K., 162
Brown, Raymond E., 81
Bruce, F. F., 25, 46, 52, 54, 56, 67, 68, 84, 88, 111, 114, 118, 121, 162, 197, 230, 232, 272, 284, 316, 325, 362, 381, 426, 430, 431, 437, 438, 446, 469, 471, 476, 479, 501, 511, 537, 538, 541, 546, 548, 557, 594, 595, 597
Bryan, David K., 206
Buckwalter, H. Douglas, xxii, 97
Burer, Michael H., 357
Burge, Gary M., 134, 143, 150, 156, 414
Burridge, Richard A., 42, 46, 48, 49, 50
Burton, Ernest DeWitt, 165

Burton, Keith A., 208
Byrskog, Samuel, 48

Cadbury, Henry Joel, 8, 24, 41, 42, 46, 47, 54, 68, 545
Caird, G. B., 488
Campbell, William S., 378
Campenhausen, Hans von, 594
Cancik, Hubert, 48
Capper, Brian J., 237
Carroll, John T., 56, 102, 449
Carson, D. A., 164, 604
Carter, C. Warren, 164, 176
Cassidy, Richard J., 54, 56, 512
Casson, Lionel, 531, 533, 534, 541, 549
Carter, Terry G., 604
Catto, Stephen K., 166
Chance, J. Bradley, 44, 89, 194
Charlesworth, James H., 173
Cheng, Ling, 93, 94
Chilton, Bruce D., 168, 175
Chrupcata, L. Daniel, 7
Clark, Andrew C., 601
Clark, Gordon H., 175
Conway, Charles Stephen, 520
Conzelmann, Hans, 47, 53, 54, 232, 425, 476
Coogan, Michael D., 171
Cook, Edward M., 173
Cowan, J. Andrew, 57
Crabbe, Kylie, 102
Creech, R. Robert, 28
Criswell, David, 572, 581, 592
Cronin, H. S., 112
Crowe, Brandon D., 99, 200, 501

Dahl, Nils, 15
Das, A. Andrew, 440
Davila, James R., 173
Dawsey, James M., 7, 47
Dayton, Wilber T., 12, 20, 386
de Jonge, Marianus, 164
Deissman, G. Adolf, 246
DeMaris, Richard E., 178
Denova, Rebecca I., 47, 97
deSilva, David A., 179, 180, 184
Dibelius, Martin, 25, 28, 47, 67, 476, 530
Dickson, John, 98
Dunn, James D. G., 93, 169, 316, 545
Dupertuís, Rubén, 114
Dupont, Jacques, 123, 270

Easley, Kendell H., 249
Easton, Burton Scott, 45, 54
Edwards, J. Christopher, 568
Edwards, James R., 84, 466
Ehrhardt, Arnold, 510, 512, 513
Ehrman, Bart D., 123
Elledge, Casey D., 501
Elliott, J. K., 568, 582
Ellis, Edward Earle, 11, 13, 242–43
Elwell, Walter A., 162
Embudo, Lora Angeline B., 98
Enslin, Morton S., 118
Epp, Eldon Jay, 127, 593
Esler, Philip Francis, 54
Estes, Douglas, xxiii
Evans, Craig A., 15, 47, 169, 554, 594
Evans, Christopher Francis, 27

Farley, Gary E., 379
Farmer, William Reuben, 594
Fee, Gordon D., 133, 134, 137, 166, 597
Feinberg, Charles L., 166, 378
Feldman, Louis H., 303
Fellows, Richard G., 413
Feltoe, C, L, 576
Ferguson, Everett, 20, 180, 498, 504, 506
Fernando, Ajith, 214, 245, 316
Filson, Floyd V., 77
Finger, Reta Halteman, 257
Finlan, Stephen, 179
Fitzgerald, John T., 531
Fitzmyer, Joseph A., 15, 23, 24, 27, 44, 116, 117, 202, 232, 245, 422, 446, 488, 501, 512, 517, 546
Foakes, Frederick J., 114
Franklin, Eric, 56, 437
French, David, 347
Frerichs, Ernest S., 164
Friesen, Steven J., 182

Gallagher, Edmon L., 595
Gamble, Harry Y., 20, 21, 28, 108, 589, 594
Garland, David E., 417
Garrison, Roman, 30
Gärtner, Bertil E., 430, 434
Gasque, W. Ward, 84
Gaventa, Beverly Roberts, 102, 446, 558
Gempf, Conrad H., 118, 386, 556
Gilchrist, J. Michael, 541
Giles, Terry, 169, 479
Gill, David W. J., 437
Gilliard, Dominique DuBois, 16
Glenny, W. Edward, 389, 391, 396
Glover, Richard T., 9
Goheen, Michael W., 99, 604
Goldingay, John, 209
Goodspeed, Edgar J., 28, 111
Goswell, Gregory, 597
Goulder, Michael D., 47, 121, 222, 530
Graves, Michael W., 491, 598
Green, Gene L., 134, 143, 150, 156
Green, Joel B., xxii, 41, 52, 100, 234, 235
Green, William Scott, 164
Green-Armytage, A. H. N., 8, 17, 32, 110, 111, 112, 305, 471, 473, 531
Gregory, Andrew F., 42, 114, 593
Gregory of Tours, 576
Grudem, Wayne A., 236
Gruen, Erich S., 440
Gurtner, Daniel M., 173

Haacker, Klaus, 444, 446
Haenchen, Ernst, 28, 45, 67, 200, 245, 425, 430, 476, 488, 501, 530, 537

Hagner, Donald A., 166, 168
Hahneman, Geoffrey Mark, 20
Hall, Ursula, 574
Hamilton, Catherine Sider, 209
Hamilton, Floyd E., 213
Hansen, G. Walter, 347, 357, 362
Harbison, Craig, 18, 19
Harland, Philip A., 179
Harnack, Adolf von, 7, 8, 12, 114, 121, 394, 557
Harris, James Rendel, 432
Harris, Murray J., 237
Harris, William V., 16
Harrison, Everett Falconer, 232, 302, 446
Harrison, R. K., 168, 173
Hays, Christopher M., 237
Hays, Richard B., 131
Head, Peter M., 129
Heard, R. G., 23
Heard, William J., 169
Hedrick, Charles W., 494, 495, 517
Heil, John Paul, 232
Hellerman, Joseph H., 179
Helyer, Larry R., 170
Hemer, Colin J., 68, 118, 316, 362, 444, 479, 531, 534, 537, 541, 546, 548, 549, 557
Hengel, Martin, 27, 28, 47, 68, 574
Hezser, Catherine, 16, 108
Hiebert, D. Edmond, 168, 414
Hill, Craig C., 257
Hobart, William Kirk, 7, 8
Hock, Ronald F., 44
Hoehner, Harold W., 162
Hoffeditz, David M., 144
Holcomb, Justin S., 376
Holladay, Carl R., 28
Holmås, Geir Otto, 234, 235
Holmes, Michael W., 127
Hornik, Heidi J., 17, 19, 593
Horsley, G. H. R., 422, 469
House, H. Wayne, 157, 162, 167
House, Paul R., 100
Houston, Walter J., 305
Hubbard, Moyer V., 176, 446, 469
Hubbard, Robert L., Jr., 137, 184
Huffman, Douglas S., 68, 82, 92, 130, 154, 491, 509, 514, 555
Hurtado, Larry, 163, 176, 183

Jeremias, Joachim, 475
Jerkins, Marcus, 280, 282
Jervell, Jacob, xxii, 8, 32, 56, 90, 92, 93, 97, 103, 596, 597
Jewett, Robert, 537
Jipp, Joshua W., 545, 547
Jocz, Jakob, 164
Johnson, Dennis E., 90
Johnson, Luke Timothy, xxii, 232, 386, 393, 396, 411, 430, 431, 446, 501, 530, 544, 547, 549, 552
Juel, Donald, 40

Kala, J. Ellsworth, 197
Kalcyk, Hansjörg, 547
Karris, Robert J., 17
Kauppi, Lynn Allan, 549
Kee, Howard Clark, 463
Keener, Craig S., 2, 13, 28, 30, 41, 44, 52, 59, 68, 111, 113, 114, 116, 118, 119, 121, 122, 184, 194, 200, 202, 232, 245, 246, 247, 258, 272, 274, 279, 280, 301, 307, 315, 316, 341, 385, 396, 411, 412, 428, 440, 447, 469, 472, 488, 491, 498, 501, 503, 504, 506, 509, 521, 531, 533, 537, 538, 544, 546, 547, 549, 557
Kelso, James L., 488
Kennedy, George A., 472
Kepple, Robert J., 501
Kilgallen, John J., 100
Kistemaker, Simon J., 76, 232, 430, 501, 509, 546
Klauck, Hans-Josef, xxi, 175, 567, 568, 583
Klein, William W., 137
Klinghardt, Matthias, 232
Kloppenborg, John S., 16, 180, 182, 183, 184, 185
Knox, John, 119
Knox, Wilfred L., 395
Kochenash, Michael, 342
Koet, Bart J., 131
Köstenberger, Andreas J., xxii
Kruger, Michael J., 14, 594, 595, 596
Kucicki, Janusz, 88
Kuecker, Aaron, 97
Kuhn, Karl Allen, xxii, 10, 16, 27, 35, 57, 80, 88, 90, 97, 102, 144

Lake, Donald M., 384
Lane, Anthony N. S., 25
Lane, William L., 357
Larkin, William J., Jr., 283, 284, 302, 353, 354, 428, 446, 488, 494, 512, 517, 547
Lawlor, Hugh Jackson, 581
Lee-Barnewall, Michelle, 168
Lentz, John Clayton, Jr., 533
Levine, Amy-Jill, 168
Levinskaya, Irina, 302
Lewis, Jack P., 216, 305
Lewis, Naphtali, 538
Ley, Anne, 549
Liefeld, Walter L., 51, 52, 53, 76, 87, 90, 132, 137
Litfin, Bryan, 589
Litwak, Kenneth D., 150
Longenecker, Bruce W., 74, 77, 182, 316, 476, 502
Longenecker, Richard N., 77, 110, 111, 213, 214, 316, 395, 417, 430, 440, 444, 446, 447, 472, 520
Lüdemann, Gerd, 67
Lund, Nils Wilhelm, 86

MacDonald, Dennis R., 44
MacDonald, Nathan, 163
Maddox, Robert L., 46, 52, 54, 57

Maier, Paul L., 51, 59
Malherbe, Abraham J., 114
Malina, Bruce J., 178, 180
Mangum, Douglas, xxiii
Marguerat, Daniel, 25, 47, 48, 59, 98, 558
Marshall, I. Howard, 28, 34, 42, 53, 57, 68, 75, 79, 90, 103, 242, 317, 377, 432, 444, 447, 500, 511, 512, 517, 518, 521, 530, 541, 543, 551
Martin, Ralph P., 11, 84
Marx, Werner G., 28, 30, 519
Mason, Steve, 114, 118, 168
Matthews, Christopher R., 34, 574
Mattill, Andrew J., Jr., 45, 66, 83, 102, 112
Mauck, John W., 45
McBirnie, William Steuart, 572, 581, 584
McCaulley, Esau, 16
McClure, M. L., 576
McDonald, Lee Martin, 594
McDowell, Sean, 574, 579, 581, 584, 587, 592
McKnight, Scot, 90, 207, 378, 386, 388
McLachlan, Herbert, 395
McRay, John, 439, 469
Meade, John D., 595
Meeks, Wayne A., 251
Meggitt, Justin J., 181
Menzies, Robert P., 202
Merkle, Benjamin L., 384
Metzger, Bruce M., 20, 42, 123, 462
Miles, Gary B., 545
Miller, Amanda C., 56, 449
Miller, John B. F., 412
Minear, Paul S., 28
Mitchell, Terence C., 282
Moessner, David P., 84
Moo, Douglas J., 357
Moore, Michael S., 184, 251
Moreau, A. Scott, 481
Morgan, Robert C., 111
Moule, C. F. D., 111, 472, 589
Mounce, William D., 589
Mount, Christopher, 519
Murphy-O'Connor, Jerome, 440, 445
Myers, Jason A., 88, 473

Nation, Hannah, 255
Neagoe, Alexandru, 45
Neufeld, Dietmar, 178
Neusner, Jacob, 164, 168
Newbigin, Lesslie, 257
Neyrey, Jerome H., 180, 517
Nickelsburg, George W. E., 170
Niemeyer, Hans Georg, 547
Nobbs, Alanna, 343
Nobel, Joshua, 237
Noll, Stephen F., 322
Nolland, John, 57, 102
Nongbri, Brent, 163
Novakovic, Lidija, 169

O'Brien, Peter T., 164, 235
Ó Fearghail, Fearghus, 47
Ogilvie, Lloyd J., 34
Olson, Mark J., 534, 538
Olsson, Birger, 166
Omanson, Roger L., 127, 533
O'Neill, John Cochrane, 57, 114
O'Reilly, Leo, 98
O'Toole, Robert F., 42, 51, 54, 84, 517, 521
Overbeck, Franz C., 113, 1117

Packer, J. I., 275
Padilla, Osvaldo, 81, 88, 98
Pahl, Michael W., 15
Painter, John, 590
Palmer, Darryl W., 47
Panayotov, Alexander, 173
Pao, David W., 75, 93, 203, 205, 280, 301, 313, 555
Pardigon, Flavien, 431, 432, 434, 435
Parker, Pierson, 110
Parsons, Mikeal C., 8, 17, 19, 27, 42, 113, 489, 504, 544, 593
Patterson, Richard D., xxii
Patzia, Arthur G., 16, 594
Payne, J. Barton, 240
Pelikan, Jaroslav, 259
Penner, Todd C., 43
Perkins, Judith, 44
Perrin, Nicholas, 156, 176
Peterson, David G., 28, 214, 232, 249, 274, 311, 317, 427, 428, 430, 431, 446, 501, 509, 517, 530, 546, 547, 557, 558
Phillips, Thomas E., 43
Pinter, Dean, 232, 302, 325, 472
Plymale, Steven F., 235
Polhill, John B., 197, 249, 425, 430, 431, 495, 501, 512, 520, 539, 546, 559, 589
Porter, Stanley E., 46, 65, 66, 67, 68, 123, 198, 207, 488
Powell, Mark Allan, 98, 185
Praeder, Susan Marie, 84, 530, 534, 539, 542, 547
Price, Robert M., 258, 259
Puskas, Charles B., 552, 553, 554

Quinn, Jerome D., 589

Ramsay, Sir William M., 68, 69
Rapske, Brian, 488, 498, 502, 503, 504, 509, 510, 520, 531, 533, 534, 538, 546, 551, 552, 553
Read-Heimerdinger, Jenny, 45, 128
Reece, Steve, 8
Reed, Annette Yoshiko, 173
Regul, Jürgen, 23
Renatus, Flavius Vegetius, 536
Ricoeur, Paul, 59
Riesner, Rainer, 322, 342, 534
Rius-Camps, Josep, 45, 128
Robbins, Gregory Allen, 20
Robbins, Vernon K., 54, 117
Robertson, A. T., 122

Roetzel, Calvin J., 144, 150
Rosner, Brian S., xxii, 47, 557, 558
Ross, Arthur M., 28, 30, 197, 410
Roth, Dieter R., 127
Rothschild, Clark K., 48
Rowe, C. Kavin, 42, 56, 98, 99. 163, 309, 430, 431, 449, 465, 468, 509, 511, 512, 593
Runesson, Anders, 150, 166
Russell, Henry G., 110

Saldarini, Anthony J., 168
Sanders, Jack T., 113
Sanders, James A., 594
Savelle, Charles Haddon, Jr., 391
Saxby, Alan, 590
Scheer, Tanja, 549
Scheidel, Walter, 182
Schirrmacher, Thomas P., 480
Schmidt, Daryl D., 47
Schmidt, Thomas E., 592
Schnabel, Eckhard J., 28, 87, 121, 162, 197, 214, 229, 232, 245, 249, 256, 258, 274, 287, 315, 317, 321, 341, 345, 396, 397, 412, 428, 430, 431, 476, 494, 495, 501, 508, 509, 517, 520, 530, 537, 538, 544, 546, 547, 548, 551, 553, 557, 558
Schreiner, Patrick, 80
Schreiner, Thomas R., 236, 357
Schubert, Paul, 92
Schwartz, Saundra, 44
Scott, J. Julius, Jr., 90, 102, 169
Scott, James M., 357
Seccombe, David, 112
Seifrid, Mark A., 164
Seland, Torrey, 173
Sell, Phillip W., 259
Selwyn, Edward Carus, 11
Shanks, Hershel, 590
Shauf, Scott, xxii, 200, 234, 235, 282, 596
Shellard, Barbara, 27, 118
Shelton, W. Brian, 574, 579, 581, 582, 584, 590
Sherwin-White, A. N., 68, 417, 423, 444, 498, 499, 521
Shipp, Blake, 89
Sievers, Joseph, 168
Sleeman, Matthew, 207
Smith, Ben C., 22, 23
Smith, Daniel Lynwood, 89
Smith, David E., 594
Smith, Dennis E., 232
Smith, James J., 68
Soards, Marion L., 88, 508
Spencer, F. Scott, 261, 282, 446, 478, 501, 504
Spencer, Patrick E., 42
Stagg, Frank, 559
Stam, John, 259
Stambaugh, John E., 178, 531, 534
Stein, Robert H., 132, 135
Sterling, Gregory E., xxii, 47
Stigers, Harold G., 164
Still, Todd D., 316, 476, 502
Stone, Robert C., 357
Stonehouse, Ned Bernard, 53, 434, 437
Storm, Mel, 90, 99, 197, 216, 229, 249, 271, 286
Storms, Sam, 236
Stott, John R. W., 197, 220, 229, 236, 240, 243, 246, 267, 268, 269, 271, 286, 288, 317, 346, 366, 407, 412, 414, 423, 428, 431, 434, 437, 438
Strange, W. A., 127
Strauss, Mark L., 52, 57, 58, 91, 92, 93, 109, 163, 164, 166, 178
Strelan, Rick, 7, 8, 11, 15, 16, 26, 30, 117
Stuart, Douglas, 133, 134, 137, 597
Stutzman, Linford, 183, 530
Sundberg, Albert C., Jr., 20
Sweeting, Donald W., 33
Sweeting, George, 33
Tajra, Harry W., 54, 444, 446, 506, 509
Talbert, Charles H., 46, 83, 89, 117
Tannehill, Robert C., 41, 42, 113, 371
Tennent, Timothy C., 219
Thiessen, Matthew, 378
Thomas, David, 437
Thomas, Heath A., 356, 372, 400, 481
Thompson, Alan J., 34, 601
Thompson, Glen L., 301, 411
Tov, Emmanuel, 594
Townsend, John T., 113
Trebilco, Paul, 179, 315, 381
Trobisch, David, 595
Troftgruben, Troy M., 530, 557, 558, 559
Trompf, Garry, 545
Tuckett, Christopher M., 127, 593
Turner, Cuthbert Hamilton, 76, 77
Twelftree, Graham H., 166
Tyson, Joseph B., 89, 113

Uytanlet, Samson, 47

van Unnik, Willem C., 47, 59, 61
Vang, Preben, 604
Verheyden, Joseph, 42
Voragine, Jacobus de, 574, 578, 581

Wagner, C. Peter, 34
Walaskay, Paul, 54
Walker, Donald D., 184
Walker, Thomas, 288
Walker, William O., 118, 119
Wall, Robert W., 597
Wallace, Daniel B., 125, 357, 495
Wallace, James Buchanan, 205
Walters, Patricia, 5
Walton, John H., 222
Walton, Steve, 54, 207, 557
Waters, Guy Prentiss, 554, 557
Watson, Duane F., 180, 181, 183
Watson, JoAnn Ford, 414

Wecks, John, 401
Weima, Jeffrey A. D., 423
Weissenrieder, Annette, 546
Wenham, John, 10, 56
Wentling, Judith L., 46
White, William, Jr., 166, 282
Wifstrand, Albert, 6, 7
Wilcox, Max, 127
Williams, Charles Stephen Conway, 110, 114, 127, 317
Williams, David John, 197, 245, 249, 512, 513, 533
Williams, Matthew C., 90
Wilson, Benjamin R., 87
Wilson, Mark W., 347, 411
Wilson, Stephen G., 589
Wineland, John D., 538
Winter, Bruce W., 121, 316, 430, 434, 437, 444, 506, 507, 508
Wise, Michael Owen, 173, 284, 491
Witherington, Ben III, 28, 88, 89, 113, 114, 117, 118, 127, 148, 150, 230, 232, 249, 270, 302, 317, 341, 377, 378, 397, 420, 422, 423, 430, 431, 473, 488, 489, 494, 495, 508, 510, 512, 517, 518, 531, 533, 537, 543, 547, 551, 557, 589, 590
Wood, John A., 377
Wright, Christopher J. H., xxii, 204, 400
Wright, N. T., 58, 123, 143, 205, 255, 437, 594

Yamada, Kota, 47, 48
Yarbrough, Robert W., 162

Zeller, Edward, 113, 117
Ziesler, J. A., 245
Zwiep, Arie W., 207, 208, 213, 215